Writing is a political instrument.

James Baldwin

I write to find out what I'm thinking. I write to find out who I am. I write to understand things.

Julia Alvarez

If I had to say what writing is, we would define it essentially as an act of courage.

Cynthia Ozick

Writing is the act of saying *I*, of imposing yourself upon other people, of saying *listen to me*, *see it my way*, *change your mind*.

Joan Didion

The beautiful part of writing is that you don't have to get it right the first time — unlike, say, brain surgery.

Robert Cormier

Writing and rewriting are a constant search for what one is saying.

John Updike

Ninth Edition

The St. Martin's Guide to Writing

Rise B. Axelrod
University of California, Riverside

Charles R. Cooper
University of California, San Diego

Bedford / St. Martin's
Boston ● New York

For Bedford/St. Martin's

Senior Developmental Editor: Alexis P. Walker
Senior Production Editor: Harold Chester
Production Supervisor: Jennifer Peterson
Marketing Manager: Molly Parke
Art Director: Lucy Krikorian
Text Design: Jerilyn Bockorick
Copy Editor: Denise P. Quirk
Photo Research: Naomi Kornhauser
Cover Design: Richard DiTomassi
Composition: Nesbitt Graphics, Inc.
Printing and Binding: RR Donnelley and Sons

President: Joan E. Feinberg
Editorial Director: Denise B. Wydra
Editor in Chief: Karen S. Henry
Director of Development: Erica T. Appel
Director of Marketing: Karen R. Soeltz
Director of Editing, Design, and Production: Marcia Cohen
Assistant Director of Editing, Design, and Production: Elise S. Kaiser
Managing Editor: Shuli Traub

Library of Congress Control Number: 2009932161 (with Handbook)
2009932166 (without Handbook)

Manufactured in the United States of America.

5 4 3 2 1 0
f e d c b a

For information, write: Bedford/St. Martin's, 75 Arlington Street,
Boston, MA 02116   (617-399-4000)

ISBN-10: 0-312-53612-7   ISBN-13: 978-0-312-53612-1 (with Handbook)
ISBN-10: 0-312-53613-5   ISBN-13: 978-0-312-53613-8 (without Handbook)

Acknowledgments

Acknowledgments and copyrights appear at the back of the book on pages A1-A3, which constitute an extension of the copyright page.

Advisory Board

We owe an enormous debt to all the rhetoricians and composition specialists whose theory, research, and pedagogy have informed *The St. Martin's Guide to Writing*. We would be adding many pages if we were to name everyone to whom we are indebted.

The members of the Advisory Board for the ninth edition, a group of dedicated composition instructors from across the country, have provided us with extensive insights and suggestions for the chapters in Part One and have given us the benefit of their advice on new features. *The St. Martin's Guide to Writing* has been greatly enhanced by their contributions.

Samantha Andrus-Henry
Grand Rapids Community College

Melissa Batai
Triton College

Mary Bishop
Holmes Junior College–Ridgeland

Jo Ann Buck
Guilford Technical Community College

Kevin Cantwell
Macon State College

Anne Dvorak
Longview Community College

Leona Fisher
Chaffey College

Diana Grahn
Longview Community College

Dawn Hubbell-Staeble
Bowling Green State University

Amy Morris-Jones
Baker College of Muskegon

Gray Scott
University of California, Riverside

Susan Sebok
South Suburban College

Preface for Instructors

When we first wrote *The St. Martin's Guide to Writing*, we aimed to demystify writing and authorize students as writers. We wanted to help students learn to commit themselves to writing projects, communicate effectively with chosen readers, and question their own certainties. We also wanted them to understand that knowledge of writing comes both from analyzing writing and from working hard on their own writing. To achieve this aim, we took what we had learned from classical rhetoric and from contemporary composition theory and did our best to make it accessible to students.

The response from instructors and students was overwhelmingly positive: The first edition of *The Guide*, published in 1985, immediately became the most widely adopted text of its kind in the nation.

As with every new edition, we began work on this ninth edition with the goal of adapting the best of current composition research and practice to the needs of instructors and students. We listened closely to our Advisory Board and dozens of talented reviewers (students as well as instructors), and we were confirmed in our belief that the essential purpose and approach of *The Guide* is more relevant than ever: Students need clear guidance and practical strategies to harness their potential as writers — an achievement that will be key to their success in their other college courses, in their jobs, and in the wider world.

At the same time, we realized that we needed to reach out to these students, and help them connect with writing, in new ways.

Every aspect of the academic landscape has changed since we wrote the first edition. The texts we read and write, the tools we use to find them, the options we have for communicating, the habits of mind we rely on, even the students themselves — all are more varied and complex than in the past, sometimes overwhelmingly so. At the same time, students and instructors alike are increasingly burdened with demands on their time, attention, and energy that emanate from outside the classroom.

For all of these reasons, this edition represents a bold reimagining of our original vision. The chapters containing the Guides to Writing have been reengineered to reflect and build on the actual writing processes of students, and the Guides themselves are streamlined and more visual. Throughout the book, we attempt to help students focus on what is important, yet offer multiple options for critical reading and writing. The result of this reimagining is what you hold in your hands: a text that we believe to be more flexible, more engaging, and more pedagogically effective than any previous edition.

An Overview of the Book

The Guide offers everything you need for the writing course.

Part One: Writing Activities

Part One presents nine different genres of writing, all reflecting actual writing assignments that students may encounter both in and out of college. While the chapters can be taught in any order, we have organized Part One to move from writing based on personal experience and reflection, through writing based on research and observation, to writing about controversial issues and problems.

Each chapter follows the same organizational plan:

- Three brief illustrated **scenarios** providing examples of how the genre is used in college courses, in the community, and in the workplace
- A brief **introduction** to the genre
- A **collaborative activity** helping students start working in the genre
- An orientation to the genre's **basic features** and to questions of **purpose and audience** specific to the genre
- A set of **readings** illustrating the genre accompanied by **questions and prompts** designed to help students explore connections to their culture and experience and to analyze the basic features and writing strategies
- A **"Beyond the Traditional Essay"** section discussing examples of the genre drawn from unexpected contexts — advertising, blogs, museums, even public parks
- A **Guide to Writing,** tailored to the genre, that helps students refine their own writing processes, with activities for invention and research, easy-reference guides for drafting and revision, a Critical Reading Guide for peer review, strategies for integrating sources, and more
- **Editing and proofreading guidelines,** based on our nationwide study of errors in first-year college students' writing, to help students check for one or two sentence-level problems likely to occur in a given genre
- A section exploring how writers think about **document design,** expanding on one of the scenarios presented at the beginning of the chapter
- A look at one student **writer at work,** focusing on one or more aspects of the writing process of a student whose essay is featured in the chapter
- **Critical thinking activities** designed to help students reflect on what they learned and consider the social dimensions of the genre taught in the chapter

Part Two: Critical Thinking Strategies

Part Two consists of two chapters that present practical heuristics for invention and reading. Chapter 11, "A Catalog of Invention Strategies," covers clustering, looping, dramatizing, and questioning, among other strategies, while Chapter 12, "A Catalog of Reading Strategies," includes annotating, summarizing, exploring the significance of figurative language, and evaluating the logic of an argument.

Part Three: Writing Strategies

Part Three looks at a wide range of writers' strategies: paragraphing and coherence; logic and reasoning; and the familiar methods of presenting information, such as narrating, defining, and classifying.

In the ninth edition of *The Guide*, a new Chapter 20 provides students with criteria for analyzing visuals and illustrates them with several lengthy sample analyses and one full-length, documented student paper. Part Three concludes with a heavily illustrated chapter on document design, which provides principles to guide students in constructing a wide range of documents, along with examples of some of the most common kinds of documents they'll create in school, at work, and in their everyday lives.

Examples and exercises in Part Three have been drawn from a wide range of contemporary publications as well as reading selections appearing in Part One. The extensive cross-referencing between Parts One and Three allows instructors to teach writing strategies as students work on full essays.

Part Four: Research Strategies

Part Four discusses field as well as library and Internet research and includes thorough, up-to-date guidelines for using and documenting sources, with detailed examples of the 2009 Modern Language Association (MLA) and 2010 American Psychological Association (APA) documentation styles. An annotated sample student research paper models ways students can integrate citations into their own work in accordance with the rules for MLA documentation. The final chapter in Part Four, new to the ninth edition of *The Guide*, offers detailed guidelines for creating annotated bibliographies and literature reviews.

Part Five: Writing for Assessment

Part Five covers essay examinations, showing students how to analyze different kinds of exam questions and offering strategies for writing answers. It also addresses portfolios, helping students select, assemble, and present a representative sample of their writing.

Part Six: Writing and Speaking to Wider Audiences

Part Six includes chapters on oral presentations, collaborative learning, and service learning, offering advice to help students work together on writing projects and to write in and for their communities.

The Handbook

The Handbook offers a complete reference guide to grammar, word choice, punctuation, mechanics, common ESL problems, sentence structure, and usage. We have designed the Handbook so that students will find the answers they need quickly, and we have provided student examples from our nationwide study so that students will see errors similar to the ones in their own essays. In addition to the section on ESL problems, boxes throughout the rest of the Handbook offer specific support for ESL students.

Proven Features

While this edition of *The Guide* represents a bold reimagining of the way students work, it has retained the three central features that have made it a best-seller since its first edition: the detailed, practical guides to writing in different genres; the systematic integration of reading and writing; and continuing attention to changes in composition pedagogy.

Practical Guides to Writing

Each chapter in Part One offers practical, flexible guides that help students with different aspects of writing, such as invention or revision, as they write. Commonsensical and easy to follow, these writing guides teach students to assess a rhetorical situation, identify the kinds of information they will need, ask probing questions and find answers, and organize writing to achieve a particular purpose for chosen readers.

In the ninth edition, we've done even more to make these guides effective and easy to use, by streamlining them, by adding easy reference charts and tables, and by offering students multiple entry points into the composing process.

Systematic Integration of Reading and Writing

Each chapter in Part One introduces a single genre of writing, which students are led to consider both as readers and as writers. Chapters begin with an essay written in the genre by a student writer using *The Guide*; these essays are annotated with questions designed to encourage students to discover the ways in which the essay exemplifies that genre's basic features.

Each of three professional readings in the chapter is accompanied by carefully focused apparatus to guide purposeful, productive rereading. First is a response activity, Making Connections, which relates a central theme of the reading to students' own lives and cultural knowledge. The section following, Analyzing Writing Strategies, asks students to examine how the writer makes use of the basic features and strategies typical of the genre. Essays that include visuals are followed by an Analyzing Visuals section, which asks students to write about the way(s) in which photos, graphs, and other visual elements enhance the text. Finally, in Considering Topics for Your Own Essay, students approach the most important decision they have to make with a genre-centered assignment: choosing a workable topic that inspires their commitment to weeks of thinking and writing.

Continuing Attention to Changes in Composition

With each new edition, we have responded to new thinking and new issues in the field of composition and turned current theory and research into practical classroom activities — with a minimum of jargon. As a result, in every new edition *The Guide* incorporated new material that contributed to its continued effectiveness, including more on appropriate methods of argument, research, and working with sources; attention to new technologies for writing and researching; activities that promote group discussion and inquiry and encourage students to reflect on what they have learned; and material on document design, oral presentations, and writing in the community.

Changes in the Ninth Edition

In this edition, we have taken instructors' advice and revised the text to make it an even more effective teaching tool.

- **Streamlined and redesigned Part One chapters** provide more visual cues for students who learn visually, more "easy-reference" features for students who need help navigating a lengthy text, and more "ways in" to each assignment for students whose writing processes don't conform to an imaginary norm.

  - **The Basic Features** of each chapter's genre of writing are now **introduced at the start of the chapter,** to lay the groundwork for students' understanding of the genre and to prepare them for their work with that chapter's readings.

  - A **new color-coding system** calls out the Basic Features in the annotated student essay, the post-reading apparatus, and throughout the Guide to Writing, helping students see the connections among the chapter's various parts and more easily grasp what makes a successful example of a given genre.

  - **New "Beyond the Traditional Essay" sections** illustrate and discuss examples of that chapter's genre of writing drawn from advertising, blogs, museums — even public parks.

  - **New easy-reference charts** in each Guide to Writing — **"Starting Points"** and **"Troubleshooting Your Draft"** — help students self-assess and efficiently find the advice and models they need for overcoming individual writing challenges.

  - **Newly designed Invention activities** highlight different paths through the processes of generating and shaping material.

- **Chapter 5, newly revised as "Finding Common Ground,"** now teaches **students how to analyze opposing positions and find "common ground" between them** — a key step in analyzing and synthesizing sources and in constructing academic as well as civic arguments.

- **New material** brings the book up-to-date and teaches students what they'll need to succeed at academic writing.

  - To help students understand and evaluate the visual data that increasingly dominate our culture, we have added a **new Chapter 20, "Analyzing Visuals,"** which provides clear guidance on how to critically read and write about photos, ads, works of art, and other image-based texts. The chapter also offers a multi-stage model of a student's analysis of a photo by Gordon Parks, as well as exercises in visual analysis that students can do in class or on their own.

- To help them cope with information overload while doing research, we have added a **new Chapter 25, "Annotated Bibliographies and Literature Reviews,"** which offers detailed guidance on these important elements of the research process.
- To help them make useful connections between their previous writing experiences and the writing they will do in college, **Chapter 1** now focuses on the **literacy narrative,** encouraging students to reflect on their own literacy experiences in preparation for the reading and writing challenges they'll encounter in the course.

- **Fifteen new readings**, with at least one new reading in every Writing Assignment chapter, introduce compelling topics, multicultural perspectives, and fresh voices, including **Trey Ellis** on a family member's battle with AIDS, **Saira Shah** on finding her roots in Afghanistan, and **Amy Goldwasser** on what kids learn online — and why it matters.

Additional Resources

You Get More Help with *The St. Martin's Guide*

The benefits of using *The St. Martin's Guide* don't stop with the print text. Online, in print, and in digital format, you'll find both free and affordable premium resources to help students get even more out of the book and your course. You'll also find course management solutions and convenient instructor resources, such as sample syllabi, suggested classroom activities, and even a nationwide community of teachers. To learn more about or order any of the products below, contact your Bedford/St. Martin's sales representative, e-mail sales support (sales_support@bfwpub.com), or visit the Web site at bedfordstmartins .com/theguide/catalog.

Student Resources

The St. Martin's Guide Student Center **(bedfordstmartins.com/theguide).** Send students to free and open resources, allow them to choose an affordable e-book option, or upgrade to an expanding collection of innovative digital content — all in one place.

- **Free and open resources for *The St. Martin's Guide*** provide students with easy-to-access **book-specific materials, exercises, and downloadable content,** including electronic versions of the Critical Reading Guides, Starting Points and Troubleshooting Your Draft charts; tutorials for the sentence strategies in the Part One chapters; and additional essays on topics of contemporary debate for use with Chapter 5, "Finding Common Ground." Additional free resources include *Research and Documentation Online* **by Diana Hacker,** with clear advice on how to integrate outside material into a paper, how to cite sources correctly, and how to format the paper in MLA, APA, *Chicago*, or CSE style; and *Exercise Central,* a database of over 9,000 editing exercises designed to help identify students' strengths and weaknesses, recommend personalized study plans, and provide tutorials for common writing problems.

- The *St. Martin's Guide e-Book* **and enhanced Web site** let students do more and pay less. This flexible e-book allows users to highlight important sections, insert their own sticky notes, and customize content; the enhanced Web site includes *Marriage 101 and Other Student Essays*, a collection of 32 essays inspired by *The Guide,* and a peer-review lesson module and online role-playing game. The *St. Martin's Guide e-Book* and access to the enhanced Web site can be packaged free with the print book or purchased separately at the Student Center for less than the price of the print book. An activation code is required.

- *Re:Writing Plus,* **now with** *VideoCentral,* gathers all of Bedford/St. Martin's premium digital content for composition into one online collection. It includes hundreds of model documents and *VideoCentral,* with over 50 brief videos for the writing classroom. *Re:Writing Plus* can be purchased separately at the Student Center or packaged with the print book at a significant discount. An activation code is required.

Sticks and Stones and Other Student Essays, **Seventh Edition.** Available for packaging **free** with new copies of *The Guide, Sticks and Stones* is a collection of essays written by students across the nation using earlier editions of *The Guide.* Each essay is accompanied by a headnote that spotlights some of the ways the writer uses the genre successfully, invites students to notice other achievements, and supplies context where necessary.

Who Are We? Readings in Identity and Community and Work and Career. Available for packaging **free** with new copies of *The Guide, Who Are We?* contains selections that expand on themes foregrounded in *The Guide.* Full of ideas for classroom discussion and writing, the readings offer students additional perspectives and thought-provoking analysis.

i·series on CD-ROM. **Free** when packaged with new copies of *The St. Martin's Guide,* the *i·series* includes multimedia tutorials in a flexible CD-ROM format — because there are things you can't do in a book:

- *ix visual exercises* help students visualize and put into practice key rhetorical and visual concepts.
- *i·claim visualizing argument* offers a new way to see argument — with 6 tutorials, an illustrated glossary, and over 70 multimedia arguments.
- *i·cite visualizing sources* brings research to life through an animated introduction, four tutorials, and hands-on source practice.

Course Management

***CompClass for The St. Martin's Guide* (yourcompclass.com).** An easy-to-use online course space designed for composition students and instructors, *CompClass for The St. Martin's Guide* comes preloaded with the *St. Martin's Guide e-Book* as well as other Bedford/St. Martin's premium digital content, including *VideoCentral*. Powerful assignment and assessment tools make it easier to keep track of your students' progress. *CompClass for The St. Martin's Guide* can be purchased separately at yourcompclass.com or packaged with the print book at a significant discount. An activation code is required.

Content cartridges for WebCT, Angel, and other course management systems. Our content cartridges for course management systems — Blackboard, WebCT, Angel, and Desire2Learn — make it simple for instructors using this online learning architecture to build a course around *The Guide*. The content is drawn from the Web site and includes activities, models, reference materials, and the *Exercise Central* gradebook.

Ordering Information (Package ISBNs)

To order any of the following items with the print text you order for your students, please use the ISBNs provided below. For different packages or a more complete listing of supplements, contact your Bedford/St. Martin's sales representative, e-mail sales support at sales_support@bfwpub.com, or visit the Web site at bedfordstmartins .com/theguide/catalog.

	9th Edition (hardcover)	Short 9th Edition
The *St. Martin's Guide e-Book* and enhanced Web site	ISBN-10: 0-312-58408-3 ISBN-13: 978-0-312-58408-5	ISBN-10: 0-312-58409-1 ISBN-13: 978-0-312-58409-2
Re:Writing Plus	ISBN-10: 0-312-63790-X ISBN-13: 978-0-312-63790-3	ISBN-10: 0-312-62901-X ISBN-13: 978-0-312-62901-4
Sticks and Stones and Other Student Essays, Seventh Edition	ISBN-10: 0-312-62539-1 ISBN-13: 978-0-312-62539-9	ISBN-10: 0-312-63793-4 ISBN-13: 978-0-312-63793-4
Who Are We? Readings in Identity and Community and Work and Career	ISBN-10: 0-312-62532-4 ISBN-13: 978-0-312-62532-0	ISBN-10: 0-312-63791-8 ISBN-13: 978-0-312-63791-0
CompClass for The St. Martin's Guide	ISBN-10: 0-312-62533-2 ISBN-13: 978-0-312-62533-7	ISBN-10: 0-312-63792-6 ISBN-13: 978-0-312-63792-7

Instructor Resources

You have a lot to do in your course. Bedford/St. Martin's wants to make it easy for you to find the support you need — and to get it quickly.

Instructor's Resource Manual (ISBN-10: 0-312-58260-9/ISBN-13: 978-0-312-58260-9 (print); also available for download at bedfordstmartins.com/theguide). The *Instructor's Resource Manual* includes helpful advice for new instructors, guidelines on common teaching practices such as assigning journals and setting up group activities, guidelines on responding to and evaluating student writing, course plans, detailed chapter plans, an annotated bibliography in composition and rhetoric, and a selection of background readings.

Additional Resources for Teaching with *The St. Martin's Guide to Writing*, available for download at bedfordstmartins.com/theguide, supports classroom instruction with PowerPoint presentations offering lists of important features for each genre, critical reading guides, collaborative activities, and checklists, all adapted from the text. It also provides more than fifty exercises designed to accompany the Handbook section of the hardcover edition of *The Guide*.

The Elements of Teaching Writing (A Resource for Instructors in All Disciplines) (ISBN-10: 0-312-40683-5/ISBN-13: 978-0-312-40683-7). Written by Katherine Gottschalk and Keith Hjortshoj, *The Elements of Teaching Writing* provides time-saving strategies and practical guidance in a brief reference form. Drawing on their extensive experience training instructors in all disciplines to incorporate writing into their courses, Gottschalk and Hjortshoj offer reliable advice, accommodating a wide range of teaching styles and class sizes, about how to design effective writing assignments and how to respond to and evaluate student writing in any course.

Teaching Central (bedfordstmartins.com/teachingcentral). Designed for the convenience of instructors, this rich Web site lists and describes Bedford/St. Martin's acclaimed print series of free professional sourcebooks, background readings, and bibliographies for teachers. In addition, *Teaching Central* offers a host of free online resources, including

- *Bits,* a blog that collects creative ideas for teaching composition from a community of teachers, scholars, authors, and editors. Instructors are free to take, use, adapt, and pass the ideas around, in addition to sharing new suggestions.

- *Just-in-Time Teaching* and *Adjunct Central* — downloadable syllabi, handouts, exercises, activities, assignments, teaching tips, and more, organized by resource type and by topic

- *Take 20* — a 60-minute film for teachers, by teachers, in which 22 writing teachers answer 20 questions on current practices and emerging ideas in composition

Acknowledgments

We owe an enormous debt to all the rhetoricians and composition specialists whose theory, research, and pedagogy have informed *The St. Martin's Guide to Writing*. We would be adding many pages to an already long book if we were to name everyone to whom we are indebted; suffice it to say that we have been eclectic in our borrowing.

We must also acknowledge immeasurable lessons learned from all the writers, professional and student alike, whose work we analyzed and whose writing we used in this and earlier editions.

So many instructors and students have contributed ideas and criticism over the years. The members of the advisory board for the ninth edition, a group of dedicated composition instructors from across the country, have provided us with extensive insights and suggestions on the eighth edition and have given us the benefit of their advice on new readings and other new features for the ninth. For their many contributions, we would like to thank Samantha Andrus-Henry, Grand Rapids Community College; Melissa Batai, Triton College; Mary Bishop, Holmes Junior College–Ridgeland; Jo Ann Buck, Guilford Technical Community College; Kevin Cantwell, Macon State College; Anne Dvorak, Longview Community College; Leona Fisher, Chaffey College; Diana Grahn, Longview Community College; Dawn Hubbell-Staeble, Bowling Green State University; Amy Morris-Jones, Baker College of Muskegon; Gray Scott, University of California, Riverside; and Susan Sebok, South Suburban College.

Many other instructors have also helped us improve the book. For responding to detailed questionnaires about the eighth edition, we thank Diana Agy, Jackson Community College; James Allen, College of DuPage; Eileen Baland, Texas Baptist University; Sydney Bartman, Mt. San Antonio College; Elisabeth Beccue, Erie Community College; Maria J. Cahill, Edison College; Lenny Cavallaro, Northern Essex Community College; Chandra Speight Cerutti, East Carolina University; Connie Chismar, Georgian Court University; Marilyn Clark, Xavier University; Lori Rios Doddy, Texas Woman's University; Deborah Kay Ferrell, Finger Lakes Community College; April Gentry, Savannah State University; Diane Halm, Niagara University; Tammy Harosky, Virginia Highlands Community College; Anne Helms, Alamance Community College; Teresa Henning, Southwest Minnesota State University; Rick Jones, South Suburban College; Cristina Karmas, Graceland University; Glenda Lowery, Rappanannock Community College, Warsaw Campus; Rachel Jo Mack, Ball State University; Linda McHenry, Fort Hays State University; Jim McKeown, McLennan Community College; Michelle Metzner, Wright State University; Lisa Wiley Moslow, Erie Community College North Campus; Caroline Nobile, Edinboro University of Pennsylvania; Gordon Petry, Bradley University; Richard W. Porter, Cedarville University; Pamela J. Rader, Georgian Court University; Kim Salrin, Bradley University; Wanda Synstelien, Southwest Minnesota State University; Ruthe Thompson, Southwest Minnesota State University; Janice M. Vierk, Metropolitan Community College; Betsey Whited, Emporia State University; John M. Ziebell, College of Southern Nevada; and Susan Zolliker, Palomar College.

For this new edition of *The Guide*, we also gratefully acknowledge the special contributions of the following: Paul Tayyar, who drafted the new "Analyzing Visuals" chapter; Gray Scott, who drafted the new "Annotated Bibliographies and Literature Reviews" chapter; and Jill Markgraf, Judith Van Noate, Debbi Renfrow, Jaena Hollingsworth, and Beth Downs, who provided expert advice on the revised coverage of library and Internet research. We want especially to thank the many instructors at the University of California, Riverside, who offered advice and class tested new material, including Stephanie Kay, Leona Fisher, Gray Scott, Elizabeth Spies, Elissa Weeks, Rob d'Annibale, Kimberly Turner, Amanda Uvalle, Joshua Fenton, Benedict Jones, and Sandra Baringer. Finally, we are especially grateful to the student authors for allowing us to use their work in *Sticks and Stones, Marriage 101*, and *The Guide*.

We want to thank many people at Bedford/St. Martin's, especially Senior Editor Alexis Walker, whose wisdom, skill, and tireless enthusiasm made this edition possible, and our production team of Harold Chester, Shuli Traub, and Jenny Peterson. Denise Quirk made many valuable contributions to this revision with her careful copyediting, as did Diana Puglisi George with her meticulous proofreading. Cecilia Seiter managed and edited all of the most important ancillaries to the book: the *Instructor's Resource Manual, Sticks and Stones, Marriage 101*, and the rest of the *Guide* Web site. Without the help of Dan Schwartz, the new media supplements to *The Guide* would not have been possible.

Thanks also to the immensely talented design team — book designer Jerilyn Bockorick as well as Bedford/St. Martin's art directors Anna Palchik and Lucy Krikorian — for making the ninth edition so attractive and usable. Our gratitude also goes to Sandy Schechter and Warren Drabek for their hard work clearing permissions, and Martha Friedman and Naomi Kornhauser for imaginative photo research.

We wish finally to express our heartfelt appreciation to Nancy Perry for helping us to launch *The Guide* successfully so many years ago and continuing to stand by us. Over the years, Nancy has generously and wisely advised us on everything from planning new editions to copyediting manuscript, and now she is helping us develop the new customized publication of *The Guide*. We also want to thank Erica Appel, director of development, and Karen Henry, editor-in-chief, who offered valued advice at many critical stages in the process. Thanks as well to Joan Feinberg and Denise Wydra for their adroit leadership of Bedford/St. Martin's, and to marketing director Karen Soeltz and marketing manager Molly Parke — along with the extraordinarily talented and hardworking sales staff — for their tireless efforts on behalf of *The Guide*.

Features of *The St. Martin's Guide to Writing*, Ninth Edition, Correlated to the WPA Outcomes Statement

Desired Student Outcomes	Relevant Features of *The St. Martin's Guide*
Rhetorical Knowledge	
Focus on a purpose	Each writing assignment chapter in Part One offers extensive discussion of the purpose(s) for the genre of writing covered in that chapter.
Respond to the needs of different audiences	Each chapter in Part One discusses the need to consider one's audience for the particular genre covered in that chapter. In Chapters 6–10, which cover argument, there is also extensive discussion of the need to anticipate opposing positions and readers' objections to the writer's thesis.
Respond appropriately to different kinds of rhetorical situations	Each chapter in Part One gives detailed advice on responding to a particular rhetorical situation, from remembering an event (Chapter 2) to analyzing stories (Chapter 10).
Use conventions of format and structure appropriate to the rhetorical situation	Each chapter in Part One points out features of effectively structured writing, and the Guides to Writing help students systematically develop their own effective structures. Document design is covered in two sections in each of these chapters, as well as in a dedicated Chapter 21, "Designing Documents."
Adopt appropriate voice, tone, and level of formality	Many of the Sentence Strategies sections in each chapter in Part One deal with these issues. Also, see purpose and audience coverage mentioned previously.
Understand how genres shape reading and writing	Each chapter in Part One offers student and professional readings accompanied by annotations, questions, and commentary that draw students' attention to the key features of the genre and stimulate ideas for writing. Each chapter's Guide to Writing offers detailed, step-by-step advice for writing in the genre and for offering constructive peer criticism. In addition, "In College Courses," "In the Community," and "In the Workplace" sections that open each Part One chapter, as well as "Beyond the Traditional Essay" sections later in the chapter, show how the various genres are used outside the composition course.
Write in several genres	The Guides to Writing in each of the nine chapters in Part One offer specific advice on writing to remember an event; to profile a person, activity, or place; to explain a concept; to analyze opposing positions and find common ground; to argue a position; to propose a solution; to justify an evaluation; to speculate about causes; and to analyze literature. In addition, Chapters 22–25 cover research strategies that many students will use while writing in the genres covered in Part One.

Desired Student Outcomes	Relevant Features of *The St. Martin's Guide*
Critical Thinking, Reading, and Writing	
Use writing and reading for inquiry, learning, thinking, and communicating	Each Writing Assignment chapter in Part One emphasizes the connection between reading and writing in a particular genre: Each chapter begins with a group of readings whose apparatus introduces students to thinking about the features of the genre; then a Guide to Writing leads them through the process of applying these features to an essay of their own. Chapter 11, "A Catalog of Invention Strategies," and Chapter 12, "A Catalog of Reading Strategies" prompt students to engage actively in invention and reading. Other Part Two chapters include coverage of specific invention, reading, and writing strategies useful in a variety of genres.
Understand a writing assignment as a series of tasks, including finding, evaluating, analyzing, and synthesizing appropriate primary and secondary sources	The Guides to Writing in each chapter in Part One break writing assignments down into doable focused thinking and writing activities that engage students in the recursive process of invention and research to find, analyze, and synthesize information and ideas. "Working with Sources" sections teach specific strategies of evaluating and integrating source material. Chapter 12, "A Catalog of Reading Strategies," covers various strategies useful in working with sources, including annotating, summarizing, and synthesizing. Chapter 24, "Using Sources," offers detailed coverage of finding, evaluating, using, and acknowledging primary and secondary sources, while Chapter 25, "Annotated Bibliographies and Literature Reviews," helps students master these essential research-based tasks.
Integrate their own ideas with those of others	Chapter 24, "Using Sources," offers detailed advice on how to integrate and introduce quotations, how to cite paraphrases and summaries so as to distinguish them from the writer's own ideas, and how to avoid plagiarism. "Sentence Strategy" and "Working with Sources" in several Part One chapters offer additional support.
Understand the relationships among language, knowledge, and power	"Making Connections," a recurring section in the apparatus following the professional readings in Part One chapters, encourages students to put what they've read in the context of the world they live in. These preliminary reflections come into play in the Guides to Writing, where students are asked to draw on their experiences in college, community, and career in order to begin writing. "Thinking Critically about What You Have Learned" sections that conclude Part One chapters ask students to reconsider what they have learned, often in a social/political context.
Processes	
Be aware that it usually takes multiple drafts to create and complete a successful text	The need for a critical reading of a draft and for revision is emphasized in Chapter 1 as well as in the Guides to Writing in each chapter of Part One. Case studies of particular students' writing processes are offered in "Writer at Work" sections in each Part One chapter.

(continued)

Desired Student Outcomes	Relevant Features of *The St. Martin's Guide*
Processes (continued)	
Develop flexible strategies for generating ideas, revising, editing, and proofreading	The Guides to Writing in each Part One chapter offer genre-specific coverage of invention and research, getting a critical reading of a draft, revising, editing, and proofreading. Also in each Part One chapter, "Ways In" invention activities encourage students to start from their strengths, and "Starting Points" and "Troubleshooting Your Draft" charts offer specific, targeted advice for students with different challenges. A dedicated Chapter 11, "A Catalog of Invention Strategies," offers numerous helpful suggestions for idea generation.
Understand writing as an open process that permits writers to use later invention and rethinking to revise their work	The Guides to Writing in each Part One chapter offer extensive, genre-specific advice on rethinking and revising at multiple stages. "Ways In" activities, "Starting Points" charts, and "Troubleshooting Your Draft" charts in Part One chapters encourage students to discover, review, and revise their own process(es) of writing.
Understand the collaborative and social aspects of writing processes	Each chapter in Part One includes several opportunities for and guides to collaboration: "Practice" activities at the beginning of the chapter, "Making Connections" activities after the readings, and, in the Guides to Writing, "Testing Your Choice" activities and the Critical Reading Guide.
Learn to critique their own and others' works	The Critical Reading Guide and Revising sections in the Guides to Writing in each Part One chapter offer students specific advice on constructively criticizing — and praising — their own work and the work of their classmates. Peer review is also covered in depth in Chapter 29, "Working with Others."
Learn to balance the advantages of relying on others with the responsibility of doing their part	This goal is implicit in several collaborative activities: "Practice" activities at the beginning of the chapter, "Making Connections" activities after the readings, and, in the Guides to Writing, "Testing Your Choice" activities and the Critical Reading Guide. Group work is also covered in depth in Chapter 29, "Working with Others."
Use a variety of technologies to address a range of audiences	Each Guide to Writing in Part One chapters includes advice on using the Web for various stages of the writing process, as well as "sidebars" providing information and advice about grammar- and spell-checkers and software-based commenting tools. See also Chapter 23, "Library and Internet Research," for extensive coverage of finding, evaluating, and using print and electronic resources and of responsibly using the Internet, e-mail, and online communities for research, and Chapter 21, "Designing Documents," which offers advice on creating visuals on a computer or downloading them from the Web. Finally, *The Guide*'s electronic ancillaries include a robust companion Web site and an e-Book.

Desired Student Outcomes	Relevant Features of *The St. Martin's Guide*
Knowledge of Conventions	
Learn common formats for different kinds of texts	Document design is covered in a dedicated Chapter 21 as well as in two sections in each of the Writing Assignment chapters in Part One. Examples of specific formats for a range of texts appear on pp. 787–94 (research paper); p. 704 (memo); p. 705 (business letter); p. 706 (e-mail); p. 708 (résumé); p. 710 (job application letter); pp. 712–13 (lab report); and pp. 696–702 (table, diagrams, graphs, charts, map, and other figures).
Develop knowledge of genre conventions ranging from structure and paragraphing to tone and mechanics	Each chapter in Part One presents several basic features of a specific genre, which are introduced up front and then consistently reinforced throughout the chapter. Genre-specific issues of structure, paragraphing, tone, and mechanics are also addressed in the "Sentence Strategies" and "Editing and Proofreading" sections of each Guide to Writing.
Practice appropriate means of documenting their work	Chapter 24, "Using Sources," offers detailed advice on how to integrate and introduce quotations, how to cite paraphrases and summaries so as to distinguish them from the writer's own ideas, and how to avoid plagiarism. This chapter also offers coverage of MLA and APA documentation in addition to an annotated sample student research paper. Chapter 20, "Analyzing Visuals," also offers a complete student paper with MLA documentation. In addition, "Working with Sources" sections in each Guide to Writing in the Part One chapters help students with the details of using and appropriately documenting sources by providing genre-specific examples of what (and what not) to do.
Control such surface features as syntax, grammar, punctuation, and spelling	Genre-specific editing and proofreading advice is given in two sections in each Guide to Writing in the Part One chapters: "Sentence Strategies" and "Editing and Proofreading." The hardcover version of *The Guide* also includes a concise yet remarkably comprehensive handbook with coverage of syntax, grammar, punctuation, and spelling.

Preface for Students:
How to Use *The St. Martin's Guide*

We have written this book with you, the student reading and using it, always in the forefront of our minds. Although it is a long book that covers many different topics, at its heart is a simple message: The best way to become a good writer is to study examples of good writing, then to apply what you have learned from those examples to your own work. Accordingly, we have provided numerous carefully selected examples of the kinds of writing you are likely to do both in and out of college, and we have accompanied them with detailed advice on writing your own essays. In this Preface, we explain how the various parts of the book work together to achieve this goal.

The Organization of the Book

Following Chapter 1 — an introduction to writing that gives general advice about how to approach different parts of a writing assignment — *The St. Martin's Guide to Writing* is divided into six major parts:

Part One: Writing Activities (Chapters 2–10)

Part Two: Critical Thinking Strategies (Chapters 11 and 12)

Part Three: Writing Strategies (Chapters 13–21)

Part Four: Research Strategies (Chapters 22–25)

Part Five: Writing for Assessment (Chapters 26 and 27)

Part Six: Writing and Speaking to Wider Audiences (Chapters 28–30)

This hardcover version of the book also includes a Handbook that you can refer to for help with grammar, punctuation, word choice, common ESL problems, and similar issues.

The Part One Chapters

For now, to understand how to use the book effectively to improve your writing, you first need to know that the most important part — the part that all of the rest depends on — is Part One, Chapters 2 through 10. Each of these chapters is organized to teach you about one important specific *genre*, or type of writing:

- autobiography
- profile of a person, activity, or place

- explanation of a concept
- analysis of opposing positions seeking common ground
- argument supporting your position
- proposal to solve a problem
- evaluation
- analysis of possible causes
- analysis of a short story

Each Part One chapter follows essentially the same structure, beginning with three scenarios that provide examples of how that kind of writing could be used in a college course, in a workplace, and in a community setting such as a volunteer program or civic organization.

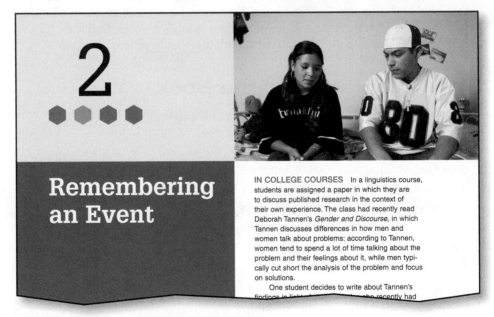

2

Remembering an Event

IN COLLEGE COURSES In a linguistics course, students are assigned a paper in which they are to discuss published research in the context of their own experience. The class had recently read Deborah Tannen's *Gender and Discourse,* in which Tannen discusses differences in how men and women talk about problems: according to Tannen, women tend to spend a lot of time talking about the problem and their feelings about it, while men typically cut short the analysis of the problem and focus on solutions.

One student decides to write about Tannen's findings in light of a conversation he recently had

Short chapter-opening scenarios provide examples of how the kind of writing covered in the chapter is used in other college courses, in your job, and in your community.

Next come a brief introduction to the genre, a collaborative activity to get you thinking about the genre, and an introduction to the genre's basic features, each of which is assigned a specific color.

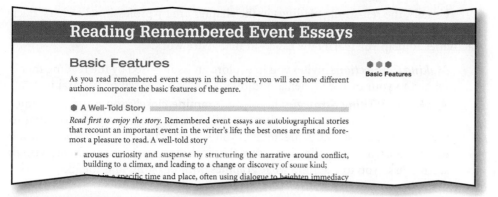

The genre's basic features are introduced toward the beginning of the chapter, so you know what to look for in the readings. Each basic feature is assigned a color, which is used whenever that basic feature is discussed later in the chapter.

Next, you'll find a series of readings, essays that will help you see how writers deploy the basic features of the genre for different purposes and audiences. The first reading in each chapter is always one written by a first-year college student who was using *The St. Martin's Guide*. These readings include color coding that highlights the writer's use of the basic features of the genre, as well as marginal questions that ask you to analyze the essay and also call your attention to particular writing strategies — such as quoting sources, using humor, providing definitions, and giving examples — that the writer used.

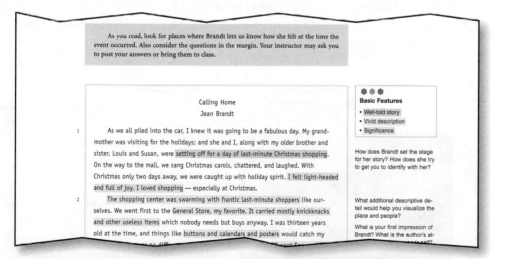

Color-coded highlighting in the chapter's first essay calls attention to the student writer's use of the basic features of the genre; questions in the margin ask you to analyze and reflect on the writer's use of various strategies.

Usually, the remaining readings in the chapter are by professional writers. Each of these additional essays is accompanied by the following groups of questions and activities to help you learn how essays in that genre work:

Making Connections invites you to explore an issue raised by the reading that is related to your own experience and often to broader social or cultural issues.

Analyzing Writing Strategies helps you examine closely some specific strategies the writer used. The questions in this section are organized according to the basic features of the genre, to help you keep track of different aspects of the essay's construction. Following essays that include visuals, an *Analyzing Visuals* section asks you to examine what graphics, photographs, and the like contribute to the written text.

Considering Topics for Your Own Essay suggests subjects that you might write about in your own essay.

Following the readings, each assignment chapter also includes the following sections:

- a "Beyond the Traditional Essay" section that provides examples of that chapter's genre of writing drawn from unexpected contexts — advertising, blogs, museums, even public parks

- a Guide to Writing that will help you write an effective essay in the genre for your particular audience and purpose. The Guides to Writing, the most important parts of the entire book, will be explained fully in the next section.

- a Writer at Work narrative showing key elements of the writing process of one student whose essay appears in the chapter

- a concluding section titled Thinking Critically about What You Have Learned, which invites you to reflect on the work you did for that chapter and to consider some of its wider social and cultural implications.

Beyond the Traditional Essay: Remembering an Event

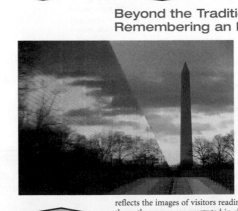

Our culture commemorates events in many ways that are likely familiar to you. Physical memorials such as statues, plaques, monuments, and buildings are traditional means of ensuring that important events remain in our collective memory: Relatively recent examples include the Vietnam Veterans Memorial in Washington, D.C., and the planned commemorative complex at the site of the 9/11 World Trade Center attack in New York City. Though such memorials function primarily visually, rather than textually, they can also be seen to exhibit the basic features we've discussed in essays remembering an event. The Vietnam memorial is a dramatic, V-shaped black granite wall partly embedded in the earth, which reflects the images of visitors reading the names of the dead and missing inscribed there; the names are [...] in chronological order, [...]

"Beyond the Traditional Essay" sections provide examples of that chapter's genre of writing drawn from unexpected contexts — advertising, blogs, museums, even public parks.

The Guides to Writing

Just as the Part One assignment chapters are the heart of the book, the heart of each assignment chapter is the Guide to Writing.

Writing an essay does not usually proceed in a smooth, predictable sequence — often, for example, a writer working on a draft will go back to what is usually an earlier step, such as invention and research, or jump ahead to what is usually a later one, such as editing and proofreading. But to make our help with the process more understandable and manageable, we have divided each Guide to Writing into the same elements that appear in the same order:

- the Writing Assignment;
- Invention and Research;
- Planning and Drafting;
- a Critical Reading Guide;
- Revising;
- and Editing and Proofreading.

The Writing Assignment. Each Guide to Writing begins with an assignment that defines the general purpose and basic features of the genre you have been studying in the chapter.

Starting Points chart. Each Guide to Writing opens with an easy-reference Starting Points chart, which is designed to help you efficiently find the advice you need for getting past writer's block and other early-stage difficulties.

Starting Points: Explaining a Concept

●●●● Basic Features

	Question	Where to Look
Choosing a Concept	How do I come up with a concept to write about?	• Considering Topics for Your Own Essay (pp. 143, 147–48, 158) • Choosing a Concept to Write About (pp. 162–63) • Testing Your Choice (pp. 165–66)
	What's my purpose in writing? How can I interest my audience?	• Reading Concept Explanations: Purpose and Audience (p. 131) • Defining Your Purpose for Your Readers (p. 167) • Refining Your Purpose and Setting Goals: Clarifying Your Purpose and Audience (p. 168)
A Focused Explanation	How can I decide on a focus for my concept?	• Reading Concept Explanations: Basic Features (pp. 129–31) • Ways In: Gaining an Overview of a Concept (p. 164) • Ways In: Focusing the Concept (p. 165)
		• Reading Concept Explanations: Basic Fe... (... ...)

Each Guide to Writing opens with an easy-reference Starting Points chart, with advice for getting started.

Invention and Research. Every Guide to Writing includes invention activities designed to help you

- find a topic
- discover what you already know about the topic
- consider your purpose and audience
- research the topic further — in the library, on the Internet, through observation and interviews, or some combination of these methods
- explore and develop your ideas, and
- compose a tentative thesis statement to guide your planning and drafting.

Because we know that different students start writing at different places, we've offered different "ways in" to many of the Invention activities: specifically, their new layout (as shown in the example below) is meant to suggest the different possible paths through the processes of generating and shaping material.

●● **Basic Features**

Ways In: Constructing a Well-Told Story

Once you've made a preliminary choice of an event, the following activities will help you begin to construct a well-told story, with vivid descriptions of people and places. You can begin with whichever basic activity you want, but wherever you begin, be sure to return to the other activities to fill in the details.

Shaping the Story	Describing the Place	Recalling Key People
Sketch the Story. *Write a quick sketch telling roughly what happened.* Don't worry about what you're leaving out; you can fill in the details later.	**Reimagine the Place.** *Identify the place where the event occurred and describe it.* What do you see, hear, or smell? Use details — shape, color, texture — to evoke the scene.	**Describe People.** *Write about people who played a role in the event.* For each person, name and detail a few distinctive physical features, mannerisms, dress, and so on.
Explore a Revealing or Pivotal Moment. *Write for a few minutes developing a moment of surprise, confrontation, crisis, change, or discovery that may become the climax of your story.* To dramatize it, try using specific narrative actions and dialogue.	**Research Visuals.** *Try to locate visuals you could include in your essay:* Look through memorabilia such as family photographs, yearbooks, newspaper articles, concert programs, ticket stubs, or T-shirts — anything that might stimulate your memory and help you reflect on the place. If you submit your essay electronically or post it online, also consider adding	**Create a Dialogue.** *Reconstruct one important conversation you had during the event.* You will probably not remember exactly what was said, but try to re-create the spirit of the interaction. Consider adding speaker tags (see p. 36) to show people's tone of voice, attitude, and gestures.
Reflect on th…		

"Ways In" activities suggest different ways of coming up with material for your essay.

The colors used correspond to the basic features of the genre that were introduced in the chapter's first few pages, which is meant to help you see how in composing in a particular genre, writers use the same basic features but may use them differently to achieve specific purposes for their readers.

Planning and Drafting. To get you started writing a draft of your essay, each Guide to Writing includes suggestions for planning your essay. The section is divided into three parts:

- *Refining Your Purpose and Setting Goals* involves reviewing what you have discovered about your subject, purpose, and audience and helps you think about your goals for the various parts of your essay.
- *Outlining Your Draft* suggests some of the ways you might organize your essay.
- *Drafting* launches you on the writing of your draft, providing both general advice and suggestions about one or two specific sentence strategies that you might find useful for the particular genre.

The Planning and Drafting section also includes a section called Working with Sources, which offers advice (using examples from one or more of the readings) on a particular issue related to incorporating materials from research sources into your essay.

Critical Reading Guide. Once you have finished a draft, you may want to make an effort to have someone else read the draft and comment on how to improve it. Each Guide to Writing includes a Critical Reading Guide, color-coded to correspond to that genre's basic features, which will help you get good advice on improving your draft as well as help you make helpful suggestions to improve others' drafts. (These Guides break out suggestions for both praise and critique — because we all sometimes need reminding that pointing out what works well can be as helpful as pointing out what needs improvement in a piece of writing.)

Critical Reading Guide

● ● ●
Basic Features

For a printable version of this Critical Reading Guide, go to bedfordstmartins .com/theguide.

Your instructor may arrange a peer review session in class or online where you can exchange drafts with your classmates and give each other a thoughtful critical reading, pointing out what works well and suggesting ways to improve the draft. This Critical Reading Guide can also be used productively by a tutor in the writing center or by a roommate or family member. A good critical reading does three things: it lets the writer know how well the reader understands the point of the story, praises what works best, and indicates where the draft could be improved.

1. Assess how well the story is told.

   Praise: Give an example in the story where the storytelling is especially effective — for example, where the speaker tags help make a dialogue dramatic or where specific narrative actions show people in action.

   Critique: Tell the writer where the storytelling could be improved — for example, where the suspense slackens, the story lacks drama, or the chronology is confusing.

2. Consider how vividly people and places are described.

Critical Reading Guides suggest ways of giving constructive criticism, as well as praise, for your classmates' drafts.

Revising. Each Guide to Writing includes a Revising section to help you get an overview of your draft, consider readers' comments, chart a plan for revision, and carry out the revisions.

A new easy-reference chart in the Revising section called "Troubleshooting Your Draft" offers specific advice for problems many students encounter at this critical stage of the writing process.

Following this chart, a section called "Thinking about Document Design" illustrates the ways in which one writer (author of one of the chapter's opening scenarios) used visuals and other elements of document design to make the essay more effective.

Troubleshooting Your Draft

● ● ● Basic Features

	Problem	Suggestions for Revising the Draft
A Well-Told Story	The story starts too slowly.	☐ Shorten the exposition. ☐ Move a bit of dialogue or specific narrative action up front. ☐ Start with something surprising. ☐ Consider beginning with a flashback or flashforward.
	The chronology is confusing.	☐ Add or change time transitions. ☐ Clarify verb tenses.
	The suspense slackens or the story lacks drama.	☐ Add remembered feelings and thoughts to heighten anticipation. ☐ Add dialogue and specific narrative action. ☐ Build rising action in stages with multiple high points. ☐ Move or cut background information and description.
	The conflict is vague or seems unconnected to the significance.	☐ Add dramatized dialogue or specific narrative actions. ☐ Clarify your remembered feelings or thoughts. ☐ Reflect on the conflict from your present perspective.
Vivid Description of People and Places	Places are hard to visualize.	☐ Name objects in the scene. ☐ Add sensory detail. ☐ Try out a comparison to evoke a particular mood. ☐ Consider adding a visual — a photograph or other memorabilia.
	People do not come alive.	☐ Describe a physical feature or mannerism that gives each person individuality. ☐ Add speaker tags to characterize people and show their feelings. ☐ Liven up the dialogue with faster repartee.
	Some descriptions weaken the dominant impression.	☐ Omit extraneous details. ☐ Add a simile or metaphor to strengthen the dominant impression. ☐ Rethink the impression you want your writing to convey and the significance it suggests.

Troubleshooting Your Draft charts offer specific advice for revising your essay.

Editing and Proofreading. Each Guide to Writing ends with a section to help you recognize and fix specific kinds of problems in grammar, punctuation, and sentence structure that are common in essays in that genre of writing.

The Other Parts of the Book

Parts Two through Five provide more help and practice with specific strategies for reading critically, analyzing visuals, designing documents, and many other key aspects of writing and research.

674   CHAPTER 20: ANALYZING VISUALS

created it? Where was it published? What audience is it addressing? What is it trying to get this audience to think and feel about the subject? How does it attempt to achieve this aim?

Let's look, for example, at the following visual text: a public service announcement (PSA) from the World Wildlife Fund (WWF).

The central image in this PSA is a photo of an attractive, smiling young couple. Most of us will immediately recognize the dress, posture, and facial expressions of the young man and woman as those of a newly married couple; the photo-mounting corners make the image seem like a real wedding album photo, as opposed to an ad agency's creation (which would be easier to ignore). After noting these things, however, we are immediately struck by what is wrong with the picture: a hurricane rages in the background, blowing hair, clothing, and the bride's veil forcefully to one side, showering the bride's pure white dress with spots (of rain? mud?), and threatening to rip the bridal bouquet from her hand.

So what do we make of the disruption of the convention (the traditional wedding photo) on which the PSA image is based? In trying to decide, most of us will look next to the text below the image: "Ignoring global warming won't make it go away." The disjunction between the couple's blissful expression and the storm raging around them turns out to be the point of the PSA: like the young couple in the picture, the PSA implies, we are all blithely ignoring the impend-

Ignoring global warming won't make it go away.
worldwildlife.org/globalwarming   WWF

Figure 20.2 "Wedding," from the WWF's 2007 "Beautiful Day U.S." Series

Chapter 20, "Analyzing Visuals," helps you approach visual texts critically and analytically.

Also included are up-to-date guidelines for choosing, using, and documenting different kinds of sources (library sources, the Internet, and your own field research); writing annotated bibliographies and literature reviews; taking essay exams; and assembling a portfolio of your writing.

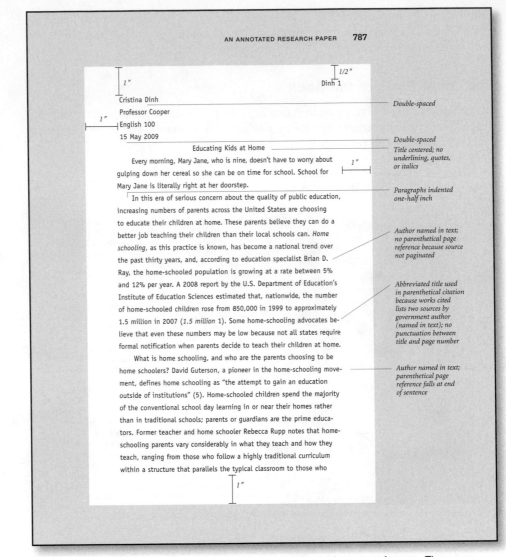

AN ANNOTATED RESEARCH PAPER   **787**

1"   1/2"
Dinh 1

Cristina Dinh   *Double-spaced*

Professor Cooper

1"   English 100

15 May 2009   *Double-spaced*

Educating Kids at Home   *Title centered; no underlining, quotes, or italics*

Every morning, Mary Jane, who is nine, doesn't have to worry about   1"
gulping down her cereal so she can be on time for school. School for
Mary Jane is literally right at her doorstep.   *Paragraphs indented one-half inch*

In this era of serious concern about the quality of public education,
increasing numbers of parents across the United States are choosing
to educate their children at home. These parents believe they can do a
better job teaching their children than their local schools can. *Home*   *Author named in text; no parenthetical page reference because source not paginated*
schooling, as this practice is known, has become a national trend over
the past thirty years, and, according to education specialist Brian D.
Ray, the home-schooled population is growing at a rate between 5%
and 12% per year. A 2008 report by the U.S. Department of Education's   *Abbreviated title used in parenthetical citation because works cited lists two sources by government author (named in text); no punctuation between title and page number*
Institute of Education Sciences estimated that, nationwide, the number
of home-schooled children rose from 850,000 in 1999 to approximately
1.5 million in 2007 (*1.5 million* 1). Some home-schooling advocates believe that even these numbers may be low because not all states require
formal notification when parents decide to teach their children at home.

What is home schooling, and who are the parents choosing to be
home schoolers? David Guterson, a pioneer in the home-schooling move-   *Author named in text; parenthetical page reference falls at end of sentence*
ment, defines home schooling as "the attempt to gain an education
outside of institutions" (5). Home-schooled children spend the majority
of the conventional school day learning in or near their homes rather
than in traditional schools; parents or guardians are the prime educators. Former teacher and home schooler Rebecca Rupp notes that home-
schooling parents vary considerably in what they teach and how they
teach, ranging from those who follow a highly traditional curriculum
within a structure that parallels the typical classroom to those who

1"

Key features of Chapter 24, "Using Sources," are color coded for easy reference. The pages tinted beige contain a sample research paper using MLA format and documentation style.

766 CHAPTER 24: USING SOURCES

The MLA System of Documentation

Citations in Text

A WORK WITH A SINGLE AUTHOR

The MLA author-page system generally requires that in-text citations include the author's last name and the page number of the passage being cited. There is no punctuation between author and page. The parenthetical citation should follow the quoted, paraphrased, or summarized material as closely as possible without disrupting the flow of the sentence.

> Dr. James is described as a "not-too-skeletal Ichabod Crane" (Simon 68).

> One reviewer compares Dr. James to Ichabod Crane (Simon 68).

Note that the parenthetical citation comes before the final period. With block quotations, however, the citation comes after the final period, preceded by a space (see p. 760 for an example). If you mention the author's name in your text, supply just the page reference in parentheses.

> Simon describes Dr. James as a "not-too-skeletal Ichabod Crane" (68).

> Simon compares Dr. James to Ichabod Crane (68).

A WORK WITH MORE THAN ONE AUTHOR

To cite a source by two or three authors, include all the authors' last names; for works with more than three authors, use all the authors' names or just the first author's name

The APA System of Documentation

Citations in Text

AUTHOR INDICATED IN PARENTHESES

The APA author-year system calls for the last name of the author and the year of publication of the original work in the citation. If the cited material is a quotation, you also need to include the page number(s) of the original. If the cited material is not a quotation, the page reference is optional. Use commas to separate author, year, and page in a parenthetical citation. The page number is preceded by *p.* for a single page or *pp.* for a range. Use an ampersand (&) to join the names of multiple authors.

> The conditions in the stockyards were so dangerous that workers "fell into the vats; and when they were fished out, there was never enough of them left to be worth exhibiting" (Sinclair, 2005, p. 134).

> Racial bias does not necessarily diminish through exposure to individuals of other races (Jamison & Tyree, 2001).

To make them easy to find, the pages explaining how to use MLA documentation have a teal stripe down the side. The pages covering APA documentation have a reddish-orange stripe down the side.

Part Six presents three brief chapters that will help you in making oral presentations, consulting and writing with others, and writing in the community.

Finding Your Way around the Book

In a book as large and complex as this one, it can sometimes be hard to tell where you are or to find the information you need on a particular topic in the book. To help you find your way around, look at the information provided at the tops of the pages: in addition to page numbers, you'll find chapter titles on the left-hand pages, and the title of the specific section you're in on the right-hand pages.

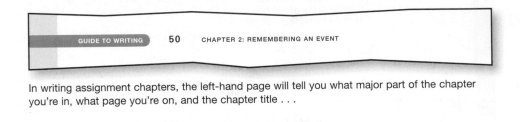

GUIDE TO WRITING   **50**   CHAPTER 2: REMEMBERING AN EVENT

In writing assignment chapters, the left-hand page will tell you what major part of the chapter you're in, what page you're on, and the chapter title . . .

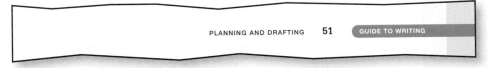

PLANNING AND DRAFTING   **51**   GUIDE TO WRITING

. . . and the right-hand page will tell you the title of the specific section you've opened to.

Also, take advantage of the following color cues used for different sections of the book:

- Guides to Writing in every chapter have yellow-edged pages.
- MLA documentation sections have teal-edged pages.
- APA documentation sections have reddish-orange-edged pages.
- Handbook pages are tinted beige.

To locate information or additional material on particular topics, besides using the table of contents in the front of the book and the index in the back, you can benefit from the cross-references that appear in the margins throughout the book. Some marginal notes refer you to the companion Web site, where related material or electronic versions of material in the book are available.

▶ Coach Kernow told me I ~~ran~~ *had run* faster than ever before.

For practice, go to bedfordstmartins.com/theguide/exercisecentral and click on The Past Perfect and/or A Common ESL Problem: Forming the Past Perfect.

ESL Note: It is important to remember that the past perfect is formed with *had* followed by a past participle. Past participles usually end in *-ed*, *-d*, *-en*, *-n*, or *-t*: *worked, hoped, eaten, taken, bent.*

▶ Before Tania went to Moscow last year, she had not really ~~speak~~ *spoken* Russian.

Marginal annotations refer to other parts of the book and to helpful online resources.

The Handbook

The Handbook offers a complete reference guide to grammar, word choice, punctuation, capitalization, use of numbers and abbreviations, spelling, ESL troublespots, sentence structure, and words that are frequently misused. We have designed the Handbook so that you can find the answers you need quickly, and we have provided examples from a nationwide study we did of college students' writing. The examples appear in regular black type, with the corrections in blue in a different font. The grammatical and other specialized terms that are used in the Handbook are all highlighted in white boxes in the text and defined in white boxes in the margins, so that you never have to look elsewhere in the book to understand the explanation. In addition to a section on ESL problems, blue boxes throughout the rest of the Handbook offer specific support for ESL students.

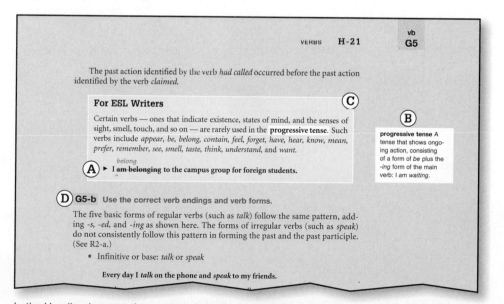

In the Handbook, corrections appear in blue type (A); white boxes in the text highlight terms that are defined in the margins (B); blue boxes offer ESL support (C); and codes for different sections offer a convenient shorthand for you and your instructor (D).

Brief Contents

Contents

● ● ● ● **PART 5** Writing for Assessment

● ● ● ● **PART 6** Writing and Speaking to Wider Audiences

GL GLOSSARY OF FREQUENTLY MISUSED
WORDS   H-132

Introduction: Thinking about Writing

Philosopher Edmund Burke once said that "reading without reflecting is like eating without digesting." We believe that what Burke said about reading applies to writing as well, and that reflecting on writing is one of the best ways to become a better and more versatile writer. That is why quotes from writers are sprinkled throughout this chapter. That is also why in this chapter and throughout this book, we ask you to write brief reflections, ultimately constructing a **literacy narrative**, a multifaceted story about yourself as a writer.

Reflection 1. A Literacy Story

Take five to ten minutes to write a story of your experience with writing. Consider the following suggestions, but do not be limited by them:

- Recall an early experience of writing: What did you write? Did anyone read it? What kind of feedback did you get? How did you feel about yourself?
- Think of a turning point when your attitude toward writing changed or crystallized. What happened? What changed?
- Recall a person — a teacher, classmate, family member, published writer, or someone else — who influenced your writing, for good or ill. How was your writing affected?
- Cast yourself as the main character of a story about writing. How would you describe yourself — as a "natural" writer; as someone who struggles to write well; or somewhere in between? Consider your trajectory or "narrative arc": Over the years, would you say you have showed steady improvement; ups and downs; more downs than ups; a decline?

Why Writing Is Important

Writing helps you think and learn, enhances your chances of success, contributes to your personal development, and strengthens your relationships with other people.

Writing Influences the Way You Think

The very act of writing encourages you to be creative as well as organized and logical in your thinking. When you write sentences, paragraphs, and whole essays, you generate ideas and connect these ideas in systematic ways. By combining words into phrases and sentences with conjunctions, you create complex new ideas: for example, *and* brings out similarities, *but* emphasizes differences, and *because* supports general ideas with specific reasons, facts, and examples.

By writing essays for different purposes as you work through *The St. Martin's Guide*, you will develop your thinking in different ways. For example, writing about a remembered event will inspire you to reflect on what happened and why it is memorable; finding common ground will deepen your ability to analyze and synthesize different points of view; arguing for a position on a controversial issue will hone your reasoning skills; and making evaluations will help you examine underlying assumptions about what you value and why.

> The mere process of writing is one of the most powerful tools we have for clarifying our own thinking. I am never as clear about any matter as when I have just finished writing about it.
> — JAMES VAN ALLEN

Writing Helps You Learn

Writing contributes to learning by helping you remember what you are studying, by leading you to analyze and connect information and ideas from different sources, and by inspiring new insights and understanding. Writing as you read — taking notes, annotating the text, and responding in writing to the text's assumptions and arguments — makes you a better reader. Reflecting in writing on what you are learning consolidates your understanding of and response to new material.

Different kinds of writing contribute to learning in different ways. Writing essays of various kinds, or **genres**, as you work through *The Guide* will help you organize and present what you have learned and, in the process, clarify and extend your own ideas. Arguing a position teaches you not only to support your reasons but also to refute objections to your argument. Researching a profile, you learn to make precise observations and ask pertinent questions. Explaining a concept requires you to inform yourself about your subject and organize the information in a way that makes it clear to readers.

> Writing has been for a long time my major tool for self-instruction and self-development.
> — TONI CADE BAMBARA

Writing Fosters Personal Development

In addition to influencing the ways you think and learn, writing can help you grow as an individual. Writing leads you to reflect on your experience, for example, when you write to understand the significance of a particular life event. Writing about a controversial issue can make you examine some of your most basic beliefs. Writing an evaluation requires that you think about what you value and how your values compare to those of others. Perhaps most important, becoming an author confers authority on you; it gives you confidence to assert your own ideas and feelings.

> In a very real sense, the writer writes in order to teach himself, to understand himself, to satisfy himself. . . .
> — ALFRED KAZIN

> Some of the things that happen to us in life seem to have no meaning, but when you write them down, you find the meanings for them. . . .
> — MAXINE HONG KINGSTON

Writing Connects You to Others

Nearly all of us use writing in one form or another — whether via e-mail, text messaging, instant messaging, blogging, Twitter, or Facebook — to keep in touch with friends and family. Many of us also use writing to take part in academic discussions and participate in civic debate and decision making. By writing about our experiences, ideas, and observations, we reach out to readers, offering them our own points of view and inviting them to share theirs in return.

The writing you do for your composition class will likewise help you connect with others. In writing an argument, for example, as you clarify your perspective and reexamine your own reasoning, you may ultimately influence other people's opinions on your topic. Their responses to your writing may, in turn, cause you to reevaluate your own ideas. Collaborative writing — as, for example, if you are assigned to write a proposal with a group of classmates — enables you to work directly with others to invent new ways of solving complex problems.

> Writing is the act of saying I, of imposing oneself upon other people, of saying listen to me, see it my way, change your mind.
> — JOAN DIDION

> It's the sense of being in contact with people who are part of a particular audience that really makes a difference to me in writing.
> — SHERLEY ANNE WILLIAMS

Writing Promotes Success in College and at Work

As a student, you are probably aware of the many ways writing can contribute to your success in school. Students who learn to write for different readers and purposes do well in courses throughout the curriculum. Eventually, you will need to use writing to advance your career by writing persuasive application letters for jobs or graduate school admission. At work, you will be expected to write effective e-mail messages, memos, and reports that present clear explanations, well-reasoned arguments, convincing evaluations, and constructive proposals.

> People think it's sort of funny that I went to graduate school as a biologist and then became a writer. . . . What I learned [in science] is how to formulate or identify a new question that hasn't been asked before and then to set about solving it, to do original research to find the way to an answer. And that's what I do when I write a book.   — BARBARA KINGSOLVER

Reflection 2. Writing That Mattered

Write a page or two describing an occasion when writing helped you accomplish something. Here are some possibilities to consider:

- an occasion when you used writing to prepare for a test or otherwise help you remember critical material
- an occasion when writing helped you better understand a difficult subject or reading
- an occasion when you worked through a personal or an intellectual problem by writing
- an occasion when you used writing to influence someone else
- an occasion when writing enabled you to express your feelings or made you feel connected
- an occasion when your writing helped you get a better grade or succeed in some way
- an occasion when your writing made others take notice

How Writing Is Learned

There are many myths about writing and writers. For example, some people assume that people who are good at writing do not have to spend a lot of time learning to write — that they just naturally know how. Others assume that "real" writers write perfectly the first time, every time, dashing off an essay with minimal effort. Writers' testimonies, however, together with extensive research on how people write and learn to write, show that writing can — indeed, must — be learned. All writers work at their writing. Some writers may be more successful and influential than others. Some may find writing easier and more satisfying than others. But no one is born knowing how to write.

> Learning to write well takes time and much effort, but it can be done.
> — MARGARET MEAD

> It's none of their business that you have to learn to write. Let them think you were born that way.
> — ERNEST HEMINGWAY

Reflection 3. How You Became Literate

Write a page or two describing how and why you became literate and what happened as a result. You may choose to write about your early memories of learning to read and write either at home or at school. Or you could think of literacy more broadly, focusing, for example, on one or more of the following:

- computer literacy — learning how to program, how to "read" the Web efficiently, or how to communicate through text messaging, blogging, and so on
- workplace literacy, perhaps including ways of talking to customers, colleagues, and managers
- academic literacy, perhaps focusing on learning to think, talk, and write as a scientist, historian, literary critic, and so on
- sports literacy, as a player, coach, or fan
- music literacy, as a musician or as a fan of certain kinds of music
- community literacy — learning to communicate with people of different ages or with people who speak different languages or dialects

In reflecting on the results of your learning to be literate, you might want to consider the following:

- how your new literacy changed you or changed your relationships
- ways in which you may have had more power in certain contexts — and perhaps less power in others
- how you felt about being bilingual or multiliterate, and how you used your new literacy

The St. Martin's Guide to Writing has helped many students become more thoughtful, effective, confident writers. From reading and analyzing an array of different kinds of essays, you will learn how other writers make their texts work. From writing for different audiences, you will learn to compose texts that readers want to read. To help you take full advantage of what you are learning, *The Guide* will also help you reflect on your learning so that you will be able to remember, apply, and build on what you have learned.

> If you want to be a writer, you must do two things above all others: read a lot and write a lot. There's no way around these two things that I'm aware of, no shortcut.
> — STEPHEN KING

Learning to Write by Reading

Believe it: Reading will help you become a better writer. In fact, most professional writers are avid readers who read not only for enjoyment and information but also to refine their craft.

Reading to Understand How Texts Work

Readers will have specific expectations of a text as soon as they recognize it as a particular genre or type of writing. For example, readers of a story about a past event in the writer's life will likely recognize it as a form of autobiography, which leads them to expect a story that changes, challenges, or complicates the writer's sense of self or connection with others. If the event seems trivial or the story lacks interest, then readers' expectations will be disappointed, and the text will not succeed. Similarly, if the text takes a position on a controversial issue, readers will recognize it as an opinion piece and expect it to not only assert and support that position, but also to refute possible objections. If the argument lacks credible support or ignores thoughtful objections or alternative points of view, readers are likely to decide that the essay is not convincing.

Although individual texts within the same genre vary a great deal — no two proposals, even those arguing for the same solution, will be identical — they nonetheless follow a general pattern that provides a certain amount of predictability without which communication would be difficult, if not impossible. But these language patterns, also called **conventions**, should not be thought of as rigid formulas. Conventions are broad frameworks within which writers are free to be creative. Most writers, in fact, find that working within a framework allows them to be more creative, not less so.

> You would learn very little in this world if you were not allowed to imitate. And to repeat your imitations until some solid grounding . . . was achieved and the slight but wonderful difference — that made you and no one else — could assert itself.
>
> — MARY OLIVER

Reading to Write Texts That Work

To learn the conventions of a particular genre, you need to read examples of that genre so that you begin to recognize its predictable patterns as well as the possibilities for innovation. At the same time, you should also practice writing in the genre.

> Read, read, read. . . . Just like a carpenter who works as an apprentice and studies the master. Read!
>
> — WILLIAM FAULKNER

The Guide provides an array of sample essays in the genres you are learning to write and helps you analyze patterns in these essays. It also helps you practice using these patterns in your own writing to achieve your own purposes. Seeing, for example, how writers define key terms and integrate quotations from their sources in an essay explaining a concept introduces you to strategies you may use when you write in this genre.

> I practiced writing in every possible way that I could. I wrote a pastiche of other people. Just as a pianist runs his scales for ten years before he gives his concert: because when he gives that concert, he can't be thinking of his fingering or of his hands, he has to be thinking of his interpretation. He's thinking of what he's trying to communicate.
>
> — KATHERINE ANNE PORTER

> I went back to the good nature books that I had read. And I analyzed them. I wrote outlines of whole books — outlines of chapters — so that

I could see their structure. And I copied down their transitional sentences or their main sentences or their closing sentences or their
lead sentences.
— Annie Dillard

Reading to Design Texts That Work

Writers have long recognized that no matter how well organized, well reasoned, or compelling a piece of writing may be, the way it looks on the page influences to some extent how well it works for readers. Today, writers have more options for designing their documents than ever before. Digital photography, scanning, and integrated word processing and graphics programs make it relatively easy for writers to heighten the visual impact of the page. For example, they can change type fonts and add colors, charts, diagrams, and photographs to written documents. In constructing Web pages or DVDs, writers can add sound, video, and active hyperlinks.

These multiple possibilities, however, do not guarantee a more effective document. In order to design effective texts, writers need to study documents that capture readers' attention and enhance understanding. As someone who has likely grown up watching television and movies, playing computer games, and surfing the Internet, you are already a sophisticated visual consumer who has unconsciously learned many of the conventions of document design for different genres and writing situations. This book will help you become aware of what you already know and help you make new discoveries about document design that you may be able to use in your own writing.

Design is a funny word. Some people think design means how it looks.
But of course, if you dig deeper, it's really how it works. — Steve Jobs

---

Reflection 4. Your Experience with Different Genres of Writing

Make two lists: one of the genres you have *read* — for example, Tweets from your friends; music reviews on iTunes — and another of genres you have *written* — for example, e-mails to your parents; job applications; or a paper for your American history class. Try to come up with at least five entries for each list. Include reading and writing you have done in school, at work, at home, and at play.

Genres You Have Read	Genres You Have Written
1.	1.
2.	2.
3.	3.
4.	4.
5.	5.
6.	6.
7.	7.

Learning Writing Strategies

It might sound strange, but it's true: One of the best ways to become a better writer is by writing. Practice will make your writing more thoughtful and productive. By offering guidance and support as you practice, *The Guide* will help you develop a richer and more flexible repertoire of writing strategies to meet the demands of different writing situations.

Strategies for Getting Started

We all know what it's like to stare at a blank computer screen or stark white page of paper waiting for inspiration. As a student, however, you're in the position of all those who write under deadlines — you can't simply sit back and wait for inspiration. Instead, you need an array of reliable thinking and writing strategies that you can use not only to write the paper by the due date, but also to help you write it analytically, critically, and creatively.

Invention is the word used since the time of Plato and Aristotle to describe the process of thinking as we compose. Invention includes deciding on your purpose in writing to a particular audience and figuring out how best to achieve your purpose; analyzing and questioning other people's ideas as well as your own; assimilating information from different sources; and organizing it logically.

As writers we cannot choose *whether* to invent; we can only choose *how* to invent. *The Guide* offers many invention strategies from which to choose, strategies that will help you meet the demands of each kind of writing you attempt.

> Inspiration usually comes during work, rather than before it.
> — MADELEINE L'ENGLE

Strategies for Discovering New Ideas

Few writers begin writing with a complete understanding of a subject. Most use writing as a means of **discovery** — that is, as a way to learn about the subject, trying out ideas and information they have collected, exploring connections and implications, and reviewing what they have written in order to expand and develop their ideas.

> When I start a project, the first thing I do is write down, in longhand, everything I know about the subject, every thought I've ever had on it. This may be twelve or fourteen pages. Then I read it through, for quite a few days . . . then I try to find out what are the salient points that I must make. And then it begins to take shape.
> — MAYA ANGELOU

Writing, then, is not something you do after thinking, but in order to help you think. Writers often reflect on this so-called **generative** aspect of writing, echoing E. M. Forster's much repeated adage: "How do I know what I think until I see what I say?" Here are some other versions of the same insight:

> Every book that I have written has been an education, a process of discovery.
> — AMITAV GHOSH

> I don't see writing as a communication of something already discovered, as "truths" already known. Rather, I see writing as a job of experiment. It's like any discovery job; you don't know what's going to happen until you try it.
> — WILLIAM STAFFORD

> Don't tear up the page and start over again when you write a bad line — try to write your way out of it. Make mistakes and plunge on. . . . Writing is a means of discovery, always.
> — GARRISON KEILLOR

Writers obviously do not give birth to a text as a whole, but must work cumulatively, focusing first on one thing, then on another. Writing therefore may seem to progress in a linear, step-by-step fashion. But in fact it almost always proceeds **recursively**, which means that writers return over and over again to ideas that they are trying to clarify or extend, or to gaps in their information or logic that they are trying to fill. Most writers plan and then revise their plans, draft and revise their drafts, write and read what they have written, and then write and revise some more. In this way, the experience of writing is less like marching in a straight line from first sentence to last and more like exploring an uphill trail with frequent switchbacks. It may appear that you are retracing old ground, but you are really rising to new levels as you learn the terrain.

> It's a matter of piling a little piece here and a little piece there, fitting them together, going on to the next part, then going back and gradually shaping the whole piece into something.
> — DAVE BARRY

Strategies for Organizing Your Ideas

Writers need strategies that make writing systematic but do not stifle inventiveness. For this reason, most writers begin drafting with some type of plan — a list, a scratch outline, or a detailed storyboard like that used by filmmakers. Outlines can be very helpful, but they must be tentative and flexible if writers are to benefit from writing's natural recursiveness.

> I began [*Invisible Man*] with a chart of the three-part division. It was a conceptual frame with most of the ideas and some of the incidents indicated.
> — RALPH ELLISON

> You are always going back and forth between the outline and the writing, bringing them closer together, or just throwing out the outline and making a new one.
> — ANNIE DILLARD

Strategies for Drafting and Revising

While composing a draft, writers benefit from frequent pauses to reread what they have written. Rereading often leads to further discovery — adding an example, choosing different words that unpack or separate ideas, filling in a gap in the logic of an argument. In addition, rereading frequently leads to substantial rethinking and revising: cutting, reorganizing, rewriting whole sections to make the writing more effective.

> You have to work problems out for yourself on paper. Put the stuff down and read it — to see if it works.   — JOYCE CARY

> As a writer, I would find out most clearly what I thought, and what I only thought I thought, when I saw it written down.   — ANNA QUINDLEN

Rereading your own writing in order to improve it can be difficult, though, because it is hard to see what the draft actually says, as opposed to what you were trying to say. For this reason, most writers also give their drafts to others to read. Students generally seek advice from their teachers and other students in the class because they understand the assignment. Published writers also share their work in progress with others. Poets, novelists, historians, scientists, newspaper reporters, magazine essayists, and even textbook writers actively seek constructive critical comments by joining writers' workshops or getting help from editors.

> I was lucky because I was always going to groups where the writers were at the same level or a little better than me. That really helped.
> — MANIL SURI

> [Ezra Pound] was a marvelous critic because he didn't try to turn you into an imitation of himself. He tried to see what you were trying to do.
> — T. S. ELIOT

Using the Guides to Writing

As you have seen, students learning to write need to be flexible and yet systematic. The Guides to Writing in Part One of this book are designed to meet this need. The first few times you write in a new genre, you can rely on these guides. They provide scaffolding to support your work until you become more familiar with the demands and possibilities of each genre. The Guides will help you develop a repertoire of strategies for creatively solving problems in your writing, such as deciding how to interest readers, how to refute opposing arguments, what to quote from a source, and how to integrate quotations into your writing.

When people engage in any new and complex activity — driving, playing an instrument, skiing, or writing — they may divide it into a series of manageable tasks. In learning to play tennis, for example, you might concentrate separately on lobbing, volleying, or serving, before putting your skills together in a game. Similarly, in writing an argument on a controversial issue, you can focus at first on separate tasks such as defining the issue, developing your reasons, and anticipating readers' objections. Dividing your writing in this way enables you to tackle a complex subject without either oversimplifying it or becoming overwhelmed.

Here is a writer's quotation that has been especially helpful for us as we have written and revised *The St. Martin's Guide to Writing*:

> You know when you think about writing a book, you think it is overwhelming. But, actually, you break it down into tiny little tasks any moron could do.
>
> — ANNIE DILLARD

Reflection 5. Your Last Writing Project

Write a couple of pages describing how you went about writing the last time you wrote an essay (or something else) that took time and effort. Use the following questions to help you recall what you did, but feel free to write about any other aspects of your writing that you think are important.

- What did you write, and when?
- Who were you writing for, and why were you writing? What did you hope to accomplish?
- What technologies did you use (a computer? a pen?), and how do you think using these technologies affected the way you wrote?
- What kinds of planning did you do, if any, before you began writing the first draft?
- If you discussed your ideas and plans with someone, how did discussing them help you? If you had someone read your draft, how did getting a response help?
- If you rewrote, moved, added, or cut anything in your first draft, describe what you changed.
- Did you write pretty much the way you usually do or did you do something differently? If you did it differently, why did you make the change?
- Were you satisfied with your writing process and with the final draft that resulted? What would you have changed if you had more time or knew what you know now?

Thinking Critically

As we said at the beginning, reflecting on your literacy experiences helps you become a better, more versatile writer. Reflecting makes you aware of what you already know and what you still need to learn. Reflecting enhances **metacognition,** which is a scholarly word for awareness of your own thinking processes.

As young children, we learn to use language primarily from hearing others talk and from being talked to. Learning language seems magical because we are not conscious of being taught. But we learn because others are modeling language use for us all the time, and sometimes they even correct our pronunciation, word choice, and grammar.

We learn the most common types of communicating such as storytelling in the same way. We listen to others tell stories and read to us; we watch stories portrayed on television, in film, and in video games; and eventually we read stories for ourselves. Being immersed in storytelling, we learn conventional ways of beginning and ending, strategies for building suspense, techniques for making time sequences clear, methods for using dialogue to develop character, and so on. As we get older, we can reinforce and increase our repertoire of storytelling strategies by analyzing stories and by consciously trying the strategies in our own oral and written stories. This is true of all literacy learning. We learn from a combination of modeling, immersion, and thinking critically about what we are learning.

In addition to modeling good writing and guiding you in writing on your own, *The St. Martin's Guide to Writing* helps you think critically about your writing. Each writing assignment chapter in Part One of the *Guide* includes many opportunities for you to think critically and reflect on your understanding of the **rhetorical situation** — the context, composed of genre, purpose, and audience — in which you are writing. In addition, a section titled Thinking Critically about What You Have Learned concludes each chapter, giving you an opportunity to look back and reflect on how you used your writing process creatively and how you expanded your understanding of the genre.

Reflection 6. Your Literacy Experience, through Metaphor and Simile

Write two or three **similes** (comparisons using *like* or *as*) or **metaphors** (implied comparisons, not using *like* or *as*) that express some aspect of your literacy experience. Then write a page or so explaining and expanding on the ideas and feelings you expressed in one or more of them. Here are some examples from professional writers:

> Writing is like exploring . . . as an explorer makes maps of the country he has explored, so a writer's works are maps of the country he has explored.
>
> — Lawrence Osgood

> The writer must soak up the subject completely, as a plant soaks up water, until the ideas are ready to sprout.
>
> — Marguerite Yourcenar

> Writing is manual labor of the mind: a job, like laying pipe.
>
> — John Gregory Dunne

> If we had to say what writing is, we would define it essentially as an act of courage.
>
> — Cynthia Ozick

To get at the meanings in your metaphors and similes, it may help also to write ones that express opposite ideas. For example, if you begin with "writing is like building a house," you could also try "writing is taking things apart, brick by brick" to get at both the constructive and analytical aspects of the process. Or you could try "writing is walking into a new house" to move from the work involved in composing to the discovery of something new.

PART 1

Writing Activities

2

Remembering an Event

IN COLLEGE COURSES In a linguistics course, students are assigned a paper in which they are to discuss published research in the context of their own experience. The class had recently read Deborah Tannen's *Gender and Discourse,* in which Tannen discusses differences in how men and women talk about problems: according to Tannen, women tend to spend a lot of time talking about the problem and their feelings about it, while men typically cut short the analysis of the problem and focus on solutions.

One student decides to write about Tannen's findings in light of a conversation she recently had with her brother about their father's drinking. Before writing, she rereads a diary entry she had written shortly after the conversation, which she found frustrating. She begins her essay by reconstructing the conversation, quoting some dialogue from her diary and paraphrasing other parts from memory. Then she analyzes the conversation, using Tannen's categories. She discovers that what bothered her about the conversation was less its content than her brother's way of communicating.

IN THE COMMUNITY As part of a local history series in a newspaper serving a small western ranching community, an amateur historian volunteers to help an elderly rancher write about the winter of 1938, when a six-foot snowstorm isolated the rancher's family for nearly a month. The historian tapes the rancher talking about how he, his wife, and his infant son survived, including an account of how he snowshoed eight miles to a logging train track in order to get a message to relatives. On a second visit, the historian and the rancher listen to the tape recording and brainstorm on further details to make the event more complete and dramatic for readers.

The historian writes a rough outline, which he and the rancher discuss, and then a draft, which the rancher reads and elaborates on. The rancher also offers several photos for possible inclusion. The historian revises and edits the story and submits it, along with two photos, to the project's editor for publication. (For more information on the layout of the published version, turn to Thinking about Document Design, p. 55).

IN THE WORKPLACE A respected longtime regional manager for a state's highway department has been asked to give the keynote speech at a meeting on workplace safety. The manager has long considered employee relations of paramount importance in keeping the workplace safe, so he decides to open his speech by recounting his recent dramatic confrontation with an unhappy employee who complained bitterly about the work schedule he had been given and threatened to harm the manager and his family if the manager did not give him a better schedule.

The manager reflects on his fear and on his frustration over not knowing how to handle the confrontation: the department's published procedures on workplace safety offered no specific advice on such a situation. Finally, the manager summarizes data he compiled on the nature and frequency of such workplace incidents nationwide and concludes by calling for new guidelines on how to handle them.

People write about their experiences in various contexts, for different purposes and audiences. For example, you may keep a private diary, a Facebook page for friends, or a public blog where you write about important events in your life. The scenarios opening this chapter show people from different walks of life reflecting on events that have significance not only for them personally, but for their readers as well. For local history buffs, stories like the rancher's reveal some the challenges of living in an earlier era. The manager uses what was undoubtedly a disturbing experience to convince colleagues that workplace safety procedures need to be revamped. The student turns an assignment into an opportunity to make sense of a family conflict. If you wrote about your personal experience in your college application, you may have tried to impress admissions officers with remembered events that show you at your best.

Not only can writing about your experiences serve different purposes, but immersing yourself in the sights, sounds, and sensations of memory can be pleasurable in itself. Even when the memories arouse mixed feelings, reflecting on the events and people important in your life can be deeply satisfying. Writing can help you understand and come to terms with the influences in your family and community that have helped shape who you are and what's important to you.

Similarly, reading about other people's experiences can be entertaining as well as challenging. As readers, we often take pleasure in seeing reflections of our own experience in other people's stories, but encountering unfamiliar experiences can also be fascinating and lead us to question some of the ways we have learned to think about ourselves and others. For example, one of the writers in this chapter remembers that when she was arrested for shoplifting she felt excited, as if she were acting in a movie. Another writer makes the eye-opening discovery that her father's cultural traditions are not her own.

From readings like these, you will learn how to make your own story interesting, even exciting to read. The Guide to Writing will support you as you compose your remembered event essay, showing you ways to use the basic features of the genre to tell your story vividly and dramatically, entertaining readers but also giving them insight into the event's significance — its meaning and importance — in your life.

A Collaborative Activity:
Practice Remembering an Event

Part 1. Take turns telling a story about an important event in your life. Each story should take just a few minutes to tell. Prepare by choosing an event you feel comfortable describing in this situation, and quickly plan how you will describe it. Then get together with two or three other students, and take turns telling your stories.

Part 2. Discuss what happened when you told about a remembered event:

- To think about your purpose and audience, see whether the students in your group understand why the event is important to you. What in your story, if anything, helped them identify with you?

- Compare your thoughts with the others in your group on what was easiest and hardest about telling the story: for example, making the story dramatic; balancing your account of what happened with your feelings and thoughts about it; deciding how much to tell about the people involved.

Reading Remembered Event Essays

Basic Features

As you read remembered event essays in this chapter, you will see how different authors incorporate the basic features of the genre.

● A Well-Told Story

Read first to enjoy the story. Remembered event essays are autobiographical stories that recount an important event in the writer's life; the best ones are first and foremost a pleasure to read. A well-told story

- arouses curiosity and suspense by structuring the narrative around conflict, building to a climax, and leading to a change or discovery of some kind;
- is set in a specific time and place, often using dialogue to heighten immediacy and drama;
- lets readers into the narrator's point of view (written in the first person *I*) and enables readers to empathize and possibly identify with the writer.

● Vivid Description of People and Places

Read for the author's description of people and places. In the essays in this chapter, notice

- the specific details describing what people look like, how they dress, gesture, and talk;
- the sensory images showing what the narrator saw, heard, smelled, touched, and tasted.

● Autobiographical Significance

Read also to understand the story's autobiographical significance. This is the point the writer is trying to make — the purpose for writing to a particular audience. Effective writers both tell and show

- by remembering feelings and thoughts from the time the event took place;
- by reflecting on the past from the present perspective;
- by choosing details and words that create a dominant impression.

Purpose and Audience

Whatever the writing situation, writers usually have various purposes in mind, including both self-discovery and self-presentation. Keep in mind, however, that the remembered event essay is a public genre meant to be read by others. Sometimes the audience is specific, as in a personal essay composed for a college or job application. Often, however, the audience is more general, as in an academic essay written in a college course to be read by the instructor and fellow students.

*As you read remembered event essays, ask yourself what seems to be the writer's **purpose** in writing about this particular experience.* For example, does the writer seem to be writing

- to understand what happened and why, perhaps to confront unconscious and possibly uncomplimentary motives;
- to relive an intense experience, perhaps to work though complex and ambivalent feelings;
- to win over readers, perhaps to justify or rationalize choices made, actions taken, words used?

You should be aware that as an insightful reader, you may be able to see larger themes or deeper implications — what we call **significance** — beyond those the writer consciously intends or even acknowledges.

*As you read, also try to grasp the writer's assumptions about the **audience.*** For example, does the writer

- expect readers to be impressed by the writer's courage, honesty, ability, and so on;
- assume readers will have had similar experiences and therefore appreciate what the writer went through and not judge the writer too harshly;
- try to convince the reader that the writer was innocent, well intended, a victim, or something else;
- hope readers will laugh with and not at the writer, seeing the writer's failings as amusing foibles and not serious shortcomings?

Readings

JEAN BRANDT wrote this essay as a first-year college student. In it, she tells about a memorable event that occurred when she was thirteen. Reflecting on how she felt at the time, Brandt writes, "I was afraid, embarrassed, worried, mad." In disclosing her tumultuous and contradictory remembered feelings, Brandt makes her story dramatic and resonant. Even if readers have not had a similar experience, they are likely to empathize with Brandt and grasp the significance of this event in her life.

As you read, look for places where Brandt lets us know how she felt at the time the event occurred. Also consider the questions in the margin. Your instructor may ask you to post your answers or bring them to class.

Calling Home
Jean Brandt

1   As we all piled into the car, I knew it was going to be a fabulous day. My grandmother was visiting for the holidays; and she and I, along with my older brother and sister, Louis and Susan, were setting off for a day of last-minute Christmas shopping. On the way to the mall, we sang Christmas carols, chattered, and laughed. With Christmas only two days away, we were caught up with holiday spirit. I felt light-headed and full of joy. I loved shopping — especially at Christmas.

2   The shopping center was swarming with frantic last-minute shoppers like ourselves. We went first to the General Store, my favorite. It carried mostly knickknacks and other useless items which nobody needs but buys anyway. I was thirteen years old at the time, and things like buttons and calendars and posters would catch my fancy. This day was no different. The object of my desire was a 75-cent Snoopy button. Snoopy was the latest. If you owned anything with the Peanuts on it, you were "in." But since I was supposed to be shopping for gifts for other people and not myself, I couldn't decide what to do. I went in search of my sister for her opinion. I pushed my way through throngs of people to the back of the store where I found Susan. I asked her if she thought I should buy the button. She said it was cute and if I wanted it to go ahead and buy it.

3   When I got back to the Snoopy section, I took one look at the lines at the cashiers and knew I didn't want to wait thirty minutes to buy an item worth less than one dollar. I walked back to the basket where I found the button and was about to drop it when suddenly, instead, I took a quick glance around, assured myself no one could see, and slipped the button into the pocket of my sweatshirt.

4   I hesitated for a moment, but once the item was in my pocket, there was no turning back. I had never before stolen anything; but what was done was done. A few seconds later, my sister appeared and asked, "So, did you decide to buy the button?" "No, I guess not." I hoped my voice didn't quaver. As we headed for the

● ● ●
Basic Features
• Well-told story
• Vivid description
• Significance

How does Brandt set the stage for her story? How does she try to get you to identify with her?

What additional descriptive detail would help you visualize the place and people?

What is your first impression of Brandt? What is the author's attitude toward her younger self?

What is the effect of all these action verbs (highlighted) in pars. 3–5?

entrance, my heart began to race. I just had to get out of that store. Only a few more yards to go and I'd be safe. As we crossed the threshold, I heaved a sigh of relief. I was home free. I thought about how sly I had been and I felt proud of my accomplishment.

An unexpected tap on my shoulder startled me. I whirled around to find a middle-aged man, dressed in street clothes, flashing some type of badge and politely asking me to empty my pockets. Where did this man come from? How did he know? I was so sure that no one had seen me! On the verge of panicking, I told myself that all I had to do was give this man his button back, say I was sorry, and go on my way. After all, it was only a 75-cent item.

Next thing I knew, he was talking about calling the police and having me arrested and thrown in jail, as if he had just nabbed a professional thief instead of a terrified kid. I couldn't believe what he was saying.

"Jean, what's going on?"

The sound of my sister's voice eased the pressure a bit. She always managed to get me out of trouble. She would come through this time too.

"Excuse me. Are you a relative of this young girl?"

"Yes, I'm her sister. What's the problem?"

"Well, I just caught her shoplifting and I'm afraid I'll have to call the police."

"What did she take?"

"This button."

"A button? You are having a thirteen-year-old arrested for stealing a button?"

"I'm sorry, but she broke the law."

The man led us through the store and into an office, where we waited for the police officers to arrive. Susan had found my grandmother and brother, who, still shocked, didn't say a word. The thought of going to jail terrified me, not because of jail itself, but because of the encounter with my parents afterward. Not more than ten minutes later, two officers arrived and placed me under arrest. They said that I was to be taken to the station alone. Then, they handcuffed me and led me out of the store. I felt alone and scared. I had counted on my sister being with me, but now I had to muster up the courage to face this ordeal all by myself.

As the officers led me through the mall, I sensed a hundred pairs of eyes staring at me. My face flushed and I broke out in a sweat. Now everyone knew I was a criminal. In their eyes I was a juvenile delinquent, and thank God the cops were getting me off the streets. The worst part was thinking my grandmother might be having the same

5

6

7

8

9

10

11

12

13

14

15

16

17

What do you learn about Brandt from her remembered thoughts in pars. 5–8?

How does your understanding of Brandt deepen or change through what she writes in pars. 16–18?

thoughts. The humiliation at that moment was overwhelming. I felt like Hester Prynne being put on public display for everyone to ridicule.

18   That short walk through the mall seemed to take hours. But once we reached the squad car, time raced by. I was read my rights and questioned. We were at the police station within minutes. Everything happened so fast I didn't have a chance to feel remorse for my crime. Instead, I viewed what was happening to me as if it were a movie. Being searched, although embarrassing, somehow seemed to be exciting. All the movies and television programs I had seen were actually coming to life. This is what it was really like. But why were criminals always portrayed as frightened and regretful? I was having fun. I thought I had nothing to fear — until I was allowed my one phone call. I was trembling as I dialed home. I didn't know what I was going to say to my parents, especially my mother.

19   "Hi, Dad, this is Jean."

20   "We've been waiting for you to call."

21   "Did Susie tell you what happened?"

22   "Yeah, but we haven't told your mother. I think you should tell her what you did and where you are."

23   "You mean she doesn't even know where I am?"

24   "No, I want you to explain it to her."

How does the dialogue in pars. 21–24 add to the drama?

25   There was a pause as he called my mother to the phone. For the first time that night, I was close to tears. I wished I had never stolen that stupid pin. I wanted to give the phone to one of the officers because I was too ashamed to tell my mother the truth, but I had no choice.

26   "Jean, where are you?"

27   "I'm, umm, in jail."

28   "Why? What for?"

29   "Shoplifting."

30   "Oh no, Jean. Why? Why did you do it?"

31   "I don't know. No reason. I just did it."

32   "I don't understand. What did you take? Why did you do it? You had plenty of money with you."

33   "I know but I just did it. I can't explain why. Mom, I'm sorry."

34   "I'm afraid sorry isn't enough. I'm horribly disappointed in you."

35   Long after we got off the phone, while I sat in an empty jail cell, waiting for my parents to pick me up, I could still distinctly hear the disappointment and hurt in my

What is the effect of interweaving storytelling and describing with remembering thoughts and feelings in par. 35?

mother's voice. I cried. The tears weren't for me but for her and the pain I had put her through. I felt like a terrible human being. I would rather have stayed in jail than confront my mom right then. I dreaded each passing minute that brought our encounter closer. When the officer came to release me, I hesitated, actually not wanting to leave. We went to the front desk, where I had to sign a form to retrieve my belongings. I saw my parents a few yards away and my heart raced. A large knot formed in my stomach. I fought back the tears.

What do you make of Brandt's account of her father's reaction? Her mother's?

Not a word was spoken as we walked to the car. Slowly, I sank into the back seat anticipating the scolding. Expecting harsh tones, I was relieved to hear almost the opposite from my father. 36

"I'm not going to punish you and I'll tell you why. Although I think what you did was wrong, I think what the police did was more wrong. There's no excuse for locking a thirteen-year-old behind bars. That doesn't mean I condone what you did, but I think you've been punished enough already." 37

How well does this ending work?

As I looked from my father's eyes to my mother's, I knew this ordeal was over. Although it would never be forgotten, the incident was not mentioned again. 38

LEARN ABOUT BRANDT'S WRITING PROCESS

To learn about Brandt's process of writing this essay, turn to A Writer at Work on pp. 57–62. How did trying out dialogues help Brandt discover the central conflict and significance of her story?

ANNIE DILLARD, professor emerita at Wesleyan University, won the Pulitzer Prize for nonfiction writing in 1975 with her first book, *Pilgrim at Tinker Creek* (1974). Since then, she has written eleven other books in a variety of genres. They include *Teaching a Stone to Talk* (1988), *The Writing Life* (1990), *The Living* (1993), *Mornings Like This* (1996), and *The Maytrees* (2007). Dillard also wrote an autobiography of her early years, *An American Childhood* (1987), from which the following selection comes.

This reading relates an event that occurred one winter morning when the seven-year-old Dillard and a friend were chased by an adult stranger. Dillard admits that she was terrified at the time, and yet she asserts that she has "seldom been happier since." As you read, think about how this paradox helps you grasp the autobiographical significance of this experience for Dillard.

AN AMERICAN CHILDHOOD

Annie Dillard

1 Some boys taught me to play football. This was fine sport. You thought up a new strategy for every play and whispered it to the others. You went out for a pass, fooling everyone. Best, you got to throw yourself mightily at someone's running legs. Either you brought him down or you hit the ground flat out on your chin, with your arms empty before you. It was all or nothing. If you hesitated in fear, you would miss and get hurt: you would take a hard fall while the kid got away, or you would get kicked in the face while the kid got away. But if you flung yourself wholeheartedly at the back of his knees — if you gathered and joined body and soul and pointed them diving fearlessly — then you likely wouldn't get hurt, and you'd stop the ball. Your fate, and your team's score, depended on your concentration and courage. Nothing girls did could compare with it.

2 Boys welcomed me at baseball, too, for I had, through enthusiastic practice, what was weirdly known as a boy's arm. In winter, in the snow, there was neither baseball nor football, so the boys and I threw snowballs at passing cars. I got in trouble throwing snowballs, and have seldom been happier since.

3 On one weekday morning after Christmas, six inches of new snow had just fallen. We were standing up to our boot tops in snow on a front yard on trafficked Reynolds Street, waiting for cars. The cars traveled Reynolds Street slowly and evenly; they were targets all but wrapped in red ribbons, cream puffs. We couldn't miss.

4 I was seven; the boys were eight, nine, and ten. The oldest two Fahey boys were there — Mikey and Peter — polite blond boys who lived near me on Lloyd Street, and who already had four brothers and sisters. My parents approved Mikey and Peter Fahey. Chickie McBride was there, a tough kid, and Billy Paul and Mackie Kean too, from across Reynolds, where the boys grew up dark and furious, grew up skinny, knowing, and skilled. We had all drifted from our houses that morning looking for action, and had found it here on Reynolds Street.

5 It was cloudy but cold. The cars' tires laid behind them on the snowy street a complex trail of beige chunks like crenellated castle walls. I had stepped on some earlier; they squeaked. We could not have wished for more traffic. When a car came, we all popped it one. In the intervals between cars we reverted to the natural solitude of children.

6 I started making an iceball — a perfect iceball, from perfectly white snow, perfectly spherical, and squeezed perfectly translucent so no snow remained all the way through. (The Fahey boys and I considered it unfair actually to throw an iceball at somebody, but it had been known to happen.)

7 I had just embarked on the iceball project when we heard tire chains come clanking from afar. A black Buick was moving toward us down the street. We all

spread out, banged together some regular snowballs, took aim, and, when the Buick drew nigh, fired.

A soft snowball hit the driver's windshield right before the driver's face. It made a smashed star with a hump in the middle. 8

Often, of course, we hit our target, but this time, the only time in all of life, the car pulled over and stopped. Its wide black door opened; a man got out of it, running. He didn't even close the car door. 9

He ran after us, and we ran away from him, up the snowy Reynolds sidewalk. At the corner, I looked back; incredibly, he was still after us. He was in city clothes: a suit and tie, street shoes. Any normal adult would have quit, having sprung us into flight and made his point. This man was gaining on us. He was a thin man, all action. All of a sudden, we were running for our lives. 10

Wordless, we split up. We were on our turf; we could lose ourselves in the neighborhood backyards, everyone for himself. I paused and considered. Everyone had vanished except Mikey Fahey, who was just rounding the corner of a yellow brick house. Poor Mikey, I trailed him. The driver of the Buick sensibly picked the two of us to follow. The man apparently had all day. 11

He chased Mikey and me around the yellow house and up a backyard path we knew by heart: under a low tree, up a bank, through a hedge, down some snowy steps, and across the grocery store's delivery driveway. We smashed through a gap in another hedge, entered a scruffy backyard and ran around its back porch and tight between houses to Edgerton Avenue; we ran across Edgerton to an alley and up our own sliding woodpile to the Halls' front yard; he kept coming. We ran up Lloyd Street and wound through mazy backyards toward the steep hilltop at Willard and Lang. 12

He chased us silently, block after block. He chased us silently over picket fences, through thorny hedges, between houses, around garbage cans, and across streets. Every time I glanced back, choking for breath, I expected he would have quit. He must have been as breathless as we were. His jacket strained over his body. It was an immense discovery, pounding into my hot head with every sliding, joyous step, that this ordinary adult evidently knew what I thought only children who trained at football knew: that you have to fling yourself at what you're doing, you have to point yourself, forget yourself, aim, dive. 13

Mikey and I had nowhere to go, in our own neighborhood or out of it, but away from this man who was chasing us. He impelled us forward; we compelled him to follow our route. The air was cold; every breath tore my throat. We kept running, block after block; we kept improvising, backyard after backyard, running a frantic course and choosing it simultaneously, failing always to find small places or hard places to slow him down, and discovering always, exhilarated, dismayed, that only bare speed could save us — for he would never give up, this man — and we were losing speed. 14

He chased us through the backyard labyrinths of ten blocks before he caught us by our jackets. He caught us and we all stopped. 15

We three stood staggering, half blinded, coughing, in an obscure hilltop backyard: a man in his twenties, a boy, a girl. He had released our jackets, our pursuer, 16 our captor, our hero: he knew we weren't going anywhere. We all played by the rules. Mikey and I unzipped our jackets. I pulled off my sopping mittens. Our tracks multiplied in the backyard's new snow. We had been breaking new snow all morning. We didn't look at each other. I was cherishing my excitement. The man's lower pants legs were wet; his cuffs were full of snow, and there was a prow of snow beneath them on his shoes and socks. Some trees bordered the little flat backyard, some messy winter trees. There was no one around: a clearing in a grove, and we the only players.

17   It was a long time before he could speak. I had some difficulty at first recalling why we were there. My lips felt swollen; I couldn't see out of the sides of my eyes; I kept coughing.

18   "You stupid kids," he began perfunctorily.

19   We listened perfunctorily indeed, if we listened at all, for the chewing out was redundant, a mere formality, and beside the point. The point was that he had chased us passionately without giving up, and so he had caught us. Now he came down to earth. I wanted the glory to last forever.

20   But how could the glory have lasted forever? We could have run through every backyard in North America until we got to Panama. But when he trapped us at the lip of the Panama Canal, what precisely could he have done to prolong the drama of the chase and cap its glory? I brooded about this for the next few years. He could only have fried Mikey Fahey and me in boiling oil, say, or dismembered us piecemeal, or staked us to anthills. None of which I really wanted, and none of which any adult was likely to do, even in the spirit of fun. He could only chew us out there in the Panamanian jungle, after months or years of exalting pursuit. He could only begin, "You stupid kids," and continue in his ordinary Pittsburgh accent with his normal righteous anger and the usual common sense.

21   If in that snowy backyard the driver of the black Buick had cut off our heads, Mikey's and mine, I would have died happy, for nothing has required so much of me since as being chased all over Pittsburgh in the middle of winter — running terrified, exhausted — by this sainted, skinny, furious redheaded man who wished to have a word with us. I don't know how he found his way back to his car.

At the beginning of the essay, Dillard tells about being taught by the neighborhood boys the joy of playing football, particularly the "all or nothing" of flinging yourself "fearlessly" (par. 1).

With other students in your class, discuss an occasion when you had an opportunity to fling yourself fearlessly into an activity that posed some challenge or risk or required special effort. For example, like Dillard, you may have been challenged by your team members at a football game or by a group of volunteers helping during a natural disaster. Or you may have felt pressured by friends to do something that went against your better judgment, was illegal, or was dangerous.

MAKING CONNECTIONS: ACTING FEARLESSLY

Take turns briefly telling what happened. Then, together, consider the following questions as you discuss what now seems significant about this particular experience:

- What made you embrace the challenge or resist it? What do you think your choice tells about you at the time of the event?
- Dillard uses the value term *courage* to describe the fearless behavior she learned playing football. What value term would you use to you describe your experience? For example, were you being *selfless* or *self-serving*; *responsible* or *irresponsible*; a *follower*, *leader*, or *self-reliant individual*?

ANALYZING WRITING STRATEGIES

Your instructor may assign these activities in class or as homework, for you to do by yourself or with classmates.

● ● ●
Basic Features

● A Well-Told Story

To construct an action sequence in writing, Dillard combines two narrating strategies: *specific narrative actions* and *prepositional phrases*. **Specific narrative actions** show people moving and gesturing through the use of

- action verbs (for example, "He *ran* after us, and we *ran* away from him. . . . we *were running* for our lives" in paragraph 10), and

For more on specific narrative action, see Chapter 14.

- modifying phrases that use the *-ing* form of the verb as a modifier (for example, "Every time I glanced back, *choking* for breath" in paragraph 13).

Prepositional phrases tell us where the action is taking place. When combined with specific narrative actions, prepositional phrases enable Dillard to create continuing movement through space. To see how she does this, look at the first sentence in paragraph 12 with the prepositional phrases highlighted:

> He chased Mikey and me around the yellow house and up a backyard path we knew by heart: under a low tree, up a bank, through a hedge, down some snowy steps, and across the grocery store's delivery driveway.

To analyze how Dillard uses specific narrative actions with prepositional phrases, do the following:

- Reread paragraphs 11–13, and find three other examples of specific narrative actions combined with prepositional phrases.
- Write a sentence about how well you think these narrating strategies work in the essay. What effect do they have?

● Vivid Description of People and Places

Describing — naming objects and detailing their colors, shape, size, textures, and other qualities — is an important writing strategy in remembered event essays. To see how writers use **naming** and **detailing** to create vivid images, look closely at Dillard's description of an iceball:

> I started making an <u>iceball</u> — a [perfect] <u>iceball</u>, from [perfectly white] <u>snow</u>, [perfectly spherical], and [squeezed perfectly translucent] so no snow remained all the way through. (par. 6)

Notice that she names two things (underlined): *iceball* and *snow*. She adds to these names descriptive details (in brackets) — *white* (color), *spherical* (shape), and *translucent* (appearance) — that help readers imagine more precisely what an iceball looks like. She also repeats the words *perfect* and *perfectly* (highlighted) to emphasize the color, shape, and appearance of this particular iceball.

To analyze Dillard's use of the describing strategies of naming and detailing to present places and people, do the following:

- Reread paragraphs 10 and 12, where she describes the man and the neighborhood through which he chases her and Mikey.

- Underline the names of people and objects (nouns).

- Put brackets around the words and phrases that modify the nouns they name.

- Write a couple of sentences explaining what you notice about the relative amount of naming and detailing Dillard uses in these paragraphs and the kinds of details she chooses to include.

To learn more about the describing strategies of naming and detailing, see Chapter 15.

● Autobiographical Significance

Writers convey significance by a combination of *showing* and *telling*. **Showing,** through the careful choice of words and details, creates an overall or *dominant impression.* **Telling** includes the narrator's *remembered feelings and thoughts* together with her *present perspective* on what happened and why it is significant.

To analyze Dillard's use of **showing** to convey significance, do the following:

- Reread paragraphs 7, 10, 13, 16, 18, 20–21, and highlight the details Dillard uses to describe the man, how he dresses, the car he drives, and especially the way he talks when he catches the kids.

- Write a couple of sentences characterizing the dominant impression you get of the man from these details and what they suggest about why he chases the kids.

To analyze Dillard's use of **telling** to convey significance, do the following:

- Reread paragraphs 15–21 and highlight the key words Dillard uses to tell readers what she thinks of the man and the chase.

- Write a couple of sentences explaining what these key words tell you about the significance of the experience for Dillard.

- Write another sentence discussing how the opening anecdote about learning to play football fearlessly and courageously helps you understand the significance of the event for Dillard.

**CONSIDERING
TOPICS FOR YOUR
OWN ESSAY**

Like Dillard, you could write about a time when an adult did something entirely unexpected during your childhood, an action that seemed dangerous or threatening to you, or something humorous, kind, or generous. List two or three of these occasions. Consider unpredictable actions of adults in your immediate or extended family, adults you had come to know outside your family, and strangers. As you consider these possible topics, think about your purpose and audience: What would you want your instructor and classmates to learn about you from reading about this particular event?

TREY ELLIS is a film professor at Columbia University and a prolific writer. He has written novels including *Right Here, Right Now* (1999), winner of the American Book Award; plays and screenplays, including *The Tuskegee Airmen* (1995); and essays published in notable newspapers and magazines such as the *Washington Post, Newsweek,* and *Salon.* He also does commentary for NPR's *All Things Considered* and blogs for the *Huffington Post* and his own Web site, *treyellis.com.* His most recent publication is *Bedtime Stories: Adventures in the Land of Single-Fatherhood* (2008), from which this essay was adapted for publication in the *New York Times.*

The reading tells what happened when Ellis was twenty-two years old and visited his father in France. Ellis includes a photograph of his father. As you read, think about what the photograph adds to your reading of the essay.

When the Walls Came Tumbling Down

TREY ELLIS

A year before his death, my dad was forced to come out to me. I thought he was in Paris for a vacation. Instead, he was there for treatment with AZT, which in 1986 was experimental and not yet approved in the United States for people infected with the virus that causes AIDS.

After my mother died when I was 16, my dad fulfilled his lifelong dream and moved us from Hamden, a suburb of New Haven, to Manhattan and there raised me alone. Moving from our modest three-bedroom in suburban Connecticut to a majestic prewar on the corner of West 81st Street and Riverside Drive made me feel like George Jefferson in the television comedy series "The Jeffersons." During my first year there, I unconsciously found myself humming the show's theme song, "Movin' On Up," every time I passed our uniformed doormen.

1

2

3

■ The author's father, Dr. William Ellis, in 1983, a few years before he became ill.

I might have had my suspicions about my father's sexuality (finding an International Male catalog, with its all-male photo layouts, under his mattress probably should have tipped me off years earlier). But back then I couldn't reconcile my love for him with my own juvenile homophobia.

4   That August, I was 22, a year out of college and visiting my father in Paris, where he had found a sublet off Place d'Italie on the Boulevard de Port Royal. He said he was interviewing for a spot as a roving State Department psychiatrist based there. The job was a world away from his work at the time, as a child psychiatrist shepherding hundreds of troubled kids at a center run by Harlem Hospital.

5   It wasn't until my father opened the door that I realized something terrifyingly life-altering was about to be revealed. Always movie star handsome, he looked older than I had remembered him, and his light green eyes had gone dull.

6   "Trey, I'm not here to work for the State Department," he said. "I wanted to, but then I got sick."

7   O.K. He's sick. He'll get better. I'll help him get better.

8   "Have you heard of ARC, AIDS-related complex?"

9   Did he just say he's got AIDS?

10   "It's not AIDS. They just don't want it to ever turn into AIDS so I came here to try this new drug called AZT."

11   "Rock Hudson came here, right? He took the same stuff and he died."

12   "Not everyone dies."

13   He told me he had been with some men, but that he thought he had always been careful.

14   I said I had to go for a walk.

15   This is impossible, I was thinking. My mom killed herself when I was still a teenager. After she died, I loved my dad so hard, for both of them. But remember it's not AIDS, I told myself, just some sort of pre-AIDS. The best scientists in the world are working on only this problem. They'll find some pill, I told myself. I'll help them find some pill. We'll get though this and say: "Phew! That was a close one!"

16   When I returned to his apartment, I was almost smiling. My bad luck would be cosmically counterbalanced by the miraculous good luck of having a father who would be the very first person in the world to recover from AIDS.

17   We never left each other's sight that week. Without his huge secret between us, we could now talk about anything. He told me about his boyfriends and girlfriends and his heartaches, and as long as he didn't give too much information I was happy to listen.

18   We became best friends. And when he returned home to New York, I was his live-in nurse for those last six months, supercharging his Cream of Wheat with heavy

cream to try to keep his weight up, emptying his dialysis bag several times a day after his kidneys failed, and sharing his king-size bed.

By Christmas he seemed better and my plan was for the cure to arrive some time in the middle of the following year. So in mid-January, when he was admitted into St. Luke's Roosevelt Hospital Center with AIDS-related pneumonia, I refused to panic. The doctors said opportunistic infections were to be expected. Sitting up in his hospital bed, my dad displayed a calm nobility I still try to remember to emulate. He explained that if the pneumonia didn't surrender to the antibiotics, he very likely would die.   19

He said that at his memorial service he wanted a childhood friend turned opera singer to sing an old spiritual, "There's a Man Goin' Round Taking Names." I took notes just to humor him, but assured him that he was just being a drama queen. Five days later, my godfather, also a physician, called me at 3 a.m. and told me to hurry back to the hospital.   20

When I showed up, my father's eyes were Caribbean clear, yet huge and eerily calm, though it was hard to see the rest of his face through all the white tape and the plastic tubing. My fingers found his, and we stared at each other as I cried.   21

I wished he could still speak, because I was in no shape to say anything more than that I loved him. I wanted to tell him that I'd be fine. That he'd raised me just perfectly right. I went home to the apartment. A few hours later he was dead, four days short of 50.   22

In those days, no one spoke about AIDS. No one outside a small circle knew for sure why my father died. Even now, 22 years later, what's left of my family has pleaded with me not to tell the truth.   23

My dad never understood how he could have contracted AIDS. He swore that he was scrupulously hygienic. I subsequently learned from a family doctor, who had checked my dad's records, that my father's AIDS must have been passed along by a tainted blood transfusion.   24

The explanation was an odd blessing. If my dad had known what caused his AIDS, he probably never would have come out to me. He would have died with so many secrets still lodged in his heart. And I would have never known my father with the fullness every child craves. Embarrassment is always the price we pay for more intimacy. Perhaps there is no such thing as too much information.   25

MAKING CONNECTIONS: INTIMACY

Ellis concludes his essay by pointing out the irony that if his father had known that he got AIDS from a blood transfusion, "he probably never would have come out to me. . . . Embarrassment is always the price we pay for more intimacy. Perhaps there is no such thing as too much information." Ellis seems to be defining intimacy as the ability to be open with another person and share the most personal information. He describes how after his father came out to him, they became "best friends" because they could "talk about anything" (pars. 17–18).

With other students in your class, discuss your experience and understanding of intimacy by describing a relationship you have with a close friend or family member. Note that we're not talking about sexual intimacy, but about strictly emotional intimacy. You may choose to talk about a relationship that has *not* become intimate, perhaps because of embarrassment, lack of trust, fear of being rejected, or the need to control. Don't feel constrained to share details; just describe the kinds of things you feel comfortable sharing.

Discuss what you learned about intimacy from this relationship. To help keep your discussion focused, consider the following questions:

- What do you look for in an intimate relationship?
- Ellis generalizes that embarrassment is a barrier to intimacy. What else could have prevented the relationship between Ellis and his father from becoming intimate?

⬢ A Well-Told Story

To keep readers' interest, even the most exciting stories, like Dillard's story of being chased through city streets and backyards, need to be organized in a way that builds suspense and tension. A common way to represent the dramatic organization of a narrative is with a pyramid:

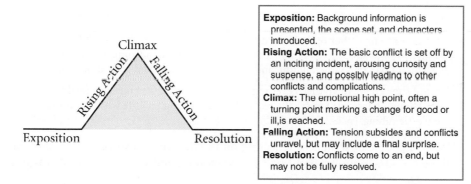

Exposition: Background information is presented, the scene set, and characters introduced.
Rising Action: The basic conflict is set off by an inciting incident, arousing curiosity and suspense, and possibly leading to other conflicts and complications.
Climax: The emotional high point, often a turning point marking a change for good or ill, is reached.
Falling Action: Tension subsides and conflicts unravel, but may include a final surprise.
Resolution: Conflicts come to an end, but may not be fully resolved.

You can use this pyramid to analyze the structure of a story you're reading or to outline a story you're planning to write (see p. 48).

If you compare the dramatic structure of Dillard's story to Brandt's, you will see that the two writers give more space to different elements of the story. After several paragraphs of exposition, Dillard devotes most of the story to the rising action as the man chases Dillard and Mikey relentlessly through streets and backyards. The climax comes when he catches the kids, but the story ends without description of the falling action or resolution. Brandt has a more complicated rising action that includes the mini-climaxes of getting caught and getting arrested before the final confrontation with her parents, followed by falling action and a briefly stated resolution.

To analyze how Ellis organizes his story, do the following:

- Skim the essay and note in the margin where you find the exposition, rising action, climax, falling action, and resolution. Does Ellis's story have one climax, or more than one?

- Write a few sentences indicating how useful it is for you to outline the story in this way. Describe another way of outlining the story if you think that it would be more useful.

⬡ Vivid Description of People

Writers of remembered event essays typically describe people sparingly, using just a few choice details. For example, Brandt names her relatives but never describes them; although she does mention looking into her parents' eyes, she doesn't describe their expressions. The only person she describes is the store detective: a "middle-aged man, dressed in street clothes, flashing some type of badge" (par. 5). Dillard, on the other hand, gives us brief descriptions of several neighborhood boys: "Mikey and Peter — polite blond boys," as well as the other boys "from across Reynolds, where the boys grew up dark and furious, grew up skinny, knowing, and skilled" (par. 4). As you've discovered in analyzing how she describes the man who chased her and Mikey, Dillard's description is brief but vivid.

To analyze how Ellis describes his father, do the following:

- Reread the following two brief descriptions, underlining the objects being described and putting brackets around the words and phrases that describe them (detailing such things as the color, shape, size, and appearance of the objects):

> It wasn't until my father opened the door that I realized something terrifyingly life-altering was about to be revealed. Always movie-star handsome, he looked older than I had remembered him, and his light green eyes had gone dull. (par. 5)

> When I showed up, my father's eyes were Caribbean clear, yet huge and eerily calm, though it was hard to see the rest of his face through all the white tape and the plastic tubing. (par. 21)

- Write a couple of sentences reflecting on the **dominant impression** created by these two descriptions, pointing out the naming and detailing that stands out for you.

⬡ Autobiographical Significance

Writers convey the significance of events by telling how they felt and what they thought at the time the event occurred and by telling what they think now as they look back on the event. Here's an example from Brandt's essay where she presents her **remembered feelings and thoughts**:

> I felt like a terrible human being. I would rather have stayed in jail than confront my mom right then. I dreaded each passing minute that brought our encounter closer. (par. 35)

The following example from Dillard's essay shows the writer's reflections looking back on the event from her **present perspective**:

> . . . what precisely could he have done to prolong the drama of the chase and cap its glory? I brooded about this for the next few years. (par. 20)

Obviously, in writing about his father's illness and death, Ellis has chosen a subject that is inherently significant — both important in his life and deeply meaningful.

To analyze how Ellis presents his remembered feelings and thoughts as well as his present perspective, follow these suggestions:

- Reread paragraphs 6–10, where Ellis alternates dialogue with thoughts he had but didn't express at the time, and highlight the remembered thoughts.

- Reread paragraphs 22–24 and highlight in another color Ellis's present reflections from his perspective.

- Write a few sentences explaining what you learn about Ellis from his remembered thoughts and from his present perspective.

ANALYZING VISUALS

PHOTOGRAPH OF TREY ELLIS'S FATHER

Write a paragraph or two analyzing the photograph Ellis includes in his remembered event essay and explaining what it contributes to the essay.

To analyze the visual, you can use the Criteria for Analyzing Visuals chart on pp. 675–77. The chart offers a series of questions you can ask yourself under two categories: Key Components and Rhetorical Context. You will see that there are a lot of questions, but don't feel you have to answer all of them. Focus on the questions that seem most productive in helping you write a short analysis. Try beginning with these questions that specifically refer to Ellis's photograph:

People

- Why do you think Ellis chose a photograph of his father alone rather than one with both of them in it?

Scene

- Why do you think Ellis chose a photograph of his father in his office rather than at home or elsewhere?

- What impression do you get of Ellis's dad from the way his office looks — for example, from the piles of files and books as well as the other objects on the desk?

Rhetorical Context

- How does the photograph's portrayal of Ellis's dad add to Ellis's description of him in paragraphs 5 and 21? Note that in the original *New York Times* article, the photo was black-and-white. What, if anything, is the effect of reproducing it in color, as we do here?

- How does seeing Ellis's father as a doctor help you understand the tone his dad adopts when he tells Ellis about his illness in paragraphs 6, 8, 10, and 12?

In one sense, the event Ellis writes about was tragic: The news his father broke to him was of an illness that led to his death a few short months later. Ellis tells us, however, that the event had an unexpectedly positive side effect: It gave him an opportunity to help his dad and get to know him in a new way. For your own essay, you, too, might consider writing about an event that had an unexpectedly positive outcome. Ellis's essay also suggests the possibility of writing about an event that challenged your pre-conceptions or prejudices. Ellis tells us that learning about his father's sexual orientation challenged his "own juvenile homophobia" (par. 3). As you consider these possible topics, think about your purpose and audience. What would you want your instructor and classmates to learn about you from reading about this particular event?

SAIRA SHAH, a British journalist and documentary filmmaker, won the Courage Under Fire and Television Journalist of the Year awards for her reporting on Afghan guerrillas fighting the Soviet occupation in the 1980s, as well as the Persian Gulf War and the conflict in Kosovo. She is best known in the United States for her undercover documentary films about the Taliban rule in Afghanistan, *Beneath the Veil* (2001) and *Unholy War* (2002), as well as for *Death in Gaza* (2004), about children caught in the Israeli-Palestinian conflict.

The following selection, adapted from Shah's autobiography, *The Storyteller's Daughter* (2003), tells what happened when, at the age of seventeen, she visited her father's Afghan relatives in Pakistan. In an interview, Shah explains: "When I was growing up, I had this secret doubt — which I couldn't even admit to myself — that I was not at all an Afghan because I was born in Britain to a mixed family." As you read, think about the way Shah conveys her anxiety about her identity.

LONGING TO BELONG

Saira Shah

The day he disclosed his matrimonial ambitions for me, my uncle sat me at his right during lunch. This was a sign of special favor, as it allowed him to feed me choice tidbits from his own plate. It was by no means an unadulterated pleasure. He would often generously withdraw a half-chewed delicacy from his mouth and lovingly cram it into mine — an Afghan habit with which I have since tried to come to terms. It was his way of telling me that I was valued, part of the family.

My brother and sister, Tahir and Safia, and my elderly aunt Amina and I were all attending the wedding of my uncle's son. Although my uncle's home was closer than I'd ever been, I was not yet inside Afghanistan. This branch of my family lived in Peshawar, Pakistan. On seeing two unmarried daughters in the company of a female chaperone, my uncle obviously concluded that we had been sent to be married. I was taken aback by the visceral longing I felt to be part of this world. I had never realized that I had been starved of anything. Now, at 17, I discovered that like a princess in a fairy tale, I had been cut off from my origins. This was the point in the tale where, simply by walking through a magical door, I could recover my gardens and palaces. If I allowed my uncle to arrange a marriage for me, I would belong.

3   Over the next few days, the man my family wished me to marry was introduced into the inner sanctum. He was a distant cousin. His luxuriant black mustache was generally considered to compensate for his lack of height. I was told breathlessly that he was a fighter pilot in the Pakistani Air Force. As an outsider, he wouldn't have been permitted to meet an unmarried girl. But as a relative, he had free run of the house. Whenever I appeared, a female cousin would fling a child into his arms. He'd pose with it, whiskers twitching, while the women cooed their admiration.

4   A huge cast of relatives had assembled to see my uncle's son marry. The wedding lasted nearly 14 days and ended with a reception. The bride and groom sat on an elevated stage to receive greetings. While the groom was permitted to laugh and chat, the bride was required to sit perfectly still, her eyes demurely lowered. I didn't see her move for four hours.

5   Watching this tableau vivant of a submissive Afghan bride, I knew that marriage would never be my easy route to the East. I could live in my father's mythological homeland only through the eyes of the storyteller. In my desire to experience the fairy tale, I had overlooked the staggeringly obvious: the storyteller was a man. If I wanted freedom, I would have to cut my own path. I began to understand why my uncle's wife had resorted to using religion to regain some control — at least in her own home. Her piety gave her license to impose her will on others.

6   My putative fiancé returned to Quetta, from where he sent a constant flow of lavish gifts. I was busy examining my hoard when my uncle's wife announced that he was on the phone. My intended was a favorite of hers; she had taken it upon herself to promote the match. As she handed me the receiver, he delivered a line culled straight from a Hindi movie: "We shall have a love-match, ach-cha?" Enough was enough. I slammed down the phone and went to find Aunt Amina. When she had heard me out, she said: "I'm glad that finally you've stopped this silly wild goose chase for your roots. I'll have to extricate you from this mess. Wait here while I put on something more impressive." As a piece of Islamic one-upmanship, she returned wearing not one but three head scarves of different colors.

7   My uncle's wife was sitting on her prayer platform in the drawing room. Amina stormed in, scattering servants before her like chaff. "Your relative . . . ," was Amina's opening salvo, ". . . has been making obscene remarks to my niece." Her mouth opened, but before she could find her voice, Amina fired her heaviest guns: "Over the telephone!"

8   "How dare you!" her rival began.

9   It gave Amina exactly the opportunity she needed to move in for the kill. "What? Do you support this lewd conduct? Are we living in an American movie? Since when have young people of mixed sexes been permitted to speak to each other on the telephone? Let alone to talk — as I regret to inform you your nephew did — of love! Since when has love had anything to do with marriage? What a dangerous and absurd concept!"

My Peshawari aunt was not only outclassed; she was out-Islamed too. "My niece is a rose that hasn't been plucked," Amina said. "It is my task as her chaperone to ensure that this happy state of affairs continues. A match under such circumstances is quite out of the question. The engagement is off." My uncle's wife lost her battle for moral supremacy and, it seemed, her battle for sanity as well. In a gruff, slack-jawed way that I found unappealing, she made a sharp, inhuman sound that sounded almost like a bark.

10

**MAKING
CONNECTIONS:
SEARCH FOR
IDENTITY**

This essay is titled "Longing to Belong" because Shah is writing about a time in her life when she felt "cut off from [her] origins" and was searching for her identity (par. 2). Shah's search took her to her father's homeland, where she discovered that she did not want to fit in, after all. With other students in your class, discuss something you have learned about your own search for identity.

Begin by telling one another about an occasion when you tried to discover or recover some part of your identity — perhaps, like Shah, by visiting or researching a place you or your parents used to live. Alternatively, you may have tried to reinvent yourself in some other interesting or unique way — such as taking on a new hobby, trying out for a play or team, doing volunteer work, or actively seeking out new acquaintances. Together, discuss what you learned from this experience of searching for identity:

- How successful was your search?
- What do you think leads people to this kind of search? What led you?
- Clearly, Shah's family, community, ethnic, or religious traditions affected her ideas about identity. What influences your ideas about identity?

**ANALYZING
WRITING
STRATEGIES**

● ● ●
Basic Features

● A Well-Told Story

Dialogue is a narrating strategy that helps writers dramatize a story. Hearing what was said and how it was said can also help readers identify with or at least understand the writer's point of view and also give us an impression of the speakers. There are two ways to present dialogue: *dramatizing* or *summarizing* it.

Dramatized dialogue reconstructs what was said. You can easily identify dramatized dialogue because it uses quotation marks. Most writers (Brandt is an exception) include speaker tags identifying the speakers and describing them in some way. Here is an example:

> It was a long time before he could speak. I had some difficulty at first recalling why we were there. My lips felt swollen; I couldn't see out of the sides of my eyes; I kept coughing.
>
> "You stupid kids," he began perfunctorily.
>
> We listened perfunctorily indeed, if we listened at all, for the chewing out was redundant, a mere formality, and beside the point. . . . (Dillard, pars. 17–19)

Summarized dialogue reports the content of what was said but doesn't report the words or use quotation marks:

> Not more than ten minutes later, two officers arrived and placed me under arrest. They said that I was to be taken to the station alone. (Brandt, par. 16)

To analyze Shah's use of dialogue, follow these suggestions:

- Find two examples of dialogue — one that is dramatized and the other summarized.

- Write a couple of sentences speculating about why Shah decided to dramatize one and summarize the other bit of dialogue.

- Add a sentence or two assessing Shah's choice. What would be the effect if the dramatized example was summarized and the summarized example was dramatized?

● A Vivid Description of People and Places

Interestingly, Shah chooses not to describe the city of Peshawar where her uncle's family lives. Nor does she describe the dining room or any of the other rooms in the house. Although she does not use the strategies of naming and detailing to give readers a visual image of the place, she does use a third describing strategy: *comparing.*

Comparing involves the use of simile or metaphor. A **simile** compares two different things explicitly by using the word *like* or *as*. **Metaphor** makes the comparison implicitly by describing one thing as though it were another thing.

To analyze Shah's use of simile or metaphor, do the following:

- Reread paragraph 2 and highlight the simile and the metaphor Shah uses.

- Write a few sentences explaining what these comparisons tell you about the place and Shah's attitude toward it.

For more on comparing strategies, including similes and metaphors, see Chapter 15, pp. 631–32.

● Autobiographical Significance

Writers often use description to create an overall or **dominant impression**. Notice, for example, how Shah builds on her "princess in a fairy tale" comparison when she describes the bride and groom sitting on "an elevated stage" with the bride "required to sit perfectly still, her eyes demurely lowered" (par. 4). She calls this image a "tableau vivant" (which literally means "living picture") of a "submissive Afghan bride" (par. 5).

To analyze how Shah conveys the significance of the event, do the following:

- Reread paragraphs 4 and 5 and consider their relation to the comparisons she uses in paragraph 2. (See the previous activity.)

- Write a couple of sentences describing the dominant impression you get from these paragraphs.

- Add another sentence or two explaining how the dominant impression helps you understand the significance of the event for Shah.

For more on creating a dominant impression, see Chapter 15, pp. 637–38.

CONSIDERING TOPICS FOR YOUR OWN ESSAY

Like Shah, consider writing about an event that you were looking forward to but that turned out differently than you had expected — perhaps turning out to be a dreadful disappointment, a delightful surprise, or, more likely, a combination of disappointment and delight. Alternatively, you might write about a time when you had thought you wanted something but then realized your desires were more complicated; a time when you were trying to fit in and discovered something unexpected about yourself or about the group to which you wanted to belong; or a time when you decided not to try to conform to someone's expectations, but to rebel and go your own way. If, like Shah's, your experience involves a clash of cultures, you might write about that aspect of your experience, how it has affected you, and what you have learned from the experience.

As you consider these possible topics, think about your purpose and audience. What would you want your instructor and classmates to learn about you from reading about this particular event?

Beyond the Traditional Essay: Remembering an Event

Our culture commemorates events in many ways that are likely familiar to you. Physical memorials such as statues, plaques, monuments, and buildings are traditional means of ensuring that important events remain in our collective memory: Relatively recent examples include the Vietnam Veterans Memorial in Washington, D.C., and the planned commemorative complex at the site of the 9/11 World Trade Center attack in New York City. Though such memorials function primarily visually, rather than textually, they can also be seen to exhibit the basic features we've discussed in essays remembering an event. The Vietnam memorial is a dramatic, V-shaped black granite wall partly embedded in the earth, which reflects the images of visitors reading the names of the dead and missing inscribed there; the names are presented in chronological order, telling the story of the conflict from start to finish in terms of the American lives that were lost. In a statement accompanying her design for the memorial, architect Maya Lin summarizes its significance: "These names, seemingly infinite in number, convey the sense of overwhelming numbers, while unifying these individuals into a whole."

Community gatherings, which often include speeches, music, and visual tributes, and community activities like the ongoing creation of the AIDs Memorial Quilt (http://www.aidsquilt.org), are also means of remembering events. Films, books, plays, poems, music albums, art exhibits, Web sites, and other forms of expression are still other means by which people in our culture retell the stories of important events, encouraging those who read, view, or listen to them to reexperience them and reflect. Just one example among countless similar examples is offered by the Exploratorium (www.exploratorium.edu), an online "museum of science, art, and human perception," which hosts a site called "Remembering Nagasaki," constructed to commemorate the fiftieth anniversary of the bombing of Nagasaki, Japan, near the end of World War II. The site features photos taken by Japanese army photographer Yosuke Yamahata immediately after the bombing, in addition to "a public forum on issues related to the atomic age."

As you work on your own project remembering an event, you might want to consult some of these alternative forms of commemoration for inspiration. If the format in which you are working allows for it — if, for example, you are creating a poster, Web site, or video — you should consider taking advantage of the strategies available to those working in multimedia: for example, by embedding artifacts that are relevant to the event you're relating. (Always remember to properly document any material you might use that was created by someone else.)

The Writing Assignment

Write an essay about an event in your life that will engage readers and that will, at the same time, help them understand the significance of the event. Tell your story dramatically and vividly.

This Guide to Writing will help you apply what you have learned about how writers invest their remembered event essays with drama, vividness, and significance. The Guide is divided into five sections with various activities in each section:

- **Invention and Research**
- **Planning and Drafting**
- **Critical Reading Guide**
- **Revising**
- **Editing and Proofreading**

The Guide is designed to escort you through the writing process, from finding an event to editing your finished essay. Your instructor may require you to follow the Guide to Writing from beginning to end. Working through the Guide to Writing in this way will help you — as it has helped many other college students — write a thoughtful, fully developed, polished essay.

If, however, your instructor gives you latitude to choose and if you have had experience writing a remembered event essay, then you can decide on the order in which you'll do the activities in the Guide to Writing. For example, the Invention and Research section includes activities to help you find an event, sketch the story, describe the people and places, and explore significance. Obviously, finding an event must precede the other activities, but you may come to the Guide with an event already in mind, and you may choose to explore its significance before sketching the story or begin by describing the place it happened because it is particularly vivid in your memory. In fact, you may find your response to one of the invention activities expanding into a draft before you've had a chance to do any of the other activities. That's a good thing — but you should later flesh out your draft by going back to the activities you skipped and layering the new material into your draft.

To learn about using the *Guide* e-book for invention and drafting, go to **bedfordstmartins.com/ theguide**.

The following chart will help you find answers to many of the questions you might have about planning, drafting, and revising a remembered event essay. The page references in the Where to Look column refer to examples from the readings and activities in the Guide to Writing.

Starting Points: Remembering an Event

●●● Basic Features

	Question	Where to Look
Choosing an Event	How do I come up with an event to write about?	• Considering Topics for Your Own Essay (pp. 28, 34, 38) • Choosing an Event to Write About (pp. 42–44) • Testing Your Choice (p. 45)
	What's my purpose in writing? How can I interest my audience?	• Defining Your Purpose and Audience (p. 47) • Refining Your Purpose and Setting Goals (pp. 47–48)
A Well-Told Story	How can I make the story of my event dramatic?	• Add specific narrative actions (p. 26) • Add dialogue (pp. 36–37) • Construct a narrative outline (pp. 31–32) • Constructing a Well-Told Story: Explore a Revealing or Pivotal Moment (p. 44) • Refining Your Purpose and Setting Goals (pp. 47–48)
	How can I help readers keep track of what happened?	• Use prepositional phrases (p. 26) • A Sentence Strategy: Time Transitions and Verb Tenses (pp. 49–50)
	How should I organize my story?	• Construct a narrative outline (pp. 31–32) • Outlining Your Draft (pp. 48–49)
Vivid Description of People and Places	How can I make my description of the place where the event happened vivid and specific?	• Use concrete naming and specific detailing (pp. 26–27) • Use comparison — metaphor and simile (p. 36) • Constructing a Well-Told Story: Describing the Place (p. 44) • Exploring Memorabilia (pp. 45–46)
	How can I create a vivid impression of people?	• Use concrete naming and specific detailing (pp. 26–27) • Add dialogue (pp. 36–37) • Constructing a Well-Told Story: Recalling Key People (p. 44) • Exploring Memorabilia (pp. 45–46)
Autobiographical Significance	How can I help readers grasp the significance of my story?	• Use showing and telling (p. 27) • Constructing a Well-Told Story: Reflect on the Conflict and Its Significance (p. 44) • Reflecting on the Event's Autobiographical Significance (p. 46) • Considering Your Thesis (p. 47) • Refining Your Purpose and Setting Goals (pp. 47–48)
	How can I make a dominant impression?	• Constructing a Well-Told Story: Create a Dominant Impression (p. 44) • Considering Your Thesis (p. 47)

Invention and Research

The following invention activities are easy to complete and take only a few minutes. Spreading out the activities over several days will stimulate your memory, enabling you to recall details and to reflect deeply on the event's meaning. Remember to keep a written record of your invention work: you'll need it when you draft the essay and later when you revise it.

Choosing an Event to Write About

List several significant past events in your life and choose one to explore. This will come more easily to some of us than to others. Bear in mind that you're looking for an event that meets the following criteria:

Criteria for Choosing an Event: A Checklist	The event should ☐ take place over a short period of time (preferably just a few hours); ☐ center on conflict (a personal struggle or an external confrontation); ☐ disclose something significant about your life; ☐ allow you to portray yourself in a way that you feel comfortable sharing with your instructor and classmates; ☐ reveal complex or ambivalent feelings (rather than superficial and sentimental ones); ☐ lead readers to think about their own experience and about the cultural forces that shape their lives.

If you're like most people, you'll need some help in coming up with a number of good options. To get your juices flowing, you might first try quickly rereading the Considering Topics for Your Own Essay activities following the readings, and recalling any events those suggestions brought to mind. Reread any notes you might have made in response to these suggestions.

For further ideas, consult the suggestions in the following sections:

Types of Events to Consider

- a difficult situation (for example, when you had to make a tough choice and face the consequences, or when you let someone down or someone you admired let you down)

- an occasion when things did not turn out as expected (for example, when you expected to be criticized but were praised or ignored instead, or when you were convinced you would succeed but failed)

- an incident that changed you in a particular way or revealed an aspect of your personality you had not seen before (for example, dependence, insecurity, ambition, jealousy, or heroism)

- an event in which an encounter with another person led you to consider seriously someone else's point of view or changed you (for example, the way you view yourself, your ideas about how you fit into a particular group or community)

- an incident in which you had a conflict with someone else or a serious misunderstanding that made you feel unjustly treated or in which you realize you mistreated someone else (for example, an incident of racial bias, sexual harassment, false accusation, or hurtful gossip)

- an incident that made you reexamine a basic value or belief (for example, when you were expected to do something that went against your values or make a decision about which you were deeply conflicted)

- an event that made you aware of your interest in or aptitude for a particular career or convinced you that you were not cut out for a particular career

- an event that revealed to you other people's surprising assumptions about you (as a student, friend, colleague, or worker)

Using the Web to Find and Explore an Event

Exploring Web sites where people write about their life experiences might inspire you by triggering memories of similar events in your own life. Moreover, the Internet provides a rich repository of cultural and historical information, including photographs and music, which you might be able to use to prime your memory and create a richly detailed, multimedia text for your readers.

Here are some suggestions:

- Investigate Web sites such as Citystories.com, StoryPreservation.com, and MemoryArchive.org where people post brief stories about their lives.

- Search sites like MySpace, Facebook, and Blogspot featuring people you are writing about, as well as sites of friends, family members, or others who have been important to you.

- Look for sites related to places or activities — such as neighborhoods, schools, workplaces, sports events, or films — that you associate with the event you are writing about.

- Take a look at narrative history sites such as Survivors' Stories, Katrina Stories, and Sixties Personal Narrative Project to see what people who experienced these events are writing about.

Make notes of any ideas, memories, or insights suggested by your online research, and download any visuals you might include in your essay, being sure to get the information necessary to cite any online sources. (See pp. 774-76 for the MLA citation format for electronic sources.)

Basic Features

Ways In: Constructing a Well-Told Story

Once you've made a preliminary choice of an event, the following activities will help you begin to construct a well-told story, with vivid descriptions of people and places. You can begin with whichever basic activity you want, but wherever you begin, be sure to return to the other activities to fill in the details.

Shaping the Story	Describing the Place	Recalling Key People
Sketch the Story. *Write a quick sketch telling roughly what happened.* Don't worry about what you're leaving out; you can fill in the details later.	**Reimagine the Place.** *Identify the place where the event occurred and describe it.* What do you see, hear, or smell? Use details — shape, color, texture — to evoke the scene.	**Describe People.** *Write about people who played a role in the event.* For each person, name and detail a few distinctive physical features, mannerisms, dress, and so on.
Explore a Revealing or Pivotal Moment. *Write for a few minutes developing a moment of surprise, confrontation, crisis, change, or discovery that may become the climax of your story.* To dramatize it, try using specific narrative actions and dialogue.	**Research Visuals.** *Try to locate visuals you could include in your essay:* Look through memorabilia such as family photographs, yearbooks, newspaper articles, concert programs, ticket stubs, or T-shirts — anything that might stimulate your memory and help you reflect on the place. If you submit your essay electronically or post it online, also consider adding music that you associate with the event. (You may need to cite where you found your sources, so keep a record.)	**Create a Dialogue.** *Reconstruct one important conversation you had during the event.* You will probably not remember exactly what was said, but try to re-create the spirit of the interaction. Consider adding speaker tags (see p. 36) to show people's tone of voice, attitude, and gestures.
Reflect on the Conflict and Its Significance. *Identify the conflict and do some exploratory writing about it.* If it was an internal conflict, a struggle within yourself, how does the event reflect what you were going through? If it was an external confrontation between you and someone else, how can you dramatize what occurred? Do exploratory writing of both kinds if the conflict was both internal and external, as it was for Brandt.		**Research People.** *Do some research and add to your invention notes any thoughts or feelings suggested by what you find.* Look for photographs, e-mails, letters, or videos from the time of the event. Contact people involved in the event. Imagine having a conversation with someone who was there: What would you say about what happened? How might the person respond?

Creating a Dominant Impression

Reread what you have written for Shaping the Story, Describing the Place, and Recalling Key People, and consider the overall or dominant impression of your descriptions. Review your word choices and descriptive details, and add language to strengthen the impression you want to make. Imagine writing a song or making a film based on this event. If you were making a film, what mood or atmosphere would you try to create? If you were writing a song, what kind would you write — blues, hip-hop, country, rock? What kind of refrain would it have? Try not to oversimplify or sugar-coat the meanings; instead, note where your description points to complexities and contradictions that could deepen your story.

Testing Your Choice

After you've made some attempts to construct the story, you should pause to decide whether you recall enough of the event and care enough about it to write about it. Test your choice using the following questions.

- *Will I be able to reconstruct enough of the story and describe the place and people with enough vivid detail to make my story dramatic and create a dominant impression?*

- *Do I feel drawn toward understanding what this event meant to me then and means to me now?* You need not yet understand the significance, but you should feel compelled to explore it — keeping in mind that you will decide what you want to disclose in your essay.

- *Do I feel comfortable writing about this event for my instructor and classmates?* You are not writing a diary entry. Rather, you are writing a public document — a fact that may give you pause, but may also inspire you.

  If you lose confidence in your choice, return to the list of possible events you made, and choose another event.

Get together with two or three other students to try out your story. Your classmates' reactions will help you determine whether you have chosen an event you can present in an interesting way.

Storytellers: Take turns telling your story briefly, describing the place and key people. Try to pique your listeners' curiosity and build suspense.

Listeners: Briefly tell each storyteller what you found most intriguing about the story. For example, consider these questions:

- Were you eager to know how the story would turn out?
- Was there a clear conflict that seemed important enough to write about?
- Were you able to identify with the storyteller?
- Could you understand why the event was significant for the storyteller?

A Collaborative Activity:
Testing Your Choice

Exploring Memorabilia

Memorabilia are visual images, video clips, recordings, and objects that can help you remember details and explore the personal and cultural significance of an event. Examples include photographs, Facebook pages, e-mails, old telephone book entries, newspaper clippings, music, and ticket stubs. Memorabilia are not required for success with this assignment, but they may prove helpful in stimulating your memory.

Look for memorabilia relevant to the event, and add to your invention notes details about the time period, places, and people that the memorabilia suggest. In addition to personal memorabilia, you could do research on the historical period or the cultural context in which the event you are writing about took place, collecting images or other records of relevant material. Consider including memorabilia in your essay by photocopying, scanning, or downloading images or other records into your electronic document. If your project will be submitted electronically, you should consider including sound, video, links, and other digital material that's relevant to your event.

Basic Features

Ways In: Reflecting on the Event's Autobiographical Significance

The following activities will help you to understand the meaning that the event holds in your life and to develop ways to convey this significance to your readers. It might help to move back and forth between your memory of the experience and how you see it now — examining changes in your attitude toward the event and your younger self. Also move between your past and present feelings and the dominant impression your description and narrative makes. Often, our word choices — what we focus on and how we describe it, especially the comparisons we draw — can tell us a lot about our feelings.

Recalling Your Remembered Feelings and Thoughts	Exploring Your Present Perspective
Write for a few minutes, exploring what you can say or show that will let readers know how you felt and what you thought at the time the event occurred.	*Write for a few minutes, exploring what you can say or show that will let readers know what you now think and feel about the event as you look back.*

Recalling Your Remembered Feelings and Thoughts

Write for a few minutes, exploring what you can say or show that will let readers know how you felt and what you thought at the time the event occurred.

- What did you feel — angry or subdued, in control or vulnerable, proud or embarrassed, or a combination of contradictory feelings?
- How did you show or express your feelings?
- What did you want others to think of you at the time?
- What did you think of yourself? If at the time you thought the event was memorable, why? If not, what made you change your mind?
- How aware were you at the time of the cultural context in which the event took place? How do you think it affected you?

Exploring Your Present Perspective

Write for a few minutes, exploring what you can say or show that will let readers know what you now think and feel about the event as you look back.

- How have your feelings changed?
- What do your actions at the time of the event say about the person you were then? How would you respond to the same event today?
- What do you understand now about the conflicts, internal and external, underlying the event? For example, did you struggle with contradictory desires? Were your needs in conflict with someone else's?
- Try to recall what else was happening in your life at the time and how it may have affected your experience. What music, movies, sports, or books did you like? What concerns did you have at home, school, work, play? What do they suggest about who you were at the time?
- How did the event relate to power — that is, to asserting yourself, pleasing someone, or being pressured by someone else?
- How can looking at the event historically or culturally help explain it? How did your situation resemble what was happening to other people at the time? How did it relate to social norms and expectations?

Defining Your Purpose and Audience

Write for several minutes exploring what you want your readers to understand about the significance in your life of the event you have chosen to write about. Use these questions to help you clarify your thoughts:

- Who are my readers, and what are they likely to think of me when they read about this event? What do I want them to think of me?

- What about this event is likely to be familiar to my readers and what might surprise them, perhaps encouraging them to think in new ways or to question some of their assumptions and stereotypes?

- What will writing about this event enable me to suggest about myself as an individual?

- What will it let me suggest about the social and cultural forces that helped shape me — for example, how people exercise power over one another, how family or community values and attitudes affect individuals, or how economic and social conditions impact our lives?

Considering Your Thesis

Review what you wrote for Reflecting on the Event's Autobiographical Significance and Defining Your Purpose and Audience, and add another two or three sentences extending your insights. These sentences must necessarily be tentative because you may not yet fully understand the event's significance.

Keep in mind that readers do not expect you to begin your remembered event essay with the kind of explicit thesis statement typical of argumentative or explanatory writing. You are not obliged to announce the significance, but you must convey it through the way you tell the story and through the dominant impression you create.

Planning and Drafting

The following activities will help you refine your purpose, set goals for your draft, and outline it. In addition, this section will help you write a draft by writing opening sentences, trying out a useful sentence strategy, and learning how to work with sources.

Refining Your Purpose and Setting Goals

Here are some questions that may help you sharpen your purpose for your audience and set goals before you start to draft. Your instructor may ask you to write out your answers to some of these questions or simply to think about them as you plan and draft your essay.

Clarifying Your Purpose and Audience

- What do I want my readers to think of me as I was then and as I am now?
- How can I avoid viewing the past with nostalgia, oversimplifying complicated feelings, or tacking on a moral?
- How can I help readers understand the event's meaning in my life — for example, how it tested or changed me, gave me insight, or made me question my assumptions?
- How can I lead readers to think in new ways or to question some of their own assumptions or stereotypes?

Crafting Your Story

- How can I present the conflict so that readers identify with me and can vicariously experience what I felt?
- How can I make my story dramatic — arousing curiosity and building suspense?
- How can I make the climax not only an emotional high point in the story but also explain it as a meaningful turning point in my life?
- How can I describe people and places vividly so that readers can imagine what it was like and also create a dominant impression that shows the event's significance?
- How can I tell readers what I thought and felt at the time, and feel now looking back, without self-justification or moralizing?

Outlining Your Draft

With your purpose and goals in mind, reread what you wrote in response to the Shaping the Story activity (p. 44). Then make an outline to plan your story. You can make a simple scratch outline or create a chart like the one that follows, which shows the elements of the dramatic narrative pyramid (see p. 31) with examples from Jean Brandt's essay.

Example: "Calling Home" by Jean Brandt (pp. 18–22)

Exposition	I want to set the stage — the time, place, people, and mood — at the very beginning: Christmas, busy mall, good mood of family. Have to mention fact that Snoopy anything was really big at the time.
Rising Action	The "inciting incident" would be my stealing the button. The action will rise in 3 stages: (1) I'm caught shoplifting; (2) I'm taken to the station; (3) I'm waiting to see my parents.
Climax	I talk to my parents on the phone.
Falling Action	I cry.
Resolution	In the end, I realize it's finally all over.

Once you have the basic storyline, you can add notes about where you might put some of your invention writing — description of people and places, dialogue, remembered feelings and thoughts, and reflections on the event from your present perspective. You also may see where you still need to fill in details. Use this outline to guide your drafting, but do not feel tied to it because you are likely to make discoveries as you draft your essay. Your outline may also be helpful when you revise your draft, so be sure to hang on to it.

Drafting

If you have not already begun to draft your essay, this section will help by suggesting how to craft your opening sentences; how to use temporal transitions and verb tenses to draft a narrative that readers will be able to follow; and how to decide when to quote, paraphrase, or summarize. Drafting isn't always a smooth process, so don't be afraid to skip the hard parts or to write notes to yourself about what you could do next. If you get stuck while drafting, go back over your invention writing. You may be able to copy and paste some of it into your evolving draft. Or you may need to do some additional invention to fill in details in your draft.

Writing the Opening Sentences

You could try out one or two different ways of beginning your story — possibly from the list that follows — but do not agonize over the first sentences because you are likely to discover the best way to begin only after you've written a rough draft. Review your invention writing to see if you have already written something that would work to launch your story. To engage your readers' interest from the start, consider setting the stage with the following opening strategies:

- a compelling graphic description of the place or a person
- a startling specific narrative action you or someone else took that would surprise readers and arouse curiosity
- a telling bit of dialogue
- your present reflections on your past self or on the context of the event
- your feelings at the time

A Sentence Strategy: Time Transitions and Verb Tenses

As you draft a remembered event essay, you will be trying to help readers follow the sequence of actions in time. To prevent readers from becoming confused about the chronology, writers use a combination of time transitions and verb tenses to help readers understand when the event occurred and when particular actions occurred in relation to other actions.

Cite calendar or clock time to establish when the event took place and to help readers follow the action over time. Writers often situate the event in terms of the date or time. Brandt, for example, establishes in the opening paragraph that the event occurred when she went to the mall for "a day of last-minute Christmas shopping." Early in her essay, Dillard identifies when the event took place: "On one weekday morning after Christmas . . ." (par. 3). Ellis also uses calendar time to establish the time the event began, but because his narrative spans months instead of hours, he gives readers a series of time cues throughout the essay so we can easily follow the progression: "A year before his death" (par. 1); "That August, I was 22" (par. 4); and so on.

Use temporal transitions combined with appropriate verb tenses to help readers follow a sequence of actions. Writers can employ temporal transitions such as *after, before, in the meantime,* and *simultaneously* to help readers keep track of the sequence of actions:

> *When* I got back to the Snoopy section, I took one look at the lines. . . . (Brandt, par. 3)

In this example, *when* signals that one action followed another in time: Brandt did not take a look at the lines until she got back to the Snoopy section. Here's another example of a simple one-thing-and-then-another time progression:

> We all spread out, banged together some regular snowballs, took aim, and, *when* the Buick drew nigh, fired. (Dillard, par. 7)

In this example, the word *when* together with a series of simple past-tense verbs indicates that a sequence of actions took place in a straightforward chronological order: they took their positions, made snowballs, aimed, the Buick came near, they threw their snowballs.

Transitions can also signal a more complicated relationship between the actions:

> *As* we all piled into the car, *I knew* it was going to be a fabulous day. (Brandt, par. 1)

In this example, *as* indicates that the first action (piling into the car) occurred at the same time as the second action (I knew).

In many cases, the transition itself makes clear the order of the actions. But in some cases, readers have to pay attention to the verb tenses as well as the transitional word:

> *When I returned* to his apartment, *I was almost smiling.* (Ellis, par. 16)

In this example, Ellis uses *when* to indicate that both actions (returning and smiling) took place at the same time. Ellis's first verb — *returned* — is in simple past tense, indicating that the action began and ended in the past, but his second verb — *was . . . smiling* — is in the past progressive tense, indicating that the action began and continued. In other words, he began smiling before he returned and continued to do so after he returned.

For more on temporal transitions, go to bedfordstmartins.com/ theguide and click on Sentence Strategies; see also p. 611 in Chapter 13, Cueing the Reader.

Working with Sources:
Quoting, Paraphrasing, and Summarizing

The primary source for remembered event essays is the writer's memory of what was said at the time the event occurred. Although writers may not remember exactly what was said, they often reconstruct dialogue in order to make their stories dramatic. Quoting tends to be more dramatic than either paraphrasing or summarizing, but you can use any of these strategies as you draft and revise your remembered event essay.

When you quote, you must enclose the words, phrases, or sentences within quotation marks. You may present a sequence of quotations, each in its own paragraph, as in this example of turn-taking:

"Excuse me. Are you a relative of this young girl?"

"Yes, I'm her sister. What's the problem?"

"Well, I just caught her shoplifting and I'm afraid I'll have to call the police."

"What did she take?"

"This button."

In this example from paragraphs 9–13, Brandt is careful to present the dialogue in a way that lets readers know who is speaking during each turn. Sometimes writers identify the speakers in the paragraphs that come before the turn-taking, as in this example:

There was a pause as he called my mother to the phone. For the first time that night, I was close to tears. I wished I had never stolen that stupid pin. I wanted to give the phone to one of the officers because I was too ashamed to tell my mother the truth, but I had no choice.

"Jean, where are you?"

"I'm, umm, in jail." (Brandt, pars. 25–27)

You can also use speaker tags to identify the speaker, as Dillard does in the single quote she includes in her essay:

"You stupid kids," he began perfunctorily. (par. 18)

You can learn more about speaker tags in the Working with Sources section in Chapter 3, pp. 112–13.

Whereas Brandt lets her quotations stand by themselves, writers often encase quotes in description and narration, as in this example:

My uncle's wife was sitting on her prayer platform in the drawing room. Amina stormed in, scattering servants before her like chaff. "Your relative . . . ," was Amina's opening salvo, ". . . has been making obscene remarks to my niece." Her mouth opened, but before she could find her voice, Amina fired her heaviest guns: "Over the telephone!"

"How dare you!" her rival began.

It gave Amina exactly the opportunity she needed to move in for the kill. "What? Do you support this lewd conduct? Are we living in an American movie? . . ." (Shah, pars. 7–9)

Paraphrasing and summarizing are alternatives to quoting that you should consider in cases where your readers need only a sense of what was said. Whereas quoting presents the words as if they had been spoken, paraphrase and summary use the writer's own words without quotation marks. Here are several examples of paraphrasing:

> Next thing I knew, he was talking about calling the police and having me arrested and thrown in jail . . . (Brandt, par. 6)

> I was told breathlessly that he was a fighter pilot in the Pakistani Air Force. (Shah, par. 3)

> He explained that if the pneumonia didn't surrender to the antibiotics, he very likely would die. (Ellis, par. 19)

> He said that at his memorial service he wanted a childhood friend turned opera singer to sing an old spiritual, "There's a Man Goin' Round Taking Names." (Ellis, par. 20)

Notice that these paraphrases essentially repeat the substance of what was said without representing it as the speaker's words. Now look at two examples of summarizing:

> He told me about his boyfriends and girlfriends and his heartaches. . . . (Ellis, par. 17)

> The day he disclosed his matrimonial ambitions for me. . . . (Shah, par. 1)

To learn more about quoting, paraphrasing, and summarizing, see Chapter 24, pp. 756-64.

Notice that these summaries identify the topics, giving the gist but none of the details of what was said.

Critical Reading Guide

Your instructor may arrange a peer review session in class or online where you can exchange drafts with your classmates and give each other a thoughtful critical reading, pointing out what works well and suggesting ways to improve the draft. This Critical Reading Guide can also be used productively by a tutor in the writing center or by a roommate or family member. A good critical reading does three things: it lets the writer know how well the reader understands the point of the story, praises what works best, and indicates where the draft could be improved.

Basic Features

For a printable version of this Critical Reading Guide, go to bedfordstmartins.com/theguide.

1. Assess how well the story is told.

   Praise: Give an example in the story where the storytelling is especially effective — for example, where the speaker tags help make a dialogue dramatic or where specific narrative actions show people in action.

   Critique: Tell the writer where the storytelling could be improved — for example, where the suspense slackens, the story lacks drama, or the chronology is confusing.

2. Consider how vividly people and places are described.

   Praise: Give an example in the story where the description is particularly vivid — for example, where sensory description is particularly powerful or an apt comparison makes an image come alive.

Critique: Tell the writer where the description could be improved — for example, where objects in the scene are not named or described with specific sensory detail, where the description is sparse or seems to contradict rather than reinforce the significance.

3. Evaluate how well the autobiographical significance is conveyed.

Summarize: Tell the writer what you understand is the story's basic conflict and significance.

Praise: Give an example where the significance comes across effectively — for example, where remembered feelings are poignant, the present perspective seems insightful, or the description creates a strong dominant impression that reinforces the significance.

Critique: Tell the writer where the significance could be strengthened — for example, if the conflict is too easily resolved, if a moral seems tacked on at the end, or if a more interesting meaning could be drawn out of the experience.

4. If the writer has expressed concern about anything in the draft that you have not discussed, respond to that concern.

Making Comments Electronically Most word processing software offers features that allow you to insert comments directly into the text of someone else's document. Many readers prefer to make their comments this way because it tends to be faster than writing on hard copy and space is virtually unlimited; it also eliminates the process of deciphering handwritten comments. Where such features are not available, simply typing comments directly into a document in a contrasting color can provide the same advantages.

Revising

Very likely you have already thought of ways to improve your draft, and you may even have begun to revise it. In this section is a Troubleshooting chart that may help. Before using the chart, however, it is a good idea to

- review critical reading comments from your classmates, instructor, or writing center tutor, and
- make an outline of your draft so that you can look at it analytically.

You may have made an outline before writing your draft, but after drafting you need to see what you actually wrote, not what you intended to write. You can outline the draft quickly by noting in the margin the elements of the dramatic narrative pyramid — exposition, rising action, climax, falling action, and resolution — and highlighting the basic features — storytelling, describing people and places, and indicating significance.

For an electronic version of the Troubleshooting Chart, go to **bedfordstmartins** .com/theguide.

Troubleshooting Your Draft

● ● ● **Basic Features**

	Problem	Suggestions for Revising the Draft
A Well-Told Story	The story starts too slowly.	☐ Shorten the exposition. ☐ Move a bit of dialogue or specific narrative action up front. ☐ Start with something surprising. ☐ Consider beginning with a flashback or flashforward.
	The chronology is confusing.	☐ Add or change time transitions. ☐ Clarify verb tenses.
	The suspense slackens or the story lacks drama.	☐ Add remembered feelings and thoughts to heighten anticipation. ☐ Add dialogue and specific narrative action. ☐ Build rising action in stages with multiple high points. ☐ Move or cut background information and description.
	The conflict is vague or seems unconnected to the significance.	☐ Add dramatized dialogue or specific narrative actions. ☐ Clarify your remembered feelings or thoughts. ☐ Reflect on the conflict from your present perspective.
Vivid Description of People and Places	Places are hard to visualize.	☐ Name objects in the scene. ☐ Add sensory detail. ☐ Try out a comparison to evoke a particular mood. ☐ Consider adding a visual — a photograph or other memorabilia.
	People do not come alive.	☐ Describe a physical feature or mannerism that gives each person individuality. ☐ Add speaker tags to characterize people and show their feelings. ☐ Liven up the dialogue with faster repartee.
	Some descriptions weaken the dominant impression.	☐ Omit extraneous details. ☐ Add a simile or metaphor to strengthen the dominant impression. ☐ Rethink the impression you want your writing to convey and the significance it suggests.
Auto-biographical Significance	Readers do not identify or empathize with the writer.	☐ Tell about your background or the particular context. ☐ Give readers a glimpse of the continuing significance of the event years later. ☐ Reveal the cultural influences acting on you or emphasize the historical period in which the event occurred.
	Readers do not under-stand the significance.	☐ Try explaining the significance directly by explaining your present perspective.
	The significance seems too pat or simplistic.	☐ Develop contradictions or show ambivalences. ☐ Stress the social or cultural dimensions of the event. ☐ Try to develop a more complex and interesting significance.

As the amateur historian and rancher were working on the newspaper article described in the scenario at the beginning of this chapter (see p. 15), they considered visual and textual elements appropriate to writing about remembered events, including photographs of the area and quotations from the rancher's tape-recorded story.

Thinking About Document Design:
Integrating Visuals

Selecting Visuals

To begin, the historian and rancher discussed what visuals might accompany the final written piece. The historian found old snow-day photographs from the newspaper's archives, and the rancher selected a compelling photo of his wife standing on the roof of the family home after the storm. The historian and the rancher also considered including a painting of an isolated homestead and an early snapshot that the rancher had taken of his house in 1931, but decided that the painting was too abstract for a newspaper story, and the snapshot did not capture the snowstorm, which was the focus of the newspaper's special supplement. They narrowed their selection to two black-and-white photos — the photo of his wife standing on the house and a family photo taken in the spring — both of which emphasized the key point they wanted readers to get from the story: the importance of family in the face of adversity.

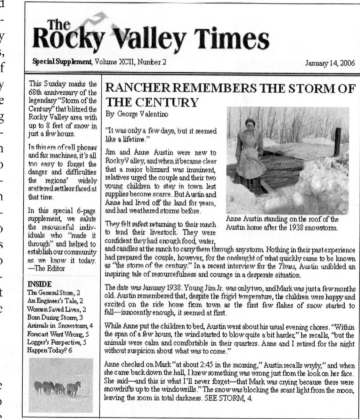

Pulling Revealing Quotations

After reviewing the draft of their article, the amateur historian and the rancher chose two potential "pull-quotes" (inset or otherwise highlighted quotations) from the story that they thought would capture readers' attention and convey some of the story's drama: "It was only a few days, but it seemed like a lifetime" and "I knew I had to make a decision — to continue on through the storm, or to head back to the house." The idea was not to summarize the rancher's story in these quotations, but to emphasize to readers the significance of the event as well as to leave readers with a good understanding of the event as they finished reading the piece. The newspaper selected the first quotation as the story lead.

A Note on Grammar and Spelling Checkers
These tools can be helpful, but don't rely on them exclusively to catch errors in your text: Spelling checkers cannot catch misspellings that are themselves words, such as *to* for *too*. Grammar checkers miss some problems, sometimes give faulty advice for fixing problems, and can flag correct items as wrong. Use these tools as a second line of defense after your own (and, ideally, another reader's) proofreading/editing efforts.

Editing and Proofreading

Several errors occur often in essays about remembered events: missing commas after introductory elements, fused sentences, and misused past-perfect verbs. The following guidelines will help you check your essay for these common errors.

Missing Commas after Introductory Elements

The Problem: Remembered-event essays often include sentences with introductory elements, especially temporal transitions to indicate calendar or clock time and to show when one action occurred in relation to other actions. A comma after such an element tells readers that the main part of the sentence is about to begin. If the introductory element is lengthy or complex, leaving the comma out can make your sentence confusing.

How to Correct It: Add a comma for clarity.

For practice, go to bedfordstmartins.com/theguide/exercisecentral and click on Commas after Introductory Elements.

▶ Through the nine-day run of the play, the acting just kept getting better and better.

▶ Knowing that the struggle was over, I felt through my jacket to find tea bags and cookies the robber had taken from the kitchen.

▶ As I stepped out of the car, I knew something was wrong.

Using the Past Perfect

The Problem: One common problem in writing about a remembered event is the failure to use the past perfect when it is needed, which can sometimes make your meaning unclear (what happened when, exactly?).

How to Correct It: Check passages where you recount events to be sure you are using the past perfect to indicate an action that was completed at the time of another past action (she *had finished* her work when we saw her).

▶ I had three people in the car, something my father ^had^ told me not to do on several occasions.

▶ Coach Kernow told me I ~~ran~~ ^had run^ faster than ever before.

For practice, go to bedfordstmartins.com/theguide/exercisecentral and click on The Past Perfect and/or A Common ESL Problem: Forming the Past Perfect.

ESL Note: It is important to remember that the past perfect is formed with *had* followed by a past participle. Past participles usually end in *-ed, -d, -en, -n,* or *-t: worked, hoped, eaten, taken, bent.*

▶ Before Tania went to Moscow last year, she had not really ~~speak~~ ^spoken^ Russian.

Fused Sentences

The Problem: When you write about a remembered event, you try to re-create a scene. This sometimes results in fused sentences, where two independent clauses are joined with no punctuation or connecting word between them.

How to Correct It:

- Rewrite the sentence, subordinating one clause.
- Make the clauses separate sentences.
- Join the two clauses with a comma and *and, but, or, nor, for, so,* or *yet.*
- Join the two clauses with a semicolon.

> The
> ▶ Sleet glazed the windshield. ~~the~~ wipers were frozen stuck.

> , and
> ▶ Sleet glazed the windshield the wipers were frozen stuck.

> ;
> ▶ Sleet glazed the windshield the wipers were frozen stuck.

> As sleet   became
> ▶ ~~Sleet~~ glazed the windshield the wipers ~~were~~ frozen stuck.

For practice, go to **bedfordstmartins.com/ theguide/exercisecentral** and click on Fused Sentences.

A Writer at Work

Jean Brandt's Essay from Invention to Revision

In this section, we look at the writing process that Jean Brandt followed in composing her essay, "Calling Home." You will see some of her invention writing and her complete first draft, which you can then compare to the final draft printed on pp. 19–22.

Invention

Brandt's invention work produced about nine pages, but it took her only two hours, spread out over four days, to complete. She began by choosing an event and then reimagining the place with specific sensory details and recalling the other people involved.

Creating a Dialogue

She also wrote two dialogues, one with her sister Sue and the other with her father. Following is the dialogue between her and her sister:

SUE: Jean, why did you do it?

ME: I don't know. I guess I didn't want to wait in that long line. Sue, what am I going to tell Mom and Dad?

SUE: Don't worry about that yet, the detective might not really call the police.

ME: I can't believe I was stupid enough to take it.

SUE: I know. I've been there before. Now when he comes back, try crying and acting like you're really upset. Tell him how sorry you are and that it was the first time you ever stole something, but make sure you cry. It got me off the hook once.

ME: I don't think I can force myself to cry. I'm not really that upset. I don't think the shock's worn off. I'm more worried about Mom.

SUE: Who knows? Maybe she won't have to find out.

ME: God, I hope not. Hey, where's Louie and Grandma? Grandma doesn't know about this, does she?

SUE: No, I sort of told Lou what was going on so he's just taking Grandma around shopping.

ME: Isn't she wondering where we are?

SUE: I told him to tell her we would meet them in an hour.

ME: How am I ever going to face her? Mom and Dad might possibly understand or at least get over it, but Grandma? This is gonna kill her.

SUE: Don't worry about that right now. Here comes the detective. Now try to look like you're sorry. Try to cry.

Brandt wrote this dialogue quickly, trying to capture the language of excited talk, keeping the exchanges brief. She included a version of this dialogue in her first draft (see pp. 60–61), but excluded it from the final essay. Even though she eventually decided to leave it out, this invention dialogue helped her work out her thoughts about the event and enabled her to evaluate how to dramatize it.

Recalling Remembered Feelings and Thoughts

In an attempt to bring the autobiographical significance of the event into focus, Brandt explored her remembered as well as her current feelings and thoughts about the experience:

> Being arrested for shoplifting was significant because it changed some of my basic attitudes. Since that night I've never again considered stealing anything. This event would reveal how my attitude toward the law and other people has changed from disrespectful to very respectful.

Reading this statement might lead us to expect a moralistic story of how someone learned something the hard way. As we look at the subsequent invention activities, however, we will see how her focus shifts to her relations with other people.

> I was scared, humiliated, and confused. I was terrified when I realized what was happening. I can still see the manager and his badge and remember what I felt when I knew who he was. I just couldn't believe it. I didn't want to run. I felt there wasn't anything I could do--I was afraid, embarrassed, worried, mad that it happened. I didn't show my feelings at all. I tried to look very calm on the outside, but inside I was extremely nervous. The nervousness might have come through in my voice a little. I wanted the people around me to think I was tough and that I could handle the situation. I was really disappointed with myself. Getting arrested made me realize how wrong my actions were. I felt very ashamed. Afterward I had to talk to my father about it. I didn't say much of anything except that I was wrong and I was sorry. The immediate consequence was being taken to jail and then later having to call my parents and tell them what happened. I hated to call my parents. That was the hardest part. I remember how much I dreaded that. My mom was really hurt.

Naming specific feelings, Brandt focuses here on the difference between what she felt and how she acted. She remembers her humiliation at being arrested as well as the terrible moment when she had to tell her parents. As we will see, this concern with her parents' reaction, more than her own humiliation, becomes the focus of her remembered feelings and thoughts.

Exploring Her Present Perspective

In exploring her first response to the event, Brandt wrote quickly, jotting down memories as they came to mind. Next, she reread this first exploration and attempted to state briefly what the incident really revealed about her:

> I think it reveals that I was not a hard-core criminal. I was trying to live up to Robin Files's (supposedly my best girlfriend) expectations, even though I actually knew that what I was doing was wrong.

Stopping to focus her thoughts like this helped Brandt see the point of what she had just written and discover the autobiographical significance of the event. Next, she wrote about her present perspective on the event.

> At first I was ashamed to tell anyone that I had been arrested. It was as if I couldn't admit it myself. Now I'm glad it happened, because who knows where I'd be now if I hadn't been caught. I still don't tell many people about it. Never before have I written about it. I think my response was appropriate. If I'd broken down and cried, it wouldn't have helped me any, so it's better that I reacted calmly. My actions and responses show that I was trying to be tough. I thought that that was the way to gain respectability. If I were to get arrested now (of course it wouldn't be for shoplifting), I think I'd react the same way because it doesn't do any good to get emotional. My current feelings are ones of appreciation. I feel lucky because

> I was set straight early. Now I can look back on it and laugh, but at the same time
> know how serious it was. I am emotionally distant now because I can view the event
> objectively rather than subjectively. My feelings are settled now. I don't get upset
> thinking about it. I don't feel angry at the manager or the police. I think I was more
> upset about my parents than about what was happening to me. After the first part of
> it was over I mainly worried about what my parents would think.

In writing about her present perspective, Brandt reassures herself that she feels
comfortable enough to write for class about this event: she no longer feels humiliated, embarrassed, or angry. She is obviously pleased to recall that she did not lose
control and show her true feelings. Staying calm, not getting emotional, looking
tough — these are the personal qualities Brandt wants others to see in her. Exploring
her present perspective seems to have led to a new, respectable self-image she can
proudly display to her readers:

> My present perspective shows that I'm a reasonable person. I can admit when
> I'm wrong and accept the punishment that was due me. I find that I can be con-
> cerned about others even when I'm in trouble.

Clarifying Her Purpose and Audience

Next, Brandt reflected on what she had written and restated the event's significance,
with particular emphasis on her readers' likely reactions:

> The event was important because it entirely changed one aspect of my charac-
> ter. I will be disclosing that I was once a thief, and I think many of my readers will
> be able to identify with my story, even though they won't admit it.

This writing reveals that Brandt is now confident that she has chosen an event with
personal significance. She knows what she will be disclosing about herself and feels
comfortable doing it. In her brief focusing statements, she begins by moralizing ("my
attitude . . . changed") and blaming others ("Robin Files") but concludes by acknowledging what she did. She is now prepared to disclose it to readers ("I was once a thief").
Also, she thinks readers will like her story because she suspects many of them will recall
doing something illegal and feeling guilty about it, even if they never got caught.

The First Draft

The day after completing the invention writing, Brandt reviewed her invention and
composed her first draft on a word processor. It took her about an hour to write
the draft, and she wrote steadily without doing a lot of rearranging or correcting of
obvious typos and grammatical errors. She knew this would not be her only draft.

> It was two days before Christmas and my older sister and brother, my grand-   1
> mother, and I were rushing around doing last-minute shopping. After going to a few
> stores we decided to go to Lakewood Center shopping mall. It was packed with other
> frantic shoppers like ourselves from one end to the other. The first store we went to
> (the first and last for me) was the General Store. The General Store is your typical
> gift shop. They mainly have the cutesy knick-knacks, posters, frames and that sort.

The store is decorated to resemble an old-time western general store but the appearance doesn't quite come off.

We were all browsing around and I saw a basket of buttons so I went to see what the different ones were. One of the first ones I noticed was a Snoopy button. I'm not sure what it said on it, something funny I'm sure and besides I was in love with anything Snoopy when I was 13. I took it out of the basket and showed it to my sister and she said "Why don't you buy it?" I thought about it but the lines at the cashiers were outrageous and I didn't think it was worth it for a 75 cent item. Instead I figured just take it and I did. I thought I was so sly about it. I casually slipped it into my pocket and assumed I was home free since no one pounced on me.

Everyone was ready to leave this shop so we made our way through the crowds to the entrance. My grandmother and sister were ahead of my brother and I. They were almost to the entrance of May Co. and we were about 5 to 10 yards behind when I felt this tap on my shoulder. I turned around already terror struck, and this man was flashing some kind of badge in my face. It happened so fast I didn't know what was going on. Louie finally noticed I wasn't with him and came back for me. Jack explained I was being arrested for shoplifting and if my parents were here then Louie should go find them. Louie ran to get Susie and told her about it but kept it from Grandma.

By the time Sue got back to the General Store I was in the back office and Jack was calling the police. I was a little scared but not really. It was sort of exciting. My sister was telling me to try and cry but I couldn't. About 20 minutes later two cops came and handcuffed me, led me through the mall outside to the police car. I was kind of embarrassed when they took me through the mall in front of all those people. When they got me in the car they began questioning me, while driving me to the police station. Questions just to fill out the report — age, sex, address, color of eyes, etc.

Then when they were finished they began talking about Jack and what a nuisance he was. I gathered that Jack had every single person who shoplifted, no matter what their age, arrested. The police were getting really fed up with it because it was a nuisance for them to have to come way out to the mall for something as petty as that. To hear the police talk about my "crime" that way felt good because it was like what I did wasn't really so bad. It made me feel a bit relieved. When we walked into the station I remember the desk sergeant joking with the arresting officers about "well we got another one of Jack's hardened criminals." Again, I felt my crime lacked any seriousness at all.

Next they handcuffed me to a table and questioned me further and then I had to phone my mom. That was the worst. I never was so humiliated in my life. Hearing the disappointment in her voice was worse punishment than the cops could ever give me.

Brandt's first draft establishes the main sequence of actions. About a third of it is devoted to the store manager, an emphasis that disappears by the final draft. What ends up having prominence in the final draft — Brandt's feelings about telling her parents and her conversations with them — appears here only in a few lines at the very end. But mentioning the interaction suggests its eventual importance.

Critical Reading and Revision

Brandt revised this first draft for another student to read critically. In this revised draft, she includes dialogues with her sister and with the police officers. She also provides more information about her actions as she considered buying the Snoopy button and then decided to steal it instead. She includes visual details of the manager's office. This draft is not much different in emphasis from the first draft, however, and still ends with a long section about the police officers and the station. The parents are mentioned briefly only at the very end.

The reader told Brandt how much he liked her story and admired her frankness. However, he did not encourage her to develop the dramatic possibilities in calling her parents and meeting them afterward. In fact, he encouraged her to keep the dialogue with the police officers about the manager and to include what the manager said to the police.

In her final version, "Calling Home," Brandt's final revision shows that she did not take her reader's advice. She reduces the role of the police officers, eliminating any dialogue with them. She greatly expands the role of her parents: The last third of the essay is now focused on her remembered feelings about calling them and seeing them afterward. In terms of dramatic importance, the phone call home now equals the arrest. When we recall Brandt's earliest invention writings, we can see that she was headed toward this conclusion all along, but she needed invention, two drafts, a critical reading, a final revision, and about two weeks to get there.

Thinking Critically About What You Have Learned

In this chapter, you have learned a great deal about this genre from reading several autobiographical stories and writing one of your own. To consolidate your learning, it is helpful to think metacognitively; that is, to reflect not only on what you learned but on how you learned it. Following are two brief activities your instructor may ask you to do.

Reflecting on Your Writing

Your instructor may ask you to turn in with your essay and process materials a brief metacognitive essay or letter reflecting on what you have learned about writing your essay remembering an event. Choose among the following invention activities those that seem most productive for you.

- Explain how your purpose and audience — what you wanted your readers to learn about you from reading your story — influenced *one* of your decisions as a writer, such as what you put in the exposition section of your story, how you used dialogue to intensify the drama of the climax, or how you integrated your remembered thoughts and feelings into your storytelling.

- Discuss what you learned about yourself as a writer in the process of writing this particular essay. For example, what part of the process did you find most challenging, or did you try something new like getting a critical reading of your draft or outlining your draft in order to revise it?

- If you were to give advice to a friend who was about to write a remembered event essay, what would you say?

- Which of the readings in this chapter influenced your essay? Explain the influence, citing specific examples from your essay and the reading.

- If you got good advice from a critical reader, explain exactly how the person helped you — perhaps by questioning the conflict in a way that enabled you to refocus your story's significance or pointing out passages that needed clearer time markers to better orient readers.

Considering the Social Dimensions: Autobiography and Self-Discovery

If writing a remembered event essay leads to self-discovery, what do we mean by the "self"? Should we think of the self as our "true" essence or as the different roles we play in different situations? If we accept the idea of an essential self, writing about significant events in our lives can help us in the search to discover who we truly are. Given this idea of the self, we might see Jean Brandt, for example, as searching to understand whether she is the kind of person who breaks the law and only cares when she is caught and has to face her parents' disapproval. If, on the other hand, we accept the idea that the various roles we play are what create the self, then writing about a remembered event allows us to reveal the many sides of our personalities. This view of the self assumes that we present different self-images to different people in different situations. Given this idea, we might see Brandt as presenting her sassy teenage side to the police but keeping her vulnerability hidden from them.

1. ***Consider how your remembered event essay might be an exercise in self-discovery.*** Planning and writing your essay, did you see yourself as discovering your true self or examining how you reacted in a particular situation? Do you think your essay reveals your single, essential, true self, or does it show only an aspect of the person you understand yourself to be?

2. ***Write a page or so explaining your ideas about self-discovery and truth in remembered event essays.*** Connect your ideas to your own essay and to the readings in this chapter.

3
●●●●

Writing Profiles

IN COLLEGE COURSES To fulfill a requirement for an upper-division education course, a student who plans to teach sixth grade decides to study collaborative learning in action. The student arranges to visit an elementary school class that is beginning a project on immigration. On three separate visits, she observes a group of three students working together on the project and interviews them individually and as a group. She also interviews the teacher about her goals for the project and her views of the advantages and challenges of collaborative learning.

After reviewing the notes from her observation and the tapes of her interviews, the student roughs out outlines for both narrative and topical organizations of her profile. After considering both, she decides that a narrative plan would be likely to engage her readers more effectively. She then writes a draft based on her outline. To keep the focus on students and their progress, she reports as a spectator, weaving her insights about collaborative learning into a detailed narrative of a typical half-hour meeting. From her profile emerges the central idea that sixth graders' collaborative work is unlikely to succeed unless the students, along with their teacher, frequently reflect on what they are learning and on how they can work together more productively.

After completing her project, she decides to publish it online so that classmates and others interested in collaborative learning can read her work. (See Thinking about Document Design on p. 118.)

IN THE COMMUNITY

A newspaper reporter is assigned to write a profile of a large-scale mural project recently commissioned by the city for a wall sheltering a section of the city's central park.

Having scheduled an appointment, the reporter visits the studio of the local artist in charge of the project. They discuss the artist's career, the specifics of the mural project, and the artist's views of other notable civic art projects. The artist invites the reporter to spend the following day at the mural site. Before he leaves, the reporter takes several digital photos of the artist and the studio.

The next day when the reporter arrives at the mural site, the artist puts him to work alongside two volunteers. This firsthand experience, informal interviews with volunteers, and photos of the process help the reporter describe the mural painting from a participant-observer's point of view.

Later, writing for the Sunday local affairs section of the paper, the reporter organizes the profile around different topics: the artist's background and goals for the project; the experience of volunteers working on it; and the mural's function as civic art. As the reporter presents each topic, he uses photos and vivid description of the artist, his helpers, and the mural itself, seeking to capture the civic spirit that pervades the entire project.

IN THE WORKPLACE

For a company newsletter, a public-relations officer profiles the corporation's new chief executive officer (CEO). He follows the CEO from meeting to meeting, taking photographs and observing her interactions. Between meetings, he interviews her about her management philosophy and her five-year plan for the corporation. With her permission, he records these brief interviews. Immediately after the interviews he listens to the recordings, making notes and writing down questions to ask in a follow-up interview.

A day later, the CEO invites the writer to visit her at home. He stays for dinner and then watches the CEO help her daughter with homework. He converses with her husband. He also takes more photographs.

The writer reviews his notes, the recordings of their interviews, and the photos he took. He decides to illustrate the profile with two images, one showing the CEO at a meeting and the other showing her with her daughter. As he reports on some of the immediate challenges she anticipates for the corporation, he tries to convey the ease and confidence she shows both at work and at home.

The writers in the scenarios that open this chapter profile a group of young students involved in a complex learning activity, an artist and neighborhood volunteers creating a public mural, and a high-ranking business executive going about her daily activities. Whatever their subject, profile writers strive most of all to enable readers to imagine the person, place, or activity that is the focus of the profile. Writers succeed only through specific and vivid details: how the person dresses, gestures, and talks; what the place looks, sounds, and smells like; what the activity requires of those who participate in it. Not only must the details be vivid, but they also must help to convey a writer's perspective, offering some insight, idea, or interpretation of the subject's cultural significance.

Because profiles share many features — including description, narration, and dialogue — with essays about remembered events, you may use many of the strategies learned in Chapter 2: Remembering Events when you write your profile. The differences are also important, however. To write about a remembered event, you look inside for memories in order to write about yourself and your experiences with other people. To write a profile, you look outside for fresh observations of an unfamiliar subject in order to understand it better. Still, both remembered event and profile require you to strive for understanding, to recognize significance, and to gain a new perspective.

The scope of your profile may be large or small, depending on your subject. You could attend a single event such as a parade, dress rehearsal for a play, or city council meeting and write your observations of the place, people, and activities. Or you might conduct an interview with a person who has an unusual occupation and write a profile based on your interview notes. If you have the time to do more extensive research, you might write a more complete profile based on several visits to a place and interviews with various people there.

Reading profiles and writing your own profile will make you a more insightful reader of the cultural practices of everyday life. Doing the various kinds of research needed to write a profile will also give you confidence in your observational skills and your ability to ask probing questions. You will learn how to break through the façade and better understand the inner workings of your subject. At the same time, you will learn how to write engagingly, to interest readers and keep them reading.

A Collaborative Activity:

Practice Conducting an Interview

Part 1. Get together in a small group and ask someone to volunteer to be the interviewee while the rest of the group acts as interviewers. The interviewers should spend a couple of minutes preparing questions and then, after choosing an interviewer to begin, take turns asking questions. When you act as interviewer, be sure to listen to what the interviewee says and ask follow-up questions. All interviewers should take notes quoting and summarizing what the interviewee says as well as describing the interviewee's tone of voice, facial expressions, and gestures.

Part 2. Discuss these questions as a group:

- What was the hardest part of interviewing: thinking of questions, following up, taking notes, or something else?

- If you were to write a brief profile based on this interview to present to the rest of the class, what information would you emphasize? What would you quote? How would you describe the interviewee? What would guide these choices?

Reading Profiles

Basic Features

As you read the profiles in this chapter, you will see how different authors incorporate the basic features of the genre.

● Detailed Information about the Subject

Read first to identify the subject of the profile. Profiles are about the following subjects:

- a place where something interesting happens (such as a hospital emergency room)
- an activity (such as the mural project in the second scenario)
- a person (such as the CEO profiled in the third scenario)
- a group of people (such as the students profiled in the first scenario)

Much of the pleasure of reading a profile comes from the way the writer presents *detailed information* about the subject. To make the information entertaining as well as readable and interesting, profile writers interweave bits of information into a tapestry that includes vivid descriptions, lively anecdotes, and arresting quotations.

Because profile writers get their information primarily from observing and interviewing, and because they try to give readers a vivid picture of the subject, *describing* is perhaps the most important writing strategy for presenting information. **Describing** includes the following activities:

- *detailing* what people look like, how they dress, gesture, and talk
- *showing* what the observer saw, heard, smelled, touched, and tasted
- *quoting, summarizing,* or *paraphrasing* the people interviewed

Look also for these other ways of presenting information about the subject: *classifying, defining new terms, comparing and contrasting, identifying causes or effects,* and *giving examples.*

● A Clear Organizational Plan

Profiles can be organized according to two different plans:

- a **narrative plan** that interweaves the information with elements of a story
- a **topical plan** that groups the information into topics and moves from one topic to another

Whereas a narrative plan may be more engaging, a topical plan may deliver information more efficiently. *As you read the profiles in this chapter, consider why the writer might have chosen one plan or the other.* What was gained? Was anything lost?

◆ A Role for the Writer

Look also at the role that the writer assumes in relation to his or her subject:

- As a **spectator** or **detached observer**, the writer's position is like that of the reader, an outsider looking in on the people and their activities (such as the college student in the first scenario).

- As a **participant observer**, the writer participates in the activity being profiled and acquires insider knowledge (such as the reporter in the second scenario profiling the mural project).

◆ A Perspective on the Subject

All of the basic features listed above — detailed information; the plan of the profile; and the writer's role — support the writer's **perspective on the subject**, the main idea or cultural significance that the writer wants readers to take away from reading the profile. Profiles, like remembered event essays, seldom state the thesis directly. Instead, they convey it by creating a *dominant impression* from the descriptive details and other kinds of information together with the writer's thoughts and comments.

Purpose and Audience

Profiles are a popular way to learn about interesting people, activities, and places. You can find profiles in many different venues — blogs, television, and radio, as well as in traditional magazines, newspapers, and books. Academic disciplines such as cultural studies, anthropology, and literacy studies often use a type of profile called an *ethnography*. Ethnographies use the same field research methods and employ the same writing strategies as more traditional journalistic profiles. They differ in that ethnographers do their research over an extended period of time and usually study groups of people who identify themselves as members of a particular community (for example, a group of Twitter users, Facebook friends, or students who share a dorm room or belong to the same club). Depending on their academic interest, ethnographers may focus on the group's patterns of communication, how newcomers are initiated into the group, how conflicts are handled, how relationships form and dissolve, and so on. Though you will not have the time or resources to study your subject in as much depth as an ethnographer normally does, any of these topics could become the focus of the profile you write for this course.

*As you read profiles, ask yourself what seems to be the writer's **purpose** in writing about this particular subject.* For example, does the writer seem to be writing

- to inform readers about some aspect of everyday life — the places and activities that surround us but that we may not notice, let alone get to know intimately;

- to give readers an in-depth, behind-the-scenes look at an intriguing or unusual activity — for example, a fascinating hobby or challenging career;
- to surprise readers by presenting unusual subjects or familiar ones in new ways;
- to give readers a new way to look at and think about the cultural significance of the subject;
- to present vivid descriptions and engaging stories showing how people communicate and work together, construct their identities, and define their values?

As you read, also try to grasp the writer's assumptions about the **audience**. For example, does the writer

- assume readers will know nothing or very little about the subject;
- expect readers to be interested and possibly amused by a particular aspect of the subject;
- hope readers will be intrigued by the perspective the writer takes or fascinated by certain quotes or descriptive details?

Readings

■ A recent photo of Goodbody Mortuary, the subject of Cable's profile. Does this photo match Cable's description? Would the addition of such a photo, or other photos of the mortuary, have strengthened Cable's profile?

BRIAN CABLE wrote this profile of a neighborhood mortuary when he was a first-year college student. "Death," as he explains in the opening sentence, "is a subject largely ignored by the living," so it is not surprising that he notices people averting their eyes as they walk past the mortuary on a busy commercial street. Cable, however, walks in and takes readers on a guided tour of the premises. As he presents information he learned from observing how the mortuary works — from the reception room up front to the embalming room in back — and from interviewing the people who work there, Cable lets us know his feelings and his thoughts on cultural attitudes about death.

●●●●
Basic Features
- Detailed Information
- Organizational Plan
- Writer's Role
- Perspective on the Subject

As you read, notice how Cable uses humor to defuse the inherent seriousness of the place. Also consider the questions in the margin. Your instructor may ask you to post your answers or bring them to class.

The Last Stop

Brian Cable

Let us endeavor so to live that when we come to die even the undertaker will be sorry.

— Mark Twain

What expectations do the title and epigraph (opening quote) raise for you?

Death is a subject largely ignored by the living. We don't discuss it much, not as children (when Grandpa dies, he is said to be "going away"), not as adults, not even as senior citizens. Throughout our lives, death remains intensely private. The death of a loved one can be very painful, partly because of the sense of loss, but also because someone else's mortality reminds us all too vividly of our own.

Cable begins by sharing his thoughts and observations. What impression does this opening create?

More than a few people avert their eyes as they walk past the dusty-pink building that houses the Goodbody Mortuaries. It looks a bit like a church — tall, with gothic arches and stained glass — and somewhat like an apartment complex — low, with many windows stamped out of red brick.

It wasn't at all what I had expected. I thought it would be more like Forest Lawn, serene with lush green lawns and meticulously groomed gardens, a place set apart from the hustle of day-to-day life. Here instead was an odd pink structure set in the middle of a business district. On top of the Goodbody Mortuaries sign was a large electric clock. What the hell, I thought. Mortuaries are concerned with time, too.

What organizational plan for the profile emerges in pars. 4 and 5?

I was apprehensive as I climbed the stone steps to the entrance. I feared rejection or, worse, an invitation to come and stay. The door was massive, yet it swung open easily on well-oiled hinges. "Come in," said the sign. "We're always open." Inside was a cool and quiet reception room. Curtains were drawn against the outside glare, cutting the light down to a soft glow.

I found the funeral director in the main lobby, adjacent to the reception room. Like most people, I had preconceptions about what an undertaker looked like. Mr. Deaver fulfilled my expectations entirely. Tall and thin, he even had beady eyes and a bony face. A low, slanted forehead gave way to a beaked nose. His skin, scrubbed of all color, contrasted sharply with his jet black hair. He was wearing a starched white shirt, gray pants, and black shoes. Indeed, he looked like death on two legs.

What does the detailed description of Deaver in pars. 5 and 6 contribute to Cable's profile of the mortuary?

What role has Cable adopted in writing the profile? When does it become clear?

He proved an amiable sort, however, and was easy to talk to. As funeral director, Mr. Deaver ("Call me Howard") was responsible for a wide range of services. Goodbody Mortuaries, upon notification of someone's death, will remove the remains from the hospital or home. They then prepare the body for viewing, whereupon

1

2

3

4

5

6

features distorted by illness or accident are restored to their natural condition. The body is embalmed and then placed in a casket selected by the family of the deceased. Services are held in one of three chapels at the mortuary, and afterward the casket is placed in a "visitation room," where family and friends can pay their last respects. Goodbody also makes arrangements for the purchase of a burial site and transports the body there for burial.

7   All this information Howard related in a well-practiced, professional manner. It was obvious he was used to explaining the specifics of his profession. We sat alone in the lobby. His desk was bone clean, no pencils or paper, nothing — just a telephone. He did all his paperwork at home; as it turned out, he and his wife lived right upstairs. The phone rang. As he listened, he bit his lips and squeezed his Adam's apple somewhat nervously.

8   "I think we'll be able to get him in by Friday. No, no, the family wants him cremated."

9   His tone was that of a broker conferring on the Dow Jones. Directly behind him was a sign announcing "Visa and Master Charge Welcome Here." It was tacked to the wall, right next to a crucifix.

10   "Some people have the idea that we are bereavement specialists, that we can handle emotional problems which follow a death: Only a trained therapist can do that. We provide services for the dead, not counseling for the living."

11   Physical comfort was the one thing they did provide for the living. The lobby was modestly but comfortably furnished. There were several couches, in colors ranging from earth brown to pastel blue, and a coffee table in front of each one. On one table lay some magazines and a vase of flowers. Another supported an aquarium. Paintings of pastoral scenes hung on every wall. The lobby looked more or less like that of an old hotel. Nothing seemed to match, but it had a homey, lived-in look.

12   "The last time the Goodbodies decorated was in '59, I believe. It still makes people feel welcome."

13   And so "Goodbody" was not a name made up to attract customers but the owner's family name. The Goodbody family started the business way back in 1915. Today, they do over five hundred services a year.

14   "We're in *Ripley's Believe It or Not*, along with another funeral home whose owners' names are Baggit and Sackit," Howard told me, without cracking a smile.

15   I followed him through an arched doorway into a chapel that smelled musty and old. The only illumination came from sunlight filtered through a stained glass ceiling. Ahead of us lay a casket. I could see that it contained a man dressed in a black suit.

Why do you think Cable summarizes the information in par. 6 instead of quoting Howard?

What does this observation reveal about Cable's perspective?

Why do you think he quotes Howard in par. 10, instead of paraphrasing or summarizing?

What does this observation contribute to the dominant impression?

How does Cable make the transition from topic to topic in pars. 15-18?

Wooden benches ran on either side of an aisle that led to the body. I got no closer. From the red roses across the dead man's chest, it was apparent that services had already been held.

"It was a large service," remarked Howard. "Look at that casket — a beautiful work of craftsmanship." 16

I guess it was. Death may be the great leveler, but one's coffin quickly reestablishes one's status. 17

We passed into a bright, fluorescent-lit "display room." Inside were thirty coffins, lids open, patiently awaiting inspection. Like new cars on the showroom floor, they gleamed with high-gloss finishes. 18

"We have models for every price range." 19

Indeed, there was a wide variety. They came in all colors and various materials. Some were little more than cloth-covered cardboard boxes, others were made of wood, and a few were made of steel, copper, or bronze. Prices started at $400 and averaged about $1,800. Howard motioned toward the center of the room: "The top of the line." 20

This was a solid bronze casket, its seams electronically welded to resist corrosion. Moisture-proof and air-tight, it could be hermetically sealed off from all outside elements. Its handles were plated with 14-karat gold. The price: a cool $5,000. 21

A proper funeral remains a measure of respect for the deceased. But it is expensive. In the United States the amount spent annually on funerals is about $2 billion. Among ceremonial expenditures, funerals are second only to weddings. As a result, practices are changing. Howard has been in this business for forty years. He remembers a time when everyone was buried. Nowadays, with burials costing $2,000 a shot, people often opt instead for cremation — as Howard put it, "a cheap, quick, and easy means of disposal." In some areas of the country, the cremation rate is now over 60 percent. Observing this trend, one might wonder whether burials are becoming obsolete. Do burials serve an important role in society? 22

For Tim, Goodbody's licensed mortician, the answer is very definitely yes. Burials will remain in common practice, according to the slender embalmer with the disarming smile, because they allow family and friends to view the deceased. Painful as it may be, such an experience brings home the finality of death. "Something deep within us demands a confrontation with death," Tim explained. "A last look assures us that the person we loved is, indeed, gone forever." 23

How does the comparison to a new car showroom in pars. 18–21 reveal Cable's perspective?

Where does the information in pars. 22–23 come from?

What is the function of this rhetorical question?

24   Apparently, we also need to be assured that the body will be laid to rest in comfort and peace. The average casket, with its inner-spring mattress and pleated satin lining, is surprisingly roomy and luxurious. Perhaps such an air of comfort makes it easier for the family to give up their loved one. In addition, the burial site fixes the deceased in the survivors' memory, like a new address. Cremation provides none of these comforts.

Whose perspective does this statement reflect? How do you know?

25   Tim started out as a clerk in a funeral home but then studied to become a mortician. "It was a profession I could live with," he told me with a sly grin. Mortuary science might be described as a cross between pre-med and cosmetology, with courses in anatomy and embalming as well as in restorative art.

Is Tim's definition of mortuary science helpful? Why or why not?

26   Tim let me see the preparation, or embalming, room, a white-walled chamber about the size of an operating room. Against the wall was a large sink with elbow taps and a draining board. In the center of the room stood a table with equipment for preparing the arterial embalming fluid, which consists primarily of formaldehyde, a preservative, and phenol, a disinfectant. This mixture sanitizes and also gives better color to the skin. Facial features can then be "set" to achieve a restful expression. Missing eyes, ears, and even noses can be replaced.

Which of the information in par. 26 comes from observation and which comes from interviewing Tim? How do you know?

27   I asked Tim if his job ever depressed him. He bridled at the question: "No, it doesn't depress me at all. I do what I can for people and take satisfaction in enabling relatives to see their loved ones as they were in life." He said that he felt people were becoming more aware of the public service his profession provides. Grade-school classes now visit funeral homes as often as they do police stations and museums. The mortician is no longer regarded as a minister of death.

28   Before leaving, I wanted to see a body up close. I thought I could be indifferent after all I had seen and heard, but I wasn't sure. Cautiously, I reached out and touched the skin. It felt cold and firm, not unlike clay. As I walked out, I felt glad to have satisfied my curiosity about dead bodies, but all too happy to let someone else handle them.

How effective is this ending?

To learn about how Cable conducted his interview with the funeral director and wrote up his notes, turn to A Writer at Work on pp. 120–24. Compare the write-up to paragraphs 5–23 of the essay where Cable reports on what he learned from this interview. How did writing up his notes help him draft part of the essay?

LEARN ABOUT CABLE'S WRITING PROCESS

JOHN T. EDGE directs the Southern Foodways Symposium, which is part of the Center for the Study of Southern Culture at the University of Mississippi, and edits the *Encyclopedia of Southern Culture*. He has written *A Gracious Plenty: Recipes and Recollections from the American South* (1999); *Southern Belly* (2000), a portrait of southern food told through profiles of people and place; and a series of books on specific foods, including *Fried Chicken* and *Apple Pie* (2004) and *Hamburgers and Fries* (2005).

Edge also contributes to a number of magazines, newspapers, and radio and television programs, including NPR's *All Things Considered, Gourmet* magazine, the *Atlanta Journal-Constitution,* and the *Oxford American,* in which this profile originally appeared. In it, Edge profiles Farm Fresh Food Supplier, a small business located in Mississippi, and introduces readers to its pickled meat products. As you read, enjoy Edge's struggle to eat a pickled pig lip, but notice also how much you are learning about this bar snack as Edge details his discomfort in trying to eat it.

I'm Not Leaving Until I Eat This Thing

John T. Edge

It's just past 4:00 on a Thursday afternoon in June at Jesse's Place, a country juke 17 miles south of the Mississippi line and three miles west of Amite, Louisiana. The air conditioner hacks and spits forth torrents of Arctic air, but the heat of summer can't be kept at bay. It seeps around the splintered doorjambs and settles in, transforming the squat particleboard-plastered roadhouse into a sauna. Slowly, the dank barroom fills with grease-smeared mechanics from the truck stop up the road and farmers straight from the fields, the soles of their brogans thick with dirt clods. A few weary souls make their way over from the nearby sawmill. I sit alone at the bar, one empty bottle of Bud in front of me, a second in my hand. I drain the beer, order a third, and stare down at the pink juice spreading outward from a crumpled foil pouch and onto the bar.

I'm not leaving until I eat this thing, I tell myself.

Half a mile down the road, behind a fence coiled with razor wire, Lionel Dufour, proprietor of Farm Fresh Food Supplier, is loading up the last truck of the day, wheeling case after case of pickled pork offal out of his cinder-block processing plant and into a semitrailer bound for Hattiesburg, Mississippi.

His crew packed lips today. Yesterday, it was pickled sausage; the day before that, pig feet. Tomorrow, it's pickled pig lips again. Lionel has been on the job since 2:45 in the morning, when he came in to light the boilers. Damon

Landry, chief cook and maintenance man, came in at 4:30. By 7:30, the production line was at full tilt: six women in white smocks and blue bouffant caps, slicing ragged white fat from the lips, tossing the good parts in glass jars, the bad parts in barrels bound for the rendering plant. Across the aisle, filled jars clatter by on a conveyor belt as a worker tops them off with a Kool-Aid-red slurry of hot sauce, vinegar, salt, and food coloring. Around the corner, the jars are capped, affixed with a label, and stored in pasteboard boxes to await shipping.

Unlike most offal — euphemistically called "variety meats" — lips belie their provenance. Brains, milky white and globular, look like brains. Feet, the ghosts of their cloven hoofs protruding, look like feet. Testicles look like, well, testicles. But lips are different. Loosed from the snout, trimmed of their fat, and dyed a preternatural pink, they look more like candy than like carrion.

"Lips are all meat," Lionel told me earlier in the day. "No gristle, no bone, no nothing. They're bar food, hot and vinegary, great with a beer."

At Farm Fresh, no swine root in an adjacent feedlot. No viscera-strewn killing floor lurks just out of sight, down a darkened hallway. These pigs died long ago at some Midwestern abattoir. By the time the lips arrive in Amite, they are, in essence, pig Popsicles, 50-pound blocks of offal and ice.

"Lips are all meat," Lionel told me earlier in the day. "No gristle, no bone, no nothing. They're bar food, hot and vinegary, great with a beer. Used to be the lips ended up in sausages, headcheese, those sorts of things. A lot of them still do."

Lionel, a 50-year-old father of three with quick, intelligent eyes set deep in a face the color of cordovan, is a veteran of nearly 40 years in the pickled pig lips business. "I started out with my daddy when I wasn't much more than 10," Lionel told me, his shy smile framed by a coarse black mustache flecked with whispers of gray. "The meatpacking business he owned had gone broke back when I was 6, and he was peddling out of the back of his car, selling dried shrimp, napkins, straws, tubes of plastic cups, pig feet, pig lips, whatever the bar owners needed. He sold to black bars, white bars, sweet shops, snowball stands, you name it. We made the rounds together after I got out of school, sometimes staying out till two or three in the morning. I remember bringing my toy cars to this one joint and racing them around the floor with the bar owner's son while my daddy and his father did business."

For years after the demise of that first meatpacking company, the Dufour family sold someone else's product. "We used to buy lips from Dennis Di Salvo's company down in Belle Chasse," recalled Lionel. "As far as I can tell, his mother was the one who came up with the idea to pickle and pack lips back in the '50s, back when she was working for a company called Three Little Pigs over in Houma. But pretty soon, we were selling so many lips that we had to almost beg Di Salvo's for product. That's when we started cooking up our own," he told me, gesturing toward the cast-iron kettle that hangs from the rafters by the front door of the plant. "My daddy started cooking lips in that very pot." 9

Lionel now cooks lips in 11 retrofitted milk tanks, dull stainless-steel cauldrons shaped like oversized cradles. But little else has changed. Though Lionel's father has passed away, Farm Fresh remains a family-focused company. His wife, Kathy, keeps the books. His daughter, Dana, a button-cute college student who has won numerous beauty titles, takes to the road in the summer, selling lips to convenience stores and wholesalers. Soon, after he graduates from business school, Lionel's younger son, Matt, will take over operations at the plant. And his older son, a veterinarian, lent his name to one of Farm Fresh's top sellers, Jason's Pickled Pig Lips. 10

"We do our best to corner the market on lips," Lionel told me, his voice tinged with bravado. "Sometimes they're hard to get from the packing houses. You gotta kill a lot of pigs to get enough lips to keep us going. I've got new customers calling every day; it's all I can do to keep up with demand, but I bust my ass to keep up. I do what I can for my family — and for my customers." 11

"When my customers tell me something," he continued, "just like when my daddy told me something, I listen. If my customers wanted me to dye the lips green, I'd ask, 'What shade?' As it is, every few years we'll do some red and some blue for the Fourth of July. This year we did jars full of Mardi Gras lips — half purple, half gold," Lionel recalled with a chuckle. "I guess we'd had a few beers when we came up with that one." 12

Meanwhile, back at Jesse's Place, I finish my third Bud, order my fourth. *Now,* I tell myself, my courage bolstered by booze, *I'm ready to eat a lip.* 13

They may have looked like candy in the plant, but in the barroom they're carrion once again. I poke and prod the six-inch arc of pink flesh, peering up from my reverie just in time to catch the barkeep's wife, Audrey, staring straight at me. She fixes me with a look just this side of pity and asks, "You gonna eat that thing or make love to it?" 14

Her nephew, Jerry, sidles up to a bar stool on my left. "A lot of people like 'em with chips," he says with a nod toward the pink juice pooling on the bar in front of me. I offer to buy him a lip, and Audrey fishes one from a jar behind the counter, wraps it in tinfoil, and places the whole affair on a paper towel in front of him. 15

I take stock of my own cowardice, and, following Jerry's lead, reach for a bag of potato chips, tear open the top with my teeth, and toss the quivering hunk of 16 hog flesh into the shiny interior of the bag, slick with grease and dusted with salt. Vinegar vapors tickle my nostrils. I stifle a gag that rolls from the back of my throat, swallow hard, and pray that the urge to vomit passes.

With a smash of my hand, the potato chips are reduced to a pulp, and I feel the cold lump of the lip beneath my fist. I clasp the bag shut and shake it hard in an effort to ensure chip coverage in all the nooks and crannies of the lip. The technique that Jerry uses — and I mimic — is not unlike that employed by home cooks mixing up a mess of Shake 'n Bake chicken.   17

I pull from the bag a coral crescent of meat now crusted with blond bits of potato chips. When I chomp down, the soft flesh dissolves between my teeth. It tastes like a flaccid cracklin', unmistakably porcine, and not altogether bad. The chips help, providing texture where there was none. Slowly, my brow unfurrows, my stomach ceases its fluttering.   18

Sensing my relief, Jerry leans over and peers into my bag. "Kind of look like Frosted Flakes, don't they?" he says, by way of describing the chips rapidly turning to mush in the pickling juice. I offer the bag to Jerry, order yet another beer, and turn to eye the pig feet floating in a murky jar by the cash register, their blunt lips bobbing up through a pasty white film.   19

Edge uses the words *courage* (par. 13) and *cowardice* (par. 16) to describe his squeamishness about eating pickled pig lip. And when he finally eats a bite of pig lip, he feels queasy. Although his nausea is undoubtedly real, it may be caused more by anxiety than by anything sickening in the food itself.

With other students, discuss the kinds of food you feel uncomfortable eating — foods you have anxiety eating, foods that gross you out, or foods you stay away from for some other reason such as a religious dietary restriction or a moral conviction. Begin by briefly telling each other about the kinds of foods you avoid. Then, together consider the following questions as you discuss the reasons for your strong feelings about certain kinds of food:

- What role do factors such as family, ethnic, or religious traditions play in your food choices? If your food aversions are unusual in your family or community, consider how other family or community members regard your choice — for example, as a quirk or as a rejection of something they value. If you find it hard to try foods from different cultures, why do you think that is?

- Early in the essay, Edge makes clear that he is squeamish about eating a pickled pig lip even though he is a Southerner and it is a popular southern delicacy. How does his difficulty eating the pig lip set him apart from the other people in the bar? What else separates him from them?

MAKING CONNECTIONS: AVERSION TO NEW FOODS

● Detailed Information about the Subject

Profiles present information primarily from the writer's direct observation of the subject, plus what was learned from interviews and from background Internet and library research. Because profile writers get much of their information from observation and because they try to give readers a vivid picture of the subject, *describing* is their most important writing strategy.

Edge probably assumes that most of his readers have never seen a pickled pig lip, much less eaten one. Therefore, he describes this product carefully. To describe an object like a pickled pig lip, writers use **naming**, **detailing**, and **comparing** to create vivid images. Consider, for example, Edge's description of the brine in which the pig lips swim as "Kool-Aid-red slurry" (par. 4). *Slurry*, which Edge uses to *name* the mixture of ingredients in the brine, is also descriptive, because the term *slurry* derives from mining and other industrial uses, where it denotes a slimy liquid or thin mud. The *detail* "Kool-Aid-red," with its implied *comparison* with the popular, artificially colored children's drink, creates a vivid visual image for anyone familiar with Kool-Aid. Descriptive details such as these provide sensory information — color, shape, smell, taste, or texture — and may also identify qualities and make evaluations (for example, the "good" and "bad" parts of the pig lip in par. 4).

Writers use the following familiar figures of speech when they make comparisons:

■ **Simile**, in which two things are *explicitly* compared using the words *like* or *as.*

■ **Metaphor**, in which two things are *implicitly* compared by calling one thing something else.

For example, Edge uses simile when he writes that pig lips "look more <u>like</u> candy than <u>like</u> carrion" (par. 5), and he employs metaphor when he describes the temperature of the air conditioning at Jesse's Place as "Arctic" (par. 1).

To analyze Edge's use of the describing strategies of naming, detailing, and comparing, do the following:

■ Reread paragraphs 5–7, 14, and 16–18. Underline two things Edge names, put brackets around four descriptive details, and circle any similes and metaphors that he uses to help readers imagine eating a pig lip.

■ Write a few sentences about the overall or **dominant impression** Edge's description of pickled pig lips makes. If you have never seen a pickled pig lip, what more do you need to know to imagine what it looks, smells, feels, tastes, and sounds like when you chomp down on it? Which details make a lip seem appealing to you? Which ones make it seem unappealing?

● A Clear Organizational Plan

A profile may be presented **narratively**, as a sequence of events observed by the writer during an encounter with the place, person, or activity; or it may be presented

topically, as a series of topics of information gathered by the writer about the person, place, or activity. Sometimes profile writers, like Edge, use both narrative and topical organization. Edge frames (begins and ends) his profile with a story about his attempt to eat a pig lip.

To analyze how Edge uses both a narrative and topical organization, do the following:

- Reread paragraphs 16–18 and highlight places where the sequence of actions involved in eating a pig lip are narrated.

- Skim paragraphs 3–12 and note in the margin where Edge presents the following topics: the production process, the various products produced by Farm Fresh, the source of the products, and the history of the Farm Fresh business.

- Write a few sentences explaining what, if anything, you learn from Edge's narrative that you can't find out from the topics he presents in paragraphs 3–12.

● A Role for the Writer

Profile writers can choose to adopt the role of a *spectator* or the role of a *participant*. For example, in the preceding essay, Cable takes the role of spectator when he talks to Howard and Tim and takes a tour of the Goodbody mortuary. To take on a participant role, Cable would have had to help the funeral director or embalmer in his daily activities.

To analyze how Edge uses both roles in this essay, do the following:

- Skim the essay and note in the margin where Edge uses the spectator role and where he uses the participant role.

- Write a few sentences giving an example of each role and explaining how the examples show which role he is using. How does he keep the two roles separate?

● A Perspective on the Subject

Profile writers do not merely present information about the subject; they also offer their insights. They may convey a perspective on their subject by stating it explicitly or by implying it through the descriptive details and information they choose to include in the essay. Brian Cable, for example, by comparing the display of caskets to shiny new cars in a showroom, shares his realization about Americans' denial of death and our inclination to profit from it.

To analyze Edge's perspective in this essay, do the following:

- Reread paragraph 1 and highlight the descriptions of the patrons of Jesse's Place, noting particularly information suggesting the kinds of work they do and their socioeconomic class.

- Skim paragraph 15, where Jerry shows Edge how people like to eat pickled pig lips.
- Write a few sentences explaining Edge's perspective on this popular Southern bar snack and how it may reflect his own class position.

ANALYZING VISUALS

❯ **PHOTOGRAPH OF A PIG**

Write a paragraph or two analyzing the photograph Edge includes in his essay and explain what it contributes to the profile.

To analyze the visual, you can use the Criteria for Analyzing Visuals chart in Chapter 20 on pp. 675–77. The chart offers a series of questions you can ask yourself under two categories: Key Components and Rhetorical Context. You will see that there are a lot of questions, but don't feel you have to answer all of them. Focus on the questions that seem most productive in helping you write a short analysis. Try beginning with these questions:

Composition

- Edge could have used a full-body photograph of a pig, a photo of pigs at play, or some other composition. Why do you think he chose a close-up of a pig's face taken from one particular angle?

Rhetorical Context

- Given his purpose and audience, why do you think Edge chose a photograph of a pig instead of a photograph of pig lips in a jar or of lips being eaten in a site like Jesse's Place? Why did he not choose a photograph of the Farm Fresh company or the Dufour family? What does the choice of visual suggest about the subject and the writer's perspective?

CONSIDERING TOPICS FOR YOUR OWN ESSAY

❯ Consider writing about a place that serves, produces, or sells something unusual, perhaps something that, like Edge, you could try yourself for the purpose of further informing and engaging your readers. There are many possibilities: producer or packager of a special ethnic or regional food or a local café that serves it, licensed acupuncture clinic, caterer, novelty and toy balloon store, microbrewery, chain saw dealer, boat builder, talent agency, manufacturer of ornamental iron, bead store, nail salon, pet fish and aquarium supplier, detailing shop, tattoo parlor, scrap metal recycler, fly-fishing shop, handwriting analyst, dog or cat sitting service. If none of these appeal to you, try browsing the Yellow Pages in print or online at yellow.com. Remember that relating your experience with the service or product is a good idea but not a requirement for a successful profile.

SUSAN ORLEAN is a staff writer for the *New Yorker* and widely recognized as a master of the profile genre. The 2002 Academy Award-nominated film *Adaptation* was based on Orlean's book *The Orchid Thief*, which began as "Orchid Fever," a *New Yorker* profile originally published in 1995. Some of Orlean's other profiles have been reprinted in *The Bullfighter Checks Her Makeup: My Encounters with Extraordinary People* (2001) and *My Kind of Place: Travel Stories from a Woman Who's Been Everywhere* (2004). A dog lover, Orlean claims to have co-written *Throw Me a Bone: 50 Healthy, Canine Taste-Tested Recipes for Snacks, Meals, and Treats* (2003) with her Welsh Springer Spaniel, Cooper. Presumably without Cooper's help, she is currently writing a biography of the movie and television star Rin Tin Tin.

"Show Dog," as you will see, begins with an attention-grabbing, playful opening sentence. As you read, consider how Orlean's tone changes throughout the essay and how effective these changes in tone are in keeping your interest.

Show Dog

Susan Orlean

If I were a bitch, I'd be in love with Biff Truesdale. Biff is perfect. He's friendly, good-looking, rich, famous, and in excellent physical condition. He almost never drools. He's not afraid of commitment. He wants children — actually, he already has children and wants a lot more. He works hard and is a consummate professional, but he also knows how to have fun. 1

What Biff likes most is food and sex. This makes him sound boorish, which he is not — he's just elemental. Food he likes even better than sex. His favorite things to eat are cookies, mints, and hotel soap, but he will eat just about anything. Richard Krieger, a friend of Biff's who occasionally drives him to appointments, said not long ago, "When we're driving on I-95, we'll usually pull over at McDonald's. Even if Biff is napping, he always wakes up when we're getting close. I get him a few plain hamburgers with buns — no ketchup, no mustard, and no pickles. He loves hamburgers. I don't get him his own French fries, but if I get myself fries I always flip a few for him into the back." 2

If you're ever around Biff while you're eating something he wants to taste — cold roast beef, a Wheatables cracker, chocolate, pasta, aspirin, whatever — he will stare at you across the pleated bridge of his nose and let his eyes sag and his lips tremble and allow a little bead of drool to percolate at the edge of his mouth until you feel so crummy that you give him some. This routine puts the people who know him in a quandary, because Biff has to watch his weight. Usually, he is as skinny as 3

> **If you're ever around Biff while you're eating something he wants to taste . . . he will stare at you across the pleated bridge of his nose and let his eyes sag and his lips tremble . . .**

Kate Moss, but he can put on three pounds in an instant. The holidays can be tough. He takes time off at Christmas and spends it at home, in Attleboro, Massachusetts, where there's a lot of food around and no pressure and no schedule and it's easy to eat all day. The extra weight goes to his neck. Luckily, Biff likes working out. He runs for fifteen or twenty minutes twice a day, either outside or on his Jog-Master. When he's feeling heavy, he runs longer, and skips snacks, until he's back down to his ideal weight of seventy-five pounds.

Biff is a boxer. He is a show dog — he performs under the name Champion Hi-Tech's Arbitrage — and so looking good is not mere vanity; it's business. A show dog's career is short, and judges are unforgiving. Each breed is judged by an explicit standard for appearance and temperament, and then there's the incalculable element of charisma in the ring. When a show dog is fat or lazy or sullen, he doesn't win; when he doesn't win, he doesn't enjoy the ancillary benefits of being a winner, like appearing as the celebrity spokesmodel on packages of Pedigree Mealtime with Lamb and Rice, which Biff will be doing soon, or picking the best-looking bitches and charging them six hundred dollars or so for his sexual favors, which Biff does three or four times a month. Another ancillary benefit of being a winner is that almost every single weekend of the year, as he travels to shows around the country, he gets to hear people applaud for him and yell his name and tell him what a good boy he is, which is something he seems to enjoy at least as much as eating a bar of soap.

Pretty soon, Biff won't have to be so vigilant about his diet. After he appears at the Westminster Kennel Club's show, this week, he will retire from active show life and work full time as a stud. It's a good moment for him to retire. Last year, he won more shows than any other boxer, and also more than any other dog in the purebred category known as Working Dogs, which also includes Akitas, Alaskan malamutes, Bernese mountain dogs, bullmastiffs, Doberman pinschers, giant schnauzers, Great Danes, Great Pyrenees, komondors, kuvaszok, mastiffs, Newfoundlands, Portuguese water dogs, Rottweilers, St. Bernards, Samoyeds, Siberian huskies, and standard schnauzers. Boxers were named for their habit of standing on their hind legs and punching with their front paws when they fight. They were originally bred to be chaperones — to look forbidding while being pleasant to spend time with. Except for show dogs like Biff, most boxers lead a life of relative leisure. Last year at Westminster, Biff was named Best Boxer and Best Working Dog, and he was a serious contender for Best in Show, the highest honor any show dog can hope for. He is a contender to win his breed and group again this year, and is a serious contender once again for Best in

4

5

Show, although the odds are against him, because this year's judge is known as a poodle person.

Biff is four years old. He's in his prime. He could stay on the circuit for a few more years, but by stepping aside now he is making room for his sons Trent and Rex, who are just getting into the business, and he's leaving while he's still on top. He'll also spend less time in airplanes, which is the one part of show life he doesn't like, and more time with his owners, William and Tina Truesdale, who might be persuaded to waive his snacking rules.

6

Biff has a short, tight coat of fox-colored fur, white feet and ankles, and a patch of white on his chest roughly the shape of Maine. His muscles are plainly sketched under his skin, but he isn't bulgy. His face is turned up and pushed in, and has a dark mask, spongy lips, a wishbone-shaped white blaze, and the earnest and slightly careworn expression of a small-town mayor. Someone once told me that he thought Biff looked a little bit like President Clinton. Biff's face is his fortune. There are plenty of people who like boxers with bigger bones and a stockier body and taller shoulders — boxers who look less like marathon runners and more like weight-lifters — but almost everyone agrees that Biff has a nearly perfect head.

7

"Biff's head is his father's," William Truesdale, a veterinarian, explained to me one day. We were in the Truesdales' living room in Attleboro, which overlooks acres of hilly fenced-in fields. Their house is a big, sunny ranch with a stylish pastel kitchen and boxerabilia on every wall. The Truesdales don't have children, but at any given moment they share their quarters with at least a half-dozen dogs. If you watch a lot of dog-food commercials, you may have seen William — he's the young, handsome, dark-haired veterinarian declaring his enthusiasm for Pedigree Mealtime while his boxers gallop around.

8

"Biff has a masculine but elegant head," William went on. "It's not too wet around the muzzle. It's just about ideal. Of course, his forte is right here." He pointed to Biff's withers, and explained that Biff's shoulder-humerus articulation was optimally angled, and bracketed his superb brisket and forelegs, or something like that. While William was talking, Biff climbed onto the couch and sat on top of Brian, his companion, who was hiding under a pillow. Brian is an English toy Prince Charles spaniel who is about the size of a teakettle and has the composure of a hummingbird. As a young competitor, he once bit a judge — a mistake Tina Truesdale says he made because at the time he had been going through a little mind problem about being touched. Brian, whose show name is Champion Cragmor's Hi-Tech Man, will soon go back on the circuit, but now he mostly serves as Biff's regular escort. When Biff sat on him, he started to quiver. Biff batted at him with his front leg. Brian gave him an adoring look.

9

"Biff's body is from his mother," Tina was saying. "She had a lot of substance."

10

"She was even a little extreme for a bitch," William said. "She was rather buxom. I would call her zaftig."

11

"Biff's father needed that, though," Tina said. "His name was Tailo, and he was fabulous. Tailo had a very beautiful head, but he was a bit fine, I think. A bit slender."

"Even a little feminine," William said, with feeling. "Actually, he would have been a really awesome bitch."

The first time I met Biff, he sniffed my pants, stood up on his hind legs and stared into my face, and then trotted off to the kitchen, where someone was cooking macaroni. We were in Westbury, Long Island, where Biff lives with Kimberly Pastella, a twenty-nine-year-old professional handler, when he's working. Last year, Kim and Biff went to at least one show every weekend. If they drove, they took Kim's van. If they flew, she went coach and he went cargo. They always shared a hotel room.

While Kim was telling me all this, I could hear Biff rummaging around in the kitchen. "Biffers!" Kim called out. Biff jogged back into the room with a phony look of surprise on his face. His tail was ticking back and forth. It is cropped so that it is about the size and shape of a half-smoked stogie. Kim said that there was a bitch downstairs who had been sent from Pennsylvania to be bred to one of Kim's other clients, and that Biff could smell her and was a little out of sorts. "Let's go," she said to him. "Biff, let's go jog." We went into the garage, where a treadmill was set up with Biff's collar suspended from a metal arm. Biff hopped on and held his head out so that Kim could buckle his collar. As soon as she leaned toward the power switch, he started to jog. His nails clicked a light tattoo on the rubber belt.

Except for a son of his named Biffle, Biff gets along with everybody. Matt Stander, one of the founders of *Dog News*, said recently, "Biff is just very, very personable. He has a *je ne sais quoi* that's really special. He gives of himself all the time." One afternoon, the Truesdales were telling me about the psychology that went into making Biff who he is. "Boxers are real communicators," William was saying. "We had to really take that into consideration in his upbringing. He seems tough, but there's a fragile ego inside there. The profound reaction and hurt when you would raise your voice at him was really something."

"I *made* him," Tina said. "I made Biff who he is. He had an overbearing personality when he was small, but I consider that a prerequisite for a great performer. He had such an *attitude!* He was like this miniature man!" She shimmied her shoulders back and forth and thrust out her chin. She is a dainty, chic woman with wide-set eyes and the neck of a ballerina. She grew up on a farm in Costa Rica, where dogs were considered just another form of livestock. In 1987, William got her a Rottweiler for a watchdog, and a boxer, because he had always loved boxers, and Tina decided to dabble with them in shows. Now she makes a monogrammed Christmas stocking for each animal in their house, and she watches the tape of Biff winning at Westminster approximately once a week. "Right from the beginning, I made Biff think he was the most fabulous dog in the world," Tina said.

"He doesn't take after me very much," William said. "I'm more of a golden retriever." 18

"Oh, he has my nature," Tina said. "I'm very strong-willed. I'm brassy. And Biff is an egotistical, self-centered, selfish person. He thinks he's very important and special, and he doesn't like to share." 19

Biff is priceless. If you beg the Truesdales to name a figure, they might say that Biff is worth around a hundred thousand dollars, but they will also point out that a Japanese dog fancier recently handed Tina a blank check for Biff. (She immediately threw it away.) That check notwithstanding, campaigning a show dog is a money-losing proposition for the owner. A good handler gets three or four hundred dollars a day, plus travel expenses, to show a dog, and any dog aiming for the top will have to be on the road at least a hundred days a year. A dog photographer charges hundreds of dollars for a portrait, and a portrait is something that every serious owner commissions, and then runs as a full-page ad in several dog-show magazines. Advertising a show dog is standard procedure if you want your dog or your presence on the show circuit to get well known. There are also such ongoing show-dog expenses as entry fees, hair-care products, food, health care, and toys. Biff's stud fee is six hundred dollars. Now that he will not be at shows, he can be bred several times a month. Breeding him would have been a good way for him to make money in the past, except that whenever the Truesdales were enthusiastic about a mating they bartered Biff's service for the pick of the litter. As a result, they now have more Biff puppies than Biff earnings. "We're doing this for posterity," Tina says. "We're doing it for the good of all boxers. You simply can't think about the cost." 20

On a recent Sunday, I went to watch Biff work at one of the last shows he would attend before his retirement. The show was sponsored by the Lehigh Valley Kennel Club and was held in a big, windy field house on the campus of Lehigh University, in Bethlehem, Pennsylvania. The parking lot was filled with motor homes pasted with life-size decals of dogs. On my way to the field house, I passed someone walking an Afghan hound wearing a snood, and someone else wiping down a Saluki with a Flintstones beach towel. Biff was napping in his crate — a fancy-looking brass box with bright silver hardware and with luggage tags from Delta, USAir, and Continental hanging on the door. Dogs in crates can look woeful, but Biff actually likes spending time in his. When he was growing up, the Truesdales decided they would never reprimand him, because of his delicate ego. Whenever he got rambunctious, Tina wouldn't scold him — she would just invite him to sit in his crate and have a time-out. 21

On this particular day, Biff was in the crate with a bowl of water and a gourmet Oinkeroll. The boxer judging was already over. There had been thirty-three in competition, and Biff had won Best in Breed. Now he had to wait for several hours . . . for Best in Show. . . . 22

While he was napping, I pawed through his suitcase. In it was some dog food; towels; an electric nail grinder; a whisker trimmer; a wool jacket in a lively 23 pattern that looked sort of Southwestern; an apron; some antibiotics; baby oil; coconut-oil coat polish; boxer chalk powder; a copy of *Dog News*; an issue of *Showsight* magazine, featuring an article subtitled "Frozen Semen — Boon or Bane?" and a two-page ad for Biff, with a full-page, full-color photograph of him and Kim posed in front of a human-size toy soldier; a spray bottle of fur cleanser; another Oinkeroll; a rope ball; and something called a Booda Bone. The apron was for Kim. The baby oil was to make Biff's nose and feet glossy when he went into the ring. Boxer chalk powder — as distinct from, say, West Highland-white-terrier chalk powder — is formulated to cling to short, sleek boxer hair and whiten boxers' white markings. . . .

Typically, dog contestants first circle the ring together; then each contestant poses individually for the judge, trying to look perfect as the judge lifts its lips for a dental exam, rocks its hindquarters, and strokes its back and thighs. The judge at Lehigh was a chesty, mustached man with watery eyes and a grave expression. He directed the group with hand signals that made him appear to be roping cattle. The Rottweiler looked good, and so did the giant schnauzer. I started to worry. Biff had a distracted look on his face, as if he'd forgotten something back at the house. Finally, it was his turn. He pranced to the center of the ring. The judge stroked him and then waved his hand in a circle and stepped out of the way. Several people near me began clapping. A flashbulb flared. Biff held his position for a moment, and then he and Kim bounded across the ring, his feet moving so fast that they blurred into an oily sparkle, even though he really didn't have very far to go. He got a cookie when he finished the performance, and another a few minutes later, when the judge wagged his finger at him, indicating that Biff had won again.   24

You can't help wondering whether Biff will experience the depressing letdown that retired competitors face. At least, he has a lot of stud work to look forward to, although William Truesdale complained to me once that the Truesdales' standards for a mate are so high — they require a clean bill of health and a substantial pedigree — that "there just aren't that many right bitches out there." Nonetheless, he and Tina are optimistic that Biff will find enough suitable mates to become one of the most influential boxer sires of all time. "We'd like to be remembered as the boxer people of the nineties," Tina said. "Anyway, we can't wait to have him home." . . .   25

Just then, Biff, who had been on the couch, jumped down and began pacing. "Going somewhere, honey?" Tina asked.   26

He wanted to go out, so Tina opened the back door, and Biff ran into the back yard. After a few minutes, he noticed a ball on the lawn. The ball was slippery and a little too big to fit in his mouth, but he kept scrambling and trying to grab it. In the meantime, the Truesdales and I sat, stayed for a moment, fetched ourselves turkey sandwiches, and then curled up on the couch. Half an hour passed, and Biff was still happily pursuing the ball. He probably has a very short memory, but he acted as if it were the most fun he'd ever had.   27

William and Tina Truesdale talk about Biff as if they were his natural, rather than his adoptive parents:

> "He doesn't take after me very much," William said. "I'm more of a golden retriever."
> "Oh, he has my nature," Tina said. "I'm very strong-willed. I'm brassy. And Biff is an egotistical, self-centered, selfish person. He thinks he's very important and special, and he doesn't like to share." (pars. 18–19)

Referring to an animal as if it were a human being is called *anthropomorphism*. Tina does this when she describes Biff's personality as being like her own, as if he inherited certain characteristics from her. William goes even further by describing himself as a dog. Tina and William identify with Biff so thoroughly that the differences between the species seem to evaporate for them.

With other students in your class, discuss your own attitudes toward animals with whom you have lived or the attitudes of other people you have observed. In what ways do people identify with and anthropomorphize their pets? Begin by briefly telling each other what you have experienced or observed. Then, together consider the following questions as you discuss your ideas about people's attitudes toward animals:

- Although we may feel attached to our pets, many of us eat other animals. How do you think people reconcile anthropomorphizing pets while they treat other species (in)differently?

- In addition to being a member of the family, Biff is big business for the Truesdales. How does his being a show dog affect the Truesdales' attitudes toward Biff? Is there any evidence in the essay that they treat him differently because he's a moneymaker as well as a pet?

MAKING CONNECTIONS: ATTITUDES TOWARD ANIMALS

● Detailed Information about the Subject

Most of the information in profile writing comes from direct observation and interview, although some may also come from background library or Internet research. Brian Cable, for example, describes what he sees as he tours the Goodbody Mortuary, but much of the information about the mortuary business and the embalming process he gathers from interviews with the funeral director and mortician. He presents the interview information by quoting and paraphrasing what they told him.

To analyze Orlean's use of observation, interview, and background research, do the following:

- Skim the essay and find at least one example of information from each of the following categories: (1) observation, (2) interview, and (3) background library or Internet research. Be sure that at least one of your examples is a *quotation*,

ANALYZING WRITING STRATEGIES

■ ■ ■ ■
Basic Features

and at least one is a *summary* or *paraphrase*. (A **summary** very briefly gives the gist of what was said, while a **paraphrase** provides more detail. Both summary and paraphrase are written essentially in the writer's own words, although a word or phrase may be quoted.)

- Write a couple of sentences explaining what in your examples enables you to identify whether the information comes from observation, interview, or background research.

- Analyze Orlean's use of quotation by circling the quotation marks, underlining the punctuation, and putting brackets around the **speaker tags** — words and phrases that identify the speaker and characterize how the words were spoken. (To learn more about speaker tags, turn to Working with Sources on pp. 112–13.) Write a sentence or two speculating about why Orlean chose to quote, when she uses quotation, rather than summarize or paraphrase the information.

A Clear Organizational Plan

Orlean's plan for her profile is primarily topical. Her essay moves from topic to topic until paragraph 21, where she signals to readers that she is switching to narrative with the opening phrase: "On a recent Sunday. . . ." In paragraphs 21–24, she recounts what happened to Biff on that particular day.

To analyze the topical organization, follow these suggestions:

- Reread paragraphs 2–5, 7–13, 16–19, and 20, and note the topic of each of these groups of paragraphs. (Some of these paragraphs are about more than one thing, so choose the topic that seems most important.)

- Write a couple of sentences reflecting on how well these topics answer your questions about Biff's life as a show dog.

- Add another sentence or two explaining what the narrative in paragraphs 21–24 contributes to the profile.

A Role for the Writer

Even when profile writers refer to themselves and express their preconceptions, surprise, or other reaction to the subject, they may still be playing a detached observer role. Such is the case in Brian Cable's profile of the Goodbody Mortuary. He uses the personal pronoun *I* throughout his essay and places himself in various scenes: for example, "I found the funeral director in the main lobby. . . . I followed him through an arched doorway" (pars. 5, 15). Cable also explicitly tells us what he thought and felt: "It wasn't at all what I had expected. I thought it would be more like Forest Lawn . . ." (par. 3). To have played a participant observer role, however, Cable would have had to work alongside the funeral director or mortician — in other words, he would have had to acquire insider knowledge. Instead, by playing the spectator role, Cable makes it easy for readers to identify with his point of view.

To analyze the role Susan Orlean plays in her essay, follow these suggestions:

- Reread the following scenes, noting where Orlean uses *I*, locates herself in the scene, or indicates what she was thinking and feeling: the first time she met Biff at Kim's house on Long Island (pars. 14–15); the scene at the Lehigh Valley Kennel Club show in Pennsylvania (pars. 21–24); or the scene at the Truesdales' home (pars. 25–27).

- Write a few sentences giving examples from your analysis of these scenes and reflecting on the effectiveness of the spectator role in enabling you to look over Orlean's shoulder as she learns about Biff's life as a show dog.

● A Perspective on the Subject

Profile writers convey their perspective through the choices they make about the kinds of information they include in the essay. But they may also frame the essay at the beginning with comments that give readers a sense of what they think about their subject. Cable, for example, begins by noting that pedestrians "avert their eyes when they walk past" the mortuary. He, on the other hand, walks in and faces his fears. In fact, Cable concludes the essay by describing what it feels like to touch a dead body.

To analyze how Orlean conveys her perspective, do the following:

- Reread paragraphs 1–2, noting how Orlean introduces Biff.

- Reread paragraphs 25–27, noting that Orlean asks and seems to answer her own question about how Biff will handle his retirement. What do you think her point is here?

- Write a few sentences analyzing Orlean's perspective in the opening and concluding paragraphs of the essay. Consider how the kind of anthropomorphizing discussed in the Making Connections activity for this reading plays out in these two passages.

CONSIDERING TOPICS FOR YOUR OWN ESSAY

Some profiles are about a particular individual who has an unusual job or hobby, or has accomplished something special. In profiling Biff, Orlean is writing this kind of profile. Even though she can't interview Biff, she spends time with him in several different locations and interviews people who live and work with him. You might consider writing about somebody you find intriguing, perhaps someone who does the kind of work you are interested in learning more about — for example, a police officer, attorney, or judge; a high school or college coach; an independent contractor or a small business owner; a newspaper editor, blogger, or poet; or a performance artist, graffiti artist, or musician.

AMANDA COYNE, an award-winning staff writer for the *Anchorage Press*, earned an MFA in nonfiction writing from the University of Iowa. Coauthor of *Alaska Then and Now* (2008), a profile of Alaska across the decades, Coyne has written for the *New York Times Magazine* and *Newsweek*, among other national publications. Coyne also blogs on the Huffington Post and contributes to National Public Radio's *All Things Considered* and PRI's *This American Life*. "The Long Good-Bye," her first piece of published writing, originally appeared in *Harper's Magazine*.

Coyne's "Long Good-Bye" takes a more ethnographic turn than the other profiles in this chapter, in that she uses direct observation and interview over an extended period of time to study the behavior of a particular community. In this profile, Coyne examines women who have been incarcerated and separated from their children to see how the mothers and children negotiate their difficult relationships. As you read, think about what you learn about the stresses on these parent-child relationships. Which of these stresses seem particular to the situation Coyne describes? Are any of the factors present recognizable in the relationships of parents and children where prison is not a factor?

The Long Good-Bye: Mother's Day in Federal Prison

Amanda Coyne

You can spot the convict-moms here in the visiting room by the way they hold and touch their children and by the single flower that is perched in front of them — a rose, a tulip, a daffodil. Many of these mothers have untied the bow that attaches the flower to its silver-and-red cellophane wrapper and are using one of the many empty soda cans at hand as a vase. They sit proudly before their flower-in-a-Coke-can, amid Hershey bar wrappers, half-eaten Ding Dongs, and empty paper coffee cups. Occasionally, a mother will pick up her present and bring it to her nose when one of the bearers of the single flower — her child — asks if she likes it. And the mother will respond the way that mothers always have and always will respond when presented with a gift on this day. "Oh, I just love it. It's perfect. I'll put it in the middle of my Bible." Or, "I'll put it on my desk, right next to your school picture." And always: "It's the best one here." 1

But most of what is being smelled today is the children themselves. While the other adults are plunking coins into the vending machines, the mothers take deep whiffs from the backs of their children's necks, or kiss and smell the backs of their knees, or take off their shoes and tickle their feet and then pull them close to their noses. They hold them tight and take in their own second 2

> **While the other adults are plunking coins into the vending machines, the mothers take deep whiffs from the backs of their children's necks, or kiss and smell the backs of their knees, or take off their shoes and tickle their feet and then pull them close to their noses.**

scent — the scent assuring them that these are still their children and that they still belong to them.

The visitors are allowed to bring in pockets full of coins, and today that Mother's Day flower, and I know from previous visits to my older sister here at the Federal Prison Camp for women in Pekin, Illinois, that there is always an aberrant urge to gather immediately around the vending machines. The sandwiches are stale, the coffee weak, the candy bars the ones we always pass up in a convenience store. But after we hand the children over to their mothers, we gravitate toward those machines. Like milling in the kitchen at a party. We all do it, and nobody knows why. Polite conversation ensues around the microwave while the popcorn is popping and the processed-chicken sandwiches are being heated. We ask one another where we are from, how long a drive we had. An occasional whistle through the teeth, a shake of the head. "My, my, long way from home, huh?" "Staying at the Super 8 right up the road. Not a bad place." "Stayed at the Econo Lodge last time. Wasn't a good place at all." Never asking the questions we really want to ask: "What's she in for?" "How much time's she got left?" You never ask in the waiting room of a doctor's office either. Eventually, all of us — fathers, mothers, sisters, brothers, a few boyfriends, and very few husbands — return to the queen of the day, sitting at a fold-out table loaded with snacks, prepared for five or so hours of attempted normal conversation.

Most of the inmates are elaborately dressed, many in prison-crafted dresses and sweaters in bright blues and pinks. They wear meticulously applied makeup in corresponding hues, and their hair is replete with loops and curls — hair that only women with the time have the time for. Some of the better seamstresses have crocheted vests and purses to match their outfits. Although the world outside would never accuse these women of making haute-couture fashion statements, the fathers and the sons and the boyfriends and the very few husbands think they look beautiful, and they tell them so repeatedly. And I can imagine the hours spent preparing for this visit — hours of needles and hooks clicking over brightly colored yards of yarn. The hours of discussing, dissecting, and bragging about these visitors — especially the men. Hours spent in the other world behind the door where we're not allowed, sharing lipsticks and mascaras, and unraveling the occasional hair-tangled hot roller, and the brushing out and lifting and teasing . . . and the giggles that abruptly change into tears without warning — things that define any female-only world. Even, or especially, if that world is a female federal prison camp.

While my sister Jennifer is with her son in the playroom, an inmate's mother comes over to introduce herself to my younger sister, Charity, my brother, John, and me. She tells us about visiting her daughter in a higher-security prison before she was transferred here. The woman looks old and tired, and her shoulders sag under the weight of her recently acquired bitterness.

"Pit of fire," she says, shaking her head. "Like a pit of fire straight from hell. Never seen anything like it. Like something out of an old movie about prisons." Her voice is getting louder and she looks at each of us with pleading eyes. "My *daughter* was there. Don't even get me started on that place. Women die there."

John and Charity and I silently exchange glances.

"My daughter would come to the visiting room with a black eye and I'd think, 'All she did was sit in the car while her boyfriend ran into the house.' She didn't even touch the stuff. Never even handled it."

She continues to stare at us, each in turn. "Ten years. That boyfriend talked and he got three years. She didn't know anything. Had nothing to tell them. They gave her ten years. They called it conspiracy. Conspiracy? Aren't there real criminals out there?" She asks this with hands outstretched, waiting for an answer that none of us can give her.

The woman's daughter, the conspirator, is chasing her son through the maze of chairs and tables and through the other children. She's a twenty-four-year-old blonde, whom I'll call Stephanie, with Dorothy Hamill hair and matching dimples. She looks like any girl you might see in any shopping mall in middle America. She catches her chocolate-brown son and tickles him, and they laugh and trip and fall together onto the floor and laugh harder.

Had it not been for that wait in the car, this scene would be taking place at home, in a duplex Stephanie would rent while trying to finish her two-year degree in dental hygiene or respiratory therapy at the local community college. The duplex would be spotless, with a blown-up picture of her and her son over the couch and ceramic unicorns and horses occupying the shelves of the entertainment center. She would make sure that her son went to school every day with stylishly floppy pants, scrubbed teeth, and a good breakfast in his belly. Because of their difference in skin color, there would be occasional tension — caused by the strange looks from strangers, teachers, other mothers, and the bullies on the playground, who would chant after they knocked him down, "Your Momma's white, your Momma's white." But if she were home, their weekends and evenings would be spent together transcending those looks and healing those bruises. Now, however, their time is spent eating visiting-room junk food and his school days are spent fighting the boys in the playground who chant, "Your Momma's in prison, your Momma's in prison."

He will be ten when his mother is released, the same age my nephew will be when his mother is let out. But Jennifer, my sister, was able to spend the first five years of Toby's life with him. Stephanie had Ellie after she was incarcerated. They let her hold him for eighteen hours, then sent her back to prison. She has done the "tour," and her son is a well-traveled six-year-old. He has spent weekends visiting his mother in prisons in Kentucky, Texas,

Connecticut (the Pit of Fire), and now at last here, the camp — minimum security, Pekin, Illinois.

Ellie looks older than his age. But his shoulders do not droop like his grandmother's. On the contrary, his bitterness lifts them and his chin higher than a child's should be, and the childlike, wide-eyed curiosity has been replaced by defiance. You can see his emerging hostility as he and his mother play together. She tells him to pick up the toy that he threw, say, or to put the deck of cards away. His face turns sullen, but she persists. She takes him by the shoulders and looks him in the eye, and he uses one of his hands to swat at her. She grabs the hand and he swats with the other. Eventually, she pulls him toward her and smells the top of his head, and she picks up the cards or the toy herself. After all, it is Mother's Day and she sees him so rarely. But her acquiescence makes him angrier, and he stalks out of the playroom with his shoulders thrown back.

Toby, my brother and sister and I assure one another, will not have these resentments. He is better taken care of than most. He is living with relatives in Wisconsin. Good, solid, middle-class, churchgoing relatives. And when he visits us, his aunts and his uncle, we take him out for adventures where we walk down the alley of a city and pretend that we are being chased by the "bad guys." We buy him fast food, and his uncle, John, keeps him up well past his bedtime enthralling him with stories of the monkeys he met in India. A perfect mix, we try to convince one another. Until we take him to see his mother and on the drive back he asks the question that most confuses him, and no doubt all the other children who spend much of their lives in prison visiting rooms: "Is my Mommy a bad guy?" It is the question that most seriously disorders his five-year-old need to clearly separate right from wrong. And because our own need is perhaps just as great, it is the question that haunts us as well.

Now, however, the answer is relatively simple. In a few years, it won't be. In a few years we will have to explain mandatory minimums, and the war on drugs, and the murky conspiracy laws, and the enormous amount of money and time that federal agents pump into imprisoning low-level drug dealers and those who happen to be their friends and their lovers. In a few years he might have the reasoning skills to ask why so many armed robbers and rapists and child-molesters and, indeed, murderers are punished less severely than his mother. When he is older, we will somehow have to explain to him the difference between federal crimes, which don't allow for parole, and state crimes, which do. We will have to explain that his mother was taken from him for five years not because she was a drug dealer but because she made four phone calls for someone she loved.

But we also know it is vitally important that we explain all this without betraying our bitterness. We understand the danger of abstract anger, of being disillusioned with your country, and, most of all, we do not want him to inherit that legacy. We would still like him to be raised as we were, with the idea that we live in the best country in the world with the best legal system in the world — a legal system carefully designed to be immune to political mood swings and public hysteria; a system that promises to fit the punishment to the crime. We want him to be a good citizen. We want him to have absolute faith that he lives in a fair country, a country that watches over and protects its most vulnerable citizens: its women and children.

So for now we simply say, "Toby, your mother isn't bad, she just did a bad thing. Like when you put rocks in the lawn mower's gas tank. You weren't bad then, you just did a bad thing." 17

Once, after being given this weak explanation, he said, "I wish I could have done something really bad, like my Mommy. So I could go to prison too and be with her." 18

It's now 3:00. Visiting ends at 3:30. The kids are getting cranky, and the adults are both exhausted and wired from too many hours of conversation, too much coffee and candy. The fathers, mothers, sisters, brothers, and the few boyfriends, and the very few husbands are beginning to show signs of gathering the trash. The mothers of the infants are giving their heads one last whiff before tucking them and their paraphernalia into their respective carrying cases. The visitors meander toward the door, leaving the older children with their mothers for one last word. But the mothers never say what they want to say to their children. They say things like, "Do well in school," "Be nice to your sister," "Be good for Aunt Berry, or Grandma." They don't say, "I'm sorry I'm sorry I'm sorry. I love you more than anything else in the world and I think about you every minute and I worry about you with a pain that shoots straight to my heart, a pain so great I think I will just burst when I think of you alone, without me. I'm sorry." 19

We are standing in front of the double glass doors that lead to the outside world. My older sister holds her son, rocking him gently. They are both crying. We give her a look and she puts him down. Charity and I grasp each of his small hands, and the four of us walk through the doors. As we're walking out, my brother sings one of his banana songs to Toby. 20

"Take me out to the — " and Toby yells out, "Banana store!" 21

"Buy me some — " 22

"Bananas!!" 23

"I don't care if I ever come back. For it's root, root, root for the — " 24

"Monkey team!" 25

I turn back and see a line of women standing behind the glass wall. Some of them are crying, but many simply stare with dazed eyes. Stephanie is holding both of her son's hands in hers and speaking urgently to him. He is struggling, and his head is twisting violently back and forth. He frees one of his hands from her grasp, balls up his fist, and punches her in the face. Then he walks with purpose through the glass doors and out the exit. I look back at her. She is still in a crouched position. She stares, unblinking, through those doors. Her hands have left her face and are hanging on either side of her. I look away, but before I do, I see drops of blood drip from her nose, down her chin, and onto the shiny marble floor. 26

Coyne reflects near the end of the essay that she wishes her nephew Toby would "have absolute faith that he lives in a fair country" (par. 16). Yet, she expects that, like Stephanie's son Ellie, Toby will become bitter and angry when he understands that "his mother was taken from him for five years not because she was a drug dealer but because she made four phone calls for someone she loved" (par. 15).

With other students in your class, discuss an occasion when you broke a rule or neglected to fulfill an obligation and believe your punishment did not fit the crime. Perhaps you broke a school regulation, violated a rule at work or on a team, or failed to meet a reasonable expectation of your parents or a friend. Perhaps you failed someone who trusted you and whose trust you valued. Although you willingly admit having done it, you may still feel the punishment was unjustified. Begin by briefly telling each other what you did and why you think the punishment was unfair. Then, together consider the following questions as you discuss your ideas about what is fair and unfair:

- Why do you think the punishment was unfair? Were the rules or expectations that you broke clear and reasonable? Were they applied to everyone or only applied selectively or at the whim of those in power?

- Coyne uses the value term *fair* to describe what's wrong with the punishment her sister and some of the other women received. Why do you think Coyne believes her sister's punishment is unfair? Why does Stephanie's mother think her punishment was unfair? Do you agree or disagree?

MAKING CONNECTIONS: UNFAIR PUNISHMENT

● Detailed Information about the Subject

Coyne conveys a lot of information about her sister and the other inmates. She focuses, however, on the effects of separation on mothers and children. The most powerful effects are revealed in Coyne's *anecdotes* portraying what happened between Stephanie and her son Ellie during this particular visit. **Anecdotes** are brief narratives about one-time events.

To analyze how Coyne uses anecdotes to present information about the effects of separation, do the following:

- Reread paragraphs 13 and 26, underlining the words that Coyne uses to present Ellie's hostile actions and putting brackets around the words Coyne uses to present his mother's reactions.

- Write a few sentences explaining what you learn from these anecdotes about the effects on Stephanie and Ellie of enforced separation.

ANALYZING WRITING STRATEGIES

Basic Features

● A Clear Organizational Plan

Coyne's plan for her profile is narrative, spanning visiting hours at the Federal Prison Camp on one particular day, Mother's Day. The essay begins early in the visit and stops a few hours later, when the visiting period ends. But it does not follow a strict chronological order. Some events occur at the same time as other events. For example, paragraphs 1 to 3 present actions that occur at the same time: while mothers are getting reacquainted with their children (pars. 1 and 2), the family members are using the vending machines and chatting with one another.

To analyze Coyne's organizational plan, follow these suggestions:

- Reread the rest of the essay, noting in the margin when the events are happening in relation to the events in earlier paragraphs and highlighting any words, phrases, or sentences that let you know the time of the events.
- Write a few sentences analyzing and evaluating the effectiveness of this plan. Coyne could have chosen to organize her essay topically, by presenting a series of insights and impressions from the many visits she made instead of focusing on this particular Mother's Day. How does the focus Coyne chose help you understand the situation of the women and their families?

⬣ A Role for the Writer

Profile writers usually adopt either the role of a participant or the role of a spectator. Sometimes, they manage to use both roles, as Edge does. Because Coyne made her observations during a family visit to her sister, she has the opportunity to use both the spectator and participant role in her essay.

To analyze the way Coyne uses the two roles, do the following:

- Skim the essay, looking for passages where Coyne shifts from the spectator to the participant role and back again to the spectator role. Note in the margin the role she is using and highlight the words that let you know what her role is.
- Write a sentence or two describing how she uses the two roles and how she avoids confusing readers when she shifts from one role to another.

⬣ A Perspective on the Subject

Coyne seems concerned both about the difficult relationship between incarcerated mothers and their children and about the plight of women in the legal system. Coyne makes a judgment about the fairness of the laws that sent women like her sister Jennifer and Stephanie to prison, but she does not state it explicitly. Instead, she conveys her perspective indirectly through the dialogue, stories, and descriptive details she includes in the profile. Rather than *telling* readers what to think about this issue, she *shows* them what she used to reach her own conclusions, and hopes her readers will agree with her.

To analyze Coyne's perspective, do the following:

- Reread paragraphs 5–10 to see how Stephanie's mother explains her daughter's dilemma, paragraph 11 where Coyne presents a scene she imagines, and paragraph 15 to see what *Coyne speculates about*.
- Write a few sentences explaining how these three episodes convey Coyne's perspective. Give specific examples from the essay to help your readers understand why you think these episodes convey this particular perspective.

In researching her profile, Coyne spends the day in the visitor's room of a prison where she can observe and talk to prisoners and visitors, both adults and children. She has the advantage of having made many previous visits to this same prison's visitor's room, yet nearly all of the information presented in her profile comes from this one visit. You can replicate Coyne's method by profiling an activity occurring over a short period of time, in a relatively small space, and involving only a few people. You should visit the place several times beforehand, observing and talking to people on every visit, making notes in the process, and perhaps capturing a few digital images. Here are some manageable possibilities:

- the waiting room of the student health service's clinic on your campus, a day-care center, a hospital emergency room
- the practice sessions of a college sport or rehearsals of a small music ensemble
- the research lab where a small group of students is collaborating on the same project, or the campus learning or writing center where students come for help with their studies
- the broadcast room of a campus radio station or a production studio where film students are assembling a film

Beyond the Traditional Essay: Writing Profiles

One meaning of the word *profile* is the outline or shape of a person's face when viewed from the side; it shouldn't come as much of a surprise, then, that our first example of nontraditional profiles is a visual portrait.

Many formal portraits tell the viewer a great deal about the subject beyond what they look(ed) like. Clothing, attitude and posture, setting, other people and objects in the frame, and even the identity of the portraitist (as evidenced by the signature and/or characteristic style) all provide explicit markers of the significance of the individual portrayed.

For example, take a look at this portrait of Captain Charles Stewart, painted between 1811 and 1812 by American artist Thomas Sully. According the Web site of the National Gallery of Art (www.nga.gov), where the painting is displayed, "During the half-century from the War of 1812 to the Civil War, American connoisseurs judged portraits by the romantic, even theatrical, standards set by Thomas Sully. . . . Having recently won victories over French privateers, the handsome naval officer [Stewart] commissioned the work as a gift for his mother. . . . Sully lit the thirty-three-year-old captain with a fiery orange glow and depicted his feet braced apart as though planted on a rolling deck. Stewart's thumb aggressively presses down on a nautical chart, while a world globe, underneath the tablecloth, alludes to navigation."

Traditional portraiture, then, can exhibit most of the basic features of the written profile: Sully's painting offers a physical description of Stewart, provides information about his profession and station in life, and presents the artist's (and, likely, the subject's) perspective on the officer's achievements and prospects as those of a dashing, ambitious, successful adventurer. Even a role for the author of the portrait is in evidence — Sully's literal signature and his artistic style make his participation visible, while at the same time they indicate the social prominence of the subject who could afford to commission him.

By their nature, still portraits do not allow for a profile's development — either topical or narrative — over time. However, there are many other forms of profile common in our culture — films, books, plays, operas, and Web sites, among other forms of expression — that do. Michael Moore's documentaries (*Bowling for Columbine, Roger and Me, Sicko*) are examples of works that exhibit the basic features of a traditional profile, including a primarily narrative plan of development.

Many of us are probably most familiar with profiles as the self-descriptions we create on Internet sites such as Facebook, MySpace, and LinkedIn. As is the case on most such sites, the various sections of the Facebook profile — (basic) Information; Friends; Photos; the "Wall," with its various components; etc. — are customizable, to an extent, but they provide a basic template of identity that many of us find recognizable and useful, both for presenting ourselves and for understanding others.

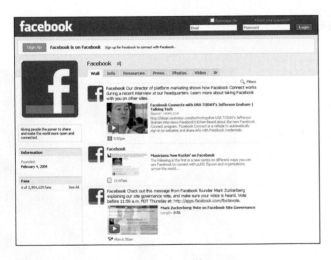

As you work on your own profile, you might want to consult some of these alternative forms of profiles for inspiration. If the format in which you are working allows for it — if, for example, you are creating a poster, Web site, or video — you should consider taking advantage of the strategies available to those working in multimedia — for example, by embedding artifacts that are relevant to the profile you're creating. (Always remember to properly document any material you might use that was created by someone else.)

Guide to Writing

The Writing Assignment

Write an essay about an intriguing person, group of people, place, or activity in your community. Observe your subject closely, and then present what you have learned in a way that both informs and engages readers.

This Guide to Writing will help you apply what you have learned about how writers make their profile essays informative and entertaining. The Guide is divided into five sections with various activities in each section:

- Invention and Research
- Planning and Drafting
- Critical Reading Guide
- Editing and Proofreading
- Revising

The Guide is designed to escort you through the writing process, from finding an event to editing your finished essay. Your instructor may require you to follow the Guide to Writing from beginning to end. Working through the Guide to Writing in this way will help you — as it has helped many other college students — write a thoughtful, fully developed, polished essay.

If, however, your instructor gives you latitude to choose and if you have had experience writing a profile essay, then you can decide on the order in which you'll do the activities in the Guide to Writing. For example, the Invention and Research section includes activities to help you find a subject, choose a role, explore your preconceptions, research the subject, and develop a perspective you want your profile essay to take on the subject. Obviously, finding a subject must precede the other activities, but you may come to the Guide with a subject and a role already in mind, and you may do some preliminary research before you explore your preconceptions or choose to explore your preconceptions and develop a perspective as you are researching the subject. In fact, you may find your response to one of the invention activities expanding into a draft before you've had a chance to do any of the other activities. Writers sometimes find that, in writing up their observation and interview notes, they are in effect drafting parts of their essay. That's a good thing — but you should later flesh out your draft by going back to the activities you skipped and layering the new material into your draft.

The following chart will help you find answers to many of the questions you might have about planning, drafting, and revising a profile. The page references in the Where to Look column refer to examples from the readings, activities in the Guide to Writing, and chapters later in the book.

To learn about using the *Guide* e-book for invention and drafting, go to **bedfordstmartins.com/theguide**.

Starting Points: Writing a Profile

◆ ◆ ◆ ◆ Basic Features

	Question	Where to Look
Choosing a Subject	How do I come up with an appropriate subject to profile?	• Considering Topics for Your Own Essay (pp. 80, 89, 97) • Choosing a Subject to Profile (pp. 101–2) • Finalizing Your Choice (pp. 103–4) • Testing Your Choice (p. 104) • Setting Up a Tentative Schedule (p. 105)
	What's my purpose in writing? How can I convince my audience that the subject is worth profiling?	• Reading Profiles: Purpose and Audience (pp. 68–69) • Exploring Your Preconceptions (p. 104) • Reflecting on Your Purpose and the Profile's Perspective (p. 108) • Refining Your Purpose and Setting Goals (pp. 109–10)
Detailed Information about the Subject	How can I gather information on my subject?	• Collecting Information from Field Research (pp. 106–7) • Chapter 22, "Field Research"
	How can I make my subject come to life?	• Reading Profiles: Basic Features (pp. 67–68) • Use naming, detailing, and comparing (metaphor and simile) (p. 74) • Quote, paraphrase, or summarize from interviews (pp. 87–88) • Use anecdotes (p. 95) • A Sentence Strategy: Absolute Phrases (p. 112) • Working with Sources: Integrating Quotations from Your Interviews (pp. 112–13)
A Clear Organizational Plan	How should I organize my profile?	• Reading Profiles: Basic Features (pp. 67–68) • Using a narrative or topical plan (pp. 78–79) • Refining Your Purpose and Setting Goals: Presenting the Information (pp. 109–10) • Outlining Your Draft (pp. 110–11)
A Role for the Writer	What role should I adopt in researching and presenting my subject?	• Reading Profiles: Basic Features (pp. 67–68) • Choose a role: spectator or participant (p. 79) • Refining Your Purpose and Setting Goals: Using Your Role (p. 110)
A Perspective on the Subject	How do I develop and express a clear perspective on the subject?	• Reading Profiles: Basic Features (pp. 67–68) • Exploring Your Preconceptions (p. 104) • Reflecting on Your Purpose and the Profile's Perspective (p. 108) • Considering Your Thesis (p. 108) • Refining Your Purpose and Setting Goals: Clarifying the Dominant Impression (p. 109)

Invention and Research

Some of the following invention activities will take only a few minutes each to complete, but the field research — making detailed observations and conducting interviews — will take more time to plan and carry out. There is much to learn about observing, interviewing, and writing about what you have discovered, and these activities will support your learning. Remember to keep a written record of your invention work: You will need it when you draft the essay and later when you revise it.

Choosing a Subject to Profile

List several possible subjects and choose one to explore. You may already have a subject in mind, perhaps one suggested by the Considering Topics for Your Own Essay activities following the readings. Reread any notes you might have made in response to those suggestions. Below are criteria you should keep in mind as you make your choice. Also consider the kinds of subjects listed below and the advice on using the Web to find a subject.

Criteria for Choosing a Profile Subject: A Checklist	Your subject — whether it's a person, a group of people, a place, or an activity — should be ☐ a subject that you can gain access to in the time allowed for researching the essay, allowing you to make detailed observations; ☐ a subject about which (or with whom) you can conduct in-depth interviews; ☐ a subject about which/whom you can find background information (if required by your instructor); ☐ a subject about which/whom you have special insight, or at least strong ideas or curiosity; ☐ a subject your readers would find interesting and informative.

Kinds of Subjects to Consider

Community-Related Subjects

- an activity that takes a "broken windows" approach to community improvement (for example, helping people in a neighborhood fix broken windows, paint their homes, plant trees, or remove graffiti)

- a facility that provides a needed service at your college or in the community (for example, a legal advice bureau, child-care center, medical clinic, or homeless shelter)

- a place where people come together because they are of the same age, gender, or ethnic group (for example, a foreign language–speaking dorm or Lesbian

Gay Bisexual Transgender club) or a place where people of different ages, genders, or ethnic groups have formed a community (for example, a Sunday morning pickup basketball game in the park, political action headquarters, or barber shop)

- a person who is a community leader, a volunteer, or an elected official with the ability to bring people together or solve local problems

Career- and Work-Related Subjects

- activities performed by researchers on your campus (for example, nanotechnology, forensics, entomology, indigenous languages, or religious studies)
- a place where people are trained for a certain kind of work (for example, a police academy, cosmetology program, or truck driving school) or a person preparing for a particular kind of work (for example, a boxer preparing for a fight, an attorney preparing for a trial, or an actor rehearsing a role)
- activities performed on your campus by a department, program, club, or center (for example, a center for crime and justice studies, medical and health career program, or center for sustainable development)
- a place where you could learn more about the kind of career you would like to pursue (for example, a law office, dental office, or television station) or where people do a kind of work you would like to know more about (for example, a clothing factory, dairy farm, or racetrack)
- a person working in the career you are thinking of pursuing or a college senior or graduate student in a major you are considering who could help you learn about the kind of preparation needed
- people working together for a particular purpose (for example, students and their teacher working together to prepare for the academic decathlon competition, employees working together to produce something, or scientists collaborating on a research project)

Using the Web to Find and Explore a Profile Subject

You could search the following Internet sites for possible subjects:

- your campus Web site for potentially intriguing places, activities, people, or programs (for example, campus freshman tours, disability services, student clubs, or the academic senate)
- a city or state Web site for interesting places or people (for example, the city council, EMS department, public records department, or a jury room)
- Google or YellowPages.com for unusual local restaurants or small businesses (like these near Riverside, California: Al Kauser Halal Meat, Association of Nigerian Physicians in the Americas, La Sierra Fire Equipment, or Scuba Bee Supplies)

Once you have found a subject, exploring the Web could help you find background information that could help you develop questions to ask in your interview:

- Google the subject to find possible sources of information. (For example, if you are planning on interviewing a local beekeeper, Googling "beekeeping" will give you a lot of information about the process and history as well as possible causes and effects of the die-off of honey bees.)
- If you are writing about a person, try searching Facebook or some other social-networking site for background on him or her.

Make notes of any information or insights suggested by your online research, and download any visuals you might include in your essay, being sure to get the information necessary to cite any online sources. (See p. 774–76 for the MLA citation format for electronic sources.)

Ways In: Finalizing Your Choice

Basic Features

To be certain that the subject you have chosen will work, you need to check that you can get access to the subject and also see whether the role you want to adopt will be possible. You may do these in either order or even at the same time.

Checking That You Can Do the Field Research
• Check to be sure that you can get access to the place or activity you want to observe and/or the people you want to interview. Observing some places and activities may not require special planning, but interviews will nearly always require advance scheduling.
• You may need to go to the place to find out who you need to get permission from, or you may be able to phone or e-mail your request. Either way, build in time for a response to your request.
• Explain that your project is for a class and why you are interested. Most people tend to be surprisingly generous with their time and eager to help students, but be prepared for occasional refusals, and always make an effort to be polite, dress properly, come on time, and conduct yourself professionally.
(See Chapter 22 for more advice on planning your observations and interviews.)

Getting Permission for Your Role
You may need to get permission to do your research from someone in authority and also from your instructor.
Participant Observer
• If you are new to the subject, ask permission to take part in a small way for a limited time (for example, by making a hamburger at a fast-food restaurant).
• If you are already an insider, ask your instructor whether you should assume your regular role; he or she may require you to find a new angle instead so that you learn something new. (For example, if you're on the football team, you might focus not on the players but the cheerleaders or the people who maintain the field.)
Spectator Role. To use this role effectively, you need to get close enough to look over the shoulder of people who are centrally involved. Ask permission from those in charge to interview participants and observe them in action.

● Exploring Your Preconceptions

Write a paragraph or two describing what you already know and think about your subject and what you would like to learn about it. The following questions will get you started:

What I Already Know about This Subject

- How can I define or describe it?
- What are its chief qualities or parts?
- Whom do I associate with it?
- What is its purpose or function?
- How does it compare with other subjects with which I am more familiar?

My Expectations about This Subject

- Why do I assume it will be interesting to me and to my readers?
- What do I hope to learn about it?
- How does this subject reflect cultural or community values and concerns?

Testing Your Choice

Decide whether you should proceed with this particular subject. Giving up on a profile subject is bound to be frustrating, but if, after doing some work on it, the subject does not seem a strong possibility for you to research and write about, starting over may be the wisest course of action. The questions that follow may help you decide whether to go on with this subject or begin looking for an alternative.

- *After reviewing my possible subjects, do I still feel that I have made the best choice, or does another subject seem more promising?*
- *Do I still feel curious about the subject?*
- *Am I confident I will be able to make the subject interesting for my readers?*
- *Do I believe that I can research this subject sufficiently in the time I have?*

A Collaborative Activity:
Testing Your Choice

Get together with two or three other students, and describe the subject you have chosen to profile.

Presenters: Take turns identifying your subjects. Explain your interest in the subject, and speculate about why you think it will interest readers.

Listeners: Briefly tell each presenter what you already know about his or her subject, if anything, and what might make it interesting to readers.

Setting Up a Tentative Schedule

Create a tentative schedule for your observations, interviews, and background research. You might use a chart like the one that follows, which you can update as you go along. Think about the order in which each activity should be completed. Sometimes it's best to start with observations; other times it's best to begin with an interview, a trip to the library, or an Internet search for background information. Notice that immediately after the observations and interviews, you need to give yourself five minutes or so to clarify and add to your notes. It's also a good idea to do write-ups for each observation and interview; your instructor may ask you to bring your write-ups to class, and you can use them when you draft your essay. (See the sections that follow for more information on making observations and conducting interviews, and refer to Chapter 22: Field Research for more detail.)

Date	Time Needed	Purpose	Preparation
10/22	30 minutes	Background Internet research	Print map, bookmark potentially useful sites
10/23	30 minutes	1st observation: Find out whom to interview, pick up any materials	Bring map, directions, paper & pen
10/23	30 minutes	Write up 1st observation (for class) & schedule interview	Review observation notes
10/24	45 minutes	1st interview. While there schedule 2nd interview	Prepare questions
10/24	20 minutes	Write up 1st interview (for class)	Review interview notes
10/25	1 hour	2nd observation and interview	Bring notes on needed details & prepare 2nd interview questions

Basic Features

◆ Ways In: Collecting Information from Field Research

The following activities will help you make observations and conduct interviews. Many writers begin with observation to get the lay of the land and decide whom to interview, but you can start with either one. You may also be able to make observations and conduct interviews during the same visit.

Making Observations	Conducting Interviews
Come Prepared. *Bring a notepad, pen, and any necessary devices (such as a phone with a camera and audio recorder) to each observational visit.*	**Come Prepared.** *Bring preliminary questions, a notepad, pen, and any necessary recording devices to each interview.*

Take Notes. *Use all of your senses — sight, hearing, smell, taste, and touch:*

- Describe the place from multiple vantage points, noting furnishings, décor, etc.
- Sketch the layout.
- Describe people's appearance, dress, gestures, and actions, but be careful not to invade people's privacy.
- Note what is happening, who does what, how people seem to feel.
- Make a record of interesting overheard conversation.
- Note your reactions, insights, and ideas, especially in relation to your preconceptions and the perspective you might take in your essay.

Take Notes. *Write down potentially important information and anything quotable.* Describe the interviewee's tone, gestures, mannerisms — anything that would provide vivid description and add to the overall impression.

- To generate **anecdotes,** ask how the interviewee got involved in the first place; if there was a high or a low point, a breakthrough, or a key event worth noting; what most concerns the interviewee; what has been the biggest influence for good or ill.
- To elicit **process narratives**, ask how it works; what happens if it breaks down; whether it was always done the same way; how it has changed; how it could be improved.
- To **classify**, **compare**, or **contrast**, ask what kind of thing it is; how it's like and unlike others of its kind; how it compares to what it was like in the past.
- To help you think about your **perspective**, ask why the interviewee thinks it is important, needed, helpful, etc., and who would agree and disagree; what the purpose of it is or how it contributes to the community; what its shortcomings are or how it could be improved.

(continued)

(continued)

Making Observations	Conducting Interviews

Collect Visuals. *Look for artifacts and consider taking photographs you could include in your profile.*

- Collect any brochures or other written material you might be able to use either to prepare for interviews or to include in your essay.
- Consider taking photographs or videos (but be sure to ask permission of the people you are photographing).
- Take a 360-degree video of the place, a pan shot scanning the scene from side to side, or a tracking shot indicating what you see as you enter or walk through the place.

Reflect on the Interview. *Take five minutes right after your interview to review your notes.* Later, you can listen to or watch any recordings you made at the scene and add to your notes. Focus now on your first impressions. Mark the promising material — for example:

- anything new or surprising that calls into question your own or your readers' likely preconceptions;
- sensory details you could use to create a vivid portrait of the place, people, and activity;
- quotable words and phrases that could help you capture the tone or mood of the subject;
- questions you still need answered;
- insights and ideas you might research further; and
- anything that could help you clarify or develop your perspective on the subject.

Reflect on Your Observations. *Take five minutes right after your visit to think about what you observed, and write a few sentences about your impressions of the subject:*

- What seems most interesting to you now?
- How did your visit confirm or change your preconceptions?
- What is your dominant impression of the subject?

Write Up Your Interview. *Write a few paragraphs, deciding what to quote, summarize, paraphrase, or leave out.* Be sure to describe the person's tone of voice, gestures, and appearance as well as any details you noticed about the place. You may decide not to include all of this material in your essay but it will help you figure out what's important and interesting.

Write Up Your Observations. *Compose a few paragraphs reporting on your visit.* Your instructor may ask you to bring these paragraphs to class, and writing up your observations may produce language you can use in your draft. It will certainly help you think about how to describe your subject, what impression you want to create, and the perspective your profile should take.

Do a Follow-up Interview. *If your interviewee said you could e-mail or phone to check your facts, follow up with questions or requests for clarification.* You might also arrange to talk to another person who has different kinds of information to share.

Do a Follow-up Observation. *Consider returning for a follow-up visit, which you could combine with a scheduled interview.* Examine other aspects of the place or activity and try to answer questions you still have. Consider whether the impression you had on the first visit holds and what else you could note that would make your description vivid.

Basic Features

Ways In: Reflecting on Your Purpose and the Profile's Perspective

The following activities, which can be done in any order, will help you deepen your analysis and think of ways to help your readers gain a better understanding of your subject's cultural significance.

Developing a Perspective	Defining Your Purpose for Your Readers
Write for five minutes exploring your perspective on the subject — what it is about the subject that seems important and meaningful. • If you are focusing on a **place,** ask yourself what is interesting to you about its culture: What rituals are practiced there? Who visits it? What is its function in the community? • If you are focusing on an **activity**, consider how it has changed over time, for good or for ill; how outsiders are initiated into the activity; who benefits from the activity; and what its value is for the community. • If you are focusing on a **person** or **group**, ask yourself what sense of identity they have; what customs and ways of communicating they follow; what their values and attitudes are; what they think about social hierarchies or gender difference; and how they see their role in the community.	*Write for five minutes exploring what you want your readers to learn about the subject.* Use these questions to help you clarify your thinking: • Who are your intended readers? What are they likely to know and think about your subject? • What about your subject will be surprising to them? • How can you make your perspective on this subject interesting to your readers? • How can you help readers examine their own preconceptions or stereotypes about the subject? • How can you lead readers to think about the subject's social and cultural significance — that is, what it implies about our shared or different values and concerns?

Considering Your Thesis

Review what you wrote under Developing a Perspective and Defining Your Purpose for Your Readers, and add a couple of sentences summarizing the main idea you want readers to take away from your essay.

Remember that readers do not expect a profile to have the kind of explicit thesis statement typical of argumentative essays, but they do need the descriptive details and other information to work together to create a dominant impression.

Designing Your Document

Think about whether visual or audio elements — photographs, postcards, menus, or snippets from films, television programs, or songs — would strengthen your profile. These are not a requirement for an effective profile, but they can be helpful. Consider also whether your readers might benefit from design features such as headings, bulleted or numbered lists, or other typographic elements that can make an essay easier to follow.

Think of the profiles you have seen in a magazine or on a Web page or television show. What visual or audio elements, if any, were used to create a strong sense of the subject being profiled? Photographs? Postcards? Menus? Signs? Song lyrics?

As you review the questions on the next few pages, especially those under "Refining Your Purpose and Setting Goals," think about the ways in which you might show as well as tell readers about your object of study. (Remember that you must cite the source of any visual or audio element you do not create yourself, and you should also request permission from the source if your essay is going to be posted on a Web site that is not password-protected.)

Planning and Drafting

The following activities will help you refine your purpose, set goals for your draft, and outline it. In addition, this section will help you write a draft by writing opening sentences, trying out a useful sentence strategy, and learning how to work with sources.

Refining Your Purpose and Setting Goals

Before starting to draft, here are some questions that may help you sharpen your purpose for your audience and set goals for your draft. Your instructor may ask you to write out your answers to some of these questions or simply to think about them as you plan and draft your essay.

Clarifying the Dominant Impression

Although you are trying to create a dominant impression with the description and information you include in your essay, you should be careful not to oversimplify or whitewash it. Readers appreciate profiles that reveal the richness and complexity of the subject. For example, even as Brian Cable shows that the Goodbody Mortuary is guided by crass commercialism, he also gets readers to think about cultural attitudes about death, perhaps exemplified in his own complex feelings.

- Review your observation and interview notes and write-ups, highlighting in one color the descriptive language that supports the dominant impression you want your essay to create.

- Highlight in a second color any descriptions that seem to create a different impression.

- Write for a few minutes exploring how these different impressions relate to one another. Consider whether they reveal complexity in the subject or ambivalence in your perspective that could be developed further in your essay.

Presenting the Information

Review your invention writing, noting in the margin which bits of information you should include in your draft and how you might present them. Consider the following:

- What special terms will I need to define for my readers?

- What comparisons or contrasts might make the information clearer and more memorable?

- Which information could be listed or categorized?
- How can I present causes or effects in a vivid way?
- From my interview(s) and background research, what lively language should I quote (instead of summarizing or paraphrasing)?

Using Your Role

Whether you chose to adopt a participant-observer or spectator role, you need to think about how you can use your role to engage readers and present the information you've chosen to include. Either role can be used to help readers identify with you. For example, if you are entering a place most of us avoid (as Cable does when he enters the mortuary) you can take us with you as you learn about the place and look over other people's shoulders to see what they're doing. Or if you act as a participant trying to learn how to do what others routinely do (as Edge does when he tries to eat a pickled pig lip), readers can imagine themselves in your shoes.

Regardless of your role, also consider how to refer to yourself in your draft. Here are some possibilities:

- Use the first-person pronoun. (For example, "While Kim was telling me all this, I could hear Biff rummaging around in the kitchen" [Orlean, par. 15].)
- Place yourself at the scene. (For example, "I followed him through an arched doorway into a chapel that smelled musty and old" [Cable, par. 15].)
- Refer to your own actions. (For example, "John and Charity and I silently exchange glances" [Coyne, par. 7].)
- Share your thoughts and feelings. (For example, "Death may be a great leveler, but one's coffin quickly reestablishes one's status" [Cable, par. 17].)

Outlining Your Draft

It may already be clear to you whether you should organize your information topically or narratively — or try to combine the two as Edge does when he uses his story about eating a pig lip as a frame for the topical presentation of the information he learned from observing and interviewing at the Farm Fresh Food Supplier plant.

If you plan to arrange your material *narratively*, plot the key events on a timeline. The following suggests one possible way to organize a narrative profile of a place:

I. Begin by describing the place from the outside.

II. Present background information.

III. Describe what you see as you enter.

IV. Introduce the people and activities.

V. Tour the place, describing what you see as you move from one part to the next.

VI. Fill in information wherever you can, and comment about the place or the people.

VII. Conclude with reflections on what you have learned about the place.

If you plan to arrange your material *topically*, use clustering or outlining to help you divide and group related information. Here is a suggested outline for a topical profile about a person:

For more on clustering and outlining, see Chapter 11, pp. 563–68.

I. Begin with a vivid image of the person in action.

II. Present the first topic. (A topic could be a characteristic of the person or one aspect of his or her work.) Use dialogue, description, narration, process description, evaluation, or interpretation to illustrate this topic.

III. Present the second topic. Use dialogue, description, narration, process description, evaluation, or interpretation to illustrate this topic.

IV. Present the third topic (and continue as above until you have presented all topics).

V. Conclude with a bit of action or dialogue.

The tentative plan you choose should reflect the possibilities in your material as well as your purpose and readers. As you begin drafting, you will almost certainly discover new ways of organizing parts of your material.

Drafting

If you have not already begun to draft your essay, this section will help by suggesting how to write your opening sentences; how to use temporal transitions and verb tense to draft a narrative that readers will be able to follow; and how to integrate quotations from your interviews. Drafting isn't always a smooth process, so don't be afraid to leave spaces where you don't know what to put in or to write notes to yourself about what you still need to do. If you get stuck while drafting, go back over your invention writing: You may be able to copy and paste some of it into your evolving draft, or you may need to do some additional invention to fill in details in your draft.

Writing the Opening Sentences

You could try out one or two different ways of beginning your essay — possibly from the list that follows — but do not agonize over the first sentences because you are likely to discover the best way to begin only as you draft your essay. Review your invention writing to see if you have already written something that would work to launch your essay. To engage your readers' interest from the start, consider the following opening strategies:

- a surprising statement (like Orlean)
- a remarkable thought or occasion that triggers your observational visit (like Cable)
- a vivid description (like Coyne)
- a compelling description of the time and place (like Edge)
- an arresting quotation
- a fascinating bit of information
- an amusing anecdote

A Sentence Strategy: Absolute Phrases

As you draft your profile, you will need to help your readers imagine your subject. A grammatical structure called an **absolute phrase** is useful for this purpose. Here is an example, with the absolute phrase in italics:

> I offer the bag to Jerry, order yet another beer, and turn to eye the pig feet floating in a murky jar by the cash register, *their blunt tips bobbing up through a pasty white film.* (Edge, par. 19)

Edge could have presented his observation of the pickled pig feet in a separate sentence, but the sentence he wrote brings together his turning and looking and what he actually saw, emphasizing the at-a-glance instant of another possible stomach flutter.

Absolute phrases modify a whole sentence or a clause, rather than a single word. They are nearly always attached to the end of a main clause, adding various kinds of details to it to create a more complex, informative sentence. They are usually introduced by a noun (like *tips*) or a possessive pronoun (like *his, its,* or *their*), followed by participial phrases (like *bobbing up . . .*). Here are three further examples of absolute phrases from this chapter's readings:

> This was a solid bronze casket, *its seams electronically welded to resist corrosion.* (Cable, par. 21)

> Slowly, the dank barroom fills with grease-smeared mechanics from the truck stop up the road and farmers straight from the fields, *the soles of their brogans thick with dirt clods.* (Edge, par. 1)

> Biff held his position for a moment, and then he and Kim bounded across the ring, *his feet moving so fast that they blurred into an oily sparkle,* even though he really didn't have very far to go. (Orlean, par. 24)

For more on using absolute phrases, go to **bedfordstmartins.com/ theguide** and click on Sentence Strategies.

Absolute phrases are certainly not required for a successful profile — experienced writers use them only occasionally — yet they do offer writers an effective sentence option. Try them out in your own writing.

Working with Sources:
Integrating Quotations from Your Interviews

One of the ways profiles present information from interviews is by quoting. These quotations can be especially revealing because they let readers hear different people speaking for themselves. Nevertheless, it is the writer who decides which quotations to use and how. Therefore, one major task you face in drafting and revising your essay is to choose quotations from your notes, present them in a timely way to reveal the style and character of people you interviewed, and integrate these quotations smoothly into your sentences.

When you directly quote (rather than paraphrase or summarize) what someone has said, you will usually need to identify the speaker. The principal way to do so is to create what is called a **speaker tag**. You may rely on a general or all-purpose speaker tag, using *said*:

> "She was even a little extreme for a bitch," William *said*. "She was rather buxom. I would call her zaftig." (Orlean, par. 11)

Other speaker tags are more specific:

> "It was a large service," *remarked* Howard. (Cable, par. 16)

> "Something deep within us demands a confrontation with death," Tim *explained*. (Cable, par. 23)

> "Take me out to the" — and Toby *yells out*, "Banana store!" (Coyne, par. 21)

As you draft your profile, consider using specific speaker tags. They give readers more help with imagining speakers' attitudes and personal styles. You may also add a word or phrase to any speaker tag to identify or describe the speaker or to reveal more about *how, where, when,* or *why* the speaker speaks:

> "We're in *Ripley's Believe It or Not*, along with another funeral home whose owners' names are Baggit and Sackit," Howard told me, *without cracking a smile*. (Cable, par. 14)

> "Kind of look like Frosted Flakes, don't they?" he says, *by way of describing the chips rapidly turning to mush in the pickling juice*. (Edge, par. 19)

> Matt Sander, one of the founders of *Dog News*, said *recently*, "Biff is just very, very personable." (Orlean, par. 16)

> *Once, after being given this weak explanation*, he said, "I wish I could have done something really bad, like my Mommy. So I could go to prison too and be with her." (Coyne, par. 18).

In addition to being carefully introduced, quotations must be precisely punctuated, and fortunately there are only two general rules:

1. Enclose all quotations in quotation marks. These always come in pairs, one at the beginning, one at the end of the quotation. Be especially careful not to forget to include the one at the end.

2. Separate the quotation from its speaker tag with appropriate punctuation, usually a comma. But if you have more than one sentence (as in the first and last examples above), be careful to punctuate the separate sentences properly.

For more on integrating quotations, go to **bedfordstmartins.com/theguide** and click on Bedford Research Room; see also Chapter 24, pp. 759–60.

Critical Reading Guide

Basic Features

For a printable version of this Critical Reading Guide, go to bedfordstmartins.com/ theguide.

Your instructor may arrange a peer review session in class or online where you can exchange drafts with your classmates and give each other a thoughtful critical reading, pointing out what works well and suggesting ways to improve the draft. This Critical Reading Guide can also be used productively by a tutor in the writing center or by a roommate or family member. A good critical reading does three things: it lets the writer know how the reader understands the point of the profile, praises what works best, and indicates where the draft could be improved.

1. Assess the quality and presentation of information about the subject.

   Summarize: Tell the writer one thing you learned about the subject from reading the essay.

   Praise: Point out one passage where the description seems especially vivid, a quotation stands out, or another writing strategy — defining, comparing or contrasting, classifying, explaining causes or effects, narrating anecdotes or processes, giving examples or lists — works particularly well to present information.

   Critique: Point out one passage where description could be added or where the description could be made more vivid, where a quotation falls flat and should be paraphrased or summarized, or where another writing strategy — defining, comparing or contrasting, classifying, explaining causes or effects, narrating anecdotes or processes, giving examples or lists — could be added or improved.

2. Analyze the organizational plan.

   Summarize: Identify the kind of plan — narrative, topical, or both — the draft uses.

   Praise: Comment on the plan's effectiveness. For example, point to a place where one topic leads logically to the next or where temporal transitions help you follow the narrative organization. Also, indicate what in the opening paragraphs grabs your attention or why you think the ending works well.

   Critique: Point to information that seems out of place or where the chronology is confusing. If you think the opening or ending could be improved, suggest an alternative passage in the essay that could work as an opening or an ending.

3. Evaluate the writer's role.

   Summarize: Identify the role — spectator or participant-observer — the writer adopts.

   Praise: Point to a passage where the spectator or participant-observer role enables you to identify with the writer, enhancing the essay's immediacy or interest.

Critique: Point out any problems with the role — for example, if the participant-observer role becomes tiresome or distracting, or if the spectator role seems too mechanical and distant.

4. Evaluate how well the author's perspective on the subject and the dominant impression are conveyed.

Summarize: State briefly what you believe to be the writer's perspective on the subject and the dominant impression you get from the essay.

Praise: Give an example where you have a strong sense of the writer's perspective through a comment, description, quotation, or bit of information.

Critique: Tell the writer if the essay does not have a clear perspective or convey a dominant impression. To help him or her find one, explain what interests you about the subject and what you think is important. If you see contradictions in the draft that could be developed to make the profile more complex and illuminating, briefly explain.

5. If the writer has expressed concern about anything in the draft that you have not discussed, respond to that concern.

Making Comments Electronically Most word processing software offers features that allow you to insert comments directly into the text of someone else's document. Many readers prefer to make their comments this way because it tends to be faster than writing on hard copy and space is virtually unlimited; it also eliminates the process of deciphering handwritten comments. Where such features are not available, simply typing comments directly into a document in a contrasting color can provide the same advantages.

Revising

Very likely you have already thought of ways to improve your draft, and you may even have begun to revise it. In this section is a Troubleshooting chart that may help. Before using the chart, however, it is a good idea to

For an electronic version of the Troubleshooting chart, go to **bedfordstmartins** **.com/theguide.**

- review critical reading comments from your classmates, instructor, or writing center tutor, and
- make an outline of your draft so that you can look at it analytically.

Making an outline of the draft, even if you made an outline before drafting, can help you see what you actually wrote as opposed to what you intended to write. Your aim should not be to make your draft conform to your original draft, but to make your draft as good as it can be.

Troubleshooting Your Draft

●●●● Basic Features

	Problem	Suggestions for Revising the Draft
Detailed Information about the Subject	People do not come alive.	☐ Describe a physical feature or mannerism that gives each person individuality. ☐ Add speaker tags to characterize how people talk. ☐ Liven up the dialogue with faster repartee. ☐ Add details to help readers see the person. ☐ Consider adding a comparison. ☐ Use anecdotes or specific narrative action to show the person in action.
	The place is hard to visualize.	☐ Name objects in the scene. ☐ Add sensory detail — sight, sound, smell, taste, touch. ☐ Say what the place is like or unlike. ☐ Consider adding a visual — a photograph or sketch, for example.
	There is too much information — it is not clear what is important.	☐ Cut extraneous information or make clearer why the information is important. ☐ Break up long blocks of informational text with description of scenes or people, narration of events, or examples. ☐ Vary the writing strategies used to present the information: for example, add a comparison or discuss known causes or effects. ☐ Consider which parts of the information would be more engaging if presented through dialogue or summarized more succinctly.
	Visuals could be added or improved.	☐ Use a photo, map, drawing, cartoon, or other visual that might make the place and people easier to imagine or the information more understandable. ☐ Consider adding textual references to any images in your essay or positioning images more effectively.
A Clear Organizational Plan	The narrative plan drags or rambles.	☐ Try adding drama through dialogue or specific narrative action. ☐ Summarize or paraphrase instead if dialogue seems pointless or uninteresting. ☐ Give the narrative shape — for example, by building suspense or tension. ☐ Make sure the narrative unfolds or develops and has a direction that is clear.
	Topically arranged essay is disorganized or out of balance.	☐ Try rearranging topics to see whether another order makes more sense. ☐ Add clearer, more explicit transitions or topic sentences. ☐ Move or condense information to restore balance.

(continued)

(continued)	**Problem**	**Suggestions for Revising the Draft**
A Clear Organizational Plan	The opening fails to engage readers' attention.	☐ Consider alternatives. Think of questions, an engaging image, or dialogue you could open with. ☐ Go back to your notes for other ideas. ☐ Recall how the writers in this chapter open their profiles: Cable stands on the street in front of the mortuary, Edge sits at a bar staring at a pig lip.
	Transitions are missing or are confusing.	☐ Add appropriate transitional words or phrases. ☐ Revise sentences to make transitions clearer or smoother.
	The ending seems weak.	☐ Consider ending earlier or moving a striking insight to the end. ☐ Review your invention and research notes to see if you overlooked something that would make for a strong ending. ☐ Recall how the writers in this chapter end their profiles: Cable touches the cold flesh of a cadaver, Edge stares at pig feet.
	Visual features are not effective.	☐ Use an image, as Edge does. Consider adding textual references to any images in your essay or positioning images more effectively. ☐ Think of other possible design features — drawings, lists, tables, graphs, cartoons, headings — that might make the place and people easier to imagine or the information more understandable.
A Role for the Writer	The spectator role is too distant.	☐ Consider placing yourself in the scene as you describe it. ☐ Add your thoughts and reactions to one of the interviews.
	Participation is distracting.	☐ Bring other people forward by adding material about them. ☐ Reduce the material about yourself.
A Perspective on the Subject	The perspective or dominant impression is unclear.	☐ Try stating it more directly by adding your thoughts or someone else's. ☐ Be sure that the descriptive and narrative details reinforce the dominant impression you want your essay to convey. ☐ If your perspective is complex, you may need to discuss more directly the contradictions or complications you see in the subject.
	Readers don't find my perspective interesting.	☐ Consider how you can appeal to readers' interests. ☐ Reconsider what you think is important about the subject in light of readers' ideas, and consider expanding your ideas. ☐ Elaborate on your perspective, helping readers understand why you think it is culturally significant.

Thinking About Document Design:
Creating Web-Based Essays

The education student writing on collaborative learning (see p. 64) published her essay online so that classmates and other interested people could read her work. Web-based publishing allowed her not only to include photographs and materials from her research, but also to show her final product to the sixth graders and the teacher she had profiled.

Web documents can be more visually complex and interactive than essays written for print. In her Web-based essay, the education student incorporated photographs, links, and color highlights to make the material both more interesting and helpful to her readers. As the screen shot on this page shows, she embedded links on the left side of the page so readers could easily move through her essay and used a graphic (the dark blue circle) to mark the current page. Since Web readers tend to skim, surf, and bounce around, the student provided several different points of entry into her post: a table of contents ("Contents"); an introduction with information about the assignment and some context for the site ("Introduction"); a page summarizing the work she researched, read, and reviewed for the project ("Background Reading"); a section reporting on her research ("Findings"); and a page including photos taken during the project ("Gallery"). She also included a "Bibliography" page listing the scholarly essays she used for background reading, with links to material available online. In addition, the student writer included links to the sixth-grade class's Web site, which contained the final projects that resulted from the Internet research she had watched the children engage in. She encouraged readers to view these projects as evidence of the advantages of collaborative learning.

Because her topic was collaboration, she wanted a photograph showing children working together. However, since the children were minors, she would have needed parent and teacher permission to take and include their photographs. Instead, she used graphic software to alter a picture of four children so that the children's faces were not identifiable. At key points in her essay, the student writer also included quotes from the sixth graders. She used these quotes as subtitles for individual sections of her essay, and to draw more attention to the quotes, she used a font larger than that of the body of the essay — a technique borrowed from print publishing.

Editing and Proofreading

Now is the time to check your revised draft for errors in grammar, punctuation, and mechanics. Our research has identified several errors that occur often in profiles, including problems with the punctuation of quotations and the order of adjectives. The following guidelines will help you check your essay for these common errors.

Checking the Punctuation of Quotations

Because most profiles are based in part on interviews, you probably have quoted one or more people in your essay. When you quote someone's exact words, you must enclose these words in quotation marks and observe strict conventions for punctuating them.

What to Check For:

- All quotations should have quotation marks at the beginning and the end.

  ▶ "What exactly is civil litigation?" I asked.

- Commas and periods go *inside* quotation marks.

  ▶ "I'm here to see Anna Post," I replied nervously.

  ▶ Tony explained, "Fraternity boys just wouldn't feel comfortable at the Chez Moi Café."

- Question marks and exclamation points go *inside* closing quotation marks if they are a part of the quotation, *outside* if they are not.

  ▶ After a pause, the patient asked, "Where do I sign?"

  ▶ Willie insisted, "You can *too* learn to play Super Mario!"

  ▶ When was the last time someone you just ticketed said to you, "Thank you, Officer, for doing a great job?"

- Use commas with speaker tags (*he said, she asked,* etc.) that accompany direct quotations.

  ▶ "This sound system costs only four thousand dollars," Jorge said.

  ▶ I asked, "So where were these clothes from originally?"

A Note on Grammar and Spelling Checkers
These tools can be helpful, but don't rely on them exclusively to catch errors in your text: Spelling checkers cannot catch misspellings that are themselves words, such as *to* for *too*. Grammar checkers miss some problems, sometimes give faulty advice for fixing problems, and can flag correct items as wrong. Use these tools as a second line of defense after your own (and, ideally, another reader's) proofreading/editing efforts.

For practice, go to **bedfordstmartins.com/ theguide/exercisecentral** and click on Punctuation of Quotations.

A Common ESL Problem: Adjective Order

The Problem: In trying to present the subject of your profile vividly and in detail, you probably have included many descriptive adjectives. When you include more than one adjective in front of a noun, you may have difficulty sequencing them. For example, do you write *a large old ceramic pot* or *an old large ceramic pot*?

How to Correct It: The following list shows the order in which adjectives are ordinarily arranged in front of a noun:

1. *Amount* (a/an, the, six)
2. *Evaluation* (good, beautiful, ugly, serious)
3. *Size* (large, small, tremendous)
4. *Shape, length* (round, long, short)
5. *Age* (young, new, old)

6. *Color* (red, black, green)

7. *Origin* (Asian, Brazilian, German)

8. *Material* (wood, cotton, gold)

9. Noun used as an adjective (computer [as in *computer program*], cake [as in *cake pan*])

    1.   *3.*   *6.*
Seventeen small green buds appeared on my birch sapling.

    1. 2. 5. 6. 9.
He tossed his daughter a nice new yellow tennis ball.

 1. 4.   7.   8.
The slender German-made gold watch cost a great deal of money.

For practice, go to bedfordstmartins.com/theguide/exercisecentral and click on A Common ESL Problem: Adjective Order.

A Writer at Work

Brian Cable's Interview Notes and Write-Up

Most profile writers take notes when interviewing people. Later, they may summarize their notes in a short write-up. In this section, you will see some of the interview notes and a write-up that Brian Cable prepared for his mortuary profile, "The Last Stop," printed on pp. 69–73.

Cable arranged to tour the mortuary and conduct interviews with the funeral director and mortician. Before each interview, he wrote out a few questions at the top of a sheet of paper and then divided it into two columns; he used the left-hand column for descriptive details and personal impressions and the right-hand column for the information he got directly from the person he interviewed. Following are Cable's notes and write-up for his interview with the funeral director, Howard Deaver.

Cable used three questions to guide his interview with Howard and then took brief notes during the interview. He did not concern himself too much with notetaking because he planned to spend a half-hour directly afterward to complete his notes. He focused his attention on Howard, trying to keep the interview comfortable and conversational and jotting down just enough to jog his memory and catch especially meaningful quotations. A typescript of Cable's interview notes follows.

The Interview Notes

QUESTIONS

1. How do families of the deceased view the mortuary business?

2. How is the concept of death approached?

3. How did you get into this business?

Descriptive Details & Personal Impressions	Information
weird-looking	Howard Deaver, funeral director,
tall	Goodbody Mortuaries
long fingers	"Call me Howard"
big ears	How things work: Notification, pick up
low, sloping forehead	body at home or hospital, prepare for
Like stereotype — skin colorless	viewing, restore distorted features —
	accident or illness, embalm, casket —
	family selects, chapel services (3 in bldg.),
	visitation room — pay respects, family & friends.
	Can't answer questions about death —
	"Not bereavement specialists. Don't
	handle emotional problems. Only a
	trained therapist can do that." "We
	provide services for dead, not counseling
	for the living." (great quote) Concept of
	death has changed in last 40 yrs
	(how long he's been in the business)
	Funeral cost: $500–$600, now $2,000
plays with lips	Phone call (interruption)
blinks	"I think we'll be able to get him in
plays with Adam's apple	on Friday. No, no, the family wants
desk empty — phone, no	him cremated."
paper or pen	Ask about Neptune Society — cremation
	Cremation "Cheap, quick, easy means of
angry	disposal."
disdainful of the	
Neptune Society	Recent phenomenon. Neptune Society — erroneous
	claim to be only one.
	"We've offered them since the beginning. It's only
	now it's come into vogue."
	Trend now back toward burial.
	Cremation still popular in sophisticated areas
	60% in Marin Co. and Florida
	Ask about paperwork — does it upstairs,
	lives there with wife, Nancy.
musty, old stained glass	Tour around (happy to show me around)
sunlight filtered	Chapel — large service just done,
	Italian.

man in black suit	"Not a religious institution — a
roses	business."
wooden benches	casket — "beautiful craftsmanship" —
	admires, expensive
contrast brightness	Display room — caskets, about 30 of them
fluorescent lights	Loves to talk about caskets "models in every price
Plexiglas stands	range" glossy (like cars in a showroom) cardboard
	box, steel, copper, bronze $400 up to $1,800.
	Top of line: bronze, electronically welded, no
	corrosion — $5,000

Cable's interview notes include many descriptive details of Howard as well as of various rooms in the mortuary. Though most entries are short and sketchy, much of the language found its way into the final essay. In describing Howard, for example, Cable noted that he fits the stereotype of the cadaverous undertaker, a fact that Cable emphasized in his essay.

He put quotation marks around Howard's actual words, some of them written in complete sentences, others in fragments. We will see how Cable filled these quotes in when he wrote up the interview. In only a few instances did he take down more than he could use. Even though profile writers want good quotes, they should not use quotes to present information that can be more effectively expressed in their own words. In profiles, writers use direct quotation both to provide information and to capture the mood or character of the person speaking.

As you can see, Howard was not able to answer Cable's questions about the families of the deceased and their attitudes toward death or mortuaries. The gap between these questions and Howard's responses led Cable to recognize one of his own misperceptions about mortuaries — that they serve the living by helping people adjust to the death of loved ones. This misperception would become an important theme of his essay.

Immediately after the interview, Cable filled in his notes with details while they were still fresh in his mind. Next, he took some time to reflect on what he had learned from his interview with Howard. Here are some of his thoughts:

> I was surprised by how much Howard looked like the undertakers in scary movies. Even though he couldn't answer some of my questions, he was friendly enough. It's obviously a business for him (he loves to talk about caskets and to point out all their features, like a car dealer kicking a tire). Best quote: "We offer services to the dead, not counseling to the living." I have to bring up these issues in my interview with the mortician.

The Interview Write-Up

Writing up an account of the interview a short time afterward helped Cable fill in more details and reflect further on what he had learned. His write-up shows him already beginning to organize the information he had gained from his interview with the funeral director.

I. His physical appearance.

Tall, skinny, with beady blue eyes embedded in his bony face. I was shocked to see that he looks just like the undertakers in scary movies. His skin is white and colorless, from lack of sunshine. He has a long nose and a low, sloping forehead. He was wearing a clean white shirt. A most unusual man — have you ever seen those Ames Home Loan commercials? But he was friendly, and happy to talk with me. "Would I answer some questions? Sure."

II. What people want from a mortuary.

A. Well first of all, he couldn't answer my second question, about how families cope with the loss of a loved one. "You'd have to talk to a psychologist about that," he said. He did tell me how the concept of death has changed over the last ten or so years.

B. He has been in the business for forty years(!). One look at him and you'd be convinced he'd been there at least that long. He told me that in the old times, everyone was buried. Embalmed, put in a casket, and paid final homage before being shipped underground forever. Nowadays, many people choose to be cremated instead. Hence comes the success of the Neptune Society and others specializing in cremation. You can have your ashes dumped anywhere. "Not that we don't offer cremation services. We've offered them since the beginning," he added with a look of disdain. It's just that they've become so popular recently because they offer a "quick, easy, and efficient means of disposal." Cheap too — I think it is a reflection of a "no nonsense" society. The Neptune Society has become so successful because it claims to be the only one to offer cremations as an alternative to expensive burial. "We've offered it all along. It's just only now come into vogue."

Sophisticated areas (I felt "progressive" would be more accurate) like Marin County have a cremation rate of over 60 percent. The phone rang. "Excuse me," he said. As he talked on the phone, I noticed how he played with his lips, pursing and squeezing them. He was blinking a lot, too. I meant to ask him how he got into this business, but I forgot. I did find out his name and title: Mr. Howard Deaver, funeral director of Goodbody Mortuaries (no kidding, that's the real name). He lives on the premises, upstairs with his wife. I doubt if he ever leaves the place.

III. It's a business!

Some people have the idea that mortuaries offer counseling and peace of mind — a place where everyone is sympathetic and ready to offer advice. "In some mortuaries, this is true. But by and large, this is a business. We offer services to the dead, not counseling to the living." I too had expected to feel an awestruck respect for the dead upon entering the building. I had also expected green lawns, ponds with ducks, fountains, flowers, peacefulness — you know, a "Forest Lawn" type deal. But it was only a tall, Catholic-looking building. "Mortuaries do not sell plots for burial," he was saying. "Cemeteries do that, after we embalm the body and select a casket. We're not a religious institution." He seemed hung up on caskets — though maybe he was just trying to impress upon me the differences between caskets. "Oh, they're very important. A good casket is a sign of respect. Sometimes if the family doesn't have enough money, we rent them a nice one.

People pay for what they get just like any other business." I wondered when you had to return the casket you rented.

I wanted to take a look around. He was happy to give me a tour. We visited several chapels and visiting rooms — places where the deceased "lie in state" to be "visited" by family and friends. I saw an old lady in a "fairly decent casket," as Mr. Deaver called it. Again I was impressed by the simple businesslike nature of it all. Oh yes, the rooms were elaborately decorated, with lots of shrines and stained glass, but these things were for the customers' benefit. "Sometimes we have up to eight or nine corpses here at one time, sometimes none. We have to have enough rooms to accommodate." Simple enough, yet I never realized how much trouble people were after they died. So much money, time, and effort go into their funerals.

As I prepared to leave, he gave me his card. He'd be happy to see me again, or maybe I could talk to someone else. I said I was going to interview the mortician on another day. I shook his hand. His fingers were long and his skin was warm.

Writing up the interview helped Cable probe his subject more deeply. It also helped him express a humorous attitude toward his subject. Cable's interview notes and write-up were quite informal; later, he integrated this material more formally into his full profile of the mortuary.

Thinking Critically About What You Have Learned

In this chapter, you have learned a great deal about this genre from reading several profiles and writing one of your own. To consolidate your learning, it is helpful to think metacognitively — that is, to reflect not only on what you learned but on how you learned it. Following are two brief activities your instructor may ask you to do.

Reflecting on Your Writing

Your instructor may ask you to turn in with your essay and process materials a brief metacognitive essay or letter reflecting on what you have learned about writing your profile. Choose among the following invention activities those that seem most productive for you:

- Explain how your purpose and audience — what you wanted your readers to learn about your subject from reading your profile — influenced *one* of your decisions as a writer, such as what kinds of descriptive detail you included, what method of organization you used, or the role you adopted in writing about your subject.

- Discuss what you learned about yourself as a writer in the process of writing this profile. For example, what part of the process did you find most challenging?

Did you try anything new, like getting a critical reading of your draft or outlining your draft in order to revise it? If so, how well did it work?

- If you were to give advice to a friend who was about to write a profile, what would you say?

- Which of the readings in this chapter influenced your essay? Explain the influence, citing specific examples from your profile and the reading.

- If you got good advice from a critical reader, explain exactly how the person helped you — perhaps by questioning your perspective in a way that enabled you to refocus your profile's dominant impression or pointing out passages that needed more information or clearer chronology to better orient readers.

Considering the Social Dimensions: Entertaining Readers, or Showing the Whole Picture?

Profiles broaden our view of the world by entertaining and informing us with portraits of people, places, or things. It is important to recognize, however, that profiles — even effective ones — sometimes offer a limited view of their subjects. For example, the impulse to entertain readers may lead a profile writer to focus exclusively on the dramatic, colorful, or humorous aspects of a person, a place, or an activity, ignoring the equally important humdrum, routine, or otherwise less appealing aspects. Imagine a profile that focuses on the dramatic moments in an emergency-room doctor's shift but ignores the routine cases and the slow periods when nothing much is happening. Such a profile would provide a limited and distorted picture of an emergency-room doctor's work.

In addition, by focusing on the dramatic or glamorous aspects of a subject, profile writers tend to ignore economic or social consequences and to slight supporting players. Profiling the highly praised chef in a trendy new restaurant, a writer might not ask whether the chef participates in the city's leftover-food-collection program for the homeless or find out who the kitchen workers and wait staff are, how the chef treats them, or how much they are paid. Profiling the campus bookstore, a writer might become so caught up in the details of ordering books for hundreds of courses and selling them efficiently to hordes of students during the first week of a semester that he or she could forget to ask about textbook costs, pricing policies, profit margins, and payback on used textbooks.

1. ***Consider whether any of the profiles you have read glamorize or sensationalize their subjects.*** Do they ignore less colorful but centrally important everyday activities? Is this a problem with your own profile?

2. ***Write a page or so explaining what the omissions signify.*** What do they suggest about the readers' desires to be entertained and the profile writer's reluctance to present the subject in a more complete way?

4

Explaining a Concept

IN COLLEGE COURSES For a linguistics course, a student is assigned a paper explaining the development in children's control of sentences, or *syntax*. To get started, she reviews the relevant sections in her linguistics textbook and then goes to the library and finds a few sources recommended by the textbook. She then goes to her professor's office hours and asks for advice on other articles or books she should consult.

From these sources, she learns about stages that children go through as they gain control of syntax, beginning with the one-word or holophrastic stage (*mommy*) and progressing through the two-word or duose stage (*baby sleep* or *want toy*), and multiword or telegraphic stages (*no sit there*). After presenting this initial research to her peer group in class, she takes their advice and decides to organize her essay around these stages. Even though she is writing for her professor, who is an expert in child language development, she carefully defines key terms to show that she understands what she is writing about.

IN THE COMMUNITY A manager at a marketing research firm has been tutoring fifth-grade students in math for a few hours each month. Aware of the manager's market research expertise, the teacher asks her to do a presentation to the class on *surveying*, an important research method in the social sciences.

The manager begins the first part of her presentation by having students fill out a brief survey on their television-watching habits. When they are done, she asks them to speculate on what they expect their answers to show, and how this data might be used by advertisers and television programmers. Then, with the students' help, she begins to analyze the data by selecting the variables that seem significant: the respondents' gender and place in the family structure, the number of hours spent watching television, and the types of shows watched.

At home, using PowerPoint, the manager prepares charts and graphs from the data. At the next class meeting, she distributes the data and asks the students to see whether it matches their initial assumptions about what the data might show.

She concludes by giving examples of questions from other surveys and explaining who does them, what they hope to learn, and how they report and use the results. Finally, she passes out a quiz so that she and each student can find out how much has been learned about surveys.

IN THE WORKPLACE At a seminar on the national security implications of satellite photography, the CEO of a space-imaging company takes part in the debate about *symmetrical transparency*, which involves using satellite photography to make everything on the planet visible at one-meter resolution — enough detail to reveal individual cars in parking lots and individual shrubs and trees planted in parks.

Aware of the financial implications for his company, on his return the executive drafts a presentation that will succinctly explain the relevant issues to his employees. He begins by providing an overview of the impact of changing technologies and the politics of global terrorism; he then gives a brief overview of key issues in the debate on symmetrical transparency. He accompanies his remarks with PowerPoint slides that highlight statistics and lend emphasis to the key points of his presentation.

Concepts are the special terms, the jargon, that insiders use and that anyone who wants to become part of the conversation needs to learn. That's why explaining concepts plays such an important role in education, as the scenarios about the linguistics student, the classroom volunteer, and even the CEO demonstrate. The student needs to use concepts she is learning, such as *syntax*, to show she understands them. The CEO teaches his employees about the concept of *symmetrical transparency* in order to prepare for impending business challenges. Finally, the tutor needs to explain concepts such as *surveying* to teach students about marketing research.

We encounter explanatory writing all the time — in blogs, books, brochures, magazines, and many other contexts. Explaining concepts is especially important when you are trying to learn or teach a new subject. You probably know a fair amount about some concepts that are not general knowledge and that would interest your instructor and classmates. For example, if you know a lot about music, you might be able to explain concepts such as *breaking, krumping, counterpoint*, or *harmonics*. If you are an avid video game player, you could explain *game mechanics* or a particular genre such as *real-time strategy (RTS)* games. If you are a sports enthusiast, you could clarify a concept such as the *curve ball* in baseball or the *Wing-T offense* in football. Concepts like these would make excellent topics for an explanatory essay.

Alternatively, your instructor may ask you to write about an academic concept you are just now learning in one of your courses. Every field of study has concepts that students must learn and be able to explain and apply — textbooks are full of them. For example, philosophy has *existentialism, metaphysics*, and *logical positivism*; physics has *string theory, entropy*, and *quantum mechanics*; economics has *Keynesian theory, macroeconomics*, and *monetary policy*; social psychology has *altruism, aggression, prejudice*, and so on.

In this chapter, you will read essays explaining the concepts of *cannibalism* (an anthropological concept), *romantic love* (a cultural concept), *hyperthymia* (a psychological concept), and *morality* (a philosophical concept). One of these essays — the explanation of hyperthymia — was written by an expert on the subject, research psychologist Richard A. Friedman. The other essays were written by student Linh Kieu Ngo, science reporter Anastasia Toufexis, and journalist Jeffrey Kluger, all of whom explain concepts they have learned about from doing research.

These readings illustrate the basic features and strategies writers typically use when composing concept explanations. The activities following the readings will help you consider what is particular to one writer's approach and what strategies you might want to try out in writing your own concept explanation. The Guide to Writing will support you as you compose your own concept explanation, showing you ways to use the basic features of the genre to focus your concept, to explain it both readably and effectively, and to smoothly integrate sources supporting your explanation.

Learning to explain a concept is especially important for you as a college student. It will prepare you to write a common type of exam and paper assignment; it will help you read critically; and it will acquaint you with the basic strategies common to all types of expository writing — defining, classifying, comparing and contrasting, and describing and narrating processes. Moreover, it will sharpen your skill in researching and using sources, abilities essential for success in college, whatever your major.

Part 1. Choose one concept to explain to two or three other students. When you have chosen a concept, think about what others in the group are likely to know about it. Consider how you will define the concept and what other strategies you might use — description, comparison, and so on — to explain it in an interesting, memorable way.

Get together with two or three other students, and explain your concepts to one another.

Part 2. Discuss what happened when you explained your concept:

- To think about your purpose and audience, take turns asking the students in your group whether they were interested in and understood your explanation. In particular, find out whether your explanation would have been clearer with examples, definitions, comparisons with more familiar concepts, or something else.

- Compare your thoughts with the others in your group on what was easiest and hardest about explaining a concept: for example, focusing the concept; appealing to your listeners' interests; or organizing the explanation.

Reading Concept Explanations

Basic Features

As you read the essays in this chapter, you will see how different authors incorporate the basic features of concept explanations.

● A Focused Explanation

Read first to identify the concept. A concept may be any of the following:

- a principle, an ideal, or a value (such as the American dream or equal justice)
- a theory (such as theory of mind, relativity, or evolution)
- an idea (such as utilitarianism, panopticism, or realism)
- a condition (such as the state of flow, paranoia, or neurosis)
- a specialized or technical term (such as markedness in linguistics, path dependence in economics, or high intensity interval training (HIIT) in sports medicine)

Concepts are typically general notions that mean different things to different people (such as friendship, happiness, or family). Effective writers narrow the general concept, providing an explanation that is focused on an aspect of the concept likely to be of interest to readers. Some concepts, for example, benefit from being examined in terms of their cultural context (such as the Asian concept of face) or their historical context (such as the changing customs of calling, dating, and hooking up).

● A Readable Plan

Effective concept explanations have to be readable. *As you read the essays in this chapter, notice how each writer develops a plan that does the following:*

- divides the information into clearly distinguishable topics
- forecasts the topics
- presents the topics in a logical order
- gives readers cues or road signs to guide them, such as topic sentences, transitions, and summaries

● Appropriate Explanatory Strategies

Writers of essays explaining a concept typically present information using a number of different strategies, such as the following:

- defining key terms
- classifying or grouping together related material
- comparing and contrasting
- narrating anecdotes or processes
- illustrating with examples, visuals, or lists of facts and details
- reporting established causes and effects

As you read the essays in this chapter, notice how they make use of these strategies. Note that essays explaining concepts depend especially on clear definitions; any key terms that are likely to be unfamiliar or misunderstood must be explicitly defined. Illustrations usually also play a key role because examples, visuals, and other details can help make abstract concepts understandable.

● Smooth Integration of Sources

Finally, as you read, think about how the writer establishes authority by smoothly integrating sources into the explanation. Although writers often draw on their own experiences and observations, they almost always do additional research into what others have to say about their subject.

How writers treat sources depends on the writing situation. Certain formal situations, such as college assignments or scholarly publications, have rules for citing and documenting sources. Students and scholars are expected to cite their sources formally because readers judge their work in part by what the writers have read and how they have used their reading. For more informal writing — magazine articles, for example — readers do not expect or want page references or publication information, but they do expect sources to be identified and their expertise established in some way.

Purpose and Audience

*As you read concept explanations, ask yourself what seems to be the writer's **purpose** in explaining this concept.* For example, does the writer seem to be writing

- to teach readers about an unfamiliar concept;
- to engage readers' interest in the concept;
- to better understand the concept by explaining it to others;
- to demonstrate knowledge of the concept and the ability to apply it?

*As you read, also try to determine what the writer assumes about the **audience**.* For example, does the writer

- expect the readers to be generally well informed but not knowledgeable about this particular concept;
- assume the readers may not be especially interested in the concept;
- know that the only or primary reader is an instructor who knows more about the concept than the writer does and who is evaluating the writer's knowledge;
- anticipate that readers will be unfamiliar with the concept, so that the essay will serve as an introduction;
- anticipate that readers will know something about the concept, so that the essay may add to their prior knowledge or provide a new perspective?

Readings

LINH KIEU NGO wrote this essay as a first-year college student. In it, he explains the concept of cannibalism, the eating of human flesh by other humans. Most Americans know about survival cannibalism — eating human flesh to avoid starvation — but Ngo also explains the historical importance of dietary and ritual cannibalism.

As you read, notice how he uses examples to illustrate the three types of cannibalism. Also consider the questions in the margin. Your instructor may ask you to post your answers or bring them to class.

Basic Features

- A Focused Explanation
- A Readable Plan
- Appropriate Explanatory Strategies
- Smooth Integration of Sources

Cannibalism: It Still Exists

Linh Kieu Ngo

Fifty-five Vietnamese refugees fled to Malaysia on a small fishing boat to escape communist rule in their country following the Vietnam War. During their escape attempt, the captain was shot by the coast guard. The boat and its passengers managed to outrun the coast guard to the open sea, but they had lost the only person who knew the way to Malaysia, the captain.

The men onboard tried to navigate the boat, but after a week fuel ran out, and they drifted farther out to sea. Their supply of food and water was gone; people were starving, and some of the elderly were near death. The men managed to produce a small amount of drinking water by boiling salt water, using dispensable wood from the boat to create a small fire near the stern. They also tried to fish but had little success.

A month went by, and the old and weak died. At first, the crew threw the dead overboard, but later, out of desperation, they turned to human flesh as a source of food. Some people vomited as they attempted to eat it, while others refused to resort to cannibalism and see the bodies of their loved ones sacrificed for food. Those who did not eat died of starvation, and their bodies in turn became food for others. Human flesh was cut out, washed in salt water, and hung to dry for preservation. The liquids inside the cranium were drunk to quench thirst. The livers, kidneys, hearts, stomachs, and intestines were boiled and eaten.

Five months passed before a whaling vessel discovered the drifting boat, looking like a graveyard of bones. There was only one survivor.

Cannibalism, the act of human beings eating human flesh (Sagan 2), has a long history and continues to hold interest and create controversy. Many books and research reports offer examples of cannibalism, but a few scholars have questioned whether it actually was ever practiced anywhere, except in cases of ensuring survival in times of famine or isolation (Askenasy 43–54). Recently, some scholars have tried to understand why people in the West have been so eager to attribute cannibalism to non-Westerners (Barker, Hulme, and Iversen). Cannibalism has long been a part of American popular culture. For example, Mark Twain's "Cannibalism in the Cars" tells a humorous story about cannibalism by well-to-do travelers on a train stranded in a snowstorm, and cannibalism is still a popular subject for jokes ("Cannibal Jokes").

1

2

3

4

5

How effectively does this anecdote about a one-time event introduce the concept to readers?

Ngo shifts from narrating to presenting research in this paragraph. How does he introduce his sources?

6   If we assume there is some reality to the reports about cannibalism, how can we best understand this concept? Cannibalism can be broken down into two main categories: exocannibalism, the eating of outsiders or foreigners, and endocannibalism, the eating of members of one's own social group (Shipman 70). Within these categories are several functional types of cannibalism, three of the most common being survival cannibalism, dietary cannibalism, and religious and ritual cannibalism.

7   Survival cannibalism occurs when people trapped without food have to decide "whether to starve or to eat fellow humans" (Shipman 70). In the case of the Vietnamese refugees, the crew and passengers on the boat ate human flesh to stay alive. They did not kill people to get human flesh for nourishment but instead waited until the people had died. Even after human carcasses were sacrificed as food, the boat people ate only enough to survive. Another case of survival cannibalism occurred in 1945, when General Douglas MacArthur's forces cut supply lines to Japanese troops stationed in the Pacific Islands. In one incident, Japanese troops were reported to have sacrificed the Arapesh people of northeastern New Guinea for food in order to avoid death by starvation (Tuzin 63). The most famous example of survival cannibalism in American history comes from the diaries, letters, and interviews of survivors of the California-bound Donner Party, who in the winter of 1846 were snowbound in the Sierra Nevada Mountains for five months. Thirty-five of eighty-seven adults and children died, and some of them were eaten (Hart 116–117; Johnson).

8   Unlike survival cannibalism, in which human flesh is eaten as a last resort after a person has died, in dietary cannibalism humans are purchased or trapped for food and then eaten as a part of a culture's traditions. In addition, survival cannibalism often involves people eating other people of the same origins, whereas dietary cannibalism usually involves people eating foreigners.

9   In the Miyanmin society of the west Sepik interior of Papua, New Guinea, villagers do not value human life over that of pigs or marsupials because human flesh is part of their normal diet (Poole 7). The Miyanmin people observe no differences in "gender, kinship, ritual status, and bodily substance"; they eat anyone, even their own dead. In this respect, then, they practice both endocannibalism and exocannibalism; and to ensure a constant supply of human flesh for food, they raid neighboring tribes and drag their victims back to their village to be eaten (Poole 11). Perhaps, in the history of this society, there was at one time a shortage of wild game to be hunted for food, and because people were more plentiful than fish, deer, rabbits, pigs, or cows, survival cannibalism

How effectively does Ngo introduce the thesis and forecast the topics of the essay?

How do Ngo's anecdotes and examples here and later in the essay help you understand the concept?

How do Ngo's topic sentences fulfill the promise of the forecast in par. 6 and help you follow the explanation?

What writing strategy is Ngo using in pars. 9–10?

How does Ngo's use of the terms *endo-* and *exocannibalism* here help orient the reader?

was adopted as a last resort. Then, as their culture developed, the Miyanmin may have retained the practice of dietary cannibalism, which has endured as a part of their culture.

Similar to the Miyanmin, the people of the Leopard and Alligator societies in South America eat human flesh as part of their cultural tradition. Practicing dietary exocannibalism, the Leopard people hunt in groups, with one member wearing the skin of a leopard to conceal the face. They ambush their victims in the forest and carry their victims back to their village to be eaten. The Alligator people also hunt in groups, but they hide themselves under a canoelike submarine that resembles an alligator, then swim close to a fisherman's or trader's canoe to overturn it and catch their victims (MacCormack 54).

10

Religious or ritual cannibalism is different from survival and dietary cannibalism in that it has a ceremonial purpose rather than one of nourishment. Sometimes only a single victim is sacrificed in a ritual, while at other times many are sacrificed. For example, the Bangala tribe of the Congo River in central Africa honors a deceased chief or leader by purchasing, sacrificing, and feasting on slaves (Sagan 53). The number of slaves sacrificed is determined by how highly the tribe members revered the deceased leader.

11

Ritual cannibalism among South American Indians often serves as revenge for the dead. Like the Bangalas, some South American tribes kill their victims to be served as part of funeral rituals, with human sacrifices denoting that the deceased was held in high honor. Also like the Bangalas, these tribes use outsiders as victims. Unlike the Bangalas, however, the Indians sacrifice only one victim instead of many in a single ritual. For example, when a warrior of a tribe is killed in battle, the family of the warrior forces a victim to take the identity of the warrior. The family adorns the victim with the deceased warrior's belongings and may even force him to marry the deceased warrior's wives. But once the family believes the victim has assumed the spiritual identity of the deceased warrior, the family kills him. The children in the tribe soak their hands in the victim's blood to symbolize their revenge of the warrior's death. Elderly women from the tribe drink the victim's blood and then cut up his body for roasting and eating (Sagan 53–54). The people of the tribe believe that by sacrificing a victim, they have avenged the death of the warrior and the soul of the deceased can rest in peace.

12

In the villages of certain African tribes, only a small part of a dead body is used in ritual cannibalism. In these tribes, where the childbearing capacity of women is highly valued, women are obligated to eat small, raw fragments of genital parts during fertility rites. Elders of the tribe supervise this ritual to ensure that the women will be fertile. In the Bimin-Kuskusmin tribe, for instance, a widow eats a small, raw fragment

13

How does this topic sentence help you understand how the information in pars. 11–13 fits into Ngo's plan? What other words or phrases help you follow his comparisons and contrasts?

of flesh from the penis of her deceased husband in order to enhance her future fertility and reproductive capacity. Similarly, a widower may eat a raw fragment of flesh from his deceased wife's vagina along with a piece of her bone marrow; by eating her flesh, he hopes to strengthen the fertility of his daughters borne by his dead wife, and by eating her bone marrow, he honors her reproductive capacity. Also, when an elder woman of the village who has shown great reproductive capacity dies, her uterus and the interior parts of her vagina are eaten by other women who hope to benefit from her reproductive power (Poole 16–17).

14   Members of developed societies in general practice none of these forms of cannibalism, with the occasional exception of survival cannibalism when the only alternative is starvation. It is possible, however, that our distant-past ancestors were cannibals who through the eons turned away from the practice. We are, after all, descended from the same ancestors as the Miyanmin, the Alligator, and the Leopard people, and survival cannibalism shows that people are capable of eating human flesh when they have no other choice.

Works Cited

Askenasy, Hans. *Cannibalism: From Sacrifice to Survival*. Amherst, NY: Prometheus, 1994. Print.

Barker, Francis, Peter Hulme, and Margaret Iversen, eds. *Cannibalism and the New World*. Cambridge: Cambridge UP, 1998. Print.

Brown, Paula, and Donald Tuzin, eds. *The Ethnography of Cannibalism*. Washington: Society of Psychological Anthropology, 1983. Print.

"Cannibal Jokes." *Bored.com*. N.p., n.d. Web. 22 Sept. 2008.

Hart, James D. *A Companion to California*. Berkeley: U of California P, 1987. Print.

Johnson, Kristin. *New Light on the Donner Party*. Kristin Johnson, 5 Nov. 2006. Web. 28 Sept. 2008.

MacCormack, Carol. "Human Leopard and Crocodile." Brown and Tuzin 54–55.

Poole, Fitz John Porter. "Cannibals, Tricksters, and Witches." Brown and Tuzin 16–17.

Sagan, Eli. *Cannibalism*. New York: Harper, 1976. Print.

Shipman, Pat. "The Myths and Perturbing Realities of Cannibalism." *Discover* Mar. 1987: 70+. Print.

Tuzin, Donald. "Cannibalism and Arapesh Cosmology." Brown and Tuzin 61–63.

Twain, Mark. "Cannibalism in the Cars." *The Complete Short Stories of Mark Twain*. Ed. Charles Neider. New York: Doubleday, 1957. 9–16. Print.

What does Ngo hope to achieve in this conclusion? How well does it work for you?

What makes Ngo's sources seem authoritative (or not)?

What can you learn about creating a Works-Cited list from this example?

**LEARN ABOUT
LINH KIEU NGO'S
WRITING PROCESS**

To learn about Linh Kieu Ngo's process of writing this essay, turn to A Writer at Work on pp. 181–82. How did Ngo combine quotation with paraphrase to integrate source material into his essay and avoid simply stringing quotes together?

ANASTASIA TOUFEXIS has been an associate editor of *Time*, senior editor of *Discover*, and editor in chief of *Psychology Today*. She has written on subjects as diverse as medicine, health and fitness, law, environment, education, science, and national and world news. Toufexis has won a number of awards for her writing, including a Knight-Wallace Fellowship at the University of Michigan and an Ocean Science Journalism Fellowship at Woods Hole Oceanographic Institution. She has also lectured on science writing at Columbia University, the University of North Carolina, and the School of Visual Arts in New York.

The following essay was originally published in 1993 in *Time* magazine. As you read, notice how Toufexis brings together a variety of sources of information to present a neurochemical perspective on love.

Love: The Right Chemistry

Anastasia Toufexis

> Love is a romantic designation for a most ordinary biological — or, shall we say, chemical? — process. A lot of nonsense is talked and written about it.
> — Greta Garbo to Melvyn Douglas in *Ninotchka*

O.K., let's cut out all this nonsense about romantic love. Let's bring some scientific precision to the party. Let's put love under a microscope. 1

When rigorous people with Ph.D.s after their names do that, what they see is not some silly, senseless thing. No, their probe reveals that love rests firmly on the foundations of evolution, biology and chemistry. What seems on the surface to be irrational, intoxicated behavior is in fact part of nature's master strategy — a vital force that has helped humans survive, thrive and multiply through thousands of years. Says Michael Mills, a psychology professor at Loyola Marymount University in Los Angeles: "Love is our ancestors whispering in our ears." 2

It was on the plains of Africa about 4 million years ago, in the early days of the human species, that the notion of romantic love probably first began to blossom or at least that the first cascades of neurochemicals began flowing from the brain to the bloodstream to produce goofy grins and sweaty palms as men and women gazed deeply into each other's eyes. When mankind graduated from scuttling 3 around on all fours to walking on two legs, this change made the whole person visible to fellow human beings for the first time. Sexual organs were in full display, as were other characteristics, from the color of eyes to the span of shoulders. As never before, each individual had a unique allure.

> **While Western culture holds fast to the idea that true love flames forever . . . nature apparently meant passions to sputter out in something like four years.**

When the sparks flew, new ways of making love enabled sex to become a romantic encounter, not just a reproductive act. Although mounting mates from the rear was, and still is, the method favored among most animals, humans began to enjoy face-to-face couplings; both looks and personal attraction became a much greater part of the equation.

Romance served the evolutionary purpose of pulling males and females into long-term partnership, which was essential to child rearing. On open grasslands, one parent would have a hard — and dangerous — time handling a child while foraging for food. "If a woman was carrying the equivalent of a 20-lb. bowling ball in one arm and a pile of sticks in the other, it was ecologically critical to pair up with a mate to rear the young," explains anthropologist Helen Fisher, author of *Anatomy of Love*.

While Western culture holds fast to the idea that true love flames forever (the movie *Bram Stoker's Dracula* has the Count carrying the torch beyond the grave), nature apparently meant passions to sputter out in something like four years. Primitive pairs stayed together just "long enough to rear one child through infancy," says Fisher. Then each would find a new partner and start all over again.

What Fisher calls the "four-year itch" shows up unmistakably in today's divorce statistics. In most of the 62 cultures she has studied, divorce rates peak around the fourth year of marriage. Additional youngsters help keep pairs together longer. If, say, a couple have another child three years after the first, as often occurs, then their union can be expected to last about four more years. That makes them ripe for the more familiar phenomenon portrayed in the Marilyn Monroe classic *The Seven-Year Itch*.

If, in nature's design, romantic love is not eternal, neither is it exclusive. Less than 5% of mammals form rigorously faithful pairs. From the earliest days, contends Fisher, the human pattern has been "monogamy with clandestine adultery." Occasional flings upped the chances that new combinations of genes would be passed on to the next generation. Men who sought new partners had more children. Contrary to common assumptions, women were just as likely to stray. "As long as prehistoric females were secretive about their extramarital affairs," argues Fisher, "they could garner extra resources, life insurance, better genes and more varied DNA for their biological futures. . . ."

Lovers often claim that they feel as if they are being swept away. They're not mistaken; they are literally flooded by chemicals, research suggests. A meeting of eyes, a touch of hands or a whiff of scent sets off a flood that starts in the brain and races along the nerves and through the blood. The results are familiar: flushed skin, sweaty palms, heavy breathing. If love looks suspiciously like stress, the reason is simple: the chemical pathways are identical.

Above all, there is the sheer euphoria of falling in love — a not-so-surprising reaction, considering that many of the substances swamping the newly smitten are chemical cousins of amphetamines. They include dopamine, norepinephrine and especially phenylethylamine (PEA). Cole Porter knew what he was talking about when he wrote, "I get a kick out of you." "Love is a natural high," observes Anthony Walsh, author of *The Science of Love: Understanding Love and Its Effects on Mind and Body.* "PEA gives you that silly smile that you flash at strangers. When we meet someone who is attractive to us, the whistle blows at the PEA factory." 10

But phenylethylamine highs don't last forever, a fact that lends support to arguments that passionate romantic love is short-lived. As with any amphetamine, the body builds up a tolerance to PEA; thus it takes more and more of the substance to produce love's special kick. After two to three years, the body simply can't crank up the needed amount of PEA. And chewing on chocolate doesn't help, despite popular belief. The candy is high in PEA, but it fails to boost the body's supply. 11

Fizzling chemicals spell the end of delirious passion; for many people that marks the end of the liaison as well. It is particularly true for those whom Dr. Michael Liebowitz of the New York State Psychiatric Institute terms "attraction 12

1 IMPRINTING
Evolution, genetics, psychological experiences and even **smells** can trigger romantic reactions to another person. Scientists have recently found that animals may have an innate aesthetic sense and experience attraction.

2 ATTRACTION
The brain is revved up by **phenylethylamine** (PEA) and possibly the neurochemicals **dopamine** and **norepinephrine,** all natural amphetamines. These produce feelings of euphoria and elation. This stage can last for two to three years, then starts to wane.

3 ATTACHMENT
During this stage, larger amounts of **endorphins** (chemically similar to morphine) flow into the brain, leaving lovers with a sense of security, peace and calm.

"CUDDLE CHEMICAL"
The brain's pituitary gland secretes **oxytocin** ("the cuddle chemical"), which stimulates sensations during lovemaking and produces feelings of relaxed satisfaction and attachment.

junkies." They crave the intoxication of falling in love so much that they move frantically from affair to affair just as soon as the first rush of infatuation fades.

Still, many romances clearly endure beyond the first years. What accounts for that? Another set of chemicals, of course. The continued presence of a partner gradually steps up production in the brain of endorphins. Unlike the fizzy amphetamines, these are soothing substances. Natural pain-killers, they give lovers a sense of security, peace and calm. "That is one reason why it feels so horrible when we're abandoned or a lover dies," notes Fisher. "We don't have our daily hit of narcotics." 13

Researchers see a contrast between the heated infatuation induced by PEA, along with other amphetamine-like chemicals, and the more intimate attachment fostered and prolonged by endorphins. "Early love is when you love the way the other person makes you feel," explains psychiatrist Mark Goulston of the University of California, Los Angeles. "Mature love is when you love the person as he or she is." It is the difference between passionate and compassionate love, observes Walsh, a psychobiologist at Boise State University in Idaho. "It's Bon Jovi vs. Beethoven." 14

Oxytocin is another chemical that has recently been implicated in love. Produced by the brain, it sensitizes nerves and stimulates muscle contraction. In women it helps uterine contractions during childbirth as well as production of breast milk, and seems to inspire mothers to nuzzle their infants. Scientists speculate that oxytocin might encourage similar cuddling between adult women and men. The versatile chemical may also enhance orgasms. In one study of men, oxytocin increased to three to five times its normal level during climax, and it may soar even higher in women. 15

Chemicals may help explain (at least to scientists) the feelings of passion and compassion, but why do people tend to fall in love with one partner rather than a myriad of others? Once again, it's partly a function of evolution and biology. "Men are looking for maximal fertility in a mate," says Loyola Marymount's Mills. "That is in large part why females in the prime childbearing ages of 17 to 28 are so desirable." Men can size up youth and vitality in a glance, and studies indeed show that men fall in love quite rapidly. Women tumble more slowly, to a large degree because their requirements are more complex; they need more time to check the guy out. "Age is not vital," notes Mills, "but the ability to provide security, father children, share resources and hold a high status in society are all key factors." 16

Still, that does not explain why the way Mary walks and laughs makes Bill dizzy with desire while Marcia's gait and giggle leave him cold. "Nature has wired us for one special person," suggests Walsh, romantically. He rejects the idea that a woman or a man can be in love with two people at the same time. Each person carries in his or her mind a unique subliminal guide to the ideal partner, a "love map," to borrow a term coined by sexologist John Money of Johns Hopkins University. 17

Drawn from the people and experiences of childhood, the map is a record of whatever we found enticing and exciting — or disturbing and disgusting. Small feet, curly hair. The way our mothers patted our head or how our fathers told a joke. A fireman's uniform, a doctor's stethoscope. All the information gathered while growing up is imprinted in the brain's circuitry by adolescence. Partners never 18 meet each and every requirement, but a sufficient number of matches can light up the wires and signal, "It's love." Not every partner will be like the last one, since lovers may have different combinations of the characteristics favored by the map.

O.K., that's the scientific point of view. Satisfied? Probably not. To most people — with or without Ph.D.s — love will always be more than the sum of its natural parts. It's a commingling of body and soul, reality and imagination, poetry and phenylethylamine. In our deepest hearts, most of us harbor the hope that love will never fully yield up its secrets, that it will always elude our grasp.

¹⁹

MAKING CONNECTIONS: LOVE MAPS

The chemistry of love is easily summarized: Amphetamines fuel romance; endorphins and oxytocin sustain lasting heterosexual relationships. As Toufexis makes clear, however, these chemical reactions do not explain why specific people are initially attracted to each other. Toufexis observes that an initial attraction occurs because each of us carries a "unique subliminal guide" or "love map" (par. 17) that leads us unerringly to a partner.

With two or three other students, discuss these explanations for attraction between the sexes. Begin by briefly taking turns describing the qualities you are attracted to in a partner. Then, consider together the following questions as you discuss your love map:

- What role do factors such as family, friends, community, the media, and advertising play in constructing your love map?

- Do you think an individual's love map can change over time? If so, what might contribute to such changes?

- According to Toufexis, men typically look for "maximal fertility," whereas women look for security, resources, status, and a willingness to father children (par. 18). Does this explanation seem convincing to you? Why or why not?

ANALYZING WRITING STRATEGIES

◆◆◆◆

Basic Features

● **A Focused Explanation of the Concept**

Obviously, essays explaining concepts cannot communicate everything that is known about a concept. Writers must limit the scope of their explanation. They choose a focus in part by considering the rhetorical situation — the purpose and audience — in which they are writing. Linh Kieu Ngo, for example, is writing for a college composition course, where he can expect his readers not to know very much about anthropology or research on cannibalism. For this reason, Ngo chose to give readers a rather simple overview of the research by explaining the three "most common" types of cannibalism (par. 6). To set up his explanation, Ngo uses an anecdote about survival cannibalism, the type his readers are most likely to have heard about. Beginning his essay by describing a familiar type of cannibalism confirms for readers what they already know and at the same time arouses curiosity and makes them want to learn more.

To analyze how Toufexis focuses her explanation and engages her readers, do the following:

- Write a sentence or two describing how she focuses her explanation.

- Add another couple of sentences explaining how she tries to capture her readers' interest and assessing how effective her strategy is for you as a reader.

⬡ A Readable Plan

Experienced writers know that readers often have a hard time making their way through new and difficult material and sometimes give up in frustration. To avoid this problem, effective writers construct a reader-friendly plan by dividing the information into clearly distinguishable topics. They also give readers cues or road signs to guide them through the explanation.

Early in the essay, the **thesis statement** announces the concept. It also may **forecast** the topics, giving readers a preview so that they know where they are headed. For example, in paragraphs 5–6 of his essay, Ngo announces that he is writing about the much written-about concept of cannibalism and forecasts the topics he uses to organize his essay, the three types of cannibalism: survival, dietary, and ritual cannibalism.

To analyze how Toufexis constructs a readable plan, try the following:

- Skim the essay and note in the margin where she announces her concept and forecasts the topics she uses to organize her essay. Highlight the point at which she begins discussing each topic.

- Write a sentence or two assessing how well her forecast works to make her essay readable.

- Add another sentence explaining how Toufexis connects the topic of "love maps" (pars. 16–18) to the topics she discussed earlier in the essay.

For more on constructing a readable plan, see Chapter 13.

⬤ Appropriate Explanatory Strategies

When writers organize and present information, they rely on writing strategies that are the building blocks of explanatory essays: **defining**, **classifying** or **dividing**, **comparing and contrasting**, **narrating** anecdotes or processes, **illustrating** with examples or lists of facts and details, and reporting known **causes and effects**. Toufexis uses classification along with comparison and contrast when she explains the roles played by two types of chemicals: amphetamine-like chemicals, especially phenylethylamine (PEA), and endorphins, such as oxytocin. But her primary writing strategy is reporting causes and effects.

To analyze how Toufexis reports causes and effects, do the following:

- Reread paragraph 5 where she explains the causes and effects of the rush of amphetamine-like chemicals, and highlight the causes in one color and the effects in another color (or underline one and put brackets around the other).

For more on these explanatory strategies, see Chapters 14–18.

- Reread paragraphs 13 and 15 and highlight the effects of endorphins.
- Write a sentence or two assessing how well Toufexis explains causes and effects.

● Smooth Integration of Sources

Writers of explanatory essays have to convince readers that the information they've used to explain the concept is trustworthy. They do this by acknowledging their expert sources. Academic writers provide detailed information about their sources so that scholars can consult the original sources. For example, the essay by Linh Kieu Ngo written for a college composition course demonstrates the MLA style of citing sources. Writing for college courses, you will be expected to cite your sources in a conventional academic way — with parenthetical citations in the body of your essay keyed to a works-cited list at the end.

Writing for a nonacademic publication, Toufexis does not need to cite sources using the MLA or another academic style sheet. But she does need to reassure readers that her sources are authoritative.

To analyze how Toufexis cites sources, follow these steps:

For more on integrating sources, see pp. 759–65. For more on MLA documentation, see pp. 766–78.

- Skim the essay and underline the name of each source she mentions.
- Write a few sentences describing the kinds of information she gives readers about her sources and assessing how well she establishes their authority.

ANALYZING VISUALS

USING A FLOWCHART

Analyze the visual Toufexis includes in her essay, and write a few sentences explaining how you read the visual and assessing how well it helps you understand her explanation of the concept.

Toufexis's visual is a flowchart, a diagram that shows the steps in a process. To determine how effective this visual is, consider the following questions:

- When you initially read the essay, did you stop to study the visual, just glance at it in passing, go back to it after finishing the essay, or not look at it at all?
- How does the flowchart clarify the role played by each element of the diagram? Are there any seemingly extraneous elements?
- Is the flowchart easy to read or too complicated; attractive or dull; eye-candy or actually useful? Explain your answer.
- If the flowchart repeats information already presented in the text of the essay, what does it contribute to the explanation?
- If the flowchart adds new information not presented in the text of the essay, how effective is it?

Like Toufexis, you could write an essay about love or romance, but you could choose a different focus: its history (how and when did romantic love develop as an idea in the West?), its cultural characteristics (how is love regarded currently among different American ethnic groups or world cultures?), its excesses or extremes, or the phases of falling in and out of love. Also consider writing about other concepts involving personal relationships, such as jealousy, codependency, idealization, stereotyping, or homophobia.

 RICHARD A. FRIEDMAN is a professor of clinical psychiatry and director of the psychopharmacology clinic at the New York Weill Cornell Medical Center. Specializing in clinical depression, anxiety, and mood disorders, he has published his research in distinguished academic journals such as the *American Journal of Psychiatry,* the *Journal of Affective Disorders,* and the *Journal of Clinical Psychopharmacology.* He also writes a regular column on health issues in the *New York Times,* which is where this article originally appeared. As you read, notice how Friedman makes the concept of hyperthymia accessible to readers who may not be knowledgeable about science.

Born to Be Happy, Through a Twist of Human Hard Wire

RICHARD A. FRIEDMAN

In the course of the last year, the woman lost her husband to cancer and then her job. But she did not come to my office as a patient; she sought advice about her teenage son who was having trouble dealing with his father's death. Despite crushing loss and stress, she was not at all depressed — sad, yes, but still upbeat. I found myself stunned by her resilience. What accounted for her ability to weather such sorrow with buoyant optimism? So I asked her directly. "All my life," she recalled recently, "I've been happy for no good reason. It's just my nature, I guess." But it was more than that. She was a happy extrovert, full of energy and enthusiasm who was indefatigably sociable. And she could get by with five or six hours of sleep each night. 1

Like this woman, a journalist I know realized when she was a teenager that she was different from others. "It's actually kind of embarrassing to be so cheerful and happy all 2 the time," she said. "When I was in high school I read the Robert Browning poem 'My Last Duchess.' In it, the narrator said he killed his wife, the duchess, because 'she had a heart — how shall I say — too soon made glad?' And I thought, uh-oh, that's me."

These two women were lucky to be born with a joyous temperament, which in its most extreme form is called hyperthymia. Cheerful despite life's misfortunes, energetic and productive, they are often the envy of all who know them because they don't even have to work at it. In a sense, they are the psychiatric mirror image of people who suffer from a chronic, often lifelong, mild depression called dysthymia, which affects about 3 percent of American adults. Always down, dysthymics experience little pleasure and battle through life with a dreary pessimism. Despite whatever fortune comes their way, they remain glum. But hyperthymia certainly doesn't look like an illness; there appears to be no disadvantage to being a euphoric extrovert, except, perhaps, for inspiring an occasional homicidal impulse from jealous friends or peers. But little is actually known about people with hyperthymia for the simple reason that they don't see psychiatrists complaining that they are happy.

3

If dysthymia is hyperthymia's dark twin, then hyperthymia may not always be so rosy. That is because about 90 percent of dysthymic people experience episodes of more severe depression in their lifetimes. Are hyperthymics at risk of some mood disorders, too?

4

If hyperthymics bear a kinship with any psychiatric illness, it may be bipolar disorder. Bipolar patients live on a roller coaster of depressive troughs and manic peaks. But unlike hyperthymia, mania is an inherently unstable state of euphoria, irritability and often psychosis that causes profound morbidity and impaired functioning. Some researchers believe hyperthymics may be at increased risk of depression or hypomania, a mild variant of mania. And they may have high rates of affective disorders in their closest relatives. Hyperthymic and bipolar people may also share a tendency to be highly creative, given the strong association between bipolar disorder and creativity. For example, a 1987 study of creative writers at the University of Iowa Writers' Workshop by Dr. Nancy Andreasen showed that writers had bipolar illness at a rate four times as high as control group members who were not writers.

5

Of course, the notion of a hyperthymic temperament is hardly new. Some 2,400 years ago, Hippocrates proposed that a mixture of four basic humors — blood, phlegm, yellow bile and black bile — determined human temperament; depending on which humor predominates, one's nature is happy, phlegmatic, irritable or sad. Modern science has renamed the humors neurotransmitters, like serotonin and dopamine, and tried to link them to abnormal mental states. For example, depression was thought to result from a functional deficit of serotonin or norepinephrine in the brain. But one problem with this theory is that antidepressants increase the levels of these neurotransmitters within days, yet their clinical effects take several weeks. If the theory were correct, then depression should clear up within days of taking an antidepressant, not weeks. Still, many dysthymic people respond to antidepressants and watch their unhappiness melt away in a matter of weeks. If a lifelong depressive state like dysthymia can be erased in some cases with medication, is it possible then to make a person better than well, let's say hyperthymic?

6

Of course, humans have experimented with various recreational drugs for this purpose since recorded history without much success. Cocaine, to name one, produces an instant and intense euphoria by flooding the brain with dopamine. But the pleasure of cocaine is fleeting because the neurons that are activated by dopamine become rapidly desensitized to it, leading to a state of apathy and depression. Ecstasy can induce tranquil euphoria, largely by enhancing brain serotonin activity, but it is short-lived. And it can permanently damage serotonin-containing neurons in animals, hardly good news for humans. In fact, the pleasure brought on by all recreational drugs will fade sooner or later because of the brain's own homeostatic mechanisms. 7

What about psychotropic medications? A study by Dr. Brian Knutson at the University of California at San Francisco looked at the effects of the serotonin-enhancing antidepressant Paxil among normal volunteers, randomly assigned to either Paxil or a placebo. Neither the volunteers nor the researchers knew who was taking Paxil and who was taking the placebo. Compared with the placebo, Paxil reduced hostile feelings and slightly increased social affiliation. But Paxil did not make the normal people any happier. 8

In short, no drug — recreational or prescribed — comes close to creating the stable euphoria of hyperthymic people. Of course, antidepressants, unlike recreational drugs, are nonaddicting and retain their benefits over time. So if some people are just born happy and stay happy for no good reason, does this mean that happiness is nothing more than a lucky combination of neurotransmitters? For most people, no. Circumstance and experience count for a lot, and being happy takes work. But hyperthymic people have it easy: they have won the temperamental sweepstakes and may be hard-wired for happiness. 9

MAKING CONNECTIONS: TEMPERAMENT

Everyone has good and bad moods and everyone suffers setbacks that have emotional consequences, but Friedman explains that some people also tend to be either **dysthymic** or **hyperthymic**. That is, they are temperamentally inclined either to be mildly depressed or to be relatively happy and resilient regardless of the circumstances.

With two or three other students, discuss Friedman's categories. Begin by briefly taking turns describing someone you know who seems to display a hyperthymic or dysthymic temperament. Then, together consider the following questions as you discuss temperament:

- Friedman's title asserts that temperament is hard-wired, or genetic. Who in your family do you take after in terms of temperament? Could you have consciously or unconsciously imitated this behavior and outlook, or do you think you were born like him or her?

- At the end of the essay, Friedman tells us that for most of us "being happy takes work" (par. 9). What do you think he means? What kind of work do you do to make yourself happy?

● A Focused Explanation of the Concept

In choosing to explain hyperthymia, Friedman could have focused his explanation in any number of ways. For example, he could have written about the history of the concept, showing how it began in the early nineteenth century as a type of personality disorder and has become regarded in the twenty-first century as simply a type of temperament or personality.

To analyze how Friedman focuses his explanation of hyperthymia, do the following:

- Skim the essay and note in the margin where he first identifies the concept.
- Write a couple of sentences explaining how the anecdotes in the two opening paragraphs prepare readers for his explanation.
- Add another sentence or two speculating about how writing the essay for the *New York Times* might have influenced Friedman's choice on how to focus the explanation.

● A Readable Plan

Writers sometimes use *rhetorical questions* both to engage readers and signal a change to a new topic. **Rhetorical questions** are questions the writer poses but does not expect readers to answer. Instead, the writer goes on to answer the question in the next sentence or paragraph. Here are a few examples of rhetorical questions from the other concept explanation essays in this chapter:

> If we assume there is some reality to the reports about cannibalism, how can we best understand this concept? (Ngo, par. 6)

> Chemicals may help explain (at least to scientists) the feelings of passion and compassion, but why do people tend to fall in love with one partner rather than a myriad of others? (Toufexis, par. 16)

> Where do those intuitions come from? And why are we so inconsistent about following where they lead us? (Kluger, par. 7)

To analyze how Friedman uses rhetorical questions, follow these steps:

- Skim the essay and note where Friedman uses rhetorical questions.
- Write a sentence or two explaining how each rhetorical question works as a topic sentence to let readers know what the following paragraph or set of paragraphs will be about.
- Add another sentence speculating about how the rhetorical questions may work to engage readers and how effective they are.

● Appropriate Explanatory Strategies

Defining is probably the most important writing strategy for explaining a concept. In fact, the concept explanation essay can be seen as an extended definition. Unfamiliar terms are often best defined by giving **synonyms**, words that have similar meanings but are likely to be more familiar to readers than the term being defined. We can see how synonyms work in the following example where the term being defined is underlined and the synonyms are highlighted: "These two women were lucky to be born with a joyous temperament, which in its most extreme form is called hyperthymia. Cheerful despite life's misfortunes, energetic and productive..." (par. 3). In addition to synonyms, **antonyms** — words that are opposite in meaning — may also be used to clarify a definition. Here is an example of Friedman's use of antonyms (underlined) to define hyperthymia: "Some researchers believe hyperthymics may be at increased risk of depression or hypomania, a mild variant of mania" (par. 5). Friedman, as you will see, gives readers an array of synonyms and antonyms with which they can create a multifaceted understanding of what the concept hyperthymia means.

For more on defining, see Chapter 16.

To analyze how Friedman uses synonyms and antonyms to define his concept, do the following:

- Reread paragraphs 1–3. Highlight the synonyms, and underline the antonyms.
- Write a few sentences identifying a few of the synonyms and antonyms that help you understand the meaning of hyperthymia.

● Smooth Integration of Sources

Writers of concept explanation essays may quote sources directly or choose to *summarize* or *paraphrase* sources. Linh Kieu Ngo primarily uses summary and paraphrase, as does Friedman. In paragraphs 1 and 2, however, he quotes two sources with whom he spoke. He does not identify these sources by name, but he does identify the two researchers whose studies he summarizes. Whether they are writing for an academic audience (as Ngo was in writing for a college class) or for a more general audience (as Friedman was in writing an essay for the *New York Times*), writers typically identify researchers from whom they got important information because they know that readers may need to find the research reports. By including the author, title, publication, and date, academic styles of documentation make it especially easy for readers to find reports.

For more on summary, paraphrase, and quotation, see Chapter 24, pp. 756–65.

To analyze how Friedman uses sources, try the following:

- Reread paragraphs 5 and 8 where he refers to two different research studies: put brackets around the information he gives to identify the study, highlight his description of what was done, and underline his summary of the results.
- Write a couple of sentences describing how Friedman presents these two studies.
- Add another sentence or two speculating about why he does not include any information about the sources he quotes in paragraphs 1 and 2 or the statistics he cites in paragraphs 3 and 4.

Friedman mentions several concepts you might think about exploring further for your own essay, such as pessimism, extroversion (or introversion), apathy, addiction, psychosis, and the placebo effect. Other psychological concepts you might consider writing about include agoraphobia, obsessive-compulsive disorder, seasonal

CONSIDERING TOPICS FOR YOUR OWN ESSAY

affective disorder, malingering, kleptomania, dyslexia, or attention deficit disorder (ADD). Alternatively, you could focus on the history of psychology and write about Freudian concepts such as psychoanalysis, ego, id, superego, repression, or libido; Jungian concepts such as anima, archetype, or collective unconscious; behavioral psychology concepts such as conditioning, or positive and negative reinforcement; or social psychology concepts such as socialization, conformity, "the looking-glass self," altruism, narcissism, empathy, or codependency.

Jeffrey Kluger has written several books, including *Splendid Solution: Jonas Salk and the Conquest of Polio* and *Lost Moon: The Perilous Voyage of Apollo 13*, upon which the 1995 film *Apollo 13* was based. He has written for *Discover, Science Digest,* and the *New York Times' Business World Magazine.* A staff writer for *Time* magazine, Kluger wrote this essay in November 2007.

As you read, notice how the visuals contribute to the essay.

What Makes Us Moral

Jeffrey Kluger

If the entire human species were a single individual, that person would long ago have been declared mad. The insanity would not lie in the anger and darkness of the human mind — though it can be a black and raging place indeed. And it certainly wouldn't lie in the transcendent goodness of that mind — one so sublime, we fold it into a larger "soul." The madness would lie instead in the fact that both of those qualities, the savage and the splendid, can exist in one creature, one person, often in one instant.

We're a species that is capable of almost dumbfounding kindness. We nurse one another, romance one another, weep for one another. Ever since science taught us how, we willingly tear the very organs from our bodies and give them to one another. And at the same time, we slaughter one another. The past 15 years of human history are the temporal equivalent of those subatomic particles that are created in accelerators and vanish in a trillionth of a second, but in that fleeting instant, we've visited untold horrors on ourselves — in Mogadishu, Rwanda, Chechnya, Darfur, Beslan, Baghdad, Pakistan, London, Madrid,

> **The deeper that science drills into the substrata of behavior, the harder it becomes to preserve the vanity that we are unique among Earth's creatures.**

1

2

Lebanon, Israel, New York City, Abu Ghraib, Oklahoma City, an Amish schoolhouse in Pennsylvania — all of the crimes committed by the highest, wisest, most principled species the planet has produced. That we're also the lowest, cruelest, most blood-drenched species is our shame — and our paradox.

The deeper that science drills into the substrata of behavior, the harder it becomes to preserve the vanity that we are unique among Earth's creatures. We're the only species with language, we told ourselves — until gorillas and chimps mastered sign language. We're the only one that uses tools — but that's if you don't count otters smashing mollusks with rocks or apes stripping leaves from twigs and using them to fish for termites. 3

What does, or ought to, separate us then is our highly developed sense of morality, a primal understanding of good and bad, of right and wrong, of what it means to suffer not only our own pain — something anything with a rudimentary nervous system can do — but also the pain of others. That quality is the distilled essence of what it means to be human. Why it's an essence that so often spoils, no one can say. 4

Morality may be a hard concept to grasp, but we acquire it fast. A preschooler will learn that it's not all right to eat in the classroom, because the teacher says it's not. If the rule is lifted and eating is approved, the child will happily comply. But if the same teacher says it's also O.K. to push another student off a chair, the child hesitates. "He'll respond, 'No, the teacher shouldn't say that,'" says psychologist Michael Schulman, coauthor of *Bringing Up a Moral Child*. In both cases, somebody taught the child a rule, but the rule against pushing has a stickiness about it, one that resists coming unstuck even if someone in authority countenances it. That's the difference between a matter of morality and one of mere social convention, and Schulman and others believe kids feel it innately. 5

Of course, the fact is, that child will sometimes hit and won't feel particularly bad about it either — unless he's caught. The same is true for people who steal or despots who slaughter. "Moral judgment is pretty consistent from person to person," says Marc Hauser, professor of psychology at Harvard University and author of *Moral Minds*. "Moral behavior, however, is scattered all over the chart." The rules we know, even the ones we intuitively feel, are by no means the rules we always follow. 6

Where do those intuitions come from? And why are we so inconsistent about following where they lead us? Scientists can't yet answer those questions, but that hasn't stopped them from looking. Brain scans are providing clues. Animal studies are providing more. Investigations of tribal behavior are providing still more. None of this research may make us behave better, not right away at least. But all of it can help us understand ourselves — a small step up from savagery perhaps, but an important one. 7

The Moral Ape

The deepest foundation on which morality is built is the phenomenon of empathy, the understanding that what hurts me would feel the same way to you. And human ego notwithstanding, it's a quality other species share. 8

It's not surprising that animals far less complex than we are would display a trait that's as generous of spirit as empathy, particularly if you decide there's no spirit involved in it at all. Behaviorists often reduce what we call empathy to a mercantile business known as reciprocal altruism. A favor done today — food offered, shelter given — brings a return favor tomorrow. If a colony of animals practices that give-and-take well, the group thrives.

9

But even in animals, there's something richer going on. One of the first and most poignant observations of empathy in nonhumans was made by Russian primatologist Nadia Kohts, who studied nonhuman cognition in the first half of the 20th century and raised a young chimpanzee in her home. When the chimp would make his way to the roof of the house, ordinary strategies for bringing him down — calling, scolding, offers of food — would rarely work. But if Kohts sat down and pretended to cry, the chimp would go to her immediately. "He runs around me as if looking for the offender," she wrote. "He tenderly takes my chin in his palm…as if trying to understand what is happening."

10

You hardly have to go back to the early part of the past century to find such accounts. Even cynics went soft at the story of Binta Jua, the gorilla who in 1996 rescued a 3-year-old boy who had tumbled into her zoo enclosure, rocking him gently in her arms and carrying him to a door where trainers could enter and collect him. "The capacity of empathy is multilayered," says primatologist Frans de Waal of Emory University, author of *Our Inner Ape*. "We share a core with lots of animals."

11

While it's impossible to directly measure empathy in animals, in humans it's another matter. Hauser cites a study in which spouses or unmarried couples underwent functional magnetic resonance imaging (fMRI) as they were subjected to mild pain. They were warned before each time the painful stimulus was administered, and their brains lit up in a characteristic way signaling mild dread. They were then told that they were not going to feel the discomfort but that their partner was. Even when they couldn't see their partner, the brains of the subjects lit up

12

MORAL DILEMMA
The Sinking Lifeboat

You are adrift in a life raft after your cruise ship has sunk. There are too many survivors for the life rafts, and yours is dangerously overloaded. The raft is certain to sink, and even with life vests on, all the passengers are sure to die because of the frigid temperature of the water. One person on the boat is awake and alert but gravely ill and will not survive the journey no matter what. Throwing that person overboard would prevent the raft from sinking. Could you be the one who tosses the person out?

I COULD THROW A SURVIVOR OVERBOARD

❏ Yes
❏ No

precisely as if they were about to experience the pain themselves. "This is very much an 'I feel your pain' experience," says Hauser.

The brain works harder when the threat gets more complicated. A favorite scenario that morality researchers study is the trolley dilemma. You're standing near a track as an out-of-control train hurtles toward five unsuspecting people. There's a switch nearby that would let you divert the train onto a siding. Would you do it? Of course. You save five lives at no cost. Suppose a single unsuspecting man was on the siding? Now the mortality score is 5 to 1. Could you kill him to save the others? What if the innocent man was on a bridge over the trolley and you had to push him onto the track to stop the train?

Pose these dilemmas to people while they're in an fMRI, and the brain scans get messy. Using a switch to divert the train toward one person instead of five increases activity in the dorsolateral prefrontal cortex — the place where cool, utilitarian choices are made. Complicate things with the idea of pushing the innocent victim, and the medial frontal cortex — an area associated with emotion — lights up. As these two regions do battle, we may make irrational decisions. In a recent survey, 85% of subjects who were asked about the trolley scenarios said they would not push the innocent man onto the tracks — even though they knew they had just sent five people to their hypothetical death. "What's going on in our heads?" asks Joshua Greene, an assistant professor of psychology at Harvard University. "Why do we say it's O.K. to trade one life for five in one case and not others?"

How We Stay Good

Merely being equipped with moral programming does not mean we practice moral behavior. Something still has to boot up that software and configure it properly, and that something is the community. Hauser believes that all of us carry what he calls a sense of moral grammar — the ethical equivalent of the basic grasp of speech that most linguists believe is with us from birth. But just as syntax is nothing until words are built upon it, so too is a sense of right and wrong useless until someone teaches you how to apply it.

It's the people around us who do that teaching — often quite well. Once again, however, humans aren't the ones who dreamed up such a mentoring system. At the Arnhem Zoo in the Netherlands, de Waal was struck by how vigorously apes enforced group norms one evening when the zookeepers were calling their chimpanzees in for dinner. The keepers' rule at Arnhem was that no chimps would eat until the entire community was present, but two adolescents grew willful, staying outside the building. The hours it took to coax them inside caused the mood in the hungry colony to turn surly. That night the keepers put the delinquents to bed in a separate area — a sort of protective custody to shield them from reprisals. But the next day the adolescents were on their own, and the troop made its feelings plain, administering a sound beating. The chastened chimps were the first to come in that evening. Animals have what de Waal calls "oughts" — rules that the group must follow — and the community enforces them.

Human communities impose their own oughts, but they can vary radically from culture to culture. Take the phenomenon of Good Samaritan laws that

13

14

15

16

17

require passersby to assist someone in peril. Our species has a very conflicted sense of when we ought to help someone else and when we ought not, and the general rule is, Help those close to home and ignore those far away. That's in part because the plight of a person you can see will always feel more real than the problems of someone whose suffering is merely described to you. But part of it is also rooted in you from a time when the welfare of your tribe was essential for your survival but the welfare of an opposing tribe was not — and might even be a threat.

In the 21st century, we retain a powerful remnant of that primal dichotomy, which is what impels us to step in and help a mugging victim — or, in the astonishing case of Wesley Autrey, New York City's so-called Subway Samaritan, jump onto the tracks in front of an oncoming train to rescue a sick stranger — but allows us to decline to send a small contribution to help the people of Darfur. "The idea that you can save the life of a stranger on the other side of the world by making a modest material sacrifice is not the kind of situation our social brains are prepared for," says Greene.

₁₈

Throughout most of the world, you're still not required to aid a stranger, but in France and elsewhere, laws now make it a crime for passersby not to provide at least the up-close-and-personal aid we're good at giving. In most of the U.S., we make a distinction between an action and an omission to act. Says Hauser: "In France they've done away with that difference."

₁₉

But you don't need a state to create a moral code. The group does it too. One of the most powerful tools for enforcing group morals is the practice of shunning. If membership in a tribe is the way you ensure yourself food, family and protection from predators, being blackballed can be a terrifying thing. Religious believers as diverse as Roman Catholics, Mennonites and Jehovah's Witnesses have practiced their own forms of shunning — though the banishments may go by names like *excommunication* or *disfellowshipping*. Clubs, social groups and fraternities expel undesirable members. and the U.S. military retains the threat of discharge as a

₂₀

MORAL DILEMMA
The Runaway Trolley

A runaway trolley is heading down the tracks toward five workmen who can't be warned in time. You are standing near a switch that would divert the trolley onto a siding, but there is a single unsuspecting workman there. Would you throw the switch, killing one to save five? Suppose the workman was on a bridge with you and you could save the men only by pushing him onto the tracks? (He's large enough to stop the train; you're not.) Suppose you could throw a switch dropping him through a trapdoor — thus not physically pushing him?

DIVERT TRAIN	PUSH MAN	USE TRAPDOOR
❏ Yes	❏ Yes	❏ Yes
❏ No	❏ No	❏ No

disciplinary tool, even grading the punishment as "other than honorable" or "dishonorable," darkening the mark a former service person must carry for life.

Sometimes shunning emerges spontaneously when a society of millions recoils at a single member's acts. O.J. Simpson's 1995 acquittal may have outraged people, but it did make the morality tale surrounding him much richer, as the culture as a whole turned its back on him, denying him work, expelling him from his country club, refusing him service in a restaurant. In November his erstwhile publisher, who was fired in the wake of her and Simpson's disastrous attempt to publish a book about the killings, sued her ex-employer, alleging that she had been "shunned" and "humiliated." That, her former bosses might well respond, was precisely the point.

"Human beings were small, defenseless and vulnerable to predators," says Barbara J. King, biological anthropologist at the College of William and Mary and author of *Evolving God.* "Avoiding banishment would be important to us."

Why We Turn Bad

With so many redundant moral systems to keep us in line, why do we so often fall out of ranks? Sometimes we can't help it, as when we're suffering from clinical insanity and behavior slips the grip of reason. Criminal courts are stingy about finding such exculpatory madness, requiring a disability so severe, the defendant didn't even know the crime was wrong. That's a very high bar that prevents all but a few from proving the necessary moral numbness.

Things are different in the case of the cool and deliberate serial killer, who knows the criminality of his deeds yet continues to commit them. For neuroscientists, the iciness of the acts calls to mind the case of Phineas Gage, the Vermont railway worker who in 1848 was injured when an explosion caused a tamping iron to be driven through his prefrontal cortex. Improbably, he survived, but he exhibited stark behavioral changes — becoming detached and irreverent, though never criminal. Ever since, scientists have looked for the roots of serial murder in the brain's physical state.

A study published last year in the journal *NeuroImage* may have helped provide some answers. Researchers working through the National Institute of Mental Health scanned the brains of 20 healthy volunteers, watching their reactions as they were presented with various legal and illegal scenarios. The brain activity that most closely tracked the hypothetical crimes — rising and falling with the severity of the scenarios — occurred in the amygdala, a deep structure that helps us make the connection between bad acts and punishments. As in the trolley studies, there was also activity in the frontal cortex. The fact that the subjects themselves had no sociopathic tendencies limits the value of the findings. But knowing how the brain functions when things work well is one good way of knowing where to look when things break down.

Fortunately, the overwhelming majority of us never run off the moral rails in remotely as awful a way as serial killers do, but we do come untracked in smaller ways. We face our biggest challenges not when we're called on to behave ourselves within our family, community or workplace but when we have to apply the same moral care to people outside our tribe.

The notion of the "other" is a tough one for *Homo sapiens*. Sociobiology has been criticized as one of the most reductive of sciences, ascribing the behavior of all living things — humans included — as nothing more than an effort to get as many genes as possible into the next generation. The idea makes sense, and all creatures can be forgiven for favoring their troop over others. But such bias turns dark fast.

Schulman, the psychologist and author, works with delinquent adolescents at a residential treatment center in Yonkers, New York, and was struck one day by the outrage that swept through the place when the residents learned that three of the boys had mugged an elderly woman. "I wouldn't mug an old lady. That could be my grandmother," one said. Schulman asked whom it would be O.K. to mug. The boy answered, "A Chinese delivery guy." Explains Schulman: "The old lady is someone they could empathize with. The Chinese delivery guy is alien, literally and figuratively, to them."

This kind of brutal line between insiders and outsiders is evident everywhere — mobsters, say, who kill promiscuously yet go on rhapsodically about "family." But

27

28

29

MORAL DILEMMA
The Crying Baby

It's wartime, and you're hiding in a basement with your baby and a group of other people. Enemy soldiers are outside and will be drawn to any sound. If you're found, you will all be killed immediately. Your baby starts to cry loudly and cannot be stopped. Smothering him to death is the only way to silence him and save the lives of everyone in the room. Could you do so? Assume the baby is not yours, the parents are unknown and there will be no penalty for killing him. Could you be the one who smothers this baby if no one else would?

YOUR BABY	SOMEONE ELSE'S BABY
❏ Yes	❏ Yes
❏ No	❏ No

it has its most terrible expression in wars, in which the dehumanization of the outsider is essential for wholesale slaughter to occur. Volumes have been written about what goes on in the collective mind of a place like Nazi Germany or the collapsing Yugoslavia. While killers like Adolf Hitler or Slobodan Milosevic can never be put on the couch, it's possible to understand the xenophobic strings they play in their people.

"Yugoslavia is the great modern example of manipulating tribal sentiments to create mass murder," says Jonathan Haidt, associate professor of psychology at the University of Virginia. "You saw it in Rwanda and Nazi Germany too. In most cases of genocide, you have a moral entrepreneur who exploits tribalism for evil purposes." 30

That, of course, does not take the stain of responsibility off the people who follow those leaders — a case that war-crimes prosecutors famously argued at the Nuremberg trials and a point courageous people have made throughout history as they sheltered Jews during World War II or refuse to murder their Sunni neighbor even if a militia leader tells them to. 31

For grossly imperfect creatures like us, morality may be the steepest of all developmental mountains. Our opposable thumbs and big brains gave us the tools to dominate the planet, but wisdom comes more slowly than physical hardware. We surely have a lot of killing and savagery ahead of us before we fully civilize ourselves. The hope — a realistic one, perhaps — is that the struggles still to come are fewer than those left behind. 32

Kluger explains that the community plays a central role in disciplining us so that we practice moral behavior. Most of us, however, belong to more than one community, which may each have different and possibly contradictory standards and expectations — for example, parents versus friends, or college friends versus neighborhood or high school friends.

With two or three other students, discuss how community enforces morality. Begin by briefly taking turns telling each other about a conflict you encountered in the moral codes of different groups or a case where someone was disciplined by other members of a particular community. Then, consider together the following questions:

- If you have experienced a conflict between different community expectations, how did you deal with it?

- If someone was disciplined by a community, what kind of discipline was it and how effective was it?

- To explain the power of *shunning*, Kluger quotes Barbara J. King, who makes the point that avoiding banishment from the group was especially important when we were "small, defenseless and vulnerable to predators" (par. 22). Do you fear shunning? If so, what makes shunning powerful for you and your friends today?

MAKING CONNECTIONS: COMMUNITY MORALITY

ANALYZING WRITING STRATEGIES

● ● ● ●
Basic Features

● A Focused Explanation of the Concept

To focus his essay and interest readers, Kluger introduces his explanation by establishing what he calls at the end of paragraph 2 "our *paradox*." A **paradox** is a statement that contradicts itself. For example, the statement "I always lie" is a paradox because if the statement is true, it also must be false. Paradoxes work by setting up an apparent opposition (such as telling the truth and lying) that upon closer examination may not be contradictory after all.

To analyze how Kluger introduces the concept and focuses his explanation, do the following:

- Reread paragraphs 1–7 and note in the margin the oppositions Kluger uses to set up his explanation.

- Write a few sentences identifying the oppositions and summarizing the paradox Kluger presents in this introductory section of the essay.

- Add another sentence or two explaining how he focuses his explanation and how well this focus helps you understand what Kluger acknowledges is "a hard concept to grasp" (par. 5).

● A Readable Plan

To learn more about cueing strategies, see Chapter 13: Cueing the Reader.

Writers of essays explaining concepts seek to make the information easy for readers to follow. To do so, they employ various cues, such as a *thesis statement*, *topic sentences*, *headings*, and various *transitional words and phrases*. Writers also use an array of cohesive devices including *word repetition* and *synonyms*.

To analyze how Kluger uses some of these cues, do the following activities:

Topic Sentences and Headings

- Reread the second section (pars. 8–14). Highlight the sentence or sentences that announce the topic of these paragraphs.

- Write a few sentences explaining why you think the text you highlighted serves as this section's topic sentence(s).

- Add a sentence speculating about why Kluger uses the heading "The Moral Ape" for this section.

Word Repetition and Synonyms

- Skim paragraphs 15 and 16 to see how Kluger uses word repetition and synonyms as cohesive devices to help readers follow the movement from topic to topic. For example, the last sentence in paragraph 15 uses the word *teaches* and the first two sentences of paragraph 16 use repetition (*teaching*) and a synonym (*mentoring system*).

- Reread paragraphs 20–22 and underline the word repetitions and synonyms Kluger uses.
- Write a sentence or two describing the word repetitions and synonyms Kluger uses in paragraphs 20–22.

● Appropriate Explanatory Strategies

Kluger uses many of the explanatory strategies we've seen in the other essays explaining a concept, but he relies primarily on *examples* from research studies. To present these examples, he has to summarize the study succinctly so that readers can see how the example illustrates the topic he's discussing. For example, in paragraph 10, Kluger relates the anecdote that summarizes Nadia Kohts's research finding about the ability of chimpanzees to experience and act on empathy. (Interestingly, Kluger ends his brief summary with a quotation that could raise questions about the subjectivity of Kohts's interpretation of the chimp's behavior.)

To analyze Kluger's use of examples, do the following:

- Reread the examples in paragraphs 11–14.
- Write a sentence or two explaining how each example relates to Kluger's explanation.

● Smooth Integration of Sources

When writers integrate source material into their concept explanations, they have choices to make about what to quote and what to summarize or paraphrase. Because he is reporting several research reports, Kluger quotes and summarizes a lot. Let's look at an example:

> While it's impossible to directly measure empathy in animals, in humans it's another matter. Hauser cites a study in which spouses or unmarried couples underwent functional magnetic resonance imaging (fMRI) as they were subjected to mild pain. They were warned before each time the painful stimulus was administered, and their brains lit up in a characteristic way signaling mild dread. They were then told that they were not going to feel the discomfort but that their partner was. Even when they couldn't see their partner, the brains of the subjects lit up precisely as if they were about to experience the pain themselves. "This is very much an 'I feel your pain' experience," says Hauser. (par. 12)

The first sentence (highlighted) is the topic sentence announcing what the paragraph is about. The next four sentences summarize Hauser's research study, beginning with a brief process narrative explaining how the study was conducted and concluding with a sentence (underlined) summarizing the results of the experiment. The final sentence of the paragraph, a quotation from the researcher, comments on the results using down-to-earth language to discuss what the experiment reveals about empathy, the topic of the paragraph. This is a clear, efficient, and interesting way to present information.

For more on summary, paraphrase, and quotation, see
Chapter 24, pp. 756-65.

To analyze how Kluger integrates sources into his essay, do the following:

- Choose one of the following paragraphs to read, and analyze it using the method presented in the sample analysis above: paragraph 5, 10, 14, or 16.
- Write a few sentences describing the results of your analysis.

ANALYZING VISUALS

"MORAL DILEMMAS"

The visuals included in this essay accompany brief scenarios called "Moral Dilemmas." Examine each "Moral Dilemma" carefully, and then write a few sentences describing them and explaining what they contribute to Kluger's explanation of the concept. In performing your analysis, consider the following questions:

- When you initially read the essay, did you stop to study any of the scenarios, just glance at them in passing, go back to them after finishing the essay, or not look at them at all?
- What purpose do the scenarios serve?
- The scenarios use words as well as illustrations. What do the illustrations contribute to the scenarios?
- Do the scenarios repeat information already presented in the text of the essay, or do they add new information?
- Each "Moral Dilemma" invites readers to answer questions. Online, this was an interactive feature of the essay, and the original print publication directed readers to the online activity. How effective is this type of visual in a print publication compared to an online one?

CONSIDERING TOPICS FOR YOUR OWN ESSAY

Kluger mentions several concepts you might think about exploring further for your own essay: empathy, reciprocal altruism, nonhuman cognition, tribalism, shunning, clinical insanity, sociobiology, and xenophobia. Alternatively, you could focus on one of the many research studies Kluger refers to, explaining in depth one of the key concepts the study investigates, or you could focus on relevant research Kluger does not mention, such as the famous experiment on obedience to authority conducted by psychologist Stanley Milgram in the early 1960s, or the recent re-staging of this experiment done by Jerry Burger at Santa Clara University. You could also consider writing about a different concept from Western philosophy such as metaphysics, truth, epistemology, idealism, pragmatism, logical positivism, or existentialism, or you could examine a concept related to an Eastern philosophy such as Confucianism, Taoism, karma, nirvana, or Zoroastrianism.

Beyond the Traditional Essay: Explaining a Concept

Perhaps more than for any other kind of writing, visuals — especially graphs, charts, diagrams, and tables — are common components of concept explanations. So-called "infographics" like the "Mapping Memory" interactive feature reproduced here from the *National Geographic* online are used more and more frequently in print, televised, and online news media to help explain complex concepts.

You should definitely use illustrations, either self-created or borrowed (and, as always, appropriately documented), to help your reader understand something you're trying to explain, even if you're submitting your essay in print form.

You're likely familiar with many other kinds of concept explanations that fall outside the bounds of traditional essays. Most of us have made use of Web tutorials that use video, audio, illustrations, and text to explain concepts — for example, tutorials that help us use tools like Microsoft Word, or the one shown here from the National Library of Medicine (www.nlm.nih.gov/) on evaluating Internet health information. Such tutorials typically share all or many of the basic features of essays that explain concepts, including presenting a focused concept (often breaking complex systems down into concrete, highly specific steps), a readable plan and clear definitions, and use of internal and external links for further information.

As you work on your own project, you might want to consult some of these alternative forms of explaining a concept for inspiration. If the format in which you are working allows for it — if, for example, you are creating a poster, Web site, or video — you should consider taking advantage of the strategies available to those working in multimedia — for example, by embedding artifacts that are relevant to the concept you're explaining. (Always remember to properly document any material you might use that was created by someone else.)

Guide to Writing

The Writing Assignment

Write an essay about a concept that interests you and that you want to study further. When you have a good understanding of the concept, explain it to your readers, considering carefully what they already know about it and how your essay might add to what they know.

This Guide to Writing will help you apply what you have learned about how writers create concept explanations that are focused, readable, well explained, and supported by credible sources. The Guide is divided into five sections with various activities in each section:

- **Invention and Research**
- **Planning and Drafting**
- **Critical Reading Guide**
- **Editing and Proofreading**
- **Revising**

The guide is designed to escort you through the writing process, from finding a concept to editing your finished essay. Your instructor may require you to follow the Guide to Writing from beginning to end. Working through the Guide to Writing in this way will help you — as it has helped many other college students — write a thoughtful, fully developed, polished essay.

If, however, your instructor gives you latitude to choose and if you have had experience writing a concept explanation, then you can decide on the order in which you'll do the activities in the Guide to Writing. For example, the Invention and Research section includes activities to help you find a concept, get an overview of it, focus it, research your focus, and consider explanatory strategies. Obviously, finding a concept must precede the other activities, but you may come to the Guide with a concept already in mind, and you may choose to do research on it before you focus your explanation. In fact, you may find your response to one of the invention activities expanding into a draft before you've had a chance to do any of the other activities. That's a good thing — but you should later flesh out your draft by going back to the activities you skipped and layering the new material into your draft.

To learn about using the *Guide* e-book for invention and drafting, go to **bedfordstmartins.com/ theguide.**

The following chart will help you find answers to many of the questions you might have about planning, drafting, and revising a concept explanation. The page references in the Where to Look column refer to examples from the readings, activities in the Guide to Writing, and chapters later in the book.

Starting Points: Explaining a Concept

●●●○ Basic Features

	Question	Where to Look
Choosing a Concept	How do I come up with a concept to write about?	• Considering Topics for Your Own Essay (pp. 143, 147–48, 158) • Choosing a Concept to Write About (pp. 162–63) • Testing Your Choice (pp. 165–66)
	What's my purpose in writing? How can I interest my audience?	• Reading Concept Explanations: Purpose and Audience (p. 131) • Defining Your Purpose for Your Readers (p. 167) • Refining Your Purpose and Setting Goals: Clarifying Your Purpose and Audience (p. 168)
A Focused Explanation	How can I decide on a focus for my concept?	• Reading Concept Explanations: Basic Features (pp. 129–31) • Ways In: Gaining an Overview of a Concept (p. 164) • Ways In: Focusing the Concept (p. 165)
A Readable Plan	How should I arrange my explanation so that it's logical and easy to read? What kinds of cues should I provide?	• Reading Concept Explanations: Basic Features (pp. 129–31) • Use forecasting (p. 141) • Use rhetorical questions (p. 146) • Use cues and cohesive devices (pp. 156–57) • Formulating a Tentative Thesis Statement (pp. 167–68) • Refining Your Purpose and Setting Goals: Presenting the Information and the Ending (pp. 168–69) • Outlining Your Draft (pp. 169–70)
Appropriate Explanatory Strategies	What's the best way to explain my concept? What kinds of writing strategies should I use?	• Reading Concept Explanations: Basic Features (pp. 129–31) • Use explanatory writing strategies (pp. 141–42) • Use synonyms to define (pp. 146–47) • Use examples (p. 157) • Doing In-Depth Research on Your Focused Concept (p. 166) • Considering Explanatory Strategies (pp. 166–67) • Designing Your Document (p. 167) • Thinking about Document Design: Designing Surveys and Presenting Results (pp. 178–79)
	How do I write clear definitions?	• Use synonyms to define (pp. 146–47) • A Sentence Strategy: Appositives (pp. 170–71)
Smooth Integration of Sources	How should I integrate sources so that they support my argument?	• Reading Concept Explanations: Basic Features (pp. 129–31) • Use summary and paraphrase (pp. 147; 157–58) • Working with Sources: Using Descriptive Verbs to Introduce Information (p. 172)

Invention and Research

The following invention activities are easy to complete and take only a few minutes. Spreading out the activities over several days will stimulate your creativity, enabling you to find a concept and an approach to explaining it that works for both you and your readers. Remember to keep a written record of your invention work: you'll need it when you draft the essay and later when you revise it.

Choosing a Concept to Write About

List several concepts that you might like to explore. Include concepts you already know something about as well as some you know only slightly and would like to research further — the longer your list, the more likely you are to find the right concept, and should your first choice not work out, you will have a ready list of alternatives. Bear in mind that you're looking for a concept that meets the following criteria.

Criteria for Choosing a Concept:

A Checklist

The concept should be:
- ☐ a concept that you feel eager to learn more about;
- ☐ a concept that will interest your readers;
- ☐ a concept that you can research sufficiently in the allotted time;
- ☐ a concept that you can explain fully and clearly in the length prescribed by your instructor.

If you're like most people, you'll need some help in coming up with a number of good options. To get your juices flowing, you might first try quickly rereading the Considering Topics for Your Own Essay activities following the readings, and thinking about any concepts those suggestions brought to mind. Reread any notes you might have made in response to the suggestions. Consider also any concepts related to your hobbies or special interests.

For further ideas, consult the suggestions in the following sections.

Possible Concepts to Consider

Your work in this or your other courses can provide concepts you might be interested in exploring. Try skimming through your class notes and your textbooks. Here are a few possibilities, by discipline:

- **Literature:** irony, semiotics, hero, dystopia, picaresque, the absurd, canon, modernism, identity politics, queering

- **Philosophy:** nihilism, logical positivism, determinism, metaphysics, ethics, natural law, Zeno's paradox, epistemology, ideology
- **Business management:** quality circle, cybernetic control system, management by objectives, zero-based budgeting, liquidity gap
- **Psychology:** assimilation/accommodation, social cognition, moratorium, intelligence, operant conditioning, the Stroop effect
- **Government:** majority rule, minority rights, federalism, popular consent, exclusionary rule, hegemony
- **Biology:** photosynthesis, mitosis, karyotype analysis, morphogenesis, electron transport, plasmolysis, phagocytosis, homozygosity, diffusion
- **Art:** cubism, Dadaism, surrealism, expressionism, perspective, collage
- **Math:** polynomials, boundedness, null space, permutations and combinations, factoring, Rolle's theorem, continuity, derivative, indefinite integral
- **Physical sciences:** matter, mass, weight, energy, gravity, atomic theory, law of definite proportions, osmotic pressure, first law of thermodynamics, entropy
- **Public health:** addiction, seasonal affective disorder, contraception, prenatal care, toxicology, glycemic index
- **Environmental studies:** acid rain, recycling, ozone depletion, toxic waste, endangered species, sustainability
- **Sports:** squeeze play (baseball), power play (hockey), wishbone offense (football), serve and volley (tennis), inside game (basketball)
- **Personal finance:** reverse mortgage, budget, insurance, deduction, revolving credit, interest rates, dividend, bankruptcy, socially conscious investing
- **Law:** tort, contract, garnishment, double indemnity, reasonable doubt, class action suits, product liability, lemon law
- **Sociology:** norm, deviance, role conflict, ethnocentrism, class, social stratification, acculturation, Whorf-Sapir hypothesis, machismo

Also consider exploring concepts that relate to issues of **identity and community**, such as self-esteem, character, autonomy, narcissism, multiculturalism, ethnicity, race, racism, social contract, community policing, social Darwinism, identity politics, special-interest groups, colonialism, public space, the other, or agency.

Finally, consider exploring concepts that relate to your **work experiences and career aspirations,** such as free enterprise, minimum wage, affirmative action, stock option, glass ceiling, downsizing, collective bargaining, service sector, entrepreneur, bourgeoisie, underclass, working class, middle class, monopoly, automation, robotics, management style, deregulation, or multinational corporation.

Ways In: Gaining an Overview of a Concept

Your research efforts for a concept essay can be divided into three stages. First, you must gain an overview of the concept; next, you will identify an aspect of it to focus on; finally, you will do in-depth research in order to gather information. The activities below will help you gain an overview of your concept. You can begin with whichever activity you want, but wherever you begin, be sure to return to the other activities to gather sufficient information.

Discovering What You Already Know	Doing Research	Doing a General Internet Search
Take a few minutes to write about what you already know about the concept. Consider, too, why you have chosen the concept and why you find it interesting. Write quickly, without planning or organizing. Note questions you have about the concept. Also, check any materials you have at hand that explain your concept. (If you are considering a concept from one of your other courses, for example, check your textbook or your lecture notes first.)	*To find comprehensive, up-to-date information on your concept, locate relevant articles, books, and encyclopedias through your library.* Chapter 23, Library and Internet Research, has general information that will help you do research productively. When you find potentially useful information, take accurate notes, make a photocopy, or save the information electronically, always being sure to record exact source information for your Works Cited list. Depending on your topic, you might also consider consulting experts on campus or in the community, and visiting other potential sources of information such as museums or research centers.	*Do an Internet search to help you find a focus for your essay.* Try entering the word "overview" or "definition" together with the name of your concept, in order to confine your results to introductions and overviews. Bookmark Web sites you find that invite more than a quick glance, and copy or save any potentially useful information — making sure to include the URL, the title of the site, the date the information was posted (if available), and the date you accessed the site. As always, if your first searches don't turn up much of use, be sure to try variations on the search terms you use.

Ways In: Focusing the Concept

Basic Features

The following activities will help you determine a focus for your concept. Concepts can be approached from many perspectives (for example, history, definition, known causes or effects), and you cannot realistically explain every aspect of any concept, so you must limit your explanation to reflect both your special interest in the concept and your readers' likely knowledge and interest.

Exploring Your Own Interests	Analyzing Your Readers
Make a list of two or three aspects of the concept that could become a focus for your essay, and evaluate what you know about each aspect. Under each possible focus in your list, make notes about why it interests you, what you know about it already, and what questions you want to answer about it.	*Take a few minutes to write about your readers.* Ask yourself the following: • Who are your readers likely to be? • What do they already know about the concept? about related concepts? • Are they likely to be interested in the concept, or related concepts? If not, how could you interest them? • What would be useful for them to know about this concept — perhaps something that could relate to their life or work? Even if you are writing only for your instructor, you should give some thought to what he or she knows and thinks about the concept.

After doing the activities above, choose an aspect of your concept on which to focus, and write a sentence justifying its appropriateness.

Testing Your Choice

After you've chosen a concept and attempted to focus it, you should pause to decide whether you should write about it. As painful as it may be to consider, starting over with a new concept is better than continuing with an unworkable one. Test your choice using the questions that follow.

- *Can I learn what I need to know in the time I have available to write a concept explanation with this focus?*
- *Am I likely to understand the concept well enough to make it clear to my readers?*
- *Do I feel a personal interest in the concept and the particular focus I have chosen? If so, what is the basis for this interest? Is the concept so interesting to me that I am willing to spend the next two or three weeks on an essay explaining it?*

- *Do I think I can make the concept and the focus I have chosen interesting to readers? Can I relate the concept to something readers already know? Can I think of any anecdotes or examples that will make the concept more meaningful to them?*

If you lose confidence in your choice, return to the list of possible concepts you made and choose another one.

A Collaborative Activity:
Testing Your Choice

Get together with two or three other students to find out what your readers are likely to know about your subject and what might interest them about it.

Presenters: Take turns briefly explaining your concept, describing your intended readers, and identifying the aspect of the concept that you will focus on.

Listeners: Briefly tell the presenter whether the focus sounds appropriate and interesting for the intended readers. Share what you think readers are likely to know about the concept and what information might be especially interesting to them.

● Doing In-Depth Research on Your Focused Concept

Having chosen a concept and a focus for your explanation of it, begin your in-depth search of the library, Internet, and other relevant sources for information on your concept. You will want to keep careful records of all sources you believe will contribute in any way to your essay. If possible, scan or make photocopies of print sources, and save other sources electronically. If you must rely on notes, be sure to copy any quotations exactly and enclose them in quotation marks. Since you do not know which sources you will ultimately use, keep careful records of the author, title, publication information, page numbers, and other required information for each source you gather so that you can acknowledge your sources. Check with your instructor about whether you should follow the documentation style of the Modern Language Association (MLA), the American Psychological Association (APA), or a different style.

● Considering Explanatory Strategies

Before you move on to plan and draft your essay, consider some possible ways of presenting the concept. Try to answer each of the following questions in a sentence or two. Questions that you can answer readily may identify the best strategies for presenting your focused concept.

- What term is typically used to name the concept, and what does it mean? (*definition*)

- How is this concept like or unlike related concepts with which your readers may be more familiar? (*comparison and contrast*)

- How can an explanation of this concept be divided into parts to make it easier for readers to understand? (*classification*)

- How does this concept happen, or how does one go about doing it? (*process narration*)

- What are this concept's known causes or effects? (*cause and effect*)

- What examples or anecdotes can make the concept less abstract and more memorable? (*example* or *anecdote*)

Designing Your Document

Think about whether visual elements — tables, graphs, drawings, photographs — would make your explanation clearer. These are not a requirement, but they could be helpful. Consider also whether your readers might benefit from design features such as headings, bulleted or numbered lists, or other elements that would present information efficiently or make your explanation easier to follow. You could construct your own graphic elements (using word processing software to create bar graphs or pie charts, for example), download materials from the Internet, copy images from television or DVDs, or scan visuals from books and magazines. Remember that you must cite the source of any visual you do not create yourself, and you should also request permission from the source of the visual if your paper is going to be posted on a Web site that is not password-protected.

Defining Your Purpose for Your Readers

Write a few sentences that define your purpose in writing about this particular concept for your readers. Remember that you have already identified and analyzed your readers and that you have begun to research and develop your explanation with these readers in mind. Try now to define your purpose in explaining the concept to them. Use these questions to focus your thoughts:

- *Are my readers familiar with the concept?* If not, how can I relate it to what they already know? If so, will my focus allow my readers to see the familiar concept in a new light?

- *If I suspect that my readers have misconceptions about the concept, how can I correct the misconceptions without offending my readers?*

- *Will I need to arouse readers' interest in information that may seem at first to be less than engaging?*

- *Do I want readers to see that the information I have to report is relevant to their lives, families, communities, work, or studies?*

Formulating a Tentative Thesis Statement

Write one or more sentences, stating your focused concept, that could serve as a thesis statement. You might also want to forecast the topics you will use to explain the concept.

Anastasia Toufexis begins her essay with this thesis statement:

> O.K., let's cut out all this nonsense about romantic love. Let's bring some scientific precision to the party. Let's put love under a microscope.
>
> When rigorous people with Ph.D.s after their names do that, what they see is not some silly, senseless thing. No, their probe reveals that love rests firmly on the foundations of evolution, biology and chemistry.

Toufexis's concept is *love,* and her focus is the scientific explanation of love — specifically the evolution, biology, and chemistry of love. In announcing her focus, she forecasts the order in which she will present information from the three most relevant academic disciplines — anthropology (which includes the study of human evolution), biology, and chemistry. These discipline names become her topics.

In his essay on cannibalism, Linh Kieu Ngo offers his thesis statement in paragraph 6:

> Cannibalism can be broken down into two main categories: exocannibalism, the eating of outsiders or foreigners, and endocannibalism, the eating of members of one's own social group (Shipman 70). Within these categories are several functional types of cannibalism, three of the most common being survival cannibalism, dietary cannibalism, and religious and ritual cannibalism.

Ngo's concept is *cannibalism,* and his focus is on three common types of cannibalism. He carefully forecasts how he will divide the information to create topics and the order in which he will explain each of the topics.

As you draft your own tentative thesis statement, take care to make the language clear. Although you may want to revise your thesis statement as you draft your essay, trying to state it now will give your planning and drafting more focus and direction. Keep in mind that the thesis in an explanatory essay merely announces the subject; it never asserts a position that requires an argument to defend it.

Planning and Drafting

The following guidelines will help you get the most out of your invention notes, determine specific goals for your essay, and write a first draft. In addition, this section will help you write a draft by writing opening sentences, trying out a useful sentence strategy, and learning how to work with sources.

Refining Your Purpose and Setting Goals

Successful writers are always looking beyond the next sentence to larger goals. Indeed, the next sentence is easier to write if you keep larger goals in mind. The following questions can help you set these goals. Consider each one now, and then return to them as necessary while you write.

Clarifying Your Purpose and Audience

- How can I build on my readers' knowledge?
- What new information can I present to them?
- How can I organize my essay so that my readers can follow it easily?
- What tone would be most appropriate? Would an informal tone like Toufexis's or a formal one like Ngo's be more appropriate to my purpose?

Presenting the Information

- Should I name and define my concept early in the essay, as Ngo, Toufexis, and Friedman do? Or should I lead up to it gradually by providing illustrations, as Kluger does?

- Could I develop my explanation by dividing my concept into different categories, as Ngo does? By comparing my concept to related concepts, like Friedman?

- How can I establish the authority of my sources? Should I simply give their names and credentials, as Friedman does, or also refer to specific publications or research, as Ngo, Toufexis, and Kluger do? Will my instructor require me to use APA style, MLA style — as Ngo's instructor did — or some other documentation style?

- How can I make it easy for readers to follow my explanation? Should I simply use clear and explicit transitions when I move from one topic to another, as Ngo does, or also include rhetorical questions, like Toufexis, Friedman, and Kluger?

- Should I use visuals, like Toufexis and Kluger?

The Ending

- Should I end with speculation, as Ngo does, or by suggesting what is special about the concept, as Friedman does?

- Should I frame the essay by relating the ending to the beginning, as Toufexis and Kluger do?

Outlining Your Draft

The goals that you have set should help you draft your essay, but first you might want to make a quick scratch outline. In your outline, list the main topics into which you have divided the information about your concept. Use this outline to guide your drafting, but do not feel tied to it. As you draft, you may find a better way to sequence the action and integrate these features.

An essay explaining a concept is made up of four basic parts:

- an attempt to engage readers' interest
- the thesis statement, announcing the concept, its focus, and its topics
- an orientation to the concept, which may include a description or definition of the concept
- information about the concept

Here is a possible outline for an essay explaining a concept:

  I. Introduction (attempt to gain readers' interest in the concept)
 II. Thesis statement
III. Definition of the concept
 IV. Topic 1 with illustration
  V. Topic 2 with illustration
     (Topic 3, etc.)
 VI. Conclusion

An attempt to gain readers' interest could take as little as two or three sentences or as many as four or five paragraphs. The thesis statement and definition are usually quite brief — sometimes only a few sentences. A topic illustration may occupy one or several paragraphs, and there can be few or many topics, depending on how the information has been divided up. A conclusion might summarize the information presented, give advice about how to use or apply the information, or speculate about the future of the concept.

Drafting

If you have not already begun to draft your essay, this section will help by suggesting how to choose an opening sentence strategy; how to use appositive phrases; and how to use descriptive verbs to introduce information from sources. Drafting isn't always a smooth process, so don't be afraid to leave spaces where you don't know what to put in or write notes to yourself about what you could do next. If you get stuck while drafting, go back over your invention writing: You may be able to copy and paste some of it into your evolving draft, or you may need to do some additional invention to fill in details in your draft.

Writing the Opening Sentences

You could try out one or two different ways of beginning your essay — possibly from the list that follows — but do not agonize over the first sentences because you are likely to discover the best way to begin only after you've written a rough draft. Review your invention writing to see if you have already written something that would work to launch your essay. To engage your readers' interest from the start, consider the following opening strategies:

- a surprising or provocative quotation (like Toufexis)
- an anecdote illustrating the concept (like Ngo and Friedman)
- a paradox or surprising aspect of the concept (like Kluger)
- a fascinating bit of information
- a comparison or contrast
- a concrete example
- an announcement of the concept
- a forecast of the topics

A Sentence Strategy: Appositives

As you draft an essay explaining a concept, you have a lot of information to present, such as definitions of terms and credentials of experts. Appositives provide an efficient, clear way to integrate these kinds of information into your sentences. An appositive is a noun or pronoun that, along with modifiers, gives more information about another noun or pronoun. Here is an example from Ngo's concept essay (the appositive is in italics and the noun it refers to is underlined):

> Cannibalism, *the act of human beings eating human flesh* (Sagan 2), has a long history and continues to hold interest and create controversy. (par. 5)

By placing the definition in an appositive phrase right after the word it defines, this sentence locates the definition exactly where readers need it.

Writers explaining concepts rely on appositives because they serve many different purposes needed in concept essays, as the following examples demonstrate. (Again, the appositive is in italics and the noun it refers to is underlined.)

Defining a New Term

Some researchers believe hyperthymics may be at increased risk of depression or hypomania, *a mild variant of mania* (Friedman, par. 5)

The deepest foundation on which morality is built is the phenomenon of empathy, *the understanding that what hurts me would feel the same way to you.* (Kluger, par. 8)

Introducing a New Term

Each person carries in his or her mind a unique subliminal guide to the ideal partner, a *"love map."* (Toufexis, par. 17)

Behaviorists often reduce what we call empathy to a mercantile business known as *reciprocal altruism.* (Kluger, par. 9)

Giving Credentials of Experts

"Love is a natural high," observes Anthony Walsh, *author of The Science of Love: Understanding Love and Its Effects on Mind and Body.* (Toufexis, par. 10)

"He'll respond, 'No, the teacher shouldn't say that,'" says psychologist Michael Schulman, *coauthor of Bringing Up a Moral Child.* (Kluger, par. 5)

Identifying People and Things

"When I was in high school I read the Robert Browning poem 'My Last Duchess.' In it, the narrator said he killed his wife, *the duchess.* . . ." (Friedman, par. 2)

Even cynics went soft at the story of Binta Jua, *the gorilla who in 1996 rescued a 3-year-old boy who had tumbled into her zoo enclosure.* . . . (Kluger, par. 11)

Giving Examples or Specifics

Some 2,400 years ago, Hippocrates proposed that a mixture of four basic humors — *blood, phlegm, yellow bile and black bile* — determined human temperament . . . (Friedman, par. 6)

Notice that this last example uses dashes instead of commas to set off the appositive from the rest of the sentence. Although commas are more common, either punctuation will do the job. Dashes are often used if the writer wants to give the appositive more emphasis or if the appositive itself contains commas, as in this example.

For more on appositives, go to **bedfordstmartins .com/theguide** and click on Appositives.

Working with Sources:
Using Descriptive Verbs to Introduce Information

When explaining concepts, writers usually need to present information from different sources. There are many verbs writers can choose to introduce the information they quote or summarize. Here are a few examples from the concept essays in this chapter (the verbs are in italics):

> "That is one reason why it feels so horrible when we're abandoned or a lover dies," *notes* Fisher. (Toufexis, par. 13)

> In one incident, Japanese troops *were reported* to have sacrificed the Arapesh people of northeastern New Guinea for food in order to avoid death by starvation (Tuzin 63). (Ngo, par. 7)

> "This is very much an 'I feel your pain' experience," *says* Hauser. (Kluger, par. 12)

Toufexis's verb *notes*, Ngo's *were reported*, and Kluger's *says* indicate that they are not characterizing or judging their sources, but simply reporting them. Often, however, writers are more descriptive — even evaluative — when they introduce information from sources, as these examples demonstrate:

> "As long as prehistoric females were secretive about their extramarital affairs," *argues* Fisher, "they could garner extra resources, life insurance, better genes and more varied DNA for their biological futures. . . ." (Toufexis, par. 8)

> Some researchers *believe* hyperthymics may be at increased risk of depression or hypomania, a mild variant of mania. And they may have high rates of affective disorders in their closest relatives. (Friedman, par. 5)

The verbs in these examples — *argues* and *believe* — describe the particular role played by the source in explaining the concept. Verbs like *argues* emphasize that what is being reported is an interpretation that others may disagree with. Friedman chooses *believe* to designate a conclusion or speculation made by researchers.

As you refer to sources in your concept explanation, you will want to choose carefully among a wide variety of precise verbs. You may find this list of verbs helpful in selecting the right verbs to introduce your sources when you are explaining a concept: *suggests, reveals, questions, brings into focus, finds, notices, observes, emphasizes.*

Notice that Ngo tends not to introduce his sources in the body of his essay; instead, he simply integrates the information from them into his sentences, and readers can see from the parenthetical citation and the works-cited list where the information came from. Here is an example from paragraph 9 in which Ngo includes a quotation together with information he paraphrases from his source:

> The Miyanmin people observe no differences in "gender, kinship, ritual status, and bodily substance"; they eat anyone, even their own dead. In this respect, then, they practice both endocannibalism and exocannibalism; and to ensure a constant supply of human flesh for food, they raid neighboring tribes and drag their victims back to their village to be eaten (Poole 11).

This strategy of integrating source material allows Ngo to emphasize the information and downplay the source. (To learn more about Ngo's use of quoting and paraphrasing, see A Writer at Work on pp. 181–82.)

You can find more information about integrating sources into your sentences and constructing signal phrases in Chapter 24: Using Sources.

Your instructor may arrange a peer review session in class or online where you can exchange drafts with your classmates and give each other a thoughtful critical reading, pointing out what works well and suggesting ways to improve the draft. This Critical Reading Guide can also be used productively by a tutor in the writing center or by a roommate or family member. A good critical reading does three things: It lets the writer know how well the reader understands the concept explanation, praises what works best, and indicates where the draft could be improved.

1. Evaluate how effectively the concept is focused.

   Summarize: Tell the writer, in one sentence, what you understand the concept to mean.

   Praise: Give an example of something in the draft that you think will especially interest the intended readers.

   Critique: Tell the writer about any confusion or uncertainty you have about the concept's meaning. Does the focus seem too broad or too narrow for the intended readers? Can you think of a more interesting way to focus the explanation?

2. Assess how readable the explanation is.
   Look at the way the essay is organized by making a scratch outline.

   - Does the information seem to be logically divided?
   - Does the *beginning* pull readers into the essay and make them want to continue? Does it adequately forecast the direction of the essay?
   - Do *transitions* helpfully guide the reader from part to part?
   - Is the *ending* effective?

   Praise: Give an example of where the essay succeeds in being readable — for instance, in its overall organization, its use of transitions, its beginning, or its ending.

   Critique: Tell the writer where the readability could be improved. Can you suggest a better way of sequencing the information, for example? Can the use of transitions be improved, or transitions added where they are lacking? Can you suggest a better beginning or more effective ending?

3. Consider how effectively explanatory strategies are used.

   Praise: Give an example of the effective use of writing strategies such as defining, classifying or dividing, comparing and contrasting, narrating anecdotes or processes, illustrating with examples or lists of facts and details, and reporting causes and effects. Point out places where definitions succeed in conveying information clearly, and places where visuals (if visuals are present) aid in helping readers understand important concepts.

   Critique: Tell the writer where a different writing strategy might help in conveying information effectively. Point out places where definitions might be

Critical Reading Guide

Basic Features

For a printable version of this Critical Reading Guide, go to bedfordstmartins.com/ theguide.

needed or existing definitions need clarification or expansion. Suggest places where additional information is needed. Note places in the essay where the addition of visuals such as charts, graphics, or tables could help in making the concept clearer.

4. Evaluate how smoothly sources are integrated.

Praise: Give an example of the effective use of sources — a particularly well-integrated quotation, paraphrase, or summary that supports the writer's claims. Note any especially descriptive verbs used to introduce information.

Critique: Tell the writer where a quote, paraphrase, or summary could be more smoothly integrated. Suggest places where it would be better to summarize or paraphrase than to quote, or vice versa. If the list of sources used is less balanced than it should be, suggest types of sources that would strengthen it, or suggest sources that would be better left out.

5. If the writer has expressed concern about anything in the draft that you have not discussed, respond to that concern.

Making Comments Electronically Most word processing software offers features that allow you to insert comments directly into the text of someone else's document. Many readers prefer to make their comments this way because it tends to be faster than writing on hard copy and space is virtually unlimited; it also eliminates the process of deciphering handwritten comments. Where such features are not available, simply typing comments directly into a document in a contrasting color can provide the same advantages.

Revising

For an electronic version of this Troubleshooting chart, go to **bedfordstmartins.com/ theguide**.

Very likely you have already thought of ways to improve your draft, and you may even have begun to revise it. In this section is a Troubleshooting chart that may help. Before using the chart, however, it is a good idea to

- review critical reading comments from your classmates, instructor, or writing center tutor, and
- make an outline of your draft so that you can look at it analytically.

You may have made an outline before writing your draft, but after drafting you need to see what you actually wrote, not what you intended to write. You can outline the draft quickly by highlighting the basic features — focus, readability, use of explanatory strategies, and integration of sources.

Troubleshooting Your Draft

●●●● **Basic Features**

	Problem	Suggestions for Revising the Draft
A Focused Explanation	I have too much to cover. (The focus is too broad.)	☐ Narrow your concept to a specific cultural or historical context — for example, instead of "dating," try "U.S. dating conventions in the mid-20th century." ☐ Ask yourself what about the concept drew you to it. Refocus based on your initial interest. ☐ Consider what aspects of your concept would be of particular interest to your audience. Refocus accordingly. ☐ Look up your concept in your library catalog or online and browse for subtopics related to it, or sites that treat a narrowed aspect of it. ☐ If your concept comes from another course you're taking, check your textbook or lecture notes for a way to focus it.
	I don't have enough to write about. (The focus is too narrow.)	☐ Broaden your concept by adding cultural or historical comparisons and contrasts. ☐ Look up your concept in your library catalog or online and browse for larger concepts that include it. ☐ If your concept comes from another course you're taking, check your textbook or lecture notes for broader, related topics.
	My focus is not interesting to readers.	☐ Try providing more information likely to be of value and interest to your readers or consider using humor, anecdotes, or visuals to engage their interest. ☐ Ask yourself whether the focus is interesting to *you*. If it isn't, choose a different focus. If it is, ask yourself how you can communicate your enthusiasm to your readers — perhaps with anecdotes, examples, or illustrations?
A Readable Plan	The organization is not logical.	☐ Outline your material to be sure that it's divided into clear topics that are parallel conceptually and presented in a logical order. ☐ Reread your thesis statement to be sure that it clearly announces the concept and forecasts the topics in the order they appear in the essay. ☐ Look for topic sentences in each paragraph. (If you find them difficult to locate, your reader will, too.) Clarify where necessary.
	The beginning does not draw readers in.	☐ Review your opening paragraphs to be sure that you clearly introduce your concept and your focus. ☐ Try starting with an anecdote, interesting quotation, surprising aspect of the concept, concrete example, or a similar lead-in. ☐ Consider stating explicitly what makes the concept worth thinking about and how it relates to your readers' interests.

(continued)

(continued)

A Readable Plan	The essay doesn't flow smoothly from one part to the next.	☐ Outline your essay, dividing it into major parts — introduction, main topics, and conclusion. Reread the end of each major part and the beginning of the next, looking for transitions (for example, repeated words or phrases; synonyms; or rhetorical questions). If there are none, add them. ☐ Consider adding headings to make the connections among parts clearer.
	The ending falls flat.	☐ Consider ending by speculating on what the future will bring — how the concept might be redefined, for example. ☐ Consider relating the ending to the beginning — for example, by recalling an example or a comparison.
Appropriate Explanatory Strategies	The information isn't getting through to readers as clearly as it should.	☐ Consider whether you have used the best writing strategies — defining, classifying, comparing and contrasting, narrating, illustrating, describing, and explaining cause and effect — for your topic. ☐ Recheck your definitions for clarity. Be sure that you have explicitly defined any key terms your readers might not know. ☐ Consider adding explicit forecasting, transitional cues (repetition, rhetorical questions, etc.) and/or organizational markers (headings, bulleted lists, and so on).
	Readers want more information about certain aspects of the concept.	☐ Reread existing definitions and illustrations, and expand or clarify where necessary. ☐ Do additional research on your topic and cite it in your essay.
	Definitions need work.	☐ Consider providing synonyms or antonyms for terms you are defining. ☐ Consider supplementing definitions with illustrations or examples. ☐ Consider using appositives to define terms efficiently and clearly.
	Readers want visuals to help them understand certain concepts.	☐ Check whether your sources use visuals (tables, graphs, drawings, photographs, and the like) that might be appropriate for your explanation. ☐ Consider drafting your own charts, tables, or graphs or adding your own photographs or illustrations.

(continued)

(continued)

Smooth Integration of Sources	Summaries lack oomph; paraphrases are too long or too close to original source; quotations are too long or uninteresting.	☐ If a summary is too long-winded, try providing only the necessary source information and the single key idea that illuminates your topic. ☐ If a paraphrase is too long or too close to the original, try to restate it more succinctly. If you feel you're losing essential information by paraphrasing, consider using a quotation instead. ☐ If a quotation is too long, locate the essential information in it and consider excerpting that information only, using ellipses to make it flow naturally with your prose. ☐ If a quotation is uninteresting, paraphrase or summarize the information instead.
	Quotes, summary, and/or paraphrase don't flow smoothly with the rest of the essay.	☐ Reread all passages where you quote outside sources. Ask yourself whether the sentences would read smoothly if the material were entirely original, rather than quoted. If not, rewrite, using appropriate introductory or interrupting phrases. ☐ Check to be sure that you have appropriately commented on all cited material, making its relation to your own ideas absolutely clear. ☐ Consider using descriptive verbs to give your readers more information about what your source is saying and why you are referring to it.
	My list of sources is too limited.	☐ Categorize your sources by author, medium (print; electronic database; open Web; other); and type (book; journal article; magazine or newspaper article; Web site; other). Do additional research to balance your list, taking particular care that you have an adequate number of scholarly sources. ☐ If you have difficulty finding appropriate material, ask your instructor or a reference librarian for help.
	Some sources are inappropriate or not credible.	☐ Clearly identify all sources, and fully state the credentials of all cited authorities. ☐ Provide expanded or clarified accounts of research that your readers find unconvincing on grounds apart from the credibility of the source. ☐ Eliminate sources that are clearly identified and well integrated but that are not considered credible or otherwise appropriate by your instructor or other readers.

Thinking About Document Design:

Designing Surveys and Presenting Results

Effective document design is an important factor for the marketing manager who volunteers to teach fifth graders about surveys (see p. 127). Because the marketer is teaching students about surveys by having them take one, she knows that the design of the survey will be crucial to the students' understanding.

She recognizes that students need to be interested in the questionnaire and able to fill it out quickly; she also knows that it is important that they not feel intimidated by its appearance. After first drafting the questionnaire, she realizes that although the questions all fit on one page (cutting down on paper and photocopying costs), the page is very cluttered and difficult to read.

First Draft of Survey (excerpt)

1. What is your gender? _____
2. Where do you fall in terms of birth order in your family — youngest, oldest, in the middle, or only child? _____
3. How frequently are you able to watch the television programming you want to watch — all of the time, most of the time, some of the time, hardly ever, or never? _____

Before getting started on the redesign, she considers her audience — ten- and eleven-year-olds — and refers to workbooks and other print material designed for this age group. In this case, the convenience to her audience (their ability to easily read and answer the questions) outweighs the time and expense of photocopying multiple pages. She thinks that the students will be able to fill out the survey more easily if each question has more space around it.

Final Draft of Survey (excerpt)

1. I am
   - ❏ male   ❏ female
2. In my family, I am
   - ❏ the youngest child   ❏ the oldest child
   - ❏ a middle child   ❏ the only child
3. When I'm at home, I can watch the TV shows I want to watch
   - ❏ all of the time   ❏ hardly ever
   - ❏ most of the time   ❏ never
   - ❏ some of the time

The appearance of the survey is only her initial design consideration, however. After the students complete the survey, she guides the class in tabulating the survey results. Explaining that the information from the questionnaire is best presented graphically so that the viewers will understand the results, she discusses with the class which information best fits in a pie chart (in this case, aggregate data broken into percentages) and which in a bar graph (data with multiple variables). She creates the data displays using a PowerPoint program. Two of the slides are shown here.

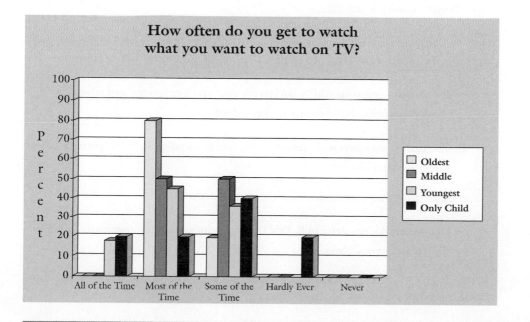

Editing and Proofreading

A Note on Grammar and Spelling Checkers
These tools can be helpful, but don't rely on them exclusively to catch errors in your text: Spelling checkers cannot catch misspellings that are themselves words, such as *to* for *too*. Grammar checkers miss some problems, sometimes give faulty advice for fixing problems, and can flag correct items as wrong. Use these tools as a second line of defense after your own (and, ideally, another reader's) proofreading/editing efforts.

Two kinds of errors occur often in concept explanations: punctuation around adjective clauses, and commas around interrupting phrases. The following guidelines will help you check your essay for these common errors.

Using Punctuation with Adjective Clauses

What Is an Adjective Clause? Adjective clauses include both a subject and a verb. They give information about a noun or a pronoun. They often begin with *who*, *which*, or *that*. Here is an example from a student essay explaining the concept of *schizophrenia*, a type of mental illness:

> It is common for schizophrenics to have delusions *that they are being persecuted.*

Because adjective clauses add information about the nouns they follow — defining, illustrating, or explaining — they can be useful in writing that explains a concept.

The Problem: Adjective clauses may or may not need to be set off with a comma or commas. To decide, first you have to determine whether the clause is essential to the meaning of the sentence. Clauses that are essential to the meaning of a sentence should not be set off with a comma; clauses that are not essential to the meaning must be set off with a comma.

How to Correct It: Mentally delete the clause. If taking out the clause does not change the basic meaning of the sentence or make it unclear, add a comma or commas.

> ▶ **Postpartum neurosis, which can last for two weeks or longer, can adversely affect a mother's ability to care for her infant.**

> ▶ **The early stage starts with memory loss, which usually causes the patient to forget recent life events.**

If the clause follows a proper noun, add a comma/commas.

> ▶ **Nanotechnologists defer to K. Eric Drexler, who speculates imaginatively about the use of nonmachines.**

If taking out the clause changes the basic meaning of the sentence or makes it unclear, do **not** add a comma or commas.

> ▶ **Seasonal affective disorders are mood disturbances, that occur with a change of season.**

> ▶ **The coaches, who do the recruiting should be disciplined.**

For practice, go to bedfordstmartins.com/ theguide/exercisecentral and click on Adjective Clauses.

Using Commas with Interrupting Phrases

What Is an Interrupting Phrase? When writers are explaining a concept, they need to supply a great deal of information. They add much of this information in phrases that interrupt the flow of a sentence, as in the following example:

> **People on the West Coast, especially in Los Angeles, have always been receptive to new ideas.**

Interrupting phrases are typically set off with commas.

The Problem: Forgetting to set off an interrupting phrase with commas can make sentences difficult to read or unclear.

How to Correct It: Add a comma on either side of an interrupting phrase.

▶ **People on the West Cost ˏ especially in Los Angeles ˏ have always been receptive to new ideas.**

▶ **Alzheimer's disease ˏ named after the German neuropathologist Alois Alzheimer ˏ is a chronic degenerative illness.**

▶ **These examples ˏ though simple ˏ present equations in terms of tangible objects.**

For practice, go to **bedfordstmartins.com/ theguide/exercisecentral** and click on Interrupting Phrases.

A Writer at Work

Linh Kieu Ngo's Use of Sources

This section describes how student writer Linh Kieu Ngo selected information from a source and integrated it into one part of his essay on cannibalism.

One paragraph from Ngo's essay illustrates a sound strategy for integrating sources into your essay, relying on them fully — as you nearly always must do in explanatory writing — and yet making them your own. Here is paragraph 9 from Ngo's essay (the five sentences are numbered for ease of reference):

(1) In the Miyanmin society of the west Sepik interior of Papua, New Guinea, villagers do not value human life over that of pigs or marsupials because human flesh is part of their normal diet (Poole 7). (2) The Miyanmin people observe no differences in "gender, kinship, ritual status, and bodily substance"; they eat anyone, even their own dead. (3) In this respect, then, they practice both endocannibalism and exocannibalism; and to ensure a constant supply of human flesh for food, they raid neighboring tribes and drag their victims back to their village to be eaten (Poole 11). (4) Perhaps, in the history of this society, there was at one time a shortage of wild game to be hunted for food, and because people were more plentiful than fish, deer, rabbits, pigs, or cows, survival cannibalism was adopted as

a last resort. (5) Then, as their culture developed, the Miyanmin may have retained the practice of dietary cannibalism, which has endured as a part of their culture.

Most of the information in this paragraph comes from a twenty-six-page research report by an anthropologist, Fitz John Porter Poole. Given Ngo's purpose in this paragraph — to illustrate some forms of dietary cannibalism — he selects only a limited amount of information from small sections of text on two different pages of the Poole report. Notice first that Ngo quotes only once, in sentence 2, using a phrase that emphasizes what indiscriminate dietary cannibals the Miyanmin people are.

Otherwise, Ngo paraphrases information from Poole. (When you **paraphrase**, you construct your own sentences and phrases but rely necessarily on the key words in your source.) For example, in his sentence 1, Ngo paraphrases this sentence: "For Miyanmin, they claim, humans do indeed become food in an ordinary sense and are seen as comparable to pigs and marsupials." Toward the end of sentence 3, Ngo again paraphrases Poole. By contrast, Ngo's sentences 4 and 5 seem to be his own speculations about the possible origins of Miyanmin cannibalism because this information does not appear in Poole.

The paragraph illustrates a careful balance between a writer's ideas and information gleaned from sources. Ngo is careful not to let the sources take over the explanation. The paragraph also illustrates judicious use of quotations and paraphrases. Ngo avoids stringing quotes together to illustrate an explanation.

Thinking Critically About What You Have Learned

In this chapter, you have learned a great deal about this genre from reading several concept explanations and writing one of your own. To consolidate your learning, it is helpful to think **metacognitively** — that is, to reflect not only on what you learned but on how you learned it. Following are two brief activities your instructor may ask you to do.

Reflecting on Your Writing

Your instructor may ask you to turn in with your essay and process materials a brief metacognitive essay or letter reflecting on what you have learned about writing your concept explanation. Choose among the following invention activities those that seem most productive for you:

- Explain how your purpose and audience — what you wanted your readers to learn from reading your concept explanation — influenced *one* of your decisions as a writer, such as how you focused the concept, how you organized your explanation, how you used writing strategies to convey information, or how you integrated sources into your essay.

- Discuss what you learned about yourself as a writer in the process of writing this particular essay. For example, what part of the process did you find most challenging, or did you try something new like getting a critical reading of your draft or outlining your draft in order to revise it?

- If you were to give advice to a friend who was about to write a concept explanation, what would you say?

- Which of the readings in this chapter influenced your essay? Explain the influence, citing specific examples from your essay and the reading.

- If you got good advice from a critical reader, explain exactly how the person helped you — perhaps by questioning your definitions, your use of visuals, the way you began or ended your essay, or the kinds of sources you used.

Considering the Social Dimensions: Concept Explanations and the Nature of Knowledge

Concepts are the building blocks of knowledge, essential to its creation and acquisition. We use concepts to name and organize ideas and information in areas as diverse as snowboarding and psychiatry. Academic disciplines and most professions are heavily concept-based, enabling newcomers to be introduced efficiently, if abstractly, to the basic knowledge they need to begin learning. As you have learned from your reading, research, and writing for this chapter, writers explaining concepts present knowledge as established and uncontested. They presume to be unbiased and objective, and they assume that readers will not doubt or challenge the truth or the value of the knowledge they present. This stance encourages readers to feel confident about the validity of the explanation. However, explanatory writing should not always be accepted at face value.

Textbooks and reference materials, in particular, sometimes present a limited view of knowledge in an academic discipline. Because introductory textbooks must be highly selective, they necessarily leave out certain sources of information and types of knowledge.

1. *Consider the claim that concept explanations attempt to present their information as uncontested truths.* Identify a reading in this chapter that particularly seems to support this claim, and then think about how it does so. Do the same for a chapter or section in a textbook you are reading for another course.

2. *Reflect on how concept explanations present established knowledge.* How do you think knowledge gets established in academic disciplines such as biology, psychology, and history? How might the prominent researchers and professors in a discipline go about deciding what is to be considered established knowledge for now? How might they decide when that established knowledge needs to be revised? If possible, ask these questions of a professor in a subject you are studying.

3. *Write a page or two explaining your initial assumptions about the knowledge or information you presented about a concept in your essay.* When you were doing research on the concept, did you discover that some of the information was being challenged by experts? Or did the body of knowledge seem settled and established? Did you at any point think that your readers might question any of the information you were presenting? How did you decide what information might seem new or even surprising to readers? Did you feel comfortable in your roles as the selector and giver of knowledge?

5

Finding Common Ground

IN COLLEGE COURSES For a course in science research ethics, a biology major writes a paper on the debate over stem cell research. She begins with a surprising quote: "Catholic and evangelical Christian leaders are welcoming the National Institute of Health's (NIH's) new draft guidelines for federal financing of embryonic stem cell research, in recognition of their common interest in establishing strong ethical parameters in scientific research." She explains that groups with seemingly irreconcilable views on these issues had found common ground in the NIH's guidelines, which provide that research be limited to stem cells from embryos that would have been destroyed because they are no longer needed for in vitro fertilization. In addition, the rules bar research on embryos created solely for stem cell research and require donors to give their consent.

The student points out that the NIH guidelines represent a compromise and that not everyone is happy. Some scientists argue that they will be a serious impediment because developing matched organs for transplantation would only be possible if banned techniques like therapeutic cloning or somatic cell nuclear transfer were allowed. Opponents of stem cell research such as the National Right to Life Committee make a slippery slope counterargument, claiming that the new guidelines are "part of an incremental strategy to desensitize the public to the concept of killing human embryos for research purposes." The student concludes by pointing out that, despite continuing points of disagreement, support for the guidelines among parties traditionally opposed to such research represents a step toward an eventual resolution of the issue.

IN THE COMMUNITY The chair of the School Uniform Committee of a middle school's Parent Teacher Association (PTA) writes an e-mail to the members reporting on a recent meeting about whether to adopt school uniforms. She begins by summarizing outside research undertaken by the committee: anecdotal information, primarily from school administrators, supports the claim that school uniforms can have a positive effect on discipline, achievement, and safety; however, studies by sociologist David Brunsma, among others, have found no positive correlation between uniforms and school safety or academic achievement.

The committee chair then presents the arguments made at the meeting by those on both sides of the issue. She reports that those who support the adoption of uniforms argued that they encourage school spirit, eliminate unnecessary social tensions by obscuring differences in socioeconomic background, and forestall gang violence by eliminating the use of gang colors. Those opposed agreed that reducing class distinctions and forestalling gang violence are worthy goals, but expressed concern that school uniforms stifle individuality and are costly and wasteful because they would not be worn outside of school.

Proponents recommended a compromise — to substitute ordinary casual clothes (such as polo shirts and jeans) for expensive formal uniforms. Although this suggestion has appeal to some people, a few voiced the concern that wealthy students would still wear designer jeans. At the conclusion of the meeting, a subcommittee was formed to make specific recommendations for a dress code that would exclude gang colors and achieve a desirable degree of uniformity without incurring undue expense or inviting displays of privilege.

IN THE WORKPLACE Major population growth and haphazard development in a previously rural area in southwest Washington State threaten a watershed that supplies several local communities and supports endangered salmon species. Longtime residents, including Native Americans who live on tribal land adjacent to areas slated for development; developers; and county planning officials come together to discuss a plan for sustainable growth in the area. They agree to hire a consulting firm to write a report that analyzes the positions of the stakeholders and outlines a plan for development.

Whereas the residents' interest is in maintaining quality of life and protecting the environment, the developers want access to building sites, and the county officials need to build infrastructure to support the growing population. The consulting firm analyzes these competing needs and recommends changes to developers' original proposals, calling for higher-density development that would be situated further from tribal lands and from the endangered watershed but at the same time cost less to build and support with transportation and utilities. The plan also channels money from the economic growth enabled by development to environmental upkeep.

The U.S. Environmental Protection Agency (EPA) nominates the plan for a National Award in Smart Growth Achievement. The consulting firm and the EPA co-present a session on the project for the 2009 New Partners for Smart Growth Conference. While the presenters encounter some skepticism, many audience members leave the presentation believing that public-private partnerships for sustainable growth can work.

No one is exempt from the call to find common ground.
— Barack Obama, *The Audacity of Hope*

A debate is raging in Congress, on the airwaves, and in the blogosphere over the president's proposals for health-care reform. Many citizens are listening in, and some are participating in the discussion. Mostly, those who do tune in witness people with different points of view arguing, sometimes vehemently, but seldom listening to what others are saying. What is too often lacking is a fair and dispassionate overview of the issue, a careful sorting out of the main arguments on various sides, and ideas about where agreement might be possible — in other words, what is lacking is the search for common ground. In this chapter, you will be reading essays that seek common ground and, as you work through the chapter, you will be writing an essay of your own in which you analyze arguments on a controversial issue and suggest where they might find common ground.

Controversial issues are inevitable in any society, and many people shy away from entering public debate because it tends to be loud, raucous, and confusing. Reasoned argument, however, is the lifeblood of a democracy. Free and open discussion offers us insight into why people favor certain policies and resist others, and it helps us establish and refine informed positions of our own. Sometimes the disagreement is local and relatively trivial — whether, for example, traffic should flow two ways or one way on a busy city street. Sometimes the controversy has broader and longer-term implications — for example, whether to build a new campus for a state university system. Sometimes the debate takes on global significance — as, for example, in the question of whether to permit torture as a means of interrogation.

Essays that analyze arguments to find common ground aim to inform and educate readers. To write a common ground essay, you need to avoid thinking of argument as a zero-sum game in which one side wins and the other sides lose. Where values and concerns are shared, where interests and priorities overlap, win-win thinking takes the place of zero-sum thinking, and it becomes possible to find common ground.

For example, the opening scenario about stem cell research suggests that people may be able to come together over certain shared values and concerns even when they continue to disagree on some fundamental aspects of the issue. As long as the stem cells come from embryos that would be destroyed anyway, many pro-life advocates seem willing to accept their use for research designed to save human lives devastated by disease. The shared value of human life together with the common interest in curing diseases like Alzheimer's and Parkinson's make agreement possible.

Similarly, the second scenario about school uniforms suggests that everyone at the PTA meeting agrees that instituting some policies on clothing makes sense; they share concerns about gang-related violence and about the negative effects of obvious socioeconomic differences among students. They have not yet figured out how to accomplish the shared goal of making students' lives safer and more harmonious, but they have agreed to try. Finding common ground is often just the beginning of the process, but it is a crucial and challenging first step.

Learning to write a clear and unbiased explanation of points of agreement and disagreement on a controversial issue can be especially helpful when you are embarking on a new research project and may be a required part of a prospectus or research proposal. Obviously, honing your ability to analyze arguments, understand differences, and find potential areas of agreement can also be helpful personally and professionally.

In this chapter, you will read student essays analyzing different positions on controversial issues: whether steroids should be banned from baseball, whether the United States should use torture as a means of interrogation, and whether the No Child Left Behind Act needs to be changed to improve public education. These readings illustrate the basic features and strategies writers typically use when analyzing opposing positions to find common ground among them. The questions and activities following the readings will help you consider what is particular to one writer's approach and what strategies you might want to try out in writing your own common ground essay.

The Guide to Writing that follows the readings will support you as you compose your own essay, showing you ways to use the basic features of the genre to write a probing and creative analysis of opposing positions on an issue that interests you.

Finally, the Appendix to this chapter offers seven readings taking positions on two different issues: torture and same-sex marriage. (Additional essays on different topics can be found at bedfordstmartins.com/theguide.) You might want to use the arguments presented in these readings as the basis of the essay you write for this chapter.

A Collaborative Activity: Practice Finding Common Ground

To get a sense of what is involved in trying to find common ground on a controversial issue, get together with two or three other students, and explore the possibilities for agreement among those who argue about the issue.

Part 1. Select an issue with which you are familiar. Here are a few possibilities to consider:

- Should there be a community service requirement for graduation from college?
- Should sororities and fraternities be banned from college campuses?
- Should college athletes be paid?
- Should intelligent design be taught in science classes as an alternative theory to evolution?
- Should oil drilling in places like the Arctic National Wildlife Refuge be allowed?
- Should private cars be taxed to support mass transit?
- Should the drinking age be lowered?
- Should marijuana be legalized?

- Identify the positions people have taken on the issue and the arguments they typically put forward to support their position. (You do not have to agree or disagree; you simply have to recall what others have said or written on the issue. Doing a quick Google search could be helpful here, though it would be best at this point to stick to arguments with which you are familiar.)

- Identify a couple of shared concerns, needs, priorities, values, or beliefs that you think could potentially be the basis for agreement among those who have taken a position on the issue.

Part 2. Discuss what you learned about analyzing arguments on a controversial issue and trying to find possible common ground.

- How would you try to convince people who argue about this particular issue that the potential points of agreement you have identified could be the basis for a productive discussion toward building common ground?
- Since debates over controversial issues normally emphasize points of disagreement rather than potential points of agreement, how did you go about finding areas of possible agreement?

Reading Essays That Seek Common Ground

Basic Features

Basic Features

As you read essays that analyze opposing positions to find common ground, you will see how different authors incorporate the basic features of the genre.

● An Informative Introduction to the Issue and Opposing Positions

Read first to see how the writer presents the issue. Look, for example, at whether the writer assumes that readers are already well informed or need background information, and whether they will be interested in the issue or will need to have their interest piqued. To inform and interest readers, writers may provide material such as the following:

- a political or historical context
- facts or statistics
- examples or anecdotes
- quotations from authorities

Consider also how the writer introduces the opposing positions and their authors. The writer usually provides the following information:

- the authors' names
- their professional affiliation or credentials
- the titles of the essays that are being analyzed

- where and when the essays were originally published or posted
- who sponsored the original publication

● A Probing Analysis

Read next to see how the writer analyzes the arguments. Keep in mind that the purpose of the common ground essay is not primarily to *summarize* the arguments, but to *analyze* them in order to discover ways of bridging significant differences.

*Consider whether the writer's treatment of the arguments is both **analytical** and **constructive*** — that is, whether it examines the arguments advanced by each side to understand the points of disagreement as well as the points of potential agreement (analytical) and whether it suggests ways to build common ground on shared values and concerns, needs and interests (constructive).

Think, too, about what the writer has chosen to focus on and what has been left out. Because of time and space constraints, essays finding common ground cannot be exhaustive: writers must select only two or three points of comparison, among which the following are perhaps most common:

- values (for example, freedom, justice, equality)
- moral, ethical, or religious principles (for example, the sense of right and wrong, "do unto others," social responsibility, stewardship of the natural environment)
- ideology (a system of ideas and ideals — for example, the ideas in the Declaration of Independence that everyone is created equal and has the right to life, liberty, and the pursuit of happiness)
- needs and interests (for example, food, shelter, work, respect, privacy, choice)
- fears and concerns (for example, regarding safety, socioeconomic status, power)
- priorities or agendas about what is most important or urgent (for example, whether law and order is more important than securing justice and equality)

In reading the essay, try to decide whether the writer has selected points of comparison that are likely to be seen by readers as significant.

Look also at how the writer tries to frame (or reframe) the issue. A sincere attempt at finding common ground will frame the issue so that it can be perceived anew as potentially unifying and productive. For example, the opening scenario about stem cell research indicates how the issue was productively reframed in terms of the ethics of scientific research — an area where interests and concerns overlap — rather than as a pro-life/pro-choice issue, where values and priorities seem irreconcilable. Similarly, the scenario about school uniforms shows how people constructively framed the issue as an attempt to reduce tensions among students — a shared priority on which agreement could be forged. Finally, the scenario about sustainable development shows how some individuals are seeking a way out of the "either (we make money) or (we do good in the community)" binary thinking traditionally assumed by many to be the principle by which capitalism functions.

● A Fair and Impartial Presentation

Read carefully to see whether the writer comes across as fair and unbiased. A common ground essay is not a passive summary merely repeating what others have said. It is a probing examination seeking to understand not only on what points people agree and disagree, but *why* they agree and disagree and *how* they might come to an agreement on at least some points. Therefore, it is necessary for the writer to be perceived as unbiased, equitable, even impartial. To win and hold readers' confidence, the writer normally does the following:

- refrains from taking a position on the issue
- represents the opposing sides fairly and accurately
- avoids judging either side's arguments
- gives roughly equal attention to the opposing viewpoints

● A Readable Plan

Finally, read to see how the writer provides a readable plan by dividing the essay into clearly distinguishable points of agreement and disagreement. Examine the strategies the writer uses to make the essay easy to follow, such as:

- providing a clear thesis and forecasting statement
- using topic sentences for paragraphs or groups of paragraphs
- labeling the positions consistently (for example, with the authors' last names)
- repeating key words to identify the points of agreement and disagreement
- signaling similarities and differences with clear comparative transitional words and phrases

Purpose and Audience

*As you read common ground essays, ask yourself what seems to be the writer's **purpose**.* For example, does the writer seem to be writing for any of the following reasons:

- to inform readers about a controversial issue
- to explain the kinds of arguments particular writers have made and possibly the kinds of arguments that are typically made on the issue
- to clarify different points of view on the issue
- to examine ways in which people already agree on the issue
- to suggest where there may be potential for significant common ground between different points of view

*As you read, also try to decide what the writer assumes about the **audience**.* For example, does the writer

- expect the readers to be generally well informed but not knowledgeable about this particular issue;
- assume the readers may not be especially interested in the issue;
- anticipate readers will be unfamiliar with the issue, so that the essay will serve as an introduction;
- anticipate readers will know something about the arguments typically made on the issue, so that the essay may open new possibilities; or
- expect some readers will already have strong views about the issue?

Readings

JEREMY BERNARD is an avid baseball fan who has closely followed the many steroid scandals. He asked his instructor if he could write about the issue and use as his two main texts George Mitchell's report and a Web site written in response to it. Even though these two texts are too long and complex to cover in depth, his instructor gave Bernard permission to use them if he met two criteria: he had to make sure his essay stayed within the page limit and he had to refrain from stating his own position on the issue. His instructor gave him the opportunity to write his next essay, a position paper, on the steroids issue. Moreover, he was told — as was the rest of the class — that he could use the research he did for the common ground essay for his position essay. He could even quote from his common ground essay in his position paper so long as he cited it correctly.

Bernard jumped at the chance to write two essays on baseball. As you read this essay, consider whether Bernard successfully kept his opinion to himself. (Bernard's sources are available online at **bedfordstmartins.com/theguide.**)

◼◼◼⬡
Basic Features

- An Informative Introduction
- A Probing Analysis
- A Fair and Impartial Presentation
- A Readable Plan

Lost Innocence

Jeremy Bernard

In a nation committed to better living through chemistry — where Viagra-enabled men pursue silicone-contoured women — the national pastime has a problem of illicit chemical enhancement.

— George Will

1   Many American writers have waxed poetic about baseball. Walt Whitman, the great nineteenth-century poet, sang its praises: "It's our game — the American game." "More than anything," remarked Pete Hamill, the twentieth-century journalist and novelist,

Why does Bernard begin with the epigraph and quotes by Whitman and Hamill?

"it's a game of innocence" (Andrijeski). The age of innocence in baseball seems to have ended in the 1990s when "the Steroid Era" began and players from Mark McGwire to Roger Clemmons, Barry Bonds, and Alex Rodriguez were identified as using performance enhancing drugs (PEDs). Such substances as anabolic steroids and human growth hormone are a concern in other sports as well, but the steroid scandal has been especially painful in baseball, possibly because of its special status as America's national pastime.

In 2006, the concern was so great that George Mitchell, the former Senate Majority Leader and peace negotiator, was enlisted to investigate. "The minority of players who used [performance enhancing] substances were wrong," the *Mitchell Report* concludes. "They violated federal law and baseball policy, and they distorted the fairness of competition by trying to gain an unfair advantage over the majority of players who followed the law and the rules" (310).

An opposing position has been presented by respected baseball authority Eric Walker on his Web site, *Steroids, Other "Drugs," and Baseball*. Walker concedes that using PEDs is against the law and against the rules of baseball. But he argues that the real issue is whether PEDs ought to be "illegal and banned" by Major League Baseball (MLB). He addresses many of Mitchell's arguments, but I will focus here on two of Mitchell's main reasons supporting the ban on PEDs: the health risk and fairness.

Should PEDs Be Banned from Baseball Because They Constitute a Significant Health Risk?

The health risks of using PEDs would seem to be a question of fact on which everyone should be able to agree. Mitchell and Walker do agree, but not on everything. They agree that the medical evidence is inconclusive. More importantly, they agree that there is a risk of side effects from PEDs. They agree that the medical risks to adolescents are, as Walker puts it, "substantial and potentially grave." But they disagree on the significance of the risks to adults, and they disagree on who should decide whether the risks are worth taking.

Mitchell and Walker consider the medical evidence for a variety of PEDs. They each cite reputable scientists and research studies. While Walker concludes that "PEDs are by no means guaranteed harmless," he argues that the side effects tend to be mild and reversible. Mitchell takes a more negative view, arguing that there is "sufficient data to conclude that there is an association between steroid abuse and significant adverse side effects" (6). Nevertheless, it is notable that when discussing each of the possible side effects, he is careful to use hedging words like *can* and *may* and to acknowledge that clinical trial data is limited. So it's possible that Mitchell and Walker are closer on the health risks than their arguments suggest.

Margin notes:

Why is this information worth presenting to readers?

How does Bernard frame the debate in pars. 2 and 3? How fair does he seem?

Skim the essay to see how Bernard uses these key terms to forecast his main points.

How do the repeated words and sentence structure help readers understand the two positions?

Where does Bernard choose to quote and paraphrase? Are these choices appropriate?

What do these highlighted transitions signal?

Paragraph numbers: 2, 3, 4, 5

6   However, Mitchell and Walker seem to be miles apart when it comes to the question of who should decide whether the risks are worth taking. Walker argues that adults ought to have the responsibility to decide for themselves. To support this ethical argument, Walker cites authorities such as Dr. Norman Fost, Director of the Program in Medical Ethics at the University of Wisconsin. Fost asserts in "Steroid Hysteria: Unpacking the Claims" that "even if steroids did have . . . dire effects, it wouldn't follow that a competent adult should be prohibited from assuming those risks in exchange for the possible benefits. We allow adults to do things that are far riskier than even the most extreme claims about steroids, such as race car driving, and even playing football."

How does citing Fost get at a potential basis for agreement between Walker and Mitchell?

7   Although Mitchell does not address this ethical question directly, he clearly thinks Major League Baseball should make the decision for the players by banning PEDs. While Mitchell expresses other ethical concerns (discussed in the sections below), he seems not to have considered the ethics of who should decide whether the risks are worth taking. Perhaps he and Walker would be able to find common ground if they discussed this question directly and if the players themselves made their opinions known.

How does Bernard avoid taking a position here?

Should PEDs Be Banned from Baseball Because They Give an Unfair Advantage to Athletes Willing to Take the Risk?

How do the headings help you as a reader?

8   You'd think anyone interested in sports would value fairness. But fairness turns out to be rather complicated, at least for Walker. For Mitchell, it's pretty straightforward. As I explained earlier, Mitchell claims performance enhancing substances are wrong simply because they give some players an "unfair advantage" over those who play by the rules (310). Walker concedes this point. In fact, he says "that is why PEDs are banned."

How effectively does Bernard transition to and introduce his second point?

9   However, Walker disagrees with Mitchell's way of defining "a level playing field" as one where "success and advancement . . . is the result of ability and hard work" (Mitchell 5). According to Walker, Mitchell makes a false distinction between what is natural and unnatural. Whereas certain aids to performance — such as better bats, chemical-filled drinks like Gatorade, Tommy John and Lasik surgery — are considered natural and therefore allowable, other aids — particularly PEDs — are deemed unnatural and banned. To support his argument, Walker cites Fost again. "Here's what Fost wrote in 'Steroid Hysteria': 'There is no coherent argument to support the view that enhancing performance is unfair. If it were, we should ban coaching and training. Competition can be unfair if there is unequal access to such enhancements.'"

How do the highlighted transitions help you as a reader?

10   In other words, unequal access is the key to the unfairness argument. On this point, Mitchell and Walker seem to agree. The argument is really about making sure that there is a level playing field. Mitchell puts his finger on it when he explains that

Why does Bernard indent this quotation?

> the illegal use of these substances by some players is unfair to the majority of players who do not use them. These players have a right to expect a level playing field where success and advancement to the major leagues is the result of ability and hard work. They should not be forced to choose between joining the ranks of those who illegally use these substances or falling short of their ambition to succeed at the major league level. (5)

Ethicists call this a coercion argument. "Steroids are coercive," Fost explains, because "if your opponents use them, you have to" as well or you risk losing. Walker has a simple solution: allow PEDs to be "equally available to any who might want them." He argues that there are lots of requirements or expectations that athletes regularly make choices about. He sees "no logical or ethical distinction between — just for example — killer workouts and PEDs." Therefore, Walker concludes, each athlete has to decide for him- or herself what's "appropriate or necessary."

How effectively does Bernard analyze the argument about fairness?

Mitchell, on the other hand, assumes it should be the responsibility of Major League Baseball to set rules that protect the athletes and protect the sport. He acknowledges that players "are responsible for their actions" (311). But he insists that "Commissioners, club officials, the Players Association, and players" should share "responsibility for the steroids era" and "should join in" the "effort to bring the era of steroids and human growth hormone to an end" (311).   11

How effective is this way of ending the essay?

By saying that everyone involved in Major League Baseball shares some responsibility for its future well being, Mitchell appears also to be reaching out to critics like Walker who share a common love of the sport. It seems that they may not really be that far apart after all.   12

Works Cited

Andrijeski, Peter. *Pete's Baseball Quotes*. Peter Andrijeski, n. d. Web. 24 Apr. 2009.

Fost, Norman. "Steroid Hysteria: Unpacking the Claims." *Virtual Mentor* 7.11 (Nov. 2005): n. pag. Web. 24 Apr. 2009.

Mitchell, George J. *Report to the Commissioner of Baseball of an Independent Investigation into the Illegal Use of Steroids and Other Performance Enhancing Substances by Players in Major League Baseball*. Office of the Commissioner of Baseball, 2007. Web. 25 Apr. 2009.

Walker, Eric. *Steroids, Other "Drugs," and Baseball*. The Owlcroft Company, 2008. Web. 23 Apr. 2009.

Will, George. "George Will Quotes." *The Baseball Almanac*. Baseball Almanac, 2009. Web. 25 Apr. 2009.

What can you learn from these citations for your own essay?

MELISSA MAE asked her instructor if she could analyze the controversy about the U.S. government's treatment of detainees under the Bush administration. She read two published essays on torture recommended by her instructor, one coauthored by law professor Mirko Bagaric and law lecturer Julie Clarke (reprinted in this chapter on pp. 233–34), the other by retired Army chaplain Kermit D. Johnson (pp. 235–38). Mae decided to focus her essay more on their commonalities than on the obvious differences between them.

As you read Mae's essay, consider how well she succeeds in finding areas of potential common ground between the authors she is analyzing.

Laying Claim to a Higher Morality
Melissa Mae

1   In 2004, when the abuse of detainees at Abu Ghraib became known, many Americans became concerned that the government was using torture as part of its interrogation of war-on-terror detainees. Although the government denied a torture program existed, we now know that the Bush Administration did order what they called "enhanced interrogation techniques" such as waterboarding and sleep deprivation. The debate over whether these techniques constitute torture continues today.

2   In 2005 and 2006, when Kermit D. Johnson wrote "Inhuman Behavior" and Mirko Bagaric and Julie Clarke wrote "A Case for Torture," this debate was just heating up. Bagaric and Clarke, professor and lecturer, respectively, in the law faculty at Australia's Deakin University, argued that torture is necessary in extreme circumstances to save innocent lives. Major Johnson, a retired Army chaplain, wrote that torture should never be used for any reason whatsoever. Although their positions appear to be diametrically opposed, some common ground exists, because the authors of both essays share a goal — the preservation of human life — as well as a belief in the importance of morality.

3   The authors of both essays present their positions on torture as the surest way to save lives. Bagaric and Clarke write specifically about the lives of innocent victims threatened by hostage-takers or terrorists and claim that the use of torture in such cases to forestall the loss of innocent life is "universally accepted" as "self-defense." Whereas Bagaric and Clarke think saving lives justifies torture, however, Johnson believes renouncing torture saves lives. Johnson asserts: "A clear-cut repudiation of torture or abuse is . . . essential to the safety of the troops" (26), who need to be able to "claim the full protection of the Geneva Conventions . . . when they are captured, in this or any war" (27).

This underlying shared value — human life is precious — represents one important aspect of common ground between the two positions. In addition to this, however, the authors of both essays agree that torture is ultimately a moral issue, and that morality is worth arguing about. For Bagaric and Clarke, torture is morally defensible under certain, extreme circumstances when it "is the only means, due to the immediacy of the situation, to save the life of an innocent person"; in effect, Bagaric and Clarke argue that the end justifies the means. Johnson argues against this common claim, writing that "whenever we torture or mistreat prisoners, we are capitulating morally to the enemy — in fact, adopting the terrorist ethic that the end justifies the means" (26). Bagaric and Clarke, in their turn, anticipate Johnson's argument and refute it by arguing that those who believe (as Johnson does) that "torture is always wrong" are "misguided." Bagaric and Clarke label Johnson's kind of thinking "absolutist," and claim it is a "distorted" moral judgment.

It is not surprising that, as a chaplain, Johnson would adopt a religious perspective on morality. Likewise, it should not be surprising that, as faculty at a law school, Bagaric and Clarke would take a more pragmatic and legalistic perspective. It is hard to imagine how they could bridge their differences when their moral perspectives are so different, but perhaps the answer lies in the real-world application of their principles.

The authors of essays refer to the kind of situation typically raised when a justification for torture is debated: Bagaric and Clarke call it "the hostage scenario," and Johnson refers to it as the "scenario about a ticking time bomb" (26). As the Parents

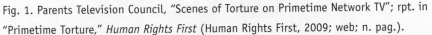

Fig. 1. Parents Television Council, "Scenes of Torture on Primetime Network TV"; rpt. in "Primetime Torture," *Human Rights First* (Human Rights First, 2009; web; n. pag.).

Television Council has demonstrated (see Figure 1), scenes of torture dominated television in the period the authors were writing about, and may have had a profound influence on the persuasive power of the scenario.

7   Johnson rejects the scenario outright as an unrealistic "Hollywood drama" (26). Bagaric and Clarke's take on it is somewhat more complicated. First, Bagaric and Clarke ask the rhetorical question: "Will a real-life situation actually occur where the only option is between torturing a wrongdoer or saving an innocent person?" They initially answer, "Perhaps not." Then, however, they offer the real-life example of Douglas Wood, a 63-year-old engineer taken hostage in Iraq and held for six weeks until he was rescued by U.S. and Iraqi soldiers.

8   At first glance, they seem to offer this example to refute Johnson's claim that such scenarios don't occur in real life. However, a news report about the rescue of Wood published in the *Age*, where Bagaric and Clarke's essay was also published, says that the soldiers "effectively 'stumbled across Wood' during a 'routine' raid on a suspected insurgent weapons cache" ("Firefight"). The report's wording suggests that the Wood example does not really fit the Hollywood-style hostage scenario; Wood's rescuers appear to have acted on information they got from ordinary informants rather than through torture.

9   By using this example, rather than one that fits the ticking time bomb scenario, Bagaric and Clarke seem to be conceding that such scenarios are exceedingly rare. Indeed, they appear to prepare the way for a potentially productive common-ground-building discussion when they conclude: "Even if a real-life situation where torture is justifiable does not eventuate, the above argument in favour of torture in limited circumstances needs to be made because it will encourage the community to think more carefully about moral judgments. . . ."

10   Although Bagaric and Clarke continue to take a situational view of torture (considering the morality of an act in light of its particular situation) and Johnson does not waver in seeing torture in terms of moral absolutes, a discussion about real-world applications of their principles could allow them to find common ground. Because they all value the preservation of life, they already have a basis for mutual respect and might be motivated to work together to find ways of acting for the greatest good — to "lay claim to a higher morality" (26).

Works Cited

Bagaric, Mirko, and Julie Clarke. "A Case for Torture." *theage.com.au*. The Age, 17 May 2005. Web. 1 May 2009.

"Firefight as Wood Rescued." *theage.com.au*. The Age, 16 June 2005. Web. 2 May 2009.

Johnson, Kermit D. "Inhuman Behavior: A Chaplain's View of Torture." *Christian Century* 18 Apr. 2006: 26–27. *Academic Search Premier*. Web. 2 May 2009.

**LEARN ABOUT
MAE'S
WRITING PROCESS**

To see how Melissa Mae developed her essay, take a look at the Writer at Work section on pp. 232–41, which shows her progress in moving from close analysis of each position essay to a draft of her finished paper.

**MAKING
CONNECTIONS:
HOLLYWOOD AND
THE TICKING TIME
BOMB SCENARIO**

The post-9/11 television series *24* brought the ticking time bomb scenario into our homes on a weekly basis. Other popular programs such as *Lost* and *Law & Order*, as well as many films, also sometimes show scenes of torture.

In her essay, Mae includes a bar graph she found on the Web site *Human Rights First* to show how prevalent scenes of torture became during the period her authors are writing about, and she asks us to think about whether the hostage and ticking time bomb scenarios so often used to justify torture are Hollywood dramas or real-life situations.

With two or three other students, discuss your views about torture. Begin by sharing memories of films and television shows you have seen where someone is tortured. Was the torturer the "good guy" or the "bad guy"? Was torture quick and effective? Was it depicted as justifiable, even patriotic?

Then, consider the following questions:

- Have your views on torture been influenced by the way torture has been portrayed on television and in film?

- How do you think torture should be portrayed, if at all?

**ANALYZING
WRITING
STRATEGIES**

■ ■ ■ ◆
Basic Features

● **An Informative Introduction to the Issue and Opposing Positions** ▭▭

Common ground essays typically situate the issue in time, as Jeremy Bernard does when he locates the end of the "age of innocence" and the beginning of "the Steroid Era" (par. 1) in the 1990s and suggests that it came to a head in 2006 with the *Mitchell Report*. To engage readers' interest, Bernard drops the names of star players who were involved in the steroid scandals — sluggers Mark McGwire and Barry Bonds, award-winning pitcher Roger Clemens, and Alex Rodriguez, considered one of the best all-around players. Baseball fans — indeed anyone interested in sports celebrities — would be likely to recognize these names and want to know more about the controversy surrounding them.

To analyze how Melissa Mae introduces her issue and opposing positions, try the following:

- Reread paragraph 1 to see how Mae situates the issue in time and tries to engage readers' interest. Why do you think she chose to mention Abu Ghraib? What, if anything, do you know about it?

- Look also at how she introduces the two essays she analyzes. Underline the information she gives about each author in paragraph 2, and then skim paragraph 5 where she refers again to their backgrounds. How does Mae use the information to introduce the authors and also to help readers understand their different points of view?

■ Write a few sentences explaining how Mae introduces the issue and the opposing positions.

● A Probing Analysis

In analyzing an argument and attempting to find common ground, writers usually focus on just a few important areas of disagreement. Doing so gives them the space to unpack the arguments and identify underlying values and interests that could be used to bridge differences.

In his essay about the baseball steroid controversy, for example, Jeremy Bernard addresses two points of disagreement: health risks and fairness. He discovers that Walker and Mitchell basically agree on the risk of adverse side effects from using performance-enhancing drugs like steroids. But his analysis leads Bernard to pinpoint where they disagree, namely on the ethical question of responsibility: Should professional athletes make their own decisions about health risks, or should Major League Baseball decide for them? Clarifying the argument in this way may not resolve the disagreement, but it reframes the issue in a way that could lead to fruitful discussion.

To examine Mae's analysis of the argument about torture, try the following:

■ Reread paragraphs 4–9 to think about how Mae analyzes the authors' arguments on the morality of torture and tries to see their disagreement in a constructive way. Focus especially on their different views of the hostage and time bomb scenarios.

■ Write a couple of sentences explaining how Mae tries to reframe their debate and find a way to bridge their differences. Add another sentence or two assessing how effective you think Mae's efforts are likely to be for most readers.

● A Fair and Impartial Presentation

Writers try to adopt an impartial stance when analyzing opposing arguments. One method Bernard uses is to quote an authority to critique one of the authors he is analyzing, rather than doing so directly himself. We can see this strategy in paragraphs 9 and 10 of Bernard's essay, where Bernard quotes Dr. Norman Fost to provide a critical perspective on Mitchell's argument about unfairness: "There is no coherent argument to support the view that enhancing performance is unfair . . ." (par. 9). Bernard makes it clear that Walker also cites Fost, but Bernard found and quoted from Fost's original article in the American Medical Association's *Virtual Mentor*, a highly respected publication.

To examine whether Mae is fair and unbiased, try the following:

■ Reread paragraphs 6–8, where Mae presents information on the Douglas Wood hostage situation. As you read, consider whether Mae's use of the

Wood example is comparable to Bernard's strategy. How does the Wood example help Mae remain impartial as she questions Bagaric and Clarke's argument?

- Write a sentence or two explaining how Mae tries to appear fair and impartial, and also assess how effective her strategy seems to be.

 A Readable Plan

Writers of common ground essays usually try to make the analysis clear and direct. Fairly early in the essay, they typically state the essay's thesis about the possibility of finding common ground and forecast the main points of disagreement and agreement. Bernard, for example, states his plan explicitly at the end of paragraph 3 when he explains, "I will focus here on two of Mitchell's main reasons supporting the ban on PEDs: the health risk and fairness." He organizes his essay around these two topics, introducing each of them with a heading in the form of a rhetorical question that he goes on to answer in some detail.

To analyze how Mae makes the plan of her essay visible to readers, try the following:

- Reread paragraph 2 and highlight her thesis statement. What are the two topics Mae plans to discuss in the essay?
- Skim the rest of the essay and note in the margin where these two topics are brought up and whether they are used in topic sentences that introduce the paragraph or set of paragraphs that follow.
- Write a few sentences assessing how well Mae orients readers and keeps them on track.

ANALYZING VISUALS

GRAPHICAL PRESENTATION OF DATA

Write a few sentences on Mae's use of the graph in her essay. Before you start, consider the following questions:

- When you initially read the essay, did you stop to study the visual, just glance at it in passing, go back to it after finishing the essay, or not look at it at all?
- What element(s) of Mae's subject does it illuminate?
- How does Mae's description of the graph in paragraph 6 help you read it? Is the information the graph conveys intelligible? If not, how might it have been improved?
- Is the information the graph conveys easier to understand in graph form, or could it have been conveyed just as well using words only?
- Do you think Mae's essay would have benefited from the addition of other visual elements? If so, what kind(s)?

Consider writing about an aspect of the torture debate or about a different political issue, such as what, if anything, should be done about the Patriot Act, which expanded the ability of the government to monitor communications and medical and financial records without a court order. Other issues might relate to the government's handling of the economy, foreign affairs, health care, and so on.

CONSIDERING TOPICS FOR YOUR OWN ESSAY

ATHENA ALEXANDER is a sociology major who hopes to become a doctor. When she began work on this essay in her composition class, she did not know anything about the No Child Left Behind Act (NCLB). She wrote the essay in part to understand what it was all about. On the advice of her instructor, she chose two essays — one by Rod Paige, and one by Reg Weaver — that took sharply different positions on the debate. Before analyzing the essays, however, she did some background research, beginning with the Web site of the U.S. Department of Education. From there, she discovered that to find out what happens to schools that do not show improvement under the requirements of the act, she would have to search the sites of individual state departments of education, which is how she happened to find and quote from the Georgia state Web site. As you read the opening paragraphs of Alexander's essay, notice how she uses the information she got from these two sources.

The two position essays by Rod Paige and Reg Weaver that Alexander uses as the basis of her essay are available on this book's companion Web site (**bedfordstmartins.com/theguide**).

No Child Left Behind: "Historic Initiative" or "Just an Empty Promise"?
Athena Alexander

1   In 2001, an overwhelming bipartisan majority in Congress approved President George W. Bush's No Child Left Behind Act (NCLB), designed to improve the quality of education in American schools. Under this law, every state must test public school students in grades 3–8 annually to assess their progress in reading and math. The NCLB also sets "adequate yearly progress" (AYP) goals for schools to meet. According to the Executive Summary of the act posted on *ED.gov,* the U.S. Department of Education's Web site, "schools that fail to make adequate yearly progress toward statewide proficiency goals will, over time, be subject to improvement, corrective action, and restructuring measures aimed at getting them back on course to meet State standards" (United States).

2   Each state determines how its own failing schools will be handled. For example, according to the Georgia State Department of Education's Web site, low performing Georgia schools must meet AYP goals within five years. After a school has fallen below the AYP target for two years, school administrators are "required to seek outside expert assistance." This is also the point at which parents are permitted to transfer their

children to a higher-performing school; if they choose a private school, they are given vouchers to pay the tuition. If the problem persists after three years, additional actions may be taken. For example, students may be given additional tutoring. After four or five years, more severe measures may go into effect, such as replacing teachers, administrators, or both; putting the failing school under "private management"; or even permanently closing it (Georgia).

As the effects of the law began to be felt at the state and local level, the debate about it intensified. One particular pair of opposing essays appeared in *Insight on the News* in 2004. In "Testing Has Raised Students' Expectations, and Progress in Learning Is Evident Nationwide," Rod Paige, the secretary of education under President George W. Bush from 2001 to 2005, defends NCLB, claiming that major improvements in schools have resulted in the short time the law has been in effect. Reg Weaver, president of the National Education Association, a union representing teachers, argues the opposite position in his essay, "NCLB's Excessive Reliance on Testing Is Unrealistic, Arbitrary and Frequently Unfair." Weaver calls for changes in the law, arguing that in its present form, NCLB will destroy the public education system in America. Paige and Weaver differ on the role standardized testing should play in assessing students' progress and the NCLB's effectiveness. Ultimately, however, their disagreement is political — with Paige accusing NCLB critics of being cynical and Weaver accusing its supporters of having a hidden agenda.

Whether testing should be the only, or even the most important, diagnostic tool for assessing the rate of learning is a central topic of debate between Paige and Weaver. Paige defends the NCLB's reliance on standardized testing, claiming that testing is an integral "part of life." He compares testing of students to tests that certify drivers, pilots, doctors, and teachers. Furthermore, he argues that testing is essential because it indicates "whether the system is performing as it should."

Weaver, however, disagrees with Paige on the role standardized testing should play in assessment. He argues that the NCLB should not rely on "only one type of assessment" because "good teachers" know that "judgments about what has been learned" should be based on "a variety of assessments." He also points out that teachers complain about the reliance on standardized testing because it makes preparing students for the test the focus of coursework, "push[ing] more and more of the important things that prepare us for life . . . off the curriculum plate." He reports that the majority of teachers believe that "teaching to the test 'inevitably stifles real teaching and learning'." In addition, Weaver questions the "one-size-fits-all approach" standardized testing imposes on special needs students, who he says require more "complex and multifaceted assessment" procedures. Therefore, unlike Paige, who defends standardized tests as "scientifically based research techniques," Weaver calls for a change in the NCLB's method of assessing adequate yearly progress.

6   Although Weaver and Paige both agree that, as Weaver puts it, the "focus should be on helping the individual student," they appear to have different information about whether NCLB, in fact, is being used for this purpose. Weaver apparently believes the tests are used only to compare schools and not to diagnose individual students' problems. He asserts: "Measuring this year's fourth-graders against next year's fourth-graders tells us little that we need to know about the improvement of individual students." Paige, on the other hand, confidently affirms that the tests identify "problems" individual students have "so that they can be fixed." To support his claim that the law is helping individual students, Paige points to the example of Cheltenham, Pennsylvania, "where the district provides schools with specific information about each student's abilities and weaknesses in specific academic areas" that teachers use to develop their lesson plans for the coming school year. Another example Paige cites shows that school administrators are using grant money to invest in computerized assessment programs like "Yearly Progress Pro" to track individual student progress. Whether such grants are funded by NCLB or in some other way is not clear from Paige's essay. But what is clear from both Paige and Weaver's essays is that they both agree the goal of any assessment should be to help individual students receive the teaching they need to improve.

7   Indeed, the need to improve America's educational system is unquestioned by both writers. But whereas Paige argues passionately that the NCLB is not only necessary but effective, Weaver contends that it fails to deliver on its promise. Paige makes a strong economic argument for the need to improve high school education so that students are prepared for the "fastest-growing occupations in the United States" and can compete in the new "global economy." To support his argument, Paige cites statistics from the National Assessment of Educational Progress and quotes from authorities like Federal Reserve Chairman Alan Greenspan. He also refers to a research study that claims the "vast majority of employers sadly expect that a high-school graduate will not write clearly or have even fair math skills." Perhaps most important, Paige argues that "the status quo result of a decades-old education system before the NCLB" results in a disparity in student performance along race and ethnic lines: "only one in six African Americans and one in five Hispanics are proficient in reading by the time they are high-school seniors." These are impressive and depressing statistics. But, according to studies Paige cites, the NCLB is making progress in reversing this trend. For example, he explains that the "Beating the Odds IV report showed that since NCLB has been imple-

mented, public-school students across the country" — and especially those in large metropolitan school systems — "have shown a marked improvement in reading."

Weaver also cites authorities, studies, and statistics, but his purpose is to question the NCLB's effectiveness in solving the problem. He focuses his criticism on the concept of "adequate yearly progress" that is used by the NCLB to measure progress. Weaver claims that the AYP sets an unrealistic standard for schools. He bases this argument on economic scenarios or projections, together with preliminary results after two years under the NCLB Act. As he says, "the prediction became reality last summer when nearly 25 percent of schools in Connecticut were identified as having failed to make AYP." Projections also estimate that at the end of twelve years, 93 percent (744 of 802) of Connecticut's elementary and middle schools will have failed to reach AYP targets. Weaver's point is that if Connecticut, "a state that is regarded nationally as a high performer[,] is not adequate to meet the statistical demands of this law," there must be something wrong with the AYP standard.

The problem, according to Weaver, is that the "current formula for AYP fails to consider the difference between where you start and how quickly you must reach the goal." He therefore calls the formula "irresponsible." He criticizes the NCLB's grouping of English-language learners and special-education students with the general student population, and its requirement that all students progress at the same rate. Moreover, he asserts that using standardized tests to determine progress is "totally inappropriate and emotionally injurious" for some of these groups of students.

Paige refutes Weaver's argument by labeling critics of the NCLB "cynics" and claiming that they exercise what President Bush has called the "soft bigotry of low expectations." He argues that "pessimism" sets up a self-fulfilling prophecy, in which the expectation a teacher has of a student affects the performance of that student. Paige adamantly insists that such "excuses must stop" and that every child should be treated equally. He reminds readers of NCLB's theme: "If you challenge students, they will rise to the occasion." Paige is making a political argument here, implying that if you oppose the law, you do not cherish the American ideal of equal opportunity for all, or you are prejudiced in your assumptions about the abilities of students.

Weaver, in turn, counters Paige's political argument with a political argument of his own. He suggests that the NCLB Act has a hidden agenda to privatize education in America by replacing public schools with private schools funded by government vouchers. He presents this argument gingerly through rhetorical questions: "Is this all the law of unintended consequences? Or is there, as many believe, an insidious intent to discredit public education, paving the way for a breakup of the current system — an opening of the door to a boutique system with increased privatization and government vouchers?" Weaver contends that if the goal is really to improve "student achievement," then before encouraging parents to abandon a school that is failing according to NCLB measures, "shouldn't we offer tutoring to struggling students first?" But vouchers are offered, in Georgia at least, only after two years of failing to meet AYP targets, and tutoring is not offered until the third year. Weaver seems to think that by making AYP goals so hard to reach, the NCLB will frighten parents into taking their children out of public schools and with the help of vouchers put them into private schools that are likely to have higher scores because they have more selective enrollments and are not required to take in English-language learners, disabled students, and others who bring down the school average. Private schools, in any case, are not held to NCLB requirements.

12   If you look up school vouchers on the Internet, you see that the debate over them has been going on for years. Many of the arguments that were made about vouchers in the past are echoed in the arguments about the No Child Left Behind Act. Wikipedia, for example, points out that whereas supporters of vouchers, like Paige, argue they "promote competition among schools of all types," opponents, like Weaver, contend that the funding for vouchers would compete with the funding for public education. Similarly, although proponents of vouchers argue that the poor would benefit by being able to "attend private schools that were previously inaccessible," opponents fear that "vouchers are tantamount to providing taxpayer subsidized white flight from urban public schools, whose student bodies are predominantly non-white in most large cities" ("Education Voucher"). Readers who are aware of the history of this debate over school vouchers cannot fail to see how these same arguments support the opposing positions Weaver and Paige take on No Child Left Behind.

13   Even though Paige and Weaver are part of a long history of debate on how to improve American education, they do agree with the sentiment behind the slogan "no child left behind." Both support "high standards and accountability." But they disagree on the means to achieve these goals. For Weaver, adequate yearly progress as measured by standardized tests — the backbone of the law — is a stumbling block rather than a building block to quality education for all. He recommends significant changes in the law that he believes would make it more effective and fairer. Paige, on the other hand, characterizes Weaver's recommendations as "complaints of the unwilling," arguing that instead of changing the NCLB Act, we should give it time and "work to make the law successful." Time will tell whether No Child Left Behind is viewed as an "historic initiative," as Paige predicts, or as "just an empty promise," as Weaver warns.

Works Cited

"Education Voucher." *Wikipedia*. Wikimedia, 27 Apr. 2006. Web. 29 Apr. 2006.

Georgia. Dept. of Education. "Consequences for Schools and Districts Not Making Adequate Yearly Progress (AYP)." *Georgia Department of Education*. Georgia Dept. of Education, 2006. Web. 5 Apr. 2006.

Paige, Rod. "Testing Has Raised Students' Expectations, and Progress in Learning Is Evident Nationwide." *Insight on the News* 11 May 2004: n. pag. Web. 17 Apr. 2006.

United States. Dept. of Education. "The No Child Left Behind Act of 2001: Executive Summary." *ED.gov*. U.S. Dept. of Education, 10 Feb. 2004. Web. 5 Apr. 2006.

Weaver, Reg. "NCLB's Excessive Reliance on Testing Is Unrealistic, Arbitrary and Frequently Unfair." *Insight on the News* 11 May 2004: n. pag. Web. 17 Apr. 2006.

MAKING CONNECTIONS: IMPROVING SCHOOLS

Everyone seems to agree that schools in the United States need improvement. Whether you attended public or private schools or both — and even if you were schooled at home or in another country — you have had extensive experience in schooling and could be considered an expert.

In her essay, Athena Alexander indicates that in passing the No Child Left Behind Act, Congress thought that the biggest problem with schooling was the quality of education, particularly in math, reading, and writing. With two or three classmates, discuss what you consider the most pressing problem in the public school system, based on your experience and/or observation. Begin by taking turns briefly saying what you think needs to be solved. Then, together discuss the following questions:

- Does your group agree on what the most pressing problem is?
- If the group disagrees, what is the basis of your disagreement — experience, values, ideals, goals, or something else?
- If you agree, why do you agree? Is it because you share the same experience, values, ideals, goals, or something else?

ANALYZING WRITING STRATEGIES

◼◼◼◼
Basic Features

● An Informative Introduction to the Issue and Opposing Positions

If an issue is current and controversial, there is a good chance that readers will already be familiar with it and will not need much of an introduction. Nevertheless, writers of common ground essays tend to explain the issue anyway. They do so because they want to reframe the issue for readers in a way that prepares them for the analysis to come.

For example, Jeremy Bernard introduces the argument about banning steroids in baseball by reminding readers of the nostalgia surrounding baseball and its association with a more innocent, perhaps simpler period in American history. This association of baseball, America, and innocence sets the stage for the debate about ethics. It even makes the metaphor of a level playing field seem to be literally about baseball.

To analyze how Alexander frames her issue, try the following:

- Reread paragraphs 1–2 and highlight the information Alexander provides. Focus especially on how she explains the criterion of "adequate yearly progress" (AYP) and how she uses the example of Georgia.

- Then reread paragraphs 8–10 to see how Alexander's analysis of the argument between Weaver and Paige depends on her earlier explanation of AYP.

- Write a few sentences about Alexander's way of framing the issue around the concept of AYP. What does she tell readers in the opening paragraphs that prepares them for her later analysis of the argument about AYP?

◆ A Probing Analysis

Although common ground essays seek ways to bridge differences, sometimes the analysis does nothing more than reveal how deep the disagreement is because it is based on fundamental values and beliefs, political ideology, or moral principles. For example, in her essay on torture, Melissa Mae discovered that the authors of the two essays she chose to analyze have very different philosophical or ideological perspectives on torture. Johnson thinks in terms of moral absolutes: Torture is simply wrong, always, in every situation. Bagaric and Clarke, on the other hand, advocate situational ethics: They think that the situation or context determines whether torture is right or wrong. These ways of thinking about morality appear to be irreconcilable.

To examine Alexander's analysis, try the following:

- Reread paragraphs 11 and 12, where Alexander analyzes Weaver's political argument about school vouchers. What ideologies and/or value systems seem to underlie opposing positions on vouchers?

- Notice that in addition to analyzing Weaver's essay, Alexander also looked up background information on school vouchers in Wikipedia. Many people think Wikipedia is not a reliable source because it is not written by experts and can easily be changed by readers with a political agenda of their own. As you examine this part of Alexander's analysis, consider whether she uses the information she gleaned from Wikipedia responsibly, and whether she should have used it at all.

- Write a couple of sentences explaining what you learned from Alexander's analysis of Weaver's argument about school vouchers. Add another sentence or two evaluating Alexander's use of Wikipedia as a source.

● A Fair and Impartial Presentation

To establish themselves as fair and impartial in their analysis, writers of common ground essays try to use neutral language in describing the people whose arguments they are discussing.

All the writers in this chapter describe the authors respectfully, with a few simple words identifying their professions. Melissa Mae, for example, describes Mirko Bagaric as a law professor, Julie Clarke as a law lecturer, and Kermit D. Johnson as "a retired Army Chaplain" (par. 2). Similarly, Alexander describes Rod Paige as "the secretary of education under President George W. Bush from 2001 to 2005" and Reg Weaver as the "president of the National Education Association, a union representing teachers" (par. 3). Alexander's descriptions establish the authors' credentials without evaluation or comment. But she does let readers know something about the authors' political affiliations, information that is significant because of the politics surrounding the No Child Left Behind Act. Paige, as she explains, wrote his essay defending the No Child Left Behind Act when he was the secretary of education; Weaver wrote his when he was president of the teachers' union. As spokesmen for these different constituencies, Paige and Weaver represent two important political points of view.

Writers also try to use descriptive but unbiased language when they introduce quotations. For example, Jeremy Bernard uses verbs like *concludes*, *argues*, *cites*, *expresses*, and *assumes*. Melissa Mae uses *writes*, *thinks*, *asserts*, *argues*, and *labels*. With these descriptive verbs, Bernard and Mae do not reveal their attitude toward the authors or what they wrote. They express no judgments, but act as impartial reporters.

To assess Alexander's fairness and impartiality, try the following:

- Reread paragraphs 4–6 and highlight the verbs Alexander uses to describe Weaver's and Paige's writing. Consider whether Alexander's word choices reveal her attitude or judgment and whether she comes across as fair and unbiased.

- Write a sentence or two explaining what you learned from analyzing Alexander's word choices.

● A Readable Plan

To help readers track the points of agreement and disagreement, writers often use **comparative transitions**, words and phrases that identify similarities or differences in the texts being analyzed. Transitions indicating similarity include *both*, *like*, *similarly*, and *in the same way*. Transitions to indicate difference include *unlike*, *however*, *although*, and *alternatively*. Here are a few examples from Jeremy Bernard and Melissa Mae's essays:

> Mitchell, on the other hand, . . . (Bernard, par. 11)

> Whereas Bagaric and Clarke think saving lives justifies torture, however, Johnson believes renouncing torture saves lives. (Mae, par. 3)

Bagaric and Clarke, in their turn, . . . (Mae, par. 4)

Bagaric and Clarke's take on it is somewhat more complicated. (Mae, par. 7)

Note that in these examples, Bernard and Mae use the authors' last names as a shortcut to help readers keep track of who wrote what. Occasionally, however, a writer will use pronouns, as in this example:

They agree that the medical evidence is inconclusive. . . . But they disagree on . . . (Bernard, par. 4).

Occasionally, writers also use labels (highlighted) to identify different positions:

Although Bagaric and Clarke continue to take a situational view of torture (considering the morality of an act in light of its particular situation) and Johnson does not waver in seeing torture in terms of moral absolutes. . . . (Mae, par. 10)

Using labels like these can be helpful if the writer goes on to discuss the different positions. (But you can see that even in this example, Mae is careful to use the authors' names so as not to confuse readers.)

In addition to comparative transitions, writers often use **transitional words and phrases** to introduce the following:

- an additional item: *as well as, in addition to, first . . . second*
- an illustration: *for example, specifically*
- a restatement or clarification: *that is, in other words, to put it differently*
- a cause or result: *because, therefore, consequently, so*
- a conclusion or summary: *in conclusion, clearly, thus*

To analyze Alexander's use of transitional words and phrases to make her essay readable, try the following:

- Reread paragraphs 5 and 6 and highlight the transitions Alexander uses. For each transition you highlight, note its function.
- Write a sentence or two explaining what you have learned about Alexander's use of transitions in these paragraphs.

CONSIDERING TOPICS FOR YOUR OWN ESSAY

You might be interested in writing about other issues related to NCLB — for example, the quality of teaching in the public schools, the value of standardized testing, private versus public schooling, or school vouchers. What basis for common ground might bridge differences on one of these topics? The Collaborative Activity on pp. 187–88 also raises a number of school issues you might consider: sororities and fraternities, college athletics, community service, and the teaching of evolution. Your group discussion about one of these issues could become the basis for your common ground essay.

Beyond the Traditional Essay: Finding Common Ground

The search for common ground is in evidence in many areas of our culture. Professional mediators are in constant demand for a wide range of business negotiations and for resolution of conflicts ranging from the personal (as, for example, when a counselor helps a couple resolve marital difficulties) to the global (for instance, when the United Nations weighs in on an international conflict). Of course, efforts to find common ground require the prior, full expression of opposing viewpoints.

Perhaps the most familiar examples of the expression of opposing points of view come from television, where talk shows like *Washington Week, Real Time with Bill Maher,* and *The View* are explicitly presented as contexts for a wide-ranging discussion of current issues. Online, sites such as bloggingheads.tv and Opposing Views (www.opposingviews.com) offer commentary from experts with opposing perspectives on current issues. While these media projects vary in their commitment to a "fair and unbiased" presentation, most of them do exhibit the other basic features common in traditional essays that search for common ground: a moderator or host typically introduces the issue and often highlights points of similarity and difference in the views expressed by participants; the structure of the show or site and the host's commentary provide a logical (or at least conventionally perceptible) plan.

As you work on your own project, you might want to consult some of these projects, both for factual information and for inspiration. If the format in which you are working allows for it — if, for example, you are creating a poster, Web site, or video — you should consider taking advantage of the strategies available to those working in multimedia — for example, by embedding artifacts that are relevant to the positions you are explaining. (Always remember to properly document any material you might use that was created by someone else.)

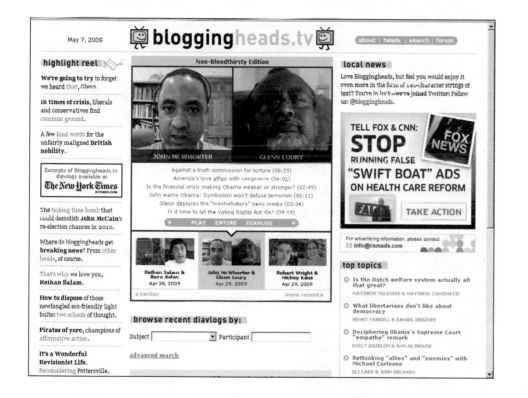

Guide to Writing

The Writing Assignment

Write an essay analyzing two or more essays taking different positions on an issue. Your purpose is to analyze the essays to understand their authors' main points of disagreement and to suggest ways to build common ground on shared values, concerns, needs, and interests.

This Guide to Writing will help you apply what you have learned about how writers present an issue, analyze the positions others take on it, strive for fairness in presenting their analysis, and write a readable essay communicating their ideas. The Guide is divided into five sections with various activities in each section:

- **Invention and Research**
- **Planning and Drafting**
- **Critical Reading Guide**
- **Revising**
- **Editing and Proofreading**

The Guide to Writing is designed to support you through the writing process, from finding an issue and essays arguing different positions on it, to editing your finished essay. Your instructor may require you to follow it from beginning to end. Working through the Guide in this way will help you — as it has helped many other college students — write a thoughtful, fully developed, polished essay.

If, however, your instructor allows it, you can decide on the order in which you will do the activities in the Guide to Writing. For example, the Invention and Research section includes activities to help you choose a set of argument essays to write about, analyze them, and research the issue, among other things. Obviously, choosing essays must precede the other activities, but you may come to the Guide with essays already in mind, and you may choose to research the issue further before turning to an analysis of the essays. In fact, you may find your response to one of the invention activities expanding into a draft before you have had a chance to do any of the other activities. That is a good thing — but you should later flesh out your draft by going back to the activities you skipped and layering the new material into your draft.

The following chart will help you find answers to many of the questions you might have about planning, drafting, and revising an essay finding common ground. The page references in the Where to Look column refer to examples from the readings and activities in the Guide to Writing.

To learn about using the *Guide* e-book for invention and drafting, go to **bedfordstmartins.com/ theguide**.

Starting Points: Finding Common Ground

◆ ◆ ◆ ◆ **Basic Features**

	Question	Where to Look
Choosing an Issue and Opposing Arguments to Write About	How do I come up with an issue to write about?	Choosing a Set of Argument Essays to Write About (p. 214) Using the Web to Find a Set of Arguments on an Issue (p. 214) Considering Topics for Your Own Essay (pp. 201, 209)
	What is my purpose in writing?	Defining Your Purpose for Your Readers (p. 220) Clarifying Your Purpose and Readers (p. 221)
An Informative Introduction to the Issue and Opposing Positions	How do I interest and inform readers about the issue?	Analyzing Writing Strategies (pp. 198–99, 206–7) Thinking about Your Readers (p. 217) Introducing the Issue and Opposing Positions (p. 221) Writing the Opening Sentences (pp. 224–25)
	How can I give readers an overview of the debate?	Analyzing the Essays (pp. 216–19) Researching the Issue (pp. 219–20)
A Probing Analysis	How do I find points of disagreement and agreement to analyze?	Annotate the Essays: Criteria for Analyzing the Essays (pp. 216–17) List Promising Points (p. 219)
	How do I analyze them?	Analyzing Writing Strategies (pp. 199–207) Analyzing the Essays (pp. 216–19) Exploring Points of Agreement and Disagreement (p. 219) Try Out an Analysis (p. 219)
A Fair and Impartial Presentation	How do I avoid entering the debate myself?	Analyzing Writing Strategies (pp. 199, 208)
A Readable Plan	How can I make my essay clear?	Analyzing Writing Strategies (pp. 200, 208–9)

Invention and Research

The following invention activities are easy to complete and take only a few minutes. Spreading out the activities over several days will stimulate your creativity, enabling you to analyze the arguments thoughtfully and discover ways to bridge their disagreements. Remember to keep a written record of your invention work: you will need it when you draft the essay and later when you revise it.

Choosing a Set of Argument Essays to Write About

If your instructor has not assigned one of the debates from the Appendix to this chapter or from the companion Web site for this book at bedfordstmartins.com/theguide, choose one that you already know about, that connects to your personal experience or interests, or that you think is especially important.

Getting an Overview

Read the essays to get a basic understanding of each author's position and supporting argument. Do not expect to understand everything on your first reading, even if you are already fairly knowledgeable about the issue and the way people typically argue about it. As you read, make notes about the following:

- points on which the authors disagree and points on which they agree
- values, ideals, interests, and concerns that seem to be important to each author
- ideas you have about how the authors might come together around shared values and ideals or common concerns, interests, and goals

Criteria for Choosing a Set of Arguments to Analyze: A Checklist	The set of argument essays should ☐ address the same controversial issue, which must be arguable — that is, a matter of opinion on which there is no absolute proof or authority on which everyone can rely; ☐ take different positions on the issue; ☐ offer thoughtful arguments supporting the position; ☐ anticipate and respond to opposing arguments; ☐ be interesting to you and worth the time and effort you will need to invest.

Using the Web to Find or Explore a Set of Arguments on an Issue

Your instructor may allow or even require you to find your own argument essays to analyze, rather than assigning those in the Appendix or on the companion

Web site, in which case the Internet will likely prove an important resource. However, even if you are working from essays we recommend, exploring the Internet can enrich your understanding of the issue. Moreover, the Web provides a rich repository of information, including photographs and music, which you might be able to use to create a richly detailed, multimedia text for your readers.

Here are some suggestions:

- Search Web sites such as ProCon.org, publicagenda.org, cqresearcher.org, or usa.gov for information and arguments.
- Do a Google search including keywords such as *current debates, controversial issues, arguments* or *debate* plus your issue.

Download or copy any information or quotations you might be able to use as well as any visuals you might include in your essay, being sure to get the information necessary to cite any online sources. (See p. 774–76 for the MLA citation format for electronic sources.)

Testing Your Choice

If you have the option of choosing a set of argument essays to analyze, pause now to decide whether you want to stay with the essays you have chosen or consider choosing different essays.

Consider these questions:

- Does the issue continue to engage your interest?
- Do you have a basic understanding of the issue and the arguments made in these essays?
- Have you found points on which the authors disagree and points on which they agree or could potentially agree?
- Have you begun to understand the motivating factors such as values, ideals, interests, and concerns in each author's argument?

Get together with two or three other students and take turns discussing your choice.

Presenters: Begin by identifying the issue and briefly summarizing the position argued in each of the essays you are analyzing.

Listeners: Tell the presenter what seem to be the motivating factors such as the values, concerns, or interests at the heart of the debate and where you see the possibility of finding common ground.

A Collaborative Activity:
Testing Your Choice

● Analyzing the Essays

To understand the points of disagreement and to find common ground in the argument essays you have chosen, you need to read them closely and critically. The following activities will help you find and annotate the essays' key features and motivating factors and keep track of what you find by filling in a chart. This process of annotating and charting will be helpful as you plan, organize, and draft your essay. Keep in mind that most writers need to reread all or parts of the essays several times to get all they can out of their analysis.

Annotate the Essays

Either on paper or electronically, annotate the essays you have chosen, identifying and labeling the key features of each essay, along with the author's motivating factors, listed in the "Criteria for Analyzing the Essays" box below. (Do not feel you must annotate every item on these two lists — some might not be relevant, or might not be present in a particular essay.)

CRITERIA FOR ANALYZING THE ESSAYS

Features of the Argument

- ISSUE. How does the writer define or frame the issue?
- POSITION. What is the writer's opinion (thesis statement)?
- ARGUMENT. What are the main reasons and kinds of evidence (facts, statistics, examples, authorities, and so on) the writer uses to support his/her position?
- COUNTERARGUMENT. What opposing arguments does the writer anticipate? Does the writer **concede** (agree with) or **refute** (disagree with) these arguments?

Motivating Factors

Factors such as the following may be stated explicitly or implied. If you find any other factor that you consider important but that is not on the list, give it a name and include it in your annotations.

- VALUES — MORAL, ETHICAL, OR RELIGIOUS PRINCIPLES (for example, justice, equality, the public good, "do unto others," social responsibility, stewardship of the natural environment)
- IDEOLOGY AND IDEALS (for example, democratic ideals — everyone is created equal and has the right to life, liberty, and the pursuit of happiness; capitalist ideals; socialist ideals; feminist ideals)
- NEEDS AND INTERESTS (for example, food, shelter, work, respect, privacy, choice)
- FEARS AND CONCERNS (for example, regarding safety, socioeconomic status, power, consequences of actions taken or not taken)

- **PRIORITIES** AND **AGENDAS** about what is most important or urgent (for example, whether law and order is more important than securing justice and equality; whether the right to life trumps all other concerns; whether combating global warming ought to be a principal concern of our government)

- **BINARY THINKING** (the assumption that things are "either/or" — for example, that only one of two outcomes is possible; that there can only be winners or losers in a situation; that only two positions are possible; that the world is divided into "us" against "them")

Fill in the Chart

Creating a chart like the one on p. 218 will make it easy for you to locate points of agreement and disagreement in the essays you are analyzing:

1. At the top of the second and third columns, identify the essays you are analyzing. (If you are analyzing more than two essays, add another column.)

2. Begin by charting the argument's key features. Add paragraph numbers directing you to the places in each essay where the key feature is evident. Add brief notes or jot down key phrases to jog your memory.

3. Chart the argument's motivating factors, adding paragraph numbers and notes (if appropriate and helpful).

4. Chart any additional significant factors you might find, naming them appropriately.

Remember that you will not necessarily find evidence of *every* key feature or motivating factor in each essay.

An electronic version of the blank chart is available on the companion Web site at **bedfordstmartins.com/ theguide.**

To see an example of student writer Melissa Mae's annotations chart, turn to pp. 239–40 of the Writer at Work section.

Thinking about Your Readers

Now that you have a good understanding of the argument essays you will be discussing, take a few minutes to write about your readers. The following questions will help you identify them and develop a better understanding of them:

- Who are my readers?

- What are they likely to know and think about the issue?

- How can I interest them in it — for example, by connecting it to their experience or concerns, or by citing statistics or vivid anecdotes?

- Are there specialized terms or concepts I will have to explain to them? Do the essays give me enough information to define these terms, or will I have to search out further information?

My Annotations Chart

		Essay 1:	Essay 2:
Features of the Argument	**ISSUE**		
	POSITION (THESIS)		
	ARGUMENT (Main supporting reasons and evidence)		
	COUNTERARGUMENT (Refutation, concession)		
Motivating Factors	**VALUES** (Moral, ethical, religious)		
	IDEOLOGY AND **IDEALS** (Cultural, legal, political)		
	NEEDS AND **INTERESTS**		
	FEARS AND **CONCERNS**		
	PRIORITIES AND **AGENDAS**		
	BINARY THINKING		
Other Factors			

● Exploring Points of Agreement and Disagreement

These activities will help you find points of agreement and disagreement in the essays and try out your analysis on one or two of them. As you write about the points, you may find you are actually writing parts of a rough draft. Do not censor yourself, but go ahead and see where your exploratory writing leads you.

List Promising Points

Make a list of promising points of agreement and disagreement in the essays you are analyzing. For your analysis, you probably will not need to discuss more than two or three interesting points because you will need to examine them in some detail. Nevertheless, generating a substantial list of points now will give you the luxury of choice.

Generating a substantial list may also lead you to discover less obvious potential points of agreement that will help your readers see the issue in a new way. The most effective analyses often go beyond the obvious, finding common ground where most people would imagine agreement is impossible.

You might begin your list by reviewing the notes you wrote for the Getting an Overview activity (p. 213). Also, review your Annotations Chart. Look for places where the same reasons, evidence, or motivational factors are used in both essays. For example, you may find, as Melissa Mae did, that the essays use a similar scenario to argue different positions or that they both make a moral argument. Or you may find, as Jeremy Bernard did, that both writers are concerned about fairness.

Try Out an Analysis

Choose a point of agreement or disagreement that looks promising, and write a page analyzing it. If the point appears to be one on which the writers disagree, consider whether the disagreement when examined might reveal a potential shared value, concern, or interest. If the point is one on which the writers already agree, think about the significance of the agreement and whether it could be extended to include other points as well.

You will probably need to go back into both essays and reread the relevant paragraphs. As you do, consider the following:

- how the key feature or motivating factor fits into the essay as a whole
- how it is used to advance the argument
- whether it is central or peripheral
- whether the writers use it in similar or different ways
- whether the writers use comparable words, examples, and details
- whether there are words, phrases, or sentences you could quote (and what you would say about the quotes you use)

Researching the Issue

It may help to gather some background information about the issue and the authors. Researching the history of the issue may help you introduce it in a way that captures your readers' interest. As you try out your analysis and draft other parts of the essay, you may also discover that you have questions that can be answered with library or Internet research. For example, Athena Alexander noticed that both writers referred to "vouchers," a word she did not understand. She Googled the word and found information that helped her understand the central role vouchers play in the politics of the argument on reforming public education.

Consider beginning research in your college library, where a librarian can give you advice about the online catalog and databases. Also consult Chapters 23 and 24 for help finding and citing sources.

Designing Your Document

Think about whether your readers might benefit from design features such as headings or numbered or bulleted lists or from visuals such as drawings, graphs, tables, or photographs. Earlier in the chapter, for example, Jeremy Bernard uses headings to introduce his two main points and Melissa Mae displays a graph to illustrate an observation brought up by one of the authors she is writing about. You might also look back at the scenario on p. 185 describing a proposal for "smart growth" in a formerly rural area in Washington State, and then read the Thinking about Document Design on p. 228 to see how this proposal was presented at a conference.

For more information on document design, see Chapter 21.

Defining Your Purpose for Your Readers

Write a few sentences defining your purpose. Recall that in an earlier invention activity you identified your readers and considered what they know and think about the issue you are analyzing. Given these readers, try now to define your purpose by considering the following questions:

- How can I interest my readers?
- If they are likely to have their own opinions about the issue, how much resistance should I expect they will have to my analysis of the points of disagreement?
- How can I make my ideas about the potential for common ground intriguing for my readers?

Formulating a Tentative Thesis Statement

Write one or more sentences that could serve as a thesis statement for your essay. These sentences from the end of paragraph 3 in Athena Alexander's essay assert her thesis:

> Paige and Weaver differ on the role standardized testing should play in assessing students' progress and the NCLB's effectiveness. Ultimately, however, their disagreement is political — with Paige accusing NCLB critics of being cynical and Weaver accusing its supporters of having a hidden agenda.

As you write your own tentative thesis statement, think about how you could help readers see the important ways the writers disagree and also possibly on what basis they might be able to agree. Although you may want to revise your thesis statement as you draft your essay, trying to state it now will give you focus and direction as you plan and draft your essay.

Planning and Drafting

The following guidelines will help you get the most out of your invention work, determine specific goals for your essay, and write a promising first draft.

Refining Your Purpose and Setting Goals

Successful writers are always looking beyond the next sentence to their larger goals for the whole essay. Indeed, that next sentence is easier to write if you keep larger goals in mind. The following questions can help you set these goals. Consider each one now, and then return to them as necessary while you write.

Clarifying Your Purpose and Readers

- Who are my readers, and what can I realistically hope to accomplish by analyzing this issue?
- Should I assume my readers may not understand the points on which people disagree?
- Should I assume they have not considered seriously points on which people may agree?
- Can I inspire readers to think critically about their own position on the issue by helping them understand some of the motivating factors that could be used as common ground?
- How can I gain readers' confidence? Can I keep my own views to myself and present the opposing positions in a fair and balanced way, as all of the writers in this chapter try to do?

Introducing the Issue and Opposing Positions

- Should I place the issue in a historical context and indicate also that the issue is still unresolved, as all of the writers in this chapter try to do?
- Should I quote famous people readers may have heard of to help establish the issue's importance, as Bernard does?
- Should I try to clarify the issue by giving concrete examples, as Bernard and Mae do, or by defining terms, as Bernard and Alexander do?
- Should I introduce the authors of the opposing positions by name and also give their credentials, as all the writers do?

Presenting Your Analysis

- Can I help readers understand what the significant points of disagreement and potential or actual points of agreement are, as all the writers try to do?
- Can I suggest that a point of disagreement may actually be based on shared values, as Mae does when she focuses on the importance of saving lives and Bernard does when he discusses fairness?

- Should I call attention to common needs and concerns, as Alexander does when she notes that both writers want to improve education?
- Should I mark where the writers are motivated by different political agendas, as Alexander does when she discusses privatizing education through school vouchers?
- Can I point to places where the writers rely on similar scenarios, as Mae does, or other kinds of support, as Bernard and Alexander do?

Striving for Fairness

- Can I avoid discussing my own view of the issue?
- Should I try to give roughly equal space to each position?
- Should I quote others rather than speak in my own voice?

Making Your Plan Readable

- Should I forecast my main points early on, as all three writers do?
- Should I use the authors' names and repeat key words to help readers follow my analysis?
- Should I use comparative transitions to make it easy to see when I am comparing and contrasting the different arguments?

The Ending

- Should I end by summarizing the major differences, as Alexander does?
- Should I remind readers of the common ground that exists between the different positions, as all the writers do?
- Should I discuss the possibilities for the future, as all the writers do?

Outlining Your Draft

The goals that you have set should help you draft your essay, but first you might want to make a quick scratch outline of the points of agreement and disagreement between the authors that you expect to focus on. Your Annotations Chart plus the list you made under Exploring Points of Agreement and Disagreement should be particularly helpful. Use your outline to guide your drafting, but do not feel tied to it.

Here is an outline of Jeremy Bernard's essay. Remember that he divides his essay into two points — the health risk and fairness of using steroids — and under each point, he explains the ways in which the writers agree and disagree.

> *Introduction*
>
> > *From age of innocence to steroids era*
> >
> > *Issue: Should PEDs be banned by MLB?*
> >
> > > *Yes — George Mitchell, the MLB-sponsored Mitchell Report*
> > >
> > > *No — Eric Walker's independent Web site, "Steroids, Other 'Drugs,' and Baseball"*

Point 1. Health Risk: Should PEDs be banned because their health risk is significant?

    Agreement

        Medical evidence inconclusive

        Risk of side effects exists

        Risk to adolescents particularly serious

    Disagreement

        Risk to adults is likely grave (Mitchell) / likely not grave (Walker)

        Adults should be prohibited from undergoing risk (Mitchell) / should be allowed to choose (Walker)

Point 2. Fairness/Level Playing Field: Should PEDs be banned because players who take them have an unfair advantage?

    Agreement

        Use of PEDs gives athletes an advantage

        Unequal access is unfair, not a level playing field

    Disagreement

        Whose responsibility? MLB should set rules (Mitchell) / let athletes decide what's best for themselves (Walker)

        The distinction between "natural" and "unnatural" advantages is clear and should be maintained (Mitchell) / the distinction is arbitrarily determined and needs rethinking (Walker)

Conclusion

    Possibility of common ground based on shared love of baseball

And here is an outline of the points of agreement and disagreement in the two essays Melissa Mae addresses in her analysis:

Introduction

    History: Abu Ghraib–present

    Issue: Should the U.S. ever torture?

    Yes — Mirko Bagaric and Julie Clarke, "A Case for Torture"

    No — Kermit D. Johnson, "Inhuman Behavior"

Points of agreement (shared values)

    Human life is precious

    Torture is a moral issue

    Morality is worth arguing about

Points of disagreement

    Torture can be considered self-defense and therefore moral when innocent lives will be saved through its use (Bagaric and Clarke) / Torture is never moral (Johnson)

    Torture saves lives (Bagaric and Clarke) / Torture endangers lives (Johnson)

The "ticking time bomb scenario" is real, though rare (Bagaric and Clarke) / The
scenario is a Hollywood-fueled fantasy (Johnson)

Conclusion

Summarize: Bagaric and Clarke's situational ethics v. Johnson's moral absolutes
Common ground possible based on shared values and morality

The introduction to the issue, positions, and debaters could take from one to four paragraphs — Bernard's introduction takes two paragraphs and Mae's takes three. What is important is that the introductory paragraphs not dominate your analysis. The thesis statement is usually brief — sometimes only a sentence or two — and often serves also to forecast the main points of disagreement and agreement that the essay will address. The concluding paragraph in each of these essays is brief and evolves from the preceding discussion. In neither case does the writer simply summarize the main points of agreement and disagreement that were discussed in detail, although that could be useful for readers. What they do, though, is probably more important because it focuses on underlying motivating factors and the possibility of building on this foundation of common ground.

Consider any outlining that you do before you begin drafting to be tentative. As you draft, expect that your essay will likely depart from your original outline. In fact, it may help, especially if you are drafting the essay over several hours or days, to revise your outline to correspond with the changes you are making.

Drafting

If you have not already begun to draft your essay, this section will help by suggesting how to write your opening sentences, and how to use the sentence strategy of introducing a quotation with a colon. Drafting is not always a smooth process, so do not be afraid to leave spaces where you do not know what to put in or to write notes to yourself about what you could do next. If you get stuck while drafting, go back over your invention writing: You may be able to copy and paste some of it into your evolving draft, or you may find that you need to do some additional invention to fill in details in your draft.

Writing the Opening Sentences

You could try out one or two different ways of beginning your essay — possibly from the list that follows — but do not agonize over the first sentences because you are likely to discover the best way to begin only after you have written a rough draft. Again, you might want to review your invention writing to see if you have already written something that would work to launch your essay.

To engage your readers' interest from the start, consider the following opening strategies:

- an interesting and relevant quotation (like Bernard)
- an assertion of a topic's larger cultural relevance (like Bernard)

- an assertion of an issue's increasing significance (like Mac and Alexander)
- an anecdote or personal reminiscence
- a surprising statement
- statistics
- a research study
- a scenario
- an historical analogy

A Sentence Strategy: Introducing a Quotation with a Colon

As you draft an essay finding common ground, you will need to quote frequently from the two opposing positions. Quoting does more than prove the fairness and accuracy of your report. If you allow readers to see some of the writers' actual language, you help them understand the debaters as writers and thinkers. There are several strategies available to you for inserting writers' language directly into the sentences of your own essay.

You may use speaker tags alone — "Johnson *says*" or "Lopez *claims*" — or you may rely on the word *that*, as in "Kynard counters *that* 'Graff greatly exaggerates the amount of damage this hurricane will cause.'" And there is another way, not necessarily better but a very useful alternative: setting up or preparing for a quotation from the beginning of a sentence that leads the reader towards a colon, with the quotation immediately following the colon. Here is an example:

> He [Paige] reminds readers of NCLB's theme: "If you challenge students, they will rise to the occasion." (Alexander, par. 10)

Alexander might have written a different sentence: "NCLB's theme is something he wants to remind you of when he says, 'if you challenge students, they will rise to the occasion.'" The advantage to the sentence she did write is that it is more precise, and it puts the mention of a theme right next to the quotation that illustrates or defines it.

Here are three more examples:

> He [Weaver] presents this argument gingerly through rhetorical questions: "Is this all the law of unintended consequences? . . ." (Alexander, par. 11)

> Walt Whitman, the great nineteenth-century poet, sang its praises: "It's our game — the American game." (Bernard, par. 1)

> Johnson asserts: "A clear-cut repudiation of torture or abuse is . . . essential to the safety of the troops" (26), who need to be able to "claim the full protection of the Geneva Conventions . . . when they are captured, in this or any war" (27). (Mae, par. 3)

Your essay seeking common ground is based on sources: the position essays you have studied and your background research on the issue. In nearly every sentence of your essay, you will be quoting, summarizing, or paraphrasing these sources. When you quote from them, you have many options for integrating a quotation smoothly into your explanation.

Working with Sources:

Weaving Quoted Materials into Your Own Sentences

One familiar, common strategy is to create a noun clause beginning with *that*, as in this example:

> Johnson argues against this common claim, writing that "whenever we torture or mistreat prisoners, we are capitulating morally to the enemy — in fact, adopting the terrorist ethic that the end justifies the means" (26). (Mae, par. 4)

> But he insists that "Commissioners, club officials, the Players Association, and players" should share "responsibility for the steroids era" and "should join in" the "effort to bring the era of steroids and human growth hormone to an end" (311). (Bernard, par. 11)

Another common strategy is to introduce the quotation with a verb like *say*, or alternatives to it like *assert, claim, ask, argue, explain*:

> "Steroids are coercive," Fost explains, because "if your opponents use them, you have to" as well or you risk losing. (Bernard, par. 10)

> "More than anything," remarked Pete Hamill, the twentieth-century journalist and novelist, "it's a game of innocence" (Andrijeski). (Bernard, par. 1)

> As he says, "the prediction became reality last summer when nearly 25 percent of schools in Connecticut were identified as having failed to make AYP." (Alexander, par. 8)

> Therefore, Walker concludes, each athlete has to decide for him- or herself what's "appropriate or necessary." (Bernard, par. 10)

Beyond relying on *that* or a verb alone, you can weave the quotations right into your own sentence structures. This option is especially useful when the material you want to quote is a phrase rather than a clause or a complete sentence.

> He sees "no logical or ethical distinction between — just for example — killer workouts and PEDs." Therefore, Walker concludes, each athlete has to decide for him- or herself what's "appropriate or necessary." (Bernard, par. 10)

> Johnson puts down the scenario outright as an unrealistic "Hollywood drama" (26). (Mae, par. 7)

This approach allows you to easily accommodate two or more quotations in one of your own sentences:

> Paige makes a strong economic argument for the need to improve high school education so that students are prepared for the "fastest-growing occupations in the United States" and can compete in the new "global economy." (Alexander, par. 7)

> Paige, on the other hand, characterizes Weaver's recommendations as "complaints of the unwilling," arguing that instead of changing the NCLB Act, we should give it time and "work to make the law successful." (Alexander, par. 13)

For more help on using sources in your writing, turn to Chapter 24.

Your instructor may arrange a peer review session in class or online where you can exchange drafts with your classmates and give each other a thoughtful critical reading — pointing out what works well and suggesting ways to improve the draft. Remember, a good critical reading does three things: it lets the writer know how well the reader understands the analysis, praises what works best, and indicates where the draft could be improved.

Basic Features

1. Evaluate how effectively the issue and opposing positions are introduced.

   Summarize: Briefly tell the writer what you understand the issue to be about and what the different positions are on the issue.

   Praise: Indicate where the writer does a good job explaining the issue, introducing the authors, or engaging readers' interest.

   Critique: Describe any confusion or uncertainty you have about the issue, why it is important, or what positions are usually taken on it.

2. Consider whether the analysis is sufficiently probing.

   Summarize: Tell the writer what you think are the main points of disagreement and agreement (actual or potential).

   Praise: Identify one or two passages where the analysis seems especially interesting and original — for example, where the arguments seem opposed but are shown to be based on the same reasoning, evidence, or motivational factor, such as a shared value.

   Critique: Give the writer suggestions on how the analysis could be improved — for example, indicate where one of the writer's points needs additional explanation or where adding an example would make the point easier to grasp. Let the writer know if you detect any other motivating factors that might be used to establish common ground.

3. Consider whether the writer's presentation is fair and impartial.

   Praise: Note any passages where the writer comes across as being especially fair and impartial.

   Critique: Tell the writer if the authors and their positions are presented unfairly or if one side seems to be favored over the other.

4. Assess the essay's readability.

   Praise: Pick one or two places where the essay is especially clear and easy to follow — for example, where comparative transitions signal similarities and differences.

   Critique: Let the writer know where the readability could be improved — for example, where a topic sentence could be clearer or where a transition is needed. Can you suggest a better beginning or more effective ending?

5. If the writer has expressed concern about anything in the draft that you have not discussed, respond to that concern.

Making Comments Electronically Most word processing software offers features that allow you to insert comments directly into the text of someone else's document. Many readers prefer to make their comments this way because it tends to be faster than writing on hard copy and space is virtually unlimited; it also eliminates the process of deciphering handwritten comments. Where such features are not available, simply typing comments directly into a document in a contrasting color can provide the same advantages.

Revising

Very likely you have already thought of ways to improve your draft, and you may even have begun to revise it. The Troubleshooting Chart on p. 230 will help. Before using the chart, however, it is a good idea to do the following:

- Review critical reading comments from your classmates, instructor, or writing center tutor.
- Make an outline of your draft so that you can look at it analytically.

You may have made an outline before writing your draft, but after drafting you need to see what you actually wrote, not what you intended to write. You can outline the draft quickly by highlighting the basic features — presenting the issue, analyzing the opposing positions, effectively presenting an impartial account of the opposing arguments, and making the essay readable.

Thinking About Document Design:
Helping Readers Visualize a Solution

In the presentation cosponsored by an engineering consulting firm and the EPA at the New Partners for Smart Growth Conference (see the chapter-opening scenario on p. 185), document design played an important role in helping attendees visualize the proposed plan for development. The greatest challenge for the presenters was to design materials that would make clear the complexities of the competing needs of the stakeholders, and the proposed resolution of them, in a relatively short session.

Their first impulse was to present the precise statistical data that the consulting firm had gathered to persuade stakeholders that their solution was best for all parties. When they drafted PowerPoint slides that contained such data, however, they realized that the information was too detailed and too text-based to be effective in the conference setting: depending on where they were sitting, attendees would not necessarily be able to read all the detail, and they wouldn't have enough time to absorb it. Instead, the presenters designed a series of slides that conveyed the challenges and alternative solutions concisely and in a visually compelling way.

For example, to introduce one of their key concepts — the large difference between high- and low-density development in terms both of environmental impact and dollar costs — they began by engaging their audience with a simple question, set in an eye-catching yellow font, which they illustrated simply using contrasting photographs:

They proceeded to answer their own question with statistics showing that low-density lots cost more to supply with water and basic utilities:

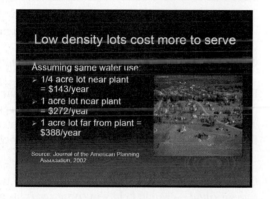

Next, they used a simple illustration showing the differences in environmental impact from high-, medium-, and low-density developments:

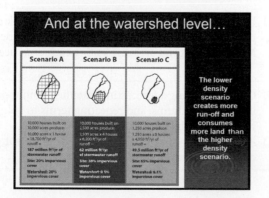

The simplicity and visual appeal of the PowerPoint slides they created were instrumental in conveying their ideas clearly and persuasively.

Troubleshooting Your Draft

⬡ ⬡ ⬡ ⬡ **Basic Features**

	Problem	Suggestions for Revising the Draft
An Informative Introduction to the Issue and Opposing Positions	My readers are not clear about the issue or the opposing positions.	☐ State the issue explicitly as a *should* question. ☐ Use a comparative transition (i.e., *whereas* X . . . , Y . . . ; or X . . . *but* Y . . .) to sharpen the contrast between the opposing positions. ☐ Explain the positions in more depth, perhaps providing examples or anecdotes to make them more concrete. ☐ Consider adding visuals, graphs, tables, or charts, if these would help clarify the issue and opposing positions.
	My readers are not interested or do not appreciate the issue's importance.	☐ Add additional information about the issue and authors. ☐ Contextualize the issue in history, politics, socioeconomics, or cultural phenomena or trends. ☐ Quote notable authorities on the issue. ☐ Cite polls or research studies.
A Probing Analysis	My readers do not understand what my main points are.	☐ Determine whether you are trying to cover too many points without going into detail about any of them. ☐ Consider which points can be cut or categorized under other points.
	My analysis seems more like a summary than a probing analysis.	☐ Reexamine each argument to get at the underlying motivating factors that could explain the agreement or disagreement. ☐ Try reorganizing your analysis by grouping related points — on the basis of shared values, common concerns, political agenda, etc.
A Fair and Impartial Presentation	I reveal my own position.	☐ Consider where changing your word choice — perhaps adding *may* or *could* — would help you come across as impartial. ☐ Cut passages where you evaluate the opposing positions, or quote others to critique weak arguments.
	My presentation is not unbiased or balanced.	☐ If you favor one side over the other, try to balance your presentation by discussing how the other essay deals with the point. ☐ Make sure that you are representing each essay accurately and fairly.
A Readable Plan	My readers are confused by my essay, or find it difficult to read.	☐ Consider adding a forecasting statement and topic sentences to introduce key terms, and repeating terms to help readers track your main points. ☐ Add or clarify comparative transitions when you are comparing or contrasting the opposing arguments.

Editing and Proofreading

Our research indicates that particular errors occur often in common ground essays: incorrect comma usage in sentences with interrupting phrases, and vague pronoun reference. The following guidelines will help you check your essay for these common errors.

Using Commas around Interrupting Phrases

What is an interrupting phrase? When writers are analyzing opposing positions, they need to supply a great deal of information, precisely and accurately. They add much of this information in phrases that interrupt the flow of a sentence, as in the following example:

> The concern was so great that George Mitchell, the former Senate Majority Leader and peace negotiator, was enlisted to investigate.

Such *interrupting phrases*, as they are called, are typically set off with commas.

The Problem. Forgetting to set off an interrupting phrase with commas can make sentences difficult to read or unclear.

How to Correct It. Add a comma on either side of an interrupting phrase.

> ▶ **Live Nation, without hesitating, paid $350 million to buy HOB Entertainment, which owns the popular House of Blues clubs.**

> ▶ **Virtual football, to hold onto its fans and gain more, soon has to move beyond solitary players to teams of players on the Internet.**

Correcting Vague Pronoun Reference

The Problem. *Pronouns* replace and refer to nouns, making writing more efficient and cohesive. If the reference is vague, however, rather than clear and precise, this advantage is lost. A common problem is vague use of *this, that, it,* or *which.*

How to Correct It. Scan your writing for pronouns, taking special note of places where you use *this, that, it,* or *which.* Check to be sure that it is crystal clear what *this, that, it, which,* or another pronoun refers to. If it is not, revise your sentence.

> *This habit*
> ▶ **Television evangelists seem to be perpetually raising money, ~~which~~ makes some viewers question their motives.**

A Note on Grammar and Spelling Checkers
These tools can be helpful, but do not rely on them exclusively to catch errors in your text: Spelling checkers cannot catch misspellings that are themselves words, such as *to* for *too.* Grammar checkers miss some problems, sometimes give faulty advice for fixing problems, and can flag correct items as wrong. Use these tools as a second line of defense after your own (and, ideally, another reader's) proofreading/editing efforts.

For practice, go to
bedfordstmartins.com/
theguide/exercisecentral
and click on Commas around
Interrupting Phrases.

▶ By the late 1960s, plate tectonics emerged as a new area of study.

Tectonics was based on the notion of the earth's crust as a collection

of plates or land masses above and below sea level, constantly in motion.

startling new geological theory
This took a while for most people to accept. ~~because of its unexpected novelty.~~
　　　　　　　　　　　　　　　　　　　　　　　　　　　^

▶ Inside the Summit Tunnel the Chinese laborers were using as much as

500 kegs a day of costly black powder to blast their way through the

　　　　　The unexpected expense
solid rock. ~~It~~ was straining the Central Pacific's budget.
　　　　　　^

For practice, go to
bedfordstmartins.com/
theguide/exercisecentral
and click on Vague Pronoun
Reference.

A Writer at Work

Melissa Mae's Analysis

Annotating and Charting Annotations

In this section, you can learn how one writer, Melissa Mae, prepared to write "Laying Claim to a Higher Morality" (see pp. 195–97 in the Readings section of this chapter). In this essay, Mae analyzes two essays taking opposing positions on the issue of whether the United States should use torture in the interrogation of suspected terrorists. Following the Guide to Writing, Mae first annotated the key features of the essays' arguments and their motivating factors. Then she entered the results of her analysis on a chart that helped her see at a glance where the points of agreement and disagreement were located in both essays.

To learn from this Writer at Work demonstration, first read the two essays Mae analyzed. Then, look at Mae's Annotation Chart and a passage she annotated.

The Essays Melissa Mae Analyzed

Below are the two essays Mae used for her finding common ground essay. (For three additional essays on the issue of torture, along with a short overview of the issue, see pp. 243–63.)

"A Case for Torture" is the summary of an article written for the *University of San Francisco Law Review* by MIRKO BAGARIC, professor and coordinator of the Graduate Law Program at the Deakin Law School in Melbourne, Australia, and JULIE CLARKE, lecturer in the same program. Bagaric's recent books include *How to Live: Being Happy and Living with Moral Dilemmas* (2006) and *Criminal Laws of Australia*, with Ken Arenson (2004). Clarke's most recent publications include *Contract Law: Commentaries, Cases and Perspectives* (2008), with Philip Clarke and Ming Zhou. Together, Bagaric and Clarke also wrote *Torture: When the Unthinkable Is Morally Permissible* (2006). "A Case for Torture" was published in 2005 in the *Age*, a Melbourne, Australia, newspaper.

A Case for Torture

MIRKO BAGARIC AND JULIE CLARKE

1   Recent events stemming from the "war on terrorism" have highlighted the prevalence of torture. This is despite the fact that torture is almost universally deplored. The formal prohibition against torture is absolute — there are no exceptions to it.

2   The belief that torture is always wrong is, however, misguided and symptomatic of the alarmist and reflexive responses typically emanating from social commentators. It is this type of absolutist and short-sighted rhetoric that lies at the core of many distorted moral judgements that we as a community continue to make, resulting in an enormous amount of injustice and suffering in our society and far beyond our borders.

3   Torture is permissible where the evidence suggests that this is the only means, due to the immediacy of the situation, to save the life of an innocent person. The reason that torture in such a case is defensible and necessary is because the justification manifests from the closest thing we have to an inviolable right: the right to self-defence, which of course extends to the defence of another. Given the choice between inflicting a relatively small level of harm on a wrongdoer and saving an innocent person, it is verging on moral indecency to prefer the interests of the wrongdoer.

4   The analogy with self-defence is sharpened by considering the hostage-taking scenario, where a wrongdoer takes a hostage and points a gun to the hostage's head, threatening to kill the hostage unless a certain (unreasonable) demand is met. In such a case it is not only permissible, but desirable for police to shoot (and kill) the wrongdoer if they get a "clear shot." This is especially true if it's known that the wrongdoer has a history of serious violence, and hence is more likely to carry out the threat.

5   There is no logical or moral difference between this scenario and one where there is overwhelming evidence that a wrongdoer has kidnapped an innocent person and informs police that the victim will be killed by a co-offender if certain demands are not met.

6   In the hostage scenario, it is universally accepted that it is permissible to violate the right to life of the aggressor to save an innocent person. How can it be wrong to

violate an even less important right (the right to physical integrity) by torturing the aggressor in order to save a life in the second scenario?

There are three main [objections] to even the above limited approval of torture. The first is the slippery slope argument: if you start allowing torture in a limited context, the situations in which it will be used will increase.   7

This argument is not sound in the context of torture. First, the floodgates are already open — torture is used widely, despite the absolute legal prohibition against it. Amnesty International has recently reported that it had received, during 2003, reports of torture and ill-treatment from 132 countries, including the United States, Japan and France. It is, in fact, arguable that it is the existence of an unrealistic absolute ban that has driven torture beneath the radar of accountability, and that legalisation in very rare circumstances would in fact reduce instances of it.   8

The second main argument is that torture will dehumanise society. This is no more true in relation to torture than it is with self-defence, and in fact the contrary is true. A society that elects to favour the interests of wrongdoers over those of the innocent, when a choice must be made between the two, is in need of serious ethical rewiring.   9

A third [objection] is that we can never be totally sure that torturing a person will in fact result in us saving an innocent life. This, however, is the same situation as in all cases of self-defence. To revisit the hostage example, the hostage-taker's gun might in fact be empty, yet it is still permissible to shoot. As with any decision, we must decide on the best evidence at the time.   10

Torture in order to save an innocent person is the only situation where it is clearly justifiable. This means that the recent high-profile incidents of torture, apparently undertaken as punitive measures or in a bid to acquire information where there was no evidence of an immediate risk to the life of an innocent person, were reprehensible.   11

Will a real-life situation actually occur where the only option is between torturing a wrongdoer or saving an innocent person? Perhaps not. However, a minor alteration to the Douglas Wood situation illustrates that the issue is far from moot. If Western forces in Iraq arrested one of Mr. Wood's captors, it would be a perverse ethic that required us to respect the physical integrity of the captor, and not torture him to ascertain Mr. Wood's whereabouts, in preference to taking all possible steps to save Mr. Wood.   12

Even if a real-life situation where torture is justifiable does not eventuate, the above argument in favour of torture in limited circumstances needs to be made because it will encourage the community to think more carefully about moral judgements we collectively hold that are the cause of an enormous amount of suffering in the world.   13

First, no right or interest is absolute. Secondly, rights must always yield to consequences, which are the ultimate criteria upon which the soundness of a decision is gauged. Lost lives hurt a lot more than bent principles.   14

Thirdly, we must take responsibility not only for the things that we do, but also for the things that we can — but fail to — prevent. The retort that we are not responsible for the lives lost through a decision not to torture a wrongdoer because we did not create the situation is code for moral indifference.   15

Equally vacuous is the claim that we in the affluent West have no responsibility for more than 13,000 people dying daily due to starvation. Hopefully, the debate on torture will prompt us to correct some of these fundamental failings.   16

"Inhuman Behavior" was written by Major General KERMIT D. JOHNSON, a retired chaplain in the U.S. Army. Johnson is a graduate of the U.S. Military Academy, the Princeton Theological Seminary, the U.S. Command and General Staff College, and the U.S. Army War College. As an infantry officer, he commanded a heavy mortar company in the Korean War. As a chaplain, he served in the United States, Germany, and Vietnam, completing his service as Chief of Chaplains from 1979 to 1982.

"Inhuman Behavior" was published in 2006 in *the Christian Century*, a national magazine concerned with "faithful living, critical thinking."

Inhuman Behavior: A Chaplain's View of Torture

Kermit D. Johnson

1 The historian Arnold Toynbee called war "an act of religious worship." Appropriately, when most people enter the cathedral of violence, their voices become hushed. This silence, this reluctance to speak, is based in part on not wishing to trivialize or jeopardize the lives of those who have been put in harm's way. We want to support the men and women in our armed forces, whether we are crusaders, just warriors or pacifists.

2 Furthermore, those who interrupt this service of worship become a source of public embarrassment, if not shame. The undercurrent seems to be that dissent or critique in the midst of war is inherently unpatriotic because it violates a sacred wartime precept: support our troops.

3 > **If war causes us to suppress our deepest religious, ethical and moral convictions, then we have indeed caved in to a "higher religion" called war.**

From the standpoint of Christian faith, how do we respond? I would say that if war causes us to suppress our deepest religious, ethical and moral convictions, then we have indeed caved in to a "higher religion" called war.

4 Since this obeisance to war is packaged in the guise of patriotism, it is well to admit to the beauty of patriotism, the beauty of unselfishness and love of country, land, community, family, friends and, yes, our system of government. But this fabulous beauty makes us appreciate all the more what Reinhold Niebuhr called the "ethical paradox in patriotism." The paradox is that patriotism can transmute individual unselfishness into national egoism. When this happens, when the critical attitude of the individual is

squelched, this permits the nation, as Niebuhr observed, to use "power without moral constraint."

I believe this has been the case, particularly since 9/11, in the treatment of prisoners under U.S. custody.

We must react when our nation breaks the moral constraints and historic values contained in treaties, laws and our Constitution, as well as violating the consciences of individuals who engage in so-called "authorized" inhuman treatment. Out of an unsentimental patriotism we must say no to torture and all inhuman forms of interrogation and incarceration. It is precisely by speaking out that we can support our troops and at the same time affirm the universal values which emanate from religious faith.

A clear-cut repudiation of torture or abuse is also essential to the safety of the troops. If the life and rule of Jesus and his incarnation is to be normative in the church, then we must stand for real people, not abstractions: for soldiers, their families, congregations to which they belong, and the chaplains and pastors who minister to their needs from near and far. By "real people" we also mean that tiny percentage of the armed forces who are guards and interrogators and the commanders responsible for what individuals and units do or fail to do in treating prisoners.

Too often the topic of torture is reduced to a Hollywood drama, a theoretical scenario about a ticking time bomb and the supposed need to torture someone so the bomb can be discovered and defused in the nick of time. Real torture is what takes place in the daily interchange between guards, interrogators and prisoners, and in the everyday, unglamorous, intricate job of collecting intelligence.

U.S. troops in Iraq are fighting an insurgency. It is a battle for the "hearts and minds" of the people. Mao Zedong referred to guerrillas or insurgents as the fish and the supporting population as the water. This is an asymmetrical battle. As a weaker force, the insurgents cannot operate without the support of the people. So the classic formula for combating an insurgency is to drain the swamp — cut the insurgents off from their life support. Both sides are trying to win the "hearts and minds" of the people.

Imagine, then, the consequences when people learn that U.S. forces have tortured and abused captives. A strengthened and sustained insurgency means danger and death for U.S. forces. Never mind that the other side routinely tortures. It is we who lay claim to a higher morality.

Nor should we take comfort that we do not chop off heads or field suicide bombers. What we must face squarely is this: whenever we torture or mistreat prisoners, we are capitulating morally to the enemy — in fact, adopting the terrorist ethic that the end justifies the means. And let us not deceive ourselves: torture is a form of terrorism. Never mind the never-ending debate about the distinctions between "cruel, inhuman and degrading treatment" and "torture." The object of all such physical and mental torment is singularly clear: to terrify prisoners so they will yield information. Whenever this happens to prisoners in U.S. control, we are handing terrorists and insurgents a priceless ideological gift, known in wartime as aid and comfort to the enemy.

12   As for individual guards or interrogators, whenever they are encouraged or ordered to use torture, two war crimes are committed: one against the torturer and the other against the prisoner. The torturer and the tortured are both victims, unless the torturer is a sadist or a loose cannon who needs to be court-martialed. This violation of conscience is sure to breed self-hatred, shame and mental torment for a lifetime to come.

13   Finally, the most obvious reason for repudiating torture and inhuman treatment is that our nation needs to claim the full protection of the Geneva Conventions on behalf of our troops when they are captured, in this or any war.

14   The congressional votes for and the presidential capitulation to the amendment offered by Senator John McCain prohibiting torture and inhuman treatment have to be seen as positive (despite the president's statement in signing it, in which he claimed an exception to the rule when acting as commander in chief). But reasons for concern remain.

- The most passionate defenders of the Geneva Conventions, the judge advocate generals, the military lawyers, were completely cut off from providing input on the torture issue.

- The government has denigrated international treaties that the U.S. has signed and that constitute U.S. law regarding torture and inhuman treatment.

- The definition of torture has been reinterpreted by the Justice Department as follows: "Physical pain amounting to torture must be equivalent in intensity to the pain accompanying serious physical injury, such as organ failure, impairment of bodily function, or even death."

- There is no indication that the outsourcing or "rendition" of brutal treatment will cease. Is it not odd that some of the countries the U.S. State Department faults for torture are the very countries we utilize in outsourcing interrogations? What credence can we put in their assurances that they will not torture?

- In Senate testimony, Senator Jack Reed (D., R.I.) asked the military this question: "If you were shown a video of a United States Marine or an American citizen [under the] control of a foreign power, in a cell block, naked with a bag over their head, squatting with their arms uplifted for 45 minutes, would you describe that as a good interrogation technique or a violation of the Geneva Convention?" The chairman of the Joint Chiefs of Staff, Marine General Peter Pace, answered: "I would describe it as a violation." The next question might be: Why have these and other violations of the Geneva Conventions been certified as legal when employed by the U.S.?

- The public has been dragged through a labyrinth of denials, retractions, redefinitions and tortured arguments, all designed to justify and rationalize lowered moral standards in the treatment of prisoners, not to strengthen and defend high ethical standards.

In a letter to Senator McCain, Captain Ian Fishback, a West Point graduate in the 82nd Airborne Division, said, "Some argue that since our actions are not as horrifying as al-Qaeda's we should not be concerned. When did al-Qaeda become any type of standard by which we measure the morality of the United States? I strongly urge you to do justice to your men and women in uniform. Give them clear standards of conduct that reflect the ideals they risk their lives for." Torture is not one of those ideals.

15

How Mae Analyzed the Debate between Bagaric/Clarke and Johnson

As Mae reread each essay, she highlighted the text and made notes in the margin where she found the key features of the argument and several motivating factors. At the same time, she entered the paragraph numbers and brief summaries of what she found into her Annotations Chart (see pp. 239–40).

Analyzing both essays took a few hours of intense close reading, but when she was done, Mae felt she understood both essays very well and had many ideas about which points of disagreement and agreement she could discuss in her essay. In fact, Mae felt confident that she had found more material than she could use in an essay her instructor limited to one thousand words.

Mae found it easy to identify the issue and position in each essay. After some careful analysis, she also located the main reasons and supporting evidence for each argument, as well as all counterarguments and possible objections the authors acknowledged, along with how they responded to them (either by conceding or refuting them).

The trickiest part for Mae was identifying the authors' motivating factors. Her instructor had forewarned the class that this would likely be the case, because the motivating factors were likely not to be explicitly stated. After rereading key passages a few times, Mae felt satisfied that she had found the major motivating factors for both essays in paragraphs she had already annotated.

An example of Mae's annotations of one portion of the Bagaric and Clarke essay and her completed Annotations Chart are shown in this section.

Position (thesis)	Torture is permissible where the evidence suggests that this is the only means, due to the immediacy of the situation, to save the life of an innocent person. The reason that torture in such a case is defensible and necessary is because the justification manifests from the closest thing we have to an inviolable right: the right to self-defence, which of course extends to the defence of another. Given the choice between inflicting a relatively small level of harm on a wrongdoer and saving an innocent person, it is verging on moral indecency to prefer the interests of the wrongdoer.	3 *Torture sometimes OK — analogy to self-defense (par. 3)*
Ideology: self-defense is inviolable right		*Moral value: human life*
		Priority: saving innocent life outweighs harming wrongdoer
Hostage-taking scenario (pars. 4-6)	The analogy with self-defence is sharpened by considering the hostage-taking scenario, where a wrongdoer takes a hostage and	4

points a gun to the hostage's head, threatening to kill the hostage unless a certain (unreasonable) demand is met. In such a case it is not only permissible, but desirable for police to shoot (and kill) the wrongdoer if they get a "clear shot." This is especially true if it's known that the wrongdoer has a history of serious violence, and hence is more likely to carry out the threat.

"Logically" and "morally," terrorist like wrongdoer

5   There is no logical or moral difference between this scenario and one where there is overwhelming evidence that a wrongdoer has kidnapped an innocent person and informs police that the victim will be killed by a co-offender if certain demands are not met.

Logic: If right to kill to save life, then right to torture

6   In the hostage scenario, it is universally accepted that it is permissible to violate the right to life of the aggressor to save an innocent person. How can it be wrong to violate an even less important right (the right to physical integrity) by torturing the aggressor in order to save a life in the second scenario?

Ideology: right to life more imp. than right to physical integrity

Melissa Mae's Annotations Chart

		Essay 1: Bagaric/Clarke	Essay 2: Johnson
Features of the Argument	**ISSUE**	*1 (war on terrorism)*	*1-5 (post 9/11 wartime ethics/ politics)*
	POSITION (THESIS)	*3 ("Torture permissible . . . only means . . . to save the life of an innocent person.")*	*6 ("We must react when our nation breaks the moral constraints and historic values . . . say no to torture . . . ")*
	ARGUMENT (Main supporting reasons and evidence)	*Torture sometimes OK* *3 (analogy: self-defense)* *4-6 (analogy: hostage-taking scenario → b/c If it's right to kill to save innocent life, then it's right to torture)* *13 (b/c it's necessary in real life — Wood example)* *14 (b/c "no right or interest is absolute")*	*Torture never OK* *6-7 (b/c it endangers our troops & against "universal values" & "religious faith")* *9-10 (b/c it's counterproductive, loses "hearts & minds")* *11 (b/c we become terrorists)* *12 (b/c torturers also "victims")* *13 (b/c our troops need Geneva Conventions protection)* *14 (b/c it's against the law)*

(continued)

(continued)

		Essay 1: Bagaric/Clarke	Essay 2: Johnson
Motivating Factors	COUNTERARGUMENT (Refutation or concession?)	*1-2 (Refutes "absolute" prohibition against torture argument)* *7-10 (Refutes slippery slope, dehumanizes society, & info untrustworthy arguments.)* *11 (Concedes cases torture is wrong → therefore qualifies thesis: not when punitive, only in immediate risk.)*	*1-6 (Refutes dissent is "unpatriotic" argument b/c it's morally necessary & saves troops)* *8 (Refutes ticking time bomb scenario b/c it's "Hollywood drama," not realistic)* *15 (Refutes U.S. behavior "not as horrifying as al-Qaeda's" b/c we have our own moral standards)*
	VALUES (Moral, ethical, religious)	*2-3 (save innocent life)* *13-16 (need "to think more carefully about moral judgments")*	*1-4 (Niebuhr's "ethical paradox in patriotism" → "power w/o moral constraint")* *6 ("affirm universal values which emanate from religious faith")* *11 ("terrorist ethic that the end justifies the means")*
	IDEOLOGY AND IDEALS (Cultural, legal, political)	*3 (right to self defense)* *6 ("universally accepted . . . to violate the right to life of the aggressor to save an innocent person")* *14 ("Lost lives hurt a lot more than bent principles.")*	*11 (U.S. torturing — "ideological gift" to terrorists)* *1-6 (morality absolute: end doesn't justify the means?)* *15 ("Torture is not one of those ideals.")*
	FEARS AND CONCERNS	*1 (post 9/11 fear of terrorism)*	*14 ("reasons for concern")*
	PRIORITIES AND AGENDAS	*3 (save innocent life)*	*6-7 (save troops lives)* *10-11 (preserve U.S. ideals & morals)*
	BINARY THINKING	*12 ("only option [is] between torturing a wrongdoer or saving an innocent person? Perhaps not. However . . .")*	*1-6 (morality, Religious principles, Law v. Pragmatism; Ends v. Means)*

How Mae Used the Annotations Chart to Plan and Draft Her Essay

Mae relied on the Annotations Chart as a guide to planning her essay (see pp. 195–97). It seemed logical to her to start her essay where she started the chart: by identifying the *issue* and the *positions* on the issue presented by each essay.

In her first paragraph, she provides some context for the issue, noting that the disclosure in 2004 of detainee abuse at Abu Ghraib first led many Americans to become concerned about torture and that the debate over "enhanced inter-rogation techniques" such as waterboarding and sleep deprivation continues today. Like Mae, you may turn up relevant details in your background research about the issue — facts, history, current news — that you can use to present it to readers.

In her second paragraph, Mae introduces the two opposing position essays by title and date of publication, gives some background on the writers, and briefly states the positions they take in their essays. She concludes the paragraph by suggesting that common ground exists between what seem at first glance to be starkly opposing perspectives.

In her third and fourth paragraphs, Mae continues to make good use of her chart in presenting key aspects of the authors' main arguments. To represent their arguments fairly and accurately and to identify the language she would paraphrase, she first consulted her chart and then looked again at her highlighted and annotated essays. You can see from the chart that she made use of information from several paragraphs in both readings. Her patience in charting the topics ensured that she would not overlook any important material that would help her compare and contrast these writers' essays.

As you read the rest of Mae's essay, note that she does not cover every element in her chart but selected those that enable her to represent fairly what she considers to be the most interesting and important points of agreement and disagreement between the two writers.

Thinking Critically About What You Have Learned

Now that you have read and discussed several common ground essays and written one of your own, take some time to think critically and write about what you have learned. To think critically means to use all of your new genre knowledge — acquired from the information in this chapter, your own writing, the writing of other students, and class discussions — to reflect deeply on your work for this assignment. It also requires that you consider the social implications of your new knowledge.

Critical thinking is sustained by analysis — a thoughtful, patient survey of all of the materials you have read and produced during your work in this chapter. The benefit is proven and important: You will remember longer what you have learned, ensuring that you will be able to put it to good use well beyond this writing course.

Reflecting on Your Writing

Your instructor may ask you to turn in with your essay and process materials a brief metacognitive essay or letter reflecting on what you have learned in writing your essay finding common ground. Choose among the following invention activities those that seem most productive for you.

- Explain how your purpose and audience — what you wanted your readers to understand about why people disagree and where they might find common ground — influenced *one* of your decisions as a writer, such as how you framed the issue, how you introduced the authors, which points of disagreement and agreement you chose to discuss, or the motivating factors you emphasized.

- Discuss what you learned about yourself as a writer in the process of writing this particular essay. For example, what part of the process did you find most challenging. Did you try something new, like annotating the essays and making a chart of your annotations or listing the points of disagreement and agreement?

- If you were to give advice to a friend who was about to write an essay finding common ground, what would you say?

- Which of the readings in this chapter influenced your essay? Explain the influence, citing specific examples from your essay and the reading.

- If you got good advice from a critical reader, explain exactly how the person helped you — perhaps by suggesting a motivating factor, a shared concern or value that your analysis was hinting at but not addressing directly or by noting passages where comparative transitions or clearer labeling was needed to help readers keep track of the similarities or differences between the arguments.

Considering the Social Dimensions: Being Fair and Impartial

Essays that attempt to understand the basis for disagreement and find common ground on controversial topics are unquestionably helpful for writers and readers alike. They help us to understand complicated arguments and discover ways to move forward amicably and constructively. They are especially important in a democracy because they enable us to perform our role as citizens conscientiously, informing ourselves about important issues.

Traditionally, journalists and academics have served as authors of analytical essays that seek to help us understand differences and find common ground on controversial social, cultural, and political issues. For example, the Committee of Concerned Journalists identifies the news media as "the common carriers of public discussion" and asserts that it bears a responsibility "to fairly represent the varied viewpoints and interests in society, and to place them in context rather than highlight only the conflicting fringes of debate." Most importantly, they make clear that "[a]ccuracy and truthfulness require that as framers of the public discussion we not neglect the points of common ground where problem solving occurs" ("A Statement of Shared Purpose," www.concernedjournalists.org/node/380).

Journalists and academic analysts, however, recognize that maintaining accuracy and trustworthiness can be quite challenging on highly contentious issues. They wrestle with the requirement that analysis be impartial. They often make a distinction between impartiality — which can be defined as not partial or biased, but fair and just — and objectivity — which assumes that it is possible to examine a controversy scientifically, without being influenced by personal feelings, experiences, values, or prior knowledge. Most analysts, however, acknowledge that while objectivity may not be possible, writers can strive to be fair in the way they represent different viewpoints, even-handed and balanced in giving each side its voice, and unbiased in avoiding judgmental language.

1. ***Consider how challenging it was to make your analysis fair and impartial.*** As you were analyzing the argument essays and writing your finding common ground essay, in what ways, if any, did you have difficulty maintaining your impartiality? How did you try to make sure you were being fair? What strategies did you use in your writing to come across to readers as a trustworthy analyst?

2. ***Write a page or so about the goal of trying to be fair and impartial as an analyst.*** Based on your own experience as a writer of a finding common ground essay (as well as other writing you may have done in the past), what have you learned about the goal of trying to be fair and impartial? Is it an achievable goal? Is it a worthwhile goal? Why or why not?

Add to your discussion any ideas you have from your experience as a consumer of analytical writing and talk. How critical are you as a reader or listener? How important do you think it is for you as a citizen and student to feel confident that the analysis you are consuming comes across as fair, unbiased, impartial, even objective? Be sure to distinguish between op-ed style commentary intended to express opinions and judgments and journalism or academic style analysis intended to be fair and impartial.

Appendix: Two Debates

Following are two clusters of essays taking positions on two different issues: torture and same-sex marriage. These essays are also available electronically on the companion Web site for this book, bedfordstmartins.com/theguide, which also includes several other debates for you or your instructor to choose from.

Debate 1: Torture

"Thinking about Torture" by Ross Douthat (pp. 245–48)

**"Committing War Crimes for the 'Right Reasons'"
by Glenn Greenwald (pp. 248–51)**

"An End to Torture" by Maryann Cusimano Love (pp. 251–55)

See also:

"A Case for Torture" by Mirko Bagaric and Julie Clarke (pp. 233–34)

"Inhuman Behavior" by Kermit D. Johnson (pp. 235–38)

Understanding the Torture Debate

The United States ratified the United Nations Convention against Torture (1987), which asserts that "[n]o exceptional circumstances whatsoever, whether a state of war or a threat of war, internal political instability or any other public emergency may be invoked as a justification for torture." People differ on what constitutes torture, but the U.N. defined torture as

> any act by which severe pain or suffering, whether physical or mental, is inten-
> tionally inflicted on a person for such purposes as obtaining from him, or a
> third person, information or a confession, punishing him for an act he or a third
> person has committed or is suspected of having committed, or intimidating or
> coercing him or a third person, or for any reason based on discrimination of any
> kind, when such pain or suffering is inflicted by or at the instigation of or with
> the consent or acquiescence of a public official or other person acting in an offi-
> cial capacity.

Since the terrorist attacks of September 11, 2001, and the subsequent revelations of abuse of prisoners by the U.S. military and others at the Abu Ghraib and Guantanamo Bay prisons and elsewhere, however, torture has again become a subject of intense debate in the United States. For example, writers have debated whether torture is effective in obtaining the truth, affects the torturers, threatens the international standing of the United States, or undermines justice. Other contested issues include what qualifies as torture, whether the United States must observe international laws forbidding torture, or whether the United States should set an example by not torturing. The five essays in this chapter take different approaches to the issue, but they all make arguments that are worth examining.

ROSS DOUTHAT is the author of *Privilege: Harvard and the Education of the Ruling Class* (2005) and the coauthor, with Reihan Salam, of *Grand New Party: How Republicans Can Win the Working Class and Save the American Dream* (2008). He is the film critic for *National Review*, and his work has appeared in the *Wall Street Journal*, the *Weekly Standard, GQ, Slate*, and other publications. Currently a columnist for the *New York Times*, Douthat was a senior editor at the *Atlantic* until April 2009. He posted "Thinking about Torture" to his blog on the *Altantic .com* on December 16, 2008.

Thinking about Torture

ROSS DOUTHAT ▼

1   I haven't written anything substantial, ever, about America's treatment of detainees in the War on Terror. There are good reasons for this, and bad ones. Or maybe there's only one reason, and it's probably a bad one — a desire to avoid taking on a fraught and desperately importantly subject without feeling extremely confident about my own views on the subject.

2   I keep waiting, I think, for somebody else to write a piece about the subject that eloquently captures my own inarticulate mix of anger, uncertainty and guilt about the Bush Administration's interrogation policy, so that I can just point to their argument and say go read *that*. But so far as I know, nobody has. There's been straightforward outrage, obviously, from many quarters, and then there's been a lot of evasion — especially on the Right, where occasional defenses of torture in extreme scenarios have coexisted with a remarkable silence about the broad writ the Bush Administration seems to have extended to physically-abusive interrogation, and the human costs thereof. But to my knowledge, nobody's written something that captures the sheer *muddiness* that surrounds my own thinking (such as it is) on the issue.

3   That muddiness may reflect moral and/or intellectual confusion on my part, since the grounds for straightforward outrage are pretty obvious. There's a great deal of political tendentiousness woven into Jane Mayer's *The Dark Side*, for instance, but it's very difficult to come away from her reportage unpersuaded that this Administration's counterterrorism policies exposed significant numbers of people — many guilty, but some innocent — to forms of detention and interrogation that we would almost certainly describe as torture if they were carried out by a lawless or dictatorial regime. For a less vivid but also somewhat less partisan analysis that reaches the same conclusion, you can read the executive summary of the just-released Levin-McCain report. (And of course both Mayer's book and the Arms

Services Committee report are just the latest in a line of similar findings, by reporters and government investigations alike.)

Now it's true that a great deal of what seems to have been done to detainees arguably falls into the category of what Mark Bowden, in his post-9/11 *Atlantic* essay on "The Dark Art of Interrogation," called "torture lite": It's been mostly "stress positions," extreme temperatures, and "smacky-face," not thumbscrews and branding irons. But it's also clear now, in a way that it wasn't when these things were still theoretical to most Americans, that the torture/torture lite distinction gets pretty blurry pretty quickly in practice. It's clear from the deaths suffered in American custody. It's clear from the testimony that Mayer puts together in her book. And it's clear from the outraged response, among conservatives and liberals alike, to the photographs from Abu Ghraib, which were almost all of practices closer to "torture-lite" than outright torture but which met, justly I think, with near-universal condemnation nonetheless. (And while it still may be true that in some sense, the horrors of Abu Ghraib involved individual bad apples running amok, they clearly weren't running all that *far* amok, since an awful lot of the things they photographed themselves doing — maybe not the human pyramids, but the dogs, the hoods, the nudity and so forth — showed up on lists of interrogation techniques approved by the Secretary of Defense himself.)

So as far as the bigger picture goes, then, it seems indisputable that in the name of national security, and with the backing of seemingly dubious interpretations of the laws, this Administration pursued policies that delivered many detainees to physical and mental abuse, and not a few to death. These were wartime measures, yes, but war is not a moral blank check: If you believe that Abu Ghraib constituted a failure of *jus in bello*, then you have to condemn the decisions that led to Abu Ghraib, which means that you have to condemn the President and his Cabinet. . . .

Given this reality, whence my uncertainty about how to think about the issue? Basically, it stems from the following thought: That while the Bush Administration's policies clearly failed a just-war test, they didn't fail it in quite so *new* a way as some of their critics suppose . . . and moreover, had I been in their shoes I might have failed the test as well. . . .

For instance: The use of the atomic bomb. I think it's very, very difficult to justify Harry Truman's decision to bomb Hiroshima and Nagasaki in any kind of plausible just-war framework, and if that's the case then the nuclear destruction of two Japanese cities — and indeed, the tactics employed in our bombing campaigns against Germany and Japan more broadly — represents a "war crime" that makes Abu Ghraib look like a trip to Pleasure Island. (And this obviously has implications for the justice of our entire Cold War nuclear posture as well.) But in so thinking, I also have to agree with Richard Frank's argument that "it is hard to imagine anyone who could have been president at the time (a spectrum that includes FDR, Henry Wallace, William O. Douglas, Harry Truman, and Thomas Dewey) failing to authorize use of the atomic bombs" — in so small part because I find it hard to imagine *myself* being in Truman's shoes and deciding the matter differently, my beliefs about just-war principle notwithstanding.

8   The same difficulty obtains where certain forms of torture are concerned. If I find it hard to condemn Harry Truman for incinerating tens of thousands of Japanese civilians, even though I think his decision probably violated the moral framework that should govern the conduct of war, I *certainly* find it hard to condemn the waterboarding of, say, a Khalid Sheikh Muhammed in the aftermath of an event like 9/11, and with more such attacks presumably in the planning stages. I disagree with Charles Krauthammer, who has called torture in such extreme circumstances a "moral duty"; rather, I would describe it as a kind of immorality that we cannot expect those charged with the public's safety to always and everywhere refrain from. (Perhaps this means, as some have suggested, that we should ban torture, but issue retroactive pardons to an interrogator who crosses the line when confronted with extreme circumstances and high-value targets. But I suspect that this "maybe you'll get retroactive immunity, wink wink" approach probably places too great a burden on the individual interrogator, and that ultimately some kind of mechanism is required whereby the use of extreme measures in extreme circumstances is brought within the law.)

9   Yet of course the waterboarding of al Qaeda's high command, despite the controversy it's generated, is not in fact the biggest moral problem posed by the Bush Administration's approach to torture and interrogation. The biggest problem is the sheer scope of the physical abuse that was endorsed from on high — the way it was routinized, extended to an ever-larger pool of detainees, and delegated ever-further down the chain of command. Here I'm more comfortable saying straightforwardly that *this should never have been allowed* — that it should be considered impermissible as well as immoral, and that it should involve disgrace for those responsible, the Cheneys and Rumsfelds as well as the people who actually implemented the techniques that the Vice President's office promoted and the Secretary of Defense signed off on.

10   But here, too, I have uncertainty, mixed together with guilt, about how strongly to condemn those involved — because in a sense I know that what they were doing was what I wanted to them to do. . . .

11   Some of the most passionate torture opponents have stated that they never, ever imagined that the Bush Administration would even consider authorizing the sort of interrogation techniques described above, to say nothing of more extreme measures like waterboarding. I was not so innocent, or perhaps I should I say I was more so: If you had listed, in the aftermath of 9/11, most of the things that have been done to prisoners by representatives of the U.S. government, I would have said that *of course* I expected the Bush Administration to authorize "stress positions," or "slapping, shoving and shaking," or the use of heat and cold to elicit information. After all, there was a war on! I just had no idea — until the pictures came out of Abu Ghraib, and really until I started reading detailed accounts of how detainees were being treated — what these methods could mean in practice, and especially as practiced on a global scale. A term like "stress positions" sounds like one thing when it's sitting, bloodless, on a page; it sounds like something else when somebody dies from it.

Now obviously what I've said with regard to the financial crisis is also true in this arena: With great power comes the responsibility to exercise better judgment than, say, my twenty-three year old, pro-torture-lite self. But with great power comes a lot of pressures as well, starting with great fear: The fear that through *inaction* you'll be responsible for the deaths of thousands or even millions of the Americans whose lived you were personally charged to protect. This fear ran wild the post-9/11 Bush Administration, with often-appalling consequences, but it wasn't an irrational fear — not then, and now. It doesn't excuse what was done by our government, and in our name, in prisons and detention cells around the world. But anyone who felt the way I felt after 9/11 has to reckon with the fact that what was done in our name was, in some sense, done for us — not with our knowledge, exactly, but arguably with our blessing. I didn't get what I wanted from this administration, but I think you could say with some justification that I got what I asked for. And that awareness undergirds — to return to where I began this rambling post — the mix of anger, uncertainty and guilt that I bring to the current debate over what the Bush Administration has done and failed to do, and how its members should be judged.

GLENN GREENWALD worked as a constitutional law and civil rights lawyer in New York before becoming a columnist for *Salon*, where he focuses on legal and political issues. Greenwald, whose writing also appears in such publications as the *American Conservative*, the *National Interest*, and *In These Times*, is the author of three books: *How Would a Patriot Act? Defending American Values from a President Run Amok* (2006), *A Tragic Legacy: How a Good v. Evil Mentality Destroyed the Bush Presidency* (2007), and *Great American Hypocrites: Toppling the Big Myths of Republican Politics* (2008). The following article, a response to Ross Douthat's blog post "Thinking about Torture," was published on *Salon* on December 17, 2008.

Committing War Crimes for the "Right Reasons"

GLENN GREENWALD   ▼

The Atlantic's Ross Douthat has a post today — "Thinking about Torture" — which, he acknowledges quite remarkably, is the first time he has "written anything substantial, ever, about America's treatment of detainees in the War on Terror." He's abstained until today due to what he calls "a desire to avoid taking on a fraught and desperately importantly (sic) subject without feeling extremely confident about my own views on the subject."

2   I don't want to purport to summarize what he's written. It's a somewhat meandering and at times even internally inconsistent statement. Douthat himself characterizes it as "rambling" — befitting someone who appears to think that his own lack of moral certainty and borderline-disorientation on this subject may somehow be a more intellectually respectable posture than those who simplistically express "straightforward outrage." In the midst of what is largely an intellectually honest attempt to describe the causes for his ambiguity, he actually does express some "straightforward outrage" of his own. About the widespread abuse, he writes: "it should be considered impermissible as well as immoral" and "should involve disgrace for those responsible, the Cheneys and Rumsfelds as well as the people who actually implemented the techniques that the Vice President's office promoted and the Secretary of Defense signed off on."

3   Nonetheless, Douthat repeatedly explains that he is burdened by "uncertainty, mixed together with guilt, about how strongly to condemn those involved," and one of the central reasons for that uncertainty — one that is commonly expressed — is contained in this passage:

> But with great power comes a lot of pressures as well, starting with great fear: The fear that through inaction you'll be responsible for the deaths of thousands or even millions of the Americans whose lived you were personally charged to protect. This fear ran wild the post-9/11 Bush Administration, with often-appalling consequences, but it wasn't an irrational fear — not then, and now. It doesn't excuse what was done by our government, and in our name, in prisons and detention cells around the world. But anyone who felt the way I felt after 9/11 has to reckon with the fact that what was done in our name was, in some sense, done for us — not with our knowledge, exactly, but arguably with our blessing. I didn't get what I wanted from this administration, but I think you could say with some justification that I got what I asked for. And that awareness undergirds — to return to where I began this rambling post — the mix of anger, uncertainty and guilt that I bring to the current debate over what the Bush Administration has done and failed to do, and how its members should be judged.

4   This is the Jack Goldsmith argument: while what Bush officials did may have been misguided and wrong, they did it out of a true fear of Islamic enemies, with the intent to protect us, perhaps even consistent with the citizenry's wishes. And while Douthat presents this view as some sort of candid and conflicted complexity, it isn't really anything more than standard American exceptionalism — more accurately: blinding American narcissism — masquerading as a difficult moral struggle.

5   The moral ambiguity Douthat thinks he finds is applicable to virtually every war crime. It's the extremely rare political leader who ends up engaging in tyrannical acts, or commits war crimes or other atrocities, simply for the fun of it, or for purely frivolous reasons. Every tyrant can point to real and legitimate threats that they feared.

Ask supporters of Fidel Castro why he imprisoned dissidents and created a police state and they'll tell you — accurately — that he was the head of a small, defenseless island situated 90 miles to the South of a huge, militaristic superpower that repeatedly tried to overthrow his government and replace it with something it preferred. Ask Hugo Chavez why he rails against the U.S. and has shut down opposition media stations and he'll point out — truthfully — that the U.S. participated to some extent in a coup attempt to overthrow his democratically elected government and that internal factions inside Venezuela have done the same. 6

Iranian mullahs really do face internal, foreign-funded revolutionary groups that are violent and which seek to overthrow them. Serbian leaders — including those ultimately convicted of war crimes — had legitimate grievances about the treatment of Serbs outside of Serbia proper and threats posed to Serbian sovereignty. The complaints of Islamic terrorists regarding U.S. hegemony and exploitation in the Middle East are grounded in factual truth, as are those of Gazan terrorists who point to the four-decades-old Israeli occupation. Georgia really did and does face external threats from Russia, and Russia really did have an interest in protecting Russians and South Ossetians under assault from civilian-attacking Georgian artillery. The threat of Israeli invasion which Hezbollah cites is real. Some Muslims really have been persecuted by Hindus. 7

But none of those facts justify tyranny, terrorism or war crimes. There are virtually always "good reasons" that can be and are cited to justify war crimes and acts of aggression. It's often the case that nationalistic impulses — or genuine fears — lead the country's citizens to support or at least acquiesce to those crimes. War crimes and other atrocities are typically undertaken in defense against some real (if exaggerated) threat, or to target actual enemies, or to redress real grievances. 8

But we don't accept that justifying reasoning when offered by others. In fact, those who seek merely to explain — let alone justify — the tyranny, extremism and/or violence of Castro, or Chavez, or Hamas, or Slobodan Milosevic or Islamic extremists are immediately condemned for seeking to defend the indefensible, or invoking "root causes" to justify the unjustifiable, or offering mitigating rationale for pure evil. 9

Yet here we have American leaders who now, more openly than ever, are literally admitting to what has long been known — that they violated the laws of war and international treaties which, in the past, we've led the way in advocating and enforcing. And what do we hear even from the most well-intentioned commentators such as Douthat? Yes, it was wrong. True, they shouldn't have done it. But they did it for good reasons: they believed they had to do it to protect us, to guard against truly bad people, to discharge their heavy responsibility to protect the country, because we were at war. 10

All of the same can be said for virtually every tyrant we righteously condemn and every war criminal we've pursued and prosecuted. The laws of war aren't applicable only in times of peace, to be waived away in times of war or crisis. To the contrary, they exist precisely because the factors Douthat cites to explain and 11 mitigate what our leaders did always exist, especially when countries perceive themselves at war. To cite those factors to explain away war crimes — or to render them morally ambiguous — is to deny the very validity of the concept itself.

12   The pressures and allegedly selfless motivations being cited on behalf of Bush officials who ordered torture and other crimes — even if accurate — aren't unique to American leaders. They are extremely common. They don't mitigate war crimes. They are what typically motivate war crimes, and they're the reason such crimes are banned by international agreement in the first place — to deter leaders, through the force of law, from succumbing to those exact temptations. What determines whether a political leader is good or evil isn't their nationality. It's their conduct. And leaders who violate the laws of war and commit war crimes, by definition, aren't good, even if they are American.

MARYANN CUSIMANO LOVE teaches graduate and undergraduate courses in politics and ethics at both the Pentagon and Catholic University, as well as serving on the U.S. Catholic Conference of Bishops' International Policy Committee and, since 1998, on the Council on Foreign Relations. Her recent books include *Beyond Sovereignty: Issues for a Global Agenda* (3rd edition, 2006) and *Morality Matters: Ethics and the War on Terrorism* (forthcoming). "An End to Torture" was published in the December 1, 2008 issue of *America.*

An End to Torture

Maryann Cusimano Love

1   Sixty years ago, Eleanor Roosevelt and the U.S. government worked doggedly to create the Universal Declaration of Human Rights. Mrs. Roosevelt knew many successes in her long years of public service, yet she regarded the writing and passage of the Universal Declaration of Human Rights as her greatest accomplishment. She envisioned it as an international Magna Carta and Bill of Rights for people everywhere. She worked so hard (and drove others hard as well) that one delegate charged that the length of the drafting committee meetings violated his own human rights.

2   Like all other human organizations, the United States has a less than pure record on human rights. The same U.S. founding documents that set some souls soaring with language of universal rights also enslaved other human beings and defined them as property, while also excluding the female majority of the population

Protecting human rights and prohibiting torture is practical and advances U.S. interests, especially security interests. By contrast, using torture undermines security.

entirely. We the people have spent the last 232 years working to live up to the best and undo the worst of those founding documents. Protecting human rights and prohibiting torture is practical and advances U.S. interests, especially security interests. By contrast, using torture undermines security.

Whatever one thinks of Barack Obama, Sarah Palin or Hillary Clinton, the 2008 presidential election campaign was a historic move to open up our political life and leadership to all. Eleanor Roosevelt was no starry-eyed idealist. As a woman, an advocate for the poor and the wife of a man with a disability, she knew that U.S. rhetoric on human rights often did not match reality. Lest she forget it, the Soviet and other Communist delegates to the United Nations continually reminded her. As she recounted it, they would point out some failure of human rights in the United States and ask, "'Is that what you consider democracy, Mrs. Roosevelt?' And I am sorry to say that quite often I have to say, 'No, that isn't what I consider democracy. That's a failure of democracy, but there is one thing in my country: we can know about our failures and those of us who care can work to improve our democracy!'" Mrs. Roosevelt placed her faith in the transparency of our society and in the ready supply of everyday prophets who would challenge and overcome injustices.

What Would Eleanor Do?

What would Mrs. Roosevelt make of the current U.S. debate over the use of torture in the war on terrorism? Article 5 of the Universal Declaration of Human Rights prohibits torture, unequivocally stating, "No one shall be subjected to torture or to cruel, inhuman or degrading treatment or punishment." So serious was this basic human right that the drafters placed it at the very beginning of the document, right after the articles stating that all human beings are free and equal and enjoy "the right to life, liberty and security of person." Articles 6 to 11 guaranteed a person's legal rights, including freedom from arbitrary arrest or detention, a right to an impartial trial and a presumption of innocence; these were the "easy" articles from the U.S. perspective. The harder rights for the United States, with its laissez-faire, capitalist economic system, were the social and economic rights tucked in at the end of the document, particularly Articles 23 and 25, which guarantee the right to a job, adequate compensation and an adequate standard of living, "including food, clothing, housing and medical care and necessary social services, and the right to security in the event of unemployment, sickness, disability, widowhood, old age or other lack of livelihood in circumstances beyond his control." Throughout the cold war, the United States repeatedly criticized violations by Soviet and Communist countries of the legal and political rights enumerated in the declaration. These countries returned fire by noting their "iron rice bowl," a state-supported social safety net that they charged was lacking in the

United States and other capitalist states.

5   The current torture debate has turned this history on its head. After the terrorist attacks of Sept. 11, 2001, the Bush administration retreated from the traditional U.S. stance against torture and argued instead for an American exception. Lawyers like John Yoo argued that a "new kind of war" against an enemy that has no regard for human rights excused the United States of its responsibilities as outlined in the Universal Declaration of Human Rights and in the Geneva Conventions. While never admitting to practicing torture, the Bush administration allowed and undertook what it characterized as "aggressive interrogation techniques," including waterboarding, sexual humiliation, attacks by dogs, sleep deprivation and so on. While some of the practices were later decried, particularly those atrocities captured on photos at the Abu Ghraib prison in Iraq, many others were doggedly defended (particularly by Vice President Dick Cheney) as necessary and helpful in the war on terror.

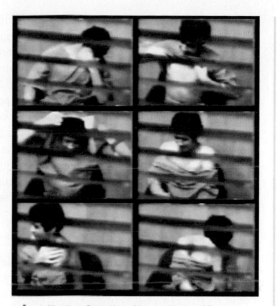

■ Omar Khadr, a Canadian citizen who was 16 years old at the time, appears in multiple video screen grabs during a February 2003 interview in the Guantánamo Bay prison. His attorney and some human rights groups allege that Khadr was tortured.

6   Not all members of the government defense and security communities were so convinced. Then-Secretary of State Colin Powell and State Department lawyers, as well as military JAG lawyers, fought the administration's interpretations. They believed such interrogation techniques were illegal and counterproductive, undermining military morale and discipline, exposing U.S. troops and citizens to the risk of same or similar treatment, and undermining the standing of the United States around the world. So concerned were C.I.A. employees that they purchased insurance policies and urged Congressional action to protect them from lawsuits and legal liability should the political winds change and the actions they were being ordered to undertake be declared illegal.

7   Congress and the public largely acquiesced. Polls showed that pluralities of Americans (and among them, Catholics) believed torture to be permissible. Congressional action to rein in the administration was tepid. In order to avoid a presidential veto, Congress watered down more vigorous anti-torture legislation, never declared waterboarding and other administration-approved methods to be torture, and granted legal protections to government agents who used these aggressive techniques.

President Obama's administration will have to take up the torture debate. Most of the debate centered on whether particular "aggressive interrogation techniques" constituted torture, and whether particular actions taken by agents of the U.S. government (Defense Intelligence Agency, Central Intelligence Agency, military interrogators and government contractors) were legal, including foreign renditions to countries suspected of torture. Religious leaders like the U.S. Conference of Catholic Bishops and the National Religious Campaign Against Torture addressed the morality of torture by emphasizing the fundamental dignity of all human life, as expressed in the Universal Declaration, over the utilitarian view (that the ends of protecting the United States from acts of terror justified the means of violating the rights of suspected terrorists). Torture is a particularly problematic form of violence because it is inflicted by the very state that is supposed to be the protector and guarantor of human rights.

8

Points Missing in the Public Debate

First, torture is ineffective. Philosophers and television shows erroneously propagate the scenario of the "bomb in a baby carriage": government agents apprehend a terrorist who knows when and where the next attack will take place; agents must stop the imminent attack; so they use torture to extract information quickly from the attacker. This model is wrong in almost all respects. Such "exquisite" intelligence as is depicted in prime time never exists in the real world. Instead, government agents never know exactly whom they have caught and what such persons know. Torture does not work because individuals respond in different ways to pain. Aggressive interrogation techniques can yield false information made up to satisfy interrogators and stop the pain. Instead of actionable intelligence that could stop the next attack, such false information wastes scarce government resources on wild goose chases. Even when government agents catch real terrorists, the application of coercive techniques may play into their apocalyptic visions of martyrdom, rather than "loosening lips."

9

Second, torture is immoral, even in a utilitarian calculus. Others besides suspected terrorists are harmed by torture. Arriving at the conclusion that "the end" of saving innocents from terrorist attack justifies the means of torture grossly underestimates the costs of torture to society, to our nation's military and legal institutions and to our role in the world. Those we ask to do the torturing are also harmed, sometimes irreparably. Our legal and political systems are harmed, as professionalism in the military and in law enforcement suffers. For this reason, military lawyers are among the strongest critics of torture. As Shannon E. French, formerly of the U.S. Naval Academy, notes in her book *The Code of the Warrior*, military professionals need ethical codes to work effectively and to differentiate themselves from barbarians and murderers. The United States has the strongest military on earth, and others come from far and wide to study and emulate U.S. military professionalism and codes of conduct. The ethical frameworks of the Universal Declaration of Human Rights, the military code of conduct and the Geneva Conventions protect not only innocent civilians but military personnel

10

themselves. Violating those norms puts Americans at risk for similar treatment. According to his killers, contractor Nicholas Berg was beheaded in retaliation for torture at Abu Ghraib.

11   *Third, torture is impractical.* Protecting human rights and prohibiting torture is practical and advances U.S. interests, especially U.S. security interests. By contrast, using torture undermines U.S. security. The National Religious Campaign Against Torture acknowledges this in its call for the new president to issue an executive order banning torture (www.nrcat.org). The war against terror is primarily a battle of ideas. Al Qaeda fights for the idea of the bankruptcy of modern and secular Islamic states allied with the West, while the United States fights for the idea that the tactic of terrorism, of intentionally killing civilians, is impermissible. The United States cannot effectively fight for a global norm while ignoring normative constraints. The United States cannot champion human rights abroad while ignoring them at Guantánamo. The United States certainly cannot do this with the world watching.

12   Military force is not the source of American power in the world today. The strength and attractiveness of U.S. ideals are at the basis of U.S. "soft power," and torture undermines those. The debate is not between realists keen on protecting U.S. citizens and idealists who place human rights ahead of security concerns. As Eleanor Roosevelt knew 60 years ago, and a new administration must rediscover now, advancing human rights also advances U.S. interests and security.

Debate 2: Same-Sex Marriage

"Interracial Marriage: Slippery Slope?" by La Shawn Barber (pp. 256–57)

"The Loving Decision" by Anna Quindlen (pp. 258–60)

"The Future of Marriage," Editorial from *National Review* (pp. 260–61)

"The Right's Contempt for Gay Lives" by Andrew Sullivan (pp. 261–63)

Understanding the Debate over Same-Sex Marriage

Same-sex marriage — the right of gay couples to marry and enjoy all the legal rights and protections of married couples — has been the source of heated debate in the United States for decades. Much of the current conversation about same-sex marriage has centered around recent activity at the ballot box, in state legislatures, and in the courts. Ballot measures in November 2008 in California, Florida, and Arizona explicitly defined marriage as between one man and one woman or otherwise attempted to forestall measures designed to allow same-sex marriage. In early

2009, judicial and legislative decisions in Iowa, Vermont, and Maine specifically allowed same-sex marriage in those states.

As a result, some of the discussion around same-sex marriage — both in the articles collected here and elsewhere — centers around the relative merits of "majority rule" versus "judicial activism" when it comes to establishing or protecting rights. A good deal of discussion, particularly among opponents of same-sex marriage, rests on perceptions of what marriage has meant and should mean and how it differs from civil unions.

The issue is complex, and passions run high. In reading the four articles presented here, try to put aside your own preconceptions and weigh each argument on its own merits. The need to find common ground on this issue is more than just a classroom activity — most people would agree that, as with other divisive but significant issues, our future direction as a society depends on finding a resolution we can all live with.

LA SHAWN BARBER is a freelance writer whose writing about politics, faith, and culture has appeared in a variety of publications including the *Washington Post*, the *Washington Times*, *Christianity Today*, Beliefnet.com, and *National Review Online*. Barber has appeared on CNN's "Reliable Sources" as well as MSNBC, National Public Radio, and Bill O'Reilly's "The Radio Factor." She also blogs at the American Civil Rights Institute blog and her own Web site, La Shawn Barber's Corner (www.lashawnbarber.com). On her "Who Am I?" page, Barber tells us how to introduce her: "Don't call her 'African American.' She *hates* that term. If you must refer to her race, call her 'black.' And La Shawn is not a Republican. She's an independent conservative." She posted the following essay arguing her position on same-sex marriage at Townhall.com on June 11, 2007.

Interracial Marriage: Slippery Slope?

LA SHAWN BARBER ▼

Tomorrow marks the 40th anniversary of *Loving v. Virginia*, the landmark Supreme Court case that declared Virginia's law against interracial marriage unconstitutional.   1

Mildred Jeter and Richard Loving had to leave their home state to marry. They exchanged vows in Washington, D.C., in June 1958, where there was no prohibition against interracial marriage. Shortly after returning to Virginia, the couple was arrested in their home and charged with "unlawful cohabitation."   2

3   The court suspended sentence on the condition that the two leave the state and not return together for 25 years. In 1963, the Lovings filed a motion to vacate the judgment and set aside the sentence. Almost a year later, the court still hadn't ruled on the motion, and the couple filed a class action suit in federal court. The case eventually made its way to Virginia's highest court, which upheld the state's law against miscegenation and affirmed the convictions.

4   On June 12, 1967, the U.S. Supreme Court declared Virginia's anti-miscegenation statute unconstitutional. As marriage is defined as a union between a man and a woman, there was no "legitimate overriding purpose" to outlaw marriage between a white man and a black woman other than blatant racial discrimination. Racial classifications are suspect. For courts to uphold such classifications, states must demonstrate a "permissible state objective, independent of the racial discrimination which it was the object of the Fourteenth Amendment to eliminate."

5   The court also found that Virginia's anti-miscegenation law violated the Due Process Clause: "To deny this fundamental freedom on so unsupportable a basis as the racial classifications embodied in these statutes . . . is surely to deprive all the State's citizens of liberty without due process of law."

6   Ironically, Democrats created laws prohibiting interracial marriage. After the Civil War, states enacted laws called Black Codes in response to the emancipation of slaves, which restricted the rights of newly freed slaves to own or rent farmland, vote, sit on juries, testify against white men, sue, enter into contracts, and intermarry with whites. Republicans opposed the laws and wanted to pass the Civil Rights Bill, but Democratic president Andrew Johnson refused. The rest is well documented history.

7   Homosexuals have cited Loving v. Virginia and the modern civil rights movement to argue for marriage between two men. Aside from the moral outrage this should generate in the black community but doesn't, marriage between a man and woman of different races and marriage between people of the same sex aren't comparable at all.

8   The goal of interracial marriage bans and legalized segregation was to maintain a subordinate class of citizens based on race. The goal of same-sex marriage bans is to protect traditional marriage, not maintain a subordinate class based on "sexual orientation." One would be hard-pressed to argue that homosexuals in America are second-class citizens.

9   Marriage is a legal union and social institution recognized by the states as serving fundamental purposes: providing structure for family formation and rearing children, and acting as a stabilizing influence that benefits the whole society. Changing the definition to include the union of two men and two women opens the door to legalizing increasingly deviant unions. Marriage will cease to have any meaning at all.

10   For instance, if we extend marriage to same-sex couples, on what grounds can we deny the same to three people? Or 10? Or close relatives? Or adults and children? It makes a mockery of marriage.

11   Individuals are worthy of equal treatment under the law, regardless of race, but an individual's lifestyle choices are not.

ANNA QUINDLEN is a prolific and nationally acclaimed writer. She has written many novels for adults and children, including *One True Thing* (1994) and *Black and Blue* (1998), both of which were also made into movies. Among Quindlen's nonfiction books are *A Short Guide to a Happy Life* (2000) and several collections of essays reprinted from her Pulitzer Prize–winning *New York Times* column. As a contributing editor for *Newsweek* magazine, Quindlen writes a regular column in which the following essay arguing her opinion on same-sex marriage originally appeared on November 12, 2008.

The Loving Decision

Anna Quindlen

Same-sex marriage was beaten back at the ballot box. Now here's a history lesson on why victory is inevitable in the long run.

One of my favorite supreme court cases is *Loving v. Virginia*, and not just because it has a name that would delight any novelist. It's because it reminds me, when I'm downhearted, of the truth of the sentiment at the end of "Angels in America," Tony Kushner's brilliant play: "The world only spins forward."

> **Same-sex marriage was beaten back at the ballot box. Now here's a history lesson on why victory is inevitable in the long run.**

Here are the facts of the case, and if they leave you breathless with disbelief and rage it only proves Kushner's point, and mine: Mildred Jeter and Richard Loving got married in Washington, D.C. They went home to Virginia, there to be rousted out of their bed one night by police and charged with a felony. The felony was that Mildred was black and Richard was white and they were therefore guilty of miscegenation, which is a $10 word for bigotry. Virginia, like a number of other states, considered cross-racial matrimony a crime at the time.

It turned out that it wasn't just the state that hated the idea of black people marrying white people. God was onboard, too, according to the trial judge, who wrote, "The fact that He separated the races shows that he did not intend for the races to mix." But the Supreme Court, which eventually heard the case, passed over the Almighty for the Constitution, which luckily has an equal-protection clause. "Marriage is one of the basic civil rights of man," the unanimous opinion striking down the couple's conviction said, "fundamental to our very existence and survival."

That was in 1967.

1

2

3

4

5

6   Fast-forward to Election Day 2008, and a flurry of state ballot propositions to outlaw gay marriage, all of which were successful. This is the latest wedge issue of the good-old-days crowd, supplanting abortion and immigration. They really put their backs into it this time around, galvanized by court decisions in three states ruling that it is discriminatory not to extend the right to marry to gay men and lesbians.

7   The most high-profile of those rulings, and the most high-profile ballot proposal, came in California. A state court gave its imprimatur to same-sex marriage in June; the electorate reversed that decision on Nov. 4 with the passage of Proposition 8, which defines marriage as only between a man and a woman. The opponents of gay marriage will tell you that the people have spoken. It's truer to say that money talks. The Mormons donated millions to the anti effort; the Knights of Columbus did, too. Like the judge who ruled in the Loving case, they said they were doing God's bidding. When I was a small child I always used to picture God on a cloud, with a beard. Now I picture God saying, "Why does all the worst stuff get done in my name?"

8   Just informationally, this is how things are going to go from here on in: two steps forward, one step back. Courts will continue to rule in some jurisdictions that there is no good reason to forbid same-sex couples from marrying. Legislatures in two states, New York and New Jersey, could pass a measure guaranteeing the right to matrimony to all, and both states have governors who have said they would sign such legislation.

9   Opponents will scream that the issue should be put to the people, as it was in Arizona, Florida and California. (Arkansas had a different sort of measure, forbidding unmarried couples from adopting or serving as foster parents. This will undoubtedly have the effect of leaving more kids without stable homes. For shame.) Of course if the issue in Loving had been put to the people, there is no doubt that many would have been delighted to make racial intermarriage a crime. That's why God invented courts.

10   The world only spins forward.

11   "I think the day will come when the lesbian and gay community will have its own *Loving v. Virginia*," says David Buckel, the Marriage Project director for Lambda Legal.

12   Yes, and then the past will seem as preposterous and mean-spirited as the events leading up to the Loving decision do today. After all, this is about one of the most powerful forces for good on earth, the determination of two human beings to tether their lives forever. The pitch of the opposition this year spoke to how far we have already come — the states in which civil unions and domestic partnerships are recognized, the families in which gay partners are welcome and beloved.

13   The antis argued that churches could be forced to perform same-sex unions, when any divorced Roman Catholic can tell you that the clergy refuse to officiate whenever they see fit. They argued that the purpose of same-sex marriage was the indoctrination of children, a popular talking point that has no basis in reality. As Ellen DeGeneres, who was married several months ago to the lovely Portia de Rossi (great dress, girl), said about being shaped by the orientation of those around you, "I was raised by two heterosexuals. I was surrounded by heterosexuals. Just everywhere I looked: heterosexuals. They did not influence me." As for

the notion that allowing gay men and lesbians to marry will destroy conventional marriage, I have found heterosexuals perfectly willing to do that themselves.

The last word here goes to an authority on battling connubial bigotry. On the anniversary of the Loving decision last year, the bride wore tolerance. Mildred Loving, mother and grandmother, who once had cops burst into her bedroom because she was sleeping with her own husband, was quoted in a rare public statement saying she believed all Americans, "no matter their race, no matter their sex, no matter their sexual orientation, should have that same freedom to marry." She concluded, "That's what *Loving*, and loving, are all about." 14

National Review describes itself as "America's most widely read and influential magazine and web site for Republican/conservative news, commentary, and opinion." It was founded by William F. Buckley Jr. and is currently edited by Rich Lowry. The following essay was published in the *National Review Online* on April 8, 2009. A slightly different version was published in the May 4, 2009, print edition of the *National Review* under the title "Marriage and Civilization."

The Future of Marriage

NATIONAL REVIEW EDITORIAL	▼

One of the great coups of the movement for same-sex marriage has been to plant the premise that it represents the inevitable future. This sense has inhibited even some who know perfectly well that marriage is by nature the union of a man and a woman. They fear that throwing themselves into the cause of opposing it is futile — worse, that it will call down the judgment of history that they were bigots. 1

Contrary to common perception, however, the public is not becoming markedly more favorable toward same-sex marriage. Support for same-sex marriage rose during the 1990s but seems to have frozen in place (at least according to Gallup) since the high court of Massachusetts invented a right to same-sex marriage earlier this decade. 2

Our guess is that if the federal judiciary does not intervene to impose same-sex marriage on the entire country, we are not going to see it triumph from coast to coast. Rather, we will for some time have a patchwork of laws. The division will not be so much between socially liberal and conservative states as between those states where voters can amend their state constitutions easily and those where they cannot. Thus same-sex marriage is likely to stay the law of the land in Massachusetts, Iowa, and Vermont, and perhaps also in New Hampshire. 3

4   In two of those states, at least, democratic procedure is now being respected. Vermont has chosen to recognize same-sex marriages legislatively, and New Hampshire may do so. Other states, such as Connecticut, have legislated recognition of civil unions for same-sex couples. While free from the taint of lawlessness, these decisions seem to us unwise. Few social goods will come from recognizing same-sex couples as married. Some practical benefits may accrue to the couples, but most of them could easily be realized without changing marriage laws. Same-sex couples will also receive the symbolic affirmation of being treated by the state as equivalent to a traditional married couple — but this spurious equality is a cost of the new laws, not a benefit. One still sometimes hears people make the allegedly "conservative" case for same-sex marriage that it will reduce promiscuity and encourage commitment among homosexuals. This prospect seems improbable, and in any case these do not strike us as important governmental goals.

5   Both as a social institution and as a public policy, marriage exists to foster connections between heterosexual sex and the rearing of children within stable households. It is a non-coercive way to channel (heterosexual) desire into civilized patterns of living. State recognition of the marital relationship does not imply devaluation of any other type of relationship, whether friendship or brotherhood. State recognition of those other types of relationships is unnecessary. So too is the governmental recognition of same-sex sexual relationships, committed or otherwise, in a deep sense pointless.

6   No, we do not expect marriage rates to plummet and illegitimacy rates to skyrocket in these jurisdictions over the next decade. But to the extent same-sex marriage is normalized here, it will be harder for American culture and law to connect marriage and parenthood. That it has already gotten harder over the last few decades is no answer to this concern. In foisting same-sex marriage on Iowa, the state's supreme court opined in a footnote that the idea that it is best for children to have mothers and fathers married to each other is merely based on "stereotype."

7   If worse comes to worst, and the federal courts sweep aside the marriage laws that most Americans still want, then decades from now traditionalists should be ready to brandish that footnote and explain to generations yet unborn: That is why we resisted.

ANDREW SULLIVAN, a self-identified gay Catholic conservative, has written extensively about politics and culture. He has written several books, including *The Conservative Soul: Fundamentalism, Freedom, and the Future of the Right* (2006), and edited *Same-Sex Marriage: Pro and Con* (2004), a collection of argument essays. He is a senior editor at the *New Republic* and writes a popular blog, "The Daily Dish," which originally appeared at Time.com and is now published by the *Atlantic* online. He has appeared on numerous television and radio talk shows, including *The Colbert Report, Meet the Press, The O'Reilly Factor,* and *Real Time with Bill Maher.* He wrote the following blog post on April 8, 2009, in response to the *National Review* editorial that appears on pp. 260–61.

The Right's Contempt for Gay Lives

ANDREW SULLIVAN   ▼

National Review's new editorial comes out firmly against even civil unions for gay couples, and continues to insist that society's exclusive support for straight couples is designed "to foster connections between heterosexual sex and the rearing of children within stable households." [1]

This is an honest and revealing point, and, in a strange way, it confirms my own analysis of the theocon position. It reaffirms, for example, that infertile couples who want to marry in order to adopt children have no place within existing marriage laws, as *NR* sees them. Such infertile and adoptive "marriages" rest on a decoupling of actual sex and the rearing of children. The same, of course, applies much more extensively to any straight married couple that uses contraception: they too are undermining what *National Review* believes to be the core reason for civil marriage. Now, you could argue — and I suspect *NR*'s editors would — that society nonetheless has a role in providing moral, social and legal support for couples with children, however those children came about, and to provide "a non-coercive way to channel (heterosexual) desire into civilized patterns of living." I agree with this, actually, which is why I do not want to alter or weaken traditional marriage in any way, and regard it as a vital social institution that deserves our support. [2]

But what of "channeling homosexual desire into civilized patterns of living?" Ah, there's the rub. [3]

National Review clearly believes that gays exist beyond the boundaries of civilized life, or even social life, let alone the purview of social policy. But, of course, a total absence of social policy is still a social policy. And such a social policy — leaving gay people outside of existing social institutions, while tolerating their existence — has led to some rather predictable consequences. We have, for example, lived through a period in which around 300,000 young Americans died of a terrible disease that was undoubtedly compounded by the total lack of any social incentives for stable relationships. Imagine what would happen to STD rates or legitimacy rates if heterosexual marriage were somehow not in existence. Do you think that straight men would be more or less socially responsible without the institution of civil marriage? [4]

This is not to deny the responsibility of those of us who contracted HIV. It is to make the core conservative case that culture matters, and that in so far as we can non-coercively encourage and support committed relationships, society, which includes gay people, will be better off. But *National Review*, stunningly, regards the well-being, health and flourishing of gay people as unworthy of any attention at all. Here is the passage that reflects the core homophobia — and yes, I see no alternative to using that word — in that magazine: [5]

> Same-sex couples will also receive the symbolic affirmation of being treated by the state as equivalent to a traditional married couple — but this spurious

equality is a cost of the new laws, not a benefit. One still sometimes hears people make the allegedly "conservative" case for same-sex marriage that it will reduce promiscuity and encourage commitment among homosexuals. This prospect seems improbable, and in any case these do not strike us as important governmental goals.

Ponder those sentences for a moment. The fact that gay Americans may feel equal because of inclusion within their own families and societies is now a cost to society, not a benefit. Encouraging commitment, fewer partners, and greater responsibility are important governmental goals with respect to heterosexuals but not with respect to homosexuals. As far as *National Review* is concerned, homosexuals can go to hell. Their interests and views cannot even be accorded respect. They are non-persons to *National Review*: means, not ends.

6   Flip this around and you see what the theocon right actually believes: that society has no interest in the welfare of its gay citizens, and an abiding interest in ensuring that they remain unequal, feel unequal and suffer the consequences of a culture where family and commitment and fidelity are non-existent. And they write this within living memory of an appalling and devastating plague. This is how the social right is responding to our times, and to put it personally, my life and the lives and deaths of countless others. One day, they will understand the callousness and bitterness and willful ignorance they currently represent. As civilized society leaves them increasingly behind.

6

Arguing a Position

IN COLLEGE COURSES For a political science course, a student writes an essay arguing in favor of the controversial Employee Free Choice Act (EFCA). She begins by explaining that the EFCA would reform current labor law by allowing workers to unionize if a majority simply signed a card requesting it; by contrast, under current law, if workers express interest in forming a union, their employer can require a secret ballot. Those who oppose the new law claim that without a secret ballot, workers could be intimidated by union representatives into voting for the union.

The student's essay acknowledges that supporting the new law in the name of free choice might seem counterintuitive because it does away with the secret ballot, a staple of democracy. She argues, however, that under existing law, employers routinely make use of the time required to set up a secret ballot by dissuading workers from voting to unionize, using such tactics as videotaping people going into union meetings and then harassing them at work and at home, or requiring employees to attend meetings during which they are bombarded with anti-union propaganda, including threats of mass firing. To support her argument, she cites statistics from the National Labor Relations Board and other sources showing, among other things, that 88 percent of the unfair labor practice citations in 2006 and 2007 were against employers, not unions; 25 percent of employers illegally fire at least one worker for union activity; 92 percent of employers force employees to attend mandatory closed-door meetings against the union; and 51 percent of companies threaten to shut down if the union wins the election.

IN THE COMMUNITY   In a letter to the school board, a group of parents writes a petition in favor of a proposal to institute a Peacemakers program at the local middle school. Their argument refutes the claims made by another group of parents who oppose the idea.

They begin with anecdotal reports of bullying at the school to underscore the need for action. They emphasize that the program's primary goal — teaching children not to avoid conflict but to manage conflict constructively — is one all parents could endorse, and they argue that those who oppose the program misunderstand it. To support this claim, they quote a parent who described the Peacemakers' objectives as teaching children "to become passive and submissive rather than thinking adults who can make their way in the world and speak up for what is right." To clarify the Peacemakers' true objectives, they quote the program's Web site as well as research studies of schools where the program has been in effect.

In addition, they refute parents' misunderstanding of the program's methods — for example, the ideas that students must keep their hands clasped behind their backs when walking down the halls and that students cannot play contact sports like basketball and football. To clarify the Peacemakers' actual methods, they briefly describe the negotiation procedure children are taught that involves articulating what they want, listening to what others want, and cooperatively inventing ways of resolving the conflict. They conclude by claiming that learning negotiation skills like these will help children in their personal, professional, and civic lives.

IN THE WORKPLACE   An executive in the financial industry writes a blog entry defending American International Group (AIG) for paying out $165 million in bonuses after the company was saved from bankruptcy by an infusion of taxpayer money. The executive, whose company is not affiliated with AIG, begins by acknowledging the justifiable public indignation at the situation. Nevertheless, he argues that, legally, AIG had no choice but to honor the contracts that guaranteed the bonuses. He claims that efforts by the government to void the contracts would set a dangerous precedent. He warns, too, that punitively taxing the bonuses would make companies less likely to accept government help, even when doing so is in the nation's best interests, as in the case of AIG.

He refutes charges that Congress acted inconsistently in allowing AIG executives' contracts to stand while requiring the autoworkers' union to renegotiate their contracts with bailed-out automakers: The AIG situation, he points out, refers to past contracts, whereas the autoworkers' situation refers to future contracts. He concludes by reminding his readers of what he assumes is a shared value: not getting paid for work already performed is un-American.

To his surprise, his blog entry provokes nearly two hundred responses, most of which disagree with his defense of the bonuses, arguing that incompetence and greed should not be federally subsidized.

You may associate arguing with quarreling or with the in-your-face debating we hear so often on radio and television talk shows. These ways of arguing may let you vent strong feelings, but they seldom lead you to consider seriously other points of view or to reflect on your own thinking.

This chapter presents a more deliberative way of arguing that we call **reasoned argument** because it depends on giving reasons rather than raising voices. Like the college student supporting the Employee Free Choice Act, the parents arguing in favor of the Peacemakers program, and the financial industry executive defending AIG bonuses, writers advocating controversial positions know that they will have a better chance of convincing others, or at least getting a fair hearing for their opinions, if they offer plausible reasons and acknowledge other points of view.

Controversial issues are, by definition, issues about which people may have strong feelings. The issue may involve a practice that has been accepted for some time, like allowing college athletes to register for their courses before all other students to accommodate practice and travel schedules, or it may concern a newly proposed or recently instituted policy, like the U.S. military's use of "enhanced interrogation" techniques to get information from suspected terrorists. People may agree about goals but disagree about the best way to achieve them, as in the perennial debate over how to make a public-college education affordable to all qualified students. Or they may disagree about fundamental values and beliefs, as in the debate over gay marriage or granting citizenship to immigrants who have entered the United States illegally.

As you can see from these examples, controversial issues have no obvious right answer, no truth that everyone accepts, no single authority on which everyone relies. Writers cannot offer absolute proof in debates about controversial issues because such issues are matters of opinion and judgment. Simply gathering information — finding the facts or learning from experts — will not settle disputes like these. (Of course, the more you know about an issue, the more informed your position on it will be.)

Although it is not possible to prove that a position on a controversial issue is right or wrong, it is possible through reasoned argument to convince others to accept or reject the position. To be convincing, an argument must not only present convincing reasons and plausible support for its position, but also should anticipate readers' likely objections and opposing arguments, conceding those that are reasonable and refuting those that are not. Vigorous debate that sets forth arguments and counterarguments on all sides of an issue can advance everyone's thinking.

Learning to make reasoned arguments on controversial issues and to evaluate our own as well as others' arguments is not a luxury; it is a necessity if our form of government is to survive and flourish. As citizens in a democracy, we have a special duty to inform ourselves about pressing issues and to participate constructively in the public debate. Improving our research and reasoning strategies also has practical advantages in school, where we often are judged by our ability to write convincingly, and in the workplace, where we may want to take a stand on issues concerning working conditions, environmental impact, or pay and promotional policies.

To get a sense of the complexities and possibilities involved in arguing a position, get together with two or three other students, and discuss an issue you have strong feelings about. Here are some guidelines to follow:

Part 1.

- As a group, choose one issue from the following list, or think of a different college issue you all know about:

    - Should admission to college be based solely on high school grade-point average?
    - Should there be a community service requirement for graduation from college?
    - Should college students be required to take courses outside of their major?
    - Should the federal government subsidize everyone's college education?
    - Should sororities and fraternities be banned from college campuses?
    - Should drinking alcohol on college campuses be permitted?
    - Should college students living in residence halls be allowed to have pets?
    - Should college athletes be paid?

- Decide which audience you are trying to convince of your position on this particular issue — college administrators, your parents, or your fellow students.
- Divide into two teams — pro (those in favor) and con (those opposed) — and take a few minutes to think of reasons why your audience should accept your position.
- Take turns presenting your argument. You may have only a few minutes each, so set a phone alarm or countdown timer.

Part 2. Discuss what you learned about making an argument for your position on a controversial issue.

- How did knowing whether you were addressing administrators, parents, or students affect which reasons you used and how you presented them? Why did you expect your audience to accept your reasons?
- To set up a debate, we asked you to think in pro/con terms, but there are usually more than two points of view on most controversial issues. What values, priorities, or interests do you think are most important to your audience when they think about this issue? What is most important to you?

A Collaborative Activity:
Practice Arguing a Position

Reading Essays Arguing a Position

Basic Features

As you read essays in this chapter arguing a position, you will see how different authors incorporate the basic features of the genre.

Basic Features

● A Well-Presented Issue

Read first to see how the writer presents the issue. Is the issue controversial and clearly arguable — a matter on which people can reasonably disagree — or is the issue not arguable because opinions are based on belief, faith, or personal taste?

Writers may also use a variety of strategies to present the issue. Their choice of strategies depends in part on what they assume readers already know and what they want readers to think about the issue. For current, hotly debated issues, the title may be enough to identify the issue, but for less well-known issues, the writer may need to establish that the issue exists and is serious enough to deserve readers' attention. To inform readers about the issue's seriousness and arouse readers' concern, writers may

- give examples or statistics that show how many people are affected by the issue and how they are affected;
- use scenarios or anecdotes that resonate with readers' own experience and raise their concern; or
- quote authorities or research studies to show that the issue deserves attention.

Do not assume that the writer's presentation of the issue is objective. Writers almost always try to define or *frame* the issue in a way that promotes their position, usually by emphasizing values, priorities, and interests that are important to the reader. So as you read essays in this chapter, be attentive to how the writers frame the issues, and consider how this framing affects your response to the essays.

● A Well-Supported Position

Find where the essay states and supports the writer's position on the issue. Very often writers declare their position in a thesis statement early in the essay. If you cannot at first find a direct statement of the writer's position, consider the title and the first and last paragraphs, and then read the entire essay through. Once you have decided what position the author is arguing, determine whether the argument is plausible by assessing whether the supporting reasons and evidence clearly back up the writer's claims and come from trustworthy sources. For example, consider the following questions:

- Are statements asserted to be *facts* widely accepted as true and complete?
- Are *examples* and *anecdotes* representative or idiosyncratic and are they illustrative or manipulative?
- Are cited *authorities* credible and trustworthy?
- Are *statistics* taken from reliable sources and representative population samples?

● An Effective Counterargument

Read also to see how the writer responds to possible objections readers might raise as well as to opposing positions. Writers may counterargue in one or more of the following ways:

- by acknowledging readers' concerns and points of view
- by conceding an objection and modifying the argument to accommodate it
- by refuting readers' objections or by arguing against opposing positions

● A Readable Plan

Finally, examine the essay to see whether the writer provides a readable plan. Essays arguing a position need to explain the issue, provide a reasoned argument for the position, and counterargue objections and alternative positions, backing everything up with solid support and clear citations. Therefore, it is especially important to have a readable plan that helps readers follow the twists and turns of the argument.

To make their essays easy to read, writers usually include some or all of the following:

- a forecast of the argument
- key words introduced in the thesis and forecasting statement
- topic sentences introducing paragraphs or groups of paragraphs
- repeated use of key words and synonyms throughout the essay, particularly in topic sentences
- clear transitional words and phrases

Purpose and Audience

People sometimes write position essays to clarify their own reasons for taking a particular position, but most position essays are written to influence readers' thinking on the issue. *As you read essays arguing a position, ask yourself what seems to be the writer's* **purpose** *in writing.* For example, does the writer seem to be writing

- to change readers' minds
- to confirm readers' opinions
- to supply readers with reasons and evidence to support the writer's position
- to convince readers to look at the issue in a new way
- to move readers to take action
- to establish common ground on which people might be able to agree
- to win readers' respect for a different point of view?

As you read, also try to guess what the writer assumes about the **audience**. For example, does the writer assume readers will

- be only mildly interested or know little about the issue
- care deeply about the issue and have strong convictions
- oppose or be skeptical of the writer's position
- have their own position on the issue
- have serious objections to the writer's argument?

Readings

● ● ● ●

Basic Features

- A Well-Presented Issue
- A Well-Supported Position
- An Effective Counterargument
- A Readable Plan

JESSICA STATSKY wrote the following essay about children's competitive sports for her college composition course. Before reading, recall your own experiences as an elementary student playing competitive sports, either in or out of school. If you were not actively involved yourself, did you know anyone who was? Looking back, do you think that winning was unduly emphasized? What value was placed on having a good time? On learning to get along with others? On developing athletic skills and confidence?

As you read, consider the questions in the margin. Your instructor may ask you to post your answers or bring them to class.

Children Need to Play, Not Compete
Jessica Statsky

How does Statsky present the issue in a way that prepares readers for her argument?

Over the past three decades, organized sports for children have increased dramatically in the United States. And though many adults regard Little League Baseball and Peewee Football as a basic part of childhood, the games are not always joyous ones. When overzealous parents and coaches impose adult standards on children's sports, the result can be activities that are neither satisfying nor beneficial to children. 1

How does she qualify her position in par. 2?

I am concerned about all organized sports activities for children between the ages of six and twelve. The damage I see results from noncontact as well as contact sports, from sports organized locally as well as those organized nationally. Highly organized competitive sports such as Peewee Football and Little League Baseball are too often played to adult standards, which are developmentally inappropriate for children and can be both physically and psychologically harmful. Furthermore, because they eliminate many children from organized sports before they are ready to compete, they are actually counterproductive for developing either future players or fans. Finally, because they emphasize competition and winning, they unfortunately provide occasions for some parents and coaches to place their own fantasies and needs ahead of children's welfare. 2

What reasons does she forecast here, and in which paragraphs does she discuss each reason?

One readily understandable danger of overly competitive sports is that they entice children into physical actions that are bad for growing bodies. Although the official Little League Web site acknowledges that children do risk injury playing baseball, it insists that "severe injuries...are infrequent," the risk "far less than the risk of riding a skateboard, a bicycle, or even the school bus" ("What about My Child?"). 3

Nevertheless, Leonard Koppett in *Sports Illusion, Sports Reality* claims that a twelve-year-old trying to throw a curve ball, for example, may put abnormal strain on developing arm and shoulder muscles, sometimes resulting in lifelong injuries (294). Contact sports like football can be even more hazardous. Thomas Tutko, a psychology professor at San Jose State University and coauthor of the book *Winning Is Everything and Other American Myths*, writes:

> I am strongly opposed to young kids playing tackle football. It is not the right stage of development for them to be taught to crash into other kids. Kids under the age of fourteen are not by nature physical. Their main concern is self-preservation. They don't want to meet head on and slam into each other. But tackle football absolutely requires that they try to hit each other as hard as they can. And it is too traumatic for young kids. (qtd. in Tosches A1)

4 As Tutko indicates, even when children are not injured, fear of being hurt detracts from their enjoyment of the sport. The Little League Web site ranks fear of injury as the seventh of seven reasons children quit ("What about My Child?"). One mother of an eight-year-old Peewee Football player explained, "The kids get so scared. They get hit once and they don't want anything to do with football anymore. They'll sit on the bench and pretend their leg hurts..." (qtd. in Tosches A1). Some children are driven to even more desperate measures. For example, in one Peewee Football game, a reporter watched the following scene as a player took himself out of the game:

> "Coach, my tummy hurts. I can't play," he said. The coach told the player to get back onto the field. "There's nothing wrong with your stomach," he said. When the coach turned his head the seven-year-old stuck a finger down his throat and made himself vomit. When the coach turned back, the boy pointed to the ground and told him, "Yes there is, coach. See?" (Tosches A33)

5 Besides physical hazards and anxieties, competitive sports pose psychological dangers for children. Martin Rablovsky, a former sports editor for the *New York Times*, says that in all his years of watching young children play organized sports, he has noticed very few of them smiling. "I've seen children enjoying a spontaneous pre-practice scrimmage become somber and serious when the coach's whistle blows," Rablovsky says. "The spirit of play suddenly disappears, and sport becomes joblike" (qtd. in Coakley 94). The primary goal of a professional athlete — winning — is not appropriate for children. Their goals should be having fun, learning, and being with friends. Although winning does add to the fun, too many adults lose sight of what matters and make winning the most important goal. Several studies have shown that

How does Statsky try to establish the credibility of her sources in pars. 3–5?

Why do you think she uses block quotations instead of integrating these quotes into her own sentences?

when children are asked whether they would rather be warming the bench on a winning team or playing regularly on a losing team, about 90 percent choose the latter (Smith, Smith, and Smoll 11).

How does Statsky try to refute this objection?

Winning and losing may be an inevitable part of adult life, but they should not be part of childhood. Too much competition too early in life can affect a child's development. Children are easily influenced, and when they sense that their competence and worth are based on their ability to live up to their parents' and coaches' high expectations — and on their ability to win — they can become discouraged and depressed. Little League advises parents to "keep winning in perspective" ("Your Role"), noting that the most common reasons children give for quitting, aside from change in interest, are lack of playing time, failure and fear of failure, disapproval by significant others, and psychological stress ("What about My Child?"). According to Dr. Glyn C. Roberts, a professor of kinesiology at the Institute of Child Behavior and Development at the University of Illinois, 80 to 90 percent of children who play competitive sports at a young age drop out by sixteen (Kutner).

6

How effective do you think Statsky's argument in par. 7 is? Why?

This statistic illustrates another reason I oppose competitive sports for children: because they are so highly selective, very few children get to participate. Far too soon, a few children are singled out for their athletic promise, while many others, who may be on the verge of developing the necessary strength and ability, are screened out and discouraged from trying out again. Like adults, children fear failure, and so even those with good physical skills may stay away because they lack self-confidence. Consequently, teams lose many promising players who with some encouragement and experience might have become stars. The problem is that many parent-sponsored, out-of-school programs give more importance to having a winning team than to developing children's physical skills and self-esteem.

7

In criticizing some parents' behavior in pars. 8–9, Statsky risks alienating her readers. How effective is this part of her argument?

Indeed, it is no secret that too often scorekeeping, league standings, and the drive to win bring out the worst in adults who are more absorbed in living out their own fantasies than in enhancing the quality of the experience for children (Smith, Smith, and Smoll 9). Recent newspaper articles on children's sports contain plenty of horror stories. *Los Angeles Times* reporter Rich Tosches, for example, tells the story of a brawl among seventy-five parents following a Peewee Football game (A33). As a result of the brawl, which began when a parent from one team confronted a player from the other team, the teams are now thinking of hiring security guards for future games. Another example is provided by a *Los Angeles Times* editorial about a Little League manager who intimidated the opposing team by setting fire to one of their team's jerseys on the pitcher's mound before the game began. As the editorial writer commented, the manager showed his young team that "intimidation could substitute for playing well" ("The Bad News").

8

9   Although not all parents or coaches behave so inappropriately, the seriousness of the problem is illustrated by the fact that Adelphi University in Garden City, New York, offers a sports psychology workshop for Little League coaches, designed to balance their "animal instincts" with "educational theory" in hopes of reducing the "screaming and hollering," in the words of Harold Weisman, manager of sixteen Little Leagues in New York City (Schmitt). In a three-and-one-half-hour Sunday morning workshop, coaches learn how to make practices more fun, treat injuries, deal with irate parents, and be "more sensitive to their young players' fears, emotional frailties, and need for recognition." Little League is to be credited with recognizing the need for such workshops.

How effective is Statsky's use of concession and refutation here?

10   Some parents would no doubt argue that children cannot start too soon preparing to live in a competitive free-market economy. After all, secondary schools and colleges require students to compete for grades, and college admission is extremely competitive. And it is perfectly obvious how important competitive skills are in finding a job. Yet the ability to cooperate is also important for success in life. Before children are psychologically ready for competition, maybe we should emphasize cooperation and individual performance in team sports rather than winning.

11   Many people are ready for such an emphasis. In 1988, one New York Little League official who had attended the Adelphi workshop tried to ban scoring from six- to eight-year-olds' games — but parents wouldn't support him (Schmitt). An innovative children's sports program in New York City, City Sports for Kids, emphasizes fitness, self-esteem, and sportsmanship. In this program's basketball games, every member on a team plays at least two of six eight-minute periods. The basket is seven feet from the floor, rather than ten feet, and a player can score a point just by hitting the rim (Bloch). I believe this kind of local program should replace overly competitive programs like Peewee Football and Little League Baseball. As one coach explains, significant improvements can result from a few simple rule changes, such as including every player in the batting order and giving every player, regardless of age or ability, the opportunity to play at least four innings a game (Frank).

12   Authorities have clearly documented the excesses and dangers of many competitive sports programs for children. It would seem that few children benefit from these programs and that those who do would benefit even more from programs emphasizing fitness, cooperation, sportsmanship, and individual performance. Thirteen- and fourteen-year-olds may be eager for competition, but few younger children are. These younger children deserve sports programs designed specifically for their needs and abilities.

How effectively does Statsky conclude her argument?

Are Statsky's sources adequate to support her position, in number and kind? Has she documented them clearly and accurately?

Works Cited

"The Bad News Pyromaniacs?" Editorial. *Los Angeles Times* 16 June 1990: B6. *LexisNexis*. Web. 16 May 2008.

Bloch, Gordon B. "Thrill of Victory Is Secondary to Fun." *New York Times* 2 Apr. 1990, late ed.: C12. *LexisNexis*. Web. 14 May 2008.

Coakley, Jay J. *Sport in Society: Issues and Controversies*. St. Louis: Mosby, 1982. Print.

Frank, L. "Contributions from Parents and Coaches." *CYB Message Board*. AOL, 8 July 1997. Web. 14 May 2008.

Koppett, Leonard. *Sports Illusion, Sports Reality*. Boston: Houghton, 1981. Print.

Kutner, Lawrence. "Athletics, through a Child's Eyes." *New York Times* 23 Mar. 1989, late ed.: C8. *LexisNexis*. Web. 15 May 2008.

Schmitt, Eric. "Psychologists Take Seat on Little League Bench." *New York Times* 14 Mar. 1988, late ed.: B2. *LexisNexis*. Web. 14 May 2008.

Smith, Nathan, Ronald Smith, and Frank Smoll. *Kidsports: A Survival Guide for Parents*. Reading: Addison, 1983. Print.

Tosches, Rich. "Peewee Football: Is It Time to Blow the Whistle?" *Los Angeles Times* 3 Dec. 1988: A1+. *LexisNexis*. Web. 22 May 2008.

"What about My Child?" *Little League Online*. Little League Baseball, Incorporated, 1999. Web. 30 May 2008.

"Your Role as a Little League Parent." *Little League Online*. Little League Baseball, Incorporated, 1999. Web. 30 May 2008.

LEARN ABOUT STATSKY'S WRITING PROCESS

To learn about Statsky's process of writing this essay, turn to A Writer at Work on pp. 315–17. How did anticipating readers' possible objections strengthen the presentation of her argument?

RICHARD ESTRADA, best known as a thoughtful, independent-minded commentator on immigration and social issues, was the associate editor of the *Dallas Morning News* editorial page and a syndicated columnist whose essays appeared regularly in the *Washington Post*, the *Los Angeles Times*, and other major newspapers. Before joining the *Dallas Morning News* in 1988, Estrada worked as a congressional staff member and as a researcher at the Center for Immigration Studies in Washington, D.C. In the 1990s, he was appointed to the U.S. Commission on Immigration Reform. The Richard Estrada Fellowship in Immigration Studies was established in his honor after his death in 1999.

(continued)

(continued)

In this essay, Estrada argues his position on naming sports teams using words associated with Native Americans. Several high schools and at least one university, Stanford, have changed the names of their sports teams because of this ongoing controversy. A coworker remarked that in his newspaper columns, Estrada "firmly opposed separating the American people into competing ethnic and linguistic groups." As you read this essay, think about his purpose in writing this position essay and how he constructs his argument on common ground that could bring different groups together.

Sticks and Stones and Sports Team Names

RICHARD ESTRADA

When I was a kid living in Baltimore in the late 1950s, there was only one professional sports team worth following. Anyone who ever saw the movie *Diner* knows which one it was. Back when we liked Ike, the Colts were the gods of the gridiron and Memorial Stadium was their Mount Olympus.

Ah, yes: The Colts. The Lions. Da Bears. Back when defensive tackle Big Daddy Lipscomb was letting running backs know exactly what time it was, a young fan could easily forget that in a game where men were men, the teams they played on were not invariably named after animals. Among others, the Packers, the Steelers and the distant 49ers were cases in point. But in the roll call of pro teams, one name in particular always discomfited me: the Washington Redskins. Still, however willing I may have been to go along with the name as a kid, as an adult I have concluded that using an ethnic group essentially as a sports mascot is wrong.

The Redskins and the Kansas City Chiefs, along with baseball teams like the Atlanta Braves and the Cleveland Indians, should find other names that avoid highlighting ethnicity.

By no means were such names originally meant to disparage Native Americans. The noble symbols of the Redskins or college football's Florida State Seminoles or the Illinois Illini are meant to be strong and proud. Yet, ultimately, the practice of using a people as mascots is dehumanizing. It sets them apart from the rest of society. It promotes the politics of racial aggrievement at a moment when our storehouse is running over with it.

The World Series between the Cleveland Indians and the Atlanta Braves reignited the debate. In the chill night air of October, tomahawk chops and war chants suddenly became far more familiar to millions of fans, along with the ridiculous and offensive cartoon logo of Cleveland's "Chief Wahoo."

The defenders of team names that use variations on the Indian theme argue that tradition should not be sacrificed at the altar of political correctness. In truth, the nation's No. 1 P.C. [politically correct] school, Stanford University, helped matters some when it changed its team nickname from "the Indians" to "the Cardinals." To be sure, Stanford did the right thing, but the school's status as P.C. without peer tainted the decision for those who still need to do the right thing. 6

Another argument is that ethnic group leaders are too inclined to cry wolf in alleging racial insensitivity. Often, this is the case. But no one should overlook genuine cases of political insensitivity in an attempt to avoid accusations of hypersensitivity and political correctness. 7

The real world is different from the world of sports entertainment. I recently heard a father who happened to be a Native American complain on the radio that his child was being pressured into participating in celebrations of Braves baseball. At his kid's school, certain days are set aside on which all children are told to dress in Indian garb and celebrate with tomahawk chops and the like. 8

That father should be forgiven for not wanting his family to serve as somebody's mascot. The desire to avoid ridicule is legitimate and understandable. Nobody likes to be trivialized or deprived of their dignity. This has nothing to do with political correctness and the provocations of militant leaders. 9

Against this backdrop, the decision by newspapers in Minneapolis, Seattle and Portland to ban references to Native American nicknames is more reasonable than some might think. 10

What makes naming teams after ethnic groups, particularly minorities, reprehensible is that politically impotent groups continue to be targeted, while politically powerful ones who bite back are left alone. How long does anyone think the name "Washington Blackskins" would last? Or how about "the New York Jews"? 11

With no fewer than 10 Latino ballplayers on the Cleveland Indians' roster, the team could change its name to "the Banditos." The trouble is, they would be missing the point: Latinos would correctly object to that stereotype, just as they rightly protested against Frito-Lay's use of the "Frito Bandito" character years ago. 12

It seems to me that what Native Americans are saying is that what would be intolerable for Jews, blacks, Latinos and others is no less offensive to them. Theirs is a request not only for dignified treatment, but for fair treatment as well. For America to ignore the complaints of a numerically small segment of the population because it is small is neither dignified nor fair. 13

MAKING CONNECTIONS: NAME-CALLING

As children, we may say, "Sticks and stones will break my bones, but words will never hurt me." Most children, however, recognize the power of words, especially words that make them feel different or inferior.

With two or three other students, discuss the power of name-calling. Begin by making a list of words that are used to refer to groups with which you identify. Try to think of words associated with your body, ethnicity, religion, gender, interests, geographic region, or any other factor. Then, together consider the following questions:

- Which of the words on your list seem to you to be most hurtful? How does the identity of the person who uses the word or the situation in which it is used affect its power to hurt?

- Why do you think words like these have the power to hurt?

- How does name-calling compare to what Estrada calls "the practice of using a people as mascots," a practice he thinks is "dehumanizing" (par. 4)?

A Well-Presented Issue

ANALYZING
WRITING
STRATEGIES

● ● ● ●
Basic Features

At the center of every position essay is a controversial issue — a question on which people disagree, sometimes vehemently. Controversial issues have no definitive answers because they cannot be proven by facts alone, although convincing readers what the facts are may be a necessary part of the argument. Disagreement over controversial issues usually depends on a difference of values, principles, and priorities. Therefore, writers not only need to identify the issue early in the essay, but they also must present it in a way that sets the stage for the argument. To do so effectively, they need to think about their *purpose* and *audience* — to consider how much their readers are likely to know about the issue and what they are likely to think about it.

Estrada wrote this essay during the World Series between the Atlanta Braves and the Cleveland Indians, when team mascots and fans wearing headdresses and war paint rallied their teams with the "tomahawk chop" and the "Indian chant." The controversy over these practices revitalized a long-standing debate over naming sports teams with words associated with Native Americans. Writing at this time, Estrada could assume readers of his *Dallas Morning News* column would be familiar with the issue. But knowing that his readers tended to be politically conservative, Estrada could also assume they would not be very sympathetic to his point of view on this issue. Therefore, in presenting the issue, he tries to define or *frame* it for readers.

Writers frame issues (and reframe issues that have already been framed) to influence how readers think about the issue. **Framing** an issue is like putting a frame around a picture, or in digital terms, using an editing program to crop and resize a photograph to focus the viewer's eye on the part of the picture you think is most important. Framing, like cropping, cuts some parts out altogether or moves them to the margins. Framing an issue essentially does the same thing by focusing attention on a certain way of seeing the issue.

For example, Jessica Statsky's title "Children Need to Play, Not Compete" frames the issue as a story about what children need. She clarifies this story in the first paragraph by asserting that the parents and coaches have taken over young children's sports, imposing their own "adult standards" of competition, and that these standards are not appropriate, "neither satisfying nor beneficial to children."

In "Sticks and Stones and Sports Team Names," Estrada refers in paragraph 6 to the way in which the issue of sports team names has already been framed by political conservatives, who use the label "political correctness" to belittle concerns about the issue. The label makes it sound as though those who object are just being overly sensitive. Estrada tries to reframe the issue — changing it from a story about oversensitivity to a story about bullying.

To analyze how Estrada reframes the issue, try the following:

- Consider what each of the following elements contributes to the story he is trying to tell about bullying:
  - the title
  - Estrada's remembered experience of being upset by the name "the Washington Redskins" (par. 1–2)
  - the anecdote about the Native American father upset about the practice at his son's school of celebrating Braves' victories with Indian costumes and tomahawk chops (par. 8)
- Write a few sentences speculating about how effective Estrada's reframing of the issue was for his original readers and is today for readers like you.

● A Well-Supported Position

To argue a position effectively, writers need to state the position clearly and provide supporting reasons and evidence. Very often writers declare the position early in the essay, as Jessica Statsky does in the opening paragraphs of her essay. At the end of the first paragraph, she indicates her position: "When overzealous parents and coaches impose adult standards on children's sports, the result can be activities that are neither satisfying nor beneficial to children." In paragraph 2, she elaborates on what "neither satisfying nor beneficial" means by specifying two of her reasons: "adult standards . . . can be both physically and psychologically harmful." Taking each reason in turn — physical harm in paragraphs 3–4 and psychological harm in paragraphs 5–6 — Statsky then supports her position with expert testimony, anecdotes, and statistics.

To analyze how Estrada presents and supports his position, try the following:

- Reread paragraphs 1–3 and highlight the sentence where Estrada first states his position.
- Skim the essay and note in the margin where he states his reasons for this position.
- Notice that in paragraphs 11–13, Estrada offers hypothetical examples of team names for ethnic groups. How do these examples support Estrada's position? Given his original *Dallas Morning News* readers, how convincing do you think the examples are likely to be? How convincing are they for you?
- Write a few sentences explaining what you discovered in analyzing Estrada's argument.

● An Effective Counterargument

Writers of position essays try to anticipate other widely held positions on the issue as well as objections and questions readers might raise to their argument. Writers have three options in anticipating readers' alternative positions and objections:

- they can simply acknowledge readers' views;
- they can accommodate them by making concessions; or
- they can try to refute them.

Anticipating readers' positions and objections can enhance the writer's credibility and strengthen the argument. When readers holding an opposing position recognize that the writer takes their position seriously, they are more likely to listen to what the writer has to say. It can also reassure readers that they share certain important values and interests with the writer, building a bridge of common concerns among people who have been separated by difference and antagonism.

To analyze how Estrada anticipates and counterargues opposing positions, try the following:

- Reread paragraphs 6 and 7, where Estrada introduces two opposing arguments to his position. Highlight the sentence in each paragraph that best states an opposing position.

- Examine paragraphs 6–9 to see how Estrada counterargues these two opposing arguments. For example, notice that he both concedes and refutes, and consider why he would attempt to do both. What seems to be his attitude toward those who disagree with him or, at least, object to parts of his argument?

- Write a few sentences reflecting on Estrada's way of counterarguing.

● A Readable Plan

Writers of position essays usually try to make their arguments easy for readers to follow. They typically preview their main reasons early in the essay and clearly mark each reason as it comes up. For example, notice how directly Statsky announces her reason in the topic sentence of paragraph 7: "This statistic illustrates another reason I oppose competitive sports for children: because they are so highly selective, very few children get to participate." Similarly, in the topic sentence of paragraph 10, she announces an objection readers are likely to raise to her argument: "Some parents would no doubt argue. . . ." Inexperienced writers are sometimes reluctant to be this explicit, but readers tend to appreciate the directness because it makes reading easier.

To analyze how Estrada makes his reasoning explicit, try the following:

- Reread paragraphs 6 and 7, and highlight the language Estrada uses to announce two objections likely to be raised by those who disagree with his position on the issue.

- Write a sentence or two explaining what you discovered about how Estrada tries to help readers follow his argument.

List some issues that involve what you believe to be unfair treatment of any group. For example, should a law be passed to make English the official language in this country, requiring that election ballots and drivers' tests be printed only in English? Should teenagers be required to get their parents' permission to obtain birth-control

CONSIDERING TOPICS FOR YOUR OWN ESSAY

information and contraception? What is affirmative action, and should it be used in college admissions for underrepresented groups? Should schools create and enforce guidelines to protect individuals from bullying and discrimination? Should everyone, regardless of their sexual orientation, be allowed to marry?

AMITAI ETZIONI is a sociologist who has taught at Columbia, Harvard, and George Washington Universities, where he currently directs the Institute for Communitarian Policy Studies. He has written numerous articles and more than two dozen books reflecting his commitment to peace in a nuclear age (for example, *Winning without War* [1964]); overcoming excessive individualism through communitarianism (for example, *The Spirit of Community: The Reinvention of American Society* [1983]); limiting the erosion of privacy in an age of technological surveillance (for example, *The Limits of Privacy* [2004]); and most recently, rethinking foreign policy in an age of terrorism (for example, *Security First: For a Muscular, Moral Foreign Policy* [2007]).

The following essay was originally published in the *Miami Herald*. The original headnote identifies Etzioni as the father of five sons, including three teenagers, and points out that his son Dari helped Etzioni write this essay — although it does not say what Dari contributed.

As you read, think about what you learned from the various summer and school-year jobs you have held.

Working at McDonald's

AMITAI ETZIONI

McDonald's is bad for your kids. I do not mean the flat patties and the white-flour buns; I refer to the jobs teen-agers undertake, mass-producing these choice items.   1

As many as two-thirds of America's high school juniors and seniors now hold down part-time paying jobs, according to studies. Many of these are in fast-food chains, of which McDonald's is the pioneer, trend-setter and symbol.   2

At first, such jobs may seem right out of the Founding Fathers' educational manual for how to bring up self-reliant, work-ethic-driven, productive youngsters. But in fact, these jobs undermine school attendance and involvement, impart few skills that will be useful in later life, and simultaneously skew the values of teen-agers — especially their ideas about the worth of a dollar.   3

It has been a longstanding American tradition that youngsters ought to get paying jobs. In folklore, few pursuits are more deeply revered than the newspaper route and the sidewalk lemonade stand. Here the youngsters are to learn how sweet are the   4 fruits of labor and self-discipline (papers are delivered early in the morning, rain or shine), and the ways of trade (if you price your lemonade too high or too low . . .).

Roy Rogers, Baskin Robbins, Kentucky Fried Chicken, *et al.* may at first seem nothing but a vast extension of the lemonade stand. They provide very large numbers of teen jobs, provide regular employment, pay quite well compared to many other teen jobs and, in the modern equivalent of toiling over a hot stove, test one's stamina.

Closer examination, however, finds the McDonald's kind of job highly uneducational in several ways. Far from providing opportunities for entrepreneurship (the lemonade stand) or self-discipline, self-supervision and self-scheduling (the paper route), most teen jobs these days are highly structured — what social scientists call "highly routinized."

True, you still have to have the gumption to get yourself over to the hamburger stand, but once you don the prescribed uniform, your task is spelled out in minute detail. The franchise prescribes the shape of the coffee cups; the weight, size, shape and color of the patties; and the texture of the napkins (if any). Fresh coffee is to be made every eight minutes. And so on. There is no room for initiative, creativity, or even elementary re-arrangements. These are breeding grounds for robots working for yesterday's assembly lines, not tomorrow's high-tech posts.

There are very few studies on the matter. One of the few is a 1984 study by Ivan Charper and Bryan Shore Fraser. The study relies mainly on what teen-agers write in response to questionnaires rather than actual observations of fast-food jobs. The authors argue that the employees develop many skills such as how to operate a food-preparation machine and a cash register. However, little attention is paid to how long it takes to acquire such a skill, or what its significance is.

What does it matter if you spend 20 minutes to learn to use a cash register, and then — "operate" it? What "skill" have you acquired? It is a long way from learning to work with a lathe or carpenter tools in the olden days or to program computers in the modern age.

A 1980 study by A. V. Harrell and P. W. Wirtz found that, among those students who worked at least 25 hours per week while in school, their unemployment rate four years later was half of that of seniors who did not work. This is an impressive statistic. It must be seen, though, together with the finding that many who begin as part-time employees in fast-food chains drop out of high school and are gobbled up in the world of low-skill jobs.

Some say that while these jobs are rather unsuited for college-bound, white, middle-class youngsters, they are "ideal" for lower-class, "non-academic," minority youngsters. Indeed, minorities are "over-represented" in these jobs (21 percent of fast-food employees). While it is true that these places provide income, work and even some training to such youngsters, they also tend to perpetuate their disadvantaged status. They provide no career ladders, few marketable skills, and undermine school attendance and involvement.

The hours are often long. Among those 14 to 17, a third of fast-food employees (including some school dropouts) labor more than 30 hours per week, according to the Charper-Fraser study. Only 20 percent work 15 hours or less. The rest: between 15 and 30 hours.

Often the stores close late, and after closing one must clean up and tally up. In affluent Montgomery County, Md., where child labor would not seem to be a widespread economic necessity, 24 percent of the seniors at one high school in 1985 worked as much as five to seven days a week; 27 percent, three to five. There is just no way such amounts of work will not interfere with school work, especially homework. In an informal survey published in the most recent yearbook of the high school, 58 percent of seniors acknowledged that their jobs interfere with their school work.

13

The Charper-Fraser study sees merit in learning teamwork and working under supervision. The authors have a point here. However, it must be noted that such learning is not automatically educational or wholesome. For example, much of the supervision in fast-food places leans toward teaching one the wrong kinds of compliance: blind obedience, or shared alienation with the "boss."

14

Supervision is often both tight and woefully inappropriate. Today, fast-food chains and other such places of work (record shops, bowling alleys) keep costs down by having teens supervise teens with often no adult on the premises.

15

There is no father or mother figure with which to identify, to emulate, to provide a role model and guidance. The work-culture varies from one place to another: Sometimes it is a tightly run shop (must keep the cash registers ringing); sometimes a rather loose pot party interrupted by customers. However, only rarely is there a master to learn from, or much worth learning. Indeed, far from being places where solid adult work values are being transmitted, these are places where all too often delinquent teen values dominate. Typically, when my son Oren was dishing out ice cream for Baskin Robbins in upper Manhattan, his fellow teen-workers considered him a sucker for not helping himself to the till. Most youngsters felt they were entitled to $50 severance "pay" on their last day on the job.

16

The pay, oddly, is the part of the teen work-world that is most difficult to evaluate. The lemonade stand or paper route money was for your allowance. In the old days, apprentices learning a trade from a master contributed most, if not all, of their income to their parents' household. Today, the teen pay may be low by adult standards, but it is often, especially in the middle class, spent largely or wholly by the teens. That is, the youngsters live free at home ("after all, they are high school kids") and are left with very substantial sums of money.

17

Where this money goes is not quite clear. Some use it to support themselves, especially among the poor. More middle-class kids set some money aside to help pay for college, or save it for a major purchase — often a car. But large amounts seem to flow to pay for an early introduction into the most trite aspects of American consumerism: flimsy punk clothes, trinkets and whatever else is the last fast-moving teen craze.

18

One may say that this is only fair and square; they are being good American consumers and spend their money on what turns them on. At least, a cynic might add, these funds do not go into illicit drugs and booze. On the other hand, an educator might bemoan that these young, yet unformed individuals, so early in life driven to buy objects of no intrinsic educational, cultural or social merit, learn so quickly the dubious merit of keeping up with the Joneses in ever-changing fads, promoted by mass merchandising.

19

Many teens find the instant reward of money, and the youth status symbols it buys, much more alluring than credits in calculus courses, European history or foreign languages. No wonder quite a few would rather skip school — and certainly homework — and instead work longer at a Burger King. Thus, most teen work these days is not providing early lessons in the work ethic; it fosters escape from school and responsibilities, quick gratification and a short cut to the consumeristic aspects of adult life.

Thus, parents should look at teen employment not as automatically educational. It is an activity — like sports — that can be turned into an educational opportunity. But it can also easily be abused. Youngsters must learn to balance the quest for income with the needs to keep growing and pursue other endeavors that do not pay off instantly — above all education.

Go back to school.

20

21

22

Etzioni argues that fast-food jobs do not qualify as meaningful work experience because they do not teach young people the skills and habits they will need for fulfilling careers: "entrepreneurship . . . self-discipline, self-supervision and self-scheduling" (par. 6).

With two or three other students, discuss what you have learned from your summer and after-school jobs. Begin by taking turns briefly describing the various jobs you have held. If you have never held a job, describe other significant activities you have participated in that required time and effort. Then, together consider the following questions:

- Which, if any, of the skills and habits Etzioni lists as important did you practice at your job or through the activities in which you participated?

- Why do you think these skills and habits are worth learning? If you think other skills and habits are as important or even more important, explain what they are and why you think so.

MAKING CONNECTIONS: JOB SKILLS

● A Well-Presented Issue

From the first sentence, it is clear that Etzioni's primary audience is parents of teenagers, rather than the teenagers themselves. Given his readers, it may seem fitting that Etzioni refers to "a longstanding American tradition that youngsters ought to get paying jobs" and what he calls the "folklore" associated with "the newspaper route and the sidewalk lemonade stand" (par. 4). In other words, Etzioni begins his essay by assuming the issue has already been *framed* for his audience through their associations and experience.

Framing, as we explained on p. 277, refers to the way the issue is defined. To get these readers to listen to his argument, Etzioni has to *reframe* the issue — to show that today's McDonald's-type jobs are not the same as the newspaper route and lemonade stand of yesteryear.

ANALYZING WRITING STRATEGIES

● ● ● ●
Basic Features

To analyze how Etzioni tries to reframe the issue, try the following:

- Reread paragraphs 1–7, highlighting the qualities — values and skills — associated with traditional jobs and with McDonald's-type jobs, at least according to Etzioni.

- Write a couple of sentences explaining how Etzioni tries to reframe the issue and whether you think the story he tells about McDonald's-type jobs compared to traditional jobs is likely to make his readers reconsider their assumption that McDonald's-type jobs are good for kids.

● A Well-Supported Position

Writers may use various kinds of support for their arguments. Like Statsky, Etzioni cites authorities. For example, Statsky quotes the official Little League Web site, professors, journalists, and parents. She carefully identifies her sources by supplying their credentials — for example, "Thomas Tutko, a psychology professor at San Jose State University and coauthor of the book *Winning Is Everything and Other American Myths*" (par. 3).

While Statsky cites credible authorities and tends to present their evidence confidently, she also *qualifies* it where appropriate — that is, she presents it tentatively when there can be reasonable debate about whether it qualifies as fact. For example, she reports that "Leonard Koppett in *Sports Illusion, Sports Reality* claims that a twelve-year-old trying to throw a curve ball . . . may put abnormal strain on developing arm and shoulder muscles, sometimes resulting in lifelong injuries" (par. 3). Notice that Statsky uses the word *claims* to indicate that the statement's status as fact is not certain, and she also uses the words *may* and *sometimes* to emphasize that throwing a curve ball is not necessarily injurious. This is the kind of careful qualification of sources that readers deserve and academic audiences typically require.

To analyze how Etzioni uses **statistics**, numerical data about a given population sample, to support his position, try the following:

- Reread paragraphs 8–15 where Etzioni reports on two research studies. Both studies provide Etzioni with statistics. Underline the statistics, and note what each statistic is being used to illustrate or prove. Why do you think Etzioni relies on statistics?

- Write a few sentences reporting what you have learned about Etzioni's use of statistics to argue for his position on a controversial issue.

● An Effective Counterargument

At key points throughout his essay, Etzioni acknowledges readers' likely objections and then counterargues them. In paragraph 3, he acknowledges that some readers will believe that McDonald's-type jobs are good because they teach teenagers to become "self-reliant, work-ethic-driven, productive youngsters." Although he agrees with his readers that these are valuable objectives, Etzioni makes clear that he disagrees about how well fast-food jobs fulfill these goals.

To analyze how Etzioni counterargues, try the following activity:

- Examine how Etzioni refutes findings of the Charper-Fraser study — specifically, the claims that employees in McDonald's-type jobs develop many skills (pars. 8 and 9) and that they learn how to work under supervision (pars. 14–16). Highlight places where he presents the claims and note how he asserts and supports his refutation.

- Write a couple of sentences explaining how Etzioni refutes the findings of this particular research study. Add another sentence assessing the effectiveness of Etzioni's counterargument.

● A Readable Plan

The *thesis statement* in a position essay is particularly important because it asserts the writer's position on the issue. Most writers also use the thesis statement to forecast the reasons they will develop and support in the essay. Jessica Statsky, for example, asserts her position in paragraph 1 and uses paragraph 2 to qualify and clarify the position and to forecast her three reasons for it.

To analyze how Etzioni forecasts his argument, try the following:

- Etzioni states his thesis in the opening sentence of paragraph 1. But he does not preview his reasons until paragraph 3. Find and underline the forecasting statement in which he does so.

- Skim the essay and note in the margin where Etzioni supports his reasons.

- Write a couple of sentences indicating whether Etzioni's method of forecasting his reasons makes his argument easy to follow.

Etzioni focuses on a single kind of part-time work, takes a position on how worthwhile it is, and recommends against it. You could write a similar kind of essay. For example, you could take a position for or against students' participating in other kinds of part-time work or recreation during the high school or college academic year — for example, playing on an interscholastic or collegiate sports team, doing volunteer work, or taking an elective class. You might pursue a different argument, taking a position on students' doing a certain kind of work or recreation during the summer months — say, working or volunteering in a job related to a career they would like to pursue; focusing on learning something important to them, such as another language or a musical instrument; or participating in an exercise program. If you work to support yourself and pay for college, you could focus on why the job either strengthens or weakens you as a person, given your life and career goals. Writing for other students, you would either recommend the job or activity to them or discourage them from pursuing it, giving reasons and support for your position. Like Etzioni, you might enrich your argument by citing studies or by interviewing students who participate in the activity.

CONSIDERING TOPICS FOR YOUR OWN ESSAY

AMY GOLDWASSER is a writer and editor. Her writing has appeared in a wide array of journals and Web sites including the *New Yorker, Vogue,* and *Salon,* where this essay first appeared. She has served as the executive editor of *Elle* and *Seventeen,* features editor of *New York Magazine,* and staff editor at *Outside.* A volunteer at the Lower Eastside Girls Club in New York, Goldwasser founded a writing and blogging program that led to her editing a collection of essays called *Red: The Next Generation of American Writers — Teenage Girls — on What Fires Up Their Lives Today* (2007). "I came to realize," Goldwasser observed in an interview, "how much more excited I was about the writing I was getting from the girls than the writing I was getting from professional writers in my day job." You can learn about the book and the authors at www.redthebook.com.

This position essay was occasioned by the publication of a 2008 survey called "Still at Risk: What Students Don't Know, Even Now" (http://www.aei.org/docLib/20080226_ CommonCorereport.pdf). As Goldwasser indicates, the report is the latest in a series of critiques of the Millennial or Google generation, as it is sometimes called. As you read, think about why Goldwasser uses the pronouns *we* and *they* repeatedly throughout the essay.

What's the Matter with Kids Today?

AMY GOLDWASSER ▼

The other week was only the latest takedown of what has become a fashionable segment of the population to bash: the American teenager. A phone (land line!) survey of 1,200 17-year-olds, conducted by the research organization Common Core and released Feb. 26, found our young people to be living in "stunning ignorance" of history and literature. 1

This furthered the report that the National Endowment for the Arts came out with at the end of 2007, lamenting "the diminished role of voluntary reading in American life," particularly among 13-to-17-year-olds, and Doris Lessing's condemnation, in her acceptance speech for the Nobel Prize in literature, of "a fragmenting culture" in which "young men and women . . . have read nothing, knowing only some specialty or other, for instance, computers." 2

Kids today — we're telling you! — don't read, don't write, don't care about anything farther in front of them than their iPods. The Internet, according to 88-year-old Lessing (whose specialty is sturdy typewriters, or perhaps pens), has "seduced a whole generation into its inanities." 3

Or is it the older generation that the Internet has seduced — into the inanities of leveling charges based on fear, ignorance and old-media, multiple-choice testing? So much so that we can't see that the Internet is only a means of communication, and one that has created a generation, perhaps the first, of writers, activists, storytellers? When the world worked in hard copy, no parent or teacher 4 ever begrudged teenagers who disappeared into their rooms to write letters to friends — or a movie review, or an editorial for the school paper on the first president they'll vote for. Even 15-year-old boys are sharing some part of their feelings with someone out there.

We're talking about 33 million Americans who are fluent in texting, e-mailing, blogging, IM'ing and constantly amending their profiles on social network sites — which, on average, 30 of their friends will visit every day, hanging out and writing for 20 minutes or so each. They're connected, they're collaborative, they're used to writing about themselves. In fact, they choose to write about themselves, on their own time, rather than its being a forced labor when a paper's due in school. Regularly, often late at night, they're generating a body of intimate written work. They appreciate the value of a good story and the power of a speech that moves: Ninety-seven percent of the teenagers in the Common Core survey connected "I have a dream" with its speaker — they can watch Dr. King deliver it on demand — and eight in 10 knew what "To Kill a Mockingbird" is about.

This is, of course, the kind of knowledge we should be encouraging. The Internet has turned teenagers into honest documentarians of their own lives — reporters embedded in their homes, their schools, their own heads.

But this is also why it's dangerous, why we can't seem to recognize that it's just a medium. We're afraid. Our kids know things we don't. They drove the presidential debates onto YouTube and very well may determine the outcome of this election. They're texting at the dinner table and responsible for pretty much every enduring consumer cultural phenomenon: iPod, iTunes, iPhone; Harry Potter, "High School Musical"; large hot drinks with gingerbread flavoring. They can sell ads on their social network pages, and they essentially made MySpace worth $580 million and "Juno" an Oscar winner.

Besides, we're tired of having to ask them every time we need to find Season 2 of "Heroes," calculate a carbon footprint or upload photos to Facebook (now that we're allowed on).

Plus, they're blogging about us.

So we've made the Internet one more thing unknowable about the American teenager, when, really, it's one of the few revelations. We conduct these surveys and overgeneralize — labeling like the mean girls, driven by the same jealousy and insecurity.

Common Core drew its multiple-choice questions for teens from a test administered by the federal government in 1986. Twenty-plus years ago, high school students didn't have the Internet to store their trivia. Now they know that the specific dates and what-was-that-prince's-name will always be there; they can free their brains to go a little deeper into the concepts instead of the copyrights, step back and consider what Scout and Atticus were really fighting for. To criticize teenager's author-to-book title matching on the spot, over the phone, is similar to cold-calling over-40s and claiming their long-division skills or date of "Jaws" recall is rusty. This is what we all rely on the Internet for.

That's not to say some of the survey findings aren't disturbing. It's crushing to hear that one in four teens could not identify Adolf Hitler's role in world history, for instance. But it's not because teenagers were online that they missed this. Had a parent introduced 20 minutes of researching the Holocaust to one month of their teen's Internet life, or a teacher assigned "The Diary of Anne Frank" (arguably a 13-year-old girl's blog) — if we worked with, rather than against, the way this generation voluntarily takes in information — we might not be able to pick up the phone and expose tragic pockets of ignorance.

The average teen chooses to spend an average of 16.7 hours a week reading and writing online. Yet the NEA report did not consider this to be "voluntary" reading and writing. Its findings also concluded that "literary reading declined significantly in a period of rising Internet use". The corollary is weak — this has as well been a period of rising franchises of frozen yogurt that doesn't taste like frozen yogurt, of global warming, of declining rates of pregnancy and illicit drug use among teenagers, and of girls sweeping the country's most prestigious high school science competition for the first time.   13

Teenagers today read and write for fun; it's part of their social lives. We need to start celebrating this unprecedented surge, incorporating it as an educational tool instead of meeting it with punishing pop quizzes and suspicion.   14

We need to start trusting our kids to communicate as they will online — even when that comes with the risk that they'll spill the family secrets or campaign for a candidate who's not ours.   15

Once we stop regarding the Internet as a villain, stop presenting it as the enemy of history and literature and worldly knowledge, then our teenagers have the potential to become the next great voices of America. One of them, 70 years from now, might even get up there to accept the very award Lessing did — and thank the Internet for making him or her a writer and a thinker.   16

MAKING CONNECTIONS: THE INFORMATION AGE

It is often said that we live in an Age of Information. But, as Goldwasser suggests, there may now be a generational shift in the way information is thought of and accessed.

With two or three other students, discuss your own experience. Begin by taking turns listing the ways you use technology to transmit and retrieve information on a typical day. Then, together consider the following questions:

- Goldwasser reports that the National Endowment for the Arts laments "the diminished role of voluntary reading in American life" (par. 2). How much time do you spend reading in a typical day? What kinds of things do you read?

- What kinds of information do you typically look up in the course of a day? How do you most commonly look it up? Would your answers to these questions be different if you did not have easy access to the Internet?

- Goldwasser distinguishes between "concepts" (for example, "Adolf Hitler's role in world history" [par. 12] and "what 'To Kill a Mockingbird' is about" [par. 5]) and "copyrights" or "trivia" (for example, dates and author-to-book title matching [par. 11]). Why do you think she distinguishes between what you should know and what you could just as easily look up when you need it? What do you think about Goldwasser's distinction?

● A Well-Presented Issue

Like the other writers in this chapter, Goldwasser tries to reframe the issue for her readers. Her title, "What's the Matter with Kids Today?," is the title of a song from *Bye Bye Birdie*, a late-1950s musical. The lyrics tell the story of how the issue has traditionally been framed:

> Why can't they be like we were,
> Perfect in every way?
> What's the matter with kids today?

To analyze how Goldwasser tries to reframe the issue, try the following:

- Reread paragraph 7 to determine what story Goldwasser is telling about the generational divide. How does this story reframe the issue?

- Who are the *we* and the *they* in this paragraph? Assuming Goldwasser is addressing the *we*, how effective do you think this way of reframing the issue is likely to be for these particular readers?

● A Well-Supported Position

In arguing for a position, writers may provide various kinds of supporting evidence, including facts, statistics, examples, anecdotes, and quotes from authorities.

- **Facts** are statements that can be proven to be true. However, a statement that is not true or only partially true may be asserted as fact. Therefore, readers may need to be reassured that an asserted fact is reliable and comes from a trustworthy source.

- **Statistics** are sometimes mistaken for facts, but they are only interpretations or correlations of numerical data. Their reliability depends on how and by whom the information was collected and interpreted.

- **Examples** and **anecdotes** illustrate what may be true in certain situations; effective writers do not usually offer them as hard-and-fast evidence of the universal truth of their positions. Using them can, however, make an argument less abstract and enable readers to identify with those affected by the issue.

- **Quotes from authorities** can carry weight if readers see them as knowledgeable and trustworthy.

To analyze how Goldwasser supports her position, try the following:

- Reread the essay and highlight at least two places where Goldwasser presents different kinds of supporting evidence. Examine each instance to determine how she uses the evidence to support her argument, and consider how effective the evidence is likely to be in convincing her readers.

- Write a few sentences explaining what you discovered about Goldwasser's use of supporting evidence in this essay.

An Effective Counterargument

Some position essays are essentially organized as a defense or refutation. This is the case with Goldwasser's essay. As she explains in the opening paragraph, it has become "fashionable" to "bash" teenagers, and her essay attempts to defend against this "latest takedown." One object of her counterargument is the Common Core phone survey, but she also counterargues the claims made by the National Endowment for the Arts (NEA) and Doris Lessing in her Nobel Prize acceptance speech.

Before examining how Goldwasser tries to refute these authorities, however, look at one passage where she makes a concession. In paragraph 12, she begins by acknowledging that "some of the survey findings" are "disturbing." In fact, she calls it "crushing" that "one in four teens could not identify Adolf Hitler's role in world history." Not only does this concession allow her to express her strong feelings, but it is also a smart rhetorical strategy in that it shows readers that she shares their values about the kinds of knowledge that really are important for everyone to learn.

To analyze Goldwasser's counterargument, try the following:

- Reread paragraphs 4–5 where she tries to defend teenagers' use of the Internet against Doris Lessing's criticism.

- Notice that one of her strategies is to support her counterargument with the same Common Core survey that was used to attack teenagers' use of the Internet. How effective is this strategy likely to be for her readers? Ask yourself what these statistics allow Goldwasser to demonstrate.

- Write a few sentences describing what you have learned about Goldwasser's use of counterargument.

A Readable Plan

Writers of position essays sometimes repeat in the conclusion language or ideas introduced in the opening paragraphs of the essay. For example, Statsky comes back in the last paragraph to her concerns about "the excesses and dangers" of competitive sports, ideas she introduced in her first two paragraphs. Similarly, Estrada uses actual names of sports teams in his opening paragraphs and lists imagined sports team names in his last few paragraphs.

To analyze how Goldwasser uses this strategy, try the following:

- Reread the opening and closing paragraphs of Goldwasser's essay, and highlight any language or ideas that are repeated.

- Write a few sentences describing what you found and discussing whether you think this strategy of repeating material makes her essay more readable.

You could consider writing a position essay on some other aspect of contemporary culture and its effects on relationships, education, work, or recreation. For example, social-networking sites cost businesses a lot of money in lost productivity: Should they be banned at workplaces? Social-networking sites are increasingly being used by school administrations, law-enforcement officials, and human-resources departments to check up on students, parolees and suspects, and job applicants: Should the information on these sites be protected from such uses? Should music lyrics be censored for violence and exploitation? Should the legal drinking age be lowered? Should community service be required of all high school or college students? Is video gaming a harmless hobby or a health hazard?

CONSIDERING
TOPICS FOR YOUR
OWN ESSAY

Beyond the Traditional Essay: Arguing a Position

Reasoned argument takes many forms in our culture. Among the most common forms of written argument are the editorials found in major newspapers. These editorials usually exhibit the basic features of argument — a well-presented issue, a well-supported position, effective counterargument, and a readable plan — found in formal academic essays. Formal debates and courtroom summations are the classic forms of oral argument found in our culture, and these, too, tend to exhibit the basic features of the academic argument essay. Examples of argument that exhibit at least some of the basic features can commonly be found in advertisements, brochures, Web sites, documentaries, and many other forms of expression that present specific positions or perspectives.

As an example, consider the public service announcement (PSA) reproduced on p. 292. Cosponsored by the AdCouncil and the U.S. Department of Transportation, the ad achieves a surprising amount with a single image and relatively few words. The "recipe" presented is a recipe for disaster: fatigue, an icy road, and a seemingly harmless "few rounds with the guys" result in a totalled car. The enticing visual, the familiar and nonthreatening recipe format, and the use of realistic language expressing a seemingly moderate perspective ("It's only another beer"; "just a few") reach out to average adults, who likely do not think of themselves as reckless or irresponsible, and remind them that it can be a short step from an ordinary evening relaxing with friends to a catastrophic accident.

As you work on your own project, you might want to consult some of these alternative forms of argument for inspiration. If the format in which you are working allows for it — if, for example, you are creating a poster, Web site, or video — you should consider taking advantage of the strategies available to those working in multimedia — for example, by embedding artifacts that are relevant to the position you are arguing. Always remember to properly document any material you might use that was created by someone else.

**The "It's Only Another Beer"
Black and Tan**

8 oz. pilsner lager
8 oz. stout lager
1 frosty mug
1 icy road
1 pick-up truck
1 10-hour day
1 tired worker
A few rounds with the guys

Mix ingredients.
Add 1 totalled vehicle.

**Never underestimate 'just a few.'
Buzzed driving is drunk driving.**

Ad
Council

U.S. Department of Transportation

Guide to Writing

The Writing Assignment

Write an essay on a controversial issue. Learn more about the issue, and take a position on it. Present the issue to readers, and develop a well-supported argument for the purpose of confirming, challenging, or changing your readers' views on the issue.

This Guide to Writing will help you apply what you have learned about how writers clearly present an issue, argue effectively for their position on it, present counterarguments to opposing positions, and deliver their argument in a readable manner. The Guide is divided into five sections with various activities in each section:

- **Invention and Research**
- **Planning and Drafting**
- **Critical Reading Guide**
- **Revising**
- **Editing and Proofreading**

The Guide is designed to escort you through the writing process, from finding an issue to editing your finished essay. Your instructor may require you to follow the Guide to Writing from beginning to end. Working through the Guide to Writing in this way will help you — as it has helped many other college students — write a thoughtful, fully developed, polished essay.

If, however, your instructor gives you latitude to choose and if you have had experience writing an essay in which you argue a position, then you can decide on the order in which you will do the activities in the Guide to Writing. For example, the Invention and Research section includes activities to help you find an issue to write about, explore it, analyze and define your audience and purpose, and formulate a tentative position on it, among other things.

Obviously, finding an issue must precede the other activities, but you may come to the Guide with an issue already in mind, and you may choose to define your audience and purpose before turning to a fuller exploration of the issue itself. In fact, you may find your response to one of the invention activities expanding into a draft before you have had a chance to do any of the other activities. That is a good thing — but you should later flesh out your draft by going back to the activities you skipped and layering the new material into your draft.

The chart on p. 294 will help you find answers to many of the questions you might have about planning, drafting, and revising an essay arguing a position. Because we know different students will start at different places, we designed the chart so you could find the information you need, when you need it. The page references in the Where to Look column refer to examples from the readings and activities in the Guide to Writing.

To learn about using the *Guide* e-book for invention and drafting, go to **bedfordstmartins.com/ theguide**.

Starting Points: Arguing a Position

●●●● Basic Features

	Question	Where to Look
A Well-Presented Issue	How do I come up with an issue to write about?	• Considering Topics for Your Own Essay (pp. 279–80, 285, 291) • Choosing an Issue to Write About (pp. 295–96) • Testing Your Choice (p. 298)
	What is my purpose in writing? How can I convince my audience that the issue is real and serious?	• Reading Essays Arguing a Position (pp. 267–69) • Ways In: Bringing the Issue and Your Audience into Focus (p. 297) • Framing the Issue for Your Readers (p. 298) • Defining Your Purpose for Your Readers (pp. 301–2) • Refining Your Purpose and Setting Goals (pp. 303–4)
	How can I effectively frame the issue for my readers?	• Framing (concept) (pp. 268, 277, 283, 289) • Framing the Issue for Your Readers (p. 298)
A Well-Supported Position	How do I come up with a plausible position?	• Ways In: Bringing the Issue and Your Audience into Focus (p. 297) • Ways In: Developing Your Argument and Counterargument (pp. 299–300)
	How do I construct an argument supporting my position?	• Ways In: Developing Your Argument and Counterargument (pp. 299–300) • Researching Your Argument (p. 301) • Formulating a Tentative Thesis Statement (p. 302)
An Effective Counterargument	How do I counter possible objections to my position?	• Counterarguing Readers' Objections (pp. 299–300) • A Sentence Strategy: Concession Followed by Refutation (pp. 306–7)
	How do I respond to possible alternative positions?	• Counterarguing Opposing Positions (pp. 299–300) • Working with Sources: Fairly and Accurately Quoting Opposing Positions (pp. 307–8)
A Readable Plan	How can I help my readers follow my argument?	• Designing Your Document (p. 301) • Outlining Your Draft (pp. 304–5) • Drafting: Writing the Opening Sentences (pp. 305–6) • Revising (pp. 309–10) • Editing and Proofreading (pp. 312–14)

Invention and Research

The following activities should take only a few minutes to complete. Spreading them out over several days will stimulate your creativity, enabling you to consider many more potential issues to address and possible ways in which to address them. Remember to keep a record of your invention work: you will need it when you draft and revise your essay.

Choosing an Issue to Write About

List several issues that you might like to write about. You may already have an issue in mind, possibly one suggested by the topics you considered following the readings. If you want to try writing about that issue, make sure it meets the criteria below and, if so, go on to the next section. If you are not ready to make a choice, the suggestions below may help you think of issues to consider.

The issue should be
☐ controversial — an issue that people disagree about, sometimes passionately;
☐ arguable — a matter of opinion on which there is no absolute proof or authority;
☐ one about which you already know something, or about which you want to know more;
☐ one that you can research, if necessary, in the time you have; and
☐ one that you care about.

> **Criteria for Choosing an Issue:**
>
> A Checklist

Listing Issues

Make a list of issues you might consider writing about. Begin your list now, and add to it over the next few days. It might help you generate ideas if, at first, you focus on three categories: school, community, and work. Put the issues you come up with in the form of questions, as in the following examples.

School

- Should boys and girls be educated in single-sex schools or classrooms?
- Should local school boards be allowed to ban books from school libraries or block access to selected Internet sites?
- Should students attending public colleges be required to pay higher tuition fees if they have been full-time students but have not graduated within four years?

Community

- Should businesses remain loyal to their communities, or should they move wherever labor costs, taxes, or other conditions are most favorable?

- Should materials related to voting, driving, and income-tax reporting be written only in English or also in other languages read by members of the community?
- Should the racial, ethnic, or gender makeup of a police force resemble the makeup of the community it serves?

Work

- When people choose careers, should they look primarily for jobs that are well paid or for jobs that are personally fulfilling, morally acceptable, or socially responsible?
- Should the state or federal government provide job training or temporary employment to people who are unemployed but willing to work?
- Should drug testing be mandatory for people such as bus drivers, heavy-equipment operators, and airplane pilots?

Going Local

Proposing to write on an issue directly related to a community to which you belong gives you an important advantage: You know something about the history of the issue and you might already have taken a position on it. Equally important, you will know your readers, and you can interview them to get their views of the issue and your position on it. From such knowledge and authority comes confident, convincing writing.

If you want to argue your position on an issue of national scope, try to concentrate on one with which you have some direct experience. Even better, focus on unique local aspects of the issue. For example, instead of writing generally about school boards that block access to Internet sites, write about efforts to do so at your former high school. If you are concerned about the effect of megachains like Wal-Mart and Home Depot on small businesses nationwide, you could write your argument about whether a new big-box store should be allowed in your area.

Using the Web to Find or Explore an Issue

Exploring Web sites can provide you with an idea of what to write about, if you have not already chosen an issue, and it can enrich your understanding of an issue you have already chosen. Moreover, the Web provides a rich repository of cultural and historical information, including photographs and music, which you might be able to use to create a richly detailed, multimedia text for your readers.

Here are some suggestions:

- Look for sites related to the community, workplace, or group you are writing about. See what issues are of concern to members of those groups and whether you might write about one of them.
- Consider getting in touch with others who are concerned about the issue that concerns you. If your conversation is fruitful, ask their permission to include their insights in your project.

- Do a Google search on a particular issue, and try to get a sense of how common it might be — or, on the other hand, of how specific it might be to your local community, campus, or workplace.

Make notes of any ideas or insights suggested by your online research, and download any visuals you might include in your essay, being sure to get the information necessary to cite any online sources.

(See pp. 774–76 for the MLA citation format for electronic sources.)

Ways In: Bringing the Issue and Your Audience into Focus

Once you have made a preliminary choice of an issue, the following activities will help you explore what you know now about it, determine what else you need to find out, and discover ways of presenting the issue to your readers. You can begin with whichever activity you want, but wherever you begin, be sure to return to the other activities to bring the issue and your readers fully into focus.

Basic Features

Exploring the Issue	Identifying Your Possible Readers
Define the Issue. *Write for a few minutes explaining how you think people currently understand the issue.* Focus on clarifying the issue by considering questions like these: • Who has taken a position on this issue, and what positions have they taken? What position are you inclined to take? • What typically causes people to disagree about this issue? On what about the issue, if anything, do people agree? • What is the issue's history? How long has it been an issue? Has it changed over time? What makes it important now? **Learn More about the Issue.** *If you do not know very much about the issue, do some preliminary research to help you decide whether you want to write about it.* You might start by talking to other people about the issue and their opinions; doing a search online; or searching your school's library for information. If you find that you are not interested in an issue, do not have the time to research it fully, or do not have a strong opinion yourself, you should switch to another issue. Return to your list of possible issues, and make another choice.	*Write several sentences describing the readers to whom you will be addressing your argument.* Begin by briefly identifying your readers; then use the following questions to help you describe them: • What do my readers know about the issue? In what contexts are they likely to have encountered it? In what ways might the issue affect them personally or professionally? • What positions will my readers likely take on this issue? How strongly do they hold these positions? Which of my readers' values, priorities, and interests might influence their views? • How far apart on the issue are my readers and I? What fundamental differences in worldview or experience might keep us from agreeing? What shared values and concerns might enable us to find common ground? • What could I realistically hope to achieve with these particular readers — convincing them to adopt my point of view, getting them to reconsider their own position, confirming or challenging some of their underlying beliefs and values?

● Framing the Issue for Your Readers

Write several sentences exploring ways you might frame or reframe the issue for your readers. If the issue has already been framed for your readers in a particular way, you may want to reframe it. Specifically, ask yourself what the argument over this issue has tended to be about and what you think it *should* be about. What values, priorities, and interests are at stake? For example, Statsky assumed her readers would be uncritically in favor of Little League–type sports for children because they are healthy and fun, so she tried to reframe the issue in terms of the potential physical and psychological damage they can have for young children.

Testing Your Choice

Test your choice by asking yourself the following questions:

- Do I now know enough about the issue, or can I learn what I need to know in the time I have remaining?

- Have I begun to understand the issue well enough to present it to readers — to frame or reframe it in a way that might make readers open to my point of view?

- Do I feel a personal need to reach a deeper understanding of the issue? Do I want to learn about other people's points of view on the issue and to develop an argument that addresses our shared concerns as well as our different perspectives?

- Does the issue matter to other people? If the issue is not currently one of widespread concern, would I be able to argue convincingly at the beginning of my essay that it *ought* to be of concern?

As you plan and draft your argument, you will probably want to consider these questions again. If at any point you cannot answer them with a confident *yes*, you may want to consider taking a different position on the issue or choose a different issue to write about. If you have serious doubts, consider discussing them with your instructor.

A Collaborative Activity:
Testing Your Choice

Get together with two or three other students and take turns discussing the issues you have tentatively chosen.

Presenters: Begin by identifying your issue, and briefly explaining the values, priorities, and interests you think are at stake.

Listeners: Tell the presenter how you understand the issue — the values, priorities, or interests that are at stake for you.

Ways in: Developing Your Argument and Counterargument

● ●
Basic Features

The following activities will help you develop your argument and counterargument by finding plausible reasons and evidence for your position and by anticipating readers' objections to your argument. You can begin with whichever activity you want, but wherever you begin, be sure to return to the other activities to explore all possibilities.

You may need more information to fully develop your argument. If so, you could start with these activities to develop the outlines of an argument and then do research, using the suggestions on p. 301, to fill in the details. Alternatively, you could start with research and return to these activities afterwards. Wherever you start, keeping careful notes will make it easy to fill in details and ideas as you develop your essay.

Developing Your Argument	Counterarguing Readers' Objections	Counterarguing Opposing Positions
State Your Tentative Position. *Briefly state your current position on the issue.* As you develop your argument and counterargument, you will refine this claim and decide how to formulate it effectively for your readers. For now, say as directly as you can where you stand on the issue.	**List Possible Objections.** *Look for places where your argument is vulnerable.* For example, think of an assumption that you are making that others might not accept or a value others might not share. Imagine how people in different situations — different neighborhoods, occupations, age groups, living arrangements — might react to each of your reasons.	**Consider Other Positions.** *Identify one or more widely held opposing positions and consider the one you think most likely to be attractive to your particular readers.* Try to represent the argument accurately and fairly. Decide whether you need to do research to find out more about this opposing position.
List Possible Reasons. *List the reasons for your position.* Try to come up with as many reasons as you can. Later, you may add reasons or modify the ones you have listed.	**Accommodate a Legitimate Objection.** *Choose one objection that makes sense to you, and write for a few minutes on how you could accommodate it into your argument.* You may be able simply to acknowledge an objection and explain why you think it does not negatively affect your argument. If the criticism is more serious, consider conceding the point and qualifying your position or changing the way you argue for it. If the criticism seems so damaging that you cannot accommodate it into your argument, however, you may need to rethink your position.	**List Reasons for the Opposing Position.** *List as many reasons as you can think of that your readers are likely to give in support of this position.*

(continued)

(continued)

Developing Your Argument	**Counterarguing Readers' Objections**	**Counterarguing Opposing Positions**

Collect Evidence. *Make notes of the evidence — such as authorities, facts, anecdotes, and statistics — you might be able to use to support your reasons.* You may already have some evidence you could use. If you need to do research, make notes of sources you could consult.

Refute an Illegitimate Objection. *Choose one objection that seems to challenge or weaken your argument, and write for a few minutes on how you could refute it.* Do not choose to refute only the weakest objection while ignoring the strongest one. Consider whether you can show that the objection is based on a misunderstanding or that it does not really damage your argument. You may also need to modify your position to make sure the objection is not valid.

Accommodate a Plausible Reason. *Choose one reason that makes sense to you, and write for a few minutes on how you could accommodate it into your argument.* Consider whether you can concede the point and yet put it aside as not really damaging to your central argument. You may also have to consider qualifying your position or changing the way you argue for it.

Choose the Most Plausible Reasons. *Write several sentences explaining why you think each reason would be likely to convince your particular readers to take your argument seriously.* Then identify your most plausible reasons. If you decide that none of your reasons seems very plausible, you might need to reconsider your position, do some more research, or choose another issue.

Refute an Implausible Reason. *Choose one reason that you do not accept, and write for a few minutes on how you could refute it.* Consider trying one of these strategies: argue that readers' values are better served by your position; point out where the reasoning is flawed (for instance, that it commits a straw-man fallacy by refuting your weakest reason and ignoring stronger ones); show that the argument lacks convincing support (for instance, that an example applies only to certain people in certain situations or that alternative authorities disagree). If you do not have all the information you need, make a note of what you need and where you might find it. (Note: Do not choose to refute a position no one takes seriously. Also, be careful not to misrepresent other people's positions or to criticize people personally.)

● Researching Your Argument

Do some library and Internet research to find out how others have framed the issue and what positions they have taken. If you are writing on an issue relating to your school, community, or workplace, you may also want to conduct interviews to see how people view the issue, what they know about its history, what positions they take, and how they react to your position.

Searching the Web can be a productive way of learning more about arguments other people have made on your issue and gathering additional information. Here are some suggestions for conducting an efficient search:

- Enter keywords — words or brief phrases related to the issue or your position — into a search tool such as Google. For example, Statsky could have tried keywords such as *children's competitive sports*, or she could have tried the question *Should children participate in competitive sports?* You could also try Googling your keywords plus *statistics, anecdotes,* or *facts.*

- If you think your issue has been dealt with by a government agency, you could try entering your keywords on FirstGov.gov, the U.S. government's official Web portal. If you want to see whether the issue has been addressed in your state or by local government, you can go to the Library of Congress Internet Resource Page on State and Local Governments (www.loc.gov/global/state/) and follow the links.

Bookmark or keep a record of the URLs of promising sites. You may want to download or copy information you could use in your essay, including visuals; if so, remember to record source information.

For more information on library and Internet research, see Chapter 23.

Designing Your Document

Think about whether your readers might benefit from design features such as headings or numbered or bulleted lists or from visuals such as drawings, photographs, tables, or graphs. Elements like these often make the presentation of an issue easier to follow and an argument more convincing. For an example, look back at the scenario on p. 264 describing a student's argument on the Employee Free Choice Act and then read Thinking about Document Design on pp. 311–12 to see how she used visuals to bolster its impact.

For more on document design, see Chapter 21.

Defining Your Purpose for Your Readers

Write a few sentences defining your purpose. Remember that you have already identified your readers and developed a tentative argument with these readers in mind. Try now to define your purpose by considering the following questions:

- If my readers are likely to be sympathetic to my point of view, what is my aim in writing — to give them reasons to commit to my position, to suggest arguments they can use, and/or to win their respect and admiration?

- If my readers are likely to be hostile to my point of view, what is my aim in writing — to get them to take my point of view seriously, to make them defend their reasons, to show them how knowledgeable and committed I am to my position, or to show them how well I can argue?

- If my readers are likely to take an opposing position but are not staunchly committed to it, what should I try to do — make them question or doubt the reasons and the kinds of support they have for their position, show them how my position serves their interests better, appeal to their values and sense of responsibility, or make them reconsider their preconceptions and prejudices against my position?

Formulating a Tentative Thesis Statement

Write a few sentences that could serve as a thesis — that is, a statement that tells your readers simply and directly what you want them to think about the issue and why. You might also forecast your reasons, mentioning them in the order in which you will take them up in your argument.

Estrada states his thesis at the end of paragraph 2: "Still, however willing I may have been to go along with the name as a kid, as an adult I have concluded that using an ethnic group essentially as a sports mascot is wrong." Perhaps the most explicit and fully developed thesis statement in this chapter's readings is Jessica Statsky's. She asserts her thesis at the end of paragraph 1 and then qualifies it and forecasts her reasons in paragraph 2:

> When overzealous parents and coaches impose adult standards on children's sports, the result can be activities that are neither satisfying nor beneficial to children.
>
> I am concerned about all organized sports activities for children between the ages of six and twelve. The damage I see results from noncontact as well as contact sports, from sports organized locally as well as those organized nationally. Highly organized competitive sports such as Peewee Football and Little League Baseball are too often played to adult standards, which are developmentally inappropriate for children and can be both physically and psychologically harmful. Furthermore, because they eliminate many children from organized sports before they are ready to compete, they are actually counterproductive for developing either future players or fans. Finally, because they emphasize competition and winning, they unfortunately provide occasions for some parents and coaches to place their own fantasies and needs ahead of children's welfare.

For more on thesis and forecasting statements, see Chapter 19.

As you draft your own thesis, pay attention to the language you use. It should be clear and unambiguous, emphatic but appropriately qualified. Although you will probably refine your thesis as you draft and revise your essay, trying now to articulate it will help give your planning and drafting direction and impetus.

Planning and Drafting

The following activities will help you refine your purpose, set goals for your draft, and outline it. In addition, this section will help you write a draft with advice on writing opening sentences, using effective sentence strategies, and working with sources.

Refining Your Purpose and Setting Goals

Before starting to draft, here are some questions that may help you sharpen your purpose for your audience and set goals for your draft. Your instructor may ask you to write out your answers to some of these questions or simply to think about them as you plan and draft your essay.

Clarifying Your Purpose and Audience

- Who are my readers, and what can I realistically hope to accomplish by addressing them?
- Should I write primarily to change readers' minds, to get them to consider my arguments seriously, to confirm their opinions, to urge them to do something about the issue, or to accomplish some other purpose?
- How can I present myself so that my readers will consider me informed, knowledgeable, and fair?

Presenting the Issue

- Should I place the issue in a historical context or in a personal context, as Estrada does?
- Should I use examples — real or hypothetical — to make the issue concrete for readers, as Estrada does?
- Should I try to demonstrate that the issue is important by citing statistics, quoting authorities, or describing its negative effects, as Statsky and Goldwasser do?
- Should I try to reframe the issue by showing how first impressions are wrong, as Etzioni does?

Making Your Argument and Counterargument

- How can I present my reasons so that readers will see them as plausible, logically supporting my position?
- If I have more than one reason, how should I sequence them?
- Should I forecast my reasons or counterarguments early in the essay, as Statsky does?
- Which objections should I anticipate? Can I concede any objections without undermining my argument, as Estrada and Goldwasser do?
- Should I refute any objections, as Etzioni and Goldwasser do?
- Which opposing positions should I anticipate?
- Can I counterargue by showing that the statistics offered by others are not relevant, as Etzioni does?

- Can I support my reasoning by narrating anecdotes (Estrada), pointing out benefits (Goldwasser), stressing benefits and losses (Etzioni, Statsky), or quoting research (Etzioni, Statsky)?

The Ending

- How can I conclude my argument effectively? Should I reiterate my position, as Estrada and Etzioni do?
- Should I try to unite readers with different allegiances by reminding them of values we share, as Estrada does?
- Could I conclude by looking to the future or by urging readers to take action or make changes, as Statsky and Goldwasser do?
- Should I conclude with a challenge, as Etzioni does?

Outlining Your Draft

With your purpose and goals in mind, you might want to make a quick scratch outline that includes the following:

I. Presentation of the issue

II. A clear position

III. Reasons and support

IV. Anticipation of opposing positions and objections

This simple plan is nearly always complicated by other factors, however. In outlining your material, you must take into consideration whether your readers are likely to agree or disagree with your position, which will determine how you will present the issue and how much attention you should give to readers' likely objections and to alternative solutions.

If most or all of your readers are likely to disagree with you, for example, you might try to redefine the issue so that these readers can see the possibility that they may share some common values with you after all. To reinforce your connection to readers, you could go on to concede the wisdom of an aspect of their position before presenting the reasons and support for your position. You would conclude by reiterating the shared values on which you hope to build agreement. In this case, an outline might look like this:

I. Presentation of the issue

II. Accommodation of some aspect of an opposing position

III. Thesis statement

IV. First reason with support

V. Second reason with support (etc.)

VI. Conclusion

If you have decided to write primarily for readers who agree rather than disagree with you, then you might choose to strengthen your readers' convictions by organizing your argument as a refutation of opposing arguments, and you might conclude by calling your supporters to arms. Here is an outline showing what this kind of essay might look like:

    I. Presentation of the issue

   II. Thesis statement

  III. Your most plausible reasons

  IV. First opposing argument with refutation

   V. Second opposing argument with refutation (etc.)

  VI. Conclusion

Your outline will, of course, reflect your own writing situation. Once you have a working outline, you should not hesitate to change it as necessary while drafting and revising. For instance, you might find it more effective to hold back on presenting your own position until you have discussed alternative but unacceptable positions. Or you might find a better way to order the reasons for supporting your position. The purpose of an outline is to identify the basic components of your argument and to help you organize them effectively, not to lock you into a particular structure.

For more on outlining, see Chapter 11

Drafting

If you have not already begun to draft your essay, this section will help by suggesting how to write your opening sentences; how to use the sentence strategy of concession followed by refutation; and how to cite opposing arguments. Drafting is not always a smooth process, so do not be afraid to leave spaces where you do not know what to put in or to write notes to yourself about what you could do next. If you get stuck while drafting, go back over your invention writing: You may be able to copy and paste some of it into your evolving draft, or you may find that you need to do some additional invention to fill in details in your draft.

Writing the Opening Sentences

You could try out one or two different ways of beginning your essay — possibly from the list that follows — but do not agonize over the first sentences because you are likely to discover the best way to begin only after you have written a rough draft. Again, you might want to review your invention writing to see if you have already written something that would work to launch your essay.

To engage your readers' interest from the start, consider the following opening strategies:

- an anecdote or personal reminiscence (like Estrada)
- a surprising statement (like Etzioni)
- an assertion of an issue's increasing significance (like Statsky)
- statistics (like Etzioni)

- a research study (like Goldwasser)
- a scenario
- an historical analogy
- criticism of an alternative position

A Sentence Strategy: Concession Followed by Refutation

As you draft, you will need to move back and forth smoothly between arguments for your position and counterarguments against your readers' likely objections and preferred positions. One useful strategy for making this move is to *concede* the value of a likely criticism and then to *refute* it immediately, either in the same sentence or in the next one.

The following sentences from Jessica Statsky's essay illustrate several ways to make this move (the concessions are in italics, the refutations in bold):

> The primary goal of a professional athlete — winning — is not appropriate for children. Their goals should be having fun, learning, and being with friends. *Although winning does add to the fun,* **too many adults lose sight of what matters and make winning the most important goal.** (par. 5)

> *And it is perfectly obvious how important competitive skills are in finding a job.* **Yet the ability to cooperate is also important for success in life.** (par. 10)

In both these examples from different stages in her argument, Statsky concedes the importance or value of some of her readers' likely objections, but then firmly refutes them. (Because these illustrations are woven into an extended argument, you may be better able to appreciate them if you look at them in context by turning to the paragraphs where they appear.) The following examples come from other readings in the chapter:

> *The authors argue that the employees develop many skills such as how to operate a food-preparation machine and a cash register.* **However, little attention is paid to how long it takes to acquire such a skill, or what its significance is.** (Etzioni, par. 8)

> *Another argument is that ethnic group leaders are too inclined to cry wolf in alleging racial insensitivity. Often, this is the case.* **But no one should overlook genuine cases of political insensitivity in an attempt to avoid accusations of hypersensitivity and political correctness.** (Estrada, par. 7)

> *That's not to say some of the survey findings aren't disturbing. It's crushing to hear that one in four teens could not identify Adolf Hitler's role in world history, for instance.* **But it's not because teenagers were online that they missed this. Had a parent introduced 20 minutes of researching the Holocaust to one month of their teen's Internet life, or a teacher assigned "The Diary of Anne Frank" (arguably a 13-year-old girl's blog) . . . we might not be able to pick up the phone and expose tragic pockets of ignorance.** (Goldwasser, par. 12)

The concession-refutation move, sometimes called the "yes-but" strategy, is important in most arguments. Following is an outline of some other kinds of language authors rely on to introduce their concession-refutation moves:

Introducing the Concession	*Introducing the Refutation That Follows*
I understand that ____.	What I think is ____.
I cannot prove ____.	But I think ____.
X claims that ____.	As it happens ____.
It is true that ____.	But my point is ____.
Another argument ____.	But ____.
It has been argued that ____.	Nevertheless, ____.
We are told that ____.	My own belief is ____.
Proponents argue that ____.	This argument, however, ____.
This argument seems plausible ____.	But experience and evidence show ____.
One common complaint is ____.	In recent years, however, ____.
I am not saying ____, nor am I saying ____.	But I am saying ____.
Activists insist ____.	Still, in spite of their good intentions ____.
A reader might ask ____.	But the real issue ____.

For more on concession followed by refutation, go to **bedfordstmartins.com/ theguide** and click on Sentence Strategies.

Working with Sources: Fairly and Accurately Quoting Opposing Positions

How you represent the views of those who disagree with your position is especially important because it affects your credibility with readers. If you do not represent your opponents' views fairly and accurately, readers very likely will — and probably should — question your honesty. One useful strategy is to quote your sources.

Compare the sentence from paragraph 3 of Statsky's essay to the passage from her source, the Little League Web site. The words Statsky quotes are highlighted.

Quote: Although the official Little League Web site acknowledges that children do risk injury playing baseball, it insists that "severe injuries . . . are infrequent," the risk "far less than the risk of riding a skateboard, a bicycle, or even the school bus" ("What about My Child?").

Source: (1) We know that injuries constitute one of parents' foremost concerns, and rightly so. (2) Injuries seem to be inevitable in any rigorous activity, especially if players are new to the sport and unfamiliar with its demands. (3) But because of the safety precautions taken in Little League, severe injuries such as bone fractures are infrequent. (4) Most injuries are sprains and strains, abrasions and cuts and bruises. (5) The risk of serious injury in Little League Baseball is far less than the risk of riding a skateboard, a bicycle, or even the school bus.

Statsky accurately condenses her source's second sentence ("Injuries seem to be inevitable in any rigorous activity, especially if players are new to the sport and unfamiliar with its demands") into one clause ("children do risk injury playing baseball"). She makes clear in the second part of her sentence that although the Little League agrees with her on the risk of injury, it disagrees about the seriousness of that risk. By quoting ("it insists that 'severe injuries . . . are infrequent,' 'far less than the risk of riding a skateboard, a bicycle, or even the school bus'"), she assures readers she has not distorted the Little League's position.

Quoting Appropriately to Avoid Plagiarism

In an earlier, rough draft, Statsky omitted the quotation marks in her sentence. Below is part of her draft sentence, followed by the source with the quoted words highlighted.

> . . . it insists that severe injuries are infrequent, the risk far less than the risk of riding a skateboard, a bicycle, or even the school bus ("What about My Child?").

> . . . severe injuries such as bone fractures are infrequent. Most injuries are sprains and strains, abrasions and cuts and bruises. The risk of serious injury in Little League Baseball is far less than the risk of riding a skateboard, a bicycle, or even the school bus.

For more information on integrating language from sources into your own sentences, see pp. 759–60 in Chapter 24.

For more help avoiding plagiarism, go to **bedfordstmartins.com/ theguide** and click on Avoiding Plagiarism Tutorial.

Even though Statsky cites the source, this failure to use quotation marks around language that is borrowed amounts to plagiarism. Use quotation marks whenever you use phrases from your source *and* indicate your source. Doing one or the other is not enough; you must do both.

Critical Reading Guide

◆ ◆ ◆ ◆
Basic Features

For a printable version of this Critical Reading Guide, go to **bedfordstmartins.com/ theguide.**

Your instructor may arrange a peer review session in class or online where you can exchange drafts with your classmates and give each other a thoughtful critical reading — pointing out what works well and suggesting ways to improve the draft. This Critical Reading Guide can also be used productively by a tutor in the writing center or by a roommate or family member.

A good critical reading does three things: It lets the writer know how the reader understands the point of the story, praises what works best, and indicates where the draft could be improved.

1. Evaluate how well the issue is presented.

   Summarize: Tell the writer what you understand the issue to be about. If you were already familiar with it and understand it differently, briefly explain.

   Praise: Give an example from the essay where the issue and its significance come across effectively.

   Critique: Tell the writer where more information about the issue is needed, where more might be done to establish its seriousness, or how the issue could be reframed in a way that would better prepare readers for the argument.

2. Assess how well the position is supported.

   Summarize: Underline the thesis statement and the main reasons.

   Praise: Give an example in the essay where the argument is especially effective — for example, indicate which reason is especially convincing or which supporting evidence is particularly compelling.

Critique: Tell the writer where the argument could be strengthened — for example, indicate how the thesis statement could be made clearer or more appropriately qualified, how the argument could be developed, or where additional support is needed.

3. **Consider how effectively objections and alternative positions are counterargued.**

Praise: Give an example in the essay where a concession seems particularly well done or a refutation is convincing.

Critique: Tell the writer how a concession or refutation could be made more convincing; what objection or alternative position should be counterargued; or where common ground could be sought.

4. **Assess how readable the argument is.**

Praise: Give an example of where the essay succeeds in being especially easy to read, either in its overall organization, clear presentation of the thesis, clear transitions, an effective opening or closing, or by other means.

Critique: Tell the writer where the readability could be improved. Can you, for example, suggest better forecasting, clearer transitions, or a more effective ending? If the overall organization of the essay needs work, make suggestions for rearranging parts or strengthening connections.

5. If the writer has expressed concern about anything in the draft that you have not discussed, respond to that concern.

Making Comments Electronically Most word processing software offers features that allow you to insert comments directly into the text of someone else's document. Many readers prefer to make their comments this way because it tends to be faster than writing on hard copy and space is virtually unlimited; it also eliminates the process of deciphering handwritten comments. Where such features are not available, simply typing comments directly into a document in a contrasting color can provide the same advantages.

Revising

Very likely you have already thought of ways to improve your draft, and you may even have begun to revise it. In this section is a Troubleshooting chart that may help. Before using the chart, however, it is a good idea to

- review critical reading comments from your classmates, instructor, or writing center tutor, and
- make an outline of your draft so that you can look at it analytically.

You may have made an outline before writing your draft, but after drafting you need to see what you actually wrote, not what you intended to write. You can outline the draft quickly by highlighting the basic features — presenting the issue, supporting a position, effectively anticipating counterarguments and alternative positions, and making the argument readable.

For an electronic version of this Troubleshooting chart, go to **bedfordstmartins.com/ theguide.**

Troubleshooting Your Draft

● ● ● ● **Basic Features**

	Problem	Suggestions for Revising the Draft
A Well-Presented Issue	The issue is not clear to readers.	☐ Add information — statistics, examples, anecdotes, and so on. ☐ Consider adding visuals, graphs, tables, or charts.
	Readers understand the issue differently than I do.	☐ Show the limitations of how the issue has traditionally been understood. ☐ Reframe the issue by showing how it relates to values, concerns, needs, and priorities you share with readers. ☐ Give concrete examples or anecdotes, facts, and details that could help readers see the issue as you see it.
A Well-Supported Position	My readers are not convinced that my position is reasonable and/or persuasive.	☐ Explain your reasons. ☐ Add additional supporting evidence. ☐ Ask yourself whether you have inadvertently offended or alienated readers. If so, change the way you have presented your position. ☐ Consider whether your position is in fact arguable. If you cannot provide reasons and support for it, consider modifying your position or writing about a different issue.
	My readers do not understand my position.	☐ Go over the way you present your position; if necessary, explain it and your supporting reasons more clearly. ☐ Try outlining your argument; if the organization or coherence is weak, try reorganizing it.
An Effective Counterargument	My readers continue to raise objections to my position.	☐ Address the objections directly in your argument. If possible, refute them, using clear reasons and support. ☐ If objections cannot be completely refuted, acknowledge them but demonstrate that they do not make your position invalid. Try using sentence openers like *It is true that . . . , but my point is . . . .* ☐ If you can neither refute nor accommodate objections, rethink your position or add qualifications.
	My readers have proposed opposing positions that I do not discuss in my argument.	☐ Address opposing positions directly. Establish common ground with opponents, if possible, but use clear reasons and support to show why their positions are not as reasonable as yours. ☐ If you cannot show that your position is preferable, rethink it.
A Readable Plan	My readers are confused by my essay or find it difficult to read.	☐ Outline your essay. If necessary, move, add, or delete sections to strengthen coherence. ☐ Consider adding a forecasting statement with key terms that are repeated in topic sentences throughout the essay. ☐ Check for appropriate transitions between sentences, paragraphs, and major sections of your essay. ☐ Review your opening and closing paragraphs. Be sure that your thesis is clearly expressed and that you review your main points in your closing.

In her paper arguing that the Employee Free Choice Act (EFCA) should become law (see the scenario described on p. 264), the student decides to reinforce her written argument with visuals because she believes her readers may have difficulty absorbing information from text that is densely packed with numerical data.

First, she considers downloading visual aids directly from the National Labor Relations Board (NLRB). After examining the material she finds online at www .nrlb.gov, however, she decides that the available charts and tables are too detailed to make a strong visual impact. Eventually, she locates "Dropping the Ax," a March 2009 report written by John Schmitt and Ben Zipperer for the Center for Economic and Policy Research, which condenses some of this NLRB data in easy-to-comprehend charts, tables, and graphs. She decides to reproduce one of these graphs in her paper.

**Thinking About
Document
Design:**
Adding Visuals

Fig. 1. Probability that a Pro-Union Worker Is Fired During a Union Election Campaign, 1976–2007

In the sections of her paper where she deals with the perspectives of those who oppose the EFCA, the student decides to reproduce an ad from the Coalition for a Democratic Workplace, which offers a summary of the results of a January 2009 survey it commissioned. (See p. 312.) After doing some research on the survey, the student explains why the statistics do not persuade her that the EFCA is a bad idea. In addition, she analyzes the ad as a visual text using the criteria for analysis from Chapter 20 (pp. 675–77) and explains how it illustrates the (in her view, misguided) attitudes and strategies of those who actively campaign against the EFCA.

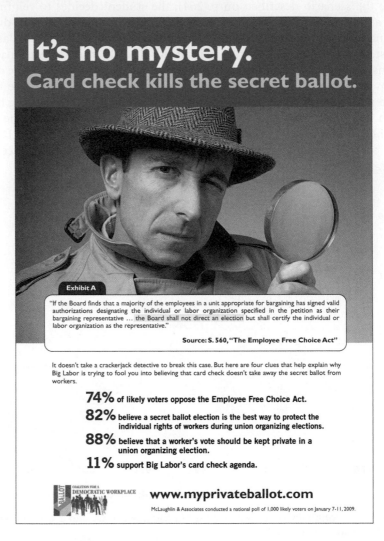

Editing and Proofreading

Our research indicates that particular errors occur often in essays that argue a position: incorrect comma usage in sentences with coordinating conjunctions and punctuation errors in sentences that use conjunctive adverbs. The following guidelines will help you check your essay for these common errors.

Using Commas before Coordinating Conjunctions

The Problem. In essays that argue a position, writers often link related ideas by joining independent clauses — groups of words that can stand alone as complete sentences — with coordinating conjunctions (*and, but, for, or, nor, so, yet*). Consider this example from Jessica Statsky's essay:

> Winning and losing may be an inevitable part of adult life, but they should not be part of childhood. (par. 6)

In this sentence, Statsky links two complete ideas: (1) that winning and losing may be part of adult life, and (2) that they should not be part of childhood. She links these ideas using a comma and the coordinating conjunction *but*.

A common error in sentences like these is the omission of the comma, which makes it difficult for the reader to see where one idea stops and the next one starts.

How to Correct It. Add a comma before coordinating conjunctions that join two independent clauses, as in the examples below:

▶ The new immigration laws will bring in more skilled people, but their presence will take jobs away from other Americans.

▶ Sexually transmitted diseases are widespread, and many students are sexually active.

Note: Do *not* use a comma when coordinating conjunctions join phrases that are not independent clauses, as in the following examples:

▶ Newspaper reporters have visited pharmacies/ and observed pharmacists selling steroids illegally.

▶ We need people with special talents/ and diverse skills to make the United States a stronger nation.

Using Punctuation with Conjunctive Adverbs

The Problem. When writers take a position, the reasoning they need to employ invites the use of conjunctive adverbs (*consequently, furthermore, however, moreover, therefore, thus*) to connect sentences and clauses. Sentences that use conjunctive

A Note on Grammar and Spelling Checkers
These tools can be helpful, but do not rely on them exclusively to catch errors in your text: Spelling checkers cannot catch misspellings that are themselves words, such as *to* for *too*. Grammar checkers miss some problems, sometimes give faulty advice for fixing problems, and can flag correct items as wrong. Use these tools as a second line of defense after your own (and, ideally, another reader's) proofreading/editing efforts.

For practice, go to **bedfordstmartins.com/ theguide/exercisecentral** and click on Commas before Coordinating Conjunctions.

adverbs require different punctuation, depending on how the conjunctive adverbs are used. Incorrect use of punctuation can make the sentences grammatically incorrect and/or difficult to understand.

How to Correct It. Conjunctive adverbs that open a sentence should be followed by a comma:

> ▶ Consequently, many local governments have banned smoking.

> ▶ Therefore, talented teachers will leave the profession because of poor working conditions and low salaries.

If a conjunctive adverb joins two independent clauses, it must be preceded by a semicolon and followed by a comma:

> ▶ The recent vote on increasing student fees produced a disappointing turnout; moreover, the presence of campaign literature on ballot tables violated voting procedures.

> ▶ Children watching television recognize violence but not its intention; thus, they become desensitized to violence.

Conjunctive adverbs that fall in the middle of an independent clause should be set off with commas:

> ▶ Due to trade restrictions, however, sales of Japanese cars did not surpass sales of domestic cars.

For practice, go to **bedfordstmartins.com/ theguide/exercisecentral** and click on Punctuation of Conjunctive Adverbs.

A Common ESL Problem: Subtle Differences in Meaning

Because the distinctions in meaning among some common conjunctive adverbs are subtle, nonnative speakers often have difficulty using them accurately. For example, the difference between *however* and *nevertheless* is small; each is used to introduce a statement that contrasts with what precedes it. But *nevertheless* emphasizes the contrast, whereas *however* softens it. Check usage of such terms in an English dictionary rather than a bilingual one. *The American Heritage Dictionary of the English Language* has special usage notes to help distinguish frequently confused words.

For practice, go to **bedfordstmartins.com/ theguide/exercisecentral** and click on A Common ESL Problem: Subtle Differences in Meaning.

A Writer at Work

Jessica Statsky's Response to Opposing Positions

In this section, we look at how Jessica Statsky tried to anticipate opposing positions and respond to them. To understand Statsky's thinking about her possible counter-argument, look first at the invention writing she did while analyzing her potential readers.

> I think I will write mainly to parents who are considering letting their children get involved in competitive sports and to those whose children are already on teams and who don't know about the possible dangers. Parents who are really into competition and winning probably couldn't be swayed by my arguments anyway. I don't know how to reach coaches (but aren't they also parents?) or league organizers. I'll tell parents some horror stories and present solid evidence from psychologists that competitive sports can really harm children under the age of twelve. I think they'll be impressed with this scientific evidence.
>
> I share with parents one important value: the best interests of children. Competition really works against children's best interests. Maybe parents' magazines (don't know of any specific ones) publish essays like mine.

Notice that Statsky lists three potential groups of readers here — parents, coaches, and league organizers — but she is already leaning toward making parents her primary audience. Moreover, she divides these parents into two camps: those who are new to organized sports and unaware of the adverse effects of competition and those who are really into winning. Statsky decides early on against trying to change the minds of parents who place great value on winning. But as you will see in the next excerpt from her invention writing, Statsky gave a lot of thought to the position these parents would likely favor.

Listing Reasons for the Opposing Position

In continuing her invention writing, Statsky listed the following reasons she thought others might have for their position that organized competitive sports teach young children valuable skills:

    --because competition teaches children how to succeed in later life
    --because competition--especially winning--is fun
    --because competition boosts children's self-esteem
    --because competition gives children an incentive to excel

This list appears to pose serious challenges to Statsky's argument, but she benefited considerably before she drafted her essay by considering the reasons her readers might give for opposing her position. By preparing this list, she gained insight into how she had to develop her own argument in light of these predictable arguments, and she could begin thinking about which reasons she might accommodate and which she had to refute. Her essay ultimately gained authority because she could demonstrate a good understanding of the opposing arguments that might be offered by her primary readers — parents who have not considered the dangers of competition for young children.

Accommodating a Plausible Reason

Looking over her list of reasons, Statsky decided that she could accommodate readers by conceding that competitive sports can sometimes be fun for children — at least for those who win. Here are her invention notes:

> It is true that children do sometimes enjoy getting prizes and being recognized as winners in competitions adults set up for them. I remember feeling very excited when our sixth-grade relay team won a race at our school's sports day. And I felt really good when I would occasionally win the candy bar for being the last one standing in classroom spelling contests. But when I think about these events, it's the activity itself I remember as the main fun, not the winning. I think I can concede that winning is exciting to six- to twelve-year-olds, while arguing that it's not as important as adults might think. I hope this will win me some friends among readers who are undecided about my position.

We can see this accommodation in paragraph 5 of Statsky's revised essay (p. 271), where she concedes that sports should be fun but quotes an authority who argues that even fun is jeopardized when competition becomes intense.

Refuting an Implausible Reason

Statsky recognized that she had to attempt to refute the other objections in her list. She chose one and tried out the following refutation to the first reason in her list:

> It irritates me that adults are so eager to make first and second graders go into training for getting and keeping jobs as adults. I don't see why the pressures on adults need to be put on children. Anyway, both my parents tell me that in their jobs, cooperation and teamwork are keys to success. You can't get ahead unless you're effective in working with others. Maybe we should be

training children and even high school and college students in the skills necessary for cooperation, rather than competition. Sports and physical activity are
important for children, but elementary schools should emphasize achievement
rather than competition--race against the clock rather than against each other.
Rewards could be given for gains in speed or strength instead of for defeating
somebody in a competition.

This brief invention activity led to the argument in paragraph 10 of the revised
essay (p. 273), where Statsky acknowledges the importance of competition for success in school and work, but goes on to argue that cooperation is also important.
To support this part of her argument, she gives examples in paragraph 11 of sports
programs that emphasize cooperation over competition.

You can see from Statsky's revised essay that her refutation of this opposing argument runs through her entire essay. The invention activities Statsky did advanced
her thinking about her readers and purpose; they also brought an early, productive
focus to her research on competition in children's sports.

Thinking Critically About What You Have Learned

In this chapter, you have learned a great deal about this genre from reading several
essays that argue a position and from writing one of your own. To consolidate your
learning, it is helpful to think metacognitively — that, is to reflect not only on
what you learned but on how you learned it. Following are two brief activities your
instructor may ask you to do.

Reflecting on Your Writing

Your instructor may ask you to turn in with your essay and process materials a
brief metacognitive essay or letter reflecting on what you have learned about writing your essay arguing a position. Choose among the following invention activities
those that seem most productive for you.

- Explain how your purpose and audience influenced *one* of your decisions
  as a writer, such as how you presented the issue, the strategies you used in
  arguing your position, or the ways in which you attempted to counter possible objections.

- Discuss what you learned about yourself as a writer in the process of writing this particular essay. For example, what part of the process did you find most challenging? Did you try anything new, like getting a critical reading of your draft or outlining your draft in order to revise it?

- If you were to give advice to a friend who was about to write an essay arguing a position, what would you say?

- Which of the readings in this chapter influenced your essay? Explain the influence, citing specific examples from your essay and the reading.

- If you got good advice from a critical reader, explain exactly how the person helped you — perhaps by questioning the way you addressed your audience or the kinds of evidence you offered in support of your position.

Considering the Social Dimensions: Suppressing Dissent

Some critics argue that society privileges reasoned argument over other ways of arguing in order to control dissent. Instead of expressing what may be legitimate outrage and inciting public concern through passionate language, dissenters are urged to be dispassionate and reasonable. They may even be encouraged to try to build their arguments on shared values even though they are arguing with people whose views they find repugnant. While it may help prevent violent confrontation, this emphasis on calmly giving reasons and support may also prevent an honest and open exchange of differences. In the end, trying to present a well-reasoned, well-supported argument may serve to maintain the status quo by silencing the more radical voices within the community.

1. *In your own experience of writing an essay arguing a position on a controversial issue, did having to give reasons and support discourage you from choosing any particular issue or from expressing strong feelings?* Reflect on the issues you listed as possible subjects for your essay and how you made your choice. Did you reject any issues because you could not come up with reasons and support for your position? When you made your choice, did you think about whether you could be dispassionate and reasonable about it?

2. *Consider the readings in this chapter and the essays you read by other students in the class.* Do you think any of these writers felt limited by the need to give reasons and support for their position? Which of the essays you read, if any, seemed to you to express strong feelings about the issue? Which, if any, seemed dispassionate?

3. *Consider the kind of arguing you typically witness in the media — radio, television, newspapers, magazines, the Internet.* We have said that society privileges reasoned argument, but in the media, have giving reasons and support and anticipating readers' objections been replaced with a more contentious, in-your-face style of arguing? Think of media examples of these two different ways of arguing. What do these examples lead you to conclude about the contention that reasoned argument can stifle dissent?

4. *Write a page or two explaining your ideas about whether the requirement to give reasons and support suppresses dissent.* Connect your ideas to your own essay and to the readings in this chapter.

7

Proposing a Solution

IN COLLEGE COURSES In an early childhood education class, a student becomes interested in the potential of television for educational purposes. Online, he learns about the Communications Act of 1934, which requires publicly owned airwaves to serve the public interest, and the Children's Television Act of 1990, which was designed to encourage commercial stations to provide educational children's programming. The student reviews current programming and discovers that commercial networks actually offer little in the way of educational programming for children and nothing targeted to English-language learners.

He decides to develop a proposal that would require television networks to provide programming specifically designed to help preschool children learn English. After consulting his professor and the college reference librarian for advice on resources, the student finds statistics that establish the need for such programming and sources on early education theory to support his proposal. In addition, he interviews via e-mail both an educational researcher who specializes in the impact of media on children's language acquisition and the programming coordinator for a national television network. In writing his proposal, he counters possible objections that his proposal is impractical by citing two model programs, public television's *Sesame Street* and cable's *Mi Casita (My Little House)*.

320

IN THE COMMUNITY A social services administrator in a large northeastern city becomes increasingly concerned about what he perceives to be a dramatic rise in the number of adolescents in jail. In search of data to support his observations, he visits the library of a local university and locates a number of recent studies, from which he concludes that the problem is in fact national in scope and growing in urgency. He reflects on his research and experience and comes to the conclusion that a partial solution to the problem would be to intervene at the first sign of delinquent behavior in eight- to twelve-year-olds.

In developing a proposal to circulate among decision makers in the local police department, juvenile justice system, school system, and business and religious communities, the administrator begins by describing the consequences of jailing young criminals, focusing on the costs of incarceration and the high rate of return to criminal activity by juveniles after their release. To bring his description to life, he provides the case histories of several juvenile offenders he has worked with over the years. He then discusses the major components of his early intervention program, which include finding mentors for young people who are beginning to fail in school, placing social workers with troubled families, and hiring neighborhood residents to work full-time on the streets to counter the influence of gangs. The administrator acknowledges the costs of the program but points to lowered costs for incarceration if it is successful. He also suggests sources of grant money to fund it.

IN THE WORKPLACE A driver of a heavy diesel tractor-and-trailer truck has an idea for a solution to the perennial shortage of well-qualified drivers at her trucking company. She convinces two coworkers to help her write a proposal suggesting that the company actively recruit more women. The driver talks to the owner of her company and to the few other women drivers she knows and concludes that women tend to be turned off by truck-driving schools, which cater to and are largely run by men. In trucking industry magazines, one of her coauthors finds statistics they can use to argue for a new training program that would exceed the Professional Truck Driver Institute standard, which requires a minimum of forty-four hours of driving time. They propose that after an initial off-road training period, recruits would be assigned to experienced drivers serving as paid mentors. The students would not have to attend a truck-driving school, thus saving the $4,000-plus cost of tuition, but they would be required to sign a contract agreeing to drive for the company at a reduced salary for a minimum number of months after the training period.

In the final draft of the proposal, the coauthors argue that everyone benefits. The company gets a skilled workforce. The experienced drivers get additional income. The recruits get hands-on experience without the up-front cost of tuition. The three coauthors give the proposal to the company president, and it is eventually published in an online industry newsletter, where it generates many comments, some of which propose that the plan be made available to men, too.

As the chapter-opening scenarios suggest, people write proposals in many different contexts and for a variety of purposes and audiences. The college student, for example, writes a proposal designed to support the creation of educational television programming for children. The social services administrator proposes an intervention program for at-risk children in the city where he works. Finally, in order to redress a shortage of qualified drivers, three employees of a trucking company draft a proposal for a recruitment program aimed at women.

Proposals are in fact vital to a democracy. By reading proposals, citizens learn about problems affecting their well-being and explore possible solutions to them. By writing proposals, citizens can significantly affect the ways in which individuals, families, and communities function. In the scenarios, for example, the proposals for more educational television programming and for intervention programs for at-risk children address problems of broad social import. Proposals, however, do not have to be about large social problems. Many proposals, like the one to train women as truck drivers, concern business-related or other problems that are narrower in scope.

As a special form of argument, proposals have much in common with position papers, described in Chapter 6. Both take a stand on a subject about which there is disagreement and both make a reasoned argument, acknowledging readers' likely objections. Proposals, however, go further: They urge readers to take specific action. They argue for a proposed solution to a problem, and they succeed or fail by the strength of that argument.

Good proposals are creative as well as convincing. Problem-solving depends on a questioning attitude — wondering about alternative approaches to bringing about change and posing challenges to the status quo. To solve a problem, you need to look at it from new angles and in new contexts.

Because a proposal tries to convince readers that its way of defining and solving the problem makes sense, proposal writers must be sensitive to readers' needs and expectations. Readers may be wary of costs, demands on their time, and grand schemes. Consequently, readers need to know details of the solution and to be convinced that it will solve the problem and can be implemented. If readers initially favor a different solution, knowing why the writer rejects it will help them decide whether to support or reject the writer's proposal.

In this chapter, you will read proposals designed to change the ways in which students are evaluated in college courses; to address the problems of childcare faced by families with multiple wage-earners; to increase the number of good jobs available to Americans; and to expand and improve the pool of applicants for teaching jobs. These readings illustrate the basic features and strategies writers typically use when writing proposals. The questions and activities following the readings will help you consider what is particular to one writer's approach and which strategies might be most effective for your proposal.

The Guide to Writing that follows the readings will support you as you compose a proposal, showing you ways to use the basic features of the genre to write a creative and convincing argument for change. Like the student who advocates more children's educational television programming, you may be asked in a course to propose a solution to a problem addressed in the course material, or you may decide on your own to address a problem in a class you are taking, as Patrick O'Malley does in proposing a solution to the problem of "high-stakes exams."

As you plan and draft a proposal, you will have to determine whether your readers are aware of the problem and whether they recognize its seriousness, and you will have to consider their views on possible alternative solutions. Knowing what your readers know — their understanding of the problem, their assumptions and attitudes toward change, and the kinds of arguments likely to appeal to them — is a central part of proposal writing.

A Collaborative Activity:

Practice Proposing a Solution to a Problem

To get a sense of the complexities and possibilities involved in proposing solutions, think through a specific problem with two or three other students, and try to come up with a **feasible** proposal — one that could actually help solve the problem and be implemented:

Part 1. Select a problem in your college community that you know something about — for example, overly complicated registration procedures or noisy residence halls.

- Discuss possible solutions and identify one solution that seems feasible. (You need not all be equally enthusiastic about this solution.)

- Determine who can act on your proposed solution and how to convince them that it could be implemented and would indeed help solve the problem.

Part 2. As a group, discuss your efforts.

- How did you think of possible solutions — for example, did you consider comparable problems and borrow their solutions, try to figure out what caused the problem and how to eliminate it, or use some other strategies?

- What seemed most challenging about constructing an argument to convince people to take action on your proposed solution — for example, showing how your solution could be implemented, proving it would help solve the problem, or something else?

Reading Essays Proposing a Solution

Basic Features

As you read essays proposing a solution in this chapter, you will see how different authors incorporate the basic features of the genre.

Basic Features

● A Well-Defined Problem

Read first to see how the writer presents the problem. Writers try to define the problem in a way that establishes the need to find a solution. Notice which strategies, such as the following, the writer uses to present the problem as real and serious:

- giving examples to make the problem specific
- using scenarios or anecdotes to dramatize the problem
- quoting testimony from those affected by the problem
- citing statistics to show the severity of the problem
- vividly describing the problem's negative consequences

● A Well-Argued Solution

To find where the essay advocates a solution, look for the thesis statement. A good thesis statement in an essay proposing a solution makes clear exactly what is being proposed and may also forecast the reasons for it that will be developed and supported in the essay. Check to see that the argument for the proposed solution offers concrete reasons and support showing that the solution is feasible — meaning it meets the following criteria:

- it will help solve the problem;
- it can be implemented; and
- it is worth the expense, time, and effort.

For example, a writer might demonstrate that

- the proposed solution would reduce or eliminate a major cause of the problem;
- a similar solution has worked elsewhere;
- the necessary steps to put the solution into practice can be taken without excessive cost or inconvenience; or
- stakeholders could come together behind the proposal.

● An Effective Counterargument

Read also to see how the writer responds to possible objections and alternative solutions. Writers may counterargue in one or more of the following ways:

- by acknowledging an objection
- by conceding the point and modifying the proposal to accommodate it
- by refuting criticism — for example, by arguing that an alternative solution would be more costly or less likely to solve the problem than the proposed solution.

● A Readable Plan

Finally, read to see how clearly the writer presents the proposal. Essays proposing a solution tend to be rather complicated because the writer has to establish the problem, argue for the proposed solution, and counterargue against objections and alternative solutions — all of which must be backed with solid support and clear citations. Therefore, it is especially important to have a readable plan that helps readers follow the twists and turns of the argument.

To make their essays easy to read, writers usually include some or all of the following:

- a forecast of the argument
- key words introduced in the thesis and forecasting statement
- topic sentences introducing paragraphs or groups of paragraphs
- repeated use of key words and synonyms throughout the essay, particularly in topic sentences
- clear transitional words and phrases
- headings that explicitly identify different sections of the essay
- visuals, including charts that present information in an easy to read format

Purpose and Audience

An effective proposal is one that is taken seriously by readers and that stands a chance of convincing them to support or act on the proposed solution. To be effective, a writer must establish credibility by anticipating readers' needs and concerns and by representing readers' views fairly.

As you read essays proposing solutions, ask yourself what seems to be the writer's purpose in writing. For example, does the writer seem to be writing primarily

- to convince readers that the problem truly exists and needs immediate action;
- to assure readers that the problem can indeed be solved;
- to persuade readers that the writer's proposed solution is better than alternative solutions;
- to inspire readers to take action; or
- to rekindle readers' interest in a long-standing problem?

As you read, also try to determine what the writer assumes about the audience. For example, does the writer assume most readers will

- be unaware of the problem;
- recognize the existence of the problem but fail to take it seriously;
- think the problem has already been solved;
- feel it is someone else's problem and not of concern to them;
- be skeptical about the cost and possibility of implementing the proposed solution; or
- prefer an alternative solution?

● ● ● ●
Basic Features

- A Well-Defined Problem
- A Well-Argued Solution
- An Effective Counterargument
- A Readable Plan

PATRICK O'MALLEY wrote the following proposal while he was a first-year college student frustrated by what he calls "high-stakes exams." O'Malley interviewed two professors (his writing instructor and the writing program director), talked with several students, and read published research on the subject of testing. Notice how he anticipates professors' likely objections to his proposed solution and argues against their preferred solutions to the problem. Where do you think his argument is strongest? Weakest?

As you read, consider the questions in the margin. Your instructor may ask you to post your answers or bring them to class.

More Testing, More Learning
Patrick O'Malley

What is the function of this opening paragraph?

It's late at night. The final's tomorrow. You got a C on the midterm, so this one will make or break you. Will it be like the midterm? Did you study enough? Did you study the right things? It's too late to drop the course. So what happens if you fail? No time to worry about that now — you've got a ton of notes to go over. 1

How does defining the problem this way set up the solution?

Although this last-minute anxiety about midterm and final exams is only too familiar to most college students, many professors may not realize how such major, infrequent, high-stakes exams work against the best interests of students both psychologically and intellectually. They cause unnecessary amounts of stress, placing too much importance on one or two days in the students' entire term, judging ability on a single or dual performance. They don't encourage frequent study, and they fail to inspire students' best performance. If professors gave additional brief exams at frequent intervals, students would be spurred to study more regularly, learn more, worry less, and perform better on midterms, finals, and other papers and projects. 2

How does O'Malley use the key terms introduced here throughout the essay?

What does par. 3 contribute to the argument?

Ideally, a professor would give an in-class test or quiz after each unit, chapter, or focus of study, depending on the type of class and course material. A physics class might require a test on concepts after every chapter covered, while a history class could necessitate quizzes covering certain time periods or major events. These exams should be given weekly or at least twice monthly. Whenever possible, they should consist of two or three essay questions rather than many multiple-choice or short-answer questions. To preserve class time for lecture and discussion, exams should take no more than 15 or 20 minutes. 3

4   The main reason professors should give frequent exams is that when they do and when they provide feedback to students on how well they are doing, students learn more in the course and perform better on major exams, projects, and papers. It makes sense that in a challenging course containing a great deal of material, students will learn more of it and put it to better use if they have to apply or "practice" it frequently on exams, which also helps them find out how much they are learning and what they need to go over again. A 2006 study reported in *Psychological Science* journal concluded that "taking repeated tests on material leads to better long-term retention than repeated studying," according to the study's coauthors, Henry L. Roediger and Jeff Karpicke. When asked what the impact of this breakthrough research would be, they responded: "We hope that this research may be picked up in educational circles as a way to improve educational practices, both for students in the classroom and as a study strategy outside of class" (ScienceWatch.com, 2008). "Incorporating more frequent classroom testing into a course," the study concludes, "may improve students' learning and promote retention of material long after a course has ended" (qtd. in Science Blog, 2006). Many students already recognize the value of frequent testing, but their reason is that they need the professor's feedback. A Harvard study notes students' "strong preference for frequent evaluation in a course." Harvard students feel they learn least in courses that have "only a midterm and a final exam, with no other personal evaluation." They believe they learn most in courses with "many opportunities to see how they are doing" (Light, 1990, p. 32). In a review of a number of studies of student learning, Frederiksen (1984) reports that students who take weekly quizzes achieve higher scores on final exams than students who take only a midterm exam and that testing increases retention of material tested.

5   Another, closely related argument in favor of multiple exams is that they encourage students to improve their study habits. Greater frequency in test taking means greater frequency in studying for tests. Students prone to cramming will be required — or at least strongly motivated — to open their textbooks and notebooks more often, making them less likely to resort to long, kamikaze nights of studying for major exams. Since there is so much to be learned in the typical course, it makes sense that frequent, careful study and review are highly beneficial. But students need motivation to study regularly, and nothing works like an exam. If students had frequent exams in all their courses, they would have to schedule study time each week and gradually would develop a habit of frequent study. It might be argued that students are adults who have to learn how to manage their own lives, but learning history or physics is more complicated than learning to drive a car or balance a checkbook. Students need coaching and practice

How does O'Malley introduce this reason? What kinds of support does he offer?

How does O'Malley integrate sources into his text and cite them?

How does O'Malley support this reason? Why does he include it?

How does O'Malley introduce and respond to this possible objection?

in learning. The right way to learn new material needs to become a habit, and I believe that frequent exams are key to developing good habits of study and learning. The Harvard study concludes that "tying regular evaluation to good course organization enables students to plan their work more than a few days in advance. If quizzes and homework are scheduled on specific days, students plan their work to capitalize on them" (Light, 1990, p. 33).

By encouraging regular study habits, frequent exams would also decrease anxiety by reducing the procrastination that produces anxiety. Students would benefit psychologically if they were not subjected to the emotional ups and downs caused by major exams, when after being virtually worry-free for weeks they are suddenly ready to check into the psychiatric ward. Researchers at the University of Vermont found a strong relationship among procrastination, anxiety, and achievement. Students who regularly put off studying for exams had continuing high anxiety and lower grades than students who procrastinated less. The researchers found that even "low" procrastinators did not study regularly and recommended that professors give frequent assignments and exams to reduce procrastination and increase achievement (Rothblum, Solomon, & Murakami, 1986, pp. 393–394).

6

Research supports my proposed solution to the problems I have described. Common sense as well as my experience and that of many of my friends support it. Why, then, do so few professors give frequent brief exams?

7

Some believe that such exams take up too much of the limited class time available to cover the material in the course. Most courses meet 150 minutes a week — three times a week for 50 minutes each time. A 20-minute weekly exam might take 30 minutes to administer, and that is one-fifth of each week's class time. From the student's perspective, however, this time is well spent. Better learning and greater confidence about the course seem a good trade-off for another 30 minutes of lecture. Moreover, time lost to lecturing or discussion could easily be made up in students' learning on their own through careful regular study for the weekly exams. If weekly exams still seem too time-consuming to some professors, their frequency could be reduced to every other week or their length to 5 or 10 minutes. In courses where multiple-choice exams are appropriate, several questions could be designed to take only a few minutes to answer.

8

Another objection professors have to frequent exams is that they take too much time to read and grade. In a 20-minute essay exam, a well-prepared student can easily write two pages. A relatively small class of 30 students might then produce 60 pages, no small amount of material to read each week. A large class of 100 or more students would produce an insurmountable pile of material. There are a number of responses

9

Side questions:

How effectively does O'Malley use this source?

What is the purpose of this question?

How does O'Malley argue against possible objections in pars. 8 and 9?

to this objection. Again, professors could give exams every other week or make them very short. Instead of reading them closely they could skim them quickly to see whether students understand an idea or can apply it to an unfamiliar problem; and instead of numerical or letter grades they could give a plus, check, or minus. Exams could be collected and responded to only every third or fourth week. Professors who have readers or teaching assistants could rely on them to grade or check exams. And the Scantron machine is always available for instant grading of multiple-choice exams. Finally, frequent exams could be given *in place of* a midterm exam or out-of-class essay assignment.

10   Since frequent exams seem to some professors to create too many problems, however, it is reasonable to consider alternative ways to achieve the same goals. One alternative solution is to implement a program that would improve study skills. While such a program might teach students how to study for exams, it cannot prevent procrastination or reduce "large test anxiety" by a substantial amount. One research team studying anxiety and test performance found that study skills training was not effective in reducing anxiety or improving performance (Dendato & Diener, 1986, p. 134). This team, which also reviewed other research that reached the same conclusion, did find that a combination of "cognitive/relaxation therapy" and study skills training was effective. This possible solution seems complicated, however, not to mention time-consuming and expensive. It seems much easier and more effective to change the cause of the bad habit rather than treat the habit itself. That is, it would make more sense to solve the problem at its root: the method of learning and evaluation.

How effectively does O'Malley present alternative solutions in pars. 10–12?

11   Still another solution might be to provide frequent study questions for students to answer. These would no doubt be helpful in focusing students' time studying, but students would probably not actually write out the answers unless they were required to. To get students to complete the questions in a timely way, professors would have to collect and check the answers. In that case, however, they might as well devote the time to grading an exam. Even if it asks the same questions, a scheduled exam is preferable to a set of study questions because it takes far less time to write in class, compared to the time students would devote to responding to questions at home. In-class exams also ensure that each student produces his or her own work.

How do the highlighted words and phrases make the argument easy to follow?

12   Another possible solution would be to help students prepare for midterm and final exams by providing sets of questions from which the exam questions will be selected or announcing possible exam topics at the beginning of the course. This solution would have the advantage of reducing students' anxiety about learning every fact in the textbook, and it would clarify the course goals, but it would not motivate students to study

carefully each new unit, concept, or text chapter in the course. I see this as a way of complementing frequent exams, not as substituting for them.

How effective is this conclusion?

From the evidence and from my talks with professors and students, I see frequent, brief in-class exams as the only way to improve students' study habits and learning, reduce their anxiety and procrastination, and increase their satisfaction with college. These exams are not a panacea, but only more parking spaces and a winning football team would do as much to improve college life. Professors can't do much about parking or football, but they can give more frequent exams. Campus administrators should get behind this effort, and professors should get together to consider giving exams more frequently. It would make a difference.

13

References

Dendato, K. M., & Diener, D. (1986). Effectiveness of cognitive/relaxation therapy and study skills training in reducing self-reported anxiety and improving the academic performance of test-anxious students. *Journal of Counseling Psychology, 33*, 131–135.

Frederiksen, N. (1984). The real test bias: Influences of testing on teaching and learning. *American Psychologist, 39*, 193–202.

Light, R. J. (1990). *Explorations with students and faculty about teaching, learning, and student life.* Cambridge, MA: Harvard University Graduate School of Education and Kennedy School of Government.

Rothblum, E. D., Solomon, L., & Murakami, J. (1986). Affective, cognitive, and behavioral differences between high and low procrastinators. *Journal of Counseling Psychology, 33*, 387–394.

ScienceBlog. (2006, March 7). To learn something, testing beats studying. [Blog posting]. Retrieved from http://www.scienceblog.com/cms/to_learn_something_testing_beats_studying_10161.html

ScienceWatch.com. (2008, February). Fast Breaking Papers - 2008. [Interview with authors Henry L. Roediger & Jeff Karpicke about journal article Test-enhanced learning: Taking memory tests improves long-term retention]. Retrieved from http://sciencewatch.com/dr/fbp/2008/08febfbp/08febfbpRoedigerETAL/

Why do you think O'Malley assumes these sources would carry weight with his readers?

LEARN ABOUT O'MALLEY'S WRITING PROCESS

To learn about O'Malley's process of writing this essay, turn to A Writer at Work on pp. 379–81. How did revision help O'Malley strengthen the presentation of his argument?

KAREN KORNBLUH earned a B.A. in economics and English and an M.A. from Harvard University's Kennedy School of Government. She worked in the private sector as an economist and management consultant and in the public sector as director of the office of legislative and intergovernmental affairs at the Federal Communications Commission before becoming the deputy chief of staff at the Treasury Department in the Clinton administration. Kornbluh has been a senior adviser to President Barack Obama since 2004.

As director of the Work and Family Program of the New America Foundation, a nonprofit, nonpartisan institute that sponsors research and conferences on public policy issues, Kornbluh led an effort to change the American workplace to accommodate what she calls the new "juggler family," in which parents have to juggle their time for parenting and work. Her book *Running Harder to Stay in Place: The Growth of Family Work Hours and Incomes* was published in 2005 by the New America Foundation, and Kornbluh's articles have appeared in such distinguished venues as the *New York Times*, the *Washington Post*, and the *Atlantic Monthly*. The following proposal was published in 2005 by the Work and Family Program.

As you read, think about your own experiences as a child, a parent, or both and how they affect your response to Kornbluh's proposal. Have you or your parents had to juggle time for parenting and work — and if so, how did you or they manage it?

WIN-WIN FLEXIBILITY

Karen Kornbluh

Introduction

Today fully 70 percent of families with children are headed by two working parents or by an unmarried working parent. The "traditional family" of the breadwinner and homemaker has been replaced by the "juggler family," in which no one is home full-time. Two-parent families are working 10 more hours a week than in 1979 (Bernstein and Kornbluh).

To be decent parents, caregivers, and members of their communities, workers now need greater flexibility than they once did. Yet good part-time or flex-time jobs remain rare. Whereas companies have embraced flexibility in virtually every other aspect of their businesses (inventory control, production schedules, financing), full-time workers' schedules remain largely inflexible. Employers often demand workers be available around the clock. Moreover, many employees have no right to a minimum number of sick or vacation days; almost two thirds of all workers — and an even

1

2

larger percentage of low-income parents — lack the ability to take a day off to care for a family member (Lovell). The Family and Medical Leave Act (FMLA) of 1993 finally guaranteed that workers at large companies could take a leave of absence for the birth or adoption of a baby, or for the illness of a family member. Yet that guaranteed leave is unpaid.

Many businesses are finding ways to give their most valued employees flexibility but, all too often, workers who need flexibility find themselves shunted into part-time, temporary, on-call, or contract jobs with reduced wages and career opportunities — and, often, no benefits. A full quarter of American workers are in these jobs. Only 15 percent of women and 12 percent of men in such jobs receive health insurance from their employers (Wenger). A number of European countries provide workers the right to a part-time schedule and all have enacted legislation to implement a European Union directive to prohibit discrimination against part-time workers.   3

In America, employers are required to accommodate the needs of employees with disabilities — even if that means providing a part-time or flexible schedule. Employers may also provide religious accommodations for employees by offering a part-time or flexible schedule. At the same time, employers have no obligation to allow parents or employees caring for sick relatives to work part-time or flexible schedules, even if the cost to the employer would be inconsequential.   4

In the 21st Century global economy, America needs a new approach that allows businesses to gain flexibility in staffing without sacrificing their competitiveness and enables workers to gain control over their work-lives without sacrificing their economic security. This win-win flexibility arrangement will not be the same in every company, nor even for each employee working within the same organization. Each case will be different. But flexibility will not come for all employees without some education, prodding, and leadership. So, employers and employees must be required to come to the table to work out a solution that benefits everyone. American businesses must be educated on strategies for giving employees flexibility without sacrificing productivity or morale. And businesses should be recognized and rewarded when they do so.   5

America is a nation that continually rises to the occasion. At the dawn of a new century, we face many challenges. One of these is helping families to raise our next generation in an increasingly demanding global economy. This is a challenge America must meet with imagination and determination.   6

Background: The Need for Workplace Flexibility

Between 1970 and 2000, the percentage of mothers in the workforce rose from 38 to 67 percent (Smolensky and Gootman). Moreover, the number of hours worked by dual-income families has increased dramatically. Couples with children worked a full 60 hours a week in 1979. By 2000 they were working 70 hours a week (Bernstein and Kornbluh). And more parents than ever are working long hours. In 2000, nearly 1 out of every 8 couples with children was putting in 100 hours a   7 week or more on the job, compared to only 1 out of 12 families in 1970 (Jacobs and Gerson).

In addition to working parents, there are over 44.4 million Americans who provide care to another adult, often an older relative. Fifty-nine percent of these caregivers either work or have worked while providing care ("Caregiving").

In a 2002 report by the Families and Work Institute, 45 percent of employees reported that work and family responsibilities interfered with each other "a lot" or "some" and 67 percent of employed parents report that they do not have enough time with their children (Galinksy, Bond, and Hill).

Over half of workers today have no control over scheduling alternative start and end times at work (Galinksy, Bond, and Hill). According to a recent study by the Institute for Women's Policy Research, 49 percent of workers — over 59 million Americans — lack basic paid sick days for themselves. And almost two-thirds of all workers — and an even larger percentage of low-income parents — lack the ability to take a day off to care for a family member (Lovell). Thirteen percent of non-poor workers with caregiving responsibilities lack paid vacation leave, while 28 percent of poor caregivers lack any paid vacation time (Heymann). Research has shown that flexible arrangements and benefits tend to be more accessible in larger and more profitable firms, and then to the most valued professional and managerial workers in those firms (Golden). Parents with young children and working welfare recipients — the workers who need access to paid leave the most — are the least likely to have these benefits, according to research from the Urban Institute (Ross Phillips).

In the US, only 5 percent of workers have access to a job that provides paid parental leave. The Family and Medical Leave Act grants the right to 12 weeks of unpaid leave for the birth or adoption of a child or for the serious illness of the worker or a worker's family member. But the law does not apply to employees who work in companies with fewer than 50 people, employees who have worked for less than a year at their place of employment, or employees who work fewer than 1,250 hours a year. Consequently, only 45 percent of parents working in the private sector are eligible to take even this unpaid time off (Smolensky and Gootman).

Workers often buy flexibility by sacrificing job security, benefits, and pay. Part-time workers are less likely to have employer-provided health insurance or pensions and their hourly wages are lower. One study in 2002 found that 43 percent of employed parents said that using flexibility would jeopardize their advancement (Galinksy, Bond, and Hill).

Children, in particular, pay a heavy price for workplace inflexibility (Waters Boots 2004). Almost 60 percent of child care arrangements are of poor or mediocre quality (Smolensky and Gootman). Children in low-income families are even less likely to be in good or excellent care settings. Full-day child care easily costs $4,000 to $10,000 per year — approaching the price of college tuition at a public university. As a result of the unaffordable and low quality nature of child care in this country, a disturbing number of today's children are left home alone: Over 3.3 million children age 6–12 are home alone after school each day (Vandivere et al).

Many enlightened businesses are showing the way forward to a 21st century flexible workplace. Currently, however, businesses have little incentive to provide families with the flexibility they need. We need to level the playing field and remove the competitive disadvantages for all businesses that do provide workplace flexibility.

This should be a popular priority. A recent poll found that 77 percent of likely voters feel that it is difficult for families to earn enough and still have time to be with their families. Eighty-four percent of voters agree that children are being shortchanged when their parents have to work long hours. . . .

Proposal: Win-Win Flexibility

A win-win approach in the US to flexibility . . . might function as follows. It would be "soft touch" at first — requiring a process and giving business an out if it would be costly to implement — with a high-profile public education campaign on the importance of workplace flexibility to American business, American families, and American society. A survey at the end of the second year would determine whether a stricter approach is needed.

Employees would have the right to make a formal request to their employers for flexibility in the number of hours worked, the times worked, and/or the ability to work from home. Examples of such flexibility would include part-time, annualized hours,[1] compressed hours,[2] flex-time,[3] job-sharing, shift working, staggered hours, and telecommuting.

The employee would be required to make a written application providing details on the change in work, the effect on the employer, and solutions to any problems caused to the employer. The employer would be required to meet with the employee and give the employee a decision on the request within two weeks, as well as provide an opportunity for an internal appeal within one month from the initial request.

The employee request would be granted unless the employer demonstrated it would require significant difficulty or expense entailing more than ordinary costs, decreased job efficiency, impairment of worker safety, infringement of other employees' rights, or conflict with another law or regulation.

The employer would be required to provide an employee working a flexible schedule with the same hourly pay and proportionate health, pension, vacation, holiday, and FMLA benefits that the employee received before working flexibly and would be required thereafter to advance the employee at the same rate as full-time employees.

Who would be covered: Parents (including parents, legal guardians, foster parents) and other caregivers at first. Eventually all workers should be eligible in our flexible, 24×7 economy. During the initial period, it will be necessary to define non-parental "caregivers." One proposal is to define them as immediate relatives or other caregivers

---

[1] *Annualized hours* means working different numbers of hours a week but a fixed annual total.

[2] *Compressed hours* means working more hours a day in exchange for working fewer days a week.

[3] *Flex-time* means working on an adjustable daily schedule.

of "certified care recipients" (defined as those whom a doctor certifies as having three or more limitations that impede daily functioning — using diagnostic criteria such as Activities of Daily Living [ADL]/Instrumental Activities of Daily Living [IADL] — for at least 180 consecutive days). . . .

Public Education: Critical to the success of the proposal will be public education along the lines of the education that the government and business schools conducted in the 1980s about the need for American business to adopt higher quality standards to compete against Japanese business. A Malcolm Baldridge–like award[4] should be created for companies that make flexibility win-win. A public education campaign conducted by the Department of Labor should encourage small businesses to adopt best practices of win-win flexibility. Tax credits could be used in the first year to reward early adopters.

22

Works Cited

Bernstein, Jared, and Karen Kornbluh. *Running Faster to Stay in Place: The Growth of Family Work Hours and Incomes.* Washington: New America Foundation, 2005. *New America Foundation.* Web. 22 May 2008.

Galinsky, Ellen, James Bond, and Jeffrey E. Hill. *Workplace Flexibility: What Is It? Who Has It? Who Wants It? Does It Make a Difference?* New York: Families and Work Institute, 2004. Print.

Golden, Lonnie. *The Time Bandit: What U.S. Workers Surrender to Get Greater Flexibility in Work Schedules.* Washington: Economic Policy Institute, 2000. *Economic Policy Institute.* Web. 18 May 2008.

Heyman, Jody. *The Widening Gap: Why America's Working Families Are in Jeopardy — and What Can Be Done About It.* New York: Basic, 2000. Print.

Jacobs, Jerry, and Kathleen Gerson. *The Time Divide: Work, Family and Gender Inequality.* Cambridge: Harvard UP, 2004. Print.

Lovell, Vickey. *No Time to Be Sick: Why Everyone Suffers When Workers Don't Have Paid Sick Leave.* Washington: Institute for Women's Policy Research, 2004. *Institute for Women's Policy Research.* Web. 20 May 2008.

National Alliance for Caregiving and AARP. *Caregiving in the U.S.* Bethesda: NAC, 2004. *National Alliance for Caregiving.* Web. 20 May 2008.

Ross Phillips, Katherine. *Getting Time Off: Access to Leave among Working Parents.* Washington: Urban Institute, 2004. *Urban Institute.* Web. 21 May 2008. New Federalism: National Survey of America's Families B-57.

Smolensky, Eugene, and Jennifer A. Gootman, eds. *Working Families and Growing Kids: Caring for Children and Adolescents.* Washington: The National Academies P, 2004. Print.

Vandivere, Sharon, et al. *Unsupervised Time: Family and Child Factors Associated with Self-Care.* Washington: Urban Institute, 2003. *Urban Institute.* Web. 21 May 2008. Assessing the New Federalism 71.

---

[4] The Malcolm Baldridge National Quality Award is given by the U.S. President to outstanding businesses.

Waters Boots, Shelley. *The Way We Work: How Children and Their Families Fare in a 21st Century Workplace*. Washington: New America Foundation, 2004. *New America Foundation*. Web. 22 May 2008.

Wenger, Jeffrey. *Share of Workers in "Nonstandard" Jobs Declines*. Briefing Paper. Washington: Economic Policy Institute, 2003. *Economic Policy Institute*. Web. 18 May 2008.

MAKING CONNECTIONS: THE PROBLEM OF CHILD CARE

Many of you have probably grown up during the period Kornbluh is describing, and your family may have been configured more as a "juggler" than as a "traditional family" (par. 1). Kornbluh asserts in paragraph 13 that it is the children in juggler families who "pay a heavy price." She is particularly critical of child care, which she says is very expensive and of low quality, especially for low-income families. She cites Vandivere et al. to argue that more than "3.3 million children age 6–12 are home alone after school each day" (par. 13).

With two or three other students, discuss how well Kornbluh's argument compares with your experiences as a child. Begin by taking turns telling whether you attended after-school programs, were a "latchkey child," or had some other arrangement. Then, together consider the following questions:

- Kornbluh cites research claiming that "60 percent of child care arrangements are of poor or mediocre quality" (par. 13). Looking back, how would you rate your child-care arrangements?

- Based on your experience, what kinds of child-care arrangements do you think would serve children and their parents best today?

ANALYZING WRITING STRATEGIES

◉ ◉ ◉ ◉
Basic Features

Your instructor may assign these activities in class or as homework for you to do by yourself or with classmates.

⬢ A Well-Defined Problem

Every proposal begins with a problem. What writers say about the problem and how much space they devote to it depend on what they assume their readers already know and think about the problem.

Some problems require more explanation than others. For problems that are new to readers, writers not only need to explain the problem but also to convince readers that it exists and is serious enough to justify taking the actions the writer thinks are necessary to solve it. Kornbluh assumes readers will not be familiar with key aspects of the problem she is writing about, so she spends the first part of her essay introducing the problem and the second part establishing the problem's existence and seriousness.

To analyze how Kornbluh defines the problem, do the following:

- Skim the first two sections, highlighting each time she uses some form of the word *flexibility*.

- Write a few sentences explaining how Kornbluh establishes that there is a lack of workplace flexibility for the "juggler family" and why it is a serious problem that needs to be solved.

● A Well-Argued Solution

You have seen that O'Malley gives three reasons why he thinks a greater number of brief exams will solve the problem he addresses and how he supports each reason with published research studies as well as his own experience. Kornbluh does not have to prove that her proposed solution would help solve the problem because it is obvious that a flexible work schedule would help juggler families juggle their responsibilities. But she does have to argue that her solution is feasible (possible). Readers of essays proposing a solution to a problem need to be told precisely what the solution is that the writer is advocating. Therefore, writers describe the proposed solution simply and directly in a way that readers cannot miss.

O'Malley presents his solution in his title, as does Kornbluh. But they both go on to describe the solution and to argue for it by trying to convince readers that the proposed solution would help solve the problem, is feasible, and could be implemented within a reasonable time and budget.

To analyze how Kornbluh argues that her solution can be implemented, try the following:

- Reread paragraph 5, where she sets out some general principles, and paragraphs 16–22, where she details what is needed to implement her solution. As you read, highlight the guidelines for what employees as well as what employers should do, and also underline the *would*, *should*, and *could* verb forms.

- Write a few sentences explaining how well you think the procedure she outlines satisfies the goals Kornbluh sets out in paragraph 5. What, if anything, do you think is missing?

- Add a sentence speculating about why Kornbluh uses *would*, *should*, and *could* verb forms, as O'Malley does in paragraph 3 of his essay.

● An Effective Counterargument

Writers of essays proposing solutions need to anticipate other solutions their readers may prefer. O'Malley, for example, brings up several alternative solutions his readers might prefer: implementing programs to improve students' study skills, giving students frequent study questions, and handing out possible exam topics to help students prepare. He acknowledges the benefits of some of these solutions but also points out their shortcomings, arguing that his solution is preferable to the alternatives.

To analyze how Kornbluh anticipates alternative solutions and counterargues, do the following:

- Reread paragraphs 10–12.

- Write a sentence or two for each alternative solution she brings up, explaining what the solution is and how effectively she handles it.

● A Readable Plan

Writers sometimes use headings to make it easy for readers to follow the argument. In long proposals, headings can be especially helpful. But what do you think they add to a short essay like this one?

To analyze how Kornbluh uses headings, follow these suggestions:

- Skim the essay, noting how each heading functions.
- Write a few sentences describing the function of the headings and indicating whether you think they are helpful.
- Add another sentence or two comparing Kornbluh's headings to the headings in Robert Kuttner's essay (pp. 346–52), if you have read that essay as well.

CONSIDERING TOPICS FOR YOUR OWN ESSAY

If you are interested in the problem Kornbluh describes, you might suggest other ways of helping parents juggle their parenting and work responsibilities. For example, consider writing a proposal for increasing opportunities for one or more parents to work at home via telecommuting. Alternatively, you might consider ways of improving preschool or after-school child-care arrangements. Would it be feasible, for instance, for high schools or community colleges to train interested students who could provide child care at supervised facilities on campus? You might interview people in your community to explore alternative ways of funding after-school programs. Perhaps you could propose that local businesses sponsor sports teams or offer after-school internships to students.

MATT MILLER has a B.A. in economics and a law degree, is a nationally syndicated columnist, hosts the public radio program *Left, Right, and Center,* is a commentator on *Morning Edition,* and has a Web site, mattmilleronline.com. His articles have appeared in the *Wall Street Journal,* the *New Yorker, Time,* the *New York Times Magazine, Fortune,* and *Slate.* Miller has written one book, *The Two Percent Solution: Fixing America's Problems in Ways Liberals and Conservatives Can Love* (2003), and edited a second, *Presidential Campaigns: Sins of Omission* (2001), with Kathleen Hall Jamieson. He is a senior fellow at the Center for American Progress and was a senior adviser to the White House Office of Management and Budget in the Clinton administration.

"A New Deal for Teachers" first appeared in the *Atlantic Monthly* in 2003 and was drawn from *The Two Percent Solution.* As you read, think about your experiences with teachers in grade school and high school. What do you think motivated them to teach? How would you rate the quality of your teachers? Would you ever consider teaching as a career? Why or why not?

A New Deal for Teachers

Matt Miller

No one should need convincing that schools in the nation's poor districts are in crisis. A recent Department of Education study found that fourth-grade students in low-income areas tested three grade levels behind students in higher-income areas. "Most 4th graders who live in U.S. cities can't read and understand a simple children's book," a special report in *Education Week* concluded a few years ago, "and most 8th graders can't use arithmetic to solve a practical problem." 1

There are probably a hundred things these schools need, and ten things that could make a very big difference, but if we had to focus on only one thing, the most important would be improving teacher quality. Owing to rising enrollments and a coming wave of retirements, more than two million teachers must be recruited over the next decade — 700,000 of them in poor districts. That means fully two thirds of the teacher corps will be new to the job. Finding top talent and not simply warm bodies is a tall order, especially in urban districts, where half of new teachers quit within three years (and studies suggest that it's the smarter half). Research shows that much of the achievement gap facing poor and minority students comes not from poverty or family conditions but from systemic differences in teacher quality; thus recruiting better teachers for poor schools is not only the biggest issue in education but the next great frontier for social justice. 2

> **Research shows that much of the achievement gap facing poor and minority students comes not from poverty or family conditions but from systemic differences in teacher quality.**

The obstacles to improving teacher quality are great. Good teachers in urban schools have told me with dismay of the incompetence of many of their colleagues. The state competency requirements that aspiring teachers must meet are appallingly low. The late Albert Shanker, the legendary president of the American Federation of Teachers, once said that most of the state tests are so easy to pass that they keep only "illiterates" out of teaching. Yet even these minimal standards are routinely waived so that districts can issue "emergency credentials"; in our biggest cities as many as half of new hires, and up to a quarter of city teachers overall, aren't properly trained or credentialed. 3

The situation may soon get even worse, because many of the teachers now reaching retirement age are among the best in the system. Until the 1960s and 1970s schools attracted talented women and minority members to whom most higher-paying careers weren't open. Now people who might once have taught 4 science or social studies become doctors, lawyers, and engineers. Salaries that start, on average, at $29,000 simply can't compete with the pay in other professions. In 1970 in New York City a lawyer starting out at a prestigious firm and a teacher going into public education had a difference in their salaries of about $2,000. Today that lawyer makes $145,000 (including bonus), whereas the teacher earns roughly $40,000. Sandra Feldman, the president of the American Federation of Teachers, is quite open about the problem. "You have in the schools right now, among the teachers who are going to be retiring, *very* smart people," she told me. "We're not getting in the same kinds of people. In some places it's disastrous."

How should we address this crisis? Most discussion so far has revolved around improving the skills of the teachers we already have. But upgrading the skills of current teachers can get us only so far when so many new teachers will be needed. Although changing the kind of person who goes into teaching may be hopelessly beyond the power of local school budgets and policies, we need to seize this moment of generational turnover in the teaching ranks to lure top college graduates to our toughest classrooms.

How to do this? Let's stipulate first that pay isn't everything. Teachers are the only category of people I've ever met who routinely say, without irony, that their jobs are so fulfilling they hardly care how little they make. For many of them, too, job security, good health benefits and pensions, and free summers offset the low income. But fulfillment and fringe benefits will never suffice to attract and retain hundreds of thousands of talented new teachers for poor districts.

There's no way to get large numbers of top people without paying up. Conservatives rightly worry that pouring more money into the system will subsidize mediocrity rather than lure new talent — especially when union rules make it next to impossible to fire bad teachers. "Dismissing a tenured teacher is not a process," one California official has said. "It's a career." The effort can take years and involve hundreds of thousands of dollars. Rather than being fired, bad teachers are shuffled from school to school. In a recent five-year period only sixty-two of the 220,000 tenured teachers in California were dismissed.

A grand bargain could be struck between unions and conservatives: make more money available for teachers' salaries in exchange for flexibility in how it is spent. For instance, the standard "lockstep" union pay scale, whereby a teacher with a degree in biochemistry has to be paid the same as one with a degree in physical education if both have the same number of years in the classroom (even though the biochemist has lucrative options outside teaching) should be scrapped. Better-performing teachers should make more than worse ones. And dismissing poor performers — who, even union leaders agree, make up perhaps 10 percent of urban teachers — should be made much easier.

If the quality of urban schools is to be improved, teaching poor children must become the career of choice for talented young Americans who want to make a difference with their lives and earn a good living too. To achieve that the federal government should raise the salary of every teacher in a poor school by at least *50 percent*. But this increase would be contingent on two fundamental reforms: teachers' unions would have to abandon the lockstep pay schedules, so that the top-performing half of the teacher corps could be paid significantly more; and the dismissal process for poor-performing teachers would have to be condensed to four to six months.

In Los Angeles teachers currently earn about $40,000 to start and top out, after thirty years and a Ph.D., at about $70,000. Under this new deal those teachers would start at $60,000, and the top-performing half of teachers would make $85,000 to $90,000 a year, on average. A number of the best teachers could earn close to $150,000 a year. The plan is designed to pay America's best teachers of poor students salaries high enough to allow them to put aside a million dollars in savings by the end of their careers.   10

How much would this plan cost? Roughly $30 billion a year, which would lift the federal share of K–12 spending from seven percent to 14 percent of the total nationwide — only right, given that on their own poor districts can't afford the skilled teachers they need. This federal investment looks modest beside the $80 billion a year that some representatives of corporate America say they spend training ill-prepared high school graduates to work in modern industry. The plan could be administered through a program similar to Title I, which provides supplementary federal funds to poor schools. We might call it Title I for Teachers.   11

To find out whether this basic plan is politically feasible, I presented it to big-city superintendents, high-ranking union leaders, and assorted education experts and teachers.   12

"I'd endorse something like that in a hot minute," said Day Higuchi, the president of the Los Angeles teachers' union from 1996 to 2002. "Right now L.A. Unified is the employer of last resort. People who can't get jobs elsewhere come here. If we did this, we'd become the employer of first resort. High-powered college students will be taking the job." Arne Duncan, the CEO of the Chicago Public Schools, told me that now there's "very little incentive outside of pure altruism" to get someone into teaching. This proposal "would dramatically change the face of the teacher profession," he said.   13

To gauge the conservative reaction, I spoke with Chester E. Finn Jr., a longtime school reformer on the right. Finn is the president of the Thomas B. Fordham Foundation and served as an assistant secretary of education in the Reagan Administration. He expressed several concerns. "The troubling part of this proposal," he said, "is a 50 percent boost for just showing up for work, without any reference to whether anybody you teach learns a damned thing."   14

I replied that the offer was designed to make it worthwhile for the unions to accept real reform in pay and dismissal practices. And the pay increase would subsidize mediocrity only briefly, because under the new dismissal rules bad teachers could much more easily be fired.   15

Finn had his own variation to offer. "If you wanted to make this plan really interesting," he told me, "job security and tenure would be traded for this raise. The   16 swap here ought to be that you take a risk with your employment and you don't have to be retained if you're not good at what you do. If you are good and you get retained, you get paid a whole lot more money. If current teachers can't swallow that tradeoff, make this a parallel personnel system for new ones coming in and for the existing ones who want to do it."

How might that work? I asked.

17

"Any current teacher is free to join this new system on its terms," Finn said, "or to stick with the old arrangement, in which they have high security and low pay. That's just a political accommodation to an existing work force for whom this might be too abrupt a shift. Over time you'll get a very different kind of person into teaching."

18

"It sounds tempting from a union point of view," Sandra Feldman told me of Finn's parallel approach. "The more voluntary you can make a system like this, the easier it is to sell. But I worry that something like that could create resentment between the people in the different tracks." Other union and district leaders, however, told me they thought that virtually every new hire would opt for the new system, as would perhaps a quarter of the senior teachers — meaning that most of the urban teacher corps would be on the plan within five years.

19

That union leaders think it makes sense to move toward serious pay differentials for teachers is important. But educators are concerned about two related questions. In determining pay rates, who will decide which teachers are better performers? And what standards will be used to assess teachers?

20

I asked Sandra Feldman if there was a consensus in the faculty lounges at most schools about who the best teachers were. "Absolutely," she said. The question is how to evaluate performance in a way that is objective and untainted by cronyism.[1]

21

The superintendents and conservative reformers I spoke to agreed that serious weight should be given to students' test scores. In theory, so-called "value-added analysis" — the effort to track the impact of teachers on student achievement each year — is the holy grail of accountability, and thus the ideal basis for performance pay. But in reality, many people think it has serious limits. "There's just no reliable way of doing that right now," Feldman told me. This isn't only a union view. Joseph Olchefske, the superintendent of schools in Seattle, has studied the issue; he believes it would be hard to measure the value added by individual teachers. Others, however, think individual value-added analysis may soon be practical. Day Higuchi, the former L.A. union leader, argues that in elementary school, where each child has essentially one teacher, the right testing could constructively measure that teacher's impact.

22

Finn and others suggested a blended approach to teacher assessment. "You could have value-added analysis at the school level, which is clearly going to be done," Finn said, "combined with some other kind of performance

23

---

[1] partiality to friends

reviews." Adam Urbanski, the president of the Rochester Teachers Association, who has spearheaded union-reform efforts for two decades, said, "It would be a fatal mistake not to include student learning outcomes as the ultimate test of this. It would be equally fatal to use only test scores, because you would have a huge invitation to cheating and manipulation." He and others proposed that various indicators regarded as germane to teacher assessment by educators and the public — such as dropout rates, graduation rates, peer review, specialized training, teaching technique, and student work — be considered along with test scores.

The superintendents all told me that principals should be the final arbiters   24
of teacher performance. This is a sticking point with the unions. The problem with giving principals control is that many teachers think principals don't know the first thing about good teaching. Jene Galvin, a teacher who has worked in the Cincinnati school system for twenty-seven years, told me, "We don't really believe that the principals are the experts on pedagogy or classroom teaching or classroom management. The reason is they just didn't do it very long." The solution might be to have peer evaluators — mentor and master teachers — do the evaluations along with principals.

Experts I spoke with, including Finn, thought that all these challenges ulti-   25
mately seemed surmountable. Finn said that a key to his supporting such a plan would be "that it included the ability for managers of schools to have a whole lot of control over who is working in their school."

If this agenda were presented as a federal challenge, in which the President   26
or congressional leaders said, "We're putting this pot of money on the table for those communities that can come together around a plan that meets its conditions and make it work," school districts would almost surely step forward. If unions declined to come to the table, local media and business leaders could ask why they were balking at billions of dollars. Rank-and-file teachers, who might earn an extra $20,000 to $50,000 a year, would obviously have a huge stake in the plan's adoption. They might tell union leaders they supported finding ways of speedily dismissing poor performers.

Some Republicans may resist. After all, teachers' unions are big Democratic   27
donors and the chief foes of Republican efforts to introduce school vouchers. The last thing we need, these Republicans might say, is a bunch of teachers with more money to spend on making sure that Republicans never get elected.

But some savvy Republicans think the time for a plan like this is ripe. Rick   28
Davis, a political adviser to Senator John McCain, believes that such a plan may be inevitable. "Anybody who has looked at teacher pay as an element of the overall problem in education realizes that money matters," Davis told me. "Other than the voucher debate, we've exhausted the Republican position on education. So sooner or later we're going to get to teacher pay, because we can't be against teachers' making money. The American public is going to figure out that their teachers make less than their garbage collectors, and they're not going to be for that."

Miller explains that "more than two million teachers must be recruited over the next decade — 700,000 of them in poor districts" (par. 2). "Teachers," he also says, "are the only category of people [he's] ever met who routinely say, without irony, that their jobs are so fulfilling they hardly care how little they make" (par. 6).

With two or three other students, discuss whether you can imagine becoming a teacher yourself. Begin by taking turns telling each other what your current career goals are, and whether or not becoming a teacher is one of them. Then, together discuss the following questions:

- What could entice you to become a teacher?
- What would discourage you from becoming a teacher?
- Would any of the changes Miller considers in this proposal influence you either way?

● A Well-Defined Problem

Miller opens his essay by identifying the general problem that there is what he calls a "crisis" in our nation's schools, especially in "poor districts" (par. 1). But instead of trying to address such a large problem, he focuses on a specific aspect of the problem: "teacher quality" (par. 2). Narrowing the focus of a proposal can be a smart strategy because many problems, such as the quality of public education, are big and complicated. They need a many-pronged solution. But focusing on one aspect of the problem and proposing a way of remedying that part of the problem can also assure readers that the proposed solution is feasible — both beneficial and implementable.

To analyze how Miller tries to establish that the problem exists and is serious, try the following:

- Reread paragraphs 2–4 and note in the margin how he supports his assertion that teacher quality is the "most important" aspect of the broader problem.
- Write a sentence or two explaining how he supports this assertion and what values he assumes his readers share with him.

● A Well-Argued Solution

Essays proposing a solution, especially ones attempting to solve a problem that is highly controversial and much debated, must meet a feasibility test: That is, the solution has to be possible or realistic. Miller himself acknowledges this requirement when he writes that he sought "[t]o find out whether this basic plan is politically feasible" (par. 12).

To analyze how Miller argues for the feasibility of his proposed solution, follow these suggestions:

■ Reread paragraph 12 and note what categories of people he says he consulted. Skim the rest of the essay, highlighting the names of the people he consulted, and determine whether he actually talked to individuals who represent these particular categories.

■ Reread paragraph 26 and write a few sentences explaining what he is arguing in this paragraph and how it relates to his need to establish that his proposed solution is "politically feasible."

● An Effective Counterargument

Proposal writers usually try to anticipate readers' objections and questions and respond to them by counterarguing. Writers have three strategies for counterarguing: (1) they can simply acknowledge that they are aware of critics' concerns but do nothing else to respond; (2) they can accommodate the criticism, modifying their argument by making concessions; or (3) they can defend their proposed solutions and try to refute criticism. Those seeking to convince readers to take action to solve a problem nearly always try to respond by accommodating or refuting.

How writers handle objections and questions affects their credibility. Readers expect writers to be respectful of other points of view and to take criticism seriously, but readers also understand that it is important that proposal writers assertively argue for and defend their solution. Miller knows that he faces tough opposition because change in something as entrenched and widely accepted as our public education system calls for a significant change in thinking. His proposal also involves money, and people are sometimes reluctant to spend money on public education. Miller therefore devotes a large part of his proposal to counterargument. Throughout his essay, Miller raises questions and objections, addressing each of them in turn.

To analyze how Miller counterargues, consider how he deals with possible questions and objections regarding the raising of teachers' pay:

■ Reread paragraphs 14–18 and write a few sentences summarizing the conservative reaction to Miller's basic proposal and suggested variations of it.

■ Reread paragraphs 19–21 and write another sentence or two summarizing the teachers' union's view of the conservative suggestion.

■ Add another couple of sentences assessing how successfully Miller addresses both conservative and union points of view about raising teacher pay. What questions or objections, if any, do you think Miller overlooked in this part of his argument?

● A Readable Plan

Topic sentences — particularly ones placed at the top of a paragraph — are important tools for orienting readers. For example, look at how Patrick O'Malley structures these topic sentences:

The main reason professors should give frequent exams is that . . . (par. 4)

Another, closely related argument in favor of multiple exams is that . . . (par. 5)

Each topic sentence announces a reason that the rest of the paragraph goes on to explain and support in some detail. The topic sentence not only states the reason, but it also reminds readers what the proposed solution is — frequent or multiple exams. The word *another* also makes a clear transition alerting readers from the start that a new reason is being introduced.

To analyze how Miller uses topic sentences, try the following:

- Choose two topic sentences that you think help to make the essay readable.
- Write a couple of sentences explaining how the topic sentences you chose help readers.

CONSIDERING TOPICS FOR YOUR OWN ESSAY

Consider making a proposal to improve the operation of an organization, a business, or a club to which you belong. For example, you might propose that your college keep administrative offices open in the evenings or on weekends to accommodate working students or that a child-care center be opened for students who are parents of young children. For a business, you might propose a system to handle customer complaints or a fairer way for employees to arrange their schedules. If you belong to a club that has a problem with the collection of dues, you might propose a new collection system or suggest alternative ways of raising money.

ROBERT KUTTNER is a journalist and economist who cofounded the Economic Policy Institute as well as the journal the *American Prospect*, of which he is also a coeditor. A regular columnist for *Business Week* and the *Boston Globe*, his essays have appeared in such distinguished publications as the *New York Times Magazine*, the *Atlantic*, the *New Yorker*, *Harvard Business Review*, and the *New England Journal of Medicine*. His most recent books include *The Squandering of America: How the Failure of Our Politics Undermines Our Prosperity* (2007), and *Obama's Challenge: America's Economic Crisis and the Power of a Transformative Presidency* (2008). He has taught at various colleges including Harvard's Institute of Politics and the University of California at Berkeley.

This proposal originally appeared in the *American Prospect* in May 2008, months before the "severe recession" he predicts was in full swing. As you read Kuttner's essay, consider whether any of his ideas have been implemented since he wrote it, and if so, how effective they have been.

Good Jobs for Americans Who Help Americans

Robert Kuttner

For three decades, the supply of good jobs has been dwindling. The causes include globalization, deregulation, and weaker worker protections, such as minimum-wage laws and government defense of the right to unionize. Now, after three decades of stagnant incomes, we are heading for a severe recession. Higher unemployment will reduce worker bargaining power even further. The cure will require a much more active government role in the economy — both as a regulator and as a source of funds. [1]

In the same 30 years, the service sector has exploded as a source of jobs. The American work force has gone from 28 percent factory workers and 72 percent service workers in 1978 to 16 percent factory workers and 84 percent service workers today. But the service sector encompasses tens of millions of bad jobs — in routine clerical work, retail sales, fast food, low-end human services — and a relatively small number of very well compensated professional positions, among them doctor, lawyer, scientist, and investment banker. [2]

> Let's have a national policy to make every human-service job a good job.

Here is a very straightforward proposal. Let's have a national policy to make every human-service job a good job — one that pays a living wage with good benefits, and includes adequate training, professional status, and the prospect of advancement — a career rather than casual labor. [3]

Don't Mourn — Professionalize

These, after all, are jobs caring for our parents, our children, and ourselves. Transforming all human-service work into good jobs would not merely replenish the supply of decent work. It would vastly improve the quality of care delivered to the elderly at home or in institutions; to young children in pre-kindergartens or day-care facilities; and to sick people whether in hospitals, hospices, outpatient settings, or their homes. [4]

These are also the jobs that cannot be outsourced. Even if we succeed in reviving American manufacturing, the process of automation means that America is almost certain to become even more of a service economy over time. Good service-sector jobs can help replace good factory jobs. [5]

Many economists once thought that widening income inequality was caused in part by the shift to a service economy. Factory jobs, the argument went, tended to pay above the median wage because each job added a lot of value. The more [6] productive and capital-intensive the machinery became over time, the more value each job added. So by the mid-20th century, industrial workers could command middle-class wages and good fringe benefits. By contrast, human-service jobs were hands-on and labor intensive. A nursing-home worker or a pre-k teacher was low-tech. So the pay was low, too.

We now know that this picture was highly misleading. How do we know? Just look at the global economy. Autoworkers in Mexico use the same production technology as workers in Michigan, but their pay is about $2 an hour. In China, autoworkers may earn 50 cents a day. American autoworkers were paid middle-class wages not because of something inherent about making cars but because the United Auto Workers had the power to negotiate good wages. Conversely, Scandinavia has no low-wage human-service workers because it has made a decision that everyone who takes care of the sick, the old, or the young is a professional or at least a paraprofessional and is compensated as such.

Since most human-service costs are paid socially, choices about how to compensate workers are social decisions. In the United States, with our meager social outlay, we define these human-service positions as low-wage, casual jobs. In the Nordic countries, the people who work in pre-kindergartens or child-care centers are either teachers or apprentice teachers. In France, to work in a *crèche maternelle*,[1] you need more qualifications than a public school teacher — additional courses in child development and public health. When I recently interviewed Michel Rocard, who served as French prime minister from 1988–1991, he told me that his proudest success in resisting austerity demands was preventing the budget-cutters from reducing the qualifications and pay of pre-kindergarten teachers.

But in America, how can we possibly make all human-service jobs into good jobs? And aren't some of these jobs inherently low-skill? How much training, after all, does it take to empty a bedpan or change linen?

All It Takes Is Money

Start with the fact that at least 60 percent of the funding for these jobs is ultimately public money. Government pays upward of half of all health-care costs through Medicare, Medicaid, the State Children's Health Insurance Program, the Veterans Administration, and the health insurance of public employees. Forty-five percent of nursing-home care is paid by Medicaid. Home care is heavily subsidized by public agencies. And in early childhood education and day care, while the affluent may have nannies or private day-care arrangements, Head Start is a public program, and state, local, and federal agencies subsidize day care through a variety of social-service programs.

Clearly, the government has the leverage to set standards. The federal Davis-Bacon Act is a rough model. It was enacted in 1931 to assure that nonunion construction contractors would not undercut prevailing wage scales. Davis-Bacon

---

[1] A French communal nursery or child-care facility for children from birth to three years old.

requires that all federally funded construction pay prevailing wages, which in practice turns out to mean union-scale wages.

Davis-Bacon, of course, has its critics. There was a time when union bargaining power was accused of stimulating inflation by driving contract settlements that increased wages and benefits in excess of the rate of productivity growth. But whatever the reality of that long-ago charge, that time is long gone. Today, the problem is the opposite — wages lag far behind productivity increases, and the gains go instead to the top.   12

America needs a good-jobs strategy. And human-service jobs are a good place to begin.   13

How would such a transformation happen? Congress could require that any job in the human services supported in whole or in part by federal funds would have to pay a professional wage and be part of a career track. A minimum starting annual salary might be $24,000 a year, or about $12 an hour, an increase from the current common wage of around $9 an hour for nurse's-aide and home-care workers, and a sharp jump from the median wage of $7.69 for direct child-care providers. Opportunities for genuine advancement with pay increases would have to be part of the plan. For example, instead of defining a nurse's aide as a high-turnover, low-qualification, low-pay occupation, the job would require substantially more training, much of which could be done on the job. Such jobs would also be entry points to higher-level positions, such as licensed practical nurse. With more training and qualifications, these workers could be entrusted with more responsibilities, and nursing-home residents would get better care.   14

In the area of pre-kindergarten and day care, all such jobs would be teaching jobs rather than the high-turnover, largely custodial jobs of the current system. Raising the qualifications and pay of pre-k teachers, at least to the level of public school teachers, would be part of a national strategy of universal pre-kindergarten. 15

What of the argument that you don't need much training to baby-sit kids or provide basic care to senescent old folks? In fact, the development of young children and the quality of life of the elderly are profoundly affected by the quality of their caregivers. One of the best established findings of recent research on child development is that a dollar invested in early childhood education is one of the most cost-effective investments we can make. (See the Prospect's December 2007 special report, "Life Chances: The Case for Early Investment in Our Kids.") The difference between child-development and baby-sitting, of course, is the availability of well-trained professionals who work with young children. Likewise, in the care of the elderly, having well-trained people improves not just seniors' comfort but seniors' physical health, cognitive stimulation, and capacity to live fulfilling lives.   16

We have seen a rough model of this kind of upgrading and professionalization in the strategies of unions that represent home-care workers. Home-care workers are often classified as independent contractors. As a result, they have no bargaining power, and public and nonprofit agencies often try to solve their own budget problems by paying home-care workers as little as possible. This creates a vicious 17 circle of burnout and high turnover, even though the vast majority of these workers are conscientious and eager to perform well. Recently, in several states led by California, the Service Employees International Union (SEIU) and the American Federation of State, County and Municipal Employees succeeded in persuading legislatures and governors to approve laws or executive orders establishing public agencies with which home-care workers could bargain collectively. In California, the typical wage went from minimum wage to $10 an hour.

Another pressing need is public subsidy to help low-wage human-service workers ascend career ladders. In some occupations, these ladders exist in principle, and there are heartening individual stories of the nurse's aide who graduated to licensed practical nurse, or the classroom aide who went to night school and earned a teaching credential. Despite a few model programs, our society seems determined to make this path as arduous as possible. Almost by definition, someone working for $6 or $7 an hour, often with family responsibilities, has an extreme shortage of time as well as money. Though some rare individuals do succeed, it takes uncommon tenacity and self-sacrifice, and sometimes the sacrifice of one's own children. Why should we make this so hard? Other societies provide subsidies for living expenses during training.

This effort would be part of two broader labor-policy shifts that America sorely needs. First, we need to reverse the trend toward casualization of labor that has been occurring for three decades. One of the great advances of the 20th century was regularization of the employment relationship. Through successful social struggle, growth of unions, and enactment of legislation, most jobs came to provide decent wages and fringe benefits. Workers could not be fired without cause. Loyalty to the firm was reciprocated. Grievance systems were created and respected. Economists termed these jobs primary labor-market jobs. Casual, secondary labor-market jobs, which paid less and offered no such guarantees, continued to exist, but they were the exception. In recent years, however, the shift to casual jobs has become the norm, and in low-paid human-service work, casual, high-turnover jobs are the industry standard.

Second, the upgrading of human-service work would reverse another insidious trend — the employer's habit of trying to increase the efficiency of labor by fragmenting jobs into separate tasks and paying the lowest possible wage for each task — a strategy known as Taylorism, after the early 20th-century "efficiency expert," Fredrick Winslow Taylor, who first recommended it.

However, when it comes to human services, many of the supposed gains of Taylorism are false economies. Studies of nursing homes have shown that better trained and paid workers can head off expensive conditions such as bedsores. Whereas registered nurses once performed a multiplicity of tasks and became very familiar with each patient, many hospitals have created a plethora of lower-wage occupations — phlebotomists to draw blood, technicians to perform tests, nurse's aides to take blood pressures — leaving the RN to cover more patients and do a far narrower range of tasks. But when the Massachusetts General Hospital ran an experiment, putting all care on one floor directly in the hands of RNs, the results were better patient outcomes and a more efficient use of human resources. The upgrading of human-service work would be part of an overdue process of reversing Taylorism. More workers would use a broader range of human skills to care for whole human beings.

But How Much Money?

A rough estimate of the cost of upgrading all low-wage human-service work into decent professional career paths is about $150 billion a year. A generally accepted figure of the cost of providing universal, high-quality pre-kindergarten and child care is about $50 billion a year. Upgrading existing jobs in day care for older children, care of seniors, and low-wage hospital-based work, would cost roughly another $100 billion.

22

Isn't that a lot of money? It certainly is, if you're invoking conventional budget assumptions that predate the current recession and financial collapse — though it's not a lot of money compared to the cost of military operations in Iraq and Afghanistan, which is now budgeted at $188 billion annually. To put this in perspective, $150 billion a year is approximately 1 percent of gross domestic product.

23

But for the rest of this decade, and perhaps well beyond, the American economy faces two huge challenges. The first is to dig out of the most serious financial collapse since the Great Depression and its spillover effects into the rest of the economy. The second is to restore the income of American workers.

24

A strategy that increases Americans' purchasing power can take a variety of forms. Besides good human-service jobs, it could include massive public spending on deferred public infrastructure needs, as well as a green recovery path, creating new alternative-energy industries and jobs retrofitting homes and offices. Both strategies would also create decent job opportunities. Enacting the Employee Free Choice Act, protecting collective bargaining rights, would also increase the ability of workers to bargain for a decent share of the pie.

25

Voters are only going to embrace serious public spending if we think big. The promise of millions of good service-sector jobs that can't be exported — providing superior care to our children, our parents, and ourselves — is an example of the kind of idea that could capture the national imagination and rekindle the necessary political support for serious public outlay. This is the kind of idea that could be embraced by a broad coalition of experts, opinion leaders, editorial writers, grass-roots groups — and the next administration. It touches a national nerve of anxiety about where the good jobs will be for our children — and who will take care of us as we age.

26

I don't mean to suggest that we should ignore the upgrading of other service jobs. As our friends at the SEIU have shown, collective bargaining can improve janitor jobs as well as jobs of home-care workers, just as unions once upgraded factory jobs. The labor union UNITE-HERE has turned low-wage hotel jobs into middle-class jobs. We need a decent-work strategy for the whole economy. But human services are one place where the federal government has direct leverage.

27

Before this recession is over, we will need to find several hundred billion dollars a year for a recovery strategy — and what better place to begin than by restoring workers' paychecks? We can find that money by reclaiming progressive

28

taxation, by defending deficit spending in a deep recession, by shifting federal dollars from a pointless war to a domestic recovery, and reviving trade unionism. The political situation is comparable to the one that Franklin Roosevelt faced in 1933. Policies that were unthinkable yesterday are just the bare beginning of an adequate response today.

MAKING CONNECTIONS: PROFESSIONALIZING SERVICE JOBS

Although Kuttner focuses on human-service jobs, he starts out by talking more generally about the explosion of jobs in the "service sector." These include jobs in fast-food restaurants and in stores like Walmart, jobs with which you may have experience. You may also have experience babysitting or doing other human-service jobs.

With two or three other students, discuss Kuttner's argument that such jobs should be professionalized, with jobholders given "adequate training" and "the prospect of advancement" as well as being paid a "living wage" (par. 3). Begin by taking turns briefly telling about your experience in the service sector, or any other work experience that you think is relevant — for example, as a camp counselor or tutor. Then, together consider the following questions:

- Were you given adequate training, possibilities for advancement, and/or a living wage? If you were not given any of them, why not? Should you have been given them?

- How does the practice of Taylorism that Kuttner explains in paragraphs 20–21 apply to the work you have done? Do you agree with Kuttner that Taylorism ought to be eliminated?

ANALYZING WRITING STRATEGIES

◆◆◆◆
Basic Features

● A Well-Defined Problem

One of the most persuasive strategies for writing a proposal is to define the problem in terms of its causes and then to propose a solution that eliminates those causes. Kornbluh employs this strategy when she cites a lack of flexibility in the workplace as a principal cause of the "juggler family" problem and then, logically, argues that the problem can be fixed by adding flexibility to the workplace. Similarly, by identifying the primary cause of the "crisis" in the schools as the quality of the teaching, Miller sets the stage for his proposed solution.

To analyze how Kuttner defines the problem in terms of its possible causes, try the following:

- Reread the first three paragraphs, noting where he talks about the causes of the problem and forecasts his proposed "cure."

- Write a couple of sentences explaining the connection between one or more of the causes he lists and the cure or solution he proposes.

● A Well-Argued Solution

Like the other writers in this chapter, Kuttner argues for his solution, in part, by demonstrating that it is feasible because it can be implemented. For example, in paragraph 14, he explicitly raises the question likely to be on readers' minds: "How would such a transformation happen?" He then offers specific details and examples to show how his proposed solution could be put into effect. Similarly, in paragraph 17, Kuttner argues that his proposal is workable by pointing out that it has already been done for "home-care workers."

In addition to arguing that the solution is feasible, proposal writers also usually offer reasons claiming that the proposed solution is a good idea because it has this or that particular benefit. For example, O'Malley's main reason for frequent exams is that students learn more and do better on subsequent assignments (par. 4). He assumes that, like him, his readers place a high value on learning. This value is the common ground on which he tries to build a logical argument. If he can convince readers that frequent exams do indeed foster better learning, then he is likely also to convince them to accept his solution.

To analyze how Kuttner argues for his solution, follow these suggestions:

- Reread paragraphs 4–5 and write a sentence or two summarizing the two reasons Kuttner offers for his proposed solution.

- Choose one of these reasons and add a few sentences explaining the value that underlies Kuttner's argument and why he assumes the argument based on it will be likely to convince his readers.

● An Effective Counterargument

Writers often announce objections and questions they are counterarguing. Kuttner, for example, introduces an objection in paragraph 6 this way: "Many economists once thought. . . ." In the next paragraph, he begins his counterargument with "We now know. . . ." He then uses the rhetorical question "How do we know?" to anticipate the question readers are likely to be thinking themselves.

To answer the question and support his argument, Kuttner compares American wages for factory and human-service workers to those of other countries, showing that there is no universal agreement about the value of one kind of work over another and that "choices about how to compensate workers are social decisions" (par. 8). Convincing readers of this point is crucial because if wages are based on "choices," then we can do what he proposes in paragraph 3 — set a new "national policy to make every human-service job a good job."

To analyze how Kuttner responds to possible objections, follow these suggestions:

- Reread paragraphs 11–12 and 16 and write a few sentences briefly summarizing the objections Kuttner anticipates in these paragraphs and assessing how he refutes them.

- Alternatively, reread paragraphs 20–21 and write a couple of sentences explaining Taylorism and how Kuttner argues against it. What is the implicit objection that he is counterarguing?

● A Readable Plan

Because proposals present a complex, multipart argument — to establish the seriousness of the problem, to convince readers that the proposed solution is feasible, and to refute objections and persuade readers that the proposed solution is better than alternatives — writers try to make it easy for readers to navigate the essay. Among the cueing strategies writers use to orient readers are the use of transitional words and phrases, and rhetorical questions.

Transitions or connectives help readers understand the logical connection between one paragraph or sentence and the one that follows. Here is a brief chart showing several transitions and the logical relationships they signal:

Function	Transitional Words and Phrases
To introduce another item in a series	first . . . second; in addition; moreover; furthermore
To introduce an example or illustration	for example; that is; in particular; specifically
To counterargue	but; however; nevertheless; in contrast; neither
To concede an objection	granted; of course; to be sure; certainly
To resume the argument after acknowledging an objection or alternative solution	nonetheless; even though; still; all the same

For a more complete discussion of transitions, see Chapter 13, Cueing the Reader.

For additional uses of rhetorical questions in essays proposing solutions, see A Sentence Strategy: Rhetorical Questions on pp. 369–71.

In addition to logical transitions, writers may also use rhetorical questions to orient readers. Rhetorical questions are questions writers pose but then go on to answer themselves. For example, Patrick O'Malley uses this rhetorical question to make a transition from arguing for his proposed solution to counterarguing possible objections: "Why, then, do so few professors give frequent exams?" (par. 7).

To analyze how Kuttner uses logical transitions and/or rhetorical questions to make his argument easy to follow, consider these suggestions:

- Find two examples in Kuttner's essay of logical transitions or rhetorical questions (or one example of each), and determine how each example functions.

- Write a couple of sentences describing how they work.

CONSIDERING TOPICS FOR YOUR OWN ESSAY

Kuttner's topic suggests a type of proposal you might want to consider for your essay — a proposal to improve the living or working conditions of a group of people. You could focus on a particular category of people and a problem they face. For example, think of ways to help elderly and infirm people in your community who need transportation or elementary-school kids who have no after-school programs. Think, too, about solutions to problems that affect students — for example, the creation of job-training or referral programs to help college students find work on or near campus, or recycling and "green" energy solutions that will help students living in dorms limit their impact on the environment.

Beyond the Traditional Essay: Proposing a Solution

Proposals take many forms in our culture. Formal written proposals are often required in business, government, and academia in order to procure funding and/or authorization for projects. The presentation of proposals for a particular solution to a problem is also common in these settings (as, for example, when an employee, department, or committee presents a plan for controlling costs or increasing revenue). Effective proposals tend to exhibit all of the basic features of the proposal essay — a well-defined problem; a well-argued solution; an effective counterargument; and a readable plan — discussed in this chapter.

Open, or publicly addressed, proposals to problems of concern to a community or a nation also have a long tradition, perhaps most famously embodied in Jonathan Swift's satirical "A Modest Proposal" recommending cannibalism as a remedy for the desperate poverty of eighteenth-century Irish peasants. Self-help literature, such as *The Secret* or *The Seven Habits of Highly Effective People*, tends to exhibit many if not all of the basic features of the proposal essay. Many advertisements also propose solutions. While ads do not generally exhibit all of the basic features present in formal proposals, the best ones use images and text efficiently in order to define a problem — as, for example, poor money management, in the ad reproduced here — and suggest a solution (in this case, packing your lunch rather than buying it).

As you work on your own project, you might want to consult some of these alternative forms of proposals for inspiration. If the format in which you are working allows for it — if, for example, you are creating a poster, Web site, or video — you should consider taking advantage of the strategies available to those working in multimedia — for example, by embedding artifacts that are relevant to the solution you're proposing. (Always remember to properly document any material you might use that was created by someone else.)

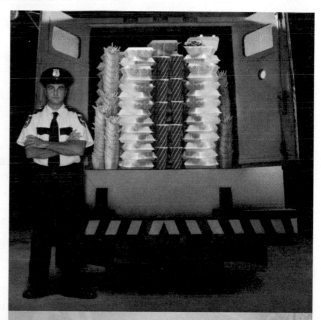

That 9 dollar lunch is worth more than you think. Like 19,000 dollars more.

Pack your own lunch instead of going out. $6 saved a day x 5 days a week x 10 years x 6% interest = $19,592. That could be money in your pocket. Small changes today. Big bucks tomorrow. Go to feedthepig.org for free savings tips.

Guide to Writing

The Writing Assignment

Write an essay proposing a solution to a problem. Choose a problem faced by a community or group to which you belong, and address your proposal to one or more members of the group or to outsiders who might help solve the problem.

This Guide to Writing will help you apply what you have learned about how proposal writers clearly define a problem, argue effectively for a particular solution, and present counterarguments to possible objections and alternative solutions. The Guide is divided into five sections with various activities in each section:

- **Invention and Research**
- **Planning and Drafting**
- **Critical Reading Guide**
- **Revising**
- **Editing and Proofreading**

The Guide is designed to escort you through the writing process, from deciding which problem to address to editing your finished essay. Your instructor may require you to follow the Guide to Writing from beginning to end. Working through the Guide in this way will help you — as it has helped many other college students — write a thoughtful, fully developed, polished essay.

If, however, your instructor gives you latitude to choose and if you have had experience writing a proposal, then you can decide on the order in which you'll do the activities in the Guide to Writing. For example, the Invention and Research section includes activities to help you find a problem to write about, analyze and define it, identify your readers, and find a tentative solution, among other things. Obviously, choosing a problem to write about must precede the other activities, but you may come to the Guide with a problem already in mind and want to focus first on exploring how you would solve it before deciding how to establish that the problem exists and is serious. In fact, you may find your response to one of the invention activities expanding into a draft before you've had a chance to do any of the other activities. That's a good thing — but you should later flesh out your draft by going back to the activities you skipped and layering the new material into your draft.

The following chart will help you find answers to many of the questions you might have about planning, drafting, and revising an essay proposing a solution to a problem. The page references in the Where to Look column refer to examples from the readings and activities in the Guide to Writing.

To learn about using the *Guide* e-book for invention and drafting, go to **bedfordstmartins.com/ theguide.**

Starting Points: Proposing a Solution

●●●● Basic Features

	Question	Where to Look
Choosing a Problem to Write About	How do I come up with a problem to write about?	• Considering Topics for Your Own Essay (pp. 338, 346, 354) • Choosing a Problem to Write About (pp. 358–60) • Testing Your Choice (p. 363)
A Well-Defined Problem	How can I best define the problem for my readers?	• Ways In: Bringing the Problem and Your Audience into Focus (p. 361) • Refining Your Purpose and Setting Goals: Defining the Problem (pp. 366–67) • Working with Sources: Establishing the Problem's Existence and Seriousness (pp. 371–73)
A Well-Argued Solution	How do I come up with a plausible solution?	• Listing Possible Solution (p. 362) • Refining Your Purpose and Setting Goals: Describing the Proposed Solution (p. 367)
	How do I construct an argument supporting my solution?	• Ways In: Exploring Your Tentative Solution: Constructing an Argument (pp. 362–63) • Researching Your Proposal (p. 364)
An Effective Counterargument	How do I counter possible objections to my solution?	• Ways In: Exploring Your Tentative Solution: Planning a Counterargument (pp. 362–63) • Refining Your Purpose and Setting Goals: Counterarguing Readers' Objections (p. 367)
	How do I respond to possible alternative solutions?	• Ways In: Counterarguing Alternative Solutions (p. 364) • Researching Your Proposal (p. 364) • Refining Your Purpose and Setting Goals: Counterarguing Alternative Solutions (p. 367)
A Readable Plan	How can I help my readers follow my argument?	• Formulating a Tentative Thesis Statement (pp. 365–66) • Outlining Your Draft (p. 368) • A Sentence Strategy: Rhetorical Questions (pp. 369–71) • Thinking about Document Design: Following Formatting Conventions (pp. 376–77)

Invention and Research

The following invention activities are easy to complete and take only a few minutes. Spreading out the activities over several days will stimulate your creativity, enabling you to consider many more potential problems to address and possible ways in which to address them.

Remember to keep a written record of your invention work: you'll need it when you draft the essay and later when you revise it.

Choosing a Problem to Write About

List several problems that you might like to explore. This will come more easily to some of us than to others. As you explore possibilities, bear in mind that you're looking for a problem that meets the following criteria:

Criteria for Choosing a Problem: A Checklist	The problem should be ☐ important to you and of concern to others; ☐ solvable, at least in part; ☐ one that you can research in the time you have; ☐ one that you can explore in detail and are willing to discuss in writing.

If you're like most people, you'll need some help in coming up with a number of good options. To get your juices flowing, you might first try rereading the Considering Topics for Your Own Essay activities following the readings and recalling any problems those suggestions brought to mind. Reread any notes you might have made in response to these suggestions. For further ideas, consult the suggestions in the following sections.

Making a Chart

Divide a piece of paper or your computer screen into two columns. In the left-hand column, list communities you are part of (for example, your residence hall, gym, or hometown), groups you have joined (for example, a sports team, multiplayer online game site, or garage band), organizations to which you belong (for example, your high school, church, or a local photography museum), and places you have worked (for example, a coffee shop, community pool, or college radio station). In the right-hand column, list any problems that exist within each context. Here is how such a chart might look:

Community/Group/Work	Problem
School	lousy food noisy residence halls lack of enough sections of required courses no school spirit too few computers in library
My Neighborhood	need for traffic signal at dangerous intersection run down lack of safe places for children to play terrible zoning laws (factory next to housing development)
Work (radio station)	inadequate training conflicts with supervisor unfair shift assignments unsatisfactory facilities
Still Alive (band)	too little time to practice no good place to practice too few venues for performance crazy expenses for equipment
Volunteer Work (tutoring)	disorganized schedules no money for materials no training apathetic students

Proposing to solve a problem in a group or community to which you belong or a workplace with which you are familiar gives you an important advantage: You can write as an expert. You know the history of the problem, have felt the urgency to solve it, and perhaps have already thought of possible solutions. Equally important, you will know to whom to address the proposal, and you can interview others in the group to get their views of the problem and your solution. From such a position of knowledge and authority comes confident, convincing writing.

Should you want to propose a solution for a problem of national scope, concentrate on one with which you have direct experience and for which you can suggest a detailed plan of action. Even better, focus on unique local aspects of the problem. For example, if you are concerned about the rise of smoking among young people, you can offer a solution for a particular location or organization — for example, you could organize an information campaign on campus.

Using the Web to Find or Explore a Problem

While we encourage you to "go local" with the problem you treat in this essay, exploring Web sites where people write about similar problems and about potential solutions might inspire you. Moreover, the Web provides a rich repository of cultural and historical information, including photographs and music, which you might be able to use to create a richly detailed, multimedia text for your readers.

Here are some suggestions:

- Look for sites related to the community, workplace, or group you are writing about. See if others have noted problems that are the same as or similar to those you have noted. Do they offer solutions? Do these solutions seem viable, or at least worth exploring?

- Consider getting in touch with others who are concerned about the problem that concerns you. If your conversation is fruitful, ask their permission to include their insights in your project.

- Do a Google search on a particular problem, and try to get a sense of how common it might be — or, on the other hand, of how specific it might be to your local group or workplace.

Make notes of any ideas, memories, or insights suggested by your online research, and download any visuals you might include in your essay, being sure to get the information necessary to cite any online sources. (See p. 774 for the MLA citation format for electronic sources.)

Ways in: Bringing the Problem and Your Audience into Focus

● **Basic Features**

Once you've made a preliminary choice of a problem, try the following activities to help you understand the problem, determine what else you need to find out about it, and discover ways of defining the problem for your readers. You can begin with whichever activity you want, but wherever you begin, be sure to return to the other activities to fill in the details.

Identifying Your Possible Readers

In a few sentences, explore your readers. In addition to your instructor and classmates, think about writing to people who are affected by the problem or those in a position to take action to solve it. The following questions will help you develop an understanding of your readers:

- How informed are my readers likely to be about the problem? Have they shown any awareness of it?
- Why would my readers care about solving this problem?
- Have my readers supported any other proposals to solve this problem? If so, what do those proposals have in common with mine?
- What values and concerns do my readers and I share that could bring us together to solve the problem?

Analyzing the Problem

Explore What You Know. *Figure out what you know now about the problem and what you still need to find out by jotting down answers to the questions below:*

- How do I know the problem exists and that it is serious?
- What could cause a problem like this?
- Who suffers from the problem? What evidence of it have I seen or experienced myself?
- Who, if anyone, would benefit from *not* changing the way things work now?

Identify Research Questions.

- Where can I find a history of the problem, details describing its negative consequences, statistics, or expert analyses?
- Are there people I could interview to get additional information?
- If an institution or organization is part of the problem, can I find public information about its funding or budget and about the way it operates? Can I interview its leadership, employees, and customers or clients?

● Defining the Problem

Write a paragraph or two describing the problem for your readers. Be as specific and vivid in your explanation as possible given the information you currently have. Writing a very rough draft of this part of your essay should help clarify what additional information you will need.

● Listing Possible Solutions

It usually helps to consider several possible solutions before focusing on one solution, so problem solving requires creativity. *Use the following questions to help you make a list of creative solutions you could consider for your essay:*

- Can you adapt a solution that has already been tried or proposed for related problems?
- What smaller, more manageable aspect of the larger problem could you solve?
- Could re-imagining the goal help you make fundamental changes?
- Could the problem be solved from the bottom up instead of from the top down?
- Could an ongoing process help solve the problem?

● Making a Tentative Choice

In a sentence or two, describe the solution you want to explore further. You cannot know for certain whether you will be able to construct a convincing argument to support this solution, but you should choose a solution that you feel motivated to pursue.

Basic Features

●● Ways in: Exploring Your Tentative Solution

These activities will help you decide whether you can support your tentative solution and respond to your readers' likely objections. You can begin with whichever activity you want, but wherever you begin, be sure to return to the other activities to fill in the details.

Constructing an Argument	Planning a Counterargument
Explain Why It Would Solve the Problem. *Write for a few minutes explaining why you think this solution could solve the problem.* For example, would it • eliminate one or more causes? • change people's attitudes? • re-imagine the objective? • reduce anxiety and tension?	**Anticipate Objections.** *Write a few sentences responding to the following objections you think are most likely:* • We can't afford it. • It would take too long. • People would not do it. • Too few would benefit. • You would benefit personally. • We already tried that, with unsatisfactory results.

(continued)

(*continued*)

Constructing an Argument	Planning a Counterargument
Show Why It Is Possible. *Write for a few minutes explaining why people could agree to put the solution into effect.* For example, what would it cost them in time or money?	**Plan Follow-Up Research.** Add notes about the kinds of information you think would help make your counterargument convincing for your readers and where you think you can find this information.
Explain How It Could Be Implemented. *Write down the major stages or steps necessary to carry out your solution.* This list of steps will provide an early test of whether your solution can, in fact, be implemented.	
Plan Follow-Up Research. Add notes about the kinds of information you think would help make your argument convincing for your readers and where you think you can find this information.	

Testing Your Choice

Now test your choice by asking yourself the following questions:

- Do I understand the problem well enough to convince my readers that it really exists and is serious?
- Do I have some idea of how to argue that my solution is feasible — that it really can solve the problem and that it can be implemented?
- Will I be able to answer objections readers are likely to raise?
- Do I know enough about the problem or can I learn what I need to know in the time remaining?

As you plan and draft your proposal, you will probably want to consider these questions again. If at any point you cannot answer them with a confident yes, you may want to consider proposing a different solution to the problem or choose a different problem to write about. If you have serious doubts, consider discussing them with your instructor.

Get together with two or three other students, and present your proposal to one another.

Presenters: Take turns briefly defining the problem you hope to solve, identifying your intended readers, and describing your proposed solution.

Listeners: Tell the presenter whether the proposed solution seems feasible for the situation and intended readers. Suggest objections you have or the intended readers are likely to have. Tell the writer if you know of any alternative solutions to the problem.

A Collaborative Activity:
Testing Your Choice

● **Basic Features**

Ways in: Counterarguing Alternative Solutions

These activities will help you counterargue your readers' alternative solutions. You can begin with whichever activity you want, but wherever you begin, be sure to return to the other activities to fill in the details.

Using the Web to Research Alternative Solutions	Considering Alternative Solutions	Developing Your Counterargument
Do online research to identify at least two alternative solutions to your problem and gather information to evaluate them. To search, try the following: • entering various keywords into a search engine such as Google. • adding the word *government* to a Google search. • entering your keywords on FirstGov.gov. • going to the Library of Congress Internet Resource Page on State and Local Governments (www .loc.gov/global/state/). Bookmark promising sites. If you download or copy information, record source information.	*List two or three alternative solutions that others have proposed or tried.* You may have discovered these alternatives during interviews or in your library research. You do not have to list every solution that has been mentioned, but you should include the most popular or serious alternatives. If you include only obviously weak solutions in your argument, your credibility will be harmed and you could be accused of committing the *straw man fallacy*, which involves directing your counterargument against an alternative that nobody takes seriously anyway.	*Write a paragraph for each alternative solution you think you should include in your argument.* Describe the alternative solution fairly, quoting supporters if possible. Then work out the reasons you believe the alternative solution • would not be feasible, • would not solve the problem, • would not be approved, • would be hard to implement, or • would be too costly, disruptive, or time-consuming to put into effect.

Researching Your Proposal

You may have already identified research questions about the problem and made notes about the kinds of information you need to support your argument and counterargument. Doing research with your questions and notes in mind will help you work efficiently. But researching sometimes is most productive when you have the time to go into unexplored territory. You may find support for your argument, but you also may find contradictory evidence and decide to change your plans as a result.

If you are proposing a solution to a problem about which others have written, you will want to do library and Internet research to find out how they have defined the problem and what solutions they have proposed or tried. If you are proposing a solution to a problem in a group or workplace, you may want to conduct interviews to see how people are affected by the problem, what they know about its history, what solutions they prefer, and how they react to your solution.

Designing Your Document

Think about whether your readers might benefit from design features such as headings or numbered or bulleted lists or from visuals such as drawings, photographs, tables, or graphs. Elements like these often make the presentation of a problem easier to follow and a solution more convincing. Earlier in this chapter, for example, Karen Kornbluh's and Robert Kuttner's proposals use headings to introduce the major sections.

Consider reviewing other published proposals to see how they use design elements and visuals to support and strengthen their arguments. Look back at the scenario on p. 321 describing the proposal for recruiting more female truck drivers, and then read "Thinking about Document Design" on pp. 376–77 to see how its authors used visuals to bolster its impact.

For more on document design, see Chapter 21. For guidelines on acknowledging the sources of visuals, see Chapter 24.

Defining Your Purpose for Your Readers

Write a few sentences defining your purpose. Remember that you have already identified your readers and developed your proposal with these readers in mind. Try now to define your purpose by considering the following questions:

- Do I seek incremental, moderate, or radical change? Am I being realistic about what my readers are prepared to support? How can I overcome their likely resistance to change?

- How can I ensure that my readers will not remain indifferent to the problem?

- Whom can I count on for support, and what can I do to secure that support? Who will oppose my solution? Shall I write them off or seek common ground with them?

- What exactly do I want my readers to do — take my proposed solution as a starting point for further discussion? Take action immediately? Take preliminary steps, like seeking funding or testing the feasibility of the solution?

Formulating a Tentative Thesis Statement

Write one or more sentences to serve as your tentative thesis statement. In most essays proposing solutions to problems, the thesis statement is a concise announcement of the solution. Think about how emphatic you should make the thesis and whether you should forecast your reasons.

Review the readings in this chapter to see how other writers construct their thesis statements. For example, recall that Patrick O'Malley states his thesis in paragraph 2:

> If professors gave additional brief exams at frequent intervals, students would be spurred to study more regularly, learn more, worry less, and perform better on midterms, finals, and other papers and projects.

O'Malley's thesis announces his solution — brief, frequent exams — and lists the reasons students would benefit from the solution. (A forecast of reasons is not a requirement in a thesis, but it does enable readers to predict the stages of the argument, thereby increasing their understanding.)

As you draft your own thesis, pay attention to the language you use. It should be clear and unambiguous, emphatic but appropriately qualified. Although you will probably refine your thesis as you draft and revise your essay, trying now to articulate it will help give your planning and drafting direction and impetus.

For more on thesis and forecasting statements, see Chapter 13.

Planning and Drafting

The following activities will help you refine your purpose, set goals for your draft, and outline it. In addition, this section will help you write a draft by writing opening sentences, trying out a useful sentence strategy, and learning how to work with sources.

Refining Your Purpose and Setting Goals

Before starting to draft, here are some questions that may help you sharpen your purpose for your audience and set goals for your draft. Your instructor may ask you to write out your answers to some of these questions or simply to think about them as you plan and draft your essay.

Clarifying Your Purpose and Audience

- What do my readers already know about this problem? Should I assume, as O'Malley does, that my readers are unfamiliar with the problem? Or should I assume, as Kornbluh does, that my readers know about the problem but do not realize how serious it is?

- How can I gain readers' enthusiastic support? Can I convince them that solving the problem is in everyone's interest, as Kornbluh and Kuttner try to do?

- How can I present myself so that I seem both reasonable and authoritative?

- Should I aim to show that I am not dictating a one-size-fits-all solution but trying to get those involved to find solutions that work for them, as O'Malley and Kornbluh try to do?

Defining the Problem

- How can I demonstrate that the problem really exists? Can I present statistics, as Kornbluh and Kuttner do?

- How can I show the seriousness and urgency of the problem? Should I stress negative consequences, as all the writers do? Can I use quotations or cite research to stress the problem's importance, as Kornbluh and Kuttner do?

- Will reporting or speculating about the problem's causes or history help readers understand why it needs attention? Can I use comparison and contrast, as Kornbluh does?

- How much space should I devote to defining the problem? Only a little space (like O'Malley) or a lot of space (like Kornbluh)?

Describing the Proposed Solution

- How can I describe my solution so that it will look like the best way to proceed?
- Should I give examples to show how solutions like mine have worked, as Kuttner does? Or should I focus on my reasons to support it, as O'Malley does?
- Should I make the solution seem easy to implement, as O'Malley does, or should I acknowledge that the solution will require effort and compromise, as Kornbluh does?

Counterarguing Readers' Objections

- How do I decide which objections to include?
- Should I accommodate or concede certain objections by modifying my proposal, as O'Malley does?
- How can I support my refutation? Should I cite statistics or research studies, as Kuttner does?

Counterarguing Alternative Solutions

- How do I decide which alternative solutions to mention?
- How can I support my refutation of alternative solutions? Can I argue that they are too expensive and time-consuming, as O'Malley does, or that they will not really solve the problem, as Kornbluh does?
- How can I reject these other solutions without seeming to criticize their proponents? Can I provide reasons, as O'Malley does, or marshal statistics, as Kornbluh does?

The Ending

- How should I conclude? Should I end by summarizing my solution and its advantages, as O'Malley and Kuttner do? Should I end with a scenario suggesting the consequences of a failure to solve the problem? Can I end with an inspiring call to action? Might a shift to humor or satire provide an effective ending?
- Is there something special about the problem that I should remind readers of at the end, as Kornbluh does when she urges that an award be given to the companies that lead the way?

Outlining Your Draft

With your purpose and goals in mind, you might want to make a quick scratch outline that includes the following:

- a clear statement of the problem
- your thesis statement, announcing the proposed solution and forecasting your reasons for it
- your argument for the solution, giving reasons and support
- anticipation of counterarguments and a response to objections readers might have about the proposed solution

This simple plan is nearly always complicated by other factors, however. In outlining your material, you must take into consideration whether readers already recognize the problem, how much agreement exists on the need to solve the problem, and how much attention must be given to readers' likely objections and to alternative solutions.

Here is a possible outline for a proposal where readers may not understand the problem fully:

    I. Presentation of the problem

       A. Its existence

       B. Its seriousness

       C. Its causes

    II. Consequences of failing to solve the problem

   III. Description of the proposed solution

   IV. List of steps for implementing the solution

    V. Reasons and support for the solution

       A. Acknowledgment of objections

       B. Accommodation or refutation of objections

   VI. Consideration of alternative solutions and their disadvantages

  VII. Restatement of the proposed solution and its advantages

For more on outlining, see Chapter 11.

Your outline will of course reflect your own writing situation. Once you have a working outline, you should not hesitate to change it as necessary while drafting and revising. For instance, you might find it more effective to hold back on presenting your own solution until you have discussed alternative but unacceptable solutions. Or you might find a better way to order the reasons for adopting your proposal. The purpose of an outline is to identify the basic features of your proposal and to help you organize them effectively, not to lock you into a particular structure.

Drafting

If you have not already begun to draft your essay, this section will help by suggesting how to write your opening sentences; how to use rhetorical questions; and how to cite sources to define the problem. Drafting isn't always a smooth process, so don't be afraid to leave spaces where you don't know what to put in or write notes to yourself about what you could do next. If you get stuck while drafting, go back over your invention writing: You may be able to copy and paste some of it into your evolving draft, or you may find that you need to do some additional invention to fill in details in your draft.

Writing the Opening Sentences

You could try out one or two different ways of beginning your essay — possibly from the list below — but do not agonize over the first sentences because you are likely to discover the best way to begin only after you've written a rough draft. Again, you might want to review your invention writing to see if you have already written something that would work to launch your essay.

To engage your readers' interest from the start, consider the following opening strategies:

- a scenario (like O'Malley)
- statistics (like Kornbluh)
- a research study (like Miller)
- an historical analogy (like Kuttner)
- a comparison to other places where the solution has been tried successfully
- a preview of the negative consequences if the problem goes unsolved
- criticism of an alternative solution

A Sentence Strategy: Rhetorical Questions

As you draft an essay proposing a solution to a problem, you will want to connect with your readers. You will also want readers to become concerned with the seriousness of the problem and thoughtful about the challenge of solving it. Sentences that take the form of *rhetorical questions* can help you achieve these goals.

A **rhetorical question** is conventionally defined as a sentence posing a question to which the writer expects no answer from the reader. In proposals, however, rhetorical questions do important rhetorical work — that is, they assist a writer in realizing a particular purpose and they influence readers in certain ways. Here are three examples from Matt Miller's proposal:

> How should we address this crisis? (par. 5)

> How to do this? (par. 6)

> How much would this plan cost? (par. 11)

These questions, each placed at the beginning of a paragraph, function like headings. They announce the main parts of the proposal. The first question makes a transition from defining the problem to describing the solution, and the word *we* reaches out to include readers. The second question introduces the plan to implement the writer's proposed solution: the word *this* refers back to the sentence that immediately precedes the question and states the thesis of the essay. Similarly, the last question lets readers know that the focus is shifting to Miller's argument about the feasibility of his proposed solution.

Below are two more rhetorical questions from Miller's essay:

> In determining pay rates, who will decide which teachers are better performers? And what standards will be used to assess teachers? (par. 20)

Unlike the earlier examples, these rhetorical questions are positioned at the end of a paragraph, where they serve as a transition to readers' concerns about how Miller's proposed solution will be implemented. In fact, he frames them as questions that have been raised by "educators." Nevertheless, he treats them as rhetorical questions because he goes on to explore answers to them.

Miller uses rhetorical questions, then, to engage readers by voicing questions they are likely to have — and that others have expressed — about his proposed solution. They also help orient readers by making transitions from one topic to the next.

Other writers in this chapter also use rhetorical questions for these and similar purposes:

- *Engaging readers' attention to or interest in the problem or the proposed solution.*

> Will it be like the midterm? Did you study enough? Did you study the right things? It's too late to drop the course. So what happens if you fail? (O'Malley, par. 1)

O'Malley uses his rhetorical questions to dramatize the plight of students studying for a high-stakes exam in order to engage his primary readers — professors capable of implementing his solution — and put them in a receptive frame of mind.

- *Orienting readers to a proposal and forecasting the plan of the argument or parts of it.*

> Why, then, do so few professors give frequent brief exams? (O'Malley, par. 7)

O'Malley uses his rhetorical question as a transition to his anticipating objections that professors are likely to have to his proposed solution.

> But in America, how can we possibly make all human-service jobs into good jobs? And aren't some of these jobs inherently low-skill? How much training, after all, does it take to empty a bedpan or change linen? (Kuttner, par. 9)

Kuttner uses these three questions at the end of the first section of his proposal to forecast the topics he will address in the next section.

- *Acting as a topic sentence.*

> How would such a transformation happen? (Kuttner, par. 14)

> Isn't that a lot of money? (Kuttner, par. 23)

Kuttner uses each of these rhetorical questions not only as a topic sentence to introduce the topic of a paragraph or group of paragraphs, but to anticipate readers' likely questions. By writing these simple and direct questions, Kuttner seeks to reassure readers that he knows what concerns them and will answer their questions in a straightforward manner.

Writers sometimes vary their way of presenting rhetorical questions. Kornbluh uses a subheading worded like a question and followed by a colon — "Who would be covered:" — after which she introduces the "answer" (par. 21).

Miller, on the other hand, presents a question indirectly:

> The question is how to evaluate performance in a way that is objective and untainted by cronyism. (par. 21)

He also inserts a rhetorical question into his recounting of a part of the conversation between himself and the people he interviewed:

> How might that work? I asked. (par. 17)

Except for Kornbluh, all of the authors in this chapter use direct rhetorical questions. Two of them — Miller and O'Malley — use five questions, and if we count the two indirect ones, Miller uses seven, and Kuttner uses eight. Miller spreads his throughout the essay, while O'Malley bunches most of his questions in the opening paragraph. Clearly, then, rhetorical questions are useful, but they are not a requirement for a successful proposal. They should be used for a specific purpose, and they should not be overused, because readers may begin to find them annoying. Who can blame them?

In addition to using rhetorical questions, you can strengthen your proposal with other kinds of sentences, such as those that introduce concession and refutation (pp. 306–7) and that signal explicitly the logical relationship to a previous sentence.

Statistics can be helpful in establishing that the problem exists and is serious. For example, Patrick O'Malley cites research to support his assertion that students prefer frequent exams to fewer high-stakes exams: "A Harvard study notes students' 'strong preference for frequent evaluation in a course'" (par. 4). But his argument would have been stronger and possibly more convincing if he had cited statistics to support the study's conclusion. All of the other writers in this chapter cite statistics in their proposals. Let us look at some of the ways Karen Kornbluh uses statistics to define the problem.

> Today fully 70 percent of families with children are headed by two working parents or by an unmarried working parent. The "traditional family" of the breadwinner and homemaker has been replaced by the "juggler family," in which no one is home full-time. (par. 1)

Kornbluh begins with an impressive statistic, "fully 70 percent." But what does it mean? Seventy percent of how many? She does not answer this question with a number, but she does make clear that she is talking about nearly three-quarters of

Working with Sources:

Establishing the Problem's Existence and Seriousness

all "families with children," a number that we can infer is very large. At other points in the essay, Kornbluh does provide the raw numbers along with statistics such as percentages. Here are a couple of examples:

> In addition to working parents, there are over 44.4 million Americans who provide care to another adult, often an older relative. Fifty-nine percent of these caregivers either work or have worked while providing care ("Caregiving"). (par. 8)

> Over half of workers today have no control over scheduling alternative start and end times at work (Galinksy, Bond, and Hill). According to a recent study by the Institute for Women's Policy Research, 49 percent of workers — over 59 million Americans — lack basic paid sick days for themselves. (par. 10)

Because of the raw numbers, readers can see at a glance that the percentages Kornbluh cites are truly significant: 59 percent of 44.4 million people (who have worked while providing care to another adult) and 59 million people (who lack sick leave). Note that Kornbluh spells out some of the numbers she provides and uses numerals for others, depending on whether the number begins a sentence.

Kornbluh also compares different time periods to show that the problem has worsened over the last thirty years. Here are several examples from paragraph 7. Note that Kornbluh presents statistics in three different ways: percentages, numbers, and proportion.

> Between 1970 and 2000, the percentage of mothers in the workforce rose from 38 to 67 percent (Smolensky and Gootman). Moreover, the number of hours worked by dual-income families has increased dramatically. Couples with children worked a full 60 hours a week in 1979. By 2000 they were working 70 hours a week (Bernstein and Kornbluh). And more parents than ever are working long hours. In 2000, nearly 1 out of every 8 couples with children was putting in 100 hours a week or more on the job, compared to only 1 out of 12 families in 1970 (Jacobs and Gerson).

To establish that there is a widespread perception among working parents that the problem is serious, Kornbluh cites survey results:

> In a 2002 report by the Families and Work Institute, 45 percent of employees reported that work and family responsibilities interfered with each other "a lot" or "some" and 67 percent of employed parents report that they do not have enough time with their children (Galinksy, Bond, and Hill).

This example, from paragraph 9, shows that a large percentage, nearly half of all employees surveyed, are aware of interference between work and family responsibilities. The readers Kornbluh is addressing — employers — are likely to find this statistic important because it suggests that their employees are spending time worrying about or attending to family responsibilities instead of focusing on work.

For statistics to be persuasive, they must be from sources that readers consider reliable. Researchers' trustworthiness, in turn, depends on their credentials as experts in the field they are investigating and also on the degree to which they are disinterested, or free from bias.

Kornbluh provides a Works Cited list of sources that readers can follow up on to check whether the sources are indeed reliable. The fact that some of her sources are books published by major publishers (Harvard University Press and Basic Books, for example) helps establish their credibility. Other sources she cites are research institutes (such as New America Foundation, Economic Policy Institute, and Families and Work Institute) that readers can easily check out. Another factor that adds to the appearance of reliability is that Kornbluh cites statistics from a range of sources instead of relying on only one or two. Moreover, the statistics are current and clearly relevant to her argument.

Your instructor may arrange a peer review session in class or online where you can exchange drafts with your classmates and give each other a thoughtful critical reading, pointing out what works well and suggesting ways to improve the draft. This critical reading guide can also be used productively by a tutor in the writing center or by a roommate or family member.

A good critical reading does three things: It lets the writer know how the reader understands the point of the draft, praises what works best, and indicates where the draft could be improved.

1. Evaluate how well the problem is defined.

   Summarize: Tell the writer what you understand the problem to be.

   Praise: Give an example where the nature of the problem and its significance to readers comes across effectively.

   Critique: Tell the writer where the readers might need more information about the problem's causes and consequences, or where more might be done to establish its seriousness.

2. Assess how well the solution is argued.

   Summarize: Tell the writer what you understand the proposed solution to be.

   Praise: Give an example in the essay where support for the solution is presented especially effectively — for example, note particularly strong reasons; writing strategies that engage readers; or design or visual elements that make the solution clear and accessible.

   Critique: Tell the writer where the argument for the solution could be strengthened — for example, where steps for implementation could be laid out more clearly; where the practicality of the solution could be established more convincingly; or where additional support for reasons should be added.

Critical Reading Guide

● ● ● ●
Basic Features

For a printable version of this Critical Reading Guide, go to **bedfordstmartins .com/theguide.**

3. Consider how effectively counterarguments are addressed and alternative solutions are offered.

    Praise: Give an example in the essay where the writer effectively responds to a likely objection to the argument, and where reasons against accepting other solutions are most effectively presented.

    Critique: Tell the writer where concessions and refutations could be more convincing; where possible objections or reservations should be taken into account, or alternative solutions discussed; where reasons against accepting other solutions need to be strengthened; or where common ground should be sought with advocates of other positions.

4. Assess how readable the proposal is.

    Praise: Give an example of where the essay succeeds in being readable — for example, in its overall organization; its use of forecasting statements or key terms introduced in its thesis and strategically repeated elsewhere; its use of topic sentences or transitions; an especially effective opening or closing; or by other means.

    Critique: Tell the writer where the readability could be improved. Can you point to places where key terms would help or where a topic sentence could be made clearer, for example? Can the use of transitions be improved, or transitions added where they are lacking? Can you suggest a better beginning or more effective ending?

5. If the writer has expressed concern about anything in the draft that you have not discussed, respond to that concern.

Making Comments Electronically Most word processing software offers features that allow you to insert comments directly into the text of someone else's document. Many readers prefer to make their comments this way because it tends to be faster than writing on a hard copy and space is virtually unlimited; it also eliminates the process of deciphering handwritten comments. Where such features are not available, simply typing comments directly into a document in a contrasting color can provide the same advantages.

Revising

Very likely you have already thought of ways to improve your draft, and you may even have begun to revise it. In this section is a Troubleshooting Chart that may help. Before using the chart, however, it is a good idea to

For an electronic version of this Troubleshooting Chart, go to **bedfordstmartins .com/theguide.**

- review critical reading comments from your classmates, instructor, or writing center tutor, and
- make an outline of your draft so that you can look at it analytically.

    You may have made an outline before writing your draft, but after drafting you need to see what you actually wrote, not what you intended to write. You can outline your draft by highlighting the basic features — a well-defined problem, a clearly argued solution, response to counterarguments, and a readable plan.

Troubleshooting Your Draft

● ● ● ● **Basic Features**

	Problem	Suggestions for Revising the Draft
A Well-Defined Problem	My readers are not convinced of the seriousness and/or the existence of the problem.	☐ Consider changing the way you present the problem to more directly address your audience's concerns. ☐ Add additional information — statistics, examples, description, etc. — likely to be of interest to your audience. ☐ Consider adding visuals, graphs, tables, or charts if these would help clarify the nature of the problem for your audience.
A Well-Argued Solution	My readers are not convinced that my solution is a good one.	☐ Try to explain the solution more convincingly, perhaps by discussing similar solutions used elsewhere or by more clearly demonstrating how it will solve the problem. ☐ Add additional support for your reasons. ☐ Go over the way you present the steps needed to put your solution into place; if necessary, lay them out more clearly.
An Effective Counter-argument	My readers continue to raise objections to my solution.	☐ Address the objections directly in your proposal. If possible, refute them, using solid reasons and support or citing authorities. ☐ If objections cannot be completely refuted, modify your solution to accommodate valid criticism. ☐ If you can neither refute nor accommodate objections, rethink your solution.
	My readers have proposed alternative solutions that I do not discuss in my proposal.	☐ Address the alternative solutions directly. Establish common ground with those who propose alternatives, if possible, but show why their solutions will not work as well as yours. ☐ If you cannot demonstrate that your solution is preferable, consider arguing that both solutions deserve serious consideration.
A Readable Plan	My readers are confused by my proposal or find it difficult to read.	☐ Try outlining your proposal to be sure that the overall organization is strong; if not, try rearranging parts, moving, adding, or deleting sections to strengthen coherence. ☐ Consider adding a forecasting statement and using key terms in your thesis and repeating them when you introduce and later when you discuss main points. ☐ Check to see that your main points are introduced clearly through the use of topic sentences and that you provide appropriate transitions, particularly in places where readers indicate the greatest trouble in following your argument.

Thinking About Document Design:
Following Formatting Conventions

The trucking company employees who wrote the proposal for recruiting and training more women (see the "In the Workplace" scenario described on p. 321) drafted and designed their document on the computer. They were familiar with some key features of their word processing software, such as the ability to create headings, format lists, and include photographs, and they recognized that these elements could serve persuasive purposes in the document they wanted to produce. They also searched the Web for similar proposals that they could use as models. After looking them over, they found that the proposals all used the same formatting conventions: They were single-spaced, had descriptive headings, and included visuals (tables, charts, and photographs).

The employees decided to format their document similarly, using single-spacing and headings and incorporating graphs and tables gathered from several trucking industry magazines and newsletters. To stress that carriers must increase their fleets to remain competitive within the industry, they used the line graph below showing how the skyrocketing demand for carriers over the next ten years would make the current driver shortage much worse. They used a second visual,

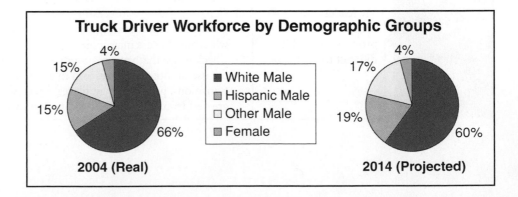

the pie chart on p. 376, to show that current projections indicate that women will remain an underutilized group in the truck driver workforce. And to show how the trucking industry can attract women on the basis of salary, they also included a table contrasting the amount of money a woman truck driver could earn after one year, after five years, and so on, with how much women in other fields could earn over the same periods of time.

The coworkers knew that the preferred hiring solution of many companies is to recruit from truck-driving schools. However, they also knew that the region's divorced and single-parent women would likely not be able to afford such training. Therefore, they included a list comparing truck-driving school tuition rates with income statistics for women in the region to illustrate their lack of access. As an alternative solution, they proposed that companies offer after-hours training programs at various community centers in the region, which they admitted would require the companies to spend some money up front but would allow them to help the community, support the training of women, and recruit from the pool of qualified women in the region.

Finally, the proposal authors used photographs as a framing device. They knew from their own experience that people respond to photographs and are compelled by appropriate images. Thus, toward the beginning of the proposal, they scanned in a snapshot showing the lead author in the double-bottom dump truck that she first learned to drive, which helped establish her authority as a trucker. Toward the end of the proposal, they included a variety of photographs like the one at right, showing women truck drivers competently performing their jobs; each of these images attested to the feasibility of their proposed solution.

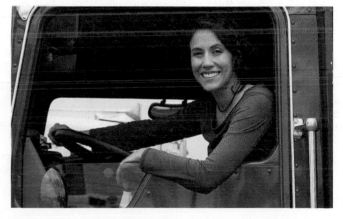

Editing and Proofreading

Several errors occur often in essays that propose solutions: ambiguous use of *this* and *that*, and sentences that lack an agent. The following guidelines will help you check your essay for these common errors.

Avoiding Ambiguous Use of *This* and *That*

The Problem. Because you must frequently refer to the problem and the solution in a proposal, you will often use pronouns to avoid the monotony or wordiness of

A Note on Grammar and Spelling Checkers
These tools can be helpful, but do not rely on them exclusively to catch errors in your text: Spelling checkers cannot catch misspellings that are themselves words, such as *to* for *too*. Grammar checkers miss some problems, sometimes give faulty advice for fixing problems, and can flag correct items as wrong. Use these tools as a second line of defense after your own (and, ideally, another reader's) proofreading/editing efforts.

repeatedly referring to them by name. Using *this* and *that* vaguely to refer to other words or ideas, however, can confuse readers.

How to Correct It. Add a specific noun after *this* or *that*. For example, in his essay in this chapter, Patrick O'Malley writes:

> Another possible solution would be to help students prepare for midterm and final exams by providing sets of questions from which the exam questions will be selected. . . . *This solution* would have the advantage of reducing students' anxiety about learning every fact in the textbook. . . . (par. 12)

O'Malley avoids an ambiguous *this* in the second sentence by repeating the noun *solution*. (He might just as well have used *preparation* or *action* or *approach*.)

▶ Students would not resist a reasonable fee increase of about $40 a year.

      increase

This would pay for the needed dormitory remodeling.

▶ Compared with other large California cities, San Diego has the weakest

              neglect

programs for conserving water. This and our decreasing access to Colorado

River water give us reason to worry.

                                  alternative

▶ Compared with other proposed solutions to this problem, that is clearly the most feasible.

For practice, go to bedfordstmartins.com/theguide/exercisecentral and click on Ambiguous Use of *This* and *That*.

Revising Sentences That Lack an Agent

The Problem. A writer proposing a solution to a problem usually needs to indicate who exactly should take action to solve it. Such actors — those who are in a position to take action — are called "agents." Look, for example, at this sentence from O'Malley's proposal:

> To get students to complete the questions in a timely way, professors would have to collect and check the answers. (par. 11)

In this sentence, *professors* are the agents. They have the authority to assign and collect study questions, and they would need to take this action in order for this solution to be successfully implemented.

Had O'Malley instead written "the answers would have to be collected and checked," the sentence would lack an agent. Failing to name an agent would have made his argument less convincing, because it would have left unclear one of the key parts of any proposal: who is going to take action.

How to Correct It. When you revise your work, ask yourself *who* or *what* performed the action in any given sentence. If there's no clear answer, rewrite the sentence to give it an agent. Watch in particular for forms of the verb *to be* (the balls *were* dropped, exams should *be* given, etc.), which often signal agentless sentences.

> *Your staff should plan a survey*
> ▶ ~~A survey could be planned~~ to find out more about students' problems in scheduling the courses they need.

> *The registrar should extend*
> ▶ ~~Extending~~ the deadline to mid-quarter. ~~would make sense.~~

Note: Sometimes, however, it is appropriate to write agentless sentences, as in the following examples from O'Malley's essay:

These exams should be given weekly or at least twice monthly. (par. 3)

Exams could be collected and responded to only every third or fourth week. (par. 3)

Still another solution might be to provide frequent study questions for students to answer. (par. 11)

Even though these sentences do not name explicit agents, they are all fine because it is clear from the larger context who will perform the action: a professor.

For practice, go to bedfordstmartins.com/theguide/exercisecentral and click on Sentences That Lack an Agent.

A Writer at Work

Patrick O'Malley's Revision Process

This section focuses on student writer Patrick O'Malley's successful efforts to strengthen his argument for the solution he proposes in his essay, "More Testing, More Learning." Read the following three paragraphs from his draft; then compare them with paragraphs 4–6 of his final essay on pp. 327–28. As you read, take notes on the differences you observe between the draft and final versions.

The predominant reason students perform better with multiple exams is that they improve their study habits. Greater regularity in test taking means greater regularity in studying for tests. Students prone to cramming will be forced to open their textbooks more often, keeping them away from long, "kamikaze" nights of studying. Regularity prepares them for the "real world" where you rarely take on large tasks at long intervals. Several tests also improve study habits by reducing procrastination. An article about procrastination from the *Journal of Counseling*

Psychology reports that "students view exams as difficult, important, and anxiety provoking." These symptoms of anxiety leading to procrastination could be solved if individual test importance was lessened, reducing the stress associated with the perceived burden.

With multiple exams, this anxiety decrease will free students to perform better. Several, less important tests may appear as less of an obstacle, allowing the students to worry less, leaving them free to concentrate on their work without any emotional hindrances. It is proven that "the performance of test-anxious subjects varies inversely with evaluation stress." It would also be to the psychological benefit of students if they were not subjected to the emotional ups and downs of large exams where they are virtually worry-free one moment and ready to check into the psychiatric ward the next.

Lastly, with multiple exams, students can learn how to perform better on future tests in the class. Regular testing allows them to "practice" the information they learned, thereby improving future test scores. In just two exams, they are not able to learn the instructor's personal examination style, and are not given the chance to adapt their study habits to it. The *American Psychologist* concludes: "It is possible to influence teaching and learning by changing the type of tests."

One difference you may have noted between O'Malley's draft and revision paragraphs is the sequencing of specific reasons that readers should accept the solution and take action on it. Whereas the draft moves in three paragraphs from improving study habits to decreasing anxiety to performing better on future tests, the revision moves from learning more and performing better on major exams to improving study habits to decreasing anxiety. O'Malley made the change after a response from a classmate and a conference with his instructor helped him see that his particular readers (professors) would probably be most convinced by the improved quality of students' learning, not by improvements in their study habits and feelings. As he continued thinking about his argument and discovering further relevant research, he shifted his emphasis from the psychological to the intellectual benefits of frequent exams.

You may also have noticed that the paragraphs of the revision are better focused than in the draft. The psychological benefits (reduced anxiety as a result of less procrastination) are now discussed mainly in a single paragraph (the third), whereas in the draft they are mixed in with the intellectual benefits in the first two paragraphs. O'Malley also uses more precise language in his revision; for example, changing "future tests" to "major exams, projects, and papers."

Another change you may have noticed is that all of the quoted research material in the draft has been replaced in the revision. Extending his library research to support his argument, O'Malley discovered the very useful Harvard report. As he found a more logical sequence, more precise terms, and more support for his argument, he saw different ways to use the research studies he had turned up initially and quoted in the draft.

A final difference is that in the revision, O'Malley argues his reasons more effectively. Consider the draft and revised paragraphs on improved study habits. In the draft paragraph, O'Malley shifts abruptly from study habits to procrastination to anxiety. Except for study habits, none of these topics is developed, and the quotation adds nothing to what he has already said. By contrast, the revised paragraph focuses strictly on study habits. O'Malley keeps the best sentences from the draft for the beginning of the revised paragraph, but he adds several new sentences to help convince readers of the soundness of his argument that frequent exams improve students' study habits. These new sentences serve several functions: They anticipate a possible objection ("It might be argued . . ."), note a contrast between complex academic learning and familiar survival skills, and assert claims about the special requirements of regular academic study. The quotation from the Harvard report provides convincing support for O'Malley's claims and an effective way to conclude the paragraph.

Thinking Critically About What You Have Learned

In this chapter, you have learned a great deal about this genre from reading several proposals and writing one of your own. To consolidate your learning, think metacognitively — that is, to reflect not only on what you learned but on how you learned it. Following are two brief activities your instructor may ask you to do.

Reflecting on Your Writing

Your instructor may ask you to turn in with your essay and process materials a brief metacognitive essay or letter reflecting on what you have learned about writing your essay proposing a solution. Choose among the following invention activities those that seem most productive for you.

- Explain how your purpose and audience influenced *one* of your decisions as a writer, such as how you defined the problem, the strategies you used in presenting your solution, or the ways in which you attempted to counter possible objections.

- Discuss what you learned about yourself as a writer in the process of writing this particular essay. For example, what part of the process did you find most challenging? Did you try anything new, like getting a critical reading of your draft or outlining your draft in order to revise it?

- If you were to give advice to a friend who was about to write an essay proposing a solution to a problem, what would you say?

- Which of the readings in this chapter influenced your essay? Explain the influence, citing specific examples from your essay and the reading.

- If you got good advice from a critical reader, explain exactly how the person helped you — perhaps by questioning the way you addressed your audience or the kinds of support you offered in support of your proposed solution.

Considering the Social Dimensions: The Frustrations of Effecting Real Change

No matter how well researched and well argued, many proposals are simply never carried out. The head of a personnel department might spend weeks drawing up a persuasive and feasible proposal for establishing a company day-care center, only to have upper management decide not to commit the necessary resources. A team of educators and social scientists might spend several years researching and writing a comprehensive, book-length proposal for dealing with the nation's drastic illiteracy rate but never see their solutions carried out because of a lack of coordination among the country's various educational institutions and governing bodies. In fact, it might be argued that the most successful proposals often operate on the smallest scale. For example, a proposal suggesting ways for a single community to increase literacy rates would probably have a better chance of implementation and ultimate success than the more far-reaching national proposal. (Yet this observation does not rule out the value of the national proposal, on which the local proposal might, in fact, be based.)

Further, in choosing among competing alternative proposals, decision makers — who usually hold the power of the purse strings and necessarily represent a fairly conservative position — often go for the one that is cheapest, most expedient, and least disruptive. They may also choose small, incremental changes over more fundamental, radical solutions. While sometimes the most pragmatic choice, such immediately feasible solutions may also merely patch over a problem, failing to solve it structurally. They may even inadvertently maintain the status quo. Worse, they can cause people to give up all attempts to resolve a problem after superficial treatments fail.

1. *Consider how proposals invite writers to select problems that are solvable and how they might inadvertently attempt to solve a minor problem that is actually only a small part of a major problem.* Do any of the proposals you have read and written reveal this misdirection? If so, which ones, and what do you think is the major problem in each case? Do you think the minor problem is worth solving as a first step toward solving the major problem, or is it perhaps an unfortunate diversion?

2. ***Consider how the proposals you have read and written challenge the status quo.*** What existing situation do they challenge, and just how do they challenge it? What roadblocks might deter these challenges? Might the proposals be more successfully carried out on a local scale?

3. ***Reflect on commentators' arguments that we should not try to solve fundamental social problems by "throwing money at them."*** Do you think this objection is a legitimate criticism of most proposals to solve social problems, or is it a manipulative justification for allowing the rich and powerful to maintain the status quo? What else, besides money, is required to solve serious social problems? Where are these other resources to come from?

4. ***Write a page or two explaining your ideas about the frustrations of effecting real change.*** Connect your ideas to your own essay and to the readings in this chapter.

8

Justifying an Evaluation

IN COLLEGE COURSES For a research paper in a literature-in-film course, a student sets out to evaluate the 1995 film *Clueless*, an adaptation of Jane Austen's novel *Emma* set in modern-day Beverly Hills. He had already seen the film but decides to watch it again on DVD before reading the novel. Then, while he is reading the novel, he reviews key scenes in the film to see how they have been translated to the screen. He also looks closely at differences in how the main characters are portrayed in novel and film.

While considering how to approach his evaluation, he does an Internet search for reviews of *Clueless* and discovers that there is a 1996 film called *Emma* set in early nineteenth-century England like the novel. He rents the DVD and decides that his paper would be more interesting if he could write about both the more historically accurate film and the looser adaptation. He goes to his professor's office to see if there is any problem evaluating two film versions of a novel instead of one. His professor responds enthusiastically.

The student then spends several days drafting his essay and selecting stills from the two films to illustrate his argument that *Clueless* is a more effective adaptation than *Emma*. He offers two main reasons for this judgment: *Emma*, while beautifully filmed, looks like a museum piece, and viewers cannot identify with the main characters. In contrast, he argues, the familiar setting and characters in *Clueless* engage viewers, allowing them to better appreciate Austen's social commentary.

IN THE COMMUNITY   A motorcycle enthusiast rides to York, Pennsylvania, to tour the Harley-Davidson factory there. He decides to take notes and photographs for a review of the tour that he plans to post on his blog. Before the tour begins, he and about twenty other visitors wander through the Vaughn L. Beals Tour Center, marveling at the dozens of vintage motorcycles on display, including special police and war-era bikes. He watches a short film that relates the history of the company, which was founded in 1903, and then explores exhibits describing the plant and the manufacturing process he is about to observe.

Before entering the plant, he is given safety glasses and a headset so he can hear the tour guide on the noisy factory floor. The factory is housed in an immense building of more than 230 acres with over a thousand workers on each shift. He takes pictures and makes notes describing each part of the manufacturing and assembly process. He notes with amazement that workers add a new part to each bike every three minutes as it moves along a conveyor belt and is ultimately rolled off the assembly line into the crating area.

On the way home, he reflects on what he has seen and decides to title his review "Hog Heaven." At home, he spends a couple of days writing the review, enthusiastically recommending the tour as free, fun, and educational. He illustrates his review with his photographs and supplements it with links to additional information online.

IN THE WORKPLACE   For a conference panel on innovations in education, an elementary school teacher decides to give a talk on *Schoolhouse Rock!*, an animated television series developed in the 1970s and 1980s. She had enjoyed the series when she was a child, so she bought the DVD and started showing segments to her students, who seemed to enjoy them as much as she had.

To prepare for her talk, she plays four songs for her class: two from the "Grammar Rock" lessons ("Conjunction Junction" and "A Noun Is a Person, Place or Thing") and two from "Multiplication Rock" ("Three Is a Magic Number" and "The Good 11"). Following each, she gives her students a quiz to see how well they have learned the lesson. Finally, she conducts an informal opinion poll to see whether the kids find this kind of learning enjoyable.

In her panel presentation, she describes her research and gives two reasons why the series is an effective educational tool: The witty lyrics and catchy tunes make the information memorable, and the cartoon visuals make the lessons vivid and enjoyable. She supports her evaluation by screening and discussing the segments she played in class, presenting the results of the follow-up quizzes, and quoting from the opinion poll. She ends by expressing her hope that teachers and developers of multimedia educational software will learn from the example of *Schoolhouse Rock!*

Evaluation involves making judgments. Many times each day, people make judgments about subjects as diverse as the weather, food, music, computer programs, sports events, politicians, and films. In everyday conversation, you often express judgments casually ("I like it" or "I don't like it"), only occasionally giving your reasons (for example, "I hate cafeteria food because it is bland and overcooked") or supporting them with specific examples ("Take last night's spaghetti. That must have been a tomato sauce because it was red, but it didn't have the tang of tomatoes. And the noodles were so overdone that they were mushy.").

When you write an evaluation, however, readers expect you to provide reasons and support for your judgment. In the scenario about the Harley-Davidson factory tour, for example, the writer gives three reasons for recommending the tour, supporting them with details and photographs. Similarly, the student evaluating two film versions of Jane Austen's novel gives two reasons for arguing that *Clueless* is a more effective adaptation than *Emma* and supports his argument with still images and examples from both films and references to the novel. The teacher who gives a presentation on *Schoolhouse Rock!* uses examples of the songs as well as her quiz grades and survey results to support her reasons for praising the old educational series.

Readers also need to agree that your criteria are appropriate for evaluating the subject. For example, in an evaluation of an action film like *Mission Impossible III*, you would want to show that you are judging the film according to standards most people would use in evaluating action films, as James Berardinelli does in his *ReelViews* review (www.reelviews.net/movies/m/mission3.html). Berardinelli first places the film in its general category ("a flashy, leave-your-brain-at-the-door summer movie"). Then he goes on to argue that even though it has all the characteristics of a summer blockbuster ("It's loud, raucous, frenetic, and blows things up real good"), he found the film disappointing because "it's testosterone without adrenaline, danger without suspense." Berardinelli understands that readers expect him to judge the film as an example of its genre, so he bases his judgment on qualities such as the film's special effects, action sequences, and most important, its ability to generate excitement. He even makes a point of saying that he is not criticizing the film's "plot contrivances" because "they go with the territory."

Showing readers you understand how your particular subject relates to other subjects in the same general category demonstrates that your judgment is based on criteria readers will recognize as appropriate. Readers may disagree with you, but they will understand and respect your argument.

A Collaborative Activity:
Practice Evaluating a Subject

To get a sense of the complexities and possibilities involved in writing an evaluation, get together with two or three other students, and discuss your judgments of a subject with which you are all familiar. Here are some guidelines to follow:

Part 1.

- Select a subject you all know well — for example, a film, Web site, recent performance, or sports event.

- Discuss what you consider the pluses and minuses, what is good and what is bad about your subject. You do not have to agree; take notes on what you agree and disagree about.

Part 2. Talk about one or two occasions when your group disagreed, and try to determine what caused the disagreement:

- the standards or criteria used in evaluating a subject of this particular kind (for example, in evaluating a Web site, the relative importance of the information provided, ease of navigation, or credibility); or
- differing judgments on how the subject measured up to the standards (for example, whether the site was in fact easy to navigate, and why)

Reading Essays Justifying Evaluations

Basic Features

● A Well–Presented Subject

●●●●
Basic Features

Read first to see how the writer presents the **subject**. For familiar subjects, writers may need only to identify the subject by name. Most often, however, writers provide some details to describe the subject — for example, identifying what kind of film is being reviewed, who is in it, and what it is about. Identifying the kind of subject being evaluated is especially important because the criteria or standards writers use to judge a subject depend on how people normally judge subjects of that kind. If a writer chooses to apply a standard readers consider unusual, it may be harder to convince readers that the writer's judgment can be relied upon.

● A Well-Supported Judgment

Look for the overall **judgment** *and the argument supporting it.* The judgment usually appears in a thesis statement early in the essay, and may be repeated at other points in the essay. A good thesis statement in an evaluative essay makes a clear and unambiguous assertion about how the writer values the subject — whether it is good or bad, or better or worse than something else of the same kind. But writers also know that readers of evaluative essays appreciate measured or balanced judgments that are not exaggerated but carefully qualified, acknowledging the subject's strengths as well as its flaws.

Examine the argument, noting how each reason is explained and the kinds of evidence offered as backing, such as the following:

- examples
- facts
- statistics
- textual evidence in the form of quotations, summaries, or paraphrases

- expert testimony
- research studies

Determine whether the support is relevant and comes from reliable sources. Note also any comparisons and how well they demonstrate the appropriateness of the criteria being applied or substantiate the writer's judgment of the relative value of the subject compared to other similar subjects.

● An Effective Counterargument

*Read also to see how the writer responds to possible objections to the argument or alternative judgments with **an effective counterargument**.* Writers of evaluation often counterargue by simply acknowledging other judgments. More substantial counterargument could include making concessions — for example, conceding an objection and modifying the judgment to accommodate it — or refuting readers' possible objections or alternative judgments.

● A Readable Plan

*Finally, examine the essay to see how the writer provides **a readable plan**.* Evaluative essays tend to analyze the subject in detail; so it is helpful to have a readable plan that gives readers a clear overview of the argument. To make their essays easy to read, writers usually include some or all of the following:

- a forecast of the argument
- key words introduced in the thesis and forecasting statement and repeated in topic sentences
- clear transitional words and phrases
- headings that explicitly identify different sections of the essay

Purpose and Audience

Although many evaluative essays seek to influence readers' judgments, their primary purpose is usually to explain and justify the writer's judgment. Readers may or may not find the argument convincing, but a well-written evaluation will be interesting and informative. It may also lead thoughtful readers to examine the values or criteria they think are important and to wonder why these particular values have become so important.

*As you read evaluation essays, ask yourself what seems to be the writer's **purpose** in writing.* The following purposes are common in evaluative essays:

- to convince readers that the writer's judgment is correct or preferable to other people's judgments
- to influence readers' judgments and possibly their actions
- to encourage readers to examine the values they use as criteria for judging subjects of this kind

- to get readers to look at the subject in a new way
- to stimulate readers' interest in the subject

*As you read, also try to guess what the writer assumes about the **audience**.* Which of the following assumptions about audience might apply?

- The audience will accept the writer's judgment.
- The audience will use the review to make their own independent, informed judgments of the subject.
- The audience will already have an independent judgment of the subject.
- The audience will have serious objections to the writer's argument.

Readings

WENDY KIM, a business administration major, immigrated to the United States from South Korea when she was eight years old. For a composition course, she decided to research RateMyProfessors.com, a Web site she uses regularly to decide which classes to take. You may already be familiar with this site or with comparable resources that evaluate professors. If not, you may want to take a look at the Web site (which has been redesigned since Kim wrote her description) to see whether you think her judgment is sound. (RateMyProfessors .com, like other online professor evaluation services, is free, but you do have to register.)

● ● ● ●
Basic Features

- A Well-Presented Subject
- A Well-Supported Judgment
- An Effective Counterargument
- A Readable Plan

Grading Professors

Wendy Kim

1   "Where the Students Do the Grading" is the tagline for the Web site www .RateMyProfessors.com (RMP). Users just choose their state and find their school among the more than 6,000 campuses listed, and they're ready to start grading their professors. The home page proudly displays the numbers: last I looked, there were more than 6,200,000 ratings, covering more than 770,000 professors in the United States and Canada. In fact, RMP has been so successful that it has expanded to Australia, Ireland, and the United Kingdom, and its sister-site for high school students, RateMyTeachers .com, already has a user base of 3 million students (RateMyProfessors). While not everyone agrees that these ratings provide an entirely accurate assessment, many students, like me, routinely consult RMP at the beginning of every term to decide which classes to take. Overall, the Web site is well designed, extremely helpful, and amusing.

Is this opening effective? Why or why not?

How does this information help readers?

How well does Kim forecast her reasons here? Find where each reason is developed in the essay.

Why does Kim mention the class she took?

The design of RateMyProfessors.com makes the site attractive and easy to browse (see Fig. 1). In my senior year of high school, I took a class that taught me how to make a good Web site and learned that Web site design requires care in picking colors and in organizing the layout. The layout of RMP's home page is smart, with information grouped in clearly defined rectangular boxes. Across the top is a banner with the name in easy-to-read letters. Below the banner, the page is divided into boxes, three across and two down, with plenty of white space along the left and right borders and bottom so that the page looks neatly organized and uncluttered. The top box on the left has the main menu in blue lettering against a white background with links to "Hot or Not," "Funny Ratings," "Signup Now," "Recent Press," and "Forum," five areas likely to be of most use to users. The placement of the menu is smart because readers of English are used to reading from left to right as well as top to bottom. Below the menu a box titled "Statistics" (which I cited in the first paragraph) reveals how many students use the ratings.

What purpose does her detailed description of the site in pars. 2 and 3 and the addition of Fig. 1 serve?

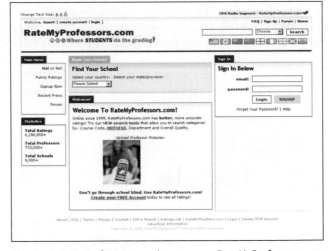

Fig. 1. *RateMyProfessors.com* home page; RateMyProfessors.com, 2006; Web; 13 May 2006.

How does Kim support her judgments about the site's design?

The viewer's eye is drawn to the center box, which is twice as wide as the boxes on the sides and includes the all-important search function (set off against a distinctive yellow background). The box below this, which includes eye-catching graphics, serves as a portal to the Welcome page. The box in the top right-hand portion of the screen allows users to sign in conveniently. Ads fill the space in the lower right-hand portion of the screen; however, they coordinate in color with the rest of the elements on the page, so they're not too distracting. The placement of information seems just right.

2

3

4   The navigation system is smooth and fast. When you log in, you get the main member page; from there, you easily link to your school's page. On the member page, you can edit your ratings, go to the message board, or manage your account. Your school's page is the destination for checking out professors whose classes you are considering, entering your own rating of a professor, or adding a professor not already listed. Finding a particular professor is quick and easy because professors' names are listed in alphabetical order. The list is easy to skim and contains lots of valuable information. To the left of each name is a face icon (which I will explain in a minute) followed by a check icon that you can click on to add your own rating. To the right of the name is the professor's department, the date he or she was last rated, the number of ratings, and the vital average ratings for overall quality and ease. Clicking on a name takes you to the professor's page, which presents even more information: a box with averages in each rating category and a list of individual users' ratings, starting with the most recent. These ratings identify the class, give the student's rating in each category, and often include a comment. You can add your own rating of the professor or respond to other users' ratings. Every page displays the information clearly, without distractions. Even though there are ads, they do not flicker or get in the way. This is not the kind of Web site that takes minutes just to find what you need. Not only is it easy to browse, but it also doesn't lag because there are no large files or images to slow it down. For me, the longest it took to get to another page was two seconds using a cable modem.

5   Most important, RateMyProfessors.com is full of useful information that can help students make informed decisions when it comes to choosing teachers and preparing for a class they are about to take. A student debating whether to take a history or a sociology class, for example, can go to the Web site, first look at the overall ratings of each professor and then find user ratings for the classes being considered. Assuming the professor has been graded by other students, a great deal can be learned about the professor and possibly also about the specific class.

6   Professors are rated in several categories on a scale of 1 (worst) to 5 (best). The scores on clarity and helpfulness are averaged for the "Overall Quality rating," the overall rating that determines which icon is placed next to the professor's name: A yellow smiley face indicates "good quality," a bluish-gray sad face "poor quality," and an indifferent-looking green face "average quality." The numerical rating in each category is displayed along with the face so that students and professors can see the breakdown. In addition to evaluating the professor's clarity and helpfulness, students also rate the difficulty of the course. This rating, however, has no effect on assigning the face icon because, as the site explains, "an Easiness rating of 5 may actually mean the teacher

Why do you think Kim introduces the next reason with this transition?

How do transitions like these help readers follow her argument?

is TOO easy." Although RMP acknowledges that easiness is "definitely the most controversial" reason for judging a class, they still present it because "many students decide what class to take based on the difficulty of the teacher." Another category that is not included in the overall rating is "Rater Interest." To explain this category the Web site quotes from a study that found student "motivation correlated with the overall evaluation," meaning that the more motivated a student was to succeed in a course, the higher the professor's overall quality score. "Instructors," however, as RMP acknowledges, "usually have little control over student motivation" (RateMyProfessors).

The faces and numbers are informative, but I think the comments help the most because they are so detailed. Not surprisingly, the comments on RateMyProfessors .com tend to address many of the same issues that my college's course evaluation forms do. For example, one question on my campus evaluation form asks if the instructor presented the material in "an organized, understandable manner." Many of the RMP comments answer this question: from high praise ("lectures are interesting, and he's happy to answer whatever questions you could ask") to severe criticism ("lectures are BORING and POINTLESS" or "totally disorganized!! boring and reads off the power point!!"). Another question on my campus form asks if the instructor was "concerned about students learning and understanding the course material." This issue also draws many comments on RMP, from highly positive ("he wrote a personal whole-page to each of my papers. So I knew exactly what he liked and how to improve on my writing") to slams ("Kinda scary and intimidating" or "He does not care if the students are learning the basic concepts. He teaches as if he were teaching a Graduate level class. This is an INTRO class, let us learn the basics 1st"). In addition to these kinds of comments, RMP also posts information that course evaluations do not include — advice on how to pass the course ("If you keep up w/ your notes and the reading, you should be fine. Pop quizzes every week." or "Has notes available online. Tests are extremely difficult and require a lot of reading from the book to be successful as well as attending class. Gives surprise quizzes"). The site also gives students warnings ("He's ****in' hard. Fails half his class." or "OMG, one of the worst teachers I've ever had . . . Does not know how to teach and wears the tightest pants ever . . . gross.")

And as this last comment suggests, we can't forget the last rating category: Is your professor hot or not? The answer to this question makes the Web site amusing. "Hot" professors are marked with a red chili pepper beside their names. Some students also include comments in this area: "good lookin guy, nice body" and "this chick [the professor] totally blew my mind. She was sooo hot. I'm serious take this class just to check her out. SEXY!!!!" In fact, this issue may not be just a sideline to ones that supposedly are more

7

8

How effectively does she refute these objections?

Why do you think Kim refers to her college's student evaluation forms?

How well does putting examples in parentheses work?

What purpose does this observation serve?

Why do you think Kim presents this reason last?

serious. Students give professors higher overall ratings if they are hot, according to a *New York Times* article, "The Hunk Differential," which the RMP site provides as the answer to its FAQ question "Why do you have the 'hot' category?" The article, written by a professor of business, economics, and information management, reports a study that found "good-looking professors got significantly higher teaching scores" than those who did not rate as high on a beauty scale (Varian). So it may be that a professor who is considered "hot" on the site may be judged on a more lenient scale of teaching effectiveness.

9   This question about the possible effect of the teacher's appearance on student response and learning leads to a more basic question about the credibility of the evaluations on RateMyProfessors.com: Are the ratings statistically valid? The simple answer, the Web site itself admits, is "Not really. They are a listing of opinions and should be judged as such" (RateMyProfessors). The results are statistically invalid, as one psychology professor explained, because the users are self-selected and not selected randomly (Harmon). And the fewer student ratings an instructor has been given, the less reliable the overall evaluation. Nevertheless, RMP claims "we often receive emails stating that the ratings are uncannily accurate, especially for schools with over 1000 ratings" (RateMyProfessors). RMP also refers readers to an article reporting a study at the University of Waterloo, Canada (UW), that found fifteen of the sixteen Distinguished Teacher Award winners at UW also had yellow smiley faces on RateMyProfessors.com (TRACE). While this correlation is reassuring, students should not approach the ratings uncritically. And evidence suggests most don't. As one college newspaper reporter put it, "students claim they do not blindly follow the comments" (Espach). A recent study of RMP published in the *Journal of Computer-Mediated Communication* found that students "are aware that ratings and comments on the site could reflect students exacting revenge or venting" (Kindred and Mohammed). As one student explained: "If half the ratings are bad, I will ask around about the professor. If every rating is poor I won't take the teacher" (Espach).

10   There are other Internet professor evaluation sites, but none is as widely used or as easy to use as RateMyProfessors.com. I compared RMP with three competitors: Professor Performance, Reviewum.com, and RatingsOnline. The user base of the first two sites looks too small to provide reliable information. Professor Performance has 73,040 evaluations at 1,742 colleges and universities, and Reviewum.com claims to have 20,098 records for 137 campuses. In addition, for the limited number of professors who are listed, there are only a small number of evaluations, not enough to enable students to make informed judgments.

11   Although RatingsOnline does not appear to display its statistics, it claims to have ratings for "thousands of professors." However, there are only 19 professors from

What objection does Kim anticipate here? How well does she counter it?

How effectively does Kim use sources to support her counterargument here?

Why do you think Kim compares RMP to other sites?

my campus among the 1,252 listed on RMP. Still, RatingsOnline is better designed and includes more helpful information than the other two competitors, and it may even be better than RMP in terms of helpfulness. Students not only identify the class and term it was taken, but also are asked to list the grade they received. Of course, this information about the grade is no more reliable than any other information a user gives, but it could help students judge the user's credibility. The ratings categories on RatingsOnline also seem more specific than on RMP: prepared, enthusiastic, focused, available, material, exam prep, quality. In addition, students are prompted to indicate the percentage given to homework, quizzes, and exams in determining the final grade. This information could be useful in helping students decide which classes to take, but only if there are enough reviews posted. In its design and potential helpfulness, RatingsOnline is a very good site but not likely to be as good as RMP because its user base appears to be smaller.

How effective are these final sentences?

When you have the option of choosing a teacher, wouldn't you really like some information? RateMyProfessors.com allows you to see what other students have to say about professors and courses you may be considering as well as to voice your opinion. As a Web site, it is not only helpful and easy to use, but it is also amusing to read.   12

Do Kim's sources seem credible and appropriate for the kind of argument she's making and the situation in which she is writing?

Works Cited

Espach, Alison. "RateMyProfessors.com — Blessing or Bluffing?" *Cowl*. Providence College, 27 Apr. 2006. Web. 15 May 2006.

Harmon, Christine. "Professors Rate Reliability of RateMyProfessors.com." *Daily Forty-Niner*. California State U., Long Beach, 2 May 2006. Web. 15 May 2006.

Kindred, Jeannette, and Shaheed N. Mohammed. "'He Will Crush You Like an Academic Ninja!': Exploring Teacher Ratings on RateMyProfessors.com." *Journal of Computer-Mediated Communication* 10.3 (2005): n. pag. Web. 15 May 2006.

Professor Performance. Professorperformance.com, n.d. Web. 19 May 2006.

"ratemyprofessors.ca." *Teaching Matters Newsletter*. U. of Waterloo Teaching Resources Office, Sept. 2001. Web. 13 May 2005.

RateMyProfessors.com. Ratemyprofessors.com, 2006. Web. 13 May 2006.

RatingsOnline. Ratingsonline.com, n.d. Web. 19 May 2006.

Reviewum.com. Reviewum.com, 2006. Web. 19 May 2006.

Varian, Hal R. "The Hunk Differential." *New York Times*. New York Times, 28 Aug. 2003. Web. 14 May 2006.

ANN HULBERT writes often about cultural issues. Her latest book, *Raising America: Experts, Parents, and a Century of Advice about Children* (2003), examines the political and social history of child-rearing advice books. She also writes regularly for newspapers and magazines, online and in print, including the *New Yorker*, the *New York Times*, and the *New York Times Magazine*. She was a senior editor and writer for the *New Republic*, and is now a contributing editor for *Slate*, where this film review originally appeared. If you have seen *Juno*, consider how well Hulbert's evaluation of the film corresponds to your own evaluation. If you have not seen the film, consider whether or not Hulbert's review makes you want to see *Juno*.

Juno and the Culture Wars

ANN HULBERT ▼

I braced for a skirmish in the culture wars when reviews of *Juno* appeared the very same week that newspaper headlines announced a rise in the teenage birth rate — the first uptick in a decade and a half. "Not many [movies] are so daring in their treatment of teenage pregnancy, which this film flirts with presenting not just as bearable but attractive," wrote the *New York Times*' A. O. Scott, who added a wry homily: "Kids, please! Heed the cautionary whale." If the critic at liberal-media headquarters was mildly clucking, it was only a matter of time before anti-Hollywood moralizers would be up in arms about the corruption of youth (at the hands of a former-stripper-turned-screenwriter, Diablo Cody, no less). But among *Juno*'s distinctive charms

1

is that it seems to have disarmed both sides of the family values debate. And the feat gets pulled off in the wry style of the eponymous hero: The film doesn't offer up a formulaic or fervent call for family harmony. Instead, it takes idiosyncratic aim at everybody's pieties.

One by one, polarized positions on the hot-button issues get defused by a 16-year-old girl who has evidently never considered marching with any crowd — an approach hard enough to manage in life, never mind in high school. Let's start with Juno MacGuff's own profile. She has a blue-collar background, complete with parents who've never heard of Pilates and hoard kitsch in their house. But there isn't much sign of the red-America attitudes that either radio talk-show hosts, or snooty liberals, assume go with the pedigree. A heartland family, hers is not an intact one. An off-beat girl, she's a very good daughter whose dad adores her.

Supersmart but neither a teacher's pet nor a pariah, Juno eludes hip vs. square student stereotypes, too. Early on, she jokes about herself as the kind of freaky girl — "with horn-rimmed glasses and vegan footwear and Goth makeup" or Converse All-Stars and cello skills — whom jocks secretly want. But in fact she and her friend Bleeker, in his dweebily short running shorts, confound their peers' social categories altogether — and adults' preconceptions, too. Subverting age and gender expectations, Juno seems at once peculiarly mature and oddly child-like as she fearlessly figures things out for herself; she's neither the suave teen whom liberal types invoke nor the old-fashioned innocent whom the Christian right celebrates. And with her funky get-ups and wit, Juno is in no way sexualized, but she isn't de-sexed either, as her ever-bigger belly shows us.

Her take on the roster of family values issues is as heterodox as her image. Consider her sendup of the term *sexually active*, a trope of the sex-ed wars. Liberal advocates of honest, open sexual communication with teens embrace the epithet as though it were part and parcel of puberty. Abstinence promoters invoke it as the plague to be avoided at all costs. For Juno, it's ridiculous, an Orwellian phrase that in no way speaks to her actual experience (sex, once, in a chair) — as is surely true, when you stop and think about it, for the majority of high-school juniors who aren't virgins.

The real flashpoint issue in the film, of course, could have been abortion. Here Cody's politics (presumably pro-choice) are at odds with her plot needs (a birth) and, who knows, maybe commercial dictates, too, if studios worry about antagonizing the evangelical audience. It's a tension the screenplay finesses deftly, undercutting both pro-life and pro-choice purism. Pregnant Juno at first reflexively embraces abortion as the obvious option, and her best friend is at the ready with phone numbers; she's helped other classmates through this. But just when pro-lifers might be about to denounce this display of secular humanist decadence, Juno stomps out of the clinic, unable to go through with it.

She isn't moved by thoughts of the embryo's hallowed rights, however, but by a sense of her own autonomy. And for her, that doesn't mean a right to privacy, or to protect her body ("a fat suit I can't take off," she calls it at one point).

Juno is driven by the chance to make her own unconventional choice. Parental notification doesn't quite follow the liberal or conservative scripts, either: Juno confides in her father and stepmother, initially portrayed as stock down-home folks who are completely surprised, not least to find themselves asking her if she's "considered, you know, the alternative" — not that they'd presume to pressure her. These are neither old-style authoritarians nor enlightened empathizers. They emerge as people who respect, and would do anything to support, their independent-minded kid.

Here *Juno* moves into the realm of marriage and childrearing, by way of the vexed terrain of assisted reproduction in its most traditional form, adoption. When Juno finds the perfect yuppie adoptive couple for her unborn baby — fussy Vanessa and mellow Mark — the film gets to address a bundle of politically charged questions: class mores, parenting styles, gender relations, and family structure. On every count, *Juno* skewers the assumptions of ideologues on both sides. She refuses to be either an exploited female at the service of the affluent, or a sacrificial vessel of life. She counters Vanessa's materialist and hyper-maternalist solicitude with her own hard-boiled attitude; appalled by the notion of open adoption (or compensation), she tells the couple she'd love to give over the kid immediately, but figures it needs more "cooking" until it gets cuter. And she quickly starts bonding with the laid-back husband, who is still nursing rock band dreams, where the uptight wife, worrying over the color palette for the nursery, turns her off. 7

Juno has a fun-loving adolescent's enthusiasm for the prospect of what sounds like a permissive family with a cool dad — until Mark suddenly upsets that ideal vision of the future. He — spoiler alert — stages a display of just the kind of egotistical guy regression that regularly induces female groans on the right and left, and that *Slate*'s Meghan O'Rourke recently examined in this piece about *Knocked Up*. (Suffice it to say, Vanessa finds herself stranded.) Stunned, Juno is suddenly furious at the infantile male and frantic that what she calls "the big-ass bump" end up in a family "not shitty and broken like everyone else's." 8

But *Juno* doesn't end there. Another twist, and the film closes with a celebration of single parenthood — anathema to family traditionalists. Yet Juno, in deciding to hand her baby over to a now-solo Vanessa, doesn't endorse the dour, who-needs-men-when-we-can-go-it-alone ethos of progressives who defend "permeable" arrangements, either. A great comic scene in a bustling mall has convinced Juno — and us in the audience — that Vanessa isn't actually a vain control freak whose life plan won't be complete without a perfect little appurtenance. Juno has stumbled on a woman who actually finds kids, of all things, fun and lovable. That is a figure whom both liberals and conservatives often seem to have forgotten, or lost faith in, as they endlessly lament the embattled family. If sharp-eyed girls can spot her in the fraught landscape, though, there's reason to hope the culture wars will wane and the American family, in its many forms, won't. 9

MAKING
CONNECTIONS:
DEFUSING
"HOT-BUTTON
ISSUES"

Ann Hulbert writes that when *Juno* first appeared, she "braced for a skirmish in the culture wars. . . . But among *Juno*'s distinctive charms is that it seems to have disarmed both sides of the family values debate" (par. 1). What fascinates her is the way *Juno* defuses such polarized issues as abortion by taking "idiosyncratic aim at everybody's pieties" (par. 2).

With two or three other students, discuss the "culture wars" and the possibility of finding common ground. Begin by taking turns telling about a time people were arguing about a polarized issue and someone (perhaps you) tried to defuse the argument. What did the person do and what was the result? Then, together consider the following questions:

- Hulbert assumes undercutting stereotypes and breaking down polarized thinking is a good thing. Do you agree or disagree? Why?

- What strategies do you think work best in helping people find common ground on highly controversial issues?

ANALYZING
WRITING
STRATEGIES

◆ ◆ ◆ ◆
Basic Features

◆ A Well-Presented Subject

Film reviews are one of the most familiar types of evaluation. Like other kinds of evaluation essays, film reviews begin by presenting the subject. If it is a well-publicized new film, readers may only need the name to identify it. But writers often provide additional information such as the director and main actors. They may also include one or more still photographs showing the main characters, as Hulbert does in this essay. (For more on the photograph, see Analyzing Visuals on p. 401.)

Reviewers usually begin by telling what the film is about and indicating the kind of film it is. Hulbert, for example, names the film in the title and opening sentence. She uses the phrase "culture wars" (also repeated in the title and opening sentence) to categorize *Juno* as a film about social problems. She also lets readers know that although the film treats a serious subject, it does so with humor or "wry style" (par. 1).

In describing a film, reviewers are guided by the *rhetorical situation* in which they are writing. In other words, they have to balance the needs and expectations of their readers against their own purposes in writing. Because reviewers know that most people read reviews primarily to decide whether or not to see the movie, they tend to be careful not to give away too much of the plot for fear of spoiling the surprise.

But not all film reviews share the same rhetorical situation. When you write for a course, you may be able to assume your readers are already familiar with the film or that they will not be concerned if you reveal the plot. Similarly, although Hulbert is writing for a Web site that features reviews of current films, she does not write a typical film review.

To analyze how Hulbert presents the film, try the following:

- Reread the opening paragraph and write a few sentences suggesting how Hulbert conveys to readers that her essay is not a typical film review.

- Skim the essay, highlighting some of the plot details she chooses to reveal. (Note, for example, paragraphs 8 and 9, where she reveals plot twists and uses the phrase *spoiler alert.*)

- Write a few sentences identifying any plot details that you would not expect in a typical film review and speculating on why Hulbert chooses to reveal this information in her essay.

● A Well-Supported Judgment

The center of an evaluation is the argument supporting the writer's judgment. Writers usually assert their overall judgment in a thesis statement early in the essay. Wendy Kim, for example, presents her judgment of RateMyProfessors.com at the end of the opening paragraph: "While not everyone agrees that these ratings provide an entirely accurate assessment[,] . . . [o]verall, the Web site is well designed, extremely helpful, and amusing." By acknowledging that the Web site's ratings cannot be relied on as "accurate," Kim shows readers her judgment is thoughtful and measured. She also shows readers that her judgment is based on criteria or standards of judgment that readers would be likely to consider appropriate for judging the kind of subject being evaluated. As she develops her argument, Kim takes up each criterion in the order she introduced it. For example, her first reason is articulated in the opening sentence of paragraph 2: "The design of RateMyProfessors.com makes the site attractive and easy to browse." This sentence serves as the topic sentence for paragraphs 2–4. Paragraphs 5–7 address her second reason, and paragraph 8 develops her third reason.

An important way writers establish criteria is through comparison. In paragraphs 10-11, for example, Kim compares RateMyProfessor.com to three other professor evaluation Web sites. Whereas Kim makes an in-depth comparison, Hulbert makes only a passing reference to *Knocked Up*, another social problem film about unplanned pregnancy (par. 8). She uses the comparison to support her argument about the complexity of *Juno*'s plot and its thoughtful representation of marriage and child-rearing.

Hulbert's argument is built on a single criterion which she asserts in her opening paragraph: "But among *Juno*'s distinctive charms is that it seems to have disarmed both sides of the family values debate." She goes on in the beginning of the next paragraph to claim that the film defuses "polarized positions on the hot-button issues" related to this debate. For readers to take her argument seriously, they need first to regard the standard she is using as appropriate to evaluating a film about a vexing social issue. Then, they have to determine if the film succeeds according to the standard being applied.

To analyze how Hulbert supports her judgment of *Juno,* try the following:

- Consider whether it is appropriate that a film like *Juno*, which is about a heated cultural issue, should be judged by how effectively it undermines stereotypes and assumptions on all sides of the issue, "undercutting" what Hulbert calls "pro-life and pro-choice purism" (par. 5).

- Write a few sentences explaining why you think Hulbert's criterion is or is not appropriate for judging a film like *Juno*.

● An Effective Counterargument

Most film reviews appear when the film is initially released. Consequently, they seldom refer to other reviews. Hulbert's review, however, appeared some time after *Juno*'s release, so she is able to acknowledge other reviews (the original *Slate* Web page included a link) and to quote one of them, A. O. Scott's *New York Times* review. Moreover, when she refers to the "newspaper headlines" (another link) that "announced a rise in the teenage birth rate," Hulbert describes the special context for her evaluation — what she calls "the family values debate."

To see how Hulbert acknowledges alternative judgments of *Juno*, try the following:

- Reread paragraph 1 where Hulbert sets up an opposition between what she labels the "liberal-media headquarters" (the *New York Times*) and "anti-Hollywood moralizers."

- Reread paragraphs 2–5 underlining the other labels Hulbert uses to categorize opposing points of view.

- Write a few sentences describing how Hulbert represents the cultural division in American society regarding the family values debate. Add another sentence or two giving an example of how, according to Hulbert, *Juno* attempts to break down these oppositional categories.

● A Readable Plan

Writing for *Slate*, Hulbert can expect readers to be fairly well-educated and knowledgeable about current political and cultural issues. Consequently, she can assume her readers will know what she's talking about when she titles her essay "*Juno* and the Culture Wars" and refers to "the family values debate." She can also assume that if they do not know some of her vocabulary (such as *wry*, *eponymous*, and *pieties* in par. 1), they will look up the words with which they are unfamiliar. Hulbert cannot assume, however, that her readers will be able to follow her argument if she does not provide signposts along the way to signal when she is shifting from one topic to another.

To analyze how Hulbert uses transitions to help readers follow her argument, try these suggestions:

- Reread the first sentence of paragraph 4, where Hulbert provides a transition that identifies the topic she is about to discuss ("the roster of family values issues") as well as the topic she has just addressed (Juno's "image").

- Look back at the preceding paragraphs and note in the margin where Hulbert discusses the topic of Juno's image.

- Skim paragraphs 4–6 and note in the margin where Hulbert brings up several different family values issues.

- Write a few sentences describing how effectively Hulbert guides the reader through the argument.

STILL PHOTOGRAPH OF *JUNO*'S MAIN CHARACTERS

Write a paragraph or two in which you analyze the photograph Hulbert includes in her evaluation essay and explain what it contributes to the essay.

To analyze the photo, start with the questions below (adapted from the Criteria for Analyzing Visuals in Chapter 20 on pp. 675–77):

People

- Why do you think Hulbert chose a still photograph that shows the two main characters, Juno and Bleeker?

- If you have not seen the film, what would you infer about Juno and Bleeker and their relationship from this picture?

- How would you describe their age, gender, subculture, ethnicity, and socio-economic class?

- What do the facial expressions and body language tell you about power relationships and attitudes?

Composition

- What is the focal point of the photograph — the place your eyes are drawn to?

- What does this focal point bring to your attention? What does it suggest about the characters or their relationship?

- How is color used — for example, to draw your attention, to connect images, or something else?

Rhetorical Context

- How does the photograph's portrayal of Juno and Bleeker correspond to Hulbert's descriptions of them in paragraphs 2 and 3?

- If you have seen the film, what is happening in the scene depicted in this photograph? What ideas and feelings do you think readers familiar with the film are likely to experience as they look at the photograph and read Hulbert's essay?

ANALYZING VISUALS

List several movies that you have seen recently, and choose one from your list that you recall especially well and about which you already have a strong overall judgment. Then consider how you would argue for your judgment. Specifically, what reasons do you think you would give your readers? Why do you assume that your readers would accept these reasons as appropriate for evaluating this particular kind of film? (Note that if you were actually to write about this movie, you would need to see it at least twice to develop your reasons and find supporting examples. For this activity, however, you do not have to view your film again.)

CONSIDERING TOPICS FOR YOUR OWN ESSAY

CHRISTINE ROMANO wrote the following essay when she was a first-year college student. In it she evaluates another student's argument essay, Jessica Statsky's "Children Need to Play, Not Compete," which appears in Chapter 6 of this book (pp. 270–74). Romano focuses not on the writing strategies or basic features of an essay arguing a position but rather on its logic — on whether the argument is likely to convince its intended readers — according to the standards presented in Chapter 12. You might want to review these standards on pp. 594–96 before you read Romano's evaluation. Also, if you have not already read Statsky's essay, you might want to do so now, thinking about what seems most and least convincing to you about her argument that competitive sports can be harmful to young children.

To learn about Romano's writing process, see A Writer at Work, pp. 443–44.

"Children Need to Play, Not Compete," by Jessica Statsky: An Evaluation
Christine Romano

Parents of young children have a lot to worry about and to hope for. In "Children Need to Play, Not Compete," Jessica Statsky appeals to their worries and hopes in order to convince them that organized competitive sports may harm their children physically and psychologically. Statsky states her thesis clearly and fully forecasts the reasons she will offer to justify her position: Besides causing physical and psychological harm, competitive sports discourage young people from becoming players and fans when they are older and inevitably put parents' needs and fantasies ahead of children's welfare. Statsky also carefully defines her key terms. By *sports*, for example, she means to include both contact and noncontact sports that emphasize competition. The sports may be organized locally at schools or summer sports camps or nationally, as in the examples of Peewee Football and Little League Baseball. She is concerned only with children six to twelve years of age. [1]

In this essay, I will evaluate the logic of Statsky's argument, considering whether the support for her thesis is appropriate, believable, consistent, and complete. While her logic *is* appropriate, believable, and consistent, her argument also has weaknesses. I will focus on two: Her argument seems incomplete because she neglects to anticipate parents' predictable questions and objections and because she fails to support certain parts of it fully. [2]

Statsky provides appropriate support for her thesis. Throughout her essay, she relies for support on different kinds of information (she cites eleven separate sources, including books, newspapers, and Web sites). Her quotations, examples, and statistics all support the reasons she believes competitive sports are bad for children. For [3] example, in paragraph 3, Statsky offers the reason that "overly competitive sports" may damage children's fragile bodies and that contact sports, in particular, may be especially hazardous. She supports this reason by paraphrasing Koppett's claim that muscle strain or even lifelong injury may result when a twelve-year-old throws curve balls. She then quotes Tutko on the dangers of tackle football. The opinions of both experts are obviously appropriate. They are relevant to her reason, and we can easily imagine that they would worry many parents.

Not only is Statsky's support appropriate, but it is also believable. Statsky quotes or summarizes authorities to support her argument in paragraphs 3–6, 8, 9, and 11. The question is whether readers would find these authorities credible. Since Statsky relies almost entirely on authorities to support her argument, readers must believe these authorities for her argument to succeed. I have not read Statsky's sources, but I think there are good reasons to consider them authoritative. First of all, the newspaper authors she quotes write for two of America's most respected newspapers, the *New York Times* and the *Los Angeles Times*. These newspapers are read across the country by political leaders and financial experts and by people interested in the arts and popular culture. Both have sports reporters who not only report on sports events but also take a critical look at sports issues. In addition, both newspapers have reporters who specialize in children's health and education. Second, Statsky gives background information about the authorities she quotes, which is intended to increase the person's believability in the eyes of parents of young children. In paragraph 3, she tells readers that Thomas Tutko is "a psychology professor at San Jose State University and coauthor of the book *Winning Is Everything and Other American Myths*." In paragraph 5, she announces that Martin Rablovsky is "a former sports editor for the *New York Times*," and she notes that he has watched children play organized sports for many years. Third, she quotes from two Web sites — the official Little League site and a message board. Parents are likely to accept the authority of the Little League site and be interested in what other parents and coaches (most of whom are also parents) have to say.

In addition to quoting authorities, Statsky relies on examples and anecdotes to support the reasons for her position. If examples and anecdotes are to be believable, they must seem representative to readers, not bizarre or highly unusual or completely unpredictable. Readers can imagine a similar event happening elsewhere. For anecdotes to be believable, they should, in addition, be specific and true to life. All of Statsky's examples and anecdotes fulfill these requirements, and her readers would find them believable. For example, early in her argument, in paragraph 4, Statsky reasons that fear of being hurt greatly reduces children's enjoyment of contact sports. The anecdote

4

5

comes from Tosches's investigative report on Peewee Football as does the quotation by the mother of an eight-year-old player who says that the children become frightened and pretend to be injured in order to stay out of the game. In the anecdote, a seven-year-old makes himself vomit to avoid playing. Because these echo the familiar "I feel bad" or "I'm sick" excuse children give when they do not want to go somewhere (especially school) or do something, most parents would find them believable. They could easily imagine their own children pretending to be hurt or ill if they were fearful or depressed. The anecdote is also specific. Tosches reports what the boy said and did and what the coach said and did.

Other examples provide support for all the major reasons Statsky gives for her position: 6

- That competitive sports pose psychological dangers — children becoming serious and unplayful when the game starts (par. 5)
- That adults' desire to win puts children at risk — parents fighting each other at a Peewee Football game and a coach setting fire to an opposing team's jersey (par. 8)
- That organized sports should emphasize cooperation and individual performance instead of winning — a coach banning scoring but finding that parents would not support him and a New York City basketball league in which all children play an equal amount of time and scoring is easier (par. 11)

All of these examples are appropriate to the reason they support. They are also believable. Together, they help Statsky achieve her purpose of convincing parents that organized, competitive sports may be bad for their children and that there are alternatives.

If readers are to find an argument logical and convincing, it must be consistent and complete. While there are no inconsistencies or contradictions in Statsky's argument, it is seriously incomplete because it neglects to support fully one of its reasons, it fails to anticipate many predictable questions parents would have, and it pays too little attention to noncontact competitive team sports. The most obvious example of this support comes in paragraph 11, where Statsky asserts that many parents are ready for children's team sports that emphasize cooperation and individual performance. Yet the example of a Little League official who failed to win parents' approval to ban scores raises serious questions about just how many parents are ready to embrace noncompetitive sports teams. The other support, a brief description of City Sports for Kids in New York City, is very convincing but will only be logically compelling to those parents who are already inclined to agree with Statsky's position. Parents inclined to disagree with Statsky would need additional evidence. Most parents know that big cities 7 receive special federal funding for evening, weekend, and summer recreation. Brief descriptions of six or eight noncompetitive teams in a variety of sports in cities, rural areas, suburban neighborhoods — some funded publicly, some funded privately — would be more likely to convince skeptics. Statsky is guilty here of failing to accept the burden of proof, a logical fallacy.

Statsky's argument is also incomplete in that it fails to anticipate certain objections and questions that some parents, especially those she most wants to convince, are almost sure to raise. In the first sentences of paragraphs 6, 9, and 10, Statsky does show that she is thinking about her readers' questions. She does not go nearly far enough, however, to have a chance of influencing two types of readers: those who themselves are or were fans of and participants in competitive sports and those who want their six- to twelve-year-old children involved in mainstream sports programs despite the risks, especially the national programs that have a certain prestige. Such parents might feel that competitive team sports for young children create a sense of community with a shared purpose, build character through self-sacrifice and commitment to the group, teach children to face their fears early and learn how to deal with them through the support of coaches and team members, and introduce children to the principles of social cooperation and collaboration. Some parents are likely to believe and to know from personal experience that coaches who burn opposing team's jerseys on the pitching mound before the game starts are the exception, not the rule. Some young children idolize teachers and coaches, and team practice and games are the brightest moments in their lives. Statsky seems not to have considered these reasonable possibilities, and as a result her argument lacks a compelling logic it might have had. By acknowledging that she was aware of many of these objections — and perhaps even accommodating more of them in her own argument, as she does in paragraph 10, while refuting other objections — she would have strengthened her argument.

Finally, Statsky's argument is incomplete because she overlooks examples of non-contact team sports. Track, swimming, and tennis are good examples that some readers would certainly think of. Some elementary schools compete in track meets. Public and private clubs and recreational programs organize competitive swimming and tennis competitions. In these sports, individual performance is the focus. No one gets trampled. Children exert themselves only as much as they are able to. Yet individual performances are scored, and a team score is derived. Because Statsky fails to mention any of these obvious possibilities, her argument is weakened.

The logic of Statsky's argument, then, has both strengths and weaknesses. The support she offers is appropriate, believable, and consistent. The major weakness is

8

9

10

incompleteness — she fails to anticipate more fully the likely objections of a wide range of readers. Her logic would prevent parents who enjoy and advocate competitive sports from taking her argument seriously. Such parents and their children have probably had positive experiences with team sports, and these experiences would lead them to believe that the gains are worth whatever risks may be involved. Many probably think that the risks Statsky points out can be avoided by careful monitoring. For those parents inclined to agree with her, Statsky's logic is likely to seem sound and complete. An argument that successfully confirms readers' beliefs is certainly valid, and Statsky succeeds admirably at this kind of argument. Because she does not offer compelling counterarguments to the legitimate objections of those inclined not to agree with her, however, her success is limited.

MAKING CONNECTIONS: COMPETITIVE TEAM SPORTS AND SOCIAL COOPERATION

Romano reasons in paragraph 8 that some parents "feel that competitive team sports for young children create a sense of community with a shared purpose, build character through self-sacrifice and commitment to the group, teach children to face their fears early and learn how to deal with them through the support of coaches and team members, and introduce children to the principles of social cooperation and collaboration."

With two or three other students, discuss this view of the role that sports plays in developing a child's sense of social cooperation.

- Begin by telling one another about your own, your siblings', or your children's experiences with team sports between the ages of six and twelve.
- Explain how participating in sports at this young age did or did not teach social cooperation. If you think team sports failed to teach cooperation or had some other effect, explain the effect it did have.

ANALYZING WRITING STRATEGIES

Basic Features

● A Well-Presented Subject

Christine Romano is writing for a uniquely academic rhetorical situation in that she has to assume that her readers — primarily her instructor, but also possibly other students — will have read the essay she is writing about and may even reread it with her evaluation in mind. Because she is responding to a specific assignment to evaluate a reading in the textbook, Romano can simply name the reading by title and author. Following her teacher's instructions, she refers to paragraphs rather than page numbers, and she does not include a formal works-cited page. If your instructor gives you the option of evaluating a reading — such as an essay, a story, or a poem — you may be required to cite the text using MLA style. For example, your list of works cited would cite Romano's essay this way:

Romano, Christine. "'Children Need to Play, Not Compete,' by Jessica Statsky: An
Evaluation." *The St. Martin's Guide to Writing.* 9th ed. Ed. Rise B. Axelrod and
Charles R. Cooper. Boston: Bedford, 2010. 402–06. Print.

For more information on citing sources, see Chapter 24.

In addition to identifying her subject, Romano begins her essay by summarizing Statsky's argument. To analyze how Romano represents the essay she is evaluating, try the following:

- Reread paragraph 1 and note in the margin the kinds of information about
  Statsky's essay Romano includes.

- Write a couple of sentences indicating the kinds of information Romano uses
  in her introductory paragraph. Add a sentence or two explaining why you think
  Romano chose to begin with this information.

● A Well-Supported Judgment

Writers who use textual evidence choose summarizing over quoting when they
want to emphasize a text's ideas rather than its language. They choose summarizing
over paraphrasing when they want to stress the source's main ideas or information
and skip the details.

Kim and Romano are both writing about texts, and they therefore rely primarily on textual evidence in the form of quotation, paraphrase, and summary. Kim,
for example, opens her essay by quoting the tagline for the RateMyProfessors.com
Web site: "Where the students do the grading." She also quotes extensively from
comments posted on the Web site in paragraph 7 to support her assertion that they
may be the most informative parts of the site. To acknowledge readers' concerns, she
quotes from several external sources in paragraphs 8 and 9.

In contrast, Romano quotes minimally and refers to no outside sources (following her teacher's instructions to focus solely on the text being evaluated): She
chooses instead to summarize or paraphrase passages from the text she is evaluating. Here is an example where Romano uses summary:

> In the anecdote, a seven-year-old makes himself vomit to avoid playing. (par. 5)

The original passage (Statsky, par. 4) includes dialogue and detail that Romano
decided was not needed to make her point. Her summary is concise, significantly
shorter than Statsky's original (ten instead of sixty-nine words, a reduction of more
than 85 percent). Here's an example of Romano's use of paraphrase:

> Besides causing physical and psychological harm, competitive sports discourage
> young people from becoming players and fans when they are older and inevitably
> put parents' needs and fantasies ahead of children's welfare. (par. 1)

Romano's paraphrase does not leave out very much detail or drastically condense
Statsky's original passage from paragraph 2 (thirty-one words in the paraphrase
compared to fifty-nine in the original, slightly less than a 50 percent reduction).

For additional information on using these strategies for presenting textual evidence, see Chapter 6, Working with Sources, pp. 307–8, Chapter 19, Arguing, pp. 667–68, and Chapter 24, Using Sources, pp. 759–64.

More important than whether the writer quotes, summarizes, or paraphrases is how the writer explains how the textual evidence supports the point being made. To analyze Romano's use of summary to support her evaluation, try the following:

- Reread paragraph 5 where the summary quoted above is presented, and examine Romano's explanation of what the summary demonstrates. Notice how many sentences Romano uses before and after the summary to introduce and explain it.
- Write a couple of sentences about how Romano introduces the summary and explains what it demonstrates. Why do you think she devotes so much space to explaining the summary rather than letting it speak for itself?

● An Effective Counterargument

Writers of evaluation sometimes need to respond to readers' possible objections to the argument, which they may either concede or refute. Wendy Kim, for example, anticipates several concerns readers are likely to raise about RateMyProfessors.com. In paragraphs 6 and 8, she concedes criticism of the Easiness and Hot categories, both of which she acknowledges are controversial, but she refutes the implicit claim that these categories really affect what students learn from the site. Similarly, she concedes that the ratings are not statistically valid, and while quoting the Web site's claim that they are nevertheless "uncannily accurate" (par. 9), she concludes that "students should not approach the ratings uncritically."

To analyze how Romano attempts to anticipate readers' possible objections and develop an effective counterargument, try the following:

- Read the Writer at Work section on pp. 443–44 to see how Romano was made aware by her classmates that readers might raise certain objections to Statsky's argument. Then reread paragraph 8 of her essay where Romano tries to counterargue. Which of the three strategies for counterarguing does she use — conceding the objection, accommodating it by making it part of her argument, or refuting it?
- Write a few sentences describing her counterargument strategy and why you think it is or is not effective.

● A Readable Plan

Writers of evaluative essays usually try to make their argument clear and direct. To do so, they typically state their essay's thesis and forecast their reasons early on. Romano, for example, states her plan explicitly in paragraph 2: "In this essay, I will evaluate the logic of Statsky's argument, considering whether the support for her thesis is appropriate, believable, consistent, and complete." Although Romano could have skipped this sentence, it does help readers understand the criteria she intends to apply.

The next sentence states her judgment that Statsky's argument meets the first three criteria, but falls short in the fourth criterion of completeness. This forecast of the reasons she will develop in the essay serves as a helpful map readers can use as they read her argument. Notice that Romano is careful to introduce these reasons in the order she first listed them — examining the appropriateness of Statsky's support in paragraph 3, believability in paragraphs 4–6, and consistency and completeness in paragraphs 7–9.

Romano also uses topic sentences and transitional words and phrases to make the organizational plan of her essay visible to readers.

To analyze how Romano helps her readers follow her argument, try the following:

- Reread paragraphs 3–9, and highlight the words *appropriate, believable, consistent,* and *complete.* (Highlight the words in any form they appear, for example, *incomplete*).

- Notice where these words appear in each paragraph, and whether they are used in topic sentences, transitions, or summaries.

- Write a couple of sentences assessing how well these key words help to keep readers oriented. Add a sentence or two describing where Romano tends to place them in a paragraph and why.

List several written texts you would consider evaluating. For example, you might include in your list an essay from one of the chapters in this book. If you choose an argument from Chapters 6–10, you could evaluate its logic, its use of emotional appeals, or its credibility. You might prefer to evaluate a children's book that you read when you were young or that you now read to your own children, a magazine for people interested in a particular topic like computers or cars, a scholarly article you read for a research paper, or a short story from Chapter 10. You need not limit yourself to texts written on paper; also consider texts available online. Choose one possibility from your list, and come up with two or three reasons why it is a good or bad text.

CONSIDERING TOPICS FOR YOUR OWN ESSAY

CHRISTINE ROSEN is a senior editor of the *New Atlantis: A Journal of Technology and Society,* where she writes about the social impact of technology, bioethics, and the history of genetics. Rosen has written several books, including *My Fundamentalist Education* (2005), *Preaching Eugenics* (2004), and *The Feminist Dilemma* (2001). She frequently appears on National Public Radio, CNN, and other news programs. Her essays have appeared in such prestigious venues as the *New York Times Magazine,* the *Washington Post,* the *Wall Street Journal,* and the *National Review.*

In this essay, which originally appeared in the *New Atlantis,* Rosen evaluates multitasking. As you read, think about your own experience with multitasking and what you think are its advantages and disadvantages.

The Myth of Multitasking

Christine Rosen

In one of the many letters he wrote to his son in the 1740s, Lord Chesterfield offered the following advice: "There is time enough for everything in the course of the day, if you do but one thing at once, but there is not time enough in the year, if you will do two things at a time." To Chesterfield, singular focus was not merely a practical way to structure one's time; it was a mark of intelligence. "This steady and undissipated attention to one object, is a sure mark of a superior genius; as hurry, bustle, and agitation, are the never-failing symptoms of a weak and frivolous mind."

In modern times, hurry, bustle, and agitation have become a regular way of life for many people — so much so that we have embraced a word to describe our efforts to respond to the many pressing demands on our time: *multitasking*. Used for decades to describe the parallel processing abilities of computers, multitasking is now shorthand for the human attempt to do simultaneously as many things as possible, as quickly as possible, preferably marshalling the power of as many technologies as possible.

> **Numerous studies have shown the sometimes-fatal danger of using cell phones and other electronic devices while driving, for example, and several states have now made that particular form of multitasking illegal.**

In the late 1990s and early 2000s, one sensed a kind of exuberance about the possibilities of multitasking. Advertisements for new electronic gadgets — particularly the first generation of handheld digital devices — celebrated the notion of using technology to accomplish several things at once. The word *multitasking* began appearing in the "skills" sections of résumés, as office workers restyled themselves as high-tech, high-performing team players. "We have always multitasked — inability to walk and chew gum is a time-honored cause for derision — but never so intensely or self-consciously as now," James Gleick wrote in his 1999 book *Faster*. "We are multitasking connoisseurs — experts in crowding, pressing, packing, and overlapping distinct activities in our all-too-finite moments." An article in the *New York Times Magazine* in 2001 asked, "Who can remember life before multitasking? These days we all do it." The article offered advice on "How to Multitask" with suggestions about giving your brain's "multitasking hot spot" an appropriate workout.

But more recently, challenges to the ethos of multitasking have begun to emerge. Numerous studies have shown the sometimes-fatal danger of using cell phones and other electronic devices while driving, for example, and several states have now made that particular form of multitasking illegal. In the business world, where concerns about time-management are perennial, warnings about workplace distractions spawned by a multitasking culture are on the rise. In 2005, the BBC reported on a research study, funded by Hewlett-Packard and conducted by the Institute of Psychiatry at the University of London, that found, "Workers distracted by e-mail and phone calls suffer a fall in IQ more than twice that found in marijuana smokers." The psychologist who led the study called this new "info-mania" a serious threat to workplace productivity. One of the *Harvard Business Review*'s "Breakthrough Ideas" for 2007 was Linda Stone's notion of "continuous partial attention," which might be understood as a subspecies of multitasking: using mobile computing power and the Internet, we are "constantly scanning for opportunities and staying on top of contacts, events, and activities in an effort to miss nothing."

Dr. Edward Hallowell, a Massachusetts-based psychiatrist who specializes in the treatment of attention deficit/hyperactivity disorder and has written a book with the self-explanatory title *CrazyBusy*, has been offering therapies to combat extreme multitasking for years; in his book he calls multitasking a "mythical activity in which people believe they can perform two or more tasks simultaneously." In a 2005 article, he described a new condition, "Attention Deficit Trait," which he claims is rampant in the business world. ADT is "purely a response to the hyper-kinetic environment in which we live," writes Hallowell, and its hallmark symptoms mimic those of ADD. "Never in history has the human brain been asked to track so many data points," Hallowell argues, and this challenge "can be controlled only by creatively engineering one's environment and one's emotional and physical health." Limiting multitasking is essential. Best-selling business advice author Timothy Ferriss also extols the virtues of "single-tasking" in his book, *The 4-Hour Workweek*. 5

Multitasking might also be taking a toll on the economy. One study by researchers at the University of California at Irvine monitored interruptions among office workers; they found that workers took an average of twenty-five minutes to recover from interruptions such as phone calls or answering e-mail and return to their original task. Discussing multitasking with the *New York Times* in 2007, Jonathan B. Spira, an analyst at the business research firm Basex, estimated that extreme multitasking — information overload — costs the U.S. economy $650 billion a year in lost productivity. 6

Changing Our Brains

To better understand the multitasking phenomenon, neurologists and psychologists have studied the workings of the brain. In 1999, Jordan Grafman, chief of cognitive neuroscience at the National Institute of Neurological Disorders and Stroke (part of the National Institutes of Health), used functional magnetic resonance imaging (fMRI) scans to determine that when people engage in "task-switching" — that is, multitasking behavior — the flow of blood increases to a region of the frontal cortex called Brodmann area 10. (The flow of blood to particular regions of the brain is taken as a proxy indication of activity in those regions.) "This is presumably the last part of the brain to evolve, the most mysterious and exciting part," Grafman 7 told the *New York Times* in 2001 — adding, with a touch of hyperbole, "It's what makes us most human."

It is also what makes multitasking a poor long-term strategy for learning. Other studies, such as those performed by psychologist René Marois of Vanderbilt University, have used fMRI to demonstrate the brain's response to handling multiple tasks. Marois found evidence of a "response selection bottleneck" that occurs when the brain is forced to respond to several stimuli at once. As a result, task-switching leads to time lost as the brain determines which task to perform. Psychologist David Meyer at the University of Michigan believes that rather than a bottleneck in the brain, a process of "adaptive executive control" takes place, which "schedules task processes appropriately to obey instructions about their relative priorities and serial order," as he described to the *New Scientist*. Unlike many other researchers who study multitasking, Meyer is optimistic that, with training, the brain can learn to task-switch more effectively, and there is some evidence that certain simple tasks are amenable to such practice. But his research has also found that multitasking contributes to the release of stress hormones and adrenaline, which can cause long-term health problems if not controlled, and contributes to the loss of short-term memory.

In one recent study, Russell Poldrack, a psychology professor at the University of California, Los Angeles, found that "multitasking adversely affects how you learn. Even if you learn while multitasking, that learning is less flexible and more specialized, so you cannot retrieve the information as easily." His research demonstrates that people use different areas of the brain for learning and storing new information when they are distracted: brain scans of people who are distracted or multitasking show activity in the striatum, a region of the brain involved in learning new skills; brain scans of people who are not distracted show activity in the hippocampus, a region involved in storing and recalling information. Discussing his research on National Public Radio recently, Poldrack warned, "We have to be aware that there is a cost to the way that our society is changing, that humans are not built to work this way. We're really built to focus. And when we sort of force ourselves to multitask, we're driving ourselves to perhaps be less efficient in the long run even though it sometimes feels like we're being more efficient."

If, as Poldrack concluded, "multitasking changes the way people learn," what might this mean for today's children and teens, raised with an excess of new entertainment and educational technology, and avidly multitasking at a young age? Poldrack calls this the "million-dollar question." Media multitasking — that is, the simultaneous use of several different media, such as television, the Internet, video games, text messages, telephones, and e-mail — is clearly on the rise, as a 2006 report from the Kaiser Family Foundation showed: in 1999, only 16 percent of the time people spent using any of those media was spent on multiple media at once; by 2005, 26 percent of media time was spent multitasking. "I multitask every single second I am online," confessed one study participant. "At this very moment I am watching TV, checking my e-mail every two minutes, reading a newsgroup about who shot JFK, burning some music to a CD, and writing this message."

8

9

10

The Kaiser report noted several factors that increase the likelihood of media multitasking, including "having a computer and being able to see a television from it." Also, "sensation-seeking" personality types are more likely to multitask, as are those living in "a highly TV-oriented household." The picture that emerges of these pubescent multitasking mavens is of a generation of great technical facility and intelligence but of extreme impatience, unsatisfied with slowness and uncomfortable with silence: "I get bored if it's not all going at once, because everything has gaps — waiting for a website to come up, commercials on TV, etc." one participant said. The report concludes on a very peculiar note, perhaps intended to be optimistic: "In this media-heavy world, it is likely that brains that are more adept at media multitasking will be passed along and these changes will be naturally selected," the report states. "After all, information is power, and if one can process more information all at once, perhaps one can be more powerful." This is techno-social Darwinism, nature red in pixel and claw.

Other experts aren't so sure. As neurologist Jordan Grafman told *Time* magazine: "Kids that are instant messaging while doing homework, playing games online and watching TV, I predict, aren't going to do well in the long run." "I think this generation of kids is guinea pigs," educational psychologist Jane Healy told the *San Francisco Chronicle*; she worries that they might become adults who engage in "very quick but very shallow thinking." Or, as the novelist Walter Kirn suggests in a deft essay in *The Atlantic*, we might be headed for an "Attention-Deficit Recession."

Paying Attention

When we talk about multitasking, we are really talking about attention: the art of paying attention, the ability to shift our attention, and, more broadly, to exercise judgment about what objects are worthy of our attention. People who have achieved great things often credit for their success a finely honed skill for paying attention. When asked about his particular genius, Isaac Newton responded that if he had made any discoveries, it was "owing more to patient attention than to any other talent."

William James, the great psychologist, wrote at length about the varieties of human attention. In *The Principles of Psychology* (1890), he outlined the differences among "sensorial attention," "intellectual attention," "passive attention," and the like, and noted the "gray chaotic indiscriminateness" of the minds of people who were incapable of paying attention. James compared our stream of thought to a river, and his observations presaged the cognitive "bottlenecks" described later by neurologists: "On the whole easy simple flowing predominates in it, the drift of things is with the pull of gravity, and effortless attention is the rule," he wrote. "But at intervals an obstruction, a set-back, a log-jam occurs, stops the current, creates an eddy, and makes things temporarily move the other way."

To James, steady attention was thus the default condition of a mature mind, an ordinary state undone only by perturbation. To readers a century later, that placid portrayal may seem alien — as though depicting a bygone world. Instead, today's multitasking adult may find something more familiar in James's description of the youthful mind: an "extreme mobility of the attention" that "makes the child seem to belong less to himself than to every object which happens to catch his notice." For some people, James noted, this challenge is never overcome; such people only get their work done "in the interstices of their mind-wandering." Like Chesterfield, James believed that the transition from youthful distraction to mature attention was in large part the result of personal mastery and discipline — and so was illustrative of character. "The faculty of voluntarily bringing back a wandering attention, over and over again," he wrote, "is the very root of judgment, character, and will."

Today, our collective will to pay attention seems fairly weak. We require advice   16
books to teach us how to avoid distraction. In the not-too-distant future we may even employ new devices to help us overcome the unintended attention deficits created by today's gadgets. As one *New York Times* article recently suggested, "Further research could help create clever technology, like sensors or smart software that workers could instruct with their preferences and priorities to serve as a high tech 'time nanny' to ease the modern multitasker's plight." Perhaps we will all accept as a matter of course a computer governor — like the devices placed on engines so that people can't drive cars beyond a certain speed. Our technological governors might prompt us with reminders to set mental limits when we try to do too much, too quickly, all at once.

Then again, perhaps we will simply adjust and come to accept what James   17
called "acquired inattention." E-mails pouring in, cell phones ringing, televisions blaring, podcasts streaming — all this may become background noise, like the "din of a foundry or factory" that James observed workers could scarcely avoid at first, but which eventually became just another part of their daily routine. For the younger generation of multitaskers, the great electronic din is an expected part of everyday life. And given what neuroscience and anecdotal evidence have shown us, this state of constant intentional self-distraction could well be of profound detriment to individual and cultural well-being. When people do their work only in the "interstices of their mind-wandering," with crumbs of attention rationed out among many competing tasks, their culture may gain in information, but it will surely weaken in wisdom.

MAKING CONNECTIONS: ADVANTAGES AND DISADVANTAGES OF MULTITASKING

Rosen cites research studies that show multitasking can have a number of negative effects, such as increasing stress, making learning less flexible, having difficulty focusing attention on a single task, and tending to be easily distracted, impatient, and bored.

With two or three other students, discuss whether your experience with multitasking confirms these studies:

- Begin by telling one another how you typically multitask — what kinds of tasks you usually juggle at one time.
- Explain what you see as the advantages and disadvantages of multitasking, and whether you have experienced any of the negative effects Rosen writes about.

- Consider whether multitasking is better for certain kinds of tasks than others, and whether you limit multitasking or practice what Timothy Ferriss calls "single-tasking" for any particular kind of task or situation.

ANALYZING WRITING STRATEGIES

●●●●
Basic Features

A Well-Presented Subject

Whereas the other writers in this chapter evaluate various kinds of texts — Kim reviews the effectiveness of a Web site, Hulbert judges the quality of a film, and Romano assesses the logic of an essay arguing a position — the subject of Rosen's evaluative essay is a phenomenon that she can confidently expect her readers to know firsthand. Nevertheless, she presents the subject by defining *multitasking* and giving examples of it.

To analyze how Rosen presents her subject, try the following:

- Reread paragraph 2 and highlight the definition of multitasking.
- Skim the rest of the essay, highlighting examples of multitasking.
- Write a sentence or two explaining how Rosen defines multitasking. Add another sentence indicating whether her explanation of what constitutes multitasking is the same as yours. (Do not comment now on how she judges multitasking; focus only on how she defines it.)

A Well-Supported Judgment

To support their arguments, writers of evaluative essays provide various kinds of evidence such as statistics, quotations from authorities, research reports, and examples. Here are some of the ways the other writers in this chapter use examples.

Kim uses parentheses to give a series of examples in paragraph 7:

> The site also gives students warnings ("He's ****in' hard. Fails half his class." or "OMG, one of the worst teachers I've ever had . . .").

Hulbert uses dashes to set out her examples:

> Early on, she jokes about herself as the kind of freaky girl — "with horn-rimmed glasses and vegan footwear and Goth makeup" or Converse All-Stars and cello skills — whom jocks secretly want. (par. 3)

Romano also uses dashes but she combines them with a bulleted list of items cited from Statsky, including this example (from paragraph 6 of Romano's essay):

- That adults' desire to win puts children at risk — parents fighting each other at a Peewee Football game and a coach setting fire to an opposing team's jersey (par. 8).

She also simply refers readers to several passages in the essay she's evaluating to illustrate her point:

> "In the first sentences of paragraphs 6, 9, and 10, Statsky. . . ." (par. 8).

Rosen relies primarily on authorities and research studies to support her argument about the value of multitasking. Because she is not writing for an academic audience, she does not include formal citations. But she does provide readers with enough information about her sources — the lead researcher's name and academic affiliation, often together with the publication in which the report appeared — so that they could do further research.

To analyze how Rosen uses authorities and research studies to support her argument, try the following:

- Reread paragraphs 4–9 and highlight the names of authorities and the research studies Rosen cites.

- Choose two sources and determine how Rosen uses them to support her argument.

- Write a couple of sentences explaining how Rosen uses sources to support her evaluative argument. Add another sentence or two speculating on how convincing these sources are likely to be for Rosen's readers.

⬢ An Effective Counterargument

Writers reviewing certain kinds of subjects such as films and live performances can usually assume their readers will be less familiar with the subject than they are, and that readers may not have formed a judgment themselves or even be aware of the arguments supporting alternative judgments of the subject. Writing about a phenomenon that her readers are likely to have experienced firsthand, however, Rosen has to assume that many of her readers will have a judgment of multitasking that differs from the one she is advocating. Consequently, Rosen's entire essay can be seen as an attempt to refute alternative judgments.

To refute a judgment she expects readers to favor, Rosen tries to *reframe* the argument about the value of multitasking. Reframing is a common strategy writers use when they expect their readers' ideas have been strongly influenced. To help readers see the subject in a new way, Rosen tries to set up an opposition between focused attention and multitasking that makes multitasking seem less preferable. She uses Lord Chesterton's letters advising his son and William James's ideas about psychology to associate focused attention with maturity and intelligence, and multitasking with immaturity and a lack of intelligence or at least the inability to think properly.

To analyze how Rosen uses reframing to counterargue the alternative judgment, try the following:

- Reread paragraphs 1–3 and 13–17, highlighting the words Rosen uses to develop this opposition.

- To analyze the system of oppositions Rosen sets up, you could try using a critical reading strategy described in Chapter 12: making a two-columned chart (pp. 592–93). List the words Rosen associates with focused attention in one column and the words she associates with multitasking in the other column; then put an asterisk next to the word that Rosen values more highly — for example, *maturity* as opposed to *immaturity*.

■ Write a couple of sentences describing how Rosen uses this system of oppositions to reframe readers' ideas about multitasking.

● A Readable Plan

Writers sometimes use headings to make it easy for readers to follow the argument. In long or complicated essays, headings can be especially helpful.

To analyze how Rosen uses headings, try the following:

■ Skim the essay, noting how each heading functions.

■ Write a few sentences describing the function of the headings and indicating whether you think they are helpful.

List several trends that interest you and that engender debate — for example, our increasing reliance on the Internet for research (Wikipedia) and news (Google News), social networking (Facebook), blogging, and microblogging (Twitter); the use of emoticons in formal writing; our fascination with reality television; and so forth. Choose one trend from your list about which you already have a strong overall judgment. Then consider how you would argue for your judgment. Specifically, what reasons do you think you would give your readers for evaluating the trend as you do? Why do you assume that your readers would accept these reasons as appropriate?

CONSIDERING TOPICS FOR YOUR OWN ESSAY

Beyond the Traditional Essay: Justifying an Evaluation

Most of us have opinions on anything that interests us, and many of us offer these opinions readily, in writing, through speech, or even by gesture (a "thumbs up" or a simple grimace can be remarkably effective in making an opinion known). As you've seen so far in this chapter, however, more than a simple opinion is required for an evaluation: Effective examples of evaluation include a well-presented subject; a clear, well-supported overall judgment; an effective counterargument; and a readable plan.

Evaluations are nevertheless among the most common and popular forms of written expression: reviews of movies, restaurants, books, theater, sports events, and so on, are ubiquitous in print and online. Many reviews are written by experts; increasingly,

Choosing the right shoe

Like ordinary shoes, running shoes consist of an upper and a sole. But there the similarity ends, as the cutaway of the shoe below shows.

1 The upper. These days, leather is out; most running shoes have breathable synthetic mesh. The toe box should be roomy enough to let toes spread. The heel counter should keep your heel from slipping excessively.

2 The midsole. Or middle layer provides most of the cushioning. The midsole is usually made of shock-absorbing foam and may incorporate gel or air sacs and plastic torsion supports.

3 The insole. Or sock liner, is the layer nearest the foot, provides added shock absorption and arch support. It's removable and washable in all the shoes we tested.

The sole. The bottom layer, usually carbon rubber, is segmented for flexibility and grooved for traction.

4 The reflector. Some uppers have large reflective areas, for those who run after dark.

5 Lacing. Fabric, plastic, or metal speed-lacing loops make tightening easier. Extra top eyelets provide a snug fit at the ankle.

send to a friend   print this article

Used with permission from Consumers Union of United States, Inc.

however, especially online, nonexperts — ordinary people who use the products or otherwise take a special interest in them — also contribute evaluations of a wide range of products and services. Sites such as Trip Advisor (www.tripadvisor.com) advertise themselves as an online community of "real travelers," as opposed to experts and industry insiders, who rate hotels, destinations, and the like from a perspective that closely matches that of other travelers. Most online shopping sites also allow consumers to evaluate products online for the benefit of those who have not yet hit "buy." Typically, such sites allow for "objective" ratings (for example, a score from 1 to 10) and prose commentary. In an interesting acknowledgment that not all evaluations are created equal, some of these sites encourage visitors to rate another individual's ratings (as, for example, "helpful" or "not helpful").

As you work on your own project, you might want to consult some of these alternative forms of evaluation for inspiration. If the format in which you are working allows for it — if, for example, you are creating a poster, Web site, or video — you should consider taking advantage of the strategies available to those working in multimedia — for example, by embedding artifacts that are relevant to the evaluation you are making. In some cases — as, for example, in the example here from *Consumer Reports.org,* which explains the criteria used for *Consumer Reports'* ratings of athletic shoes — the addition of an illustration can be invaluable. (Always remember to properly document any material you might use that was created by someone else.)

Guide to Writing

The Writing Assignment

Write an essay evaluating a specific subject. Examine your subject closely, and make a judgment about it. Give reasons for your judgment that are based on widely recognized criteria or standards for evaluating a subject like yours. Support your reasons with examples and other details primarily from your subject.

This Guide to Writing will help you apply what you have learned about how writers clearly present a subject; make a clear, well-supported judgment about it; present an effective counterargument to objections and alternative judgments; and make the whole thing readable. The Guide is divided into five sections with various activities in each section:

- Invention and Research
- Planning and Drafting
- Critical Reading Guide
- Revising
- Editing and Proofreading

The Guide is designed to escort you through the writing process, from finding a subject to editing your finished essay. Your instructor may require you to follow the Guide to Writing from beginning to end. Working through the Guide to Writing in this way will help you — as it has helped many other college students — write a thoughtful, fully developed, polished essay.

If, however, your instructor gives you latitude to choose and if you have had experience writing an essay in which you justify an evaluation, then you can decide on the order in which you will do the activities in the Guide to Writing. For example, the Invention and Research section includes activities to help you find a subject to write about, explore it, analyze and define your audience and purpose, and formulate a tentative judgment of it, among other things. Obviously, finding a subject must precede the other activities, but you may come to the Guide with a subject already in mind, and you may choose to make a tentative judgment before considering your own and your readers' likely criteria. In fact, you may find your response to one of the invention activities expanding into a draft before you have had a chance to do any of the other activities. That is a good thing — but you should later flesh out your draft by going back to the activities you skipped and layering the new material into your draft.

The following chart will help you find answers to many of the questions you might have about planning, drafting, and revising an essay justifying an evaluation. The page references in the Where to Look column refer to examples from the readings and activities in the Guide to Writing.

To learn about using the *Guide* e-book for invention and drafting, go to **bedfordstmartins.com/ theguide.**

Starting Points: Justifying an Evaluation

●●●● **Basic Features**

	Question	Where to Look
A Well-Presented Subject	How do I come up with a subject to write about?	• Considering Topics for Your Own Essay (pp. 401, 409, 417) • Choosing a Subject to Write About (pp. 421–23) • Testing Your Choice (p. 425) • Clarifying Your Purpose and Audience (p. 429)
	What is my purpose in writing? How can I present my subject clearly and convincingly?	• Reading Essays Justifying Evaluations: Purpose and Audience (pp. 388–89) • Defining Your Purpose for Your Readers (p. 428) • Presenting the Subject (pp. 429–30)
A Well-Supported Judgment	How do I come up with a reasonable evaluation?	• Ways In: Bringing the Subject and Your Audience into Focus (pp. 423–24) • Making a Tentative Judgment (p. 425) • Researching Your Argument (p. 427)
	How do I construct an argument supporting my judgment?	• Ways In: Developing Your Argument and Counterargument (p. 426) • Your Reasons and Support (p. 430) • Working with Sources: Using Summary (pp. 434–35)
An Effective Counterargument	How do I respond to possible objections and to alternative judgments?	• Ways In: Developing Your Argument and Counterargument (p. 426) • Your Counterargument of Objections or Alternative Judgments (p. 430) • Two sentence strategies (pp. 432–33)
A Readable Plan	How can I help my readers follow my argument?	• Designing Your Document (p. 427) • Formulating a Tentative Thesis Statement (p. 428) • Outlining Your Draft (pp. 431–32) • Writing the Opening Sentences (p. 432) • Thinking about Document Design: Using Images to Support an Argument (pp. 439–41)

Invention and Research

The following invention activities are easy to complete and take only a few minutes. Spreading out the activities over several days will stimulate your creativity, enabling you to consider many more potential issues to address and possible ways in which to address them. Remember to keep a written record of your invention work: you'll need it when you draft the essay and later when you revise it.

Choosing a Subject to Write About

List several subjects that you might like to explore. This will come more easily to some of us than to others. As you explore possibilities, bear in mind that you are looking for a subject that meets the following criteria:

Criteria for Choosing a Subject: A Checklist	The subject should be ☐ one that has strengths and/or weaknesses you could write about; ☐ one that you can examine closely, that you can view and review; ☐ one typically evaluated according to criteria or standards of judgment that you understand.

If you are like most people, you will need some help in coming up with a number of good options. Review the Considering Topics for Your Own Essay activities following the readings, and recall any subjects those suggestions brought to mind. For further ideas, consult the suggestions in the following sections.

Listing Subjects

Make a list of subjects you might consider writing about. Because you will need to spend considerable time analyzing your subject, consider subjects that you can examine and reexamine, such as Web sites, DVDs, written texts, software programs, and the like. To get started, consider the suggestions below, organized by broad category:

- *Culture:* Film or television series, computer game, recorded performance, artist, individual work of art, museum, amusement park
- *Written work:* Essay, poem, short story, Web site, magazine, textbook, campus publication
- *Education:* Your high school, a particular program or major you are considering, a science lab, a teacher
- *Government:* Elected official or candidate for public office, proposed or existing law, agency, or program

- *A Particular Community:*
  - Evaluate how well one of the following meets the needs of residents of your town or city: the public library, health clinic, neighborhood watch or block parent program, meals-on-wheels program, theater or symphony.
  - Evaluate how well one of the following serves the members of your religious community: a religious school, youth or senior group, choir, building.
- *A Particular Career/Workplace:*
  - Evaluate a job you have had or currently have, or evaluate someone else you have observed closely, such as a coworker or supervisor.
  - Evaluate a local job-training program, either one in which you have participated or one where you can observe and interview trainees.

Using the Web to Find or Explore a Subject

Exploring Web sites can provide you with an idea of what to write about, if you have not already chosen a subject, and it can enrich your understanding of a subject you have already chosen. Moreover, the Web provides a rich repository of cultural and historical information, including photographs and music, which you might be able to use to create a richly detailed, multimedia text for your readers.

Here are some suggestions:

- If you do not yet have a subject but have an idea of what broad category interests you — films, music, books, computer games, software, technology, etc. — look for sites that evaluate such things and get a sense of what criteria people usually use when evaluating them.
- If you have already chosen a subject to evaluate, find out how others have judged it and the criteria they have used in their evaluation. You may find points on which you agree as well as disagree that you can use in your essay to support your judgment or to counterargue.

Make notes of any ideas suggested by your online research, and download any visuals you might include in your essay, being sure to get the information necessary to cite any online sources. (See pp. 774–76 for the MLA citation guidelines for electronic sources.)

Familiarizing Yourself with the Subject

Before making a choice, take some time to study your subject and take notes on what seem to be its strengths and weaknesses. The best subject is one you can view and review — for example, a DVD, Web site, printed text, software program, or piece of equipment. If you plan to evaluate a film or recorded performance, for example, you will want to have it on DVD or in digital form so that you can reexamine parts and possibly capture stills or a video clip.

Be aware that some subjects will require special planning. Evaluating a one-time performance or sports event that cannot be recorded is especially challenging because it requires advance planning (such as considering the criteria you expect to apply as you judge the performance), careful note-taking during the performance, and time devoted right after the performance to adding to and clarifying your notes. If you are evaluating something like a government agency or a campus program or lab, you will need to get permission to do field research, making observations and interviewing people.

Ways In: Bringing the Subject and Your Audience into Focus

Basic Features

Once you've made a preliminary choice of a subject, the following activities will help you explore what you already know about your subject, determine what else you need to find out, and discover ways of presenting the subject to your readers. You can begin with whichever activity you want, but wherever you begin, be sure to return to the other activities to fill in the details.

Exploring What You Know about the Subject	Exploring What Your Readers Know about the Subject
Examine Your First Impressions of the Subject. *Write for a few minutes about what you currently know and think about your subject. Focus your writing by trying to answer one or both of these questions:* • What do I like and dislike about this subject? • What are the subject's strengths and weaknesses? Try to identify specific aspects of the subject and explain what it is about them that you think is good or bad, or strong or weak. What is important is not just your judgment (which may change as you think about the subject), but the kinds of things you choose to focus on. For example, if you were evaluating a particular sports event such as the Super Bowl, you might focus on the drama of the game, the quality of the defense, the performance of particular players, and so on.	**Identify Your Readers.** *Write several sentences describing your readers by answering the following questions:* • For what particular readers am I writing this evaluation? • What are these readers likely to know about my subject? Will I be introducing the subject to them (as in a typical film or book review), or will they already be familiar with it? • If my readers are already familiar with the subject, what do I expect them to like and dislike about it? • How might such factors as my readers' age, gender, education, socioeconomic status, work experience, religious or political affiliation affect their judgment of the subject?

(continued)

(continued)

Exploring What You Know about the Subject	Exploring What Your Readers Know about the Subject

Consider Your Criteria. Write for a few minutes considering your subject in light of the criteria or standards of judgment you typically apply to such subjects. The following questions may help you develop your thinking:

- *What kind of subject is it?* For example, if it is a film, what kind of film is it? Sometimes, subjects fit into more than one category — *Juno*, for instance, is a social problem film, but it is also an unconventional romantic comedy. Your judgment may depend on how you classify the subject and whether you appreciate that it pushes against conventional boundaries or stays within them.
- *What criteria or standards of judgment do you usually apply in evaluating a subject of this kind?* For example, you might evaluate a film like *Juno* in term of its plot, humor, acting, its realistic representation of "real" life situations and people, or, like Hulbert, on the way it handles controversial subject matter.
- *What other subjects of this kind does this particular subject make you think of and how do they compare to the subject you are evaluating now?*

Consider Your Readers' Likely Criteria. Write for a few minutes considering the criteria or standards of judgment your readers are likely to apply to subjects like yours. The following questions may help you develop your analysis:

- *How have your readers judged similar subjects in the past?* For example, if you are evaluating a film like *Juno*, consider whether your readers tend to like films about social issues, films with a strong female character, films with a quirky sense of humor, and so on.
- *Can you predict your readers' reaction to a subject like yours?* For example, given your readers' age, are they likely to appreciate films about teenagers? Given their religious or political affiliations, are they likely to appreciate films that challenge their point of view?
- *Can you predict the criteria your readers are likely to apply to your subject?* For example, if your readers live in the suburbs, a small town, or the inner city, how might they judge a pregnant teenager with an attitude like Juno's?
- *Which of your readers' criteria do you share?* Can you build an argument for your judgment based on these criteria?
- *If your readers are not likely to share your criteria, how will you be able to explain and defend your judgment?*

Making a Tentative Judgment

Write a few sentences stating your current judgment of the subject. Try answering these two basic questions:

- In what ways is it a good example of this kind of subject?
- In what ways does it fall short?

Testing Your Choice

Now test your choice by asking yourself the following questions:

- Do I know enough about the subject, or can I learn enough in the time I have, to write an argument supporting my judgment?
- Are my readers likely to share my criteria, or will I be able to justify my criteria in a way that will assure my readers that my judgment makes sense even if they don't agree with me?

As you plan and draft your argument, you will probably want to consider these questions again. If at any point you cannot answer them with a confident *yes*, you may want to consider revising your evaluation or choosing a different subject to evaluate. If you have serious doubts, consider discussing them with your instructor.

A Collaborative Activity:
Testing Your Choice

Get together with two or three other students, and discuss the subjects you have tentatively chosen.

Presenters: Take turns briefly describing your subject and the judgment you plan to argue for.

Listeners: Explain to each presenter what criteria or standards of judgment you would use to evaluate a subject of this kind and how you think you would judge it. For example, would you judge a science-fiction film by the acting, ideas, special effects, or something else? Would you judge a lecture course by how organized the lectures are, whether images are shown, whether the tests reflect the lectures, or something else? In other words, tell the presenter what criteria you would apply to his or her particular subject.

Basic Features

●● Ways In: Developing Your Argument and Counterargument

The following activities will help you develop your argument by collecting reasons and evidence for your judgment and also develop your counterargument by anticipating readers' objections and alternative judgments. You can begin with whichever activity you want, but wherever you begin, be sure to return to the other activities to explore the possibilities.

Depending on what you already know about your subject, you could use the activities to develop an outline of your argument and then do research to fill in the details, or you could start with research (see p. 427).

Developing Your Argument	Counterarguing Readers' Likely Objections or Alternative Judgments

List Possible Reasons. *Write down at least two or three reasons for your judgment, but try for as many as five.* Some of these reasons will turn out to be more promising than others. Try listing your reasons as *because* statements — for example,

RateMyProfessors.com is good *because* it is well designed

or *because* it has useful information.

Anticipate a Likely Objection or Alternative Judgment. *Write a few sentences describing an objection or an alternative judgment you expect some readers to raise.* Consider whether readers base their criticism on different criteria or analyze the subject differently than you do.

Collect Evidence. *Make notes of the evidence — such as examples, authorities, textual evidence, images, statistics, and comparisons — you might be able to use to support each reason.* You may already have some evidence you could use. If you lack evidence for any of your reasons, you may need to collect additional material. (Make notes of your sources, perhaps in a working bibliography.)

Consider Whether to Concede or Refute the Objection. *Write a few sentences trying out a possible counterargument.* You may be able simply to acknowledge an objection or alternative judgment. If the criticism is serious, consider conceding the point and qualifying your judgment. You might also try to refute it by arguing that the standards you are using are appropriate and important. (For example, Hulbert could have expected some readers to argue that *Juno* is a conventional romantic film, based primarily on Juno's quirky character and the seemingly happy ending. If you were to counterargue, you might concede the point about Juno's character but refute the idea that the film has a happy, romantic ending.)

Choose Your Strongest Reasons. *Write several sentences on each reason, trying out the evidence you have that supports it.* Then identify the reasons you think are compelling. These may be the ones most likely to be convincing to your particular readers, but some of your best reasons may be based on criteria your readers have not thought of or may not value as highly as you do.

● Researching Your Argument

You may have identified questions you have about your subject and made notes about the kinds of information you need to support your argument and counterargument. Doing research with your questions and notes in mind will help you work efficiently. But researching sometimes is most productive when you have the time to go into unexplored territory. You may find support for the judgment you have made, but you also may find convincing opposing opinions and decide to modify your argument as a result.

If you are evaluating a subject that others have evaluated, you will want to do library and Internet research to find out what judgments they have made. If you are writing on an issue related to your school, community, or workplace, you may want to conduct interviews to see how people in those venues view the subject and how they react to your judgment.

If you do not know the criteria usually used to evaluate your subject, do some research. For example, if you are reviewing a particular kind of film, read a few recent reviews of the same kind of film you are reviewing, noting the standards that reviewers typically use and the reasons that they assert for liking or disliking that kind of film. If you are evaluating a soccer team, you could read about coaching or playing soccer or talk to an experienced soccer coach or player to learn about what makes an excellent team. If you are evaluating a civic, governmental, or religious program, look for information online or in the library about what makes a good program of its type. If you are evaluating an essay in this book, consult the standards suggested in the Purpose and Audience and the Basic Features sections of the chapter where the essay appears. If you are evaluating an argument essay from Chapters 6–10, you will find additional standards in Evaluating the Logic of an Argument, Recognizing Emotional Manipulation, and Judging the Writer's Credibility in Chapter 12 (pp. 594–98).

Designing Your Document

Think about whether your readers might benefit from design features such as headings or numbered or bulleted lists or from visuals such as drawings, photographs, tables, or graphs. Elements like these often make the presentation of a subject easier to follow and an argument more convincing. In thinking about possible visual aids to your argument, consider the ways in which effective speakers and writers draw upon visual information and evidence to support their claims. You might think back to compelling speeches or lectures you have heard, or to interesting debates or slide shows or campaign ads you have watched. You might also review Web pages for organizations making specific claims on their Web sites.

Also consider reviewing published essays to see how they use design elements and visuals to support and strengthen their arguments. Look back at the scenario on p. 384 describing a student's paper on the movies *Emma* and *Clueless,* and then read "Thinking about Document Design" on pp. 439–41 to see how the student used visuals to bolster its impact.

For more on document design, see Chapter 21. For guidelines on acknowledging sources, see Chapter 24.

Defining Your Purpose for Your Readers

Write a few sentences defining your purpose. Remember that you have already identified your readers and developed a tentative argument with these readers in mind. Try now to define your purpose by considering the following questions:

- If my readers are likely to agree with my overall judgment, what is my aim in writing — to confirm them in their judgment by giving them well-supported reasons for it; to help them refute others' judgments; or to suggest how they might respond to questions and objections?

- If my readers and I share criteria for making judgments of this kind but differ in the judgment we make about the subject, what is my aim in writing — to convince them to adopt my judgment or just to compel them to admit that my judgment is a legitimate one?

- If my readers have different standards of judgment, should I try to convince them to consider seriously the criteria I am using?

Formulating a Tentative Thesis Statement

Write several sentences that could serve as your thesis statement. Think about how you should state your overall judgment — how emphatic you should make it, whether you should qualify it, and whether you should include in the thesis a forecast of your reasons and support. Remember that a strong thesis statement should be clear, arguable, and appropriately qualified. As you consider your overall judgment, keep in mind that readers of evaluative essays expect writers to present a balanced evaluation of a subject by pointing out strengths as well as weaknesses. At the same time, however, readers expect to encounter a definitive judgment, not a vague, wishy-washy, or undecided judgment.

Review the readings in this chapter to see how other writers construct thesis statements. For example, Romano uses the thesis statement to forecast her reasons as well as to express her overall judgment. She begins by indicating the standards she thinks are appropriate for evaluating her subject. Her thesis statement shows that she bases her reasons on these standards. In addition, it lets readers know in advance what she likes about the subject she is evaluating as well as what she does not like: "While [Statsky's] logic *is* appropriate, believable, and consistent, her argument also has weaknesses" (par. 2). Romano makes her thesis statement seem thoughtful and balanced, but there is no ambivalence or confusion about her judgment. She is clear and emphatic, not vague or wishy-washy.

As you draft your own tentative thesis statement, think carefully about the language you use. It should be clear and unambiguous, emphatic but appropriately qualified. Although you will most likely refine your thesis statement as you draft and revise your essay, trying now to articulate it will help give direction and impetus to your planning and drafting.

For more on thesis and forecasting statements, see Chapter 19.

Planning and Drafting

The following activities will help you review what you have accomplished so far, refine your purpose, set goals for your draft, and outline it. In addition, this section will help you draft, with advice on writing opening sentences, using effective sentence strategies, and working with sources.

Refining Your Purpose and Setting Goals

Before starting to draft, review the questions below, which are designed to help you sharpen your purpose for your audience and set goals for your draft. Your instructor may ask you to write out your answers to some of these questions or simply to think about them as you plan and draft your essay.

Clarifying Your Purpose and Audience

- What do I want my readers to think about the subject after reading my evaluation? Do I want them to appreciate the subject's strengths and weaknesses, as Kim, Rosen, and Romano do? Or do I want them to see why it succeeds (as Hulbert does) or fails?

- Should I assume, like Hulbert and Rosen, that my readers may have read other evaluations of my subject? Or should I assume that I am introducing readers to the subject, as Kim and Romano seem to do?

- How should I present myself to my readers — as someone who is an expert on the subject (perhaps like Hulbert) or as someone who has examined the subject closely (like Kim and Romano)? Should I convey enthusiasm (as Kim and Hulbert do) or strike a more balanced, distanced tone (as Rosen and Romano do)?

The Beginning

- How can I capture readers' attention from the start? Should I begin by naming and describing the subject, as Kim and Romano do? Should I open with a quote (like Rosen) or a reference to current events (like Hulbert)?

- When should I state my judgment — at the beginning of the opening paragraph; in the middle, like Romano; at the end, like Kim and Hulbert; or should I wait until later in the essay, as Rosen does?

- Should I forecast the reasons for my judgment in the first couple of paragraphs, as Kim, Romano, and Hulbert do?

Presenting the Subject

- How should I identify the subject? In addition to naming it, as all the writers in this chapter do, should I place it in a recognizable category or genre, as Kim does when she talks about "Internet professor evaluation sites" (par. 10) or Hulbert does when she talks about "the culture wars" (title and par. 1)?

- What about the subject should I describe? Can I use visuals to illustrate, as Kim and Hulbert do? Should I place the subject historically, as Rosen does, or politically, as Hulbert does?
- If the subject has a story, how much of it should I tell? Should I simply set the scene and identify the characters, or should I give details of the plot, even at the risk of spoiling the surprise, as Hulbert does?

Your Overall Judgment

- How should I state my thesis? Should I forecast my reasons early in the essay, as Kim, Romano, and Hulbert do? Should I place my thesis at the beginning or wait until after I have provided a context, as Rosen does?
- How can I convince readers to consider my overall judgment seriously even if they disagree with it? Should I try to present a balanced judgment by praising some things and criticizing others, as all the writers but Hulbert do?

Your Reasons and Support

- How can I present my reasons and the criteria on which they are based? Should I try to justify my criteria, as Romano does by asserting the authority of her textbook; as Kim does by telling readers she took a class in Web site design; or as Rosen does by citing research studies and other experts? Can I assume that my readers will share my criteria, as Hulbert does when she praises the film for taking "aim at everybody's pieties"?
- If I have more than one reason, how should I order them? Should I begin with my strongest reason or with the one I think is most likely to appeal to my readers, as Kim does when she begins with the Web site's design and navigability? In an evaluation that is generally positive, should I begin with the strengths of my subject and end with its weaknesses, as Romano does?
- How can I support my reasons — with example, paraphrase, and summary, as all the writers do? Should I quote the text, as Kim, Romano, and Hulbert do? Can I call on authorities and cite statistics, as Kim and Rosen do?

Your Counterargument of Objections or Alternative Judgments

- What objections or alternative judgments should I anticipate? Should I assume that my readers will favor a subject I am criticizing, as Rosen does?
- Should I concede legitimate objections and qualify my judgment, as Romano and Kim do? Or should I devote my essay to refuting the alternative judgment, as Rosen does?

The Ending

- How should I conclude? Should I try to frame the essay by echoing something from the opening or from another part of the essay, as Rosen and Hulbert do?

- Should I conclude by restating my overall judgment, as all the writers do?
- Should I include a rhetorical question at the end, as Kim does?

Outlining Your Draft

An evaluative essay contains as many as four basic parts:

1. Presentation of the subject
2. Judgment of the subject
3. Presentation of reasons and support
4. Consideration of readers' objections and alternative judgments

These parts can be organized in various ways. If, for example, you expect readers to disagree with your judgment, you could show them what you think they have overlooked or misjudged about the subject. You could begin by presenting the subject; then you could assert your thesis, present your reasons and support, and anticipate and refute readers' likely objections, as illustrated in the following rough outline:

   I. Presentation of the subject
  II. Thesis statement (judgment)
 III. First reason and support
  IV. Anticipation and refutation of objection
   V. Second reason and support
  VI. Anticipation and accommodation of objection
 VII. Conclusion

If you expect some of your readers to disagree with your negative judgment even though they base their judgment on the same standards on which you base yours, you could try to show them that the subject really does not satisfy your shared standards. You could begin by restating these standards and then demonstrating how the subject fails to meet them:

   I. Establish shared standards
  II. Acknowledge alternative judgment
 III. State thesis (judgment) that subject fails to meet shared criteria
  IV. First reason and support showing how subject falls short
   V. Second reason and support
      (etc.)
  VI. Conclusion

There are, of course, many other possible ways to organize an evaluative essay, but these outlines should help you start planning your own essay.

Consider any outlining you do before you begin drafting to be tentative. Never be a slave to an outline. As you draft, you will usually see ways to improve your

For more on outlining, see Chapter 11.

original plan. Be ready to revise your outline, shift parts around, or drop or add parts as you draft. If you use the outlining function of your word processing program, changing your outline will be simple, and you may be able to write the essay simply by expanding the outline.

Drafting

If you have not already begun to draft your essay, this section will help by suggesting how to write your opening sentences; how to use the sentence strategies of comparison and contrast and balance; and how to summarize your subject. Drafting is not always a smooth process, so do not be afraid to leave spaces where you do not know what to put in or to write notes to yourself about what you could do next. If you get stuck while drafting, go back over your invention writing. You may be able to copy and paste some of it into your evolving draft, or you may find that you need to do some additional invention to fill in details in your draft.

Writing the Opening Sentences

You could try out one or two different ways of beginning your essay — possibly from the list below — but do not agonize over the first sentences because you are likely to discover the best way to begin only after you have written a rough draft. Again, you might want to review your invention writing to see if you have already written something that would work to launch your essay.

To engage your readers' interest from the start, consider the following opening strategies:

- an anecdote, quote, or personal reminiscence (like Rosen)
- a surprising or provocative statement (like Romano)
- an assertion of an issue's increasing or immediate significance (like Hulbert)
- statistics (like Kim)
- a research study
- a scenario
- an historical analogy
- criticism of an alternative position

Two Sentence Strategies

Comparing and Contrasting Your Subject with Similar Ones. As you draft an essay evaluating a subject, you may want to compare or contrast your subject with similar subjects to provide a frame of reference for them and to establish for readers your authority to evaluate the subject. To do so, you will need to use sentences that clearly and efficiently express comparisons or contrasts. These sentences often make use of key comparative terms like *more, less, most, least, as, than, like, unlike, similar,* or *dissimilar.*

Let us begin with three examples from Wendy Kim's essay "Grading Professors":

> Still, RatingsOnline is *better* designed and includes *more helpful* information than the other two competitors, and it may even be *better* than RMP in terms of helpfulness. (par. 11)

> The ratings categories on RatingsOnline also seem *more specific* than on RMP. (11)

> In its design and potential helpfulness, RatingsOnline is a very good site but *not* likely to be *as good as* RMP because its user base appears to be *smaller*. (11)

In these sentences Kim compares Web sites that allow students to evaluate their instructors. The first sentence compares RatingsOnline and three other sites, including RateMyProfessors.com (RMP). In the second and third examples, she narrows the match-up to what she considers the two best Web sites, pointing out their relative strengths and weaknesses.

In the following example, Hulbert describes an event in *Juno* by referring to a similar event in the film *Knocked Up*:

> He — spoiler alert — stages a display of *just the kind of* egotistical guy regression that regularly induces female groans on the right and left, and that *Slate*'s Meghan O'Rourke recently examined in <u>this piece</u> about *Knocked Up*. (par. 8)

Note that Hulbert leaves the task of making the full comparison to the reader, which in the original version she facilitates by inserting a hyperlink (underlined) to another online review.

Balance Criticism and Praise. You should in most cases try to present a balanced evaluation of your subject, by criticizing one or more aspects of it if you generally praise it or by praising one or more aspects of it if you generally criticize it. To do so, you will need to use sentences that clearly and efficiently express comparisons or contrasts. In general, sentences that do this rely on words expressing contrast — *but, although, however, while,* and so on — to set up the shift between the two responses.

Praise followed by criticism:

> This information could be useful in helping students decide which classes to take, *but* only if there are enough reviews posted. (Kim, par. 11)

> . . . Statsky does show that she is thinking about her readers' questions. She does not go nearly far enough, *however,* to have a chance of influencing two types of readers. (Romano, par. 8)

> The picture that emerges of these pubescent multitasking mavens is of a generation of great technical facility and intelligence *but* of extreme impatience, unsatisfied with slowness and uncomfortable with silence. (Rosen, par. 11)

Criticism followed by praise:

> Here Cody's politics (presumably pro-choice) are at odds with her plot needs (a birth) and, who knows, maybe commercial dictates, too, if studios worry about antagonizing the evangelical audience. It's a tension the screenplay finesses deftly, undercutting both pro-life and pro-choice purism. (Hulbert, par. 5)

For more on using sentences of comparison and contrast in evaluations, go to **bedfordstmartins .com/theguide** and click on Sentence Strategies. For illustrations of comparisons and contrasts in different kinds of writing, see Chapter 18.

For more on using sentences that balance criticism and praise in evaluations, go to **bedfordstmartins .com/theguide** and click on Sentence Strategies.

Notice that the last example does not use an explicitly comparative term to set up the contrast. In her first sentence, Hulbert implies that there is a contradiction in the film that some would consider a flaw; in her second sentence, however, Hulbert states that the screenplay resolves the seeming contradiction in a way that makes it, in her view, more successful.

In addition to using sentences that make comparisons or contrasts with other subjects and sentences that balance criticism and praise, you can strengthen your evaluation with other kinds of sentences as well. You may want to review the information about using appositives (pp. 170–71) and writing sentences introducing concession and refutation (pp. 306–7).

Working with Sources:
Using Summary to Support Your Evaluative Argument

Writers of evaluation often use summary to support their argument. As the following examples show, evaluations may summarize an expert source (as Kim does in her Web site evaluation and Rosen does in her article on multitasking), the plot of a film or video game (as Hulbert does in her film review), or an aspect of an essay or story (as Romano does in her evaluation of another essay in this book), to name just a few of the more common uses of summary.

> The results are statistically invalid, as one psychology professor explained, because the users are self-selected and not selected randomly (Harmon). (Kim, par. 9)

> In 2005, the BBC reported on a research study, funded by Hewlett-Packard and conducted by the Institute of Psychiatry at the University of London, that found, "Workers distracted by e-mail and phone calls suffer a fall in IQ more than twice that found in marijuana smokers." (Rosen, par. 4)

> In the anecdote, a seven-year-old makes himself vomit to avoid playing. (Romano, par. 5)

> Pregnant Juno at first reflexively embraces abortion as the obvious option, and her best friend is at the ready with phone numbers. . . . But just when pro-lifers might be about to denounce this display of secular humanist decadence, Juno stomps out of the clinic, unable to go through with it. (Hulbert, par. 5)

To get a better understanding of how summaries can support an evaluative argument, let us look closely at another example of summarizing, from paragraph 3 of Christine Romano's essay. This summary, highlighted below, supports Romano's argument that Statsky provides "appropriate" support:

> Her quotations, examples, and statistics all support the reasons she believes competitive sports are bad for children. For example, in paragraph 3, Statsky offers the reason that "overly competitive sports" may damage children's fragile bodies and that contact sports, in particular, may be especially hazardous. She supports this reason by paraphrasing Koppett's claim that muscle strain or even lifelong injury may result when a twelve-year-old throws curve balls. She then quotes Tutko on the dangers of tackle football. The opinions of both experts are obviously appropriate. They are relevant to her reason, and we can easily imagine that they would worry many parents.

To understand how this summary works, compare it to the original:

Statsky's Original (paragraph 3)

One readily understandable danger of overly competitive sports is that they entice children into physical actions that are bad for growing bodies. Although the official Little League Web site acknowledges that children do risk injury playing baseball, they insist that severe injuries . . . are infrequent, the risk "far less than the risk of riding a skateboard, a bicycle, or even the school bus" ("What about My Child?"). Nevertheless, Leonard Koppett in *Sports Illusion, Sports Reality* claims that a twelve-year-old trying to throw a curve ball, for example, may put abnormal strain on developing arm and shoulder muscles, sometimes resulting in lifelong injuries (294). Contact sports like football can be even more hazardous. Thomas Tutko, a psychology professor at San Jose State University and coauthor of the book *Winning Is Everything and Other American Myths*, writes:

> I am strongly opposed to young kids playing tackle football. It is not the right stage of development for them to be taught to crash into other kids. Kids under the age of fourteen are not by nature physical. Their main concern is self-preservation. They don't want to meet head on and slam into each other. But tackle football absolutely requires that they try to hit each other as hard as they can. And it is too traumatic for young kids. (qtd. in Tosches A1)

Romano not only repeats Statsky's main ideas in a condensed form (reducing 220 words to 105), but she also describes Statsky's moves as a writer:

Statsky offers the reason . . .

She supports this reason by paraphrasing Koppett's claim . . .

She then quotes Tutko . . .

Romano's description of each step in Statsky's argument shows readers exactly how Statsky uses her sources in constructing her argument.

Notice that in her summary, Romano puts quotation marks around only one of the phrases she borrows from Statsky ("overly competitive sports"). The most likely reason for this is that Romano considers the designation "overly competitive sports" debatable. She may have decided not to use quotation marks around other borrowed phrases such as *contact sports* and *tackle football* because they are common expressions and not specific to Statsky.

Because Romano makes it perfectly clear when she is re-presenting her source's language and ideas, and also includes careful citations to indicate where in the original text the material comes from, she could not be accused of plagiarism. Remember, though, that putting quotation marks around quoted words and phrases will eliminate any possible misunderstanding. If you are unsure about whether you need quotation marks, consult your instructor.

For additional information on summary, quotation, and paraphrase, see Chapter 24, Using Sources, pp. 756–64.

Critical Reading Guide

Basic Features

For a printable version of this Critical Reading Guide, go to **bedfordstmartins** **.com/theguide.**

Your instructor may arrange a peer review session in class or online where you can exchange drafts with your classmates and give each other a thoughtful critical reading, pointing out what works well and suggesting ways to improve the draft. This Critical Reading Guide can also be used productively by a tutor in the writing center or by a roommate or family member.

A good critical reading does three things: it lets the writer know how the reader understands the point of the essay, praises what works best, and indicates where the draft could be improved.

1. Evaluate how well the subject is presented.

   Summarize: Tell the writer what you understand the specific subject of the evaluation to be and the kind of subject it is.

   Praise: Point to a place where the subject is presented effectively — for example, where it is described vividly and accurately, where it is named, or where it is clearly placed in a recognizable genre or category.

   Critique: Tell the writer where readers might need more information about the subject, and whether any information about it seems inaccurate or possibly only partly true. Suggest how the writer could clarify the kind of subject it is, either by identifying the category by name or giving examples of familiar subjects of the same type.

2. Assess how well the judgment is supported.

   Summarize: Tell the writer what you understand the overall judgment to be and the criteria on which it is based.

   Praise: Identify a passage in the essay where support for the judgment is presented effectively — for example, note particularly strong supporting reasons; appeals to criteria readers are likely to share; or especially compelling evidence.

   Critique: Let the writer know if you cannot find a thesis statement or think it is vague or overstated. Tell the writer where the argument could be improved — for example, suggest another reason that could be added; propose a way to justify one of the criteria on which the argument is based; or recommend a source or an example that could be used to bolster the support for the argument.

3. Consider how effectively objections and alternative judgments are counterargued.

   Praise: Identify a passage in the essay where the writer counterargues an objection or alternative judgment effectively. An effective counterargument may include making a concession — for example, agreeing that a subject the writer is primarily criticizing has some good points, or the subject has weaknesses as well as strengths.

Critique: Tell the writer where counterargument is needed or could be made more effective — for example, suggesting a likely objection or alternative judgment that should be taken into account, helping the writer understand the criteria behind an alternative judgment, or pointing to an example that could be used to refute an objection.

4. Assess how readable the argument is.

Praise: Give an example of where the essay succeeds in being readable — in its overall organization; clear presentation of the thesis; an effective opening or closing; or by other means.

Critique: Tell the writer where the readability could be improved. Can you, for example, suggest a better beginning or more effective ending? If the overall organization of the essay needs work, make suggestions for rearranging parts or strengthening connections.

5. If the writer has expressed concern about anything in the draft that you have not discussed, respond to that concern.

Making Comments Electronically Most word processing software offers features that allow you to insert comments directly into the text of someone else's document. Many readers prefer to make their comments this way because it tends to be faster than writing on hard copy and space is virtually unlimited; it also eliminates the process of deciphering handwritten comments. Where such features are not available, simply typing comments directly into a document in a contrasting color can provide the same advantages.

Revising

Very likely you have already thought of ways to improve your draft, and you may even have begun to revise it. In this section is a Troubleshooting chart that may help. Before using the chart, however, it is a good idea to do the following:

- Review critical reading comments from your classmates, instructor, or writing center tutor.
- Make an outline of your draft so that you can look at it analytically.

You may have made an outline before writing your draft, but after drafting you need to see what you actually wrote, not what you intended to write. You can outline the draft quickly by highlighting the basic features — presenting the subject, making and supporting an evaluation, effectively anticipating objections and alternative judgments, and making the argument readable.

For an electronic version of this Troubleshooting chart, go to **bedfordstmartins** **.com/theguide.**

Troubleshooting Your Draft

● ● ● ● Basic Features

	Problem	Suggestions for Revising the Draft
A Well-Presented Subject	The subject is not identified or is vague.	☐ Identify the subject by name — such as the title and author, or director and main characters. ☐ Describe the subject — summarize what it is about, cite statistics that establish its importance, or give examples to make it concrete. ☐ Consider adding visuals — photographs, graphs, tables, or charts — if these would help clarify the subject.
	It is not clear what kind of subject it is.	☐ Classify the subject by naming the genre or category a subject of this kind fits into. ☐ Refer to other reviews or reviewers of subjects of this kind. ☐ Compare your subject to other, better known subjects of the same kind.
A Well-Supported Evaluation	My thesis or overall judgment is not clear.	☐ State your thesis early in the essay. ☐ Clarify the language in your thesis statement to indicate what your judgment is overall. ☐ Qualify your thesis if it seems overstated or does not correspond to your argument. ☐ Consider whether your judgment is in fact arguable. If you cannot provide reasons and support, then your judgment probably is not arguable. Consult your instructor about modifying your judgment or writing about a different subject.
	My readers are not convinced that my evaluation is reasonable and/or persuasive.	☐ Clarify the criteria on which you base your argument and try to justify them — by citing authorities or other reviews of similar subjects, by making comparisons, or by explaining why your criteria are appropriate and perhaps preferable to other criteria readers may be more familiar with. ☐ Add additional support for your reasons — quoting respected experts or research studies, providing facts or statistics, giving specific examples, or citing textual evidence in the form of quotation, summary, or paraphrase.
	My readers do not understand my evaluation.	☐ Go over the way you present your evaluation; if necessary, explain it and your supporting reasons more clearly. ☐ Try outlining your argument to be sure that the overall organization and coherence is strong; if it is not, try rearranging parts or strengthening connections.

(continued)

(continued)

An Effective Counter-argument	My readers raise objections I haven't considered or find fault with my counterargument.	☐ Consider whether new objections need to be answered. Not every objection requires a response, so think about whether you can ignore it or dismiss it as only a minor concern. ☐ Take seriously important objections that undermine your argument. Try to refute them — showing they are not based on widely held or appropriate criteria, or that they misunderstand your argument or the subject. ☐ If objections cannot be refuted, acknowledge them but demonstrate that they do not make your evaluation invalid. Try using sentence openers like *I understand that . . . , but what I think is,* and *It is true that . . . , but my point is. . . .*
	My readers have proposed alternative judgments or find fault with my handling of alternatives.	☐ Address the alternative judgments directly in your essay. Concede good or bad qualities of the subject others emphasize, even if you disagree on the overall value of the subject. ☐ Point out where you and your readers agree on criteria but perhaps disagree on how well the subject meets the criteria. ☐ Where you and your readers disagree on criteria, try to justify the standards you are applying by citing authorities or establishing your own authority.
A Readable Plan	My readers are confused by my essay, or find it difficult to read.	☐ Review the overall organization of your essay by outlining it. If necessary, move, add, or delete sections to strengthen coherence. ☐ Consider adding a forecasting statement early in your essay. ☐ Repeat your key terms to keep readers oriented. ☐ Check to see that your reasons are introduced clearly through the use of topic sentences. ☐ Check to be sure that you provide appropriate transitions between sentences, paragraphs, and sections of your essay. Pay particular attention to these transitions at points where your readers indicate the greatest trouble in following your argument. ☐ Review your opening and closing paragraphs. Be sure that your overall judgment is clear and appropriately qualified.

In his comparison of the films *Emma* and *Clueless*, the student author described on p. 384 of this chapter selected movie stills to accompany his written text. He collected a number of stills from each film and chose two contrasting images that would best illustrate his argument that *Emma*, the film, looks more like Austen's England, but that *Clueless*, with its emphasis on today's social and cultural norms and its setting in contemporary suburban California, better captures the satirical spirit of the novel.

The writer used the still from *Emma* of Emma and Knightley dancing to emphasize the film's attention to aesthetics and romance. Details such as the hanging

Thinking About Document Design:

Using Images to Support an Argument

garlands, the ornate woodwork, the women's similar pale-toned dresses, the style of dancing, and the musicians in the background create an image of aristocratic wealth and elegance that, the student argues, satisfies audience expectations for a romantic period piece but obscures an important part of the novel's message.

To illustrate the flavor of *Clueless*, the student chose the picture of Cher descending the stairs wearing a minidress and an outrageous hat, with shopping bags, water bottle in its holder, and cell phone. This over-the-top satiric image in *Clueless*,

Perillo 3

Emma the film (1996) is better at capturing the feel of the period than the intricacies of social dynamics. (See Fig. 1.) Though the characters come from a range of social classes, their homes and clothing look more similar than not: in the end, social distinctions get paved over for the audience's aesthetic expectations of a romance and of a period piece.

Fig. 1. *Emma*, dir. Douglas McGrath, perf. Gwyneth Paltrow, Toni Colette, Alan Cumming, and Jeremy Northam (Miramax, 1996; film).

Clueless (1995), though it could not look less like Austen's England, better captures the spirit of the novel. Cher, who never leaves her cell phone at home and shops on Rodeo Drive, is both the consummate brat and the consummate charmer. (See Fig. 2.) In its portrayal of Cher, the film parallels the novel's attention to *Emma*'s preoccupation with social status.

Fig. 2. *Clueless*, dir. Amy Heckerling, perf. Alicia Silverstone, Stacey Dash, Brittany Murphy, and Paul Rudd (Paramount, 1995; film).

the student argued, was designed to emphasize the social and economic distinctions in the novel. The image captures the ridiculousness of Cher in her obvious displays of wealth and posturing. While admired and well liked by her peers, she is also naive and too well-off for her own good.

The student builds to a concluding point that Cher's interest in reforming Tai is a result of her confidence that she could help someone to become as stylish and savvy as herself. Just as the novel makes fun of Emma for her lack of critical self-awareness, the student argued, so does *Clueless* make fun of Cher.

Editing and Proofreading

Our research indicates that particular errors occur often in essays that justify an evaluation: incomplete and illogical comparisons, and short, choppy sentences. The following guidelines will help you check your essay for these common errors.

Complete, Correct Comparisons

The Problem. In essays that justify an evaluation, writers often engage in comparison — showing, for example, that one film is stronger than another, a new recording is inferior to an earlier one, or one restaurant is better than another. When comparisons are expressed incompletely, illogically, or incorrectly, however, the point of the comparison can be dulled or lost completely.

How to Correct It. Reread your comparisons, checking for completeness, logic, and correctness.

A comparison is complete if two terms are introduced, and the relationship between them clearly expressed:

▶ *Jazz* is as good, ^as^ if not better than, Morrison's other novels.

▶ I liked the Lispector story because it's so different ^*from anything else I've ever read.*^

A comparison is **logical** if the terms compared are parallel (and therefore comparable):

▶ Will Smith's Muhammad Ali is more serious than any ^other^ role he's played.

▶ Ohio State's offense played much better than ~~Michigan.~~ ^*Michigan's did.*^

Note that *different from* is correct; *different than*, while commonly used, is incorrect:

▶ Carrying herself with a confident and brisk stride, Katherine Parker seems

different ^*from*^ ~~than~~ the other women in the office.

▶ Films like *Pulp Fiction* that glorify violence for its own sake are different ^*from*^ ~~than~~ films like *Apocalypse Now* that use violence to make a moral point.

A Note on Grammar and Spelling Checkers
These tools can be helpful, but do not rely on them exclusively to catch errors in your text: Spelling checkers cannot catch misspellings that are themselves words, such as *to* for *too*. Grammar checkers miss some problems, sometimes give faulty advice for fixing problems, and can flag correct items as wrong. Use these tools as a second line of defense after your own (and, ideally, another reader's) proofreading/editing efforts.

For practice, go to bedfordstmartins.com/ theguide/exercisecentral and click on Comparisons.

Combining Sentences

The Problem. When writers justify an evaluation, they generally present their subject in some detail — defining it, describing it, placing it in some context. Inexperienced writers often present such details one after another, in short, choppy sentences. These sentences can be difficult or irritating to read, and they provide the reader with no help in determining how the different details relate to each other.

How to Correct It. Combine sentences to make your writing more readable, and to clarify the relationships among ideas. Two common strategies for sentence combining involve converting full sentences into **appositive phrases** (a noun phrase that renames the noun or pronoun that immediately precedes it) or **verbal phrases** (phrases using words derived from verbs that function as adjectives, adverbs, or nouns). Consider the following example:

► In paragraph 5, the details provide a different impression, ~~It is a comic or~~
    based on
perhaps even pathetic impression, ~~The impression comes from~~ the boy's

attempts to dress up like a real westerner.

From three separate sentences, this writer smoothly combines details about the "different impression" into a single sentence, using an appositive phrase ("a comic or perhaps even pathetic impression") and a verbal phrase ("based on the boy's attempts to dress up like a real westerner").

Here are two additional examples of the first strategy (conversion into an appositive phrase):

► "Something Pacific" was created by Nam June Paik, ~~He is~~ a Korean artist who is considered a founder of video art.

"Talkin' John Birch Paranoid Blues,"
► One of Dylan's songs ridiculed the John Birch Society. ~~This song was called "Talkin' John Birch Paranoid Blues."~~

Finally, here are two additional examples of the second strategy (conversion into a verbal phrase):

carrying
► Spider-Man's lifesaving webbing sprung from his wristbands, ~~They carried~~ Mary Jane Watson and him out of peril.

enticing
► The coffee bar flanks the bookshelves, ~~It entices~~ readers to relax with a book.

For practice, go to
bedfordstmartins.com/ theguide/exercisecentral
and click on Combining Sentences.

A Writer at Work

Christine Romano's Counterargument of Objections

In this section, we look at how Christine Romano tried to anticipate her readers' objections. The final revision of Romano's evaluation essay appears in this chapter on pp. 402-06; Statsky's argument essay (which Romano evaluates) appears in Chapter 6 (pp. 270–74).

Using the Exploring What Your Readers Know about the Subject activities (pp. 423–24) in this chapter's Guide to Writing, Romano identified two kinds of readers: her instructor, whom she assumed would approve of her using the textbook standards, and parents of young children, the same audience that Statsky addresses. Romano acknowledged that parents would not know the textbook standards, but she speculated that they, like her, would be impressed by the way Statsky supports her position. Romano noted also that she expected parents to be sympathetic to Statsky's position because they would not want their children to be hurt playing sports. Because she was applying the criteria for evaluating logical arguments that are presented in Chapter 12 of this textbook, she felt confident that the criteria on which she based her overall judgment of Statsky's argument would also be important to her readers, especially her instructor and fellow students.

After writing for a few minutes on the Testing Your Choice activity (p. 425), Romano worked with a group of students in class on A Collaborative Activity: Testing Your Choice (p. 425). One of her group's members told her that he had been hurt playing in a Little League baseball game and had wanted to quit but that his dad had made him continue playing. He remembered crying and trying to get out of going to the next game. But looking back on the experience now, he said he was glad his father insisted because years later, when playing on the high school football team, he realized that being a serious athlete meant facing up to the fear and pain of injury. He said this was an important lesson, one that applied to everything in life, not just to playing sports. Therefore, the student told Romano, his criterion for judging competitive sports for young children was how well the experience taught them to stick it out to conquer their pain and fear.

This student's choice of criteria made Romano realize that Statsky's argument does not adequately address this compelling alternative judgment. When Romano planned and wrote her first draft, she tried to accommodate this student's point of view and others like it. In addition to praising the appropriateness, believability, and consistency of Statsky's argument, she criticized the argument for being incomplete: "[Statsky] neglects to anticipate parents' predictable questions and objections" (par. 2).

A few days later, Romano received some helpful advice from another student who read her draft. Using the Critical Reading Guide in this chapter (pp. 436–37), the student noted that she could not find a clear statement of the thesis (overall judgment) in the draft. She guessed that it might be hinted at in the final paragraph, but she was not sure what Romano's judgment was and urged Romano to state it clearly. Here is the draft version of Romano's final paragraph that the student reader commented on:

I have been able to point out both strengths and weaknesses in the logic of Statsky's support for her argument. The strengths are appropriateness, believability, and consistency. The major weakness is incompleteness — a failure to anticipate more fully the likely objections of a wide range of readers. I have been able to show that her logic would prevent certain kinds of parents from taking her argument seriously, parents whose experience and whose children's experience of team sports lead them to believe that the gains are worth whatever risks may be involved and who believe that many of the risks Statsky points out can be avoided by careful monitoring. For parents inclined to agree with her, however, her logic is likely to seem sound and complete. An argument that successfully confirms readers' beliefs is certainly valid, and Statsky succeeds admirably at this kind of argument.

The student reader also noted that she thought Romano's draft essay was well supported by textual evidence and examples. She said she found the praise of the strengths of Statsky's argument convincing but found the criticism of its weaknesses equally convincing. Therefore, she concluded by asking Romano to clarify her overall judgment.

This request hit home because Romano had been trying to give Statsky's essay a mixed review but was not sure how well her own judgment was coming across. Romano was reassured that her critical reader thought her argument was convincing, but she saw that she needed to clarify which criteria carried the most weight for her. She revised the last paragraph, adding this final sentence to make her thesis more explicit and let readers see exactly which standards were most important in her evaluation of Statsky's argument:

Because she does not offer compelling counterarguments to the legitimate objections of those inclined not to agree with her, however, her success is limited.

Thinking Critically About What You Have Learned

In this chapter, you have learned a great deal about this genre from reading several essays that justify an evaluation and from writing one of your own. To consolidate your learning, it is helpful to think metacognitively; that is, to reflect not only on what you learned but on how you learned it. Following are two brief activities your instructor may ask you to do.

Reflecting on Your Writing

Your instructor may ask you to turn in with your essay and process materials a brief metacognitive essay or letter reflecting on what you have learned about writing your essay justifying an evaluation. Choose among the following invention activities those that seem most productive for you.

- Explain how your purpose and audience influenced *one* of your decisions as a writer, such as how you presented the subject, the strategies you used in justifying your evaluation, or the ways in which you attempted to counter possible objections.

- Discuss what you learned about yourself as a writer in the process of writing this particular essay. For example, what part of the process did you find most challenging? Did you try anything new, like getting a critical reading of your draft or outlining your draft in order to revise it?

- If you were to give advice to a friend who was about to write an essay justifying an evaluation, what would you say?

- Which of the readings in this chapter influenced your essay? Explain the influence, citing specific examples from your essay and from the reading.

- If you got good advice from a critical reader, explain exactly how the person helped you — perhaps by questioning the way you addressed your audience or the kinds of support you offered in support of your position.

Considering the Social Dimensions: Evaluators' Hidden Assumptions

Good evaluative writing provides readers with reasons and support for the writer's judgment. However, the writer's personal experiences, cultural background, and political ideology are also reflected in written evaluations. Even the most fair-minded evaluators write from the perspective of their particular ethnicity, religion, gender, age, social class, sexual orientation, academic discipline, and so on. Writers seldom make their assumptions explicit, however. Consequently, while the reasons for an evaluation may make it seem fair and objective, the writer's judgment may result from hidden assumptions that even the writer has not examined critically.

1. *Choose one reading from this chapter, and try to identify one of the hidden assumptions of its writer.* Think of a personal or cultural factor that may have influenced the writer's judgment of the subject. For example, how do you imagine that Romano's gender may have influenced her judgment of Statsky's essay on competitive sports for children?

2. *Reflect on your own experience of writing an evaluation essay.* How do you think factors such as gender, age, social class, ethnicity, religion, geographical region, or political perspective may have influenced your own evaluation? Recall the subjects that you listed as possibilities for your essay and how you chose one to evaluate. Also recall how you arrived at your overall judgment and how you decided which reasons to use and which not to use in your essay.

3. *Write a page or two explaining your ideas about how hidden assumptions play a role in evaluation essays.* Connect your ideas to the readings in this chapter and to your own essay.

9

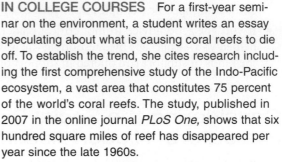

Speculating about Causes

IN COLLEGE COURSES For a first-year seminar on the environment, a student writes an essay speculating about what is causing coral reefs to die off. To establish the trend, she cites research including the first comprehensive study of the Indo-Pacific ecosystem, a vast area that constitutes 75 percent of the world's coral reefs. The study, published in 2007 in the online journal *PLoS One,* shows that six hundred square miles of reef has disappeared per year since the late 1960s.

To plan her argument, she examines a number of research studies in scientific journals as well as popular newsmagazine reports and discovers significant disagreement on the causes of the decline. After reviewing the evidence, she decides that increasing global warming is the most significant cause of the trend.

To gather support for this position, she does further research and eventually refines her argument, focusing on two effects of global warming — rising ocean temperatures and increasing carbon dioxide concentrations in the atmosphere — that she believes account for much of the die-off of coral reefs. In making her argument, she acknowledges that there are also some lesser but still important causes, such as overfishing, pollution runoff from agriculture, and damage from shipping.

IN THE COMMUNITY   In an op-ed piece for a community newspaper, the captain of a neighborhood watch committee speculates on the causes of neighborhood deterioration. He knows that there are a number of larger economic and sociological causes for the problem, but he thinks there might also be causes that neighbors could do something about. He has heard of the "broken windows" effect, so he goes to the public library and searches the Internet for information. Broken windows theory, he discovers, argues that small things like not fixing broken windows or cleaning up graffiti has a snowball effect that accelerates the deterioration of neighborhoods. He finds the March 1982 *Atlantic Monthly* article that introduced the theory as well as several books written subsequently. One book by a police commissioner argues strongly in support of the theory, while other books by political scientists and sociologists tend to be mixed, reporting statistical correlations but no definitive cause-effect relationship between things like unrepaired windows and serious crime.

In his op-ed piece, he is careful not to overstate his argument, but he cites his research and his own long experience in the neighborhood to support his claim that letting individual homes deteriorate has a negative effect on the neighborhood. He concludes that with foreclosure rates increasing and housing values decreasing, it is especially important that neighbors join together to help clean up the neighborhood, suggesting that a side effect would be to strengthen community ties.

IN THE WORKPLACE   After an incident in which her twelve-year-old son is disciplined in school, a science reporter comes up with an idea for an article speculating on the reasons for increasing intolerance in the United States of what she calls "boyish behavior." After getting the go-ahead from her editor, she begins reviewing recent research in medical journals, where she reads that boys are being diagnosed with various behavioral disorders at a far higher rate than girls. While reading, she notes that Tom Sawyer would today be diagnosed with attention-deficit hyperactivity disorder (ADHD) and put on medication — an idea that later becomes the opener for her article.

Drawing on her prior knowledge of the research on biological differences between boys and girls, she contends that these differences cannot account for the disparity in diagnoses. Instead, she argues that social, cultural, and economic changes explain it. She speculates that adults attempt to stamp out any early signs of aggression in boys, such as shouting or roughhousing, because our society has become extremely fearful of crime. In addition, because classrooms are increasingly group-oriented, boys' expressions of individuality are perceived by teachers as disruptive. Finally, the writer speculates that boys' fidgeting at their desks is seen as a threat to success in an economy that increasingly values sitting still and concentrating for seven or more hours a day.

Within a week after her article is published, she receives twenty-six e-mail responses from teachers accusing her of having no understanding of what it is like to try to teach in a rowdy classroom and only nine responses from teachers or parents praising her speculations as insightful.

447

We all quite naturally try to explain causes. Because we assume that everything has a cause, we predictably ask "Why?" when we notice something new or unusual or puzzling. The opening scenarios illustrate three contexts in which such questioning was worked out in writing. The college student concerned about the environment decided to try to explain why coral reefs are declining around the world. Prompted by an incident involving her son, the science reporter wondered whether some diagnoses of behavioral disorders in boys reflect cultural judgments rather than medical conditions and eventually wrote an article suggesting that they do. Finally, the neighborhood watch captain wondered whether the "broken windows" theory made any sense in neighborhoods like his own, did some research, and ultimately wrote an article suggesting that it could.

Many things can be fully and satisfactorily explained. It is possible to provide a conclusive answer to a question such as "Why is the sky blue?" But we can answer other questions only tentatively — for example, "Why have the college graduation rates for women surpassed the rates for men in the last fifty years?" or "Why are unemployment rates for African Americans higher than for other groups?" Questions such as these have only plausible, not definitive, explanations because often cause-effect relationships cannot be scientifically proven. Some have suggested, for example, that a possible cause for the gender disparity in college completion is that men watch more television than women do. Although there may be a statistical correlation between television watching and not completing college, a causal connection cannot be proven and, of course, there may be other possible causes that are more plausible. When we cannot offer a definitive causal explanation, we make arguments speculating about causes we think are the most **plausible** — that is, causes that likely play a significant role in bringing about the effect.

The essays that you will read in this chapter speculate about the causes of a *phenomenon* or *trend*. A **phenomenon** is a notable attitude or behavior among people — for example, the political influence of evangelical Christians or bullying among schoolchildren. A **trend** is a significant change that occurs over a period of time — for example, the *rise or decline* in the political influence of evangelical Christians or bullying among schoolchildren. Some of the writers in this chapter attempt to explain phenomena, such as the well-known master of horror fiction Stephen King, who tries to explain why the U.S. public loves horror movies. Other writers examine the possible causes of trends, such as Erica Goode, an award-winning journalist with a master's degree in social psychology, who tries to explain the recent epidemic of obesity in the United States. What is most interesting about these essays is their creativity. The writers have done their homework; they know about and acknowledge the predictable explanations. But their main purpose is to go beyond what their readers already think and offer new ways of understanding what may have caused the phenomenon or trend.

The readings in this chapter illustrate the basic features and strategies that writers typically use when speculating about causes. The activities following the readings will help you consider what is particular to one writer's approach and what strategies you might want to try out in writing your own essay. Finally, the Guide to Writing that follows the readings will support you as you compose your own essay speculating about causes. In your essay, you will establish that the phenomenon or trend exists and argue that one or more causes you propose are indeed plausible by offering your reasons and support and by countering readers' possible objections or preferred causes.

A Collaborative Activity:

Practice Speculating about Causes

To get a sense of this special kind of argument, choose a current trend or phenomenon and speculate about its causes.

Part 1. Get together with two or three other students and select one person to take notes.

- Choose a trend or phenomenon about which your group has ideas. For example, why do you think the rate of teenage smoking is declining (according to the December 2008 University of Michigan "Monitoring the Future" study)? Why do you think voter turnout was so heavy in the 2008 presidential election?

- Together, list as many likely causes for this trend or phenomenon as you can, including economic, cultural, and psychological causes.

- Select two or three causes that seem most plausible — in other words, causes that are most likely to be convincing.

Part 2. As a group, discuss your efforts.

- Where did your ideas about causes come from — the Internet, television, your own experience, or elsewhere?

- How did you determine which causes to reject and which to accept as plausible?

- Where do you think you might find support for the plausibility of these causes?

Reading Essays That Speculate About Causes

Basic Features

●●●●
Basic Features

As you read essays that speculate about causes in this chapter, you will see how different authors incorporate the basic features of the genre.

● A Well-Presented Subject

Read first to see how the writer presents the subject — a phenomenon or a trend that has no definite established cause. Notice which kinds of strategies the writer uses to establish that the phenomenon or trend exists, for example:

- giving examples that make the subject concrete
- using scenarios or anecdotes that may resonate with readers' own experience

  - quoting authorities and research findings
  - citing statistics to show a significant increase or decrease over time

● Plausible Causes and Support

Next, examine the essay for its presentation and support of plausible causes. Start by looking for the thesis statement. A good thesis statement in an essay speculating about causes makes clear exactly what causes are being proposed. The argument for these causes seeks to demonstrate that they are plausible, which means that the best available evidence and experience suggest they are likely to have caused the phenomenon or trend. Causal arguments may show that a potential cause is one or more of the following:

  - sufficient — that is, it *could* have the effect
  - necessary — that is, without it, there would be no such phenomenon or trend
  - a contributing cause but not sufficient in itself
  - a background cause (early in a chain of causes) or an immediate cause (possibly the last link in the chain)
  - a perpetuating cause (keeping the phenomenon or trend going)

● An Effective Counterargument

Read also to see how the writer responds to possible objections and alternative causes. Writers may counterargue in the following ways:

  - by acknowledging a cause readers may prefer
  - by conceding an objection and modifying the argument to accommodate it
  - by refuting readers' objections to the proposed causes or by arguing against alternative causes readers may prefer

● A Readable Plan

Finally, examine the essay to see how readable it is. Essays speculating about causes tend to be rather complicated because the writer has to establish the phenomenon or trend, argue for the proposed causes, and counterargue against objections and alternative causes, backing up everything with solid support and clear citations. Therefore, it is especially important to have a readable plan that helps readers follow the twists and turns of the argument.

To make their essays easy to read, writers usually include some or all of the following:

  - a forecast of the argument
  - topic sentences introducing paragraphs or groups of paragraphs
  - repeated use of key words and synonyms throughout the essay, introduced in the thesis and forecasting statement and reiterated in topic sentences

- clear transitional words and phrases
- headings that explicitly identify different sections of the essay
- visuals, including charts that present information in an easy-to-read format

Purpose and Audience

The fundamental purpose of writing a causal argument is to engage readers in making sense of the world. The possible causes of puzzling phenomena or trends are worth thinking about and irresistibly interesting. Indeed, humans are probably unable *not* to speculate about causes, since so much of what we want to understand can never be known definitively.

As you read essays speculating about causes, ask yourself what seems to be the writer's **purpose** *in writing*. The following purposes are common in speculative essays:

- to convince readers that the proposed causes are plausible
- to persuade readers that the proposed causes are more likely than their preferred causes
- to get readers to look at a phenomenon or trend in a new way
- to urge readers to go beyond obvious or familiar causal explanations
- to spark change in behaviors that have bad effects

As you read, also try to guess what the writer assumes about the **audience***.* For example, does the writer assume readers will

- be only mildly curious about the subject;
- know little about the subject;
- oppose or be skeptical of the proposed causes;
- have their own preferred causes; or
- have serious objections to the argument?

Readings

SHEILA McCLAIN wrote this causal-speculation essay for her first-year college composition course. In it, she speculates about the causes of the U.S. public's growing interest in health and fitness. She carefully documents the trend and then offers four possible causes to explain it. As you read, reflect on your own efforts as well as those by friends and family to achieve physical fitness and evaluate how plausibly McClain explains its growing appeal.

⬡⬡⬡⬡
Basic Features

• A Well-Presented
  Subject
• Plausible Causes
  and Support
• An Effective
  Counterargument
• A Readable Plan

How does McClain establish the fact that the trend exists?

Take a look at the words and phrases McClain repeats in par. 2. Why does she repeat them?

Fitness Culture: A Growing Trend in America

Sheila McClain

Twenty years ago the exercise and fitness industry catered to a small, select group of hard-core athletes and bodybuilders. Now the interest in physical fitness has an increasingly broad appeal to people of all ages, and the evidence can be seen everywhere (Merritt). These days a person cannot turn on the television without seeing an infomercial featuring the latest exercise machine. Yoga, Tai Chi, and other popular forms of exercise are depicted in movies and on television and are advertised across the country. Products such as herbs and muscle-building supplements, fitness wear, exercise mats, workout videos, and new age music for meditation line the shelves of department stores. As one source points out, sales of fitness equipment for use at home have been booming since the early 1990s, and wholesalers in this market saw an increase in profits from just under $1 billion in 1990 to nearly $3 billion in 2001. Furthermore, health club memberships among people 55 and older jumped 273 percent between 1987 and 2001 ("Wellness"). Several causes have contributed to the growth of this "fitness culture" in America.

One of the most obvious causes is the increase in public awareness about the benefits of health and fitness. As noted in a 1992 report (Leepson), numerous clinical studies and scientific reports confirm that exercise together with a proper diet helps prevent heart disease as well as many other serious health problems. In fact, a healthy lifestyle may even reverse the effects of certain ailments. Because "clinical studies in 1989 done by the United States Preventive Services Task Force, a government appointed panel of experts, found 'a strong association between physical activity and decreased risk of several medical conditions, as well as overall mortality'" (Leepson), the federal government has attempted to increase awareness about the benefits of exercise. It, along with some state governments, has also implemented programs designed to increase the health and fitness of the public. With doctors, health experts, and even the government supporting the health and fitness trend, employers and health insurance providers are encouraging the "wellness culture" as well. There are now well-recognized economic benefits for companies that sponsor fitness programs, because healthy people are more productive and make fewer insurance claims (Goldberg). Increasingly, companies even pay for employee fitness club memberships, and some insurance companies give price breaks to businesses that encourage their employees to make healthy lifestyle changes.

1

2

Increased public awareness about health and fitness is also seen in our nation's schools, where health and physical education are today required subjects. As a nation, we are now much more aware of the ways that physical fitness contributes to health, longevity, and productivity.

3   We all know the benefits of being healthy, but why the popularity of fitness clubs and group activities? The answer may be in part that these fulfill the basic human desire for a sense of community and belonging. Social institutions small and large, from local book clubs to national campaigns to protect endangered forests or wild animal species, were once widespread in the United States. Instead of joining others in such activities, people these days may be more likely to stay at home to watch television, play video games, search for entertainment online, or use up generous calling-time allowances on their cell phones. In families, both parents may be working full time, with little time left for volunteer activities. As a result, Americans have become more solitary and family oriented. At the same time, they are growing more aware that they must stay fit to be healthy and realize that fitness classes and health clubs can have the added advantage of bringing them into contact with others. Glenn Colarossi, co-owner of the Stamford (Connecticut) Athletic Club, says this about why people join clubs and attend classes: "People like to belong to something. They like the support and added incentive of working out with others" (qtd. in Glenn). Catherine Larner, a writer on health and lifestyle issues, considers "increasing one's circle of friends" among the benefits of going to the gym (1). Group exercise creates positive peer pressure that keeps many going where they might give up were they exercising alone. A sense of community and belonging to a group also creates a sense of responsibility toward that community, enabling the members to encourage one another and drawing them closer together, fulfilling the need for companionship as well as the need to keep fit.

4   Another, somewhat surprising cause of the increase in popularity of fitness activities may be the fear and anxiety people feel from threats of terrorism along with the stress of modern life. The fact that exercise provides a release of built-up negative emotions and that exercising regularly can reduce stress has long been recognized. As Mary Sisson notes in an article in *Crain's New York Business*, health club chains saw an increase in revenues immediately after 9/11 and even expanded, one of them opening four new clubs, despite an economic downturn for most other industries. This article gives several plausible reasons why fear and stress cause people to exercise more and

How effective is this rhetorical question?

How do these sources support McClain's argument?

Why does McClain call this cause "somewhat surprising"?

How does she use this source to support her argument?

to do so together: (1) under stressful conditions people want the sense of community provided by gyms and classes, (2) working out gives people a sense of empowerment which counteracts feelings of helplessness, (3) traveling less provided many people with more leisure time to fill after 9/11, and (4) people make personal reassessments after a major catastrophe. For example, one woman descended forty flights of stairs evacuating the World Trade Center. Thereafter, realizing how out-of-shape she was, she took up regular exercise (Sisson). Nurturing class instructors and the meditation techniques used in many popular fitness classes also contribute to their stress-relieving properties.

How does McClain refute this objection?

I have a friend who is very cynical about the fitness trend because she suspects it is fueled mainly by women who want bodies like celebrity movie and HBO actresses. It is not fitness and good health these women desire but rather eye-catching, man-enticing bodies, she insists. I tried this skeptical idea out on my exercise physiology professor, and she agreed that some people purchase celebrity-endorsed health products and are motivated to begin exercise programs by the desire to reshape their bodies, not to become more fit and healthy. She doubted that people with these motives could explain the huge increase in attendance at fitness gyms and clubs, however, because research in her field has shown that people with these motives are more likely to become discouraged easily and drop out of fitness classes (Harton).

How do these words and phrases make the argument clear?

Therefore, only increased awareness of the health benefits of physical fitness, not a desire for a more beautiful body, could be sustaining the long-term trend of participation in fitness programs. In addition, attitudes towards exercise are changing. It used to be seen as hard work involving lots of pain and little gain. Moreover, people often exercised so sporadically that the only noticeable change was increased muscle soreness. These days the forms of exercise available are more engaging, more interesting, and gentler than in the past, and they vary greatly to appeal to a wide range of people. Consider classes in belly dancing (you know what that is), strip tease aerobics (look it up!), and spinning (indoor group stationary cycling, led by an instructor) — these are just a few examples. People's attitudes change when they stick with exercise long enough to experience the body's release of endorphins, hormones known to induce "runner's high." David Glenn, writing in a business journal, points to the impacts of these life-changing attitudes: "People look to personal fitness as a lifestyle and a way to enjoy life, not as a way to look like Arnold Schwarzenegger." Gabriela Lukas, a New Yorker who has been exercising regularly since 2001, finds it emotionally satisfying and says it makes her "feel alive" (qtd. in Sisson). More and more people are

5

6

changing their attitudes about physical fitness as they recognize that they feel better, have more energy, and are actually improving the quality of their lives by exercising regularly.

7   The "fitness culture" in America continues to grow and shows no signs of slowing down anytime soon. As we become increasingly aware of the costs of ill health and a lack of physical fitness — and daily newspapers and popular magazines still seem determined to make us aware — and as we experience more stress and anxiety, we are bound to have ever more need of friendship, community, and the endorphins provided by our bodies when we exercise. As more and more people continue to experience the benefits of exercise, the good news about regular exercise spreads wider. As people talk up the pleasures of belonging to a club or fitness center where familiar people welcome them, more will join. Together, these causes snowball, ensuring the continued growth of the fitness industry.

How effective is this way of ending?

What is one thing you learn from this works-cited list?

Works Cited

Glenn, David J. "Exercise Activities Mellowing Out." *Fairfield County Business Journal* 2 June 2003: 22. *Regional Business News*. Web. 19 May 2006.

Goldberg, Carol. "Fitness Industry: Shaping Up for a Good Run." *Long Island Business News* 16 Dec. 1996: 21–2. *Regional Business News*. Web. 20 Apr. 2006.

Harton, Dorothy. Personal interview. 9 May 2006.

Larner, Catherine. "Will Gym Fix It for You?" *Challenge Newsline* 31.1 (2003): 1–2. *Academic Search Premier*. Web. 2 May 2006.

Leepson, Marc. "Physical Fitness." *CQ Researcher* 2.41 (1992): 955–74. *Academic Search Premier*. Web. 2 May 2006.

Merritt, Greg. "The 20 Biggest Changes of the Past 20 Years." *FLEX* Nov. 2003: 286–92. *Health Source*. Web. 5 May 2006.

Sisson, Mary. "Gyms Dandy." *Crain's New York Business* 26 Aug. 2002: 1–2. *Regional Business News*. Web. 6 May 2006.

"Wellness: Finally a Well-Rooted Concept." *American Fitness* 21.1 (2003). *Academic Search Premier*. Web. 2 May 2006.

To learn about Sheila McClain's process of writing this essay, turn to A Writer at Work on pages 500–1. How did McClain determine which possible causes for her trend were plausible enough to advance? How did she decide on the order in which to introduce them?

LEARN ABOUT McCLAIN'S WRITING PROCESS

STEPHEN KING is America's best-known writer of horror fiction. In 2003, he won a Lifetime Achievement Award from the Horror Writers Association, and he has also won many other awards, including the 2003 National Book Foundation Medal for Distinguished Contribution to American Letters. A prolific writer in many genres, King has recently published the novel *Duma* (2008), the short-story collection *Just after Sunset* (2008), and the graphic novel series *Dark Tower*. Many films and television movies have been based on King's work, including the classics *The Shawshank Redemption* (1994) and *Stand by Me* (1986). King offers this wise advice to beginning writers in *On Writing* (2000): "You have to read a lot and write a lot. There's no way around these two things . . . no shortcut."

In this essay, King speculates about the popular appeal of horror movies. Before you begin reading, think about your own attitude toward horror films. Do you enjoy them? "Crave" them? Dislike them? Or are you indifferent to them? As you read, notice how King goes beyond the obvious in explaining why the culture at large appears never to tire of them.

Why We Crave Horror Movies

Stephen King

I think that we're all mentally ill; those of us outside the asylums only hide it a little better — and maybe not all that much better, after all. We've all known people who talk to themselves, people who sometimes squinch their faces into horrible grimaces when they believe no one is watching, people who have some hysterical fear — of snakes, the dark, the tight place, the long drop . . . and, of course, those final worms and grubs that are waiting so patiently underground.

When we pay our four or five bucks and seat ourselves at tenth-row center in a theater showing a horror movie, we are daring the nightmare.

Why? Some of the reasons are simple and obvious. To show that we can, that we are not afraid, that we can ride this roller coaster. Which is not to say that a really good horror movie may not surprise a scream out of us at some point, the way we may scream when the roller coaster twists through a complete 360 or plows through a lake at the bottom of the drop. And horror movies, like roller coasters, have always been the special province of the young; by the time one turns 40 or 50, one's appetite for double twists or 360-degree loops may be considerably depleted.

We also go to re-establish our feelings of essential normality; the horror movie is innately conservative, even reactionary. Freda Jackson as the horrible melting woman in *Die, Monster, Die!* confirms for us that no matter how far we

The mythic horror movie, like the sick joke, has a dirty job to do. It deliberately appeals to all that is worst in us.

may be removed from the beauty of a Robert Redford or a Diana Ross, we are still light-years from true ugliness.

And we go to have fun.

Ah, but this is where the ground starts to slope away, isn't it? Because this is a very peculiar sort of fun, indeed. The fun comes from seeing others menaced — sometimes killed. One critic has suggested that if pro football has become the voyeur's version of combat, then the horror film has become the modern version of the public lynching.

It is true that the mythic, "fairy tale" horror film intends to take away the shades of gray. . . . It urges us to put away our more civilized and adult penchant for analysis and to become children again, seeing things in pure blacks and whites. It may be that horror movies provide psychic relief on this level because this invitation to lapse into simplicity, irrationality, and even outright madness is extended so rarely. We are told we may allow our emotions a free rein . . . or no rein at all.

If we are all insane, then sanity becomes a matter of degree. If your insanity leads you to carve up women like Jack the Ripper or the Cleveland Torso Murderer, we clap you away in the funny farm (but neither of those two amateur-night surgeons was ever caught, heh-heh-heh); if, on the other hand, your insanity leads you only to talk to yourself when you're under stress or to pick your nose on your morning bus, then you are left alone to go about your business . . . though it is doubtful that you will ever be invited to the best parties.

The potential lyncher is in almost all of us (excluding saints, past and present; but then, most saints have been crazy in their own ways), and every now and then, he has to be let loose to scream and roll around in the grass. Our emotions and our fears form their own body, and we recognize that it demands its own exercise to maintain proper muscle tone. Certain of these emotional muscles are accepted — even exalted — in civilized society; they are, of course, the emotions that tend to maintain the status quo of civilization itself. Love, friendship, loyalty, kindness—these are all the emotions that we applaud, emotions that have been immortalized in the couplets of Hallmark cards and in the verses (I don't dare call it poetry) of Leonard Nimoy.

When we exhibit these emotions, society showers us with positive reinforcement; we learn this even before we get out of diapers. When, as children, we hug our rotten little puke of a sister and give her a kiss, all the aunts and uncles smile and twit and cry, "Isn't he the sweetest little thing?" Such coveted treats as chocolate-covered graham crackers often follow. But if we deliberately slam the rotten little puke of a sister's fingers in the door, sanctions follow — angry remonstrance from parents, aunts, and uncles; instead of a chocolate-covered graham cracker, a spanking.

But anticivilization emotions don't go away, and they demand periodic exercise. We have such "sick" jokes as "What's the difference between a truckload of bowling balls and a truckload of dead babies?" ("You can't unload a truckload of bowling balls with a pitchfork" . . . a joke, by the way, that I heard originally from a ten-year-old.) Such a joke may surprise a laugh or a grin out of us even as we recoil, a possibility that confirms the thesis: If we share a brotherhood of man, then we also share an insanity of man. None of which is intended as a defense of either the sick joke or insanity but merely as an explanation of why the best horror films, like the best fairy tales, manage to be reactionary, anarchistic, and revolutionary all at the same time.

The mythic horror movie, like the sick joke, has a dirty job to do. It deliberately appeals to all that is worst in us. It is morbidity unchained, our most base instincts let free, our nastiest fantasies realized . . . and it all happens, fittingly enough, in the dark. For those reasons, good liberals often shy away from horror films. For myself, I like to see the most aggressive of them — *Dawn of the Dead*, for instance — as lifting a trap door in the civilized forebrain and throwing a basket of raw meat to the hungry alligators swimming around in that subterranean river beneath. 12

Why bother? Because it keeps them from getting out, man. It keeps them down there and me up here. It was Lennon and McCartney who said that all you need is love, and I would agree with that. 13

As long as you keep the gators fed. 14

MAKING CONNECTIONS: MEDIA VIOLENCE

"The potential lyncher is in almost all of us," says Stephen King, ". . . and every now and then, he has to be let loose to scream and roll around in the grass" (par. 9). King seems to say that horror films perform a social function by allowing us to exercise (or possibly exorcise) our least civilized emotions. Some religious groups and politicians believe, on the contrary, that media violence — of any kind, in any medium — inspires people, especially the impressionable young, to commit violence.

With two or three other students, discuss these different views of the effects of violence in the media. Begin by taking turns briefly explaining how you feel about horror films or other violent media. Use specific examples. Then, consider the following questions:

- Do you think that media violence inspires real violence or, as King argues, that it exorcizes violent impulses?

- If you think media violence inspires real violence, do you support censorship of movies, television programs, books, or Internet sites that portray violence? If so, should this material be censored just for children or for all viewers? If you oppose outright censorship, do you support movie rating systems or the television V-chip, which gives parents some control over what their children watch? Explain your responses.

ANALYZING WRITING STRATEGIES

◆◆◆◆

Basic Features

● **A Well-Presented Subject**

Essays speculating about causes usually address either social phenomena or trends. Stephen King, for example, writes about a phenomenon — our culture's craving for horror movies — while Sheila McClain is writing about a trend — the growing interest in physical fitness. King could have presented his subject as a trend if he had evidence that the appeal of horror movies was increasing or decreasing, and if he had wanted to speculate on why people's attitudes were changing at this particular time. Similarly, McClain could have written about her subject as a phenomenon — the fitness culture — rather than as a trend, but she chose to examine the trend because she was curious primarily about what brought about the change.

Whether you present your subject as a phenomenon or a trend, you need to start out by convincing readers that it exists. To prove there is a growing fitness trend, McClain devotes her opening paragraph to documenting a threefold increase in fitness industry profits and memberships. King, however, cites no sources to prove that there are people who crave horror movies.

To analyze how King does present his subject, try the following:

- Notice King's use of the pronoun *we*, and write a sentence or two speculating on why he uses this particular pronoun. How does his use of *we* help establish the phenomenon he is writing about?

- Skim the essay, highlighting the titles of the horror films he mentions, and write a few additional sentences explaining why you think he names them and whether he names enough films to achieve his purpose.

● Plausible Causes and Support

Essays speculating about causes do not report cause-effect relationships that have been established as fact. Instead, they present the writer's opinion about possible causes and an argument supporting those causes.

The kinds of support writers rely on range from anecdotal evidence to expert testimony and scientific research. For example, McClain cites a research report in paragraph 2 that confirms the link between exercise, diet, and the prevention of heart disease. In paragraph 3, she cites two authorities — a health club owner and a health writer — to explain why people join fitness clubs and participate in group activities. Of course, some kinds of support may carry more weight than others.

To analyze how King supports his argument, try the following:

- Reread paragraphs 3 and 12 and identify the *analogy* in each paragraph. (An **analogy** is a special kind of comparison in which one part of the comparison is used to explain the other. In arguing by analogy, the writer reasons that if two situations are alike, their causes will be similar.)

- Write a few sentences explaining the reasoning behind each analogy.

● An Effective Counterargument

When causes cannot be known for certain, there is bound to be disagreement. Consequently, writers try to anticipate possible objections readers might raise to their argument. Reaching out to readers and acknowledging that they may disagree helps the writer establish credibility. Most important, however, is how the writer represents alternative points of view and responds to criticism. One strategy is to use words like *may* and *might* to signal awareness that others may not agree.

McClain does this when she writes: "The answer *may be* in part . . ." and "Another, somewhat surprising cause . . . *may be*" (pars. 3 and 4). King uses this strategy in paragraph 7, where he writes: "It *may be* that . . . ." He also occasionally inserts rhetorical questions designed to engage readers, for example in the opening sentence of paragraph 6. Both of these strategies help create a tone that is thoughtful and assertive, but not combative or belittling to those who may disagree.

To analyze how King counterargues, try the following:

- Reread paragraphs 10 and 11 and write a sentence or two explaining how his choice of examples is calculated to help convince skeptical readers that they also have what he calls "anticivilization emotions."

- Reread paragraphs 12–14 and write a few additional sentences analyzing how he reaches out at the end of the essay to readers who may disagree with his contention that they should indulge their craving for horror movies.

● A Readable Plan

Writers of essays speculating about causes sometimes rely on certain kinds of sentence patterns that present cause-effect relationships. Two such types of sentences can be seen in King's essay:

> When we exhibit these emotions, society showers us with positive reinforcement; we learn this even before we get out of diapers. When, as children, we hug our rotten little puke of a sister and give her a kiss, all the aunts and uncles smile and twit and cry, "Isn't he the sweetest little thing?" Such coveted treats as chocolate-covered graham crackers often follow. But if we deliberately slam the rotten little puke of a sister's fingers in the door, sanctions follow — angry remonstrance from parents, aunts, and uncles; instead of a chocolate-covered graham cracker, a spanking. (par. 10)

King repeats the same pattern in the first two sentences. Each of these sentences basically says: *when this occurs, then that will be the result.* The last sentence of the paragraph illustrates a second sentence pattern: *if . . . then . . . .* (Even though King leaves out the word *then*, it is implied and readers fill it in themselves.) Both of these sentence patterns establish a chronological relationship — one thing happens and then another thing happens. They also establish a causal relationship. (Chronology and causality do not always go together, however. See pp. 469 and 672 for more on the *post hoc, ergo propter hoc* fallacy.)

To analyze how King uses the *if . . . then* pattern, try the following:

- Reread paragraphs 6, 8, and 11, and put brackets around the *if . . . then* sentences.

- Write a few sentences explaining how King uses this sentence pattern to present a cause-effect relationship.

- Add another sentence or two commenting on the effect of his repeating the same sentence pattern so often in this essay.

Consider speculating about a popular cultural phenomenon that interests you. For instance, have you ever wondered why romance novels, comic books, a dance craze, a type of music, a television series, or a style of dress is so popular? How about a type of television show — police procedurals, soap operas, reality TV? Coffee houses or drive-through fast-food restaurants? Video games, roller derby, or professional football? A board game, toy, or doll? Science fiction novels about alien invaders or the genomics revolution? Christian pop? Think about how you might present the phenomenon to your readers. What obvious and not-so-obvious causes might you propose to explain the popularity of the phenomenon?

CONSIDERING TOPICS FOR YOUR OWN ESSAY

ERICA GOODE is an award-winning journalist currently on the staff of the *New York Times.* After earning a master's degree in social psychology in 1979, Goode was awarded a mass-media fellowship sponsored by the American Association for the Advancement of Science. She then spent six years as a general assignment reporter and a science writer at the *San Francisco Chronicle,* a year on a fellowship at the Center for Advanced Study in the Behavioral Sciences at Stanford University, and several years as senior writer and assistant managing editor at *U.S. News & World Report.* Goode has also written for publications such as *Vogue, Self,* and *Mirabella,* and she has edited a book called *Letters for Our Children* (1996). She has won awards for her writing from the National Mental Health Association and the American Psychiatric Association.

"The Gorge-Yourself Environment" was published in the *New York Times* in 2003. As you read it, you will see that Goode relies on research studies in nutrition and public health to support her speculations. Even though she does not use an academic style of citing sources, as student Sheila McClain does and as you will be expected to do, notice that she gives readers enough information to find the research reports and other publications that she cites.

The Gorge-Yourself Environment

ERICA GOODE

From giant sodas to supersize burgers to all-you-can-eat buffets, America's approach to food can be summed up by one word: Big. Plates are piled high, and few crumbs are left behind. Today's blueberry muffin could, in an earlier era, have fed a family of four.

But social norms change. Free love has given way to safe sex. Smokers have become pariahs. The gin fizz and the vodka gimlet have yielded to the mojito and the cosmopolitan. Now many health experts are hoping that, in the service of combating an epidemic of obesity, the nation might be coaxed into a similar cultural shift in its eating habits.

Traditionally, the prescription for shedding extra pounds has been a sensible diet and increased exercise. Losing weight has been viewed as a matter of personal responsibility, a private battle between dieters and their bathroom scales. But a growing number of studies suggests that while willpower obviously plays a role, people do not gorge themselves solely because they lack self-control.

Rather, social scientists are finding, a host of environmental factors — among them, portion size, price, advertising, the availability of food and the number of food choices presented — can influence the amount the average person consumes. "Researchers have underestimated the powerful importance of the local environment on eating," said Dr. Paul Rozin, a professor of psychology at the University

■ More Food, More Choices, More Eating
In an affluent society, decisions about what and how much to eat are dictated by many factors besides hunger. Bigger, cheaper, and more varied meals, heavily advertised and widely available, may induce people to eat more than they need to.

Portion size

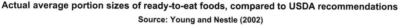

Actual average portion sizes of ready-to-eat foods, compared to USDA recommendations
Source: Young and Nestle (2002)

of Pennsylvania, who studies food preferences. Give moviegoers an extra-large tub of popcorn instead of a container one size smaller and they will eat 45 to 50 percent more, as Dr. Brian Wansink, a professor of nutritional science and marketing at the University of Illinois, showed in one experiment. Even if the popcorn is stale, they will still eat 40 to 45 percent more. Keep a tabletop in the office stocked with cookies and candy, and people will nibble their way through the workday, even if they are not hungry. Reduce prices or offer four-course meals instead of single tasty entrees, and diners will increase their consumption.

In a culture where serving sizes are mammoth, attractive foods are ubiquitous, bargains are abundant and variety is not just the spice but the staple of life, many researchers say, it is no surprise that waistlines are expanding. Dr. Kelly D. Brownell, a professor of psychology at Yale and an expert on eating disorders, has gone so far as to label American society a "toxic environment" when it comes to food.

Health experts and consumer advocates point to the studies of portion size and other environmental influences in arguing that fast-food chains and food manufacturers must bear some of the blame for the country's weight problem. "The food industry has used portion sizes and value marketing as very effective tools to try to increase their sales and profits," said Margo Wootan, the director of nutrition policy at the Center for Science in the Public Interest, an advocacy group financed by private foundations.

Trial lawyers met in Boston last month to discuss legal approaches to obesity, including lawsuits against fast-food chains and food manufacturers on grounds like false advertising, failure to provide labeling about caloric content or even fostering food addiction. At least seven such lawsuits have been filed, with varying success, said John F. Banzhaf III, a professor of public interest law at George Washington University. Professor Banzhaf, who led the way in litigation against tobacco companies, is now channeling similar energy into reforming fast food.

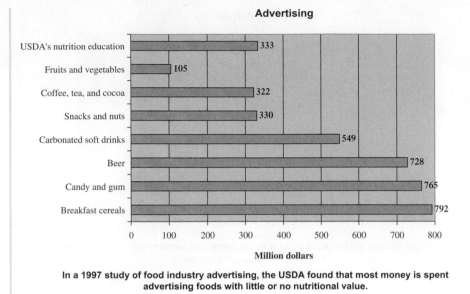

Advertising

In a 1997 study of food industry advertising, the USDA found that most money is spent advertising foods with little or no nutritional value.

Source: USDA/ Economic Research Service

The food industry, however, dismisses such suits as a device to deposit more money in lawyers' bank accounts. The onus for eating healthfully, industry spokesmen say, rests entirely with the consumer. "If you don't want a large hamburger in a restaurant, usually there is a smaller hamburger," said Steven Anderson, the president and chief executive of the National Restaurant Association. "You can get a grilled chicken sandwich in almost any restaurant I've ever been in. There are the options there and it's for the individual to decide." Still, at least one company, Kraft Foods, the maker of Oreos and Lunchables, recently announced its intention to "help encourage healthy lifestyles" by reducing portion sizes for some products.

Some scientists have mixed feelings about taking the obesity issue into court. "Whenever trial lawyers get hold of an issue, I worry," said Dr. Adam Drewnowski, the director for the Center for Public Health Nutrition at the University of Washington. But none dispute that an increasing number of studies show that how food is served, presented and sold plays at least some role in what and how much people eat.

Price is a powerful influence. In a series of studies, researchers at the University of Minnesota have demonstrated that the relative cost of different products has an even more potent effect on food choice than nutritional labeling. Dr. Simone French, an associate professor of epidemiology, and her colleagues manipulated the prices of high-fat and low-fat snacks in vending machines at 12 high schools and 12 workplaces. In some cases, the snacks were labeled to indicate their fat content. "The most interesting finding was that the price changes were whopping in effect," compared with the labels, Dr. French said. Dropping the price of the low-fat snacks by even a nickel spurred more sales. In contrast, orange stickers signaling low-fat content or cartoons promoting the low-fat alternatives had little influence over which snacks were more popular.

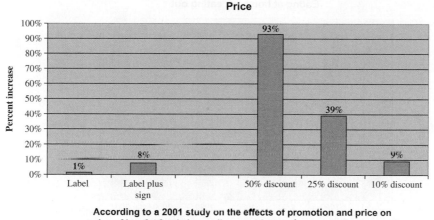

Price

According to a 2001 study on the effects of promotion and price on
sales of low-fat foods in vending-machines, price was by far the most
significant factor in persuading consumers to buy.

Source: French, et al (2001)

Packaging can change the amount people consume. Dr. Wansink and his colleagues have showed that, fooled by a visual illusion, people drink more from short,
wide glasses than thinner, taller ones, but they think they are drinking less.

Having more choices also appears to make people eat more. In one study, Dr. Barbara
Rolls, whose laboratory at Pennsylvania State University has studied the effects of the
environment on eating, found that research subjects ate more when offered sandwiches
with four different fillings than they did when they were given sandwiches with their single
favorite filling. In another study, participants served a four-course meal with meat, fruit,
bread and a pudding — foods with very different tastes, flavors and textures — ate
60 percent more food than those served an equivalent meal of only their favorite course.

To anyone who has survived Christmas season at the office, it will come as no surprise that the availability of food has an effect as well. Dr. Wansink and his colleagues varied the placement of chocolate candy in work settings over three weeks. When the candy
was in plain sight on workers' desks, they ate an average of nine pieces each. Storing the
sweets in a desk drawer reduced consumption to six pieces. And chocolates lurking out of
sight, a couple of yards from the desk, cut the number to three pieces per person.

Researchers have long suspected that large portions encourage people to eat more,
but studies have begun to confirm this suspicion only in the last several years. There
is little question that the serving size of many foods has increased since McDonald's
introduced its groundbreaking Big Mac in 1968. For her doctoral dissertation, Dr. Lisa
Young, now an adjunct assistant professor in the department of nutrition, food studies
and public health at New York University, tracked portion sizes in national restaurant
chains, in foods like cakes, bread products, steaks and sodas and in cookbook recipes
from the 1970's to the late 1990's. The amount of food allotted for one person
increased in virtually every category Dr. Young examined. French fries, hamburgers and
soda expanded to portions that were two to five times as great as they had been at the

11

12

13

14

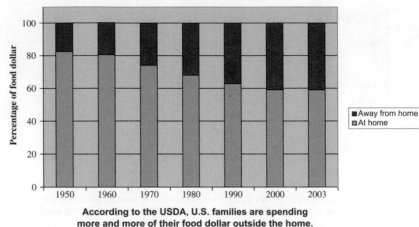

Eating at home vs. eating out

According to the USDA, U.S. families are spending
more and more of their food dollar outside the home.

Source: USDA / Economic Research Service

beginning of the period Dr. Young studied. Steaks, chocolate bars and bread products grew markedly. Cookbooks specified fewer servings (and correspondingly larger portions) for the same recipe appearing in earlier editions. "Restaurants are using larger dinner plates, bakers are selling larger muffin tins, pizzerias are using larger pans and fast-food companies are using larger drink and French fry containers," Dr. Young wrote in a paper published last year in *The American Journal of Public Health*. Even the cup holders in automobiles have grown larger to make room for giant drinks, Dr. Young noted.

She and other experts think it is no coincidence that obesity began rising sharply   15
in the United States at the same time that portion sizes started increasing. But cause and effect cannot be proved. And the food industry rejects the idea of a connection. Mr. Anderson of the restaurant association, for example, says that lack of exercise, poor eating habits and genetic influences are largely responsible for Americans' struggle with extra fat. Still, in cultures where people are thinner, portion sizes appear to be smaller. Take France, where the citizenry is leaner in body mass and where only 7.4 percent of the population is obese, a contrast to America, where 22.3 percent qualify. Examining similar restaurant meals and supermarket foods in Paris and Philadelphia, Dr. Rozin and colleagues at Penn found that the Parisian portions were significantly less hefty. Cookbook portions were also smaller. Even some items sold at McDonald's — the chicken sandwich, for example — are smaller than their American counterparts.

"There is a disconnect between people's understanding of portions and the idea   16
that a larger portion has more calories," said Dr. Marion Nestle, chairwoman of the N.Y.U. nutrition and food policy department and the author of "Food Politics: How the Food Industry Influences Nutrition and Health." The Double Gulp, a 64-ounce soft drink sold by 7-Eleven, Dr. Nestle noted, has close to 800 calories, more than a third of many people's daily requirement, but she said people were often shocked to learn this.

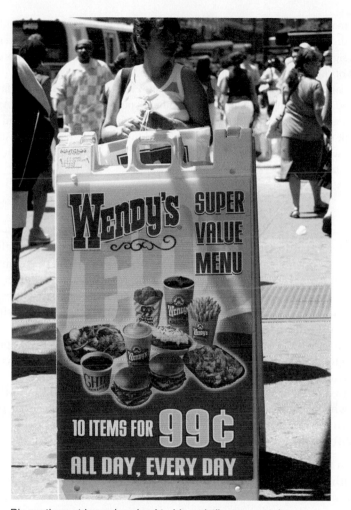

Big portions at low prices lead to big waistlines, researchers say.

And, as studies by Dr. Rolls, Dr. Wansink and others suggest, faced with larger portions, people are likely to consume more, an effect, Dr. Rolls noted, that is not limited to people who are overweight. "Men or women, obese or lean, dieters, nondieters, plate-cleaners, non-plate-cleaners — it's pretty much across the board," she said. In one demonstration of this, Dr. Rolls and her colleagues varied the portions of ziti served at an Italian restaurant, keeping the price for the dish the same but on some days increasing the serving by 50 percent. On the days of the increase, Dr. Rolls said, customers ate 45 percent more, and while diners rated the bigger portion size as a better value, they deemed both servings appropriate. The researchers have also shown that after downing large plates of food, people do not usually compensate by eating less at their next meal.

Very young children, studies suggest, are relatively immune to the pressures that huge food seems to impose on adults. Three-year-olds served three different portion sizes of macaroni and cheese for lunch on three different days, Dr. Rolls and her colleagues discovered, ate the same amount each time. Five-year-olds, however, already showed signs of succumbing to adult overindulgence, eating more when more was put in front of them.

Researchers have yet to cement the link between larger portions and a fatter public. But add up the studies, Dr. Rolls and other experts say, and it is clear Americans might have more success slimming down if plates were not quite so large and a tempting snack did not await on every corner. Obviously, people have responsibility for deciding what to eat and how much, Dr. Rolls said. "The problem is," she said, "they're not very good at it."

19

MAKING CONNECTIONS: THE FRESHMAN FIFTEEN

Have you ever heard of the "freshman fifteen?" The phrase refers to the fact that many college students gain as much as fifteen pounds in their first year of college. Some researchers attribute this typical student weight gain to increased alcohol drinking, all-you-can-eat campus cafeterias, around-the-clock socializing, and even the stress of writing papers and studying for exams. These are "environmental" causes similar to those Goode discusses in her essay, such as portion size and price. Other environmental causes might be the kinds of foods available at places where people congregate and socialize — for example, fast-food restaurants, coffee shops, and sports arenas.

With two or three other students, consider your eating habits and the environments in which you normally eat. Begin by taking turns telling each other about one place you usually hang out with friends and what you eat or drink there. Then, together discuss the following questions:

- Do you tend to eat and drink more than you normally eat and drink when you are with a group of friends? Are the foods you eat more or less healthy when you're with friends?

- Some cities require restaurants to list the calories in the foods they serve; however, Goode reports University of Minnesota studies showing that nutritional labeling is less of an influence on people than price (par. 10). Would caloric or nutritional information change what you order, or is price, habit, or something else more important?

ANALYZING WRITING STRATEGIES

■ ■ ■ ■
Basic Features

● **A Well-Presented Subject**

Examples and anecdotes or brief stories can be effective strategies for presenting a subject. For example, McClain refers to an experience many of her readers have had of turning on the television and encountering an "infomercial featuring the latest exercise machine" (par. 1). She also lists examples of frequently advertised products such as "muscle-building supplements" and "fitness wear" that are associated with exercise.

To analyze how Goode presents the subject, try the following:

- Reread her opening paragraph and highlight the examples.
- Look carefully at the visual headed "More Food, More Choices, More Eating" on page 462.
- Write a sentence or two explaining how the examples in the opening paragraph and in the visual help to present the subject.

● Plausible Causes and Support

Writers seldom consider only one possible cause because they know that most puzzling phenomena and trends have more than one contributing cause. On the other hand, they also avoid presenting every possible cause they can think of because they don't want to bore or confuse readers. Effective writers focus only on the causes they judge *necessary* to bring about the effect; at the same time, they must present causes *sufficient* to bring about the effect.

Obviously, for a cause to be plausible, it must come before the effect. But writers should be wary of a common logical fallacy that confuses chronology with causality by assuming that because one thing preceded another, it *caused* it. This fallacy is often called by its Latin name *post hoc, ergo propter hoc,* meaning "after this, therefore because of this."

The most interesting essays either suggest causes that will surprise readers or argue for familiar causes in new ways. McClain, for example, offers four causes, one of which she describes as "obvious" (par. 2), another as "surprising" (par. 4). Similarly, King calls one of the three causes he offers "simple and obvious" (par. 3) but he ends with a cause that is far from simple or obvious. In addition, effective essays present multiple causes in such a way that readers can understand what piece of the puzzle they represent. McClain, for example, characterizes one cause she cites as being able to sustain the trend over the long term and implies that a different cause may not be very long lasting (par. 6).

To analyze how Goode presents her argument, consider the following suggestions:

- Reread paragraph 4 and highlight the causes Goode forecasts.
- Reread paragraphs 10–14 and highlight each cause as it is introduced.
- Write several sentences offering a possible justification for the plausibility of these causes, the way Goode sequences the causes, and the amount of space she devotes to each cause.

● An Effective Counterargument

Writers speculating about causes sometimes anticipate readers' possible objections to their argument or causes that their readers are likely to prefer. Presenting a well-argued refutation that exposes the weakness of an objection or the unlikeliness of a preferred cause can make the argument more convincing to other readers and even to those readers inclined to disagree. For example, McClain brings up a cause others have proposed — that "the fitness trend . . . is fueled mainly by women who want bodies like celebrity movie and HBO actresses" (par. 5). She spends the entire paragraph refuting this possible cause, ultimately dismissing it as not having a lasting effect. Her way of counterarguing is to bring in other voices — a friend, her exercise physiology professor, and a research study — to demonstrate that although the cause may be real, it tends to be temporary and therefore not very significant. Counterarguing this way shows respect for readers' preferences, yet also makes a strong argument against the cause.

To analyze how Goode counterargues, try the following:

- Reread paragraphs 3 and 6–9. Write a few sentences summarizing the cause some of her readers undoubtedly prefer and explaining how Goode refutes it.

- Alternatively, reread paragraphs 14–19 and write a few sentences summarizing the objection and analyzing how Goode refutes it.

● A Readable Plan

Because essays speculating about causes often discuss multiple causes, writers need to help readers follow the argument for each of the causes. Important strategies for keeping readers oriented include

- forecasting the causes early in the essay;
- using key terms as labels for the causes;
- repeating the same key terms or synonyms as each cause is discussed in the essay.

To analyze how Goode uses these strategies, try the following:

- Identify the forecasting statement and track the key terms to see how effectively they help to orient readers.

- Write a couple of sentences explaining how the strategies work together to make the essay easy for readers to follow.

ANALYZING VISUALS

PHOTOS, CHARTS, AND GRAPHS IN "THE GORGE-YOURSELF ENVIRONMENT"

Write a paragraph or two in which you explain what the visuals — the photos on p. 462 and p. 467, as well as the charts and graphs on pp. 463–66 — contribute to Goode's article.

To analyze the visuals, you can use the Criteria for Analyzing Visuals in Chapter 20 on pp. 675–77. Consider these questions in particular:

Composition

- What objects are presented in the photos? How are they arranged?
- What colors are used? Are there obvious special effects employed? Is there a frame, or are there any additional graphical elements? If so, what do these elements contribute to your "reading" of the images?

Words

- What role does text (words and numbers) play in the images?

Contexts

- Who is the author/composer of the photos? What was their original purpose? What purpose do they serve in Goode's essay?

- What elements of Goode's subject do the charts and graphs illuminate? Is the information the graphs convey easier to understand in visual form, or could it have been conveyed just as well using words only?

- How do the photos relate to each other? How do the photos and the graphs/charts relate?

- How do the visuals relate to the text of the article? What effect do they have on the reader?

CONSIDERING TOPICS FOR YOUR OWN ESSAY

Like Goode, consider writing about the causes of a current social problem. Your guiding question is either *what causes something to occur* or *why is it increasing or decreasing over time*. For example: What causes juvenile suicides? Or, why have juvenile suicides been increasing or decreasing over a particular period of time? Consider these current social problems, or others in which you are especially interested: domestic violence, child abuse, access to health insurance, decay of a particular neighborhood in your city, crime rates, rates of incarceration, unequal funding of public schools, hunger, identity theft, gambling addiction, or teen pregnancy.

JEREMY HSU is a science and technology writer with an undergraduate degree in the history and sociology of science and a graduate degree in science, health, and environmental reporting. A staff writer for *LiveScience, Scienceline.com,* and *Space.com,* Hsu has also published in such popular journals as *USA Today, U.S. News & World Report, Popular Science,* and *Scientific American Mind,* where this essay first appeared in 2008.

As you read this essay, think about the headings — specifically, their wording and how they work for you as a reader.

The Secrets of Storytelling:
Why We Love a Good Yarn

Jeremy Hsu

When Brad Pitt tells Eric Bana in the 2004 film *Troy* that "there are no pacts between lions and men," he is not reciting a clever line from the pen of a Hollywood screenwriter. He is speaking Achilles' words in English as Homer wrote them in Greek more than 2,000 years ago in the *Iliad*. The tale of the Trojan War has captivated generations of audiences while evolving from its origins as an oral epic to written versions and, finally, to several film adaptations. The power of this story to transcend time, language and culture is clear even today, evidenced by *Troy's* robust success around the world.

Popular tales do far more than entertain, however. Psychologists and neuroscientists have recently become fascinated by the human predilection for storytelling. Why does our brain seem to be wired to enjoy stories? And how do the emotional and cognitive effects of a narrative influence our beliefs and real-world decisions?

The answers to these questions seem to be rooted in our history as a social animal. We tell stories about other people and for other people. Stories help us to keep tabs on what is happening in our communities. The safe, imaginary world of a story may be a kind of training ground, where we can practice interacting with others and learn the customs and rules of society. And stories have a unique power to persuade and motivate, because they appeal to our emotions and capacity for empathy.

A Good Yarn

Storytelling is one of the few human traits that are truly universal across culture and through all of known history. Anthropologists find evidence of folktales everywhere in ancient cultures, written in Sanskrit, Latin, Greek, Chinese, Egyptian and Sumerian. People in societies of all types weave narratives, from oral storytellers in hunter-gatherer tribes to the millions of writers churning out books, television shows and movies. And when a characteristic behavior shows up in so many different societies, researchers pay attention: its roots may tell us something about our evolutionary past. . . .

Whether fiction or nonfiction, a narrative engages its audience through psychological realism — recognizable emotions and believable interactions among

The safe, imaginary world of a story may be a kind of training ground, where we can practice interacting with others and learn the customs and rules of society.

characters. "Everyone has a natural detector for psychological realism," says Raymond A. Mar, assistant professor of psychology at York University in Toronto. "We can tell when something rings false." But the best stories — those retold through generations and translated into other languages — do more than simply present a believable picture. These tales captivate their audience, whose emotions can be inextricably tied to those of the story's characters. Such immersion is a state psychologists call "narrative transport."

Researchers have only begun teasing out the relations among the variables that can initiate narrative transport. A 2004 study by psychologist Melanie C. Green, now at the University of North Carolina at Chapel Hill, showed that prior knowledge and life experience affected the immersive experience. Volunteers read a short story about a gay man attending his college fraternity's reunion. Those who had friends or family members who were homosexual reported higher transportation, and they also perceived the story events, settings and characters to be more realistic. Transportation was also deeper for participants with past experiences in fraternities or sororities. "Familiarity helps, and a character to identify with helps," Green explains.

Other research by Green has found that people who perform better on tests of empathy, or the capacity to perceive another person's emotions, become more easily transported regardless of the story. "There seems to be a reasonable amount of variation, all the way up to people who can get swept away by a Hallmark commercial," Green says.

In Another's Shoes

Empathy is part of the larger ability humans have to put themselves in another person's shoes: we can attribute mental states — awareness, intent — to another entity. Theory of mind, as this trait is known, is crucial to social interaction and communal living — and to understanding stories.

Children develop theory of mind around age four or five. . . . Perhaps because theory of mind is so vital to social living, once we possess it we tend to imagine minds everywhere, making stories out of everything. A classic 1944 study by Fritz Heider and Mary-Ann Simmel, then at Smith College, elegantly demonstrated this tendency. The psychologists showed people an animation of a pair of triangles and a circle moving around a square and asked the participants what was happening. The subjects described the scene as if the shapes had intentions and motivations — for example, "The circle is chasing the triangles." Many studies since then have confirmed the human predilection to make characters and narratives out of whatever we see in the world around us.

But what could be the evolutionary advantage of being so prone to fantasy? "One might have expected natural selection to have weeded out any inclination to engage in imaginary worlds rather than the real one," writes Steven Pinker, a Harvard University evolutionary psychologist, in the April 2007 issue of *Philosophy and Literature*. Pinker goes on to argue against this claim, positing that stories are an important tool for learning and for developing relationships with others in one's social group. And most scientists are starting to agree: stories have such a powerful and universal appeal that the neurological roots of both telling tales and enjoying them are probably tied to crucial parts of our social cognition.

11

As our ancestors evolved to live in groups, the hypothesis goes, they had to make sense of increasingly complex social relationships. Living in a community requires keeping tabs on who the group members are and what they are doing. What better way to spread such information than through storytelling?

12

Indeed, to this day people spend most of their conversations telling personal stories and gossiping. A 1997 study by anthropologist and evolutionary biologist Robin Dunbar, then at the University of Liverpool in England, found that social topics accounted for 65 percent of speaking time among people in public places, regardless of age or gender. Anthropologists note that storytelling could have also persisted in human culture because it promotes social cohesion among groups and serves as a valuable method to pass on knowledge to future generations. But some psychologists are starting to believe that stories have an important effect on individuals as well — the imaginary world may serve as a proving ground for vital social skills.

13

"If you're training to be a pilot, you spend time in a flight simulator," says Keith Oatley, a professor of applied cognitive psychology at the University of Toronto. Preliminary research by Oatley and Mar suggests that stories may act as "flight simulators" for social life. A 2006 study hinted at a connection between the enjoyment of stories and better social abilities. The researchers used both self-report and assessment tests to determine social ability and empathy among 94 students, whom they also surveyed for name recognition of authors who wrote narrative fiction and nonnarrative nonfiction. They found that students who had had more exposure to fiction tended to perform better on social ability and empathy tests. Although the results are provocative, the authors caution that the study did not probe cause and effect — exposure to stories may hone social skills as the researchers suspect, but perhaps socially inclined individuals simply seek out more narrative fiction.

14

In support for the idea that stories act as practice for real life are imaging studies that reveal similar brain activity during viewings of real people and animated characters. In 2007 Mar conducted a study using *Waking Life*, a 2001 film in which live footage of actors was traced so that the characters appear to be animated drawings. Mar used functional magnetic resonance imaging to scan volunteers' brains as they watched matching footage of the real actors and the corresponding animated characters. During the real footage, brain activity spiked strongly in the superior temporal sulcus and the temporoparietal junction, areas associated with processing biological motion. The same areas lit up to a lesser extent for the animated footage. "This difference in brain activation could be how we distinguish between fantasy and reality," Mar says. . . .

Happily Ever After

The power of stories does not stop with their ability to reveal the workings of our minds. Narrative is also a potent persuasive tool, according to Hogan and other researchers, and it has the ability to shape beliefs and change minds.

15

Advertisers have long taken advantage of narrative persuasiveness by sprinkling likable characters or funny stories into their commercials. A 2007 study by marketing researcher Jennifer Edson Escalas of Vanderbilt University found that a test audience responded more positively to advertisements in narrative form as compared with straightforward ads that encouraged viewers to think about the arguments for a product. Similarly, Green co-authored a 2006 study that showed that labeling information as "fact" increased critical analysis, whereas labeling information as "fiction" had the opposite effect. Studies such as these suggest people accept ideas more readily when their minds are in story mode as opposed to when they are in an analytical mind-set. 16

Works of fiction may even have unexpected real-world effects on people's choices. Merlot was one of the most popular red wines among Americans until the 2005 film *Sideways* depicted actor Paul Giamatti as an ornery wine lover who snubbed it as a common, inferior wine. Winemakers saw a noticeable drop in sales of the red wine that year, particularly after *Sideways* garnered national attention through several Oscar nominations. 17

As researchers continue to investigate storytelling's power and pervasiveness, they are also looking for ways to harness that power. Some such as Green are studying how stories can have applications in promoting positive health messages. "A lot of problems are behaviorally based," Green says, pointing to research documenting the influence of Hollywood films on smoking habits among teens. And Mar and Oatley want to further examine how stories can enhance social skills by acting as simulators for the brain, which may turn the idea of the socially crippled bookworm on its head. 18

One thing is clear — although research on stories has only just begun, it has already turned up a wealth of information about the social roots of the human mind — and, in science, that's a happy ending. 19

MAKING CONNECTIONS: STORYTELLING AND TECHNOLOGY

Hsu reports research showing that "people spend most of their conversations telling personal stories and gossiping" (par. 12). This impulse to make stories of our everyday experiences and to share these stories with others seems to be reflected in the increasing popularity of such real-time communication technologies as social-networking sites, texting, and Twitter.

With two or three other students, discuss these technologies and their impact on your life. Begin by taking turns briefly telling which of these technologies you prefer and how you typically use them. Then together consider the following questions:

- When you use one of these technologies, are you basically sharing a kind of narrative of your day with your friends or are you more likely to use it to discuss ideas, work out problems, or for some other reason?

- According to Hsu, anthropologists think that storytelling "promotes social cohesion," meaning it makes people feel closely connected to others in a group (par. 12). Do you think telling about daily experiences more or less as they are happening is important? If so, why? If not, why do you think so many people do it?

A Well-Presented Subject

The subject of an essay speculating about causes may be best thought of in terms of the "why" question. For example, you could read Sheila McClain's essay as answering the question, "Why is fitness a growing trend in America?" King explicitly uses the word *why* in his title — "Why We Crave Horror Movies" — and repeats it in the beginning of paragraph 3.

To analyze how Hsu presents the subject, try the following:

- Reread the title and paragraph 1 to see how Hsu introduces the subject.
- Write a couple of sentences explaining the role that the title and opening paragraph play in presenting the subject.

Plausible Causes and Support

Writers often forecast possible causes in the opening paragraphs and then go on later in the essay to take up each cause in turn. Forecasting, using the same or similar names for the causes, and maintaining the same order helps readers follow the argument. Like Erica Goode, Hsu forecasts his proposed causes early in the essay (pars. 2 and 3) and discusses each cause later in the essay.

To analyze how Hsu presents his argument, try the following:

- Reread paragraphs 2 and 3 and highlight the causes Hsu forecasts, and then skim paragraphs 11–19 and highlight each cause as it is mentioned again. Write a couple of sentences offering a possible justification for how Hsu sequences the causes and the amount of space he devotes to each cause.
- Alternatively, reread the intervening paragraphs 4–10 and write a few sentences speculating about how Hsu uses them to advance his argument.

An Effective Counterargument

To counterargue causes that are not very interesting or original, writers usually simply *acknowledge* them but quickly pass on to other, more interesting causes. We can see an example of this strategy in King's essay where he mentions the cause of reestablishing "our feelings of essential normality" and gives a few quick examples (par. 4). Another strategy is to *concede* or *accommodate* a commonplace cause into your own argument but then go on to make it more interesting. McClain uses this strategy where she brings up what she calls "[o]ne of the most obvious causes" — "the increase in public awareness about the benefits of health and fitness" (par. 2). Not only does she cite the kinds of research studies readers would expect, but she also develops the cause in unexpected ways by discussing the economic benefits that have led companies to "sponsor fitness programs" and "even pay for employee fitness club memberships."

To analyze how Hsu presents his counterargument, try the following:

- Reread paragraph 10 to see how Hsu anticipates and responds to an objection to his argument.
- Write a sentence or two explaining how he counterargues and whether his refutation seems effective or not.

⬢ A Readable Plan

Writers sometimes use headings to make it easy for readers to follow the argument. In long essays, headings can be especially helpful. But what do you think they add to a short essay like this one?

To analyze how Hsu uses headings, try the following:

- Skim the essay, noting how each heading functions.
- Write a sentence or two describing the function of the headings and indicating whether you think they are helpful.

Like Hsu, you could consider writing about the causes and/or the effects on society of a phenomenon such as hooking up, texting, or gossiping. You might also consider explaining the social aspects of a trend such as the increasing cost of a college education, the growing gap in income between rich Americans and the rest of the population, or our increasing reliance on technology.

CONSIDERING TOPICS FOR YOUR OWN ESSAY

Beyond the Traditional Essay: Speculating about Causes

Speculating on what happened, and why, is a favorite pastime of many people. Just as expressing an opinion differs from justifying an evaluation, however, idle speculation is very different from a reasoned presentation of a plausible cause. As you have learned in this chapter, an effective essay speculating about causes needs to establish the existence of the phenomenon or trend, argue for the plausibility of the proposed causes, and counterargue readers' objections and alternate causes.

In causal arguments, graphs, charts, diagrams, or tables can be especially useful in establishing a trend, as in this graphic from *CNN.com* that illustrates the rise in obesity in the United States over time:

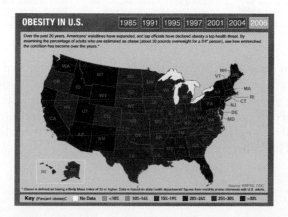

Similarly, animated "infographics" like the "Catastrophic Collapse" sequence reproduced here from *USAToday.com* take full advantage of the Web's interactivity in effectively conveying a logical sequence of causes:

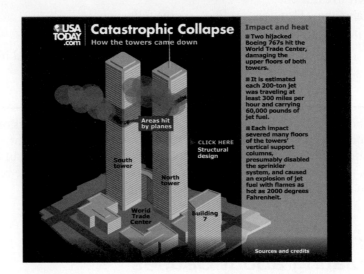

While lacking interactivity, the "Failing System" sequence from the *New York Times* online clearly lays out the sequence of events preceding the 2008 mortgage crisis in the United States:

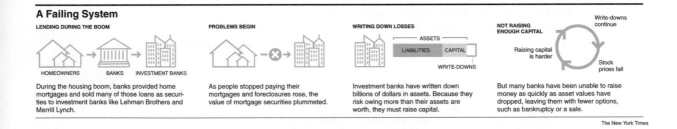

As you work on your own project, you might want to use similar explanatory graphics to present your trend or phenomenon and to support your causes. If the format in which you are working allows for it — if, for example, you are creating a Web site, PowerPoint presentation, or video — you should consider using interactive graphics. (Always remember to properly document any material you might use that was created by someone else.)

Guide to Writing

The Writing Assignment

Write an essay about an important or intriguing phenomenon or trend, and speculate about why it might have occurred. Demonstrate that the subject exists and argue for the plausibility of certain causes, while anticipating your readers' likely objections to your argument, as well as their preferred causes.

This Guide to Writing will help you apply what you have learned about how writers create causal argument essays that are focused, readable, well explained, and supported by credible sources. The Guide is divided into five sections with various activities in each section:

- **Invention and Research**
- **Planning and Drafting**
- **Critical Reading Guide**
- **Revising**
- **Editing and Proofreading**

The Guide is designed to escort you through the writing process, from finding a phenomenon or trend and plausible causes for it to editing your finished essay. Your instructor may require you to follow the Guide to Writing from beginning to end. Working through the Guide to Writing in this way will help you — as it has helped many other college students — write a thoughtful, fully developed, polished essay.

If, however, your instructor gives you latitude to choose and if you have had experience writing an essay in which you speculate about causes, then you can decide on the order in which you'll do the activities in the Guide to Writing. For example, the Invention and Research section includes activities to help you find a subject to write about, explore what you know about it, consider possible causes, research your subject and causes, and develop your argument. Obviously, finding a subject must precede the other activities, but you may come to the Guide with a phenomenon or trend already in mind, and you may choose to do research on it before you consider possible causes. Similarly, you may begin by analyzing causes and then do research followed by further analysis, or you might begin by doing research and then analyze the causes you have researched. In fact, you may find your response to one of the invention activities expanding into a draft before you've had a chance to do any of the other activities. That's a good thing — but you should later flesh out your draft by going back to the activities you skipped and layering the new material into your draft.

The following chart will help you find answers to many of the questions you might have about planning, drafting, and revising an essay speculating about causes. The page references in the Where to Look column refer to examples from the readings and activities in the Guide to Writing.

To learn about using *The Guide* e-book for invention and drafting, go to **bedfordstmartins.com/theguide.**

Starting Points: Speculating about Causes

●●●● Basic Features

	Question	Where to Look
Choosing a Subject	How do I come up with a subject to write about?	• Considering Topics for Your Own Essay (pp. 461, 471, 477) • Considering Subjects and Their Possible Causes (pp. 481–83) • Testing Your Choice (p. 484)
	What's my purpose in writing? How can I interest my audience?	• Analyzing Your Readers (p. 484) • Defining Your Purpose for Your Readers (p. 486) • Refining Your Purpose and Setting Goals: Clarifying Your Purpose and Audience (pp. 487–88)
A Well-Presented Subject	How can I present my subject clearly and effectively?	• Exploring What You Know and Need to Find Out about Your Subject (p. 483) • Refining Your Purpose and Setting Goals: The Presentation of the Subject (pp. 487–88)
Plausible Causes and Support	How do I come up with a list of possible causes to explore?	• Considering Subjects and Their Possible Causes (pp. 481–83)
	How can I convince my readers that I have identified necessary and sufficient causes to explain the phenomenon or trend I'm writing about?	• Ways In: Developing Your Argument and Counterargument (pp. 485–86) • Refining Your Purpose and Setting Goals: The Causal Argument (p. 488) • Working with Sources (p. 492)
An Effective Counterargument	How do I deal with readers' objections to my argument and preferred causes?	• Analyzing Your Readers (p. 484) • Ways In: Developing Your Argument and Counterargument (pp. 485–86)
A Readable Plan	How can I help my readers follow my argument?	• Designing Your Document (p. 486) • Formulating a Tentative Thesis Statement (p. 487) • Refining Your Purpose and Setting Goals: The Ending (p. 488) • Outlining Your Draft (pp. 488–89) • Drafting (pp. 489–92) • Thinking about Document Design (pp. 496–98)

Invention and Research

The following activities are easy to complete. Spreading them out over several days will enable you to think about and research a phenomenon or trend and consider its possible causes. Remember to keep a written record of your invention work: you will need it when you draft the essay and later when you revise it.

Considering Subjects and Their Possible Causes

You may already have a subject in mind — a phenomenon or trend — and some ideas about what could have caused it. Writers often find it helpful to consider several subjects and try to think of possible causes before choosing a subject to research more fully. Below are several activities to help you think of subjects and possible causes. *Keep track of the subjects and causes you are considering* by *filling in a chart like this one:*

Subject	Possible Causes
Why is intolerance of "boyish behavior" increasing?	Increasing awareness of medical problems like attention-deficit hyperactivity disorder leads to classifying "normal" boisterousness as illness.
	Actions by a few disgruntled boys (e.g., Columbine) make people hypersensitive.
Why do people procrastinate?	Fear of failure
	Not starting until they are in the mood
	Underestimating how long it will take

Listing Subjects and Their Possible Causes

Add to your list phenomena and trends you have some ideas about and would enjoy researching further. You might first try rereading the Considering Topics for Your Own Essay activities following the readings and recalling any subjects those suggestions brought to mind. Remember also that some subjects can be approached as either phenomena *or* trends. For example, you could speculate about why the suicide rate among young people went up or down during a particular period (a trend), or you could ignore the change over time and simply speculate about why young people commit suicide (a phenomenon).

For further ideas, consult the suggestions in the following chart.

Type of Subject	Phenomena	Trends
Education	• Why some parents choose to home school their children • Why some people choose to go to community college instead of a four-year college or university • Why a certain part of the student body lacks school spirit • Why a particular instructor or course is popular or unpopular • Why so many students on your campus choose a certain major	• Why the rate of home schooling is increasing or decreasing • Why the rate of community college enrollment is increasing or decreasing • Why the percentage of men attending college is rising or falling • Why political activism rose on campus during the 2008 presidential election • Why communications (or some other field) is one of the fastest growing majors at your college or in the United States
Entertainment and Lifestyle	• Why hooking up has replaced dating for many people • Why people of all ages join social networking sites • Why many people watch the shopping network or do-it-yourself television programs • Why twelve-step programs work for some people • Why dieters often put back on the weight they lost • Why tattoos or lip rings are popular	• Why the popularity of a certain type of music (for example, jazz) or film (science fiction or musical) is declining or increasing • Why the number of people buying lottery tickets and gambling online is increasing or decreasing • Why interest in playing and watching soccer is increasing in the United States • Why arts education has declined in primary and secondary schools • Why obesity is increasing among children
Society and Politics	• Why some athletes use steroids • Why health care benefits have traditionally been linked to employment • Why economic recessions are often worldwide phenomena • Why negative campaigning is popular • Why young people traditionally choose not to vote	• Why the marriage or divorce rate is increasing or decreasing • Why the rate of teenage pregnancy is increasing or decreasing • Why the number of children living with their grandparents has increased since the last census • Why "real wages" (wages adjusted for inflation) have declined or risen over a certain period

Using the Web to Find a Subject and Possible Causes

Search the Internet and add any interesting possibilities you find to your list. Here are some suggestions:

- Look at your city, county, or state government's Web site.

- Try the federal government's Web site (usa.gov) or the Web site of a particular bureau or department, such as the U.S. Census (factfinder.census.gov); the Bureau of Justice Statistics (www.ojp.usdoj.gov/bjs); the Environmental Protection Agency (epa.gov); or the National Center for Education Statistics (ncs.ed.gov).

- Do a Google search for "current trends," "current trends in [education, media, etc.]," "increasing rate," or "decreasing rate" and see what comes up.

In addition to helping you find a phenomenon or a trend, searching the Web can help you establish the existence of the trend and read about possible causes for it.

As always, prefer sites that are backed by reputable institutions and that present the subject in an unbiased manner. (For more on evaluating Web sites, see pp. 752–54.) Make notes of any information or insights suggested by your online research, and download any visuals you might include in your essay, being sure to get the information necessary to cite any online sources. (See pp. 774–76 for MLA guidelines for citing electronic sources.)

Making a Tentative Choice of a Subject to Write About

Choose one of the trends or phenomena you have uncovered. You cannot know for certain at this stage whether you will be able to construct a convincing causal argument for it, but you should choose a subject that meets the following criteria:

> ☐ You will be able to demonstrate that the phenomenon or trend exists.
> ☐ There is no definitive or certain explanation of what caused it.
> ☐ You have ideas about what might have caused it.
> ☐ You have time to do research.

Criteria for Choosing a Phenomenon or Trend:

A Checklist

Exploring What You Know and Need to Find Out about Your Subject

Write a page or so about the phenomenon or trend you have chosen, the possible causes you listed, and any notes you added. Your objective now is to see what you currently know about it and what you need to find out. (When you start writing, you may be surprised at how much you do know.)

Before discussing the possible causes you have thought of so far, you could briefly explain why you are interested in this trend or phenomenon. As you discuss the causes, note how you might support them. For example, if you were writing about procrastination, you could make a questionnaire for your classmates, interview someone at the learning center, or look for psychological or management research. Thinking about the research you may need to do will help you decide whether you should continue with this subject given the time you have for this paper.

Analyzing Your Readers

In a few sentences, consider what your readers are likely to think about your subject and its possible causes. If you are writing primarily for your classmates, you will be able to ask a few of them what they think when you do the next Collaborative Activity for Testing Your Choice. For now, use the following questions to help you develop an understanding of your readers:

- Who are my readers, and what are they likely to know about my subject? (For example, King could assume his readers would be interested in the phenomenon of horror movies even if they were not fans themselves.)
- Will I have to prove to them that the phenomenon or trend exists or will they already think it exists?
- Will they be interested in the subject and its possible causes?
- What causes would they likely think of themselves?
- Would any of the causes I am considering surprise them?

Testing Your Choice

Test your choice using these questions:

- Will my readers be interested in the phenomenon or trend I have chosen?
- Will I be able to demonstrate that the phenomenon or trend exists?
- Have I found plausible causes for the phenomenon or trend?
- Do I know enough or can I learn what I need to know in the time remaining to make a strong argument?

As you plan and draft your essay, you will probably want to consider these questions again. If at any point you cannot answer them with a confident yes, you may want to consider proposing different causes or choose a different subject to write about. If you have serious doubts, consider discussing them with your instructor.

A Collaborative Activity:
Testing Your Choice

Get together with two or three other students to try out your ideas.

Presenters: Take turns describing the phenomenon or trend, and then briefly explaining the two or three causes you think are most likely.

Listeners: Tell the presenter which causes seem most plausible, briefly explaining why the other causes seem unlikely. If you think of an alternative cause that you think is more plausible, let the presenter know.

Ways in: Developing Your Argument and Counterargument

These activities will help you decide how to argue for your most promising causes and prepare a counterargument. You may begin by first analyzing what you already know and then doing some research, or you may begin with the research — just be sure you do both at some point. To keep track of your developing argument and counterargument, you could use a chart like the following one:

Possible Causes	Analysis
Cause #1	[Your analysis of plausibility, possible objections, etc.]
Cause #2	

Turn to the Writer at Work on pp. 500–1 to see how Sheila McClain used this chart.

Analyzing Causes and Anticipating Objections

Categorize Each Cause. *Write a few sentences explaining why you put the cause into one or more of the following categories:*

- an obvious, hidden, and/or surprising cause
- a *necessary* cause — no phenomenon or trend without it
- a *sufficient* cause — it alone could have been the cause
- a link in a chain of causes or a contributing cause among many
- a *perpetuating* cause — it keeps the phenomenon or trend going
- a *result* rather than a *cause* of the phenomenon or trend

Consider Support for Each Cause. *Note any support you have thought of — quotations, studies, statistics, visuals, and so on — or reasons you think might convince readers the cause is plausible.* You may need to explain how a particular cause is not just something that happened before the phenomenon or trend, but something that actually could have caused it.

Researching Causes

Do Library and Internet Research. *To locate relevant articles, books, and Web sites, visit your library or access your library system online.* Chapter 23, Library and Internet Research, has general information that will help you do research productively. When you find potentially useful information, take accurate notes, make a photocopy, or save the information electronically, always being sure to record exact source information for your works cited list.

Look particularly for the following kinds of information:

- evidence that the subject exists, especially to establish a trend
- support for the plausibility of your causes
- objections readers might raise to the causes you think are plausible
- alternative causes, which you may decide either to adopt or argue against

Consider Using Personal Experience and/or Doing Field Research. *Consider using interviews and direct observation to learn about people's experiences with the phenomenon or trend.* For example, researching procrastination, you could create a questionnaire to distribute among students and/or learning-center tutors.

(continued)

(*continued*)

Analyzing Causes	Researching Causes

Anticipate Objections. *Summarize possible objections to your causes, and make notes about how you might counterargue.* Consider whether you should acknowledge, concede, or refute any objections.

Find Visuals. *Capture useful visuals — graphs, photographs, tables — that could help you establish the existence of the trend or phenomenon or help you argue for the plausibility of your causes.* (For an example, see Goode's essay on pp. 461–68.) Be sure to keep the source information for your works-cited list.

Anticipate Alternative Causes. *Make notes about alternative causes your readers might have in mind.* Consider whether you might adopt or argue against any of them — for example, by arguing that an alternative cause is too obvious or did not cause a trend to increase or decrease.

Designing Your Document

For more information on document design, see Chapter 21. For more information about including visuals in your work, see Chapter 20.

Think about whether you could use design features such as headings or visuals such as photographs or line graphs to make your essay easy to follow. Visuals are not a requirement for an essay speculating about causes, but they can be helpful, as you can see in Erica Goode's essay (pp. 461–68). Look back at the scenario on p. 446 describing the first-year seminar student's work on endangered coral reefs, and then read Thinking about Document Design on pp. 496–98 to see how she used visuals in her final paper.

Defining Your Purpose for Your Readers

Write a few sentences defining your purpose. Recall that in an earlier invention activity you identified your readers and considered what they know about your subject. Given these readers, try now to define your purpose by considering the following questions:

- How can I interest readers in my subject?

- Will I have to persuade my readers to take a fresh look at a phenomenon or trend that they may not have strong feelings about? Will I have to dissuade them from their present way of thinking about a phenomenon or trend that is already of significant concern to them?

- How much resistance should I expect from my readers to the causes I want to propose? Will the readers be largely receptive? Skeptical but convincible? Resistant and perhaps even antagonistic?

- How can I respond to my readers' likely questions and objections and to alternative causes they may prefer to my own? How can I refute my readers' ideas without seeming dismissive of them?

- If I am analyzing a trend, do I need to demonstrate that it is not just a fluctuation or a fad, as McClain does?

The Causal Argument

- How many causes should I propose? Should I have a main cause, as King does, or several causes, as Goode does?

- How can I present my proposed causes in the most effective sequence? Should I arrange them from most to least important, as Goode does; from least to most important, as Hsu does; or from most obvious to least obvious, as McClain and King do?

- Do I need to make other distinctions among causes, such as differentiating a cause that starts a trend from one that keeps it going? Can I demonstrate that a particular cause is necessary or sufficient?

- How much and what kind of support do I need to offer to make each cause plausible to my readers? Are any causes so obvious that support is unnecessary?

- Do I need to demonstrate to readers that all of my causes existed before the phenomenon or trend began?

- How can I anticipate readers' objections to my proposed causes? Should I just acknowledge the existence of some objections without responding to them? concede other objections, as King does? refute other objections, as Goode does?

- How can I anticipate alternative causes readers might propose? Should I acknowledge one or more of these causes? concede the plausibility of other causes? refute other causes as not worth taking seriously, as McClain does?

The Ending

- How should I end my essay? Should I summarize my causes, as McClain does; restate the main cause, as King does; conclude with a conjecture about larger implications, as Hsu does; or look forward to further research, as Goode does?

Outlining Your Draft

A causal analysis may contain as many as four basic parts:

1. A presentation of the subject
2. Plausible causes, logically sequenced
3. Convincing support for each cause
4. A consideration of readers' questions, objections, and alternative causes

These parts can be organized in various ways. If your readers are not likely to think of any causes other than the ones you are proposing, you may want to begin by describing the subject and indicating its importance or interest. Then state your first proposed cause, supporting it convincingly and accommodating, conceding, or refuting

Formulating a Tentative Thesis Statement

Write a sentence or two that could serve as your thesis statement. In an essay speculating about causes, the thesis statement focuses on the subject and announces the causes that are argued for in the piece. You will already have described the trend or phenomenon that is your subject. Though forecasting is optional, readers will often benefit from knowing in advance what causes you will argue for.

Readings in this chapter illustrate effective thesis statements. For instance, Erica Goode presents her thesis this way: "But a growing number of studies suggests that while willpower obviously plays a role, people do not gorge themselves solely because they lack self-control. Rather, social scientists are finding, a host of environmental factors — among them, portion size, price, advertising, the availability of food and the number of food choices presented — can influence the amount the average person consumes" (pars. 3–4). Goode refers back to her subject — "an epidemic of obesity" (par. 2) — and then lists the contributing environmental causes she will go on to argue for in the essay.

Planning and Drafting

The following activities will help you refine your purpose, set goals for your draft, and outline it. In addition, this section will help you draft your essay, with advice on writing opening sentences, developing a useful sentence strategy, and working with sources.

Refining Your Purpose and Setting Goals

Before starting to draft, use the questions below to help you sharpen your purpose for your audience and set goals for your draft. Your instructor may ask you to write out your answers to some of these questions or simply to think about them as you plan and draft your essay.

Clarifying Your Purpose and Audience

- How can I show readers that I am knowledgeable about the subject? Can I cite sources, as McClain and Goode do? What can I do to convince readers that I am a credible authority on the subject, as King does?

- How can I organize my essay to make it easy to follow? Should I use headings, as Hsu does? Should I use forecasting, topic sentences, and repetition of key terms, along with visuals, as Goode does?

- If readers are likely to resist my way of thinking about the phenomenon or trend, will I be able to get them to have an open mind, as King strives to do?

The Presentation of the Subject

- Do I need to demonstrate that my phenomenon or trend really exists, as Goode and McClain do, or can I assume that readers will be familiar with my subject, as King and Hsu do?

readers' likely questions and objections. Follow the same pattern for any other causes you propose. Your conclusion could then mention — and elucidate — the lack of other explanations for your subject:

I. Presentation of the subject
II. First proposed cause with support and consideration of objections, if any
III. Second proposed cause with support and consideration of objections, if any (etc.)
IV. Conclusion

If you need to account for alternative causes that are likely to occur to readers, you could discuss them first and give your reasons for conceding or rejecting them before offering your own proposed causes. Many writers save their own causes for last, hoping that readers will remember them best:

I. Presentation of the subject
II. Alternative causes and consideration of them
III. Proposed causes with support and consideration of objections, if any
IV. Conclusion

Another option is to put your own causes first, followed by alternatives. This pattern helps you show the relative likelihood of your causes over the others. You might then end with a restatement of your causes:

I. Presentation of the subject
II. Proposed causes with support and consideration of objections, if any
III. Alternative causes compared with your causes
IV. Concluding restatement of your proposed causes

There are, of course, many other possible ways to organize a causal analysis, but these outlines should help you start planning your own essay.

   Consider any outlining you do before you begin drafting to be tentative. Never be a slave to an outline. As you draft, you will usually see ways to improve on your original plan. Be ready to revise your outline, shift parts around, or drop or add parts as you draft. If you use the outlining function of your word processing program, changing your outline will be simple, and you may be able to write the essay simply by expanding the outline.

Drafting

If you have not already begun to draft your essay, this section will help by suggesting how to write your opening sentences, how to use topic sentences and parallel examples, and how to cite a variety of sources. Drafting is not always a smooth process, so do not be afraid to leave spaces where you do not know what to put in or to write notes to yourself about what you could do next.

   If you get stuck while drafting, go back over your invention writing: You may be able to copy and paste some of it into your evolving draft, or you may need to do some additional invention to fill in details in your draft. You might also try returning to the appropriate exploratory writing activities in the Invention and Research section of this chapter.

As you draft, keep the following tips in mind:

- Remember that in writing about causes, you are dealing with probabilities rather than certainties. Therefore, resist the urge to claim that you have the final, conclusive answer; instead, simply assert that your explanation is plausible. Qualify your statements, and acknowledge readers' objections and alternative causes.

- Causal analysis is potentially rather dry, so try to enliven your writing and to appeal to your readers' interests and concerns.

Writing the Opening Sentences

While drafting, do not agonize over the first sentences, because you are likely to discover the best way to begin only after you've written a rough draft. When you feel ready to write your opening, however, you might start by reviewing your invention writing to see if you have already written something that would work to launch your essay. You might also consider the following opening strategies:

- a surprising assertion (like King)
- a historical perspective (like McClain)
- one or more specific examples (like Hsu and Goode)
- statistics
- quoting a research study
- a scenario or an anecdote
- firsthand experience

Try out one or two different ways of beginning your essay. If possible, try them out on classmates or friends to gauge their effectiveness in engaging your readers' interest from the start.

Sentence Strategies: Topic Sentences and Parallel Examples

As you draft an essay speculating about the causes of a phenomenon or trend, you will want to ensure that your readers can readily recognize the stages of your argument and that they can easily understand the support you offer for each of your proposed causes. Two sentence strategies that can help you achieve these goals are using clear topic sentences and using grammatically parallel sentences to present examples.

Using Topic Sentences to Signal Stages in Your Argument. Topic sentences are usually placed first or very early in a paragraph. They can announce a new cause, introduce counterargument (the writer's response to readers' likely questions or alternative causes), or identify different parts of the support for a cause or counterargument. They may include key terms that the writer has introduced in a thesis statement at the beginning of the essay, and they may take identical or similar sentence forms so that readers can recognize them more easily. Here are examples from Stephen King's essay. They identify what King believes to be the three main causes for many moviegoers' attraction to horror movies:

> Why? Some of the reasons are simple and obvious. To show that we can, that we are not afraid, that we can ride this roller coaster. (par. 3)
>
> We also go to re-establish our feelings of essential normality. (4)
>
> And we go to have fun. . . . The fun comes from seeing others menaced — sometimes killed. (5–6)

King assists readers in identifying each new stage of his argument by introducing the grammatical subject *we* in the first topic sentence and then repeating it to signal the next two stages: *we can, We also go, And we go*. You will find similarly prominent topic sentences in the essays by McClain, Goode, and Hsu.

Do not hesitate to make your sequences of causes very visible and accessible to your readers. Readers like to follow a logical, step-by-step argument. You can avoid frustrating their expectations by taking care to satisfy them — chiefly through the content of your argument, but also with visible signals.

Presenting Examples in Parallel Grammatical Form. Presenting examples in parallel form helps readers understand that the examples are related. Here is a sequence of three related examples from paragraph 4 of Erica Goode's causal argument:

> Give moviegoers an extra-large tub of popcorn instead of a container one size smaller and they will eat 45 to 50 percent more. . . .
>
> Keep a tabletop in the office stocked with cookies and candy, and people will nibble their way through the workday. . . .
>
> Reduce prices or offer four-course meals instead of single tasty entrees, and diners will increase their consumption.

Note how Goode relates these examples by beginning each sentence with a verb in the imperative mood (*Give, Keep, Reduce*) and in the second clause predicting what will happen if the imperative is carried out using a future tense verb (*will eat, will nibble, will increase*). The three sentences are almost exactly parallel grammatically.

In the following examples from paragraph 12, Goode again links two related examples by opening her sentences with grammatically similar constructions:

> In one study, Dr. Barbara Rolls . . . found that research subjects ate more . . .
>
> In another study, participants served a four-course meal . . .

The repetition of grammatical form (as well as the content of the sentences) tells readers that the examples are related, making the ideas easier to follow and contributing to the effectiveness of the argument.

For more on using topic sentences to signal the main stages of a causal argument, go to **bedfordstmartins.com/ theguide** and click on Sentence Strategies.

For more on relating examples to one another by repeating grammatical forms, go to **bedfordstmartins .com/theguide** and click on Sentence Strategies.

In addition to using topic sentences that help readers follow the stages of your argument and using parallel grammatical form to present related examples, you can strengthen your causal argument with other kinds of sentences as well. You may want to review the information about sentences with appositives (pp. 170–71) and sentences that introduce concession and refutation (pp. 306–7).

Working with Sources:
Citing a Variety of Sources to Support Your Causal Speculations

For further help working with sources, go to **bedfordstmartins.com/ theguide.**

Writers of essays speculating about the causes of a phenomenon or trend must establish that the causes they offer are plausible. To do so, they often rely on evidence from experts or others who have researched and thought about the topic. But using too few sources or sources that are too narrow in scope can undercut the effectiveness of the argument because readers may feel they are being provided with only a limited vision of it. Consequently, it can be important to offer information from a number of sources and from sources that reflect a variety of areas of expertise.

Look, for example, at the sources that Erica Goode refers to in speculating about the extent to which environmental factors can affect how much people eat in her essay "The Gorge-Yourself Environment" (pp. 461–68). She cites a professor of psychology with an interest in food preferences and a professor of nutritional science and marketing in paragraph 4, a professor of psychology with an interest in eating disorders in paragraph 5, the director of nutrition policy at an advocacy group in paragraph 6, and the chair of a university's nutrition and food policy department in paragraph 16. She also cites the specific findings of at least six academic research projects (paragraphs 10, 11, 12, 14, 17, and 18). All together, the number of expert research projects she cites is impressive, and the variety of her sources adds to her credibility.

In her essay "Fitness Culture: A Growing Trend in America" (pp. 451–55), Sheila McClain cites two articles from fitness magazines (one by Greg Merritt from *FLEX* and one titled "Wellness: Finally a Well-Rooted Concept" from *American Fitness*). But a look at her works-cited list reveals that she does not rely solely — or even primarily — on such sources, which because of their editorial mission might be biased toward the position she is taking. Rather, much of the expert testimony she cites comes from business publications (*Fairfield County Business Journal, Long Island Business News, Crain's New York Business*), an online general interest publication with a focus on religious issues (*Challenge Newsline*), and a government publication (*The CQ Researcher Online*). She also cites an interview with her exercise physiology professor — whom she identifies in the text of her essay — to help refute a counterargument. Again, the number of sources and their variety in terms of approach to the subject lend credibility to the writer's speculations.

As you determine how many and what kinds of sources to cite in your essay, keep in mind that readers of essays speculating about causes are more likely to be persuaded if the sources you rely on are neither too few nor too narrowly focused. If, when you begin to draft, you find that your research seems skimpy, you may need to do further research.

Your instructor may arrange a peer review session in class or online where you can exchange drafts with your classmates and give each other a thoughtful critical reading — pointing out what works well and suggesting ways to improve the draft. This Critical Reading Guide can also be used productively by a tutor in the writing center or by a roommate or family member. A good critical reading does three things: It lets the writer know how well the reader understands the presentation of the subject and the causal argument, praises what works best, and indicates where the draft could be improved.

1. Evaluate how effectively the subject is presented.

   Summarize: Briefly tell the writer what you understand the phenomenon or trend to be, and what in the draft helped convince you it exists.

   Praise: Give an example of something in the draft that you think will especially interest the intended readers and help them understand the phenomenon or trend.

   Critique: Tell the writer if you have any confusion or uncertainty about the nature and/or the significance of the phenomenon or trend. Could the organization of the information be improved? What further explanation, detail, examples, or statistics do you need to believe that the phenomenon or trend exists and/or to understand it fully? Can you think of a more interesting way to present it? Do you think readers will be persuaded of its significance?

2. Assess how plausible and well-supported the causal argument is. Look first at the proposed causes, and list them.

   Praise: Give an example of a cause that is argued effectively. Try to be specific about what element of the argument (for example, an anecdote, an example, a statistic, or a reference to authority) works particularly well.

   Critique: Tell the writer if there seem to be too many or too few causes presented. Do any of the causes seem either too obvious (not worth mentioning) or too obscure (remote in time or overly complicated)? Do any of the causes require more support to be convincing? If so, what kind would work best? Do any causes presented seem to fall into the *post hoc, ergo propter hoc* fallacy (being presented as a cause just because they occurred before or at the start of the phenomenon or trend)? Are any of the proposed causes of the subject actually *effects* of the subject? Is the sequence in which the causes are presented logical?

3. Consider how effectively and respectfully counterarguments are made.

   Praise: Identify a counterargument that works well. Look for places where the writer respectfully and effectively acknowledges readers' possible objections to or questions about the proposed causes. Similarly, point out places where the writer acknowledges alternative causes and refutes or accommodates them convincingly.

Critical Reading Guide

● ■ ● ◆
Basic Features

For a printable version of this Critical Reading Guide, go to **bedfordstmartins** **.com/theguide.**

Critique: Tell the writer if a likely objection or alternative cause should be taken more seriously. If necessary, help the writer see more effective and respectful ways of either accommodating or refuting objections. If there are other likely questions or objections the writer has overlooked, point them out. If you can think of alternative causes the writer has not taken into account, suggest that the writer acknowledge them.

4. Assess how readable the causal argument is.

Praise: Give an example of where the essay succeeds in being readable — in its overall organization; in the key terms introduced in its thesis and forecasting statements and carried through the essay in topic sentences and elsewhere; in the use of transitions; or in its beginning or ending.

Critique: Tell the writer where the readability could be improved. Can you point to places where key terms would help or where a topic sentence could be made clearer, for example? Can the use of transitions be improved, or transitions added where they are lacking? Can you suggest a better beginning or more effective ending?

5. If the writer has expressed concern about anything in the draft that you have not discussed, respond to that concern.

Making Comments Electronically Most word processing software offers features that allow you to insert comments directly into the text of someone else's document. Many readers prefer to make their comments this way because it tends to be faster than writing on hard copy and space is virtually unlimited; it also eliminates the process of deciphering handwritten comments. Where such features are not available, simply typing comments directly into a document in a contrasting color can provide the same advantages.

Revising

For an electronic version of this Troubleshooting Chart, go to **bedfordstmartins .com/theguide.**

Very likely you have already thought of ways to improve your draft, and you may even have begun to revise it. In this section is a Troubleshooting Chart that may help. Before using the chart, however, it is a good idea to do the following:

- Review critical reading comments from your classmates, instructor, or writing center tutor.
- Make an outline of your draft so that you can look at it analytically.

You may have made an outline before writing your draft, but after drafting you need to see what you actually wrote, not what you intended to write. You can outline the draft quickly by highlighting the basic features — a clear and complete presentation of the subject; a plausible and well-supported causal argument; and respectful handling of readers' objections and alternative explanations.

Troubleshooting Your Draft

● ● ● ● **Basic Features**

	Problem	Suggestions for Revising the Draft
A Well-Presented Subject	My readers don't fully understand my subject.	☐ Try providing examples or anecdotes that make the subject concrete. ☐ Do some additional research and provide additional explanation.
	My readers aren't convinced that the phenomenon or trend exists.	☐ Use scenarios or anecdotes that readers might recognize from their own experience. ☐ Quote authorities or research findings, including statistics that show change over time.
Plausible Causes and Support	I've found too many causes that seem plausible. (My readers are confused about which causes are most important.)	☐ Be sure that you present the causes in some logical order — for example, from most to least familiar (or vice versa), most to least important (or vice versa), most to least recent (or vice versa) — and make this order apparent to the reader. ☐ Clearly identify each of the causes you present as necessary, sufficient, contributing, background, or perpetuating. Be sure to explain where each cause fits in to the big picture. ☐ Consider presenting only those causes that are necessary and, together, sufficient to explain your phenomenon or trend.
	I need to find additional plausible causes. (My readers are unconvinced.)	☐ Do some additional research on possible causes for your phenomenon or trend. ☐ Try a simple Web search on + "[your subject]" + *cause*, skimming the results for ideas. ☐ Talk to someone who has experience in the phenomenon or trend you're writing about. ☐ Return to your invention notes. If you haven't already done one, make a simple chart with two columns ("Subject" and "Possible Causes"). Don't censor your ideas at this stage: Try to write as many causes as you can think of without stopping. ☐ Try brainstorming with friends or classmates who are familiar with the phenomenon or trend you're explaining.
	The support I've found for my causes is skimpy or weak.	☐ Do some additional research. If you can't come up with sufficient evidence to support a cause, reconsider it as a cause. ☐ Check to be sure that you've presented support from a sufficient *variety* of sources: In addition to library and Internet research, consider personal experience, interviews, and other kinds of field research.
	I haven't established a clear connection between a cause and the phenomenon or trend.	☐ Be sure that your sentences are clearly constructed to show cause-and-effect relationships — for example, *when-then and if-then*. ☐ Check your essay for the *post hoc, ergo propter hoc* fallacy — that is, check to be sure that you are not confusing causation (this caused that) and simple chronology (this happened, then that happened).

(continued)

(continued)

Problem	Suggestions for Revising the Draft
An Effective Counter-argument — My readers aren't convinced by my refutation of some objections or alternative causes.	☐ Consider conceding the objections or alternative causes, and then modifying your argument to accommodate them. ☐ Do some additional research to be sure that you can answer objections confidently. Do some research on alternative causes to be sure they're less plausible than the ones you propose. Present your findings in your paper.
My readers tell me that I'm ridiculing or dismissing valid counterarguments or objections.	☐ However you introduce them — by conceding, refuting, or simply acknowledging them — be sure to treat all objections and counterarguments respectfully. ☐ Use qualified language — *may* and *might*, for example — to signal awareness that what you're presenting is reasoned opinion, not objective fact, and that not all readers will agree with you.
My readers have raised objections and/or alternative causes that I haven't addressed in my draft.	☐ Address the objections and alternative causes explicitly, and either refute, concede, or acknowledge them.
A Readable Plan — My readers are having trouble following my argument.	☐ Reread your introduction and thesis, and be sure that you have clearly introduced your subject and proposed the cause(s) that explain it. ☐ Consider adding additional forecasting, key words, topic sentences, repetition, transitional words and phrases, headings, and/or visuals. ☐ Try outlining your essay if you have not already done so; if you have, see how well your outline matches what you've written so far. If you see gaps, add additional explanation and support. If there is material there that is not clearly related to your main point, delete it.

Thinking About Document Design:
Adding Graphs and Photos

In her paper on the possible causes of the global demise of coral reefs (described on p. 446), the first-year seminar student incorporated several visuals, including a map that depicts endangered reefs in the Indo-Pacific region (Figure 9.1) and a bar chart that shows the percentage change in reef size over time in various Indo-Pacific sub-regions (Figure 9.2). The map and chart, taken from a 2007 study by John F. Bruno and Elizabeth R. Selig, present detailed information that would have been difficult if not impossible to express using words alone. The student also incorporated photos of healthy and dying reefs (Figures 9.3 and 9.4) to give her readers a vivid sense of the urgency of the problem.

As seen in these examples, visuals like maps, tables, graphs, charts, diagrams, and photos can be used both to convey information quickly and efficiently and to bolster the persuasiveness of an argument. In some cases, in fact, selecting the right

Figure 9.1 Map of study region, subregions, and the 2667 surveyed reefs (green dots).

Figure 9.2 Regional trends in coral cover between 1968 and 2004. (* indicates that data are unavailable.)

Figure 9.3 Healthy reef, Florida Keys National Marine Park.

Figure 9.4 Dead tire on dead reef near Guam's Mariana Islands.

For more on document design, see Chapter 21. For more on analyzing visuals, see Chapter 20.

visuals can be as important as selecting the right words to convey your ideas. Clarity, succinctness, vividness, accuracy, and relevance are all as important in visuals as in text. In selecting both, you want your choices to enhance readers' understanding of and interest in the argument you are making.

Keep in mind, however, that while visuals can help convey information and make an argument, they cannot do all the work for writers. Visuals can represent information but cannot interpret it. As a writer, it is your job to comment on the information illustrated in visuals — for example, by referring directly to a visual in text, explaining why the information is important, and suggesting what the implications of such information might be.

Editing and Proofreading

A Note on Grammar and Spelling Checkers
These tools can be helpful, but do not rely on them exclusively to catch errors in your text: Spelling checkers cannot catch misspellings that are themselves words, such as *to* for *too*. Grammar checkers miss some problems, sometimes give faulty advice for fixing problems, and can flag correct items as wrong. Use these tools as a second line of defense after your own (and, ideally, another reader's) proofreading/editing efforts.

Two kinds of errors occur often in essays speculating about causes: mechanical errors in using numbers, and use of the construction *the reason is because*. The following guidelines will help you check your essay for these common errors.

Checking Your Use of Numbers

Whether they are indicating the scope of a phenomenon or citing the increase or decrease of a trend, writers who are speculating about causes often cite dates, percentages, fractions, and other numbers. Academic writing prescribes conventional ways of writing such numbers. Look, for example, at these sentences from an essay about increasing reports of sexual harassment in the workplace:

> According to a 1994 survey conducted by the Society for Human Resource Management, the percentage of human resource professionals who have reported that their departments handled at least one sexual harassment complaint rose from 35 percent in 1991 to 65 percent in 1994. The jury awarded Weeks $7.1 million in punitive damages, twice what she sought in her lawsuit.

The writer follows the convention of spelling out numbers (*one*) that can be written as one or two words and using a combination of numerals and words for a large number (*$7.1 million*). (She could also have used numerals for the large number: *$7,100,000.*) She uses numerals for dates and percentages.

The Problem. Ignoring the rules for writing dates, percentages, fractions, and other numbers in academic writing can confuse your readers and/or make them question your attention to detail.

What to Do.

- Spell out numbers and fractions of one or two words.

  ▶ According to the World Health Organization, as many as 1̶ person in every 5̶0̶ may be infected with HIV.

  one ... fifty

> *two-thirds*
> ▶ Maybe ~~2/3~~ of the smoke from a cigarette is released into the air.

- Use numbers when fractions and numbers are more than two words.

> *4,837*
> ▶ That year the Japanese automobile industry produced only ~~four thousand eight hundred thirty-seven~~ vehicles, mostly trucks and motorbikes.

> *5 ⅓*
> ▶ This study shows that Americans spend an average of ~~five and one-third~~ hours a day watching television.

- Write percentages and dates with figures.

> ▶ Comparing 1980 to 1960, we can see that time spent viewing television
> *28*
> increased ~~twenty-eight~~ percent.

- Spell out numbers that begin a sentence.

(For practice, go to **bedfordstmartins.com/ theguide/exercisecentral** and click on Numbers.)

> *Thirty*
> ▶ ~~30~~ percent of commercial real estate in Washington, D.C., is owned by foreigners.

Checking for *Reason Is Because* Constructions

When you speculate about causes, you need to offer reasons and support for your speculations. Consequently, essays that speculate about causes often contain sentences constructed around a *reason is because* pattern, as in the following example:

> The *reason* we lost the war *is because* troop morale was down.

The Problem. Since *because* means "for the reason that," such sentences say essentially that "the reason is the reason."

How to Correct It. Rewrite the sentence so that it uses either *the reason . . . is* or *because*, but not both:

> The *reason* we lost the war *is* that troop morale was down.

> We lost the war *because* troop morale was down.

> *that*
> ▶ Her research suggests that one reason women attend women's colleges is ~~because~~ they want to avoid certain social pressures.

> *Older*
> ▶ ~~A reason older~~ Americans watch so much television ~~is~~ because they tend to be sedentary.

A Writer at Work

Sheila McClain's Analysis of Possible Causes

When a writer is planning an essay that speculates about causes, identifying and analyzing possible causes are the most important parts of developing an argument and counterargument. Here we look at a table of possible causes that Sheila McClain developed for "Fitness Culture: A Growing Trend in America," which appears in this chapter on pp. 451–55.

McClain worked on this invention in stages, and her table of causes shows how her ideas about her subject evolved. She began the activity with the idea that she wanted to explain the increase in the number of Americans joining health clubs. Later, as she did research and considered her subject in more detail, she decided it was too narrow and modified it to focus on an increase in interest in fitness and exercise more broadly, with the increase in health-club memberships being one element of this trend for which she could also speculate about causes. As you read through her table, notice how the causes and her analysis of them reflect McClain's developing ideas about her subject. With her initial subject in mind, she entered the first three causes in the table and a partial analysis. Then, after she researched her subject and decided to focus on fitness and exercise, she added the other three causes and completed the analysis.

Once McClain had analyzed these possible causes, she could decide how to use them to make her causal argument convincing. She decided to focus first on cause 4 because it seemed the most fundamental to the trend of increased interest in exercise and fitness, then to write about cause 1 and cause 5, and finally to combine her analyses of causes 2 and 6 because they were closely related. She thought her readers would find these causes plausible, and she knew she had enough statistics and examples to support them. After discussing her ideas with a friend, she reevaluated cause 3 and realized that it was really an objection to her claim that there is an increasing interest in "fitness culture." Citing the response of her exercise physiology professor to this objection, she tried with at least some success to refute it.

Table of Possible Causes and Analysis

Possible Causes	Analysis
1. Sense of community in going to the gym	Obvious cause. Positive peer pressure keeps people going — they are more likely to exercise on a regular basis and have a greater sense of commitment than if exercising alone. Also, going to a gym substitutes for social activities many people don't have time for. My mom joined a gym because she said it was motivation for her to do something outside of the home and office. This could be considered a perpetuating cause.

(continued)

(*continued*)

Possible Causes	Analysis
2. Variety of equipment and activities offered by gyms	Traditional exercises are boring and hard work. At a gym, people have the opportunity to work out as strenuously or as gently as they want, depending on the kind of equipment and classes they choose. Many types of exercise offered by gyms, such as aerobics, are actually considered fun. This could be seen as a sufficient cause for the popularity of gyms.
3. Desire to look better	An increasing emphasis on body image in the media means that people want to look like models and film stars. This is really a potential objection — refute with evidence from prof and Harton (= weak motivation to exercise).
4. Greater awareness of the benefits of fitness and exercise	Government studies on the benefits of physical activity in the late 1980s led both federal and state governments to make the public more aware of these benefits. This remote cause led to a perpetuating cause. Employers and insurance companies have jumped on the bandwagon — encouraged by insurers, many more companies now pay for employee health-club memberships, leading many more people to participate in exercise. Health and phys ed required in more schools also (but many schools cut b/c of $).
5. Reaction to 9/11	Definitely a hidden and surprising cause. Sisson shows an increase in the number of health clubs since the terrorist attacks on the World Trade Center for several reasons — stress leads people to want to be part of a group, working out can empower people feeling helpless, and the tragedy led people to reassess their lives and look for ways of improving themselves.
6. Changing attitudes toward exercise	Combine with #2. Inside and outside of gyms, more people are beginning to recognize the emotional benefits of exercise, the endorphin release known as runner's high. As Glenn says, exercise is now seen as "a way to enjoy life."

Thinking Critically About What You Have Learned

In this chapter, you have learned a great deal about this genre from reading several essays speculating about causes and from writing one of your own. To consolidate your learning, it is helpful to think metacognitively; that is, to reflect not only on what you learned but on how you learned it. Following are two brief activities your instructor may ask you to do.

Reflecting on Your Writing

Your instructor may ask you to turn in with your essay and process materials a brief metacognitive essay or letter reflecting on what you have learned about writing your causal argument. Choose among the following invention activities those that seem most productive for you.

- Explain how your purpose and audience influenced *one* of your decisions as a writer, such as how you explained the phenomenon or trend, the causes you presented as plausible, how you organized your presentation of these causes, the kinds of support you used for them, or how you counterargued objections or alternative explanations.

- Discuss what you learned about yourself as a writer in the process of writing this particular essay. For example, what part of the process did you find most challenging? Did you try anything new, like getting a critical reading of your draft or outlining your draft in order to revise it?

- If you were to give advice to a friend who was about to write an essay speculating about causes, what would you say?

- Which of the readings in this chapter influenced your essay? Explain the influence, citing specific examples from your essay and the reading.

- If you got good advice from a critical reader, explain exactly how the person helped you — perhaps by questioning your use of support, your use of visuals, the way you began or ended your essay, or the kinds of sources you used.

Considering the Social Dimensions: Causal Speculation and the Power of Authority and Ideology

We need to keep in mind that what seems to be the best *current* explanation for the causes of a trend or phenomenon is not necessarily the *only* explanation. Speculating about causes tends to give greater voice to certain interests and to minimize or silence others. Some analyses — particularly those of experts such as economists, psychologists, and popular authors — are often granted more authority than analyses favored by parents, teachers, community and religious leaders, and other persons most directly affected.

In addition, we need to remember that causal reasoning is always shaped by the analyst's ideology — the beliefs, values, and attitudes that determine a person's worldview. For example, Stephen King — a horror writer — has a real interest in establishing the horror movie as a legitimate literary and cinematic form; not surprisingly, then, he emphasizes the psychological benefits of horror movies. Erica Goode, whose educational background is in social psychology, is clearly sympathetic to the work of the various psychologists and social scientists she quotes to support her claim that subtle environmental factors contribute to how much people eat. For reasons of their own, spokespersons for the fast-food industry blame very different factors — such as lack of exercise and genetic makeup — for increasing obesity among Americans.

Even the way we define a phenomenon or a trend can affect our explanation of its causes. For example, when four white Los Angeles police officers were videotaped beating a black motorist but acquitted of assault charges in the spring of 1992, many people took to the streets, starting fires, looting, and killing 55 people and injuring 2,383. While some observers called the disturbance a "riot," others used a more sympathetic term — "uprising." These two terms reflect two ways of understanding what happened in the city that spring, pointing to entirely different sets of possible causes. A great deal is at stake when society must decide whether the causes of violent crimes were linked to frustration with racism and unequal justice, on the one hand, or to lack of an adequate police "presence" and respect for the law, on the other hand.

1. ***Consider how the readings and your own essay are exercises in exerting authority.*** We have said that because causal speculation deals with possibilities instead of certainties, writers must be somewhat tentative about their speculations. However, if causal argument is to be convincing, it cannot be too timid. Writers who have studied a subject carefully may feel that they are justified in exerting their authority. Compare the Erica Goode and Stephen King essays. Which seems more assertive? What accounts for your response? What seems to you assertive or unassertive about your own essay? Was it your knowledge or your ideology (your way of looking at the world), or both, that gave you the confidence to be authoritative?

2. ***Consider how easy it is to accept a causal explanation.*** We have also said that if readers are not alert, they may begin to think that the explanation offered is the only possible one. Is either Goode's or King's argument so seductive that you find yourself accepting it without question? Explain briefly.

3. ***Write a page or two explaining your ideas about authority and ideology in essays speculating about causes.*** Connect your ideas to your own essay and to the readings in this chapter.

10

Analyzing Stories

Stories have a special place in most cultures. Sharing stories strengthens the bonds of family and community: Elders relate family and cultural history through stories; children learn lessons through fables and parables; people of all ages use stories to express feelings, work out conflicts, and entertain themselves and others. Reading stories stimulates our feelings and imagination, allowing us to escape our everyday routine and become aware of the wider world around us. Stories can lead us to look at others with sensitivity and, for a brief time, to see the world through another person's eyes. They can also lead us to see ourselves differently, to gain insight into our innermost feelings and thoughts.

The short stories presented in this chapter may in some respects remind you of the essays about remembered events you read and wrote in Chapter 2. As you may remember, essays about remembered events convey significance primarily through vivid descriptive detail showing people in particular places engaged in some kind of dramatic action. Fictional stories work the same way, except that the people in them are called *characters*, places are called *setting*, the dramatic action is called *plot*, and the significance is called *theme* or *meaning*.

Good stories tend to be enigmatic in that they usually do not reveal themselves fully on first reading. That is why it can be so enjoyable and enlightening to analyze stories and discuss them with other readers. Even very short stories can elicit fascinating analyses. For example, Ernest Hemingway wrote this six-word story that he reportedly claimed was his best work:

> For sale: baby shoes, never worn.

Upon first reading, you might think you have gotten everything there is to get from the story. But consider the following questions:

- It looks like an ad, but who would try to sell baby shoes, and why? What is the relationship between the person trying to sell the shoes and the baby for whom the shoes were originally bought?
  - If the person is a parent, what does selling the shoes suggest?
  - If the person is someone unrelated to the baby, how did that person get the shoes and why is he or she selling them?
  - Could the person be someone who wanted but never had or lost a baby, or is it more likely to be someone who simply bought the wrong size shoes and didn't return them?

- Who would be a potential buyer for the shoes?
- If the story is about the death of a child, how old was the child and what were the circumstances of his/her death? If there is no death involved, what *are* the circumstances: Is the baby unable to walk or wear shoes? Was he or she taken away from the person who placed the ad? Or were the shoes simply a bad purchase?
- Where and when was the ad written? (In a country where there are land mines? At a time of severe economic depression?)
- Why is the story so short? Could the brevity say something about the inability of language to express emotion? Could the fact that the story is written in the form of an advertisement suggest something about commercialism?

As these questions suggest, even the shortest story can be analyzed and discussed in ways that enhance its possible meanings and enrich your reading experience.

In this chapter, you will be reading and writing essays analyzing a story. The essays you will read illustrate the basic features and strategies writers typically use when writing about stories. The questions and activities following these essays will help you consider what is particular to one writer's analysis and what strategies you might want to try out in writing your own analysis.

The Guide to Writing that follows the readings will support you as you compose your own essay, showing you ways to use the basic features of the genre to write a creative and convincing analysis. Even though this genre is a special kind of academic writing, you do not have to be an English major to write a successful analysis. You will be able to use your experience of listening to, viewing, reading, and telling stories to write insightfully about the story you analyze for this chapter's assignment.

To get a sense of the possibilities involved in analyzing stories, work together on an analysis of one story with two or three other students. Here are some guidelines to follow:

Part 1.

- Get together with students who have read the same story from the Anthology of Short Stories that begins on p. 546.
- Begin by discussing one question from the Questions for Analysis following the story your group reads. (During the discussion, you may go on to answer other questions as well.)

Part 2. After you have discussed the story for half of the time allotted for this activity, reflect on the process of analyzing the story in your group:

- Before you began, what were your expectations of how the group would work together? For example, did you think your group should or would agree on one "right answer" to the questions, or did you expect significant disagreement? What actually happened once you began to discuss the story?
- How did the discussion affect your attitude about the story, or about the process of analyzing stories? What, if anything, did you learn?

A Collaborative Activity:
Practice Analyzing a Story

Basic Features

As you read essays that analyze stories in this chapter, you will see how different writers incorporate the basic features of the genre.

Most essays analyzing a story begin with several sentences or paragraphs of introduction. Most writers identify the story being analyzed by giving the title, the author, and possibly some historical, biographical, or cultural context. Depending on whether the essay was written in response to a specific question or an open-ended assignment, the writer may then give some context to his or her argument by

- responding to the instructor's question(s);

- briefly summarizing the conversation to which the essay is responding — for example, a class discussion of the story or ideas presented in another essay, article, or book; and/or

- positioning the analysis — disagreeing with or expanding on established ways of understanding the story or applying a new idea or critical approach to the story.

● A Clear, Arguable Thesis

Read first to find the thesis statement, which may be a single sentence but may also be several paragraphs long. A good thesis statement in an essay analyzing a story

- asserts the main idea or claim;

- is arguable, not a simple statement of fact (such as, the boy in "Araby" lives in Dublin) or an obvious conclusion (such as, the boy has a crush on Mangan's sister);

- is appropriately qualified, not overgeneralized or exaggerated (such as, "Araby" shows how a Catholic education inevitably distorts boys' attitudes toward girls and sexuality);

- is clearly stated, not vague or ambiguous.

Thesis statements usually also preview the argument, identifying the reasons that will be presented in the rest of the essay. The thesis statement may include or be followed by a **forecasting statement** that introduces certain key terms that are used throughout the essay to identify the reasons as they are brought up and developed.

● Support for the Argument

*Consider how the writer provides **support** for the argument.* Because essays analyzing stories usually present new ideas that are not obvious and that readers may disagree with, writers need to make an argument that includes

- reasons — the supporting ideas or points that develop the essay's thesis or main claim;
- examples from the story;
- explanations or analyses showing how the examples support the argument.

In addition, writers may provide other kinds of support — for example, citing expert readers or referring to historical, biographical, or cultural evidence. But textual evidence is the primary support readers expect.

Evidence from the text can take the form of *quotation* as well as *summary* or *paraphrase*. Quoting is the most important method of providing support for essays that analyze short stories, but quoting alone is not enough. The language of the short story must be analyzed to show how words' connotations, their figurative use in images and metaphors, or their symbolism enrich the story's meanings. When reading essays that analyze short stories, notice how the essayist analyzes the language of the story and how this analysis is used to support the writer's thesis.

For more on quotation, summary, and paraphrase, see Chapter 24, pp. 756–64.

⬢ A Readable Plan

*Read also to see how the writer provides a **readable plan** to help readers follow the argument.* To make their essays easy to read, writers usually include some or all of the following:

- a forecast of the argument in the introduction
- key words introduced in the thesis and/or the forecasting statement, and repeated strategically elsewhere in the essay
- topic sentences introducing paragraphs or groups of paragraphs
- clear transitional words and phrases

Inexperienced writers sometimes are afraid to ruin the surprise by forecasting their argument at the beginning of their essays. But explicit forecasting is a convention of literary analysis, similar in purpose to the abstract that precedes many articles in scientific journals. Forecasting will make your argument clearer and meet readers' expectations.

Purpose and Audience

Although writing about stories is an important academic kind of discourse, many people enjoy discussing stories and writing about how a story resonates in their lives. That is why book clubs, reading groups, and online discussion forums are so popular. Talking and writing about stories we have read and seen can help us understand why a particular story may be moving, disturbing, or uplifting. Sharing the experience with others exposes us to different ways of interpreting and responding to stories — expanding our openness to new perspectives, deepening our insight, and enhancing our pleasure.

In the classroom, the process of discussing and writing about stories can make you feel closer to your classmates and instructors. Sharing the reading experience can tighten the bonds of community as each reader contributes to a mosaic of meanings. But analyzing stories can also be challenging because readers sometimes disagree. That is why each essay analyzing a story presents an argument.

As you read essays analyzing stories, ask yourself what seems to be the writer's **purpose**. For example, consider whether the writer seems to be writing for one or more of the following purposes:

- to illuminate the story
- to change or expand the way readers understand the story
- to impress readers with the writer's insight and close reading

As you read, also try to grasp the writer's assumptions about the **audience**. The essays you will read as you work through this chapter were written by students in a college course where the entire class had read the same story. These writers also assumed that their primary reader, the instructor, had not only read the story but also knew a fair amount about its context and the conversation surrounding it — enough, at least, to be able to judge whether the essayist read the story with sufficient care and thought. In cases such as these, plot summaries and recitals of well-known facts about the short story and its author are not necessary. Be aware, however, that if such an essay were to be published for a wider audience, this kind of basic information might be required for a full understanding of the writer's argument.

Readings

The following essays by students Sally Crane and David Ratinov analyze the short story "Araby," by James Joyce (see pp. 549–53). As Crane points out in her opening paragraph, many readers have focused on the ending of the story and have come to different conclusions about its meaning. You, too, may have puzzled over the story's ending and asked yourself what, if anything, the boy discovers. Crane and Ratinov disagree. By reading their essays, you will learn a great deal about how writers argue for their own particular analyses of a story. (Note: In citing passages from "Araby," Crane and Ratinov followed their instructors' directions rather than following MLA style, which would have required them to cite page numbers instead of paragraph numbers.)

SALLY CRANE wrote this essay for a freshman composition course. Notice that she takes her title from the concluding image of "Araby." As you read Crane's essay, think about how well the title captures her main idea. Also consider the questions in the margin. Your instructor may ask you to post your answers or bring them to class.

● ● ●
Basic Features
• Arguable Thesis
• Support
• Readable Plan

Gazing into the Darkness

Sally Crane

1   Readers of "Araby" often focus on the final scene as the key to the story. They assume the boy experiences some profound insight about himself when he gazes "up into the darkness" (par. 37). I believe, however, that the boy sees nothing and learns nothing — about either himself or others. He's not self-reflective; he's merely self-absorbed.

2   Joyce uses imagery of blindness and the ironic point of view of the narrator to show the boy's failure of sight and insight. There can seem to be a profound insight at the end of the story only if we empathize with the boy and adopt his point of view. In other words, we must assume that the young boy is narrating his own story. But if the real narrator is the grown man looking back at his early adolescence, then it becomes possible to read the narrative as ironic and to see the boy as confused and blind.

3   The story opens and closes with images of blindness — a framing device that shows the boy does not change but ends up with the same lack of understanding that he began with. The street is "blind" with an "uninhabited house . . . at the blind end" (par. 1). As he spies on Mangan's sister, from his own house, the boy intentionally limits what he is able to see by lowering the "blind" until it is only an inch from the window sash (par. 4). At the bazaar in the closing scene, "the light was out," and the upper part of the hall was "completely dark" (par. 36). The boy is left "gazing up into the darkness," seeing nothing but an inner torment that burns his eyes (par. 37).

4   This blindness appears to be caused by the boy's obsession with Mangan's sister. When he tries to read at night, for example, the girl's "image [comes] between [him] and the page," in effect blinding him (par. 12). In fact, he seems blind to everything except this "image" of the "brown-clad figure cast by [his] imagination" (par. 16). The girl's "brown-clad figure" is also associated with the houses on "blind" North Richmond Street, with their "brown imperturbable faces" (par. 1). The houses stare back at the boy, unaffected by his presence and gaze.

5   He is obsessed with Mangan's sister but he can't see her for who she really is. His description of her and interpretation of the few words she says to him can be seen as further evidence of his blindness. He sees only what he wants to see, the "image" he has in his mind's eye (par. 5). This image comes more from what he's read than from

What do these opening paragraphs try to do, and how well do they do it?

Why do you think Crane quotes these words and phrases? Are the quotes effective?

Highlight the topic sentences in paragraphs 3–5. How well do they work?

anything he's observed. He casts her simultaneously in the traditional female roles of angel and whore:

> While she spoke she turned a silver bracelet round and round her wrist. She could not go, she said, because there would be a retreat that week in her convent. . . . She held one of the spikes, bowing her head towards me. The light from the lamp opposite our door caught the white curve of her neck, lit up her hair that rested there and, falling, lit up the hand upon the railing. It fell over one side of her dress and caught the white border of a petticoat, just visible as she stood at ease. (par. 9)

How does Crane help readers understand how this indented quotation supports her argument?

Her angelic qualities are shown in her plans to attend a convent retreat and in her bowed head. Her whorish qualities come through in the way she flirtatiously plays with the bracelet, as if she were inviting him to buy her an expensive piece of jewelry at the bazaar. The "white curve of her neck" and the "white border of a petticoat" combine the symbolic color of purity, associated with the Madonna, with sexual suggestiveness (par. 9). The point is that there is no suggestion here or anywhere else in the story that the boy is capable of seeing Mangan's sister as a real person. She only exists as the object of his gaze. In fact, no one seems to have any reality for him other than himself.

How does this paragraph connect to Crane's thesis?

He is totally self-absorbed. But at the same time, he is also blind to himself. He says repeatedly that he doesn't understand his feelings: "Her name sprang to my lips at moments in strange prayers and praises which I myself did not understand. My eyes were often full of tears (I could not tell why)" (par. 5). His adoration of her is both "confused" and confusing to him. He has no self-understanding (par. 5).

6

The best insight we have into the boy comes from the language he uses. Much of his language seems to mimic the old priest's romantic books: "Her name was like a summons to all my foolish blood" (par. 4); "I imagined that I bore my chalice safely through a throng of foes" (par. 5); "my body was like a harp and her words and gestures were like fingers running upon the wires" (par. 5). Language like this sounds as though it comes out of a popular romance novel, something written by Danielle Steele perhaps. The mixing of romance with soft porn is unmistakable. Perhaps the boy has spent too much time reading the priest's sexually seductive stories from *The Memoirs of Vidocq* (par. 2).

7

How effectively does Crane use what she learned from Chapter 2, Remembering an Event?

Joyce uses this kind of language ironically to point to the fact that the narrator is not the young boy himself but the young boy now grown and looking back at how "foolish" he was (par. 4). This interpretation becomes likely when you think of "Araby" as a fictionalized autobiography. In autobiographical stories, remembered feelings and thoughts are combined with the autobiographer's present perspective. The remembered

8

feelings and thoughts in this story could be seen as expressing the boy's point of view, but we read them ironically through the adult narrator's present perspective. The romantic, gushy language the boy uses is laughable. It reveals the boy's blindness toward everyone, including himself. He sees himself as Sir Galahad, the chivalric hero on his own grail quest to Araby. The greatest irony comes at the end when his quest is exposed as merely a shopping trip and Araby as merely a suburban mall.

> Why do you think Crane does not explain the references to "Sir Galahad," "chivalric hero," and "grail quest"? Should she?

9   Most people interpret the ending as a moment of profound insight, and the language certainly seems to support this interpretation: "Gazing up into the darkness I saw myself as a creature driven and derided by vanity; and my eyes burned with anguish and anger" (par. 37). But here again we see the narrator using inflated language that suggests an ironic stance. So even in the moment of apparent insight, the boy is still playing a heroic role. He hasn't discovered his true self. He's just as self-absorbed and blind in the end as he was at the beginning.

> What are the strengths of this ending? How could it be improved?

DAVID RATINOV used the Questions for Analysis (p. 554) and the Suggestions for Analysis in the Guide to Writing (pp. 522–23) to read "Araby" as a coming-of-age story, or what he calls in his title "an initiation." We have not annotated or highlighted his essay but you may want to do so as you read it and as you respond to the suggestions in the Analyzing Writing Strategies section that follows the essay. As you read, notice how Ratinov's analysis differs from Crane's.

From Innocence to Insight: "Araby" as an Initiation Story
David Ratinov

1   "Araby" tells the story of an adolescent boy's initiation into adulthood. The story is narrated by a mature man reflecting on his adolescence and the events that forced him to face the disillusioning realities of adulthood. The minor characters play a pivotal role in this initiation process. The boy observes the hypocrisy of adults in the priest and Mrs. Mercer; and his vain, self-centered uncle introduces him to another disillusioning aspect of adulthood. The boy's infatuation with the girl ultimately ends in disillusionment, and Joyce uses the specific example of the boy's disillusionment with love as a metaphor for disillusionment with life itself. From the beginning, the boy

deludes himself about his relationship with Mangan's sister. At Araby, he realizes the parallel between his own self-delusion and the hypocrisy and vanity of the adult world.

From the beginning, the boy's infatuation with Mangan's sister draws him away from childhood toward adulthood. He breaks his ties with his childhood friends and luxuriates in his isolation. He can think of nothing but his love for her: "From the front window I saw my companions playing below in the street. Their cries reached me weakened and indistinct and, leaning my forehead against the cool glass, I looked over at the dark house where she lived" (par. 16). The friends' cries are weak and indistinct because they are distant emotionally as well as spatially. Like an adult on a quest, he imagines he carries his love as if it were a sacred object, a chalice: "Her image accompanied me even in places the most hostile to romance. . . . I imagined that I bore my chalice safely through a throng of foes" (par. 5). Even in the active, distracting marketplace, he is able to retain this image of his pure love. But his love is not pure.

Although he worships Mangan's sister as a religious object, his lust for her is undeniable. He idolizes her as if she were the Virgin Mary: "her figure defined by the light from the half-opened door. . . . The light from the lamp opposite our door caught the white curve of her neck, lit up her hair that rested there and, falling, lit up the hand upon the railing" (par. 3, 9). Yet even this image is sensual with the halo of light accentuating "the white curve of her neck." The language makes obvious that his attraction is physical rather than spiritual: "Her dress swung as she moved her body and the soft rope of her hair tossed from side to side" (par. 3). His desire for her is strong and undeniable: "her name was like a summons to all my foolish blood" (par. 4); "my body was like a harp and her words and gestures were like fingers running upon the wires" (par. 5). But in order to justify his love, to make it socially acceptable, he deludes himself into thinking that his love is pure. He is being hypocritical, although at this point he does not know it.

Hypocrisy is characteristic of the adults in this story. The priest is by far the most obvious offender. What is a man of the cloth doing with books like *The Abbot* (a romantic novel) and *The Memoirs of Vidocq* (a collection of sexually suggestive tales)? These books imply that he led a double life. Moreover, the fact that he had money to give away when he died suggests that he was far from saintly. Similarly, at first glance Mrs. Mercer appears to be religious, but a closer look reveals that she too is materialistic. Her church work — collecting used stamps for some "pious purpose" (presumably to sell for the church) — associates her with money and profit (par. 17). Even her name, Mercer, identifies her as a dealer in merchandise. In addition, her husband is a pawnbroker, a profession that the church frowns on. Despite being linked to money, she pretends to be pious and respectable. Therefore, like the priest, Mrs. Mercer is hypocritical.

The uncle, as the boy's only living male relative, is a failure as a role model and the epitome of vanity. He is a self-centered old man who cannot handle responsibility: When the boy reminds him on Saturday morning about the bazaar, the uncle brushes him off, devoting all his attention to his own appearance. After being out all afternoon the uncle returns home at 9:00, talking to himself. He rocks the hallstand when hanging up his overcoat. These details suggest that he is drunk. "I could interpret these signs" indicates that this behavior is typical of his uncle (par. 19). The uncle is the only character in the story the boy relies on, but the uncle fails him. Only after the aunt persuades him does the uncle give the boy the money he promised. From the priest, Mrs. Mercer, and his uncle, the boy learns some fundamental truths about adulthood, but it is only after his visit to Araby that he is able to recognize what he has learned.

Araby to the adolescent represents excitement, a chance to prove the purity of his love and, more abstractly, his hope; however, Araby fulfills none of these expectations. Instead, the boy finds himself in utter disillusionment and despair. Araby is anything but exciting. The trip there is dreary and uneventful, lonely and intolerably slow — not the magical journey he had expected. When he arrives, Araby itself is nearly completely dark and in the process of closing. With his excitement stunted, he can barely remember why he came there (to prove the purity of his love by buying a gift for Mangan's sister).

The young lady selling porcelain and her gentleman friends act as catalysts, causing the boy to recognize the truth of his love for Mangan's sister. Their conversation is flirtatious — a silly lovers' game that the boy recognizes as resembling his own conversation with Mangan's sister. He concludes that his love for her is no different than the two gentlemen's love for this "lady" (par. 26). Neither love is pure. He too had only been playing a game, flirting with a girl and pretending that it was something else and that he was someone else.

His disillusionment with love is then extended to life in general. Seeing the last rays of hope fading from the top floors of Araby, the boy cries: "I saw myself as a creature driven and derided by vanity; and my eyes burned with anguish and anger" (par. 37). At last he makes the connection — by deluding himself, he has been hypocritical and vain like the adults in his life. Before these realizations he believed that he was driven by something of value (such as purity of love), but now he realizes that his quest has been in vain because honesty, truth, and purity are only childish illusions and he can never return to the innocence of childhood.

LEARN ABOUT RATINOV'S WRITING PROCESS

To learn about how Ratinov used the Suggestions for Analysis, turn to A Writer at Work on pp. 541–44. Notice how he annotated the story with the suggestions for analyzing character in mind. Compare his exploratory writing about the hypocrisy of Mrs. Mercer and the boy's uncle with what he wrote in paragraphs 3 and 4 of his essay. How did his annotating and exploratory writing help Ratinov develop his ideas and draft part of his essay?

ANALYZING WRITING STRATEGIES

⬣ ⬣ ⬣

Basic Features

● A Clear, Arguable Thesis

Writers analyzing stories sometimes begin by giving a *context* for their argument, as Crane does when she refers to other readers of the story in the opening words of her essay. Ratinov does not explicitly refer to other readers, but by opening with the claim that "Araby" is an "initiation story," Ratinov sets the stage for his argument by indicating that he is taking a position in an ongoing conversation among readers of the story. After asserting his thesis in the opening sentence, he uses the rest of the first paragraph to spell out his argument and forecast the reasons he will develop in the rest of the essay.

To analyze Ratinov's thesis and forecasting statement, try the following:

- Reread the opening paragraph and mark the key terms he introduces.
- Skim the rest of the essay, marking any repetition of these key terms.
- Write a few sentences summarizing Ratinov's argument and assessing how well the opening paragraph forecasts the argument developed in the rest of the essay.

● Support for the Argument

Essays analyzing a story rely primarily on **textual evidence** — that is, on a close reading of the story itself — to support the argument. Crane's essay shows how writers may quote individual words, phrases, whole sentences, and occasionally, even whole paragraphs. But effective writers do not expect a quotation to do the work by itself. Instead, they discuss the quotation, demonstrating how it supports the point they're making.

Look at two examples in Crane's essay. In paragraph 3, she makes an assertion about the prevalence of images of blindness in the story, briefly explaining what she thinks they mean. In the next four paragraphs, she gives examples of such images, showing specifically how the image connotes lack of insight or understanding. In paragraph 7, Crane uses a variation on this strategy, preceding related quotations with an introduction and following them with analysis. There are many ways to present quotations effectively; what is important is that the writer not expect the quotations to speak for themselves because different readers are likely to interpret the quotations differently.

In addition to quoting, writers also may summarize or paraphrase parts of the story they are using as support. For example, Ratinov uses summary when he refers to the fact that the priest gave money away when he died (par. 4). He uses paraphrase in paragraph 6 when he describes the hall at Araby as "nearly completely dark and in the process of closing," in which he echoes James Joyce's language: "Nearly all the stalls were closed and the greater part of the hall was in darkness" ("Araby," par. 25).

To analyze how Ratinov uses quotation, summary, and paraphrase to support his argument, try the following:

- Reread paragraph 2, underlining the two quotations and examining how they support Ratinov's argument.

- Reread paragraphs 6–7 to see how Ratinov uses summary and paraphrase to describe what happened at Araby.

- Write a few sentences explaining what these examples show about Ratinov's use of quotation, summary, and paraphrase to support his argument.

● A Readable Plan

As we have seen, writers try to help readers follow their argument by making their plan or organization legible for readers. One way to do this is by beginning with a thesis and a forecasting statement that previews the reasons that will be developed and supported in the essay. Writers also use key terms and repeat them, or use synonyms to recall them, when they bring up the reasons later in the essay. In the first activity, you traced Ratinov's key terms to see how accurately his opening paragraph forecasts his argument. Here, we focus on the related strategy of using *topic sentences* to help readers follow the argument.

Topic sentences identify the topic of a single paragraph or sequence of paragraphs developing the same topic. Writers tend to place topic sentences at or near the top of a paragraph because topic sentences help readers make sense of the details, examples, and explanations that come next. Here is an example from Crane's essay showing the last sentence of one paragraph and the first two sentences of the next paragraph:

> . . . In fact, no one seems to have any reality for him other than himself.
>   He is totally self-absorbed. But at the same time, he is also blind to himself.
> (pars. 5–6)

The first sentence of paragraph 6 makes a transition between paragraphs 5 and 6. The statement that the boy is "self-absorbed" supports the conclusion of the preceding paragraph that no one is real to the boy "other than himself." The second sentence of paragraph 6 is the topic sentence of the paragraph. It asserts the new point that the boy "is also blind to himself." The rest of the paragraph works to support this assertion.

To analyze how Ratinov uses topic sentences, follow these suggestions:

- Reread paragraphs 3–5 and underline the topic sentences.
- Write several sentences explaining how each topic sentence works and assessing how well they help you follow the argument as it is developed and supported in these paragraphs.

Beyond the Traditional Essay: Analyzing Stories

While the traditional essay that analyzes short stories has, as you have seen, very specific basic features, responses to short stories and other forms of literature can take many other forms. Responses to literature in other media, such as visual art, live performance, film, and music, are common: the play *The Elephant Vanishes*, depicted here, is a theatrical interpretation of short stories by Japanese writer Haruki Murakami; the 2007 opera *Grapes of Wrath* is based on the Steinbeck novel of the same name; and Fitzgerald's *The Great Gatsby* has inspired numerous film versions, including *G*, in which the character of Gatsby is portrayed as an African American rap music mogul. In a sense, any performance, staged or read, of a work of literature (including, but not necessarily limited to, plays and poems) can be called an interpretation. While these works are not formal academic analyses, the way(s) in which the creators re-present the works certainly present ideas about the meanings of the literature that are at the heart of analysis.

Closer to home for many of us are the fan fiction (or "fanfic") projects — including sequels, extensions, revisions, parodies, and other "retellings" of published literature — that have become pervasive in recent years, in part as a response to the open forum for such work provided by the Internet. Hyperlinked fiction, another trend made possible by the Internet, is essentially a high-tech form of footnotes, with links inserted to related sites and to explanatory text that enriches the reading experience. Like the other forms of response discussed here, hyperlinking is not formal analysis, but it certainly illuminates the work for readers.

As you work on your own project, you might want to consult some of these alternative forms of response for inspiration. If the format in which you are working allows for it — if, for example, you are creating a poster, Web site, or video — you should consider taking advantage of the strategies available to those working in multimedia — for example, by embedding artifacts that are relevant to the story you are interpreting. (Always remember to properly document any material you might use that was created by someone else.)

Guide to Writing

The Writing Assignment

Write an essay analyzing one or more aspects of a story. Aim to convince readers that your interpretation adds to the conversation among those who read stories and write about them. Back up your analysis with reasons and support from the story.

This Guide to Writing will help you apply what you have learned about how writers make their essays analyzing stories interesting and well supported. The Guide is divided into five sections with various activities in each section:

- Invention and Research
- Planning and Drafting
- Critical Reading Guide
- Revising
- Editing and Proofreading

The Guide is designed to escort you through the writing process, from finding a story to editing your finished essay. Your instructor may require you to follow the Guide to Writing from beginning to end. Working through the Guide to Writing in this way will help you — as it has helped many other college students — write a thoughtful, fully developed, polished essay.

If, however, your instructor gives you latitude to choose and if you have had experience writing essays analyzing stories, then you can decide on the order in which you will do the activities in the Guide to Writing. For example, the Invention and Research section includes activities to help you choose a story, annotate it using one or more of the suggestions for analysis, do exploratory writing about your annotations and about the connections among your ideas, formulate and refine your thesis statement, and find additional support. Obviously, choosing a story must precede the other activities, but you may come to the Guide knowing that readers disagree about the story and you may even have an idea or a tentative thesis you want to test as you reread and annotate the story. Or you may analyze the story with the help of several Suggestions for Analysis before you begin to grab hold of an idea you can develop in your essay. In fact, you may find your response to one of the invention activities expanding into a draft before you have had a chance to do any of the other activities. Writers sometimes find that in exploring their annotations or developing connections among their ideas, they are in effect drafting parts of their essay. That is a good thing — but you should later flesh out your draft by going back to the activities you skipped and layering the new material into your draft.

The following chart will help you find answers to many of the questions you might have about planning, drafting, and revising an essay analyzing a story. The page references in the Where to Look column refer to examples from the readings and activities in the Guide to Writing.

To learn about using the *Guide* e-book for invention and drafting, go to **bedfordstmartins.com/ theguide.**

517

Starting Points: Analyzing Stories

●●● Basic Features

	Question	Where to Look
Choosing a Story and Approach to Analyzing It	What kind of story should I write about? How can I find a good one?	• Finding a Story to Write About (pp. 519–20) • Testing Your Choice (p. 525)
	What's my purpose in writing? How can I interest my audience in what I write?	• Refining Your Purpose and Setting Goals: Clarifying Your Purpose and Audience (p. 528)
	What does it mean to analyze a story? How do I get started?	• Analyzing the Story: Choosing a Suggestion for Analysis (p. 521)
	Once I have chosen an analytical approach, how do I apply it?	• Analyzing the Story: Annotating with the Suggestions for Analysis in Mind (pp. 522–23)
A Clear, Arguable Thesis	How do I decide on a main idea?	• Formulating a Tentative Thesis Statement: Finding a Main Idea (pp. 525–26)
	How do I shape my main idea into an arguable thesis?	• Giving a context for your argument (p. 514) • Formulating a Tentative Thesis Statement: Stating Your Thesis (pp. 526–27) • Refining Your Purpose and Setting Goals: Presenting a Clear, Arguable Thesis (p. 529)
Support for the Argument	How do I support my ideas?	• Citing and discussing textual evidence (pp. 514–15) • Ways In: Developing Your Analysis (p. 524) • Refining Your Purpose and Setting Goals: Providing Support for Your Argument (p. 529) • A Sentence Strategy: Using Short Quotations . . . (pp. 531–33) • Working with Sources (pp. 533–35)
	Do I need to do outside research?	• Researching Your Story (p. 527)
A Readable Plan	How should I organize my argument so that my audience can follow it easily?	• Using topic sentences to help your reader follow your argument (p. 515) • Refining Your Purpose and Setting Goals: Making Your Plan Readable and The Ending (pp. 529–30) • Outlining Your Draft (p. 530) • Drafting: Writing the Opening Sentences (p. 531)

Invention and Research

The following activities will help you choose a short story, analyze it, write to explore your annotations, test your choice, formulate a tentative thesis statement, revise your thesis statement, find additional support in the story for your thesis, and design your document. To make these activities as useful as possible, spread them out over several days, and keep a written record of all of your invention work.

Finding a Story to Write About

Your instructor may have given you a list of stories to choose from or assigned a particular story for the class to write about. If so, go on to the next section, Analyzing the Story.

If you need to find a story on your own, browse any literature anthology or short-story collection you can find in the library or bookstore. (At the library, do a keyword search on "short stories.") You can also search online for stories by Googling the keyword "short stories." Some magazines, like the *New Yorker* and *Esquire*, make some of their current fiction available online. Other online sites feature stories that have not been published in print. Still others, such as the following, offer collections of classic stories in the public domain:

- The Short Story Library at American Literature (http://www
  .americanliterature.com/SS/SSINDX.HTML)
- Classic Short Stories (http://www.classicshorts.com/)
- Classic Reader: Short Stories (http://www.classicreader.com/browse/6/)
- Short Story Archive (http://www.shortstoryarchive.com/)

You should look for a story that meets your instructor's approval and satisfies *at least one* of the following criteria:

☐ It deals with a culturally, politically, or historically significant theme.
☐ It surprises or puzzles you with apparent contradictions.
☐ It leads you to wonder what is left out of the story—the backstory or context.
☐ It raises questions about characters' motivations, relationships, or development.
☐ It uses conventional story motifs, setting, or other formal features in unconventional ways.
☐ It resonates emotionally, perhaps giving you insight into human frailty or moral ambiguity.

Criteria for Choosing a Story to Analyze:

A Checklist

The rest of this section suggests specific stories to consider.

Short Stories to Consider

Stories Related to Identity and Community. "A Good Story" (pp. 557–60), "Araby" (pp. 549–53), or "The Story of an Hour" (pp. 547–49) would all make good choices if you are interested in issues of identity and community. If you would like to look further, here are a few other widely anthologized stories you might consider writing about:

"The Monkey Garden," by Sandra Cisneros

"The Open Boat," by Stephen Crane

"Fleur," by Louise Erdrich

"A Rose for Emily," by William Faulkner

"My Kinsman, Major Molineux," by Nathaniel Hawthorne

"A Clean, Well-Lighted Place," by Ernest Hemingway

"The Lottery," by Shirley Jackson

"The Metamorphosis," by Franz Kafka

"The Ones Who Walk Away from Omelas," by Ursula Le Guin

"A Pair of Tickets," by Amy Tan

"My Father's Chinese Wives," by Sandra Tsing Loh

"Everyday Use," by Alice Walker

Stories Related to Work and Career. "The Use of Force" (pp. 554–57) would be one good choice if you are interested in writing about the topic of work and career. Here are some additional stories you might consider for exploring this topic:

"Sonny's Blues," by James Baldwin

"The Yellow Wallpaper," by Charlotte Perkins Gilman

"The Birthmark," by Nathaniel Hawthorne

"Reena," by Paule Marshall

"Shiloh," by Bobbie Ann Mason

"Bartleby the Scrivener," by Herman Melville

"Picasso," by Gertrude Stein

"The Catbird Seat," by James Thurber

"A&P," by John Updike

"Why I Live at the P.O.," by Eudora Welty

Analyzing the Story

To help you analyze the story, this section offers suggestions designed to help you find potentially meaningful details and ideas for your essay. You should try out more than one Suggestion for Analysis before making a decision on your focus. Rereading the story with different suggestions in mind can help you to discover how different aspects of the story work together and can lead you to construct a more fully developed thesis.

Choosing a Suggestion for Analysis

Think about aspects of the story that seem significant to you or about which you have questions. Then, consult the corresponding Suggestion for Analysis on pp. 522–23.

Questions Raised by the Story	Suggestions for Analysis to Consult
Why a character acts in a particular way	Character
How gender or ethnicity affects relationships	
Whether characters change or grow	
Whether we should approve of a character's actions or accept his/her justifications	
Whether the time and place matter	Setting
What the description symbolizes	
How the setting affects characters	
What the ending means	Plot Structure
Whether there is a turning point in the story	
How a subplot relates to the main plot	
Whether the narrator can be believed	Point of View
Whose values and interests are represented	
How readers' sympathies are manipulated	
Whether the story is about the development of an artist, the initiation into adulthood, or some other common literary motif	Literary Motif or Theme
What the story says about war, poverty, love, alienation, or some other general theme	
How the story illuminates an historical or current issue	

Annotating with the Suggestions for Analysis in Mind

The Suggestions for Analysis in the following chart are designed to help you read the story closely and critically. They will not cover everything you find, but are meant to be suggestive, to get you started not just reading but analyzing the story. Use these suggestions to annotate the story by highlighting key passages and noting your ideas and questions.

Suggestions for Analysis

Element to Analyze	Approach	What to Do
Character	Psychological	Consider whether the character changes or learns anything in the course of the story.
		Focus on how the character relates to other characters, noting how the character deals with intimacy, commitment, and responsibility.
		Note whether the character seems depressed, manic, abusive, fearful, egotistical, or paranoid.
		Look for another character who may represent the character's double or opposite.
	Ethical or moral	Decide what you consider to be the character's virtues and/or vices.
		Consider what influences your judgment of the character — something in the story (such as what the narrator or another character says), something you bring to the story (your views of right and wrong, based on your family upbringing or religious teachings), or something else.
		See whether any of the other characters have different moral values that could be compared and contrasted to the character's values.
	Social	Consider how the character fits into and is defined by society, in terms of race, ethnicity, socioeconomic class, sexual orientation, age, or gender.
		Notice who in the story exercises power over whom, what causes the difference in power, what its effects are, and whether the balance of power changes during the story.
Setting	In relation to the action, mood, or characters	Consider how the setting signals what is happening and whether it comments (possibly ironically) on the action.
		Notice how the setting affects the mood — for example, how it heightens suspense or foreboding.
		Look for cause-and-effect connections between the setting and what characters are thinking, doing, or feeling.
	Historical or cultural	Think of how the historical period or cultural context in which the story is set might affect what happens and does not happen and why.
		Imagine how the meaning might be different if the historical time or cultural situation were different.
	Metaphoric or symbolic	Assume that the setting is a projection of the thoughts and feelings of the narrator, and then consider what the setting tells you about the narrator's state of mind.
		Assume that the setting symbolizes the social relations among characters in the story, and then consider what the setting tells you about these relationships.

(continued)

Element to Analyze	Approach	What to Do
Setting (continued)	Metaphoric or symbolic (continued)	Assume that the setting stands for something outside the characters' control (such as nature, God, or some aspect of society), and then consider what the setting tells you about the pressures and rules under which the characters function.
Plot Structure	As realistic (as resembling real-life experience)	Think of the story as a sequence of stages or steps leading somewhere, mark where each new stage begins, and consider how the sequence could be understood.
		Think of the story as having not only a main plot but also subplots that mirror, undercut, or comment in some way on the main plot.
	As surrealistic (as having symbolic rather than literal meaning)	Think of the story as a series of images, more like a collage or a dream rather than a realistic portrayal of actual events.
		Look for a logic to the arrangement of these images.
Point of View	In terms of what the narrator actually sees	Consider whether the narrator is a character in the story or an all-knowing, disembodied voice who knows what every character thinks, feels, and does.
		Identify any important insights or ideas the narrator has.
		Consider how factors such as the narrator's gender, age, and ethnicity may influence what he or she notices as important.
		Consider what the narrator is not able to see or what the narrator distorts — for example, certain truths about himself or herself, about other characters, or about what happens in the story.
	In terms of how the narrator represents what he or she sees	Characterize the narrator's tone at various points in the story — for example, as satirical, celebratory, angry, bitter, or optimistic.
		Infer what there is about the narrator (or about the situation) that could account for each tone you identify.
		Consider what special agenda or motive may have led the narrator to this particular way of describing characters and scenes or telling the story.
Literary Motif or Theme	In terms of a traditional story motif (or an ironic reversal of the tradition)	Analyze the text as . . . an initiation (or coming-of-age or rite-of-passage) story. . . . a heroic quest (for love, truth, fame, fortune, or salvation of oneself or the community). . . . a story about a character's disillusionment or fall from innocence. . . . a story about family or surrogate families. . . . a story about storytelling (or some other art) or about becoming a writer or an artist.
	In terms of a common literary theme	Focus on the theme of . . . the American dream. . . . the social construction of femininity or masculinity. . . . race relations in America. . . . alienation. . . . the urban or suburban experience. . . . surveillance.

Basic Features

Ways in: Developing Your Analysis

After reading and annotating the story with the help of the Suggestions for Analysis, you should have made many observations about specific passages in the story, and you probably also have some general ideas about the story's meaning. To generate more of both, you can work **inductively** (reasoning from specific examples to a general idea about them) or **deductively** (stating a general idea and finding specific instances of it). Most experienced writers alternate between the two methods.

The following activities will help you use both methods to develop your analysis. You can start with either induction or deduction, but be sure to try all of the activities.

Working Inductively: Moving from Specific Details to General Ideas	Working Deductively: Moving from General Ideas to Specific Details

Write about Quotations. *Select two or three quotations and write several sentences answering this question:* What idea or ideas does each quotation suggest, and what in the quotation makes you think so?

Examine Patterns in the Story. *Write a paragraph analyzing one or more patterns you found in the story.* Here are a few patterns to get started:

- imagery (for example, the images of blindness in "Araby" that Crane analyzes)
- characters as doubles (for example, the hypocrites in "Araby" that Ratinov discusses)
- events that echo or reverse one another (for example, the boy's shopping in Dublin and at the Araby bazaar)

List Ideas. *Compose a list of ideas you thought of as you analyzed the story.* Do not worry about how these ideas relate to one another or whether they are contradictory. Simply write down every idea about the story that still interests you. For example, here are two ideas about "Araby" that Ratinov listed (see A Writer at Work, p. 544):

All the adult characters are hypocrites.
He realizes how self-deluded he was.

Look for Additional Support. *Review your annotated story to find quotations or other details you could use as examples to illustrate your ideas.*

Explore Your Key Terms. *Write for a few minutes about the most interesting key terms in your list of ideas and how they connect to one another.* For example, in exploring his ideas about "Araby," Ratinov connected the key terms *hypocrites* and *self-deluded* to develop his main claim that the boy discovers he is a hypocrite too.

Testing Your Choice

Decide whether you should proceed with the ideas you have been exploring. The questions that follow may help you decide whether to go on with these ideas or look for a different focus.

- *Have I been able to generate some interesting ideas about the story?*
- *Can I find examples in the story to support my ideas?*
- *Do my ideas go beyond what will be obvious to most anyone reading the story?*

A Collaborative Activity:
Testing Your Choice

Get together with two or three other students who have read your story and offer responses to one another's ideas.

Presenters: Take turns telling each other your two or three most promising ideas, giving an example to support each idea.

Listeners: Briefly respond to each presenter's ideas, indicating which idea seems most interesting. Also tell the writer if you disagree with any of the ideas and briefly explain why.

Formulating a Tentative Thesis Statement

Finding a Main Idea

Write for ten minutes about your most promising ideas. After writing, read what you have written and see if you can find one main idea or claim that can serve as the thesis for your essay. Focus your exploratory writing on questions like these:

- How can you understand a character's internal conflict or apparent change?
- How is the story's theme reflected in the way the story is told, the way the setting is described, how characters relate to one another, or some other aspect of the story?
- How does the language used to describe the setting illuminate such things as the main character's internal conflict, the relationship between characters, or the theme? (For example, Ratinov argues that the theme of self-delusion is reflected in "Araby's" images of blindness.)
- What does the trajectory of the story (the plot structure) say about the characters? (Crane, for example, asked why the boy is so eager to go to Araby and argues that the quest motif is ironic because the main character experiences no development or self-discovery in the end.)
- How does the setting comment on the historical, cultural, or political context? (For example, if you were analyzing "Araby," you might ask why the bazaar is set outside the bustling city center, why it is given that particular name, and why it is significant that the sales girl and young men at the bazaar speak with "English accents," given the colonial relationship between England and Ireland.)

- What, if anything, does the story say about such things as what may be universally true about people and society versus what may result from specific historical, economic, or cultural conditions; about what is usually considered normal versus what is considered abnormal; about how some groups exert power or exhibit resistance or subversion, and how others are excluded or oppressed?

Stating Your Thesis

Your thesis statement serves as the main claim of your argument. To think about your ideas in terms of an argument, here are a few suggestions:

- ***Present your ideas as links in a chain leading to some general conclusion about the story.*** For example, David Ratinov links two ideas — (1) that the boy in "Araby" is *self-deluded* about his crush on Mangan's sister and (2) that adults are *hypocrites* — to his main idea or claim — that the boy completes his "initiation into . . . the disillusioning realities of adulthood" at Araby when he realizes that he is a hypocrite too because he has been lying to himself about the purity of his love of Mangan's sister. Notice that in his thesis paragraph, Ratinov presents each link in the chain. He is *not* simply retelling the story; he is stating his ideas about what happens in the story:

  > "Araby" tells the story of an adolescent boy's initiation into adulthood. The story is narrated by a mature man reflecting on his adolescence and the events that forced him to face the disillusioning realities of adulthood. The minor characters play a pivotal role in this initiation process. The boy observes the hypocrisy of adults in the priest and Mrs. Mercer; and his vain, self-centered uncle introduces him to another disillusioning aspect of adulthood. The boy's infatuation with the girl ultimately ends in disillusionment, and Joyce uses the specific example of the boy's disillusionment with love as a metaphor for disillusionment with life itself. From the beginning, the boy deludes himself about his relationship with Mangan's sister. At Araby, he realizes the parallel between his own self-delusion and the hypocrisy and vanity of the adult world.

- ***Present your ideas as a response to someone who disagrees with you.*** For example, here is Sally Crane's thesis paragraph. Notice that she begins by explaining how other readers interpret the final scene in the story, and in her final sentence states her opposing interpretation:

  > Readers of "Araby" often focus on the final scene as the key to the story. They assume the boy experiences some profound insight about himself when he gazes "up into the darkness" (par. 37). I believe, however, that the boy sees nothing and learns nothing — about either himself or others. He's not self-reflective; he's merely self-absorbed.

- ***Present your ideas as a response to a question — either a question your instructor asked or one you composed for yourself.*** For example, here's a question we posed in the Questions for Analysis for "Araby" (p. 554):

  > "Araby" can be read as a coming-of-age story about an adolescent boy's first crush. If you read it on this level, what changes would you say the boy goes through? What, if anything, does he learn?

You could answer this question in lots of ways, but here is one possible thesis paragraph:

> "Araby" shows an adolescent boy's confusion over his sexual awakening. Because of his strict Catholic upbringing, his reading of romantic literature, and the lack of adult mentoring, the boy represses his sexual feelings and turns them into a kind of religious adoration of Mangan's sister. It is only when he sees himself and Mangan's sister mirrored in the tawdry flirtatiousness of the sales girl and young men at Araby that the boy finally realizes how foolish he has been.

Researching Your Story

Many analyses of short stories rely on the author's text alone; close reading and critical thinking are the only tools brought to bear on the work. Some approaches to analysis, however, would benefit from outside research: for example, inquiries into the author's biography, his or her other work, and other critical responses to the short story in question. If your analysis runs counter to the general trend in analysis or to particular analyses others have written, you might want to do library and Internet research to find out how these contrary positions are defended. If you are curious about some aspect of the text that you do not understand — or that you suspect your readers do not understand — you might want to do historical or linguistic research and include your findings in your essay.

Here are a few suggestions for getting started:

- Search the open Web by doing a Google search, using keywords relevant to your analysis. If you want more information about the reservation portrayed in Sherman Alexie's "A Good Story," for example, you could try keywords such as *Spokane Indian reservation*.

- To see what others have said about an author's work, you can try a Google search, entering keywords such as *Sherman Alexie criticism*. You are much more likely to find useful results, however, by doing a search on a specialized periodical database such as the *MLA Bibliography*, which specializes in academic writing about languages and literature. You should have access to periodical databases like these through your school's library: If you are not sure how to use them, see Chapter 23, pp. 740–43. As always, be sure to ask a reference librarian for help if you encounter problems.

As you work, bookmark or keep a record of promising sites. You may want to download or copy information you could use in your essay, including visuals; if so, remember to record source information.

If your approach does require outside research, you may have already identified research questions and made notes about the kinds of information you might need. Doing research with your questions and notes in mind will help you work efficiently. But researching sometimes is most productive when you have the time to go into unexplored territory. You may find support for your analysis, but you also may find contradictory evidence and decide to change your plans as a result.

Designing Your Document

While many essays that analyze short stories focus exclusively on the words of the story and the words of others who have responded to the story, some analyses make use of factors such as social and historical context that invite the use of drawings, photographs, tables, or graphs.

Suppose, for example, that you are interested in the history of reader response to "Araby." In doing research on where reviews of the story were first published, and what they said, you might devise a system of classifying them (say, according to geography and level of approval/disapproval) best communicated in a simple graph. If, on the other hand, you are interested in what Joyce's Dublin looked like in his youth, and in comparing this reality to the perception of it held by most contemporary readers, you might include archival photos and discuss how seeing them might alter or otherwise affect a contemporary reader's understanding of the story. (If you have sufficient time and energy, you might do a survey of your classmates first, to test their perception of what "Araby," downtown Dublin, a street with a "blind" end, etc., were actually like, and include the results of your survey in a simple chart or table.)

As always, consider reviewing other analyses of the short story you are studying or of other stories to see how they use design elements and visuals to support and strengthen their arguments.

For more on document design, see Chapter 21. For guidelines on acknowledging the sources of visuals, see Chapter 24.

Planning and Drafting

The following activities will help you refine your purpose, set goals for your draft, and outline it. In addition, this section will help you write a draft by writing opening sentences, trying out a useful sentence strategy, and learning how to work with sources.

Refining Your Purpose and Setting Goals

Before starting to draft, here are some questions that may help you sharpen your purpose for your audience and set goals for your draft. Your instructor may ask you to write out your answers to some of these questions or simply to think about them as you plan and draft your essay.

Clarifying Your Purpose and Audience

- Do I need to identify the story early in my essay? Is it enough simply to name the story, as both Crane and Ratinov do? Should I also identify the author?
- How much do I need to tell my readers about what happens in the story? Should I assume, as both Crane and Ratinov do, that my readers have read the story?
- Should I consider placing this particular story in the context of the author's other writing or in its historical context?

Presenting a Clear, Arguable Thesis

- Should I remind readers, as Crane does, that some readers of the story disagree with my analysis? Or should I simply assert my ideas, as Ratinov does, and assume some readers will disagree?

- How can I present ideas so that they are not simple statements of fact or obvious conclusions? For example, Ratinov does not just assert what is obvious — that the boy has a crush on Mangan's sister. He goes on to assert a cause-effect relationship between the boy's first love and his increasing isolation from "his childhood friends" (par. 2).

- How can I appropriately qualify my ideas so as to avoid overgeneralizing? For example, Crane writes at one point that the main character is "totally self-absorbed" (par. 6). While she provides a good deal of evidence and analysis to support the assertion that he is self-absorbed, she does not have access to every aspect of his being, so she probably should not claim that he is *totally* anything.

- How can I state my ideas clearly and unambiguously? Should I elaborate by adding specifics that help explain what I mean, as Crane does when she writes: "The boy sees nothing and learns nothing — about either himself or others. He's not self-reflective; he's merely self-absorbed" (par. 1)?

Providing Support for Your Argument

- How can I present my ideas as reasons supporting my central claim, the essay's thesis? Can I use the thesis paragraph to present each idea as a chain of reasons in the way that Ratinov does? Can I follow Crane's lead and use topic sentences to weave my ideas together ?

- How can I use examples from the story to support my ideas? Should I quote words and short phrases, as Crane does in paragraphs 3 and 4, to show how images of blindness are used in the story to reveal how little the boy sees and understands? If I quote any long passages in a block quote, should I repeat selected words or phrases to explain how I am interpreting the passage, as Crane does in paragraph 5?

- How can I use plot details to support my ideas rather than merely to retell the story? For example, in paragraph 5, Ratinov introduces plot details with several sentences stating his ideas (such as "The uncle . . . is a failure as a role model and the epitome of vanity"); he then tells what happens in the story (for example, "After being out all afternoon the uncle returns . . . talking to himself . . ."); finally, he makes his analysis explicit with a statement beginning: "These details suggest . . ."

Making Your Plan Readable

- Can my topic sentences repeat the key terms introduced in my thesis and forecasting statements?

- What synonyms could I use to avoid repeating my key terms too often?

- How can I use logical transitions to help readers see how one point connects to the next? For example, could I use transitions that announce contrasts, such as *but*, *although*, and *yet*, which Ratinov uses at the end of paragraph 2 and beginning of paragraph 3?

The Ending

- Can I end by framing my essay — that is, by repeating something at the end that was introduced in the beginning? Crane, for example, does this when she refers again at the end of her essay to the idea she is refuting (that the boy has a moment of insight at the end of the story).

- Should I reiterate my main idea, as Ratinov does when he ties his ideas together in the final paragraph, showing how the boy gives up his "childish illusions" and "innocence"?

- Should I consider ending with a new idea that grows out of my argument? Could I, for example, expand on the cultural or historical implications of my reading of the story?

Outlining Your Draft

With your purpose and goals in mind, you might want to make an outline that lays out your argument in a series of *because* sentences. For example, here's how Sally Crane might have outlined her argument:

I. The story uses recurring images of blindness because the main character in "Araby" sees nothing and learns nothing,
   A. The boy is blind to what is really around him because he is obsessed with Mangan's sister.
   B. The boy is blind to his real feelings about Mangan's sister because of the cultural traditions — religious and literary — that have shaped him.
II. Readers who think the ending reveals a moment of insight are wrong because the ending is ironic.
   A. The ending is ironic because the boy is just as blind at the end as at the beginning.
   B. The boy's perspective at the end is expressed in stilted, inflated language because he is still playing a heroic role and is just as self-absorbed as he was at the beginning.

Once you have a working outline, you should not hesitate to change it as necessary while drafting and revising. For instance, you might find you left out an important idea that is needed to make the chain of reasoning complete: If so, add it, and your essay will become stronger. Remember that the purpose of an outline is to help you organize your ideas logically, not to lock you into a particular structure.

Drafting

If you have not already begun to draft your essay, this section will help by suggesting how to write your opening sentences; how to use short quotations and comment on them; and how to quote from the story to support your argument. Drafting is not always a smooth process, so do not be afraid to leave spaces where you do not know what to put in or to write notes to yourself about what you could do next. If you get stuck while drafting, go back over your invention writing: You may be able to copy and paste some of it into your evolving draft. You may also find that you need to do some additional invention to fill in details in your draft, so do not hesitate to do so.

Writing the Opening Sentences

Formulating a Tentative Thesis Statement on pp. 525–27 suggests several ways to present your thesis. Be aware of a common mistake students sometimes make. You may have been taught how to write what is commonly called a "funnel paragraph." This kind of paragraph begins with a broad generalization and through a series of sentences becomes more and more focused and narrow, culminating in what is usually the essay's thesis statement. The problem with this kind of paragraph structure is that broad generalizations tend to be not worth stating and not directly relevant. They are off-putting to readers and delay the start of the argument. Look, for example, at this modified version of David Ratinov's opening paragraph:

> *As all of us know, adolescence is not an easy time. Adolescents have to go through many changes and learn many things before they can take their place as mature adults.* "Araby" tells the story of an adolescent boy's initiation into adulthood. The story is narrated by a mature man reflecting on his adolescence and the events that forced him to face the disillusioning realities of adulthood.

The two sentences in italics that we added to the opening make generalizations no one would disagree with, but they also are not very interesting and add nothing to the essay. It is best simply to begin by presenting your ideas about the story.

A Sentence Strategy: Using Short Quotations and Commenting on Quotations or Paraphrases

As you draft an essay analyzing a short story, you will need to support your analysis with quotations and paraphrases (restatements of quotations using mostly your own words) and with comments on them. In order to do so effectively, you will need to become adept at frequently quoting single words and brief phrases, rather than whole sentences or passages, and at using language that refers directly to your quotations and paraphrases.

Use Short Quotations Frequently to Support Your Analysis of the Story. Brief quotations are not in themselves superior to sentence-length and longer quotations, but they allow you to focus more intensively on the words of the story, which makes your argument more lively and interesting. They also enable you to efficiently bring evidence together from different parts of a story to support one part of your argument.

Here are examples of short quotations from this chapter's two student essays:

> At the bazaar in the closing scene, "the light was out," and the upper part of the hall was "completely dark." (Crane, par. 3)

> Her church work — collecting used stamps for some "pious purpose" (presumably to sell for the church) — associates her with money and profit. (Ratinov, par. 4)

Crane and Ratinov do occasionally quote complete sentences, and Crane once quotes a relatively lengthy passage, set off as a block quotation (par. 5). The majority of their quotations, however, are brief phrases and single words from the stories they are analyzing. These additional examples illustrate the wide range of possibilities:

> The "white curve of her neck" and the "white border of a petticoat" combine the symbolic color of purity, associated with the Madonna, with sexual suggestiveness. (Crane, par. 5)

> Yet even this image is sensual with the halo of light accentuating "the white curve of her neck." (Ratinov, par. 3)

> He concludes that his love for her is no different than the two gentlemen's love for this "lady." (Ratinov, par. 7)

These word and phrase quotations are integrated smoothly into the writers' sentences, but you may also separate quoted language from your own sentence that introduces it, as in this example:

> Most people interpret the ending as a moment of profound insight, and the language certainly seems to support this interpretation: "Gazing up into the darkness I saw myself as a creature driven and derided by vanity; and my eyes burned with anguish and anger." (Crane, par. 9)

Comment Directly on Your Quotations or Paraphrases So That Readers Will Understand Their Relevance to Your Analysis of the Story. The relevance of your quotations and paraphrases will rarely be obvious to your readers unless you provide a context for them by adding a comment in which you directly connect the quotation or paraphrase to the idea you are trying to support. Two effective strategies that writers rely on in their comments are referring to quotations or paraphrases with *this* and *these* and repeating key nouns in them.

Referring to Quotations or Paraphrases with This *and* These

- After mentioning images of looking, seeing, and blindness, Sally Crane comments, "*This blindness* appears to be caused by the boy's obsession with Mangan's sister" (par. 4).

- After quoting three of the boy's romantic thoughts about the girl, Crane comments, "*Language like this* sounds as though it comes out of a popular romance novel, something written by Danielle Steele perhaps" (par. 7).

- After paraphrasing the uncle's activities, David Ratinov comments, "*These details* suggest that he is drunk" (par. 5).

Referring to Quotations or Paraphrases by Repeating Key Nouns

- After quoting the image of North Richmond Street houses with their "brown imperturbable faces," Crane comments, "*The houses* stare back at the boy, unaffected by his presence and gaze" (par. 4).

- After quoting three sentences that describe the boy's observations of his friends as they play in the street below his house, a quotation that mentions the friends' "cries," or shouts, Ratinov comments, "*The friends' cries* are weak and indistinct because they are distant emotionally as well as spatially" (par. 2).

- After paraphrasing information in the story about the priest, Mrs. Mercer, and the boy's uncle, Ratinov comments, "From *the priest, Mrs. Mercer, and his uncle*, the boy learns some fundamental truths about adulthood, but it is only after his visit to Araby that he is able to recognize what he has learned" (par. 5).

The primary source writers analyzing stories use is the story itself. They may also use secondary sources providing information about the author or the period in which the story was written or set in addition to sources offering alternative interpretations of the story. Neither Sally Crane nor David Ratinov used secondary sources; instead, their instructors required them to focus solely on the story itself. Their essays illustrate the many different ways writers use quotations from the text they are analyzing to support their argument.

Crane and Ratinov both quote the same passage in "Araby" but they use it to support different arguments. By looking closely at how Crane and Ratinov use quotations differently, we can see why writers cannot simply drop quotations into their essays and expect them to speak for themselves. Like all writers analyzing stories, Crane and Ratinov need to show how they understand the language they quote and why they think the quotations demonstrate their argument about the story's meaning.

Here is the original passage from "Araby" followed by a side-by-side comparison showing how Crane and Ratinov quote from it:

"Araby" (paragraphs 7–11)

> At last she spoke to me. When she addressed the first words to me I was so confused that I did not know what to answer. She asked me was I going to Araby. I forgot whether I answered yes or no. It would be a splendid bazaar, she said she would love to go.
>
> "And why can't you?" I asked.
>
> While she spoke she turned a silver bracelet round and round her wrist. She could not go, she said, because there would be a retreat that week in her convent. Her brother and two other boys were fighting for their caps and I was alone at the railings. She held one of the spikes, bowing her head towards me. The light from the lamp opposite our door caught the white curve of her neck, lit up her hair that rested there and, falling, lit up the hand upon the railing. It fell over one

7

8

9

Working with Sources:

Quoting from the Story to Support Your Analysis

side of her dress and caught the white border of a petticoat, just visible as she stood at ease.

"It's well for you," she said.   10

"If I go," I said, "I will bring you something."   11

Crane's Essay (paragraph 5)

He is obsessed with Mangan's sister but he can't see her for who she really is. His description of her and interpretation of the few words she says to him can be seen as further evidence of his blindness. He sees only what he wants to see, the "image" he has in his mind's eye (par. 5). This image comes more from what he's read than from anything he's observed. He casts her simultaneously in the traditional female roles of angel and whore:

> While she spoke she turned a silver bracelet round and round her wrist. She could not go, she said, because there would be a retreat that week in her convent. . . . She held one of the spikes, bowing her head towards me. The light from the lamp opposite our door caught the white curve of her neck, lit up her hair that rested there and, falling, lit up the hand upon the railing. It fell over one side of her dress and caught the white border of a petticoat, just visible as she stood at ease. (par. 9)

Her angelic qualities are shown in her plans to attend a convent retreat and in her bowed head. Her whorish qualities come through in the way she flirtatiously plays with the bracelet, as if she were inviting him to buy her an expensive piece of jewelry at the bazaar. The "white curve of her neck" and the "white border of a petticoat" combine the symbolic color of purity, associated with the Madonna, with sexual suggestiveness (par. 9). The point is that there is no suggestion here or anywhere else in the story that the boy is capable of seeing Mangan's sister as a real person. She only exists as the object of his gaze. In fact, no one seems to have any reality for him other than himself.

Ratinov's Essay (paragraph 3):

Although he worships Mangan's sister as a religious object, his lust for her is undeniable. He idolizes her as if she were the Virgin Mary: "her figure defined by the light from the half-opened door. . . . The light from the lamp opposite our door caught the white curve of her neck, lit up her hair that rested there and, falling, lit up the hand upon the railing" (pars. 3, 9). Yet even this image is sensual with the halo of light accentuating "the white curve of her neck." The language makes obvious that his attraction is physical rather than spiritual: "Her dress swung as she moved her body and the soft rope of her hair tossed from side to side" (par. 3). His desire for her is strong and undeniable: "her name was like a summons to all my foolish blood" (par. 4); "my body was like a harp and her words and gestures were like fingers running upon the wires" (par. 5). But in order to justify his love, to make it socially acceptable, he deludes himself into thinking that his love is pure. He is being hypocritical, although at this point he does not know it.

Both Crane and Ratinov precede and follow quotations (gray highlighting) with their own words (yellow highlighting) explaining how the quotations substantiate their arguments. Notice that whereas Crane quotes nearly all of paragraph 9 from "Araby," Ratinov quotes only one sentence from that paragraph. Because she is quoting five or more lines, Crane uses a block quotation. She also uses ellipsis marks to indicate where she has omitted a sentence from her quotation (a description of what the other boys are doing that is not relevant to the point she is making about the boy's "blindness" in regard to Mangan's sister). Ratinov also uses ellipsis marks, but cuts several paragraphs to connect two descriptions of Mangan's sister on the steps of her house. Here is the description from paragraph 3 of "Araby" with the language Ratinov quotes italicized:

> She was waiting for us, *her figure defined by the light from the half-opened door.* Her brother always teased her before he obeyed and I stood by the railings looking at her. *Her dress swung as she moved her body and the soft rope of her hair tossed from side to side.*

Ratinov chose to connect this first passage from paragraph 3 in "Araby" to the passage from paragraph 9 because they both display the boy's adoring gaze and the romantic backlit image of the girl he sees.

Crane uses the block quote from "Araby" to argue that the boy's "blindness" makes him misread Mangan's sister. Following the block quotation, Crane focuses on certain words and phrases from "Araby" — paraphrasing (underlined) and quoting (gray highlighting) — to explain why she thinks the story's language demonstrates that the boy sees the girl in contrasting "angelic" and "whorish" stereotypes. This argument supports the reason Crane is developing to support her overall thesis about the boy's lack of insight.

Ratinov uses the same passage, interpreting it similarly as revealing a combination of religious idolization with sexual desire. But instead of arguing that this combination of images reveals the boy's blindness to his own feelings, Ratinov argues that they reveal his hypocrisy. Like Crane, Ratinov repeats language that he wants to focus readers' attention on: describing the light from the doorway as a "halo of light" and repeating the quotation "the white curve of her neck" to emphasize that the boy's view of the girl confuses spirituality and sensuality. At the end of the paragraph, Ratinov explicitly states the reason he is developing and repeats key words from his essay's thesis: The boy "deludes himself" and is "hypocritical."

When you quote from the story to support your analysis, be sure to do as Crane and Ratinov do, and frame the quotation with your own language explaining your ideas about the quotation and how your reasoning relates to your overall thesis.

Critical Reading Guide

Basic Features

For a printable version of this Critical Reading Guide, go to **bedfordstmartins.com/ theguide**.

Your instructor may arrange a peer review session in class or online where you can exchange drafts with your classmates and use this Critical Reading Guide to point out what works well and to suggest ways to improve the draft. This guide can also be used productively by a tutor in the writing center or by a roommate or family member.

A good critical reading does three things: It lets the writer know how the reader understands the point of the story, praises what works best, and indicates where the draft could be improved.

1. Evaluate how well the thesis and forecasting statements are presented.

   Summarize: Tell the writer what you understand the essay's thesis to be and what its key terms are.

   Praise: Tell the writer what seems most interesting to you about the writer's main claim about the story, whether you agree with it or not.

   Critique: If you cannot find the thesis statement or cannot identify the key terms, let the writer know. Evaluate the thesis statement on the basis of whether it makes an interesting and arguable assertion (rather than a statement of fact or an obvious point); whether it is clear and precise (neither ambiguous nor vague); and whether it is appropriately qualified (neither overgeneralized nor exaggerated).

2. Assess how well the argument is developed and supported.

   Praise: Give an example in the essay where support is presented especially effectively to support a reason — for instance, note where brief quotations (words and short phrases), a longer block quote, or plot details are introduced and explained in a way that clearly illustrates a particular point that is being argued.

   Critique: Tell the writer where the connection between a reason and its support seems vague, where too much plot is being told with no apparent point, or where a quotation is left to speak for itself without explanation. Let the writer know if any part of the argument seems to be undeveloped or does not support the thesis.

3. Consider how readable the essay is.

   Praise: Give an example of where the essay succeeds in being readable — where, for example, the key terms introduced in its thesis and forecasting statements recur throughout the essay in topic sentences and elsewhere, or in the use of logical transitions.

Critique: Tell the writer where readability could be improved. Can you point to places where key terms could be added or where a topic sentence could be made clearer, for example? Can the use of logical transitions be improved or can transitions be added where they are lacking? Can you suggest a more effective way to end the essay that is less abrupt or redundant?

4. If the writer has expressed concern about anything in the draft that you have not discussed, respond to that concern.

Making Comments Electronically Most word processing software offers features that allow you to insert comments directly into the text of someone else's document. Many readers prefer to make their comments this way because it tends to be faster than writing on hard copy and space is virtually unlimited; it also eliminates the process of deciphering handwritten comments. Where such features are not available, simply typing comments directly into a document in a contrasting color can provide the same advantages.

Revising

Very likely you have already thought of ways to improve your draft, and you may even have begun to revise it. In this section is a Troubleshooting Chart that may help. Before using the chart, however, it is a good idea to

- review critical reading comments from your classmates, instructor, or writing center tutor, and
- make an outline of your draft so that you can look at it analytically.

Making an outline of the draft, even if you made an outline before drafting, can help you see what you actually wrote as opposed to what you intended to write. Your aim should not be to make your draft conform to your original outline, but to make your draft as good as it can be.

For an electronic version of this Troubleshooting Chart, go to **bedfordstmartins .com/theguide.**

Troubleshooting Your Draft

●●● **Basic Features**

	Problem	Suggestions for Revising the Draft
A Clear, Arguable Thesis	My thesis is unclear or overgeneralized.	☐ Add more explanation. ☐ Refer to the story specifically. ☐ Add qualifying words like *some* or *usually*.
	My thesis is not arguable or interesting.	☐ Respond to a question or class discussion. ☐ Summarize an alternative argument. ☐ Try additional suggestions for analysis. ☐ Connect ideas.
Support for the Argument	My argument seems superficial or thin.	☐ Develop your ideas by connecting them. ☐ Link your ideas to make a chain of reasons. ☐ Connect to a literary motif or theme.
	I don't have enough support for my argument.	☐ Add textual evidence by quoting, paraphrasing, or summarizing key passages. ☐ Focus on the writer's choice of words, explaining how particular word choices support your ideas. ☐ Consider using other kinds of support, such as information about the story's historical or cultural context.
	The connection between a reason and its support seems vague.	☐ Explain why the support illustrates the reason. ☐ Explain what the quoted words mean. ☐ Introduce quotations and follow with some explanation.
	There are contradictions or gaps in my argument.	☐ Explain more fully and clearly how your reasons relate logically to one another as well as to your thesis. ☐ Fill in the gaps. ☐ Use contradictions or gaps to extend or complicate your argument.
A Readable Plan	My essay is hard to follow.	☐ Repeat key terms from the thesis and forecasting statements. ☐ Provide explicit topic sentences. ☐ Add logical transitions.
	My ending seems abrupt.	☐ Frame your argument by echoing language from the opening in the conclusion. ☐ Explain where your ideas lead. ☐ Expand on the argument's implications.

Editing and Proofreading

Now is the time to check your revised draft for errors in grammar, punctuation, and mechanics. Our research has identified several errors that occur often in essays that analyze short stories, including problems with parallelism and the use of ellipses. The following guidelines will help you check your essay for these common errors.

Using Parallel Structure

The Problem. When you present items as a pair or in a series (for example, *I gave him x and y*, or *I gave him x, y, and z*), you must present the items in the same grammatical form — all nouns, all prepositional phrases, all adverb clauses, and so on. Mixing and matching leads to lack of clarity and lessens the impact of your prose. Take as an example one of Sally Crane's first-draft sentences:

> I believe that the boy sees nothing and is incapable of learning anything.

"[S]ees nothing" is a simple verb-object arrangement; "is incapable of learning anything," which should be a parallel item, combines a helping verb, an adjective, and a prepositional phrase. The resulting sentence is unnecessarily complicated and clumsy.

How to Correct It. Crane eventually edited the sentence above as follows:

                             learns nothing.
▶ **I believe that the boy sees nothing and ~~is incapable of learning anything.~~**

The parallelism of *sees nothing* and *learns nothing* emphasizes the relationship between these two conditions in a way that the first-draft wording did not. For more examples, see the sentences below:

                       what he's read
▶ **This image comes more from ~~his reading~~ than from anything he's observed.**

               isolation,
▶ **To Kafka, loneliness, ~~being isolated,~~ and regrets are the price of freedom.**

                      values
▶ **Sarah really cares about her brother and ~~to maintain~~ their relationship. She lets us know that she was injured by her mother's abuse but avoids saying what she felt after the incident, how others reacted to the incident, and ~~that~~ physical pain she endured.**

                                                           what

Using Ellipsis Marks Correctly

You will often quote other sources when you interpret a story, and you must be careful to use **ellipsis marks** or **ellipses** — three spaced periods — to indicate places

---

A Note on Grammar and Spelling Checkers
These tools can be helpful, but do not rely on them exclusively to catch errors in your text: Spelling checkers cannot catch misspellings that are themselves words, such as *to* for *too*. Grammar checkers miss some problems, sometimes give faulty advice for fixing problems, and can flag correct items as wrong. Use these tools as a second line of defense after your own (and, ideally, another reader's) proofreading/editing efforts.

For practice, go to **bedfordstmartins.com/ theguide/exercisecentral** and click on Parallelism.

where you delete material from a quotation. Look, for example, at the way Sally Crane uses ellipsis marks in quoting from "Araby."

ORIGINAL TEXT

North Richmond Street, being blind, was a quiet street except at the hour when the Christian Brothers' School set the boys free. An uninhabited house of two storeys stood at the blind end, detached from its neighbours in a square ground.

QUQTED WITH
ELLIPSIS MARKS

The street is "blind," with an "uninhabited house . . . at the blind end."

The Problem. Failing to use ellipsis marks to indicate the omission of material misrepresents the quote, which is a serious breach of convention. Using ellipsis marks incorrectly makes your readers doubt your knowledge of conventions. Quoting long passages, instead of the words or phrases on which you mean to focus, distracts from your point. (See A Sentence Strategy on pp. 531–33.)

How to Correct It. If you are using MLA style, follow these few simple rules about using ellipsis marks:

- When you delete words from the *middle of a quoted sentence*, add ellipsis marks, and leave a single space before and after each ellipsis point.
- When you delete words from the *end of a quoted sentence* and a grammatically complete sentence remains, add a period after the last word and then three ellipsis marks.
- Leave a single space after the period and the first two ellipsis marks. Do not leave a space between the last mark and the closing quotation mark.
- When you delete material from the middle of a passage of *two or more sentences*, use ellipsis marks where the text is omitted and a period after the preceding text if it is grammatically a complete sentence.
- When you delete words from the *beginning of a quoted sentence*, use ellipsis marks only if the remainder of the sentence begins with a capitalized word and is grammatically a complete sentence.
- Single words and brief phrases can be quoted without ellipsis marks.

    For examples of sentences edited to show correct usage, see below:

    ▶ **We learn that a former tenant of the boy's house, "⁀ a priest, had died in**

    the back drawing-room ⁀. . . He had been a very charitable priest; in his will

    he had left all his money to institutions and the furniture of his house to

    his sister."

For more on ellipsis marks, see Chapter 24, pp. 757–58.

For practice, go to
bedfordstmartins.com/ theguide/exercisecentral
and click on Ellipsis Marks.

▶ The boys lived on "a quiet street."

▶ The light shone on "… the white border of a petticoat."

A Writer at Work

David Ratinov's Invention Work

In this Writer at Work section, you will see some of the invention work that David Ratinov did for his essay interpreting "Araby," which appears earlier in this chapter (pp. 511–13). Using the Guide to Writing in this book, Ratinov chose the suggestions for interpreting character to guide his analysis of the story. As you will see, he annotated a portion of the story focusing on two characters (Mrs. Mercer and the boy's uncle), wrote to explore his annotations on the passages, and listed ideas for formulating his tentative thesis statement. You will be able to infer from his invention work how his ideas came to form the thesis he developed for his final essay.

Annotating

Ratinov annotated paragraphs 13–24 of "Araby" as he reread them with the suggestions for interpreting character in mind. The annotated passages are reproduced here. Notice the diversity of his annotations. In the text itself, he underlined key words, circled words to be defined, and connected related words and ideas. In the margin, Ratinov defined words, made comments, and posed questions. He also expressed his tentative insights, reactions, and judgments.

2nd mention of uncle fussing — vain? irritable?

rude

On Saturday morning I reminded my uncle that I wished to   13
go to the bazaar in the evening. He was fussing at the hallstand,
looking for the hatbrush, and answered me (curtly:)

"Yes, boy, I know."   14

As he was in the hall I could not go into the front parlour   15   *always unkind to the boy? uncle's effect on the boy*
and lie at the window. I left the house in bad humour and walked
slowly towards the school. The air was pitilessly raw and already
my heart misgave me.

uncle will be late sudden change in mood; big contrast

When I came home to dinner my uncle had not yet been   16
home. Still it was early. I sat staring at the clock for some time
and, when its ticking began to irritate me, I left the room. I

liberated from uncle?

isolated from friends

mounted the staircase and gained the upper part of the house. The high cold empty gloomy rooms liberated me and I went from room to room singing. From the front window I saw my companions playing below in the street. Their cries reached me weakened and indistinct and, leaning my forehead against the cool glass, I looked over at the dark house where she lived. I may have stood there for an hour, seeing nothing but the brown-clad figure cast by my imagination, touched discreetly by the lamplight at the curved neck, at the hand upon the railings and at the border below the dress.

romantic, even sensual

merchandise

boy doesn't seem to like or trust the adults

When I came downstairs again I found Mrs. Mercer sitting at the fire. She was an old garrulous woman, a pawnbroker's widow, who collected used stamps for some pious purpose. I had to endure the gossip of the tea-table. The meal was prolonged beyond an hour and still my uncle did not come. Mrs. Mercer stood up to go: she was sorry she couldn't wait any longer, but it was after eight o'clock and she did not like to be out late, as the night air was bad for her. When she had gone I began to walk up and down the room, clenching my fists. My aunt said: 17

talkative

hypocritically religious

uncle and Mercer both try to give a false impression

"I'm afraid you may put off your bazaar for this night of Our Lord." 18

aunt religious, but hypocritical?

At nine o'clock I heard my uncle's latchkey in the halldoor. I heard him talking to himself and heard the hallstand rocking when it had received the weight of his overcoat. I could interpret these signs. When he was midway through his dinner I asked him to give me the money to go to the bazaar. He had forgotten. 19

boy knows uncle is drunk

boy's fears are
justified excuses

"The people are in bed and after their first sleep now," 20
he said.

I did not smile. My aunt said to him energetically: 21

"Can't you give him the money and let him go? You've kept 22   *aunt to the rescue*
him late enough as it is."

hypocritical
what a bore!

My uncle said he was very sorry he had forgotten. He said he 23
believed in the old saying: "All work and no play makes Jack a dull
boy." He asked me where I was going and, when I had told him a
second time he asked me did I know *The Arab's Farewell to His*   *boy determined to go to*
Steed. When I left the kitchen he was about to recite the opening   *bazaar to buy girl a gift*
lines of the piece to my aunt.

I held a florin tightly in my hand as I strode down 24
Buckingham Street towards the station. The sight of the streets
thronged with buyers and glaring with gas recalled to me the   *boy focused on his task*
purpose of my journey. I took my seat in a third-class carriage
of a deserted train. After an intolerable delay the train moved   *language shows boy's*
out of the station slowly. It crept onward among ruinous houses   *impatience*
and over the twinkling river. At Westland Row Station a crowd
of people pressed to the carriage doors; but the porters moved
them back, saying that it was a special train for the bazaar. I
remained alone in the bare carriage. In a few minutes the train   *boy still isolated*
drew up beside an improvised wooden platform. I passed out
on to the road and saw by the lighted dial of a clock that it was
ten minutes to ten. In front of me was a large building which
displayed the magical name.

As you can see, annotating this section of the story with the suggestions for interpreting character in mind led Ratinov to notice how negatively Mrs. Mercer and the
uncle are portrayed by Joyce.

Examining Patterns in the Story

Following the instructions in the section on Developing Your Analysis on page 524, Ratinov explored a pattern of hypocrisy he saw in the story. Here is what he wrote:

> Mrs. Mercer may be a good neighbor to the boy's aunt, but the boy dislikes her. Joyce plants many clues that she is a hypocrite. She thinks of herself as a good religious Christian, but she is pious (an exaggerated Christian, not a believable one), she collects stamps to sell for charity instead of doing good works first-hand (my guess), and she gossips. Her husband got his money in an un-Christian way. Does the boy know all this or only the narrator much later? I'm sure the boy senses it. He says he has to endure Mrs. Mercer and her gossiping with his aunt. Now that I've looked over the evidence for the uncle's hypocrisy, it seems that his unguardianlike actions toward the boy — his irresponsibility toward him — are just as big a flaw as is his hypocrisy. He seems to be trying to hide something by drinking and being obsessive about his appearance — a failure to advance at work? He tries to impress people with a bigger house than he can afford. Says he believes in things that don't apply to his own actions. I think I can show that he's a hypocrite like Mrs. Mercer. Because the boy distrusts him, he must sense this hypocrisy.

As Ratinov wrote about the hypocrisy of Mrs. Mercer and the uncle, he became increasingly confident that he not only had an interesting idea, but one he could also find support for in the story.

Listing Ideas

Ratinov also tried out the activity in the Developing Your Analysis section called List Ideas. He listed six ideas, but notice that the first one came from the exploratory writing he did about Mrs. Mercer and the uncle (above):

> All the adult characters are hypocrites.
> If this is just a story about romance, then all the adult characters wouldn't have to be so weak and flawed.
> Mangan's sister is different from the adults, but through her the boy has to face up to what the adult world is all about.
> The adults are initiating the boy into adulthood, but he doesn't see it until the end of the story.
> He realizes how self-deluded he was.
> Growing up means being able to see the world for what it actually is, not what you want it to be.

From these ideas about hypocrisy, romance, initiation, self-delusion, and the connection between growing up and learning to see reality, Ratinov was able to devise the thesis statement he eventually used in his essay.

Thinking Critically About
What You Have Learned

In this chapter, you have learned a great deal about this genre from reading two essays that analyze a short story and by writing one of your own. To consolidate your learning, it is helpful to think metacognitively; that is, to reflect not only on what you learned but on how you learned it. In the following sections are two brief activities your instructor may ask you to do.

Reflecting on Your Writing

Your instructor may ask you to turn in with your essay and process materials a brief metacognitive essay or letter reflecting on what you have learned about writing your essay analyzing a story. Choose among the following invention activities those that seem most productive for you:

- Explain how your purpose and audience influenced *one* of your decisions as a writer, such as how you chose the Suggestions for Analysis you used, the key words you used in presenting your thesis, or how you chose quotations to support your argument.

- Discuss what you learned about yourself as a writer in the process of writing this particular essay. For example, what part of the process did you find most challenging? Did you try anything new, like getting a critical reading of your draft or outlining your draft in order to revise it? If so, would you do it again?

- If you were to give advice to a friend who was about to write an essay analyzing a story, what would you say?

- Which of the readings in this chapter influenced your essay? Explain the influence, citing specific examples from your essay and the reading.

- If you got good advice from a critical reader, explain exactly how the person helped you — perhaps by questioning the way you stated your thesis or how you explained one of your reasons.

Considering the Social Dimensions:
Writing for a Specialized Audience

Some genres, like position papers, have a broad general audience, composed of people whose knowledge of current controversial issues varies widely. Other genres, like essays analyzing stories, are highly specialized, read and written by a comparatively small group of people who share certain kinds of knowledge and interests.

Students in English courses, whether they major in English or some other field, learn certain ways of reading and writing about stories. For example, they learn that analytical essays are arguments, requiring arguable assertions, reasons, and supporting evidence. But to write effectively in this genre, students also must learn what kinds of analyses are likely to interest their particular readers — people engaged in an ongoing conversation about stories and other works of literature. They need to know some of the specialized vocabulary English majors use, as well as the critical approaches to analyzing stories they find useful. English instructors determine which approaches their students need to become familiar with, and they introduce these subjects in lecture and class discussion. They choose stories to read and assign essays to write that will give students opportunities to use these approaches.

The essays written by Sally Crane and David Ratinov reflect topics and approaches that will be familiar to students in English classes. Both student writers are concerned with the character or character development of the boy in "Araby." Both of them focus on what the boy says to himself at the end, the meaning of which is not obvious but requires analysis, and both discuss images of women.

The two analyses also differ in important ways, of course. Crane writes about the way the story is narrated, arguing that the boy is an unreliable narrator, unable to read others or himself accurately; therefore what he says is ironic, meaning the opposite of what it seems to say. Ratinov writes about a theme common to many stories, the theme of initiation. Crane and Ratinov also emphasize different aspects of the boy's cultural background: Crane emphasizes the chivalric tradition about which the boy reads, and Ratinov stresses his religious education. It is important to remember, however, that while their analyses differ, they both fit comfortably within the usual conversation among English majors.

1. List some of the subjects you and your classmates discussed in class and wrote about. Where did these subjects come from — class discussion, the Suggestions for Analysis in the Guide to Writing, your instructor's questions or lecture, other English classes?

2. Consider whether any subjects were deemed by your instructor or other students as uninteresting or not appropriate for analyzing stories. Why were these subjects rejected? Do you agree with their exclusion?

3. Write a page or two about your experience analyzing literature in this and other English classes.

An Anthology of Short Stories

In this section, you will find four short stories: "The Story of an Hour," by Kate Chopin; "Araby," by James Joyce; "The Use of Force," by William Carlos Williams; and "A Good Story," by Sherman Alexie. Each of the stories is followed by Questions for Analysis. The stories are intended for use with the Collaborative Activity: Practice Analyzing a Story on p. 505. Your instructor may also ask you to choose one of these stories for your essay analyzing a story.

KATE CHOPIN (1851–1904) was born in St. Louis and lived in Louisiana until her husband died in 1882, leaving her with six children. Encouraged by friends, Chopin wrote her first novel, *At Fault* (1890), when she was nearly forty years old. She wrote many short stories for popular magazines such as *Century, Harper's*, and *Vogue*, in which "The Story of an Hour" first appeared in 1894. She published two collections of stories and a second novel, her best-known work, *The Awakening* (1899).

THE STORY OF AN HOUR

Kate Chopin

Knowing that Mrs. Mallard was afflicted with a heart trouble, great care was taken to break to her as gently as possible the news of her husband's death.   1

It was her sister Josephine who told her, in broken sentences; veiled hints that revealed in half concealing. Her husband's friend Richards was there, too, near her. It was he who had been in the newspaper office when intelligence of the railroad disaster was received, with Brently Mallard's name leading the list of "killed." He had only taken the time to assure himself of its truth by a second telegram, and had hastened to forestall any less careful, less tender friend in bearing the sad message.   2

She did not hear the story as many women have heard the same, with a paralyzed inability to accept its significance. She wept at once, with sudden, wild abandonment, in her sister's arms. When the storm of grief had spent itself she went away to her room alone. She would have no one follow her.   3

There stood, facing the open window, a comfortable, roomy armchair. Into this she sank, pressed down by a physical exhaustion that haunted her body and seemed to reach into her soul.   4

She could see in the open square before her house the tops of trees that were all aquiver with the new spring life. The delicious breath of rain was in the air. In the street below a peddler was crying his wares. The notes of a distant song which some one was singing reached her faintly, and countless sparrows were twittering in the eaves.   5

There were patches of blue sky showing here and there through the clouds that had met and piled one above the other in the west facing her window.   6

She sat with her head thrown back upon the cushion of the chair, quite motionless, except when a sob came up into her throat and shook her, as a child who has cried itself to sleep continues to sob in its dreams.   7

She was young, with a fair, calm face, whose lines bespoke repression and even a certain strength. But now there was a dull stare in her eyes, whose gaze was fixed away off yonder on one of those patches of blue sky. It was not a glance of reflection, but rather indicated a suspension of intelligent thought.

8

There was something coming to her and she was waiting for it, fearfully. What was it? She did not know; it was too subtle and elusive to name. But she felt it, creeping out of the sky, reaching toward her through the sounds, the scents, the color that filled the air.

9

Now her bosom rose and fell tumultuously. She was beginning to recognize this thing that was approaching to possess her, and she was striving to beat it back with her will — as powerless as her two white slender hands would have been.

10

When she abandoned herself a little whispered word escaped her slightly parted lips. She said it over and over under her breath: "free, free, free!" The vacant stare and the look of terror that had followed it went from her eyes. They stayed keen and bright. Her pulses beat fast, and the coursing blood warmed and relaxed every inch of her body.

11

She did not stop to ask if it were or were not a monstrous joy that held her. A clear and exalted perception enabled her to dismiss the suggestion as trivial.

12

She knew that she would weep again when she saw the kind, tender hands folded in death; the face that had never looked save with love upon her, fixed and gray and dead. But she saw beyond that bitter moment a long procession of years to come that would belong to her absolutely. And she opened and spread her arms out to them in welcome.

13

There would be no one to live for her during those coming years; she would live for herself. There would be no powerful will bending hers in that blind persistence with which men and women believe they have a right to impose a private will upon a fellow-creature. A kind intention or a cruel intention made the act seem no less a crime as she looked upon it in that brief moment of illumination.

14

And yet she had loved him — sometimes. Often she had not. What did it matter! What could love, the unsolved mystery, count for in face of this possession of self-assertion which she suddenly recognized as the strongest impulse of her being!

15

"Free! Body and soul free!" she kept whispering.

16

Josephine was kneeling before the closed door with her lips to the keyhole, imploring for admission. "Louise, open the door! I beg; open the door — you will make yourself ill. What are you doing, Louise? For heaven's sake open the door."

17

"Go away. I am not making myself ill." No; she was drinking in a very elixir of life through that open window.

18

Her fancy was running riot along those days ahead of her. Spring days, and summer days, and all sorts of days that would be her own. She breathed a quick prayer that life might be long. It was only yesterday she had thought with a shudder that life might be long.

19

She arose at length and opened the door to her sister's importunities. There was a feverish triumph in her eyes, and she carried herself unwittingly like a goddess of Victory. She clasped her sister's waist, and together they descended the stairs. Richards stood waiting for them at the bottom.

20

one was openi~ e~ front door with a latchkey. It was Brently Mallard who 21
~ a little travel-st~ composedly carrying his gripsack and umbrella. He had
~ from the sce~ ~ccident, and did not even know there had been one. He
~amazed at Jo~ ~s piercing cry; at Richards' quick motion to screen him
~the view of ~ late.

But Richar~me they said she had died of heart disease—of joy that kills. 22

When the~ 23

Questi~ for Analysis

1. **Iron~** ~ers to a gap or discrepancy between what is said and what is true, or
    betw~ a result that is expected and what actually happens. In literature, readers
    often~perceive irony that characters are unable to see. What is the central irony of
    "The Story of an Hour"? To get started, take a look at how the story is framed in
    the opening and closing paragraphs. What gap or discrepancy do you notice? Do
    the characters share your insight?

2. What do you learn from the setting, and, in particular, the language Chopin uses to
    describe what Mrs. Mallard experiences when, beginning in paragraph 4, she sits in
    her armchair looking out the window?

3. This story was originally published at the end of the nineteenth century. With this
    context in my ~h ~hat do you thi~ Chopin is saying about marriage, gender, power,
    in American society? To get started, you could look at how Richards
    tries to "screen [Mr. Mallard] from the view of his wife" (par. 21).

JAMES JOYCE (1882–1941), a native of Dublin, Ireland, is considered
one of the most influential writers of the early twentieth century.
"Araby," one of his most often anthologized stories, first appeared in
the collection *Dubliners* in 1914. Like his novel *Portrait of the Artist as
a Young Man*, published two years later, it relies on scenes from Joyce's
own boyhood.

ARABY

James Joyce

North Richmond Street, being blind,[1] was a quiet street except at the hour when the 1
Christian Brothers' School set the boys free. An uninhabited house of two storeys
stood at the blind end, detached from its neighbours in a square ground. The other

---

[1] A dead end. The young Joyce in fact lived for a time on North Richmond Street
in Dublin.

houses of the street, conscious of decent lives within them, gazed at one another with brown imperturbable faces.

The former tenant of our house, a priest, had died in the back drawing-room. Air, musty from having been long enclosed, hung in all the rooms, and the waste room behind the kitchen was littered with old useless papers. Among these I found a few paper-covered books, the pages of which were curled and damp: *The Abbot*, by Walter Scott, *The Devout Communicant* and *The Memoirs of Vidocq*. I liked the last best because its leaves were yellow. The wild garden behind the house contained a central apple-tree and a few straggling bushes under one of which I found the late tenant's rusty bicycle-pump. He had been a very charitable priest; in his will he had left all his money to institutions and the furniture of his house to his sister.

When the short days of winter came dusk fell before we had well eaten our dinners. When we met in the street the houses had grown sombre. The space of sky above us was the colour of ever-changing violet and towards it the lamps of the street lifted their feeble lanterns. The cold air stung us and we played till our bodies glowed. Our shouts echoed in the silent street. The career of our play brought us through the dark muddy lanes behind the houses where we ran the gauntlet of the rough tribes from the cottages, to the back doors of the dark dripping gardens where odours arose from the ashpits, to the dark odorous stables where a coachman smoothed and combed the horse or shook music from the buckled harness. When we returned to the street light from the kitchen windows had filled the areas. If my uncle was seen turning the corner we hid in the shadow until we had seen him safely housed. Or if Mangan's sister came out on the doorstep to call her brother in to his tea we watched her from our shadow peer up and down the street. We waited to see whether she would remain or go in and, if she remained, we left our shadow and walked up to Mangan's steps resignedly. She was waiting for us, her figure defined by the light from the half-opened door. Her brother always teased her before he obeyed and I stood by the railings looking at her. Her dress swung as she moved her body and the soft rope of her hair tossed from side to side.

Every morning I lay on the floor in the front parlour watching her door. The blind was pulled down to within an inch of the sash so that I could not be seen. When she came out on the doorstep my heart leaped. I ran to the hall, seized my books and followed her. I kept her brown figure always in my eye and, when we came near the point at which our ways diverged, I quickened my pace and passed her. This happened morning after morning. I had never spoken to her, except for a few casual words, and yet her name was like a summons to all my foolish blood.

Her image accompanied me even in places the most hostile to romance. On Saturday evenings when my aunt went marketing I had to go to carry some of the parcels. We walked through the flaring streets, jostled by drunken men and bargaining women, amid the curses of labourers, the shrill litanies of shop-boys who stood

3

4

5

---

² *The Devout Communicant* is a collection of religious meditations. *The Abbot* is a historical romance set in the court of Mary, Queen of Scots, a Catholic, who was beheaded for plotting to assassinate her Protestant cousin, Queen Elizabeth I. *The Memoirs of Vidocq* is a collection of sexually suggestive stories about a French criminal turned detective.

on guard by the barrels of pigs' cheeks, the nasal chanting of street-singers, who sang a *come-all-you* about O'Donovan Rossa,[3] or a ballad about the troubles in our native land. These noises converged in a single sensation of life for me: I imagined that I bore my chalice safely through a throng of foes. Her name sprang to my lips at moments in strange prayers and praises which I myself did not understand. My eyes were often full of tears (I could not tell why) and at times a flood from my heart seemed to pour itself out into my bosom. I thought little of the future. I did not know whether I would ever speak to her or not or, if I spoke to her, how I could tell her of my confused adoration. But my body was like a harp and her words and gestures were like fingers running upon the wires.

One evening I went into the back drawing-room in which the priest had died. It was a dark rainy evening and there was no sound in the house. Through one of the broken panes I heard the rain impinge upon the earth, the fine incessant needles of water playing in the sodden beds. Some distant lamp or lighted window gleamed below me. I was thankful that I could see so little. All my senses seemed to desire to veil themselves and, feeling that I was about to slip from them, I pressed the palms of my hands together until they trembled, murmuring: *"O love! O love!"* many times.

At last she spoke to me. When she addressed the first words to me I was so confused that I did not know what to answer. She asked me was I going to Araby. I forgot whether I answered yes or no. It would be a splendid bazaar, she said she would love to go.[4]

"And why can't you?" I asked.

While she spoke she turned a silver bracelet round and round her wrist. She could not go, she said, because there would be a retreat that week in her convent. Her brother and two other boys were fighting for their caps and I was alone at the railings. She held one of the spikes, bowing her head towards me. The light from the lamp opposite our door caught the white curve of her neck, lit up her hair that rested there and, falling, lit up the hand upon the railing. It fell over one side of her dress and caught the white border of a petticoat, just visible as she stood at ease.

"It's well for you," she said.

"If I go," I said, "I will bring you something."

What innumerable follies laid waste my waking and sleeping thoughts after that evening! I wished to annihilate the tedious intervening days. I chafed against the work of school. At night in my bedroom and by day in the classroom her image came between me and the page I strove to read. The syllables of the word *Araby* were called to me through the silence in which my soul luxuriated and cast an Eastern enchantment over me. I asked for leave to go to the bazaar on Saturday night. My aunt was surprised and hoped it was not some Freemason affair.[5] I answered few questions

---

[3] A contemporary leader of an underground organization opposed to British rule of Ireland.

[4] Traveling bazaars featured cafés, shopping stalls, and entertainment. Araby was the name of an English bazaar that visited Dublin when Joyce was a boy.

[5] The Freemasons is a secretive fraternal order that has a long history and that has traditionally been opposed by the Catholic Church.

in class. I watched my master's face pass from amiability to sternness; he hoped I was not beginning to idle. I could not call my wandering thoughts together. I had hardly any patience with the serious work of life which, now that it stood between me and my desire, seemed to me child's play, ugly monotonous child's play.

On Saturday morning I reminded my uncle that I wished to go to the bazaar in the evening. He was fussing at the hallstand, looking for the hatbrush, and answered me curtly: 13

"Yes, boy, I know." 14

As he was in the hall I could not go into the front parlour and lie at the window. I left the house in bad humour and walked slowly towards the school. The air was pitilessly raw and already my heart misgave me. 15

When I came home to dinner my uncle had not yet been home. Still it was early. I sat staring at the clock for some time and, when its ticking began to irritate me, I left the room. I mounted the staircase and gained the upper part of the house. The high cold empty gloomy rooms liberated me and I went from room to room singing. From the front window I saw my companions playing below in the street. Their cries reached me weakened and indistinct and, leaning my forehead against the cool glass, I looked over at the dark house where she lived. I may have stood there for an hour, seeing nothing but the brown-clad figure cast by my imagination, touched discreetly by the lamplight at the curved neck, at the hand upon the railings and at the border below the dress. 16

When I came downstairs again I found Mrs. Mercer sitting at the fire. She was an old garrulous woman, a pawnbroker's widow, who collected used stamps for some pious purpose. I had to endure the gossip of the tea-table. The meal was prolonged beyond an hour and still my uncle did not come. Mrs. Mercer stood up to go: she was sorry she couldn't wait any longer, but it was after eight o'clock and she did not like to be out late, as the night air was bad for her. When she had gone I began to walk up and down the room, clenching my fists. My aunt said: 17

"I'm afraid you may put off your bazaar for this night of Our Lord." 18

At nine o'clock I heard my uncle's latchkey in the halldoor. I heard him talking to himself and heard the hallstand rocking when it had received the weight of his overcoat. I could interpret these signs. When he was midway through his dinner I asked him to give me the money to go to the bazaar. He had forgotten. 19

"The people are in bed and after their first sleep now," he said. 20

I did not smile. My aunt said to him energetically: 21

"Can't you give him the money and let him go? You've kept him late enough as it is." 22

My uncle said he was very sorry he had forgotten. He said he believed in the old saying: "All work and no play makes Jack a dull boy." He asked me where I was going and, when I had told him a second time he asked me did I know *The Arab's Farewell to His Steed*. When I left the kitchen he was about to recite the opening lines of the piece to my aunt. 23

I held a florin tightly in my hand as I strode down Buckingham Street towards the station. The sight of the streets thronged with buyers and glaring with gas recalled to me the purpose of my journey. I took my seat in a third-class carriage of 24 a deserted train. After an intolerable delay the train moved out of the station slowly. It crept onward among ruinous houses and over the twinkling river. At Westland Row Station a crowd of people pressed to the carriage doors; but the porters moved them back, saying that it was a special train for the bazaar. I remained alone in the bare carriage. In a few minutes the train drew up beside an improvised wooden platform. I passed out on to the road and saw by the lighted dial of a clock that it was ten minutes to ten. In front of me was a large building which displayed the magical name.

I could not find any sixpenny entrance and, fearing that the bazaar would be closed, I passed in quickly through a turnstile, handing a shilling to a weary-looking man. I found myself in a big hall girdled at half its height by a gallery. Nearly all the stalls were closed and the greater part of the hall was in darkness. I recognised a silence like that which pervades a church after a service. I walked into the centre of the bazaar timidly. A few people were gathered about the stalls which were still open. Before a curtain, over which the words *Café Chantant*[6] were written in coloured lamps, two men were counting money on a salver. I listened to the fall of the coins.

Remembering with difficulty why I had come I went over to one of the stalls and examined porcelain vases and flowered tea-sets. At the door of the stall a young lady was talking and laughing with two young gentlemen. I remarked their English accents and listened vaguely to their conversation.

"O, I never said such a thing!"

"O, but you did!"

"O, but I didn't!"

"Didn't she say that?"

"Yes. I heard her."

"O, there's a . . . fib!"

Observing me the young lady came over and asked me did I wish to buy anything. The tone of her voice was not encouraging; she seemed to have spoken to me out of a sense of duty. I looked humbly at the great jars that stood like eastern guards at either side of the dark entrance to the stall and murmured:

"No, thank you."

The young lady changed the position of one of the vases and went back to the two young men. They began to talk of the same subject. Once or twice the young lady glanced at me over her shoulder.

I lingered before her stall, though I knew my stay was useless, to make my interest in her wares seem the more real. Then I turned away slowly and walked down the middle of the bazaar. I allowed the two pennies to fall against the sixpence in my pocket. I heard a voice call from one end of the gallery that the light was out. The upper part of the hall was now completely dark.

Gazing up into the darkness I saw myself as a creature driven and derided by vanity; and my eyes burned with anguish and anger.

_____

[6] Literally, *singing café* (French), a music hall.

Questions for Analysis

1. "Araby" can be read as a coming-of-age story about an adolescent boy's first crush. If you read it on this level, what changes would you say the boy goes through? What, if anything, does he learn? To get started, take a look at paragraph 4.

2. The boy describes himself as carrying the "image" of Mangan's sister like a "chalice," "even in places the most hostile to romance," such as the crowded, raucous streets of early twentieth century Dublin, Ireland (par. 5). How does the boy's experience on Saturday evening shopping with his aunt compare to his experience at Araby (par. 25)? What makes the experiences so different?

3. This story is saturated with the culture of Dublin, Ireland, particularly its Catholicism and its attitudes about gender and sexuality. How are these or other important cultural influences expressed in the story? To get started, take a look at paragraph 2.

WILLIAM CARLOS WILLIAMS (1883–1963) is one of the most important poets of the twentieth century, best known for his long poem *Paterson* (1946–1958). He also wrote essays, plays, novels, and short stories. "The Use of Force" was published initially in *The Doctor Stories* (1933), a collection loosely based on Williams's experiences as a pediatrician.

THE USE OF FORCE

William Carlos Williams

They were new patients to me, all I had was the name, Olson. Please come down as soon as you can, my daughter is very sick.   1

When I arrived I was met by the mother, a big startled-looking woman, very clean and apologetic, who merely said, Is this the doctor? and let me in. In the back, she added. You must excuse us, doctor, we have her in the kitchen where it is warm. It is very damp here sometimes.   2

The child was fully dressed and sitting on her father's lap near the kitchen table. He tried to get up, but I motioned for him not to bother, took off my overcoat and started to look things over. I could see that they were all very nervous, eyeing me up and down distrustfully. As often, in such cases, they weren't telling me more than they had to, it was up to me to tell them; that's why they were spending three dollars on me.   3

The child was fairly eating me up with her cold, steady eyes, and no expression to her face whatever. She did not move and seemed, inwardly, quiet; an unusually attractive little thing, and as strong as a heifer in appearance. But her face was flushed, she was breathing rapidly, and I realized that she had a high fever. She had magnificent blonde hair, in profusion. One of those picture children often reproduced in advertising leaflets and the photogravure sections of the Sunday papers. 4

She's had a fever for three days, began the father, and we don't know what it comes from. My wife has given her things, you know, like people do, but it don't do no good. And there's been a lot of sickness around. So we tho't you better look her over and tell us what is the matter. 5

As doctors often do I took a trial shot at it as a point of departure. Has she had a sore throat? 6

Both parents answered me together, No . . . No, she says her throat don't hurt her. 7

Does your throat hurt you? added the mother to the child. But the little girl's expression didn't change nor did she move her eyes from my face. 8

Have you looked? 9

I tried, said the mother, but I couldn't see. 10

As it happens we had been having a number of cases of diphtheria in the school to which this child went during that month and we were all, quite apparently, thinking of that, though no one had as yet spoken of the thing. 11

Well, I said, suppose we take a look at the throat first. I smiled in my best professional manner and asking for the child's first name I said, come on, Mathilda, open your mouth and let's take a look at your throat. 12

Nothing doing. 13

Aw, come on, I coaxed, just open your mouth wide and let me take a look. Look, I said opening both hands wide, I haven't anything in my hands. Just open up and let me see. 14

Such a nice man, put in the mother. Look how kind he is to you. Come on, do what he tells you to. He won't hurt you. 15

At that I ground my teeth in disgust. If only they wouldn't use the word "hurt" I might be able to get somewhere. But I did not allow myself to be hurried or disturbed but speaking quietly and slowly I approached the child again. 16

As I moved my chair a little nearer suddenly with one catlike movement both her hands clawed instinctively for my eyes and she almost reached them too. In fact she knocked my glasses flying and they fell, though unbroken, several feet away from me on the kitchen floor. 17

Both the mother and father almost turned themselves inside out in embarrassment and apology. You bad girl, said the mother, taking her and shaking her by one arm. Look what you've done. The nice man . . . 18

For heaven's sake, I broke in. Don't call me a nice man to her. I'm here to look at her throat on the chance that she might have diphtheria and possibly die of it. But that's nothing to her. Look here, I said to the child, we're going to look at your throat. You're old enough to understand what I'm saying. Will you open it now by yourself or shall we have to open it for you? 19

Not a move. Even her expression hadn't changed. Her breaths however were coming faster and faster. Then the battle began. I had to do it. I had to have a throat culture 20 for her own protection. But first I told the parents that it was entirely up to them. I explained the danger but said that I would not insist on a throat examination so long as they would take the responsibility.

If you don't do what the doctor says you'll have to go to the hospital, the mother admonished her severely. 21

Oh yeah? I had to smile to myself. After all, I had already fallen in love with the savage brat, the parents were contemptible to me. In the ensuing struggle they grew more and more abject, crushed, exhausted while she surely rose to magnificent heights of insane fury of effort bred of her terror of me. 22

The father tried his best, and he was a big man, but the fact that she was his daughter, his shame at her behavior and his dread of hurting her made him release her just at the critical times when I had almost achieved success, till I wanted to kill him. But his dread also that she might have diphtheria made him tell me to go on, go on though he himself was almost fainting, while the mother moved back and forth behind us raising and lowering her hands in an agony of apprehension. 23

Put her in front of you on your lap, I ordered, and hold both her wrists. 24

But as soon as he did the child let out a scream. Don't, you're hurting me. Let go of my hands. Let them go I tell you. Then she shrieked terrifyingly, hysterically. Stop it! Stop it! You're killing me! 25

Do you think she can stand it, doctor! said the mother. 26

You get out, said the husband to his wife. Do you want her to die of diphtheria? 27

Come on now, hold her, I said. 28

Then I grasped the child's head with my left hand and tried to get the wooden tongue depressor between her teeth. She fought, with clenched teeth, desperately! But now I also had grown furious — at a child. I tried to hold myself down but I couldn't. I know how to expose a throat for inspection. And I did my best. When finally I got the wooden spatula behind the last teeth and just the point of it into the mouth cavity, she opened up for an instant but before I could see anything she came down again and gripping the wooden blade between her molars she reduced it to splinters before I could get it out again. 29

Aren't you ashamed, the mother yelled at her. Aren't you ashamed to act like that in front of the doctor? 30

Get me a smooth-handled spoon of some sort, I told the mother. We're going through with this. The child's mouth was already bleeding. Her tongue was cut and she was screaming in wild hysterical shrieks. Perhaps I should have desisted and come back in an hour or more. No doubt it would have been better. But I have seen at least two children lying dead in bed of neglect in such cases, and feeling that I must get a diagnosis now or never I went at it again. But the worst of it was that I too had got beyond reason. I could have torn the child apart in my own fury and enjoyed it. It was a pleasure to attack her. My face was burning with it. 31

The damned little brat must be protected against her own idiocy, one says to oneself at such times. Others must be protected against her. It is a social necessity. And all these things are true. But a blind fury, a feeling of adult shame, bred of a longing for muscular release are the operatives. One goes on to the end. 32

In a final unreasoning assault I overpowered the child's neck and jaws. I forced | 33
the heavy silver spoon back of her teeth and down her throat till she gagged. And there
it was — both tonsils covered with membrane. She had fought valiantly to keep me
from knowing her secret. She had been hiding that sore throat for three days at least
and lying to her parents in order to escape just such an outcome as this.

Now truly she was furious. She had been on the defensive before but now she | 34
attacked. Tried to get off her father's lap and fly at me while tears of defeat blinded
her eyes.

Questions for Analysis

1. This story is told from the doctor's point of view. How does he justify his use of force? What are the pros and cons he weighs in using it? To get started, look in particular at paragraph 34.

2. How do the sexual overtones of the story — for example, in the doctor's describing the girl as "an unusually attractive little thing" (par. 4) and admitting "I had already fallen in love with the savage brat" (par. 22) — affect your understanding and judgment of the doctor's and the girl's behavior?

3. Because this story came out of the era of the Great Depression, you might expect it to say something about the impoverished material conditions in which people lived at the time and how these hardships affected them. Are these expectations borne out? What seems to be the economic status of the family and the doctor, and how does class affect what happens in the story? To get started, take a look at paragraphs 2 and 3.

SHERMAN ALEXIE (b. 1966), a Spokane/Coeur d'Alene Indian, was born on the Spokane Indian Reservation in Wellpinit, Washington. According to Alexie's official biography (www.fallsapart.com), Alexie was educated at Gonzaga University and Washington State University, where, "after fainting numerous times in human anatomy class," he abandoned his pre-med path, enrolled in a poetry workshop, and discovered his talent for writing. To date, Alexie has published eleven poetry collections, the most recent of which is *Dangerous Astronomy* (2005); four novels, including the young adult novel *The Absolutely True Diary of a Part-Time Indian* (2007); two screenplays, *Smoke Signals* (1998) and *The Business of Fancydancing* (2003); and three short-story collections, including *Ten Little Indians* (2003) and *The Toughest Indian in the World* (2000). "A Good Story" was first published in the collection *The Lone Ranger and Tonto Fistfight in Heaven* (1993).

A GOOD STORY

Sherman Alexie

The Quilting

A quiet Saturday reservation afternoon and I pretend sleep on the couch while my mother pieces together another quilt on the living room floor. | 1

"You know," she says. "Those stories you tell, they're kind of sad, enit?" | 2

I keep my eyes closed. | 3

"Junior," she says. "Don't you think your stories are too sad?" | 4

My efforts to ignore her are useless. | 5

"What do you mean?" I ask. | 6

She puts down her scissors and fabric, looks at me so straight that I have to sit up and open my eyes. | 7

"Well," she says. "Ain't nobody cries that much, you know?" | 8

I pretend to rub the sleep from my eyes, stretch my arms and legs, make small noises of irritation. | 9

"I guess," I say. "But ain't nobody laughs as much as the people in my stories, either." | 10

"That's true," she says. | 11

I stand up, shake my pants loose, and walk to the kitchen to grab a Diet Pepsi with cold, cold ice. | 12

Mom quilts silently for a while. Then she whistles. | 13

"What?" I ask her, knowing these signals for attention. | 14

"You know what you should do? You should write a story about something good, a real good story." | 15

"Why?" | 16

"Because people should know that good things always happen to Indians, too." | 17

I take a big drink of Diet Pepsi, search the cupboards for potato chips, peanuts, anything. | 18

"Good things happen," she says and goes back to her quilting. | 19

I think for a moment, put my Diet Pepsi down on the counter. | 20

"Okay," I say. "If you want to hear a good story, you have to listen." | 21

The Story

Uncle Moses sat in his sandwich chair eating a sandwich. Between bites, he hummed an it-is-a-good-day song. He sat in front of the house he built himself fifty years before. The house sat down at random angles to the ground. The front room leaned to the west, the bedroom to the east, and the bathroom simply folded in on itself. | 22

There was no foundation, no hidden closet, nothing built into the thin walls. On the whole, it was the kind of house that would stand even years after Moses died, held up by the tribal imagination. Driving by, the Indians would look across the field toward the house and hold it upright with their eyes, remembering *Moses lived there.* | 23

It would be just enough to ensure survival.   24

Uncle Moses gave no thought to his passing on most days. Instead, he usually   25
finished his sandwich, held the last bite of bread and meat in his mouth like the last
word of a good story.

"Ya-hey," he called out to the movement of air, the unseen. A summer before,   26
Uncle Moses listened to his nephew, John-John, talking a story. John-John was back
from college and told Moses that 99 percent of the matter in the universe is invisible
to the human eye. Ever since, Moses made sure to greet what he could not see.

Uncle Moses stood, put his hands on his hips, arched his back. More and more, he   27
heard his spine playing stickgame through his skin, singing old dusty words, the words of
all his years. He looked at the position of the sun to determine the time, checked his watch
to be sure, and looked across the field for the children who would soon come.

The Indian children would come with half-braids, curiosity endless and essential.   28
The children would come from throwing stones into water, from basketball and bas-
ketry, from the arms of their mothers and fathers, from the very beginning. This was
the generation of HUD house, of car wreck and cancer, of commodity cheese and beef.
These were the children who carried dreams in the back pockets of their blue jeans,
pulled them out easily, traded back and forth.

"Dreams like baseball cards," Uncle Moses said to himself, smiled hard when he   29
saw the first child running across the field. It was Arnold, of course, pale-skinned boy
who was always teased by the other children.

Arnold ran slowly, his great belly shaking with the effort, eyes narrowed in con-   30
centration. A full-blood Spokane, Arnold was somehow born with pale, pretty skin
and eyes with color continually changing from gray to brown. He liked to sit in the
sandwich chair and wait for Uncle Moses to make him a good sandwich.

It took Arnold five minutes to run across the field, and all the while Moses   31
watched him, studied his movements, the way Arnold's hair reached out in all directions, uncombed, so close to electricity, closer to lightning. He did not wear braids,
could not sit long enough for his mother.

Be still, be still, she would say between her teeth, but Arnold loved his body too   32
much to remain still.

Big as he was, Arnold was still graceful in his movements, in his hands when he   33
touched his face listening to a good story. He was also the best basketball player in
the reservation grade school. Uncle Moses sometimes walked to the playground just
to watch Arnold play and wonder at the strange, often improbable gifts a person can
receive.

We are all given something to compensate for what we have lost. Moses felt those   34
words even though he did not say them.

Arnold arrived, breathing hard.   35

"Ya-hey, Little Man," Uncle Moses said.   36

"Hello, Uncle," Arnold replied, extending his hand in a half-shy, half-adult way, a   37
child's greeting, the affirmation of friendship.

"Where are the others?" Uncle Moses asked, taking Arnold's hand in his own.   38

"There was a field trip," Arnold answered. "All the others went to a baseball game   39
in Spokane. I hid until they left."

"Why?"   40

"Because I wanted to see you."   41

Moses smiled at Arnold's unplanned kindness. He held the child's hand a little   42
tighter and pulled him up close.

"Little Man," he said. "You have done a good thing."   43

Arnold smiled, pulled his hand away from Moses, and covered his smile, smiling   44
even harder.

"Uncle Moses," he said through his fingers. "Tell me a good story."   45

Uncle Moses sat down in the story chair and told this very story.   46

The Finishing

My mother sits quietly, rips a seam, begins to hum a slow song through her skinny lips.   47

"What you singing?" I ask.   48

"I'm singing an it-is-a-good-day song."   49

She smiles and I have to smile with her.   50

"Did you like the story?" I ask.   51

She keeps singing, sings a little louder and stronger as I take my Diet Pepsi out-   52
side and wait in the sun. It is warm, soon to be cold, but that's in the future, maybe
tomorrow, probably the next day and all the days after that. Today, now, I drink what
I have, will eat what is left in the cupboard, while my mother finishes her quilt, piece
by piece.

Believe me, there is just barely enough goodness in all of this.   53

Questions for Analysis

1. Why do you think Alexie gives his story the title "A Good Story"? What does he
   seem to say about what makes a story good? To get started, you could begin by
   looking at what the word *good* means in paragraph 15.

2. The purpose of art in society, the process of making art, and the education of the
   artist are common *motifs*, or themes, in stories and films. Who are the artist figures
   in this story? What connections exist between their art and the culture from which
   it stems? What do you learn about the purpose of art, its process, or the education
   of the artist? To get started, take a look at paragraphs 22–23.

3. Alexie grew up on the Spokane Indian Reservation in Wellpinit, Washington, which
   is where he set this story. What impression of reservation life do you get from the
   story? How significant is the setting to its meaning? To get started, take a look at
   paragraph 28.

PART 2

Critical Thinking Strategies

11

A Catalog of Invention Strategies

Writers are like scientists: They ask questions, systematically inquiring about how things work, what they are, where they occur, and how more information can be learned about them. Writers are also like artists in that they use what they know and learn to create something new and imaginative.

The invention and inquiry strategies — also known as **heuristics** — described in this chapter are not mysterious or magical. They are available to all writers, and one or more of them may appeal to your common sense and experience. These techniques represent ways creative writers, engineers, scientists, composers — in fact, all of us — solve problems. Once you have mastered these strategies, you can use them to tackle many of the writing situations you will encounter in college, on the job, and in the community.

The strategies for invention and inquiry in this chapter are grouped into two categories:

Mapping: A brief visual representation of your thinking or planning

Writing: The composition of phrases or sentences to discover information and ideas and to make connections among them

These invention and inquiry strategies will help you explore and research a topic fully before you begin drafting and then help you creatively solve problems as you draft and revise. In this chapter, strategies are arranged alphabetically within each of the two categories.

Mapping

Mapping strategies involve making a visual record of invention and inquiry. In making maps, writers usually use key words and phrases to record material they want to remember, questions they need to answer, and new sources of information they want to check. The maps show the ideas, details, and facts as well as possible ways to connect and focus them. Mapping can be especially useful for working in collaborative writing situations, for preparing oral presentations, and for creating visual aids for written or oral reports. Mapping strategies include clustering, listing, and outlining.

Clustering

Clustering is a strategy for revealing possible relationships among facts and ideas. Unlike listing (the next mapping strategy), clustering requires a brief period of initial preparation when you divide your topic into parts or main ideas. Clustering works as follows:

1. In a word or phrase, write your topic in the center of a piece of paper. Circle it.

2. Also in words or phrases, write down the main parts or ideas of your topic. Circle these, and connect them with lines to the topic in the center.

3. Next, write down facts, details, examples, or ideas related to these main parts. Connect them with lines to the relevant main parts or ideas.

Clustering can be useful in the early stages of planning an essay to find subtopics and organize information. You may try out and discard several clusters before finding one that is promising. Many writers also use clustering to plan brief sections of an essay as they are drafting or revising. (A model of clustering is shown in Figure 11.1 below.)

Software-based Diagramming Tools
Software vendors have created a variety of electronic tools to help people better visualize complex projects. These flowcharts, webs, and outlines can make it easier for you to see how to proceed at any stage of your project.

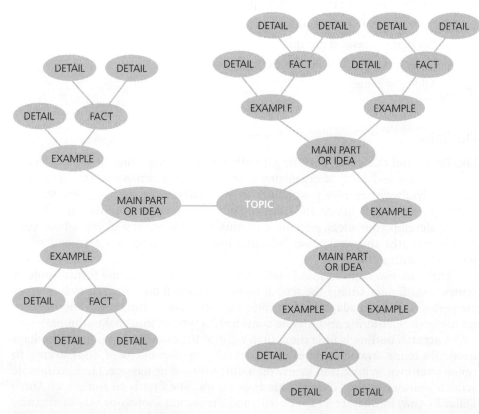

Figure 11.1 A model of clustering

Listing

Listing is a familiar activity. You make shopping lists and lists of errands to do or people to call. Listing can also be a great help in planning an essay. It enables you to recall what you already know about a topic and suggests what else you may need to find out.

A basic activity for all writers, listing is especially useful to those who have little time for planning — for example, reporters facing deadlines and college students taking essay exams. Listing lets you order your ideas quickly. It can also serve as a first step in discovering possible writing topics. Here is how listing works best for invention work:

1. Give your list a title that indicates your main idea or topic.

2. Write as fast as you can, relying on short phrases.

3. Include anything that seems at all useful. Try not to be judgmental at this point.

4. After you have finished or even as you write, reflect on the list, and organize it in the following way:
   - Put an asterisk next to the most promising items.
   - Number key items in order of importance.
   - Put items in related groups.
   - Cross out items that do not seem promising.
   - Add new items.

Outlining

Like listing and clustering, **outlining** is both a means of inventing what you want to say in an essay and a way of organizing your ideas and information. As you outline, you nearly always see new possibilities in your subject, discovering new ways of dividing or grouping information and seeing where you need additional information to develop your ideas. Because outlining lets you see at a glance where your essay's strengths and weaknesses lie, outlining can also help you read and revise your essay with a critical eye.

There are two main forms of outlining: informal outlining and formal topic or sentence outlining. Among the several types of informal outlining, scratch outlines are perhaps the most adaptable to a variety of situations. Chunking is another useful method. (Clustering also may be considered a type of informal outlining.)

A **scratch outline** is little more than a list of the essay's main points. You have no doubt made scratch outlines many times — to plan essays or essay exams, to revise your own writing, and to analyze a difficult reading passage. Here are sample scratch outlines for two different kinds of essays. The first is an outline of Annie Dillard's essay in Chapter 2 (pp. 22–25), and the second shows one way to organize a position paper (Chapter 6):

Scratch Outline: Essay about a Remembered Event

1. explains what she learned from playing football
2. identifies other sports she learned from boys in the neighborhood
3. sets the scene by describing the time and place of the event
4. describes the boys who were playing with her
5. describes what typically happened: a car would come down the street, they would throw snowballs, and then they would wait for another car
6. describes the iceball-making project she had begun while waiting
7. describes the Buick's approach and how they followed the routine
8. describes the impact of the snowball on the Buick's windshield
9. describes the man's surprising reaction: getting out of the car and running after them
10. narrates the chase and describes the man
11. explains how the kids split up and the man followed her and Mikey
12. narrates the chase and describes how the neighborhood looked as they ran through it
13. continues the narration, describing the way the man threw himself into the chase
14. continues the narration, commenting on her thoughts and feelings
15. narrates the ending or climax of the chase, when the man caught the kids
16. describes the runners trying to catch their breath
17. describes her own physical state
18. relates the man's words
19. explains her reactions to his words and actions
20. explains her later thoughts and feelings
21. explains her present perspective on this remembered event

Scratch Outline: Essay Arguing a Position

> Presentation of the issue
>
> Accommodation conceding some aspect of an opposing position
>
> Thesis statement
>
> First reason with support
>
> Second reason with support
>
> (etc.)
>
> Conclusion

Remember that the items in a scratch outline do not necessarily coincide with paragraphs. Sometimes two or more items may be developed in the same paragraph or one item may be covered in two or more paragraphs.

Chunking, a type of scratch outline commonly used by professional writers in business and industry and especially well suited to writing in the electronic age, consists of a set of headings describing the major points to be covered in the final document. What makes chunking distinctive is that the blocks of text — or "chunks" — under each heading are intended to be roughly the same length and scope. These headings can be discussed and passed around among several writers and editors before writing begins, and different chunks may be written by different authors, simply by typing notes or text on a word processor into the space under each heading. The list of headings is subject to change during the writing, and new headings may be added or old ones subdivided or discarded as part of the drafting and editing process.

The advantage of chunking in your own writing is that it breaks the large task of drafting into smaller tasks in a simple, evenly balanced way; once the headings are determined, the writing becomes just a matter of filling in the specifics that go in each chunk. Organization tends to improve as you get a sense of the weight of different parts of the document while filling in the blanks. Places where the essay needs more information or there is a problem with pacing tend to stand out because of the chunking structure, and the headings can either be taken out of the finished essay or left in as devices to help guide readers. If they are left in, they should be edited into parallel grammatical form like the items in a formal topic or sentence outline, as discussed below.

Topic outlines and **sentence outlines** are considered more formal than scratch outlines because they follow a conventional format of numbered and lettered headings and subheadings:

I. (Main topic)
   A. (Subtopic of I)
   B.
      1. (Subtopic of I.B)
      2.
         a. (Subtopic of I.B.2)
         b.
            (1) (Subtopic of I.B.2.b)
            (2)
   C.
      1. (Subtopic of I.C)
      2.

The difference between a topic and sentence outline is obvious: Topic outlines simply name the topics and subtopics, whereas sentence outlines use complete or abbreviated sentences. To illustrate, here are two partial formal outlines of an essay arguing a position, Jessica Statsky's "Children Need to Play, Not Compete," from Chapter 6 (pp. 270–74).

Formal Topic Outline

I. Organized sports harmful to children
   A. Harmful physically
      1. Curve ball (Koppett)
      2. Tackle football (Tutko)
   B. Harmful psychologically
      1. Fear of being hurt
         a. Little League Online
         b. Mother
         c. Reporter
      2. Competition
         a. Rablovsky
         b. Studies

Formal Sentence Outline

I. Highly organized competitive sports such as Peewee Football and Little League Baseball can be physically and psychologically harmful to children, as well as counterproductive for developing future players.
   A. Physically harmful because sports entice children into physical actions that are bad for growing bodies.
      1. Koppett claims throwing a curve ball may put abnormal strain on developing arm and shoulder muscles.
      2. Tutko argues that tackle football is too traumatic for young kids.
   B. Psychologically harmful to children for a number of reasons.
      1. Fear of being hurt detracts from their enjoyment of the sport.
         a. Little League Online ranks fear of injury seventh among the seven top reasons children quit.
         b. One mother says, "kids get so scared.... They'll sit on the bench and pretend their leg hurts."
         c. A reporter tells about a child who made himself vomit to get out of playing Peewee Football.
      2. Too much competition poses psychological dangers for children.
         a. Rablovsky reports: "The spirit of play suddenly disappears, and sport becomes joblike."
         b. Studies show that children prefer playing on a losing team to "warming the bench on a winning team."

In contrast to an informal outline in which anything goes, a formal outline must follow many conventions. The roman numerals and capital letters are followed by periods. In both topic and sentence outlines, the first word of each item is capitalized, but items in topic outlines do not end with a period as items in sentence outlines do. Every level of a formal outline except the top level (identified by the roman numeral *I*) must include at least two items. Items at the same level of indentation in a topic outline should be grammatically parallel — all beginning with the same part of speech. For example, *I.A.* and *I.B.* are parallel when they both begin with an adverb (*Physically harmful* and *Psychologically harmful*) or with an adjective (*Harmful physically* and *Harmful psychologically*); they would not be parallel if one began with an adverb (*Physically harmful*) and the other with an adjective (*Harmful psychologically*).

Writing

Unlike most mapping strategies, **writing strategies** invite you to produce complete sentences. Sentences provide considerable generative power. Because they are complete statements, they take you further than listing or clustering. They enable you to explore ideas and define relationships, bring ideas together or show how they differ, and identify causes and effects. Sentences can also help you develop a logical chain of thought.

Some of these invention and inquiry strategies are systematic, while others are more flexible. Even though they call for complete sentences that are related to one another, they do not require preparation or revision. You can use them to develop oral as well as written presentations.

These writing strategies include *cubing, dialoguing, dramatizing, keeping a journal, looping, questioning,* and *quick drafting*.

Cubing

Cubing is useful for quickly exploring a writing topic, probing it from six different perspectives. It is known as *cubing* because a cube has six sides. These are the six perspectives in cubing:

Describing: What does your subject look like? What size is it? What is its color? Its shape? Its texture? Name its parts.

Comparing: What is your subject similar to? Different from?

Associating: What does your subject make you think of? What connections does it have to anything else in your experience?

Analyzing: What are the origins of your subject? What are the functions or significance of its parts? How are its parts related?

Applying: What can you do with your subject? What uses does it have?

Arguing: What arguments can you make for your subject? Against it?

Here are some guidelines to help you use cubing productively.

1. Select a topic, subject, or part of a subject. This can be a person, a scene, an event, an object, a problem, an idea, or an issue. Hold it in focus.

2. Limit your writing to three to five minutes for each perspective. The whole activity should take no more than half an hour.

3. Keep going until you have written about your subject from all six perspectives. Remember that cubing offers the special advantage of enabling you to generate multiple perspectives quickly.

4. As you write from each perspective, begin with what you know about your subject. However, do not limit yourself to your present knowledge. Indicate what else you would like to know about your subject, and suggest where you might find that information.

5. Reread what you have written. Look for bright spots, surprises. Recall the part that was easiest for you to write. Recall the part where you felt a special momentum and pleasure in writing. Look for an angle or an unexpected insight. These special parts may suggest a focus or topic within a larger subject, or they may provide specific details to include in a draft.

Dialoguing

A *dialogue* is a conversation between two or more people. You can use **dialoguing** to search for topics, find a focus, explore ideas, or consider opposing viewpoints. When you write a dialogue as an invention strategy, you need to make up all parts of the conversation (unless, of course, you are writing collaboratively). To construct a dialogue independently or collaboratively, follow these steps:

See p. 58 for an example of dialogue used for invention.

1. Write a conversation between two speakers. Label the participants *Speaker A* and *Speaker B*, or make up names for them.

2. If you get stuck, you might have one of the speakers ask the other a question.

3. Write brief responses to keep the conversation moving fast. Do not spend much time planning or rehearsing responses. Write what first occurs to you, just as in a real conversation, where people take quick turns to prevent any awkward silences.

Dialogues can be especially useful with personal experience and persuasive essays because they help you remember conversations and anticipate objections.

Dramatizing

Dramatizing is an invention activity developed by the philosopher Kenneth Burke as a way of thinking about how people interact and as a way of analyzing stories and films.

Thinking about human behavior in dramatic terms can be very productive for writers. Drama has action, actors, setting, motives, and methods. Since stars and acting go together, you can use a five-pointed star to remember these five points of dramatizing: Each point on the star provides a different perspective on human behavior (see Figure 11.2).

Figure 11.2 Dramatizing

Action. An action is anything that happens, has happened, will happen, or could happen. Action includes events that are physical (running a marathon), mental (thinking about a book you have read), and emotional (falling in love).

Actor. The actor is involved in the action — either responsible for it or simply affected by it. (The actor does not have to be a person. It can be a force, something that causes an action. For example, if the action is a rise in the price of gasoline, the actor could be increased demand or short supply.) Dramatizing may also include a number of coactors working together or at odds.

Setting. The setting is the situation or background of the action. We usually think of setting as the place and time of an event, but it may also be the historical background of an event or the childhood of a person.

Motive. The motive is the purpose or reason for an action — the actor's intention. Actions may have multiple, even conflicting, motives.

Method. The method explains how an action occurs, including the techniques an actor uses. It refers to whatever makes things happen.

Each of these points suggests a simple invention question:

> *Action:* What?
>
> *Actor:* Who?
>
> *Setting:* When and where?
>
> *Motive:* Why?
>
> *Method:* How?

This list looks like the questions reporters typically ask. But dramatizing goes further: It enables us to consider relations between and among these five elements. We can think about actors' motives, the effect of the setting on the actors, the relations between actors, and so on.

You can use this invention strategy to learn more about yourself or about other significant people in your life. You can use it as well to explore, interpret, or evaluate characters in stories or movies. Moreover, dramatizing is especially useful in understanding the readers you want to inform or convince.

To use dramatizing, imagine the person you want to understand better in a particular situation. Holding this image in mind, write answers to any questions in the following list that apply. You may draw a blank on some questions, have little to say to some, and find a lot to say to others. Be exploratory and playful with the questions. Write responses quickly, relying on words and phrases, even drawings.

- What is the actor doing?
- How did the actor come to be involved in this situation?
- Why does the actor do what he or she does?
- What else might the actor do?

- What is the actor trying to accomplish?
- How do other actors influence — help or hinder — the main actor?
- What do the actor's actions reveal about him or her?
- What does the actor's language reveal about him or her?
- How does the event's setting influence the actor's actions?
- How does the time of the event influence what the actor does?
- Where does this actor come from?
- How is this actor different now from what he or she used to be?
- What might this actor become?
- How is this actor like or unlike the other actors?

Keeping a Journal

Professional writers often use **journals** to keep notes. Starting one is easy. Buy a special notebook, or open a new file on your computer, and start writing. Here are some possibilities:

- Keep a list of new words and concepts you learn in your courses. You could also write about the progress and direction of your learning in particular courses — the experience of being in the course, your feelings about what is happening, and what you are learning.

- Respond to your reading, both assigned and personal. As you read, write about your personal associations, reflections, reactions, and evaluations. Summarize or copy memorable or especially important passages, and comment on them. (Copying and commenting have been practiced by students and writers for centuries in special journals called *commonplace books.*)

- Write to prepare for particular class meetings. Write about the main ideas you have learned from assigned readings and about the relationship of these new ideas to other ideas in the course. After class, write to summarize what you have learned. List questions you have about the ideas or information discussed in class. Journal writing of this kind involves reflecting, evaluating, interpreting, synthesizing, summarizing, and questioning.

- Record observations and overheard conversations.

- Write for ten or fifteen minutes every day about whatever is on your mind. Focus these meditations on your new experiences as you try to understand, interpret, and reflect on them.

- Write sketches of people who catch your attention.

- Organize your time. Write about your goals and priorities, or list specific things to accomplish and what you plan to do.

- Keep a log over several days or weeks about a particular event unfolding in the news — a sensational trial, an environmental disaster, a political campaign, a campus controversy, or the fortunes of a sports team.

You can use a journal in many ways. All of the writing in your journal has value for learning. You may also be able to use parts of your journal for writing in your other courses.

Looping

Looping is especially useful for the first stages of exploring a topic. As its name suggests, **looping** involves writing quickly to explore some aspect of a topic and then looping back to your original starting point or to a new starting point to explore another aspect. Beginning with almost any starting point, looping enables you to find a center of interest and eventually a thesis for your essay. The steps are simple:

1. Write down your area of interest. You may know only that you have to write about another person or a movie or a cultural trend that has caught your attention. Or you may want to search for a topic in a broad historical period or for one related to a major political event. Although you may wander from this topic as you write, you will want to keep coming back to it. Your purpose is to find a focus for writing.

2. Write nonstop for ten minutes. Start with the first thing that comes to mind. Write rapidly, without looking back to reread or to correct anything. *Do not stop writing. Keep your pencil moving or keystrokes clacking.* Continuous writing is the key to looping. If you get stuck for a moment, rewrite the last sentence. Follow diversions and digressions, but keep returning to your topic.

3. After ten minutes, pause to reread what you have written. Decide what is most important — a single insight, a pattern of ideas, an emerging theme, a visual detail, anything at all that stands out. Some writers call this a "center of gravity" or a "hot spot." To complete the first loop, restate this center in a single sentence.

4. Beginning with this sentence, write nonstop for another ten minutes.

5. Summarize in one sentence again to complete the second loop.

6. Keep looping until one of your summary sentences produces a focus or thesis. You may need only two or three loops; you may need more.

Questioning

Asking questions about a subject is a way to learn about it and decide what to write. When you first encounter a subject, however, your questions may be scattered. Also, you are not likely to think right away of all the important questions you ought to ask. The advantage of having a basic list of questions for invention, like the ones for cubing and for dramatizing discussed earlier in this chapter, is that it provides a systematic approach to exploring a subject.

The questions that follow come from classical rhetoric (what the Greek philosopher Aristotle called *topics*) and a modern approach to invention called *tagmemics*. Based on the work of linguist Kenneth Pike, tagmemics provides questions about different ways we make sense of the world, the ways we sort and classify experience in order to understand it.

Here are the steps in using questions for invention:

1. In a sentence or two, identify your subject. A subject could be any event, person, problem, project, idea, or issue — in other words, anything you might write about.

2. Start by writing a response to the first question in the following list, and move right through the list. Try to answer each question at least briefly with a word or a phrase. Some questions may invite several sentences or even a page or more of writing. You may draw a blank on a few questions. Skip them. Later, when you have more experience with questions for invention, you can start anywhere in the list.

3. Write your responses quickly, without much planning. Follow digressions or associations. Do not screen anything out. Be playful.

What Is Your Subject?

- What is your subject's name? What other names does it have? What names did it have in the past?

- What aspects of the subject do these different names emphasize?

- Imagine a still photograph or a moving picture of your subject. What would it look like?

- What would you put into a time capsule to stand for your subject?

- What are its causes and effects?

- How would it look from different vantage points or perspectives?

- What particular experiences have you had with the subject? What have you learned?

What Parts or Features Does Your Subject Have, and How Are They Related?

- Name the parts or features of your subject.

- Describe each one, using the questions in the preceding subject list.

- How is each part or feature related to the others?

How Is Your Subject Similar to and Different from Other Subjects?

- What is your subject similar to? In what ways?

- What is your subject different from? In what ways?

- What seems to you most unlike your subject? In what ways? Now, just for fun, note how they are alike.

How Much Can Your Subject Change and Still Remain the Same?

- How has your subject changed from what it once was?

- How is it changing now — moment to moment, day to day, year to year?

- How does each change alter your way of thinking about your subject?
- What are some different forms your subject takes?
- What does it become when it is no longer itself?

Where Does Your Subject Fit in the World?

- When and where did your subject originate?
- What would happen if at some future time your subject ceased to exist?
- When and where do you usually experience the subject?
- What is this subject a part of, and what are the other parts?
- What do other people think of your subject?

Quick Drafting

Sometimes you know what you want to say or have little time for invention. In these situations, **quick drafting** may be a good strategy. There are no special rules for quick drafting, but you should rely on it only if you know your subject well, have had experience with the kind of writing you are doing, and will have a chance to revise your draft. Quick drafting can help you discover what you already know about the subject and what you need to find out. It can also help you develop and organize your thoughts.

A Catalog of Reading Strategies

This chapter presents strategies to help you become a thoughtful reader. A thoughtful reader is above all a patient *re*reader, concerned not only with comprehending and remembering but also with interpreting and evaluating — on the one hand, striving to understand the text on its own terms; on the other hand, taking care to question its ideas.

The reading strategies in this chapter can help you enrich your thinking as a reader and participate in conversations as a writer. These strategies include the following:

- *Annotating:* Recording your reactions to, interpretations of, and questions about a text as you read it
- *Taking inventory:* Listing and grouping your annotations and other notes to find meaningful patterns
- *Outlining:* Listing the text's main ideas to reveal how it is organized
- *Paraphrasing:* Restating what you have read to clarify or refer to it
- *Summarizing:* Distilling the main ideas or gist of a text
- *Synthesizing:* Integrating into your own writing ideas and information gleaned from different sources
- *Contextualizing:* Placing a text in its historical and cultural contexts
- *Exploring the significance of figurative language:* Examining how metaphors, similes, and symbols are used in a text to convey meaning and evoke feelings
- *Looking for patterns of opposition:* Inferring the values and assumptions embodied in the language of a text
- *Reflecting on challenges to your beliefs and values:* Examining the bases of your personal responses to a text
- *Evaluating the logic of an argument:* Determining whether an argument is well reasoned and adequately supported
- *Recognizing emotional manipulation:* Identifying texts that unfairly and inappropriately use emotional appeals based on false or exaggerated claims
- *Judging the writer's credibility:* Considering whether writers represent different points of view fairly and know what they are writing about

Although mastering these strategies will not make critical reading easy, it can make your reading much more satisfying and productive and thus help you handle even difficult material with confidence. These reading strategies will, in addition, often be useful in your reading outside of school — for instance, these strategies can help you understand, evaluate, and comment on what political figures, advertisers, and other writers are saying.

Annotating

Annotating Onscreen
Although this discussion of annotating assumes you are reading printed pages, you can also annotate many kinds of text on the computer screen by using your software's highlighting and commenting functions or simply by typing annotations into the text using a different color or font. If electronic annotation is not possible, print out the text and annotate by hand.

Annotations are the marks — underlines, highlights, and comments — you make directly on the page as you read. Annotating can be used to record immediate reactions and questions, outline and summarize main points, and evaluate and relate the reading to other ideas and points of view. Your annotations can take many forms, such as the following:

- Writing comments, questions, or definitions in the margins
- Underlining or circling words, phrases, or sentences
- Connecting ideas with lines or arrows
- Numbering related points
- Bracketing sections of the text
- Noting anything that strikes you as interesting, important, or questionable

Most readers annotate in layers, adding further annotations on second and third readings. Annotations can be light or heavy, depending on the reader's purpose and the difficulty of the material. Your purpose for reading also determines how you use your annotations.

The following selection, excerpted from Martin Luther King Jr.'s "Letter from Birmingham Jail," illustrates some of the ways you can annotate as you read. Add your own annotations, if you like.

> MARTIN LUTHER KING JR. (1929–1968) first came to national notice in 1955, when he led a successful boycott against the policy of restricting African American passengers to rear seats on city buses in Montgomery, Alabama, where he was minister of a Baptist church. He subsequently formed the Southern Christian Leadership Conference, which brought people of all races from all over the country to the South to fight nonviolently for racial integration. In 1963, King led demonstrations in Birmingham, Alabama, that were met with violence; a bomb was detonated in a black church, killing four young girls. King was arrested for his role in organizing the protests, and while in prison, he wrote his "Letter from Birmingham Jail" to justify his strategy of civil disobedience, which he called "nonviolent direct action."
>
> King begins his letter by discussing his disappointment with the lack of support he has received from white moderates, such as the group of clergy who published criticism of his organization in the local newspaper. As you read the following excerpt, try to infer what the clergy's specific criticisms might have been. Also, notice the tone King uses. Would you characterize the writing as apologetic, conciliatory, accusatory, or something else?

An Annotated Sample from "Letter from Birmingham Jail"

Martin Luther King Jr.

¶1. White moderates block progress.

I must confess that over the past few years I have been gravely disappointed with the white moderate. I have almost reached the regrettable conclusion that the Negro's [great stumbling block in his stride toward freedom] is not the White Citizen's Counciler or the Ku Klux Klanner, but the white moderate, who is more devoted to "order" than to justice; who prefers a negative peace which is the absence of tension to a positive peace which is the presence of justice; who constantly says: "I agree with you in the goal you seek, but I cannot agree with your methods of direct action"; who paternalistically believes he can set the timetable for another man's freedom; who lives by a mythical concept of time and who constantly advises the Negro to wait for a "more convenient season." Shallow understanding from people of good will is more frustrating than absolute misunderstanding from people of ill will. Lukewarm acceptance is much more bewildering than outright rejection.

Contrasts: order vs. justice, negative vs. positive peace, ends vs. means

(treating others like children)

more contrasts

¶2. What the moderates don't understand

metaphor: law and order = dams (faulty?)

I had hoped that the white moderate would understand that law and order exist for the purpose of establishing justice and that when they fail in this purpose they become the [dangerously structured dams that block the flow of social progress.] I had hoped that the white moderate would understand that the present tension in the South is a necessary phase of the transition from an [obnoxious negative peace,] in which the Negro passively accepted his unjust plight, to a [substantive and positive peace,] in which all men will respect the dignity and worth of human personality. Actually, we who engage in nonviolent direct action are not the creators of tension. We merely bring to the surface the hidden tension

repeats contrast (negative/positive)

Tension already exists: We help dispel it. (True?)

simile: hidden tension is "like a boil"

that is already alive. We bring it out in the open, where it can be seen and dealt with. [Like a boil that can never be cured so long as it is covered up but must be opened with all its ugliness to the natural medicines of air and light, injustice must be exposed, with all the tension its exposure creates, to the light of human conscience and the air of national opinion before it can be cured.]

¶3. Questions clergymen's logic: condemning his actions = condemning robbery victim, Socrates, Jesus.

In your statement you assert that our actions, even though peaceful, must be condemned because they precipitate violence. But is this a logical assertion? Isn't this like condemning (a robbed man) because his possession of money precipitated the evil act of robbery? Isn't this like condemning (Socrates) because his unswerving commitment to truth and his philosophical inquiries precipitated the act by the misguided populace in which they made him drink hemlock? Isn't this like condemning (Jesus) because his unique God-consciousness and never-ceasing devotion to God's will precipitated the evil act of crucifixion? We must come to see that, as the federal courts have consistently affirmed, it is wrong to urge an individual to cease his efforts to gain his basic constitutional rights because the question may precipitate violence. [Society must protect the robbed and punish the robber.]

3

repetition ("Isn't this like . . .")

(Yes!)

example of a white moderate's view

I had also hoped that the white moderate would reject the myth concerning time in relation to the struggle for freedom. I have just received a letter from a white brother in Texas. He writes: "All Christians know that the colored people will receive equal rights eventually, but it is possible that you are in too great a religious hurry. It has taken Christianity almost two thousand years to accomplish what it has. The teachings of Christ take time to come to earth." Such an attitude stems from a tragic misconception of time, from the strangely irrational notion that there is something in the very flow of time that will inevitably cure all ills. (Actually, time itself

4

¶14. *Time must be used to do right.*

is neutral; it can be used either destructively or constructively.) More and more I feel that the people of ill will have used time much more effectively than have the people of good will. We will have to repent in this generation not merely for the [hateful words and actions of the bad people] but for the [appalling silence of the good people.] Human progress never rolls in on [wheels of inevitability;] it comes through the tireless efforts of men willing to be co-workers with God, and without this hard work, time itself becomes an ally of the

(decay)

forces of social (stagnation.) [We must use time creatively, in the knowledge that the time is always ripe to do right.] Now is the time to make real the promise of democracy and transform our pending

metaphors (song, natural world)

[national elegy] into a creative [psalm of brotherhood.] Now is the time to lift our national policy from the [quicksand of racial injustice] to the [solid rock of human dignity.]

Silence/passivity is as bad as hateful words and actions.

metaphor (mechanical?)

5   You speak of our activity in Birmingham as extreme. At first I was rather disappointed that fellow clergymen would see my nonviolent efforts as those of an extremist. I began thinking about the fact that I stand in the middle of two opposing forces in the Negro community. One is a [force of complacency,] made up in part of Negroes who, as a result of long years of oppression, are so drained of self-respect and a sense of "somebodiness"

King accused of being an extremist.

¶15. *Puts self in middle of two extremes: complacency and bitterness.*

that they have adjusted to segregation; and in part of a few middle-class Negroes, who because of a degree of academic and economic security and because in some ways they profit by seg-regation, have become insensitive to the problems of the masses. The other [force is one of bitterness and hatred,] and it comes perilously close to advocating violence. It is expressed in the various black nationalist [groups that are springing up] across the nation, the largest and best-known being Elijah Muhammad's Muslim movement. Nourished by the Negro's frustration over

Malcolm X?

the continued existence of racial discrimination, this movement is made up of people who have lost faith in America, who have absolutely repudiated Christianity, and who have concluded that the white man is an incorrigible "devil."

¶6. Offers better choice: nonviolent protest.

I have tried to stand between these two forces, saying that we need emulate neither the "do-nothingism" of the complacent nor the hatred and despair of the black nationalist. For there is the more excellent way of love and nonviolent protest. I am grateful to God that, through the influence of the Negro church, the way of nonviolence became an integral part of our struggle.

6

(How did non-violence become part of King's movement?)

¶7. Says movement prevents racial violence. (Threat?)

If this philosophy had not emerged, by now many streets of the South would, I am convinced, be flowing with blood. And I am further convinced that if our white brothers dismiss as "rabble-rousers" and "outside agitators" those of us who employ nonviolent direct action, and if they refuse to support our nonviolent efforts, millions of Negroes will, out of frustration and despair, seek (solace) and security in black-nationalist ideologies — a development that would inevitably lead to a frightening racial nightmare.

7

(comfort)

(Oppressed people cannot remain oppressed forever.) The yearning for freedom eventually manifests itself, and that is what has happened to the American Negro. Something within has reminded him of his birthright of freedom, and something without has reminded him that it can be gained. Consciously or unconsciously, he has been caught up by the (Zeitgeist,) and with his black brothers of Africa and his brown and yellow brothers of Asia, South America and the Caribbean, the United States Negro is moving with a sense of great urgency toward the [promised land of racial justice.] If one recognizes

8

(spirit of the times)

this *[vital urge that has engulfed the Negro community,]* one should readily understand why public demonstrations are taking place. The Negro has many *[pent-up resentments]* and latent frustrations, and he must release them. So let him march; let him make prayer pilgrimages to the city hall; let him go on freedom rides — and try to understand why he must do so. If his repressed emotions are not released in nonviolent ways, they will seek expression through violence; this is not a threat but a fact of history. So I have not said to my people: "Get rid of your discontent." Rather, I have tried to say that this normal and healthy discontent can be *[channeled into the creative outlet of nonviolent direct action.]* And now this approach is being termed extremist.

Not a threat, but a fact—?

¶8. Discontent is normal, healthy, and historically inevitable, but it must be channeled.

9   But though I was initially disappointed at being categorized as an extremist, as I continued to think about the matter I gradually gained a measure of satisfaction from the label. Was not Jesus an extremist for love: "Love your enemies, bless them that curse you, do good to them that hate you, and pray for them which despitefully use you, and persecute you." Was not (Amos) an extremist for justice: "Let justice roll down like waters and righteousness like an ever-flowing stream." Was not (Paul) an extremist for the Christian gospel: "I bear in my body the marks of the Lord Jesus." Was not (Martin Luther) an extremist: "Here I stand; I cannot do otherwise, so help me God." And (John Bunyan:) "I will stay in jail to the end of my days before I make a butchery of my conscience." And (Abraham Lincoln:) "This nation cannot survive half slave and half free." And (Thomas Jefferson:) "We hold these truths to be self-evident, that all men are created equal. . . ." (So the question is not whether

¶9. Redefines "extremism."

(Hebrew prophet)

(Christian apostle)

(Founder of Protestantism)

(English preacher)

Compares self to great "extremists" — including Jesus

we will be extremists, but what kind of extremists we will be. Will we be extremists for hate or for love? Will we be extremists for the preservation of injustice or for the extension of justice? In that dramatic scene on Calvary's hill three men were crucified. We must never forget that all three were crucified for the same crime — the crime of extremism. Two were extremists for immorality, and thus fell below their environment. The other, Jesus Christ, was an extremist for love, truth and goodness, and thereby rose above his environment. Perhaps the South, the nation and the world are in dire need of creative extremists.

Disappointed in the white moderate

I had hoped that the white moderate would see this need.   10
Perhaps I was too optimistic; perhaps I expected too much. I suppose I should have realized that few members of the oppressor race can understand the deep groans and passionate yearnings of the oppressed race, and still fewer have the vision to see that [injustice must be rooted out] by strong, persistent and determined action. I am thankful, however, that some of our white brothers in the South have grasped the meaning of this social revolution and committed themselves to it. They are still all too few in quantity, but they are big in quality. Some — such

¶10. Praises whites who have supported movement.

(Who are they?)

as Ralph McGill, Lillian Smith, Harry Golden, James McBride Dabbs, Ann Braden and Sarah Patton Boyle — have written about our struggle in eloquent and prophetic terms. Others have marched with us down nameless streets of the South. They have languished in filthy, roach-infested jails, suffering

(been left unaided)

the abuse and brutality of policemen who view them as "dirty nigger-lovers." Unlike so many of their moderate brothers and sisters, they have recognized the urgency of the moment and sensed the need for [powerful "action" antidotes] to combat the

Metaphor: segregation is a disease.

[disease of segregation.]

Checklist: Annotating

1. Mark the text using notations like these:
   - Circle words to be defined in the margin.
   - Underline key words and phrases.
   - Bracket important sentences and passages.
   - Use lines or arrows to connect ideas or words.
2. Write marginal comments like these:
   - Number and summarize each paragraph.
   - Define unfamiliar words.
   - Note responses and questions.
   - Identify interesting writing strategies.
   - Point out patterns.
3. Layer additional markings on the text and comments in the margins as you reread for different purposes.

Taking Inventory

Taking inventory helps you analyze your annotations for different purposes. When you take inventory, you make various kinds of lists to explore patterns of meaning you find in the text. For instance, in reading the annotated passage by Martin Luther King Jr., you might have noticed that certain similes and metaphors are used or that many famous people are named. By listing the names (Socrates, Jesus, Luther, Lincoln, and so on) and then grouping them into categories (people who died for their beliefs, leaders, teachers, and religious figures), you could better understand why the writer refers to these particular people. Taking inventory of your annotations can be helpful if you plan to write about a text you are reading.

Checklist: Taking Inventory

1. Examine your annotations for patterns or repetitions such as recurring images, stylistic features, repeated words and phrases, repeated examples or illustrations, and reliance on particular writing strategies.
2. List the items in a pattern.
3. Decide what the pattern might reveal about the reading.

Outlining

Outlining is an especially helpful reading strategy for understanding the content and structure of a reading. **Outlining**, which identifies the text's main ideas, may be part of the annotating process, or it may be done separately. Writing an outline in the margins of the text as you read and annotate makes it easier to find information later. Writing an outline on a separate piece of paper gives you more space to work with, and therefore such an outline usually includes more detail.

The key to outlining is distinguishing between the main ideas and the supporting material such as examples, quotations, comparisons, and reasons. The main ideas form the backbone, which holds the various parts of the text together. Outlining the main ideas helps you uncover this structure.

Making an outline, however, is not simple. The reader must exercise judgment in deciding which are the most important ideas. The words used in an outline reflect the reader's interpretation and emphasis. Readers also must decide when to use the writer's words, their own words, or a combination of the two.

For more on the conventions of formal outlines, see pp. 564–68.

You may make either a formal, multileveled outline or an informal scratch outline. A *formal outline* is harder to make and much more time-consuming than a scratch outline. You might choose to make a formal outline of a reading about which you are writing an in-depth analysis or evaluation. For example, here is a formal outline a student wrote for an essay evaluating the logic of the King excerpt.

Formal Outline of "Letter from Birmingham Jail"

I. "[T]he Negro's great stumbling block in his stride toward freedom is . . . the white moderate . . ." (par. 1).

    A. White moderates are more devoted to "order" than to justice; however,

        1. law and order exist only to establish justice (par. 2).

        2. law and order *without* justice actually threaten social order ("dangerously structured dams" metaphor, par. 2).

    B. White moderates prefer "negative peace" (absence of tension) to "positive peace" (justice); however,

        1. tension already exists; it is not created by movement (par. 2).

        2. tension is a necessary phase in progress to just society (par. 2).

        3. tension must be allowed outlet if society is to be healthy ("boil" simile, par. 2).

    C. White moderates disagree with methods of movement; however,

        1. nonviolent direct action can't be condemned for violent response to it (analogies: robbed man; Socrates; Jesus, par. 3).

        2. federal courts affirm that those who seek constitutional rights can't be held responsible for violent response (par. 3).

    D. White moderates paternalistically counsel patience, saying time will bring change; however,

        1. time is "neutral"--we are obligated to use it *actively* to achieve justice (par. 4).

        2. the time for action is now (par. 4).

II. Contrary to white moderates' claims, the movement is not "extremist," in the usual sense (par. 5 ff.).
   A. It stands between extremes in black community: passivity, seen in the oppressed and the self-interested middle-class; and violent radicalism, seen in Elijah Muhammad's followers (pars. 5-6).
   B. In its advocacy of love and nonviolent protest, the movement has forestalled bloodshed and kept more blacks from joining radicals (pars. 5-7).
   C. The movement helps blacks channel urge for freedom that's part of historical trend and the prevailing *Zeitgeist* (par. 8).
III. The movement can be defined as extremist if the term is redefined: "Creative extremism" is extremism in the service of love, truth, and goodness (examples of Amos, Paul, Luther, Bunyan, Lincoln, Jefferson, Jesus, par. 9).
IV. Some whites "few in quantity, but...big in quality"--have recognized the truth of the arguments above and, unlike the white moderates, have committed themselves to the movement (par. 10).

A *scratch outline* will not record as much information as a formal outline, but it is sufficient for most reading purposes. To make a scratch outline, you first need to locate the topic of each paragraph in the reading. The topic is usually stated in a word or phrase, and it may be repeated or referred to throughout the paragraph. For example, the opening paragraph of the King excerpt (p. 577) makes clear that its topic is the white moderate.

After you have found the topic of the paragraph, figure out what is being said about it. To return to our example: King immediately establishes the white moderate as the topic of the opening paragraph and at the beginning of the second sentence announces the conclusion he has come to — namely, that the white moderate is "the Negro's great stumbling block in his stride toward freedom." The rest of the paragraph specifies the ways the white moderate blocks progress.

The annotations include a summary of each paragraph's topic. Here is a scratch outline that lists the topics:

Scratch Outline of "Letter from Birmingham Jail"

¶1. White moderates block progress
¶2. What the moderates don't understand
¶3. Questions clergymen's logic
¶4. Time must be used to do right
¶5. Puts self in the middle of two extremes: complacency and bitterness
¶6. Offers better choice: nonviolent protest
¶7. Says movement prevents racial violence
¶8. Discontent normal, healthy, and historically inevitable, but it must be channeled
¶9. Redefines "extremism," embraces "extremist" label
¶10. Praises whites who have supported movement

> ### Checklist: Outlining
>
> 1. Reread each paragraph, identifying the topic and the comments made about the topic. Do not include examples, specific details, quotations, or other explanatory and supporting material.
> 2. List the author's main ideas in the margin of the text or on a separate piece of paper.

Paraphrasing

Paraphrasing is restating a text you have read by using mostly your own words. It can help you clarify the meaning of an obscure or ambiguous passage. It is one of the three ways of integrating other people's ideas and information into your own writing, along with **quoting** (reproducing exactly the language of the source text) and **summarizing** (distilling the main ideas or gist of the source text). You might choose to paraphrase rather than quote when the source's language is not especially arresting or memorable. You might paraphrase short passages but summarize longer ones.

Following are two passages. The first is from paragraph 2 of the excerpt from King's "Letter." The second passage is a paraphrase of the first:

Original

I had hoped that the white moderate would understand that law and order exist for the purpose of establishing justice and that when they fail in this purpose they become the dangerously structured dams that block the flow of social progress. I had hoped that the white moderate would understand that the present tension in the South is a necessary phase of the transition from an obnoxious negative peace, in which the Negro passively accepted his unjust plight, to a substantive and positive peace, in which all men will respect the dignity and worth of human personality.

Paraphrase

King writes that he had hoped for more understanding from white moderates--specifically that they would recognize that law and order are not ends in themselves but means to the greater end of establishing justice. When law and order do not serve this greater end, they stand in the way of progress. King expected the white moderate to recognize that the current tense situation in the South is part of a transition process that is necessary for progress. The current situation is bad because although there is peace, it is an "obnoxious" and "negative" kind of peace based on blacks passively accepting the injustice of the status quo. A better kind of peace--one that is "substantive," real and not imaginary, as well as "positive"--requires that all people, regardless of race, be valued.

When you compare the paraphrase to the original, you can see that the paraphrase contains all the important information and ideas of the original. Notice also that the paraphrase is somewhat longer than the original, refers to the writer by name, and encloses King's original words in quotation marks. The paraphrase tries to be *neutral*, to avoid inserting the reader's opinions or distorting the original writer's ideas.

Checklist: Paraphrasing

1. Reread the passage to be paraphrased, looking up unfamiliar words in a college dictionary.

2. Translate the passage into your own words, putting quotation marks around any words or phrases you quote from the original.

3. Revise to ensure coherence.

Summarizing

Summarizing is important because it helps you understand and remember what is most significant in a reading. Another advantage of summarizing is that it creates a condensed version of the reading's ideas and information, which you can refer to later or insert into your own writing. Along with quoting and paraphrasing, summarizing enables you to integrate other writers' ideas into your own writing.

A **summary** is a relatively brief restatement, primarily in the reader's own words, of the reading's main ideas. Summaries vary in length, depending on the reader's purpose. Some summaries are very brief — a sentence or even a subordinate clause. For example, if you were referring to the excerpt from "Letter from Birmingham Jail" and simply needed to indicate how it relates to your other sources, your summary might look something like this: "There have always been advocates of extremism in politics. Martin Luther King Jr., in 'Letter from Birmingham Jail,' for instance, defends nonviolent civil disobedience as an extreme but necessary means of bringing about racial justice." If, however, you were surveying the important texts of the civil rights movement, you might write a longer, more detailed summary that not only identifies the reading's main ideas but also shows how the ideas relate to one another.

Many writers find it useful to outline the reading as a preliminary to writing a summary. A paragraph-by-paragraph scratch outline (like the one on p. 585) lists the reading's main ideas in the sequence in which they appear in the original. But summarizing requires more than merely stringing together the entries in an outline. It fills in the logical connections between the author's ideas. Notice also in the following example that the reader repeats selected words and phrases and refers to the author by name, indicating, with verbs like *expresses, acknowledges,* and *explains,* the writer's purpose and strategy at each point in the argument.

Summary

King expresses his disappointment with white moderates who, by opposing his program of nonviolent direct action, have become a barrier to progress toward racial justice. He acknowledges that his program has raised tension in the South, but he explains that tension is necessary to bring about change. Furthermore, he argues that tension already exists, but because it has been unexpressed, it is unhealthy and potentially dangerous.

He defends his actions against the clergy's criticisms, particularly their argument that he is in too much of a hurry. Responding to charges of extremism, King claims that he has actually prevented racial violence by channeling the natural frustrations of oppressed blacks into nonviolent protest. He asserts that extremism is precisely what is needed now--but it must be creative, rather than destructive, extremism. He concludes by again expressing disappointment with white moderates for not joining his effort as some other whites have.

A summary presents only ideas. While it may use certain key terms from the source, it does not otherwise attempt to reflect the source's language, imagery, or tone; and it avoids even a hint of agreement or disagreement with the ideas it summarizes. Of course, however, a writer might summarize ideas in a source like "Letter from Birmingham Jail" to show readers that he or she has read it carefully and then proceed to use the summary to praise, question, or challenge King's argument. In doing so, the writer might quote specific language that reveals word choice, imagery, or tone.

Checklist: Summarizing

1. Make a scratch outline of the reading.
2. Write a paragraph or more that presents the author's main ideas largely in your own words. Use the outline as a guide, but reread parts of the original text as necessary.
3. To make the summary coherent, fill in connections between the ideas you present.

Synthesizing

Synthesizing involves presenting ideas and information gleaned from different sources. It can help you see how different sources relate to one another. For example, one reading may provide information that fills out the information in another reading, or a reading could present arguments that challenge arguments in another reading.

When you synthesize material from different sources, you construct a conversation among your sources, a conversation in which you also participate. Synthesizing contributes most when writers use sources not only to support their ideas, but to challenge and extend them as well.

In the following example, the reader uses a variety of sources related to the King passage (pp. 577–82) and brings them together around a central idea. Notice how quotation, paraphrase, and summary are all used.

Synthesis

When King defends his campaign of nonviolent direct action against the clergymen's criticism that "our actions, even though peaceful, must be condemned because they precipitate violence" (King excerpt, par. 3), he is using what Vinit Haksar calls Mohandas Gandhi's "safety-valve argument" ("Civil Disobedience and Non-Cooperation" 117). According to Haksar, Gandhi gave a "non-threatening warning of worse things to come" if his demands were not met. King similarly makes clear that advocates of actions more extreme than those he advocates are waiting in the wings: "The other force is one of bitterness and hatred, and it comes perilously close to advocating violence" (King excerpt, par. 5). King identifies this force with Elijah Muhammad, and although he does not name him, King's contemporary readers would have known that he was referring also to his disciple Malcolm X, who, according to Herbert J. Storing, "urged that Negroes take seriously the idea of revolution" ("The Case against Civil Disobedience" 90). In fact, Malcolm X accused King of being a modern-day Uncle Tom, trying "to keep us under control, to keep us passive and peaceful and nonviolent" (*Malcolm X Speaks* 12).

Checklist: Synthesizing

1. Find and read a variety of sources on your topic, annotating the passages that give you ideas about the topic.

2. Look for patterns among your sources, possibly supporting or challenging your ideas or those of other sources.

3. Write a paragraph or more synthesizing your sources, using quotation, paraphrase, and summary to present what they say on the topic.

Contextualizing

All texts reflect historical and cultural assumptions, values, and attitudes that may differ from your own. To read thoughtfully, you need to become aware of these differences. **Contextualizing** is a critical reading strategy that enables you to make inferences about a reading's historical and cultural context and to examine the differences between its context and your own.

The excerpt from King's "Letter from Birmingham Jail" is a good example of a text that benefits from being read contextually. If you knew little about the history of slavery and segregation in the United States, it would be difficult to understand the passion expressed in this passage. To understand the historical and cultural context in which King wrote his "Letter from Birmingham Jail," you could do some library or Internet research. Comparing the situation at the time King wrote the "Letter" to situations with which you are familiar would help you understand some of your own attitudes toward King and the civil rights movement.

Here is what one reader wrote to contextualize King's writing:

Notes from a Contextualized Reading

1. I am not old enough to know what it was like in the early 1960s when Dr. King was leading marches and sit-ins, but I have seen television documentaries showing demonstrators being attacked by dogs, doused by fire hoses, beaten and dragged by helmeted police. Such images give me a sense of the violence, fear, and hatred that King was responding to.

   The tension King writes about comes across in his writing. He uses his anger and frustration creatively to inspire his critics. He also threatens them, although he denies it. I saw a film on Malcolm X, so I could see that King was giving white people a choice between his own nonviolent way and Malcolm's more confrontational way.

2. Things have certainly changed since the sixties. Legal segregation has ended, but there are still racists like the detective in the O. J. Simpson trial. African Americans like Condoleezza Rice and Barack Obama are highly respected and powerful. The civil rights movement is over. So when I'm reading King today, I feel like I'm reading history. But then again, every once in a while there are reports of police brutality because of race (think of Amadou Diallo) and of what we now call hate crimes.

Checklist: Contextualizing

1. Describe the historical and cultural situation as it is represented in the reading and in other sources with which you are familiar. Your knowledge may come from other reading, television or film, school, or elsewhere. (If you know nothing about the historical and cultural context, you could do some library or Internet research.)

2. Compare the historical and cultural situation in which the text was written with your own historical and cultural situation. Consider how your understanding and judgment of the reading are affected by your own context.

Exploring the Significance of Figurative Language

Figurative language — metaphor, simile, and symbolism — enhances literal meaning by implying abstract ideas through vivid images and by evoking feelings and associations.

Metaphor implicitly compares two different things by identifying them with each other. For instance, when King calls the white moderate "the Negro's great stumbling block in his stride toward freedom" (par. 1), he does not mean that the white moderate literally trips the Negro who is attempting to walk toward freedom. The sentence makes sense only if understood figuratively: The white moderate trips up the Negro by frustrating every effort to achieve justice.

Simile, a more explicit form of comparison, uses the word *like* or *as* to signal the relationship of two seemingly unrelated things. King uses simile when he says that injustice is "like a boil that can never be cured so long as it is covered up" (par. 2). This simile makes several points of comparison between injustice and a boil. It suggests that injustice is a disease of society as a boil is a disease of the skin and that injustice, like a boil, must be exposed or it will fester and infect the entire body.

Symbolism compares two things by making one stand for the other. King uses the white moderate as a symbol for supposed liberals and would-be supporters of civil rights who are actually frustrating the cause.

How these figures of speech are used in a text reveals something of the writer's feelings about the subject. Exploring possible meanings in a text's figurative language involves (1) annotating and then listing the metaphors, similes, and symbols you find in a reading; (2) grouping and labeling the figures of speech that appear to express related feelings or attitudes; and (3) writing to explore the meaning of the patterns you have found.

The following example shows the process of exploring figures of speech in the King excerpt.

Listing Figures of Speech

"stumbling block in his stride toward freedom" (par. 1)

"law and order...become the dangerously structured dams" (2)

"the flow of social progress" (2)

"Like a boil that can never be cured" (2)

"the light of human conscience and the air of national opinion" (2)

"the quicksand of racial injustice" (4)

Grouping and Labeling Figures of Speech

Sickness: "like a boil" (2); "the disease of segregation" (10)

Underground: "hidden tension" (2); "injustice must be exposed" (2); "injustice must be rooted out" (10)

Blockage: "dams," "block the flow" (2); "Human progress never rolls in on wheels of inevitability" (4); "pent-up resentments" (8); "repressed emotions" (8)

Writing to Explore Meaning

The patterns labeled underground and blockage suggest a feeling of frustration. Inertia is a problem; movement forward toward progress or upward toward the promised land is stalled. The strong need to break through the resistance may represent King's feelings about both his attempt to lead purposeful, effective demonstrations and his effort to write a convincing argument.

The simile of injustice being "like a boil" links the two patterns of underground and sickness, suggesting that something bad, a disease, is inside the people or the society. The cure is to expose or to root out the blocked hatred and injustice as well as to release the tension or emotion that has long been repressed. This implies that repression itself is the evil, not simply what is repressed. Therefore, writing and speaking out through political action may have curative power for individuals and society alike.

> ### Checklist: Exploring the Significance of Figurative Language
>
> 1. Annotate all the figures of speech you find in the reading—metaphors, similes, and symbols—and then list them.
>
> 2. Group the figures of speech that appear to express related feelings and attitudes, and label each group.
>
> 3. Write one or two paragraphs exploring the meaning of these patterns. What do they tell you about the text?

Looking for Patterns of Opposition

All texts carry within themselves voices of opposition. These voices may echo the views and values of readers the writer anticipates or predecessors to whom the writer is responding in some way; they may even reflect the writer's own conflicting values. Careful readers look closely for such a dialogue of opposing voices within the text.

When we think of oppositions, we ordinarily think of polarities: *yes* and *no, up* and *down, black* and *white, new* and *old.* Some oppositions, however, may be more subtle. The excerpt from King's "Letter from Birmingham Jail" is rich in such oppositions: *moderate* versus *extremist, order* versus *justice, direct action* versus *passive acceptance, expression* versus *repression.* These oppositions are not accidental; they form a significant pattern that gives a reader important information about the essay.

A careful reading will show that King always values one of the two terms in an opposition over the other. In the passage, for example, *extremist* is valued over *moderate* (par. 9). This preference for extremism is surprising. The reader should ask why, when white extremists like members of the Ku Klux Klan have committed so many outrages against African Americans, King would prefer extremism. If King is trying to convince his readers to accept his point of view, why would he represent himself as an extremist? Moreover, why would a clergyman advocate extremism instead of moderation?

Studying the **patterns of opposition** in the text enables you to answer these questions. You will see that King sets up this opposition to force his readers to examine their own values and realize that they are in fact misplaced. Instead of working toward justice, he says, those who support law and order maintain the unjust status quo. By getting his readers to think of white moderates as blocking rather than facilitating peaceful change, King brings readers to align themselves with him and perhaps even embrace his strategy of nonviolent resistance.

Looking for patterns of opposition involves annotating words or phrases in the reading that indicate oppositions, listing the opposing terms in pairs, deciding which term in each pair is preferred by the writer, and reflecting on the meaning of the patterns. Here is a partial list of oppositions from the King excerpt, with the preferred terms marked by an asterisk:

Listing Patterns of Opposition

moderate	*extremist
order	*justice
negative peace	*positive peace
absence of justice	*presence of justice
goals	*methods
*direct action	passive acceptance
*exposed tension	hidden tension

Checklist: Looking for Patterns of Opposition

1. Annotate the selection for words or phrases indicating oppositions.

2. List the pairs of oppositions. (You may have to paraphrase or even supply the opposite word or phrase if it is not stated directly in the text.)

3. For each pair of oppositions, put an asterisk next to the term that the writer seems to value or prefer over the other.

4. Study the patterns of opposition. How do they contribute to your understanding of the essay? What do they tell you about what the author wants you to believe?

Reflecting on Challenges to Your Beliefs and Values

To read thoughtfully, you need to scrutinize your own assumptions and attitudes as well as those expressed in the text you are reading. If you are like most readers, however, you will find that your assumptions and attitudes are so ingrained that you are not always fully aware of them. A good strategy for getting at these underlying beliefs and values is to identify and reflect on the ways the text challenges you, how it makes you feel — disturbed, threatened, ashamed, combative, pleased, exuberant, or some other way.

For example, here is what one student wrote about the King passage:

Reflections

In paragraph 1, Dr. King criticizes people who are "more devoted to 'order' than to justice." This criticism upsets me because today I think I would choose order over justice. When I reflect on my feelings and try to figure out where they come from, I realize that what I feel most is fear. I am terrified by the violence in society today. I'm afraid of sociopaths who don't respect the rule of law, much less the value of human life.

I know Dr. King was writing in a time when the law itself was unjust, when order was apparently used to keep people from protesting and changing the law. But things are different now. Today, justice seems to serve criminals more than it serves law-abiding citizens. That's why I'm for order over justice.

Checklist: Reflecting on Challenges to Your Beliefs and Values

1. Identify challenges by marking the text where you feel your beliefs and values are being opposed, criticized, or unfairly characterized.

2. Write a few paragraphs reflecting on why you feel challenged. Do not defend your feelings; instead, search your memory to discover where they come from.

Evaluating the Logic of an Argument

An argument includes a thesis backed by reasons and support. The **thesis** asserts a position on a controversial issue or a solution to a problem that the writer wants readers to accept. The **reasons** tell readers why they should accept the thesis, and the **support** (such as examples, statistics, authorities, and textual evidence) gives readers grounds for accepting it. For an argument to be considered logically acceptable, it must meet the three conditions of what we call the ABC test:

The ABC Test

A. The reasons and support must be *appropriate* to the thesis.

B. The reasons and support must be *believable.*

C. The reasons and support must be *consistent* with one another as well as *complete.*

For more on argument, see Chapter 19. For an example of the ABC test, see Christine Romano's essay in Chapter 8, pp. 402–6.

Testing for Appropriateness

To evaluate the logic of an argument, you first decide whether the argument's reasons and support are appropriate. To test for appropriateness, ask these questions: How does each reason or piece of support relate to the thesis? Is the connection between reasons and support and the thesis clear and compelling?

Readers most often question the appropriateness of reasons and support when the writer argues by analogy or by invoking authority. For example, in paragraph 2, King argues that when law and order fail to establish justice, "they become the dangerously structured dams that block the flow of social progress." The analogy asserts the following logical relationship: Law and order are to progress toward justice what a dam is to water. If you do not accept this analogy, the argument fails the test of appropriateness.

King uses both analogy and authority in paragraph 3: "Isn't this like condemning Socrates because his unswerving commitment to truth and his philosophical inquiries precipitated the act by the misguided populace in which they made him drink hemlock?" Not only must you judge the appropriateness of the analogy comparing the Greeks' condemnation of Socrates to the white moderates' condemnation of King, but you must also judge whether it is appropriate to accept Socrates as an authority. Since Socrates is generally respected for his teaching on justice, his words and actions are likely to be considered appropriate to King's situation in Birmingham.

For more on analogy, see Chapter 18, pp. 657–58. For invoking authorities, see Chapter 19, pp. 665–66.

Testing for Believability

Believability is a measure of your willingness to accept as true the reasons and support the writer gives in defense of a thesis.

To test for believability, ask: On what basis am I being asked to believe this reason or support is true? If it cannot be proved true or false, how much weight does it carry?

In judging facts, examples, statistics, and authorities, consider the following points.

Facts are statements that can be proved objectively to be true. The believability of facts depends on their *accuracy* (they should not distort or misrepresent reality), their *completeness* (they should not omit important details), and the *trustworthiness* of their sources (sources should be qualified and unbiased). King, for instance, asserts as fact that the African American will not wait much longer for racial justice (par. 8). His critics might question the factuality of this assertion by asking, is it true of all African Americans? How does King know what African Americans will and will not do?

Examples and **anecdotes** are particular instances that may or may not make you believe a general statement. The believability of examples depends on their *representativeness* (whether they are truly typical and thus generalizable) and their *specificity* (whether particular details make them seem true to life). Even if a vivid example or gripping anecdote does not convince readers, it usually strengthens argumentative writing by clarifying the meaning and dramatizing the point. In paragraph 5 of the King excerpt, for example, King supports his generalization that some African American extremists are motivated by bitterness and hatred by citing the specific example of Elijah Muhammad's Black Muslim movement. Conversely, in paragraph 9, he refers to Jesus, Paul, Luther, and others as examples of extremists motivated by love and Christianity. These examples support his assertion that extremism is not in itself wrong and that any judgment of extremism must be based on its motivation and cause.

Statistics are numerical data. The believability of statistics depends on the *comparability* of the data (the price of apples in 1985 cannot be compared with the price of apples in 2010 unless the figures are adjusted to account for inflation), the *precision* of the methods employed to gather and analyze data (representative samples should be used and variables accounted for), and the *trustworthiness* of the sources.

Authorities are people to whom the writer attributes expertise on a given subject. Not only must such authorities be appropriate, as mentioned earlier, but they must be credible as well — that is, the reader must accept them as experts on the topic at hand. King cites authorities repeatedly throughout his essay. He refers to religious leaders (Jesus and Luther) as well as to American political leaders (Lincoln and Jefferson). These figures are likely to have a high degree of credibility among King's readers.

Testing for Consistency and Completeness

In looking for consistency, you should be concerned that all the parts of the argument work together and that they are sufficient to convince readers to accept the thesis or at least take it seriously. To test for consistency and completeness, ask: Are any of the reasons and support contradictory? Do they provide sufficient grounds for accepting the thesis? Does the writer fail to counterargue (to acknowledge, accommodate, or refute any opposing arguments or important objections)?

For more on counter-arguing, see Chapter 19, pp. 668–71.

A thoughtful reader might regard as contradictory King's characterizing himself first as a moderate and later as an extremist opposed to the forces of violence. (King attempts to reconcile this apparent contradiction by explicitly redefining extremism in paragraph 9.) Similarly, the fact that King fails to examine and refute every legal recourse available to his cause might allow a critical reader to question the sufficiency of his argument.

Checklist: Evaluating the Logic of an Argument

Use the ABC test:

A. *Test for appropriateness* by checking that the reasons and support are clearly and directly related to the thesis.

B. *Test for believability* by deciding whether you can accept the reasons and support as likely to be true.

C. *Test for consistency and completeness* by deciding whether the argument has any contradictions and whether any important objections or opposing arguments have been ignored.

Recognizing Emotional Manipulation

Writers often try to arouse emotions in readers to excite their interest, make them care, or move them to take action. There is nothing wrong with appealing to readers' emotions. What is wrong is manipulating readers with false or exaggerated appeals. Therefore, you should be suspicious of writing that is overly sentimental, that cites alarming statistics and frightening anecdotes, that demonizes others and identifies itself with revered authorities, or that uses potent symbols (for example, the American flag) or emotionally loaded words (such as *racist*).

King, for example, uses the emotionally loaded word *paternalistically* to refer to the white moderate's belief that "he can set the timetable for another man's freedom" (par. 1). In the same paragraph, King uses symbolism to get an emotional reaction from readers when he compares the white moderate to the "Ku Klux Klanner." To get readers to accept his ideas, he also relies on authorities whose names evoke the greatest respect, such as Jesus and Lincoln. But some readers might object that comparing his own crusade to that of Jesus is pretentious and manipulative. A critical reader might also consider King's discussion of African American extremists in paragraph 7 to be a veiled threat designed to frighten readers into agreement.

Checklist: Recognizing Emotional Manipulation

1. Annotate places in the text where you sense emotional appeals are being used.

2. Assess whether any of the emotional appeals are unfairly manipulative.

Judging the Writer's Credibility

Writers try to persuade readers by presenting an image of themselves in their writing that will gain their readers' confidence. This image must be created indirectly, through the arguments, language, and system of values and beliefs expressed or implied in the writing. Writers establish credibility in their writing in three ways:

- By showing their knowledge of the subject
- By building common ground with readers
- By responding fairly to objections and opposing arguments

Testing for Knowledge

Writers demonstrate their knowledge through the facts and statistics they marshal, the sources they rely on for information, and the scope and depth of their understanding. You may not be sufficiently expert on the subject yourself to know whether the facts are accurate, the sources are reliable, and the understanding is sufficient. You may need to do some research to see what others say about the subject. You can also check credentials — the writer's educational and professional qualifications, the respectability of the publication in which the selection first appeared, and reviews of the writer's work — to determine whether the writer is a respected authority in the field. For example, King brings with him the authority that comes from being a member of the clergy and a respected leader of the Southern Christian Leadership Conference.

Testing for Common Ground

One way writers can establish common ground with their readers is by basing their reasoning on shared values, beliefs, and attitudes. They use language that includes their readers (*we*) and qualify their assertions to keep them from being too extreme. Above all, they acknowledge differences of opinion. You want to notice such appeals.

King creates common ground with readers by using the inclusive pronoun *we*, suggesting shared concerns between himself and his audience. Notice, however, his use of masculine pronouns and other references ("the Negro . . . he," "our brothers"). Although King addressed his letter to male clergy, he intended it to be published in the local newspaper, where it would be read by an audience of both men and women. By using language that excludes women, a common practice at the time the selection was written, King may have missed the opportunity to build common ground with more than half of his readers.

Testing for Fairness

Writers reveal their character by how they handle opposing arguments and objections to their argument. As a critical reader, pay particular attention to how writers treat possible differences of opinion. Be suspicious of those who ignore differences and pretend that everyone agrees with their viewpoints. When objections or opposing views are represented, consider whether they have been distorted in any way; if they are refuted, be sure they are challenged fairly — with sound reasoning and solid support.

One way to gauge the author's credibility is to identify the tone of the argument, for it conveys the writer's attitude toward the subject and toward the reader. Is the text angry? Sarcastic? Evenhanded? Shrill? Condescending? Bullying? Do you feel as if the writer is treating the subject — and you, as a reader — with fairness? King's tone might be characterized in different passages as patient (he doesn't lose his temper), respectful (he refers to white moderates as "people of good will"), or pompous (comparing himself to Jesus and Socrates).

Checklist: Judging the Writer's Credibility

1. Annotate for the writer's knowledge of the subject, how well common ground is established, and whether the writer deals fairly with objections and opposing arguments.
2. Decide what in the essay you find credible and what you question.

PART 3

Writing Strategies

13

Cueing the Reader

Readers need guidance. To guide readers through a piece of writing, a writer can provide five basic kinds of **cues**, or signals:

1. Thesis and forecasting statements, to orient readers to ideas and organization
2. Paragraphing, to group related ideas and details
3. Cohesive devices, to connect ideas to one another and bring about clarity
4. Transitions, to signal relationships or shifts in meaning
5. Headings and subheadings, to group related paragraphs and help readers locate specific information quickly

This chapter illustrates how each of these cueing strategies works.

Orienting Statements

To help readers find their way, especially in difficult and lengthy texts, you can provide two kinds of **orienting statements**: a thesis statement, which declares the main point, and a forecasting statement, which previews subordinate points, showing the order in which they will be discussed in the essay.

Thesis Statements

To help readers understand what is being said about a subject, writers often provide a thesis statement early in the essay. The **thesis statement**, which can comprise one or more sentences, operates as a cue by letting readers know which is the most important general idea among the writer's many ideas and observations. In "Love: The Right Chemistry" in Chapter 4, Anastasia Toufexis expresses her thesis in the second paragraph:

> O.K., let's cut out all this nonsense about romantic love. Let's bring some scientific precision to the party. Let's put love under a microscope.
>
> When rigorous people with Ph.D.s after their names do that, what they see is not some silly, senseless thing. No, their probe reveals that love rests firmly on the foundations of evolution, biology and chemistry.

Readers naturally look for something that will tell them the point of an essay, a focus for the many diverse details and ideas they encounter as they read. They expect to find some information early on that will give them a context for reading the essay, particularly if they are reading about a new and difficult subject. Therefore, a thesis statement, like Toufexis's, placed at the beginning of an essay enables readers to anticipate the content of the essay and helps them understand the relationships among its various ideas and details.

Occasionally, however, particularly in fairly short, informal essays and in some autobiographical and argumentative essays, a writer may save a direct statement of the thesis until the conclusion. In "Sticks and Stones and Sports Team Names," for example, from Chapter 6, Richard Estrada explicitly states his thesis in his final paragraph:

> It seems to me that what Native Americans are saying is that what would be intolerable for Jews, blacks, Latinos and others is no less offensive to them. Theirs is a request not only for dignified treatment, but for fair treatment as well. For America to ignore the complaints of a numerically small segment of the population because it is small is neither dignified nor fair.

Similarly, Trey Ellis's autobiographical essay from Chapter 2 closes with a two-sentence thesis:

> Embarrassment is always the price we pay for more intimacy. Perhaps there is no such thing as too much information.

Ending with the thesis brings together the various strands of information or supporting details introduced over the course of the essay and makes clear the essay's main idea.

Some essays, particularly autobiographical essays, offer no direct thesis statement. While this can make the point of the essay more difficult to determine, it can be appropriate when the essay is more expressive and personal than it is informative. In all cases, careful writers keep readers' needs and expectations in mind when deciding how — and whether — to state the thesis.

Exercise 13.1

In the essay by Jessica Statsky in Chapter 6, underline the thesis statement, the last sentence in paragraph 1. Notice the key terms: "overzealous parents and coaches," "impose adult standards," "children's sports," "activities . . . neither satisfying nor beneficial." Then skim the essay, stopping to read the sentence at the beginning of each paragraph. Also read the last paragraph.

Consider whether the idea in every paragraph's first sentence is anticipated by the thesis's key terms. Consider also the connection between the ideas in the last paragraph and the thesis's key terms. What can you conclude about how a thesis might assert the point of an essay, anticipate the ideas that follow, and help readers relate the ideas to each other?

Forecasting Statements

Some thesis statements include **a forecast**, which overviews the way a thesis will be developed, as in the following example.

> In the three years from 1348 through 1350 the pandemic of plague known as the Black Death, or, as the Germans called it, the Great Dying, killed at least a fourth of the population of Europe. It was undoubtedly the worst disaster that has ever befallen mankind. Today we can have no real conception of the terror under which people lived in the shadow of the plague. For more than two centuries plague has not been a serious threat to mankind in the large, although it is still a grisly presence in parts of the Far East and Africa. Scholars continue to study the Great Dying, however, as a historical example of human behavior under the stress of universal catastrophe. In these days when the threat of plague has been replaced by the threat of mass human extermination by even more rapid means, there has been a sharp renewal of interest in the history of the fourteenth-century calamity. With new perspective, students are investigating its manifold effects: demographic, economic, psychological, moral and religious.
>
> —WILLIAM LANGER, "The Black Death"

Langer's thesis statement forecasts the five main categories of effects of the Black Death his essay will examine.

As a reader would expect, Langer divides his essay into explanations of the research into these five effects, addressing them in the order in which they appear in the forecasting statement.

Exercise 13.2

Turn to Linh Kieu Ngo's essay in Chapter 4, and underline the forecasting statement in paragraph 6. Then skim the essay. Notice whether Ngo takes up every point he mentions in the forecasting statement and whether he sticks to the order he promises readers. How well does his forecasting statement help you follow his essay? What suggestions for improvement, if any, would you offer him?

Paragraphing

Paragraph cues as obvious as indentation keep readers on track. You can also arrange material in a paragraph to help readers see what is important or significant. For example, you can begin with a topic sentence, help readers see the relationship between the previous paragraph and the present one with an explicit transition, and place the most important information toward the end.

Paragraph Cues

One paragraph cue — the indentation that signals the beginning of a new paragraph — is a relatively modern printing convention. Old manuscripts show that paragraph divisions were not always marked. To make reading easier, scribes and printers began to use the symbol ¶ to mark paragraph breaks, and later, indenting became

For additional visual cues for readers, see Headings and Subheadings on pp. 613–14.

common practice. Even that relatively modern custom, however, has been abandoned by most business writers, who now distinguish one paragraph from another by leaving a line of space above and below each paragraph. Writing on the Internet is also usually paragraphed in this way.

Paragraphing helps readers by signaling when a sequence of related ideas begins and ends. Paragraphing also helps readers judge what is most important in what they are reading. Writers typically emphasize important information by placing it at the two points in the paragraph where readers are most attentive — the beginning and the end.

You can give special emphasis to information by placing it in its own paragraph.

Exercise 13.3

Turn to Patrick O'Malley's essay in Chapter 7, and read paragraphs 4–6 with the following questions in mind: Does all the material in each paragraph seem to be related? Do you feel a sense of closure at the end of each paragraph? Does the last sentence offer the most important or significant or weighty information in the paragraph?

Topic Sentence Strategies

A **topic sentence** lets readers know the focus of a paragraph in simple and direct terms. It is a cueing strategy for the paragraph, much as a thesis or forecasting statement is for the whole essay. Because paragraphing usually signals a shift in focus, readers expect some kind of reorientation in the opening sentence. They need to know whether the new paragraph will introduce another aspect of the topic or develop one already introduced.

Announcing the Topic. Some topic sentences simply announce the topic. Here are some examples taken from Barry Lopez's book *Arctic Dreams*:

> A polar bear walks in a way all its own.

> What is so consistently striking about the way Eskimos used parts of an animal is the breadth of their understanding about what would work.

> The Mediterranean view of the Arctic, down to the time of the Elizabethan mariners, was shaped by two somewhat contradictory thoughts.

The following paragraph shows how one of Lopez's topic sentences (highlighted) is developed:

> What is so consistently striking about the way Eskimos used parts of an animal is the breadth of their understanding about what would work. Knowing that muskox horn is more flexible than caribou antler, they preferred it for making the side prongs of a fish spear. For a waterproof bag in which to carry sinews for clothing repair, they chose salmon skin. They selected the strong, translucent

Lopez's topic sentences identify topics and also indicate how they will be developed in subsequent sentences.

intestine of a bearded seal to make a window for a snowhouse — it would fold up for easy traveling and it would not frost over in cold weather. To make small snares for sea ducks, they needed a springy material that would not rot in salt water — baleen fibers. The down feather of a common eider, tethered at the end of a stick in the snow at an angle, would reveal the exhalation of a quietly surfacing seal. Polar bear bone was used anywhere a stout, sharp point was required, because it is the hardest bone.

—BARRY LOPEZ, *Arctic Dreams*

Exercise 13.4

Turn to Jessica Statsky's essay in Chapter 6. Underline the topic sentence (the first sentence) in paragraphs 3 and 5. Consider how these sentences help you anticipate the paragraph's topic and method of development.

Making a Transition. Not all topic sentences simply point to what will follow. Some also refer to earlier sentences. Such sentences work both as topic sentences, stating the main point of the paragraph, and as transitions, linking that paragraph to the previous one. Here are a few topic sentences from "Quilts and Women's Culture," by Elaine Hedges, with transitions highlighted:

> Hedges uses specific transitions to tie each topic sentence to a previous statement.

Within its broad traditionalism and anonymity, however, variations and distinctions developed.

Regionally, too, distinctions were introduced into quilt making through the interesting process of renaming.

Finally, out of such regional and other variations come individual, signed achievements.

Quilts, then, were an outlet for creative energy, a source and emblem of sisterhood and solidarity, and a graphic response to historical and political change.

Sometimes the first sentence of a paragraph serves as a transition, and a subsequent sentence states the topic, as in the following example:

> The highlighted sentences serve as transitions.

. . . What a convenience, what a relief it will be, they say, never to worry about how to dress for a job interview, a romantic tryst, or a funeral!
    Convenient, perhaps, but not exactly a relief. Such a utopia would give most of us the same kind of chill we feel when a stadium full of Communist-bloc athletes in identical sports outfits, shouting slogans in unison, appears on TV. Most people do not want to be told what to wear any more than they want to be told what to say. In Belfast recently four hundred Irish Republican prisoners "refused to wear any clothes at all, draping themselves day and night in blankets," rather than put on prison uniforms. Even the offer of civilian-style dress did not satisfy them; they insisted on wearing their own clothes brought from home, or nothing. Fashion is free speech, and one of the privileges, if not always one of the pleasures, of a free world.

—ALISON LURIE, *The Language of Clothes*

Occasionally, whole paragraphs serve as transitions, linking one sequence of paragraphs with those that follow, as below:

> Yet it was not all contrast, after all. Different as they were — in background, in personality, in underlying aspiration — these two great soldiers had much in common. Under everything else, they were marvelous fighters. Furthermore, their fighting qualities were really very much alike.
>
> — BRUCE CATTON, "Grant and Lee: A Study in Contrasts"

This transition paragraph summarizes the contrasts between Grant and Lee and sets up an analysis of the similarities of the two men.

Exercise 13.5

Turn to Matt Miller's essay in Chapter 7 and read paragraphs 2–6. As you read, underline the part of the first sentence in paragraphs 3–6 that refers to the previous paragraph, creating a transition from one to the next. Notice the different ways Miller creates these transitions. Consider whether they are all equally effective.

Positioning the Topic Sentence. Although topic sentences may occur anywhere in a paragraph, stating the topic in the first sentence has the advantage of giving readers a sense of how the paragraph is likely to be developed. The beginning of the paragraph is therefore the most common position.

A topic sentence that does not open a paragraph is most likely to appear at the end. When a topic sentence concludes a paragraph, it usually summarizes or generalizes preceding information:

> Even black Americans sometimes need to be reminded about the deceptiveness of television. Blacks retain their fascination with black characters on TV: Many of us buy *Jet* magazine primarily to read its weekly television feature, which lists every black character (major or minor) to be seen on the screen that week. Yet our fixation with the presence of black characters on TV has blinded us to an important fact that *Cosby*, which began in 1984, and its offshoots over the years demonstrate convincingly: There is very little connection between the social status of black Americans and the fabricated images of black people that Americans consume each day. The representation of blacks on TV is a very poor index to our social advancement or political progress.
>
> — HENRY LOUIS GATES JR., "TV's Black World Turns — but Stays Unreal"

Gates does not explicitly state his topic until the last sentence.

When a topic sentence is used in a narrative, it often appears as the last sentence as a way to evaluate or reflect on events:

> A cold sun was sliding down a gray fall sky. Some older boys had been playing tackle football in the field we took charge of every weekend. In a few years, they'd be called to Southeast Asia, some of them. Their locations would be tracked with pushpins in red, white, and blue on maps on nearly every kitchen wall. But that afternoon, they were quick as young deer. They leapt and dodged, dove from each other and collided in midair. Bulletlike passes flew to connect them. Or the

ball spiraled in a high arc across the frosty sky one to another. In short, they were mindlessly agile in a way that captured as audience every little kid within running distance of the yellow goalposts.

—MARY KARR, *Cherry*

Karr's topic sentence reflects on narrated events described earlier in the paragraph.

It is possible for a single topic sentence to introduce two or more paragraphs. Subsequent paragraphs in such a sequence have no separate topic sentences of their own:

Tannen's topic sentence states the topic of two paragraphs: the one in which it appears and the one that follows it.

Anthropologists Daniel Maltz and Ruth Borker point out that boys and girls socialize differently. Little girls tend to play in small groups or, even more common, in pairs. Their social life usually centers around a best friend, and friendships are made, maintained, and broken by talk — especially "secrets." If a little girl tells her friend's secret to another little girl, she may find herself with a new best friend. The secrets themselves may or may not be important, but the fact of telling them is all-important. It's hard for newcomers to get into these tight groups, but anyone who is admitted is treated as an equal. Girls like to play cooperatively; if they can't cooperate, the group breaks up.

Little boys tend to play in larger groups, often outdoors, and they spend more time doing things than talking. It's easy for boys to get into the group, but not everyone is accepted as an equal. Once in the group, boys must jockey for their status in it. One of the most important ways they do this is through talk: verbal display such as telling stories and jokes, challenging and sidetracking the verbal displays of other boys, and withstanding other boys' challenges in order to maintain their own story — and status. Their talk is often competitive talk about who is best at what.

—DEBORAH TANNEN, *That's Not What I Meant!*

Exercise 13.6

Consider the variety and effectiveness of the topic sentences in your most recent essay. Begin by underlining the topic sentence in each paragraph after the first one. The topic sentence may not be the first sentence in a paragraph, though often it will be.

Then double-underline the part of the topic sentence that provides an explicit transition from one paragraph to the next. You may find a transition that is separate from the topic sentence. You may not always find a topic sentence.

Reflect on your topic sentences, and evaluate how well they serve to orient your readers to the sequence of topics or ideas in your essay.

Cohesive Devices

Cohesive devices guide readers, helping them follow your train of thought by connecting key words and phrases throughout a passage. Among such devices are pronoun reference, word repetition, synonyms, repetition of sentence structure, and collocation.

Pronoun Reference

One common cohesive device is **pronoun reference**. As noun substitutes, pronouns refer to nouns that either precede or follow them and thus serve to connect phrases or sentences. The nouns that come before the pronouns are called *antecedents*.

> In New York from dawn to dusk to dawn, day after day, you can hear the steady rumble of tires against the concrete span of the George Washington Bridge. The bridge is never completely still. It trembles with traffic. It moves in the wind. Its great veins of steel swell when hot and contract when cold; its span often is ten feet closer to the Hudson River in summer than in winter.
>
> —GAY TALESE, "New York"

> The pronouns form a chain of connection with their antecedent.

This example has only one pronoun-antecedent chain, and the antecedent comes first, so all the pronouns refer back to it. When there are multiple pronoun-antecedent chains with references forward as well as back, writers have to make sure that readers will not mistake one pronoun's antecedent for another's.

Word Repetition

To avoid confusion, writers often use **word repetition.** The device of repeating words and phrases is especially helpful if a pronoun might confuse readers:

> Some odd optical property of our highly polarized and unequal society makes the poor almost invisible to their economic superiors. The poor can see the affluent easily enough — on television, for example, or on the covers of magazines. But the affluent rarely see the poor or, if they do catch sight of them in some public space, rarely know what they're seeing, since — thanks to consignment stores and, yes, Wal-Mart — the poor are usually able to disguise themselves as members of the more comfortable classes.
>
> —BARBARA EHRENREICH, *Nickel and Dimed*

> Ehrenreich repeats words instead of using pronouns.

In the next example, several overlapping chains of word repetition prevent confusion and help the reader follow the ideas:

> Natural selection is the central concept of Darwinian theory — the fittest survive and spread their favored traits through populations. Natural selection is defined by Spencer's phrase "survival of the fittest," but what does this famous bit of jargon really mean? Who are the fittest? And how is "fitness" defined? We often read that fitness involves no more than "differential reproductive success" — the production of more surviving offspring than other competing members of the population. Whoa! cries Bethell, as many others have before him. This formulation defines fitness in terms of survival only. The crucial phrase of natural selection means no more than "the survival of those who survive" — a vacuous tautology. (A tautology is a phrase — like "my father is a man" — containing no information in the predicate ["a man"] not inherent in the subject ["my father"]. Tautologies are fine as definitions, but not as testable scientific statements — there can be nothing to test in a statement true by definition.)
>
> — STEPHEN JAY GOULD, *Ever Since Darwin*

> Gould uses repetition, with some variation of form, to keep readers focused on key concepts.

Synonyms

In addition to word repetition, you can use **synonyms**, words with identical or very similar meanings, to connect important ideas. In the following example, the author develops a careful chain of synonyms and word repetitions:

> Over time, small bits of knowledge about a region accumulate among local residents in the form of stories. These are remembered in the community; even what is unusual does not become lost and therefore irrelevant. These narratives comprise for a native an intricate, long-term view of a particular landscape. . . . Outside the region this complex but easily shared "reality" is hard to get across without reducing it to generalities, to misleading or imprecise abstraction.
>
> — BARRY LOPEZ, *Arctic Dreams*

Lopez uses a variety of synonym sequences to reinforce his point.

Note the variety of synonym sequences:

"region," "particular landscape"
"local residents," "native"
"stories," "narratives"
"accumulate," "are remembered," "does not become lost"
"intricate, long-term view," "complex . . . reality"

The result is a coherent paragraph that constantly reinforces the author's point.

Sentence Structure Repetition

Writers occasionally use **sentence structure repetition** to emphasize the connections among their ideas, as in this example:

> But the life forms are as much part of the structure of the Earth as any inanimate portion is. It is all an inseparable part of a whole. If any animal is isolated totally from other forms of life, then death by starvation will surely follow. If isolated from water, death by dehydration will follow even faster. If isolated from air, whether free or dissolved in water, death by asphyxiation will follow still faster. If isolated from the Sun, animals will survive for a time, but plants would die, and if all plants died, all animals would starve.
>
> — ISAAC ASIMOV, "The Case against Man"

Asimov repeats the same if/then sentence structure to show the relationship between his ideas.

Collocation

Collocation — the positioning of words together in expected ways around a particular topic — occurs quite naturally to writers and usually forms recognizable networks of meaning for readers. For example, in a paragraph on a high school graduation, a reader might expect to encounter such words as *valedictorian*, *diploma, commencement, honors, cap* and *gown,* and *senior class.* The paragraph that follows uses five collocation chains:

housewife, cooking, neighbor, home

clocks, calculated, progression, precise

obstinacy, vagaries, problem

sun, clear days, cloudy ones, sundial, cast its light, angle, seasons, sun, weather

cooking, fire, matches, hot coals, smoldering, ashes, go out, bed-warming pan

The seventeenth-century housewife not only had to make do without thermometers, she also had to make do without clocks, which were scarce and dear throughout the sixteen hundreds. She calculated cooking times by the progression of the sun; her cooking must have been more precise on clear days than on cloudy ones. Marks were sometimes painted on the floor, providing her with a rough sundial, but she still had to make allowance for the obstinacy of the sun in refusing to cast its light at the same angle as the seasons changed; but she was used to allowing for the vagaries of sun and weather. She also had a problem starting her fire in the morning; there were no matches. If she had allowed the hot coals smoldering under the ashes to go out, she had to borrow some from a neighbor, carrying them home with care, perhaps in a bed-warming pan.

—WAVERLY ROOT AND RICHARD DE ROUCHEMENT, *Eating in America*

Exercise 13.7

Now that you know more about pronoun reference, word repetition, synonyms, sentence structure repetition, and collocation, turn to Brian Cable's essay in Chapter 3 and identify the cohesive devices you find in paragraphs 1–4. Underline each cohesive device you can find; there will be many. You might also want to connect with lines the various pronoun, related-word, and synonym chains you find. You could also try listing the separate collocation chains. Consider how these cohesive devices help you read and make sense of the passage.

Exercise 13.8

Choose one of your recent essays, and select any three contiguous paragraphs. Underline every cohesive device you can find; there will be many. Try to connect with lines the various pronoun, related-word, and synonym chains you find. Also try listing the separate collocation chains.

You will be surprised and pleased at how extensively you rely on cohesive ties. Indeed, you could not produce readable text without cohesive ties. Consider these questions relevant to your development as a writer: Are all of your pronoun references clear? Are you straining for synonyms when repeated words would do? Do you ever repeat sentence structures to emphasize connections? Do you trust yourself to put collocation to work?

Transitions

A **transition** serves as a bridge to connect one paragraph, sentence, clause, or word with another. It also identifies the kind of connection by indicating to readers how the item preceding the transition relates to the one that follows it. Transitions help readers anticipate how the next paragraph or sentence will affect the meaning of what they have just read. There are three basic groups of transitions, based on the relationships they indicate: logical, temporal, and spatial.

Logical Relationships

Transitions help readers follow the **logical relationships** within an argument. How such transitions work is illustrated in this tightly and passionately reasoned paragraph by James Baldwin:

Baldwin uses transitions to reinforce the logic of his argument.

> The black man insists, by whatever means he finds at his disposal, that the white man cease to regard him as an exotic rarity and recognize him as a human being. This is a very charged and difficult moment, for there is a great deal of will power involved in the white man's naïveté. Most people are not naturally malicious, and the white man prefers to keep the black man at a certain human remove because it is easier for him thus to preserve his simplicity and to avoid being called to account for crimes committed by his forefathers, or his neighbors. He is inescapably aware, nevertheless, that he is in a better position in the world than black men are, nor can he quite put to death the suspicion that he is hated by black men therefore. He does not wish to be hated, neither does he wish to change places, and at this point in his uneasiness he can scarcely avoid having recourse to those legends which white men have created about black men, the most unusual effect of which is that the white man finds himself enmeshed, so to speak, in his own language which describes hell, as well as the attributes which lead one to hell, as being black as night.
>
> —JAMES BALDWIN, "Stranger in the Village"

Transitions Showing Logical Relationships

- **To introduce another item in a series:** first . . . , second; in the second place; for one thing . . . , for another; next; then; furthermore; moreover; in addition; finally; last; also; similarly; besides; and; as well as
- **To introduce an illustration or other specification:** in particular; specifically; for instance; for example; that is; namely
- **To introduce a result or a cause:** consequently; as a result; hence; accordingly; thus; so; therefore; then; because; since; for
- **To introduce a restatement:** that is; in other words; in simpler terms; to put it differently
- **To introduce a conclusion or summary:** in conclusion; finally; all in all; evidently; clearly; actually; to sum up; altogether; of course

- *To introduce an opposing point:* but; however; yet; nevertheless; on the contrary; on the other hand; in contrast; still; neither; nor
- *To introduce a concession to an opposing view:* certainly; naturally; of course; it is true; to be sure; granted
- *To resume the original line of reasoning after a concession:* nonetheless; all the same; even though; still; nevertheless

Temporal Relationships

In addition to showing logical connections, transitions may indicate **temporal relationships** — a sequence or progression in time — as this example illustrates:

> That night, we drank tea and then vodka with lemon peel steeped in it. The four of us talked in Russian and English about mutual friends and American railroads and the Rolling Stones. Seryozha loves the Stones, and his face grew wistful as we spoke about their recent album, *Some Girls.* He played a tape of "Let It Bleed" over and over, until we could translate some difficult phrases for him; after that, he came out with the phrases at intervals during the evening, in a pretty decent imitation of Jagger's Cockney snarl. He was an adroit and oddly formal host, inconspicuously filling our teacups and politely urging us to eat bread and cheese and chocolate. While he talked to us, he teased Anya, calling her "Piglet," and she shook back her bangs and glowered at him. It was clear that theirs was a fiery relationship. After a while, we talked about ourselves. Anya told us about painting and printmaking and about how hard it was to buy supplies in Moscow. There had been something angry in her dark face since the beginning of the evening; I thought at first that it meant she didn't like Americans; but now I realized that it was a constant, barely suppressed rage at her own situation.
>
> — ANDREA LEE, *Russian Journal*

Lee uses transitions to show the relationship of events transpiring over one evening.

Transitions Showing Temporal Relationships

- *To indicate frequency:* frequently; hourly; often; occasionally; now and then; day after day; every so often; again and again
- *To indicate duration:* during; briefly; for a long time; minute by minute; while
- *To indicate a particular time:* now; then; at that time; in those days; last Sunday; next Christmas; in 2003; at the beginning of August; at six o'clock; first thing in the morning; two months ago; when
- *To indicate the beginning:* at first; in the beginning; since; before then
- *To indicate the middle:* in the meantime; meanwhile; as it was happening; at that moment; at the same time; simultaneously; next; then
- *To indicate the end and beyond:* eventually; finally; at last; in the end; subsequently; later; afterward

Spatial Relationships

Transitions showing **spatial relationships** orient readers to the objects in a scene, as illustrated in these paragraphs:

> On Georgia 155, I crossed Troublesome Creek, then went through groves of pecan trees aligned one with the next like fenceposts. The pastures grew a green almost blue, and syrupy water the color of a dusty sunset filled the ponds. Around the farmhouses, from wires strung high above the ground, swayed gourds hollowed out for purple martins.
>
> The land rose again on the other side of the Chattahoochee River, and Highway 34 went to the ridgetops where long views over the hills opened in all directions. Here was the tail of the Appalachian backbone, its gradual descent to the Gulf. Near the Alabama stateline stood a couple of LAST CHANCE! bars. . . .
>
> — WILLIAM LEAST HEAT MOON, *Blue Highways*

Least Heat Moon uses transitions to track the movement of his narrative.

Transitions Showing Spatial Relationships

- ***To indicate closeness:*** close to; near; next to; alongside; adjacent to; facing
- ***To indicate distance:*** in the distance; far; beyond; away; there
- ***To indicate direction:*** up/down; sideways; along; across; to the right/left; in front of/behind; above/below; inside/outside; toward/away from

Exercise 13.9

Turn to Trey Ellis's essay in Chapter 2. Relying on the lists of transitions just given, underline the *temporal* transitions in paragraphs 1–5. Consider how the transitions relate the ideas and events from sentence to sentence. Suggest any further transitions that could be added to make the relationships even clearer.

Exercise 13.10

Select a recent essay of your own. Choose at least three paragraphs, and underline the logical, temporal, and spatial transitions. Depending on the kind of writing you were doing, you may find few, if any, transitions in one category or another. For example, an essay speculating about causes may not include any spatial transitions; writing about a remembered event might not contain transitions showing logical relationships.

Consider how your transitions relate the ideas from sentence to sentence. Compare your transitions with those in the lists in this text. Do you find that you are making full use of the repertoire? Do you find gaps between any of your sentences that a well-chosen transition would close?

Headings and Subheadings

Headings and **subheadings** — brief phrases set off from the text in various ways — can provide visible cues to readers about the content and organization of a text. Headings can be distinguished from text in numerous ways, including the selective use of capital letters, bold or italic type, or different sizes of type. To be most helpful to readers, headings should be phrased similarly and follow a predictable system.

Heading Systems and Levels

In this chapter, the headings in the section Paragraphing, beginning on p. 602, provide a good example of a system of headings that can readily be outlined:

Paragraphing

Paragraph Cues

Topic Sentence Strategies

Announcing the Topic.

Making a Transition.

Positioning the Topic Sentence.

Notice that in this example, the heading system has three levels. The first-level heading sits on its own line and is set in a large, colored (blue) font; this heading stands out most visibly among the others. (It is one of five such headings in this chapter.) The second-level heading also sits on its own line, but is set in a smaller font (also blue). The first of these second-level headings has no subheadings beneath it, while the second has three. These third-level headings, in black, do not sit on their own lines — they run into the paragraph they introduce, as you can see if you turn back to pp. 603–5.

All of these headings follow a parallel grammatical structure: nouns at the first level; nouns at the second level ("cues" and "strategies"); and "-ing" nouns at the third level.

To learn more about distinguishing headings from surrounding text and about setting up systems of headings, see p. 692 in Chapter 21, Designing Documents.

Headings and Genres

Headings may not be necessary in short essays: thesis statements, forecasting statements, well-positioned topic sentences, and transition sentences may be all the cues the reader needs. Headings are rare in some genres, such as essays about remembered events (Chapter 2) and essays profiling people and places (Chapter 3). Headings appear more frequently in genres such as concept explanations, explanations of various perspectives on an issue, position papers, public policy proposals, evaluations, and speculations about social problems (Chapters 4–9).

Frequency and Placement of Headings

Before dividing their essays into sections with headings and subheadings, writers need to make sure their discussion is detailed enough to support at least two headings at each level. The frequency and placement of headings depend entirely on the content and how it is divided and organized. Keep in mind that headings do not reduce the need for other cues to keep readers on track.

Exercise 13.11

Turn either to Jeffrey Kluger's "What Makes Us Moral" in Chapter 4 or to Robert Kuttner's "Good Jobs for Americans Who Help Americans" in Chapter 7 and survey that essay's system of headings. If you have not read the essay, read or skim it now. Consider how the headings help readers anticipate what is coming and how the argument is organized. Decide whether the headings substitute for or complement other cues for keeping readers on track. Consider whether the headings are grammatically parallel.

Exercise 13.12

Select one of your essays that might benefit from headings. Develop a system of headings, and insert them where appropriate. Be prepared to justify your headings in light of the discussion about headings in this section.

Narrating

14

Narrating is a basic strategy for representing action and events. As the term's Latin root, *gnarus* ("knowing"), implies, narrating helps people make sense of events they are involved in, as well as events they observe or read about. From earliest childhood, we use narrating to help us reflect on what has happened, to explain what is happening, and to imagine what could happen.

Narrating serves many different purposes. It can be used to report on events, present information, illustrate abstract ideas, support arguments, explain procedures, and entertain with stories. This chapter begins by describing and illustrating five basic narrating strategies and concludes by looking at two types of process narrative — explanatory and instructional.

Narrating Strategies

Strategies such as calendar and clock time, temporal transitions, verb tense, specific narrative action, and dialogue give narrative its dynamic quality, the sense of events unfolding in time. They also help readers track the order in which the events occurred and understand how they relate to one another.

Calendar and Clock Time

One of the simplest ways of constructing a clear time sequence is to place events on a timeline with years or precise dates and times clearly marked. Look, for example, at the excerpted portion of a timeline in Figure 14.1, which presents a series of events in the history of flight. A timeline is not itself a narrative, but it shares with narrative two basic elements: Events are presented in chronological order, and each event is "time-stamped," so that readers can understand clearly when events occurred in relation to one another.

Look now at a brief but fully developed narrative reconstructing the discovery of the bacterial cause of stomach ulcers. This narrative was written by Martin J. Blaser for *Scientific American*, a journal read primarily by nonspecialists interested in science. As you read, notice the same narrating strategies you saw in the

Figure 14.1 Chronology of events in the history of flight (Library of Congress)

Blaser cites specific years, months, days, and a holiday to convey the passage of time and indicate when each event occurred.

timeline in Figure 14.1: sequencing events in chronological order and specifying when each event occurred:

In 1979 J. Robin Warren, a pathologist at the Royal Perth Hospital in Australia, made a puzzling observation. As he examined tissue specimens from patients who had undergone stomach biopsies, he noticed that several samples had large numbers of curved and spiral-shaped bacteria. Ordinarily, stomach acid would destroy such organisms before they could settle in the stomach. But those Warren saw lay underneath the organ's thick mucus layer — a lining that coats the stomach's tissues and protects them from acid. Warren also noted that the bacteria were present only in tissue samples that were inflamed. Wondering whether the microbes might somehow be related to the irritation, he looked to the literature for clues and learned that German pathologists had witnessed similar organisms a century earlier. Because they could not grow the bacteria in culture, though, their findings had been ignored and then forgotten.

Warren, aided by an enthusiastic young trainee named Barry J. Marshall, also had difficulty growing the unknown bacteria in culture. He began his efforts in 1981. By April 1982 the two men had attempted to culture samples from 30-odd patients — all without success. Then the Easter holidays arrived. The hospital laboratory staff accidentally held some of the culture plates for five days instead of the usual two. On the fifth day, colonies emerged. The workers christened them *Campylobacter pyloridis* because they resembled pathogenic bacteria of the *Campylobacter* genus found in the intestinal tract. Early in 1983 Warren and Marshall published their first report, and within months scientists around the world had isolated the bacteria.

— MARTIN J. BLASER, "The Bacteria behind Ulcers"

In addition to calendar time (years, months, days), writers sometimes also refer to clock time (hours, minutes, seconds). Here is a brief narrative from an essay profiling the emergency room at Bellevue Hospital in New York City:

> 9:05 p.m. An ambulance backs into the receiving bay, its red and yellow lights flashing in and out of the lobby. A split second later, the glass doors burst open as a nurse and an attendant roll a mobile stretcher into the lobby. When the nurse screams, "Emergency!" the lobby explodes with activity as the way is cleared to the trauma room. Doctors appear from nowhere and transfer the bloodied body of a black man to the treatment table. Within seconds his clothes are stripped away.
>
> — George Simpson, "The War Room at Bellevue"

The references to clock time establish the sequence and contribute to dramatic intensity.

Exercise 14.1

Turn to the remembered-event essay "When the Walls Came Tumbling Down," by Trey Ellis, in Chapter 2, and underline the references to calendar time. How do you think these calendar time markers function in the narrative? What do they tell you about the impression Ellis wants to create about that period of his life?

Exercise 14.2

Read through "Show Dog" by Susan Orlean, in Chapter 3, and underline any references to clock time that you find. What does Orlean's use of clock time contribute to her essay?

Temporal Transitions

Whereas writers tend to use calendar and clock time sparingly, they regularly use **temporal transitions** such as *when, at that moment, before,* and *while* in order to establish a clear sequence of actions in narrating onetime or recurring events.

For a more extensive list of transitions showing temporal relationships, see Chapter 13.

Onetime Events. To see how temporal transitions work, let us look at the concluding paragraphs of a remembered-event essay in which Russell Baker recounts what happened after his final flight test, his last chance to become a pilot. The "he" Baker refers to is the flight check pilot, T. L. (nicknamed "Total Loss") Smith.

> Back at the flight line, when I'd cut the ignition, he climbed out and tramped back toward the ready room while I waited to sign the plane in. When I got there he was standing at a distance talking to my regular instructor. His talk was being illustrated with hand movements, as pilots' conversations always were, hands executing little loops and rolls in the air. After he did the falling-leaf motion with his

Baker uses temporal transitions to show what he and Smith were doing after the flight test.

hands, he pointed a finger at my instructor's chest, said something I couldn't hear, and trudged off. My instructor, who had flown only with the pre-hangover Baker, was slack-jawed when he approached me.

"Smith just said you gave him the best check flight he's ever had in his life," he said. "What the hell did you do to him up there?"

"I guess I just suddenly learned to fly," I said.

— Russell Baker, "Smooth and Easy"

Look closely at the two transitions in the first sentence. The word *when* presents actions in chronological order (first Baker stopped the plane, and then Smith got out). *While* performs a different function, showing that the next two actions occurred at the same time (Baker signed in as the check pilot returned to the ready room). There is nothing complicated or unusual about this set of actions, but it would be hard to represent them in writing without temporal transitions.

Recurring Events. Temporal transitions also enable writers to narrate recurring events. In the following narrative by Monica Sone about her daily life in an internment camp for Japanese Americans during World War II, we can see how transitions (highlighted) help the writer represent actions she routinely performed.

With the time marker *first,* Sone starts describing her typical work routine. In the third sentence, she tells of her surreptitious actions *in the first few months and every morning.*

First I typed on pink, green, blue and white work sheets the hours put in by the 10,000 evacuees, then sorted and alphabetized these sheets, and stacked them away in shoe boxes. My job was excruciatingly dull, but under no circumstances did I want to leave it. The Administration Building was the only place which had modern plumbing and running hot and cold water; in the first few months and every morning, after I had typed for a decent hour, I slipped into the rest room and took a complete sponge bath with scalding hot water. During the remainder of the day, I slipped back into the rest room at inconspicuous intervals, took off my head scarf and wrestled with my scorched hair. I stood upside down over the basin of hot water, soaking my hair, combing, stretching and pulling at it.

— Monica Sone, "Camp Harmony"

Exercise 14.3

Turn to the essay "Show Dog," by Susan Orlean, in Chapter 3. Underline the temporal transitions in paragraph 22, where Orlean relates a onetime event, and paragraph 21, where she presents a recurring event. Notice the number of transitions she uses and how each one functions. What can you conclude about Orlean's use of temporal transitions from your analysis of these two paragraphs? How well do these transitions create a sense of time passing? How effectively do they help you follow the sequence of actions?

Exercise 14.4

Turn to "Love: The Right Chemistry," by Anastasia Toufexis, in Chapter 4. Read paragraph 3, underlining the temporal transitions Toufexis uses to present the sequence of evolutionary changes that may have contributed to the development of romantic love. How important are these transitions in helping you follow her narrative?

Verb Tense

In addition to time markers like calendar time and temporal transitions, writers use **verb tense** to represent action in writing and to help readers understand when each action occurred in relation to the other actions.

Onetime Events. Writers typically use the past tense to represent onetime events that began and ended in the past. Here is a brief passage from a remembered-person essay by Amy Wu. In addition to the temporal transitions *once* and *when* in the opening sentence, which let readers know that this particular event occurred many years earlier, the writer also uses simple past-tense verbs (highlighted):

> Once, when I was 5 or 6, I interrupted my mother during a dinner with her friends and told her that I disliked the meal. My mother's eyes transformed from serene pools of blackness into stormy balls of fire. "Quiet!" she hissed, "do you not know that silent waters run deep?"
>
> — AMY WU, "A Different Kind of Mother"

Wu uses the simple past tense to indicate that actions occurred in a linear sequence.

In the next example, by Chang-Rae Lee, we see how verb tense can be used to show more complicated relationships between past actions that occurred at different times in the past:

> When Uncle Chul amassed the war chest he needed to open the wholesale business he had hoped for, he moved away from New York.
>
> — CHANG-RAE LEE, "Uncle Chul Gets Rich"

Lee employs both the simple past (*amassed, needed, moved*) and the past perfect tense (*had hoped*).

You do not have to know that *amassed* is simple past tense and *had hoped* is past perfect tense to know that the uncle's hopes came before the money was amassed. In fact, most readers of English can understand complicated combinations of tenses without knowing their names.

Let us look at another verb tense combination used frequently in narrative: the simple past and the past progressive.

> When Dinah Washington was leaving with some friends, I overheard someone say she was on her way to the Savoy Ballroom where Lionel Hampton was appearing that night — she was then Hamp's vocalist.
>
> — MALCOLM X, *The Autobiography of Malcolm X*

Malcolm X uses the simple past tense (*overheard, was*) and past progressive tense (*was leaving, was appearing*).

This combination of tenses plus the temporal transition *when* shows that the two actions occurred at the same time in the past. The first action ("Dinah Washington was leaving") continued during the period that the second action ("I overheard") occurred.

Occasionally, writers use the present instead of the past tense to narrate onetime events. Process narratives and profiles typically use the present tense to give the story a sense of "you are there" immediacy.

> Slowly, the dank barroom fills with grease-smeared mechanics from the truck stop up the road and farmers straight from the fields, the soles of their brogans thick with dirt clods. A few weary souls make their way over from the nearby sawmill.

Edge uses present-tense verbs to give readers a sense that they are in the room with him.

I sit alone at the bar, one empty bottle of Bud in front of me, a second in my hand. I drain the beer, order a third, and stare down at the pink juice spreading outward from a crumpled foil pouch and onto the bar.

I'm not leaving until I eat this thing, I tell myself.

— JOHN T. EDGE, "I'm Not Leaving Until I Eat This Thing"

Recurring Events. Verb tense, usually combined with temporal transitions, can also help writers narrate events that occurred routinely.

> Many times, walking home from work, I would see some unknowing soul venture across that intersection against the light and then freeze in horror when he saw the cars ripping out of the tunnel toward him. . . . Suddenly, the human reflex would take over, and the pedestrian would jackknife first one way, then another, arms flaying the empty air, and often the car would literally skim the man, brushing by him so close it would touch his coat or his tie. . . . On one occasion, feeling sorry for the person who had brushed against the speeding car, I hurried across the intersection after him to cheer him up a little. Catching up with him down by 32nd I said, "That was good legwork, sir. Excellent moves for a big man!" but the man looked at me with an empty expression in his eyes, and then moved away mechanically and trancelike, heading for the nearest bar.
>
> — WILLIE MORRIS, *North toward Home*

Morris uses the helping verb *would* along with temporal transitions to show recurring actions.

Notice also that Morris shifts to the simple past tense when he moves from recurring actions to an action that occurred only once. He signals this shift with the temporal transition *on one occasion*.

Exercise 14.5

Turn to the remembered-event essay "Calling Home," by Jean Brandt, in Chapter 2. Read paragraph 3, and underline the verbs, beginning with *got, took, knew,* and *didn't want* in the first sentence. Brandt uses verb tense to reconstruct her actions and reflect on their effectiveness. Notice also how verb tense helps you follow the sequence of actions Brandt took.

Specific Narrative Action

The narrating strategy we call **specific narrative action** uses active verbs and modifying phrases and clauses to present action vividly. Specific narrative action is especially suited to representing the intense, fast-moving, physical actions of sports events. The following example by George Plimpton shows how well specific narrative actions (highlighted) work to show what happened during a practice scrimmage. Plimpton participated in the Detroit Lions football training camp while writing a book profiling professional football. This is what he experienced:

Though Plimpton uses active verbs, he describes most of the action through modifying phrases and clauses.

> Since in the two preceding plays the concentration of the play had been elsewhere, I had felt alone with the flanker. Now, the whole heave of the play was toward me, flooding the zone not only with confused motion but noise — the quick stomp of feet, the creak of football gear, the strained grunts of effort, the faint *ah-ah-ah* of piston-stroke regularity, and the stiff calls of instruction, like exhalations. "Inside,

inside! Take him inside!" someone shouted, tearing by me, his cleats thumping in the grass. A call — a parrot squawk — may have erupted from me. My feet splayed in hopeless confusion as Barr came directly toward me, feinting in one direction, and then stopping suddenly, drawing me toward him for the possibility of a buttonhook pass, and as I leaned almost off balance toward him, he turned and came on again, downfield, moving past me at high speed, leaving me poised on one leg, reaching for him, trying to grab at him despite the illegality, anything to keep him from getting by. But he was gone, and by the time I had turned to set out after him, he had ten yards on me, drawing away fast with his sprinter's run, his legs pinwheeling, the row of cleats flicking up a faint wake of dust behind.

— George Plimpton, *Paper Lion*

By piling up specific narrative actions, Plimpton reconstructs for readers the texture and excitement of his experience on the football field. He uses the two most common kinds of modifiers that writers employ to present specific narrative action:

Participial phrases: tearing by me, stopping suddenly, moving past me at high speed

Absolute phrases: his cleats thumping in the grass, his legs pinwheeling, the row of cleats flicking up a faint wake of dust behind

Combined with vivid sensory description (*the creak of football gear, the strained grunts of effort, the faint* ah-ah-ah *of piston-stroke regularity*), these specific narrative actions re-create the sights and sounds of people in motion.

Exercise 14.6

Turn to paragraph 2 of the profile essay "The Long Good-Bye: Mother's Day in Federal Prison" by Amanda Coyne, in Chapter 3. Underline any specific narrative actions you find in this brief paragraph. Then reflect on how they help the reader envision the scene in the prison's visiting room.

Exercise 14.7

Make a videotape of several brief — two- or three-minute — televised segments of a fast-moving sports competition such as a football or basketball game. Then review the tape, and choose one segment to narrate using specific narrative actions to describe in detail what you see.

If you cannot videotape a televised game, narrate a live-action event (for example, people playing touch football, a dog catching a Frisbee, or a skateboarder or inline skater practicing a trick). As you watch the action, take detailed notes of what you see. Then, based on your notes, write a few sentences using specific narrative actions to describe the action you witnessed firsthand.

Dialogue

Dialogue is most often used in narratives that dramatize events. It reconstructs choice bits of conversation, rather than trying to present an accurate and complete record. In addition to showing people interacting, dialogue can give readers insight into character and relationships. Dialogue may be quoted to make it resemble the give-and-take of actual conversation, or it may be summarized to give readers the gist of what was said.

The following example from Gary Soto's *Living up the Street* shows how a narrative can combine quoted and summarized dialogue. In this passage, Soto recalls his first experience as a migrant worker in California's San Joaquin Valley.

> "Are you tired?" she asked.
>
> "No, but I got a sliver from the frame," I told her. I showed her the web of skin between my thumb and index finger. She wrinkled her forehead but said it was nothing.
>
> "How many trays did you do?"
>
> I looked straight ahead, not answering at first. I recounted in my mind the whole morning of bend, cut, pour again and again, before answering a feeble "thirty-seven." No elaboration, no detail. Without looking at me she told me how she had done field work in Texas and Michigan as a child. But I had a difficult time listening to her stories. I played with my grape knife, stabbing it into the ground, but stopped when Mother reminded me that I had better not lose it. I left the knife sticking up like a small, leafless plant. She then talked about school, the junior high I would be going to that fall, and then about Rick and Debra, how sorry they would be that they hadn't come out to pick grapes because they'd have no new clothes for the school year. She stopped talking when she peeked at her watch, a bandless one she kept in her pocket. She got up with an "Ay, Dios," and told me that we'd work until three, leaving me cutting figures in the sand with my knife and dreading the return to work.
>
> — GARY SOTO, "One Last Time"

Quoted dialogue is easy to recognize, of course, because of the quotation marks. Summarized dialogue can be harder to identify. In this case, however, Soto embeds signal phrases (*she told me* and *she then talked*) in his narrative. Summarizing leaves out information the writer decides readers do not need. In this passage about a remembered event, Soto has chosen to focus on his own feelings and thoughts rather than his mother's.

Soto uses signal phrases with the first two quotations but not with the third, where it is clear who is speaking. The fourth quotation, *thirty-seven*, is preceded by a narrative that tells what Soto did and thought before speaking and is followed by a summary of further conversation.

For more on deciding when to quote, see Chapter 2, pp. 50–52; Chapter 3, pp. 112–13; and Chapter 24. pp. 756–62.

Exercise 14.8

Read the essay "Longing to Belong" in Chapter 2, and consider Saira Shah's use of both direct quotation and summaries for reporting speech. When does Shah choose to quote directly, and why might she have made this decision?

Exercise 14.9

If you wrote a remembered-event essay in Chapter 2 or wrote a bit of narrative in some other essay, reread your essay, looking for one example of each of the following narrating strategies: calendar or clock time, temporal transitions, past-tense verbs in onetime events, specific narrative action, and dialogue. Do not worry if you cannot find examples of all of the strategies. Pick one strategy you did use and comment on what it contributes to your narrative.

Narrating a Process

Process narratives explain how something was done or instruct readers on how it could or should be done. Whether the purpose is explanatory or instructional, process narratives must convey clearly each necessary action and the exact order in which the actions occur.

Explanatory Process Narratives

Explanatory process narratives often relate particular experiences or elucidate processes followed by machines or organizations. Let us begin with an excerpt from a remembered-event essay by Mary Mebane. She uses process narrative to let readers know what happened the first time she worked on an assembly line putting tobacco leaves on the conveyor belt.

> The job seemed easy enough as I picked up bundle after bundle of tobacco and put it on the belt, careful to turn the knot end toward me so that it would be placed right to go under the cutting machine. Gradually, as we worked up our tobacco, I had to bend more, for as we emptied the hogshead we had to stoop over to pick up the tobacco, then straighten up and put it on the belt just right. Then I discovered the hard part of the job: the belt kept moving at the same speed all the time and if the leaves were not placed on the belt at the same tempo there would be a big gap where your bundle should have been. So that that when you got down lower, you had to bend down, get the tobacco, straighten up fast, make sure it was placed knot end toward you, place it on the belt, and bend down again. Soon you were bending down, up; down, up; down, up. All along the line, heads were bobbing — down, up; down, up — until you finished the barrel. Then you could rest until the men brought you another one.
>
> — Mary Mebane, "Summer Job"

Temporal transitions and simple past-tense verbs place the actions in time.

Here, specific narrative actions (*bend down, get the tobacco, straighten up fast*) become a series of staccato movements (*down, up; down, up; down, up*) that emphasize the speed and machinelike actions Mebane had to take to keep up with the conveyor belt.

The next example shows how a laser printer functions.

> To create a page, the computer sends signals to the printer, which shines a laser at a mirror system that scans across a charged drum. Whenever the beam strikes the drum, it removes the charge. The drum then rotates through a toner chamber filled with thermoplastic particles. The toner particles stick to the negatively charged areas of the drum in the pattern of characters, lines, or other elements the computer has transmitted and the laser beam mapped.
>
> Once the drum is coated with toner in the appropriate locations, a piece of paper is pulled across a so-called transfer corona wire, which imparts a positive electrical charge. The paper then passes across the toner-coated drum. The positive charge on the paper attracts the toner in the same position it occupied on the drum. The final phase of the process involves fusing the toner to the paper with a set of high-temperature rollers.
>
> — Richard Golub and Eric Brus, *Almanac of Science and Technology*

Because the objects performing the action change from sentence to sentence, the writers must construct a clearly marked chain, introducing the object's name in one sentence and repeating the name or using a synonym in the next.

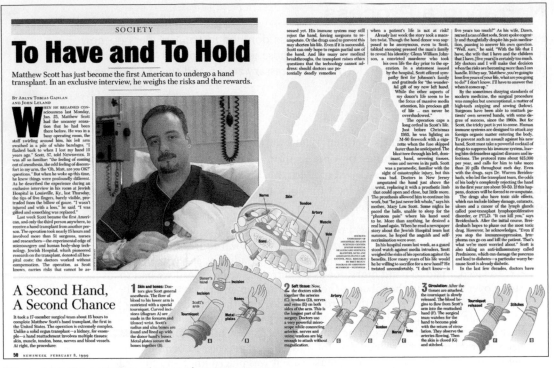

Figure 14.2 Presentation of an explanatory process
The two-page layout reproduced here shows how "A Second Hand, A Second Chance" was designed as a sidebar accompanying a longer article, "To Have and to Hold." From *Newsweek,* February 8, 1999, pp. 50–51.

Like Mebane's process narrative, this one sequences the actions chronologically from beginning ("the computer sends signals to the printer") to end ("fusing the toner to the paper"). Temporal transitions (*then, once, then, final*), present-tense verbs, and specific narrative actions (*sends, shines, scans, strikes*) convey the passage of time and place the actions clearly in this chronological sequence.

Our last explanatory process narrative is a graphic sidebar of the type commonly used in magazines and books. This one comes from a *Newsweek* magazine feature on Matthew Scott, only the third person to receive a hand transplant. "A Second Hand, A Second Chance," shown in Figure 14.2, illustrates the process narrative.

Notice that this process narrative integrates writing with graphics. The procedure is divided into three distinct steps, with each step clearly numbered and labeled (*1. Skin and bones*). In each step, the figure captions refer to the graphics with letters — *Curved incisions (diagram A)*. The graphics themselves incorporate labels — *Donor's hand, Incision, Tourniquet released*. The writer uses some basic narrating strategies to present the actions and make clear the sequence in which they were taken: temporal transitions (*now, while, after*), present-tense verbs, and

A Second Hand,
A Second Chance

It took a 17-member surgical team about 15 hours to complete Matthew Scott's hand transplant, the first in the United States. The operation is extremely complex. Unlike a solid organ transplant—a kidney, for example—a hand reattachment involves multiple tissues: skin, muscle, tendon, bone, nerves and blood vessels. At right, the procedure.

50 NEWSWEEK FEBRUARY 8, 1999

specific narrative actions, mostly in the form of active verbs (*secure, stitch, watches*). Much is left out, of course. Readers could not duplicate the procedure based on this narrative, but it does give *Newsweek* readers a clear sense of what was done during the fifteen hours of surgery.

Exercise 14.10

In Chapter 3, read paragraph 6 of Brian Cable's profile of a local mortuary, "The Last Stop." Here Cable narrates the process that the company follows once it has been notified of a client's death. As you read, look for and mark the narrating strategies discussed in this chapter that Cable uses. Then reflect on how well you think the narrative presents the actions and their sequence.

Instructional Process Narratives

Unlike explanatory process narratives, **instructional process narratives** must include all of the information a reader needs to perform the procedure presented. Depending on the reader's experience, the writer might need to define technical terms, list tools that should be used, give background information, and account for alternatives or possible problems.

For guidelines on designing your own documents, see Chapter 21.

Figure 14.3 presents a detailed instructional process narrative from the Sunset *Home Repair Handbook* that gives readers directions for replacing a broken plug.

The instructions begin with general advice on when to replace a plug, followed by a classification of three common types of plugs that also are illustrated in the accompanying graphic. Notice that even though the graphic is not referred to explicitly in the text, readers are unlikely to be confused because the graphic is right next to the relevant paragraph and is clearly titled "Types of plugs."

Paragraphs 4 and 5 briefly explain the procedure for replacing two- and three-prong plugs. These procedures are spelled out in greater detail in the accompanying graphics titled "Replacing a plug with terminal screws" and "Replacing three special types of plugs." The first of these graphics includes four steps that are clearly numbered, illustrated, and narrated. Each step presents several actions to be taken, and its graphic shows what the plug should look like when these actions have been completed. We can identify the actions by looking at the verbs. Step 1 in "Replacing

■ Replacing Plugs ■

Any plug with a cracked shell or loose, damaged, or badly bent contacts should be replaced. Also replace plugs that transmit power erratically or get warm when used. If a plug arcs when it's pushed into or pulled out of a receptacle, examine the wires; if they're not firmly attached to the terminal screws, tighten the connections.

The two kinds of common plugs are terminal-screw and self-connecting. In plugs with terminal screws, the wires are attached to screws inside the plug body. Self-connecting plugs clamp onto wires, making an automatic connection. These plugs, as well as two-prong plugs with terminal screws, are commonly used for lamps and small appliances. Three-prong grounding plugs are used for larger appliances and power tools. Detachable cords for small appliances have female plugs with terminal screws.

NOTE: Many old-style plugs with terminal screws have a removable insulating disc covering the terminals and wires. The NEC now requires "dead-front" plugs; such plugs have a rigid insulating barrier.

To replace a plug, cut off the old one plus at least an inch of the cord. For plugs that have terminal screws, split the cord insulation to separate the wires; then strip the insulation from the ends *(page 159)*.

When replacing a two-prong plug, connect the identified conductor to the silver-colored screw. For a three-prong grounding plug, attach the wires to the terminal screws as follows: white neutral wire to silver screw, black hot wire to brass screw, and green grounding wire to green terminal screw.

Types of plugs

Replacing a plug with terminal screws

Unscrew and remove the new plug's insulating barrier. Using a utility knife, split the end of the cord to separate the wires; push the cord through the plug body.

Make two loops with the wires, pass the loose ends of the wires through the loops, and pull to form an Underwriter's knot (to prevent strain on connections).

Strip ½ to ¾ inch of insulation off the wire ends, being careful not to nick the wires *(page 159)*. Unscrew the terminal screws to allow space for the wires.

Form loops on wires and wrap them clockwise three-quarters of the way around screws. Tighten the screws, trim excess wire, and reattach the barrier to the body.

Replacing three special types of plugs

Three-prong grounding plug. Unscrew the insulating barrier; push stripped wires through the plug body into the correct terminal slots. Tighten the terminal screws and reassemble the plug.

Self-connecting plug. Push the cord (don't strip it) through the shell and into the terminal block; squeeze the prongs together to grip the cord and slide into the shell.

Female appliance plug. Unscrew the plug shell; feed the cord through the spring guard. Strip the wire ends *(page 159)*, wrap them clockwise around the terminal screws, and tighten; reassemble the plug.

Figure 14.3 Replacing plugs

From *Home Repair Handbook* (Menlo Park, Calif.: Sunset, 1999), pp. 156–57.

a plug with terminal screws," for example, instructs readers to take four separate actions, each signaled by the verb (italicized here): "*Unscrew* and *remove* the new plug's insulating barrier. Using a utility knife, *split* the end of the cord to *separate* the wires; *push* the cord through the plug body." These are active verbs, and the sentences are in the form of clear and efficient commands.

The anonymous authors do not assume that readers know very much, especially on important safety matters. Paragraph 3, for example, presents a note explaining the National Electrical Code ("NEC") for old-style plugs. Also, readers are referred twice (in paragraph 4 and in step 3 of "Replacing a plug with terminal screws") to the explanation of how to strip wires safely, which appears on page 159 of the *Home Repair Handbook*.

Exercise 14.11

Write a one- to two-page instructional process narrative that tells readers how to make a peanut butter and jelly sandwich or perform some other equally simple procedure such as logging on to the Internet, hemming a pair of pants, potting a plant, or filling a fountain pen. Address your narrative to readers who have never done the procedure before.

15

Describing

The word **describing** comes from the Latin *describere*, meaning "to sketch" or "to copy in writing." Written descriptions help readers imagine what is being described. Vivid description creates an intense, distinctive image, one that seems to bring the words on the page to life. Good description can also be evocative, calling up memories or suggesting feelings associated with the subject being described. Writers can use description for many purposes: to give readers an impression of a person or place, to illustrate abstract ideas, to make information memorable, or to support an argument. This chapter presents the three basic descriptive techniques of **naming**, **detailing**, and **comparing**; surveys the words writers typically use to evoke vivid sense impressions; and examines how writers use description to create a dominant impression.

Naming

Naming calls readers' attention to observable features of the subject being described. To describe a room, for example, you might name objects you see as you look around, such as a bed, pillows, blankets, dresser, clothes, books, a CD player, and CDs. These objects suggest what kind of room it is and begin to give readers an impression of what it is like to be in this particular room.

Look closely at the following passage describing a weasel that the writer, Annie Dillard, encountered in the woods:

> He was ten inches long, thin as a curve, a muscled ribbon, brown as fruitwood, soft-furred, alert. His face was fierce, small and pointed as a lizard's; he would have made a good arrowhead. There was just a dot of chin, maybe two brown hairs' worth, and then the pure white fur began that spread down his underside. He had two black eyes I didn't see, any more than you see a window.
>
> — ANNIE DILLARD, *Teaching a Stone to Talk*

With these names, readers can begin to put together a mental image of the animal Dillard is describing. She uses simple, everyday nouns, like *chin*, to identify the weasel's features, not technical words like *maxilla* or *mandible*. The piling up of simple, concrete nouns helps readers imagine what the weasel looked like to Dillard.

Although writers most commonly name what they see, sight is not the only sense contributing to vivid descriptions, as in the following passage:

> When the sun fell across the great white pile of the new Telephone Company building, you could smell the stucco burning as you passed; then some liquid sweetness that came to me from deep in the rings of the freshly cut lumber stacked in the yards, and the fresh plaster and paint on the brand-new storefronts. Rawness, sunshiny rawness down the end streets of the city, as I thought of them then — the hot ash-laden stink of the refuse dumps in my nostrils and the only sound at noon the resonant metal plunk of a tin can I kicked ahead of me as I went my way.
>
> — ALFRED KAZIN, *A Walker in the City*

Kazin names smells, sounds, tastes, and tactile qualities.

Exercise 15.1

Go to a place where you can sit for a while and observe the scene. It might be a landscape or a cityscape, indoors or outdoors, crowded or solitary. For five minutes, list everything in the scene that you can name using nouns. (A simple way to test if a word is a noun is to see if you can put the word *the, a,* or *an* in front of the word.) Remember, you can name objects you see (*dog, hydrant*) as well as impressions such as smells or sounds you experience at the place (*stench, hiss*).

Then write a page or so that describes the scene for someone who is not there with you. Write for readers who have never been to this particular place to let them know what to expect when they get there.

Exercise 15.2

Turn to "An American Childhood," by Annie Dillard, in Chapter 2. Read paragraphs 12 and 13 and underline the names that Dillard uses to describe the circuitous route she runs while the stranger is chasing her. Begin underlining with the words *house, path, tree,* and *bank* in the opening sentence. How do you think the amount of naming Dillard does contributes to the description's vividness — measured by your ability to imagine the chase scene?

Detailing

Naming identifies the notable features of the subject being described; **detailing** makes the features more specific or particularized. Naming answers the questions "What is it?" and "What are its parts or features?" Detailing answers questions like these:

- What size is it?
- How many are there?
- What is it made of?
- Where is it located?

- What is its condition?
- How is it used?
- Where does it come from?
- What is its effect?
- What is its value?

To add details to names, add modifiers — adjectives and adverbs, phrases and clauses. *Modifiers* make nouns more specific by supplying additional information. Notice how many modifying details Dillard provides in her description of the weasel.

> He was ten inches long, thin as a curve, a muscled ribbon, brown as fruitwood, soft-furred, alert. His face was fierce, small and pointed as a lizard's; he would have made a good arrowhead. There was just a dot of chin, maybe two brown hairs' worth, and then the pure white fur began that spread down his underside. He had two black eyes I didn't see, any more than you see a window.
>
> — ANNIE DILLARD, *Teaching a Stone to Talk*

Dillard's details provide information that shows readers what this specific weasel looked like. Other details convey subjective information about Dillard's thoughts and feelings during the encounter. For example, when Dillard writes that the weasel's "face was fierce," she is making a judgment. She uses details like this to make readers see the weasel as a wild animal, not a soft and cuddly pet.

In describing people, writers often combine physical details with details characterizing aspects of the individual's personality. These characterizations or evaluations let readers know something about the writer's thoughts about the person, as the following examples illustrate:

> My father, a fat, funny man with beautiful eyes and a subversive wit . . .
>
> — ALICE WALKER, "Beauty: When the Other Dancer Is the Self"

> I was afraid of her higharched bony nose, her eyebrows lifted in half-circles above her hooded, brilliant eyes, and of the Kentucky R's in her speech, and the long steps she took in her hightop shoes. I did nothing but fear her bearing-down authority. . . .
>
> — EUDORA WELTY, "Miss Duling"

Sometimes physical details alone can be enough to symbolize a person's character or the writer's feelings toward that person, as in the following passage:

> Rick was not a friendly looking man. He wore only swim trunks, and his short, powerful legs rose up to meet a bulging torso. His big belly was solid. His shoulders, as if to offset his front-heaviness, were thrown back, creating a deep crease of excess muscle from his sides around the small of his back, a crease like a huge frown. His arms were crossed, two medieval maces placed carefully on their racks, ready to be swung at any moment. His round cheeks and chin were darkened by traces of black whiskers. His hair was sparse. Huge, black, mirrored sunglasses replaced his eyes. Below his prominent nose was a thin, sinister mustache. I couldn't believe this menacing-looking man was the legendary jovial Rick.
>
> — BRAD BENIOFF, "Rick"

Sidebar notes:

Dillard provides details about size, shape, color, and texture, as well as details that convey subjective information.

Walker uses both physical description (*fat*) and evaluative details (*funny, beautiful*) to express her feelings about her father. Welty combines physical detail (*higharched bony nose*) with subjective judgment (*bearing-down authority*) to help readers understand her fear.

The physical details suggest a powerful and threatening character.

Exercise 15.3

Return to the description you wrote in Exercise 15.1. Put brackets around the details you used to help describe the scene. Add any other details you think of now — details that indicate size, quantity, makeup, location, condition, use, source, effect, value, or any other quality that would make the description more specific and particularized for readers. Then reread your description. What do you think the detailing contributes to the description you wrote?

Exercise 15.4

Look again at paragraphs 12 and 13 of Annie Dillard's essay in Chapter 2. In Exercise 15.2, you underlined the names Dillard used. Now put brackets around the details. You might begin, for example, with the modifiers *yellow* and *backyard*. How do you think detailing contributes to Dillard's description? How do these details help you imagine Dillard's experience of the chase?

Exercise 15.5

Turn to paragraphs 10 and 13 of Amanda Coyne's essay in Chapter 3. Read and put brackets around the words that detail the description of Stephanie and her son Ellie. If you have not read the entire essay, read it now, and consider how Coyne uses these contrasting descriptions of the inmate and her son to emphasize her main point in the essay.

Comparing

In addition to naming and detailing, writers sometimes use **comparing** to make their description more vivid for readers. Look again at Annie Dillard's description of a weasel, paying attention this time to the comparisons:

> He was ten inches long, thin as a curve, a muscled ribbon, brown as fruitwood, soft-furred, alert. His face was fierce, small and pointed as a lizard's; he would have made a good arrowhead. There was just a dot of chin, maybe two brown hairs' worth, and then the pure white fur began that spread down his underside. He had two black eyes I didn't see, any more than you see a window.

> — Annie Dillard, *Teaching a Stone to Talk*

Dillard uses similes and metaphors to describe the weasel.

Dillard uses two kinds of comparison in this description: simile and metaphor, both of which point out similarities in things that are essentially dissimilar. A *simile* expresses the similarity directly by using the words *like* or *as* to announce the comparison. A *metaphor,* by contrast, is an implicit comparison in which one thing is described as though it were the other.

Similes and metaphors can enhance the vividness of a description by giving readers additional information to help them picture the subject. For example, Dillard uses the word *thin* to detail the weasel's body shape. But *thin* is a relative term, leading readers to wonder, how thin? Dillard gives readers two images for comparison, a curve and a ribbon, to help them construct a fuller mental image of the weasel.

Comparing can also convey to readers what the writer feels about the subject. The following comparison from Brad Benioff's description of Coach Rick suggests the writer's feelings: "His arms were crossed, two medieval maces placed carefully on their racks, ready to be swung at any moment." Sometimes the similes or metaphors writers use are suggestive but hard to pin down. What do you think Dillard means, for example, by comparing the weasel's eyes to a window: "He had two black eyes I didn't see, any more than you see a window"?

Exercise 15.6

Return to the description you wrote in Exercise 15.1 and may have added to in Exercise 15.3. Reread it, and mark any comparing you did. Try to add one or two similes or metaphors to your description. How do you think your use of comparing may help readers imagine the subject or get a sense of what you feel about it?

Using Sensory Description

When writers use **sensory description** to describe animals, people, or scenes, they usually rely on the sense of sight more than the other senses. In general, our vocabulary for reporting what we see is larger and more varied than our vocabulary for reporting other sense impressions. Nevertheless, writers can detail the qualities and attributes of nonvisual sensations — the loudness or tinniness or rumble of an engine, for instance. They can also use comparing to help readers imagine what something sounds, feels, smells, or tastes like.

The Sense of Sight

When people describe what they see, they identify the objects in their field of vision. Here are two brief examples of visual description.

> On Christmas Eve I saw that my mother had outdone herself in creating a strange menu. She was pulling black veins out of the backs of fleshy prawns. The kitchen was littered with appalling mounds of raw food: A slimy rock cod with bulging eyes that pleaded not to be thrown into a pan of hot oil. Tofu, which looked like stacked wedges of rubbery white sponges. A bowl soaking dried fungus back to life. A plate of squid, their backs crisscrossed with knife markings so they resembled bicycle tires.
>
> — AMY TAN, "Fish Cheeks"

She was thirty-four. She wore a white skirt and yellow sweater and a thin gold necklace, which she held in her fingers, as if holding her own reins, while waiting

Tan uses visual details to depict her mother's kitchen.

Kidder uses visual details to describe Mrs. Zajac, a grade school teacher.

for children to answer. Her hair was black with a hint of Irish red. It was cut short to the tops of her ears, and swept back like a pair of folded wings. She had a delicate cleft chin, and she was short — the children's chairs would have fit her. . . . Her hands kept very busy. They sliced the air and made karate chops to mark off boundaries. They extended straight out like a traffic cop's, halting illegal maneuvers yet to be perpetrated. When they rested momentarily on her hips, her hands looked as if they were in holsters.

— TRACY KIDDER, *Among Schoolchildren*

Exercise 15.7

Write a few sentences describing a teacher, friend, or family member. Do not rely on memory for this exercise; describe someone who is before you as you write so that you can describe in detail what you see. Later, when you are alone, reread what you have written, and make any changes you think will help make this visual description more vivid for your readers.

The Sense of Hearing

In reporting auditory impressions, writers seldom name sounds without also specifying where the sounds come from: the murmur of a voice, the rustle of the wind, the squeak of a hinge, the sputter of an engine. *Onomatopoeia* is the term for names of sounds that echo the sounds themselves: *squeak, murmur, hiss, boom, plink, tinkle, twang, jangle, rasp, chirr.* Sometimes writers make up words like *sweesh* and *cara-wong* to imitate sounds they wish to describe. Qualitative words like *powerful* and *rich* as well as relative terms like *loud* and *low* often specify sounds further. For detailing sounds, writers sometimes use the technique called *synesthesia*, applying words commonly used to describe one sense to another, such as describing sounds as *sharp* and *soft*; they sometimes also use simile or metaphor to compare one sound to another.

To write about the sounds along Manhattan's Canal Street, Ian Frazier uses many of these describing and naming techniques.

> The traffic on Canal Street never stops. It is a high-energy current jumping constantly between the poles of Brooklyn and New Jersey. It hates to have its flow pinched in the density of Manhattan, hates to stop at intersections. Along Canal Street, it moans and screams. Worn brake shoes of semitrucks go "Ooohhhh nooohhhh" at stoplights, and the sound echoes in the canyons of warehouses and Chinatown tenements. People lean on their horns from one end of Canal Street to the other. They'll honk nonstop for ten minutes at a time, until the horns get tired and out of breath. They'll try different combinations: shave-and-a-hair-cut, long-long-long, short-short-short-long. Some people have musical car horns; a person purchasing a musical car horn seems to be limited to a choice of four tunes — "La Cucaracha," "Theme from *The Godfather*," "Dixie," and "Hava Nagila."

— IAN FRAZIER, "Canal Street"

Frazier uses metaphor, onomatopoeia, and other vivid detail.

Exercise 15.8

Turn to paragraphs 3, 7, and 10 of Saira Shah's essay, "Longing to Belong," in Chapter 2, and examine the ways in which Shah describes women's voices. What do you think these descriptions of sound contribute to the essay?

Exercise 15.9

Find a noisy spot — a restaurant, a football game, a nursery school, a laundry room — where you can perch for about half an hour. Listen attentively to the sounds of the place, and make notes about what you hear. Then write a page or so describing the place through its sounds.

The Sense of Smell

The English language has a meager stock of words to express the olfactory sense. In addition to the word *smell*, fewer than a dozen commonly used nouns name this sensation: *odor, scent, vapor, fume, aroma, fragrance, perfume, bouquet, stench, stink*. Although there are other, rarer words like *fetor* and *effluvium*, few writers use them, probably for fear that their readers will not know them. Few verbs describe receiving or sending odors — *smell, sniff, waft* — but a fair number of detailing adjectives are available: *redolent, pungent, aromatic, perfumed, stinking, musty, rancid, putrid, rank, fetid, malodorous, foul, acrid, sweet*, and *cloying*.

Here is an example of how Amanda Coyne, in her essay in Chapter 3, uses smell in a description:

Coyne uses smell to describe "convict moms" and their children in a prison visiting room.

> Occasionally, a mother will pick up her present and bring it to her nose when one of the bearers of the single flower — her child — asks if she likes it. . . . But most of what is being smelled today is the children themselves. While the other adults are plunking coins into the vending machines, the mothers take deep whiffs from the backs of their children's necks, or kiss and smell the backs of their knees, or take off their shoes and tickle their feet and then pull them close to their noses. They hold them tight and take in their own second scent — the scent assuring them that these are still their children and that they still belong to them.
>
> — AMANDA COYNE, "The Long Good-Bye: Mother's Day in Federal Prison"

In addition to using *smell* as a verb, Coyne describes the repeated action of bringing the object being smelled to the nose, an act that not only signifies the process of smelling but also underscores its intimacy. To further emphasize intimacy, Coyne connects smelling with other intimate acts of kissing, tickling, pulling close, and holding tight.

Because she is not describing her own experience of smell, Coyne does not try to find words to evoke the effect the odor has on her. In the next passage, however, Frank Conroy uses comparing in addition to naming and detailing to describe how the smell of flowers affected him:

> The perfume of the flowers rushed into my brain. A lush aroma, thick with sweetness, thick as blood, and spiced with the clear acid of tropical greenery.
>
> — FRANK CONROY, *Stop-Time*

Naming the objects from which smells come can also be very suggestive.

> The odor of these houses was different, full of fragrances, sweet and nauseating. On 105th Street the smells were of fried lard, of beans and car fumes, of factory smoke and home-made brew out of backyard stills. There were chicken smells and goat smells in grassless yards filled with engine parts and wire and wood planks, cracked and sprinkled with rusty nails. These were the familiar aromas: the funky earth, animal and mechanical smells which were absent from the homes my mother cleaned.
>
> — Luis J. Rodriguez, *Always Running: Gang Days in L.A.*

Exercise 15.10

Turn to "I'm Not Leaving Until I Eat This Thing," by John T. Edge, in Chapter 3, and read paragraph 16. Underline the words describing the sense of smell. How do you think this bit of sensory description helps readers imagine the scene?

Exercise 15.11

Choose a place with noticeable, distinctive smells where you can stay for ten or fifteen minutes. You may choose an eating place (a cafeteria, a doughnut shop), a place where something is being manufactured (a sawmill, a bakery), or some other place that has strong, identifiable odors (a fishing dock, a garden, a locker room). While you are there, take notes on what you smell, and then write a page or so describing the place primarily through its smells.

The Sense of Touch

Relatively few nouns and verbs name tactile sensations besides words like *touch, feel, tickle, brush, scratch, sting, itch,* and *tingle.* Probably as a consequence, writers describing the sense of touch tend not to name the sensation directly or even to report the act of feeling. Nevertheless, a large stock of words describes temperature (*hot, warm, mild, tepid, cold, arctic*), moisture content (*wet, dry, sticky, oily, greasy, moist, crisp*), texture (*gritty, silky, smooth, crinkled, coarse, soft, leathery*), and weight (*heavy, light, ponderous, buoyant, feathery*). Read the following passages with an eye for descriptions of touch.

> A small slab of roughly finished concrete offered a place to stand opposite a square of tar from which a splintered tee protruded.
>
> — William Rintoul, "Breaking One Hundred"

> The earth was moldy, a dense clay. No sun had fallen here for over two centuries. I climbed over the brick retaining wall and crawled toward the sound of the kitten. As I neared, as it sensed my presence was too large to be its mother, it went silent and scrabbled away from the reach of my hand. I brushed fur, though, and that slight warmth filled me with what must have been a mad calm because

when the creature squeezed into a bearing wall of piled stones, I inched forward on my stomach.

— Louise Erdrich, "Beneath the House"

Here is an example of a writer recalling a childish fantasy of aggression toward her younger sister. Notice the tactile description she uses.

She was baby-soft. I thought that I could put my thumb on her nose and push it bonelessly in, indent her face. I could poke dimples into her cheeks. I could work her face around like dough.

— Maxine Hong Kingston, "The Quiet Girl"

Exercise 15.12

Do something with your hands, and then write a sentence or two describing the experience of touch. For example, you might pet a dog, dig a hole and put a plant into the earth, make a pizza, sculpt with clay, bathe a baby, or scrub a floor. As you write, notice the words you consider using to describe temperature, moisture content, texture, weight, or any other tactile quality.

Exercise 15.13

Turn to "The Last Stop," by Brian Cable, in Chapter 3, and read the last paragraph. Underline the language that describes the sense of touch. What does this detail add to your understanding of the scene, and why might Cable have chosen to save it for the last paragraph of his profile?

The Sense of Taste

Other than *taste, savor,* and *flavor,* few words name gustatory sensations directly. Certain words do distinguish among types of tastes — *sweet (saccharine, sugary, cloying); sour (acidic, tart); bitter (acrid, biting); salty (briny, brackish)* — and several other words describe specific tastes (*piquant, spicy, pungent, peppery, savory, toothsome*).

In the following passage, M. F. K. Fisher describes the surprisingly "delicious" taste of tar:

Tar with some dust in it was perhaps even more delicious than dirty chips from the iceman's wagon, largely because if we worked up enough body heat and had the right amount of spit we could keep it melted so that it acted almost like chewing gum, which was forbidden to us as vulgar and bad for the teeth and in general to be shunned. Tar was better than anything ever put out by Wrigley and Beechnut, anyway. It had a high, bright taste. It tasted the way it smelled, but better.

— M. F. K. Fisher, "Prejudice, Hate, and the First World War"

Fisher uses suggestive words not typically associated with taste.

Fisher tries to evoke the sense of taste by comparing tar that acted like chewing gum to actual Wrigley and Beechnut chewing gum. More surprisingly, she compares the taste of tar to its smell.

Ernest Hemingway, in a more conventional passage, tries to describe taste primarily by naming the foods he consumed and giving details that indicate the intensity and quality of the tastes:

> As I ate the oysters with their strong taste of the sea and their faint metallic taste that the cold wine washed away, leaving only the sea taste and the succulent texture, and as I drank their cold liquid from each shell and washed it down with the crisp taste of the wine, I lost the empty feeling and began to be happy and to make plans.
>
> — ERNEST HEMINGWAY, *A Moveable Feast*

Hemingway combines taste and touch (the feel of the food in his mouth).

Writers often use words like *juicy, chewy,* and *chunky* to evoke both the taste and the feel of food in the mouth.

Exercise 15.14

In the manner of Hemingway, take notes as you eat a particular food or an entire meal. Then write a few sentences describing the tastes you experienced.

Exercise 15.15

Turn to John T. Edge's "I'm Not Leaving Until I Eat This Thing" in Chapter 3, an essay about pickled pig's lips. Read paragraphs 7 and 18, underlining any language that describes or suggests the sense of taste. How well does this sensory description help you participate in the writer's experience?

Creating a Dominant Impression

The most effective description creates a **dominant impression,** a mood or an atmosphere that reinforces the writer's purpose. Naming, detailing, comparing, and sensory language — all the choices about what to include and what to call things — come together to create this effect, as the following passage by Mary McCarthy illustrates. Notice that McCarthy directly states the idea she is trying to convey in the last sentence of the paragraph.

> Whenever we children came to stay at my grandmother's house, we were put to sleep in the sewing room, a bleak, shabby, utilitarian rectangle, more office than bedroom, more attic than office, that played to the hierarchy of chambers the role of a poor relation. It was a room seldom entered by the other members of the family, seldom swept by the maid, a room without pride; the old sewing machine, some cast-off chairs, a shadeless lamp, rolls of wrapping paper, piles of pins, and remnants of material united with the iron folding cots put out for our use and the bare floor boards to give an impression of intense and ruthless temporality. Thin, white spreads, of the kind used in hospitals and charity institutions, and naked

McCarthy names objects and provides details that support the overall impression she seeks to convey.

blinds at the windows reminded us of our orphaned condition and of the ephemeral character of our visit; there was nothing here to encourage us to consider this our home.

— Mary McCarthy, *Memories of a Catholic Girlhood*

Everything in the room made McCarthy and her brothers feel unwanted, discarded, orphaned. The room itself is described in terms applicable to the children: Like them, it "played to the hierarchy of chambers the role of a poor relation."

Sometimes writers comment directly in a description, as McCarthy does. Often, however, writers want description to speak for itself, as in the following example.

Orwell uses language that *shows* objects and details that convey an impression.

Hanging from the ceiling there was a heavy glass chandelier on which the dust was so thick that it was like fur. And covering most of one wall there was a huge hideous piece of junk, something between a sideboard and a hall-stand, with lots of carving and little drawers and strips of looking-glass, and there was a once-gaudy carpet ringed by the slop-pails of years, and two gilt chairs with burst seats, and one of those old-fashioned armchairs which you slide off when you try to sit on them. The room had been turned into a bedroom by thrusting four squalid beds in among the wreckage.

— George Orwell, *The Road to Wigan Pier*

Exercise 15.16

Turn to Amanda Coyne's essay in Chapter 3 and read paragraph 3. What seems to you to be the dominant impression of this description? What do you think contributes most to this impression?

Defining

Defining is an essential strategy for all writing. Autobiographers, for example, must occasionally define objects, conditions, events, and activities for readers likely to be unfamiliar with particular terms, as in the following example.

> My father's hands are grotesque. He suffers from psoriasis, a chronic skin disease that covers his massive, thick hands with scaly, reddish patches that periodically flake off, sending tiny pieces of dead skin sailing to the ground.
>
> — Jan Gray, "Father"

Gray defines *psoriasis* in this example of autobiographical writing.

When writers share information or explain how to do something, they must often define important terms for readers who are unfamiliar with the subject, as in this example.

> Shifting baselines are the chronic, slow, hard-to-notice changes in things, from the disappearance of birds and frogs in the countryside to the increased drive time from L.A. to San Diego.
>
> — Randy Olson, "Shifting Baselines: Slow-Motion Disaster below the Waves"

Olson defines *shifting baselines* in this example of explanatory writing.

To convince readers of a position or an evaluation or to move them to act on a proposal, a writer must often define concepts important to an argument.

> You would come across news of a study showing that the percentage of Wisconsin food-stamp families in "extreme poverty" — defined as less than 50 percent of the federal poverty line — has tripled in the last decade to more than 30 percent.
>
> — Barbara Ehrenreich, *Nickel and Dimed*

Ehrenreich defines *extreme poverty* in this example of argument.

As these examples illustrate, there are many kinds of definitions and many forms that they can take. Some published essays and reports are concerned primarily with the definition of a little-understood or problematic concept or thing. Usually, however, definition is only a part of an essay. A long piece of writing, like a term paper, textbook, or research report, may include many kinds of brief and extended definitions, all of them integrated with other writing strategies.

This chapter illustrates various types of sentence definitions, the most common in writing. When writers use sentence definitions, they rely on various sentence patterns to provide concise definitions. The chapter also provides illustrations of multisentence extended definitions, including definition by word history, or etymology, and by stipulation.

Sentence Definitions

Coming to a new field of study, institution, or activity for the first time, a participant is often baffled by the many unfamiliar concepts and terms. In college, introductory courses in all the academic disciplines often seem like courses in definitions of new terms. In the same way, newcomers to a sport like sailing or rock climbing often need to learn a great deal of specialized terminology. Writers of textbooks and manuals that cover such topics rely on brief **sentence definitions** to explain terms and concepts.

The following examples, from introductory college textbooks, illustrate various sentence strategies an author may use to name and define terms for readers.

The most obvious sentence strategies simply announce a definition.

> A *karyotype* is a graphic representation of a set of chromosomes.

These sentences present their definitions directly.

> Then, within the first week, the cells begin to *differentiate* — to specialize in structure and function.

> Geologists refer to the processes of mountain building as *orogenesis* (from the Greek *oro*, "mountain," and *genesis*, "birth").

> *Posthypnotic suggestions* (suggestions to be carried out after the hypnosis session has ended) have helped alleviate headaches, asthma, warts, and stress-related skin disorders.

Other strategies, signaled by subordinate clauses, are less direct but still quite apparent.

The definitions in the subordinate clauses add details, express time and cause, or indicate conditions or tentativeness.

> During the *oral stage*, which lasts throughout the first 18 months, the infant's sensual pleasures focus on sucking, biting, and chewing.

> *Hemophilia* is called the bleeder's disease because the affected person's blood does not clot.

Another common defining strategy is the appositive phrase. Here one word or phrase defines another word or phrase in a brief inserted phrase called an *appositive*.

These sentences use appositives to present either the definition or the word to be defined.

> *Taxonomy*, the science of classifying groups (taxa) of organisms in formal groups, is hierarchical.

> The actual exchange of gases takes place in small air sacs, the *alveoli*, which are clustered in branches like grapes around the ends of the smallest bronchioles.

Exercise 16.1

Look up any three of the following words or phrases in a dictionary. Define each one in a sentence. Try to use a different sentence pattern for each of your definitions.

bull market	caricature	ectomorph
carcinogen	clinometer	ecumenism

edema	mnemonic	sonnet
harangue	samba	testosterone
hyperhidrosis	seasonal affective disorder	zero-based budgeting

Exercise 16.2

Turn to the essay in Chapter 4 titled "Cannibalism: It Still Exists" by student writer Linh Kieu Ngo, and analyze the sentence definitions in paragraphs 5, 6, 7, 8, and 11. Notice the different kinds of sentence patterns Ngo relies on. (You need not be able to analyze the sentences grammatically to examine their patterns.) Keeping in mind that Ngo's purpose is to introduce readers to the concept of cannibalism and its varieties, how helpful do you find these sentence definitions? How do they work with Ngo's use of examples?

Extended Definitions

At times a writer may need to go further than a brief sentence definition and provide readers with a fuller, **extended definition**, as in the following example.

> Every day, 1.5 million temps are dispatched from agencies like Kelly Services and Manpower — nearly three times as many as 10 years ago. But they are only the most visible part of America's enormous new temporary work force. An additional 34 million people start their day as other types of "contingent" workers. Some are part-timers with some benefits. Others work by the hour, the day or the duration of a project, receiving only a paycheck without benefits of any kind. The rules of their employment vary widely and so do the attempts to label them. They are called short-timers, per-diem workers, leased employees, extra workers, supplementals, contractors — or in IBM's ironic computer-generated parlance, "the peripherals." They are what you might expect: secretaries, security guards, salesclerks, assembly-line workers, analysts and CAD/CAM designers. But these days they are also what you'd never expect: doctors, high school principals, lawyers, bank officers, X-ray technicians, biochemists, engineers, managers — even chief executives.
>
> — JANICE CASTRO, "Contingent Workers"

Castro provides an extended definition of the term *contingent worker*.

Castro begins by comparing contingent workers to the more familiar temporary workers ("temps") managed by temporary employment agencies. Then she gives examples of contingent workers' working arrangements and lists many names by which these workers are known. Finally, she identifies the various categories of contingent workers. These strategies — comparisons, examples, synonyms, and classification — are often found in extended definitions and in fact in all kinds of explanatory writing. Castro never concisely defines the word *contingent* in the phrase "contingent worker" because she assumes that readers can infer that it means roughly the opposite of permanent, continuing worker.

In this next example, Marie Winn offers an extended definition of television addiction. Like Janice Castro, Winn begins with a comparison. These two experienced writers know that comparison or contrast is often the most effective way to present an unfamiliar term or concept to readers. The key is to know your readers well enough to find a term nearly all of them will know to compare to the unfamiliar term.

> People often refer to being "hooked on TV." Does this, too, fall into the lighthearted category of cookie eating and other pleasures that people pursue with unusual intensity, or is there a kind of televison viewing that falls into the more serious category of destructive addiction? . . .

In Winn's extended definition of *TV addiction,* she compares her subject to drug and alcohol addiction, describes its effects on addicts, and speculates on why breaking the addiction is so difficult.

> Let us consider television viewing in the light of the conditions that define serious addictions.
>
> Not unlike drugs or alcohol, the television experience allows the participant to blot out the real world and enter into a pleasurable and passive mental state. The worries and anxieties of reality are as effectively deferred by becoming absorbed in a television program as by going on a "trip" induced by drugs or alcohol. And just as alcoholics are only inchoately aware of their addiction, feeling that they control their drinking more than they really do ("I can cut it out any time I want — I just like to have three or four drinks before dinner"), people similarly overestimate their control over television watching. Even as they put off other activities to spend hour after hour watching television, they feel they could easily resume living in a different, less passive style. But somehow or other while the television set is present in their homes, the click doesn't sound. With television pleasures available, those other experiences seem less attractive, more difficult somehow. . . .
>
> The self-confessed television addict often feels he "ought" to do other things — but the fact that he doesn't read and doesn't plant his garden or sew or crochet or play games or have conversations means that those activities are no longer as desirable as television viewing. In a way a heavy viewer's life is as imbalanced by his television "habit" as a drug addict's or an alcoholic's. He is living in a holding pattern, as it were, passing up the activities that lead to growth or development or a sense of accomplishment. This is one reason people talk about their television viewing so ruefully, so apologetically. They are aware that it is an unproductive experience, that almost any other endeavor is more worthwhile by any human measure.
>
> Finally, it is the adverse effect of television viewing on the lives of so many people that defines it as a serious addiction. The television habit distorts the sense of time. It renders other experiences vague and curiously unreal while taking on a greater reality for itself. It weakens relationships by reducing and sometimes eliminating normal opportunities for talking, for communicating.
>
> And yet television does not satisfy, else why would the viewer continue to watch hour after hour, day after day? "The measure of health," writes Lawrence Kubie, "is flexibility . . . and especially the freedom to cease when sated." But the television viewer can never be sated with his television experiences — they do not provide the true nourishment that satiation requires — and thus he finds that he cannot stop watching.
>
> — MARIE WINN, "TV Addiction"

Extended definitions may also include *negative definitions* — explanations of what the thing being defined is *not:*

It's important to be clear about the reverse definition, as well: what dinosaurs are not. Dinosaurs are not lizards, and vice versa. Lizards are scaly reptiles of an ancient bloodline. The oldest lizards antedate the earliest dinosaurs by a full thirty million years. A few large lizards, such as the man-eating Komodo dragon, have been called "relics of the dinosaur age," but this phrase is historically incorrect. No lizard ever evolved the birdlike characteristics peculiar to each and every dinosaur. A big lizard never resembled a small dinosaur except for a few inconsequential details of the teeth. Lizards never walked with the erect, long-striding gait that distinguishes the dinosaur like ground birds today or the birdlike dinosaurs of the Mesozoic.

— ROBERT T. BAKKER, *The Dinosaur Heresies*

> Bakker uses a negative definition, explaining that *dinosaurs* are not lizards.

Exercise 16.3

Choose one term that names some concept or feature of central importance in an activity or a subject you know well. For example, if you are studying biology, you have probably encountered terms like *morphogenesis* and *ecosystem*. Choose a word with a well-established definition. Write an extended definition of several sentences for this important term. Write for readers your own age who will be encountering the term for the first time when they read your definition.

Exercise 16.4

In his essay in Chapter 4, Richard A. Friedman presents an extended definition. After reading his essay, how would you define *hyperthymia*? Reread the first five paragraphs of the essay to see which strategies he uses to define the term.

Historical Definitions

Occasionally, a writer will provide a **historical definition**, tracing the evolution of a term from its first use to its adoption into other languages to its shifting meanings over the centuries. Such a strategy can be a rich addition to an essay, bringing surprising depth and resonance to the definition of a concept.

In this example, from a special issue of *Time* magazine on the future uses of cyberspace and its potential impact on the economy, Philip Elmer-DeWitt provides a historical definition of the term *cyberspace.*

It started, as the big ideas in technology often do, with a science-fiction writer. William Gibson, a young expatriate American living in Canada, was wandering past the video arcades on Vancouver's Granville Street in the early 1980s when something about the way the players were hunched over their glowing screens struck him as odd. "I could see in the physical intensity of their postures how *rapt* the kids were," he says. "It was like a feedback loop, with photons coming off the screens into the kids' eyes, neurons moving through their bodies and electrons moving through the video game. These kids clearly *believed* in the space the games projected."

That image haunted Gibson. He didn't know much about video games or computers — he wrote his breakthrough novel *Neuromancer* (1984) on an ancient manual typewriter — but he knew people who did. And as near as he could tell, everybody who worked much with the machines eventually came to accept, almost as an article of faith, the reality of that imaginary realm. "They develop a belief that there's some kind of *actual space* behind the screen," he says. "Some place that you can't see but you know is there."

Gibson called that place "cyberspace," and used it as the setting for his early novels and short stories. In his fiction, cyberspace is a computer-generated landscape that characters enter by "jacking in" — sometimes by plugging electrodes directly into sockets implanted in the brain. What they see when they get there is a three-dimensional representation of all the information stored in "every computer in the human system" — great warehouses and skyscrapers of data. He describes it in a key passage in *Neuromancer* as a place of "unthinkable complexity," with "lines of light ranged in the nonspace of the mind, clusters and constellations of data. Like city lights, receding. . . ."

In the years since, there have been other names given to that shadowy space where our computer data reside: the Net, the Web, the Cloud, the Matrix, the Metaverse, the Datasphere, the Electronic Frontier, the information superhighway. But Gibson's coinage may prove the most enduring. By 1989 it had been borrowed by the online community to describe not some science-fiction fantasy but today's increasingly interconnected computer systems — especially the millions of computers jacked into the Internet.

— Philip Elmer-DeWitt, "Welcome to Cyberspace"

The historical definition serves Elmer-DeWitt's larger purpose in writing this essay: to help readers acquire a deeper understanding of the new technologies that continue to profoundly affect the ways in which we live our lives.

Exercise 16.5

You can consult a historical, or etymological, dictionary, such as the *Oxford English Dictionary, A Dictionary of American English,* or *A Dictionary of Americanisms,* to trace changes in the use of a word over long periods of time or to survey different theories of a word or phrase's origins. Online you can search the *Phrase Finder,* the *Urban Dictionary,* or just Google the word or phrase plus definition. Look up the historical definition of any one of the following words or a word or phrase you're curious about in one or more sources, and write several sentences on its roots and development.

bedrock	eye-opener	lobbying	rubberneck
bogus	filibuster	lynching	sashay
bushwhack	gerrymander	pep	23 skidoo
dugout	head over heels	podunk	two-bit

Stipulative Definitions

To stipulate means to seek or assert agreement on something. In a **stipulative definition**, the writer declares a certain meaning, generally not one found in the dictionary.

In her autobiography, Annie Dillard defines *football* as she understood it as a nine-year-old.

> Some boys taught me to play football. This was fine sport. You thought up a new strategy for every play and whispered it to the others. You went out for a pass, fooling everyone. Best, you got to throw yourself mightily at someone's running legs. Either you brought him down or you hit the ground flat out on your chin, with your arms empty before you. It was all or nothing. If you hesitated in fear, you would miss and get hurt: you would take a hard fall while the kid got away, or you would get kicked in the face while the kid got away. But if you flung yourself wholeheartedly at the back of his knees — if you gathered and joined body and soul and pointed them diving fearlessly — then you likely wouldn't get hurt, and you'd stop the ball. Your fate, and your team's score, depended on your concentration and courage. Nothing girls did could compare with it.
>
> — Annie Dillard, *An American Childhood*

Dillard provides a stipulative definition of *football* as she understood it when she was nine years old.

For Dillard's complete essay, see Chapter 2.

There are recognizable elements of grown-up football in Dillard's definition. Her focus is less on rules and strategy, however, than on the "concentration and courage" required to make a successful tackle and, of course, on the sheer thrill of doing it.

This next example illustrates how a newspaper columnist might create a stipulative definition of a term to support an argument.

> Ozone depletion and the greenhouse effect are human disasters. They happen to occur in the environment. But they are urgent because they directly threaten man. A sane environmentalism, the only kind of environmentalism that will win universal public support, begins by unashamedly declaring that nature is here to serve man. A sane environmentalism is entirely anthropocentric: it enjoins man to preserve nature, but on the grounds of self-preservation.
>
> A sane environmentalism does not sentimentalize the earth. It does not ask people to sacrifice in the name of other creatures. After all, it is hard enough to ask people to sacrifice in the name of other humans. (Think of the chronic public resistance to foreign aid and welfare.) Ask hardworking voters to sacrifice in the name of the snail darter, and, if they are feeling polite, they will give you a shrug.
>
> — Charles Krauthammer, "Saving Nature, but Only for Man"

Krauthammer uses his stipulative definition of *environmentalism* to argue for a more realistic approach to protecting the environment.

Exercise 16.6

Look at Karen Kornbluh's essay "Win-Win Flexibility" in Chapter 7. Kornbluh begins the argument with contrasting stipulative definitions of the "traditional" family and the "juggler" family. What is her stipulative definition of each type of family? How does she use these definitions to support her overall argument?

Exercise 16.7

Write several sentences of a stipulative definition for one of the following.

1. Define in your own way game shows, soap operas, police dramas, horror movies, or some other form of entertainment. Try for a stipulative definition of what your subject is generally like. In effect, you will be saying to your readers — other students in your class who are familiar with these entertainments — "Let's define it this way for now."

2. Define in your own way some hard-to-define concept, such as "loyalty," "love," "bravery," "shyness," or "masculinity."

3. Think of a new development or phenomenon in contemporary romance, music, television, leisure, fashion, or eating habits, or in your line of work. Invent a name for it, and write a stipulative definition for it.

17

Classifying

Classifying is an essential writing strategy for thinking about and organizing ideas, information, and experience. The process of classifying involves either grouping or dividing. Writers group related items (such as *apples, oranges, bananas, strawberries, cantaloupes,* and *cherries*) and label the general class of items they grouped together (*fruit*). Or they begin classifying with a general class (such as *fruit*) and then divide it into subclasses of particular types (*apples, oranges,* etc.).

This chapter shows how you can organize and illustrate a classification you have read about or constructed yourself.

Organizing Classification

Classifying in writing serves primarily as a means of **organization**, of creating a framework for the presentation of information, whether in a few paragraphs of an essay or in an entire book. This section surveys several examples of classifying, ranging from a simple two-level classification to a complex multilevel system.

The simplest classification divides a general topic into two subtopics. Here is an example by Edward J. Loughram from a proposal to keep at-risk teenagers out of jail and help them lead productive lives. Before he can present his proposed solution, Loughram has to get readers to see that all juvenile offenders are not the same. He does this by explaining that although statistics show that the number of juvenile offenders is rising, they do not take into account the fact that there are two distinct groups of young people getting into trouble. He classifies juvenile offenders into these two categories to argue that the problem of delinquency can be solved, at least in part, by interrupting the criminal paths of the second group.

> Two primary factors explain the growing numbers of juvenile offenders. First, there is indeed a rise in serious crime among young people, fueled by the steady stream of drugs and weapons into their hands. These dangerous offenders are committed — legitimately — to juvenile-correction agencies for long-term custody or treatment.
>
> But a second, larger group is also contributing to the increase. It consists of 11-, 12-, and 13-year-old first-time offenders who have failed at home, failed in school, and fallen through the cracks of state and community social-service

Loughram's two categories show that the basis for his classification is the seriousness of the crimes.

647

agencies. These are not serious offenders, or even typical delinquents. But they are coming into the correctional system because we have ignored the warning signs among them.

— EDWARD J. LOUGHRAM, "Prevention of Delinquency"

From Loughram's essay, we see how a writer can use a simple two-category classification to advance an argument. The next example, excerpted from a concept explanation essay by Janice Castro, presents a somewhat more complicated classification system:

Every day, 1.5 million temps are dispatched from agencies like Kelly Services and Manpower — nearly three times as many as 10 years ago. But they are only the most visible part of America's enormous new temporary work force. An additional 34 million people start their day as other types of "contingent" workers. Some are part-timers with some benefits. Others work by the hour, the day or the duration of a project, receiving only a paycheck without benefits of any kind. The rules of their employment vary widely and so do the attempts to label them. They are called short-timers, per-diem workers, leased employees, extra workers, supplementals, contractors — or in IBM's ironic computer-generated parlance, "the peripherals." They are what you might expect: secretaries, security guards, salesclerks, assembly-line workers, analysts and CAD/CAM designers. But these days they are also what you'd never expect: doctors, high school principals, lawyers, bank officers, X-ray technicians, biochemists, engineers, managers — even chief executives. . . .

Already the temping phenomenon is producing two vastly different classes of untethered workers: the mercenary work force at the top of the skills ladder, who thrive; and the rest, many of whom, unable to attract fat contract fees, must struggle to survive.

— JANICE CASTRO, "Contingent Workers"

> Castro classifies contingent workers into two categories: the well-paid and the low-paid.

Although Castro only indirectly labels these two types of contingent workers, we can see that her basis for differentiating between these two groups is the amount of money they are paid. So far, Castro's is a simple two-part classification system like Loughram's. It has two levels: the general class of contingent workers and two subclasses of well-paid and low-paid contingent workers. Castro, however, adds a third level to her classification by listing several types of jobs that fall under her two subclasses. Here is a tree diagram that graphically displays Castro's three-level classification:

Later in the essay, Castro identifies another class of workers who are not contingent workers but are "a permanent cadre of 'core workers.'" To add this class of core workers to the tree diagram, we should also add a new general class at the top that includes all of the subclasses below it. We could label this most general class "corporate workers." Here is what the expanded tree diagram would look like:

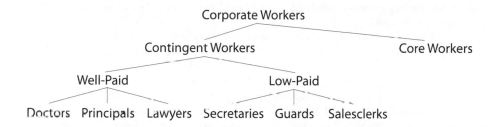

What the tree diagrams show at a glance is that in a classification system, some categories are on the same level, or *coordinate*. Some are on a higher level, or *superordinate*. And some are on a lower level, or *subordinate*. The highest level represents the most general category, and each lower level identifies increasingly specific types. If Castro took her classification to the most specific level, she would name individuals as examples of workers in each type of job.

Exercise 17.1

Turn to the concept explanation in Chapter 4, "Cannibalism: It Still Exists," and make a tree diagram of the classification in paragraphs 5–12. What do you think is Linh Kieu Ngo's basis for classification? Does each item seem to be placed in an appropriate category and on the proper level?

Exercise 17.2

Review the essays you have written so far for this class or for another class, looking for an essay in which you used classifying. What was the purpose of your essay and your basis for classifying? Construct a tree diagram of your classification to see whether each item can be placed in an appropriate category and on the proper level.

Illustrating Classification

We used tree diagrams as an **illustration** of the categories and levels of Castro's classification of workers. Writers, however, sometimes integrate graphics into their own writing to make their classification easy for readers to see at a glance.

Here is an example from *Newsweek* magazine in which Sharon Begley and Martha Brant explain the problem of drug abuse by Olympic athletes.

If doping is, as [the head of IOC's Medical Commission Prince Alexandre] de Merode noticed, suddenly "an important problem," it is partly because the newest doping agents pose the risk of serious health problems, and even death. But the larger reason is that it is ridiculously easy to dope and not get caught. Doping and detection are like an arms race. First, trainers discover a performance-enhancing drug. Then, sports officials develop a test for it. Trainers retaliate by inventing a way to elude the detectors. So far, doping has stayed a lap ahead. "Undetectable drugs are 90 percent of estimated doping cases," says Hein Verbruggen, head of international cycling.

Czech tennis pro Petr Korda tested positive for the steroid nandrolone after the Wimbledon quarterfinals last May, for instance. (Protesting that he did not know how the chemicals got into his system, he avoided the one-year suspension the International Tennis Association is supposed to impose.) But American pro Jim Courier charged that steroids are far from the worst abuse in tennis. " EPO is the problem," Courier told *Newsweek*. "I have pretty strong suspicions that guys are using it on the tour. I see guys who are out there week in and week out without taking rests. EPO can help you when it's the fifth set and you've been playing for four-and-a-half hours." Although the endurance-building effects of EPO last for about two weeks, its use can't be detected in urine at all or in blood for more than a day or so after the athlete stops taking it.

EPO is only one weapon in a pharmaceutical arsenal of performance-enhancing substances flowing through sports. Stimulants like amphetamines, ephedrine and caffeine were the first substances to land on the IOC's list of banned agents, and they're still popular. They provide a quick pop of energy, and so are a favorite of sprinters, cyclists and swimmers. They are an ingredient of many asthma medications. Exercise-induced asthma has inexplicably stricken many Olympians, including 60 percent of the U.S. team in 1994, and medical use of stimulant inhalants is allowed. Are stimulants detectable? Sure, if your trainer's IQ matches his hat size. They clear the urine in hours, so all an athlete has to do is not take them too close to her event. If you've been using too soon before your race, there are always "masking agents." Probenecid, for one, inhibits substances from reaching the urine. And urine tests are all the IOC requires: blood tests, which can detect more substances, are deemed too invasive.

Anabolic steroids, almost all of them derivatives of the hormone testosterone, are the mothers of all doping agents. They build muscles. By most estimates, an athlete can improve strength at least 5 percent by taking steroids either orally or through injection during high-intensity training. Drug-detection machines, such as the high-resolution mass spectrometer used at the Atlanta Games in 1996, can be tuned to detect any synthetic steroid; the Atlanta lab tested for 100 different types. But the Dr. Feelgoods of sport can tinker with the molecular structure of common steroids, so they slip through. "There are 72 banned steroids," says one American coach who says he developed drug regimes for athletes in Atlanta, "but the testosterone molecule is changeable in millions of ways. All you have to do is make a steroid not on the list." Or, simply by going cold turkey a few weeks before competition, an athlete can get the muscle-bulking effects without getting caught. If that seems too chancy, athletes can use a diuretic. These drugs, which are also banned, dilute the urine. That makes illicit substances virtually undetectable.

More and more athletes are turning to the source of all steroids: testosterone itself. Natural levels vary, so sports federations and the IOC try to detect doping indirectly. They measure the relative amounts of testosterone and another natural

Begley and Brant classify performance-enhancing drugs into five categories and explain what each type of drug does, how detectable it is, and what its health risks are.

Drug	What Does It Do?	Masking/Detection	Risks
Human growth hormone (hGH)	Stimulates the intracellular breakdown of body fat, allowing more to be used for energy.	This is a natural hormone, so added amounts don't show up in blood or urine tests.	Muscle and bone disfigurement — jutting forehead, elongated jaw. Also: heart and metabolic problems.
Erythropoietin (EPO)	Increases the number of red blood cells without having to "dope" using one's own blood.	It's extremely difficult to detect because the extra blood cells are the athlete's own.	Extra cells can make blood the consistency of yogurt. This can lead to a clot, heart attack or stroke.
Testosterone	Used to build muscles. It lets the body recover quickly from strenuous exercise.	Rules allow up to five times the natural body level, giving athletes latitude.	Unnatural levels can cause heart disease, liver cancer and impotence.
Steroids/ androstenedione	Anabolic steroids are incarnations of testosterone; androstenedione is a precursor molecule.	Water-based steroids (most common) are undetectable in urine after several weeks.	Synthetic testosterone carries the same risks as naturally occurring testosterone.
Stimulants	The first category that the IOC tested for. They delay the symptoms of fatigue.	Stimulants such as amphetamines can be detected; diuretics can dilute them in urine.	Fatigue is the body saying "stop" — overriding that message can be dangerous.

steroid called epitestosterone. In most people, testosterone levels are no more than twice epi levels. But to allow for individual variation, the IOC set the prohibited level at anything over 6 to 1. That means an athlete can dope himself up to, say, five times his normal testosterone levels, and get away with it. How much of an edge would that provide? A male athlete with a typical testosterone/epitestosterone ratio of 1.3 to 1 could boost that to 6 to 1, stay within the IOC limit and improve his performance at least 10 percent. Women, with a natural ratio of 2.5 to 1, could do even better, since they have less testosterone to begin with and so are more sensitive to added amounts. Testosterone can give women beards, deep voices and tough skin. It can make men's breasts swell and testicles shrivel.

The doping agents of choice today are substances that cannot be detected in urine: EPO and human growth hormone. Even though the performance-enhancing effects of hGH are unproved, many athletes believe it boosts energy. (Athletes dubbed the Atlanta Olympics "The Growth Hormone Games.") hGH can also cause grotesque skeletal deformations by stimulating abnormal bone growth. EPO, by increasing the production of red blood cells up to tenfold, can turn blood the consistency of yogurt, making it too thick to flow freely. The misuse of EPO has apparently killed at least 18 Dutch and Belgian cyclists since 1987.

— SHARON BEGLEY AND MARTHA BRANT, "The Real Scandal"

The essay's organizational plan is illustrated in the chart; the chart sometimes repeats information in the text but more often complements or adds to the text.

For more information on designing documents with graphics, see Chapter 21.

Maintaining Clarity and Coherence

The next example illustrates how writers can help readers follow a classification system by maintaining **clarity** and **coherence** — even when the subject is new and difficult. The passage comes from a book on physics by Gary Zukav. He uses classifying to explain the concept of mass. Simply defined, mass in physics is a measure of the matter in an object.

Zukav explains the concept of mass by classifying it into two types, gravitational and inertial, and provides cues to help readers understand the classification.

There are two kinds of mass, which means that there are two ways of talking about it. The first is gravitational mass. The gravitational mass of an object, roughly speaking, is the weight of the object as measured on a balance scale. Something that weighs three times more than another object has three times more mass. Gravitational mass is the measure of how much force the gravity of the earth exerts on an object. Newton's laws describe the effects of this force, which vary with the distance of the mass from the earth. . . .

The second type of mass is inertial mass. Inertial mass is the measure of the resistance of an object to acceleration (or deceleration, which is negative acceleration). For example, it takes three times more force to move three railroad cars from a standstill to twenty miles per hour (positive acceleration) than it takes to move one railroad car from a standstill to twenty miles per hour. . . . Similarly, once they are moving, it takes three times more force to stop three cars than it takes to stop the single car. This is because the inertial mass of the three railroad cars is three times more than the inertial mass of the single railroad car.

— GARY ZUKAV, *The Dancing Wu Li Masters: An Overview of the New Physics*

From this passage, we can see some of the cues writers use to make a classification clear and coherent. Zukav begins by forecasting the classification he will develop (*There are two kinds of mass*). He then introduces each category in its own paragraph, announced with the transition (*first* and *second*) and presented in the same sentence pattern (*The first is . . .* and *The second type of mass is . . .*). Careful cueing like this can help make a classification clear to readers.

Exercise 17.3

Look back at the paragraphs from Linh Kieu Ngo's essay on cannibalism that you used to make a tree diagram in Exercise 17.1 or at the example by Begley and Brant earlier in this chapter to examine the strategies these authors use to make their classifications clear and coherent. Notice how each category is introduced and the transitions are used to help readers keep track of the categories. What conclusions can you draw about how writers maintain clarity and coherence from your analysis?

Exercise 17.4

General strategies for coherence are discussed in Chapter 13.

Look back at the classification you examined in Exercise 17.2 to see how well you were able to maintain clarity and coherence in your classification. What changes would you make, if any, to improve clarity and coherence?

Comparing and Contrasting

18

Most of us compare things all the time, at work, in school, and in everyday life. You might compare two people you know well, two motorcycles you are considering buying for a cross-country tour, three Stephen King novels, four tomato plants being grown under different laboratory conditions, or two theories about the relationship between inflation and wages. But as soon as you begin to compare two things, you usually begin to contrast them as well, for rarely are two things alike in all respects. The contrasts, or differences, between the two motorcycles are likely to be more enlightening than the similarities, many of which may be so obvious as to need no analysis. **Comparison**, then, brings similar things together for examination, to see how they are alike. **Contrast** is a form of comparison that emphasizes differences. According to research on learning, we acquire new concepts most readily if we can see how they are similar to or different from concepts we already know.

Professional writers say that comparison and contrast is a basic strategy they would not want to be without. Indeed, some writing is essentially extended comparison. But for all kinds of writing situations, writers regularly alternate comparison and contrast with other writing strategies when they present information.

Chances are that you will confront many test questions and essay assignments asking you to compare and contrast — two poems, three presidents, four procedures. This strategy is popular in all academic disciplines, for it is one of the best ways to challenge students intellectually.

Two Ways of Comparing and Contrasting

There are two ways to organize comparison and contrast in writing: in chunks and in sequence. In **chunking**, each object of the comparison is presented separately; in sequencing, the items are compared point by point. For example, a chunked comparison of two motorcycles would first detail all pertinent features of the Pirsig Z-1700 XL and then consider all features of the Kawazuki 1750XL, whereas a **sequenced comparison** would analyze the Pirsig and the Kawazuki feature by feature. In a chunked comparison, the discussion is organized around each separate item being compared. In a sequenced comparison, it is organized around characteristics of the items being compared.

In the following example of chunked comparison, Jane Tompkins contrasts popular nineteenth-century "sentimental" novels with the "Western" novels that provided a reaction against them:

> The female, domestic, "sentimental" religion of the best-selling women writers — Harriet Beecher Stowe, Susan Warner, Maria Cummins, and dozens of others — whose novels spoke to the deepest beliefs and highest ideals of middle-class America, is the real antagonist of the Western.
>
> You can see this simply by comparing the main features of the Western with the sentimental novel. In these books . . . a woman is always the main character, usually a young orphan girl, with several other main characters being women too. Most of the action takes place in private spaces, at home, indoors, in kitchens, parlors, and upstairs chambers. And most of it concerns the interior struggles of the heroine to live up to an ideal of Christian virtue — usually involving uncomplaining submission to difficult and painful circumstances, learning to quell rebellious instincts, and dedicating her life to the service of God through serving others. In these struggles, women give one another a great deal of emotional and material support, and they have close relationships verging on what today we would identify as homosocial and homoerotic. There's a great deal of Bible reading, praying, hymn singing, and drinking of tea. Emotions other than anger are expressed very freely and openly. Often there are long, drawn-out death scenes in which a saintly woman dies a natural death at home. . . .
>
> The elements of the typical Western plot arrange themselves in stark opposition to this pattern, not just vaguely and generally but point for point. First of all, in Westerns (which are generally written by men), the main character is always a full-grown adult male, and almost all of the other characters are men. The action takes place either outdoors — on the prairie, on the main street — or in public places — the saloon, the sheriff's office, the barber shop, the livery stable. The action concerns physical struggles between the hero and a rival or rivals, and culminates in a fight to the death with guns. In the course of these struggles the hero frequently forms a bond with another man — sometimes his rival, more often a comrade — a bond that is more important than any relation he has with a woman and is frequently tinged with homoeroticism. There is very little free expression of the emotions. The hero is a man of few words who expresses himself through physical action — usually fighting. And when death occurs it is never at home in bed but always sudden death, usually murder.

> — JANE TOMPKINS, *West of Everything: The Inner Life of Westerns*

Schematically, a chunked comparison looks simple enough. As the preceding example shows, it is easy to block off such a discussion in a text and then provide a clean transition between the various parts. And yet it can in fact be more complicated for a writer to plan than a sequenced comparison. Sequenced comparison may be closer to the way people perceive and think about similarities or differences in things. For example, you may have realized all at once that two navy blazers are different, but you would identify the specific differences — buttons, tailoring, fabric — one at a time. A sequenced comparison would point to the differences in just this way, one at a time, whereas a chunked comparison would present all the features of one blazer and then do the same for the second. A writer using the

Tompkins discusses sentimental novels and Westerns separately, presenting each point of contrast for the two subjects in the same order (chunking).

Tompkins signals the shift from one subject to the other with a transition sentence at the start of the third paragraph.

chunked strategy, then, must organize all the points of comparison before starting to write and then be sure that the points of comparison are presented in the same order in the discussion of each item being compared. With sequencing, however, the writer can take up each point of comparison as it comes to mind.

In the next example, from a natural history of the earth, David Attenborough uses sequencing to contrast bird wings and airplane wings:

> Bird wings have a much more complex job to do than the wings of an aeroplane, for in addition to supporting the bird they must act as its engine, rowing it through the air. Even so the wing outline of a bird conforms to the same aerodynamic principles as those eventually discovered by man when designing his aeroplanes, and if you know how different kinds of aircraft perform, you can predict the flight capabilities of similarly shaped birds.
>
> Short stubby wings enable a tanager and other forest-living birds to swerve and dodge at speed through the undergrowth just as they helped the fighter planes of the Second World War to make tight turns and aerobatic manoeuvres in a dogfight. More modern fighters achieve greater speeds by sweeping back their wings while in flight, just as peregrines do when they go into a 130 kph dive, stooping to a kill. Championship gliders have long thin wings so that, having gained height in a thermal up-current, they can soar gently down for hours and an albatross, the largest of flying birds, with a similar wing shape and a span of 3 metres, can patrol the ocean for hours in the same way without a single wing beat. Vultures and hawks circle at very slow speeds supported by a thermal and they have the broad rectangular wings that very slow flying aircraft have. Man has not been able to adapt wings to provide hovering flight. He has only achieved that with the whirling horizontal blades of a helicopter or the downward-pointing engines of a vertical landing jet. Hummingbirds have paralleled even this. They tilt their bodies so that they are almost upright and then beat their wings as fast as 80 times a second producing a similar down-draught of air. So the hummingbird can hover and even fly backwards.
>
> — DAVID ATTENBOROUGH, *Life on Earth*

Attenborough finds a valid — and fascinating — basis for comparison between birds and airplanes and develops it in a way that both informs and entertains his readers. A successful comparison always has these qualities: a valid basis for comparison, a limited focus, and information that will catch a reader's attention.

Attenborough uses a limited, focused basis for the comparison of bird wings and airplane wings: their shape.

Exercise 18.1

Identify the specific items contrasted in the passage comparing sentimental novels and Westerns. Number in sequence each contrast, and underline both parts of the contrast. To get started, in the paragraph about sentimental novels, underline "a woman is always the main character, usually a young orphan girl," and number it "1" in the margin. In the paragraph about Westerns, underline "the main character is always a full-grown adult male," and number this "1" also to complete your identification of both parts of the comparison. Then look for contrast 2 and underline and number the contrasted items, and so on.

Look over your work and consider the pattern of these contrasts. Were they easy to identify? If so, what made them easy to identify? Was any contrast left incomplete? In general, how successful and informative do you find this set of contrasts?

Exercise 18.2

Identify the specific items compared in the passage comparing bird wings and aircraft wings. Underline both items, and number the pair in the margin. To get started, underline *tanager* and *fighter planes* in the first sentence of the second paragraph. In the margin, number this pair "1." Then identify pair 2 and so on.

Consider the pattern and ordering of the comparisons you have identified. Were the pairs of items easy to identify? If so, what made them easy to identify? Some comparisons begin by naming a bird, some by identifying a category of aircraft. Did this lack of predictability present problems for you? Do you see any possible justification for the writer's having given up the predictability of always beginning each comparison with either a bird or an aircraft? In general, how successful and informative did you find this comparison?

Exercise 18.3

Write a page or so comparing or contrasting any one of the following subjects. Be careful to limit the basis for your comparison, and underline the sentence that states that basis. Use chunking or sequencing to organize the comparison.

> Two ways of achieving the same goal (for example, traveling by bus or subway or using flattery or persuasion to get what you want)
>
> A good and bad job interview or date
>
> Your relationship with two friends or relatives
>
> Two or more forms of music, dance, film, or computer software
>
> Two methods of doing some task at home or on the job

Exercise 18.4

Read closely the specified comparisons in the following essays from Part One. How is each comparison organized? (It may or may not be neatly chunked or sequenced.) Why do you think the writer organizes the comparison in that way? What is the role of the comparison in the whole essay? How effective is it?

> "Love: The Right Chemistry," paragraph 14 (Chapter 4)
>
> "Born to Be Happy," paragraphs 5–6 (Chapter 4)
>
> "The Gorge-Yourself Environment," paragraph 14 (Chapter 9)

Analogy

An **analogy** is a special form of comparison in which one part of the comparison is used simply to explain the other, as in the following example.

> In like manner, geologists will sometimes use the calendar year as a unit to represent the time scale, and in such terms the Precambrian runs from New Year's Day until well after Halloween. Dinosaurs appear in the middle of December and are gone the day after Christmas. The last ice sheet melts on December 31st at one minute before midnight, and the Roman Empire lasts five seconds. With your arms spread wide . . . to represent all time on earth, look at one hand with its line of life. The Cambrian begins in the wrist, and the Permian Extinction is at the outer end of the palm. All of the Cenozoic is in a fingerprint, and in a single stroke with a medium-grained nail file you could eradicate human history. Geologists live with the geologic scale. Individually, they may or may not be alarmed by the rate of exploitation of the things they discover, but, like the environmentalists, they use these repetitive analogies to place the human record in perspective — to see the Age of Reflection, the last few thousand years, as a small bright sparkle at the end of time.
>
> — John McPhee, *Basin and Range*

McPhee uses two analogies — the 12-month calendar and the distance along two widespread arms — to explain the duration of geologic time.

Analogies are not limited to abstract, scientific concepts. Writers often use analogies to make nontechnical descriptions and explanations more vivid or to make an imaginative point of comparison that serves a larger argument. Consider the following example.

> But now that government has largely withdrawn its "handouts" [to the welfare poor], now that the overwhelming majority of the poor are out there toiling in Wal-Mart or Wendy's — well, what are we to think of them? Disapproval and condescension no longer apply, so what outlook makes sense?
>
> Guilt, you may be thinking warily. Isn't that what we're supposed to feel? But guilt doesn't go anywhere near far enough; the appropriate emotion is shame — shame at our own dependency, in this case, on the underpaid labor of others. When someone works for less pay than she can live on — when, for example, she goes hungry so that you can eat more cheaply and conveniently — then she has made a great sacrifice for you, she has made you a gift of some part of her abilities, her health, and her life. The "working poor," as they are approvingly termed, are in fact the major philanthropists of our society. They neglect their own children so that the children of others will be cared for; they live in substandard housing so that other homes will be shiny and perfect; they endure privation so that inflation will be low and stock prices high. To be a member of the working poor is to be an anonymous donor, a nameless benefactor, to everyone else. As Gail, one of my restaurant coworkers put it, "you give and you give."
>
> — Barbara Ehrenreich, *Nickel and Dimed*

Ehrenreich suggests, by analogy, that the working poor in the United States are among society's "major philanthropists."

Analogies are tricky. They can be useful, but analogies rarely are consistently accurate at all major points of comparison. For example, in the preceding analogy, the working poor can be seen as philanthropists in the sense that they have "made a great sacrifice" but not in the sense that they are selflessly sharing their wealth. Analogies can powerfully bring home a point, but skilled writers use them with caution.

Nevertheless, you will run across analogies regularly; indeed, it would be hard to find a book without at least one. For abstract information and in certain writing situations, analogy is often the writing strategy of choice.

Exercise 18.5

Write a one-paragraph analogy that explains a principle or process to a reader who is unfamiliar with it. Choose a principle or process that you know well. You might select a basic principle from the natural or social sciences, like dark matter or ethnocentrism; or you could consider a bodily movement, like running; a physiological process, like digestion; or a process from your job, like assembling a product. Look for something very familiar to compare it with that will help the reader understand the principle or process without a technical explanation.

Arguing

19

This chapter presents the basic strategies for making arguments in writing. In it, we focus on asserting a thesis, backing it up with reasons and support, and anticipating readers' questions and objections.

Asserting a Thesis

Central to any argument is the **thesis**. In a sentence or two, a thesis asserts or states the main point of any argument you want to make. It can be assertive only if you make it clear and direct. The thesis statement usually appears at the beginning of an argument essay.

There are five kinds of argument essays in Part One of this book. Each of these essays requires a special kind of assertion and reasoning:

- ***Assertion of opinion:*** What is your position on a controversial issue? (Chapter 6, "Arguing a Position")

  When overzealous parents and coaches impose adult standards on children's sports, the result can be activities that are neither satisfying nor beneficial to children.

  — JESSICA STATSKY, "Children Need to Play, Not Compete"

- ***Assertion of policy:*** What is your understanding of a problem, and what do you think should be done to solve it? (Chapter 7, "Proposing a Solution")

  Although this last-minute anxiety about midterm and final exams is only too familiar to most college students, many professors may not realize how such major, infrequent, high-stakes exams work against the best interests of students both psychologically and intellectually. . . . If professors gave additional brief exams at frequent intervals, students would be spurred to study more regularly, learn more, worry less, and perform better.

  — PATRICK O'MALLEY, "More Testing, More Learning"

- ***Assertion of evaluation:*** What is your judgment of a subject? (Chapter 8, "Justifying an Evaluation")

  Overall, the Web site is well designed, amusing, and extremely helpful.

  — WENDY KIM, "Grading Professors"

Chapters 6–10 contain essays that argue for each of these kinds of assertions, along with guidelines for constructing an argument to support such an assertion.

- *Assertion of cause:* What do you think made a subject the way it is? (Chapter 9, "Speculating about Causes")

> The mythic horror movie, like the sick joke, has a dirty job to do. It deliberately appeals to all that is worst in us. It is morbidity unchained, our most base instincts let free, our nastiest fantasies realized . . . and it all happens, fittingly enough, in the dark.
>
> — STEPHEN KING, "Why We Crave Horror Movies"

- *Assertion of interpretation:* What does a story mean, or what is significant about it? (Chapter 10, "Interpreting Stories")

> "Araby" tells the story of an adolescent boy's initiation into adulthood. . . . From the beginning, the boy deludes himself about his relationship with Mangan's sister. At Araby, he realizes the parallel between his own self-delusion and the hypocrisy and vanity of the adult world.
>
> — DAVID RATINOV, "From Innocence to Insight:
> 'Araby' as an Initiation Story"

As these different thesis statements indicate, the kind of thesis you assert depends on the occasion for which you are writing and the question you are trying to answer for your readers. Whatever the writing situation, to be effective, every thesis must satisfy the same three standards: It must be *arguable, clear*, and *appropriately qualified.*

Arguable Assertions

Reasoned argument is called for when informed people disagree over an issue or remain divided over how best to solve a problem, as is so often the case in social and political life. Hence the thesis statements in reasoned arguments make **arguable assertions**—possibilities or probabilities, not certainties.

Therefore, a statement of fact could not be an arguable thesis statement because facts are easy to verify—whether by checking an authoritative reference book, asking an authority, or observing the fact with your own eyes. For example, these statements assert facts:

> Jem has a Ph.D. in history.
>
> I am less than five feet tall.
>
> Eucalyptus trees were originally imported into California from Australia.

Each of these assertions can be easily verified. To find out Jem's academic degree, you can ask him, among other things. To determine a person's height, you can use a tape measure. To discover where California got its eucalyptus trees, you can search the library or Internet. There is no point in arguing such statements (though you might question the authority of a particular source or the accuracy of someone's measurement). If a writer asserts something as fact and attempts to support the assertion with authorities or statistics, the resulting essay is not an argument but a report.

Like facts, expressions of personal feelings are not arguable assertions. Whereas facts are unarguable because they can be definitively proved true or false, feelings are unarguable because they are purely subjective.

You can declare, for example, that you detest eight o'clock classes, but you cannot offer an argument to support this assertion. All you can do is explain why you feel as you do. If, however, you were to restate the assertion as "Eight o'clock classes are counterproductive," you could then construct an argument that does not depend solely on your subjective feelings, memories, or preferences. Your argument could be based on reasons and support that apply to others as well as to yourself. For example, you might argue that students' ability to learn is at an especially low ebb immediately after breakfast and provide scientific support for this assertion — in addition, perhaps, to personal experience and reports of interviews with your friends.

Clear and Precise Wording

The way a thesis is worded is as important as its arguability. The wording of a thesis, especially its key terms, must be **clear** and **precise**.

Consider the following assertion: "Democracy is a way of life." The meaning of this claim is uncertain, partly because the word *democracy* is abstract and partly because the phrase *way of life* is inexact. Abstract ideas like democracy, freedom, and patriotism are by their very nature hard to grasp, and they become even less clear with overuse. Too often, such words take on connotations that may obscure the meaning you want to emphasize. *Way of life* is fuzzy: What does it mean? Does it refer to daily life, to a general philosophy or attitude toward life, or to something else?

Thus a thesis is vague if its meaning is unclear; it is ambiguous if it has more than one possible meaning. For example, the statement "My English instructor is mad" can be understood in two ways: The teacher is either angry or insane. Obviously, these are two very different assertions. You would not want readers to think you mean one when you actually mean the other.

Whenever you write argument, you should pay special attention to the way you phrase your thesis and take care to avoid vague and ambiguous language.

Appropriate Qualification

In addition to being arguable and clear, an argument thesis must make **appropriate qualifications** that suit your writing situation. If you are confident that your case is so strong that readers will accept your argument without question, state your thesis emphatically and unconditionally. If, however, you expect readers to challenge your assumptions or conclusions, you must qualify your statement. Qualifying a thesis makes it more likely that readers will take it seriously. Expressions like *probably, very likely, apparently,* and *it seems* all serve to qualify a thesis.

Exercise 19.1

Write an assertion of opinion that states your position on one of the following controversial issues:

- Should English be the official language of the United States and the only language used in local, state, and federal governments' oral and written communications?
- Should teenagers be required to get their parents' permission to obtain birth control information and contraceptives?
- Should high schools or colleges require students to perform community service as a condition for graduation?
- Should marriage between same-sex couples be legal?

Constructing a persuasive argument on any of these issues would obviously require careful deliberation and research. For this exercise, however, all you need to do is construct an arguable, clear, and appropriately qualified thesis.

Exercise 19.2

Find the thesis in one of the argument essays in Chapters 6–10. Then decide whether the thesis meets the three requirements: that it be arguable, clear, and appropriately qualified.

Exercise 19.3

If you have written or are currently working on one of the argument assignments in Chapters 6–10, consider whether your essay thesis is assertive, arguable, and appropriately qualified. If you believe it does not meet these requirements, revise it appropriately.

Giving Reasons and Support

Whether you are arguing a position, proposing a solution, justifying an evaluation, or speculating about causes, you need to give **reasons** and **support** for your thesis.

Think of reasons as the main points supporting your thesis. Often they answer the question "Why do you think so?" For example, if you assert among friends that you value a certain movie highly, one of your friends might ask, "Why do you like it so much?" And you might answer, "*Because* it has challenging ideas, unusual camera work, and memorable acting." Similarly, you might oppose restrictions on students' use of offensive language at your college *because* such restrictions would make students reluctant to enter into frank debates, *because* offensive speech is hard to define, and *because* restrictions violate the free-speech clause of the First Amendment. These *because* phrases are your reasons. You may have one or many reasons, depending on your subject and your writing situation.

For your argument to succeed with your readers, you must not only give reasons but also support your reasons. The main kinds of support writers use are examples, statistics, authorities, anecdotes, and textual evidence. Following is a discussion and illustration of each kind of support, along with standards for judging its reliability.

Examples

Examples may be used as support in all types of arguments. For examples to be believable and convincing, they must be representative (typical of all the relevant examples you might have chosen), consistent with the experience of your readers (familiar to them and not extreme), and adequate in number (numerous enough to be convincing and yet not likely to overwhelm readers).

The following illustration comes from a book on illiteracy in America by Jonathan Kozol, a prominent educator and writer.

> Illiterates cannot read the menu in a restaurant.
>
> They cannot read the cost of items on the menu in the window of the restaurant before they enter.
>
> Illiterates cannot read the letters that their children bring home from their teachers. They cannot study school department circulars that tell them of the courses that their children must be taking if they hope to pass the SAT exams. They cannot help with homework. They cannot write a letter to the teacher. They are afraid to visit in the classroom. They do not want to humiliate their child or themselves.
>
> Illiterates cannot read instructions on a bottle of prescription medicine. They cannot find out when a medicine is past the year of safe consumption; nor can they read of allergenic risks, warnings to diabetics, or the potential sedative effect of certain kinds of nonprescription pills. They cannot observe preventive health care admonitions. They cannot read about "the seven warning signs of cancer" or the indications of blood-sugar fluctuations or the risks of eating certain foods that aggravate the likelihood of cardiac arrest.
>
> — JONATHAN KOZOL, *Illiterate America*

Kozol presents several examples to support his argument that the human costs of illiteracy are high.

Kozol collected these examples in his many interviews with people who could neither read nor write. Though all of his readers are literate and have never experienced the frustrations of adult illiterates, Kozol assumes they will accept that the experiences are a familiar part of illiterates' lives. Most readers will believe the experiences to be neither atypical nor extreme.

Exercise 19.4

Identify the examples in paragraphs 9 and 11 in Jessica Statsky's essay "Children Need to Play, Not Compete" and paragraphs 16–18 in Amitai Etzioni's essay "Working at McDonald's" (both in Chapter 6). If you have not read the essays, pause to skim them so that you can evaluate these examples within the context of the entire essay. How well do the examples meet the standards of representativeness, consistency with experience of readers, and adequacy in number? You will not have all the information you need to evaluate the examples—you rarely do unless you are an expert on the subject — but make a judgment based on the information available to you in the headnotes and the essays.

Statistics

In many kinds of arguments about economic, educational, or social issues, **statistics** may be essential. When you use statistics in your own arguments, you will want to ensure that they are up-to-date, relevant, and accurate. In addition, take care to select statistics from reliable sources and to cite them from the sources in which they originally appeared if at all possible. For example, you would want to get medical statistics directly from a reputable and authoritative professional periodical like the *New England Journal of Medicine* rather than secondhand from a supermarket tabloid or an unaffiliated Web site, neither of which can be relied on for accuracy. If you are uncertain about the most authoritative sources, ask a reference librarian or a professor who knows your topic.

The following selection, written by a Harvard University professor, comes from an argument speculating about the decline of civic life in the United States. Civic life includes all of the clubs, organizations, and communal activities people choose to participate in.

Putnam uses statistics to support his opinion that, since the early 1960s, Americans have devoted less and less time to civic life because they are watching more and more television.

The culprit is television.

First, the timing fits. The long civic generation was the last cohort of Americans to grow up without television, for television flashed into American society like lightning in the 1950s. In 1950 barely 10 percent of American homes had television sets, but by 1959, 90 percent did, probably the fastest diffusion of a major technological innovation ever recorded. The reverberations from this lightning bolt continued for decades, as viewing hours grew by 17–20 percent during the 1960s and by an additional 7–8 percent during the 1970s. In the early years, TV watching was concentrated among the less educated sectors of the population, but during the 1970s the viewing time of the more educated sectors of the population began to converge upward. Television viewing increases with age, particularly upon retirement, but each generation since the introduction of television has begun its life cycle at a higher starting point. By 1995 viewing per TV household was more than 50 percent higher than it had been in the 1950s.

Most studies estimate that the average American now watches roughly four hours per day (excluding periods in which television is merely playing in the background). Even a more conservative estimate of three hours means that television absorbs 40 percent of the average American's free time, an increase of about one-third since 1965. Moreover, multiple sets have proliferated: By the late 1980s three-quarters of all U.S. homes had more than one set, and these numbers too are rising steadily, allowing ever more private viewing. . . . This massive change in the way Americans spend their days and nights occurred precisely during the years of generational civic disengagement.

— Robert D. Putnam, "The Strange Disappearance of Civic America"

Chapter 23 provides help finding statistical data in the library.

These statistics come primarily from the U.S. Bureau of the Census, a nationwide count of the number of Americans and a survey, in part, of their buying habits, levels of education, and leisure activities. The Census reports are widely considered to be accurate and trustworthy. They qualify as original sources of statistics.

Exercise 19.5

In Chapter 6, underline the statistics in paragraphs 5 and 6 of Jessica Statsky's essay. If you have not read the essay, pause to skim it so that you can evaluate the writer's use of statistics within the context of the whole essay. How well do the statistics meet the standard of up-to-dateness, relevance, accuracy, and reliance on the original source? Does the writer indicate where the statistics come from? What do the statistics contribute to the argument?

Authorities

To support an argument, writers often cite experts on the subject. Quoting, paraphrasing, or even just referring to a respected **authority** can add to a writer's credibility. Authorities must be selected as carefully as facts and statistics, however. One qualification for authorities is suggested by the way we refer to them: They must be authoritative—that is, trustworthy and reputable. They must also be specially qualified to contribute to the subject you are writing about. For example, a well-known expert on the American presidency might be a perfect choice to support an argument about the achievements of a past president but a poor choice to support an argument on whether adolescents who commit serious crimes should be tried as adults. Finally, qualified authorities must have training at respected institutions or have unique real-world experiences, and they must have a record of research and publications recognized by other authorities.

The following example comes from a *New York Times* article about some parents' and experts' heightened concern over boys' behavior. The author believes that the concern is exaggerated and potentially dangerous. In the full argument, she is particularly concerned about the number of boys who are being given Ritalin, a popular drug for treating attention-deficit hyperactivity disorder (ADHD).

> Today, the world is no longer safe for boys. A boy being a shade too boyish risks finding himself under the scrutiny of parents, teachers, guidance counselors, child therapists—all of them on watch for the early glimmerings of a medical syndrome, a bona fide behavioral disorder. Does the boy disregard authority, make snide comments in class, push other kids around and play hooky? Maybe he has a conduct disorder. Is he fidgety, impulsive, disruptive, easily bored? Perhaps he is suffering from attention-deficit hyperactivity disorder, or ADHD, the disease of the hour and the most frequently diagnosed behavioral disorder of childhood. Does he prefer computer games and goofing off to homework? He might have dyslexia or another learning disorder.
>
> "There is now an attempt to pathologize what was once considered the normal range of behavior of boys," said Melvin Konner of the departments of anthropology and psychiatry at Emory University in Atlanta. "Today, Tom Sawyer and Huckleberry Finn surely would have been diagnosed with both conduct disorder and ADHD." And both, perhaps, would have been put on Ritalin, the drug of choice for treating attention-deficit disorder.
>
> — Natalie Angier, "Intolerance of Boyish Behavior"

Angier establishes Melvin Konner's professional qualifications by naming the university where he teaches and his areas of study.

For examples of two formal citation styles often used in college essays, see Chapter 24.

In this example, Angier relies on *informal* citation within her essay to introduce Melvin Konner, the authority she quotes, along with a reference to his professional qualifications. Such informal citation is common in newspapers, magazines, and some books intended for general audiences. In other books and in academic contexts, writers use *formal* citation, providing a list of works cited at the end of the essay.

Exercise 19.6

Analyze how authorities are used in paragraphs 4 and 5 of Patrick O'Malley's essay "More Testing, More Learning" in Chapter 7. Begin by underlining the authorities' contributions to these paragraphs, whether through quotation, summary, or paraphrase. On the basis of the evidence you have available, decide to what extent each source is authoritative on the subject: qualified to contribute to the subject, trained appropriately, and recognized widely. How does O'Malley establish each authority's credentials? Then decide what each authority contributes to the argument as a whole. (If you have not read the essay, take time to read or skim it.)

Anecdotes

Anecdotes are brief stories about events or experiences. If they are relevant to the argument, well told, and true to life, they can provide convincing support. To be relevant, an anecdote must strike readers as more than an entertaining diversion; it must seem to make an irreplaceable contribution to an argument. A well-told story is easy to follow, and the people and scenes are described memorably, even vividly. A true-to-life anecdote seems believable, even if the experience is foreign to readers' experiences.

The following anecdote appeared in an argument taking a position on gun control. The writer, an essayist, poet, and environmentalist who is also a rancher in South Dakota, always carries a pistol and believes that other people should have the right to do so.

To support her argument, Hasselstrom tells an engaging anecdote and, in the last paragraph, explains its relevance.

I was driving the half-mile to the highway mailbox one day when I saw a vehicle parked about midway down the road. Several men were standing in the ditch, relieving themselves. I have no objection to emergency urination, but I noticed they'd dumped several dozen beer cans in the road. Besides being ugly, cans can slash a cow's feet or stomach.

The men noticed me before they finished and made quite a performance out of zipping their trousers while walking toward me. All four of them gathered around my small foreign car, and one of them demanded what the hell I wanted.

"This is private land. I'd appreciate it if you'd pick up the beer cans."

"What beer cans?" said the belligerent one, putting both hands on the car door and leaning in my window. His face was inches from mine, and the beer fumes were strong. The others laughed. One tried the passenger door, locked; another put his foot on the hood and rocked the car. They circled, lightly thumping the roof, discussing my good fortune in meeting them and the benefits they were likely to bestow upon me. I felt very small and very trapped and they knew it.

"The ones you just threw out," I said politely.

"I don't see no beer cans. Why don't you get out here and show them to me, honey?" said the belligerent one, reaching for the handle inside my door.

"Right over there," I said, still being polite, "—there, and over there." I pointed with the pistol, which I'd slipped under my thigh. Within one minute the cans and the men were back in the car and headed down the road.

I believe this incident illustrates several important principles. The men were trespassing and knew it; their judgment may have been impaired by alcohol. Their response to the polite request of a woman alone was to use their size, numbers, and sex to inspire fear. The pistol was a response in the same language. Politeness didn't work; I couldn't match them in size or number. Out of the car, I'd have been more vulnerable. The pistol just changed the balance of power.

— LINDA M. HASSELSTROM, "Why One Peaceful Woman Carries a Pistol"

Most readers would readily agree that this anecdote is well told: It has many concrete, memorable details; there is action, suspense, climax, resolution, and even dialogue. It is about a believable, possible experience. Finally, the anecdote is clearly relevant to the author's argument about gun control.

See Chapter 14, Narrating, and Chapter 2, Remembering an Event, for more information about narrating anecdotes.

Exercise 19.7

Evaluate the way an anecdote is used in paragraph 16 of Amitai Etzioni's essay "Working at McDonald's" in Chapter 6. Consider whether the story is well told and true to life. Decide whether it seems to be relevant to the whole argument. Does the writer make the relevance clear? Does the anecdote support Etzioni's argument?

Textual Evidence

When you argue claims of value (Chapter 8) and interpretation (Chapter 10), **textual evidence** will be very important. In your college courses, if you are asked to evaluate a controversial article, you must quote, paraphrase, or summarize passages so that readers can understand why you think the author's argument is or is not credible. If you are analyzing a novel, you must include numerous excerpts to show just how you arrived at your conclusion.

For textual evidence to be considered effective support for an argument, it must be carefully selected to be relevant. You must help readers see the connection between each piece of evidence and the reason it supports. Textual evidence must also be highly selective—that is, chosen from among all the available evidence to provide the support needed without overwhelming the reader or weakening the argument with marginally relevant evidence. Textual evidence usually has more impact if it is balanced between quotation and paraphrase, and it must be smoothly integrated into the sentences of the argument.

The following example comes from a student essay in which the writer argues that the main character (referred to as "the boy") in the short story "Araby" by James Joyce is so self-absorbed that he learns nothing about himself or other people.

You can read "Araby" in Chapter 10, pp. 549–54.

Crane cites textual evidence from "Araby" to convince readers to take her argument seriously.

The story opens and closes with images of blindness — a framing device that shows the boy does not change but ends up with the same lack of understanding that he began with. The street is "blind" with an "uninhabited house . . . at the blind end" (par. 1). As he spies on Mangan's sister, from his own house, the boy intentionally limits what he is able to see by lowering the "blind"until it is only an inch from the window sash (par. 4). At the bazaar in the closing scene, the "light was out," and the upper part of the hall was "completely dark" (par. 36). The boy is left "gazing up into the darkness," seeing nothing but an inner torment that burns his eyes (par. 37).

The boy's blindness appears to be caused by his obsession with Mangan's sister. When he tries to read at night, for example, the girl's "image [comes] between [him] and the page," in effect blinding him (par. 12). In fact, he seems blind to everything except this "image" of the "brown-clad figure cast by [his] imagination" (par. 16). The girl's "brown-clad figure" is also associated with the houses on "blind" North Richmond Street, with their "brown imperturbable faces" (par. 1). The houses stare back at the boy, unaffected by his presence and gaze.

— SALLY CRANE, "Gazing into the Darkness"

For more information on paraphrasing, see pp. 586–87 in Chapter 12.

Notice how the writer quotes selected words and phrases about blindness to support her reasoning that the boy learns nothing because he is blinded. There are twelve smoothly integrated quotations in these two paragraphs, along with a number of paraphrases, all of them relevant. The writer does not assume that the evidence speaks for itself; she comments and interprets throughout.

Exercise 19.8

Analyze the use of evidence in paragraphs 2 and 3 of David Ratinov's essay "From Innocence to Insight" in Chapter 10. If you have not read this essay, read it now. Identify the quotes and paraphrases Ratinov's uses, and then try to identify the phrases or sentences that comment on or explain this evidence. Consider whether Ratinov's evidence in these two paragraphs seems relevant to his thesis and reasons, appropriately selective, well balanced between quotes and paraphrases, integrated smoothly into the sentences he creates, and explained helpfully.

Counterarguing

Asserting a thesis and backing it with reasons and support are essential to a successful argument. Thoughtful writers go further, however, by **counterarguing** — anticipating and responding to their readers' objections and questions or their alternative position or preferred solution to a problem.

To counterargue, writers rely on three basic strategies: acknowledging, accommodating or conceding, and refuting. Writers show they are aware of readers' objections and questions (acknowledge), modify their position to accept readers' concerns they think are legitimate (concede), or explicitly argue that readers' objections may be invalid or that their concerns may be irrelevant (refute). Writers may use one or more of these three strategies in the same essay. Readers find arguments more convincing when writers have anticipated their concerns in these ways.

Acknowledging Readers' Concerns

When you **acknowledge** readers' questions or objections, you show that you are aware of their point of view and you take it seriously even if you do not agree with it, as in the following example.

> The homeless, it seems, can be roughly divided into two groups: those who have had marginality and homelessness forced upon them and want nothing more than to escape them, and a smaller number who have at least in part chosen marginality, and now accept, or, in a few cases, embrace it.
>
> I understand how dangerous it can be to introduce the idea of choice into a discussion of homelessness. It can all too easily be used for all the wrong reasons by all the wrong people to justify indifference or brutality toward the homeless, or to argue that they are getting only what they deserve.
>
> And I understand, too, how complicated the notion can become: Many of the veterans on the street, or battered women, or abused and runaway children, have chosen this life only as the lesser of evils, and because, in this society, there is often no place else to go.
>
> And finally, I understand how much that happens on the street can combine to create an apparent acceptance of homelessness that is nothing more than the absolute absence of hope.
>
> Nonetheless we must learn to accept that there may indeed be people on the street who have seen so much of our world, or have seen it so clearly, that to live in it becomes impossible.
>
> — Peter Marin, "Go Ask Alice"

Marin acknowledges three doubts his readers may have regarding his argument that some of America's homeless have chosen that way of life.

You might think that acknowledging readers' objections in this way — addressing readers directly, listing their possible objections, and discussing each one — would weaken your argument. It might even seem reckless to suggest objections that not all readers would think of. On the contrary, however, most readers respond positively to this strategy because it makes you seem thoughtful and reasonable. By researching your subject and your readers, you will be able to use this strategy confidently in your own argumentative essays. And you will learn to look for it in arguments you read and use it to make judgments about the writer's credibility.

Exercise 19.9

Richard Estrada acknowledges readers' concerns in paragraphs 6 and 7 of his essay in Chapter 6. How, specifically, does Estrada attempt to acknowledge his readers' concerns? What do you find most and least successful in his acknowledgment? How does the acknowledgment affect your judgment of the writer's credibility?

Accommodating Readers' Concerns

To argue effectively, you must often take special care to **accommodate readers' concerns** by acknowledging their objections, questions, and alternative positions, causes, or solutions. Occasionally, however, you may have to go even further. Instead of merely acknowledging your readers' concerns, you may decide to accept some of them and incorporate them into your own argument. This strategy can be very disarming to readers. It is sometimes referred to as **concession**, for it seems to concede that opposing views have merit. The following example comes from an essay enthusiastically endorsing e-mail.

> To be sure, egalitarianism has its limits. The ease and economy of sending email, especially to multiple recipients, makes us all vulnerable to any bore, loony, or commercial or political salesman who can get our email address. It's still a lot less intrusive than the telephone, since you can read and answer or ignore email at your own convenience. But as normal people's email starts mounting into the hundreds daily, which is bound to happen, filtering mechanisms and conventions of etiquette that are still in their primitive stage will be desperately needed.
>
> Another supposed disadvantage of email is that it discourages face-to-face communication. At Microsoft, where people routinely send email back and forth all day to the person in the next office, this is certainly true. Some people believe this tendency has more to do with the underdeveloped social skills of computer geeks than with Microsoft's role in developing the technology email relies on. I wouldn't presume to comment on that. Whether you think email replacing live conversation is a good or bad thing depends, I guess, on how much of a misanthrope you are. I like it.
>
> — MICHAEL KINSLEY, "Email Culture"

> After supporting his own reasons for embracing e-mail, Kinsley accommodates readers' likely reservations by conceding that e-mail poses certain problems.

Notice that Kinsley's accommodation or concession is not grudging. He readily concedes that e-mail brings users a lot of unwanted messages and may discourage conversation in the workplace.

Exercise 19.10

How does Patrick O'Malley attempt to accommodate readers in paragraphs 8 and 9 of his Chapter 7 essay arguing for more frequent exams? What seems successful or unsuccessful in his argument? How do his efforts at accommodation make his argument seem more convincing?

Refuting Readers' Objections

Your readers' possible objections and views cannot always be accommodated. Sometimes they must be refuted. When you **refute readers' objections**, you assert that they are wrong and argue against them. Refutation does not have to be delivered arrogantly or dismissively, however. Because differences are inevitable, reasoned argument provides a peaceful and constructive way for informed, well-intentioned people who disagree strongly to air their differences.

In the following example, a social sciences professor refutes one argument for giving college students the opportunity to purchase lecture notes prepared by someone else.

Now, it may well be argued that universities are already shortchanging their students by stuffing them into huge lecture halls where, unlike at rock concerts or basketball games, the lecturer can't even be seen on a giant screen in real time. If they're already shortchanged with impersonal instruction, what's the harm in offering canned lecture notes?

The amphitheater lecture is indeed, for all but the most engaging professors, a lesser form of instruction, and scarcely to be idealized. Still, Education by Download misses one of the keys to learning. Education is a meeting of minds, a process through which the student educes, draws from within, a response to what the teacher teaches.

The very act of taking notes — not reading someone else's notes, no matter how stellar — is a way of engaging the material, wrestling with it, struggling to comprehend or take issue, but in any case entering into the work. The point is to decide, while you are listening, what matters in the presentation. And while I don't believe that most of life consists of showing up, education does begin with that — with immersing yourself in the activity at hand, listening, thinking, judging, offering active responses. A download is a poor substitute.

— TODD GITLIN, "Disappearing Ink"

> Gitlin first concedes a possible objection, and then even partially agrees with this view. In the second paragraph, however, he begins to refute the objection.

As this selection illustrates, writers cannot simply dismiss readers' possible concerns with a wave of their hand. Gitlin states a potential objection fully and fairly but then goes on to refute it by claiming that students need to take their own lecture notes to engage and comprehend the material that is being presented to them.

Effective refutation requires a restrained tone and careful argument. Although you may not accept this particular refutation, you can agree that it is well reasoned and supported. You need not feel attacked personally because the writer disagrees with you.

Exercise 19.11

Evaluate Robert Kuttner's use of refutation in paragraphs 11–12, 14–16, and 20–21 of "Good Jobs for Americans Who Help Americans" (Chapter 7). In each case, how does Kuttner signal or announce the refutation? How does he support the refutation? What is the tone of the refutation, and how effective do you think the tone would be in convincing readers to take the writer's argument seriously?

Logical Fallacies

Fallacies are errors or flaws in reasoning. Although essentially unsound, fallacious arguments seem superficially plausible and often have great persuasive power. Fallacies are not necessarily deliberate efforts to deceive readers. Writers may introduce a fallacy accidentally by not examining their own reasons or underlying assumptions, by failing to establish solid support, or by using unclear or ambiguous words. Here is a summary of the most common logical fallacies (listed alphabetically):

- *Begging the question:* Arguing that a claim is true by repeating the claim in different words (also called *circular reasoning*)
- *Confusing chronology with causality:* Assuming that because one thing preceded another, the former caused the latter (also called *post hoc, ergo propter hoc*—Latin for "after this, therefore because of this")
- *Either-or reasoning:* Assuming that there are only two sides to a question and representing yours as the only correct one
- *Equivocating:* Misleading or hedging with ambiguous word choices
- *Failing to accept the burden of proof:* Asserting a claim without presenting a reasoned argument to support it
- *False analogy:* Assuming that because one thing resembles another, conclusions drawn from one also apply to the other
- *Hasty generalization:* Offering only weak or limited evidence to support a conclusion
- *Overreliance on authority:* Assuming that something is true simply because an expert says so and ignoring evidence to the contrary
- *Oversimplifying:* Giving easy answers to complicated questions, often by appealing to emotions rather than logic
- *Personal attack:* Demeaning the proponents of a claim instead of refuting their argument (also called *ad hominem*—Latin for "against the man"—*attack*)
- *Red herring:* Attempting to misdirect the discussion by raising an essentially unrelated point
- *Slanting:* Selecting or emphasizing the evidence that supports your claim and suppressing or playing down other evidence
- *Slippery slope:* Pretending that one thing inevitably leads to another
- *Sob story:* Manipulating readers' emotions to lead them to draw unjustified conclusions
- *Straw man:* Directing the argument against a claim that nobody actually makes or that everyone agrees is very weak

Analyzing Visuals

We live in a highly visual world. Every day we are barraged with a seemingly endless stream of images from television, magazines, billboards, books, Web pages, newspapers, flyers, storefront signs, and more, all of them competing for our attention, and all of them loaded with information and ideas. Forms of communication that traditionally used only the written word (letters, books, term papers) or the spoken word (telephone conversations, lectures) are today increasingly enhanced with visual components (PowerPoint slides, cell-phone graphics, video, photos, illustrations, graphs, and the like) for greater impact. And most of us would agree that visuals do, indeed, have an impact: A picture, as the saying goes, is worth a thousand words.

Figure 20.1 Times Square at Dusk, February 9, 2007

In part because of their potentially powerful effect on us, visuals and visual texts[*] should be approached the way we approach written texts: analytically and critically. Whether their purpose is to sell us an idea or a car, to spur us to action or inspire us to dream, visuals invite analysis both of their key components and their rhetorical context. As we "read" a visual, therefore, we should ask ourselves a series of questions: Who

---

[*] In this chapter, we use the word *image* to refer primarily to photographs. We use the word *visual* as a broader designation for visual elements of texts (including images, but also such components as diagrams, charts, and graphs), and *visual text* for documents such as ads, brochures, and the like, in which visuals are strongly featured, but which consist of more than a single image.

Figure 20.2 "Wedding," from the WWF's 2007 "Beautiful Day U.S." Series

created it? Where was it published? What audience is it addressing? What is it trying to get this audience to think and feel about the subject? How does it attempt to achieve this purpose?

Let's look, for example, at the visual text on this page: a public service announcement (PSA) from the World Wildlife Fund (WWF).

The central image in this PSA is a photo of an attractive, smiling young couple. Most of us will immediately recognize the dress, posture, and facial expressions of the young man and woman as those of a newly married couple; the photo-mounting corners make the image seem like a real wedding album photo, as opposed to an ad agency's creation (which would be easier to ignore). After noting these things, however, we are immediately struck by what is wrong with the picture: a hurricane rages in the background, blowing hair, clothing, and the bride's veil forcefully to one side, showering the bride's pure white dress with spots (of rain? mud?), and threatening to rip the bridal bouquet from her hand.

So what do we make of the disruption of the convention (the traditional wedding photo) on which the PSA image is based? In trying to decide, most of us will look next to the text below the image: "Ignoring global warming won't make it go away." The disjunction between the couple's blissful expression and the storm raging around them turns out to be the point of the PSA: Like the young couple in the picture, the PSA implies, we are all blithely ignoring the impending disaster that global warming represents. The reputable, nonprofit WWF's logo and URL, which constitute its "signature," are meant to be an assurance that this threat is real, and not just an idea a profit-seeking ad agency dreamt up to manipulate us.

People continue to argue about how urgent the problem of climate change is and what, if anything, we need to do about it. The WWF suggests that, like the clueless young couple, too many of us have adopted a "head-in-the-sand" attitude about the problem. Lest the implied criticism be construed as an outright insult and alienate viewers, the implied connection to the couple also flatters us by implying that we are attractive, hopeful, and well-intentioned. Global warming, in the WWF's view, threatens the bright future we all like to imagine we have ahead of us.

Not everyone will be convinced by this PSA to support the work of the WWF, and some viewers may feel manipulated by the visual image. They may disagree that the problem is as dire as the depiction implicitly claims it is. They may feel that our resources and energy would be better directed toward other problems facing our nation. Nevertheless, most people would agree that, with a single cleverly constructed image, a single line of text, and a logo, the PSA delivers its message clearly and forcefully.

Criteria for Analyzing Visuals

The primary purpose of this chapter is to help you analyze visuals and write about them. In your college courses, some of you will be asked to write entire papers in which you analyze one or more visuals (a painting or a photo, for example). Some of you will write papers in which you include analysis of one or more visual texts within the context of a larger written essay (say, by analyzing the brochures and ads authorized by a political candidate, in an argument about her campaign).

Of course, learning to analyze visuals effectively can also help you gain a more complete understanding of any document that *uses* visuals but that is not entirely or predominantly composed of them. Why did the author of a remembered event essay, for example, choose a particular photo of a person mentioned in the text—does it reinforce the written description, add to it, or contradict it in some way? If there is a caption under the photo, how does it affect the way we read it? In a concept explanation, why are illustrations of one process included, but not another? How well do the charts and graphs work with the text to help us understand the author's explanation? Understanding what visuals can do for a text can also help you effectively integrate images, charts, graphs, and other visuals in your own essays, whatever your topic.

The following chart outlines key criteria for analyzing visuals and provides questions for you to ask about documents that include them.

CRITERIA FOR ANALYZING VISUALS

Key Components

Composition

- Of what elements is the visual composed?

- What is the focal point—that is, the place your eyes are drawn to?

- From what perspective do you view the focal point? Are you looking straight ahead at it, down at it, or up at it? If the visual is a photograph, what angle was the image shot from—straight ahead, looking down or up?

- What colors are used? Are there obvious special effects employed? Is there a frame, or are there any additional graphical elements? If so, what do these elements contribute to your "reading" of the visual?

People/Other Main Figures

- If people are depicted, how would you describe their age, gender, subculture, ethnicity, profession, level of attractiveness, and socioeconomic class? How do these factors relate to other elements of the image?

- Who is looking at whom? Do the people represented seem conscious of the viewer's gaze?

(continued)

- What do the facial expressions and body language tell you about power relationships (equal, subordinate, in charge) and attitudes (self-confident, vulnerable, anxious, subservient, angry, aggressive, sad)?

Scene

- If a recognizable scene is depicted, what is its setting? What is in the background and the foreground?
- What has happened just before the image was "shot"? What will happen in the next scene?
- What, if anything, is happening just outside of the visual frame?

Words

- If text is combined with the visual, what role does the text play? Is it a slogan? A famous quote? Lyrics from a well-known song?
- Does the text help you interpret the visual's overall meaning? What interpretive clues does it provide?
- What is the tone of the text? Humorous? Elegiac? Ironic?

Tone

- What tone, or mood, does the visual convey? Is it light-hearted, somber, frightening, shocking, joyful? What elements in the visual (color, composition, words, people, setting, etc.) convey this tone?

Context(s)

Rhetorical Context

- **What is its main purpose?** Are we being asked to buy a product? Form an opinion or judgment about something? Support a political party's candidate? Take some other kind of action?
- **Who is its target audience?** Children? Men? Women? Some sub- or super-set of these groups (e.g., African American men; "tweens"; seniors)?
- **Who is the author? Who sponsored its publication?** What background/ associations do the author and the sponsoring publication have? What other works have they produced?
- **Where was it published, and in what form?** Online? On television? In print? In a commercial publication (e.g., a sales brochure, billboard, ad) or an informational one (newspaper, magazine)?
- **If the visual is embedded within a document that is primarily written text, how do the written text and the visual relate to one another?** Do they convey the same message, or are they at odds in any way? Does the image seem subordinate to the written text, or is it the other way around?
- *Social Context.* **What is the immediate social and cultural context within which the visual is operating?** If we are being asked to support a

certain candidate, for example, how does the visual reinforce or counter what we already know about this candidate? What other social/cultural knowledge does the visual assume its audience already has?

- *Historical Context.* **What historical knowledge does it assume the audience already possesses?** Does the visual refer to other historical images, figures, events, or stories that the audience would recognize? How do these historical references relate to the visual's audience and purpose?

- *Intertextuality.* **How does the visual connect, relate to, or contrast with any other significant texts, visual or otherwise, that you are aware of?** How do such considerations inform your ideas about this particular visual?

A Sample Analysis

In a composition class, students were asked to do a short written analysis of a photograph of their choosing. In looking for ideas online, one student, Paul Taylor, came across the Library of Congress's *Documenting America*, an exhibit of photographs done between 1935 and 1945 for the federal government's Farm Security Administration. The work of African American photographer Gordon Parks struck Paul as particularly interesting, especially his photos of Ella Watson, a poorly paid office cleaner employed by the federal government. (See Figure 20.3.)

After studying the photographs, Paul read what the site had to say about the context from which they emerged:

> Gordon Parks was born in Kansas in 1912. . . .
> During the Depression a variety of jobs . . . took
> him to various parts of the northern United States.
> He took up photography during his travels. . . . In
> 1942, an opportunity to work for the Farm Security
> Administration brought the photographer to the
> nation's capital; Parks later recalled that "discrimi-
> nation and bigotry were worse there than any place
> I had yet seen."[1]

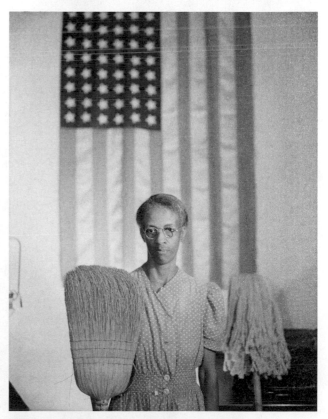

Figure 20.3 *Ella Watson*, Gordon Parks (1942)

---

[1]Martin H. Bush, "A Conversation with Gordon Parks," in *The Photographs of Gordon Parks* (Wichita, Kansas: Wichita State University, 1983), 36.

© Estate of Nan Wood Graham/VAGA, NYC.

Figure 20.4 *American Gothic,* **Grant Wood (1930)**

The exhibit also quotes Parks's recollection of his first photo session with Watson:

> She began to spill out her life's story. It was a pitiful one. She had struggled alone after her mother had died and her father had been killed by a lynch mob. . . . Her husband was accidentally shot to death two days before their daughter was born. . . . My first photograph of [Watson] was unsubtle. I overdid it and posed her, Grant Wood style, before the American flag, a broom in one hand, a mop in the other, staring straight into the camera.[2]

Paul didn't understand Parks's reference to "Grant Wood" in his description of the photo, so he did an Internet search using the terms *"Grant Wood" "Gordon Parks" "Ella Watson"* and discovered that Parks was referring to a classic painting by Wood called *American Gothic* (Figure 20.4). Reading further about the connection, he discovered that Parks's photo of Watson is itself commonly titled *American Gothic* and discussed as a parody of Grant Wood's painting.

Intrigued by what he had learned so far, Paul decided to delve into Parks's later career. A 2006 obituary of Parks in the *New York Times* reproduced his 1952 photo *Emerging Man,* which Paul decided to analyze for his assignment. First, he did additional research on the photo. Then he made notes on his responses to the photo using the criteria for analysis provided on pp. 675–77.

Figure 20.5 *Emerging Man,* **Gordon Parks (1952)**

---

[2] Gordon Parks, *A Choice of Weapons* (New York: Harper & Row, 1966), 230–31.

PAUL TAYLOR'S ANALYSIS OF *EMERGING MAN*

Key Components of the Visual

Composition

- **Of what elements is the visual composed?** It's a black-and-white photo showing the top three-quarters of a man's face and his hands (mostly fingers). He appears to be emerging out of the ground--out of a sewer? There's what looks like asphalt in the foreground, and buildings (out of focus) in the far background.

- **What is the focal point — that is, the place your eyes are drawn to?** The focal point is the face of the man staring directly into the camera's lens. There's a shaft of light angled (slightly from the right?) onto the lower-middle part of his face. His eyes appear to glisten slightly. The rest of his face, his hands, and the foreground are in shadow.

- **From what perspective do you view the focal point?** We appear to be looking at him at eye level--weird, since eye level for him is just a few inches from the ground. Was the photographer lying down? The shot is also a close-up--a foot or two from the man's face. Why so close?

- **What colors are used? Are there obvious special effects employed? Is there a frame, or are there any additional graphical elements?** There's no visible frame or any graphic elements. The image is in stark black and white, and there's a "graininess" to it: we can see the texture of the man's skin and the asphalt on the street.

People/Other Main Figures

- **If people are depicted, how would you describe their age, gender, subculture, ethnicity, profession, level of attractiveness, and socioeconomic class?** The man is African American, and probably middle-aged (or at least not obviously very young or very old). We can't see his clothing or any other marker of class, profession, etc. The fact that he seems to be emerging from a sewer implies that he's not hugely rich or prominent, of course--a "man of the people"?

- **Who is looking at whom? Do the people represented seem conscious of the viewer's gaze?** The man seems to be looking directly into the camera, and at the viewer (who's in the position of the photographer). I guess, yes, he seems to look straight at the viewer--perhaps in a challenging or questioning way.

- **What do the facial expressions and body language tell you about power relationships (equal, subordinate, in charge) and attitudes (self-confident, vulnerable, anxious, subservient, angry, aggressive, sad)?** We can only see his face from the nose up, and his fingertips. It looks like one eyebrow is slightly raised, which might mean he's questioning or skeptical. The expression in his eyes is definitely serious. The position

(continued)

of his fingers implies that he's clutching the rim of the manhole--that, and the title, indicate that he's pulling himself up out of the hole. But since we see only the fingers, not the whole hand, does his hold seem tenuous--he's "holding on by his fingertips"? Not sure.

Scene

- **If a recognizable scene is depicted, what is its setting? What is in the background and the foreground?** It looks like an urban setting (asphalt, manhole cover, buildings, and lights in the blurry distant background). Descriptions of the photo note that Parks shot the image in Harlem. Hazy buildings and objects are in the distance. Only the man's face and fingertips are in focus. The sky behind him is light gray, though--is it dawn?

- **What has happened just before the image was "shot"? What will happen in the next scene?** He appears to be coming up and out of the hole in the ground (the sewer).

- **What, if anything, is happening just outside of the visual frame?** It's not clear. There's no activity in the background at all. It's deserted, except for him.

Words

- **If text is combined with the visual, what role does the text play?** There's no text on or near the image. There is the title, though--*Emerging Man*.

- **Does the text help you interpret the visual's overall meaning?** The title is a literal description, but it might also refer to the civil rights movement--the gradual racial and economic integration--of African Americans into American society.

- **What is the tone of the text?** Hard to say. I guess, assuming wordplay is involved, it's sort of witty (merging traffic?)?

Tone

- **What tone, or mood, does the image convey? What elements in the image (color, composition, words, people, setting, etc.) convey this tone?** The tone is serious, even perhaps a bit spooky. The use of black and white and heavy shadows lend a somewhat ominous feel, though the ray of light on the man's face, the lightness of the sky, and the lights in the background counterbalance this to an extent. The man's expression is somber, though not obviously angry or grief-stricken.

Context(s)

Rhetorical Context

- **What is its main purpose?** Given Parks's interest in politics and social justice, it seems fair to assume that the image of the man emerging from underground--from the darkness into the light?--is a reference to social progress (civil rights movement) and suggests rebirth of a sort.

The use of black and white, while certainly not unusual in photographs of the era, emphasizes the division between black and white that is in part the photo's subject.

- **Who is its target audience?** Because it appeared first in *Life*, the target audience was mainstream--a broad cross-section of the magazine-reading U.S. population at mid-twentieth century.

- **Who is the author? Who sponsored its publication?** During this era, Gordon Parks was best known as a photographer whose works documented and commented on social conditions. The fact that this photo was originally published in *Life* magazine (a mainstream periodical read by white Americans throughout the country) is probably significant.

- **Where was it published, and in what form?** In *Life*, it accompanied an article on Ralph Ellison's novel *Invisible Man*.

- **If the visual is embedded within a document that is primarily written text, how do the written text and the visual relate to one another?** The photo accompanied an article about Ellison's *Invisible Man*, a novel about a man who goes underground to escape racism and conflicts within the early civil rights movement. Now the man is reentering mainstream society?

- *Social Context.* **What is the immediate social and cultural context within which the visual is operating?** The civil rights movement was gaining ground in post-World War II society.

- *Historical Context.* **What historical knowledge does it assume the audience already possesses?** For a viewer in 1952, the image would call to mind the current and past situation of African Americans. Uncertainty about what the future would hold (Would the emergence be successful? What kind of man would eventually emerge?) would be a big part of the viewer's response. Viewers today obviously feel less suspense about what would happen in the immediate (post-1952) future. The "vintage" feel of the photo's style and even the man's hair, along with the use of black and white, probably have a "distancing" effect on the viewer today. At the same time, the subject continues to be relevant--most viewers will likely think about the progress we've made in race relations, and where we're currently headed.

- *Intertextuality.* **How does the visual connect, relate to, or contrast with any other significant texts, visual or otherwise, that you are aware of?** *Invisible Man*, which I've already discussed, was a best-seller and won the National Book Award in 1953.

After writing and reviewing these notes and doing some further research to fill in gaps in his knowledge about Parks, Ellison, and the civil rights movement, Paul drafted his analysis. He submitted this draft to his peer group for comments, and then revised. His final draft follows.

Taylor 1

Paul Taylor
Professor Stevens
Writing Seminar I
4 October 2009

The Rising

Gordon Parks's 1952 photograph *Emerging Man* (Fig. 1) is as historically significant a reflection of the civil rights movement as are the speeches of Martin Luther King and Malcolm X, the music of Mahalia Jackson, and the books of Ralph Ellison and James Baldwin. Through striking use of black and white--a reflection of the racial divisions plaguing American cities and towns throughout much of the nineteenth and twentieth centuries--and a symbolically potent central subject--an African American man we see literally "emerging" from a city manhole--Parks's photo evokes the centuries of racial and economic marginalization of African Americans, at the same time as it projects a spirit of determination and optimism regarding the civil rights movement's eventual success.

In choosing the starkest of urban settings and giving the image a gritty feel, Parks alerts the viewer to the gravity of his subject and gives it a sense of immediacy. As with the documentary photographs Parks took of office cleaner Ella Watson for the Farm Security Administration in the 1940s--see Fig. 2 for one example-- the carefully chosen setting and the spareness of the treatment

Fig. 1. Gordon Parks, *Emerging Man* (1952)

Taylor 2

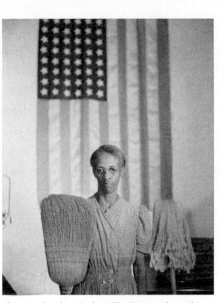

Fig. 2.   Gordon Parks, *Ella Watson* (1942)

ensure the viewer's focus on the social statement the artist is making
(*Documenting*). Whereas the photos of Ella Watson document a particular
woman and the actual conditions of her life and work, however, *Emerging
Man* strips away any particulars, including any name for the man, with
the result that the photo enters the symbolic or even mythic realm.

The composition of *Emerging Man* makes it impossible for us to focus
on anything other than the unnamed subject rising from the manhole--we
are, for instance, unable to consider what the weather might be, though
we might surmise from the relatively light tone of the sky and the empti-
ness of the street that it is dawn. Similarly, we are not given any specifics
of the setting, which is simply urban and, apart from the central figure,
unpopulated. Reducing the elements to their outlines in this way keeps
the viewer focused on the grand central theme of the piece: the role of
race in mid-twentieth-century America and the future of race relations.

The fact that the man is looking directly at the camera, in a way
that's challenging and serious but not hostile, speaks to the racial op-

timism of the period among a large cross-section of the society, African American and white alike. President Truman's creation of the President's Committee on Civil Rights in 1946 and his 1948 Executive Order for the integration of all armed services were significant steps toward the emergence of the full-blown civil rights movement, providing hope that African Americans would be able, for perhaps the first time in American history, to look directly into the eyes of their white counterparts and fearlessly emphasize their shared humanity (Leuchtenburg). The "emerging man" seems to be daring us to try to stop his rise from the manhole, his hands gripping its sides, his eyes focused intently upon the viewer.

According to several sources, Parks planned and executed the photograph as a photographic counterpart to Ralph Ellison's 1952 *Invisible Man*, a breakthrough novel about race and society that was both a bestseller and a critical success. *Invisible Man* is narrated in the first person by an unnamed African American man who traces his experiences from boyhood. The climax of the novel shows the narrator hunted by policemen controlling a Harlem race riot; escaping down a manhole, the narrator is trapped at first, but eventually decides to live permanently underground, hidden from society ("Ralph Ellison"). The correspondences between the photo and the book are apparent. In fact, according to the catalog accompanying an exhibit of Parks's photos selected by the photographer himself before his death in 2006, Ellison actually collaborated on the staging of the photo (*Bare Witness*).

More than just a photographic counterpart, however, it seems that Parks's *Emerging Man* can be read as a sequel to *Invisible Man*, with the emphasis radically shifted from resignation to optimism. The man who had decided to live underground now decides to emerge, and does so with determination. In this compelling photograph, Parks--himself an "emerging man," considering he was the first African American photographer to be hired full-time by the widely respected mainstream *Life* magazine--created a photograph that celebrated the changing racial landscape in American society.

Taylor 4

Works Cited

Bare Witness: Photographs by Gordon Parks. Catalog. Milan: Skira;
Stanford, CA: Iris & B. Gerald Cantor Center for Visual Arts at
Stanford University, 2006. Traditional Fine Arts Organization.
Resource Library. Web. 5 Dec. 2008.

Documenting America: Photographers on Assignment. 15 Dec. 1998.
*America from the Great Depression to World War II: Black-and-White
Photographs from the FSA-OWI, 1935-1945.* Prints and Photographs
Div., Lib. of Cong. Web. 3 Dec. 2008.

Leuchtenburg, William E. "The Conversion of Harry Truman." *American
Heritage* 42.7 (1991): 55-68. *America: History & Life.* Web. 5 Dec.
2008.

Parks, Gordon. *Ella Watson.* Aug. 1942. *America from the Great Depression
to World War II: Black-and-White Photographs from the FSA-OWI, 1935-
1945.* Prints and Photographs Div., Lib. of Cong. Web. 3 Dec. 2008.

---. *Emerging Man.* 1952. *PhotoMuse.* George Eastman House and ICP,
n.d. Web. 8 Dec. 2008.

"Ralph Ellison: *Invisible Man.*" *Literature and Its Times: Profiles of 300
Notable Literary Works and the Historical Events that Influenced
Them.* Ed. Joyce Moss and George Wilson. Vol. 4. Gale Research,
1997. *Literature Resource Center.* Web. 10 Dec. 2008.

Exercise 20.1

Dorothea Lange's *First-Graders at the Weill Public School* shows children of Japanese descent reciting the Pledge of Allegiance in San Francisco, California, in 1942. Following the steps below, write an essay suggesting what the image means.

1. Do some research on Lange's work. (Like Paul Taylor, you might start at the Library of Congress's online exhibit *Documenting America*, which features Lange, along with Gordon Parks and other photographers.)

2. Analyze the image using the criteria for analysis presented on pp. 675–77.

3. From this preliminary analysis, develop a tentative thesis that says what the image means and how it communicates that meaning.

■ Dorothea Lange, *First-Graders at the Weill Public School* (1942)

4. With this thesis in mind, plan your essay, using your analysis of the image to illustrate your thesis. Be aware that as you draft your essay, your thesis will develop and may even change substantially.

Exercise 20.2

Analyze one of the ads that follow by using the criteria for visual analysis on pp. 675–77. Be sure to consider the role that writing plays in the ad's overall meaning. Write an essay with a thesis that discusses the ad's central meaning and significance.

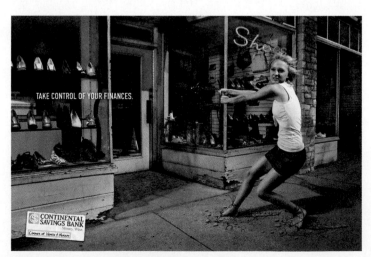

■ Magazine Ad for Continental Savings Bank (2008)

■ Billboards for Pepsi (2008)

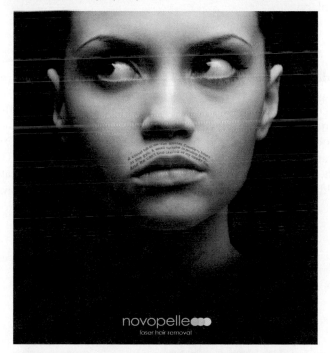

■ Magazine Ad for Novopelle Laser Hair Removal (2008)
(Text reads: "A closet full of low-cut blouses. Countless hours at the gym. A small fortune in pushup bras. And he can't stop staring at my upper lip.")

Exercise 20.3

Find an ad or public service announcement that you find compelling in its use of images. Analyze the ad by using the criteria for visual analysis on pp. 675–77. Be sure to consider the role that writing plays in the ad's overall meaning. Write an essay with a thesis that discusses the ad's central meaning and significance.

21

Designing Documents

The way a document is designed — the arrangement of text, visuals, and white space on a page — has a major impact on the readability of a document and may influence the reader's attitude toward it. This chapter introduces basic components of document design, offers guidelines for designing effective documents, and discusses some common formats for documents you may be asked to create in your college courses or in the workplace.

The Impact of Document Design

When we read a well-designed document, part of the meaning we take away from it is attributable to design. When we read a poorly designed document, however, it may be difficult to discern its meaning at all. We can probably all agree that effectively written documents are easy to navigate, and their meanings accessible to the intended audience. Good design should accordingly make readability easier and make the intended meaning clearer and more vivid.

The ways in which design affects the way we read documents can be illustrated fairly simply. Consider the following familiar phrase, rendered in four different ways:

I   l   o   v   e   y   o   u

I love you

The words in each rendering are the same, but the different uses of fonts, colors, and white space encourage us to read them very differently. The first message is vaguely unsettling (is that a ransom note? a message from a stalker?); the second seems conventionally sweet; the third carries no emotional or context clues, but the spacing makes it irritatingly difficult to read; and the fourth offers no tone or context clues at all (though this in itself might strike us as odd, given the meaning of the words). Thus design does far more than add visual interest: It actually directs how we read and to a certain extent determines the meaning we derive from texts.

The freedom you have in terms of using design elements and visuals in your college writing projects will vary quite a bit, depending on your instructors' preferences and the nature of the projects. As you write, however, you should always remain aware of the impact document design can have on your reader. And, any time you read a document — whether it is a textbook, a blog, or even an ad on the subway — you should stop to think about how that document was designed, and how that design affects your reading of it.

Considering Context, Audience, and Purpose

Context, audience, and purpose are the key components to consider in designing any document. For instance, if you are writing an essay for a college course, you can expect that your instructor and/or your classmates will read it carefully. Your design decisions should therefore make sustained reading as easy as possible; fonts that are too small to read easily or print that is too light to see clearly will make the reader's job unnecessarily difficult. Additionally, instructors usually ask students to submit hard-copy work that is double-spaced text with one-inch margins to give the instructor and/or a classmate room to write comments on the page.[*]

In most college courses, guidelines on design have traditionally followed a "less is more" rule — written assignments were generally expected to be printed on white, 8.5×11-inch paper, and the use of colors, extravagant fonts, sheerly decorative visuals, and the like, was in most cases discouraged. However, in many college classrooms, what constitutes an acceptable course "paper" or project is in transition; many instructors now allow or in some cases require the creation of multimodal projects — Web sites, video, PowerPoint presentations, playlists, and the like — in place of traditional papers.

Developments like these, driven largely by advances in technology, have obviously required some adjustments to traditional notions of acceptable design for college writing. "Less is more" still applies, however, in principle. Good design gives priority

---

[*] It is important to note that MLA, APA, and other style systems have specific rules regarding such things as spacing, margins, and heading formats. Be sure to ask your instructor whether you will be expected to adhere closely to these rules; if so, your choices regarding document design will be limited. For more on MLA and APA style, see pp. 776–88.

to clarity: Whatever the project, you should use design not for its own sake, but only in order to make your points as clearly, effectively, and efficiently as possible.

Of course, the same principle of clarity applies to most *non*academic documents you will write. In writing for nonacademic audiences, however, you cannot necessarily expect all readers to read your writing closely. Some readers may skim through your blog entries looking for interesting points; others might scan a report or memo for information important specifically to them. Design elements such as headings, bullets, and chunking will help these readers find the information of most interest to them.

Frequently, too, your document design decisions will be predetermined by the kind of document you are preparing. Business letters and memos, for example, traditionally follow specific formats. Because your readers will bring certain expectations to these kinds of documents, altering an established format can cause confusion and should therefore be avoided.

To analyze the context in which a document is read or used, ask yourself the following questions:

- ***Where will my document be read?*** Will the document be read on paper in a well-lighted, quiet room, or in another context — perhaps on a laptop in a noisy, dimly lit coffee shop?

- ***Do my readers have specific expectations for this kind of document?*** Am I writing a memo, letter, or report that requires certain design conventions? Does my instructor expect me to follow MLA style, APA style, or another system?

- ***How will the information be used?*** Are my readers reading to learn, or to be entertained? Do I expect them to skim the document or to read it carefully?

Elements of Document Design

Readable fonts, informative headings, bulleted or numbered lists, and appropriate use of color, white space, and visuals like photographs, charts, and diagrams all help readers learn from your document.

Font Style and Size

Typography is a design term for the letters and symbols that make up the print on a page or a screen. You are already using important aspects of typography when you use capital letters, italics, boldface, or different sizes of type to signal a new sentence, identify the title of a book, or distinguish a heading from body text.

Word processing programs enable you to use dozens of different fonts, or typefaces; bold and italic versions of these fonts; and a range of font sizes. Fortunately, you can rely on some simple design principles to make good typographic choices for your documents.

Perhaps the most important advice for working with typography is to choose fonts that are easy to read. Some fonts are meant for decorative or otherwise very minimal use, and are hard to read in extended passages. Font style, font size, and combinations of style and size are features that can add to or detract from readability.

Considering Font Style. For most academic and business writing, you will probably want to choose a traditional font that is easy to read, such as Arial or Times New Roman. This book is set in Minion. Sentences and paragraphs printed in fonts that imitate *calligraphy* (typically called script fonts) or those that mimic Handwriting are not only difficult to read but also too informal in appearance for most academic and business purposes.

Some Fonts Appropriate for Academic and Business Writing

> Arial
> Georgia
> Tahoma
> Times New Roman
> Verdana

Considering Font Size. To ensure that your documents can be read easily, you also need to choose an appropriate font size (traditionally measured in units called **points**). For most types of academic writing, a 12-point font is standard for the main (body) text. For Web pages, however, you should consider using a slightly larger font to compensate for the difficulty of reading from a computer monitor. For computer-projected displays, you should use an even larger font size (such as 32-point, and typically no smaller than 18-point) to ensure that the text can be read from a distance.

Combining Font Styles and Sizes. Although computers now make hundreds of font styles and sizes available to writers, you should avoid confusing readers with too many different fonts in one document. Limit the fonts in a document to one or two that complement each other well. A common practice, for instance, is to choose one font for all titles and headings (such as Arial, 14-pt, boldface) and another for the body text (such as Times New Roman, 12-pt), as shown in the example here.

This Is an Example Heading

This is body text. This is body text.
This is body text. This is body text.
This is body text. This is body text.

This Is an Example Heading

This is body text. This is body text.
This is body text. This is body text.
This is body text. This is body text.

Headings and Body Text

Titles and headings are often distinguished from body text by boldface, italics, or font size. Headings are helpful in calling attention to certain parts or sections of a piece of writing and in offering readers visual cues to its overall organization. Always check with your instructor about the conventions for using (or not using) these elements in the particular discipline you are studying.

Distinguishing between Headings and Subheadings. Typically, headings for major sections (level-one headings) must have more visual impact than those subdividing these sections (level-two headings), which should be more prominent than headings within the subdivisions (level-three headings). The typography should reflect this hierarchy of headings. Here is one possible system for distinguishing among three levels of headings:

LEVEL-ONE HEADING
Level-Two Heading
Level-Three Heading

Notice that the level-one and level-two headings are given the greatest prominence by the use of boldface and that they are distinguished from one another by the use of all capital letters for the major heading versus capital and lowercase letters for the subheading. The third-level heading, italicized but not boldfaced, is less prominent than the other two headings but can still be readily distinguished from body text. Whatever system you use to distinguish headings and subheadings, be sure to apply it consistently throughout your document.

For more on selecting appropriate headings and subheadings, see Chapter 13, pp. 613–14.

Positioning Headings Consistently. In addition to keeping track of the font size and style of headings, you need to position headings in the same way throughout a piece of writing. You will want to consider the spacing above and below headings and determine whether the headings should be aligned with the left margin, indented a fixed amount of space, or centered. In this book, headings like the one that begins this paragraph — **Positioning Headings Consistently** — are aligned with the left margin and followed by a period and a fixed amount of space.

Using Type Size to Differentiate Headings from Text. In documents that do not need to observe the MLA or APA style, which have specific rules about formatting, you may wish to use font size to help make headings visually distinct from the body of the text. If you do so, avoid making the headings too large. To accompany 12-point body text, for instance, a 14-point heading will do. The default settings for heading and body text styles on most word processing and desktop publishing programs are effective, and you may want to use them to autoformat your heading and text styles.

Numbered and Bulleted Lists

Lists are often an effective way to present information in a logical and visually coherent way. Use a **numbered list** (1, 2, 3) to present the steps in a process or to list items that readers will need to refer back to easily (for instance, see the sample e-mail message on p. 706). Use a **bulleted list** (marking each new item with a "bullet" — a dash, circle, or box) to highlight key points when the order of the items is not significant (for instance, see the sample memo on p. 704). Written instructions, such as recipes, are typically formatted using numbered lists, whereas a list of supplies, for example, is more often presented in the form of a bulleted list.

Colors

Color printers, photocopiers, and online technology facilitate the use of color, but color does not necessarily make text easier to read. In most academic print documents, the only color you should use is black. While color is typically used more freely in academic writing produced in other media (for example, Web pages or slideshow presentations), it should still be used in moderation and always with the aim of increasing your readers' understanding of what you have to say. Always consider, too, whether your readers might be color-blind and whether they will have access to a full-color version of the document.

Although the slideshow design in Figure 21.1 is visually interesting and the heading is readable, the bulleted text is very hard to read because there is too little contrast between the text color and the background color.

Figure 21.1 A Document with Too Little Color Contrast

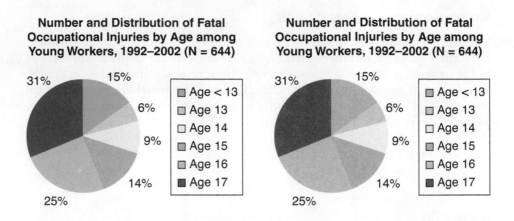

Figure 21.2 A Pie Chart That Requires a Color Printer to Be Understandable

Source: National Institute for Occupational Safety and Health, "Data on Young Worker Injuries and Illnesses in Worker Health" (2004).

In Figure 21.2, it is clear that the person who created the pie chart carefully chose the colors to represent the different data. What the person did not consider, however, is how the colors would look when printed out on a black-and-white printer. It is nearly impossible to associate the labels with the slices of the pie and thus to read the chart.

Also consider the meanings associated with different colors. For example, in the United States and other Western cultures, white typically is associated with goodness and purity; in China, however, white represents grief and mourning. Although your use of color in an essay, a Web page, or a slideshow presentation might not carry such deep meaning, bear in mind that most people have emotional or psychological responses to colors and color combinations.

White Space

Another basic element of document design, white space, is the open, or blank, space surrounding the text. White space is usually used between a heading, for instance, and the paragraph that follows the heading. You also use white space when you set the margins on the page, and even when you double-space between lines of text. In all of these cases, the space makes your document easier to read. When used generously, white space facilitates reading by keeping the pages of a document uncluttered and by helping the eye find and follow the text.

Chunking. Chunking, the breaking up of text into smaller units, also facilitates reading. Paragraphing is a form of chunking that divides text into units of closely related information. In most academic essays and reports, text is double-spaced, and paragraphs are distinguished by indenting the first line one-half inch.

In single-spaced text, you may want to make reading easier by adding extra space between paragraphs, rather than indenting the first lines of paragraphs. This format, referred to as **block style**, is often used in memos, letters, and electronic documents. When creating electronic documents, especially Web pages, you might consider chunking your material into separate "pages" or screens, with links connecting the chunks.

Margins. Adequate margins are an important component of general readability. If the margins are too small, your page will seem cluttered. Generally, for academic essays, use one-inch margins on all sides unless your instructor (or the style manual you are following) advises differently. Some instructors ask students to leave large margins to accommodate marginal comments.

Visuals

Tables, graphs, charts, diagrams, photographs, maps, and screen shots add visual interest and are often more effective in conveying information than prose alone. Be certain, however, that each visual has a valid role to play in your work; if the visual is merely a decoration, leave it out or replace it with a visual that is more appropriate.

You can create visuals on a computer, using the drawing tools of a word processing program, the charting tools of a spreadsheet program, or software specifically designed for creating visuals. You can also download visuals from the Internet or photocopy or scan visuals from print materials. If your essay is going to be posted on the Web on a site that is not password-protected and a visual you want to use is from a source that is copyrighted, you should request written permission from the copyright holder (such as the photographer, publisher, or site sponsor). For any visual that you borrow from or create based on data from a source, be sure to cite the source in the caption, your bibliography, or both, according to the guidelines of the documentation system you are using.

Choose Appropriate Visuals and Design the Visuals with Their Final Use in Mind

Select the types of visuals that will best suit your purpose. The following list identifies various types, explains what they are best used for, and provides examples. If you plan to incorporate a visual into a computer-projected display, try to envision the original version as it would appear enlarged on a screen. Similarly, if you intend the visual for use on a Web page, consider how it will appear when displayed on a computer screen.

- *Tables.* A table is used to display numerical or textual data that is organized into columns and rows to make it easy to understand. A table usually includes several items as well as variables for each item. For example, the first column of Table 21.1 includes cities and states; the next two columns show the city

Table 21.1 Population Change for the Ten Largest U.S. Cities, 1990 to 2000

| City and State | Population | | Change, 1990 to 2000 | |
	April 1, 2000	April 1, 1990	Number	Percentage
New York, NY	8,008,278	7,322,564	685,714	9.4
Los Angeles, CA	3,694,820	3,485,398	209,422	6.0
Chicago, IL	2,896,016	2,783,726	112,290	4.0
Houston, TX	1,953,631	1,630,553	323,078	19.8
Philadelphia, PA	1,517,550	1,585,577	−68,027	−4.3
Phoenix, AZ	1,321,045	983,403	337,642	34.3
San Diego, CA	1,223,400	1,110,549	112,851	10.2
Dallas, TX	1,188,580	1,006,877	181,703	18.0
San Antonio, TX	1,144,646	935,933	208,713	22.3
Detroit, MI	951,270	1,027,974	−76,704	−7.5

Source: U.S. Census Bureau, Census 2000; 1990 Census, Population and Housing Unit Counts, United States (1990 CPH-2-1).

population in 1990 and in 2000; and the final two columns show the change in population from 1990 to 2000 in number and percentage.

- *Bar graphs.* A bar graph typically compares numerical differences, often over time, for one or more items. For example, Figure 21.3 shows the rise in Internet access across five years (1997–2001) for U.S. households of varying incomes.

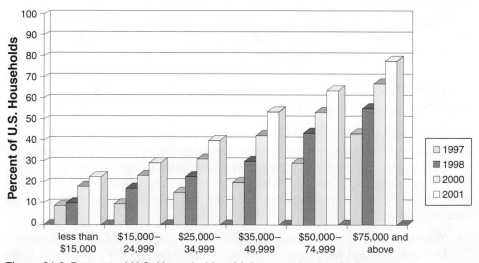

Figure 21.3 Percent of U.S. Households with Internet Access by Income

Source: U.S. Department of Commerce.

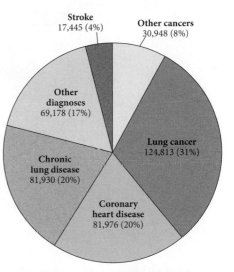

Figure 21.5 Average Annual U.S. Deaths Attributable to Cigarette Smoking, 1995–1999

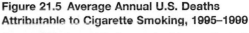

Source: Data from U.S. Centers for Disease Control.

Note: Total annual average is 406,290 deaths.

Figure 21.4 Title I Spending for Low-Income Children (in constant dollars)

Source: U.S. Department of Education.

- **Line graphs.** A line graph charts change over time, typically with only one variable represented (unlike in Figure 21.3, where the bar chart data are organized into six variables). For example, Figure 21.4 shows the amount of government spending for low-income children between 1966 and 2002.

- **Pie charts.** A pie chart shows the sizes of parts making up a whole. For instance, the whole (100 percent) in the chart shown in Figure 21.5 is the average annual number of deaths in the United States attributable to cigarette smoking; the parts are the specific causes of death, such as lung cancer (31 percent) and coronary heart disease (20 percent).

- **Flowcharts.** A flowchart shows a process broken down into parts or stages. Flowcharts are particularly helpful for explaining a process or facilitating a decision based on a set of circumstances, as shown, for instance, in Figure 21.6.

- **Organization charts.** An organization chart does what its name suggests — it creates a map of lines of authority within an organization, such as a company. Typically, the most important person — the person to whom most employees report — appears at the top of the chart, as seen in Figure 21.7, where the managing editor, who oversees the entire daily newspaper, appears at the top.

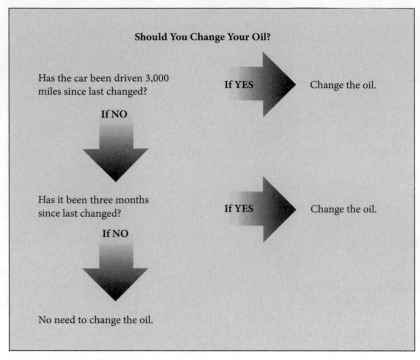

Figure 21.6 Oil-Changing Decision Process

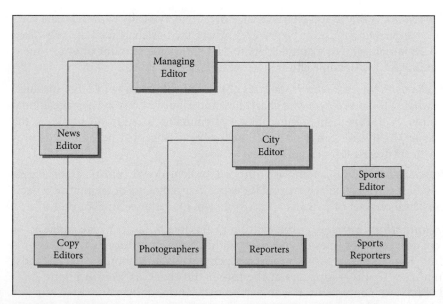

Figure 21.7 The Newsroom of a Typical Small Daily Newspaper

cerebral hemisphere

pituitary gland

brainstem

cerebellum

spinal cord

Figure 21.8 A Cross-Section of the Human Brain

- *Diagrams.* A diagram depicts an item or its properties, often using symbols. It is typically used to show relationships or how things function. (See Figure 21.8.)

- *Drawings and cartoons.* A drawing shows a simplified version or an artist's interpretation of an object or situation. Cartoons, like the one in Figure 21.9, are drawings typically used to make an argumentative point, usually in a humorous way.

- *Photographs.* Photographs are used when an author wants to represent a real and specific object, place, or person, often for its emotional impact. For instance, a student selected Figure 21.10, a photo of a burrowing owl, to be included in a report about the ways in which local development was affecting endangered species. Although photographic images are generally assumed to duplicate what the eye sees, a photograph may, in fact, be manipulated in a variety of ways for special effects. Photographs that have been altered should be so identified.

Figure 21.9 A Cartoon That Makes an Argument about Using Native American Names for Sports Teams

Figure 21.10 The Burrowing Owl

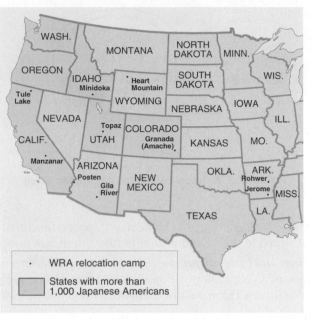

Figure 21.11 Western Relocation Authority Centers

- *Maps.* Maps are used to show geographical areas, lay out the spatial relationships of objects, or make a historical or political point. Figure 21.11 identifies World War II-era Western Relocation Authority Centers and states that had a high Japanese American population during World War II. The map reveals that though they posed no threat to U.S. security, many Japanese Americans were relocated a great distance from their homes during the war.

- *Screen shots.* A screen shot duplicates the appearance of a specific computer screen or of a window or other section within it. Screen shots can be used to capture a Web page to include in a print document or to describe steps or instructions for using a piece of software (see Figure 21.12).

Figure 21.12 Screen Capture to Accompany Written Instructions, "How to Insert a Chart into a Word Processing Document"

Number and Title Your Visuals

Number your visuals in sequential order and give each one a title. Refer to tables as *Table 1, Table 2,* and so on, and to other types of visuals as *Figure 1, Figure 2,* and so on. (In a long work with chapters or sections, you may also need to include the chapter or section number [*Figure 21.1*], as is done in this chapter of this book.)

Make sure each visual has a title that reflects the subject of the visual (for example, income levels) and its purpose (to compare and illustrate changes in those income levels): *Figure 1. Percentage of U.S. Households in Three Income Ranges, 1990–2000.* Notice that MLA style requires that the title for a table be placed above the table and the title for a figure be placed below the figure.

Label the Parts of Your Visuals and Include Descriptive Captions

To help readers understand a visual, clearly label all of its parts. In a table, for instance, give each column a heading; likewise, label each section of a pie chart with the percentage and the item it represents. You may place the label on the chart itself if it is readable and clear; if that is not practical, place a legend next to the chart.

Some visuals may require a caption that provides a fuller description than the title alone does. Your caption might also include an explanation helpful to understand the visual, as in Figure 21.11.

Cite Your Visual Sources

Finally, if you borrow a visual from another source or create a visual from borrowed information, you must cite the source, following the guidelines for the documentation style you are using (see Figure 21.2 and Table 21.1 for examples). In addition, be sure to document the source in your list of works cited or references at the end of your document.

Integrate the Visual into the Text

Visuals should facilitate, not disrupt, the reading of the body text. To achieve this goal, you need to first introduce and discuss the visual in your text and then insert the visual in an appropriate location.

Introducing the Visual. Ideally, you should introduce each visual by referring to it in your text immediately *before* the visual appears. An effective textual reference answers the following questions:

- What is the number of the visual?
- Where is it located?
- What kind of information does it contain?
- What important point does it make or support?

Here is an example of an effective introduction for the line graph shown earlier (Figure 21.4):

> Note the sharp increase between 1990 and 2002 in federal spending for disadvantaged children (see Figure 21.4), which rose steadily over this period despite fluctuations in partisan control of Congress and the White House.

Placing the Visual in an Appropriate Location. MLA style requires and APA style recommends that you place a visual in the body of your text as soon after the discussion as possible, particularly when the reader will need to consult the visual. In APA style, visuals can also be grouped at the end of an essay if they contain supplemental information that may not be of interest to the reader or if the visuals take up multiple pages. (See Figure 21.13 for a page from a sample student paper with a figure included. Note that the figure is mentioned in the text and placed directly after this introduction, and that it includes a descriptive title with source information.)

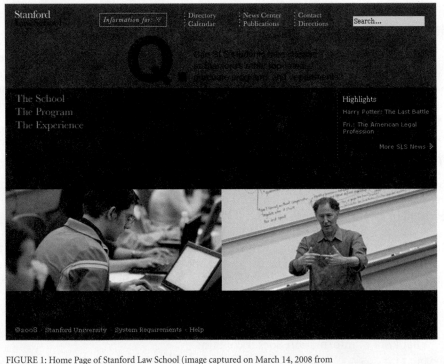

Stanford University anchors the reputation and identity of their law school via their Web site (see Figure 1). The page features strongly contrasting colors—red, black, and light grey—and includes graphics that change each time the page is reloaded: photos of students and professors, in class and on campus, as well as questions whose answers are likely to be of interest to prospective students and other visitors to the site. These rotating graphics are meant to represent the various facets of Stanford Law School.

FIGURE 1: Home Page of Stanford Law School (image captured on March 14, 2008 from http://www.law.stanford.edu).

The question and photos are the most prominent features of the page, but the basic information about the law school (linked from "The School," "The Program," and "The Experience" at left) is easy to locate.

Figure 21.13 Excerpt from Sample Student Paper with Figure

Use Common Sense When Creating Visuals on a Computer

If you use a computer program to create visuals, keep this advice in mind:

- *Make the decisions that your computer cannot make for you.* A computer can automatically turn spreadsheet data into a pie chart or bar graph, but only you can decide which visual — or what use of color, if any — is most appropriate for your purpose.

- *Avoid "chart junk."* Many computer programs provide an array of special effects that can be used to alter visuals, including three-dimensional renderings, textured backgrounds, and shadowed text. Such special effects often detract from the intended message of the visual by calling attention to themselves instead. Use them sparingly, and only when they emphasize key information.

- *Use clip art sparingly, if at all.* Clip art consists of icons, symbols, and other simple, typically abstract, copyright-free drawings. Because clip art simplifies ideas, it is of limited use in conveying the complex information contained in most academic writing.

Sample Documents

Earlier in this chapter you saw examples of various types of visuals; in this section you will take a look at various types of documents that you may be asked to prepare. Each sample document is accompanied by a discussion of appropriate design conventions.

As you examine the documents, try also to analyze the way that typography, color, white space, and visuals are used to guide the reader's eye across the page. What design features make the documents easy to read? What features make finding specific information within the documents easy? What features make the document easy to use?

In addition to examining the sample documents with these questions in mind, look at the sample research paper in Chapter 24, pp. 787–94.

Memos

Memos, such as the one shown in Figure 21.14, are documents sent between employees of the same organization (in contrast to business letters, which are sent to people outside the organization). The following conventions for writing a memo are well established and should rarely be altered. In addition, some organizations have specific guidelines for memos (such as the use of letterhead).

- *Heading.* A memo should carry the major heading *Memorandum* or *Memo.* If you are using letterhead stationery, position the heading just below the letterhead. The heading may be centered on the page or positioned at the left margin (depending on your organization's guidelines). In either case, the heading should be distinguished in some way from the rest of the body text, such as by a large font size, boldface type, or capital letters.

- *Content headings.* Just below the heading and separated by at least one line of space are the content headings: *Date, To, From,* and *Subject.* Place the content headings at the left margin and in the same size font as the body text.

- *Body text.* The main text of a memo is usually presented in block style: single-spaced with an extra line of space between paragraphs. (Do not indent the first

Subject line states clearly what the memo is about.

Main point stated in first sentence; key information highlighted in bold

Bulleted list

Request for action

"Copies" line identifies additional recipients of the memo.

SMITH AND KLEIN ASSOCIATES
MEMORANDUM

DATE: February 24, 2010
TO: Mary Reynolds, Vice President
FROM: Fred Rivera, Account Manager
SUBJECT: Staley Pharmaceutical Presentation

The president and advertising director for Staley Pharmaceutical will review ideas and preliminary sketches on **Tuesday, March 7.** The presentation will be held in the ninth-floor conference room from **9:30 a.m. until noon.** We have prepared a complete campaign for their new cold tablet, including television and radio spots and print advertisements. We can expect them to raise the following issues during the meeting.

- **Budget:** Our proposed budget is significantly higher than the original estimate (see the figures attached). The higher numbers reflect their additional requests after the estimate was prepared.
- **Schedule:** Staley plans to bring the product to market on November 1. The advertising campaign is scheduled to begin in mid-October. This schedule will be tight, and we may not be able to meet our deadlines without increasing our costs.

Please let me know if you will be available to attend all or part of the meeting on March 7.

cc: Greg Miller, Senior Designer
      Nora Katz, Sales Manager

Figure 21.14 A Sample Memo

line of paragraphs in block style.) If you need to call attention to specific information, consider presenting it in a numbered or bulleted list, or highlight the information visually by using boldface or extra white space above and below it. In a memo announcing a meeting, for example, you might boldface the date, time, and place of the meeting so the reader can quickly find the information, or you might set off the date, time, and place on separate lines.

Letters

The **business letter** (such as the one shown in Figure 21.15) is the document most often used for correspondence between representatives of one organization and representatives of another, though e-mail messages are increasingly being used in place of business letters. Business letters are written to obtain information about a company's products, to register a complaint, to respond to a complaint, or to introduce other documents (such as a proposal) that accompany the letter. As with memos, the design conventions for letters are long-established, although letters have more variations. Check to see whether there are specific business letter guidelines for your organization.

MetroType
409 South 8th Street
Pawkett, KY 45397

Phone: 502.555.1234
Fax: 502.555.4321
Email: type@micran.net

> Letterhead providing full contact information

January 26, 2010

Mr. Carl Boyer
Boyer Advertising Co.
1714 North 20th Street, Suite 16
Pawkett, KY 45397

> Full-block format: Each new line starts at left margin.

Dear Mr. Boyer:

Thank you for your letter of January 16, 2010. You asked whether MetroType could provide one of your clients with mail-merged letters after first converting your client's files from Corel WordPerfect to Microsoft Word. We certainly can. As I mentioned on the phone earlier today, creating mail-merge documents is one of our key services, and we frequently convert word-processing files for customers who are moving from one program to another.

> The author refers to earlier correspondence to state purpose of letter.

Much of the file conversion is done automatically; however, we have noticed that some parts of a file (such as accented characters and graphics) aren't always converted accurately. For this reason, we will compare a printout of your client's original files to a printout of the converted files and then make whatever corrections are necessary. For an additional fee, we can also proofread the final documents. If your client is interested in having us proofread the documents, I would be happy to furnish you with a quote.

> Letter is single-spaced, with double-spacing between paragraphs and other major parts.

> Elaboration, support, and detail

If you have any other questions, please call me at (502) 555-1234. In the meantime, I'll look forward to hearing from you again.

Sincerely yours,

Trudy L. Philips

> Signature

Trudy L. Philips
Owner/Director
TLP/dmp

> Author's initials, followed by typist's (if typist is not author)

Figure 21.15 A Sample Business Letter

The heading of a business letter consists of the contact information for both the sender and the recipient of the letter. Block style is the most commonly used format for business letters.

Be sure to state the purpose of your letter in the first few lines and to provide supporting information in the paragraphs that follow. Always maintain a courteous and professional tone throughout a business letter. Include enough information to identify clearly any documents you refer to in the letter.

E-mail

Increasingly, students and instructors rely on electronic mail to exchange information about assignments and schedules as well as to follow up on class discussions (see Figure 21.16 below). **E-mail** messages are usually concise, direct,

Accurate, informative subject line

Salutation (frequently omitted)

Casual but professional tone

Numbered list

> **Suggested Questions for the Panelists Visiting SW-312 - Message (Rich Text)**
>
> File   Edit   View   Insert   Format   Tools   Actions   Help
>
> Arial   ▾ 10 ▾ **A** | **B** *I* U | ≡ ≡ ≡ | ⋮≡ ⋮≡ ⋮≡
>
> Send | 🖫 🖨 | ✂ 🗈 🖺 | 📇 🔗 📎 📄 Attach as Adobe PDF | 📖 🔖 | 🗐 ❗ ↓ ▼
>
> | To... | Kevin S. Manderino <kmand@varnay.idbsu.edu> |
> | Cc... | Kay Warner <kwarn@varnay.idbsu.edu>; Renee Peña <rpena@varnay.idbsu.edu> |
> | Subject: | Suggested Questions for the Panelists Visiting SW-312 |
>
> Hello, everyone.
>
> Just a reminder that Professor Haberer asked our group to come up with some questions for the three social workers who will be visiting SW-312. Since the next class is only a couple of days away, I thought I would get the discussion going by sending you some suggested questions. I took a quick look at the chapter on career opportunities and came up with the following questions:
>
> 1. What education and experience are necessary for the work you do?
> 2. What is a typical day on the job like for you?
> 3. What do you like best about the work you do? What do you like least?
> 4. What projects are you currently working on? What challenges or problems do those projects pose?
> 5. How has the work you do changed over the last few years? How do you expect it to change in the next few years?
>
> That's about all I can come up with. Feel free to add to the list or change these questions. E-mail me your suggestions, and I'll put together a final list. I think we'll need at least ten questions, but that's just a guess.
>
> See you in class.
>
> *Paula*
>
> pgarr@varnay.idbsu.edu

Figure 21.16 A Sample E-Mail Message

relatively informal, and limited to a single subject. Effective e-mails include a clear subject line.

In many organizations, e-mail messages are replacing handwritten or typed memos. When you send a memo electronically, make sure the headings automatically provided by the e-mail program convey the same essential information as the content headings in a traditional memo. If you are part of a large or complex organization, you may want to repeat your name and add such information as your job title, division, and telephone extension in a "signature" at the end of the document.

E-mail is a broader medium of communication than the business memo. Nevertheless, in anything other than quick e-mails to friends, you should maintain a professional tone. Avoid sarcasm and humor, which may not come across as you intend, and be sure to proofread and spell-check your message before sending it. Also, because e-mail messages are accessible to many people other than the person to whom you are writing, always be careful about what you write in an e-mail message.

While e-mail messages are among the simplest forms of electronic documents, new software programs allow you to attach files, insert hypertext links, and even insert pictures and graphics into your e-mail documents. As a matter of courtesy, check to be sure that the recipient of your e-mail message has the software to read these electronic files before you include them with the message.

Résumés

A **résumé** is used to acquaint a prospective employer with your work experience, education, and accomplishments. All résumés contain such basic information as your name, address, phone number, and e-mail address.

The résumé is a good example of why the context in which a document is read is so important. An employer may receive dozens of résumés for one position. Your résumé may not be read closely in a first screening. Consequently, your résumé should highlight your important qualifications visually so that the reader can quickly find the pertinent information by scanning the page.

The format of résumés varies among disciplines and professions. Some professions require traditional formatting, while others allow for some flexibility in design. Be sure to research your field and the potential employers to see if a particular résumé format is preferred; consider consulting recently published reference books that show examples of good résumés. Also consider whether posting your résumé on a Web site such as Monster.com might be advisable. Always tailor your résumé to the job for which you are applying.

Résumés may also vary in terms of what is emphasized — educational or work experience, for example. If you have little work experience, focus your résumé on your grade-point average, the courses you have taken, the projects you have completed, and the applicable skills and abilities you have acquired in college. (For an example of such a résumé, see Figure 21.17.) If you have extensive, relevant, and continuous work experience, consider a reverse-chronological résumé, listing the jobs you have held (beginning with the most recent job) and describing the duties, responsibilities, and accomplishments associated with each one. If you have shifted

Contact information

Kim Hua
Current Address: MS 1789, Union College, Union, PA 55342
Permanent Address: 702 Good Street, Borah, ID 83702
Phone: (412) 555-1234 E-mail: khua@mailer.union.edu

EDUCATION

| Union College | Bachelor of Arts, | Anticipated May 2011 |
| Union, PA | Child Development | GPA: 3.7 |

Relevant Courses: Lifespan Human Development, Infancy and Early Childhood, Parent-Child Relations, Fundamentals of Nutrition, Education of the Preschool Child

Relevant Projects: Coordinator, collaborative research project analyzing educational goals for local Head Start program. Lead writer, report on parent-child relations, delivered to the Borah, Idaho, School Board.

CHILD DEVELOPMENT WORK EXPERIENCE

Work experience begins with most current employment

- *Summer 2009, Union College Child-Care Center, Union College, Union, PA*
  Child Care Provider: Provided educational experiences and daily care for three 2-year-olds and four 3-year-olds. Prepared daily activity agendas.

- *Summer 2008, St. Alphonsus Day Care Center, St. Alphonsus Hospital, Union, PA*
  Child Care Provider: Provided educational experiences and daily care for a group of nine children ages six through ten.

Relevant volunteer work

- *Fall 2007, Governor's Commission for the Prevention of Child Abuse, Union, PA*
  Intern: Located online resources relevant to the prevention of child abuse. Recommended which resources to include in the Web site of the Governor's Commission.

OTHER WORK EXPERIENCE

Other experience showing dependability and responsibility

2007 to present, Union Falls Bed & Breakfast, Union, PA
Payroll Manager: Maintain daily payroll records for all employees, compile daily and weekly reports of payroll costs for the manager, and ensure compliance with all applicable state and federal laws governing payroll matters.

PROFESSIONAL AFFILIATIONS

Past President, Union College Child and Family Studies Club; Student Member, American Society of Child Care Professionals; Member, National Child Care Providers

Figure 21.17 A Sample Résumé

directions during your adult life, consider organizing your résumé in a way that emphasizes the strengths and skills you have acquired and used in different settings — for instance, your experience speaking in front of groups, handling money, or working with specific software programs.

Do not include such personal information as your height, weight, and age. Mention personal interests or hobbies only if they are relevant to the position. Finally, proofread your résumé carefully; it must be error-free. Your résumé is the first impression you make on a potential employer. Do everything you can to make a good first impression.

Job-Application Letters

A **job-application letter** (sometimes called a **cover letter**) is sent with a résumé when you apply for a job. The primary purpose of the job-application letter is to persuade your reader that you are a qualified candidate for employment and to introduce your résumé. For college students and recent graduates, most job-application letters (such as the one shown in Figure 21.18) consist of four paragraphs:

1. The *first paragraph* identifies the position you are applying for and how you became aware of its availability. If you are not applying for a particular position, the first paragraph expresses your desire to work for the particular organization.
2. The *second paragraph* briefly describes your education, focusing on specific achievements, projects, and relevant course work.
3. The *third paragraph* briefly describes your work experience, focusing on relevant responsibilities and accomplishments.

Note that the second and third paragraphs should not merely restate what is in your résumé; rather, they should help persuade your reader that you are qualified for the job.

4. The *fourth paragraph* expresses your willingness to provide additional information and to be interviewed at the employer's convenience.

Lab Reports

A **lab report** is written to summarize the results of an experiment or test, and generally consists of the following five sections:

1. The *Introduction* provides background information: the hypothesis of the experiment, the question to be answered, how the question arose.
2. The *Methods* section describes how the research was conducted or how the experiment was performed.
3. The *Results* section describes what happened as a result of your research or experiment.
4. The *Discussion* section consists of your explanation of and reasoning about your results.
5. The *References* section cites the sources used in conducting the research, performing the experiment, or writing the report.

Modified block format:
Address, date, and signature
block begin five spaces to
the right of center.

308 Fairmont Street
Warren, CA 07812
June 9, 2009

Ms. Ronda Green
Software Engineer
Santa Clara Technology
P.O. Box 679
Santa Clara, CA 09145

Dear Ms. Green:

Purpose of the letter

I am responding to your February 10 posting on Monster.com (reference #91921) announcing that Santa Clara Technology is accepting résumés for an entry-level engineer position in the Quality Assurance Department. I think that my experience as an intern in quality assurance and my educational background qualify me for this position.

Education paragraph

As my résumé states, I graduated this past May from the University of Southern California (USC) with a Bachelor of Science degree in Interdisciplinary Studies. The Interdisciplinary Studies program at USC allows students to develop a degree plan spanning at least two disciplines. My degree plan included courses in computer science, marketing, and technical communication. In addition to university courses, I have completed courses in team dynamics, project management, and C, C++, and C# programming offered by the training department at PrintCom, a manufacturer of high-end laser printers.

Work-experience
paragraph

Throughout last summer, I worked as an intern in the quality-assurance department of PrintCom. I assisted quality-assurance engineers in testing printer drivers, installers, and utilities. In addition, I maintained a database containing the results of these tests and summarized the results in weekly reports. This experience gave me valuable knowledge of the principles of quality assurance and of the techniques used in testing software.

Concluding paragraph

I would appreciate the opportunity to discuss further the education, skills, and abilities I could bring to Santa Clara Technology. You can reach me any workday after 3 p.m. (PDT) at (907) 555-1234 or by e-mail at sstur17@axl.com.

Sincerely yours,

Shelley Sturman

Shelley Sturman

Enclosure: résumé

Figure 21.18 A Sample Job-Application Letter

The content and format of a lab report may vary from discipline to discipline or from course to course. Before writing a lab report, be certain that you understand your instructor's requirements. The sample in Figure 21.19 (see pp. 713–14) shows excerpts from a lab report written by two students in a soils science course. It uses the documentation format advocated by the Council of Science Editors (CSE).

Web Pages

While Web pages offer the potential for expanded use of color and visuals (including animation and video), the general principles of design used for paper documents can be applied to them. Again, you will want to evaluate the context in which the document will be read. Will your reader be reading from a computer screen or printing the document on paper for reading? If the reading takes place on a computer screen, how big is the screen and how good is its resolution? Reading from a computer screen can be more difficult than reading on paper, so you will want to avoid small fonts and confusing backgrounds that distract from the core content.

Web pages and other electronic texts differ from print texts in large part because of the links they can include to additional text or graphics, to other Web pages, or to short clips of video, animation, or sound. As an author, you must consider that, because of these links, readers may navigate your text in a nonlinear fashion, starting almost anywhere they like and branching off whenever a link piques their curiosity. To help readers find their way around, Web authors often provide a navigation scheme, usually in the form of site maps or "index" pages.

HTML (hypertext markup language) is the standard language used for creating Web pages. Software programs called **HTML editors** provide novices with an easy way to create Web pages, and most word processing programs allow a document to be converted into HTML and saved as a Web page.

As you design a Web page, beware of letting unnecessary graphics and multimedia elements distract from your message. Yes, you *can* add a textured background to the screen that will make it look like marble or cloth, but will that background make reading the text easier? Will a sound file improve communication of your main points, or are you adding sound simply because you can? Consider the following guidelines when designing a Web page:

- *Make sure your text is easy to read.* Many Web pages are difficult to read because of textured and brightly colored backgrounds. Keep the background of a Web page light in tone so that your text can be read with ease. Because color type can also be difficult to read, avoid vibrant colors for long blocks of text. Bear in mind that most readers are used to reading dark (typically black) text on a light (typically white) background.

- *Chunk information carefully and keep your Web pages short.* Because many people have difficulty reading long documents on a computer screen, be sure to chunk your information into concise paragraphs. Also, readers often find it difficult to read a Web page that requires extensive scrolling down the screen. Break up long text blocks into separate Web pages that require no more than one or two screens of scrolling. Use hypertext links to connect the text blocks and to help readers navigate across the pages.

- *Limit the file size of your Web pages.* A Web page that is filled with visuals and sound files can be slow and clunky to load, especially for users with old computers or dial-up connections to the Internet. Limiting your use of visuals and sound files so that your pages load quickly will help ensure that your documents are read.

- *Use hypertext links effectively.* Make sure that all of your links work correctly and that all the pages of your Web site include a link back to your home page so that readers can access it easily. You can make your text easier to read by judiciously limiting the number of links you embed in it. In addition to embedded text links, consider including a list of important links on a separate page for readers' convenience.

- *Use the elements of document design.* Remember what you have learned in this chapter about typography, white space, color, and visuals when you create Web pages. Most principles of good print document design apply to Web page design as well.

Bulk Density and Total Pore Space

Joe Aquino and Sheila Norris

Soils 101

Lab Section 1

February 22, 2010

Introduction

Soil is an arrangement of solids and voids. The voids, called pore spaces, are important for root growth, water movement, water storage, and gas exchange between the soil and atmosphere. A medium-textured soil good for plant growth will have a pore-space content of about 0.50 (half solids, half pore space). The total pore space is the space between sand, silt, and clay particles (micropore space) plus the space between soil aggregates (macropore space).[1]

[The Introduction continues with a discussion of the formulas used to calculate bulk density, particle density, and porosity.]

Methods

To determine the bulk density[2] and total pore space of two soil samples, we hammered cans into the wall of a soil pit (Hagerstown silt loam). We collected samples from the Ap horizon and a Bt horizon. We then placed a block of wood over the cans so that the hammer did not smash them. After hammering the cans into the soil, we dug the cans, now full of soil, out of the horizons; we trimmed off any excess soil. The samples were dried in an oven at 105°C for two days and weighed. We then determined the volume of the cans by measuring the height and radius, as follows:

$$volume = 1/4 \, r^2 h$$

We used the formulas noted in the Introduction to determine bulk density and porosity of the samples. Particle density was assumed to be 2.65 g/cm^3. The textural class of each horizon was determined by feel; that is, we squeezed and kneaded each sample and assigned it to a particular textural class.

Background information that the reader will need to understand the experiment

Detailed explanation of the methods used

Figure 21.19 A Sample Lab Report   (*continued*)

Presents the results of the experiment, with a table showing quantitative data

Results

We found both soils to have relatively light bulk densities and large porosities, but the Bt horizon had greater porosity than the Ap. Furthermore, we determined that the Ap horizon was a silt loam, whereas the Bt was a clay (see Table 1).

Table 1 Textural class, bulk density, and porosity of two Hagerstown soil horizons

Textural Class	Ap Silt Loam	Bt Clay
Bulk density (g/cm³)	1.20	1.08
Porosity	0.55	0.59

[The Results section continues with sample calculations.]

Explains what was significant about the results of the research

Discussion

Both soils had bulk densities and porosities in the range we would have expected from the discussions in the lab manual and textbook. The Ap horizon is a medium-textured soil and is considered a good topsoil for plant growth, so a porosity around 0.5 is consistent with those facts. The Bt horizon is a fine-textured horizon (containing a large amount of clay), and the bulk density is in the predicted range.

[The Discussion section continues with further discussion of the results.]

[The References section begins on a new page.]

The references are in the format recommended by the Council of Science Editors (CSE)

References

1. Brady NC, Weil RR. The nature and properties of soils. 11th ed. New York: Prentice-Hall; 1996. 291 p.
2. Blake GR, Hartge KH. Bulk density. In: Klute A, editor. Methods of soil analysis. Part 1. 2nd ed. Agronomy 1986;9:363-376.

PART 4

Research Strategies

22

Field Research

For more on service learning, see Chapter 30.

In universities, government agencies, and the business world, field research can be as important as library research or experimental research. If you major in education, communication, or one of the social sciences, you will probably be asked to do writing based on your own observations, interviews, and questionnaire results. You will also read large amounts of information based on these methods of learning. You might also use observations or interviews to help you select or gain background for a service-learning project.

Observations and interviews are essential for writing profiles (Chapter 3). Interviewing could be helpful, as well, in documenting a trend or phenomenon and exploring its causes (Chapter 9): You might interview an expert or conduct a survey to investigate a trend, for example. In proposing a solution to a problem (Chapter 7), you might want to interview people involved; or if many people are affected, you might find it useful to prepare a questionnaire. In writing to explain an academic concept (Chapter 4), you might want to interview a faculty member who is a specialist on the subject. As you consider how you might use such research most appropriately, ask your instructor whether your institution requires you to obtain approval for your field research.

Observations

This section offers guidelines for planning an observational visit, taking notes on your observations, writing them up, and preparing for follow-up visits. Some kinds of writing are based on observations from single visits — travel writing, social workers' case reports, insurance investigators' accident reports — but most observational writing is based on several visits. An anthropologist or a sociologist studying an unfamiliar group or activity might observe it for months, filling several notebooks with notes. If you are profiling a place (Chapter 3), you almost certainly will want to make more than one observational visit, some of them perhaps combined with interviews.

Planning the Visit

To ensure that your observational visits are productive, you must plan them carefully.

Getting Access. If the place you propose to visit is public, you will probably have easy access to it. If everything you need to see is within view of anyone passing by or using the place, you can make your observations without any special arrangements. However, most observational visits require special access. Hence, you will need to call ahead or stop by to introduce yourself and to make an appointment, if necessary.

Announcing Your Intentions. State your intentions directly and fully. Say who you are, where you are from, and what you hope to do. You may be surprised at how receptive people can be to a college student on assignment. Not every place you wish to visit will welcome you, however. In addition, private businesses as well as public institutions place a variety of constraints on visitors.

Taking Your Tools. Take a pen and a notebook with a firm back so that you will have a steady writing surface. Some writers dictate their observations, but because transcribing takes a lot of time, we recommend simply writing your notes.

Observing and Taking Notes

Here are some basic guidelines for observing and taking notes.

Observing. Your purposes in observing are twofold: to describe what you observe and to analyze the activity or place, discovering a perspective that enables you to reveal insights into its meaning and significance.

Some activities invite the observer to watch from multiple vantage points, whereas others may limit the observer to a single perspective. Take advantage of every perspective available to you. Study the scene from a stationary position, and then try to move around it. The more varied your perspectives, the more details you are likely to observe.

Try initially to be an innocent observer: Pretend that you have never seen anything like this activity or place before. Then consider your own and your readers' likely preconceptions. Ask yourself which details are surprising and which confirm expectations.

Taking Notes. Perhaps the most important advice about notetaking during an observational visit is to record as many details as possible about the place or activity and to write down your insights (ideas, interpretations, judgments) as they come to mind. You will undoubtedly find your own style of notetaking, but here are a few pointers.

- Take notes in words or phrases.
- Draw diagrams or sketches if they will help you recall details later on. Take photos if you are given permission to do so, but be aware that some people do not want their pictures taken.
- Use abbreviations as much as you like, but use them consistently and clearly.
- Note any impressions, ideas, questions, or personal insights that occur to you.

- If you are expecting to see a certain behavior, try not to let this expectation influence what you actually do see. But note how your expectations are overturned.
- Use quotation marks around any overheard remarks or conversations you record.

Do not worry about covering every aspect of the activity or place. At the same time, however, you want to be sure to include details about the setting, the people, and your reactions.

■ ***The Setting.***   Describe the setting: Name or list objects you see there, and record details about them — their color, shape, size, texture, function, relation to similar or dissimilar objects. Although your notes will probably contain mainly visual details, you might also want to record sounds and smells. Be sure to include some notes about the shape, dimensions, and layout of the place as a whole. How big is it? How is it organized?

■ ***The People.***   Note the number of people you observe, their activities, their movements and behavior, and their appearance or dress. Record parts of overheard conversations. Indicate whether you see more men than women, more members of one nationality or ethnic group than another, more older than younger people. Most important, note anything surprising, interesting, or unusual about the people and how they interact with each other.

Reflecting on Your Observations

Immediately after your visit (within a few minutes, if possible), find a quiet place to reflect on what you saw, review your notes, and fill in any gaps. Give yourself at least a half-hour to add to your notes and to write a few sentences about your perspective on the place or activity. Ask yourself the following questions:

- What did I learn?
- How did what I observed fit my own or my readers' likely preconceptions of the place or activity? Did it upset any of my preconceptions?
- What interests me the most about the activity or place? What are my readers likely to find interesting about it?
- What, if anything, seemed contradictory or out of place?

Writing Up Your Notes

Clustering is described in Chapter 11, p. 563. Inventory-taking is described in Chapter 12, p. 583.

See Chapter 15 for a full discussion of describing strategies.

Your instructor may ask you to write up your notes, as Brian Cable did after visiting the Goodbody Mortuaries for his profile essay (Chapter 3). If so, review your notes, looking for a meaningful pattern. You might find clustering or taking inventory useful for discovering patterns in your notes.

Assume that your readers have never been to the place, and decide on the perspective of the place you want to convey. Choose details that will convey this, and then draft a brief description of the place.

Exercise 22.1

Arrange to meet with a small group (three or four students) for an observational visit somewhere on campus, such as the student center, campus gym, cafeteria, or restaurant. Assign each person in your group a specific task; one person can take notes on the appearance of the people, for example; another can take notes on their activities; another on their conversations; and another on what the place looks and smells like. After twenty to thirty minutes, report to each other on your observations. Discuss any difficulties that arise.

Preparing for Follow-Up Visits

It is important to develop a plan for your follow-up visits: questions to be answered, insights to be tested, types of information you would like to discover. If possible, do some interviewing and reading before a repeat visit so that you will have a greater understanding of the subject. For additional ideas on what to aim for in a follow-up visit, you might want to present your notes from your first visit to your instructor or to your class.

Interviews

Like making observations, interviewing tends to involve four basic steps: (1) planning and setting up the interview, (2) taking notes during the interview, (3) reflecting on the interview, and (4) writing up your notes.

Planning and Setting Up the Interview

The initial steps in interviewing involve choosing an interview subject and then arranging and planning for the interview.

Choosing an Interview Subject. For a profile of an individual, most or all of your interviews would be with that person. If you are writing about some activity in which several people are involved, however, choose subjects representing a variety of perspectives. For instance, you might interview several members of an organization to gain a more complete picture of its mission or activities. You should be flexible because you may be unable to speak with the person you initially targeted and may wind up interviewing someone else — the person's assistant, perhaps. Do not assume that this interview subject will be of little use to you. With the right questions, you might even learn more from the assistant than you would from the person you had originally expected to see.

Arranging an Interview. You may be nervous about calling up a busy person and asking for some of his or her time. Indeed, you may get turned down. But if so, it is possible that you will be referred to someone who will see you, perhaps someone whose job it is to talk to the public.

Do not feel that just because you are a student, you do not have the right to ask for people's time. Most people are delighted to be asked about themselves, particularly if you reach them when they are not feeling harried. Since you are a student on assignment, some people may even feel that they are performing a public service by talking with you.

When introducing yourself to arrange the interview, give a brief description of your project. If you talk too much, you could prejudice or limit the interviewee's response. At the same time, it is a good idea to exhibit some sincere enthusiasm for your project. If you lack enthusiasm, the person may see little reason to talk with you.

Keep in mind that the person you want to interview will be donating valuable time to you. Be certain that you call ahead to arrange a specific time for the interview. Arrive on time. Dress appropriately. Bring all the materials you need. Express your thanks when the interview is over. Finally, try to represent your institution well, whether your interview is for a single course assignment or part of a larger service-learning project.

Planning for the Interview. The best interview is generally the well-planned interview. Making an observational visit and doing some background reading beforehand can be helpful. In preparation for the interview, you should consider your objectives:

- Do you want details, or a general orientation (the "big picture") from this interview?
- Do you want this interview to lead you to interviews with other key people?
- Do you want mainly facts or opinions?
- Do you need to clarify something you have observed or read? If so, what?

The key to good interviewing is flexibility. You may be looking for facts, but your interview subject may not have any to offer. In that case, you should be able to shift gears and go after whatever your subject is in a position to discuss. Be aware that the person you are interviewing represents only one point of view. You may need to speak with several people to get a more complete picture.

Composing Questions. In addition to determining your objectives, you should prepare your questions in advance. Good questions can be the key to a successful interview.

Good questions come in two basic types: open and closed. **Open questions** give the respondent range and flexibility. They also generate anecdotes, personal revelations, and expressions of attitudes. **Closed questions** usually request specific information.

Suppose you are interviewing a small-business owner. You might begin with a specific (closed) question about when the business was established and then follow up with an open-ended question such as, "Could you take a few minutes to tell me something about your early days in the business? I'd be interested to hear how it got started, what your hopes were, and what problems you had to face." Consider asking directly for an anecdote ("What happened when your employees threatened to strike?"), encouraging reflection ("What do you think has helped you most? What has hampered you?"), or soliciting advice ("What advice would you give to someone trying to start a new business today?"). Here are some examples of open and closed questions:

Open Questions

- What do you think about (*name a person or an event*)?
- Describe your reaction when (*name an event*) happened.
- Tell me about a time you were (*name an emotion*).

Closed Questions

- How do you (*name a process*)?
- What does (*name a word or phrase*) mean?
- What does (*name a person, object, or place*) look like?
- How was (*name a product, process, etc.*) developed?

The best questions encourage the subject to talk freely but to the point. If an answer strays too far from the point, you may need to ask a follow-up question to refocus the talk. Another tack you might want to try is to rephrase the subject's answer, to say something like "Let me see if I have this right" or "Am I correct in saying that you feel . . . ?" Often, a person will take the opportunity to amplify the original response by adding just the anecdote or quotable comment you have been looking for.

Avoid questions that place unfair limits on respondents. These include forced-choice questions and leading questions.

Forced-choice questions impose your terms on respondents. If you are interviewing a counselor at a campus rape crisis center and want to know what he or she thinks is the motivation for rape, you could ask this question: "Do you think rape is about control or about rage?" But the counselor might not think that either control or rage satisfactorily explains the motivation for rape. A better way to phrase the question would be as follows: "People often fall into two camps on the issue of rape. Some think it is an expression of control, while others argue that it is an expression of rage. Do you think it is either of these? If not, what is your opinion?" Phrasing the question in this way allows interviewees to react to what others have said but also gives them freedom to set the terms for their response.

Leading questions assume too much. An example of this kind of question is this: "Do you think the number of rapes has increased because women are perceived as competitors in a highly competitive economy?" This question assumes that there is an increase in the occurrence of rape, that women are perceived (apparently by rapists) as economic competitors, and that the state of the economy is somehow related to acts of rape. A better way of asking the question might be to make the assumptions more explicit by dividing the question into its parts: "Has the occurrence of rape increased in recent years? If so, what could have caused this increase? I've heard some people argue that the state of the economy has something to do with rape. Some have suggested that rapists perceive women as competitors for jobs, and that this perception is linked to rape. Do you think there might be any truth to this?"

Bringing Your Tools. As for an observational visit, when you interview someone, you will need a pen and a notebook with a firm back so you can write in it easily without the benefit of a table or desk. You might find it useful to divide several pages into two columns by drawing a line about one-third of the width of the page from the left margin. Use the left-hand column to note details about the scene, the person, the mood of the interview, and other impressions. Head this column *Details and Impressions.* At the top of the right-hand column, write several questions. You may not use them, but they will jog your memory. This column should be titled *Information.* In it, you will record what you learn from answers to your questions.

For an example of notes of this sort, see Chapter 3. pp. 120–22.

Taking Notes during the Interview

In taking notes, your goals are to gather information and to record a few quotations, key words and phrases, and details of the scene, the person, and the mood of the interview. Remember that how something is said is as important as what is said. Look for material that will give texture to your writing — gesture, verbal inflection, facial expression, body language, physical appearance, dress, hair, or anything that makes the person an individual. In general, it is probably a good idea to do more listening than notetaking. You may not have much confidence in your memory, but if you pay close attention, you are likely to recall a good deal of the conversation afterward.

Reflecting on the Interview

As soon as you finish the interview, find a quiet place to reflect on it and review your notes. This reflection is essential because so much happens in an interview that you cannot record at the time. Spend at least a half-hour adding to your notes and thinking about what you learned.

At the end of this time, write a few sentences about your main impressions from the interview. Ask yourself these questions:

- What did I learn?
- What seemed contradictory or surprising about the interview?
- How did what was said fit my own or my readers' likely expectations about the person, activity, or place?
- How can I summarize my impressions?

Writing Up Your Notes

Your instructor may ask you to write up your interview notes. If so, review them for useful details and ideas. Decide what perspective you want to take on this person. Choose details that will contribute to this perspective. Select quotations and paraphrases of information you learned from the person.

You might also review notes from any related observations or from other interviews, especially if you plan to combine these materials in a profile, ethnographic study, or other project.

Questionnaires

Questionnaires let you survey the opinions and knowledge of large numbers of people. Compared to one-on-one interviews, they have the advantages of economy, efficiency, and anonymity. Some questionnaires, such as the ones you filled out when entering college, just collect demographic information: your name, age, sex, hometown, religious preference, intended major. Others, such as the Gallup and Harris polls, collect opinions on a wide range of issues. Before elections, we are bombarded with the results of such polls. Still other kinds of questionnaires, such as those used in academic research, are designed to help answer important questions about personal and societal problems.

This section briefly outlines procedures you can follow to carry out an informal questionnaire survey of people's opinions or knowledge.

Focusing Your Study

A questionnaire survey usually has a limited focus. You might need to interview a few people to find this focus, or you may already have a limited focus in mind. If you are developing a questionnaire as part of a service-learning project, discuss your focus with your supervisor or other staff members.

As an example, let us assume that you go to your campus student health clinic and have to wait over an hour to see a doctor. Sitting in the waiting room with many other students, you decide that this long wait is a problem that would be an ideal topic for an assignment you have been asked to do for your writing class, an essay proposing a solution to a problem (Chapter 7).

You do not have to explore the entire operation of the clinic to study this problem. You are not interested in how nurses and doctors are hired or in how efficient the clinic's system of ordering supplies is, for example. Your primary interests are how long students usually wait for appointments, what times are most convenient for students to schedule appointments, how the clinic accommodates students when demand is high, and whether the long wait discourages many students from getting the treatment they need. With this limited focus, you can collect valuable information using a fairly brief questionnaire. To be certain about your focus, however, you should talk informally with several students to find out whether they also think there is a problem with appointment scheduling at the clinic. You might want to talk with staff members, too, explaining your plans and asking for their views on the problem.

Whatever your interest, be sure to limit the scope of your survey. Try to focus on one or two important questions. With a limited focus, your questionnaire can be brief, and people will be more willing to fill it out. In addition, a survey based on a limited amount of information will be easier to organize and report on.

Writing Questions

The same two basic types of questions used for interviews, closed and open, are also useful in questionnaires. Figure 22.1 illustrates how these types of questions may be

This is a survey about the scheduling of appointments at the campus Student Health Clinic. Your participation will help determine how long students have to wait to use clinic services and how these services might be more conveniently scheduled. The survey should take only 3 to 4 minutes to complete. All responses are confidential. Thank you for your participation.

Two-way question —————

1. Have you ever made an appointment at the clinic?   (Circle one.)

   Yes   No

2. How frequently have you had to wait more than 10 minutes at the clinic for a scheduled appointment?   (Circle one.)

   Always   Usually   Occasionally   Never

Multiple-choice questions —————

3. Have you ever had to wait more than 30 minutes at the clinic for a scheduled appointment?   (Circle one.)

   Yes   No   Uncertain

4. From your experience so far with the clinic, how would you rank its system for scheduling appointments?   (Circle one.)

Ranking scale —————

	0	1	2	3	4	5
	no experience	inadequate	poor	adequate	good	outstanding

5. Given your present work and class schedule, when are you able to visit the clinic?   (Check all applicable responses.)

Checklist —————

   _____ 8–10 a.m.   _____ 1–3 p.m.
   _____ 10 a.m.–Noon   _____ 3–5 p.m.
   _____ 12–1 p.m.

6. Given your present work and class schedule, which times during the day (Monday through Friday) would be the most and least convenient for you to schedule appointments at the clinic?   (Rank the four choices from 1 for most convenient time to 4 for least convenient time.)

Ranking scale —————

   _____ Morning (7 a.m.–Noon)   _____ Dinnertime (5–7 p.m.)
   _____ Afternoon (12–5 p.m.)   _____ Evening (7–10 p.m.)

7. How would you evaluate your most recent appointment at the clinic?

8. Based on your experiences with scheduling at the clinic, what advice would you give to other students about making appointments?

Open questions —————

9. What do you believe would most improve the scheduling of appointments at the clinic?

10. If you have additional comments about scheduling at the clinic, please write them on the back of this page.

Figure 22.1 Sample Questionnaire: Scheduling at the Student Health Clinic

employed in the context of a questionnaire about the student health clinic problem. Notice that the questionnaire uses several forms of *closed questions* (in items 1–6): two-way questions, multiple-choice questions, ranking scales, and checklists. You will probably use more than one form of closed question in a questionnaire to collect different kinds of information. The sample questionnaire also uses several *open questions* (items 7–10) that ask for brief written answers. You may want to combine closed and open questions in your questionnaire because both offer advantages: Closed questions will give you definite answers, while open questions can elicit information you may not have anticipated as well as provide lively quotations for your essay explaining what you have learned.

Whatever types of questions you develop, try to phrase them in a fair and unbiased manner so that your results will be reliable and credible. As soon as you have a collection of possible questions, try them out on a few typical respondents. You need to know which questions are unclear, which seem to duplicate others, and which provide the most interesting responses. These tryouts will enable you to assess which questions will give you the information you need. Readers can also help you come up with additional questions.

Designing the Questionnaire

Begin your questionnaire with a brief, clear introduction stating the purpose of your survey and explaining how you intend to use the results. Give advice on answering the questions, and estimate the amount of time needed to complete the questionnaire (see Figure 22.1 for an example). You may opt to give this information orally if you plan to hand the questionnaire to groups of people and have them fill it out immediately. However, even in this case, your respondents will appreciate a written introduction that clarifies what you expect.

Select your most promising questions, and decide how to order them. Any logical order is appropriate. You might want to arrange the questions from least to most complicated or from general to specific. You may find it appropriate to group the questions by subject matter or format. Certain questions may lead to others. You might want to place open questions at the end (see Figure 22.1 for an example).

Design your questionnaire so that it looks attractive and readable. Make it look easy to complete. Do not crowd questions together to save paper. Provide plenty of space for readers to answer questions, especially open questions, and encourage them to use the back of the page if they need more space.

Testing the Questionnaire

Make a few copies of your first-draft questionnaire, and ask at least three readers to complete it. Time them as they respond, or ask them to keep track of how long they take to complete it. Discuss with them any confusion or problems they experience. Review their responses with them to be certain that each question is eliciting the information you want it to elicit. From what you learn, reconsider your questionnaire, and make any necessary revisions to your questions and design or format.

Administering the Questionnaire

Decide whom you want to fill out your questionnaire and how you can arrange for them to do so. The more respondents you have, the better, but constraints of time and expense will almost certainly limit the number. You can mail or e-mail questionnaires, distribute them to dormitories, or send them to campus or workplace mailboxes, but the return will likely be low. Half the people receiving questionnaires in the mail usually fail to return them. If you do mail the questionnaire, be sure to mention the deadline for returning it. Give directions for its return, and include a stamped, self-addressed envelope, if necessary. Instead of mailing the questionnaire, you might want to arrange to distribute it yourself to groups of people in class or around campus, at dormitory meetings, or at work. Some colleges and universities have restrictions about the use of questionnaires, so you should check your institution's policy before sending one out.

Note that if you want to do a formal questionnaire study, you will need a scientifically representative group of readers (a random or stratified random sample). Even for an informal study, you should try to get a reasonably representative group. For example, to study satisfaction with appointment scheduling at the clinic, you would want to include students who have been to the clinic as well as those who have avoided it. You might even want to include a concentration of seniors rather than first-year students because, after four years, seniors would have made more visits to the clinic. If many students commute, you would want to be sure to have commuters among your respondents. Your essay will be more convincing if you demonstrate that your respondents represent the group whose opinions or knowledge you claim to be studying. As few as twenty-five respondents could be adequate for an informal study.

Writing Up the Results

Once you have the completed questionnaires, how do you write up the results?

Summarizing the Results. Begin by tallying the results from the closed questions. Take an unused questionnaire, and tally the responses next to each choice. Suppose that you had administered the student health clinic questionnaire to twenty-five students. Here is how the tally might look for the checklist in question 5 of Figure 22.1.

5. Given your present work and class schedule, when are you able to visit the clinic? (Check all applicable responses.)

_____ 8–10 a.m. ꙶꙶꙶ III *(18)*	_____ 1–3 p.m. III *(3)*
_____ 10 a.m.–Noon ꙶ II *(7)*	_____ 3–5 p.m. ꙶ IIII *(9)*
_____ 12–1 p.m. ꙶꙶ III *(13)*	

Each tally mark represents one response to that item. The totals add up to more than twenty-five because respondents were asked to check all the times when they could make appointments.

You can give the results from the closed questions as percentages, either within the text of your paper or in one or more tables or graphs. Conventional table formats for the social sciences are illustrated in the *Publication Manual of the American Psychological Association*, 6th edition (Washington, DC: American Psychological Association, 2010). For larger surveys, you can use computer spreadsheet programs to tabulate the results and even generate the tables and graphs.

Next, consider the open questions. Read all respondents' answers to each question separately to see the kinds and variety of responses they gave. Then decide whether you want to code any of the open questions so that you can summarize results from them quantitatively, as you would with closed questions. For example, you might want to classify the types of advice given as responses to question 8 in the clinic questionnaire: "Based on your experiences with scheduling at the clinic, what advice would you give to other students about making appointments?" You could then report the numbers of respondents (of your twenty-five) who gave each type of advice. For an opinion question (for example, "How would you evaluate your most recent appointment at the clinic?"), you might simply code the answers as positive, neutral, or negative and then tally the results accordingly for each kind of response. However, you'll probably want to use the responses to most open questions as a source of quotations for your report or essay.

Because readers' interests can be engaged more easily with quotations than with percentages, plan to use open responses in your essay, perhaps weaving them into your discussion like quoted material from published sources.

For strategies for integrating quoted material, see Chapter 24, pp. 759–60.

Organizing the Write-Up. In organizing your results, you might want to consider a plan that is commonly followed in the social sciences.

Reporting Your Survey

Statement of the problem
> Context for your study
> Question or questions you wanted to answer
> Need for your survey
> Brief preview of your survey and plan for your report

Review of other related surveys (if you know of any)

Procedures
> Questionnaire design
> Selection of participants
> Administration of the questionnaire
> Summary of the results

Results: Presentation of what you learned, with limited commentary or interpretation

Summary and discussion
> Brief summary of your results
> Brief discussion of their significance (commenting, interpreting, exploring implications, and possibly comparing with other related surveys)

23

Library and Internet Research

Research requires patience, careful planning, hard work, and even luck. The rewards are many, however. Each new research project leads you to unexplored regions of the library or of cyberspace. You may find yourself in a rare-book room reading a manuscript written hundreds of years ago or involved in a lively discussion on the Internet with people hundreds of miles away. One moment you may be surfing the Web, and the next you may be threading a microfilm reader, watching a DVD, or squinting at the fine print in a periodical index.

This chapter is designed to help you learn how to use all of the resources available to you. It gives advice on how to use the library and the Internet, develop efficient search strategies, keep track of your research, locate appropriate sources, and read them productively. Chapter 24 provides guidelines for using and acknowledging these sources in an essay and presents a sample research paper on home schooling.

Orienting Yourself to the Library

To conduct research in most college libraries, you will need to become familiar with a wide variety of resources. Library catalogs, almost all of them now electronic, provide information on books, journals, and other materials (such as DVDs) held by the library. Periodical databases and indexes, used to locate magazine and journal articles, are available in electronic format, in print, or both. The material you find may be in print, in downloadable electronic format, or on microfilm or microfiche.

Taking a Tour

Most college libraries are more complex than typical high school or public libraries, so make a point of getting acquainted with your school's library. Your instructor may arrange a library orientation tour for your composition class. If not, find out whether the library offers tours, and, if so, take one. Otherwise, design your own tour (for suggestions of important resources to look for in your college library, see Table 23.1).

When you visit the library in person, make the most of your time there. Pick up copies of any available pamphlets and guidelines, including a floor map of materials and facilities. See whether your library offers any special workshops or presentations that might help you in your work.

You don't have to visit in person, though, to find out what your college library offers. Most libraries have useful Web sites describing their resources and services,

Table 23.1   Designing Your Self-Guided Library Tour

Library Resource	*What This Resource Does for You*
Circulation desk	Check out materials, place holds and recalls, pay fees or fines.
Reference desk/room	Obtain help from reference librarians to locate and use library resources. Find reference materials such as encyclopedias, dictionaries, handbooks, atlases, bibliographies, statistics, and periodical indexes and abstracts.
Reserves	Gain access to books and journal articles that are on reserve for specific classes.
Interlibrary loan	Request materials not available on site. *(Note: Many libraries now offer this service online only.)*
Open-access computers	Gain access to the library catalog, electronic periodical indexes, the campus network, and the Internet.
Periodicals	Locate bound and unbound current issues of newspapers, journals, and magazines. *(Note: Many periodicals are now available electronically through the library databases.)*
Government publications	Locate publications from federal, state, and local government agencies.
Multimedia resources	Locate nonprint materials such as videos, CD-ROMs, and audiotapes.
Microforms	Locate materials on microfilm (reels) and microfiche (cards).
Special collections/Rare-book room	Find rare or highly specialized materials not readily available in most library collections *(In larger libraries only.)*
Archives	Find collections of papers from important individuals and organizations that provide source material for original research *(In larger libraries only.)*
Maps and atlases	Locate maps and atlases (housed in a special location because of their size and format).
Copiers, printers, and scanners	Make copies, print, and/or scan material. *(Note: Be aware that you almost always pay for copies by the page, and some libraries charge for printing or require students to supply their own paper.)*
Reading areas	Read in quiet, comfortable areas.
Study rooms	Study in rooms reserved for individuals or small groups.
Computer labs	Use networked computers for word processing, research, and other functions.

and many offer virtual tours. Many of these sites also offer access to online databases, tutorials for using the library's resources, expert advice on doing research and writing, and more.

Consulting Librarians

Think of college librarians as instructors whose job is to help you understand the library and get your hands on resources you need to complete your research projects. Most librarians have years of experience answering the very questions you are likely to ask. You should not hesitate to approach them with any questions you have about getting started, locating sources, or completing your research project. Remember, however, that they can be most helpful when you can explain your research assignment clearly and ask questions that are as specific as possible. You need not do so face-to-face: Many libraries now offer e-mail, phone, or internet chat or messaging options to connect library users to a reference librarian.

Getting Started

Let's say you have just been given a writing assignment that requires significant research. You already have a sense of how your college library is organized, and you think you know what you want to write about. If you are like most students, you will still be wondering at this point, "But where do I start?" The sections below provide an answer to that common question.

Knowing Your Research Task

Before you start a research project, learn as much as you can about the assignment. How long should the paper be? How much time do you have to do it? Does your instructor specify how many sources you will need, or which kinds? Ask your instructor to clarify any confusing terms and to define the purpose and scope of the project. Asking a question or two in advance can prevent hours — or even days — of misdirected work.

Finding Out What Your Library Offers

You should try to get to the library or do a thorough search of its resources online as soon as you understand the assignment. If many of your classmates will be working on similar projects, you may be competing with them for a limited number of books and other resources. More importantly, for your library research to be manageable and productive, you will want to work carefully and systematically, and this takes time. Although specific search strategies may vary to fit the needs of individual research tasks, the general process presented in Figure 23.1 should help you organize your time. Remember that you will be constantly refining and revising your research strategy as you find out more about your topic.

At this early stage, you need an overview of your topic. If you are researching a concept or an issue in a course you are taking, your textbook and your course materials provide the obvious starting point. Your instructor and/or a reference librarian can advise you about other sources that provide overviews of your topic. If your topic is currently in the news, you will want to consult newspapers, magazines, or Web sites. For all other topics, encyclopedias and bibliographies are often the place to start.

Consulting Encyclopedias

General encyclopedias, such as the *Encyclopaedia Britannica* and the *Columbia Encyclopedia,* provide basic information about many topics. Like many encyclopedias, these works are available online and in print. Wikipedia, too, offers a wealth of information, and it is often the first stop for students who are accustomed to consulting the open Internet first for information. Be aware, though, that Wikipedia is user-generated, rather than traditionally published, and, for this reason, the quality of information found there can be inconsistent. Many academics do not consider Wikipedia to be a reliable source, so you should ask your instructor for advice on consulting it at this stage. Whichever general encyclopedia you consult, bear in mind that general encyclopedias should be used only for an overview of a topic; on their own, they are not adequate resources for college research.

Know your research task and your resources.

Find out what your library offers.

Get an overview of your topic.

- Look in encyclopedias and bibliographies.
- Review textbooks and other course materials.
- Explore newspapers, magazines, and Internet sites.
- Consult with your instructor and/or a reference librarian.
- Construct a list of keywords and subject headings.
- Develop a preliminary topic statement.

Keep track of what you learn.

- Keep a working bibliography.
- Take notes.

Search for in-depth information on your topic.

Conduct a preliminary search for sources, using keywords and subject headings.

- Check the online catalog for books.
- Check periodical databases for articles.
- Check Internet sites.

Evaluate and refine your search by asking yourself:

- Is this what I expected to find?
- Am I finding enough?
- Am I finding too much?
- Do I need to modify my keywords?
- Do I need to recheck background sources?
- Do I need to modify my topic statement?

Refine your search based on the answers.

Locate sources.

- Books
- Magazine and journal articles
- Newspaper articles
- Internet sites
- Government and statistical sources
- Other sources appropriate to your topic

Evaluate your sources.

- For information
- For relevance
- For accuracy
- For comprehensiveness
- For bias
- For currency

Continue to evaluate and refine your search strategy based on the research results.

Figure 23.1 Overview of an Information Search Strategy

Specialized encyclopedias cover topics in more depth than general encyclopedias do. In addition to providing an overview of a topic, they often include an explanation of issues related to the topic, definitions of specialized terminology, and selective bibliographies of additional sources.

As starting points, specialized encyclopedias have two distinct advantages: (1) They provide a comprehensive introduction to key terms related to your topic, terms that will help you find related material in catalogs and indexes, and (2) they provide a comprehensive presentation of a subject, enabling you to see many possibilities for focusing your research.

The following list identifies some specialized encyclopedias in the major academic disciplines:

ART	*Dictionary of Art*
BIOLOGY	*Concise Encyclopedia Biology*
CHEMISTRY	*Concise Encyclopedia Chemistry*
COMPUTERS	*Encyclopedia of Computer Science and Technology*
ECONOMICS	*Fortune Encyclopedia of Economics*
EDUCATION	*Encyclopedia of Educational Research*
ENVIRONMENT	*Encyclopedia of the Environment*
FOREIGN RELATIONS	*Encyclopedia of U.S. Foreign Relations*
	Encyclopedia of the Third World
HISTORY	*Encyclopedia USA*
	New Cambridge Modern History
LAW	*Corpus Juris Secundum*
	American Jurisprudence
LITERATURE	*Encyclopedia of World Literature in the Twentieth Century*
	Encyclopedia of Literature and Criticism
MEDICINE	*American Medical Association's Complete Medical Encyclopedia*
MUSIC	*New Grove Dictionary of Music and Musicians*
NURSING	*Miller-Keane Encyclopedia and Dictionary of Medicine, Nursing, and Allied Health*
PHILOSOPHY	*Routledge Encyclopedia of Philosophy*
PSYCHOLOGY	*Encyclopedia of Psychology*
RELIGION	*Encyclopedia of Religion*
SCIENCE	*McGraw-Hill Encyclopedia of Science and Technology*
SOCIAL SCIENCES	*International Encyclopedia of the Social Sciences*
SOCIOLOGY	*Encyclopedia of Sociology*
WOMEN'S STUDIES	*Women's Studies Encyclopedia*

Many of these specialized encyclopedias are available both online and in print. You can locate them in the library by doing a title search in your library's catalog. Find other specialized encyclopedias by doing a keyword search using the name of the discipline, such as *psychology*, and adding the word *encyclopedia* or *dictionary*. As always, it is a good idea to consult with a reference librarian for further suggestions.

Consulting Bibliographies

A **bibliography** is simply a list of publications on a given subject. All researched articles and books include bibliographies to document their sources of information. In addition, separately published, book-length bibliographies exist for many subjects that have attracted significant amounts of writing. These are useful for in-depth research. Some bibliographies are annotated with brief summaries and evaluations of the entries.

Even if you attend a large research university, your library is unlikely to hold every book or journal article that a bibliography might direct you to. If a source looks likely to be useful but your library does not have a copy, ask a reference librarian about the possibility of acquiring it from another library through interlibrary loan.

Keeping Track of Your Research

As you research your topic, you will want to keep a careful record of all the sources you locate by setting up a working bibliography. You will also want to take notes on your sources in some systematic way.

Keeping a Working Bibliography

A **working bibliography** is a preliminary, ongoing record of books, articles, Web sites, and other sources of information you discover as you research your subject. In addition, you can use your working bibliography to keep track of any encyclopedias and bibliographies you consult, even though these general reference tools are usually not cited in an essay.

Each entry in a working bibliography is called a **bibliographic citation**. The information you record in each bibliographic citation will help you to locate the source in the library and then, if you end up using it in your paper, to *cite* or *document* it in the list of references or works cited you provide at the end of an essay. *Recording this information for each possible source as you identify it, rather than reconstructing it later, will save you hours of work.* In addition to the bibliographic information, note the library location where the source is kept, the name of the database or other reference work where you learned about it, and the date you accessed it, just in case you have to track it down again. (See Figures 23.2 and 23.3 for guidelines on what to record for a book or a print periodical article. For guidelines for Internet sources, see Figure 23.6 on p. 748.)

Author	
Title	
Place of publication	
Publisher	
Date of publication	
Location	
Notes	

Figure 23.2 Information for Working Bibliography — Books

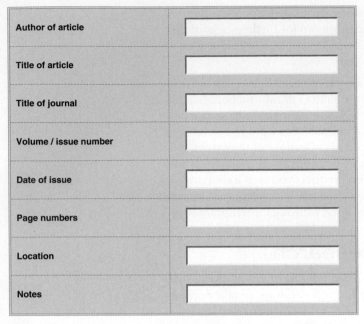

Author of article	
Title of article	
Title of journal	
Volume / issue number	
Date of issue	
Page numbers	
Location	
Notes	

Figure 23.3 Information for Working Bibliography — Periodical Articles

Chapter 24 presents two common documentation styles — one adopted by the Modern Language Association (MLA) and widely used in the humanities, and the other advocated by the American Psychological Association (APA) and used in the social sciences. Other disciplines have their own preferred styles of documentation. Confirm with your instructor which documentation style is required for your assignment so that you can follow that style for all the sources you put into your working bibliography.

Practiced researchers keep their working bibliography in a computer file, in a notebook, or on index cards. Researchers who record the information in a computer file use either standard software (such as Word or Excel) or specialized software (such as RefWorks, EndNote, Zotero, or the Bedford Bibliographer) designed for creating bibliographies. Others find index cards convenient because they are portable and easy to arrange in the alphabetical order required for the list of works cited or references. Still others find cards too easy to lose and prefer instead to keep everything — working bibliography, notes, and drafts — in a notebook.

Whatever method you use for your working bibliography, your entries need to be accurate and complete. If the call number you record for a book is incomplete or inaccurate, for example, you may not be able to find the book easily on the shelves. If the author's name is misspelled, you may have trouble finding the book in the catalog. If the volume number for a periodical is incorrect, you may not be able to locate the article. If you initially get some bibliographic information from a catalog or an index, check it again for accuracy when you examine the source directly.

Taking Notes

After you have found some useful sources, you will want to begin taking notes.

When you find a useful **electronic source**, print it out and/or download the material to a flash drive or network drive, if possible. It is also a good idea to e-mail it to yourself. Be sure your electronic version includes all the source information required by the documentation system you are using. To take notes on a document you have downloaded, you can either print it out and annotate by hand, copy and paste relevant passages into a separate document, or (depending on the format in which you download it) annotate it electronically.

When you find a useful **print source**, photocopying it can be helpful, because you can make notes directly on the photocopied page and highlight material you may wish to quote, summarize, or paraphrase. Photocopying also allows you to reread and analyze important sources at your leisure. While these advantages make photocopying in many ways an ideal option, it can be costly, so you will want to be selective. If you do choose to photocopy, be sure to copy title pages or other publication information for each source, or otherwise record this information on your copy of the text.

Some libraries now offer the option of scanning documents. As with photocopying, this can be expensive, so you will need to be selective. Once you have scanned a document, however, you can print and annotate it, or, depending on the format in which you have scanned it, annotate it electronically or cut and paste key information into another document. Be sure your scanned version includes all the source information required by the documentation system you are using.

If you can neither photocopy, download, nor scan a source, you will have to record source information, notes, and quotations carefully in a separate document. *If you record notes separately, be sure to include the page numbers where you find information, so that you can go back and reread if necessary.* You will also need to give page numbers when you cite sources within your essay and in your list of works cited.

Be sure *never* to copy an author's phrases and sentences without enclosing them in quotation marks and noting the source, and always double check all your notes for accuracy. Messy or inaccurate notes can lead to **plagiarism**, the unacknowledged and therefore improper use of another's phrases and sentences or ideas.

Outlining, paraphrasing, and summarizing are discussed in Chapter 12, and quoting is discussed in Chapter 24. For tips on avoiding plagiarism, see Chapter 24, p. 756.

Finding Library Sources

Books and periodical articles are the two types of sources most commonly used for academic research projects. Books housed in college library collections offer several advantages to the student researcher: They provide in-depth coverage of topics, and they tend to be published by reputable presses that guarantee that the material meets standards of accuracy and reliability.

The most up-to-date information on a subject, however, is usually found not in books but in articles published in periodicals. A **periodical** is a publication such as a magazine, newspaper, or scholarly journal that is published on an ongoing basis, at regular intervals (for instance, daily, weekly, monthly, or annually), and with different content in each issue. Examples of periodicals include *Sports Illustrated* (magazine), the *New York Times* (newspaper), *Tulsa Studies in Women's Literature* (scholarly journal), *Kairos* (online journal), and *Slate* (online magazine).

Books can be found in the library's **online catalog**. Articles in periodicals, on the other hand, are not listed in the library catalog; to find them, you must use **periodical databases** or **indexes**. Much of the success of your research will depend on your ability to effectively search online library catalogs and periodical databases. The next sections will give you strategies for doing so.

General Search Strategies

Doing Basic Searches

Computerized library catalogs and periodical databases consist of thousands or even millions of records, each representing an item such as a book, an article, or a government publication. Each record is made up of different fields describing the item.

Basic search strategies include author, title, keyword, and subject searches. When you perform an **author search**, the computer looks for a match between the name you type and the names listed in the author field of all the records in the online catalog or other database. When you perform a **title search,** the computer looks for a match in the title field. When performing these searches, most systems will try to match only the exact terms you enter. Therefore, accuracy counts.

Most online catalogs now permit **keyword** searching, which is an effective way to get started in most cases. Keywords are words or phrases that describe your topic. As you read about your subject in an encyclopedia or other reference book, you should keep a list of keywords that may be useful.

For an example of an online catalog reference to a periodical, see p. 744.

As you review the results of a keyword search, look for the titles that seem to match most closely the topics that you are looking for. (It is usually a good sign, for example, if your keyword(s) appear in the title.) If you get too few relevant returns, try different keywords. When you call up the detailed information for titles that seem promising, look for the section labeled "Subject" or "Subject Heading." **Subject headings** are specific words and phrases used in library catalogs and periodical databases to categorize the contents of books and articles. In many catalogs and databases, these subject headings are links that you can click on to get a list of other materials on the same subject. Here is an example of an online catalog listing for a book on home schooling:

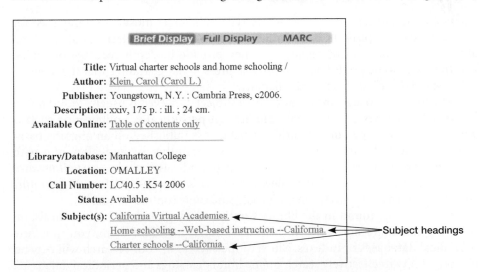

Table 23.2 on p. 737 describes some search capabilities commonly offered by library catalogs and databases.

Doing Advanced Searches and Using Boolean Operators

The real power of using online catalogs or other databases is demonstrated when you need to look up books or articles using more than one search term. For example,

Table 23.2 Common Search Capabilities Offered by Library Catalogs and Databases

Type of Search	How the Computer Conducts the Search	Things to Know
Author Search (exact) • Individual (*Guterson, David*) • Organization (*U.S. Department of Education*)	Looks in the author field for the words entered	• Names are usually, but not always, entered *last name, first name* (for example, "Shakespeare, William"). • Organizations can be considered authors. Enter the name of the organization in natural word order. • An exact-match author search is useful for finding books and articles by a particular author.
Title Search (exact) • Book title • Magazine or journal title	Looks in the title field for words in the exact order you enter them	An exact-match title search is useful for identifying the location of known items, such as when you are looking for a particular journal or book.
Subject Search (exact)	Looks in the subject heading or descriptor field for words in the exact order you enter them	An exact-match subject search is useful when you are sure about the subject heading.
Keyword Search	Looks in the title, note, subject, abstract, and text fields for the words entered	A keyword search is the broadest kind you can use. It is useful during early exploration of a subject.

suppose you want information about home schooling in California. Rather than looking through an index listing all the articles on home schooling and picking out those that mention California, you can ask the computer to do the work for you by linking your two keywords. Most online catalogs and databases offer the option of an **advanced search**, sometimes on a separate page from the main search page, that allows you to search for more than one keyword at a time, search for certain keywords while excluding others, or search for an exact phrase. Many systems allow for the use of quotation marks to specify exact phrases (for example, "home schooling"), plus signs for terms that must appear in results (+"home schooling"), or minus signs for terms that should not appear in results (−adult). Most systems also allow you to perform advanced searches by using the **Boolean operators** AND, OR, and NOT.

To understand the operation of **Boolean logic** (developed by and named after George Boole, a nineteenth-century mathematician), picture one set of articles about home schooling and another set of articles about California. A third set is formed by articles that are about both home schooling and California. The figures that follow provide an illustration of how each Boolean operator works.

AND

Returns references that contain both the term **"home schooling"** AND the term **California**

- Narrows the search
- Combines unrelated terms
- Is the default used by most online catalogs and databases

OR

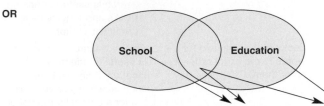

Returns all references that contain either the term **school** OR the term **education** OR both terms

- Broadens the search **("OR is more")**
- Is useful with synonyms and alternate spellings: ("home schooling" and "homeschooling")

NOT

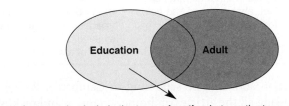

Returns references that include the term **education** but NOT the term **adult**

- Narrows the search
- Caution: By narrowing your search, you may eliminate relevant material.

Using Truncation

Another useful search strategy employs **truncation**. With this technique, you drop the ending of a word or term and replace it with a symbol, which indicates you want to retrieve records containing any term that begins the same way as your term. Truncation symbols vary with the catalog or database. The question mark (?), asterisk (*), and pound sign (#) are frequently used. Truncation is useful when you want to retrieve both the plural and singular forms of a word or any word for which you are not sure of the ending. For example, in systems using the asterisk, the term "*home school**" would return all the records that have terms such as *home school, home schooling, home schools, home schooled,* or *home schoolers.*

Table 23.3 Electronic Search Tips

If You Find Too Many Sources on Your Topic	*If You Find Insufficient Information on Your Topic*
• Use a subject search instead of a keyword search.	• Use a keyword instead of a subject.
• Add additional words to your search.	• Eliminate words from your search terms.
• Use a more precise vocabulary to describe your topic.	• Try truncated forms of your keyword.
• Use an advanced search to restrict your findings by date, format, language, or other options.	• Use different words to describe your topic.
	• Check the spelling of each term you type.

Table 23.3 offers suggestions for expanding or narrowing an electronic search.

Finding Books: Using the Online Library Catalog

Look again at the sample catalog listing for a book on home schooling:

> **Brief Display** Full Display MARC
>
> **Title:** Virtual charter schools and home schooling /
> **Author:** Klein, Carol (Carol L.)
> **Publisher:** Youngstown, N.Y. : Cambria Press, c2006.
> **Description:** xxiv, 175 p. : ill. ; 24 cm.
> **Available Online:** Table of contents only
>
> ---
>
> **Library/Database:** Manhattan College
> **Location:** O'MALLEY
> **Call Number:** LC40.5 .K54 2006
> **Status:** Available
> **Subject(s):** California Virtual Academies.
> Home schooling --Web-based instruction --California.
> Charter schools --California.

Whether you performed your search by author, title, subject, or keyword, each record you find will provide the following standard information.

1. *Title:* The title appears exactly as it does on the title page of the book, except that only the first word and proper nouns and adjectives are capitalized.
2. *Author:* The author's name usually appears last name first, sometimes followed by birth and (if applicable) death dates. For books with multiple authors, the record includes an author entry under each author's name.

3. *Publication information:* The place of publication, the publisher, and the year of publication are listed. If the book was published simultaneously in the United States and abroad, both places and publishers are indicated.

4. *Physical description:* This section provides information about the book's page length and size. A roman numeral indicates the number of pages devoted to front matter (such as a preface, table of contents, and acknowledgments).

5. *Location:* While a call number explains where a book is shelved in relation to other books, large library systems might be divided across more than one physical location. If that's the case, the name of that location will be listed.

6. *Call number:* Most college libraries use the Library of Congress system, and most public libraries use the Dewey decimal system. Call numbers provide an exact location for every book in the library, and because they are assigned according to subject classifications, they group together books on the same topic. When you go to the stacks to locate the book, therefore, always browse for other useful material on the shelves around it.

7. *Status:* Most catalogs will tell you whether a book is on the shelf, already checked out, lost, etc. Some will allow you to reserve or hold a book.

8. *Subject headings:* These headings indicate how the book is categorized in terms of subject. Often, these subject headings are active links; clicking on them will bring up a list of other books on the same subject.

If your search for books in your college library turns up little that is useful to you, do not give up. Most college libraries belong to one or more **interlibrary networks** that can be useful to you in your search. Known by different names in different regions, these networks allow you to search in the catalogs of colleges and universities in your area and across the country. Also consider using a relatively new Internet source called WorldCat (http://www.worldcat.org), which searches through some ten thousand libraries in the United States. WorldCat links directly to the library's catalog if a specific library has the book. In many cases, you can request a book by interlibrary loan, although it may take several weeks to be delivered to your library.

Examples of records in online catalogs are shown on pp. 736 and 745.

Finding Articles

Using Periodical Databases or Indexes

Traditionally available in print, in microform, or on CD-ROM, most major periodical indexes are now available online. (Keep in mind, however, that some of these online databases cover only the last fifteen to twenty years; for some research projects, you may need to consult older printed versions of indexes as well.) Some of the general databases serve mainly as indexes. Others, however, include **abstracts** or short summaries of articles, and some give you access to the **full text** of articles.

On the next page you will find a list of some of the most common periodical databases, divided into three categories: general, newspaper, and subject-specific. Your college library will likely subscribe to some but not all of these databases. Note that many online databases listed here are delivered via one of three major online reference database services — EBSCOhost, InfoTrac, and WilsonWeb — which allow you to search multiple databases in a single search. Many libraries also offer access to a separate **federated search engine**, which allows you to search multiple databases across database services.

General guidelines for searching online databases are given on pp. 735–39. Because online databases contain so much information, however, you may want to consult with a librarian to develop an efficient search strategy.

General Databases and Indexes. These indexes are a good place to start your research because they cover a broad range of subjects in popular periodicals and scholarly journals.

Academic OneFile (InfoTrac) provides full text for more than 11,000 peer-reviewed journals.

Academic Search Premier (EBSCOhost) provides full text for more than 4,500 academic journals, including more than 3,700 peer-reviewed titles.

CQ Researcher offers an overview, background, and bibliography on newsworthy or controversial topics (e.g,. terrorism, global warming, stem-cell research) in public health, social trends, criminal justice, international affairs, education, the environment, technology, and the economy.

General OneFile (*InfoTrac*) offers full text for more than 11,000 general-interest magazines.

JSTOR offers a high quality, interdisciplinary archive of over 1,000 academic journals across the humanities, social sciences, and sciences.

MasterFILE (*EBSCOhost*) provides full text for over 1,800 general-interest, business, consumer health, general science, and multicultural periodicals, in addition to indexing and abstracts for over 2,500 other periodicals.

Project Muse offers scholarly journals in the arts and humanities, social sciences, and mathematics; currently the database includes 385 journals by 91 publishers.

The example in Figure 23.4 from *Academic Search Premier* is typical of entries found in general periodical databases.

Figure 23.4 *Academic Search Premier* **Database Search Result**

Newspaper Databases and Indexes. Newspapers provide useful information for research topics in such areas as foreign affairs, economics, public opinion, and social trends. Libraries used to photograph newspapers and store them in miniature form on microfilm (reels) or microfiche (cards) that must be placed in viewing machines to be read. Now much of this material is available online. Newspaper indexes such as the *Los Angeles Times Index*, *New York Times Index*, and *London Times Index*, which are available online as well as in print, can help you locate specific articles on your topic. Many include the full text of articles going back a number of years. Your library may also subscribe to the following:

Alt-PressWatch offers full-text access to selected newspapers, magazines, and journals of the alternative and independent press.

LexisNexis provides full-text access to documents from over 5,600 news, business, legal, medical, and reference publications, including U.S. and international newspapers, magazines, wire services, newsletters, trade journals, company and industry analyst reports, and broadcast transcripts.

NewsBank provides full-text newspaper articles from the *New York Times*, *Los Angeles Times*, *Washington Post*, *Atlanta Journal-Constitution*, *Chicago Tribune*, *Christian Science Monitor*, and many others. *NewsBank* is especially useful for local and regional (United States) papers.

Newspaper Source provides cover-to-cover full text for 35 national and international newspapers and selective full text for 375 regional (U.S.) newspapers, in addition to full-text television and radio news transcripts.

Proquest Newspapers provides full-text access to articles from U.S. national newspapers, international English-language newspapers, and selected regional/state newspapers.

Subject-Specific Databases and Indexes. These databases list or summarize articles from periodicals devoted to specific fields of study. Here is a list of some of the more common subject-specific periodical databases:

America: History and Life indexes 1,700 journals from 1964 to present, covering the history and culture of the United States and Canada, from prehistory to the present.

Business Source Premier (*EBSCOhost)* provides full text for more than 2,300 marketing, management, MIS, POM, accounting, finance and economics journals, including more than 1,100 peer-reviewed titles.

ERIC (*Educational Resource Information Center*) contains links to more than 224,000 full-text documents and more than 1,243,000 records of education-related literature, including coverage of conferences, meetings, government documents, theses, dissertations, reports, audiovisual media, bibliographies, directories, books, and monographs.

Humanities Index offers full text (starting 1995) plus abstracts and bibliographic indexes (starting 1984) of scholarly sources in the humanities.

MEDLINE allows users to search abstracts from over 4,600 current biomedical journals covering the fields of medicine, nursing, dentistry, veterinary medicine, the healthcare system, pre-clinical sciences, and more.

MLA (Modern Language Association) International Bibliography indexes 3,000 English language and foreign periodicals as well as books, book chapters, and dissertations dating back to the 1920s.

PAIS International indexes articles, books, conference proceedings, government documents, book chapters, and statistical directories in the area of public affairs. Topics include business, government, international relations, banking, environment, health, social sciences, demographics, law and legislation, political science, public administration, finance, agriculture, education, and statistics.

PsycINFO contains over 2.5 million citations to and summaries of peer-reviewed articles and other documents in the field of psychology dating as far back as the early 1800s.

Science Full Text offers full text, indexing, and abstracts from over 320 journals in the fields of zoology, biology, earth science, environmental science, genetics, botany, and chemistry.

Social Sciences Index covers concepts, trends, opinions, theories, and methods from more than 350 English-language periodicals in the social sciences.

Distinguishing Scholarly Journals and Popular Magazines

Although they are both called periodicals, journals and magazines have important differences.

Journals publish articles written by experts in a particular field of study, frequently professors or researchers in academic institutions. Journals are usually specialized in their subject focus, research oriented, and peer reviewed (that is, extensively reviewed by specialists) prior to publication. They are intended to be read by experts and students conducting research. **Magazines**, in contrast, usually publish articles written to entertain and educate the general public.

Journals contain a great deal of original research. For example, a scientist might publish an article in a medical journal about the results of a new treatment protocol for breast cancer. Articles in magazines report on and summarize original research to inform the general public about new and interesting developments in scientific and other areas of research. In most college courses requiring research, original research published in journals is preferred to the accounts of research and other trends published in magazines. For this reason, it is important to note that many periodical databases will let you limit a search to scholarly journals.

Table 23.4 on p. 744 summarizes some of the important differences between scholarly journals and popular magazines.

Table 23.4   How to Distinguish a Scholarly Journal from a Popular Magazine

Scholarly Journal	Popular Magazine
• It is usually published once every other month or four times per year.	• It is published frequently, usually once a week or once a month.
• The authors of articles have *Ph.D.* or academic affiliations after their names.	• The authors of articles are journalists or reporters.
• Many articles have more than one author.	• Most articles have a single author but may quote experts.
• A short summary (abstract) of an article may appear on the first page.	• A headline or engaging description may precede the article.
• Most articles are fairly long, five to twenty pages.	• Most of the articles are fairly short, one to five pages.
• The articles may include charts, tables, figures, and quotations from other scholarly sources.	• The articles have color pictures and sidebar boxes.
• The articles have a bibliography (list of references to other books and articles) at the end.	• The articles do not include a bibliography.

Locating Periodicals in the Library

Let us say that you have identified a promising magazine, journal, or newspaper article in a periodical index or database. If that article is not available in full text electronically, you must go to the library's online catalog or online periodicals list to learn whether the library subscribes to the periodical, whether the issue is available, and, if so, where you can find it. No library can subscribe to every periodical, so as you go through indexes and databases, be sure to identify more articles than you actually need. This will save you from having to repeat your search later.

Although every library arranges its print periodicals differently, recent issues are usually arranged alphabetically by title on open shelves. Older issues may be bound like books or filmed and available in microform.

Suppose you want to look up the following article from the *Journal for the Scientific Study of Religion* that you found indexed in *Academic Search Premier*:

Alternative Schooling Strategies and *the Religious Lives* of American Adolescents.
By: UECKER, JEREMY E.. *Journal for the Scientific Study of Religion*, Dec2008, Vol. 47 Issue 4, p563-584, 22p;
DOI: 10.1111/j.1468-5906.2008.00427.x; (*AN 35052364*)
Add to folder | Cited References: (24)

Since the article is not available online, you need to do a bit more digging to find a copy. You start with the library's online catalog or online periodicals list, searching by the title of the journal, and you find the following record:

```
┌─────────────────────────────────────────────────┐
│                                                  │──── Title of the journal
│        Title: Journal for the scientific study of religion.
│    Publisher: [Storrs, Conn., etc., Society for the Scientific Study of Religion]
│   Description: 28 cm.                    ▲
│                                          │       │──── Publisher of journal
│              ─────────────────────
│
│  Library/Database: Manhattan College
│         Location: Bound Periodicals Collection HAYES ◄──── Location of bound
│      Call Number: PER                                           copies
│           Status: No information available
│       Library has: 8- (1969-) ◄──────────────────│──── Issues in library's
│        Subject(s): Religion --Periodicals.       │       collection, by vol-
│                                                  │       ume and year
└─────────────────────────────────────────────────┘
```

From this record, you would learn that the library does subscribe to the journal and that you could locate the December 2008 issue in the library's periodicals collection. If your library does not subscribe to a journal you are looking for, consult a reference librarian for other ways to access it (interlibrary loan, for example).

Finding Government and Statistical Information

Federal, state, and local governments now make many of their publications and reference services available directly through the Web, though most college libraries still maintain print collections of government publications. Ask a reference librarian for assistance in locating governmental sources and other sources of statistical information in the library or on the Web. The following sources can be useful in finding information on political subjects and national trends:

Congressional Quarterly (CQ.com) is a news and analysis service that includes up-to-date summaries of congressional committee actions, congressional votes, and executive branch activities as well as overviews of current policy discussions and other activities of the federal government.

Google U.S. Government Search (www.google.com/unclesam) is a search engine for federal, state, and local government material.

GPO Access, a service of the U.S. Government Printing Office, provides free electronic access to documents produced by the federal government.

Statistical Abstract of the United States is a publication of the Bureau of the Census, providing a variety of social, economic, and political statistics from 1878 to the present, including tables, graphs, charts, and references to additional sources of information.

WorldAlmanac presents information on a variety of subjects drawn from many sources, including a chronology of the year, climatological data, and lists of inventions and awards.

Finding Other Library Sources

Libraries hold vast amounts of useful materials other than books, periodicals, and government documents. Some of the following may be appropriate for your research:

- *Digital collections:* Materials that have been scanned or otherwise saved in digital format and made available online
- *Special collections:* Manuscripts, rare books, and materials of local interest
- *Audio collections:* Records, audiotapes, music CDs, readings, and speeches
- *Video collections:* Slides, filmstrips, videotapes, and DVDs
- *Art collections:* Drawings, paintings, and engravings
- *Computer resources:* Interactive computer programs that combine text, video, and audio resources in history, literature, business, and other disciplines

Determining the Most Promising Sources

As you search for sources in your library's catalog and databases, you will discover many seemingly relevant books and articles. How do you decide which ones to track down? You may have little to go on but author, title, date, and publisher or periodical name, but these details actually provide useful clues. Look again, for example, at the online catalog listing for *Virtual Charter Schools and Home Schooling* (p. 739). Note that the publication date, 2006, is fairly recent. From the subject headings, you can see that the geographic focus of the book is California.

Finally, from the title and subject headings, you can see that the book emphasizes online (or virtual) learning.

Now look at Figure 23.5, which shows search results from *ERIC*, an electronic periodical database of education journals, searched through EBSCOhost. The search on the term *home schooling* yielded 689 articles. Looking just at the titles of the article and the journal, you can surmise that the first article is a government publication on home schooling in Pennsylvania between 2006 and 2007; the second expresses a librarian's point of view; and the third and fourth address different technological aspects of the issue. With such variety in only the first four

Figure 23.5 ERIC Database Search Results

articles, you will clearly have to be careful to stay focused. In fact, it might be a good idea at this point to limit your search by adding another search term.

Each entry contains the information that you will need to locate it in a library, and some databases provide links to the full text of articles from selected periodicals. Here is what each piece of information means:

Always consider the following points when deciding whether you should track down a particular source:

- **Relevance to your topic:** Examine the title, subtitle, subject headings, and abstract (if provided) to determine whether the source addresses your topic.

- **Publication date:** How recent is the source? For current controversies, emerging trends, and scientific or technological developments, consult recent material. For historical or biographical topics, start with present-day perspectives but consider exploring older sources that offer authoritative perspectives.

- **Description:** Does the length of the source indicate a brief treatment of the topic or an extended treatment? Does the work include illustrations that may illuminate concepts discussed? Does the source include a bibliography that could lead you to other works or an index that could give you an overview of the text?

From among the sources that look promising, select publications that seem to address different aspects of your topic or to approach it from different perspectives. Avoid selecting sources that are mostly by the same author, from the same publisher, or in the same journal.

For a discussion of periodical indexes, see pp. 740–41.

Using the Web for Research

In this section, we discuss the open Web — the open-access areas of the Internet that exclude proprietary subscription services like the databases available through your library. By now, most of you are familiar with searching the Web. This section introduces you to some tools and strategies that will help you use it more efficiently.

Keep the following concerns and guidelines in mind:

- **Many significant electronic sources require a paid subscription or other fees.** Electronic periodical indexes, full-text article databases, and other valuable electronic resources are often available only by subscription. If your college subscribes to these resources, your tuition grants you access to them. For these reasons (as well as the ones discussed in this section), you should plan to use the resources available via your library's Web site for much of your electronic research.

■ ***Open-access Web sources may be less reliable than print sources or electronic sources to which your library or campus subscribes.*** Because it is relatively easy for anyone to publish on the Web, judging the reliability of online information is a special concern. Depending on your topic, purpose, and audience, the sources you find on the Web may not be as credible or authoritative as print sources or subscription electronic sources, which have usually been screened by publishers, editors, librarians, and authorities on the topic. For some topics, most of what you find on the Web may be written by highly biased or amateur authors, so you will need to balance or supplement these sources with information from print sources. When in doubt about the reliability of an online source for a particular assignment, check with your instructor. (See Evaluating Sources on pp. 752–54 for more specific suggestions.)

Citing Internet sources using MLA style is discussed in Chapter 24, pp. 774–76; APA style is discussed on pp. 783–84.

■ ***Web sources may be less stable than print sources or the electronic sources to which your library or campus subscribes.*** A Web site that existed last week may no longer be available today, or its content may have changed.

■ ***Web sources must be documented.*** You will need to follow appropriate conventions for quoting, paraphrasing, summarizing, and documenting the online sources you use, just as you do for print sources. Because a Web source can change or disappear quickly, be sure to record the information for the working-bibliography entry when you first find the source. Whenever possible, download and print out the source to preserve it. Make sure your download or printout includes all the items of information required for the entry, or at least all those you can find. (See Figure 23.6 for guidelines on what to record for an Internet source.)

Author(s) of work	
Title of work	
Title of site	
Sponsor of site	
URL (address)	
Date of electronic publication or of latest update	
Date you accessed source	
Publication information for print version of work (if any)	
Notes	

Figure 23.6 Information for Working Bibliography — Internet Sources

Finding the Best Information Online

Search tools like Google and Yahoo! are important resources for searching the Web for information on your topic. To use these tools effectively, you should understand their features, strengths, and limitations.

Search engines like Google are based on keywords. They are simply computer programs that scan the open Web — or that part of the Web that is in the particular search engine's database — looking for the keyword(s) you have entered. Search engines are useful whenever you have a good idea of the appropriate keywords for your topic or if you are not sure under what category the topic falls.

Google deserves special mention among search engines for the pace at which it has been evolving. In addition to its general Web search, at the time of this writing Google offers subsearches of images, maps, videos, and many other categories of potentially useful material. Of particular interest to the academic writer are Google Scholar, which searches peer-reviewed articles from forty-five scholarly databases including JSTOR, Project Muse, Wiley, Sage, etc., and Google Book Search, which searches a wide range of general-interest and scholarly books. Both Google Scholar and Google Book Search offer overviews and, in some cases, full text of indexed material.

Subject directories like Yahoo! are based on categories, like the subject headings in a library catalog or periodical index. Beginning with a menu of general subjects, you click on increasingly narrow subjects (for example, going from Science to Biology to Genetics to DNA Mapping), until you reach either a list of specific Web sites or a point where you have to do a keyword search within the narrowest subject you have chosen. Subject directories can help quickly narrow your search to those parts of the Web that are likely to be most productive and thus avoid keyword searches that produce hundreds or thousands of results.

Always click on the link called Help, Hints, or Tips on a search tool's home page to find out more about the recognized commands and advanced-search techniques for that specific search tool. Most search engines allow searches using the Boolean operators discussed on pp. 736–38. (In fact, Google automatically assumes an "AND" between multiple search terms.) Most recognize the use of quotation marks to limit results to pages containing an exact phrase. Many also let you limit a search to specific dates, languages, or other criteria.

As with searches of library catalogs and databases, the success of a Web search depends to a great extent on the keywords you choose. Remember that many different words often describe the same topic. If your topic is "ecology," for example, you may find information under the keywords *ecosystem, environment, pollution,* and *endangered species*, as well as a number of other related keywords, depending on the focus of your research. When you find a source that seems promising, be sure to create a bookmark for the Web page so that you can return to it easily later on.

No matter how precise your keywords are, search engines can be unreliable, and you may not find the best available resources. You might instead begin your search at the Web site of a relevant and respected organization. If you want photos of constellations, for example, go to the NASA Web page. If you want public laws, go to a government Web page like GPO Access. In addition, be sure to supplement your Internet research with other sources from your library, including books, reference works, and articles from appropriate periodicals.

The following open-access sources can also be of use to you in some research projects:

American Memory from the Library of Congress (memory.loc.gov) is a gateway to the Library of Congress's vast digitized collection of American historical and cultural materials, including manuscripts, prints, photographs, posters, maps, sound recordings, motion pictures, books, pamphlets, and sheet music. Comprising more than 9 million items, American Memory is organized into more than 100 thematic collections based on format, subject matter, and other criteria.

Project Gutenberg (gutenberg.org), a pioneer in the development of and distribution of ebooks, was founded in 1971 and now offers over 25,000 digitized public-domain texts.

Wikimedia Commons (commons.wikimedia.org/wiki/Main_Page) consists of a collection of over 3.5 million images and other media that are in the public domain.

WorldCat.org is an enormous online network of library content and services that allows you to search for books, DVDs, CDs, audiobooks, research articles, and other content and either download them directly or locate them in a library nearby.

YouTube (youtube.com), a phenomenally popular video-sharing site, offers some resources of interest to academic writers. Be aware that YouTube is an open site that attracts a great deal of material of questionable quality. Also, remember that any YouTube material you do wish to introduce in your projects must be fully cited.

Two other sources of online information are **blogs** and **RSS**. A blog, or Web log, is a Web site, often based on a particular topic, that is maintained by an individual or organization and updated on a regular basis, often many times a day. Blogs may contain postings written by the sponsor(s) of the site; information such as news articles, press releases, and commentary from other sites; and comments posted by readers. Blogs are usually organized chronologically, with the newest post at the top. Because they are not subjected to the same editorial scrutiny as published books or periodical articles and may reflect just one person's opinions and biases, it is a good idea to find several blogs from multiple perspectives about your subject. Some Web sites, such as Blogwise (www.blogwise.com) and Blogger (www.blogger.com), provide directories and search functions to help you find blogs on a particular topic. You can search the content of literally millions of blog posts by using blog search engines such as technorati.com or blogsearch.google.com.

If you are researching a very current topic and need to follow constantly updated news sites and blogs, you can use a program called an **aggregator**, which obtains news automatically from many sources and assembles it through a process called RSS (Really Simple Syndication). Using an aggregator, you can scan the information from a variety of sources by referring to just one Web page or e-mail and then click on links to the news stories to read further. Many aggregators, such as NetNewsWire, NewsGator, and SharpReader, are available as software that you can download to your computer; others are Web sites you can customize to your own preferences, such as Bloglines (www.bloglines.com) and NewsIsFree (www.newsisfree.com). Google Alerts offers Google account holders updates on news, Web pages, blogs, and videos relevant to key terms entered into their Alerts homepage.

Using E-mail and Online Communities for Research

You may find it possible to use your computer to do research in ways other than those already discussed in this chapter. In particular, if you can find out the e-mail address of an expert on your topic, you may want to contact the person and ask whether he or she would agree to a brief online (or telephone) interview. In addition, several kinds of electronic communities available on the Internet may possibly be helpful. Many Web sites consist of or incorporate tools known as **message boards**, in which anyone who registers may post messages to and receive them from other members. Older Internet servers known as news servers also provide access to message boards or variants called **newsgroups**. Another kind of community, **mailing lists**, are groups of people who subscribe to and receive e-mail messages shared among all the members simultaneously. **Chat rooms** allow users to meet together at the same time in a shared message space. Finally, **wikis** — of which Wikipedia is the best known example — offer content of various kinds contributed and modified collaboratively by a community of users. These can be very useful for background information, but be aware that most teachers will not accept information from wikis as sources for papers.

These different kinds of online communities often focus on a specific field of shared interest, and the people who frequent them are sometimes working professionals or academics with expertise in topics that are obscure or difficult to research otherwise. Such experts are often willing to answer both basic and advanced questions and will sometimes consent to an e-mail or telephone interview. Even if they are not authorities in the field, online community members may stimulate your thinking about the topic in new directions or save you a large amount of research time by pointing you to resources that might otherwise have taken you quite a while to uncover. Many communities provide some kind of indexing or search mechanism so that you can look for "threads" (conversation) related to your topic.

As with other sources, however, evaluate the credibility and reliability of online communities. Also be aware that while most communities welcome guests and newcomers, others may perceive your questions as intrusive or unwanted. What may seem new and exciting to you may be old news for veterans. Finally, remember that some online communities are more active than others; survey the dates of posts and frequency of activity to determine whether a given group is still lively or has gone defunct.

For most topics, you will be able to find a variety of related newsgroups; www.groups.google.com catalogs many of them (and allows you to start your own). For mailing lists, you have to register for a subscription to the list. Remember that unless a digest option (an option that compiles messages into one daily or weekly e-mail) is available, each subscription means you will be receiving a large amount of e-mail, so think about the implications before you sign up.

Evaluating Sources

From the beginning of your library and Internet search, you should evaluate potential sources that you have tracked down to determine which ones you should take the time to examine more closely and then which of these you should use in your essay. Obviously, you must decide which sources provide information relevant to the topic. But you must also decide how credible or trustworthy the sources are. Just because a book or an essay appears in print or online does not necessarily mean that an author's information or opinions are reliable.

Selecting Relevant Sources

Begin your evaluation of sources by narrowing your working bibliography to the most relevant works. Consider them in terms of scope, date of publication, and viewpoint.

Scope and Approach

To decide how relevant a particular source is to your topic, you need to examine the source in depth. Do not depend on title alone, for it may be misleading. If the source is a book, check its table of contents and index to see how many pages are devoted to the precise subject you are exploring. In most cases, you will want an in-depth, not a superficial, treatment of the subject. Read the preface or introduction to a book or the abstract or opening paragraphs of an article and any biographical information given about the author to determine the author's basic approach to the subject or special way of looking at it. As you attend to these elements, consider the following questions:

- Does the source provide a general or specialized view? General sources are helpful early in your research, but you will also need the authority or up-to-date coverage of specialized sources. Extremely specialized works, however, may be too technical.
- Is the source long enough to provide adequate detail?
- Is the source written for general readers? Specialists? Advocates? Critics?
- Is the author an expert on the topic? Does the author's way of looking at the topic support or challenge your own views? (The fact that an author's viewpoint challenges your own does not mean that you should reject the author as a source, as you will see from the discussion on viewpoints.)
- Is the information in the source substantiated elsewhere? Does its approach seem to be comparable to, or a significant challenge to, the approaches of other credible sources?

Date of Publication

Although you should always consult the most up-to-date sources available on your subject, older sources often establish the principles, theories, and data on which later work is based and may provide a useful perspective for evaluating it. If older works are considered authoritative, you may want to become familiar with them. To determine which sources are authoritative, note the ones that are cited most often in encyclopedia articles, bibliographies, and recent works on the subject. If your source is on the Web, consider whether it has been regularly updated.

Viewpoint

Your sources should represent multiple viewpoints on the subject. Just as you would not depend on a single author for all of your information, so you do not want to use only authors who belong to the same school of thought. (For suggestions on determining authors' viewpoints, see the following section on Identifying Bias.)

Using sources that represent a variety of different viewpoints is especially important when developing an argument for one of the essay assignments in Chapters 6–10. During the invention work in those chapters, you may want to research what others have said about your subject to see what positions have been staked out and what arguments have been made. You will then be able to define the issue more carefully, collect arguments supporting your position, and anticipate arguments opposing it.

Identifying Bias

One of the most important aspects of evaluating a source is identifying any bias in its treatment of the subject. Although the word *bias* may sound accusatory, most writing is not neutral or objective and does not try or claim to be. Authors come to their subjects with particular viewpoints. In using sources, you must consider carefully how these viewpoints are reflected in the writing and how they affect the way authors present their arguments.

Although the text of the source will give you the most precise indication of the author's viewpoint, you can often get a good idea of it by looking at the preface or introduction or at the sources the author cites. When you examine a reference, you can often determine the general point of view it represents by considering the following elements.

Title

Does the title or subtitle indicate the text's bias? Watch for loaded words or confrontational phrasing.

Author

What is the author's professional title or affiliation? What is the author's perspective? Is the author in favor of something or at odds with it? What has persuaded the author to take this stance? How might the author's professional affiliation affect his or her perspective? What is the author's tone? Information on the author may be available in the book, article, or Web site itself or in biographical sources available in the library. You could also try entering the author's name into a search engine and see what you learn from sites that discuss him or her.

Presentation of Argument

For more detail on these argumentative strategies, see Chapter 19.

Almost every written work asserts a point of view or makes an argument for something the author considers important. To determine this position and the reason behind it, look for the main point. What evidence does the author provide as support for this point? Is the evidence from authoritative sources? Is the evidence persuasive? Does the author make concessions to or refute opposing arguments?

Publication Information

Is the book published by a commercial publisher, a corporation, a government agency, or an interest group, or is it self-published? Is the Web site sponsored by a business, a professional group, a private organization, an educational institution, a government agency, or an individual? What is the publisher's or sponsor's position on the topic? Is the author funded by or affiliated with the publisher or sponsor? If you cannot determine the sponsor of a Web site, it is very likely not a credible source.

Editorial Slant

What kind of periodical published the article — popular, academic, alternative? If you found the article on a Web site, is the site maintained by a commercial or an academic sponsor? Does the article provide links to other Web resources? For periodicals, knowing some background about the publisher can help to determine bias because all periodicals have their own editorial slants. Where the periodical's name does not indicate its bias, reference sources may help you determine this information. Some of the most common are the following:

Encyclopedia of Associations (called *Associations Unlimited* online) is a directory of nonprofit voluntary membership organizations, such as professional societies, trade associations, labor unions, and cultural and religious organizations.

Gale Directory of Publications and Broadcast Media is a useful source providing descriptive information on newsletters, newspapers, and periodicals. Entries often include an indication of intended audience and political or other bias.

Serials Directory (EBSCOhost) offers up-to-date bibliographic information for popular U.S. and international serials from over 85,000 publishers.

Ulrich's Periodicals Directory is an international directory of approximately 210,000 current magazines, journals, annuals, irregular publications, and newspapers, as well as over 47,000 publications discontinued since 1979.

Using Sources

In your college writing, you will be expected to use and acknowledge secondary sources — books, articles, interviews, Web sites, computer bulletin boards, lectures, and other print and nonprint materials — in addition to your own ideas and insights.

When you do use material from another source, you need to acknowledge the source, usually by citing the author and page or date in your text and including a list of works cited or references at the end of your essay. Failure to acknowledge sources constitutes *plagiarism*, a serious transgression. By citing sources correctly, you give appropriate credit to the originator of the words and ideas you are using, offer your readers the information they need to consult those sources directly, and build your own credibility.

This chapter provides guidelines for using sources effectively and acknowledging them accurately. It includes model citations for both the Modern Language Association (MLA) and the American Psychological Association (APA) documentation styles and presents a sample researched essay that follows the MLA format.

Acknowledging Sources

The only types of information that do not require acknowledgment are common knowledge (John F. Kennedy was assassinated in Dallas), facts widely available in many sources (U.S. presidents used to be inaugurated on March 4 rather than January 20), well-known quotations ("To be or not to be / That is the question"), or material you created or gathered yourself, such as photographs that you took or data from surveys that you conducted. Remember that you need to acknowledge the source of any visual (photograph, table, chart, graph, diagram, drawing, map, screen shot) that you did not create yourself or of any information that you used to create your own visual. (You should also request permission from the source of a visual if your essay is going to be posted online without password protection.) When in doubt about whether you need to acknowledge a source, do so.

The documentation guidelines later in this chapter present two styles for citing sources, MLA and APA. Whichever style you use, the most important thing is that your readers be able to tell where words or ideas that are not your own begin and end. You can accomplish this most readily by taking and transcribing notes carefully, by placing parenthetical source citations correctly, and by separating your words from those of the source with **signal phrases** such as "According to Smith," "Peters claims," and "As Olmos asserts." (When you cite a source for the first time in a signal phrase, you may use the author's full name; after that, use just the last name.)

Avoiding Plagiarism

Writers — students and professionals alike — occasionally fail to acknowledge sources properly. The word **plagiarism**, which derives from the Latin word for "kidnapping," refers to the unacknowledged use of another's words, ideas, or information. Students sometimes mistakenly assume that plagiarizing occurs only when another writer's exact words are used without acknowledgment. In fact, plagiarism also applies to such diverse forms of expression as musical compositions and visual images as well as ideas and statistics. Therefore, keep in mind that you must indicate the source of any borrowed information or ideas you use in your essay, whether you have paraphrased, summarized, or quoted directly from the source or have reproduced it or referred to it in some other way.

Remember especially the need to document electronic sources fully and accurately. Perhaps because it is so easy to access and distribute text and visuals online and to copy material from one electronic document and paste it into another, some students do not realize, or may forget, that information, ideas, and images from electronic sources require acknowledgment in even more detail than those from print sources (and are often easier to detect as plagiarism if they are not acknowledged).

Some people plagiarize simply because they do not know the conventions for using and acknowledging sources. If you are unfamiliar with these conventions, this chapter makes clear how to incorporate sources into your writing and how to acknowledge your use of those sources. Others plagiarize because they keep sloppy notes and thus fail to distinguish between their own and their sources' ideas. If you keep a working bibliography and careful notes, you will not make this serious mistake.

For more on keeping a working bibliography, see Chapter 23, pp. 733–34.

Another reason some people plagiarize is that they feel intimidated by the writing task or the deadline. If you experience this anxiety about your work, speak to your instructor. Do not run the risk of failing a course or being expelled from your college because of plagiarism.

If you are confused about what is and what is not plagiarism, be sure to ask your instructor.

Quoting, Paraphrasing, and Summarizing

Writers use sources by quoting directly, by paraphrasing, and by summarizing. This section provides guidelines for deciding when to use each of these three methods and for doing so effectively. Note that all examples in this section follow MLA style for in-text citations, which is explained in detail on pp. 766–69.

Deciding Whether to Quote, Paraphrase, or Summarize

As a general rule, quote only in these situations: (1) when the wording of the source is particularly memorable or vivid or expresses a point so well that you cannot improve it, (2) when the words of reliable and respected authorities would lend support to your position, (3) when you wish to cite an author whose opinions challenge or vary greatly from those of other experts, or (4) when you are going to discuss the source's choice of words. Paraphrase passages whose details you wish to use but whose language is not particularly striking. Summarize any long passages whose main points you wish to record as support for a point you are making.

Quoting

Quotations should duplicate the source exactly. If the source has an error, copy it and add the notation *sic* (Latin for "thus") in brackets immediately after the error to indicate that it is not your error but your source's:

> According to a recent newspaper article, "Plagirism [sic] is a problem among journalists and scholars as well as students" (Berensen 62).

However, you can change quotations for the following purposes, as long as you signal your changes appropriately: (1) to emphasize particular words, (2) to omit irrelevant information, (3) to insert information necessary for clarity, or (4) to make the quotation conform grammatically to your sentence. Note that "(Berensen 62)" represents a proper MLA-style in-text citation. For explanation of the rules for in-text citations, see pp. 766–69.

Using Italics for Emphasis. You may italicize any words in the quotation that you want to emphasize; add a semicolon and the words *emphasis added* (in regular type, not italicized or underlined) to the parenthetical citation.

> In her 2001 exposé of the struggles of the working class, Ehrenreich writes, "The wages Winn-Dixie is offering--*$6 and a couple of dimes to start with*--are not enough, I decide, to compensate for this indignity" (14; emphasis added).

Using Ellipsis Marks for Omissions. A writer may decide to omit words from a quotation because they are not relevant to the point being made. When you omit words from within a quotation, you must use ellipsis marks — three spaced periods (. . .) — in place of the missing words. When the omission occurs within a sentence, include a space before the first ellipsis mark and after the closing mark.

> Hermione Roddice is described in Lawrence's *Women in Love* as a "woman of the new school, full of intellectuality and . . . nerve-worn with consciousness" (17).

When the omission falls at the end of a sentence, place a period *directly after* the final word of the sentence, followed by a space and three spaced ellipsis marks.

> But Grimaldi's commentary contends that for Aristotle rhetoric, like dialectic, had "no limited and unique subject matter upon which it must be exercised. . . . Instead, rhetoric as an art transcends all specific disciplines and may be brought into play in them" (6).

A period plus ellipsis marks can indicate the omission of the rest of the sentence as well as whole sentences, paragraphs, or even pages.

When a parenthetical reference follows the ellipsis marks at the end of a sentence, place the three spaced periods after the quotation, and place the sentence period after the final parenthesis:

> But Grimaldi's commentary contends that for Aristotle rhetoric, like dialectic, had "no limited and unique subject matter upon which it must be exercised. . . . Instead, rhetoric as an art transcends all specific disciplines . . ." (6).

When you quote only single words or phrases, you do not need to use ellipsis marks because it will be obvious that you have left out some of the original.

> More specifically, Wharton's imagery of suffusing brightness transforms Undine before her glass into "some fabled creature whose home was in a beam of light" (21).

For the same reason, you need not use ellipsis marks if you omit the beginning of a quoted sentence unless the rest of the sentence begins with a capitalized word and still appears to be a complete sentence.

Using Brackets for Insertions or Changes. Use brackets around an insertion or a change needed to make a quotation conform grammatically to your sentence, such as a change in the form of a verb or pronoun or in the capitalization of the first word of the quotation. In this example from an essay on James Joyce's short story "Araby," the writer adapts Joyce's phrases "we played till our bodies glowed" and "shook music from the buckled harness" to fit the grammar of her sentences:

> In the dark, cold streets during the "short days of winter," the boys must generate their own heat by "play[ing] till [their] bodies glowed." Music is "[shaken] from the buckled harness" as if it were unnatural, and the singers in the market chant nasally of "the troubles in our native land" (30).

You may also use brackets to add or substitute explanatory material in a quotation:

> Guterson notes that among Native Americans in Florida, "education was in the home; learning by doing was reinforced by the myths and legends which repeated the basic value system of their [the Seminoles'] way of life" (159).

Some changes that make a quotation conform grammatically to another sentence may be made without any signal to readers: (1) A period at the end of a quotation may be changed to a comma if you are using the quotation within your own sentence, and (2) double quotation marks enclosing a quotation may be changed to single quotation marks when the quotation is enclosed within a longer quotation.

Integrating Quotations

Depending on its length, a quotation may be incorporated into your text by being enclosed in quotation marks or set off from your text in a block without quotation marks. In either case, be sure to integrate the quotation into the language of your essay.

In-Text Quotations

Incorporate brief quotations (no more than four typed lines of prose or three lines of poetry) into your text. You may place the quotation virtually anywhere in your sentence:

At the Beginning

"To live a life is not to cross a field," Sutherland, quoting Pasternak, writes at the beginning of her narrative (11).

In the Middle

Woolf begins and ends by speaking of the need of the woman writer to have "money and a room of her own" (4)--an idea that certainly spoke to Plath's condition.

At the End

In *The Second Sex*, Simone de Beauvoir describes such an experience as one in which the girl "becomes an object, and she sees herself as object" (378).

Divided by Your Own Words

"Science usually prefers the literal to the nonliteral term," Kinneavy writes, "--that is, figures of speech are often out of place in science" (177).

When you quote poetry within your text, use a slash (/) with spaces before and after to signal the end of each line of verse:

Alluding to St. Augustine's distinction between the City of God and the Earthly City, Lowell writes that "much against my will / I left the City of God where it belongs" (4-5).

Block Quotations

In the MLA style, use the block form for prose quotations of five or more typed lines and for poetry quotations of four or more lines. Indent the quotation an inch (ten character spaces) from the left margin, as shown in the following example.

In "A Literary Legacy from Dunbar to Baraka," Margaret Walker says of Paul Lawrence Dunbar's dialect poems:

> He realized that the white world in the United States tolerated his literary genius only because of his "jingles in a broken tongue," and they found the

old "darky" tales and speech amusing and within the vein of folklore into which they wished to classify all Negro life. This troubled Dunbar because he realized that white America was denigrating him as a writer and as a man. (70)

In the APA style, use block form for quotations of forty words or more. Indent the block quotation one-half inch (five to seven spaces), keeping your indents consistent throughout your paper.

In a block quotation, double-space between lines just as you do in your text. *Do not* enclose the passage within quotation marks. Use a colon to introduce a block quotation, unless the context calls for another punctuation mark or none at all. When quoting a single paragraph or part of one in the MLA style, do not indent the first line of the quotation more than the rest. In quoting two or more paragraphs, indent the first line of each paragraph an extra quarter inch (three spaces). If you are using the APA style, the first line of subsequent paragraphs in the block quotation indents an additional half inch or five to seven spaces from the block quotation indent.

Note that in MLA style the parenthetical page reference follows the period in block quotations.

Introducing Quotations

Statements that introduce in-text quotations take a range of punctuation marks and lead-in words. Here are some examples of ways writers typically introduce quotations.

Introducing a Quotation Using a Colon

A colon usually follows an independent clause placed before the quotation.

As George Williams notes, protection of white privilege is critical to patterns of discrimination: "Whenever a number of persons within a society have enjoyed for a considerable period of time certain opportunities for getting wealth, for exercising power and authority, and for successfully claiming prestige and social deference, there is a strong tendency for these people to feel that these benefits are theirs 'by right'" (727).

Introducing a Quotation Using a Comma

A comma usually follows an introduction that incorporates the quotation in its sentence structure.

Similarly, Duncan Turner asserts, "As matters now stand, it is unwise to talk about communication without some understanding of Burke" (259).

Introducing a Quotation Using that

No punctuation is generally needed with *that*, and no capital letter is used to begin the quotation.

Noting this failure, Alice Miller asserts **that** "the reason for her despair was not her suffering but the impossibility of communicating her suffering to another person" (255).

Punctuating within Quotations

Although punctuation within a quotation should reproduce the original, some adaptations may be necessary. Use single quotation marks for quotations within the quotation:

Original from David Guterson's Family Matters *(pages 16–17)*

E. D. Hirsch also recognizes the connection between family and learning, suggesting in his discussion of family background and academic achievement "that the significant part of our children's education has been going on outside rather than inside the schools."

Quoted Version

Guterson claims that E. D. Hirsch "also recognizes the connection between family and learning, suggesting in his discussion of family background and academic achievement 'that the significant part of our children's education has been going on outside rather than inside the schools'" (16-17).

If the quotation ends with a question mark or an exclamation point, retain the original punctuation:

"Did you think I loved you?" Edith later asks Dombey (566).

If a quotation ending with a question mark or an exclamation point concludes your sentence, retain the question mark or exclamation point, and put the parenthetical reference and sentence period outside the quotation marks:

Edith later asks Dombey, "Did you think I loved you?" (566).

Avoiding Grammatical Tangles

When you incorporate quotations into your writing, and especially when you omit words from quotations, you run the risk of creating ungrammatical sentences. Three common errors you should try to avoid are verb incompatibility, ungrammatical omissions, and sentence fragments.

Verb Incompatibility. When this error occurs, the verb form in the introductory statement is grammatically incompatible with the verb form in the quotation. When your quotation has a verb form that does not fit in with your text, it is usually possible to use just part of the quotation, thus avoiding verb incompatibility.

he describes seeing himself

▶ The narrator suggests his bitter disappointment when "~~I saw myself~~

"as a creature driven and derided by vanity" (35).

As this sentence illustrates, use the present tense when you refer to events in a literary work.

Ungrammatical Omission. Sometimes omitting text from a quotation leaves you with an ungrammatical sentence. Two ways of correcting the grammar are (1) adapting the quotation (with brackets) so that its parts fit together grammatically and (2) using only one part of the quotation.

▶ From the moment of the boy's arrival in Araby, the bazaar is presented as a

commercial enterprise: "I could not find any sixpenny entrance and . . .

hand[ed]
~~handing~~ a shilling to a weary-looking man" (34).
  ^

▶ From the moment of the boy's arrival in Araby, the bazaar is presented as a

He
commercial enterprise: "I "could not find any sixpenny entrance ," and ~~. . .~~
  ^   ^
so had to pay a shilling to get in (34).
~~handing a shilling to a weary-looking man" (34).~~
  ^

Sentence Fragment. Sometimes when a quotation is a complete sentence, writers neglect the sentence that introduces the quote — for example, by forgetting to include a verb. Make sure that the quotation is introduced by a complete sentence.

leads
▶ The girl's interest in the bazaar ~~leading~~ the narrator to make what amounts to a
  ^
sacred oath: "If I go . . . I will bring you something" (32).

Paraphrasing and Summarizing

In addition to quoting sources, writers have the option of paraphrasing or summarizing what others have written.

Paraphrasing. In a **paraphrase**, the writer restates all the relevant information from a passage, without any additional comments or any suggestion of agreement or disagreement with the source's ideas. A paraphrase is useful for recording details of the passage when the order of the details is important but the source's wording is not. Because all the details of the passage are included, a paraphrase is often about the same length as the original passage. Paraphrasing allows you to avoid quoting too much. Anyway, it is better to paraphrase than to quote ordinary material, where the author's way of expressing things is not worth special attention.

Here is a passage from a book on home schooling and an example of an acceptable paraphrase of it:

Original Source

Bruner and the discovery theorists have also illuminated conditions that apparently pave the way for learning. It is significant that these conditions are unique to each learner, so unique, in fact, that in many cases classrooms can't provide them. Bruner also contends that the more one discovers information in a great variety of circumstances, the more likely one is to develop the inner categories required to organize that information. Yet life at school, which is for the most part generic and predictable, daily keeps many children from the great variety of circumstances they need to learn well.

— David Guterson, *Family Matters: Why Homeschooling Makes Sense*, p. 172

Acceptable Paraphrase

According to Guterson, the "discovery theorists," particularly Bruner, have found that there seem to be certain conditions that help learning to take place. Because each individual requires different conditions, many children are not able to learn in the classroom. According to Bruner, when people can explore information in many different situations, they learn to classify and order what they discover. The general routine of the school day, however, does not provide children with the diverse activities and situations that would allow them to learn these skills (172).

Readers assume that some words in a paraphrase are taken from the source. Indeed, it would be nearly impossible for paraphrasers to avoid using any key terms from the source, and it would be counterproductive to try to do so, because the original and the paraphrase necessarily share the same information and concepts. Notice, though, that of the total of 86 words in the paraphrase, the paraphraser uses only a name (*Bruner*) and a few other key nouns and verbs (*discovery theorists, conditions, children, learn[ing], information, situations*) for which it would be awkward to substitute other words or phrases. If the paraphraser had wanted to use other, more distinctive language from the source — for example, the description of life at school as "generic and predictable" — these adjectives should have been enclosed in quotation marks. In fact, the paraphraser puts quotation marks around only one of the terms from the source: "discovery theorists," a technical term likely to be unfamiliar to readers.

Paraphrasers must, however, avoid borrowing too many words from a source and repeating the sentence structures of a source. Here is an unacceptable paraphrase of the first sentence in the Guterson passage:

Unacceptable Paraphrase: Too Many Borrowed Words and Phrases

Apparently, some conditions, which have been illuminated by Bruner and other discovery theorists, pave the way for people to learn.

If you compare the source's first sentence and the paraphrase of it, you will see that the paraphrase borrows almost all of its key language from the source sentence, including the entire phrase *pave the way for*. Even if you cite the source, this heavy borrowing would be considered plagiarism.

Here is another unacceptable paraphrase of the same sentence:

Unacceptable Paraphrase: Sentence Structure Repeated Too Closely

Bruner and other researchers have also identified circumstances that seem to ease the path to learning.

If you compare the source's first sentence and this paraphrase of it, you will see that the paraphraser has borrowed the phrases and clauses of the source and arranged them in an identical sequence, simply substituting synonyms for most of the key terms: *researchers* for *theorists, identified* for *illuminated, circumstances* for *conditions, seem to* for *apparently,* and *ease the path to* for *pave the way for.* This paraphrase would also be considered plagiarism.

Summarizing.   Unlike a paraphrase, a **summary** presents only the main ideas of a source, leaving out examples and details.

Here is one student's summary of five pages from *Family Matters.* You can see at a glance how drastically summaries can condense information, in this case from five pages to five sentences. Depending on the summarizer's purpose, the five pages could be summarized in one sentence, the five sentences here, or two or three dozen sentences.

In looking at different theories of learning that discuss individual-based programs (such as home schooling) versus the public school system, Guterson describes the disagreements among "cognitivist" theorists. One group, the "discovery theorists," believes that individual children learn by creating their own ways of sorting the information they take in from their experiences. Schools should help students develop better ways of organizing new material, not just present them with material that is already categorized, as traditional schools do. "Assimilationist theorists," by contrast, believe that children learn by linking what they don't know to information they already know. These theorists claim that traditional schools help students learn when they present information in ways that allow children to fit the new material into categories they have already developed (171-75).

Summaries like this one are more than a dry list of main ideas from a source. They are instead a coherent, readable new text composed of the source's main ideas. Summaries provide balanced coverage of a source, following the same sequence of ideas and avoiding any hint of agreement or disagreement with them.

Documenting Sources

Although there is no universally accepted system for acknowledging sources, most documentation styles use parenthetical in-text citations keyed to a separate list of works cited or references. The information required in the in-text citations and the order and content of the works-cited entries vary across academic disciplines. This section presents the basic features of two styles: the author-page system that is advocated by the Modern Language Association (MLA) and widely used in the humanities (for example, literature and history) and the author-year system that is advocated by the American Psychological Association (APA) and widely used in the social sciences (for example, psychology and economics).

In Part One of this book, you can find examples of student essays that follow the MLA style and the APA style. (See p. 786 for a full list.) For more information about these documentation styles, consult the *MLA Handbook for Writers of Research Papers,* Seventh Edition (2009), or the *Publication Manual of the American Psychological Association,* Sixth Edition (2010).

Check with your instructor about which of these styles you should use or whether you should use some other style. A list of common documentation style manuals is provided in Table 24.1.

Table 24.1 Some Commonly Used Documentation Style Manuals

Subject	Style Manual	Online Source
General	*The Chicago Manual of Style.* 15th ed. 2003.	http://www.chicagomanualofstyle.org
	A Manual for Writers of Research Papers, Theses, and Dissertations. 7th ed. 2007.	http://www.turabian.org
Online sources	*Columbia Guide to Online Style.* 2nd ed. 2006.	http://cup.columbia.edu/book/978-0-231-13210-7/the-columbia-guide-to-online-style
Biological sciences	*Scientific Style and Format: The CSE Manual for Authors, Editors, and Publishers.* 7th ed. 2006.	http://www.councilscienceeditors.org/publications/style.cfm
Chemistry	*The ACS Style Guide.* 3rd ed. 2006.	http://www.pubs.acs.org/page/books/styleguide/index.html
Government documents	*The Complete Guide to Citing Government Documents.* Rev. ed. 1993.	http://exlibris.memphis.edu/resource/unclesam/citeweb.html
Humanities	*MLA Handbook for Writers of Research Papers.* 7th ed. 2009. *MLA Style Manual and Guide to Scholarly Publishing.* 3rd ed. 2008.	http://www.mla.org
Psychology/ Social sciences	*Publication Manual of the American Psychological Association.* 6th ed. 2010.	http://www.apastyle.apa.org

The MLA System of Documentation

Citations in Text

A WORK WITH A SINGLE AUTHOR

The MLA author-page system generally requires that in-text citations include the author's last name and the page number of the passage being cited. There is no punctuation between author and page. The parenthetical citation should follow the quoted, paraphrased, or summarized material as closely as possible without disrupting the flow of the sentence.

> Dr. James is described as a "not-too-skeletal Ichabod Crane" (Simon 68).

> One reviewer compares Dr. James to Ichabod Crane (Simon 68).

Note that the parenthetical citation comes before the final period. With block quotations, however, the citation comes after the final period, preceded by a space (see pp. 759–60 for an example). If you mention the author's name in your text, supply just the page reference in parentheses.

> Simon describes Dr. James as a "not-too-skeletal Ichabod Crane" (68).

> Simon compares Dr. James to Ichabod Crane (68).

A WORK WITH MORE THAN ONE AUTHOR

To cite a source by two or three authors, include all the authors' last names; for works with more than three authors, use all the authors' names or just the first author's name followed by *et al.*, meaning "and others," in regular type (not italicized or underlined).

> Dyal, Corning, and Willows identify several types of students, including the "Authority-Rebel" (4).

> The Authority-Rebel "tends to see himself as superior to other students in the class" (Dyal, Corning, and Willows 4).

> The drug AZT has been shown to reduce the risk of transmission from HIV-positive mothers to their infants by as much as two-thirds (Van de Perre et al. 4-5).

TWO OR MORE WORKS BY THE SAME AUTHOR

To cite one of two or more works by the same author, include the author's last name, a comma, a shortened version of the title you are citing, and the page number(s).

> When old paint becomes transparent, it sometimes shows the artist's original plans: "a tree will show through a woman's dress" (Hellman, *Pentimento* 1).

A WORK WITH AN UNKNOWN AUTHOR

Use a shortened version of the title, beginning with the word by which the title is alphabetized in the works-cited list. ("Awash in Garbage" was the title in the following example.)

An international pollution treaty still to be ratified would prohibit all plastic garbage from being dumped at sea ("Awash" 26).

TWO OR MORE AUTHORS WITH THE SAME LAST NAME CITED IN YOUR ESSAY

In addition to the last name, include each author's first initial in the citation. If the first initials are also the same, spell out the authors' first names.

Chaplin's *Modern Times* provides a good example of montage used to make an editorial statement (E. Roberts 246).

A CORPORATE OR GOVERNMENT AUTHOR

In a parenthetical citation, give the full name of the author if it is brief or a shortened version if it is long. If you name the author in your text, give the full name even if it is long.

A tuition increase has been proposed for community and technical colleges to offset budget deficits from Initiative 601 (Washington State Board 4).

According to the Washington State Board for Community and Technical Colleges, a tuition increase . . . from Initiative 601 (4).

A MULTIVOLUME WORK

When you use two or more volumes of a multivolume work in your paper, include the volume number and the page number(s), separated by a colon and one space, in each citation.

According to Forster, modernist writers valued experimentation and gradually sought to blur the line between poetry and prose (3: 150).

If you cite only one volume, give the volume number in the works cited (see p. 771) and include only the page number(s) in the parenthetical citation.

A LITERARY WORK

For a novel or other prose work available in various editions, provide the page numbers from the edition used as well as other information that will help readers locate the quotation in a different edition, such as the part or chapter number.

In *Hard Times,* Tom reveals his utter narcissism by blaming Louisa for his own failure: "'You have regularly given me up. You never cared for me'"(Dickens 262; bk. 3, ch. 9).

For a play in verse, such as a Shakespearean play, indicate the act, scene, and line numbers instead of the page numbers.

At the beginning, Regan's fawning rhetoric hides her true attitude toward Lear: "I profess / myself an enemy to all other joys . . . / And find that I am alone felicitate / In your dear highness' love" (*King Lear* 1.1.74-75, 77-78).

For a poem, indicate the line numbers and stanzas or sections (if they are numbered), instead of the page numbers. If the source gives only line numbers, use the term *lines* in the first citation and give only the numbers in subsequent citations.

> In "Song of Myself," Whitman finds poetic details in busy urban settings, as when he describes "the blab of the pave, tires of carts . . . the driver with his interrogating thumb" (8.153-54).

A RELIGIOUS WORK

For the Bible, indicate the book, chapter, and verse instead of the page numbers. Abbreviate books with names of five or more letters in your parenthetical citation, but spell out full names of books in your text.

> She ignored the admonition "Pride goes before destruction, and a haughty spirit before a fall" (*New Oxford Annotated Bible,* Prov. 16.18).

A WORK IN AN ANTHOLOGY

Use the name of the author of the work, not the editor of the anthology, but use the page number(s) from the anthology.

> In "Six Days: Some Rememberings," Grace Paley recalls that when she was in jail for protesting the Vietnam War, her pen and paper were taken away and she felt "a terrible pain in the area of my heart--a nausea" (191).

A QUOTATION FROM A SECONDARY SOURCE

Include the secondary source in your list of works cited. In your parenthetical citation, use the abbreviation *qtd. in* (in regular type, not italicized or underlined) to acknowledge that the original was quoted in a secondary source.

> E. M. Forster says "the collapse of all civilization, so realistic for us, sounded in Matthew Arnold's ears like a distant and harmonious cataract" (qtd. in Trilling 11).

AN ENTIRE WORK

Include the reference in the text without any page numbers or parentheses.

> In *The Structure of Scientific Revolutions,* Thomas Kuhn discusses how scientists change their thinking.

A WORK WITHOUT PAGE NUMBERS

If a work has no page numbers or is only one page long, you may omit the page number. If a work uses paragraph numbers instead, use the abbreviation *par.* (or *pars.,* plural) in regular type, not italicized or underlined, and use a comma after the author's name.

The average speed on Montana's interstate highways, for example, has risen by only 2 miles per hour since the repeal of the federal speed limit, with most drivers topping out at 75 (Schmid).

Whitman considered African American speech "a source of a native grand opera" (Ellison, par. 13).

TWO OR MORE WORKS CITED IN THE SAME PARENTHESES

When two or more different sources are used in the same passage of your essay, it may be necessary to cite them in the same parentheses. Separate the citations with a semicolon. Include any specific pages, or omit pages to refer to the whole work.

A few studies have considered differences between oral and written discourse production (Scardamalia, Bereiter, and Goelman; Gould).

MATERIAL FROM THE INTERNET

Give enough information in the citation to enable readers to locate the Internet source in the list of works cited. If the author is not named, give the document title. Include page, section, paragraph, or screen numbers, if available.

In handling livestock, "many people attempt to restrain animals with sheer force instead of using behavioral principles" (Grandin).

List of Works Cited

The list of works cited provides full information for all the sources the writer uses. Entries are alphabetized according to the first author's last name or by the title if the author is unknown. Every source cited in the text must refer to an entry in the list of works cited. Conversely, every entry in the list of works cited must correspond to at least one in-text citation.

In the MLA style, multiple works by the same author (or same group of authors) are alphabetized by title. The author's name is given for the first entry only; in subsequent entries, three hyphens and a period are used.

Kingsolver, Barbara. *High Tide in Tucson: Essays from Now or Never*. New York: HarperCollins, 1995. Print.

---. *Small Wonder*. New York: HarperCollins, 2002. Print.

The information presented in a works-cited entry for a book follows this order: author, title, publication source, year of publication, and medium of publication. The MLA style requires a "hanging indent," which means that the first line of a works-cited entry is not indented but subsequent lines of the entry are. The MLA specifies an indent of half an inch or five character spaces.

Note that in the list of works cited, publishers' names are given in shortened form. Compound or hyphenated names are usually limited to the first name only (with "Bedford," for example, used for "Bedford/St. Martin's"). The words "University" and "Press" are shortened to "U" and "P," respectively.

Books

Here is an example of a basic MLA-style entry for a book:

Double-space between lines

Author, last name first

Title (and subtitle, if any), italicized

Ehrenreich, Barbara. *Nickel and Dimed: On (Not) Getting by in America.*

New York: Metropolitan, 2001. Print.

Indent second and subsequent lines 1/2 inch

Publisher's city and name, year of publication

Medium of publication

A BOOK BY A SINGLE AUTHOR

Lamb, Sharon. *The Secret Lives of Girls*. New York: Free, 2002. Print.

A BOOK BY AN AGENCY OR A CORPORATION

American Medical Association. *Family Medical Guide*. 4th ed. Hoboken: Wiley, 2004. Print.

A BOOK BY MORE THAN ONE AUTHOR

Saba, Laura, and Julie Gattis. *The McGraw-Hill Homeschooling Companion*. New York: McGraw, 2002. Print.

Wilmut, Ian, Keith Campbell, and Colin Tudge. *The Second Creation: Dolly and the Age of Biological Control*. New York: Farrar, 2000. Print.

A WORK BY MORE THAN THREE AUTHORS

The MLA lists all the authors' names *or* the name of the first author followed by *et al.* (in regular type, not italicized or underlined).

Hunt, Lynn, et al. *The Making of the West: Peoples and Cultures*. Boston: Bedford, 2001. Print.

A BOOK BY AN UNKNOWN AUTHOR

Use the title in place of the author.

Rand McNally Commercial Atlas and Marketing Guide. Skokie: Rand, 2003. Print.

A BOOK WITH AN AUTHOR AND AN EDITOR

If you refer to the author's text, begin the entry with the author's name.

Arnold, Matthew. *Culture and Anarchy*. Ed. Samuel Lipman. New Haven: Yale UP, 1994. Print.

If you cite the editor in your paper, begin the entry with the editor's name.

Lipman, Samuel, ed. *Culture and Anarchy*. By Matthew Arnold. 1869. New Haven: Yale UP, 1994. Print.

AN EDITED COLLECTION

Waldman, Diane, and Janet Walker, eds. *Feminism and Documentary*. Minneapolis: U of
Minnesota P, 1999. Print.

A WORK IN AN ANTHOLOGY OR A COLLECTION

Lahiri, Jhumpa. "Nobody's Business." *The Best American Short Stories 2002*. Ed. Sue
Miller. Boston: Houghton, 2002. 136-72. Print.

TWO OR MORE WORKS FROM THE SAME ANTHOLOGY

To avoid repetition, you may create an entry for the collection and cite the collection's editor to cross-reference individual works to the entry.

Boyd, Herb, ed. *The Harlem Reader*. New York: Three Rivers, 2003. Print.

Wallace, Michelle. "Memories of a Sixties Girlhood: The Harlem I Love." Boyd 243-50. Print.

ONE VOLUME OF A MULTIVOLUME WORK

If only one volume from a multivolume set is used, indicate the volume number
after the title.

Freud, Sigmund. *The Standard Edition of the Complete Psychological Works of Sigmund
Freud*. Vol. 8. Trans. and ed. James Strachey. New York: Norton, 2000. Print.

TWO OR MORE VOLUMES OF A MULTIVOLUME WORK

Sandburg, Carl. *Abraham Lincoln*. 6 vols. New York: Scribner's, 1939. Print.

A BOOK THAT IS PART OF A SERIES

After the medium of publication, include the series title in regular type (not italicized or in quotation marks), followed by the series number and a period. If the word *Series* is part of the name, include *Ser.* before the number. Common abbreviations may be used for selected words in the series title.

Zigova, Tanya, et al. *Neural Stem Cells: Methods and Protocols*. Totowa: Humana, 2002.
Print. Methods in Molecular Biology 198.

A REPUBLISHED BOOK

Provide the original year of publication after the title of the book, followed by publication information for the edition you are using.

Alcott, Louisa May. *An Old-Fashioned Girl*. 1870. New York: Puffin, 1995. Print.

A LATER EDITION OF A BOOK

Rottenberg, Annette T., and Donna Haisty Winchell. *The Structure of Argument*. 6th ed.
Boston: Bedford, 2009. Print.

A BOOK WITH A TITLE IN ITS TITLE

Do not italicize a title normally italicized when it appears within a book title.

Hertenstein, Mike. *The Double Vision of* Star Trek: *Half-Humans, Evil Twins, and Science Fiction*. Chicago: Cornerstone, 1998. Print.

O'Neill, Terry, ed. *Readings on* To Kill a Mockingbird. San Diego: Greenhaven, 2000. Print.

Use quotation marks around a work normally enclosed in quotation marks when it appears within the title of a book.

Miller, Edwin Haviland. *Walt Whitman's "Song of Myself": A Mosaic of Interpretation*. Iowa City: U of Iowa P, 1989. Print.

A TRANSLATION

If you refer to the work itself, begin the entry with the author's name.

Tolstoy, Leo. *War and Peace*. Trans. Constance Garnett. New York: Modern, 2002. Print.

If you cite the translator in your text, begin the entry with the translator's name.

Garnett, Constance, trans. *War and Peace*. By Leo Tolstoy. 1869. New York: Modern, 2002. Print.

A DICTIONARY ENTRY OR AN ARTICLE IN A REFERENCE BOOK

"Homeopathy." *Webster's New World College Dictionary*. 4th ed. 1999. Print.

Rowland, Lewis P. "Myasthenia Gravis." *The Encyclopedia Americana*. 2001 ed. Print.

AN INTRODUCTION, PREFACE, FOREWORD, OR AFTERWORD

Graff, Gerald, and James Phelan. Preface. *Adventures of Huckleberry Finn*. By Mark Twain. 2nd ed. New York: Bedford, 2004. iii-vii. Print.

Articles

AN ARTICLE FROM A SCHOLARLY JOURNAL

Here is an example of a basic MLA-style entry for an article in a scholarly journal:

Author, last name first | *Article title, in quotation marks*

Simon, Robin W. "Revisiting the Relationship among Gender, Marital Status, and Mental Health." *American Journal of Sociology* 107.4 (2002): 1065-96. Print.

Double-space between lines; indent second and subsequent lines 1/2 inch | *Periodical title, italicized* | *Volume and issue number* | *Date, in parentheses, followed by colon* | *Page numbers* | *Medium of publication*

Scholarly journals are typically identified using their volume and issue numbers, separated by a period. If a journal does not use volume numbers, provide the issue number only, following the title of the journal.

Fee, Margery. "Predators and Gardens." *Canadian Literature* 197 (2008): 6-9. Print.

If the article is not on a continuous sequence of pages, give the first page number followed by a plus sign, as in the following example.

AN ARTICLE FROM A DAILY NEWSPAPER

Stoll, John D., et al. "U.S. Squeezes Auto Creditors." *Wall Street Journal* 10 Apr. 2009: A1+. Print.

Note that magazines and newspapers are identified not by volume and issue number but by date, with the names of most months abbreviated.

AN ARTICLE FROM A WEEKLY OR BIWEEKLY MAGAZINE

Doig, Will. "America's Real First Family." *Advocate* 17 July 2007: 46-50. Print.

AN ARTICLE FROM A MONTHLY OR BIMONTHLY MAGAZINE

Shelby, Ashley. "Good Going: Alaska's Glacier Crossroads." *Sierra* Sept.-Oct. 2005: 23. Print.

AN EDITORIAL

"Addiction behind Bars." Editorial. *New York Times* 12 Apr. 2009: A20. Print.

A LETTER TO THE EDITOR

Orent, Wendy, and Alan Zelicoff. Letter. *New Republic* 18 Nov. 2002: 4-5. Print.

A REVIEW

Cassidy, John. "Master of Disaster." Rev. of *Globalization and Its Discontents,* by Joseph Stiglitz. *New Yorker* 12 July 2002: 82-86. Print.

If the review does not include an author's name, start the entry with the title of the review and alphabetize by that title. If the review is untitled, begin with the words *Rev. of* and alphabetize under the title of the work being reviewed.

AN UNSIGNED ARTICLE

Begin with the article title, alphabetizing the entry according to the first word after any initial *A, An,* or *The.*

"A Shot of Reality." *U.S. News & World Report* 1 July 2003: 13. Print.

Electronic Sources

Much of the information required in citations of electronic sources takes the same form as in corresponding kinds of print sources. For example, if you are citing an article from an online periodical, put the article title in quotation marks and italicize the name of the periodical. If the source has been previously or simultaneously published in print, include the print publication information if it is available. You also should include information specific to electronic sources, where it is appropriate and available, including the following:

- The version or edition used.
- The publisher or sponsor of the site; if not available, use *N.p.*
- Date of publication; if not available, use *n.d.*
- Medium of publication (*Web*).
- The date you accessed the source.

Electronic content frequently changes or disappears, and because it is not organized in the ways that print books and periodicals are, finding the information needed for documentation is often difficult. If you cannot find some of this information, include what you do find. Always keep your goal in mind: to provide enough information so that your reader could track the source down later.

A DOCUMENT FROM A WEB SITE

Here is an example of a basic MLA-style entry for the most commonly cited kind of electronic source, a specific document from a Web site:

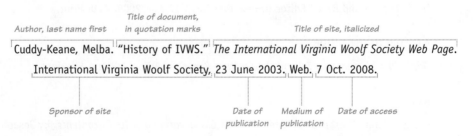

AN ENTIRE WEB SITE

Gardner, James Alan. *A Seminar on Writing Prose*. N.p., 2001. Web. 4 June 2008.

If the author's name is not known, begin the citation with the title.

The International Virginia Woolf Society Web Page. International Virginia Woolf Society, 31 Aug. 2002. Web. 21 Feb. 2008.

For an untitled personal site, put a description such as *Home page* (in regular type, not italicized), followed by a period, in the position a title would normally be cited.

Chesson, Frederick W. Home page. N.p., 1 Apr. 2003. Web. 26 Apr. 2008.

AN ONLINE SCHOLARLY PROJECT

For a complete project, provide the title, italicized, and the name of the editor, if given. Then give the electronic publication information — the version number (if any), the name of the sponsoring organization, and the date of electronic publication or latest update — followed by the medium and date of access.

> *The Darwin Correspondence Project*. Ed. Duncan Porter. Cambridge U Library, 2 June 2003.
> Web. 28 Nov. 2008.

A BOOK OR SHORT WORK WITHIN A SCHOLARLY PROJECT

Begin with the author's name and the title (italicized for a book or in quotation marks for an article, essay, poem, or other short work). Follow with the print publication information, if any, and the information about the project.

> Corelli, Marie. *The Treasure of Heaven*. London: Constable, 1906. *Victorian Women Writer's*
> *Project*. Ed. Percy Willett. Indiana U, 10 July 1999. Web. 10 Sept. 2008.

> Heims, Marjorie. "The Strange Case of Sarah Jones." *The Free Expression Policy Project*.
> FEPP, 24 Jan. 2003. Web. 13 Mar. 2006.

MATERIAL FROM AN ONLINE PERIODICAL DATABASE

If you access an article through an online database, after the print publication information, give the name of the database set in italics, the medium of publication, and the date of access.

> Braus, Patricia. "Sex and the Single Spender." *American Demographics* 15.11 (1993):
> 28-34. *Academic Search Premier*. Web. 13 Aug. 2008.

A NONPERIODICAL PUBLICATION ON A CD-ROM

> *Picasso: The Man, His Works, the Legend*. Danbury: Grolier Interactive, 1996. CD-ROM.

AN ARTICLE FROM AN ONLINE SCHOLARLY JOURNAL

Include the volume number and issue number, if given, after the title of the journal. Also include the number of pages, paragraphs, or other sections, if given, after the date of publication; if none are given, use *n. pag.*

> Cesarini, Paul. "Computers, Technology, and Literacies." *The Journal of Literacy and*
> *Technology* 4.1 (2004/2005): n. pag. Web. 12 Oct. 2008.

A POSTING TO A DISCUSSION GROUP OR NEWSGROUP

Include the author's name (if you know it), the title or subject line of the posting (in quotation marks), the group name, the sponsor, the posting date, the medium, and the access date.

> Willie, Otis. "In the Heat of the Battle." *soc.history.war.us-revolution*. Google, 27 Sept.
> 2005. Web. 7 Oct. 2008.

Martin, Francesca Alys. "Wait--Did Somebody Say 'Buffy'?" *Cultstud-L*. U of S Fl, 8 Mar. 2000. Web. 8 Mar. 2008.

AN E-MAIL MESSAGE

The subject line of the message is enclosed in quotation marks. Identify the persons who sent and received it and the date it was sent. End with the medium (*E-mail*), neither italicized nor underlined.

Olson, Kate. "Update on State Legislative Grants." Message to the author. 5 Nov. 2008. E-mail.

COMPUTER SOFTWARE

How Computers Work. Indianapolis: Que, 1998. CD-ROM.

Other Sources

A LECTURE OR PUBLIC ADDRESS

Birnbaum, Jack. "The Domestication of Computers." Conf. of the Usability Professionals Association. Hyatt Grand Cypress Resort, Orlando. 10 July 2002. Lecture.

A GOVERNMENT DOCUMENT

If the author is known, the author's name may either come first or be placed after the title, introduced with the word *By*.

United States. Dept. of Health and Human Services. *Trends in Underage Drinking in the United States, 1991-2007*. By Gabriella Newes-Adeyi, et al. Washington: GPO, 2009. Print.

A PAMPHLET

BoatU.S. Foundation for Boating Safety and Clean Water. *Hypothermia and Cold Water Survival*. Alexandria, VA: BoatU.S. Foundation, 2001. Print.

PUBLISHED PROCEEDINGS OF A CONFERENCE

If the name of the conference is part of the title of the publication, it need not be repeated. Use the format for a work in an anthology (see p. 771) to cite an individual presentation.

Duffett, John, ed. *Against the Crime of Silence*: *Proceedings of the International War Crimes Tribunal*. Nov. 1967, Stockholm. New York: Clarion-Simon, 1970. Print.

A PUBLISHED DOCTORAL DISSERTATION

Cite as you would a book, but add pertinent dissertation information before publication data.

Botts, Roderic C. *Influences in the Teaching of English, 1917-1935: An Illusion of Progress.* Diss. Northeastern U, 1970. Ann Arbor: UMI, 1971. Print.

Jones, Anna Maria. *Problem Novels/Perverse Readers: Late-Victorian Fiction and the Perilous Pleasures of Identification.* Diss. U of Notre Dame, 2001. Ann Arbor: UMI, 2001. Print.

AN UNPUBLISHED DOCTORAL DISSERTATION

Enclose the title of an unpublished dissertation in quotation marks.

Bullock, Barbara. "Basic Needs Fulfillment among Less Developed Countries: Social Progress over Two Decades of Growth." Diss. Vanderbilt U, 1986. Print.

A LETTER

Use *MS* ("manuscript") if written by hand, and *TS* ("typescript") if produced using technology.

DuHamel, Grace. Letter to the author. 22 Mar. 2008. TS.

A MAP OR CHART

Map of Afghanistan and Surrounding Territory. Map. Burlington: GiziMap, 2001. Print.

A CARTOON OR COMIC STRIP

Provide the title (if given) in quotation marks directly following the artist's name.

Cheney, Tom. Cartoon. *New Yorker.* 10 Oct. 2005: 55. Print.

AN ADVERTISEMENT

Hospital for Special Surgery. Advertisement. *New York Times* 13 Apr. 2009: A7. Print.

A WORK OF ART OR MUSICAL COMPOSITION

De Goya, Francisco. *The Sleep of Reason Produces Monsters.* 1799. Etching with water-color. Norton Simon Museum, Pasadena.

Beethoven, Ludwig van. *Violin Concerto in D Major, Op. 61.* 1809. New York: Edwin F. Kalmus, n.d. Print.

Gershwin, George. *Porgy and Bess.* 1935. New York: Alfred, 1999. Print.

If a photograph is not part of a collection, identify the subject, the name of the person who photographed it, and when it was photographed.

Washington Square Park, New York. Personal photograph by author. 24 June 2006.

A PERFORMANCE

Proof. By David Auburn. Dir. Daniel Sullivan. Perf. Mary-Louise Parker. Walter Kerr Theatre, New York. 9 Sept. 2001. Performance.

A TELEVISION PROGRAM

"Murder of the Century." *American Experience*. Narr. David Ogden Stiers. Writ. and prod. Carl Charlson. PBS. WEDU, Tampa, 14 July 2003. Television.

A FILM OR VIDEO RECORDING

Space Station. Prod. and dir. Toni Myers. Narr. Tom Cruise. IMAX, 2002. Film.

Casablanca. Dir. Michael Curtiz. Perf. Humphrey Bogart, Ingrid Bergman, and Paul Henreid. 1942. Warner Home Video, 2003. DVD.

A MUSIC RECORDING

Beethoven, Ludwig van. *Violin Concerto in D Major*, *Op. 61*. U.S.S.R. State Orchestra. Cond. Alexander Gauk. Perf. David Oistrakh. Allegro, 1980. Audiocassette.

Springsteen, Bruce. "Dancing in the Dark." *Born in the USA*. Columbia, 1984. CD.

AN INTERVIEW

Ashrawi, Hanan. "Tanks vs. Olive Branches." Interview with Rose Marie Berger. *Sojourners Magazine* Feb. 2005: 22-26. Print.

Ellis, Trey. Personal interview. 3 Sept. 2008.

The APA System of Documentation

Citations in Text

AUTHOR INDICATED IN PARENTHESES

The APA author-year system calls for the last name of the author and the year of publication of the original work in the citation. If the cited material is a quotation, you also need to include the page number(s) of the original. If the cited material is not a quotation, the page reference is optional. Use commas to separate author, year, and page in a parenthetical citation. The page number is preceded by *p.* for a single page or *pp.* for a range. Use an ampersand (&) to join the names of multiple authors.

> The conditions in the stockyards were so dangerous that workers "fell into the vats; and when they were fished out, there was never enough of them left to be worth exhibiting" (Sinclair, 2005, p. 134).

> Racial bias does not necessarily diminish through exposure to individuals of other races (Jamison & Tyree, 2001).

If you are citing an electronic source without page numbers, give the paragraph number if it is provided, preceded by the abbreviation *para*. If no paragraph number is given, give the heading of the section and the number of the paragraph within it where the material appears, if possible.

> The subjects were tested for their responses to various stimuli, both positive and negative (Simpson, 2002, para. 4).

AUTHOR INDICATED IN SIGNAL PHRASE

If the author's name is mentioned in your text, cite the year in parentheses directly following the author's name, and place the page reference in parentheses before the final sentence period. Use *and* to join the names of multiple authors.

> Sinclair (2005) wrote that workers sometimes "fell into the vats; and when they were fished out, there was never enough of them left to be worth exhibiting" (p. 134).

> As Jamison and Tyree (2001) have found, racial bias does not diminish merely through exposure to individuals of other races (Conclusion section, para. 2).

SOURCE WITH MORE THAN TWO AUTHORS

To cite works with three to five authors, use all the authors' last names the first time the reference occurs and the last name of the first author followed by *et al.* (in regular type, not italicized or underlined) subsequently. If a source has six or more authors, use only the last name of the first author and *et al.* at first and subsequent references.

First Citation in Text

> Rosenzweig, Breedlove, and Watson (2005) wrote that biological psychology is an interdisciplinary field that includes scientists from "quite different backgrounds" (p. 3).

Subsequent Citations

> Biological psychology is "the field that relates behavior to bodily processes, especially the workings of the brain" (Rosenzweig et al., 2005, p. 3).

TWO OR MORE WORKS BY THE SAME AUTHOR

To cite one of two or more works by the same author or group of authors, use the author's last name plus the year (and the page, if you are citing a quotation). When more than one work being cited was published by an author in the same year, the works are alphabetized by title and then assigned lowercase letters after the date (2005a, 2005b).

> Middle-class unemployed workers are better off than their lower-class counterparts, because "the white collar unemployed are likely to have some assets to invest in their job search" (Ehrenreich, 2005b, p. 16).

UNKNOWN AUTHOR

To cite a work listed only by its title, the APA uses a shortened version of the title.

> An international pollution treaty still to be ratified would prohibit all plastic garbage from being dumped at sea ("Awash," 1987).

SECONDARY SOURCE

To quote material taken not from the original source but from a secondary source that quotes the original, give the secondary source in the reference list, and in your essay acknowledge that the original was quoted in a secondary source.

> E. M. Forster said "the collapse of all civilization, so realistic for us, sounded in Matthew Arnold's ears like a distant and harmonious cataract" (as cited in Trilling, 1955, p. 11).

List of References

The APA follows this order in the presentation of information for each source listed: author, publication year, title, and publication source; for an article, the page range is given as well. Titles of books, periodicals, and the like should be italicized. For books and articles, capitalize only the first word of the title, proper nouns, and the first word following a colon (if any). Capitalize the titles of magazines and journals as you would normally capitalize them.

When the list of references includes several works by the same author, the APA provides the following rules for arranging these entries in the list:

- Same-name single-author entries precede multiple-author entries:

  Zettelmeyer, F. (2000).

  Zettelmeyer, F., Morton, F. S., & Silva-Risso, J. (2006).

- Entries with the same first author and a different second author are alphabetized under the first author according to the second author's last name:

  Dhar, R., & Nowlis, S. M. (2004).

  Dhar, R., & Simonson, I. (2003).

- Entries by the same authors are arranged by year of publication, in chronological order:

  Golder, P. N., & Tellis, G. J. (2003).

  Golder, P. N., & Tellis, G. J. (2004).

- Entries by the same authors with the same publication year should be arranged alphabetically by title (according to the first word after *A*, *An*, or *The*), and lowercase letters (*a*, *b*, *c*, and so on) are appended to the year in parentheses:

  Aaron, P. (1990a). *Basic* . . .

  Aaron, P. (1990b). *Elements* . . .

The APA recommends that the first line of each entry be indented one-half inch (or five spaces) in papers intended for publication but notes that student writers may use a hanging indent of five spaces. Ask your instructor which format is preferred. The following examples demonstrate a hanging indent of one-half inch.

Books

A BOOK BY A SINGLE AUTHOR

Ehrenreich, B. (2001). *Nickel and dimed: On (not) getting by in America*. New York, NY: Metropolitan.

A BOOK BY AN AGENCY OR A CORPORATION

American Medical Association. (2004). *Family medical guide*. Hoboken, NJ: Wiley.

A BOOK BY MORE THAN ONE AUTHOR

Saba, L., & Gattis, J. (2002). *The McGraw-Hill homeschooling companion*. New York, NY: McGraw-Hill.

Hunt, L., Po Chia Hsia, R., Martin, T. R., Rosenwein, B. H., Rosenwein, H., & Smith, B. G. (2001). *The making of the West: Peoples and cultures*. Boston, MA: Bedford/St. Martin's.

If there are more than seven authors, list only the first six, then insert three periods, and add the last author's name.

A BOOK BY AN UNKNOWN AUTHOR

Use the title in place of the author.

Rand McNally commercial atlas and marketing guide. (2003). Skokie, IL: Rand McNally.

When an author is designated as "Anonymous," identify the work as "Anonymous" in the text, and alphabetize it as "Anonymous" in the reference list.

A BOOK WITH AN AUTHOR AND AN EDITOR

Arnold, M. (1994). *Culture and anarchy* (S. Lipman, Ed.). New Haven, CT: Yale University Press. (Original work published 1869)

AN EDITED COLLECTION

Waldman, D., & Walker, J. (Eds.). (1999). *Feminism and documentary*. Minneapolis, MN: University of Minnesota Press.

A WORK IN AN ANTHOLOGY OR A COLLECTION

Fairbairn-Dunlop, P. (1993). Women and agriculture in western Samoa. In J. H. Momsen & V. Kinnaird (Eds.), *Different places, different voices* (pp. 211-226). London, England: Routledge.

A TRANSLATION

Tolstoy, L. (2002). *War and peace* (C. Garnett, Trans.). New York, NY: Modern Library. (Original work published 1869)

AN ARTICLE IN A REFERENCE BOOK

Rowland, R. P. (2001). Myasthenia gravis. In *Encyclopedia Americana* (Vol. 19, p. 683). Danbury, CT: Grolier.

AN INTRODUCTION, PREFACE, FOREWORD, OR AFTERWORD

Graff, G., & Phelan, J. Preface (2004). In M. Twain, *Adventures of Huckleberry Finn* (pp. iii-vii). New York, NY: Bedford/St. Martin's.

Articles

AN ARTICLE FROM A DAILY NEWSPAPER

Peterson, A. (2003, May 20). Finding a cure for old age. *The Wall Street Journal,* pp. D1, D5.

AN ARTICLE FROM A WEEKLY OR BIWEEKLY MAGAZINE

Gross, M. J. (2003, April 29). Family life during war time. *The Advocate,* 42-48.

AN ARTICLE FROM A MONTHLY OR BIMONTHLY MAGAZINE

Shelby, A. (2005, September/October). Good going: Alaska's glacier crossroads. *Sierra, 90,* 23.

AN ARTICLE IN A SCHOLARLY JOURNAL WITH CONTINUOUS ANNUAL PAGINATION

The volume number follows the title of the journal.

Shan, J. Z., Morris, A. G., & Sun, F. (2001). Financial development and economic growth: A chicken and egg problem? *Review of Economics, 9,* 443-454.

AN ARTICLE IN A SCHOLARLY JOURNAL THAT PAGINATES EACH ISSUE SEPARATELY

The issue number appears in parentheses after the volume number.

Tran, D. (2002). Personal income by state, second quarter 2002. *Current Business, 82*(11), 55-73.

AN ANONYMOUS ARTICLE

Communities blowing whistle on street basketball. (2003). *USA Today,* p. 20A.

A REVIEW

Cassidy, J. (2002, July 12). Master of disaster [Review of the book *Globalization and its discontents*]. *The New Yorker,* 82-86.

If the review is untitled, use the bracketed information as the title, retaining the brackets.

Electronic Sources

While the APA guidelines for citing online resources are still something of a work in progress, a rule of thumb is that citation information must allow readers to access and retrieve the information cited. The following guidelines are derived from the *Publication Manual of the American Psychological Association,* Sixth Edition (2010). Regular updates are posted on the APA's Web site (www.apastyle .apa.org/elecref.html).

For most sources accessed on the Internet, you should provide the following information:

- Name of author (if available).
- Date of publication or most recent update (in parentheses; if unavailable, use the abbreviation *n.d.*).
- Title of document.
- Publication information, including volume and issue numbers for periodicals.
- Retrieval information, including information necessary to locate the document. Note that the APA now requires the date of access *only* for content that is likely to be changed or updated.

For more information on using the Internet for research, see Chapter 23, pp. 747–52.

DOCUMENT FROM A WEB SITE

When you cite an entire Web site, the APA does not require an entry in the list of references. You may instead give the name of the site in your text and its Web address in parentheses. To cite a document that you have accessed through a Web site, follow these formats:

American Cancer Society. (2003). *How to fight teen smoking.* Retrieved from http://www .cancer.org/docroot/ped/content/ped_10_14_how_to_fight_teen_smoking.asp

Heins, M. (2003, January 24). *The strange case of Sarah Jones. The Free Expression Policy Project.* Retrieved from http://www.fepproject.org/commentaries/sarahjones .html

ARTICLE FROM A DATABASE

Follow the guidelines for a comparable print source, but conclude with the article's DOI (Digital Object Identifier), if one is assigned. If there is no DOI, conclude with the URL of the journal's home page.

Houston, R. G., & Toma, F. (2003). Home schooling: An alternative school choice. *Southern Economic Journal, 69*(4), 920-936. Retrieved from http://www.southerneconomic.org.

Tharp, R. G. (1989). Psychocultural variables and constants: Effects on teaching and learning in schools. *American Psychologist, 44*(2), 249-359. doi:10.1037/0003 -066X.44.2.349

AN ARTICLE FROM AN ONLINE PERIODICAL

Include the same information you would for a print article. If the article has a DOI, include it; if not, include the URL for the article or the periodical's home page.

Jauhar, S. (2003, July 15). A malady that mimics depression. *The New York Times*. Retrieved from http://www.nytimes.com

Retrieval information is always required for periodicals that are published only online.

Cesarini, P. (2004/2005). Computers, technology, and literacies. *The Journal of Literacy and Technology, 4*(1). Retrieved from http://www.literacyandtechnology.org/v4 /cesarini.htm

ONLINE POSTINGS

Include online postings in your list of references only if you can provide data that would allow retrieval of the source. Provide the author's name, the date of the posting, the subject line, and any other identifier in brackets after the title. Include the words "Retrieved from" followed by the URL where the message can be found. Include the name of the list, newsgroup, or blog, if this information is not part of the URL.

Paikeday, T. (2005, October 10). "Esquivalience" is out [Electronic mailing list message]. Retrieved from http://listserv.linguistlist.org/cgi-bin/wa?A1=ind0510b&L=ads-1#1

Ditmire, S. (2005, February 10). NJ tea party [Newsgroup message]. Retrieved from http://groups.google.com/group/TeaParty

AN E-MAIL MESSAGE

In the APA style, it is not necessary to list personal correspondence, including e-mail, in your reference list. Simply cite the person's name in your text, and in parentheses give the notation *personal communication* (in regular type, not under-lined or italicized) and the date.

COMPUTER SOFTWARE

If an individual has proprietary rights to the software, cite that person's name as you would for a print text. Otherwise, cite as you would an anonymous print text.

How Computers Work [Software]. (1998). Available from Que: http://www.howcomputerswork .net

Other Sources

A GOVERNMENT DOCUMENT

U.S. Department of Health and Human Services. (2009). *Trends in underage drinking in the United States, 1991-2007*. Washington, DC: Government Printing Office.

Note: when the author and publisher are the same, use the word *Author* (not italicized) as the name of the publisher.

AN UNPUBLISHED DOCTORAL DISSERTATION

Bullock, B. (1986). *Basic needs fulfillment among less developed countries: Social progress over two decades of growth* (Unpublished doctoral dissertation). Vanderbilt University, Nashville, TN.

A TELEVISION PROGRAM

Charlsen, C. (Writer and producer). (2003, July 14). Murder of the century [Television series episode]. In M. Samels (Executive producer), *American Experience*. Boston, MA: WGBH.

A FILM OR VIDEO RECORDING

Myers, T. (Writer and producer). (2002). *Space station* [Motion picture]. New York, NY: IMAX.

A MUSIC RECORDING

If the recording date differs from the copyright date, the APA requires that it appear in parentheses after the name of the label. If it is necessary to include a number for the recording, use parentheses for the medium; otherwise, use brackets.

Beethoven, L. van. (1806). Violin concerto in D major, op. 61 [Recorded by USSR State Orchestra]. (Cassette Recording No. ACS 8044). New York, NY: Allegro. (1980)

Springsteen, B. (1984). Dancing in the dark. On *Born in the U.S.A.* [CD]. New York, NY: Columbia.

AN INTERVIEW

When using the APA style, do not list personal interviews in your references list. Simply cite the person's name (last name and initials) in your text, and in parentheses give the notation *personal communication* (in regular type, not italicized or underlined) followed by a comma and the date of the interview. For published interviews, use the appropriate format for an article.

Some Sample Research Papers

As a writer, you will want or need to use sources on many occasions. You may be assigned to write a research paper, complete with formal documentation of outside sources. Several of the writing assignments in this book present opportunities to do library or field research — in other words, to turn to outside sources. Among the readings in Part One, the essays listed here cite and document sources. (The documentation style each follows is given in parentheses.)

"Cannibalism: It Still Exists," by Linh Kieu Ngo, Chapter 4, pp. 131–35 (MLA)

"Lost Innocence," by Jeremy Bernard, Chapter 5, pp. 191–94 (MLA)

"Laying Claim to a Higher Morality," by Melissa Mae, Chapter 5, pp. 195–97 (MLA)

"No Child Left Behind," by Athena Alexander, Chapter 5, pp. 201–6 (MLA)

"Children Need to Play, Not Compete," by Jessica Statsky, Chapter 6, pp. 270–74 (MLA)

"More Testing, More Learning," by Patrick O'Malley, Chapter 7, pp. 326–30 (APA)

"Win-Win Flexibility," by Karen Kornbluh, Chapter 7, pp. 331–36 (MLA)

"Grading Professors," by Wendy Kim, Chapter 8, pp. 389–94 (MLA)

"The Rising," by Paul Taylor, Chapter 20, pp. 682–85 (MLA)

An Annotated Research Paper

On the following pages is a student research paper speculating about the causes of a trend — the increase in home schooling. The author cites statistics, quotes authorities, and paraphrases and summarizes background information and support for her argument. She uses the MLA documentation style.

1"

1/2"
Dinh 1

1"

Cristina Dinh

Professor Cooper

English 100

15 May 2009

Educating Kids at Home

Every morning, Mary Jane, who is nine, doesn't have to worry about *1"* gulping down her cereal so she can be on time for school. School for Mary Jane is literally right at her doorstep.

In this era of serious concern about the quality of public education, increasing numbers of parents across the United States are choosing to educate their children at home. These parents believe they can do a better job teaching their children than their local schools can. *Home schooling*, as this practice is known, has become a national trend over the past thirty years, and, according to education specialist Brian D. Ray, the home-schooled population is growing at a rate between 5% and 12% per year. A 2008 report by the U.S. Department of Education's Institute of Education Sciences estimated that, nationwide, the number of home-schooled children rose from 850,000 in 1999 to approximately 1.5 million in 2007 (*1.5 million* 1). Some home-schooling advocates believe that even these numbers may be low because not all states require formal notification when parents decide to teach their children at home.

What is home schooling, and who are the parents choosing to be home schoolers? David Guterson, a pioneer in the home-schooling movement, defines home schooling as "the attempt to gain an education outside of institutions" (5). Home-schooled children spend the majority of the conventional school day learning in or near their homes rather than in traditional schools; parents or guardians are the prime educators. Former teacher and home schooler Rebecca Rupp notes that home-schooling parents vary considerably in what they teach and how they teach, ranging from those who follow a highly traditional curriculum within a structure that parallels the typical classroom to those who

1"

Double-spaced

Double-spaced
Title centered; no underlining, quotes, or italics

Paragraphs indented one-half inch

Author named in text; no parenthetical page reference because source not paginated

Abbreviated title used in parenthetical citation because works cited lists two sources by government author (named in text); no punctuation between title and page number

Author named in text; parenthetical page reference falls at end of sentence

essentially allow their children to pursue whatever interests them at their own pace (3). Home schoolers commonly combine formal instruc- tion with life skills instruction, learning fractions, for example, in terms

Work by two authors cited of monetary units or cooking measurements (Saba and Gattis 89). According to the U.S. Department of Education's 2008 report, while home schoolers are also a diverse group politically and philosophically-- libertarians, conservatives, Christian fundamentalists--most say they home school for one of three reasons: they are concerned about the quality of academic instruction, the general school environment, or the lack of religious or moral instruction (*1.5 million* 2).

The first group generally believes that children need individual at- tention and the opportunity to learn at their own pace to learn well. This group says that one teacher in a classroom of twenty to thirty children (the size of typical public-school classes) cannot give this kind of atten- tion. These parents believe they can give their children greater enrich- ment and more specialized instruction than public schools can provide. At home, parents can work one-on-one with each child and be flexible about time, allowing their children to pursue their interests at earlier ages. Many of these parents, like home schooler Peter Bergson, believe that

Quotation of more than four lines typed as a block and indented ten spaces
> home schooling provides more of an opportunity to continue the natural learning process that's in evidence in all children.

Brackets indicate alteration of quotation
> [In school,] you change the learning process from self-directed to other-directed, from the child asking questions to the teacher asking questions. You shut down areas of potential in-

Parenthetical citation of secondary source falls after period
> terest. (qtd. in Kohn 22)

This trend can be traced back to the 1960s, when many people began criticizing traditional schools. Various types of "alternative schools" were created, and some parents began teaching their children at home (Friedlander 20). Parents like this mention several reasons for their disappointment with public schools and for their decision to home school. A lack of funding, for example, leaves children without

Dinh 3

new textbooks. In a 2002 survey, 31% of teachers said that their students are using textbooks that are more than ten years old, and 29%
said that they do not have enough textbooks for all of their students
(National Education Association). Many schools also cannot afford to ———————— *Corporate author's name*
buy laboratory equipment and other teaching materials. At my own   *cited*
high school, the chemistry teacher told me that most of the lab equip-
ment we used came from a research firm he worked for. In a 2006
Gallup poll, lack of proper financial support ranked first on the list of
the problems in public schools (Rose and Gallup).

   Parents also cite overcrowding as a reason for taking their kids
out of school. The more students in a classroom, the less learning
that goes on, as Cafi Cohen discovered before choosing to home
school; after spending several days observing what went on in her
child's classroom, she found that administrative duties, including
disciplining, took up to 80% of a teacher's time with only 20% of
the day devoted to learning (6). Moreover, faced with a large group
of children, a teacher ends up gearing lessons to the students in the
middle level, so children at both ends miss out. Gifted children and
those with learning disabilities particularly suffer in this situation.
At home, parents of these children say they can tailor the material
and the pace for each child. Studies show that home-schooling
methods seem to work well in preparing children academically.
Lawrence Rudner, director of the ERIC Clearinghouse on Assessment
and Evaluation at the University of Maryland and a researcher on
home schooling, found that testing of home-schooled students
showed them to be between one and three years ahead of public
school students their age (xi). Home-schooled children have also
made particularly strong showings in academic competitions; since
the late 1990s, 10% of National Spelling Bee participants have been
home schooled, as have two National Spelling Bee and two National
Geographic Bee winners (Lyman). More and more selective colleges are

admitting, and even recruiting, home-schooled applicants (Basham, Merrifield, and Hepburn 15).

Parents in the second group--those concerned with the general school environment--claim that their children are more well-rounded than those in school. Because they don't have to sit in classrooms all day, home-schooled kids can pursue their own projects, often combining crafts or technical skills with academic subjects. Home schoolers partici- pate in outside activities such as 4-H competitions, field trips with peers in home-school support groups, science fairs, musical and dramatic pro- ductions, church activities, and Boy Scouts or Girl Scouts (Saba and Gattis 59-62). In fact, they may even be able to participate to some extent in actual school activities. A 1999 survey conducted by the U.S. Department of Education's Institute of Education Sciences found that 28% of public schools allowed home-schooled students to participate in extracurricular activities alongside enrolled students, and 20% allowed home-schooled students to attend some classes (*Homeschooling* 12).

Many home-schooling parents believe that these activities provide the social opportunities kids need without exposing their children to the peer pressure they would have to deal with as regular school students. For example, many kids think that drinking and using drugs are cool. When I was in high school, my friends would tell me a few drinks wouldn't hurt or affect driving. If I had listened to them, I wouldn't be alive today. Four of my friends were killed under the influence of alcohol. Between 1992 and 2008, the number of high school seniors surveyed who had used any illicit drug in the last year climbed from 27.1% to 36.6% (Johnston, et al. 59).

Another reason many parents decide to home school their kids is that they are concerned for their children's safety. Samuel L. Blumenfeld notes that "physical risk" is an important reason many parents remove their children from public schools as "[m]ore and more children are as- saulted, robbed, and murdered in school" and a "culture of violence, abetted by rap music, drug trafficking, . . . and racial tension, has

Work by more than three authors cited

Dinh 5

engulfed teenagers" (4). Beginning in the mid-1990s, a string of school shootings--including the 1999 massacres in Littleton, Colorado, and Conyers, Georgia, and the 2001 massacre in Santee, California--has led to increasing fears that young people are simply not safe at school.

While all of the reasons mentioned so far are important, perhaps the single most significant cause of the growing home-schooling trend is Christian fundamentalist dissatisfaction with "godless" public schools. Sociologist Mitchell L. Stevens, author of one of the first comprehensive studies of home schooling, cites a mailing sent out by Basic Christian Education, a company that markets home-schooling materials, titled "What Really Happens in Public Schools." This publication sums up the fears of fundamentalist home schoolers about public schools: that they encourage high levels of teenage sexual activity and pregnancies "out of wedlock"; expose children to "violence, crime, lack of discipline, and, of course, drugs of every kind"; present positive portrayals of communism and socialism and negative portrayals of capitalism; and undermine children's Christian beliefs by promoting "New Age philosophies, Yoga, Transcendental Meditation, witchcraft demonstrations, and Eastern religions" (51).

As early as 1988, Luanne Shackelford and Susan White, two Christian home-schooling mothers, were claiming that because schools expose children to "[p]eer pressure, perverts, secular textbooks, values clarification, TV, pornography, rock music, bad movies . . . [h]ome schooling seems to be the best plan to achieve our goal [to raise good Christians]" (160). As another mother more recently put it:

> I don't like the way schools are going. . . . What's wrong
> with Christianity all of a sudden? You know? This country was
> founded on Christian, on religious principles. [People] came
> over here for religious freedom, and now all of a sudden
> all religious references seem to be stricken out of the public
> school, and I don't like that at all. (qtd. in Stevens 67)

Brackets used to indicate changes in capitalization and addition to quotation for clarification

Ellipsis marks used to indicate words left out of quotations

Quotation cited in a secondary source

Dinh 6

Although many nonfundamentalist home schoolers make some of these same criticisms, those who cite the lack of "Christian values" in public schools have particular concerns of their own. For example, home-schooling leader Raymond Moore talks of parents who are "'sick and tired of the teaching of evolution in the schools as a cut-and-dried fact,' along with other evidence of so-called secular humanism" (Kohn 21), such as textbooks that contain material contradicting Christian beliefs. Moreover, parents worry that schools undermine their children's moral values. In particular, some Christian fundamentalist parents object to sex education in schools, saying that it encourages children to become sexually active early, challenging values taught at home. They see the family as the core and believe that the best place to instill family values is within the family. These Christian home-schooling parents want to provide their children not only with academic knowledge but also with a moral grounding consistent with their religious beliefs.

Still other home-schooling parents object to a perceived government-mandated value system that they believe attempts to override the values, not necessarily religious in nature, of individual families. For these parents, home schooling is a way of resisting what they see as unwarranted intrusion by the federal government into personal concerns (*Alliance*).

Armed with their convictions, parents such as those who belong to the Christian Home School Legal Defense Association have fought in court and lobbied for legislation that allows them the option of home schooling. In the 1970s, most states had compulsory attendance laws that made it difficult, if not illegal, to keep school-age children home from school. Today, home schooling is permitted in every state, with strict regulation required by only a few (Home School). As a result, Mary Jane is one of hundreds of thousands of American children who can start their school day without leaving the house.

Single quotation marks indicate a quotation within a quotation

Citation placed close to quotation, before comma but after quotation marks

Internet source cited by shortened form of title; author's name and page numbers unavailable

Shortened form of corporate author's name cited

1"   Dinh 7

Works Cited

Alliance for the Separation of School and State. Home page. Alliance for
　　the Separation of School and State, 26 Feb. 2009. Web. 10 Apr.
　　2009.

Basham, Patrick, John Merrifield, and Claudia R. Hepburn. *Home
　　Schooling: From the Extreme to the Mainstream*. 2nd ed. Vancouver:
　　Fraser Institute, 2007. Studies in Education Policy. *Fraser Institute*.
　　Web. 13 Apr. 2009.

Blumenfeld, Samuel L. *Homeschooling: A Parent's Guide to Teaching
　　Children*. Bridgewater: Replica, 1999. Print.

Cohen, Cafi. *And What about College?: How Home-schooling Leads to
　　Admissions to the Best Colleges and Universities*. Cambridge: Holt,
　　1997. Print.

Friedlander, Tom. "A Decade of Home Schooling." *The Home School
　　Reader*. Ed. Mark Hegener and Helen Hegener. Tonasket: Home
　　Education, 1988. 147-56. Print.

Guterson, David. *Family Matters: Why Homeschooling Makes Sense*. San
　　Diego: Harcourt, 1992. Print.

Home School Legal Defense Association. "State Action Map." HSLDA,
　　2009. Web. 5 Apr. 2009.

Johnston, Lloyd D., et al. *Monitoring the Future: National Results on
　　Adolescent Drug Use, Overview of Key Findings, 2008*. Bethesda:
　　National Institute on Drug Abuse, 2009. Web. 20 Apr. 2009.

Kohn, Alfie. "Home Schooling." *Atlantic Monthly* Apr. 1988: 20-25. Print.

Lyman, Isabel. "Generation Two." *American Enterprise* Oct./Nov. 2002:
　　48-49. *InfoTrac OneFile*. Web. 10 May 2009.

National Education Association. *2002 Instructional Materials Survey*.
　　Sept. 2002. Association of American Publishers, 2002. Web. 21
　　Apr. 2009.

Ray, Brian D. "Research Facts on Home Schooling." *National Home
　　Education Research Institute*. NHERI, 2008. Web. 10 Apr. 2009.

*Works Cited entries begin
on a new page; entries
are in alphabetical order.*

Title centered

Double-spaced

*Entries begin flush with
left margin; subsequent
lines indent one-half inch.*

*Periods separate author,
title, publication
information, medium,
and date of access.*

Dinh 8

Rose, Lowell C., and Alec M. Gallup. "The 38th Annual PDK/Gallup Poll of
the Public's Attitudes toward the Public Schools." *Phi Delta Kappan*
88.1 (2006): n. pag. *Phi Delta Kappa International*. Web. 1 May
2009.

Rudner, Lawrence. Foreword. *The McGraw-Hill Home-schooling Companion*.
By Laura Saba and Julie Gattis. New York: McGraw, 2002. Print.

Rupp, Rebecca. *The Complete Home Learning Source Book*. New York:
Three Rivers, 1998. Print.

Saba, Laura, and Julie Gattis. *The McGraw-Hill Home-schooling
Companion*. New York: McGraw, 2002. Print.

Shackelford, Luanne, and Susan White. *A Survivor's Guide to Home
Schooling*. Westchester: Crossway, 1988. Print.

Stevens, Mitchell L. *Kingdom of Children: Culture and Controversy in the
Homeschooling Movement*. Princeton: Princeton UP, 2001. Print.

United States. Dept. of Education. Institute of Education Sciences.
Homeschooling in the United States: 1999. Washington: GPO, 2001.
National Center for Education Statistics. Web. 23 Apr. 2009.

- - -. *1.5 Million Homeschooled Students in the United States in 2007*.
Washington: GPO, 2008. *National Center for Education Statistics*.
Web. 23 Apr. 2009.

Source with no pagination is marked "n. pag."

For multiple source(s) by the same author, replace author's name with three hyphens followed by a period. (The name of this government source has three separate components.)

Annotated Bibliographies and Literature Reviews

25

In college courses and in your career, you will sometimes need to read multiple sources on a subject and then consolidate what you learned in a single document, either for yourself or for an audience. For instance,

- For a research project in a philosophy course, Dominic heads to the library to learn what has been said about the topic "altruism." For each relevant source he finds, he records full source information, writes a brief summary, takes notes on how he might use the source, and copies down useful quotations. Armed with the **annotated bibliography** he has created, he sits down to write his paper. Thanks to the bibliography, he writes much more efficiently, without having to leaf through stacks of notes and photocopies whenever he needs a reminder of what a source says.

- A doctor engaged in cancer research decides to write a review of recent literature in genetics and nutrition, presenting readers in the medical profession with an up-to-date, consolidated overview of how these fields relate to cancer. He starts by preparing an **annotated bibliography** for himself, so that he has a clear idea of what the research says before he starts. Then he writes an article describing what he has learned, grouping the research topically by type of cancer. The resulting **literature review** is published in a medical journal.

- A police department captain wants to try a new approach to local drug enforcement, but, lacking the funds to implement the program she envisions, she decides to apply for a federal grant. As part of the grant proposal, she includes a **review of the literature** that summarizes current approaches to drug enforcement and recent scholarly work about the drug trade. Her goal for the literature review is to show that her approach is promising enough to support.

The terms **annotated bibliography** (sometimes also called the *annotated list of works cited*) and **literature review** (sometimes also called *review of the literature*) might sound intimidating, but, as the preceding scenarios illustrate, research projects like these come in handy in many different situations. The following diagrams will help you review their meanings.

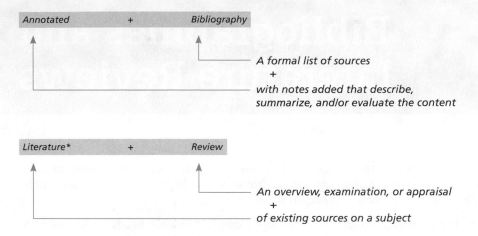

*Note: The word *literature*, as it is used here, has nothing to do with "fiction."

Annotated Bibliographies and Literature Reviews: An Overview

●●●●
Basic Features

Annotated bibliographies and literature reviews share the following basic features.

⬡ Well-Documented Sources

Regardless of the format you choose for your annotated bibliography or literature review, your readers will expect to see clear citations in recognized citation formats like MLA, APA, or *Chicago*. If your readers decide to look up a source you discuss, they need to be able to find it easily, so providing them with complete and accurate information in a familiar, readable format is critical.

⬡ An Indication of Content

Your description of sources' content will vary in terms of depth, depending on your purposes and your audience. For some projects, you might merely indicate the topic of a source, while for others you might thoroughly summarize your sources, describing their conclusions or even their methodologies in detail. Comments per source in annotated bibliographies can range in length from a sentence or two to as many as 150 words. In a literature review, four sources might be covered by a single sentence, while another source might call for several paragraphs on its own.

⬡ A Discussion of Context and Significance

Annotated bibliographies and literature reviews often go beyond summary to tell the reader something important about their central question or topic, and how each source connects to it. You might help the reader understand the significance of studies in your field generally, or you might evaluate their significance with regard to the question you are researching. In an annotated bibliography, you must discuss each source independently. In a literature review, you can group similar studies, compare and contrast sources, and reveal the chronology of a series of discoveries.

● An Assertion of One's Place in the Conversation

If you are writing your bibliography or review as part of a larger document, such as a proposal, you will want to show how your own work fits into the scholarly or professional conversation. Are you championing an underdog's vision? Are you synthesizing multiple points of view? Or is your idea new? If you have a new idea, or a new proposal, the literature review can help you show where the holes are that you intend to fill. If your argument is not new, you can show where your project fits into the existing literature. Either way, your goal is to give readers an idea of how your project relates to the field at large.

Purpose and Audience

Instructors who require you to write an annotated bibliography or a literature review usually have one or both of the following motives:

1. Both documents are a good first step in a research project, so doing them will help you write a better paper.
2. Professionals in your field need to know how to write these sorts of documents, so your professor wants you to practice them.

When you write for your instructor, you should keep these purposes in mind. Of course, some people write annotated bibliographies and literature reviews for their own purposes, rather than as a requirement. These purposes can dramatically shape the projects' format, content, and tone.

For instance, like Dominic in the opening example of this chapter, some students and researchers create annotated bibliographies for themselves because it is a good way to develop a better understanding of the field and an efficient way to write. These bibliographies are not necessarily intended for anyone else to read. However, a properly constructed annotated bibliography can be very useful beyond its immediate purpose: the author might consult it later while working on other projects and might share it with others who are also working on the topic. In many departments, graduate students preparing for comprehensive exams circulate annotated bibliographies they have created, with users adding entries as new research is published.

Other writers will create bibliographies and reviews expressly for readers who might be new to a field. In these cases, the annotated bibliography format is often preferred to literature reviews because it is easy to skim and thus fairly reader-friendly.

Professional scholars include literature reviews as part of larger documents or studies. In these cases, the literature reviews provide the reader with critical background, but perhaps more importantly, they help establish the author's credibility as an expert in the field. Readers who are already well versed in the field will read literature reviews to see how the author views the subject matter, and to evaluate those views. A paper lacking a literature review may in some cases be judged more harshly because the author will have failed to show that he or she is familiar with and understands earlier work on the topic.

Still another common use of literature reviews is to convince grant-giving agencies or authorization boards that a planned study or experiment is worth doing. These kinds of literature review tell readers what the new research will contribute to our understanding of the subject matter.

THEY'RE GOOD TO *READ*, TOO

One reason to write annotated bibliographies and literature reviews is to help your readers find more information on your subject. This works both ways: when you need to do research, you can make use of existing reviews and bibliographies on your subject. These sources can help you "catch up" on your topic, while also leading you to relevant sources you can consult for more depth. There's another benefit to reading them, too: The more often you read other people's bibliographies and reviews, the more comfortable you will be when you need to write them yourself, because as a user, you will have a better idea of readers' expectations.

Annotated Bibliographies

When you write an annotated bibliography, you choose how much to say, and what to say, about each source. Your choices will depend largely on your purpose. Are you simply trying to give the reader an idea of what each source contains? If so, a sentence or two might suffice. But if you are writing your annotated bibliography as part of an effort to analyze the field or persuade the reader, you might want to write a paragraph or so for each source, evaluating it or discussing briefly how it fits into the literature as a whole. One approach is to try to ask yourself the following three questions. The type of annotated bibliography you produce will reflect your answers, as illustrated in the discussion that follows.

- What kind of source is this?
- What does the source say?
- How can I use the source?

Most annotated bibliographies have introductions of one or more paragraphs, appearing above the list of sources. These introductions describe for the reader the subject, purpose, and scope of the annotated references. Introductions might also describe how and why the author selected those sources. For instance, an annotated reference list featuring works about computer animation might have the following introduction:

> Early animations of virtual people in computer games tended to be oblivious to their surroundings, reacting only when hit by moving objects, and then in ways that were not always appropriate--that is, a small object might generate a large effect. In the past few years, however, computer animators have turned their attention to designing virtual people who react appropriately to events around them. The sources below represent the last two years' worth of publications on the subject from the IEEE Xplore database.

Different Types of Annotation

In this section, we provide a range of sample annotations, each based on the following article about the development of an advanced carbon-based fiber. The citations are in APA format.

Source Article (from *Science News*, Aug. 30, 2008)

Carbon Tubes Leave Nano Behind

DAVIDE CASTELVECCHI

Take solace, all ye who've grown weary of carbon nanotube promises: The latest tubes are anything but nano. 1

While trying to grow better, longer nanotubes, researchers accidentally discovered a new type of carbon filament that's tens of thousands of times thicker. Christened "colossal carbon tubes," they aren't quite as strong as nanotubes but are 30 times stronger than Kevlar per unit weight, and are potentially easier to turn into applications, suggests a study to appear in *Physical Review Letters*. 2

Though exceptionally strong, nanotubes are hard to weave into larger fibers that could be used in futuristic products, such as ultralight bulletproof vests. 3

Recently at Los Alamos National Laboratory in New Mexico, materials scientist Huisheng Peng and colleagues were trying to grow "forests" of long nanotubes from carbon gas in a vacuum oven. When Peng opened the door, he saw a scene that could be compared to a barbershop floor: Thin, black hairs were scattered everywhere. 4

"At first, I thought they were a lot of carbon nanotubes bonded together," says Peng, who recently moved to Fudan University in Shanghai, China. 5

Tests revealed that the filaments, which were centimeters long and 0.1 millimeter thick, were not clumps of nanotubes, but "colossal" tubes which had the same type 6 of carbon bonds as nanotubes. The atoms were also arranged in the same hexagonal webs resembling chicken wire.

Instead of being simple cylindrical structures, the colossal tubes have two concentric layers. The researchers believe that each layer is made of many chicken wire sheets sandwiched together. Walls that are 100 nanometers thick connect the layers and divide the space between the layers into canals that run along the entire length of the tubes — similar to the gaps inside corrugated cardboard. [7]

The tubes are easily bent and stretched, and are at least twice as strong as the strongest fibers made from carbon nanotubes to date, the researchers report. The larger tubes are also good electrical conductors. [8]

László Forró of the École Polytechnique Fédérale in Lausanne, Switzerland, believes that the authors may have rushed to publication with results that are too preliminary. "At this stage it is only a cookbook," he says. "Basically, they do not know anything about the structure." [9]

More research is needed to understand how the tubes form and grow, admits senior author Quanxi Jia of Los Alamos. [10]

1. Descriptive annotation: What kind of source is this?

Descriptive (sometimes called *indicative*) annotations, which are typically very short, simply identify a source's topic. Example:

> Castelvecchi, D. (2008, August 30). Carbon tubes leave nano behind. *Science News*, *174*(5), 9-9. Retrieved from http://www.sciencenews.org

> This news article describes the accidental discovery of "colossal carbon tubes"--filaments of carbon much larger than the nanotubes studied in nanotechnology.

2. Summary annotation: What does the source say?

Summary annotations provide information on the source's content — not just the topic, but what the source does with the topic.

> Castelvecchi, D. (2008, August 30). Carbon tubes leave nano behind. *Science News*, *174*(5), 9-9. Retrieved from http://www.sciencenews.org

> This news article describes how researchers at the Los Alamos National Laboratories in New Mexico accidentally created what they dub the "colossal carbon tube"--a hair-sized structure made up of carbon atoms. Although the new fiber is not as strong as some earlier carbon structures, groups of such fibers might be easier to weave together for useful applications like bulletproof vests because of their size.

The summary approach is particularly useful if your goal is to explain something without making an argument. For instance, the above annotation might be at home in an essay explaining the role carbon plays in scientific research.

"Carbon: The Miracle Element"

[. . .] So far, we have seen why many astrobiologists expect there to be carbon-based life forms on other planets, and we have seen that our longevity on our own planet might very well depend on how much (or how little) carbon we put into the air. So carbon appears to be the stuff of life and death. But it's rapidly becoming the stuff of stuff, too. If you want to build something that has great strength but little weight-- a car, a laptop, a cable elevator to space--you'll find that much of the advanced materials research is focused on carbon. Researchers at Los Alamos National Laboratory, for instance, have come up with a kind of carbon thread that's 30 times stronger than Kevlar, but flexible enough that it might help us build a better bulletproof vest (Castelvecchi, 2008). [. . .]

The opening sentences recap earlier parts of the paper while providing a transition to the next part.

The highlighted text summarizes and clearly cites the source.

3. Evaluative annotation: How useful is this source?

If you are writing the annotated bibliography to remind yourself or tell readers what you thought of the sources, you might use an *evaluative* annotation. Sometimes, at an early stage in your research project, an instructor might ask you for an annotated bibliography in which you say how you plan to use each source you found. In this case, the result might look something like this annotation for a hypothetical criminal justice student's paper on crime-fighting technology:

Castelvecchi, D. (2008, August 30). Carbon tubes leave nano behind. *Science News, 174*(5), 9-9. Retrieved from http://www.sciencenews.org

This source, which describes a new, flexible lightweight material 30 times stronger than Kevlar and possibly useful for better bulletproof vests, provides evidence of yet another upcoming technology that might be useful to law enforcement. I can focus on the ways in which lighter, stronger bulletproof materials might change SWAT tactics, for instance, enabling them to carry more gear, protect police vehicles, or to blend into crowds better.

Notice that this annotation begins by summarizing the source and then goes on to indicate explicitly how it might be a source that could be useful in the essay the student is researching. One of the benefits of this approach is that it forces you to think about how you might use the sources ahead of time, so that you have a chance to revise or improve your ideas. You do not have to follow your annotation. If you find that your final paper uses the source differently than you had originally planned, that is fine.

For instance, this criminal justice student might later decide that since drug cartels are often better funded than police and have started to appropriate police technology for their own uses, the result of developing those carbon tubes might be a kind of arms race between law enforcement and the criminal class. In that case, her paper might eventually say something like this:

"Prospects for a Cop-Cartel Arms Race"

[. . .] The problem is that drug cartels own companies and can afford scientists, so that any high-tech edge law enforcement obtains against them is likely to be short-lived. Take, for instance, a recent discovery of a carbon thread that might yield a lighter, tougher body armor (Castelvecchi, 2008). If the technology lives up to its promise, it might appear at first glance to be good news for police: It would mean they could wear concealed armor more comfortably under street clothes or uniforms. But if it is that good, it might also mean cartels might start to armor their cars and homes with the stuff, or that crooks might wear concealed body armor to restaurants. If more drawn-out gunfights like 1997's "North Hollywood shootout" result, civilians might buy body armor, too--and then be more likely to attempt heroics or get in the way when bullets start flying. None of this, however, means the police should avoid new technologies--if they do, they'll simply be left behind. But police do need to be aware that their jobs might soon get a bit more complicated.

The opening sentence gives the author's new thesis.

This passage briefly summarizes the source. Note that the goal here is not to dwell on the information, but to move on to a discussion of its ramifications.

This passage explores the possible impacts of the discovery on police work. As with the annotation, the goal here is to evaluate. The annotation on pp. 801 reaches different conclusions because it was written earlier. If it were submitted with the paper, it would need to be revised to reflect the paper's new thesis.

4. A mixed approach

Perhaps the most common kind of annotated bibliography takes a *mixed approach*, combining description, summary, and evaluation. This is particularly true in instances when the annotated bibliography is part of a larger report or is an early step toward creating a larger report: You will want to include an element of description and/or summary so that users have an idea what the sources say, but you will also want to include evaluative comments so that they know what to do with the information, or so that the presentation supports a point you want to make about the field.

Let us assume, for instance, that Rajeev, a political-science and environmental engineering double-major, wants to evaluate proposals for "geo-engineering" — ideas for saving the planet from climate change through massive and often expensive engineering projects. Which ideas should receive government funding? Rajeev writes a paper evaluating the options and includes an annotated bibliography that combines summary and evaluation. Below is a sample annotation from this hypothetical bibliography. Notice that in this annotation, the lead sentence answers the first question — What kind of source is this, and who are the readers? — in just a few words before moving on to summary.

Castelvecchi, D. (2008, August 30). Carbon tubes leave nano behind. *Science News, 174*(5), 9-9. Retrieved from http://www.sciencenews.org

This news article for science professionals describes an accidental discovery of "colossal carbon tubes" by Los Alamos National Laboratory researchers. Although the hair-sized tubes are weaker than the nanotubes that have so far dominated carbon fiber research, they remain 30 times stronger than Kevlar and because of their size might be easier to weave together into useful materials. If true, this could be significant: Many geo-engineering plans require cables that can handle a great deal of stress. If colossal tubes are strong enough, they might help us build "space elevators"--cables that reach from the planet's surface into orbit, enabling us to implement space-based solutions to climate change more easily. The tubes even reportedly conduct electricity, which suggests they might be used both to tether floating wind turbines and to conduct power to users on the ground, simultaneously. It is not yet clear from the literature whether colossal tubes can do these jobs, but they might be the best contenders discovered so far.

Because Rajeev's purpose shapes both his annotations and his paper, his paper will also — in all likelihood — balance summary and evaluation, as in the excerpt that follows:

"Die by the Sword, Live by the Sword?"

1 [. . .] But if carbon, industrial progress, and high technology appear to be damning us to a hellish climate, they might also prove to be our salvation. In August 2008, scientists at the Los Alamos National Laboratory in New Mexico announced they had created a new carbon-based thread that is incredibly strong--30 times more so than Kevlar--and versatile enough that it might be easily woven into useful new materials. The stuff is lightweight, flexible, and even conducts electricity (Castelvecchi, 2008).

2   Why is this significant? Because many of the most ambitious plans to fix the problem require materials with these same properties: We're talking about churning out lighter, more fuel-efficient cars; creating blimp-mounted air turbines that send wind power by wire down to groundlevel; and using a space elevator to "launch" satellites that collect solar power from orbit and beam it to Earth. [. . .]

Rajeev opens with the thesis.

This passage summarizes the content of the source.

This passage begins to evaluate the significance of the discovery mentioned in the source. Note that because the text and the annotation have similar goals — to note the discovery and evaluate its impacts — they have ended up with similar structures, even though they offer slightly different details.

Writing an Annotated Bibliography

The map below walks you through the process of writing an annotated bibliography.

1. Determine Purpose and Audience

• Should your annotations describe, summarize, and/or evaluate the source?
• Is your bibliography for your own purposes, for experts, or for newcomers? Will you need to define terms and provide background information for your readers?

2. Prepare Research Questions Come up with a list of questions that you should try to answer about each source, such as the following:

• How can I tell if the source is credible? (See Chapter 23 for advice on evaluating sources.)
• How can I describe the topic?
• How can I summarize what the source says?
• How can I use it in my paper?
• How does the source relate to other sources I might use?

3. Conduct Research; Take *Good* Notes

• Research your chosen topic. Pay attention to the authors who are frequently cited by others in the field, and find their work — you will want to include it. (For help with research, see Chapter 23, p. 733.)
• Each time you find a source, create a full citation for it. (See Chapter 24 for help with citation formats.)
• Under each citation, answer the questions you came up with in the previous step.

Always: Reflect and Rethink

Has your research given you reason to rethink your purpose, audience, guiding questions, or even your topic? If so, back up and rethink or redo some steps. It is fine to backtrack as new ideas spring to mind.

4. Prepare Your Entries

• Working from your notes, draft a few sentences or paragraphs on each source, heading each annotation with a full citation.
• Decide on an organizational scheme. Most documents list entries in alphabetical order, but with a long, intensive bibliography, you might want to group your sources by subtopic, with each group listed alphabetically under its own header.
• Revise and edit your entries for space, tone, and content. If an annotation is longer than 150 words, consider tightening it.

5. Consider an Introduction

If you plan for your annotated bibliography to be a stand-alone document, you should consider giving it an introduction that tells readers what it covers, what its purpose is, and how you approached the research.

Literature Reviews

A literature review bears roughly the same relation to annotated bibliographies as a film does to a pile of still photographs — it covers similar material, but it connects the dots for the reader. One of the ways it does so is by organizing the material by topic instead of by source. For instance, a literature review on recent trends in education might focus for a paragraph or so on No Child Left Behind, comparing and contrasting several studies that have been done on it, before moving on to a paragraph that discusses articles on the merits of elective subjects like art and theater. (Chapter 5: Finding Common Ground offers good practice for this sort of writing.)

Like the annotated bibliography, the review might be motivated by a straightforward desire to help the reader catch up on a topic, or it might be prompted by the goal of persuading the reader of something. Often when the goal is persuasive, the aim of the review is to convince the reader that there is a hole in the current research that needs to be plugged. That is, the review tells the reader, "This is what the literature says so far, but here is a question that has not been answered yet, or a solution that has not been tried, and that is why I am pursuing this project."

Readers might not be able to see the hole in existing theory from an annotated bibliography, which is why the literature review is critical — by showing how the bits of knowledge fit together, it also shows where the holes are, just as putting a jigsaw puzzle together helps you discover whether pieces are missing from the box.

Below are several excerpts from real literature reviews, each with a different purpose.

1. A stand-alone review, for readers who want background on an issue

If your goal is to provide readers with helpful background on a particular question, issue, or topic, you might write a *stand-alone* literature review — a review that is self-contained, rather than part of a larger project. Below is a short excerpt from an article by Helena Catt, who describes her article as a literature review on the causes of low voter turnout in New Zealand.

Now or Never — Electoral Participation Literature Review[*]

A strong finding from Franklin's (2004) study was the persistence of early behaviour: those who voted when they first could were more likely to repeat the behaviour and those who did not vote were likely to not vote again. Surveys of non-voters consistently find that many are repeat non-voters. In the New Zealand 2002 post-election survey a third of Māori and a fifth of non-Māori non-voters said that they had not voted in the past either (Vowles et al, 2004). Some writers suggest that political participation leaves

1

---

[*]Catt, Helena. "Now or Never — Electoral Participation Literature Review." *Citizenship: Learning by Doing Symposium*. Sixth Child and Family Policy Conference. Univ. of Otago, Dunedin. July 2005. *Elections New Zealand*. Web. 12 Oct. 2008.

Notice that Catt has organized her paragraphs topically, rather than by source. (This paragraph, for example, discusses research on the role of habit in voting behavior.) This is a common organizational scheme in literature reviews.

a psychological imprint on those who act (Green & Shachar, 2000). More pragmatically, those who have voted are familiar with the process whilst for some who have not there may be apprehension at what it entails (Horwitt, 1999) and embarrassment at admitting this lack of knowledge: "Like internal efficacy, this orientation concerns one's self-confidence in a political environment" (Green & Shachar, 2000). In contrast participation by providing familiarity with the process increases confidence and thus internal efficacy (Finkel, 1985). The idea that repetition creates familiarity and confidence is commonplace.

In the underlined citation, Catt includes *two* sources. This suggests the two studies had similar conclusions. This type of multisourced citation is common in literature reviews.

There is also evidence that the practice of voting or not is passed across generations. Surveys in the UK and USA (<u>Nestle, 2003; Horwitt, 1999</u>) have found that non-voters are more likely to come from families of non-voters and that those who vote at their first election have memories of their parents voting. Discussion of politics at home also had an impact: "Half of those who often talk to their parents about politics said they voted in 1998, compared to one quarter (26%) of those who talk to their parents about politics infrequently or never" (Horwitt, 1999). This study concludes that "voting is developed as a habit. Some young people may start voting primarily out of the idealistic sense that their vote makes a difference; after an election or two, they begin to view voting as a duty and are much more likely to turn out to vote primarily because they feel it is something they should do. In this way, young people come to voting as a personal norm."

While the previous paragraph was about voting habits, this one concerns parenting's impact on voting behavior. Catt has changed subtopics, so she has also created a new paragraph to mark the change in direction.

2

2. A literature review within a larger work

Many literature reviews appear as *sections within longer essays or books*, providing readers with introductory or background information in order to show how the writer's work fits into the current conversation about the topic. For example, the text that follows is taken from a study by Rachel E. Sullivan on whether youths of different ethnicities respond differently to rap or hip-hop music. Before presenting her new research, Sullivan summarizes the contentious and controversial history of rap music, after which she presents the following digest of previous studies on rap audiences.

Rap and Race: It's Got a Nice Beat--But What about the Message?*

Notice how Sullivan chooses to show the holes in the literature: Each time she discusses a source, she also discusses how it fails to answer her primary question, thus asserting her own place in the conversation.

Given the tremendous increase in rap's popularity, it is evident that rap's White audience has grown dramatically. In the early 1990s, Public Enemy's Chuck D estimated that 60% of his audience was White (Rose, 1994). However, it is very difficult to make any precise estimates of the racial makeup of the rap audience because no specific information has been collected.

1

*Sullivan, Rachel E. "Rap and Race: It's Got a Nice Beat — But What about the Message?" *Journal of Black Studies* 33.5 (2003): 605–622. *JSTOR*. Web. 18 Oct. 2008.

2   Even though many people have made claims about rap music and its effect on its listeners, research on music effects generally focuses on young Whites and their attitudes about rock and roll, punk, or heavy metal (Arnett, 1992, 1993, 1995; Fox, 1987; Gold, 1987; Rosenbaum & Prinsky, 1991; Roe, 1995; Snow, 1987; Stack, Gundlach, & Reeves, 1994). Jonathon Epstein's (1994) collection of essays, *Adolescents and Their Music: If It's Too Loud, You're Too Old*, does include 1 essay on rap music, but this is surrounded by 13 other essays all dealing with rock and heavy metal.

Like Catt, Sullivan groups some sources into a single citation.

3   Many of the studies analyzing rap have been more qualitative and theoretical, focusing on the role of rap music in popular culture (Fenster, 1995; Martinez, 1997) and its use as a form of resistance (Berry, 1994; Martinez, 1993; Pinn, 1996; Rose, 1991). However, these studies did not examine multiracial samples and did not ask specific questions focusing on the attitudes of rap's audience. One study by Epstein, Pratto, and Skipper (1990) analyzed the relationship between behavior problems and preference for rap and heavy metal music. This study indicates that preference for heavy metal and rap was highly correlated with race: 96% of those who preferred heavy metal were White, and 98% of those who preferred rap were Black. In addition, they found that preference for both forms of music was not associated with behavior problems.

Sullivan points out that these studies do not use quantitative data.

4   Three studies have focused on young people's opinions of rap. One study written by Berry (1994) concluded that rap helps low income African American youth develop empowering beliefs that help them connect with their culture and develop positive identities. However, the weakness of this study is that it does not give a detailed analysis of students' responses or the questions students were asked, so it is difficult to gain a thorough understanding of the students' attitudes. Moreover, the sample only included low-income African Americans in an Upward Bound program.

These studies come closer to what Sullivan wants to do — she wants to ask young people how rap affects them. Nevertheless, Sullivan points out weaknesses in each study as she summarizes it.

5   The second study, from *American Demographics* magazine, reported on a survey conducted by Teenage Research Unlimited (Spiegler, 1996). This study revealed that 58% of those younger than 18 years and 59% of those 18 to 20 years *liked* or *strongly liked* rap. This study also found that several fashions associated with hip-hop were considered "in" by 12- to 19-year-olds. [. . .] The author argued that rap has expanded the market for White designers such as Tommy Hilfiger and DKNY; moreover, style of dress has become a way for Whites to connect with Blacks without actually having any face-to-face contact. Although this indicates that there are racial differences, those differences were not the focus of the survey.

This passage is a good example of a source description. It tells us who the source is (beyond just giving a citation), gives us some of the key findings, and even reports how the authors interpreted their statistics.

6   Finally, the most detailed study of rap's effect on adolescents was conducted by Kuwahara (1992). This study found that 13.3% of Black college students listened to rap all the time, and 29.7% listened to rap often. Kuwahara also found that Black men had a stronger preference for rap than Black women. The analysis of White college students revealed that 51.6% of White men and 68.9% of White women *seldom* or *never* listened to rap. [. . .] Whites and Blacks did not differ much in their reasons for listening to rap. Both groups preferred the beat most and the message second. Drawing on qualitative responses from Black students, Kuwahara argued that rap music and the styles of dance associated with it serve as forms of resistance to the dominant culture. However, findings from this study may be dated. Rap's popularity

Here Sullivan notes that the study most similar to what she wants to do is probably out-of-date.

Finally, Sullivan tightly summarizes all of her previous remarks about shortcomings in the current literature. This summary serves as a transition to her own findings.

has increased significantly since 1992, and the White audience for rap has increased (*The Source*, 1998).

Because of the rapid change in rap's popularity, it is necessary to reevaluate youth's attitudes toward rap. More literature on rap is also needed because the current writings are few and many theoretical claims have not been substantiated through empirical work.

7

3. A literature review as background for a proposal

A final way to use literature reviews is as part of a *proposal*. If you are asking for permission, assistance, or money in connection with a project, it is often a good idea to show that you know your subject's literature well, and to show how your own project contributes to that field. The following excerpt is from a literature review for a graduate student's dissertation grant proposal. The author, Gayle Reznik, is asking for $15,000 so she can add to our understanding of why women on average earn less than men.

Reznik opens with an explanation of the central thesis that undergirds the rest of the review: that income levels between similarly qualified men and women should be similar.

In her next paragraph, Reznik discusses earlier attempts to explain wage gaps. She groups sources by attempted explanation: This second paragraph discusses differences in educational background, but a later paragraph discusses differences in preferences and job tastes.

College Major and the Gender Wage Gap: A Look at the 1990's[*]

Human capital theory states that individuals with the same level of human capital (i.e., education, experience, skills, and ability) should have equal levels of earnings (Becker, 1975). Therefore human capital theory would explain the wage gap as a consequence of different levels of human capital attained by men and women. If a wage gap exists even for men and women with the same level of human capital, then perhaps this gap could be explained by discrimination against women, differences in preferences, or perhaps some other still unknown factor.

1

Two recent articles have attempted to explain the gender wage gap or at least part of the gender wage gap as being due to the different educational backgrounds of men and women. Brown and Corcoran (1997) used the *Survey of Income and Program Participation* (1984) and the *National Longitudinal Study of the High School Class of 1972* (1986 follow-up) to determine if the sex differences in wages could be attributed to sex differences in school content in high school and college. Brown and Corcoran conclude that male/female differences in high school courses and male/female differences in math and verbal achievement tests have little effect on the wage gap. However,

2

[*]Reznik, Gayle L. "College Major and the Gender Wage Gap: A Look at the 1990's." *2001 AIR Dissertation Grant Proposal*. Association for Institutional Research, 16 Jan. 2001. Web. 12 Oct. 2008.

Brown and Corcoran find that among college graduates differences in major and in the type of courses explain a significant part of the male/female wage gap. They calculate that .08-.09 of the wage gap can be attributed to these factors, after controlling for demographic and work experience variables.

3   In a similar study, Weinberger (1998) used the *1985 Survey of Recent College Graduates* to address the gender wage gap as well as the race wage gap faced by college graduates. Weinberger concludes that even after controlling for college major, college grade point average and the specific college attended, race and gender wage gaps still exist. [. . .]

4   Earlier articles also touch upon this subject. Daymont and Andrisani (1984) using data from the 1970's find that gender differences in work preferences, work expectations, and tastes for job rewards and job content are important in explaining the wage gap. In addition they find that gender differences in college major and gender differences in occupation can explain 1/3 to 2/3 of the gender wage gap. Paglin and Rufolo (1990) focus on quantitative and mathematical skills and find that differences in the distribution of scarce quantitative abilities can explain some of the unexplained differences between men and women in occupational choice and earnings. Fuller and Schoenberger (1991) using a very limited dataset of business program graduates in the mid 1980's conclude that college acquired characteristics, including college major, are significant factors for starting salary but not for current salary and that female business college graduates earn less than their male counterparts. [. . .]

> Throughout this review, Reznik comments on the methods used by previous researchers. Here, for instance, she notes that Fuller and Schoenberger's findings are based on a "limited dataset."

5   These papers conclude that part of the wage gap between men and women can be explained away by differences in the college courses, majors, and college performance of men and women. However, these previous papers examined the gender wage gap for varying cohorts in the 1970's and 1980's and not in the 1990's. I plan to update this research by examining the effect of college major on starting salaries for a cohort of recent college graduates graduating in the 1990's. I will also examine the effect of college major on the narrowing of the gap between the 1980's and the 1990's. [. . .]

> In her final paragraph, Reznik summarizes the overall findings, and then asserts her own role in the conversation by suggesting that the literature needs to be updated, particularly with respect to the impact of college majors. Her project would fill in these gaps.

4. An analytical review that draws new conclusions

By closely analyzing the existing literature of a field, it is sometimes possible to come up with *new conclusions* about the state of that field. Among reviews, such approaches are relatively rare, but they can involve some useful strategies that are worth noting.

The paragraph that follows is the conclusion of an analytical review about prediction markets, a specialized marketplace where investors bet on the probable outcomes of events like elections.

Prediction Markets: An Extended Literature Review[*]

Although this review cannot claim to be exhaustive, it does provide reasonable insights into the state of the PM [prediction markets] research. The authors feel that the results presented in this paper have several important implications.

(*a*) Undoubtedly, PM research and applications will significantly increase in future.

(*b*) There is a strong need to standardise the terminology used to refer to the PM concept.

(*c*) The formation and dissemination of a fully appropriate PM mechanism, such as the dynamic parimutuel presented by Pennock [110], could lead to the expansion of PM research and applications.

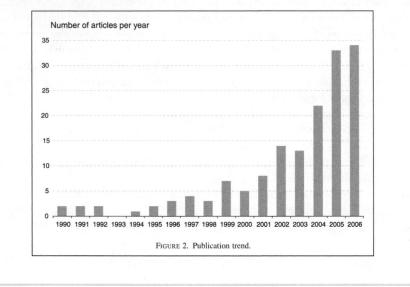

FIGURE 2. Publication trend.

Items (a), (b), and (c) are new conclusions, based on patterns the researchers noticed when they looked at the literature.

One of those patterns, seen in this graphic, is that the number of studies about prediction markets has skyrocketed in recent years.

This example shows how you can come up with new conclusions through analytical moves like charting trends in research.

[*]Tziralis, Georgios, and Ilias Tatsiopoulus. "Prediction Markets: An Extended Literature Review." *The Journal of Prediction Markets* 1.1 (Feb. 2007): 75-91. Web. 12 Oct. 2008. <www .ingentaconnect.com/content/ubpl/jpm/2007/>.

Writing a Literature Review

The map below walks you through the process of writing a literature review.

---

1. Begin by Writing an Annotated Bibliography

When creating a literature review, it often pays to create an **annotated bibliography** *first*, because many of the essential steps are the same. As with an annotated bibliography, in writing a literature review you will need to

- figure out your purpose and audience;
- figure out whether this is a stand-alone document;
- carefully describe, summarize, and/or evaluate your sources; and
- create high-quality notes.

Even if you decide not to create a formal annotated bibliography, you will need to be able to do the things listed above before moving on to the next step.

---

2. Figure Out Where You Fit

If you are writing your literature review as part of a larger document — a longer paper, or a proposal — you will need to figure out how your work fits into the literature as a whole: What have the previous sources failed to address so far, and how does your paper or proposal fill that gap?

---

3. Get Organized

Work out how the sources are related to each other. Who disagrees with whom? Which sources back each other up? What sources might be grouped by subtopic or the question they are addressing? Can the sources be divided into categories, based on purpose? Are there any recurring conclusions or themes?

Based on the analysis above, decide on an organizational scheme:

- Organizing by subtopic, the usual approach for literature reviews, enables you to show how sources agree or disagree on each subtopic or question.
- Organizing by methodology, theory, trends, or classification schemes might also be appropriate.
- Chronological order works for showing how a field has changed over time, and is sometimes used by popular science writers or journalists to "tell the story" of a field.

Create a detailed outline of your literature review, identifying where in the paper each source will be addressed. (See the formal sentence outline on p. 567 of Chapter 11 for an example of a detailed outline.)

Always: Reflect and Rethink

Has your research given you reason to rethink your purpose, audience, guiding questions, or even your topic? If so, back up and rethink or redo some steps. It is fine to backtrack as new ideas spring to mind.

4. Draft Your Review

Working from your outline and your notes, compose a draft. You might find it helpful to skip the introduction at first, going back to write it later, when you are more confident about what you are introducing. Make sure you cite your sources as you go, however, because it will help ensure that you have identified each source correctly.

5. Review Your Review, and Revise

Here is a quick checklist:

• Is your review clear enough for your audience?
• Does your review provide enough detail to be informative, without becoming overwhelming?
• Are all the sources clearly identified?
• If you are proposing new research, have you made it clear that your research is needed?

PART 5

Writing for Assessment

26

Essay Examinations

Many instructors believe that an exam that requires you to write is the best way to find out what you have learned and, more important, help you consolidate and reinforce your learning. Instructors who give essay exams want to be sure you can sort through the large body of information covered in a course, identify what is important or significant, and explain your decision. They want to see whether you understand the concepts that provide the basis for a course and whether you can use those concepts to interpret specific materials, to make connections on your own, to see relationships, to draw comparisons and find contrasts, and to synthesize diverse information in support of an original assertion. They may even be interested in your ability to justify your own evaluations based on appropriate standards of judgment and to argue your own opinions with convincing reasons and supporting evidence. All instructors want to encourage you to think more critically and analytically about a subject; many feel that a written exam provides the best demonstration that you are doing so.

As a college student, then, you will face a variety of essay exams, from short-answer identifications that require only a few sentences to take-home exams that may involve hours of planning and writing. You will find that the writing activities and strategies discussed in Parts One and Three of this book — particularly narrating, describing, defining, comparing and contrasting, classifying, and arguing — as well as the critical thinking strategies in Part Two will help you do well on these exams. This chapter provides specific guidelines for you to follow in preparing for and writing essay exams and analyzes a group of typical exam questions to help you determine which strategies will be most useful.

But you can also learn a great deal from your experiences with essay exams in the past — the embarrassment and frustration of doing poorly on one and the great pleasure and pride of doing well. Do you recall the best exam you ever wrote? Do you remember how you wrote it and why you were able to do so well? How can you approach such writing tasks confidently and complete them successfully? Keep these questions in mind as you consider the following guidelines.

Preparing for an Exam

First of all, essay exams require a comprehensive understanding of large amounts of information. The best way to ensure that you will do well on them is to keep up with readings and assignments from the very start of the course: Do the reading, go to lectures, take careful notes, participate in discussion sessions, and organize study groups with classmates to explore and review course materials throughout the term. Trying to cram weeks of information into a single night of study will never allow you to do your best.

Then, as an exam approaches, find out what you can about the form it will take. No question is more irritating to instructors than "Do we need to know this for the exam?" but it is generally legitimate to ask whether the questions will require short or long answers, how many questions there will be, whether you may choose which questions to answer, and what kinds of thinking and writing will be required of you. Some instructors may hand out study guides for exams or even lists of potential questions. However, you will often be on your own in determining how best to go about studying.

Try to avoid simply memorizing information aimlessly. As you study, you should be clarifying the important issues of the course and using these issues to focus your understanding of specific facts and particular readings. If the course is a historical survey, distinguish the primary periods, and try to see relations among the periods and the works or events that define them. If the course is thematically unified, determine how the particular materials you have been reading relate to those themes. If the course is a broad introduction to a general topic, concentrate on the central concerns of each study unit, and see what connections you can discover among the various units. Try to place all you have learned into a meaningful context. How do the pieces fit together? What fundamental ideas have the readings, the lectures, and the discussions seemed to emphasize? How can those ideas help you digest the information the course has covered?

One good way to prepare yourself for an exam is by making up questions you think the instructor might ask and then planning answers to them with classmates. Returning to your notes and to assigned readings with specific questions in mind can help enormously in your process of understanding. The important thing to remember is that an essay exam tests more than your memory of specific information; it requires you to use this information to demonstrate a comprehensive grasp of the topics covered in the course.

Reading the Exam Carefully

Before you answer a question, read the entire exam so that you can apportion your time realistically. Pay particular attention to how many points you may earn in different parts of the exam; notice any directions that suggest how long an answer should be or how much space it should take up. As you are doing so, you may wish to make tentative choices of the questions you will answer and decide on the order in which you will answer them. If you have ideas about how you would organize any of your answers, you might also jot down partial scratch outlines. But before you start to complete any answers, write down the actual clock time you expect to be working on each question or set of questions. Careful time management is crucial to your success on essay exams; giving some time to each question is always better than using up your time on only a few.

Before beginning to write your first answer, you will need to analyze the question carefully. Decide what you are being asked to do, so that you can begin to recognize the structure your answer will need to take. This tentative structure will help you focus your attention on the information that will be pertinent to your answer. Consider this question from a sociology final:

> Drawing from lectures and discussions on the contradictory aspects of American values, the "bureaucratic personality," and the behaviors associated with social mobility, discuss the problems of attaining economic success in a relatively "open," complex, post-industrial society such as the United States.

Though the question looks confusing at first, once you sort it out, you will find that it contains the key terms for the answer's thesis, as well as the main points of development. Look first at the words that give you directions: *draw from* and *discuss*. The term *discuss* invites you to list and explain the problems of attaining economic success. The categories of these problems are already identified in the opening phrases: "contradictory...values," "bureaucratic personality," and "behaviors." Therefore, you would plan to begin with an assertion (or thesis) that included the key words in the final clause ("attaining economic success in a relatively open, complex, post-industrial society") and then take up each category of problem — and perhaps other problems you can think of — in separate paragraphs.

The next section presents some further examples of the kinds of questions often found on essay exams. Pay particular attention to how the directions and the key words in each case can help you define the writing task involved.

Some Typical Essay Exam Questions

Following are nine categories of exam questions, divided according to the sort of writing task involved and illustrated by examples. Although the wording of the examples in a category may differ, the essential directions are similar.

All of the examples are unedited and were written by instructors in six different departments in the humanities and social sciences at two different universities. Drawn from short quizzes, midterms, and final exams for a variety of first- and second-year courses, these questions demonstrate the range of writing you may be expected to do on exams.

Define or Identify

See Chapter 16 for more on defining.

Some questions require you to write a few sentences defining or identifying material from readings or lectures. Such questions almost always allow you only a few minutes to complete your answer.

You may be asked for a brief overview of a large topic, as in Question 26.1. This question, from a twenty-minute quiz in a literature course, was worth as much as 15 of the 100 points possible on the quiz.

Question 26.1

Name and describe the three stages of African literature.

Answering this question would simply involve following the specific directions. A student would probably *name* the periods in historical order and then *describe* each period in a separate sentence or two.

Other questions, like Question 26.2, supply a list of specific items to identify. This example comes from a final exam in a communication course, and the answer to each part was worth as much as 4 points on a 120-point exam.

Question 26.2

Define and state some important facts concerning each of the following:

A. demographics

B. instrumental model

C. RCA

D. telephone booth of the air

E. penny press

With no more than three or four minutes for each part, students taking this exam would offer a concise definition (probably in a sentence) and briefly expand the definition with facts relevant to the main topics in the course.

Sometimes the list of items to be identified can be complicated, including quotations, concepts, and specialized terms; it may also be worth a significant number of points. The next example contains the first five items in a list of fifteen that opened a literature final. Each item was worth 3 points, for a total of 45 out of a possible 130 points.

Question 26.3

Identify each of the following items:

1. projection

2. "In this vast landscape he had loved so much, he was alone."

3. Balducci

4. *pied noir*

5. the Massif Central

Although the directions do not say so specifically, a crucial aspect of this question is not just to identify each item but also to explain its significance in terms of the overall subject. In composing a definition or an identification, always ask yourself a simple question: Why is this item important enough to be on the exam?

Recall Details of a Specific Source

For more on paraphrasing and summarizing, see Chapter 12, pp. 586–88.

Sometimes instructors will ask for a straightforward summary or paraphrase of a specific source — for example, a book or a film. To answer such questions, the student must recount details directly from the source without interpretation or evaluation. In the following example from a sociology exam, students were allowed about ten minutes and required to complete the answer on one lined page provided with the exam.

Question 26.4

In his article "Is There a Culture of Poverty?" Oscar Lewis addresses a popular question in the social sciences: What is the "culture of poverty"? How is it able to come into being, according to Lewis? That is, under what conditions does it exist? When does he say a person is no longer a part of the culture of poverty? What does Lewis say is the future of the culture of poverty?

The phrasing here invites a fairly clear-cut structure. Each of the five specific questions can be turned into an assertion and supported with illustrations from Lewis's article. For example, the first two questions could become assertions like these: "Lewis defines the culture of poverty as _____," and "According to Lewis, the culture of poverty comes into being through _____." The important thing in this case is to summarize accurately what the writer said and not waste time evaluating or criticizing his ideas.

Explain the Importance or Significance

Another kind of essay exam question asks students to explain the importance of something covered in the course. Such questions require specific examples as the basis for a more general discussion of what has been studied. This type of question often involves interpreting a literary or cinematic work by concentrating on a particular aspect of it, as in Question 26.5. This question was worth 10 out of 100 points and was to be answered in seventy-five to one hundred words.

Question 26.5

In the last scene of *Paths of Glory*, the owner of a café brings a young German woman onto a small stage in his café to sing for the French troops, while Colonel Dax looks on from outside the café. Briefly explain the significance of this scene in relation to the movie as a whole.

In answering this question, a student's first task would be to reconsider the whole movie, looking for ways in which this one brief scene illuminates or explains larger issues or themes. Then, in a paragraph or two, the student would summarize these themes and point out how each element of the specific scene fits into the overall context.

You may also be asked to interpret specific information to show that you understand the fundamental concepts of a course. The following example from a communication midterm was worth a possible 10 of 100 points and was allotted twenty minutes of exam time.

Question 26.6

Chukovsky gives many examples of cute expressions and statements uttered by small children. Give an example or two of the kinds of statements that he finds interesting. Then state their implications for understanding the nature of language in particular and communication more generally.

Here the student must start by choosing examples of children's utterances from Chukovsky's book. These examples would then provide the basis for demonstrating the student's grasp of the larger subject.

Questions like these are usually more challenging than definition and summary questions because you must decide for yourself the significance, importance, or implications of the information. You must also consider how best to organize your answer so that the general ideas you need to communicate are clearly developed.

Apply Concepts

Very often, courses in the humanities and the social sciences emphasize significant themes, ideologies, or concepts. A type of common essay exam question asks students to apply the concepts to works studied in the course. Rather than providing specific information to be interpreted more generally, such questions present you with a general idea and require you to illustrate it with specific examples from your reading.

See Chapter 4 for more on explaining a concept.

On a literature final, an instructor posed this writing task. It was worth 50 points out of 100, and students had about an hour to complete it.

Question 26.7

Many American writers have portrayed their characters or their poetic speaker as being engaged in a quest. The quest may be explicit or implicit, it may be external or psychological, and it may end in failure or success. Analyze the quest motif in the work of four of the following writers: Edwards, Franklin, Hawthorne, Thoreau, Douglass, Whitman, Dickinson, James, Twain.

On another literature final, the following question was worth 45 of 130 points. Students had about forty-five minutes to answer it.

Question 26.8

Several works studied in this course depict scapegoat figures. Select two written works and two films, and discuss how their authors or directors present and analyze the social conflicts that lead to the creation of scapegoats.

Question 26.7 instructs students to *analyze,* and Question 26.8 instructs them to *discuss;* yet the answers for both questions would be structured similarly. An introductory paragraph would define the concept — the *quest* or a *scapegoat* — and refer to the works to be discussed. Then a paragraph or two would be devoted to the works, developing specific support to illustrate the concept. A concluding paragraph would probably attempt to bring the concept into clearer focus.

Comment on a Quotation

On essay exams, an instructor will often ask students to comment on a quotation they are seeing for the first time. Usually, such quotations will express some surprising or controversial opinion that complements or challenges basic principles or ideas in the course. Sometimes the writer being quoted is identified, sometimes not. In fact, it is not unusual for instructors to write the quotation themselves.

A student choosing to answer the following question from a literature final would have risked half the exam — in points and time — on the outcome.

Question 26.9

Argue for or against this thesis: "In *A Clockwork Orange,* both the heightened, poetic language and the almost academic concern with moral and political theories deprive the story of most of its relevance to real life."

The directions here clearly ask for an argument. A student would need to set up a thesis indicating that the novel either is or is not relevant to real life and then point out how its language and its theoretical concerns can be viewed in light of this thesis.

The next example comes from a midterm exam in a history course. Students had forty minutes to write their answers, which could earn as much as 70 points on a 100-point exam.

Question 26.10

"Some historians believe that economic hardship and oppression breed social revolt; but the experience of the United States and Mexico between 1900 and 1920 suggests that people may rebel also during times of prosperity."

Comment on this statement. Why did large numbers of Americans and Mexicans wish to change conditions in their countries during the years from 1900 to 1920? How successful were their efforts? Who benefited from the changes that took place?

Although here students are instructed to "comment," the three questions make clear that a successful answer will require an argument: a clear *thesis* stating a position on the views expressed in the quotation, specific *reasons* for that thesis, and *support* for the thesis from readings and lectures. In general, such questions do not have a "correct" answer: Whether you agree or disagree with the quotation is not as important as whether you can argue your case reasonably and convincingly, demonstrating a firm grasp of the subject matter.

See Chapter 19 for more on these components of an argument.

Compare and Contrast

Instructors are particularly fond of essay exam questions that require a comparison and contrast of two or three principles, ideas, works, activities, or phenomena. To answer this kind of question, you need to explore fully the relations between the things to be compared, analyze each one separately, and then search out specific points of likeness or difference. Students must thus show a thorough knowledge of the things being compared, as well as a clear understanding of the basic issues on which comparisons and contrasts can be made.

Often, as in Question 26.11, the basis of comparison will be limited to a particular focus; here, for example, students are asked to compare two works in terms of their views of colonialism.

Question 26.11

Compare and analyze the views of colonialism presented in Memmi's *Colonizer and the Colonized* and Pontecorvo's *Battle of Algiers*. What are the significant differences between these two views?

Sometimes instructors will simply identify what is to be compared, leaving students the task of choosing the basis of the comparison, as in the next three examples from communication, history, and literature exams, respectively.

Question 26.12

In what way is the stage of electronic media fundamentally different from all the major stages that preceded it?

Question 26.13

What was the role of the United States in Cuban affairs from 1898 until 1959? How did its role there compare with its role in the rest of Spanish America during the same period?

> ### Question 26.14
>
> Write an essay on one of the following topics:
>
> 1. Squire Western and Mr. Knightley
> 2. Dr. Primrose and Mr. Elton

See Chapter 18 for more on comparing and contrasting.

Whether the point of comparison is stated in the question or left for you to define for yourself, your answer needs to be limited to the aspects of similarity or difference that are most relevant to the general concepts or themes covered in the course.

Synthesize Information from Various Sources

For more on synthesizing, see Chapter 12, pp. 588–89.

In a course with several assigned readings, an instructor may give students an essay exam question that requires them to pull together (synthesize) information from several or even all the readings.

The following example was one of four required questions on a final exam in a course in Latin American studies. Students had about thirty minutes to complete their answer.

> ### Question 26.15
>
> On the basis of the articles read on El Salvador, Nicaragua, Peru, Chile, Argentina, and Mexico, what would you say are the major problems confronting Latin America today? Discuss the major types of problems with references to particular countries as examples.

For more on forecasting statements, see Chapter 13, p. 602.

This question asks students to do a lot in thirty minutes. They must first decide which major problems to discuss, which countries to include in each discussion, and how to use material from many readings to develop their answers. To compose a coherent essay, a student will need a carefully developed forecasting statement.

Analyze Causes

See Chapter 9 for more on analyzing causes.

In humanities and social science courses, much of what students study concerns the causes of trends, actions, and events. Hence, it is not surprising to find questions about causes on essay exams. In such cases, the instructor expects students to analyze causes of various phenomena discussed in readings and lectures. These examples come from midterm and final exams in literature, sociology, cultural studies, and communication courses, respectively.

> ### Question 26.16
>
> Why do Maurice and Jean not succumb to the intolerable conditions of the prison camp (the Camp of Hell) as most of the others do?

Question 26.17

Given that we occupy several positions in the course of our lives and given that each position has a specific role attached to it, what kinds of problems or dilemmas arise from those multiple roles, and how are they handled?

Question 26.18

Explain briefly the relationship between the institution of slavery and the emergence of the blues as a new African American musical expression.

Question 26.19

Analyze the way in which an uncritical promotion of new information technology such as Twitter may support, unintentionally, the maintenance of the status quo.

Although these questions are presented in several ways ("what kinds of problems," "explain the relationship," "analyze the way"), they all require a list of causes in the answer. The causes would be organized under a thesis statement, and each cause would be argued and supported by referring to lectures or readings.

Criticize or Evaluate

Occasionally, instructors will include essay exam questions that invite students to evaluate a concept or a work. Nearly always, they want more than opinion: They expect a reasoned, documented evaluation based on appropriate criteria or standards of judgment. Such questions test students' ability to recall and synthesize pertinent information and to understand and apply criteria taught in the course.

See Chapter 8 for more on evaluation.

On a final exam in a literature course, a student might have chosen one of the following questions about novels read in the course. Each would have been worth half the total points, with about an hour to answer it.

Question 26.20

Evaluate *A Passage to India* from a postcolonial critical standpoint.

Question 26.21

A Clockwork Orange and *The Comfort of Strangers* both attempt to examine the nature of modern decadence. Which does so more successfully?

To answer either of these questions, a student would have to be very familiar with the novels under discussion and would have to establish standards for evaluating

See Chapter 18 for more on comparing and contrasting.

works of literature. The student would initially have to make a judgment favoring one novel over the other (though not necessarily casting one novel as "terrible" and the other as "perfect"). The student would then give reasons for this judgment, with supporting quotations from the novels, and probably use the writing strategies of comparison and contrast to develop the argument.

This next question was worth 10 of 85 points on a communication course midterm. Students were asked to answer "in two paragraphs."

Question 26.22

Eisenstein and Mukerji both argue that movable print was important to the rise of Protestantism. Cole extends this argument to say that print set off a chain of events that was important to the history of the United States. Summarize this argument, and criticize any part of it if you choose.

Here students are asked to criticize or evaluate an argument in several course readings. The instructor wants to know what students think of this argument and even though this is not stated, why they judge it as they do. Answering this unwritten "why" part of the question is the challenge: Students must come up with reasons and support appropriate to evaluating the argument.

Planning Your Answer

The amount of planning you do for a question will depend on how much time it is allotted and how many points it is worth. For short-answer definitions and identifications, a few seconds of thought will probably be sufficient. (Be careful not to puzzle too long over individual items. Skip over any you cannot recognize fairly quickly; often, answering other questions will help jog your memory.) For answers that require a paragraph or two, you may want to jot down several ideas and examples to focus your thoughts and give you a basis for organizing your information.

For longer answers, though, you will need to develop a much more definite strategy of organization. You have time for only one draft, so allow a reasonable period — as much as a quarter of the time allotted the question — for making notes, determining a thesis, and developing an outline. Jotting down pertinent ideas is a good way to begin; then you can plan your organization with a scratch outline (just a listing of points or facts) or a cluster.

For questions with several parts (different requests or directions, a sequence of questions), make a list of the parts so that you do not miss or minimize one part. For questions presented as questions (rather than directives), you might want to rephrase each question as a writing topic. These topics will often suggest how you should outline the answer.

For information on clustering and outlining, see Chapter 11, pp. 563–68.

You may have to try two or three outlines or clusters before you hit on a workable plan. But be realistic: You want a plan you can develop within the limited time allotted for your answer. Hence, your outline will have to be selective. It will contain not everything you know on the topic but rather what you know that you can develop clearly within the time available.

Writing Your Answer

As with planning, your strategy for writing depends on the length of your answer. For short identifications and definitions, it is usually best to start with a general identifying statement and then move on to describe specific applications or explanations. Two complete sentences will almost always suffice.

For longer answers, begin by stating your forecasting statement or thesis clearly and explicitly. In stating your point and developing your answer, use key terms from the question, and use the same key terms throughout your essay. If the question does not supply any key terms, you should provide your own in stating your main point.

If you have devised an outline for your answer, you will be able to forecast your overall plan and its subpoints in your opening sentences. Forecasting shows readers how your essay is organized and makes your answer easier to read.

See Chapter 13 for more on forecasting and transitions.

As you begin writing your answer, signal clear relations between paragraphs with transition phrases or sentences.

As you continue to write, you will certainly think of new subpoints and new ideas or facts to include later in the essay answer. Make a note of these on your original outline. If you find that you want to add a sentence or two to sections you have already completed, write them in the margin or at the top of the page, with a neat arrow pointing to where they fit in your answer. Strike out words or even sentences you want to change by drawing through them neatly with a single line. Do not stop to erase, but be as neat as you can. Instructors do not expect flawless writing, but they are put off by unnecessary messiness.

Do not pad your answer with irrelevancies and repetitions just to fill up space. Most instructors read exams carefully and are not impressed by the length of an answer alone.

Watch the clock carefully so that you do not spend too much time on one answer. You must be realistic about the time constraints of an essay exam, especially if you know the material well and are prepared to write a lot. If you write one dazzling answer on an exam with three required questions, you earn only 33 points, not enough to pass at most colleges.

If you run out of time when you are writing an answer, jot down the remaining main ideas from your outline, just to show that you know the material and with more time could have continued your exposition.

Write legibly and proofread what you write. Remember that your instructor will likely be reading a large pile of exams. Careless scrawls, misspellings, omitted words, and missing punctuation (especially missing periods needed to mark the ends of sentences) will make that reading difficult, even exasperating. A few minutes of careful proofreading can improve your grade.

Model Answers to Some Typical Essay Exam Questions

Here we analyze several successful answers and give you an opportunity to analyze one for yourself. These analyses, along with the information we have provided elsewhere in this chapter, should greatly improve your chances of writing successful exam answers.

Short Answers

A literature midterm opened with ten items to identify, each worth 3 points. Students had about two minutes for each item. Here are three of Brenda Gossett's answers, each one earning her the full 3 points.

> Rauffenstein: He was the German general who was in charge of the castle where Boeldieu, Marical, and Rosenthal were finally sent in *The Grand Illusion*. He, along with Boeldieu, represented the aristocracy, which was slowly fading out at that time.
>
> Iges Peninsula: This peninsula is created by the Meuse River in France. It is there that the Camp of Hell was created in *The Debacle*. The Camp of Hell is where the French army was interned after the Germans defeated them in the Franco-Prussian War.
>
> Pache: He was the "religious peasant" in the novel *The Debacle*. It was he who inevitably became a scapegoat when he was murdered by Loubet, La Poulle, and Chouteau because he wouldn't share his bread with them.

The instructor said only "identify the following" but clearly wanted students both to identify the item and to indicate its significance to the work in which it appeared. Gossett does both and gets full credit. She mentions particular works, characters, and events. Although she is rushed, she answers in complete sentences. She does not misspell any words or leave out any commas or periods. Her answers are complete and correct.

Paragraph-Length Answers

One question on a weekly literature quiz was worth 20 points of the total of 100. With only a few minutes to answer the question, students were instructed to "answer in a few sentences." Here is the question and Camille Prestera's answer:

> In *Things Fall Apart*, how did Okonkwo's relationship with his father affect his attitude toward his son?
>
> Okonkwo despised his father, who was lazy, cowardly, and in debt. Okonkwo tried to be everything his father wasn't. He was hardworking, wealthy, and a great warrior and wrestler. Okonkwo treated his son harshly because he was afraid he saw the same weakness in Nwoye that he despised in his father. The result of this harsh treatment was that Nwoye left home.

Prestera begins by describing Okonkwo and his father, contrasting the two sharply. Then she explains Okonkwo's relationship with his son Nwoye. Her answer is coherent and straightforward.

Long Answers

Many final exams include at least one question requiring an essay-length answer. John Pixley had an hour to plan and write this essay for a final exam in a literature course in response to Question 26.7:

> Many American writers have portrayed their characters or their poetic speaker as being engaged in a quest. The quest may be explicit or implicit, it may be external or psychological, and it may end in failure or success. Analyze the quest motif in the work of four of the following writers: Edwards, Franklin, Hawthorne, Thoreau, Douglass, Whitman, Dickinson, James, Twain.

JOHN PIXLEY'S ANSWER

1 Americans pride themselves on being ambitious and on being able to strive for goals and to tap their potential. Some say that this is what the "American Dream" is all about. It is important for one to do and be all that one is capable of. This entails a quest or search for identity, experience, and happiness. Hence, the idea of the quest is a vital one in the United States, and it can be seen as a theme throughout American literature.

Key term, quest, *is mentioned in introduction and thesis.*

2 In eighteenth-century colonial America, Jonathan Edwards dealt with this theme in his autobiographical and personal writings. Unlike his fiery and hard-nosed sermons, these autobiographical writings present a sensitive, vulnerable man trying to find himself and his proper, satisfying place in the world. He is concerned with his spiritual growth, in being free to find and explore religious experience and happiness. For example, in *Personal Narrative*, he very carefully traces the stages of religious beliefs. He tells about periods of abandoned ecstasy, doubts, and rational revelations. He also notes that his best insights and growth came at times when he was alone in the wilderness, in nature. Edwards's efforts to find himself in relation to the world can also be seen in his "Observations of the Natural World," in which he relates various meticulously observed and described natural phenomena to religious precepts and occurrences. Here, he is trying to give the world and life, of which he is a part, some sense of meaning and purpose.

First writer is identified immediately.

Edwards's work and the details of his quest are presented.

3 Although he was a contemporary of Edwards, Benjamin Franklin, who was very involved in the founding of the United States as a nation, had a different conception of the quest. He sees the quest as being one for practical accomplishment, success, and wealth. In his *Autobiography*, he stresses that happiness involves working hard to accomplish things, getting along with others, and establishing a good reputation. Unlike Edwards's, his quest is external and bound up with society. He is concerned with his morals and behavior, but, as seen in part 2 of the *Autobiography*,

Transition sentence identifies second writer. Key term (quest) is repeated.

Contrast with Edwards adds coherence to essay.

Another key term from the question, external, *is used.*

Franklin's particular kind of quest is described.

he deals with them in an objective, pragmatic, even statistical way, rather than in sensitive pondering. It is also evident in this work that Franklin, unlike Edwards, believes so much in himself and his quest that he is able to laugh at himself. His concern with society can be seen in *Poor Richard's Almanac,* in which he gives practical advice on how to find success and happiness in the world, how to "be healthy, wealthy, and wise."

Transition sentence identifies third writer. Key term is repeated.

Comparison of Whitman to Edwards and Franklin sustains coherence of essay.

Whitman's quest is defined.

Still another version of the quest can be seen in the mid-nineteenth-century poetry of Walt Whitman. The quest that he portrays blends elements of those of Edwards and Franklin. In "Song of Myself," which is clearly autobiographical, the speaker emphasizes the importance of finding, knowing, and enjoying oneself as part of nature and the human community. He says that one should come to realize that one is lovable, just as are all other people and all of nature and life. This is a quest for sensitivity and awareness, as Edwards advocates, and for great self-confidence, as Franklin advocates. Along with Edwards, Whitman sees that peaceful isolation in nature is important; but he also sees the importance of interacting with people, as Franklin does. Being optimistic and feeling good--both in the literal and figurative sense--are the objects of this quest. Unfortunately, personal disappointment and national crisis (i.e., the Civil War) shattered Whitman's sense of confidence, and he lost the impetus of this quest in his own life.

Transition: Key term is repeated, and fourth writer is identified.

Quest of James character is described.

This theme of the quest can be seen in prose fiction as well as in poetry and autobiography. One interesting example is "The Beast in the Jungle," a short story written by Henry James around 1903. It is interesting in that not only does the principal character, John Marcher, fail in his lifelong quest, but his failure comes about in a most subtle and frustrating way. Marcher believes that something momentous is going to happen in his future. He talks about his belief to only one person, a woman named May. May decides to befriend him for life and watch with him for the momentous occurrence to come about, for "the beast in the jungle" to "pounce." As time passes, May seems to know what this occurrence is and eventually even says that it has happened; but John is still in the dark. It is only long after May's death that the beast pounces on him in his recognition that the "beast" was his failure to truly love May, the one woman of his life, even though she gave him all the encouragement that she possibly, decently could. Marcher never defined the terms of his quest until it was too late. By just waiting and watching, he failed to find feeling and passion. This tragic realization, as someone like Whitman would view it, brings about John Marcher's ruin.

Conclusion repeats key term.

As seen in these few examples, the theme of the quest is a significant one in American literature. Also obvious is the fact that there are a variety of approaches to, methods used in, and outcomes of the quest. This is an appropriate theme for American literature seeing how much Americans cherish the right of "the pursuit of happiness."

Pixley's answer is strong for two reasons: He has the information he needs, and he has organized it carefully and presented it coherently.

4

5

6

Exercise 26.1

The following essay was written by Dan Hepler. He answered the same essay exam question as his classmate John Pixley. Analyze Hepler's essay to discover whether it meets the criteria of a good essay exam answer. Review the criteria mentioned earlier in this chapter in Writing Your Answer and in the annotated commentary of John Pixley's answer. Try to identify the features of Hepler's essay that contribute to or work against its success.

DAN HEPLER'S ANSWER

The quest motif is certainly important in American literature. By considering Franklin, Thoreau, Douglass, and Twain, we can see that the quest may be explicit or implicit, external or psychological, a failure or a success. Tracing the quest motif through these four authors seems to show a developing concern in American literature with transcending materialism to address deeper issues. It also reveals a drift toward ambiguity and pessimism.

1

Benjamin Franklin's quest, as revealed by his *Autobiography*, is for material comfort and outward success. His quest may be considered an explicit one because he announces clearly what he is trying to do: perfect a systematic approach for living long and happily. The whole *Autobiography* is a road map intended for other people to use as a guide; Franklin apparently meant rather literally for people to imitate his methods. He wrote with the assumption that his success was reproducible. He is possibly the most optimistic author in American literature because he enjoys life, knows exactly *why* he enjoys life, and believes that anyone else willing to follow his formula may enjoy life as well.

2

By Franklin's standards, his quest is clearly a success. But his *Autobiography* portrays only an external, not a psychological, success. This is not to suggest that Franklin was a psychological failure. Indeed, we have every reason to believe the contrary. But the fact remains that Franklin *wrote* only about external success; he never indicated how he really felt emotionally. Possibly it was part of Franklin's overriding optimism to assume that material comfort leads naturally to emotional fulfillment.

3

Henry David Thoreau presents a more multifaceted quest. His *Walden* is, on the simplest level, the chronicle of Thoreau's physical journey out of town and into the woods. But the moving itself is not the focus of *Walden*. It is really more of a metaphor for some kind of spiritual quest going on within Thoreau's mind. Most of the action in *Walden* is mental, as Thoreau contemplates and philosophizes, always using the lake, the woods, and his own daily actions as symbols of higher, more eternal truths. This spiritual quest is a success in that Thoreau is able to appreciate the beauty of nature and to see through much of the sham and false assumptions of town life and blind materialism.

4

Thoreau does not leave us with nearly as explicit a "blueprint" for success as Franklin does. Even Franklin's plan is limited to people of high intelligence, personal discipline, and sound character; Franklin sometimes seems to forget that many human beings are in fact weak and evil and so would stand little chance of success similar to his own. But at least Franklin's quest could be duplicated by another Franklin. Thoreau's quest is more problematic, for even as great a mystic and naturalist as

5

Thoreau himself could not remain in the woods indefinitely. This points toward the idea that the real quest is all internal and psychological; Thoreau seems to have gone to the woods to develop a spiritual strength that he could keep and take elsewhere on subsequent dealings with the "real world."

The quest of Frederick Douglass was explicit in that he needed physically to get north and escape slavery, but it was also implicit because he sought to discover and re-define himself through his quest, as Thoreau did. Douglass's motives were more sharply focused than either Franklin's or Thoreau's; his very humanness was at stake, as well as his physical well-being and possibly even his life. But Douglass also makes it clear that the most horrible part of slavery was the mental anguish of having no hope of freedom. His learning to read, and his maintenance of this skill, seems to have been as important as the maintenance of his material comforts, of which he had very few. In a sense, Douglass's quest is the most psychological and abstract so far because it is for the very essence of freedom and humanity, both of which were mostly taken for granted by Franklin and Thoreau. Also, Douglass's quest is the most pessimistic of the three; Douglass concludes that physical violence is the only way out, as he finds with the Covey incident. 6

Finally, Mark Twain's *Huckleberry Finn* is an example of the full range of mean-ing that the quest motif may assume. Geographically, Huck's quest is very large. But again, there is a quest defined implicitly as well as one defined explicitly, as Huck (without consciously realizing it) searches for morality, truth, and freedom. Twain's use of the quest is ambiguous, even more so than the previous writers', because while he suggests success superficially (i.e., the "happily ever after" scene in the last chapter), he really hints at some sort of ultimate hopelessness inherent in soci-ety. Not even Douglass questions the good or evil of American society as deeply as Twain does; for Douglass, everything will be fine when slavery is abolished; but for Twain, the only solution is to "light out for the territories" altogether--and when Twain wrote, he knew that the territories were no more. 7

Twain's implicit sense of spiritual failure stands in marked contrast to Franklin's buoyant confidence in material success. The guiding image of the quest, however, is central to American values and, consequently, a theme that these writers and others have adapted to suit their own vision. 8

Exercise 26.2

Analyze the following essay exam questions to decide what kind of writing task they present. What is being asked of the student as a participant in the course and as a writer? Given the time constraints of the exam, what plan would you propose for writing the answer? Following each question is the number of points it is worth and the amount of time allotted to answer it.

1. Cortazar is a producer of fantastic literature. Discuss first what fantastic literature is. Then choose any four stories by Cortazar as examples, and discuss the fantastic elements in these stories. Refer to the structure, techniques, and narrative styles that he uses in these four stories. If you like, you may refer to more than four, of course. (Points: 30 of 100. Time: 40 of 150 minutes.)

2. During the course of the twentieth century, the United States experienced three significant periods of social reform — the progressive era, the age of the Great Depression, and the decade of the 1960s. What were the sources of reform in each period? What were the most significant reform achievements of each period as well as the largest failings? (Points: 35 of 100. Time: 75 of 180 minutes.)

3. Since literature is both an artistic and ideological product, writers comment on their material context through their writing.

   a. What is Rulfo's perspective of his Mexican reality, and how is it portrayed through his stories?

   b. What particular themes does he deal with, especially in these stories: "The Burning Plain," "Luvina," "They Gave Us the Land," "Paso del Norte," and "Tell Them Not to Kill Me"?

   c. What literary techniques and structures does he use to convey his perspective? Refer to a specific story as an example.

   (Points: 30 of 100. Time: 20 of 50 minutes.)

4. Why is there a special reason to be concerned about the influence of television watching on kids? In your answer, include a statement of the following:

   a. Your own understanding of the *general communication principles* involved for any television watcher.

   b. What is special about television and kids.

   c. How advertisers and producers use this information. (You should draw from the relevant readings as well as lectures.)

   (Points: 20 of 90. Time: 25 of 90 minutes.)

5. Analyze the autobiographical tradition in American literature, focusing on differences and similarities among authors and, if appropriate, changes over time. Discuss four authors in all. In addition to the conscious autobiographers — Edwards, Franklin, Thoreau, Douglass — you may choose one or two figures from among the following fictional or poetic quasi-autobiographers: Hawthorne, Whitman, Dickinson, Twain. (Points: 50 of 120. Time: 60 of 180 minutes.)

6. How does the system of (media) sponsorship work, and what, if any, ideological control do sponsors exert? Be specific and illustrative. (Points: 33 of 100. Time: 60 of 180 minutes.)

7. Several of the works studied in this course analyze the tension between myth and reality. Select two written works and two films, and analyze how their authors or directors present the conflict between myth and reality and how they resolve it, if they resolve it. (Points: 45 of 130. Time: 60 of 180 minutes.)

8. *Man's Hope* is a novel about the Spanish Civil War written while the war was still going on. *La Guerre Est Finie* is a film about Spanish revolutionaries depicting their activities nearly thirty years after the civil war. Discuss how the temporal relationship of each of these works to the civil war is reflected in the character of the works themselves and in the differences between them. (Points: 58 of 100. Time: 30 of 50 minutes.)

9. Write an essay on one of these topics: The role of the narrator in *Tom Jones* and *Pride and Prejudice* or the characters of Uncle Toby and Miss Bates. (Points: 33 of 100. Time: 60 of 180 minutes.)

27

Writing Portfolios

A writing portfolio displays your work. Portfolios for college composition courses usually include a selection of your writing for the course and an essay reflecting on your writing and on what you learned in the course. The contents of a portfolio will, of course, vary from writer to writer and from instructor to instructor. This chapter provides some advice for assembling a writing portfolio using the resources in *The St. Martin's Guide to Writing*.

The Purposes of a Writing Portfolio

Portfolios are generally used to display an individual's accomplishments. Artists present portfolios of their work to gallery owners and patrons. Designers and architects present portfolios of their most successful and imaginative work to potential clients. Some colleges request that applicants submit portfolios of high school writing; outstanding portfolios sometimes qualify students for college credit or placement in advanced courses. Graduating seniors may be asked to submit a portfolio of their best work for evaluation, sometimes leading to special recognition or rewards. Instructors applying for new positions or advancement may compile a portfolio to demonstrate excellence in their teaching and research. No matter what the specific purpose or occasion, a portfolio presents a rich opportunity to show what you can do.

Creating a portfolio for a composition course enables you to present your best, most representative, or most extensively revised writing and, to some extent, collaborate with your instructor in assessing your work. Your instructor will assign the final grade, but how you select the materials included in your portfolio and describe them in your introductory essay may have some influence on your instructor's judgment. Most important, selecting your work and composing a reflective essay gives you an opportunity to consolidate, reinforce, and therefore better remember and apply what you have learned. Reviewing your work can increase your satisfaction with your courses as you become more aware of the specific ways in which your knowledge is growing. It can also give you insights into your own intellectual development, help you recognize your strengths and weaknesses, and discover your interests.

Whether or not you are asked to turn in a writing portfolio, you might want to consider keeping one as a personal record of an important period in your

For more on the process of thinking critically, see pp. 11–12.

intellectual development. You might even wish to update the portfolio each term, adding interesting work from all your courses or perhaps from all the courses in your major.

Assembling a Portfolio for Your Composition Course

Some instructors give students free rein in deciding what to include in their portfolio, but most specify what the portfolio should include. Instructors usually ask students to select a certain number of essays, and they may specify that certain types of essays be included, such as one based on personal experience or observation and another based on library and Internet research, along with other materials like in-class writing or responses to readings. Many instructors also ask students to include materials that reflect their writing process (such as invention work, drafts, and critical responses). In addition to a selection of course materials, instructors usually require a reflective essay or letter that introduces the portfolio and evaluates the writer's own work.

Instructors who require portfolios often do not assign grades to individual drafts or revisions but wait until the end of the term to grade the entire portfolio. In such cases, instructors may ask students to submit a midterm portfolio for an in-progress course evaluation. A midterm portfolio usually includes plans for revising one or more of the essays included.

There are many possible ways of assembling portfolios, and you will need to determine exactly what your instructor expects your portfolio to include. Here are some of the variables:

- How many essays should be included in the portfolio?
- May essays be revised further for the portfolio?
- What process work should be included?
- What other material should be included (such as exercises, notes from collaborative activities, analyses of readings, downloaded Web pages)?
- May material from other courses, workplace projects, or service-learning projects be included?

For more on service learning, see Chapter 30.

- Should the portfolio be introduced by a reflective essay or letter? If so, how long should it be? Are there any special requirements for it?
- How should the portfolio be organized?
- Will essays be graded when they are turned in, at midterm, or only at the end of the term when the final portfolio is submitted?

The following sections review specific resources in *The Guide* that can help you compose your portfolio.

Selecting Work

Even if your instructor specifies what to include in your portfolio, you have some important decisions to make. Here are some suggestions to help you:

- If you are asked to select only your best essays, begin by rereading them to see how well each one develops the basic features of its genre. Also review any critical responses you received from your instructor, classmates, writing center tutors, or other critical readers.

- If you are asked to make further revisions to one or more of your essays, reread the essay, using the Critical Reading Guide for that genre, or get a critical response to it from your instructor, a classmate, or a writing center tutor. It may also help to review any critical responses you received on earlier drafts and the Troubleshooting chart for that genre to see what else you could do to improve the essay. Be sure to edit and proofread your essays carefully.

- If you are asked to select essays based on personal experience, you might choose from the remembering events essay you wrote for Chapter 2. If you are asked for essays based on firsthand observation and analysis, look at what you wrote for the profile (Chapter 3), the story analysis (Chapter 10), or the concept explanation (Chapter 4). If you are asked to include argument essays, review the writing you did for Chapters 6–9.

- If you are asked to select essays incorporating library or Internet research, look at the essays you wrote for Chapters 4–9.

- If you are asked to select essays with a range of different purposes and audiences, you might begin by reviewing the Purpose and Audience sections of the Part One chapters you used. Then reread your invention notes defining the particular purpose and audience for each essay you wrote.

- If you are asked to include examples of your writing process work, look for your most imaginative invention work, for a first draft and one or more revisions showing significant rethinking or reorganization, for your critical reading response to another student's draft showing perceptive criticism and helpful suggestions, or for a draft you edited heavily.

- If you are asked to include a complete process for one essay, you should choose process materials that show the quality as well as quantity of work you have done. Look for examples of thoughtful invention and substantive revision you can point out in your reflective essay.

- If you are asked to select essays that show the progress you have made in the course, you may want to choose essays that underwent radical change through the term.

Reflecting on Your Work and Your Learning

Many instructors require a written statement in the form of an essay or letter introducing the portfolio. Some ask for a simple description of the work presented in your portfolio; others prefer an evaluation of your work; still others may want you to connect your learning in this course to other courses and to work you hope to do in the future. Keeping the following considerations in mind will help you write a thoughtful, well-organized statement to your instructor about what you have learned:

- *Introduce and describe your work.* Because you will need to refer to several works or parts of a work, name each item in your portfolio in a consistent way. In describing an essay, give its title, genre (using the title of the chapter in *The St. Martin's Guide*), purpose, audience, and topic.

- *Justify your choices.* When you justify what you see as your "best" work, you think critically about the standards you are using to evaluate good writing in each genre. *The Guide* sets forth clear criteria for each kind of writing in the Basic Features and Critical Reading sections in Chapters 2–10. Review these sections as you judge the success of your essay, and refer to them as you explain your choice.

  If you need help writing an evaluation, review Chapter 8.

- *Illustrate your growth as a writer with specific examples.* You may have selected work to show how you have grown as a writer, but you should not assume your readers will read the portfolio as you do without some guidance. You need to show them where they can find evidence that supports your statements by citing relevant examples from the work included in your portfolio. Summarize or quote your examples and be sure to tell readers what you think the examples illustrate. Also refer to them in a way that will help readers locate them with ease — perhaps by page and paragraph number (see the next section for some suggestions for organizing your portfolio).

- *Use* **The Guide** *to help you reflect on your learning.* Your instructor may ask you to consider what you learned in writing and revising a particular essay as well as what you learned about the process of writing that essay. In either case, it will help you to anchor your reflections in the specific work you have done using this book. Consider what you have learned analyzing and discussing the readings, inventing and researching, participating in group inquiry, planning and drafting, getting and giving critical comments, and revising and editing. Look again at the Thinking Critically about What You Have Learned sections in Chapters 2–10. There you will find questions that will help you reflect on how you solved problems when revising an essay and how your writing can be situated and understood in a larger social context. You may well be able to use your responses to these questions in your portfolio's reflective essay.

Organizing the Portfolio

Some instructors prescribe the portfolio's design and organization, while others allow students to be creative. Portfolios may be presented in an inexpensive manila folder, in a looseleaf binder, or on a Web site. Follow your instructor's specific guidelines. Here are some possibilities for organizing your portfolio:

- *Include a cover or front page.* The design of the front page may be left up to you, but be sure to indicate the class section number, the instructor's name, your own name, and the date.

- *Include a table of contents.* Portfolios, like books, need a table of contents so that readers can see at a glance what is included and where it is located. The table of contents should appear at the beginning of the portfolio, identifying all of the parts and specifying the page on which each part begins. You may decide to renumber all of the pages in the portfolio consecutively even though some of the material already has page numbers. If you add new page numbers, consider using a different color, putting the new page numbers in a new place, or using a letter- or word-number sequence (such as *Event-1, Position-1,* etc.). Whatever you decide, be consistent.

- *Label each item.* If your instructor does not specify how you should label your work, you need to develop a clear system on your own. You may need to explain your system briefly in a note on the table of contents or in your reflective essay where you refer to particular items in your portfolio. For example, you could use *The Guide* chapter number to identify each essay assignment. To indicate process materials, consider using the chapter number and title and the relevant heading from that chapter's Guide to Writing section (such as Chapter 2, Exploring Your Present Perspective). To identify different drafts, you could write on the top left margin of every page the chapter number, essay title, and draft number. For drafts that received a critical reading, you might want to add the notation "Read by S." You should also date all of your work.

- *Sequence the material.* If your instructor does not indicate how you should order the work included in your portfolio, you will have to decide yourself. If your instructor asks you to present two or more examples of your best work, you may want to begin with the essay you consider your very best. If your instructor asks you to show the progress you have made in the course, you could begin with your weakest essay and either show how you improved it or present later essays that were stronger. If your instructor asks you to demonstrate growth, you might organize your work by the particular areas that improved. For example, you could show that you learned to revise substantively by presenting earlier and later examples of revisions. Or to show that you learned to edit effectively or to avoid certain sentence errors, you could give examples of a particular error you made one or two times early on but avoided in later drafts.

PART 6

Writing and Speaking to Wider Audiences

28

Oral Presentations

At some point in your academic career, you will probably be asked to give an oral presentation. In fact, you may give many oral presentations before you graduate, and you almost certainly will give oral presentations on the job. This chapter contains practical suggestions for preparing and giving effective oral presentations.

Be Ready

Many people are terrified at the thought of public speaking, particularly people who have little experience with it. Even experienced public speakers can become jittery before giving an oral presentation. The key to defeating nervousness and anxiety is to research and prepare. If you have researched your subject thoroughly and have planned your presentation in detail, then you should be able to relax. If you find that you are still anxious, take a few slow, deep breaths before starting your presentation. It is also helpful not to think of your presentation as a performance. Remember that you are communicating a message. Think of your presentation as simply talking to an audience.

Understand the Kind of Oral Presentation You Have Been Asked to Give

The list that follows identifies the four basic types of oral presentations.

- *Impromptu presentation.* An impromptu oral presentation is given without preparation. In a history class, for example, your instructor may call on you to explain briefly a concept you are studying, such as "manifest destiny." As best you can, you would recall what you have read and summarize the information. While impromptu presentations are given without preparation, they do require knowledge of the subject matter.

- *Extemporaneous presentation.* In an extemporaneous presentation, you prepare beforehand and speak from notes or an outline. For example, in a management class, you might prepare a report on a business that you recently visited. In most academic and business situations, extemporaneous talks are preferred because they are informal yet well organized. Extemporaneous presentation often includes outlining your major points on a board or on a projector.

- *Scripted presentation.* Reading from a script is one way to ensure that you say exactly what you want to say — and that you take no more than the time you have been allotted. Because you read to your audience, a scripted presentation can be stiff and boring unless it is carefully planned and rehearsed. Scripted presentations also need to be written so that the audience can easily follow the presentation by just hearing it. Sentences often need to be shorter than in a document that is read. You will also need to provide more transitions and cues than in documents that are read. (See Use Cues to Orient Listeners, below.) A simple guideline to remember is that if your writing is difficult for you to read aloud, it will be difficult to listen to as well.

- *Memorized presentation.* This type of oral presentation is written and committed to memory beforehand. For instance, at a sales meeting, you might evaluate a new product in relation to its competition. However, most people prefer scripted talks because of the difficulty of memorizing a lengthy oral presentation.

Assess Your Audience and Purpose

To give effective oral presentations you need to assess your audience and your purpose. Even for an impromptu presentation, you should take a few moments to think about whom you are speaking to and why. To assess your audience, ask the same questions you would ask about readers: Why are the members of my audience here? What do they already know about my subject? How do they feel about my topic? What objections might they have to my argument?

Define your purpose by completing the following statement: "In this oral presentation, I want to. . . ." For instance, you may want to speculate on the causes of the recent trend of companies' hiring numerous part-time and temporary workers, or you may want to argue your position on the ethics of this new hiring policy.

Determine How Much Information You Can Present in the Allotted Time

Your presentation should be exactly as long as the time allotted. Using substantially less time will make your presentation seem incomplete or superficial; using substantially more time may alienate your audience. Plan your presentation to allocate sufficient time for an introduction, concluding remarks, and follow-up questions (if a question-and-answer session is to be part of the presentation). If you are giving a scripted presentation, each double-spaced page of text will probably take two minutes to deliver. Time yourself to be sure.

Use Cues to Orient Listeners

Listening is one of the most difficult ways to comprehend information, in part because listeners cannot look back at previous information or scan forward, as readers can. To help your audience follow your oral presentation, use the same cues you would use to orient readers — but use them more frequently and overtly. Here are four basic cues that are especially helpful for listeners.

- ■ *Thesis and forecasting statements.* Begin your presentation with thesis and forecasting statements that announce to audience members what you intend to communicate (your thesis) and the order in which you will present your material (your forecast). For instance, if you will present an argument about deregulation in the telecommunications industry, you can begin by asserting your position and preview the reasons you will offer to support your position.

- ■ *Transitions.* Provide transitions when you move from one point to the next to help your audience follow the twists and turns of your presentation. For example, when you have finished discussing your first reason, state explicitly that you are now turning to your second reason.

- ■ *Summaries.* End your oral presentation with a summary of the main points you have made. Also look for opportunities to use summaries throughout the presentation, particularly when you have spent a long time discussing something complicated. A brief summary that indicates the point you are making and its relation to your overall thesis can help listeners understand how the parts of your argument fit together to support your thesis.

- ■ *Visuals.* Visual presentation of these cues will reinforce them. Your thesis, forecasting statements, transitions, and summaries can all be presented visually.

For further discussion and illustration of orienting cues, see Chapter 13.

Prepare Effective and Appropriate Visuals

For presentations that you plan ahead of time, you can use a variety of visuals — from simple lists and graphs to sophisticated computer demonstrations — to help both you and your audience. For instance, PowerPoints listing the major points of your presentation will help your listeners understand and remember what you say.

There are many different ways to incorporate visuals. Writing on a board or flip chart has several advantages: low cost, high visibility, and simplicity for composing or altering on the spot. To present a long passage or detailed graphic, photocopied handouts are preferable, although they can be distracting.

Overhead transparencies used to be a popular way to display visuals during a presentation. An overhead transparency consists of text, graphics, or both printed on a sheet of 8½-by-11-inch film. When illuminated by an overhead projector, the material is enlarged and projected on a screen. Overhead transparencies have in most cases been replaced by the use of computer technology. With a projector, a laptop, and software such as PowerPoint, slides such as the one in Figure 28.1 can be created and displayed with relative ease. PowerPoint slides have the advantage of allowing for the use of animation, video, and audio. Just be sure that the bells and whistles don't drown you out.

If you use slides, think of them as integral to your presentation, not just decorative. They should be concise, easy to read, and uncluttered. You may use them to list the

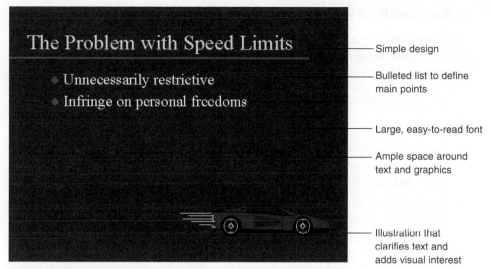

Figure 28.1 Sample PowerPoint Slide

main points of your presentation, to signal transitions from one topic to another, and to summarize information you have presented.

As you prepare visuals of any kind, keep in mind that they must be legible to everyone in your audience, including people seated in the back of the room. Use a large, easy-to-read font and generous amounts of space around text.

For more on designing documents, see Chapter 21.

Verify That You Will Have the Correct Equipment and Supplies

Well before your presentation is scheduled to begin, verify that the presentation room contains all of the equipment and supplies you will need. For example, if you plan to use a projector, make sure it is in the room, placed correctly, and working well. Anticipating your needs as well as potential problems (for example, by bringing a backup copy of any files you need) will make your presentation go smoothly and help reduce your anxiety.

Rehearse Your Presentation

Rehearsing will help you become more familiar with your material, fit the material into the allotted time, and feel more confident about speaking in public. If possible, rehearse in the same room in which you will give the presentation, using the same equipment. Also try to rehearse before an audience of colleagues or friends who can give you constructive criticism. Rehearsing a script or memorized presentation will enable you to plan your delivery. For a scripted talk, mark cues selectively on your printed text to remind yourself when to pause or emphasize a word or phrase.

Deliver the Oral Presentation Professionally

Before your presentation, try to relax: Take a few deep breaths, drink some water, or step outside for some fresh air. If someone is to introduce you, give that person information about yourself and your presentation. Otherwise, begin by introducing yourself and your title or topic.

These guidelines will help you make a professional impression:

- As you speak, try to make eye contact with the people in the room.
- Use your hands to gesture as you would in a conversation; your hands should be neither clamped rigidly at your sides nor doing something distracting such as playing with your jewelry.
- If you are behind a lectern, avoid slouching, leaning on it, or gripping it tightly throughout the presentation.
- If you are using visuals, be careful not to block the audience's view of them. After introducing a new visual, resume making eye contact with audience members; talk to the audience, not the visual.
- Try to avoid distracting vocal mannerisms, such as repeatedly saying "uh," "like," or "you know."
- Speak loudly enough so that all members of the audience can hear you, and speak clearly and distinctly. Nervousness may cause you to speak too rapidly, so watch your pace.
- Do not speak in a monotone. Instead, let the pitch of your voice rise and fall naturally, especially when giving a scripted presentation.
- Dress appropriately for your audience and the formality of the situation in which you are speaking. The focus should be on your message, not on how you are dressed.

End Your Presentation Graciously

If a question-and-answer session follows your presentation, politely invite questions by saying something like, "If you have any questions, I would be happy to try to answer them now." If no question-and-answer session is scheduled to follow your presentation, end the presentation by thanking your audience for giving you the opportunity to speak. If appropriate, offer to answer any questions in a private conversation or in a follow-up correspondence.

29

Working with Others

Writers often seek advice and feedback from friends, colleagues, or mentors on individual writing projects. For instance, they may consult a librarian for advice on research, try out an argument on a coworker or fellow student, or ask a trusted friend to check for grammar errors. On some occasions, writers also work in small groups to research, plan, and compose joint writing projects.

Working with others is often referred to as *collaboration*. Collaborating with others on individual projects and especially on joint writing projects can be challenging, but also rewarding. The following advice will help you anticipate the difficulties so that you can realize the full potential of collaboration.

Working with Others on Your Individual Writing Projects

This book assumes that you will at least to some extent be collaborating with others to write your essays. Generally speaking, your instructor is a collaborator, as are other students in your class. Class discussion of the readings will help you understand more about the genres you will be writing, and responses to your invention work and to drafts of your essays will give you ideas for writing more effectively.

Collaboration is also built directly into the activities in the writing assignment chapters, however. In every assignment chapter, four activities ask you to collaborate with other students in a purposeful way. Chapter 6, Arguing a Position, for example, has these activities:

> *A Collaborative Activity: Practice Arguing a Position.* This activity asks you to get together with a small group of your classmates to practice asserting a position, offering reasons and support for it, and anticipating likely objections to it. Afterwards, your group is encouraged to discuss the process, reflecting on what parts presented the biggest challenges, and why.

> *Making Connections.* This activity, following each of the readings, invites you to examine some of the important ideas and underlying assumptions of the reading. In small-group discussion, you can explore your responses and develop your understanding.

A Collaborative Activity: Testing Your Choice. Partway through the invention work, at a point where you need to assess realistically whether you have made a wise topic choice, this activity guides you in presenting your topic to a few other students. From discovering what you have to say about your topic in this first public tryout and from reflecting on what other students have to say, you can decide whether you have chosen a topic you can write about convincingly.

Critical Reading Guide. Once you have a draft of your essay, anyone using the Critical Reading Guide can give you a comprehensive evaluation of your work, and you can do likewise for others. Because in Chapter 6 the Critical Reading Guide reflects the particular requirements of an essay arguing a position, anyone using it to evaluate your draft will be able to give you focused, relevant advice.

In these four activities, you collaborate with others to develop your individual writing projects by discovering what you may know about a project before you get very far into it, assessing your progress after a period of initial work, and evaluating your first attempts to draft a complete essay. There are many other occasions for fruitful collaboration in the assignment chapters. For instance, in Chapter 6 you might work with other students to complete the Analyzing Writing Strategies tasks that follow the readings. You and another student might exchange revisions of your essays to help each other with final editing and proofreading. Or you might meet or exchange e-mail messages with two or three other students to work on the Considering the Social Dimensions section that concludes the chapter. Working collaboratively on these activities may make them easier or more enjoyable. Working collaboratively will also very likely be more productive, through the exchange of many more ideas than you might have come up with on your own.

Following are guidelines for successful collaboration on individual writing projects:

- Whenever you read someone else's writing, have the writer inform you about his or her purpose and readers. Collaboration is always more effective when writers focus on helping other writers achieve their purposes for their particular readers. If a writer is explaining a concept to readers who know nothing about it, as might be the case in Chapter 4, Explaining a Concept, your comments are likely to be unhelpful if you assume the essay is addressed to someone who shares your understanding of the concept.

- Know the genre the writer is working in. If a writer is proposing a solution to a problem and you are evaluating the writing as though it were an essay arguing a position, your advice is likely to be off the mark.

- When you evaluate another writer's work, be sure you know the stage of its development. Is it a set of tentative notes for a first draft? A partial draft? A complete draft? A revision? If it is a draft, you want to focus on helping the writer develop and organize ideas; if it is a revision, you might focus exclusively on cueing and coherence or editing and proofreading.

- When you evaluate someone's writing, be helpful and supportive but also frank and specific. You do a writing partner no favor if you shrink from criticizing and giving advice. If your criticism seems grounded in the purpose, audience, and genre, it will probably not seem arbitrary or personal to your partner.

- Bring as much writing as possible to a scheduled meeting with other writers. The further along your writing is, the more you can learn from the collaboration.

- Try to be receptive to criticism. Later, you can decide whether to change your essay, and how.

Working with Others on Joint Writing Projects

In addition to collaborating with others on your individual writing projects, you may be given the opportunity to work on a joint project in which you collaborate to produce a single essay. For instance, in Chapter 6, Arguing a Position, you could collaborate to construct a persuasive argument for a position you share with two or three other students. In Chapter 4, Explaining a Concept, you could work with a few other students to research and explain a concept, perhaps using graphics or hands-on activities to help others grasp the concept and its implications. In Chapter 7, Proposing a Solution, you have an opportunity to practice researching and writing proposals, by far the most common type of joint writing project in college, the workplace, and the community.

When people collaborate on joint projects, they often share responsibility for the coherence and content of the final product but divide up tasks during the invention, planning, drafting, and editing stages. For example, each team member might take on responsibilities related to his or her areas of expertise. Someone who knows the problem firsthand might work on developing ways to explain the problem to those who have not experienced it directly. People who have experience making forecasts and planning budgets might be assigned to research and draft those aspects of the proposal. Everyone in the group might suggest revisions to the draft, and individuals may be assigned parts to strengthen and clarify. When a final draft seems near, one person might be assigned the job of improving cueing and coherence, another might be in charge of editing and proofreading, and a third might work on document design. Because the team shares responsibility for the final document, most teams collectively review the final draft, so that errors do not slip through the cracks.

Consider the following workplace writing example. A pharmaceuticals company decided to invest time and money in finding a solution to a problem the company saw as damaging to its business as well as to the community. The company assigned a team of seven division managers and a technical writer, gave them a budget to pay for outside consultants, and asked them to present a written proposal to the state legislature and local school board in six months' time. The pharmaceuticals team divided the project into a series of research and writing tasks like those outlined in the Guide to Writing in Chapter 7. The team members scheduled due dates for each task and progress reports to identify problems as they arose. They assigned responsibility for each task to either individuals or small groups and identified which tasks might need consultation with outside experts.

Writing collaboratively on a joint project certainly has benefits. Collaboration not only draws on the expertise and energy of different people but can also create an outcome that is greater than the sum of its parts. One difficulty of collaborative writing projects, however, is that learning how to work effectively with others takes time and effort. Writers working on a joint project need to spend a lot of time communicating with one another. They must learn to anticipate conflicts and resolve them constructively. They should be realistic in scheduling and do their assigned tasks responsibly. They have to be flexible in their writing processes and open to different points of view.

If you are assigned a joint project in a college course, your instructor may decide how large your group should be and may even assign students to particular groups. If you are unhappy being in a particular group, discuss the situation with your instructor as soon as possible. To help group members work together constructively on joint writing projects, here are some ground rules you will want to discuss and implement:

- Begin by establishing clear and easy means of communicating with one another. Exchange e-mail addresses, but also exchange phone numbers as a backup.

- Expect to spend a lot of time planning the project together and discussing who will do what and when. Discuss how the group should divide responsibilities. Remember, however, to remain flexible and keep lines of communication open to deal with problems as they arise.

- Set a schedule of regular meetings to take place in person, online, or by phone. Agree on how to run the meetings. For example, should someone lead each discussion? Should the role of discussion leader rotate? Should notes or minutes be taken? Should each meeting have an agenda? If so, how and when should it be developed for each subsequent meeting?

- Make sure each team member has a say in major decisions, such as choosing a topic and devising a thesis statement. This isn't always easy: Some team members might be inclined to agree with whatever the team seems to want, even if they privately have concerns. However, you can get frank input from every person on the team if you periodically collect comments or votes anonymously.

- Try to treat each other with respect and consideration, but do not be surprised by disagreements and personality conflicts. Arguing can stimulate thinking — inspiring creativity as well as encouraging each person to explain ideas clearly and systematically. But arguing can also encourage aggressiveness in some people and withdrawal in others. If there is a problem in the way the group interacts, address it immediately, perhaps by calling a special meeting to work out a solution. Try to avoid placing blame. Consider, for example, whether taking turns would ensure that everyone contributes to the discussion and no one dominates. Urge everyone to refrain from characterizing other people and instead to speak only about what they themselves think and feel by making "I" rather than "you" statements.

- Keep track of everyone's progress. Consider creating a chart so that all members can see at a glance what they need to do and when. Schedule regular progress reports so that any problems can be identified immediately.

- If the group will make an oral presentation of the written proposal, plan it carefully, giving each person a role. Rehearse the presentation as a group to make sure it satisfies the time limit and other requirements of the assignment.

For more on oral presentations, see Chapter 28.

30

Writing in Your Community

Service learning combines classroom education with life experience. Through partnerships with community organizations, colleges and universities can offer students ways to see how the knowledge that they are gaining in school can be put to work beyond the campus. Such programs also provide valuable service to those who need it. If your composition class has a service-learning component, you will have an opportunity to learn more about your community, to become an active participant in that community, and to apply your writing skills to your community experience.

In service-learning programs, students are most often placed in off-campus positions with government bureaus such as local parks and recreation departments or nonprofit organizations that offer community support services such as care for the homeless. In these positions students apply what they are studying in class. Here are a few examples:

- Nursing students teach expectant mothers about prenatal and infant care.
- Chemistry students tour local elementary schools demonstrating science "magic."
- Botany students teach fourth graders about plants native to their region.
- Zoology students help researchers gather samples for a study of local amphibian populations.
- Political science students work with the local government to increase voter turnout.
- English-speaking students tutor grade school children who are having trouble learning to read and write English.

While you will probably find much to write about in your service experience, you may also find writing is a part of your service. When writing is part of your service, you move beyond having classmates and instructors as your primary audience and enter the realm of public discourse.

Using Your Service Experience as Source Material

Finding a Topic

One of the many advantages of service learning is that it can present numerous topics that might be fruitfully explored through your writing. To generate a substantial list of ideas, you need only ask yourself some simple questions:

- Who is most affected by the situation, and how are these people affected?
- How long has this situation existed?
- What forces shape the situation? Can anything be done to alter them?
- How have other organizations handled this issue? How might the situation be improved?
- What common perceptions do people hold about this situation? What are my own perceptions?
- If these perceptions are inaccurate, how might they be changed?

There are dozens of possible essay topics in any service experience. For example, if your service experience includes working at a clinic that serves low-income families without health insurance, you might write a report explaining the known long-term effects of insufficient medical care on children. You might also write a proposal to address the problem faced by people who lack medical coverage. Or perhaps you are interested in arguing a position that advocates universal health care.

Gathering Sources

For most college writing projects, research is often limited, by time and availability, to what one can find in the library or on the Internet. A service-learning environment can provide field research sources that would otherwise be difficult to tap. The most significant of these potential sources is the people who run the organization in which you are doing your service. If you have focused your writing on the kinds of issues that are relevant to your service, these people can serve as experts. Many of the people you work with will have years of experience and specialized training and probably will have researched the subject themselves. Take advantage of your opportunity to tap their knowledge. When approached courteously, people are often more than willing to share what they know.

Depending on the situation, your service site might also be a good place to circulate a questionnaire or conduct a survey to help you gather information about your subject. Of course, your own observations and experiences as you perform your service will be valuable as well. You might consider keeping a daily journal in which you record these experiences and observations. When you are ready to begin writing, you will already have done some early invention work.

For suggestions on making observations, conducting interviews, and creating questionnaires, see Chapter 22.

The service organization itself might also be a good source of information. Such organizations often collect and produce literature that is relevant to their mission. Your organization might even maintain its own small library of resource materials. Frequently such organizations are also part of a network of similar groups that share their expertise through newsletters, trade journals, Web sites, or online discussion groups. Explore these unique resources.

Keep in mind the ethical considerations that are involved. Many service-learning environments, such as those that involve counseling, tutoring, or teaching, can give you access to information that should be kept confidential, especially if you are working with minors. Be sure that you are open about your information-gathering and that everyone whom you might use as a source knows your intentions. Any questionnaires should include a disclosure stating what you intend to do with the information gathered. Any information gained from interviews should be properly attributed, but you should consider carefully maintaining the anonymity of anyone whom you cite or describe, unless you have your subjects' explicit permission to use their names. Err on the side of caution and consideration, and ask your instructor for guidance if you have any questions about how to treat sensitive material.

Writing *about* Your Service Experience

Writing in a service-learning program is really no different from other writing situations. You still must identify for yourself the kind of writing you are doing, generate ideas through invention, and refine those ideas through a process of drafting and revision. Service learning, however, may put you in a position to write for a nonacademic audience. For example, you might write an editorial for your campus or local newspaper in which you argue for increased support for your service organization or project. You might craft a letter to local government officials or even representatives to the state or national legislature suggesting a solution to a specific problem. Remember that writing is action, and as such it can be a powerful tool.

The service-learning experience can provide you with subject matter for many of the academic writing activities discussed in Part One of this textbook. While you can no doubt generate your own list of ideas, here are some to consider:

Chapter 2: Remembering an Event

- Write about your first day of service. What happened? How did you feel? What did you learn? How did it differ from what you expected to learn?
- Write about a particularly difficult day. Why was it difficult? How did you handle the situation? What would you do differently? What did you learn from the experience?

Chapter 3: Writing Profiles

- Write about the place where you are doing your service. What does it look like? How does it make you feel? How does the location reflect or affect what goes on there? What does go on there?
- Write about one of the people you have met doing your service. What is he or she like? How is he or she typical (or atypical) of other people in the same position? What makes this person special or different?

Chapter 4: Explaining a Concept

- Write about a concept with which you were unfamiliar before you did your service. What does the concept mean? How is it important in the context of your service experience? How does what you learned about this concept make you think differently now?

- Write about a concept that you knew but now understand differently because of your service. How has your understanding of the concept changed? What caused that change? How might you explain that change to someone who does not share your experience?

Chapter 5: Finding Common Ground

- Write about a debate that is relevant to the type of service you are doing and briefly describe each position in the debate. (Note that there may be more than two.) Who are the major proponents of each position? What are the main reasons and evidence given to support each position? Where is it possible to establish common ground between the positions?

Chapter 6: Arguing a Position

- Write an argument in support of the service organization you are working with. Why should people support it? How can they support it? Why is it a worthwhile endeavor?

- Write an argument about the value of service learning. What have you gained from this experience? Who should participate? What are the advantages of service learning to individuals and the community?

Chapter 7: Proposing a Solution

- Write about a process or procedure within or affecting the organization you are working with that you think needs to be improved. Why does it need to be improved? How might it be improved?

- Write about a policy, law, or practice that you think should be eliminated or revised because it negatively affects the organization you are working with. What would be the benefit of eliminating or revising it? What steps would need to be taken in order to change the policy, law, or practice?

Chapter 8: Justifying an Evaluation

- Write about how effectively the organization you are working with satisfies its objectives. How do you measure its effectiveness?

- Write about your school's service-learning program. In what ways is it most successful? In what ways could it be improved?

Chapter 9: Speculating about Causes

- Write about the causes for a problem or situation that you have encountered through your service-learning experience. What brought the problem about? What circumstances perpetuate it?

- Write about why service-learning programs have become common. What function do they serve that traditional education models do not? What demands do they meet?

Writing *for* Your Service Organization

Some service-learning situations will put you in a position not just to write *about* your service experience but also to write *as part of* your service experience. You might be asked to create flyers, brochures, press releases, or Web pages for a community organization. You might help craft presentations or reports. While these may not be academic writing activities, they are still writing activities, and the strategies presented in this text still apply. You might be asked, for example, to help write a brochure that explains the purpose and function of the organization. In effect, you would be writing an explanation, and you would need to keep in mind the basic features of this genre outlined in Chapter 4.

Such writing situations give you an opportunity to practice recognizing the kinds of writing you are asked to do. While in class you might be asked to select a topic and write an essay in which you argue a position (Chapter 6) or propose a solution (Chapter 7), in your service experience you might simply be asked to create a flyer that explains the importance of a no-kill animal shelter or a brochure that urges people to carpool as a way of cutting down traffic congestion. By identifying what kind of writing activity you are being asked to do, you can identify what basic features your readers will expect to find.

Writing in organizations is frequently a collaborative process. Everyone involved in the process is expected to do his or her part. When your written document will be used to represent your organization in any way, respect the expertise of the staff, especially when their assessment of the audience differs from your own. In some situations, your service writing may be heavily edited — or not used at all. Make sure your instructor and service-learning program administrators are aware of any instances in which you and members of the organization are having difficulty reaching a consensus.

For suggestions on how to make such collaboration run smoothly and successfully, see Chapter 29.

Finally, remember that nonacademic writing often requires greater attention to presentation than most kinds of academic writing. One-inch margins and double-spaced text simply are not enough when you are trying to create eye-catching documents such as brochures and press releases. Document design can not only make a piece of writing more visually attractive and thereby stimulate readers' interest but can also help readers with different needs identify which parts of the document are most relevant. Therefore, carefully consider the layout and configuration of your document, and take advantage of the flexibility that even a simple word processing program can give you.

For more on document design, see Chapter 21.

Handbook

How to Use This Handbook

You may be using the Handbook on your own when you edit your essays, or your instructor may guide you in using the Handbook to correct errors in your writing. If you are using the Handbook on your own, check the Handbook Contents on the next page, or look in the index for the kind of error you are concerned about — for example, "pronoun reference," "commas," "quotation marks," or "parallelism." If you cannot locate the information you need, ask your instructor or another student for advice.

Your instructor may use the Handbook's letter-and-number system to lead you directly to the page where you can learn how to correct an error. For example, the code "P1-b" indicates that a comma is needed after an introductory word, phrase, or clause. Referring to the Detailed Handbook Contents inside the back cover, you would discover that P1-b is on or near p. H-57 in the Handbook. As an alternative, you can find P1-b by flipping through the text and looking at the orange tabs at the tops of the pages. Each tab indicates the section code for that page and an abbreviation or a symbol for the topic covered on that page. If your instructor indicates errors in your sentences with conventional correction symbols such as *cap*, *frag*, or *ww*, you can find the section where the error is covered by checking the chart of correction symbols near the back of this book.

When you locate the Handbook section that will help you correct an error or make a sentence more concise or more graceful, you will find a brief explanation and a sentence or two illustrating correct usage, along with several hand-corrected sentences so you can see immediately how to edit your own sentence. Grammatical terms are defined in the margin. In addition, below the heading of each numbered Handbook section is a URL that you can use to access interactive online exercises for practice in the topics covered in that section.

We carried out extensive research in designing this Handbook. Ten college writing instructors and four professional editors worked together to identify errors* in more than five hundred student essays written in first-year composition courses by students using *The St. Martin's Guide to Writing*. These errors are listed below in order of descending frequency and can guide you in editing your own writing. The numbers in bold following each error indicate where in this Handbook you can find help with understanding and correcting each error.

---

* Spelling errors were not included.

Handbook Contents

Top 25 Errors in Student Papers

1. Wordiness **W1-a – W1-c**
2. Misused word **W2-a, W2-e**
3. Incorrect or ambiguous pronoun reference **G1**
4. Verb tense errors **G5-a, G5-b**
5. Missing comma between independent clauses **P1-a**
6. Problems with hyphens between compound adjectives **M1-a**
7. Missing comma after introductory elements **P1-b**
8. Capitalization of proper or common nouns **M2-a**
9. Unnecessary comma between compound elements **P2-a**

10. Incorrect spacing **M3**

11. Missing words **E1-a–E1-d**

12. Missing comma with nonrestrictive word groups **P1-c**

13. Comma splice or fused sentence **S1, S2**

14. Problems in using quotation marks with other punctuation **P6-b**

15. Missing or unnecessary hyphens in compound nouns **M1-b**

16. Missing comma with transitional and parenthetical expressions, absolute phrases, and contrasted elements **P1-d**

17. Problems of pronoun-antecedent agreement **G2**

18. Incorrect preposition **W2-b, L3**

19. Misuse of *who, which,* or *that* **G3**

20. Unnecessarily complex sentence structure **W1-b**

21. Spelling out or using figures for numbers incorrectly **M4**

22. Problems with apostrophes in possessive nouns **P7-a**

23. Sentence fragment **S3**

24. Missing comma in items in a series **P1-e**

25. Unnecessary comma with restrictive word groups **P2-b**

This list of the top twenty-five errors can be categorized into the following five major patterns of errors. You may find it useful to keep these patterns in mind as you edit your work.

1. Missing or unnecessary commas (**P1-a–P1-d, P2-a–P2-g**)

2. Errors in word choice (**W1-a–W1-d, W2-a–W2-d**)

3. Errors in pronoun reference, agreement, or use (**G1, G2, G3**)

4. Verb tense errors (**G5-a, G5-b**)

5. Errors in recognizing and punctuating sentences — comma splices, fused sentences, fragments (**S1, S2, S3**)

Keeping a Record of Your Own Errors

In addition to checking your work for the errors college students usually make, you will find it useful to keep a record of the errors that *you* usually make. You can then work toward avoiding them.

To use the Record of Errors form below, note the name and section number of each error you make in the left-hand column. (See the Handbook Contents on p. H-2 or the list of correction symbols at the back of the book for the names of errors.) For example, if in your first essay your instructor or another student marks a vague use of the pronoun *this* at the beginning of two of your sentences, locate the section that provides help in correcting this error (G1), and enter the error name in the left column along with the section number. Then under *Essay 1* and next to the name of the error, enter the number *2* to indicate how many times you made this error. As you edit subsequent essays, you can easily review this section in the Handbook to make sure you have avoided this pronoun problem.

By your second or third essay, you should begin to see patterns in the errors you make and to understand how to recognize and correct them.

This form is also available online at **bedfordstmartins .com/theguide.**

RECORD OF ERRORS							
Name of Error and Section Number in the Handbook	Essay 1	Essay 2	Essay 3	FREQUENCY Essay 4	Essay 5	Essay 6	Essay 7

S   Sentence Boundaries

S1   Comma Splices

For practice, go to bedfordstmartins.com/theguide/csplice

In a comma splice, two **independent clauses** are improperly joined by a comma.

┌—INDEPENDENT—┐ ┌—INDEPENDENT CLAUSE—┐
CLAUSE

COMMA SPLICE   **I know what to do, I just don't know how to do it.**

Because a comma splice can be edited in many ways, first consider how the ideas in the two independent clauses relate. For example, are they equally important, or does one depend on or explain the other? Then select the strategy below that will best clarify this relationship for a reader. To edit the example just given, for example, the writer might change the comma to a period.

▶ **I know what to do, I just don't know how to do it.**

Add a **subordinating conjunction** to one of the clauses, rewording as necessary.

After
▶ ~~The~~ New York City police began to crack down on minor offenders, a significant decrease in major crime resulted as well.

Though
▶ *Midnight Cowboy,* ~~was~~ rated X in the early 1970s, ~~it~~ contained one scene that was considered "sexually explicit," ~~yet~~ the movie was tastefully done and could not be considered pornographic by today's standards.

By beginning a clause with a subordinating conjunction, you indicate that the clause is subordinate to — and dependent on — the main clause. Usually, the **dependent clause** explains or qualifies the **independent clause**. Select the subordinating conjunction carefully so that it tells the reader how the ideas in the dependent clause relate to the ideas in the independent clause.

Separate the independent clauses with a comma and a **coordinating conjunction.**

▶ On the album *Other People's Songs,* Erasure has produced an eclectic collection
and
of cover treatments, the result highlights the group's strengths and weaknesses throughout its thirty-year recording career.

independent (main) clause A word group with a subject and a predicate that can stand alone as a separate sentence. (A predicate is the part of a clause that includes a complete verb and says something about the subject.)

subordinating conjunction A word or phrase (such as *although, because, since,* or *as soon as*) that introduces a dependent clause and relates it to an independent clause.

dependent (subordinate) clause A word group that has a subject, a predicate, and a subordinating word (such as *because*) at the beginning; it cannot stand by itself as a sentence but must be connected to an independent (main) clause.

coordinating conjunction A word that joins comparable and equally important sentence elements: *for, and, or, but, nor, yet,* or *so.*

> By 1988, the average American car had achieved a high of 26 mpg, *but* by 2003 that
>
> figure had fallen to less than 21 mpg.

The coordinating conjunction tells the reader that the ideas in the two clauses are closely related and equally important.

Separate the independent clauses with a semicolon.

> The tattoo needle appeared to be like an extension of his arm; the needle was his
>
> brush, and the human body, his canvas.

> Nate was very lucky; he lived to see his hundredth birthday.

The semicolon tells the reader that the ideas in the two clauses are closely connected, but it implies the connection rather than stating it. Occasionally, a colon may be used to introduce a second independent clause (see P4-a).

Separate the independent clauses with a semicolon or a period, and add a conjunctive adverb or a transitional phrase such as *for example* or *in other words*.

> He doesn't need the map right now; *instead* he just follows the direction Kiem pointed
>
> out to him before and checks it with the compass.

> He doesn't need the map right now. *Instead,* he just follows the direction Kiem pointed
>
> out to him before and checks it with the compass.

The semicolon tells the reader that the ideas in the two clauses are closely connected, and the conjunctive adverb describes the connection. The period shows a stronger break. Conjunctive adverbs are used more frequently in formal than in informal writing.

Note: A **subordinating conjunction** always begins a clause, but a conjunctive adverb can appear in other positions within a clause. If the conjunctive adverb appears in the middle of one clause rather than between two clauses, the semicolon is still placed between the clauses, not before the adverb.

> The importance of English as a link between those who have little else in
>
> common is clear; *in fact,* the true controversy lies in other issues.

conjunctive adverb A word or phrase (such as *finally, however,* or *therefore*) that tells how the ideas in two sentences or independent clauses are connected.

subordinating conjunction A word or phrase (such as *although, because, since,* or *as soon as*) that introduces a dependent clause and relates it to an independent clause.

Turn the independent clauses into separate sentences.

> ▶ At high noon we were off, paddling down the Potomac River, *We* ~~we~~ were two
>
> to a canoe, leaving space in the middle for our gear.

> ▶ Unfortunately, not many people realize how much scientific research with
>
> animals means to the medical world, *Only* ~~only~~ the scientists themselves and the
>
> diseased patients who suffer and hope for new cures can fully understand the
>
> importance of animal testing.

The period at the end of the first independent clause tells the reader that one complete sentence is ending and another is beginning.

Turn one independent clause into a phrase that modifies the other.

> ▶ At high noon we were off, paddling down the Potomac River, ~~we were~~ two to a
>
> canoe with space in the middle for our gear.

Eliminating the subject and verb in the second clause turns this clause into a **modifying phrase,** reducing the number of words and closely connecting the ideas.

> **modifying phrase** A word group that serves as an adjective or adverb.

S2   Fused Sentences

For practice, go to bedfordstmartins.com/theguide/fused

A fused or run-on sentence consists of two **independent clauses** run together with no punctuation.

FUSED SENTENCE	┌INDEPENDENT CLAUSE┐──────INDEPENDENT CLAUSE────────
	Her mood was good I took the opportunity to ask if she had a few minutes to answer some questions.

> **independent (main) clause** A word group with a subject and a predicate that can stand alone as a separate sentence. (A predicate is the part of a clause that includes a complete verb and says something about the subject.)

Because a fused sentence can be edited in many ways, first consider how the ideas in the two independent clauses are related, and then select the most appropriate strategy below. In the example just given, the writer might emphasize the causal relationship between the clauses.

> ▶ *Because her* ~~Her~~ mood was good, I took the opportunity to ask if she had a few minutes
>
> to answer some questions.

subordinating conjunction A word or phrase (such as *although, because, since,* or *as soon as*) that introduces a dependent clause and relates it to an independent clause.

Make one of the clauses subordinate to the other by adding a subordinating conjunction and rewording as necessary.

that
▶ Kids can be so cruel to each other ⌄ it is a wonder we all make it through childhood.

Although kids can be extremely   amazingly⌄
▶ ~~Kids can be so~~ cruel to each other ⌄ it is a wonder we all make it through childhood.

By beginning a clause with a subordinating conjunction, you indicate that the clause is subordinate to — and dependent on — the main clause. Usually, the **dependent clause** explains or qualifies the independent clause. Choose the subordinating conjunction carefully so that it tells the reader how the dependent clause relates to the independent clause.

dependent (subordinate) clause A word group that has a subject, a predicate, and a subordinating word (such as *because*) at the beginning; it cannot stand by itself as a sentence but must be connected to an independent (main) clause.

Add a comma and a coordinating conjunction to separate the independent clauses.

⌄ *and*
▶ The beast was upon me ⌄ I could feel his paws pressing down on my chest.

The coordinating conjunction tells the reader that the ideas in the two clauses are equally important.

coordinating conjunction A word that joins comparable and equally important sentence elements: *for, and, or, but, nor, yet,* or *so.*

Separate the independent clauses with a semicolon.

▶ I looked around at the different monitors ⌄ most were large color monitors, many

of which were connected to the central unit.

The semicolon tells the reader that the ideas in the two clauses are closely connected, but it implies the connection rather than stating it. Occasionally, a colon may be used to introduce a second independent clause (see P4-a).

conjunctive adverb A word or phrase (such as *finally, however,* or *therefore*) that tells how the ideas in two sentences or independent clauses are connected.

Separate the independent clauses with a semicolon or a period, and add a conjunctive adverb or a transitional phrase such as *for example* or *in other words*.

⌄ *instead⌄*
▶ Most students do not do their homework during the day ⌄ they do it in the evening.

⌄ *Instead⌄*
▶ Most students do not do their homework during the day ⌄ they do it in the evening.

The semicolon indicates that the ideas in the two clauses are closely connected, and the conjunctive adverb explains the connection. The period indicates a stronger break. Conjunctive adverbs appear more frequently in formal than in informal writing.

Note: A **subordinating conjunction** always *introduces* a clause, but a conjunctive adverb can occupy different positions within a clause. If the conjunctive adverb appears in the middle of one clause rather than between two clauses, the semicolon is still placed between the clauses, not before the adverb.

▶ Most students do not do their homework during the day they do it in the evening.

^;^   ^instead^

Turn the independent clauses into separate sentences.

▶ He was only eight. ~~his~~ *His* life hadn't even started.

▶ I couldn't believe it. I had fallen into a puddle of mud.

The period at the end of the first independent clause tells the reader that one complete sentence is ending and another is beginning.

Turn one independent clause into a phrase that modifies the other.

▶ The beast was upon me, ~~I could feel~~ his paws pressing down on my chest.

Eliminating the subject and verb in the second clause turns this clause into a **modifying phrase**, reducing the number of words and closely linking the ideas.

S3   Sentence Fragments

For practice, go to bedfordstmartins.com/theguide/frag

A fragment is either an incomplete sentence, lacking a complete **subject** or **predicate**, or a **dependent clause** punctuated as a sentence. Even though a fragment begins with a capital letter and ends with a period, it cannot stand alone as a sentence.

FRAGMENT   Tonight it's my turn. *A ride-along with Sergeant Rob Nether of the Green Valley Police Department.*

Because a fragment can often be edited in several ways, begin by considering what the fragment lacks and how its ideas relate to those in the sentences before and after it. Then use one of the following strategies to change the fragment into a complete sentence. To edit the fragment in the example, the writer might connect it to the preceding sentence.

▶ Tonight it's my turn, *for a* ~~A~~ ride-along with Sergeant Rob Nether of the Green Valley Police Department.

modifying phrase A word group that serves as an adjective or adverb.

subject The part of a clause that identifies who or what is being discussed: At the checkpoint, *we* unloaded the canoes.

predicate The part of a clause that includes a complete verb and says something about the subject: At the checkpoint, we *unloaded the canoes.*

dependent (subordinate) clause A word group that has a subject, a predicate, and a subordinating word (such as *because*) at the beginning; it cannot stand by itself as a sentence but must be connected to an independent (main) clause: *Although it was raining*, we loaded our gear onto the buses.

Connect the fragment to a complete sentence.

▶ Frank turned the tarot cards one at a time, ~~Each~~ *each* time telling me something about my future.

▶ A unique design has the distinct advantage of becoming associated with its role, ~~For~~ *for* example, the highly successful Coke bottle shape, which is now associated with soft drinks.

Eliminate the subordinating word or words that make a clause dependent.

▶ The world that I was born into demanded continuous work. ~~Where nobody~~ *Nobody* got ahead, and everyone came home tired.

Add or complete the verb or the subject to change a fragment into a complete sentence.

▶ The crowd in the lounge is basically young. The teenage and early twenties generation *gathers there.*

▶ Children are brought up in different ways. Some *grow up* around violence.

Note: Sometimes writers use fragments intentionally for emphasis or special effect.

The bare utility of the clock echoes the simplicity of the office. No sign of a large hardwood desk or a pillowy leather chair or even a wall with shelves filled with imposing law books.

Use intentional fragments cautiously. Especially in academic writing, many readers may perceive them as errors, regardless of your intentions. In the example above, for instance, the same impact might also be achieved by using a colon or dash.

G Grammatical Sentences

G1 Pronoun Reference

For practice, go to bedfordstmartins.com/theguide/pref

Make sure that each **pronoun** clearly refers to one specific **antecedent**.

> *The elderly and children* are victims when no one bothers to check on *them*.

In this example, the pronoun *them* refers to a specific antecedent, *the elderly and children*.

Rewrite to eliminate vague uses of *they, it*, or *you*.

> ▶ Lani explained that everything is completely supported by individual
> *The organization receives*
> contributions. ~~They receive~~ no tax support.
>   ^

> ▶ Often, a guest such as Martha Stewart or Tom Hanks may appear
>   *having the same guest return*
> more than once. Although ~~it~~ seems repetitious, it actually is not because the
>   ^
> guest discusses different topics each time.

> ▶ Parents argue that beginning the program in the sixth grade is too early.
> *They say that*   *encourages*
> ~~By~~ exposing teens to sex education early, ~~you encourage~~ them to go out and
> ^   ^
> have sex.

Add a noun, change the pronoun to a noun, or revise the sentence to eliminate vague uses of *this, that*, or *which*.

> ▶ Researchers have noticed that men interrupt women more than women
>   *finding*
> interrupt men. This may explain why women sometimes find it difficult to start
>   ^
> and sustain conversations with men.

>   *good grades*
> ▶ I was an *A* student, and I thought ~~that~~ should have been enough for any
>   ^
> teacher.

---

pronoun A word that replaces a specific noun (such as *she, it, his, they, them, yours, ours, myself, whose,* or *which*), points out a specific noun (such as *this, these,* or *that*), or refers to an unspecified person or object (such as *everybody* or *each*).

antecedent The word or words that a pronoun replaces and to which it refers.

▶ The brevity of the first story prevents the reader from dwelling on the plot

and caring about the outcome. ~~These~~ ^{Because these} faults are not present in "The Soft

Voice of the Serpent," ~~which makes~~ ^{is} it much more fulfilling to read.

Add a missing antecedent, or eliminate a pronoun with no clear antecedent.

▶ In addition to the cars your tenants actually drive, five or six vehicles are

always on and around the property. As a result, not only do ~~they~~ ^{your tenants} park ~~some of~~

~~them~~ in front of their neighbors' homes, but their questionable visitors park up

and down the street as well.

Adding an antecedent (specifying *your tenants* instead of *they*) and eliminating a pronoun (reducing *park some of them* to *park*) simplify and clarify the sentence.

Identify a specific antecedent if a pronoun refers vaguely to a clause or a whole sentence.

▶ After the long ride, we reached the place for our expedition at Pine Heaven

Forest in western Virginia. At my age, ~~it~~ ^{the trip} seemed to take forever.

Rewrite to eliminate an ambiguous reference to two possible antecedents.

▶ Students may now sue their schools ~~if they~~ ^{if} are underperforming.

▶ Students may now sue their schools. ^{underperforming} ~~if they are underperforming.~~

Rewrite to eliminate an implied reference.

▶ ~~This~~ ^{In this} song ^{the singer} tells about being carefree and going through life without any worries.

Years later, though, he starts to remember his past, and things do not seem so

problem-free anymore.

In this example, adding *the singer* specifies an antecedent for *he*.

Note: Sometimes the implied noun may be present in another form, such as a possessive (*Mary's* for *Mary*) or as part of another word (*child* in *childhood*).

> Radaker's ~~arguments~~ irritated everyone at the lecture because he failed to
>
> *his arguments*
> support ~~them~~ with examples or evidence.

G2   Pronoun Agreement

For practice, go to bedfordstmartins.com/theguide/pagree

Make sure that a **pronoun** and its **antecedent** agree in **number**, in **person**, and in **gender**. In the following examples, the arrows connect the pronouns and their antecedents.

The *scientists* did not know what *they* were creating.

I thought about Punita's offer while watching the movie. *My* curiosity won.

After we went back to the lab, *Punita* started concentrating on *her* work.

The form of the antecedent and the form of the pronoun must correspond — agree — so that a reader is not troubled by inconsistencies or confused about how many, who, or which gender you mean.

G2-a   Use either singular or plural forms consistently for both a pronoun and its antecedent.

If the antecedent of a pronoun is singular, the pronoun must be singular so that both agree in number. Likewise, if the antecedent is plural, the pronoun must be plural.

The *shelter* gets most of *its* cats and dogs from *owners* who cannot keep *their* pets.

When the pronoun and its antecedent do not agree, change one or the other so that both are singular or both are plural, or rewrite the sentence to eliminate the inconsistency. See also E2-b.

Change either the pronoun or its antecedent so that both are singular or plural.

he or she is
> The patient is fully aware of the decision that ~~they are~~ making.

Patients are
> ~~The patient is~~ fully aware of the decision that they are making.

Note: As an alternative, you may be able to eliminate the pronoun.

each
> The patient is fully aware of the decision that ~~they are making.~~

---

pronoun A word that replaces a specific noun (such as *she, it, his, they, them, yours, ours, myself, whose,* or *which*), points out a specific noun (such as *this, these,* or *that*), or refers to an unspecified person or object (such as *everybody* or *each*).

antecedent The word or words that a pronoun replaces and to which it refers.

number The form of a word that shows whether it refers to one thing (singular) or more than one (plural): *parent, parents; child, children.*

person The form of a word that shows whether it refers to *I* or *we* (first person), to *you* (second person), or to *he, she, it,* or *they* (third person).

gender The form of a word that shows whether it refers to a male (*he*) or a female (*she*).

Revise the sentence to eliminate the inconsistency.

▶ Roommates get agitated at always being told to clean, and the roommate

complaining
doing the yelling gets tired of ~~hearing their own voice complain.~~
                                          ^

indefinite pronoun A pronoun that does not refer to a particular person or object, such as *anybody, anyone, each, everyone, everything, somebody, something, neither, none,* or *nobody* (which take the singular); *few, many,* and *several* (which take the plural); and *all, most,* and *some* (which can take either the singular or plural).

Use a singular pronoun to refer to a singular indefinite pronoun, or reword the sentence.

▶ Whether student, teacher, faculty member, graduate, or parent, each wants

his or her
~~their~~ school to be the one that remains open.
 ^

All students, teachers, faculty members, graduates, and parents want
▶ ~~Whether student, teacher, faculty member, graduate, or parent, each wants~~
 ^

their school to be the one that remains open.

students
▶ This event would be a good chance for ~~everyone~~ to come out, socialize, and
                                              ^

enjoy themselves.

▶ This event would be a good chance for everyone to come out, socialize, and

a relaxing afternoon.
enjoy ~~themselves.~~
 ^

Consider the level of formality of your writing as you choose among your options. Participants in a casual conversation may not mind if an indefinite pronoun and its antecedent do not agree, but such errors are not acceptable in most formal writing.

collective noun A noun (such as *class* or *family*) that refers to a group as a unit and is usually considered singular.

Use a singular pronoun in most cases if the antecedent is a collective noun.

its
▶ The Santa Barbara School District has a serious problem on ~~their~~ agenda.
                                                                  ^

A collective noun may sometimes be considered plural if it refers to the group members as individuals: The *couple* decided it was time to consolidate *their* bank accounts.

See also G6-b.

antecedent The word or words that a pronoun replaces and to which it refers.

G2-b Use masculine, feminine, or gender-free forms to match a pronoun with its **antecedent.**

Match a masculine pronoun with a masculine antecedent and a feminine pronoun with a feminine antecedent so that the pronoun and its antecedent agree in **gender.**

gender The form of a word that shows whether it refers to a male (*he*) or a female (*she*).

I first met *Mark* the day *he* was hired.

If an antecedent might be either masculine or feminine, avoid using a pronoun that stereotypes by gender. See also W3-c.

Match a plural antecedent with a plural pronoun to include both sexes.

> *children are*
> Many people believe that ~~a boy or girl is~~ better off with a family that is able to provide for all of their needs than with a poverty-stricken parent.

Use a phrase that includes both masculine and feminine singular pronouns (such as *his or her*) to refer to both sexes.

> Many people believe that a child is better off with a family that is able to
>
> *his or her*
> provide for all of ~~their~~ needs than with a poverty-stricken parent.

Note: If repeating a phrase such as *his* or *her* seems cumbersome or repetitious, try using plural forms or eliminating the pronouns altogether, as the following strategy suggests.

Rewrite to eliminate unneeded or awkward pairs of masculine and feminine pronouns when you are referring to both men and women.

> *drivers*   *they are*
> This solution, of course, assumes that the bus ~~driver~~ will be where ~~he/she is~~
>
> *drivers*
> supposed to be; boredom sometimes inspires ~~a driver~~ to make up new
>
> *the*
> and exciting variations on ~~his or her~~ designated routes.

Note: Avoid using *he/she* in all but the most informal writing situations.

G3   Relative Pronouns

For practice, go to bedfordstmartins.com/theguide/relp

Use personal **relative pronouns** to refer to people: *who, whom, whoever, whomever,* and *whose.*

> This reaction is unlike the response of the boys, *who* had trouble focusing on a subject.

Use nonpersonal relative pronouns to refer to things: *which, whichever, whatever,* and *whose* (*whose* can be used as a nonpersonal relative pronoun as well as a personal one).

> **relative pronoun** A pronoun (such as *who, whom, whose, which,* or *that*) that introduces an adjective clause (a clause that modifies a noun or pronoun).

These interruptions, 75 percent of *which* come solely from males, disrupt conversations.

Use *that* for general references to things and groups.

Sensory modalities are governed by the side of the brain *that* is not damaged.

See also G6-e.

G3-a   Select *who* for references to people, *which* for nonrestrictive references to things, and *that* for restrictive references to groups and things.

My attention focused on a little dark-haired boy *who* was crying.

The tournament, *which* we had worked for all year, was the most prestigious event of the season.

Save Our Sharks tried to promote a bill *that* would forbid the killing of certain sharks.

Change *that* to *who* to refer to a person.

▶ Illness phobics have countless examinations despite the reassurance of each
        who
   physician ~~that~~ examines them.

            who
▶ It was his parents ~~that~~ made him run for student council, play the piano, and go out for sports.

Note: Rewriting a sentence to simplify its structure sometimes eliminates a problem with pronouns.

    His
▶ ~~It was his~~ parents ~~that~~ made him run for student council, play the piano, and go out for sports.

See also G3-b for information on *who* and *whom*.

Change *that* to *which* when a nonrestrictive clause supplies extra, nondefining information.

             , *which*
▶ Caroline had the prettiest jet-black hair ~~that~~ went down to the middle of her back.

(See P1-c on using commas with nonrestrictive word groups.)

---

nonrestrictive clause A clause, set off by commas, that provides extra or nonessential information and could be eliminated without changing the meaning of the noun or pronoun it modifies.

restrictive clause A clause, not set off by commas, that provides information essential to defining or identifying the noun or pronoun it modifies.

Change *which* to *that* when a restrictive clause supplies essential information defining a thing or a group.

> *that*
> ▶ From the moment we are born, we come into a society ~~which~~ assimilates us into
>
> its culture.

> *that*
> ▶ In addition to the equipment and technology ~~which~~ fill the trauma room,
>
> a team of experts assembles before the patient arrives.

(See P2-b on unnecessary commas with restrictive word groups.)

Note: Which is usually used only in nonrestrictive clauses, but sometimes writers use it in restrictive clauses as well.

G3-b Use *who* as a subject and *whom* as an object.

Two strategies can help you to figure out which word to use.

1. Mark the phrase or clause, and then arrange its words in subject-verb-object order or **preposition**-object order. In this standard order, a subject (*who*) is followed by a verb, but an object (*whom*) follows a subject and verb or follows a preposition.
2. Look for the subject of the clause. If the verb in the clause has another subject, use *whom;* if the verb in the clause has no other subject, use *who.*

SUBJECT	We remember [*who* tips well] and [*who* doesn't].
	I will always admire whom.
OBJECT OF VERB	Mr. Scott is someone [*whom* I will always admire].
OBJECT OF PREPOSITION	The university employs a large number of foreign teaching assistants [for *whom* English is a second language].

Change *who* to *whom* when the pronoun is an object within another clause that has a subject and a verb.

> *whom*
> ▶ He has the ability to attract guests ~~who~~ people want to hear.

Change *who* to *whom* when the pronoun is the object of a preposition.

> *whom*
> ▶ He also met his wife, ~~who~~ he was married to for fifty-two years.

> *to whom*
> ▶ He also met his wife, ~~who~~ he was married ~~to~~ for fifty-two years.

---

restrictive clause A clause, not set off by commas, that provides information essential to defining or identifying the noun or pronoun it modifies.

object The part of a clause that receives the action of the verb (At the checkpoint, we unloaded *the canoes*) or the part of a phrase that follows a preposition (We dragged them to *the river*).

preposition A word (such as *between, in,* or *of*) that always appears as part of a phrase and indicates the relation between a word in a sentence and the object of the preposition: The water splashed *into* the canoe.

Change *whom* to *who* when the pronoun is the subject of a clause, followed by a verb.

▶ The libraries are staffed by professionals ~~whom~~ *who* have instituted methods to keep students informed of new materials.

G4   Pronoun Case

For practice, go to bedfordstmartins.com/theguide/pcase

A pronoun can take different forms or cases, depending on its role in a sentence.

▪ Subject or **subject complement:** *I, we, you, he, she, it, they* (subjective form)

"*You*'d better be careful," *she* said.

It is *we* you owe the money to.

▪ Object of a verb or a **preposition:** *me, us, you, him, her, it, them* (objective form)

This realization spurred *me* to hasten the search.

Her dog, Peter the Great, went with *her* on the excavation in southern Siberia.

▪ Possession or ownership: *mine, ours, yours, his, hers, theirs, my, our, your, his, her, its, their* (possessive form)

I trusted *his* driving.

I finished putting *my* gear on and rolled over backward into the ocean.

See R2-a for more on pronouns.

Replace a reflexive pronoun that does not refer to another noun or pronoun in the clause.

▶ Kyle and ~~myself~~ *I* went upstairs to see how she was doing.

A reflexive pronoun does not belong in this sentence because *myself* does not refer to a preceding *I*.

Change a pronoun to the subjective form if it is part of a compound subject.

▶ Even though Annie and ~~me~~ *I* went through the motions, we didn't understand the customs of our host.

---

subject complement A word or word group that follows a linking verb (such as *seems, appears,* or *is* and other forms of *be*) and describes or restates the subject: The tents looked *old and dirty*.

preposition A word (such as *between, in,* or *of*) that always appears as part of a phrase and indicates the relation between a word in a sentence and the object of the preposition: The water splashed *into* the canoe.

reflexive pronoun A pronoun such as *myself* or *ourselves* that refers to a noun or a personal pronoun in the same clause.

compound subject Two or more words acting as a subject and linked by *and*.

Change a pronoun to the objective form if it is an object (or part of a compound object) of a preposition or a verb.

> *her*   *me*
> ▶ There was an invisible wall between ~~she~~ and ~~I~~.

Change a pronoun to the possessive form when it modifies a gerund.

> *my*
> ▶ One of the main reasons for ~~me~~ wanting to stay home with my children until they enter grade school is that I would miss so much.

Change the form of a pronoun to fit the implied or understood wording of a comparison using *than* or *as*.

> *she*
> ▶ I was still faster than ~~her~~.

Test whether a pronoun form fits by filling in the implied wording.

INCORRECT PRONOUN   I was still faster than *her* [was fast].

CORRECT PRONOUN   I was still faster than *she* [was fast].

Use *we* to precede a subject or *us* to precede an object.

We is the subjective form, and *us* is the objective form. Select the form that matches the role of the noun in the sentence.

> *we*
> ▶ Whenever ~~us~~ neighborhood kids would go out and play, I would always be goalie.

Test your choice of pronoun by reading the sentence with the noun left out.

INCORRECT PRONOUN   Whenever *us* would go out and play, I would always be goalie.

CORRECT PRONOUN   Whenever *we* would go out and play, I would always be goalie.

G5   Verbs

For practice, go to bedfordstmartins.com/theguide/verbs

Use standard verb forms in the appropriate **tense, mood,** and **voice.**

G5-a   Select the appropriate verb tense to place events in past, present, and future time.

Most of the time you will probably choose the correct verb tense without thinking about it. (See R2-a for a review of the basic verb tenses.) In a few situations, however, you will need to pay special attention to conventional usage or to the relationships among different verbs within the context of your essay.

> ### For ESL Writers
>
> See L2 for advice on how to use the correct tense in conditional clauses, two-word verbs, and helping (auxiliary) verbs and whether to use a gerund or infinitive form after a verb.

Change verbs from the past tense to the present when discussing events in a literary work or film, general truths, ongoing principles, and facts.

▶ In the "Monkey Garden," the girl ~~knew~~ *knows* it ~~was~~ *is* time to grow up but still

~~wanted~~ *wants* to play with the other kids in her make-believe world.

▶ In the film, Virginia Woolf (Nicole Kidman) ~~was~~ *is* an intensely neurotic woman

whose diet ~~seemed~~ *seems* to consist entirely of cigarettes.

Academic readers expect this use of the present tense in a literary analysis, as if the action in a work is always present and ongoing. Readers also expect general truths, facts, and ongoing principles to be stated in the present tense. See also E2-a.

GENERAL TRUTH   The family *is* the foundation for a child's education.

ONGOING
PRINCIPLE   Attaining self-sufficiency *is* one of the most important priorities of our energy policy.

FACT   The earth *is tilted* at an angle of 23 degrees.

Note: Some style guides make different recommendations about verb tense, depending on the field and its conventions. The style guide of the American Psychological Association (APA), for example, recommends using the past tense for past studies and past research procedures but using the present tense for research implications and conclusions.

APA STYLE   Davidson *stated* that father absence *is* more than twice as common now as in our parents' generation.

Change the verb from the past tense to the past perfect (using *had*) to show that one past action already had taken place before another past action occurred.

▶ The victim's roommate also claimed that she *had* called the dorm office two days

prior to the suicide attempt.

The past action identified by the verb *had called* occurred before the past action identified by the verb *claimed*.

For ESL Writers

Certain verbs — ones that indicate existence, states of mind, and the senses of sight, smell, touch, and so on — are rarely used in the **progressive tense**. Such verbs include *appear, be, belong, contain, feel, forget, have, hear, know, mean, prefer, remember, see, smell, taste, think, understand*, and *want*.

> *belong*
> ▶ I ~~am belonging~~ to the campus group for foreign students.

---

progressive tense A tense that shows ongoing action, consisting of a form of *be* plus the *-ing* form of the main verb: I *am waiting*.

G5-b Use the correct verb endings and verb forms.

The five basic forms of regular verbs (such as *talk*) follow the same pattern, adding *-s, -ed*, and *-ing* as shown here. The forms of irregular verbs (such as *speak*) do not consistently follow this pattern in forming the past and the past participle. (See R2-a.)

- Infinitive or base: *talk* or *speak*

  Every day I *talk* on the phone and *speak* to my friends.

- Third-person singular present (*-s* form): *talks* or *speaks*

  He *talks* softly, and she *speaks* slowly.

- Past: *talked* or *spoke*

  I *talked* to my parents last week, and I *spoke* to Jed on Tuesday.

- Present participle (*-ing* form): *talking* or *speaking*

  She is *talking* on the phone now, and he is *speaking* to a friend.

- Past participle (*-ed* form): *talked* or *spoken*

  I have *talked* to her many times, but she has not *spoken* to him yet.

Add an *-s* or *-es* ending to a verb when the subject is in the third-person singular (*he, she, it,* or a singular noun).

> *treats*
> ▶ The national drug control policy ~~treat~~ drug abuse as a law enforcement problem.

> *accounts*
> ▶ This group ~~account~~ for more than 10 percent of the total U.S. population.

For ESL Writers

Choosing the correct verb form is sometimes complicated by English expressions. For example, *used to* followed by the base form of the verb does not mean the same as *get used to* followed by a gerund.

> In the United States, most people *used to live* in rural areas. [This situation existed in the past but has changed.]

> My daughter *is getting used to going* to school every day. [She is getting in the habit of attending school.]

(For more on choosing correct word forms, see W2.)

Delete an *-s* or *-es* ending from a verb when the subject is in the first person (*I, we*), second person (*you*), or third-person plural (*they*).

> *suggest*
> ▶ Because I didn't tell you about the movie, I really ~~suggests~~ that you go see it.

Add a *-d* or an *-ed* ending to a regular verb to form the past tense or the past participle.

> ▶ This movie was filmed in New Orleans because it resembles the city where the
> *supposed*
> story is ~~suppose~~ to take place.

> *explained*
> ▶ As we walked through the library, she ~~explain~~ the meaning of the yellow signs.

Check to be sure you have used the correct form of an irregular verb.

If you are uncertain about a verb form, refer to the list of irregular verbs in R2-a or check your dictionary.

> *led*
> ▶ The hostess greeted us and ~~lead~~ us to our seats.

> *come*
> ▶ We could tell our food had just ~~came~~ off the grill because it still sizzled.

Note: Some verbs with different meanings are confusing because they have similar forms. For example, the verb *lie* (*lie, lay, lain, lying*) means "recline," but the verb *lay* (*lay, laid, laid, laying*) means "put or place." Check such verbs in the Glossary of Frequently Misused Words at the end of this Handbook or in a dictionary to make sure that you are using the correct forms of the word you intend.

> *lying*
> ▶ I thought everyone was going to see my car ~~laying~~ on its side.

G5-c Choose the correct form of a verb to show the indicative, imperative, or subjunctive mood.

INDICATIVE There *was* Ward, the perfect father, who *served* as sole provider for the family.

Where *are* the Cleavers today?

IMPERATIVE *Take* me to the mall.

SUBJUNCTIVE If it *were* to rain on the day of the picnic, we would simply bring everything indoors.

The subjunctive is often used in clauses with *if* or *that*. Always use the **base form** of the verb for the present subjunctive (see G5-b). For the past tense of the verb *be*, the subjunctive form is *were*, not *was*.

> *were*
> Even if this claim ~~was~~ true, it would raise a very controversial issue.

> *were*
> It was as if he ~~was~~ stretching his neck to pick leaves or fruit out of a high tree.

G5-d Use verbs primarily in the active voice.

The **active voice** calls attention to the actor performing an action. By contrast, the **passive voice** emphasizes the recipient of the action or the action itself while omitting or deemphasizing the actor.

ACTIVE The monkey *lived* in the garden.

PASSIVE The story *is told* by a girl as she reflects on her own childhood.

Change passive verbs to active in most writing situations.

Straightforward and direct, the active voice creates graceful, clear writing that emphasizes actors.

> *girl tells the story*
> The ~~story is told by the girl~~ as she reflects on her own childhood.

> *The*   *attract physicians.*
> ~~Physicians are attracted by the~~ monetary rewards of high-tech research.

Rewrite to eliminate awkward, unnecessary passive verbs.

> *^ seeking others with similar interests.*
> The guests cluster like grapes ~~as similar interests are sought~~.

indicative mood The verb form that is ordinarily used for statements and questions.

imperative mood The verb form used for commands or directions.

subjunctive mood The verb form that is used for wishes, suggestions, and conditions that are hypothetical, impossible, or unlikely.

base form The uninflected form of a verb: I *eat; to play.*

active voice The verb form that shows the subject in action: The cat *caught* the mouse.

passive voice The verb form that shows something happening to the subject: The mouse *was caught* by the cat.

Note: The passive is sometimes useful if you want to shift information to the end of a sentence. It is also frequently used in impersonal writing that focuses on an action rather than an actor, as in a scientific research report.

> When the generator *is turned on*, water *is forced* down the tunnel, and the animals swim against the current. Their metabolism *is measured*. They have participated in this experiment before, and the results from that run and this new one *will be compared*.

G6   Subject-Verb Agreement

For practice, go to bedfordstmartins.com/theguide/svagree

Use **subjects** and **verbs** that agree in **person** and **number.** Agreement problems often occur when a sentence has a complicated subject or verb, especially when the subject and verb are separated by other words.

▶ The large amounts of money that are associated with sports ~~is~~ *are* not the problem.

The plural subject, *amounts*, requires a plural verb, *are*. See also R2-a to check the correct forms of *be* and other irregular verbs.

G6-a   Make sure the subject and verb agree even if they are separated by other words.

> The *relationship* between artists and politicians *has become* a controversial issue.

First identify the subject and the verb; then change one to agree with the other.

▶ The pattern of echoes from these sound waves ~~are~~ *is* converted by computer into a visual image.

▶ The ~~pattern of~~ echoes from these sound waves are converted by computer into a visual image.

G6-b   Use a singular verb with a subject that is a **collective noun.**

> The *association distributes* information on showing bison, selling bison, and marketing bison meat.

Change the verb to a singular form if the subject is a collective noun.

---

subject The part of a clause that identifies who or what is being discussed: At the checkpoint, *we* unloaded the canoes.

verb A word or phrase that expresses action or being and, along with a subject, is a basic component of a sentence: At the checkpoint, we *unloaded* the canoes.

person The form of a word that shows whether it refers to *I* or *we* (first person), to *you* (second person), or to *he, she, it*, or *they* (third person).

number The form of a word that shows whether it refers to one thing (singular) or more than one (plural): *parent, parents; child, children.*

collective noun A noun (such as *class* or *family*) that refers to a group as a unit and is usually considered singular.

▶ If a military team ~~fight~~ without spirit and will, it will probably lose.
fights

Note: A collective noun is generally considered singular because it treats a group as a single unit. If it refers to the members of the group as individuals, however, it may be considered plural.

SINGULAR   The *staff is* amiable.
(GROUP AS A UNIT)

PLURAL   The *staff exchange* greetings and small talk as *they begin* putting
(INDIVIDUAL MEMBERS) on *their* surgical garb.

G6-c Use a verb that agrees with a subject placed after it.

In most sentences, the subject precedes the verb, but some sentences are inverted. For example, sentences beginning with *there is* and *there are* reverse the standard order, putting the subject after the verb.

VERB ┌────SUBJECT────────┐
There *are no busy lines and brushstrokes* in the paintings.

VERB ┌SUBJECT┐
There *is interaction* between central and peripheral visual fields.

In inverted sentences, change the verb so that it agrees with the subject that follows it, or rewrite the sentence.

▶ The next morning, there ~~was~~ Mike and Cindy, acting as if nothing had happened.
were

▶ The next morning, ~~there was~~ Mike and Cindy, acting as if nothing had happened.
were

G6-d Use a plural verb with a compound subject.

┌────SUBJECT────────┐ VERB
She and her husband have a partnership with her in-laws.

Two subjects joined by *and* require a plural verb.

▶ Dust and dirt ~~accumulates~~, bathrooms get mildewy, and kitchens get greasy.
accumulate

Note: If two subjects are joined by *or* or *nor*, the verb should agree with the subject that is closer to it.

Most nights, my daughter or my sons *start* dinner.

compound subject Two or more words acting as a subject and linked by *and*.

antecedent The word or words that a pronoun replaces and to which it refers.

G6-e Use a verb that agrees with the antecedent of the pronoun *who, which,* or *that.*

Its staff consists of nineteen *people* who *drive* to work in any kind of weather to make sure the station comes through for its listeners.

To check agreement, identify the antecedent of the pronoun.

▶ Within the ordered chaos of the trauma room are diagnostic tools, surgical
    are
    devices, and X-ray equipment, which ~~is~~ required for Sharp to be designated a
    trauma center.

▶ The males choose topics that enable them to establish dominance over others
    encourage
    in the group, while the females tell personally moving stories that ~~encourages~~
    others to show their feelings.

Note: With the phrase *one of the* followed by a plural noun, use a verb that agrees with the noun.

One of the *features* that *make* the monitor different is that it doubles as a television.

G6-f Use a singular verb with an indefinite pronoun.

Everything on the playground *is* child friendly.

During informal conversation, people sometimes treat indefinite pronouns as plural forms. In formal writing, however, an indefinite pronoun usually refers to a single person or object and agrees with a singular verb.

indefinite pronoun A pronoun that does not refer to a particular person or object, such as *anybody, each, one, everyone, everything, somebody, something, neither, none,* or *nobody* (which take the singular); *few, many,* and *several* (which take the plural); and *all, most,* and *some* (which can take either the singular or plural).

                                                                          seems
▶ There are two alternatives to this solution, and neither ~~seem~~ feasible.

Note: If an indefinite pronoun such as *all, none,* or *some* refers to a plural noun, use a plural form of the verb. If it refers to a singular noun, use a singular form.

Some manage to find jobs that fit their schedule, the surf schedule.

Most are respectable people.

All of the money *is* missing.

G6-g Use a verb that agrees with the subject rather than a subject complement.

The shark's favorite *diet is* elephant seals and sea lions.

When either the subject or the subject complement names a group or category, the choice between a singular or plural verb becomes confusing. Make sure that the verb agrees with the actual subject. If necessary, rewrite the sentence.

> Big blocks of color in a simple flat shape *~~is~~* his artistic trademark.
> <small>are</small>

> <small>He favors big</small>
> Big blocks of color in a simple flat shape. ~~is his artistic trademark.~~

> **subject complement**
> A word or word group that follows a linking verb (such as *seems*, *appears*, or *is* and other forms of *be*) and describes or restates the subject: The tents looked *old and dirty*.

G7   Adjectives and Adverbs

For practice, go to bedfordstmartins.com/theguide/adjadv

Distinguish **adjectives** from **adverbs** so that you select the correct forms of these **modifiers**. See also R2-a.

ADJECTIVES	Because *angry* drivers are *dangerous* drivers, it is *imperative* that the county implement *a* solution.
ADVERB	Installing traffic lights would *quickly* alleviate three important aspects of the problem.

> **adjective** A word that modifies a noun or a pronoun, adding information about it.

> **adverb** A word that modifies a verb, an adjective, or another adverb, often telling when, where, why, how, or how often.

G7-a Select an adverb, not an adjective, to modify an adjective, another adverb, or a verb.

Often ending in *-ly*, adverbs tell how, when, where, why, and how often.

Despite a *very* busy work schedule, Caesar finds time in the afternoon to come *directly* to the high school and work as a volunteer track coach.

Change an adjective that modifies another adjective, an adverb, or a verb to an adverb form.

> <small>loudly</small>
> This man yelled at me so ~~loud~~ that I began to cry.

> **modifier** A word, phrase, or clause functioning as an adjective or adverb that adds information and detail about a noun, a verb, or another word.

Note: Adjective forms that are common in informal conversation should be changed to adverb forms in more formal writing.

SPOKEN	The day was going *slow,* and I repeatedly caught my lure on the riverbed or a tree limb.

WRITTEN   The day was going *slowly*, and I repeatedly caught my lure on the riverbed or a tree limb.

G7-b Select an adjective, not an adverb, to modify a noun or a pronoun.

I am enamored of the *cool* motor, the *massive* boulder in the middle of the lake, and the sound of the wake *splashing* against the side of the two-seater.

Change an adverb that modifies a noun or a pronoun to an adjective.

traditional
▶ Working within a ~~traditionally~~ chronological plot, Joyce develops the protagonist's emotional conflict.

An adjective generally appears immediately before or after the word it modifies. When an adjective acts as a **subject complement**, however, it is separated from the word it modifies by a **linking verb**.

My grandfather is *amazing*.

Note: Some verbs act as linking verbs only in certain contexts. When one of these verbs connects a subject and its complement, use an adjective form: She looked *ill*. When the verb is modified by the word that follows it, however, use an adverb: She looked *quickly*.

> ### For ESL Writers
>
> ESL writers sometimes have trouble choosing between past and present participles (*looked*, *looking*) used as adjectives. See L6 for help in selecting the correct form.

G7-c Select the correct forms of adjectives and adverbs to show comparisons.

Add *-er* or *-est* to short words (usually of one or two syllables), and use *more, most, less*, and *least* with longer words and all *-ly* adverbs.

The southern peninsula's *smallest* kingdom was invaded continually by its two *more powerful* neighbors.

Use *-er, more,* or *less* (the comparative form) to compare two things.

I had always been a little bit *faster* than she was.

---

subject complement A word or word group that follows a linking verb (such as *seems, appears*, or *is* and other forms of *be*) and describes or restates the subject: The tents looked *old and dirty*.

linking verb *Be, seem, appear, become, taste,* or another verb that connects a subject with a subject complement that describes or modifies it: The chips *taste* salty.

Use *-est, most,* or *least* (the superlative form) to compare three or more.

An elite warrior corps grew that soon gained the respect of even its *most bitter* foes.

Change the forms of adjectives and adverbs to show comparison precisely.

▶ She has clearly been the ~~least~~ ^{less} favored child in the sense that she is not as

beautiful or as intelligent as her sister.

E Effective Sentences

E1 Missing Words

For practice, go to bedfordstmartins.com/theguide/mword

To write effective prose, you need to supply all words necessary for clarity, completeness, and logic.

> ### For ESL Writers
>
> If English is not your native language, you may have special trouble with omitted words. See also L4.

E1-a Supply small words such as prepositions, conjunctions, infinitive parts, articles, and verb parts needed for clarity and completeness.

When you forget to include these small words, the reader may be puzzled or have to pause momentarily to figure out what you mean. Proofread your essays carefully, even out loud, to catch these omitted words.

> **preposition** A word (such as *between, in,* or *of*) that always appears as part of a phrase and indicates the relation between a word in a sentence and the object of the preposition: The water splashed *into* the canoe.

Insert missing prepositions.

> ▶ The car began to skid the other direction.
>   ^in

> ▶ He graduated high school at the top of his class.
>   ^from

> ▶ A child his age shouldn't be playing outside that time of night.
>   ^at

> ### For ESL Writers
>
> If you are not a native speaker of American English, prepositions may be especially difficult for you because they are highly idiomatic. In other words, native speakers of English use prepositions in ways that do not translate directly into other languages. The best way to understand when prepositions are needed in English sentences is to read widely and study the work of other writers. See also L3.

> **conjunction** A word that relates sentence parts by coordinating, subordinating, or pairing elements, such as *and, because,* or *either . . . or.*

Insert missing conjunctions.

> ▶ Most families and patients will accept the pain, inconvenience, financial and
>   emotional strain as long as the patient can achieve a life "worth living."
>   ^and

> *or*
> The heads of these golf clubs can be made of metal, wood, graphite and often
>
> have special inserts in the part of the club that hits the ball.

A conjunction is generally needed to connect the final item in a series, such as *financial and emotional strain* in the first example and *graphite* in the second.

Restore the *to* omitted from an infinitive if it is needed for clarity.

> *to*
> They decided start the following Monday morning.
>
> *to*
> I noticed how he used his uncanny talent for acting make a dreary subject
>
> come alive.

Insert missing articles.

> *the*
> This incident ruined the party, but it was only beginning of the worst.
>
> *a*
> But such condition could be resolved by other means.

> infinitive A verb form consisting of the word *to* plus the base form of the verb: *to run, to do.*

> article An adjective that precedes a noun and identifies a definite reference to something specific (*the*) or an indefinite reference to something less specific (*a* or *an*).

For ESL Writers

Nonnative speakers of English sometimes have trouble understanding when and when not to use the articles *a*, *an*, and *the*. For more advice on the use of articles, see L1.

Insert other missing words that help clarify or complete a sentence.

> *it may*
> Malaria was once a widespread disease, and become so again.
>
> *shown*
> In these scenes, women are often with long, luxurious hair.
>
> *it*
> Finally, and I'm embarrassed to admit, I pushed Cindy against the wall.

E1-b Insert the word *that* if it is needed to prevent confusion or misreading.

CONFUSING   I would like to point out golf is not just a game for rich old men in ugly pants.

CLEARER   I would like to point out *that* golf is not just a game for rich old men in ugly pants.

Without *that*, the reader may think at first that the writer is pointing out golf and have to double back to understand the sentence. In the revised sentence, *that* tells the reader exactly where the **dependent clause** begins.

> *that*
> ▶ Dryer says, as people grow older, they may find themselves waking up early,
>
> usually at dawn.

> *that*
> ▶ Another problem parents will notice is the child leaves out certain words.

Note: If the meaning of a sentence is clear without *that*, it may be left out.

dependent (subordinate) clause A word group that has a subject, a predicate, and a subordinating word at the beginning; it cannot stand by itself as a sentence but must be connected to an independent (main) clause.

E1-c   **Add enough words to a comparison to show that the items are of the same kind and to make the comparison logical, clear, and complete.**

Because a comparison, by definition, connects two or more things for the reader, you should name both things and state the comparison fully. In addition, the items you are comparing should be of the same kind. For example, compare a person with another person, not with an activity or a situation.

> **The old student center has a *general store* that carries *as many books or supplies as* the *Saver Center*.**

This sentence compares two stores, which are entities of the same kind. See also E7-c.

Reword a comparison to specify comparable items of the same kind.

> *for her than it is for*
> ▶ Five-foot-five-inch Maria finds climbing to be more challenging ~~than~~ her six-
>
> foot-five-inch companions, who can reach the handholds more easily.

The original version of this sentence says that climbing is more challenging than companions (illogically comparing an activity to people). The edited sentence says that climbing is more challenging for Maria than it is for her companions (logically comparing one person to other people).

Reword a comparison to identify clearly and completely all items being compared.

> ▶ Danziger's article is interesting and lightly laced with facts, definitely more
>
> *than Solomon's article.*
> entertaining.

Note: In some types of comparative sentences, standard English requires the coordinated use of *as.*

Millie is *as* graceful *as,* if not more graceful than, Margot.

▶ Students opting for field experience credits would learn as much, or more, than, students who take only classes. *as;*

E1-d Supply all words needed to clarify the parts of a compound structure.

compound structure
A sentence element, such as a subject or a verb, that consists of two or more items linked by *and* or another conjunction

Although words may be left out of compound structures to avoid unnecessary repetition, these omitted words must fit in each part of the compound.

Women tend to express feelings *in the form of* requests, whereas men tend to express them *in* [*the form of*] commands.

When the same words do not fit in each part, you need to supply the missing words even if they are simply different forms of the same word.

▶ Water buffalo meat has been gaining popularity in America and being sold to the public. *is*

▶ Observable behaviors that relate to classroom assault can be dealt with prior, during, and after an attack. *to;*

E2   Shifts

For practice, go to bedfordstmartins.com/theguide/shifts

Follow the same pattern throughout a sentence or passage to avoid a shift in tense, person, number, mood, voice, or type of discourse.

E2-a Use one verb tense consistently in a sentence or passage unless a tense change is needed to show a time change.

tense The form of a verb that shows the time of the action or state of being.

▶ The nurse tried to comfort me by telling jokes and explaining that the needle wouldn't hurt. With a slight push, the long, sharp needle pierces through my *pierced* skin and finds its way to the vein. *found*

If you tend to mix verb tenses as you draft, perform a special edit of your entire essay, concentrating on this one issue.

Change the tense of any verbs that do not follow the established tense in a passage unless they show logical time changes.

▶ I noticed much activity around the base. Sailors and chiefs ~~are~~ *were* walking all over the place. At 8:00 a.m., all traffic, foot and vehicle, halted. Toward the piers, the flag ~~is rising~~ *rose* up its pole. After the national anthem ~~ends,~~ *ended*; salutes ~~are~~ *were* completed, and people ~~go~~ *went* on with what they ~~are~~ *had been* doing.

Change verbs to the present tense to discuss events in literature, general truths, facts, and other ongoing principles.

▶ In 2003, the Supreme Court ruled that antisodomy laws are unconstitutional because such laws ~~went~~ *go* against "our tradition [that] the state is not omnipresent in our homes."

▶ In the story, when the boy ~~died,~~ *dies*; Kathy ~~realized~~ *realizes* that it ~~was~~ *is* also time for her childhood to die, and so she ~~returned~~ *returns* to her South African home as an adult.

Note: The conventional use of the present tense for events in literary works and for enduring facts and principles may require tense shifts in a sentence or text. See also G5-a.

PRESENT TENSE	When Dr. Full *is introduced* in the story, he *is* very poor and dependent on alcohol.
PRESENT TENSE WITH LOGICAL SHIFT TO FUTURE	Each cell *has* forty-six chromosomes that *carry* the genetic traits the individual *will have* when he or she *is* born.

person The form of a word that shows whether it refers to *I* or *we* (first person), to *you* (second person), or to *he, she, it,* or *they* (third person).

E2-b **Change the nouns and pronouns in a passage to a consistent person and number.**

▶ Lynn informs all the members of helpful programs for ~~you and your pet.~~ *them and their pets.*

▶ Lynn informs ~~all the members~~ of helpful programs for *you* and your pet.

number The form of a word that shows whether it refers to one thing (singular) or more than one (plural): *parent, parents; child, children*.

In casual conversation, people often shift between singular and plural nouns and pronouns or between the third person and the second (or even the first). In writing, however, such shifts may be confusing or may make the essay poorly focused.

Note: Besides making sure that the nouns and pronouns are consistent in person and number within a sentence or series of sentences, consider how your choice of person suits the tone or approach of your essay. The first or second person, for example, will usually strike a reader as less formal than the third person.

E2-c Establish a consistent mood and voice in a passage.

> *knew*
> ▶ Each time I entered his house, I ~~could~~ always ~~know~~ when he was home.

The original sentence shifts from the indicative mood (*I entered*), used for statements and questions, to the subjunctive mood (*I could know*), used to indicate hypothetical, impossible, or unlikely conditions.

> *to take the test.*
> ▶ I stepped out of the car with my training permit, a necessary document ~~for the~~
>
> ~~test to be taken.~~

Although mood and voice may need to change to fit the context of a sentence, unneeded shifts may seem inconsistent. See also G5-c on mood, G5-d on voice, and L2-a on conditional clauses.

Change the verbs in a conditional clause or passage to a consistent mood.

> *would*
> ▶ If the mother should change her mind and keep the child, the couple ~~will~~ be
>
> reimbursed for their expenses.

> *changes*   *keeps*
> ▶ If the mother ~~should change~~ her mind and ~~keep~~ the child, the couple will be
>
> reimbursed for their expenses.

Change the verbs in a passage to a consistent voice, preferably the active voice.

> ▶ I will judge the song according to the following criteria: the depth with which
>
>   *the music presents each issue.*
> the lyrics treat each issue and the clarity with which ~~each issue is presented in~~
>
> ~~the music.~~

See also G5-d.

E2-d Use either direct or indirect quotation without mixing the two.

Writers use direct quotation to present statements or questions in a speaker's or another writer's own words; they use indirect quotation to present the person's words without quoting directly.

---

mood The form of a verb that shows the writer's attitude toward a statement.

voice The form of a verb that indicates (active) or deemphasizes (passive) the performer of the action.

you want to me,

▶ Do whatever ~~they wanted to her,~~ she cried,   but don't harm Reza.

They could do   *they shouldn't*

▶ ~~Do~~ whatever they wanted to her, she cried, but ~~don't~~ harm Reza.

To avoid shifts between direct and indirect quotation, make sure that your pronouns are consistent in **person** (see G2) and your verbs are consistent in **mood** (see G5-c).

E3   Noun Agreement

For practice, go to bedfordstmartins.com/theguide/nagree

In most instances, use nouns that agree in **number** when they refer to the same topic, person, or object.

> The treatment consists of *injections* of minimal *doses* of the *allergens* given at regular *intervals*.

Sometimes, however, the context calls for both singular and plural nouns.

> *Students* who want to make the most of *their* college years should pursue *a major course of study* while choosing *electives* or *a few minor courses of study* from the liberal arts.

Note: When you use a noun with a plural possessive such as *their*, the thing possessed can be expressed as a singular noun if each individual could possess only one item.

> By the time the *calves* reach two months of age, *their coat* has turned dark brown.

E3-a   Select corresponding singular or plural forms for related references to a noun.

When several nouns are used to develop a topic, they may describe and expand the characteristics of a key noun, act as synonyms for one another, or develop related points in the discussion. A sentence or passage that includes such nouns will generally be clearer and more effective if the nouns agree in number.

▶ Many people tend to "take their jobs to bed" with them and stay awake

promotions,

thinking about what needs to be done the next day. They also worry about ~~a~~

layoffs, or shifts

~~promotion, a layoff, or a shift~~ in responsibilities.

E3-b   Decide whether a noun should be singular or plural on the basis of its relationship to other words in the sentence and the meaning of the sentence as a whole.

A noun may need to agree with another word in the sentence or may need to be singular or plural to fit the context or idiomatic usage.

---

person The form of a word that shows whether it refers to *I* or *we* (first person), to *you* (second person), or to *he, she, it,* or *they* (third person).

mood The form of a verb that shows the writer's attitude toward a statement.

number The form of a word that shows whether it refers to one thing (singular) or more than one (plural): *parent, parents; child, children.*

Minnows are basically inedible because *they* have very little meat on *their bodies.*

In this sentence the writer consistently uses plural forms (*they, their,* and *bodies*) to refer to the minnows but also uses *meat,* which conventionally takes a singular form in a context like this one.

Note: Nouns such as *kind, type,* or *sort* are singular, although they have plural forms (*kinds, types*). Use *this* and *that* instead of *these* and *those* to modify the singular forms of these and similar words. Expressions with *kind of* or *sort of* are usually singular.

▶ To comprehend ~~these~~ *this* type of ~~articles,~~ *article,* it helps to have a strong background in

statistics.

▶ RAs are allowed to choose what kind of ~~programs~~ *program* they want to have.

Change a noun to singular or to plural to agree with a preceding indefinite adjective.

▶ Under some ~~circumstance,~~ *circumstances,* parents aren't there to supervise their kids.

Consider changing a noun to singular or to plural to reflect its context in the sentence.

Sometimes it is customary to treat an abstract quality (such as *justice* or *power*) as a singular noun. In other cases, a noun should be singular or plural to fit with the grammar or logic of the rest of the sentence.

▶ As soon as immigrants get to the United States, they realize that to get ~~a better job~~ *better jobs*

and better living conditions, they need to learn English.

Note: Some common idiomatic expressions mix singular and plural forms.

IDIOMATIC WORDING   The penalties set for offenders might be enough to help them see *the error of their ways* and eventually help them reform their social habits.

> **indefinite adjective** A word that modifies a noun or another adjective and indicates an unspecific quantity, such as *few, many,* or *some.*

E4   Modifiers

For practice, go to bedfordstmartins.com/theguide/mod

Put a **modifier** next to or very close to the particular word that it modifies so that the connection between the two is clear.

Fourteen teenage idealists *with nervous stomachs*

waited *for their moment in front of the onlookers.*

We had raised all the money *that we needed for the five-day trip.*

> **modifier** A word, phrase, or clause functioning as an adjective or adverb that adds information and detail about a noun, a verb, or another word.

A modifier's position in a sentence generally tells the reader what word the modifier qualifies.

E4-a **Place a word, phrase, or clause next to or close to the word that it modifies.**

My *frozen* smile faltered as my chin quivered.

The flurry *of fins, masks, weights, and wet suits* continued.

Beyond the chairs loomed the object *that I feared most* —

a beautiful, black Steinway grand piano *that gleamed under the bright stage lights.*

If a modifier is too far away from the word it modifies, a reader may assume that it modifies another word closer to it. As a result, a *misplaced modifier* can create confusion, ambiguity, or even unintended humor.

Move a modifier closer to the word it modifies.

► The ~~attempted~~ *attempted* number of suicides this semester was four.

► The women have to do all the hard work, *needed to maintain the family*, especially in subsistence culture, ~~needed to maintain the family.~~

► He and the other people start to look for any sign of a boat, an island, or an oil platform, *as hard as they can* ~~as hard as they can.~~

Rewrite to clarify the sentence.

► ~~Community~~ *In organizing meetings open to all neighbors,* community leaders should *select* ~~organize meetings open to all neighbors at~~ convenient times and locations.

► We were friends until I *turned eighteen and* became too popular and obnoxious for anyone to stand, ~~when I turned eighteen.~~

E4-b **Place a modifier so that it qualifies the meaning of a particular word in the sentence instead of dangling.**

A phrase that does not modify a specific word is called a *dangling modifier*. A dangling modifier usually occurs at the beginning of a sentence and is likely to be a **participial phrase** or a **prepositional phrase.**

participial phrase A group of words that begins with a present participle (*dancing, freezing*) or a past participle (*danced, frozen*) and modifies a noun or a pronoun: We boarded the bus, *expecting to leave immediately.*

prepositional phrase A group of words that begins with a preposition and indicates the relation between a word in a sentence and the object following the preposition: Her sunglasses slid *under the seat.*

▶ By far the best song on the album, ~~the~~ vocal performance and musical

"Don't Know Why" has a ^

that
arrangement ~~of "Don't Know Why"~~ create a perfect harmony. ^

Rewrite the sentence, placing a word that could logically be modified immediately after the modifying phrase.

▶ Rather than receiving several painful shots in the mouth before a cavity is

a patient may find that
filled, hypnosis can work just as effectively. ^

I concluded that
▶ After surveying the floor on which I live, the residents of my dorm don't care ^

much for floor programs.

Rewrite the sentence by changing the modifying phrase into a `dependent` `clause`.

Unlike a phrase, a clause includes both a **subject** and a **predicate**. By changing a phrase to a clause, you can correct a dangling modifier by supplying the information or connection that is missing. Be sure to add words and rewrite so that both the subject and the predicate are clearly stated and the clause fits the rest of the sentence.

If the school board decides to close   will
▶ ~~By closing~~ Dos Pueblos, the remaining high schools ~~would~~ have larger student ^   ^

bodies and increased budgets.

I concluded
▶ After ~~concluding~~ my monologue on the hazards of partying, she smiled broadly ^

and said, "OK, Mom, I'll be more careful next time."

E4-c **Place a `limiting modifier` just before the word it modifies to avoid ambiguity.**

A limiting modifier creates confusion or ambiguity when it is misplaced because it often could modify several words in the same sentence.

▶ Landfills in Illinois are going to be filled to capacity by 2015, and some

even
experts ~~even~~ say sooner. ^

When *even* precedes *say* in the example above, the sentence suggests that the experts are "even saying," not that the date will be even sooner.

---

dependent (subordinate) clause A word group that has a subject, a predicate, and a subordinating word (such as *because*) at the beginning; it cannot stand by itself as a sentence but must be connected to an independent (main) clause.

subject The part of a clause that identifies who or what is being discussed: At the checkpoint, *we* unloaded the canoes.

predicate The part of a clause that includes a complete verb and says something about the subject: At the checkpoint, we *unloaded the canoes.*

limiting modifier A modifier such as *almost, just,* or *only* that should directly precede the word or word group it limits.

infinitive A verb form consisting of the word *to* plus the base form of the verb: *to run*, *to do*.

limiting modifier A modifier such as *almost*, *just*, or *only* that should directly precede the word or word group it limits.

E4-d   Keep the two parts of an infinitive together.

When other words follow the *to*, they "split" the infinitive, separating *to* from the base form of the verb. These other words can usually be moved elsewhere in the sentence. Be especially alert to limiting modifiers that split infinitives. See also E4-c.

> ▶ His stomach seemed to ~~always~~ hang over his pants.
>   *always*

Note: Occasionally, moving intervening words creates a sentence more awkward than the version with the split infinitive. In such cases, leaving the split infinitive may be the better choice.

E5   Mixed Constructions

For practice, go to bedfordstmartins.com/theguide/mix

The beginning and ending of a sentence must match, and its parts should fit together. If a sentence changes course in the middle or its parts are mixed up, a reader will have to guess at the pattern or connection you intend.

E5-a   Begin and end a sentence with the same structural pattern to avoid a mixed construction.

A sentence is mixed if it combines several grammatical patterns. You usually need to rewrite a mixed construction so that its parts fit together.

> ▶ ~~The~~ more oil ~~that we save~~ now ~~means~~ much more in the future.
>   *If we save*   *we will have*

Choose one of the grammatical patterns in a mixed sentence, and rewrite to use it consistently throughout the sentence.

> ▶ School is another ~~resource for~~ children who don't have anyone to talk to can
>   *place where*
>
>   get educated about the problem of teen pregnancy.

> ▶ School is another resource for children who don't have anyone to talk to can
>   ~~get educated~~ about the problem of teen pregnancy.
>   *provide information*

Rewrite a mixed sentence if neither part supplies a workable pattern for the whole.

> ▶ ~~This is something the~~ shelter prides itself on ~~and is~~ always looking for new
>   *The*
>
>   volunteers and ideas ~~for the shelter.~~

▶ The ~~next part of the~~ essay ~~was where~~ the results of the study ~~were detailed~~
  ^*next detailed*

and ~~finally included~~ a commentary section ~~concluding the article.~~
  ^*concluded with*

E5-b   Match the **subject** and the **predicate** in a sentence so that they are compatible.

You can solve the problem of a logically mismatched subject and predicate — called *faulty predication* — by rewriting either the subject or the predicate so that the two fit together.

▶ ~~Schools~~ that prohibited paddling behaved as well as schools that permitted
  ^*Students attending schools*   ^*those at*

corporal punishment.

To test a sentence for faulty predication, ask yourself whether the subject can do what the predicate says: For example, do schools behave? If not, revise the sentence.

Revise the subject so that it can perform the action described in the predicate.

▶ Bean's service is top notch, and is striving continually to meet student needs.
  ^*the staff*

Revise the predicate so that it fits logically with the subject.

▶ Ironically, the main character's memory of Mangan's sister on the porch step

~~cannot recall the image without~~ the lamplight.
^*always includes*

E5-c   Order words logically so that the meaning of the sentence will be clear.

▶ ~~Traffic entering~~ will be dispersed into a perimeter pattern of flow.
  ^*Entering traffic*

E5-d   Eliminate the phrase *is where*, *is when*, or *the reason is because*, and then rewrite the sentence so that it is clear and logical.

Often you can replace an *is where* or *is when* phrase with a noun specifying a category or type.

▶ This ~~is where~~ the irony ~~seems to be~~ most evident.
       ^*part makes*   ^*seem*

▶ An absolutist position is ~~when someone~~ strongly opposes any restrictions on
                            ^*a stance taken by someone who*

speech.

---

subject The part of a clause that identifies who or what is being discussed.

predicate The part of a clause that includes a complete verb and says something about the subject.

To eliminate *the reason is because*, rewrite the sentence, or use *the reason is that* or *because* instead.

In addition:
▶ ~~Another reason~~ radio stations should not play songs with sexually explicit lyrics

~~is~~ because children like to sing along.

▶ Another reason radio stations should not play songs with sexually explicit

that
lyrics is ~~because~~ children like to sing along.

E6   Integrated Quotations, Questions, and Thoughts

For practice, go to bedfordstmartins.com/theguide/int

When you use sources or write dialogue, merge your quotations, questions, and thoughts smoothly into your text so that the reader can tell who is speaking, thinking, or providing information.

> The expense of being a teenager has caused many youths to join the workforce just because "they were offered a job" (Natriello 60).

> "Hello," I replied, using one of the few words I knew.

> I told myself, Don't move.

Use introductory phrases to link ideas and provide necessary background and context. Refer to the source or the speaker in the sentence, varying your words to avoid repeating *says* or *states*. See also P6 and P10.

E6-a   Introduce, connect, and cite source material with grammatically correct and logical wording when you integrate a direct quotation into a sentence.

> **direct quotation** A speaker's or writer's exact words, which are enclosed in quotation marks.

Writers often introduce quotations by mentioning the name of the person being quoted. Although *says* and *states* are acceptable, consider using more precise verbs and phrases that establish exact logical connections and provide variety. Examples include *agrees, asserts, charges, claims, confirms, discusses, emphasizes*, and *suggests*.

> In the words of American Motors President M. Paul Tippitt, "The cardinal rule of the new ballgame is change" (Sobel 259).

Readers expect quotations and text to fit gracefully so that the writer's ideas and the material from supporting sources are unified and coherent. See also E2-d.

Rewrite to cite a source smoothly, without jumping from sentences of text to quotation.

Identifying the author of your source in the main part of your sentence often supplies the context a reader needs.

▶ Most people are not even aware of the extent to which television plays a role

As Mitroff and Bennis point out,

in their lives. "Television defines our problems and shapes our actions; in

(xi),

short, how we define our world" ~~(Mitroff and Bennis xi)~~.

Mitroff and Bennis assert that most

▶ ~~Most~~ people are not even aware of the extent to which ~~television plays a role~~

"television

~~in their lives. "Television~~ defines our problems and shapes our actions; ~~in short,~~

" (xi),

~~how we define our world" (Mitroff and Bennis xi).~~

If you were writing for a magazine or newspaper, you would usually include a publication name and date in your sentence. In academic writing, however, you should cite the author's name and the date of the publication in your text and provide full publication information in a list of works cited (see Chapter 24).

FOR A MAGAZINE	Andrew DePalma's 2003 *New York Times* article, "Preparing to 'Tell Us About Yourself,'" explains this point clearly.
FOR AN ACADEMIC ESSAY OR A SCHOLARLY PUBLICATION	Andrew DePalma (2003) explains this point clearly.

Rewrite the text that introduces or integrates the quotation, and reselect the words you are quoting if necessary.

▶ The average American child ~~who~~ is "exposed to violence from every medium

and

~~. . . in addition listens to~~ "music that advocates drug use" (Hollis 624).

E6-b Integrate a question so that its source is clear.

Enclose a **direct quotation** in quotation marks, identifying the speaker and using his or her exact words. Do not use quotation marks for an **indirect quotation** or a question that you address to the reader.

DIRECT QUOTATION	"Can you get my fins?" he asked.

direct quotation A speaker's or writer's exact words, which are enclosed in quotation marks.

indirect quotation A reworded statement or question that presents a speaker's or writer's ideas without quoting directly or using quotation marks.

INDIRECT QUOTATION   Without much hesitation, I explained my mission to her and asked whether she would help me out.

QUESTION ADDRESSED TO READER   Should sex education be a required class in public schools?

As in any dialogue, begin a new paragraph to show each change of speaker.

▶   "The refrigeration system is frozen solid. Come back later," ~~Once~~ again *he said; once*

turning his back to me. ~~I asked~~

I asked;
"When would it be best for me to come back?"

E6-c   Integrate thoughts so that they are clearly identified and consistently punctuated.

If you supply the exact words that you or someone else thinks, follow the guidelines for direct quotations. Quotation marks are optional, but be consistent throughout an essay.

Go eighty feet for thirty minutes, she reminded herself.

▶   'Wife and kids?' I thought.

▶   "Wife and kids?" I thought.

E7   Parallelism

For practice, go to bedfordstmartins.com/theguide/para

Use parallel grammatical form to present items as a pair or in a series.

Imagine that you and your daughter are *walking* in the mall or *eating* in a popular restaurant.

By implementing this proposal, administrators could enhance the reputation of the university with quality *publications, plays, concerts,* and *sports teams.*

An interruption has the potential *to disrupt turns at talk, to disorganize the topic of conversation,* and *to violate the current speaker's right to talk.*

The grammatical similarity of the items in the pair or series strongly signals the reader that they are equally important, similar in meaning, and related in the same way to the rest of the sentence.

E7-a Rewrite any item in a series that does not follow the same grammatical pattern as the other items.

Items in a series are usually linked by *and* or *or*. Each item should be parallel to the others, presented as a **noun,** an **infinitive,** a **gerund,** or another grammatical form.

> ▶ The children must deal with an overprotective parent, sibling rivalry, and ~~living~~ *life* in a single-parent home.

> ▶ Drivers destined for Coronado can choose to turn left, *turn* right, or ~~proceeding~~ *proceed* straight into the city.

> **noun** A word that names a specific or general thing, person, place, concept, characteristic, or other idea.

> **infinitive** A verb form consisting of the word *to* plus the base form of the verb: *to run, to do.*

E7-b Rewrite one item in a pair so that both follow the same grammatical pattern.

Items in a pair are usually linked by *and* or *or*.

> ▶ While Simba is growing up, he is told of things he should do and things *he should* not ~~to~~ do.

> **gerund** A verb form that is used as a noun and ends in *-ing: arguing, throwing.*

E7-c Rewrite one item in a comparison using *than* or *as* so that it matches the other in grammatical form.

> ▶ They feel that using force is more comprehensible to the children than abstract *threatening* consequences.

E7-d Use parallel form for items joined by correlative conjunctions.

> ▶ At that time, the person is surprised not only about where he is but also *about* ~~unable to account for~~ what has happened.

> **correlative conjunctions** Word pairs that link sentence elements; the first word anticipates the second: *both . . . and, either . . . or, neither . . . nor, not only . . . but also.*

Besides presenting the word pairs in parallel form, position the conjunctions so that each introduces a comparable point.

E8   Coordination and Subordination

For practice, go to bedfordstmartins.com/theguide/cosub

Use coordination and subordination to indicate the relationships among sentence elements.

independent (main) clause A word group with a subject and a predicate that can stand alone as a separate sentence. (A predicate is the part of a clause that includes a complete verb and says something about the subject: At the checkpoint, we *unloaded the canoes.*)

phrase A group of words that does *not* contain both a subject and a verb and is always part of an independent clause. Common types of phrases include *prepositional* (After a flash of lightning, I saw a tree split in half) and *verbal* (Blinded by the flash, I ran into the house).

dependent (subordinate) clause A word group that has a subject, a predicate, and a subordinating word (such as *because*) at the beginning; it cannot stand by itself as a sentence but must be connected to an independent (main) clause: *Although it was raining*, we loaded our gear onto the buses.

E8-a Use coordination to join sentence elements that are equally important.

The sheriff's department lacks both the *officers* and the *equipment* to patrol every road in the county.

Most of us would agree with the evil queen's magic mirror that this Disney girl, with her *skin as white as snow, lips as red as blood*, and *hair as black as ebony*, is indeed "the fairest one of all."

Writers use coordination to bring together in one sentence two or more elements of equal importance to the meaning. These elements can be words, phrases, or clauses, including **independent clauses** within the same sentence.

The sport of windsurfing dates back only to 1969, but *it already has achieved full status as an Olympic event.*

Children like to sing along with songs they hear on the radio; consequently, *radio stations should not play songs with language that demeans women.*

E8-b Use subordination to indicate that one sentence element is more important than other elements.

After Dave finished his mutinous speech, the corners of Dan's mouth slowly formed a nearly expressionless grin.

Political liberals, *who trace their American roots to the Declaration of Independence*, insist that the federal government should attempt to reduce inequalities of income and wealth.

Writers frequently subordinate information within a single sentence. The most important information appears in an independent clause, and the less important or subordinate information appears in words, **phrases,** or **dependent clauses** attached to the independent clause or integrated into it. (Often, the most important information in a sentence will be information that is new to a reader.)

W Word Choice

Effective language is concise, exact, and appropriate for the context.

> **Tears stream down James's face as he sits scrunched up in the corner of the shabby living room, wishing that he had anyone else's life.**

> **We need traffic signals for this dangerous intersection.**

Well-chosen words engage the reader, conveying impressions or claims clearly and convincingly.

W1 Concise Sentences

For practice, go to bedfordstmartins.com/theguide/csent

Sentences with redundant phrasing, repetitive wording, wordy expressions, and unnecessary intensifiers are tiresome to read and may be difficult to understand. Concentrate on choosing words well, simplifying sentence stucture, and avoiding words that are unnecessary or evasive.

> ▶ ~~In many cases, this~~ situation may ~~be due to the fact that~~ these women ~~were~~
> *This* *occur because* *have had no*
> ~~not given the~~ opportunity to work.

Note: Even though you may need to add detail or examples to clarify your ideas, cutting out useless words will make your writing more focused and precise.

W1-a Eliminate redundancies and repetition.

Redundant phrasing adds unnecessary words to a sentence. Repetitive wording says the same thing twice.

Eliminate or rewrite redundant expressions that repeat the same point in different words.

The phrase *blue in color* is redundant because it repeats obvious information, adding a category name to a description. The following phrases do the same: *large-sized, a reluctant manner, to an extreme degree, a helpless state, a crisis-type situation, the area of population control,* and *passive kind of behavior.* In addition, expressions such as *past memories, advance planning,* and *mix together* include modifiers that repeat information already provided in the word modified. After all, all memories are of the past, planning is always done in advance, and *mix* means "put together."

Other expressions such as *the fact is true, bisect in half*, and *in my opinion, I believe* are redundant because they contain obvious implications: *Truth* is implied by *fact, bisect* means "to divide in half," and *in my opinion* says the same thing as *I believe*. Pare down these and any similar expressions.

► Many machines in the drilling area need to be ~~updated to better and more modern equipment.~~ _{modernized.}

► All these recommendations are interconnected. ~~to one another.~~

► ~~The~~ colleges ~~in the state of California~~ _{California} rely too much on the annual income of a student's parents and not enough on the parents' true financial situation.

Delete extra words from a redundant or repetitive sentence.

► In addition, there is a customer service center. _{convenient} ~~for the convenience of the customers.~~

► Student volunteers will no longer be ~~overworked, overburdened, and~~ _{exhausted} ~~overexhausted~~ from working ~~continuously at the jobs~~ without ~~any~~ breaks because of the shortage. _{labor} ~~of labor.~~

W1-b Eliminate words that do not add to the meaning of a sentence.

Rewrite a wordy sentence to reduce the number of clauses and phrases.

Concentrate on turning clauses into phrases or replacing phrases, especially strings of **prepositional phrases,** with individual words. Sometimes you can even consolidate a series of sentences into one.

prepositional phrase A group of words that begins with a preposition and indicates the relation between a word in a sentence and the object following the preposition: Her sunglasses slid *under the seat*.

► _{Michael Phelps is an excellent recent example} _{overexposed} ~~One of the best examples in recent times~~ of an athlete. ~~being completely overexposed is that of Michael Phelps.~~

► ~~It is this~~ _{This} exaggeration ~~that serves to provide the~~ _{provides the characters'} comic appeal. ~~of the characters.~~

► _{No single alternative will solve the problem of teen pregnancy, and all the possible} ~~There are many other possible alternative solutions to teen pregnancy. One solution is not going to work alone to solve the problem. But there are~~ _{solutions have disadvantages.} ~~disadvantages that come along with them.~~

Eliminate wordy expressions, or replace them with fewer words.

Extra, empty words can creep into a sentence in many ways.

▶ Demanding Eldridge's resignation ~~at this point in time~~ *now* will not solve the problem.

▶ However, in most neighorhoods, the same ~~group of~~ people who write the newsletters ~~are the ones who~~ *also* organize and participate in the activities.

Here are examples of a few common wordy phrases and clearer, more concise alternatives.

Wordy Phrases	More Concise Alternatives
due to the fact that	
in view of the fact that	
the reason for	
for the reason that	for, because, why, since
this is why	
in light of the fact that	
on the grounds that	
despite the fact that	although, though
regardless of the fact that	
as regards	
in reference to	
concerning the matter of	concerning, about, regarding
where . . . is concerned	
it is necessary that	
there is a need for	should, must
it is important that	
has the ability to	
is able to	can
is in a position to	
in order to	to
for the purpose of	
at this point in time	now
on the subject of	on, about
as a matter of fact	actually
be aware of the fact that	know [that]
to the effect that	that
the way in which	how
in the event that	if, when

Rewrite a wordy sentence to simplify its structure.

Watch particularly for *there is* or *there are* at the beginning of a sentence or for a verb in the passive voice. These indirect structures have their uses. Often, however, you can express your ideas more directly and forcefully by editing to eliminate *there is* or *there are* or by changing from the passive to the active voice.

> ▶ ~~There are always five~~ ^{Five} ^{are always} or six spots open at the ends of the rows.

> ▶ ~~The topic is initiated by a~~ ^A member who has nothing to gain by the discussion ~~of~~ ^{initiates}
>
> the topic.

Note: Often, as in these examples, the verb *be* is far less precise than another verb might be. Whenever possible, replace *am, are, is, was,* and other forms of *be* with a stronger verb that clearly defines an action.

W1-c   Rewrite a sentence to eliminate unnecessary intensifiers or hedges.

> ▶ Your choice could ~~very possibly~~ make the difference between a saved and a
>
> lost life.

Delete unnecessary intensifiers such as *very, really, clearly, quite,* and *of course*.

Although intensifiers can strengthen statements, eliminating them or substituting more forceful words is often more effective.

> ▶ The plot of this movie is ~~really great.~~ ^{thrilling.}

Some intensifiers are unnecessary because the words they modify are already as strong as possible, such as *very unique.* (Something either is or is not unique; it cannot be *very* or *slightly* unique.)

> ▶ The arrangement of the plain blocks ~~is so unique that it~~ ^{unique} makes the sculpture
>
> seem textured.

Eliminate unnecessary hedges.

Writers use hedges such as *apparently, seem, perhaps, possibly, to a certain extent, tend,* and *somewhat* to avoid making claims that they cannot substantiate. Hedges add subtlety to prose, appear careful and thoughtful, and acknowledge the possibility of important exceptions. Too many hedges, however, make writing tentative and uncertain.

> ▶ ~~In most cases, realistic~~ ^{Realistic} characteristics ~~tend to~~ ^{often} undermine comedy's primary
>
> function of making us laugh at exaggerated character traits.

W1-d Eliminate unnecessary prepositions.

▶ I went to the hospital so the clerk could admit me ~~in.~~

If the word following a preposition is the object of a verb, the preposition may be unnecessary.

▶ Nothing happened, and my doctor ordered ~~for~~ them to stop inducing labor.

▶ Consequently, student volunteers will not be inclined to leave and seek ~~for~~ smaller hospitals with less intense shifts.

Note: Another alternative is to change the verb.

▶ Consequently, student volunteers will not be inclined to leave and ~~seek~~ *look* for smaller hospitals with less intense shifts.

preposition A word (such as *between, in,* or *of*) that always appears as part of a phrase and indicates the relation between a word in a sentence and the object of the preposition: The water splashed *into* the canoe.

For ESL Writers

Prepositions also combine with verbs to form two- or three-word (or phrasal) verbs whose meaning cannot be understood literally (*handed in, longed for*). When a preposition is part of a two- or three-word verb, it is called a *particle.* See L2-b.

W2 Exact Words

For practice, go to bedfordstmartins.com/theguide/eword

Effective writers choose words carefully, paying attention to meaning, form, idiomatic phrasing, and freshness.

The central library stands like a giant concrete mushroom, towering above the surrounding eucalyptus groves. The strong, angular lines are softened by a few well-placed, sweeping curves on the stabilizing pylons and the shrouds around the low windows.

W2-a Replace incorrect words with the exact words you intend, or omit incorrect words if they are unnecessary.

Check a dictionary when you are uncertain of the meaning of a word. Watch for incorrect words and for words similar in meaning or sound. See also the Glossary of Frequently Misused Words.

▶ Louis kicked him into a river ~~invested~~ *infested* with crocodiles.

▶ How do we stop offshore oil drilling and yet offer an alternative to ~~appease~~ *alleviate* the energy crisis?

▶ Some universities have chosen to go ~~literately~~ *literally* underground to avoid public scrutiny.

W2-b Use correct prepositions.

> **preposition** A word (such as *between, in,* or *of*) that always appears as part of a phrase and indicates the relation between a word in a sentence and the object of the preposition: The water splashed *into* the canoe.

Short as they generally are, prepositions define crucial relationships for the reader.

The levels increase *in* width *from* the scrawny third floor *up to* the immense sixth story (*over* two hundred feet across).

A building's beauty must be determined *by* the harmony *of* its design.

If prepositions are a problem in your writing, note how other writers use them.

▶ Unlike many of the other pieces of art ~~about~~ *on* campus, the statues seemed to fit well.

> ### For ESL Writers
>
> If you find prepositions difficult, pay special attention to them as you read. For a review of the meanings of some common prepositions, see L3.

W2-c Use standard idioms, the conventional expressions generally used in American English.

> **idiom** An expression whose meaning cannot be determined from its parts but must be learned (*call off* for "cancel"; *look after* for "take care of").

Read and listen carefully to get a sense of standard idioms, especially the ones that consist of small words, such as **prepositions,** and verb forms.

▶ **The most serious problems of many developing countries stem ~~to~~ *from* lack of educational and economic opportunity.**

> ### For ESL Writers
>
> Idiomatic two- and three-word verbs (*put down, set up*) and combinations of verbs or adjectives and prepositions (*look for, afraid of*) can be especially troublesome for writers whose first language is not English. See L2-b for more help with these expressions.

W2-d Eliminate or rewrite clichés or overused expressions.

Readers prefer lively, original expressions to familiar, overused phrases.

▶ During ~~the thick of~~ the night, he must walk alone with only a flashlight for

company.

▶ The audience ~~is on pins and needles,~~ *erupts in gasps and nervous giggles,* wondering whose plan will falter first.

W2-e Select the correct form of the word that fits the context of your essay and conveys the meaning you intend.

If you are learning to use an unfamiliar word or are struggling to find a word whose meaning fits, you may use the wrong form of the word you intend. If so, change the word to the correct form when you discover your mistake or a reader notes it for you. Proofread your essays carefully for words written incorrectly. A good dictionary can help you determine which form of a word fits your context.

▶ The phrase "you know" ~~is an introductory to~~ *introduces* someone's opinion.

▶ I found out that becoming a ~~manicure~~ *manicurist* is increasingly popular because it takes

only a few months of training.

W2-f Use appropriate figures of speech.

Figures of speech, such as **similes** and **metaphors,** are vivid and original means of expressing comparisons. They help a reader perceive a similarity, often creating a striking image or a surprising but engaging idea.

Our dog Tiger rolls around in the warm mud and sinks his head into the soft ground like a hippo basking in the African sun.

If you think of the *Journal of the American Medical Association* article as a two-hour documentary on PBS, the *American Health* essay is a thirty-second sound bite.

A figure of speech can make a complex idea easier to understand or bring a scene or character to life for your readers. Make sure that any figure of speech that you use is clear, appropriate, and consistent.

INACCURATE
METAPHOR   The children would jump from car to car *as if they were mushrooms.* [Mushrooms cannot jump.]

---

cliché An overused expression that has lost its original freshness, such as *hard as a rock.*

figures of speech Images such as similes and metaphors that suggest a comparison (or analogy) between objects that are generally unlike each other.

simile A direct comparison that uses *like* or *as: like a tree bending in the strong wind.*

metaphor An indirect comparison that refers to or describes one thing as if it were the other: *The mob sharpened its claws.*

mixed metaphor An inconsistent metaphor, one that mixes several images rather than completing one.

Also avoid **mixed metaphors,** as in the following example, in which the soul is compared to both a criminal defendant and a plant.

| MIXED METAPHOR | Karma is an inorganic process of development in which the soul not only *pays the price* for its misdeeds but also *bears the fruit* of the *seeds sown* in former lives. |

W3   Appropriate Words

For practice, go to bedfordstmartins.com/theguide/aword

When you choose words carefully, your writing will have the appropriate level of formality, without slang, biased wording, or stuffy, pretentious language. Taken from a profile of a large city's trauma system, the following sentences illustrate how appropriate words can convey a sense of the environment.

At 6:50 p.m., the hospital's paging system comes alive.

Lying on the table, the unidentified victim can only groan and move his left leg.

All the components are in place: a countrywide trauma system, physicians and staff who care and are willing to sacrifice, and private hospitals serving the community.

Readers appreciate appropriate language choices that produce smooth, integrated writing, without sudden jumps from formal to informal language.

W3-a Use the level of formality expected in your writing situation.

Many problems with appropriate language occur when writers use language accepted in informal conversation in a more formal writing situation. For example, a phone conversation or e-mail exchange with your friend will be more informal than a memo to your employer or a report for your political science class.

| LESS FORMAL | One cool morning in May, I stood on the edge of Mount Everest, or at least that's what it seemed like to me. |
| MORE FORMAL | Mistreatment of the elderly is an unusually sensitive problem because it involves such value-laden ideas as *home* and *family*. |

Taking into account the kind of essay you are writing, reword as necessary to avoid shifts in the level of formality.

▶ What makes an excellent church, auditorium, or theater makes a ~~lousy~~ library.
                                                                       poor

> The average cost to join a gymnasium ~~can run you~~ *is* around $140 a month~~, and~~

> ~~that's only~~ when you sign a membership contract. ~~I bet~~ *Even if* you thought you

> ~~couldn't~~ *could not* afford a membership~~,~~ ~~Well,~~ you can.

W3-b Limit the use of slang in formal writing situations.

slang Informal language that tends to change rapidly.

Although slang may be appropriate in dialogue used to define a character or a situation in a narrative or description, it is likely to be out of place in more formal academic writing.

Replace inappropriate slang expressions with more formal words.

> We shouldn't ~~dis~~ *criticize* these girls.

> The cast of the movie was ~~awesome.~~ *Impressive.*

> Parties are an excellent way to ~~blow off steam~~ *relax* and take a break from the
>
> pressures of college.

Replace slang with precise, more descriptive words.

> The cast of the movie ~~was awesome.~~ *vividly embodied the historical characters.*

W3-c Use nonsexist language that includes rather than excludes.

nonsexist language Language that describes people without using words that make assumptions about gender or imply acceptance of gender-based stereotypes.

Avoid using masculine pronouns (such as *he* or *his*) to refer to people who might be either men or women. Also avoid using words referring to men to represent people in general. See also G2-b.

Revise a sentence that uses masculine pronouns to represent people in general.

Use plural forms, eliminate the pronouns, or use both masculine and feminine pronouns.

> ~~A student's~~ *Students'* eligibility for alternative loans is based on whether or not ~~his~~ *their*
>
> school decides ~~he is~~ *they are* entitled to financial aid.

▶ Abstract expressionism is art that is based on the artist's spontaneous feelings

or she   *a*
at the moment when he is creating ~~his~~ work.

Replace masculine nouns used to represent people in general with more inclusive words.

human history.
▶ Oligarchies have existed throughout ~~the history of man.~~

or her
▶ Every individual has his rightful place in the social hierarchy.

a
▶ Every individual has ~~his~~ rightful place in the social hierarchy.

Rewrite language that implies or reinforces stereotypes or discrimination.

the tribes   *outside the empire.*
▶ Oligarchies were left to ~~barbaric tribesmen~~ and herders ~~who were beyond the reach of civilization.~~

or her
▶ A doctor who did not keep up with his colleagues would be forced to update his procedures.

pretentious language
Fancy or wordy language used primarily to impress.

W3-d Replace pretentious language with simpler, more direct wording.

Using impressive words is sometimes part of the pleasure of writing, but such words may be too elaborate for the situation or may seem to be included for their own sake rather than the reader's understanding. Use words that best express your idea, and balance or replace distractingly unusual words with simpler, more familiar choices.

fear of
▶ Perhaps ~~apprehension toward instigating~~ these changes stems from financial concern.

▶ Expanded oil exploration may seem relatively innocuous, but this proposal is a
deceptive, destructive groups.
deplorable suggestion to all but the most ~~pernicious, specious entities.~~

P Punctuation

P1 Commas

For practice, go to bedfordstmartins.com/theguide/comma

Use a comma to set off and separate sentence elements.

P1-a Add a comma between independent clauses joined by a coordinating conjunction.

┌─────INDEPENDENT CLAUSE─────┐   ┌──────INDEPENDENT CLAUSE──────┐
Perhaps my father had the same dream, and perhaps my grandfather did as well.

When independent clauses are joined by a coordinating conjunction, a comma is required to tell the reader that another independent clause follows the first one.

▶ In 2002, women's ice hockey became a full Olympic medal sport, and the Canadian team brought home the gold.

▶ Researchers have studied many aspects of autism, but they readily acknowledge that they have much more to learn.

Note: If the independent clauses are brief and unambiguous, a comma is not required, though it is never wrong to include it.

The attempt fails and Spider-Man must let go.

Note: When a coordinating conjunction joins two elements other than independent clauses, no comma is needed (see P2-a).

P1-b Place a comma after an introductory word, phrase, or clause.

Sentences often begin with words, phrases, or clauses that precede the **independent clause** and modify an element within it.

Naturally, this result didn't help him any.

With a jerk, I lofted the lure in a desperate attempt to catch a fish and please my dad.

When we entered the honeymoon suite, the room smelled of burnt plastic and was the color of Pepto Bismol.

The comma following each introductory element lets the reader know where the modifying word or phrase ends and the main clause begins.

---

independent (main) clause A word group with a subject and a predicate that can stand alone as a separate sentence.

coordinating conjunction A word that joins comparable and equally important sentence elements: *for, and, or, but, nor, yet,* or *so.*

▶ In a poor family with no father‸ a boy can find the gangs more appealing than the tough life of poverty.

▶ When I picked up the receiver‸ I heard an unfamiliar voice.

▶ Forgetting my mission for a moment‸ I took time to look around.

Note: If an introductory phrase or clause is brief — four words or fewer — the comma may be omitted unless it is needed to prevent misreading.

Without hesitation I dived into the lake.

P1-c Use commas to set off a nonrestrictive word group.

To test whether a word group is *nonrestrictive* (supplemental, nondefining, and thus nonessential) or *restrictive* (defining and thus essential), read the sentence with and without the word group. If the sentence is less informative but essentially unchanged in meaning without it, the word group is nonrestrictive. Use commas to set it off. Conversely, if omitting the word group changes the meaning of the sentence by removing a definition or limitation, it is restrictive. In this case, do not use commas.

NONRESTRICTIVE   The oldest fishermen, *grizzly sea salts wrapped in an aura of experience,* led the way.

RESTRICTIVE   Blood and violence can give video games a sense of realism *that was not previously available.*

In the first sentence, the commas tell the reader that the word group presents extra information. The sentence would be essentially unchanged without the word group: *The oldest fishermen led the way.* In the second sentence, the word group is not set off with commas because it provides essential information about the realism of video games. The sentence would not have the same meaning without it.

Insert a comma to set off a nonrestrictive (nonessential) word group at the end of a sentence.

▶ We all stood‸ anxious and prepared for what he was about to say.

▶ The next period is the preoperational stage‸ which begins at age two and lasts until age seven.

▶ He was learning useful outdoor skills‸ such as how to tie knots and give first aid.

Insert a pair of commas to set off a nonrestrictive (nonessential) word group in the middle of a sentence.

▶ The most common moods are happiness, when the music is in a major key, or sadness, when the music is in a minor key.

▶ Laura, our neighbor and best friend, appeared at the kitchen window.

▶ My dog, Shogun, was lying on the floor doing what he does best, sleeping.

The last example illustrates the importance of context for deciding what is essential in a sentence. Here, the writer has only one dog, so the dog's name is nonrestrictive (nonessential) information and is placed between commas. If the writer had more than one dog, however, the name would be essential to identify which dog and would not be set off by commas.

See also P2-b.

P1-d Use commas to set off a transitional, parenthetical, or contrasting expression or an absolute phrase.

Often used to begin sentences, *transitional expressions* help the reader follow a writer's movement from point to point, showing how one sentence is related to the next. *Parenthetical comments* interrupt a sentence with a brief aside. *Contrasting expressions* generally come at the end of a sentence, introduced by *not, no,* or *nothing. Absolute phrases,* which can appear anywhere within a sentence, modify the whole clause and often include a past or present **participle** as well as modifiers.

TRANSITIONAL	*Besides*, it is summer.
PARENTHETICAL	These are all indications, *I think*, of Jan's drive for power and control.
CONTRASTING	Nick is the perfect example of a young, hungry manager trying to climb to the top, *not bothered by the feelings of others.*
ABSOLUTE	"Did I ever tell you about the time I worked with Danny Kaye at Radio City Music Hall?" she asked, *her eyes focusing dreamily into the distance.*

By using commas to set off such expressions, you signal that they are additions, supplementing or commenting on the information in the rest of the sentence.

Insert a comma to set off a transitional, parenthetical, or contrasting expression or an absolute phrase that begins or ends a sentence.

▶ For example, in our society a wedding gown is worn by the bride only once, on her wedding day.

participle A verb form showing present tense (*dancing, freezing*) or past tense (*danced, frozen*) that can also act as an adjective. In a participial phrase, a group of words begins with a present or past participle and modifies a noun or pronoun: We boarded the bus, *expecting to leave immediately.*

▶ We had an advantage, thanks to P.T.'s knowledge.

▶ My uncle talked to me as if I were a person, not a child.

▶ "Well, well," he'd grin, his crooked smile revealing his perfect white teeth.

Insert a pair of commas to set off a transitional, parenthetical, or contrasting expression or an absolute phrase that falls in the middle of a sentence.

▶ Students, therefore, often complain about their TA's inability to speak English.

▶ At every response, I defended those innocent people and emphasized that no one, absolutely no one, can decide whether or not a person is worthy of living.

▶ He uttered his famous phrase, "If you don't have time to do something right, you definitely don't have time to do it over," for the first, but not the last, time.

▶ I followed her, both of us barefoot and breathing white mist, out the door into the blood-reddened snow.

Note: If a transitional element, such as a **conjunctive adverb,** links two **independent clauses** within one sentence, add a semicolon between the clauses to avoid a **comma splice.** (See P3-d and S1.)

▶ One can see how delicate he is, yet this fragility does not detract from his masculinity; instead, it greatly enhances it.

P1-e **Use a comma to separate three or more items in a series, placing the final comma before the conjunction.**

He was wearing a camouflage hat, a yellow sweatshirt, and a pair of blue shorts.

The commas in a series separate the items for the reader.

▶ He always tells me about the loyalty, honor, and pride he feels as a Marine.

▶ Our communities would get relief from the fear and despair that come from having unremitting violence, addiction, and open-air drug markets in their midst.

Note: You will notice that newspapers, magazines, and British publications will often omit the comma before the conjunction. In your academic writing, however, you should always include it for clarity.

---

conjunctive adverb A word or phrase (such as *finally, however,* or *therefore*) that tells how the ideas in two sentences or independent clauses are connected.

independent (main) clause A word group with a subject and a predicate that can stand alone as a separate sentence.

comma splice The improper joining of two independent clauses with only a comma.

Occasionally, a writer will separate the last two items in a series with a comma but omit *and*. Or a writer may join all the items in a series with *and* or *or* and thus need no commas at all. Use such alternatives sparingly.

▶ **In her, I found a woman with character, integrity, intelligence.**

P1-f Use a comma before a trailing nonrestrictive participial phrase.

Participial phrases are generally **nonrestrictive word groups.** When they follow the **independent (main) clause** in a sentence, they should be set off with commas. (See P1-c.)

PARTICIPIAL   **The plane lifted off as he opened the package,** *expecting to find*
PHRASE   *cookies and a mushy love letter.*

The comma before the phrase signals the end of the main clause and sets off the important modifying phrase.

▶ **Every so often, a pelican agilely arcs high over the water, twisting downward gracefully to catch an unsuspecting mackerel.**

▶ **I sat down, confused and distraught.**

Note: If the participial phrase is restrictive, providing essential information, do not use a comma. (See P1-c and P2-b.)

Now at our disposal were the essential elements of life: the snow, Julie, me, and an entire pantry *stocked with food.*

I noticed his tiny form amid the crowd of vacationers *emerging from the terminal.*

Both participial phrases define or limit the nouns they modify, telling readers what kind of pantry and what kind of crowd. Consequently, they are not set off by commas.

P1-g Place a comma between a complete direct quotation and the text identifying the speaker.

I answered, "Okay, let me grab the ladder."

"Discipline is effective if you get the students to adopt your values," explained Fathman.

---

participial phrase A group of words that begins with a present participle (*dancing, freezing*) or a past participle (*danced, frozen*) and modifies a noun or a pronoun.

nonrestrictive word group A group of words, set off by commas, that provides extra or nonessential information and could be eliminated without changing the meaning of the noun or pronoun it modifies.

independent (main) clause A word group with a subject and a predicate that can stand alone as a separate sentence.

direct quotation A speaker's or writer's exact words, which are enclosed in quotation marks.

The comma, along with the quotation marks, helps the reader determine where the quotation begins and ends. See also P6.

▶ So I asked her, "Momma, who you talkin' to?"

▶ "It will be okay," Coach reassured me, as he motioned for the emergency medical technicians to bring a board.

▶ Dr. Carolyn Bailey says, "I view spanking as an aggressive act."

P1-h Add a comma (or pair of commas in the middle of a sentence) to set off expressions commonly included in dialogue.

direct address Words that are spoken directly to someone else who is named.

Use commas to set off the name of a person **directly addressed** by a speaker, words such as *yes* and *no*, and mild **interjections.** Also use a comma to set off a question added to the end of a sentence.

"Chadan, you're just too compassionate."

"Yes, sir," replied Danny.

interjection An exclamatory word that indicates strong feeling or attempts to command attention: *Shhh! Oh! Ouch!*

Boy, did we underestimate her.

That's not very efficient, is it?

A comma marks the division between the main part of the sentence and a comment that precedes or follows it:

▶ "Well, son, what are you doing?"

▶ "No, sir."

▶ So, this is to be a battle of wills, is it? Fine, I'll play.

▶ "Besides, it'll be good for me."

coordinate adjectives Two or more adjectives that modify a noun equally and independently: the *large, red* hat.

P1-i Use a comma between **coordinate adjectives**.

If you can change the order of a series of adjectives or add *and* between them without changing the meaning, they are coordinate and should be separated with a comma.

There are reasons for her *erratic, irrational* behavior.

The comma signals that the adjectives are equal, related in the same way to the word modified.

If the adjectives closest to the noun cannot logically be rearranged or linked by *and*, they are **noncoordinate adjectives** (also called *cumulative adjectives*) and should not be separated by commas.

> I pictured myself as a *professional race car* driver.

Once you have determined that adjectives are coordinate, add a comma between them.

> ▶ I can still remember the smell of his cigar and his old, greasy clothing.

> ▶ Professionals who use this five-step, systematic approach are less likely to injure or be injured during an assault.

Note: The same rule applies to coordinate adjectives that follow the noun they modify or are otherwise separated from it in the sentence.

> Skippy was a good-looking guy, *tall, blond,* and *lean.*

P1-j   Add commas where needed to set off dates, numbers, and addresses.

When you include a full date (month, day, and year), use a pair of commas to set off the year.

> ▶ In the July 8, 2002, issue of the *New Yorker,* Elizabeth Kolbert described Sidney Hook as "one of the most prominent public intellectuals of his generation" (23).

If you present a date in reverse order (day, month, and year), do not add commas.

> ▶ In the ~~July 8,~~ 8 July 2002 issue of the *New Yorker,* Elizabeth Kolbert described Sidney Hook as "one of the most prominent public intellectuals of his generation" (23).

If a date is partial (month and year only), do not add commas.

> This intriguing article appeared in the April 2003 issue of *Personnel Journal.*

In large numbers, separate groups of three digits (thousands, millions, and so forth) with commas.

> ▶ As of 2000, there were about 900,000 speakers of Korean in the United States.

When you write out an address, add commas between the parts, setting off the street address, the city, and the state with the zip code. When an address or place name is embedded in a complete sentence, add a comma after the last element.

> ▶ Mrs. Wilson relocated to Bowie, Maryland, after moving from Delaware.

P1-k **Add a comma if needed for clarity when a word is omitted, is repeated twice, or might be grouped incorrectly with the next words.**

Such instances are rare. Check the guidelines in P1 and P2 so that you do not add unnecessary or incorrect commas.

▶ The statistics reveal that in 1997₎648,000 Hispanic students (48 percent of all Hispanic students) were enrolled in Hispanic-Serving Institutions (HSIs).

P2   Unnecessary Commas

For practice, go to bedfordstmartins.com/theguide/uncom

Because commas are warranted in so many instances, it is easy to use them unnecessarily or incorrectly, particularly with compound sentence elements, with restrictive elements, and between verbs and subjects or verbs and objects.

coordinating conjunction A word that joins comparable and equally important sentence elements: *for, and, or, but, nor, yet,* or *so.*

P2-a **Omit the comma when items in a pair joined by *and* or another coordinating conjunction are not independent clauses.**

Many word pairs can be joined by *and* or another coordinating conjunction, including **compound predicates, compound objects,** and **compound subjects.** None of these pairs should be interrupted by a comma.

independent (main) clause A word group with a subject and a predicate that can stand alone as a separate sentence.

COMPOUND PREDICATE	*I grabbed my lunchbox* and *headed out to the tree.*
COMPOUND OBJECT	As for me, I wore *a pink short set with ruffles* and *a pair of sneakers.*
COMPOUND SUBJECT	My *father* and *brother* wore big hiking boots.

compound predicate Two or more verbs or verb phrases linked by *and.*

Two independent clauses joined by a coordinating conjunction require a comma (see P1-a). The comma shows the reader where one independent clause ends and the other begins. Using a comma in other situations thus sends the wrong signal.

compound object Two or more words acting as an object and linked by *and.*

▶ According to Ward, many Custer fans believe that Custer was a "hero⸴" and "represents certain endangered manly virtues."

▶ The school district could implement more programs at both the junior high and the high school⸴ and thus could offer the students more opportunities.

compound subject Two or more words acting as a subject and linked by *and.*

▶ I was running out of time⸴ and patience.

▶ Culture is not what we do, but how we do things, and why we do them in a particular way.

P2-b Omit any comma that sets off a restrictive word group.

Use commas to set off a nonrestrictive word group but not a restrictive word group. A *restrictive word group* distinguishes the noun it modifies from similar nouns or precisely defines its distinguishing characteristics. A *nonrestrictive word group* provides extra or nonessential information.

RESTRICTIVE   She demonstrates this shortcoming in her story *"Is There Nowhere Else We Can Meet?"*

NONRESTRICTIVE   The supercomputer center, *which I had seen hundreds of times,* still held many mysteries for me.

The context helps to determine which information is necessary and which is extra. In the first example, *"Is There Nowhere Else We Can Meet?"* identifies a specific story, distinguishing it from other stories by the same writer. In the second, *which I had seen hundreds of times* adds supplementary information, but the reference to the mysteries of the supercomputer center would be the same without this addition.

A comma signals that a word group is not essential to the meaning of the sentence. If a comma incorrectly sets off a restrictive word group, it undermines the meaning, suggesting to the reader that essential information is not important. See also P1-c.

▶ The ten people from the community would consist of three retired people, over the age of sixty, three middle-aged people, between the ages of twenty-five and sixty, and four teenagers.

▶ Although divorce is obviously a cause of the psychological problems, a child will face, the parents need to support their child through the anxiety and turmoil.

P2-c Omit any commas that unnecessarily separate the main elements of the sentence — subject and verb or verb and object.

Even in a complicated sentence, a reader expects the core elements — **subject, verb,** and **object** — to lead directly from one to the other. A comma that separates two of these elements confuses matters by suggesting that some other material has been added, such as an introductory or trailing element or a transitional or parenthetical expression.

subject The part of a clause that identifies who or what is being discussed.

verb A word or phrase that expresses action or being and, along with a subject, is a basic component of a sentence.

object The part of a clause that receives the action of the verb: At the checkpoint, we unloaded *the canoes.*

subject The part of a clause that identifies who or what is being discussed.

verb A word or phrase that expresses action or being and, along with a subject, is a basic component of a sentence.

object The part of a clause that receives the action of the verb: At the checkpoint, we unloaded *the canoes*.

Delete a comma that unnecessarily separates a subject and its verb.

▶ *Bilateral,̸* means that both the left and the right sides of the brain are involved in processing a stimulus.

▶ This movie's only fault,̸ is that it does not set a good example for younger children.

Delete a comma that unnecessarily separates a verb and its object.

▶ Now the voters must decide,̸ the issue of term limits.

▶ Unlike Kaoma, many other groups or solo singers try without success to incorporate in their works,̸ music from different cultures.

adverbial clause A clause that nearly always modifies a verb, indicating time, place, condition, reason, cause, purpose, result, or another logical relationship.

P2-d   Omit a comma that separates the main part of the sentence from a trailing adverbial clause.

When an adverbial clause appears at the beginning of a sentence, it is usually set off by a comma because it is an introductory element. When the clause appears at the end of a sentence, however, a comma is ordinarily not needed.

> **When** Pirates of the Caribbean *finally reaches its climax,* **the ending is full of surprises.**

> **Depp shows his charm** *when Sparrow nearly seduces the governor's daughter.*

Omitting this unnecessary comma makes the sentence flow more smoothly.

▶ I found the tables turned,̸ when he interviewed me about the reasons for my tattoo.

noncoordinate adjectives Two or more adjectives that do not modify a noun equally. Instead, one or two of the adjectives closest to the noun form a noun phrase that the remaining adjectives modify: *colorful hot-air* balloons.

P2-e   Leave out any comma that separates noncoordinate adjectives.

If you cannot rearrange the adjectives before a noun or add *and* between them, they are probably noncoordinate adjectives (sometimes called *cumulative adjectives*). Such adjectives are not equal elements; do not separate them with a comma. In contrast, **coordinate adjectives** should be separated by commas (see P1-i).

coordinate adjectives Two or more adjectives that modify a noun equally and independently: the *large, red* hat.

┌COORDINATE ADJECTIVES┐
Wearing a pair of jeans, *cutoff, bleached,* and *torn,* with an embroidered blouse
NONCOORDINATE ADJECTIVES
and *soft leather* sandals, she looked older and more foreign than Julie.

Leather modifies *sandals*, and *soft* modifies *leather sandals* as a unit. Thus the meaning is cumulative, and a comma would interrupt the connection between the adjectives and the noun.

▶ Huge, neighborhood parties could bring the people in our community together.

P2-f Omit any comma that appears before or after a series of items.

Although commas should be used to separate the items in a list, they should not be used before the first item or after the final one.

▶ Race, sex, religion, financial situation, or any other circumstance beyond the control of the applicant, should not be considered.

See also P1-e.

P2-g Omit or correct any other unnecessary or incorrect commas.

Check your essays carefully for the following typical comma problems.

Omit a comma that follows a coordinating conjunction.

> coordinating conjunction A word that joins comparable and equally important sentence elements: *for, and, or, but, nor, yet,* or *so*.

A comma is needed *before* a coordinating conjunction if it links two independent clauses but not if it links a pair of other sentence elements. A comma is never needed *after* a coordinating conjunction, however. Be especially alert to this unnecessary comma when *but* or *yet* appears at the beginning of a sentence.

▶ But, since sharks are not yet classified as endangered species, the members of Congress were not very sympathetic, and the bill was not passed.

Note: A conjunction may or may not be needed for transition or dramatic effect, depending on the context of the sentence in your essay.

▶ ~~But, since~~ *Since* sharks are not yet classified as endangered species, the members of Congress were not very sympathetic, and the bill was not passed.

Omit a comma following a coordinating conjunction joining two independent clauses, even if the conjunction is followed by a transitional or introductory expression.

▶ The ominous vision of the piano wavered before my eyes, and, before I knew it, I was at the base of the steps to the stage, steps that led to potential public humiliation.

dependent (subordinate) clause A word group that has a subject, a predicate, and a subordinating word at the beginning; it cannot stand by itself as a sentence but must be connected to an independent (main) clause.

subordinating conjunction A word or phrase that introduces a dependent clause and relates it to an independent clause.

indirect quotation A reworded statement or question that presents a speaker's or writer's ideas without quoting directly or using quotation marks.

preposition A word (such as *between*, *in*, or *of*) that always appears as part of a phrase and indicates the relation between a word in a sentence and the object of the preposition: The water splashed *into* the canoe.

prepositional phrase A group of words that begins with a preposition and indicates the relation between a word in a sentence and the object following the preposition: Her sunglasses slid *under the seat*.

▶ I had finally felt the music deep in my soul, and,⁄ when I sang, I had a great feeling of relief knowing that everything was going to be all right.

Omit a comma after the word that introduces a dependent clause.

Watch for words such as *who, which, that, whom, whose, where, when, although, because, since, though*, and other **subordinating conjunctions.**

▶ This trend was evident as I entered a college where,⁄ the first-year enrollment had been rising.

▶ The drinking age should be raised because,⁄ drunk driving has become the leading cause of death among young people between the ages of fifteen and twenty-five.

Omit a comma preceding *that* when it introduces an indirect quotation.

Unlike a direct quotation, an indirect quotation is not set off by a comma or quotation marks.

▶ After looking at my tests, the doctor said,⁄ that I had calcification.

Omit a comma immediately following a preposition.

A comma may follow a complete **prepositional phrase** at the beginning of a sentence, but a comma should not follow the preposition or interrupt the phrase.

▶ Despite,⁄ multiple recruitment and retention problems, the number of public school teachers increased by 27 percent between 1986 and 1999.

Omit unnecessary commas that set off a prepositional phrase in the middle of a sentence.

When a prepositional phrase appears in the middle of a sentence or at the end, it is usually not set off by commas. When it acts as an introductory element, however, it is generally followed by a comma.

▶ "I've seen the devil b'fore," he grumbled,⁄ in a serious tone,⁄ with his blue eyes peering into mine.

▶ The children's trauma team gathers in the Resuscitation Room,⁄ at the same time that John Doe is being treated.

Rewrite a sentence that is full of phrases and commas to simplify both the sentence structure and the punctuation.

            By   *the researchers could monitor*

▶ ~~The researchers could monitor, by~~ looking through a porthole window, how

       Noah spent

much time ~~was spent, by Noah,~~ in the dome.

P3 Semicolons

> *For practice, go to* bedfordstmartins.com/theguide/semi

Use semicolons to join closely related independent clauses and to make long sentences with commas easier to read.

P3-a Use a semicolon to join independent clauses if the second clause restates or sets up a contrast to the first.

> In fact, she always had been special; we just never noticed.

Although two independent clauses could be separated by a period, the semicolon tells the reader that they are closely related, emphasizing the restatement or sharpening the contrast.

> ▶ Davie was not an angel ; he was always getting into trouble with the teachers.

Note: When the independent clauses are linked by *and, but,* or another coordinating conjunction, use a comma rather than a semicolon (see P1-a) unless the independent clauses include internal punctuation (see P3-c).

P3-b Use semicolons to separate items in a series when they include internal commas.

> Studies of gender differences in conversational interaction include an Elizabeth Aries article titled "Interaction Patterns and Themes of Male, Female, and Mixed Groups," a study conducted in a research laboratory setting; a Pamela Fishman article titled "Interaction: The Work Women Do," a study researched by naturalistic observation; and an article by Candace West and Don Zimmerman titled "Small Insults: A Study of Interruptions in Cross-Sex Conversation between Unacquainted Persons," a study conducted in a research laboratory setting.

Because the reader expects items in a series to be separated with commas, other commas within items can be confusing. The solution is to leave the internal commas as they are but to use a stronger mark, the semicolon, to signal the divisions between items.

> **independent (main) clause** A word group with a subject and a predicate that can stand alone as a separate sentence.

▶ Appliances that use freon include air conditioners, small models as well as central systems, refrigerators, and freezers, both home and industrial types.

P3-c Use a semicolon to join a series of independent clauses when they include other punctuation.

independent (main) clause A word group with a subject and a predicate that can stand alone as a separate sentence.

Sometimes independent clauses include elements set off by internal punctuation. In such cases, use semicolons between the independent clauses if the other punctuation is likely to confuse a reader or make the sentence parts difficult to identify.

▶ He was the guide, and he was driving us in this old Ford sedan, just the two of us and him, and I had noticed early on that the car didn't have a gas cap.

Independent clauses like these could also be separated by periods, but semicolons let the reader know that the information in each clause is part of a continuing event.

P3-d Use a semicolon to join two independent clauses when the second clause contains a conjunctive adverb or a transitional expression.

conjunctive adverb A word or phrase (such as *finally, however,* or *therefore*) that tells how the ideas in two sentences or independent clauses are connected.

Because a semicolon shows a strong relationship between independent clauses, writers often use it to reinforce the connection expressed by the adverb or transition. Always place the semicolon between the two clauses, no matter where the conjunctive adverb or transitional expression appears. Place the semicolon *before* the conjunctive adverb or transition if it begins the second independent clause. See also P1-d.

transitional expression A word or group of words that expresses the relationship between one sentence and the next.

▶ Ninety-five percent of Americans recognize the components of a healthy diet, however, they fail to apply their nutritional IQ when selecting foods.

P3-e Omit or correct a semicolon used incorrectly to replace a comma or other punctuation mark.

Use semicolons to join two independent clauses or to separate the items in a series when they include other punctuation, but do not use semicolons in place of other punctuation.

Replace a semicolon with a comma to link an independent clause to a phrase or to set off an appositive.

appositive A word or word group that identifies or gives more information about a noun or pronoun that precedes it.

▶ The threat of a potentially devastating malpractice suit promotes the practice of defensive medicine, doctors ordering excessive and expensive tests to confirm a diagnosis.

Replace a semicolon with a comma to join two independent clauses linked by a coordinating conjunction.

> ▶ The ashtrays would need to be relocated to that area;, and it could then become an outdoor smoking lounge.

See also P1-a.

Replace a semicolon with a colon to introduce a list.

> ▶ Our county ditches fill up with old items that are hard to get rid of;: old refrigerators, mattresses, couches, and chairs, just to name a few.

Note: For introducing an in-text list as in this example, a dash (see P5-b) is a less formal and more dramatic alternative to the colon (see P4-a).

coordinating conjunction A word that joins comparable and equally important sentence elements: *for, and, or, but, nor, yet,* or *so.*

P4 Colons

For practice, go to bedfordstmartins.com/theguide/colon

Besides introducing specific sentence elements, colons conventionally appear in works cited or bibliography entries, introduce subtitles, express ratios and times, and follow the salutations in formal letters.

P4-a Use a colon to introduce a list, an appositive, a quotation, a question, or a statement.

Usually, a colon follows an **independent clause** that makes a general statement; after the colon, the rest of the sentence often supplies specifics — a definition, a quotation or question, or a list (generally in grammatically parallel form; see E7).

> Society's hatred, violence, and bigotry take root here: the elementary school playground.

Use the colon selectively to alert readers to closely connected ideas, a significant point, a crucial definition, or a dramatic revelation.

Note: Because a colon follows but does not interrupt an independent clause, it is not used after words such as *is, are, consists of, including, such as, for instance,* and *for example* (see P4-b).

appositive A word or word group that identifies or gives more information about a noun or pronoun that precedes it.

independent (main) clause A word group with a subject and a predicate that can stand alone as a separate sentence.

Consider using a colon to introduce a list.

You can use a colon to introduce a list if the list is preceded by an independent clause. Be careful not to interrupt the clause in the middle (see P4-b).

▶ Most young law school graduates become trial lawyers in one of three ways,/: by going to work for a government prosecutor's office, by working for a private law firm, or by opening private offices of their own.

Consider using a colon to emphasize an appositive.

appositive A word or word group that identifies or gives more information about a noun or pronoun that precedes it.

Although you can always use commas to set off an appositive, try using a colon occasionally when you need special emphasis.

▶ The oldest fishermen are followed by the younger generation of middle-aged fathers, excited by the chance to show their sons what their fathers once taught them. Last to arrive are the novices,/: the thrill seekers.

Consider using a colon to introduce a formal quotation, a question, a statement, or another independent clause.

▶ We learn that the narrator is a troublemaker in paragraph twelve,/: "I got thrown out of the center for playing pool when I should've been sewing."

▶ I ran around the office in constant fear of his questions,/: What do you have planned for the day? How many demonstrations are scheduled for this week? How many contacts have you made?

▶ Both authors are clearly of the same opinion,/: recycling scrap tires is no longer an option.

▶ I guess the saying is true,/: Absence does make the heart grow fonder.

Do not capitalize the first word following a colon that introduces an incomplete sentence. However, when the first word following a colon introduces a complete sentence, you can either capitalize the word or not, depending on your preference (see M2-b). Whichever choice you prefer, be consistent. When you introduce a quotation with a colon, always capitalize the word that begins the quotation. See also P6-b.

P4-b Delete or correct an unnecessary or incorrect colon.

As you proofread your writing, watch out for the following incorrect uses of the colon.

Omit a colon that interrupts an independent clause, especially after words such as *is, are, include, composed of, consists of, including, such as, for instance,* **and for** *example.*

▶ The tenets include; courtesy, integrity, perseverance, self-control, indomitable spirit, and modesty.

Replace an inappropriate colon with the correct punctuation mark.

▶ As I was touring the different areas of the shop, I ran into Christy, one of the owners; "Hi, Kim," she said with a smile on her face.

P5   Dashes

For practice, go to bedfordstmartins.com/theguide/dashes

A dash breaks the rhythm or interrupts the meaning of a sentence, setting off information with greater emphasis than another punctuation mark could supply. Writers often use dashes to substitute for other punctuation in quick notes and letters to friends. In many kinds of published writing, dashes are an option used sparingly — but often to good effect.

P5-a Type, space, and position a dash correctly.

Type a dash (—) as two hyphens (--) in a row with no spaces before or after. Use one dash before a word or words set off at the end of the sentence. Use two dashes — one at the beginning and one at the end — if the word or words are in the middle of the sentence.

▶ The rigid structure and asymmetrical arrangements of the sculpture blend well with three different surroundings--the trees, the library building, and the parking lots.

▶ Of all public stations in Maryland, WBJC reaches the largest audience--almost 200,000 listeners per week.

▶ And of course, the trees in the sculpture were more than just imitation--they spoke!

Note: Most word processing programs will allow you to insert a solid dash (—) instead of two hyphens (--).

Use a pair of dashes, not just one, to mark the beginning and end of a word group that needs emphasis.

> ▶ I could tell that the people in the room work in uncomfortable conditions —
>
> they all wear white lab coats, caps, and gloves, but they joke or laugh while
>
> building the guns.

If the word group includes commas or other internal punctuation, the dashes tell the reader exactly where the expression that is being set off begins and ends.

P5-b   **Consider using a dash to set off material from the rest of the sentence.**

> That smell completely cut off the outside world — the smell of the ocean, the soft
> breeze, the jubilation of young people under the sun.

Because the dash marks a strong break, it alerts the reader to the importance of the material that follows it.

Consider inserting a dash or pair of dashes to emphasize a definition, a dramatic statement, a personal comment, or an explanation.

> ▶ Binge eating, larger than normal consumption of high-calorie foods, starts with
> emotional distress and depression.

> ▶ But unlike the boys, the girls often turn to something other than violence,
> motherhood.

> ▶ In many cases it may be more humane and I personally believe it is much
>
> more humane to practice euthanasia than to cause the patient prolonged
>
> suffering and pain.

Consider inserting a dash or pair of dashes to emphasize a list.

If the list appears in the middle of the sentence, use one dash at the beginning and another at the end to signal exactly where the list begins and ends.

> ▶ Another problem is that certain toy figures The Hulk, Spider-Man, and the
>
> X-Men, to name just a few, are characters from movies that portray violence.

P5-c Rewrite a sentence that uses the dash inappropriately or excessively.

Use dashes purposefully; avoid relying on them instead of using other punctuation marks or developing clear sentences and transitions.

▶ Finally the TV people were finished with their interviewing —— *and* ~~now they~~ wanted to do a shot of the entrance to the restaurant.

If you are not sure whether you have used a dash or pair of dashes appropriately, try removing the material that is set off. If the sentence does not make logical and grammatical sense, one or both of the dashes are misused or misplaced.

▶ That's a tall order — and a reason to start ~/~ amassing some serious capital soon.

P6   Quotation Marks

For practice, go to bedfordstmartins.com/theguide/quoto

Use double quotation marks, always in pairs, to indicate direct quotations, to set off special uses of words, and to mark some types of titles. Proofread carefully to be sure that you have added quotation marks at both the beginning and the end of each quotation.

P6-a Set off direct quotations with quotation marks.

A direct quotation is set off by a pair of quotation marks and by an initial capital letter. **Indirect quotations,** however, do not use quotation marks or capital letters.

"Mary," I finally said, "I can't keep coming in every weekend."

Montgomery stated, "A good beating with a cane can have a remarkable sense of awakening on the mind and conscience of a boy" (James 13).

Ms. Goldman is saying that it's time to face the real issues.

When a phrase such as *she said* interrupts the quotation, do not capitalize the first word after the phrase unless the word actually begins a new quoted sentence.

▶ The commissioners came to the conclusion that alcohol prohibition was, in

the words of Walter Lippman, a helpless failure."

direct quotation A speaker's or writer's exact words, which are enclosed in quotation marks.

indirect quotation A reworded statement or question that presents a speaker's or writer's ideas without quoting directly or using quotation marks.

Note: In a research paper, indent a long quotation as a block, double spaced, and omit quotation marks. If you are following **MLA style**, indent a long quotation (five typed lines or more) an inch from the left margin. If you are following **APA style,** indent a long quotation (forty words or more) one-half inch.

> The mother points out the social changes over Dee's and her lifetime, contrasting the two time periods.
>
> > Who can even imagine me looking a strange white man in the eye? It seems to me I have talked to them always with one foot raised in flight, with my head turned in whichever way is farthest from them. Dee, though. She would always look anyone in the eye. (Walker 49)

P6-b Follow convention in using punctuation at the end of a quotation, after a phrase such as *he said* or *she said*, and with other punctuation in the same sentence.

Using other punctuation with quotation marks can be tricky at times.

Place a comma or a period inside the closing quotation mark.

▶ Fishman also discusses utterances such as "umm," "oh," and "yeah."

▶ Grandpa then said, "I guess you haven't heard what happened."

▶ "At that point I definitely began to have my doubts, but I tried to go on with my 'normal life.'"

In a research paper following either MLA style or APA style, the closing quotation mark should follow the last quoted word, but the period at the end of the sentence should follow the parentheses enclosing the citation.

▶ Senator Gabriel Ambrosio added that "an override would send a terrible message, particularly to the young people (Schwaneberg 60)."

Note: Place a colon or semicolon outside the closing quotation mark.

> The doctor who tells the story says that the girl is "furious"; she shrieks "terrifyingly, hysterically" as he approaches her.

Follow an introductory phrase such as *he said* with either a comma or the word *that*.

▶ I looked down and said, "I was trying on your dress blues."

MLA style Conventions set forth in the guidelines of the Modern Language Association for preparing research papers and documenting sources. See Chapter 24.

APA style Conventions set forth in the guidelines of the American Psychological Association for preparing research papers and documenting sources. See Chapter 24.

▶ Eberts and Schwirian bluntly point out that, "control attempts aimed at constraining or rehabilitating individual criminals or at strengthening local police forces are treating the symptoms or results of social conditions" (98).

When you introduce a formal quotation with an independent clause, you can instead follow the introduction with a colon. (See P4-a.)

Place a question mark or an exclamation point inside the closing quotation mark if it is part of the quotation, or outside if it is part of your own sentence.

▶ My father replied, "What have I ever done to you"?

▶ How is it possible that he could have kept repeating to our class, "You are too dumb to learn anything?"?

Note: You do not need to add a period if a question mark or an exclamation point concludes a quotation at the end of the sentence.

▶ Miriam produces a highlighter from her bookbag with an enthusiastic "Voilà!".

Supply a closing quotation mark at the end of a paragraph to show that a new quotation begins in the next paragraph.

In a dialogue, enclose each speaker's words in quotation marks, and begin a new paragraph every time the speaker changes.

▶ "Come on, James," Toby said. "Let's climb over the fence. "I don't think it's a good idea!" I replied.

Omit the closing quotation mark if a quotation continues in the next paragraph.

If a quotation from a speaker or writer continues from one paragraph to the next, omit the closing quotation mark at the end of the first paragraph, but begin the next paragraph with a quotation mark to show that the quote continues.

▶ "... I enjoy waiting on these people because they also ask about my life, instead of treating me like a servant."

"However, some customers can be rude and very impatient...."

P6-c **Consider using double quotation marks to set off words being defined.**

Set off words sparingly (see P6-f), using quotation marks only for those you define or use with a special meaning. You may also use underlining or italics rather than quotation marks to set off words. (See M5-b.)

▶ The two most popular words in the state statutes are "reasonable" and

"appropriate," used to describe the manner of administration.

Note: Occasionally, quotation marks identify words used ironically. In general, keep such use to a minimum. (See P6-f.)

P6-d Enclose titles of short works (such as articles, chapters, essays, short stories, short poems, episodes in a television program, and songs) in quotation marks.

Note: Titles of longer works are underlined or italicized. (See M5-a.)

▶ The short story The Use of Force, by William Carlos Williams, is an account of a

doctor's unpleasant experience with his patient.

▶ Charlene Marner Solomon, author of Careers under Glass, writes an excellent, in-depth article on obstacles working women encounter when trying to move up the corporate ladder.

Place the quotation marks around the exact title of the work mentioned.

▶ The "Use of Force," by William Carlos Williams, is at first just another story of a doctor's visit.

Note: When you supply your own title at the beginning of your own essay, do not enclose it in quotation marks.

P6-e Use single quotation marks inside double quotation marks to show a quotation within a quotation.

Single quotation marks indicate that the quoted words come from another source or that the source added quotation marks for emphasis.

▶ Flanagan and McMenamin say, "Housing values across the United States have

acted more like a fluctuating stock market than the 'sure' investment they

once were."

P6-f Omit or correct quotation marks used excessively or incorrectly.

Avoid using quotation marks unnecessarily when you wish to set off words or include direct or indirect quotations.

Omit unneeded quotation marks used for emphasis, irony, or distance.

Avoid using quotation marks just to emphasize certain words, to show irony, or to distance yourself from slang, clichés, or trite expressions. Reserve quotation marks for words that you define or use with a special meaning. (See P6-c.)

▶ Environmental groups can wage war in the hallways of Washington and Sacramento and drive oil companies away from our " ~~sacred~~ shores. "

Add quotation marks to show direct quotations, and omit them from indirect quotations, rewording as necessary to present material accurately.

that ˅while
▶ To start things off, he said, "While farming in Liberty, Texas, at the age of

˅inspired his move to Houston.
eighteen, the spirit of God ~~came to him to go to Houston.~~"

Whenever you quote a written source or a person you have interviewed, check your notes to make sure that you are using quotation marks to enclose only the speaker's or writer's exact words.

P7 Apostrophes

For practice, go to bedfordstmartins.com/theguide/apo

Use an apostrophe to mark the **possessive form** of nouns and some pronouns, the omission of letters or figures, and the plural of letters or figures.

P7-a Use an apostrophe to show the possessive form of a noun.

The form of a possessive noun depends on whether it is singular (one item) or plural (two or more items).

Add -'s to a singular noun to show possession.

a student's parents   the rabbit's eye   Ward's essay

Be sure to include the apostrophe and to place it before the -*s* so that the reader does not mistakenly think that the noun is plural.

apartment's
▶ The ~~apartments~~ design lacks softening curves to tame the bare walls.

library's
▶ Mrs. Johnson says that 90 percent of the ~~libraries~~ material is on the first floor.

Indicate shared or joint possession by adding -'*s* to the final noun in a list; indicate individual possession by adding -'*s* to each noun.

slang Informal language that tends to change rapidly.

cliché An overused expression that has lost its original freshness, such as *hard as a rock*.

direct quotation A speaker's or writer's exact words, which are enclosed in quotation marks.

indirect quotation A reworded statement or question that presents a speaker's or writer's ideas without quoting directly or using quotation marks.

possessive form The form that shows that a thing belongs to someone or to something.

father and mother's room (joint or shared possession)

father's and mother's patterns of conversation (individual possession)

Indicate possession by adding *-'s* to the last word in a compound.

mother-in-law's

Note: Even if a singular noun ends in *s*, add an apostrophe and *-s*. If the second *s* makes the word hard to pronounce, it is acceptable to add only an apostrophe.

Louis's life   Williams's narrator   Cisneros's story   Sophocles' plays

To show possession, add only an apostrophe to a plural noun that ends in *s* but *-'s* if the plural noun does not end in *s*.

their neighbors' homes   other characters' expressions
the children's faces   the women's team

                                females'

▶ Males tend to interrupt ~~females~~ conversations.

Note: Form the plural of a family name by adding *-s* without an apostrophe (the Harrisons); add the apostrophe only to show possession (the Harrisons' house).

P7-b **Add an apostrophe to show where letters or figures are omitted from a contraction.**

      Let's

▶ "~~Lets~~ go back inside and see if you can do it my way now."

                         '90s.

▶ Many people had cosmetic surgery in the ~~90s.~~

Note: The possessive forms of **personal pronouns** do not have apostrophes (*yours, its, hers, his, ours, theirs*) but are sometimes confused with contractions (such as *it's* for *it is*).

                                  its

▶ A huge 10- by 4-foot painting of the perfect wave in all ~~it's~~ glorious detail hangs high up on the wall of the surfing club.

P7-c **Add *-'s* to form the plural of a number, a letter, or an abbreviation.**

perfect 10's   mostly *A*'s and *B*'s   training the R.A.'s

                             3's

▶ The participants were shown a series of ~~3s~~ that configured into a large 5.

To show that a date refers to a decade, add *-s* without an apostrophe.

---

personal pronoun A pronoun that refers to a specific person or object and changes form depending on its function in a sentence, such as *I, me, my, we, us,* and *our.*

Women have come a long way in the business world since the 1950s.

Note: Some style guides, such as the MLA guide, prefer no apostrophes with plural abbreviations: *ATMs.*

P7-d Add -'s to form the possessive of an indefinite pronoun.

▶ **Everyone knows that good service can make or break ~~ones~~ dining experience.**
                                          one's

Note: The possessive forms of **personal pronouns,** however, do not have apostrophes: *my, mine, your, yours, hers, his, its, our, ours, their, theirs.*

P7-e Omit unnecessary or incorrect apostrophes.

Watch for an apostrophe incorrectly added to a plural noun ending in *s* when the noun is not a possessive.

        patients
▶ **Autistic ~~patient's~~ can be high, middle, or low functioning.**

Also remove an apostrophe added to a possessive **personal pronoun** (*yours, its, hers, his, ours, theirs*), watching especially for any forms confused with contractions (such as *it's* for *it is*). See also P7-b.

                                                          Its
▶ **That company does not use animals to develop ~~it's~~ products.**

P8   Parentheses

For practice, go to bedfordstmartins.com/theguide/paren

Parentheses are useful for enclosing material — a word, a phrase, or even a complete sentence — that interrupts a sentence. Place words in parentheses anywhere after the first word of the sentence as long as the placement is appropriate and relevant and the sentence remains easy to read.

P8-a Add parentheses to enclose additions to a sentence.

Parentheses are useful for enclosing citations of research sources (following the format required by your style guide); for enclosing an **acronym** or abbreviation at first mention; for adding dates, definitions, illustrations, or other elaborations; and for numbering or lettering a list (always using a pair of marks).

▶ **Americans are not utilizing their knowledge, and as a result, their children are**

                            (   ).

not benefiting *American Dietetic Association* 582,

    People for the Ethical Treatment of Animals
▶ **(PETA) is a radical animal liberation group.**

---

indefinite pronoun A pronoun that does not refer to a particular person or object, such as *all, anybody, anywhere, each, enough, every, everyone, everything, one, somebody, something, either, more, most, neither, none,* or *nobody.*

personal pronoun A pronoun that refers to a specific person or object and changes form depending on its function in a sentence, such as *I, me, my, we, us,* and *our.*

acronym A word formed from the first letters of the phrase that it abbreviates, such as *BART* for *Bay Area Rapid Transit.*

▶ The bill ~~called~~ (S-2232) was introduced to protect people who smoke off the job against employment discrimination.

▶ Signals would (1) prevent life-threatening collisions, (2) provide more efficient and speedy movement of traffic, and (3) decrease frustration and loss of driver judgment.

Note: Use commas to separate the items in a numbered list. If the items include internal commas, use semicolons. (See P3-b.)

P8-b   Correct the punctuation used with parentheses, and omit unnecessary parentheses.

When you add information in parentheses, the basic pattern of the sentence should remain logical and complete, and the punctuation should be the same as it would be if the parenthetical addition were removed. Delete any comma *before* a parenthesis mark.

▶ As I stood at the salad bar, a young lady asked if the kitchen had any cream cheese (normally served only at breakfast).

Parentheses are unnecessary if they enclose information that could simply be integrated into the sentence.

▶ He didn't exhibit the uncontrollable temper and the high-velocity swearing (typical of many high school coaches).

P9   Brackets

For practice, go to bedfordstmartins.com/theguide/brack

Use brackets to insert editorial notes into a quotation and to enclose parenthetical material within text that is already in parentheses. In a quotation, the brackets tell the reader that the added material is yours, not the original author's. See also P10.

▶ " 'The gang is your family,' he [Hagan] explains."

If the original quotation includes a mistake, add [sic], the Latin word for "so," in brackets to tell the reader that the error occurs in the source. Often you can reword your sentence to omit the error.

Replace inappropriate brackets with parentheses.

▶ The American Medical Society has linked "virtual" violence (violence in the

various media) to real-life acts of violence (Hollis 623).

P10   Ellipsis Marks

For practice, go to bedfordstmartins.com/theguide/ellip

Use ellipsis marks to indicate a deliberate omission within a quotation or to mark a dramatic pause in a sentence. Type ellipsis marks as three spaced periods (. . .), with a space before the first period and following the last period.

Aries also noticed this reaction in her research: "The mixed group setting seems to benefit men more than women . . . allowing men more variation in the ways they participate in discussions" (32).

If you omit the end of a quoted sentence or if you omit a sentence or more from the middle of a quoted passage, add a sentence period and a space before the first ellipsis mark. (If a quotation that ends with ellipsis marks is followed by a parenthetical citation, put the sentence period at the very end — after the closing quotation mark and the citation.)

Do not use opening or closing ellipsis marks if the quotation is clearly only part of a sentence.

▶ According to the environmental group Earthgreen, U.S. oil reserves ". . . will be economically depleted by 2018 at the current consumption rate . . ." (Miller 476).

See pp. 539–41 and pp. 757–58 for more on ellipsis marks.

P11   Slashes

For practice, go to bedfordstmartins.com/theguide/slash

Use a slash to separate quoted lines of poetry and to separate word pairs that present options or opposites.

In "A Poison Tree," William Blake gives the same advice: "I was angry with my friend: / I told my wrath, my wrath did end."

Note: When you use a slash to show the lines in poetry, leave a space before and after the mark. If you quote four lines or more, omit the quotation marks and slashes and present the poetry line for line as a block quotation, double spaced. Following **MLA style,** indent each line of a block quotation ten spaces or an inch from the left margin. See also P6-a.

P12   Periods

For practice, go to bedfordstmartins.com/theguide/period

Use a period to mark the end of a **declarative sentence,** an **indirect question,** or an abbreviation.

▶ Another significant use for clinical hypnosis would be to replace anesthesia.

▶ She asked her professor why he was not as tough on her as he was on the male students?.

▶ Mrs. Drabin was probably one of the smartest people I knew.

Note: Some abbreviations do not include periods (see M6); always check your dictionary to be sure. In addition, many specialized professional and academic fields have their own systems for handling abbreviations.

P13   Question Marks

For practice, go to bedfordstmartins.com/theguide/quest

Add a question mark after a direct question.

▶ Did they even read my information sheet/?

Avoid using question marks to express irony or sarcasm. Use them sparingly to question the accuracy of a preceding word or figure.

P14   Exclamation Points

For practice, go to bedfordstmartins.com/theguide/excl

Use an exclamation point to show strong emotion or emphasis.

He fell on one knee and exclaimed, "Marry me, my beautiful princess!"

Use exclamation points sparingly. Replace inappropriate or excessive exclamation points with periods.

▶ If parents know which disciplinary methods to use, they can effectively protect their children!.

MLA style Conventions set forth in the guidelines of the Modern Language Association for preparing research papers and documenting sources. See Chapter 24.

declarative sentence A sentence that makes a statement rather than asking a question or exclaiming.

indirect question A statement that tells what a question asked without directly asking the question.

M   Mechanics

M1   Hyphens

Hyphens are used to form **compound words** and to break words at the end of a line. Depending on the word and its position in a sentence, a compound may be written as separate words with no hyphen between them, as one word with no space or hyphen between the parts, or as a hyphenated word.

moonshine	postmaster	shipboard
vice versa	place kick	highly regarded
like-minded	once-over	all-around
father-in-law	take-it-or-leave-it	mid-December

> **compound word** A word formed from two or more words that function together as a unit.

M1-a Use a hyphen to join the parts of a compound adjective when it precedes a noun but not when it follows a noun.

> **compound adjective** An adjective formed from two or more words that function as a unit.

Before Noun	*After Noun*
after-school activities	activities after school
well-known athlete	athlete who is well known
fast-growing business	business that is fast growing

When a compound adjective precedes a noun, the hyphen clarifies that the compound functions as a unit.

▶ People usually think of locusts as hideous looking creatures that everyone dislikes and wants to squash.

▶ I was a nineteen year old second semester sophomore.

▶ People are becoming increasingly health conscious.

When two different prefixes or initial words are meant to go with the same second word, use a hyphen and a space at the end of the first prefix or word.

Over twenty people crowd the small trauma room, an army of green- and blue-hooded medical personnel.

Note: Some compound adjectives are nearly always hyphenated, before or after a noun, including those beginning with *all-* or *self-*.

all-inclusive fee	self-sufficient economy
fee that is all-inclusive	economy that is self-sufficient

▶ The use of ethanol will be a self perpetuating trend.

A compound with an -ly **adverb** preceding an **adjective** or a **participle** is always left as two words.

brilliantly clever scheme	rapidly growing business	highly regarded professor

> **adverb** A word that modifies a verb, an adjective, or another adverb, often telling when, where, why, how, or how often.

> **adjective** A word that modifies a noun or a pronoun, adding information about it.

M1-b Present a compound noun as one word, as separate words, or as a hyphenated compound.

If you are not certain about a particular compound noun, look it up in your dictionary. If you cannot find it, spell it as separate words.

Close up the parts of a compound noun spelled as one word.

▶ Another road in our county now looks like an appliance grave yard.

Omit hyphens in a compound noun spelled as separate words.

▶ First, make the community aware of the problem by writing a letter-to-the-editor.

> **participle** A verb form showing present tense (*dancing, freezing*) or past tense (*danced, frozen*) that can also act as an adjective.

> **compound noun** A noun formed from two or more words that function as a unit.

Add any hyphens needed in a hyphenated compound noun.

Hyphenate fractions, compound numbers (up to ninety-nine), and other nouns that are hyphenated in your dictionary.

▶ Almost two thirds of women who marry before age eighteen end up divorced,

twice the number of women who marry at twenty one or older.

Note: Some compound words have more than one acceptable spelling (*workforce* and *work force*, for example); if you use such a compound, choose one spelling and use it consistently. If you are unsure about whether to use a hyphen, check your dictionary, or follow the common usage of professional publications in that field.

M1-c Spell words formed with most prefixes (including *anti-*, *co-*, *mini-*, *multi-*, *non-*, *post-*, *pre-*, *re-*, *sub-*, and *un-*) as one word with no hyphen.

antismoking	coauthor	multicultural	nonviolent
postwar	repossess	submarine	unskilled

▶ This possibility is so rare as to be non-existent.

Note: Insert a hyphen in a compound noun beginning with *ex-*, *great-*, or *self-* (unless it is followed by a suffix, as in *selfhood*) or ending in *-elect* or *-in-law*. Check your dictionary in case of a question.

ex-husband   self-esteem   secretary-elect

▶ Self-sufficiency is not the only motivation.

Note: Use a hyphen in a word that includes a prefix and a **proper noun**.

un-American   anti-American   pro-American

M1-d Use a hyphen when necessary to avoid ambiguity.

Sometimes a hyphen is necessary to prevent a reader from confusing a word with a prefix (*re-cover* or *re-creation*) with another word (*recover* or *recreation*) or from stumbling over a word in which two or three of the same letters fall together (*anti-inflammatory, troll-like*).

> The police officers asked for the *recreation* facility's logbook to help them
> *re-create* the circumstances surrounding the crime.

M1-e Insert a hyphen between syllables to divide a word at the end of a line.

If you must divide a word, look for a logical division, such as between syllables, between parts of a compound word, or between the root and a prefix or suffix. If you are uncertain about where to divide a word, check your dictionary.

go-ing   height-en   mus-cu-la-ture   back-stage
dis-satis-fied   com-mit-ment   honor-able   philos-ophy

Although many word processors will automatically divide words, writing is easier to read without numerous broken words. Check with your instructor or consult the style manual used in a specific field for advice about whether to use the hyphenation function.

M2   Capitalization

Capitalize proper nouns, the first word in a sentence or a quotation that is a sentence, and the main words in a title.

M2-a Capitalize proper nouns but not common nouns.

Capitalize specific names of people, groups, places, streets, events, historical periods, monuments, holidays, days, months, and directions that refer to specific geographic areas.

proper noun The capitalized name of a specific person, group, place, or thing.

common noun The general name of a person, place, or thing.

World War II	the Great Depression	Lincoln Memorial
Independence Day	Passover	Ramadan
Monday	January	Colorado College
the Northeast	Native Americans	Magnolia Avenue

> A
> ▶ It is difficult for ^americans to comprehend the true meaning of freedom.

When a reference is general, use a common noun (uncapitalized) rather than a proper one (capitalized). Do not capitalize general names of institutions, seasons, compass directions, or words that you simply want to emphasize.

| summer vacation | last winter | university requirements |
| church service | southern exposure | western life |

> f
> ▶ The ^Federal institutions never even review the student's real financial situation.

> l   o
> ▶ I work in a ^Law ^Office that specializes in settling accident cases.

Note: Adjectives derived from proper nouns should be capitalized: *Mexican, Napoleonic.* Common nouns such as *street* and *river* are capitalized only when they are part of a proper noun: *Main Street, the Mississippi River.*

M2-b Capitalize the word that begins a sentence.

> T
> ▶ ^the garden was their world.

If a complete sentence appears within parentheses and is not part of a larger sentence, capitalize the first word.

independent (main) clause A word group with a subject and a predicate that can stand alone as a separate sentence.

Note: When you use a colon to introduce an **independent clause** — usually a dramatic or emphatic statement, a question, or a quotation — you may either capitalize the first word of the clause or not capitalize it, but be consistent within an essay. When you use a colon to introduce any other type of clause, phrase, or word, as in a list, do not capitalize the first word unless it is a proper noun. (See P4-a.)

M2-c Capitalize the first word in a quotation unless it is integrated into your own wording or continues an interrupted quotation.

Lucy Danziger says, "Forget about the glass ceiling" (81).

Marilyn describes the adult bison as having an "ugly, shaggy, brown coat."

Writers often incorporate short quotations and quotations introduced by *that* into their sentences; neither needs an initial capital letter. When a phrase such as *she said* interrupts a quotation, capitalize the first word in the quotation but not the first word after the phrase unless it begins a new sentence. See also P6.

▶ Toby said, "~~t~~rust me — we won't get caught."   *(T)*

▶ "~~r~~enting," she insists, "deprives you of big tax breaks."   *(R)*

Note: If you quote from a poem, capitalize words exactly as the poet does.

M2-d **Capitalize the first and last words in a title and subtitle plus all other words except for articles, coordinating conjunctions, and prepositions.**

War and Peace   *The Grand Canyon Suite*
Tragedy: Vision and Form   "On First Looking into Chapman's Homer"

Titles of short works are placed in quotation marks (see P6-d), and titles of long works are underlined or italicized (see M5-a).

▶ In her article "The Gun ~~I~~n ~~T~~he Closet," Straight tells of booming Riverside, *(i)* *(t)*

California, a city east of Los Angeles.

M2-e **Capitalize a title that precedes a person's name but not one that follows a name or appears without a name.**

Professor John Ganim   Aunt Alice
John Ganim, my professor   Alice Jordan, my favorite aunt

▶ At the state level, Reverend Green is ~~P~~resident of the State Congress of Christian *(p)*

Education and ~~M~~oderator of the Old Landmark Association. *(m)*

Note: References to the President (of the United States) and other major public figures are sometimes capitalized in all contexts.

M2-f **Avoid overusing capitalization for emphasis.**

Although in some writing situations a word that appears entirely in capital letters can create a desired effect, you should limit this use of capital letters to rare occasions.

The powerful SMACK of the ball on the rival's thigh brings an abrupt, anticlimactic end to the rising tension.

---

article An adjective that precedes a noun and identifies a definite reference to something specific (*the*) or an indefinite reference to something less specific (*a* or *an*).

coordinating conjunction A word that joins comparable and equally important sentence elements: *for, and, or, but, nor, yet,* or *so.*

preposition A word (such as *between, in,* or *of*) that always appears as part of a phrase and that indicates the relation between a word in a sentence and the object of the preposition: The water splashed *into* the canoe.

In most cases, follow the conventions for capitalizing described in this section.

▶ The principles are called the ~~TENETS OF TAE KWON DO.~~ *tenets of Tae Kwon Do.*

M3 Spacing

Allow standard spacing between words and punctuation marks. Writers have traditionally left two spaces after a period at the end of a sentence and one after a comma. Style guides such as **APA** now recommend leaving one space after a sentence period. **MLA** and APA also supply specific directions about spacing source citations.

M3-a Supply any missing space before or after a punctuation mark.

Although spell-checkers can help identify some misspelled words, they do not indicate spacing errors unless the error links two words or splits a word. Even if you write on a word processor, proofread carefully for spacing errors around punctuation marks.

▶ My curiosity got the best of me, so I flipped through the pages to see what would happen.

▶ "I found to my horror, " Nadine later wept, "that I was too late!"

▶ "I would die without bread!" Roberto declared. "In my village, they made fresh bread every morning."

▶ Pet adoption fees include the cost of spaying or neutering all dogs and cats four months old or older (if needed).

M3-b Close up any unnecessary space between words and punctuation marks.

▶ Karl did not know why this war was considered justifiable by the U.S. government .

▶ The larger florist shops require previous experience , but the smaller , portable wagons require only a general knowledge of flowers.

▶ Do you remember the song " The Wayward Wind" ?

M4 Numbers

Conventions for the treatment of numbers vary widely. In the humanities, writers tend to spell out numbers, but in the sciences and social sciences, writers are far more likely to use numerals.

one out of ten   1 out of 10

APA style Conventions set forth in the guidelines of the American Psychological Association for preparing research papers and documenting sources. See Chapter 24.

MLA style Conventions set forth in the guidelines of the Modern Language Association for preparing research papers and documenting sources. See Chapter 24.

M4-a Spell out whole numbers *one* through *ninety-nine,* numbers that begin sentences, and very large round numbers in most nonscientific college writing.

Five or six vehicles, in various states of disrepair, are on the property.

Forty-eight percent of students enrolling in bachelor's programs at public colleges fail to graduate.

There are more than eleven thousand regular parking spaces and almost a thousand metered spaces.

Spell out whole numbers *one* through *ninety-nine* in most nonscientific college writing.

▶ A hefty $7,000 per week is paid to Wells Fargo Security for *four* 4 guards who patrol the grounds ~~24~~ *twenty-four* hours a day.

▶ Only ~~15~~ *fifteen* years ago, it was difficult to find any public figures who were openly gay.

Note: Depending on the type of writing that you do and the conventions of your field, you may decide to spell out only numerals up to ten. Either rule is acceptable. Just be sure to follow it consistently.

Be consistent also in expressing related numbers. The following sentence expresses a range as "5 to 17." Ordinarily, *five* and *seventeen* would be spelled out, but because they appear in context with larger numbers expressed as numerals, they too are presented as numerals.

The dentists examined the mouths of 42,500 children, aged 5 to 17, at 970 schools across the nation.

Note: If two numbers occur in succession, use a combination of spelled-out words and numerals for clarity.

eight 44-cent stamps   ten 3-year-olds

Spell out a number that begins a sentence, or rewrite so that the number is no longer the first word.

▶ *Forty-one thousand* ~~41,000~~ women die from breast cancer each year.

▶ *Each year,* 41,000 women die from breast cancer ~~each year~~.

Spell out very large round numbers, or use a combination of numerals and words.

3.5 million dollars *or* $3.5 million	nearly 14 million
five thousand	a billion

M4-b **Use numerals for numbers over a hundred, in fractions and percentages, with abbreviations and symbols, in addresses and dates, and for page numbers and sections of books.**

99% 73 percent	3 cm 185 lbs.	5 a.m. 10:30 p.m.	$200
175 Fifth Avenue	May 6, 1970	the 1980s	18.5 1/2
page 44	chapter 22	volume 8	289 envelopes

▶ A woman with the same skills as her coworkers may earn an additional ~~eight~~ 8 to

~~twenty~~ 20 percent just by being well groomed.

Note: Either the word *percent* or the % symbol is acceptable as long as it is used consistently throughout a paper.

▶ The movie *Midnight Cowboy* was rated X in the late ~~nineteen sixties~~ 1960s.

M5   Underlining (Italics)

When they are printed, underlined words appear in the slanted type called *italics*. Most word processors now include an italics option, but your instructor may prefer that you continue to underline.

M5-a **Underline or italicize titles of long or self-contained works.**

Titles of books, newspapers, magazines, scholarly journals, pamphlets, long poems, movies, videotapes, CDs and DVDs, television and radio programs, long musical compositions, plays, comic strips, and works of art are underlined or italicized.

Hemingway's novel *The Sun Also Rises*	*Beowulf*	*Citizen Kane*
the *Washington Post*	*60 Minutes*	*Pride and Prejudice*

I found that the article in the *Journal of the American Medical Association* had more information and stronger scientific proof than the article in *American Health*.

Note: The Bible and its divisions are not underlined.

Titles of short works or works contained in other works, such as chapters, essays, articles, stories, short poems, and individual episodes of a television program are not underlined but are placed in quotation marks. See also P6-d.

▶ The hit Reese Witherspoon film "Legally Blonde" was based on a novel by Amanda Brown, whose most recent book is "Family Trust."

▶ The original "Star Trek" episode "The Trouble with Tribbles" was hugely popular.

M5-b Underline or italicize words used as words and letters and numbers used as themselves.

the word *committed*   three *7*'s   a *q* or a *g*

▶ Rank order is a term that Aries uses to explain the way that some individuals take the role as the leader and the others fall in behind.

M5-c Underline or italicize names of vehicles (airplanes, ships, and trains), foreign words that are not commonly used in English, and occasional words that need special emphasis.

Lindbergh's *Spirit of St. Louis*   Amtrak's *Silver Star*

Resist the temptation to emphasize words by putting them in bold type. In most writing situations, underlining provides enough emphasis.

▶ Upon every table is a vase adorned with a red carnation symbolizing amore (the Italian word for "love").

▶ This situation could exist because it is just that, **reverse** socialization.   (no bold)

M5-d Underline or italicize when appropriate, but not in place of or in addition to other conventional uses of punctuation and mechanics.

Eliminate any unusual uses of underlining or italics.

UNUSUAL   The commissioner of the NFL, Paul Tagliabue, said, *"I do not believe playing [football] in Arizona is in the best interests of the NFL."*

APPROPRIATE   The commissioner of the NFL, Paul Tagliabue, said, "I do not believe playing [football] in Arizona is in the best interests of the NFL."

M6   Abbreviations

Although abbreviations are more common in technical and business writing than in academic writing, you may sometimes want to use them to avoid repetition. Use the full word in your first reference, followed by the abbreviation in parentheses. Then use the abbreviation in subsequent references.

San Diego Humane Society (SDHS)   prisoners of war (POWs)

Abbreviations composed of all capital letters are generally written without periods or spaces between letters. When capital letters are separated by periods, do not include a space after the period, except for the initials of a person's name, which should be spaced.

USA   CNN   UPI   B.A.   Ph.D.   T. S. Eliot

M6-a Use abbreviations that your readers will recognize for names of agencies, organizations, countries, and common technical terms.

FBI   IRS   CBS   NATO   NOW   DNA   GNP   CPM

The SDHS is an independently run nonprofit organization.

Note: Do not abbreviate geographic names in formal writing unless the areas are commonly known by their abbreviations (*Washington, D.C.*).

M6-b Use a.m., p.m., *No.*, $, BC, and AD only with specific numerals or dates.

7:15 a.m.	10:30 p.m.
$172.18 *or* $38	No. 18 *or* no. 18 [item or issue number of a source]
72 BC [before Christ]	72 BCE [before the Common Era]
AD 378 [*anno Domini*]	378 CE [Common Era]

Note: AD, for *anno Domini* ("in the year of our Lord"), is placed before the date, not after it.

M6-c Use commonly accepted abbreviations for titles, degrees, and Latin terms.

Change a title or a degree to an accepted abbreviation. Avoid duplication by using a title before a person's name or a degree after the name but not both.

Rev. Jesse Jackson	Mr. Roger Smith	Ms. Martina Navratilova
Diana Lee, M.D.	Dr. Diana Lee	James Boyer, D.V.M.
Ann Hajek, Ph.D.	Ring Lardner Jr.	Dr. Albert Einstein

According to Dr. Ira Chasnoff of Northwestern Memorial, cocaine produces a dramatic fluctuation in blood pressure.

Reserve Latin terms primarily for source citations or comments in parentheses rather than using them in the text of your essay.

c. (*or* ca.)	"circa" or about (used with dates)
cf.	compare
e.g.	for example
et al.	and others (used with people)
etc.	and so forth
i.e.	that is
vs. (*or* v.)	versus (used with titles of legal cases)

Some adult rights (e.g., the right to vote) clearly should not be extended to children.

Roe v. Wade **is still the law of the land.**

M6-d Use abbreviations when appropriate, but do not use them to replace words in most writing.

In formal writing, avoid abbreviating units of measurement or technical terms (unless your essay is technical), names of time periods (months, days, or holidays), course titles or department names, names of states or countries (unless the abbreviation is the more common form), names of companies, and parts of books.

▶ **The Pets for People program gives older people the companionship they need,**
     especially
     esp. if they live alone.
      ^

         Street
▶ **I called the closest site on Hancock St. to ask for a tour.**
                ^

              September
▶ **The walkout followed an incident on Sept. 27.**
            ^

M7   Titles and Headings

Use an appropriate title and headings that follow the format required for an essay or research paper. Consult your instructor or a style guide in your field to determine whether you are expected to supply a title page, running heads, text headings, or other design features.

M7-a Place your heading and title on the first page of a research paper, following MLA style.

If you are following MLA style, do not include a title page. Instead, begin your first page with a double-spaced heading one inch from the top of the page and aligned

MLA style Conventions set forth in the guidelines of the Modern Language Association for preparing research papers and documenting sources. See Chapter 24.

with the left margin. In the heading, list your name, your instructor's name, the class name and number, and the date on separate, double-spaced lines. Double-space again and center your title, following the rules for capitalizing titles (see M2) but omitting the quotation marks.

Then begin the first paragraph of your text, indenting it and all other paragraphs one-half inch and double-spacing every part of the text (including references to sources and quotations). Throughout your paper, leave one-inch margins on all four sides of the text, except for the **running head** with the page number (see M7-b). If your computer program has a feature that aligns the right margin (called "right justification"), turn this function off because it may produce odd spaces in your text and make it hard to read. Also turn off the "auto-hyphenation" feature. You may want to refer to the format of the sample paper in Chapter 24 (pp. 787–94). See M7-b and M8-a for other MLA requirements.

If you are following **APA style**, supply a title page (see M7-c), a brief abstract, and text headings (see M7-d).

running head (header)
A heading at the top of a page that usually includes the page number and other information.

APA style Conventions set forth in the guidelines of the American Psychological Association for preparing research papers and documenting sources. See Chapter 24.

MLA style Conventions set forth in the guidelines of the Modern Language Association for preparing research papers and documenting sources. See Chapter 24.

M7-b   Use an appropriate running head to number the pages of a research paper.

If you are following **MLA style**, provide a running head on each page, starting on page 1, that includes your last name and the page number. Position this heading one-half inch below the top of the page, aligned with the right margin. (Most word processing programs have a feature that will allow you to print a running head automatically on each page.) See the sample paper in Chapter 24 (p. 787). Other style guides recommend different running heads — such as the shortened title with the page number required by **APA** — so follow any directions carefully.

M7-c   Prepare a title page for your essay or research paper if required.

Supply a separate title page if it is customary in a particular field or expected by your instructor. (If you are following MLA style, a separate title page is not required; see M7-a.) If you have not been given guidelines by your instructor, center your title about halfway down the page. Beginning about three inches up from the bottom of the page, list your name, your teacher's name, the class name and number, and the date, each on a separate line, centered and double-spaced.

M7-d   Use text headings if required to identify the sections of a research paper.

In many fields, a research paper or report is expected to follow a particular structure and to include section headings so that a reader can easily identify the parts of the discussion. The APA, for example, recommends preparing an abstract or a closing summary, an introduction, and separate sections on the method, results, and implications of the study's findings (see p. 727). References and appendixes conclude the paper. Follow whatever guidelines your instructor or department provides.

Even if specific headings are not required, a long essay may be easier for a reader to follow if headings are supplied for each section. Such headings, however, cannot replace adequate transitions within your text, and they need to reflect your audience and purpose. A heading may be centered or aligned with the left margin of the paper. It may be spaced so that it is set off from the text or be followed directly by text on the same line. Follow your instructor's advice, and be consistent so that comparable headings are set up the same way — same type size and style, same capitalization, and same position on the page. Such consistency lets the reader know that sections are of similar weight or that one section is subsidiary to another.

M8 Special Design Features

Because computers make it easy to use different typefaces, type sizes, margin widths, and indents in your documents, you may be tempted to impose an elaborate design on a simple essay and fill it with variations and special features. Resist this temptation unless your instructor specifically encourages such experimentation. Use conventional design features and layouts to make your essay easy to follow, easy to read, and easy to understand.

M8-a Prepare your essay following any required conventions.

If you are required to follow a standard style, such as **MLA** or **APA**, check with your instructor about requirements for margins, type size, and so forth. If you have not been given specific requirements, follow a fairly conservative style, like the MLA, to avoid excessive formatting that may not appeal to academic readers.

However you prepare your essay, most college instructors will hold you responsible if it should be lost. Always print a second copy, save the file on a backup disk, duplicate a typed or handwritten copy, or keep drafts so that you can replace a lost essay. Some instructors, especially in composition, require that you hand in planning materials and drafts or submit a complete portfolio at the end of the term. Keep any materials that may be needed later in the term.

For an MLA-style essay or research paper, use only one side of plain, white, nonerasable paper (8½- by 11-inch sheets). If your final version looks messy from corrections or smudges, hand in a clean duplicate made on a good copier. Make sure your printer is in good condition so that your final drafts are neat with dark, readable type. If your instructor will accept a handwritten essay or research paper, prepare it neatly, writing clearly in black or blue ink on only one side of each page. See M7-a for directions about MLA margin widths and other spacing.

MLA style Conventions set forth in the guidelines of the Modern Language Association for preparing research papers and documenting sources. See Chapter 24.

APA style Conventions set forth in the guidelines of the American Psychological Association for preparing research papers and documenting sources. See Chapter 24.

M8-b Use bold, italic, or unusual type styles or sizes sparingly.

A typical word-processor setting for text is double-spaced 12-point type. If you want to use bold or italic type, unusual fonts, or special sizes of type, check first with your instructor. Most college instructors prefer simplicity, although some might allow you to use slightly larger (14-point) type for the title, bold section headings in a long essay, additional spacing between sections, or slightly smaller (10-point) type in a crowded chart. Even so, use only features that will make your text easy to read and easy to follow. Be clear and consistent. Dramatic type variations are more suitable for a newsletter or brochure than an academic essay or report.

In **MLA style,** as in the style guides for other academic fields, the use of different type styles is essentially limited to underlining certain titles and words (see M5).

> **MLA style** Conventions set forth in the guidelines of the Modern Language Association for preparing research papers and documenting sources. See Chapter 24.

UNUSUAL	She finally let out a laughing smile and said, *"I am so happy, Shellah."*
APPROPRIATE	She finally let out a laughing smile and said, "I am so happy, Shellah."
UNUSUAL	The effect is the same: **Any violent behavior will not be tolerated.**
APPROPRIATE	The effect is the same: Any violent behavior will not be tolerated.

M8-c Use extra capital letters, icons, symbols, or other atypical features sparingly.

Although you may occasionally capitalize all of the letters in a word for emphasis, most college instructors will expect you to follow the standard conventions for capitalization (see M2). If you are preparing special tables, charts, boxes, or other visual materials, ask your instructor's advice about variations in capitalization, type size and style, special symbols, and so forth.

> ▶ When all of these components are pulled together, the lyrics become powerful,
>   *and*
> as proven by De Garmo & Key.
>   ^

M9   Spelling

Try several (or all) of the following suggestions for catching and correcting your spelling errors.

- Proofread your writing carefully to catch transposed letters (*becuase* for *because*), omitted letters (*becaus*), and other careless errors (*then* for *than*). When you proofread for spelling, read the text backward, beginning with the last word. (This strategy keeps you from reading for content and lets you focus on each word.)

- Check a good dictionary for any words you are uncertain about. When you are writing and doubt the spelling of a word, put a question mark by the word but wait to check it until you have finished drafting. (Check a misspeller's dictionary if you are unsure of the first letters of the word.)

- Keep a list of words you often misspell so that you can try to pinpoint your personal patterns. Although misspellings nearly always follow a pattern, you are not likely to misspell every word of a particular type, or you may spell the same word two different ways in the same essay.

M9-a Study the spelling rules for adding prefixes and suffixes to words.

Although English has a large number of words with unusual spellings, many follow the patterns that spelling rules describe.

Add a prefix to a root without doubling or dropping letters.

distrust	misbehave	unable
dissatisfy	misspell	unnatural

Add a suffix beginning with a vowel (such as *-ing*) in accord with the form of the root word.

Double the final consonant if the word has a single syllable that ends in a single consonant preceded by a single vowel.

begging	hidden	fitting

Do the same if the word has a final stressed syllable that ends in a single consonant preceded by a single vowel.

beginning	occurrence

The final consonant does not double if the word ends in a double consonant or has a double vowel.

acting	parted	seeming	stooped

In some cases, the stress shifts to the first syllable when a suffix is added. When it does, do not double the final consonant.

prefér:	preférring,	preférred
	préference,	préferable

Add a suffix that begins with *y* or a vowel by dropping a final silent *e*.

achieving	icy	location
grievance	lovable	continual

Note: Keep the final silent *e* to retain a soft *c* or *g* sound, to prevent mispronunciation, or to prevent confusion with other words.

changeable	courageous	noticeable
eyeing	mileage	canoeist
dyeing	singeing	

prefix A word part, such as *pre-, anti-,* or *bi-,* that is attached to the beginning of a word to form another word: *preconceived, unbelievable.*

suffix A word part, such as *-ly, -ment,* or *-ed,* that is added to the end of a word to change the word's form (*bright, brightly*) or tense (*call, called*) or to form another word (*govern, government*).

Add a suffix that begins with a consonant by keeping a final silent *e*.

achievement   discouragement   sincerely

Exceptions: acknowledgment, argument, awful, judgment, truly, wholly.

Form the plural of a singular noun in accord with its form.

If a singular noun ends in a consonant followed by *y*, change *y* to *i* and add *-es*.

baby, babies   cry, cries

Note: Simply add *-s* to names: her cousin *Mary*, both *Marys*.

If a singular noun ends in a vowel followed by *y*, add *-s*.

trolley, trolleys   day, days

If a singular noun ends in a consonant and *o*, add *-es*.

potato, potatoes   echo, echoes   veto, vetoes

Exceptions: autos, dynamos, pianos, sopranos.

If a singular noun ends in a vowel and *o*, add *-s*.

video, videos   rodeo, rodeos   radio, radios

If a singular noun ends in *s, ss, sh, ch, x,* or *z*, add *-es*.

Jones, Joneses   hiss, hisses   bush, bushes

match, matches   suffix, suffixes   buzz, buzzes

Note: The plural of *fish* is *fish;* the plural of *thesis* is *theses*.

Check the dictionary for the plural of a word that originates in another language.

criterion, criteria   datum, data

medium, mediums *or* media

hors d'oeuvre, hors d'oeuvres *or* hors d'oeuvre

M9-b **Study the spelling rules (and the exceptions) that apply to words you routinely misspell.**

Add *i* before *e* except after *c*.

Most people remember this rule because of the jingle "Write *i* before *e* / Except after *c* / Or when sounded like *ay* / As in *neighbor* and *weigh.*" *Exceptions:* either, foreign, forfeit, height, leisure, neither, seize, weird.

Spell most words ending in the sound "seed" as -cede.

precede   recede   secede   intercede

Exceptions: proceed, succeed, supersede.

> ## For ESL Writers
>
> If you have learned Canadian or British English, you may have noticed some differences in the way that words are spelled in U.S. English.
>
> | *U.S. English* | *Canadian or British English* |
> |---|---|
> | color | colour |
> | realize | realise (*or* realize in Canadian English) |
> | center | centre |
> | defense | defence |

M9-c Watch for words that are often spelled incorrectly because they sound like other words.

In English, many words are not spelled as they sound. The endings of some words may be dropped in speech but need to be included in writing. For example, speakers often pronounce *and* as *an'* or drop the *-ed* ending on verbs. Other common words sound the same but have entirely different meanings. Watch carefully for words such as the following.

already ("by now": He is *already* in class.)

all ready ("fully prepared": I'm *all ready* for the test.)

an (article: Everyone read *an* essay last night.)

and (conjunction: The class discussed the problem *and* the solution.)

its (possessive pronoun: The car lost *its* shine.)

it's ("it is": *It's* too cold to go for a walk.)

maybe ("perhaps": *Maybe* we should have tacos for dinner.)

may be (verb showing possibility: They *may be* arriving tonight.)

than (conjunction showing comparison: The house was taller *than* the tree.)

then (adverb showing time sequence: First she knocked and *then* she opened the door.)

their (possessive pronoun: They decided to sell *their* old car.)

there (adverb showing location: The car dealer is located *there* on the corner.)

they're ("they are": *They're* going to pick up the new car tonight.)

your (possessive pronoun: I can see *your* apartment.)

you're ("you are": Call me when *you're* home.)

For distinctions between other words such as *affect/effect, principal/principle,* and *to/too,* see the Glossary of Frequently Misused Words.

Watch for and correct misspelled words that sound the same as other words.

▶ I started packing my gear, still ~~vary~~ *very* excited about the trip.

▶ The campfire had ~~burn~~ *burned* down to a sizzle.

▶ I just ~~new~~ *knew* it was a bear, and I was going to be its dinner.

▶ As students pay ~~there~~ *their* fees, part of this money goes toward purchasing new books and materials.

▶ Pushing off from Anchovy Island, the boat sets its ~~coarse~~ *course*.

M9-d Watch for words that are often misspelled.

Check your essays for the following words, which are often spelled incorrectly. Look up any other questionable words in a dictionary, and keep a personal list of words that you tend to misspell.

absence	argument	commitment	especially
accidentally	arrangement	committed	every day
accommodate	attendance	competitive	exaggerated
accomplish	basically	conscience	exercise
achievement	before	conscious	exercising
acknowledge	beginning	convenient	experience
acquaintance	believe	criticize	explanation
acquire	benefited	definitely	finally
against	business	dependent	foreign
aggravate	businesses	desperate	forty
all right	calendar	develops	fourth
a lot	cannot	disappear	friend
although	categories	eighth	government
analyze	changeable	eligible	harass
apparently	choose	embarrass	height
appearance	chose	emphasize	heroes
appropriate	coming	environment	immediately

incredible	occurred	privilege	studying
indefinitely	occurrences	probably	succeed
interesting	particularly	proceed	success
irrelevant	performance	professor	successful
knowledge	phenomena	quiet	therefore
loose	phenomenon	quite	thorough
lose	physically	receive	truly
maintenance	playwright	recommend	unnecessarily
maneuver	practically	reference	until
mischievous	precede	referred	usually
necessary	preference	roommate	whether
noticeable	preferred	schedule	without
occasion	prejudice	separate	woman
occur	preparation	similar	women

L ESL Troublespots

This section provides advice about problems of grammar and standard usage that are particularly troublesome for speakers of English as a second language (ESL).

L1 Articles

For practice, go to bedfordstmartins.com/theguide/art

The rules for using articles (*a, an,* and *the*) are complicated. Your choice depends on whether the article appears before a **count, noncount,** or **proper noun.** An *article* is used before a common noun to indicate whether the noun refers to something specific (*the* moon) or whether it refers to something that is one among many or has not yet been specified (*a* planet, *an* asteroid). In addition, for some nouns, the absence of an article indicates that the reference is not specific.

count noun A noun that names people and things that can be counted: one *teacher,* two *teachers*; one *movie,* several *movies.*

noncount noun A noun that names things or ideas that are not or cannot be counted: *thunder, money, happiness.*

proper noun The capitalized name of a specific person, group, place, or thing.

L1-a Select the correct article to use with a count noun.

- Use *a* or *an* with nonspecific singular count nouns.
- Use no article with nonspecific plural count nouns.
- Use *the* with specific singular and plural count nouns.

Note: The article *a* is used before a consonant and *an* before a vowel; exceptions include words beginning with a long *u,* such as *unit.*

Use *a* or *an* before a singular count noun when it refers to one thing among many or something that has not been specifically identified.

> ▶ We, as   *a*   society, have to educate our youth about avoiding teen pregnancy.

> ▶ *A darkroom*
> ~~Darkroom~~ is a room with no light where photographs are developed.

Use *the* before a singular or plural count noun when it refers to one or more specific things.

After you have used *a* or *an* with a count noun, subsequent references to the noun become specific and are marked by *the.*

> When I walked into the office, *a* woman in her mid-forties was waiting to be called.

> As I sat down, I looked at *the* woman.

Exceptions include a second reference to one among many.

I was guided to *a* classroom. It was *a* bright room, filled with warm rays of Hawaiian sunlight.

Note: In most situations, use *the* with a count noun modified by a superlative adjective.

the most frightening moment   the smallest person

But: He gave *a* most unusual response.

Nouns such as *sun* generally refer to unique things; for instance, the only sun visible in the sky. Nouns such as *house* and *yard* often refer to things that people own. A writer may talk about *the yard* meaning his or her own yard. In most situations, both types of nouns can be preceded by the definite article *the.*

Don't look directly at *the sun.* [Only one sun could be meant.]

I spent Saturday cleaning *the house.* [The reader will infer that the writer is referring to his or her own house.]

Note: You can also introduce count nouns referring to specific entities with possessive nouns or pronouns (*Maya's* friends) or demonstrative pronouns (*these* friends). Indefinite count and noncount nouns can also be introduced by words that indicate amount (*few* friends, *some* sand).

COUNT NOUN	She stayed with *her* eight children.
NONCOUNT NOUN	Her family wanted *some* happiness.

Delete any article before a plural count noun when it does not refer to something specific.

▶ ~~The people~~ *People* like Dee cannot forget their heritage.

L1-b Select the correct article to use with a noncount noun.

The many kinds of noncount nouns include the following.

Natural phenomena: *thunder, steam, electricity*
Natural elements: *gold, air, sunlight*
Manufacturing materials: *steel, wood, cement*
Fibers: *wool, cotton, rayon*
General categories made up of a variety of specific items: *money, music, furniture*
Abstract ideas: *happiness, loyalty, adolescence, wealth*
Liquids: *milk, gasoline, water*

> **noncount noun** A noun that names things or ideas that are not or cannot be counted: *thunder, money, happiness.*

Some nouns naming foodstuffs are always noncount (*pork, rice, broccoli*); others are noncount when they refer to food as it is eaten (*We ate barbecued chicken and fruit*) but count when they refer to individual items or varieties (*We bought a plump chicken and various fruits*).

Delete any article before a noncount noun when it refers to something general.

> ► What is needed is ~~a~~ reasonable and measured legislation.

> ► The destruction caused by the war drew artists away from ~~the~~ reality, which is
>
> painful and cruel, and toward ~~the~~ abstract art that avoids a sense of despair.

Use *the* before a noncount noun when it refers to something specific or when it is specified by a prepositional phrase or an adjective clause.

> *The* coffee is probably cold by now.
> *The* water on the boat has to be rationed.
> *The* water that we have left has to be rationed.

Note: You can also introduce noncount nouns referring to specific things with possessive nouns or pronouns (*her* money) or demonstrative pronouns (*that* money). Indefinite noncount nouns can also be introduced by words that indicate amount (*some* money).

L1-c Select the correct article to use with a proper noun.

Most plural proper nouns require *the: the* United States, *the* Philippines, *the* Black Hills, *the* Clintons, *the* Los Angeles Dodgers. Exceptions include business names (Hillshire Farms, Miller Auto Sales).

Delete any article before most singular proper nouns.

In general, singular proper nouns are not preceded by an article: Dr. Livingston, New York City, Hawaii, Disneyland, Mount St. Helens, Union Station, Wrigley Field.

> ► ~~The~~ Campus Security is a powerful deterrent against parties because if you are
>
> written up twice, you can lose your housing contract.

Note: The is used before proper noun phrases that include *of* (*the* Rock of Gibraltar, *the* Gang of Four). *The* is also required before proper nouns that name the following things:

---

prepositional phrase A group of words that begins with a preposition and indicates the relation between a word in a sentence and the object following the preposition: Her sunglasses slid *under the seat*.

adjective clause A clause that modifies a noun or pronoun and is generally introduced by a relative pronoun (such as *that* or *which*).

proper noun The capitalized name of a specific person, group, place, or thing.

1. Bodies of water, except when the generic part of the name precedes the specific name: *the* Atlantic Ocean, *the* Red River, but Lake Erie

2. Geographic regions: *the* West Coast, *the* Sahara, *the* Grand Canyon

3. Vehicles for transportation: *the Concorde*

4. Named buildings and bridges: *the* World Trade Center, *the* Golden Gate Bridge

5. National or international churches: *the* Russian Orthodox Church

6. Governing bodies preceded by a proper adjective: *the* British Parliament

7. Titles of religious and political leaders: *the* Dalai Lama, *the* president

8. Religious and historical documents: *the* Bible, *the* Magna Carta

9. Historical periods and events: *the* Gilded Age, *the* Civil War

L2 Verbs

For practice, go to bedfordstmartins.com/theguide/verb

Section R2-a reviews the basic English verb forms and includes a list of common irregular verbs. As you edit your writing, pay particular attention to conditional clauses, two-word verbs, helping (auxiliary) verbs, and gerund or infinitive forms after verbs.

L2-a Select verb tenses carefully in main clauses and conditional clauses.

Conditional clauses beginning with *if* or *unless* generally indicate that one thing causes another (a factual relationship); predict future outcomes or possibilities; or speculate about the past, present, future, or impossible events or circumstances.

> ┌──────CONDITIONAL CLAUSE──────┐ ┌──────────────MAIN CLAUSE──────────────┐
> If we *use* television correctly, it *can give* us information and entertainment.

> ┌──────CONDITIONAL CLAUSE──────┐ ┌──────────────MAIN CLAUSE──────────────┐
> If we *use* television incorrectly, it *will control* our families and our community.

Change both verbs to the same tense (generally present or past) to express general or specific truths or actions that happen together habitually.

> ▶ When we moved to America, my family ~~has~~ ^had^ good communication.

Change the verb in the main clause to the future and the verb in the conditional clause to the present to express future possibilities or predictions.

> ▶ If you ask in any of her restaurants, the manager ~~would~~ ^will^ tell you about working
>
> with her all these years.

independent (main) clause A word group with a subject and a predicate that can stand alone as a separate sentence.

base form The uninflected form of a verb: I *eat*; to *play*.

Change the verb in the main clause to *would*, *could*, or *might* plus the base form and change the verb in the *if* conditional clause to the past tense to speculate about events or conditions that are unreal, improbable, or contrary to fact.

Use *were* rather than *was* in an *if* clause.

▶ Some people believe that if the Health Department ~~gives~~ *were to give* out clean needles, the number of people using drugs would increase.

participle A verb form showing present tense (*dancing, freezing*) or past tense (*danced, frozen*) that can also act as an adjective.

Change the verb in the main clause to *would have*, *might have*, *could have*, or *should have* plus the past participle, and change the verb in the *if* clause to the past perfect to speculate about actions in the past that did not in fact occur.

▶ If the computer lab *had* added more hours during finals week, students would not have had to wait to use a computer.

Note: Do not add *would have* to the *if* clause.

L2-b Learn the meanings of the idiomatic two- and three-word verbs used in English.

Idiomatic two- or three-word (or phrasal) verbs usually combine a verb with a word that appears to be a preposition or an adverb (called a *particle*). The combined meaning cannot be understood literally, and similar expressions often have very different meanings.

hand in means "submit"
hand out means "distribute"
look into means "investigate"
look out for means "watch carefully"
run away means "leave without warning"
run into means "meet by chance"
walk out on means "abandon"
want out means "desire to be free of responsibility"

Native speakers of English will notice misuses of these idiomatic verbs even though they use the verbs without thinking about their literal meanings. When you are unsure of the meaning or usage of such verbs, consult a dictionary designed for nonnative speakers of English, or ask a native speaker.

L2-c Use the correct verb forms after helping verbs.

base form The uninflected form of a verb: I *eat*; to *play*.

After the helping (auxiliary) verbs *do*, *does*, and *did*, always use the **base form** of the main verb. After the helping verbs *have*, *has*, and *had*, always use the past **participle** form of the main verb. (See R2-a and G5.)

cooperate
► They do not ~~cooperated~~ with the police.
       ^

done
► They have ~~doing~~ these things for a long time.
       ^

been
► They have doing these things for a long time.
       ^

Note: A modal such as *will* sometimes precedes *have, has,* or *had.*

By Friday I *will have finished* this project.

Following the helping verbs *be, am, is, are, was, were,* and *been* (forms of *be*), use the present participle to show ongoing action (progressive tense).

giving
► The president is ~~given~~ a speech on all major networks.
       ^

Note: Use one of the modal verbs with *be.* Use *have, has,* or *had* with *been.*

Terence *could be making* some calls while I go out.

I *have been* working hard.

After the helping verbs *am, is, are, was,* and *were* (forms of *be*), use the past participle to form the **passive voice.**

canceled
► Regular programming is ~~cancel~~ for tonight.
       ^

To form the passive, *be, being,* and *been* need another helping verb in addition to the past participle.

Tonya *will be challenged* in graduate school this fall.

After a **modal,** use the **base form.**

The Senate *might* vote on this bill next week.

L2-d Follow verbs with **gerunds** or **infinitives,** depending on the verb and your meaning.

1. Verbs that can be followed by either a gerund or an infinitive with no change in meaning

begin	continue	like	prefer
can't stand	hate	love	start

The roof *began leaking.*

The roof *began to leak.*

---

passive voice The verb form that shows something happening to the subject: The mouse *was caught* by the cat.

modals The helping verbs *can, could, may, might, must, shall, should, will,* and *would,* which must be used in conjunction with another (main) verb: I *may go* to the bank.

base form The uninflected form of a verb: I *eat;* to *play.*

gerund A verb form that is used as a noun and ends with *-ing: arguing, throwing.*

infinitive A verb form consisting of the word *to* plus the base form of the verb: *to run, to do.*

2. Verbs that change their meaning, depending on whether a gerund or an infinitive follows

    forget   remember   stop   try

    Salam *remembered going* to the park on Saturday. [Salam recalled a weekend visit to a park.]

    Salam *remembered to go* to the park on Saturday. [Salam remembered that he had to go to the park on Saturday.]

3. Verbs that can be followed by a gerund but not an infinitive

admit	deny	keep	recall
appreciate	discuss	miss	resist
avoid	dislike	postpone	risk
can't help	enjoy	practice	suggest
consider	finish	put off	tolerate
delay	imagine	quit	

    > ▶ I recall ~~to see~~ Michel there.
    > *seeing*

    Note: Not or *never* can separate the verb and the gerund.

    We discussed *not* having a party this year.

4. Verbs that can be followed by an infinitive but not a gerund

agree	expect	need	refuse
ask	fail	offer	venture
beg	have	plan	wait
choose	hope	pretend	want
claim	manage	promise	wish
decide	mean		

    > ▶ Children often only pretend ~~eating~~ food they dislike.
    > *to eat*

Note: In a sentence with a verb followed by an infinitive, the meaning changes depending on the placement of a negative word such as *not* or *never*.

I *never* promised to eat liver. [I did not make the promise.]

I promised *never* to eat candy. [I promised not to do it.]

5. Verbs that must be followed by a noun or pronoun and an infinitive

advise	encourage	order	teach
allow	force	persuade	tell
cause	instruct	remind	urge
command	invite	require	warn
convince	need		

Magda taught *her parrot to say* a few words.

Note: Use an infinitive, not *that*, following a verb such as *want* or *need*.

    ► **José wants ~~that~~ his new car ~~stays~~ in good condition.**

              to stay

6. The verbs *let, make* ("force"), and *have* ("cause") must be followed by a noun or pronoun and the **base form** of the verb (not the infinitive)

He *let me borrow* the car.

The drill sergeant *makes the recruits stand* at attention.

I *had the children draw* in their notebooks.

> **base form** The uninflected form of a verb: I *eat;* to *play.*

L3   Prepositions

For practice, go to bedfordstmartins.com/theguide/prep

Use the **prepositions** *in, on,* and *at* to indicate location and time.

Location

- *In* usually means *within a geographic place or enclosed area* (*in* Mexico, *in* a small town, *in* the park, *in* my bedroom, *in* a car).
- *On* means *on top of* (*on* the shelf, *on* a hill, *on* a bicycle); it is also used with modes of mass transportation (*on* a train, *on* the subway), streets (*on* Broadway), pages (*on* page 5), floors of buildings (*on* the tenth floor), and tracts of private land (*on* a farm, *on* the lawn).
- *At* refers to specific addresses and named locations (*at* 1153 Grand Street, *at* Nana's house, *at* Macy's), to general locations (*at* work, *at* home, *at* the beach), and to locations that involve a specific activity (*at* the mall, *at* the gym, *at* a party, *at* a restaurant).

Time

- *In* is used with months (*in* May), years (*in* 1999), and seasons (*in* the fall), as well as with *morning, afternoon,* and *evening* (*in* the morning).

> **preposition** A word (such as *between, in,* or *of*) that always appears as part of a phrase and indicates the relation between a word in a sentence and the object of the preposition: The water splashed *into* the canoe.

- *On* is used with days of the week (*on* Wednesday) and dates (*on* June 2, 2006).
- *At* is used with specific times (*at* 7:30, *at* noon, *at* midnight) and with *night* (*at* night).

Change any incorrect prepositions so that *in, on,* and *at* convey time and location correctly.

▶ People are driving at 55 or 60 miles per hour ~~in~~ *on* the highway.

Change any incorrect prepositions to idiomatic usage.

▶ Is life worse in the refugee camps or in Vietnam? You would find answers ~~from~~ *in* his article.

▶ Williams gives readers insight ~~to~~ *into* the doctor's insecurity.

L4   Omitted or Repeated Words

For practice, go to bedfordstmartins.com/theguide/oword

subject The part of a clause that identifies who or what is being discussed.

In English, every sentence, with rare exceptions, should have both a **subject** and a **verb.** If your native language allows you to omit either subject or verb, check your drafts carefully to be sure that you include both in your writing.

┌SUBJECT┐ ┌VERB┐
My brother has been very successful in his job.

Supply both a subject and a verb in each sentence, but do not repeat the subject or other words that duplicate grammatical functions.

verb A word or phrase that expresses action or being and, along with a subject, is a basic component of a sentence.

Add a missing subject.

▶ On the contrary, *the compliments* increase his irritability.

Add a missing verb.

▶ Mr. Yang *is* a man who owns a butcher shop.

Supply a missing expletive (*there* or *it*) if the subject follows the verb.

▶ ~~Are~~ *There are* many ways to help poor people get jobs.

Delete a repeated subject.

▶ The elderly woman ~~she~~ must have an eye infection.

Delete other words that repeat grammatical functions.

▶ People say that the cost of insurance ~~has~~ never goes down anymore.

▶ Only a few people ~~that~~ are rich.

L5   Adjective Order

For practice, go to bedfordstmartins.com/theguide/order

Adjectives generally appear in the following order in English sentences.

1. Article, pronoun, or other determiner: *a, an, the, that, his, their, Janine's*
2. Evaluation or judgment: *beautiful, ugly, elegant, magnificent, impressive*
3. Size or dimension: *short, tall, long, large, small, big, little*
4. Shape: *round, rectangular, square, baggy, circular, octagonal*
5. Age: *new, young, old, aged, antique*
6. Color: *pink, turquoise, gray, orange*
7. History or origin (country and religion): *Asian, Norwegian, Thai, American, Protestant, Mongolian, Buddhist, Muslim, Catholic, Jewish*
8. Material: *copper, cotton, plastic, oak, linen*
9. Noun used as a descriptive adjective: *kitchen* (sink), *bedroom* (lamp)

When you use several adjectives to modify a noun, arrange them in the order expected in English.

| 1 | 2 | 4 | 6 | | 1 | 3 | 5 |

a beautiful, round, turquoise stone   *her skinny, young* cousin

L6   Participles

For practice, go to bedfordstmartins.com/theguide/part

Use the present form of the **participle** (*-ing*) if it describes someone or something *causing* or *producing* a mental state. Use the past form (*-ed*) if it describes someone or something *experiencing* the mental state. Problem participles include the following pairs.

annoying/annoyed	exhausting/exhausted
boring/bored	pleasing/pleased
confusing/confused	surprising/surprised
disappointing/disappointed	terrifying/terrified
exciting/excited	tiring/tired

The class was *confused* by the *confusing* directions.

The teacher was *surprised* by the *surprising* number of questions.

participle A verb form showing present tense (*dancing, freezing*) or past tense (*danced, frozen*) that can also act as an adjective.

Change a participle to its present form (-*ing*) if it describes someone or something causing or producing a situation.

> ▶ Parents must not accept the ~~frightened~~ *frightening* behavior that their children learn
>
> in gangs.

Change a participle to its past form (-*ed*) if it describes someone or something experiencing a situation.

> ▶ I was not ~~pleasing~~ *pleased* with the information about religion in this article.

R   Review of Sentence Structure

As you write, your primary concern will be with rhetoric, not parts of speech or sentence structure. You will focus on learning how to develop ideas, illustrate general statements, organize an argument, and integrate information. Yet sentence structure is important. Writing clear and correct sentences is part of being a competent writer. This and the other sections in the Handbook will help you achieve that goal.*

R1   Basic Sentence Structure

This review of basic sentence structure will look first at the elements that make up simple sentences and then at how simple sentences produce compound and complex sentences.

R1-a   Words, Phrases, and Clauses

The basic building blocks of sentences are, of course, words, which can be combined into discrete groupings or *phrases*.

Words and phrases are further combined to create clauses. A *clause* is a group of at least two words that both names a topic and makes some point about that topic; every clause can be divided into a subject and a predicate. The *subject* identifies the topic or theme of the sentence — what is being discussed — while the *predicate* says something about the subject and is the focus of information in the clause. A clause can be either *independent* (that is, a complete idea in itself) or *dependent* (combined with an independent clause to create a complete idea). Dependent (or subordinate) clauses are discussed in R2-b.

R1-b   Sentence Units

To introduce the principles of sentence structure, it is useful to consider *simple sentences*, those with only a single independent clause made up of a subject and a predicate.

---

* English sentence structure has been described with scientific precision by linguists. This brief review is based on an extraordinary sentence grammar, *A Grammar of Contemporary English* (New York: Harcourt, 1972), which is available in a revised and expanded edition titled *A Comprehensive Grammar of the English Language* (New York: Addison Wesley, 1985). Two of its authors, Sidney Greenbaum and Sir Randolph Quirk, have written a shorter version, *A Student's Grammar of the English Language* (New York: Addison Wesley, 1990), which you might wish to consult for elaboration on any of the points discussed here.

Subject	Predicate
Native Americans	introduced baked beans to the New England settlers.
The Native Americans	cooked their beans in maple sugar and bear fat.
The settlers	used molasses and salt pork instead.
Both baked-bean dishes	were essentially the same.

The subject and the predicate may each be a single word or a group of words. In addition to its verb, the predicate may include **objects, complements,** and **adverbial modifiers.** Simple sentences, then, are composed of some combination of these basic units: subject, verb, direct object, indirect object, subject complement, object complement, and adverbial modifier.

Of these seven units, two — subject and verb — are required in every sentence. Note that the subject determines whether the verb in the predicate is singular or plural: In the last of the preceding examples, the plural subject *dishes* requires the plural verb *were.*

The basic sentence units can be defined as follows.

Subjects. The simplest subject can be a single noun or pronoun, but a subject may also commonly consist of a noun phrase (including adjectives and other sentence elements) or even a noun clause. Subjects may also be *compound* when two or more nouns or pronouns are linked by a conjunction. (See R2 for definitions and examples of these various elements.)

Verbs. These can be classified as *transitive*, when they occur with an object, or *intransitive*, when they occur without an object. Intransitive verbs that occur with complements are often called *linking verbs.* Like subjects, verbs may be compound.

Objects. These include *direct* and *indirect* objects, which, like subjects, can be nouns, noun phrases, noun clauses, or pronouns. Objects usually follow the subject and verb.

Complements. These are either subject complements or object complements: *Subject complements* refer to the subject, *object complements* to an object. Like subjects and objects, complements can be nouns or pronouns, noun phrases or noun clauses (sometimes referred to as *predicate nominatives*). Complements can also be adjectives or adjective phrases (sometimes called *predicate adjectives*). Like objects, complements usually follow the subject and verb. They also follow any objects.

Adverbials. These are modifiers that refer to the verb in the sentence. They can be adverbs, adverb phrases, or adverb clauses.

object The part of a clause that receives the action of the verb (At the checkpoint, we unloaded *the canoes*) or the part of a phrase that follows a preposition (We dragged them to *the river*).

complement A word or word group that describes or restates a subject or an object.

adverbial modifier A word or word group that modifies a verb, an adjective, or another adverb.

R1-c Types of Simple Sentences

The basic sentence elements listed in R1-b can be put together in various ways to produce seven general types of simple sentences. The basic units are subject (S), verb (V), direct object (DO), indirect object (IO), subject complement (SC), object complement (OC), and adverbial modifier (A).

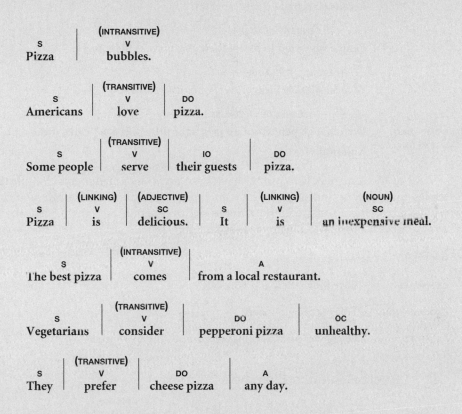

R1-d Combinations and Transformations

The simple sentence patterns shown in R1-c can be combined and transformed to produce all of the sentences writers of English need. Two or more clauses may be combined with a coordinating conjunction (such as *and* or *but*) or a pair of correlative conjunctions (such as *either . . . or*) to create a *compound sentence*. Writers create *complex sentences* by combining independent clauses with a subordinating conjunction (such as *although* or *because*) or by linking two clauses with a relative pronoun (such as *which* or *who*); clauses that contain subordinating conjunctions or relative pronouns are *dependent clauses* and cannot stand on their own as simple sentences. Clauses can also be combined to produce *compound-complex sentences* (compound sentences that contain dependent clauses). Conjunctions and dependent clauses are discussed in more detail in R2.

COMPOUND   Pizza is delicious, and it is an inexpensive meal. Either Americans love pizza, or they consider it junk food.

COMPLEX   Vegetarians consider pepperoni pizza unhealthy

┌────────DEPENDENT CLAUSE────────┐
because it is high in saturated fat.

┌────────DEPENDENT CLAUSE────────┐
People who want to please their guests serve them pizza.

┌────────DEPENDENT CLAUSE────────┐
Because pizza is inexpensive, Americans love it.

COMPOUND-
COMPLEX

┌────────────DEPENDENT CLAUSE────────────┐
Even though pepperoni pizza is unhealthy, it is a delicious meal, and Americans love it.

All of the sentences listed so far have been *declarative* statements. Simple sentences may also be transformed into *questions, commands,* and *exclamations.* In addition, sentences that are in the *active voice* can generally be transformed into the *passive voice* if they have transitive verbs and objects.

QUESTION   Why is pizza popular?

COMMAND   Bake the pizza in a brick oven.

EXCLAMATION   This pizza is delicious!

PASSIVE   Pepperoni pizza is considered unhealthy by vegetarians.

R2   Basic Sentence Elements

This section reviews the parts of speech and the types of clauses and phrases.

R2-a   Parts of Speech

There are ten parts of speech: nouns, pronouns, adjectives, adverbs, verbs, prepositions, conjunctions, articles, demonstratives, and interjections.

Nouns. Nouns function in sentences or clauses as **subjects**, **objects**, and **subject complements.** They also serve as objects of various kinds of **phrases** and as **appositives.** They can be proper (*Burger King, Bartlett pear, Julia Child, General Foods*) or common (*tomato, food, lunch, café, waffle, gluttony*). Common nouns can be abstract (*hunger, satiation, indulgence, appetite*) or concrete (*spareribs, soup, radish, champagne, gravy*). Nouns can be singular (*biscuit*) or plural (*biscuits*); they may also be collective (*food*). They can be marked to show possession (*gourmet's*

---

subject The part of a clause that identifies who or what is being discussed: At the checkpoint, *we* unloaded the canoes.

object The part of a clause that receives the action of the verb (At the checkpoint, we unloaded *the canoes*) or the part of a phrase that follows a preposition (We dragged them to *the river*).

subject complement A word or word group that follows a linking verb (such as *seems, appears,* or *is* and other forms of *be*) and describes or restates the subject: The tents looked *old and dirty.*

phrase A group of words that does *not* contain both a subject and a verb and is always part of an independent clause.

appositive A word or word group that identifies or gives more information about a noun or pronoun that precedes it.

choice, lambs' kidneys). Nouns take determiners (*that lobster, those clams*), quantifiers (*many hotcakes, several sausages*), and articles (*a milkshake, the eggnog*). They can be modified by adjectives (*fried chicken*), adjective phrases (*chicken in a basket*), and adjective clauses (*chicken that is finger-licking good*). See also E3.

Pronouns. Pronouns come in many different forms and have a variety of functions in clauses and phrases.

Personal pronouns function as replacements for nouns and come in three case forms:

1. Subjective, for use as subjects or subject complements: *I, we, you, he, she, it, they*.

2. Objective, for use as objects of verbs and prepositions: *me, us, you, him, her, it, them*.

3. Possessive: *mine, ours, yours, his, hers, theirs*. Possessive pronouns also have a determiner form for use before nouns: *my, our, your, his, her, its, their*.

Calvin Trillin says the best restaurants in the world are in Kansas City, but *he* was born there.

If *you* ever have the spareribs and french-fried potatoes at Arthur Bryant's, *you* will never forget *them*.

Your memory of that lunch at Bryant's is clearer than *mine*.

Personal pronouns come in three persons (first person: *I, me, we, us;* second person: *you;* third person: *he, him, she, her, it, they, them*), three genders (masculine: *he, him;* feminine: *she, her;* neuter: *it*), and two numbers (singular: *I, me, you, he, him, she, her, it;* plural: *we, us, you, they, them*).

Reflexive pronouns, like personal pronouns, function as replacements for nouns, nearly always replacing nouns or personal pronouns in the same clause. Reflexive pronouns include *myself, ourselves, yourself, yourselves, himself, herself, oneself, itself, themselves*.

Aunt Odessa prided *herself* on her chocolate sponge cake.

Reflexive pronouns may also be used for emphasis.

Barry baked the fudge cake *himself.*

Indefinite pronouns do not refer to a specific person or object: *each, all, everyone, everybody, everything, everywhere, both, some, someone, somebody, something, somewhere, any, anyone, anybody, anything, anywhere, either, neither, none, nobody, many, few, much, most, several, enough.*

Not *everybody* was enthusiastic about William Laird's 1698 improvement on apple cider — Jersey lightning applejack.

In the Colonies, *most* preferred rum.

Taverns usually served *both*.

Relative pronouns introduce **adjective (or relative) clauses**. They come in three forms: personal, to refer to people (*who, whom, whose, whoever, whomever*), non-personal (*which, whose, whichever, whatever*), and general (*that*).

In 1846, Nancy Johnson invented a small hand-operated machine, *which* was the forerunner of today's portable ice-cream freezer.

It was Jacob Fussell of Baltimore *who* established the first wholesale ice-cream business in 1851.

The fact *that* we had to wait until 1896 for someone to invent the ice-cream cone is surprising.

Interrogative pronouns have the same forms as relative pronouns but have different functions. They serve to introduce questions.

Who invented the ice-cream sundae?

Of chocolate and vanilla ice cream, *which* do you prefer?

The waiter asked, "*Whose* chocolate walnut sundae is this?"

Demonstrative pronouns are pronouns used to point out particular persons or things: *this, that, these, those*.

This dish is what Mandy likes best for brunch: pecan waffles with blueberry syrup.

Of everything on the menu, *these* must be most fattening.

See also G1–G4.

adjective clause A clause that modifies a noun or pronoun and is generally introduced by a relative pronoun (such as *that* or *which*).

Adjectives. Adjectives modify nouns and pronouns. Adjectives often occur immediately before or after nouns they modify. As **subject complements** (sometimes called predicate adjectives), they may be separated by the verb from nouns or pronouns they modify.

Creole cooking can be found in *many* diners along the Gulf of Mexico.

Gumbo is a *spicy* soup.

Jambalaya tastes *delicious*, and it is *cheap*.

subject complement A word or word group that follows a linking verb (such as *seems, appears,* or *is* and other forms of *be*) and describes or restates the subject: The tents looked *old* and *dirty*.

Some adjectives change form in comparisons.

Gumbo is *spicier* **than crawfish pie.**

Gumbo is the *spiciest* **Creole soup.**

Some words can be used as both pronouns and adjectives; nouns are also sometimes used as adjectives.

ADJ.   ADJ.   PRON.
Many **people love** *crawfish* **pie, and** *many* **prefer gumbo.**

See also G7-b.

Adverbs. Adverbs modify verbs (*eat* <u>well</u>), adjectives (<u>very</u> *big appetite*), and other adverbs (<u>extremely</u> *well done*). They often tell when, how, where, why, and how often.

A number of adverbs are formed by adding -*ly* to an adjective (*hearty* appetite, eat *heartily*).

Walter Jetton started the charcoal fires *early.* **[when]**

He basted the sizzling ribs *liberally* **with marinade. [how]**

Pots of beans simmered *nearby.* **[where]**

Like adjectives, adverbs can change form for comparison.

He ate the buttermilk biscuits *fast.* **[***faster* **than Bucky ate his biscuits,** *fastest* **of all the hungry diners]**

With adverbs that end in -*ly*, the words *more* and *most* are used when making comparisons.

Junior drank the first cold lemonade *quickly.* **[***more quickly* **than Billy Joe,** *most quickly* **of all those at the table]**

The *conjunctive adverb* (or simply the *connective*) is a special kind of adverb used to connect the ideas in two sentences or independent clauses. Familiar connectives include *consequently, however, therefore, similarly, besides,* and *nevertheless.*

The inspiration for Tex-Mex food came from Mexico. *Nevertheless,* **it is considered a native American cuisine.**

Finally, adverbs may evaluate or qualify the information in a sentence.

Barbecue comes from *barbacoa*, a word the Spaniards *probably* picked up from the Arawak Indians.

See also G7-a.

Verbs. Verbs tell what is happening in a sentence by expressing action (*cook, stir*) or a state of being (*be, stay*). Depending on the structure of the sentence, a verb can be **transitive** (*Jerry bakes cookies*) or **intransitive** (*Jerry bakes for a living*); an intransitive verb that is followed by a **subject complement** (*Jerry is a fine baker, and his cookies always taste heavenly*) is often called a **linking verb**.

Nearly all verbs have several forms (or principal parts), many of which may be irregular rather than follow a standard pattern. In addition, verbs have various forms to indicate *tense* (time of action or state of being), *voice* (performer of action), and *mood* (statement, command, or possibility). Studies have shown that because verbs can take so many forms, the most common errors in writing involve verbs. See also G5.

Verb Phrases. Verbs divide into two primary groups: (1) *main (lexical) verbs* and (2) *auxiliary (helping) verbs* that combine with main verbs to create verb phrases. The three primary auxiliary verbs are *do, be*, and *have*, in all their forms.

> *do:* does, did, doing, done
> *be:* am, is, are, was, were, being, been
> *have:* has, had, having

These primary auxiliary verbs can also act as main verbs in sentences. Other common auxiliary verbs (*can, could, may, might, shall, should, will, would, must, ought to, used to*), however, cannot be the main verb in a sentence but are used in combination with main verbs in verb phrases. The auxiliary verb works with the main verb to indicate tense, mood, and voice.

A favorite cheese in the United States *has* always been cheddar.

When the cheese curd forms, it *must* be separated from the whey.

After cheddar cheese is shaped into a block, it *should* be aged for at least several months.

By the year 2011, Americans *will have been* eating cheese for four hundred years.

Principal Parts of Verbs. All main verbs (as well as the primary auxiliary verbs *do, be*, and *have*) have five forms. The forms of a large number of verbs are regular, but many verbs have irregular forms.

transitive verb A verb that needs an object — something that receives the action of the verb — to make its meaning complete.

intransitive verb A verb that does not need an object to make its meaning complete.

subject complement A word or word group that follows a linking verb (such as *seems, appears,* or *is* and other forms of *be*) and describes or restates the subject: The tents looked *old* and *dirty.*

linking verb *Be, seem, appear, become, taste,* or another verb that connects a subject with a subject complement that describes or modifies it: The chips *taste* salty.

Form	Regular	Irregular
Infinitive or base	sip	drink
Third-person singular present (-*s* form)	sips	drinks
Past	sipped	drank
Present participle (-*ing* form)	sipping	drinking
Past participle (-*ed* form)	sipped	drunk

The past and past participle for most verbs in English are formed by simply adding -*d* or -*ed* (*posed, walked, pretended, unveiled*). However, a number of verbs have irregular forms, most of which are different for the past and the past participle.

For regular verbs, the past and past participle forms are the same: *sipped.* Even though regular verbs have predictable forms, they pose certain spelling problems, having to do mainly with dropping or doubling the last letter of the base form before adding -*ing,* -*d,* or -*ed.* (See M9-a.) All new verbs coming into English have regular forms: *format, formats, formatted, formatting.*

Irregular verbs have unpredictable forms. (Dictionaries list the forms of irregular verbs under the base form.) Their -*s* and -*ing* forms are generally predictable, just like those of regular verbs, but their past and past participle forms are not. In particular, be careful to use the correct past participle form of irregular verbs.

Listed here are the principal parts of fifty-three commonly troublesome irregular verbs. Check your dictionary for a more complete listing.

Base	Past Tense	Past Participle
be: am, is, are	was, were	been
beat	beat	beaten
begin	began	begun
bite	bit	bitten
blow	blew	blown
break	broke	broken
bring	brought	brought
burst	burst	burst
choose	chose	chosen
come	came	come
cut	cut	cut
deal	dealt	dealt
do	did	done
draw	drew	drawn
drink	drank	drunk
drive	drove	driven
eat	ate	eaten

Base	*Past Tense*	*Past Participle*
fall	fell	fallen
fly	flew	flown
freeze	froze	frozen
get	got	got (gotten)
give	gave	given
go	went	gone
grow	grew	grown
have	had	had
know	knew	known
lay	laid	laid
lead	led	led
lie	lay	lain
lose	lost	lost
ride	rode	ridden
ring	rang	rung
rise	rose	risen
run	ran	run
say	said	said
see	saw	seen
set	set	set
shake	shook	shaken
sink	sank	sunk
sit	sat	sat
speak	spoke	spoken
spring	sprang (sprung)	sprung
steal	stole	stolen
stink	stank	stunk
swear	swore	sworn
swim	swam	swum
take	took	taken
teach	taught	taught
tear	tore	torn
throw	threw	thrown
wear	wore	worn
win	won	won
write	wrote	written

Tense. Native speakers of English know the **tense** system and use it confidently. They comprehend time as listeners and readers. As talkers, they use the system in combination with adverbs of time to identify the times of actions. As writers, however, even native speakers may find it difficult to put together sentences that express time clearly through verbs: Time has to be expressed consistently from sentence to sentence, and shifts in time perspective must be managed smoothly. In addition, certain conventions permit time to be expressed in unusual ways: History can be written in present time to dramatize events, or characters in novels may be presented as though their actions are in present time. The following examples of verb tense provide only a partial demonstration of the complex system indicating time in English.

Present. There are three basic types of present time: timeless, limited, and instantaneous. Timeless present-tense verbs express habitual action.

> Some Americans *grow* their own fruits and vegetables.

Limited present-tense verbs express an action in process and of limited duration.

> The neighbors *are preparing* watermelon rind preserves this week.

Instantaneous present-tense verbs express action being completed at the moment.

> Laura *is eating* the last ripe strawberry.

Present-tense verbs can also be emphatic.

> I certainly *do enjoy* homemade strawberry preserves in the middle of winter.

Past. There are several kinds of past time. Some actions must be identified as having taken place at a particular time in the past.

> While he *was waiting*, Jake *ordered* a ham sandwich on whole wheat bread.

In the *present perfect tense*, actions may be expressed as having taken place at no definite time in the past or as occurring in the past and continuing into the present.

> Jake *has eaten* more ham sandwiches than he can count.

> The Downtown Deli *has sold* delicious ham sandwiches on homemade bread for as long as he can remember.

Action can even be expressed as having been completed in the past prior to some other past action or event (the *past perfect tense*).

> Before he *had taken* a bite, Jake dropped his sandwich on the floor.

tense The form of a verb that shows the time of the action or state of being.

Future. The English verb system offers writers several different ways of expressing future time. Future action can be indicated with the modal auxiliary *will.*

> **Fast-food restaurants *will grow* in popularity.**

A completed future action can even be viewed from some time farther in the future (*future perfect tense*).

> **Within a decade or two, Americans *will have given up* cooking their own meals.**

Continuing future actions can be expressed with *will be* and the *-ing* form of the verb.

> **Americans *will* soon *be eating* every second meal away from home.**

The right combination of verbs with *about* can express an action in the near future.

> **Jeremiah *is about to eat* his third hamburger.**

Future arrangements, commands, or possibilities can be expressed.

> **Junior and Mary Jo *are to be married* at McDonald's.**

> **You *have to be* there by noon to get a good table.**

> **If Junior *is to lose* weight, he must give up french fries.**

Voice. A verb is in the *active* voice when it expresses an action taken by the subject. A verb is said to be in the *passive* voice when it expresses something that happens to the subject.

In sentences with active verbs, it is apparent who is performing the action expressed in the verb.

> **The chef *disguised* the tasteless broccoli with a rich cheese sauce.**

In sentences with passive verbs, it may not be clear who is performing the action.

> **The tasteless broccoli *was disguised* with a rich cheese sauce.**

The writer could reveal the performer by adding a phrase (*by the chef*), but the revision would also create a clumsy sentence. Graceful, clear writing relies on active, rather than passive, verbs. Passive forms do fulfill certain purposes, however, such as expressing the state of something.

> **The broccoli *is disguised.***

> **The restaurant *was closed.***

Passives can give prominence to certain information by shifting it to the end of the sentence.

> ***Who* closed this restaurant? It was closed by *the Board of Health.***

Writers also use passives to make sentences more readable by shifting long **noun clauses** to the end.

ACTIVE   *That the chef disguised the tasteless broccoli* **with a cheese sauce disgusted Elvira.**

PASSIVE   **Elvira was disgusted** *that the chef disguised the tasteless broccoli* **with a cheese sauce.**

Mood. Mood refers to the writer's attitude toward a statement. There are three moods: indicative, imperative, and subjunctive. Most statements or questions are in the *indicative mood.*

> The chuck wagon *fed* cowboys on the trail.

> *Did* cowboys ever *tire* of steak and beans?

Commands or directions are given in the *imperative mood.*

> *Eat* those beans!

The *subjunctive mood* is used mainly to indicate hypothetical, impossible, or unlikely conditions.

> If I *were* you, I'd compliment the cook.

> *Had* they *been* here yesterday, they would have had hot camp bread.

Prepositions. Prepositions occur in **phrases,** followed by **objects.** (The uses of prepositional phrases are explained in R2-c.) Most prepositions are single words (*at, on, by, with, of, for, in, under, over, by*), but some consist of two or three words (*away from, on account of, in front of, because of, in comparison with, by means of*). They are used to indicate relations — usually of place, time, cause, purpose, or means — between their objects and some other word in the sentence.

> I'll meet you *at* El Ranchero *for* lunch.

> The enchiladas are stuffed *with* cheese.

> You can split an order *with* [Georgette and me].

Objects of prepositions can be single or compound nouns or pronouns in the **objective case** (as in the preceding examples) or phrases or clauses acting as nouns.

> Herman began making nachos *by* [grating the cheese].

> His guests were happy *with* [what he served].

---

noun clauses Word groups that can function like nouns, acting as subjects, objects, or complements in independent clauses.

phrase A group of words that does *not* contain both a subject and a verb and is always part of an independent clause. Common types of phrases include *prepositional* (*After a flash of lightning*, I saw a tree split in half) and *verbal* (*Blinded by the flash*, I ran into the house).

object The part of a clause that receives the action of the verb (At the checkpoint, we unloaded *the canoes*) or the part of a phrase that follows a preposition (We dragged them to *the river*).

objective case The form a pronoun takes when it is an object (receiving the action of the verb): We helped *him.*

Conjunctions. Like prepositions, conjunctions show relations between sentence elements. There are coordinating, subordinating, and correlative conjunctions.

Coordinating conjunctions (*and, but, for, nor, or, so,* or *yet*) join logically comparable sentence elements.

> **Guacamole is made with avocados, tomatoes, onions, *and* chiles.**
>
> **You may add a little lemon or lime juice, *but* be careful not to add too much.**

Subordinating conjunctions (*although, because, since, though, as though, as soon as, rather than*) introduce **dependent clauses**.

> ***As soon as* the waitress came, Susanna ordered an iced tea.**
>
> **She dived into the salsa and chips *because* she was too hungry to wait for her combination plate.**

Correlative conjunctions come in pairs, with the first element anticipating the second (*both . . . and, either . . . or, neither . . . nor, not only . . . but also*).

> **Charley wanted to order *both* the chiles rellenos *and* the enchiladas verdes.**

Articles. There are only three articles in English: *the, a,* and *an. The* is used for definite reference to something specific; *a* and *an* are used for indefinite reference to something less specific. *The Mexican restaurant in Westbury* is different from *a Mexican restaurant in Westbury.* (See L1.)

Demonstratives. *This, that, these,* and *those* are demonstratives. Sometimes called demonstrative adjectives, they are used to point to something specific.

> **Put one of *these* maraschino cherries at each end of the banana split.**
>
> **The accident left pineapple milkshake all over the front seat of *that* pickup truck.**

Interjections. Interjections indicate strong feeling or an attempt to command attention: *phew, shhh, damn, oh, yea, yikes, ouch, boo.*

R2-b Dependent Clauses

Like independent clauses, all dependent clauses have a **subject** and a **predicate** (which may also have objects, complements, and adverbial modifiers). Unlike independent clauses, however, dependent clauses cannot stand by themselves as complete sentences; they always occur with independent clauses as part of either the subject or the predicate.

INDEPENDENT   **Ribbon-shaped pasta is popular in northern Italy.**

---

dependent (subordinate) clause A word group that has a subject, a predicate, and a subordinating word (such as *because*) at the beginning; it cannot stand by itself as a sentence but must be connected to an independent (main) clause.

subject The part of a clause that identifies who or what is being discussed: At the checkpoint, *we* unloaded the canoes.

predicate The part of a clause that includes a complete verb and says something about the subject: At the checkpoint, we *unloaded the canoes.*

DEPENDENT   . . . , *while tubular-shaped pasta is popular in southern Italy.*

. . . , *which is generally made by hand,* . . .

Although it originally comes from China, . . .

There are three types of dependent clauses: adjective, adverb, and noun.

Adjective Clauses. Also known as *relative clauses*, adjective clauses modify nouns and pronouns in independent clauses. They are introduced by relative pronouns (*who, whom, which, that, whose*) or adverbs (*where, when*), and most often they immediately follow the noun or pronoun they modify. Adjective clauses can be either *restrictive* (essential to defining the noun or pronoun they modify) or *nonrestrictive* (not essential to understanding the noun or pronoun); nonrestrictive clauses are set off by commas, and restrictive clauses are not (see P1-c and P2-b).

Vincent bought a package of agnolotti, *which is a pasta used in soup.*

We went back to the restaurant *where they serve that delicious veal.*

Everyone *who likes Italian cooking* knows Romano cheese well.

Adverb Clauses. Introduced by subordinating conjunctions (such as *although, because,* and *since*), adverb clauses nearly always modify verbs in independent clauses, although they may occasionally modify other elements (except nouns). Adverb clauses are used to indicate a great variety of logical relations with their independent clauses: time, place, condition, concession, reason, cause, circumstance, purpose, result, and so on. They are generally set off by commas.

Although the finest olive oil in Italy comes from Lucca, good-quality olive oil is produced in other regions of the country. [concession]

When the tomato sauce comes to a boil, reduce the heat and simmer. [time]

If you know mushrooms, you probably prefer them fresh. [condition]

Ken carefully watches the spaghetti *because he does not like it to be overcooked.* [reason]

Noun Clauses. Like nouns, noun clauses can function as **subjects, objects,** or **complements** (or predicate nominatives) in independent clauses. They are thus essential to the structure of the **independent clause** in which they occur and so, like restrictive adjective clauses, are not set off by commas. A noun clause usually begins with a **relative pronoun,** but the introductory word may sometimes be omitted.

┌────────SUBJECT────────┐
That we preferred the sausage surprised us.

┌────────OBJECT────────┐
Harold did not know for sure *whether baloney came from Bologna.*

---

subject The part of a clause that identifies who or what is being discussed: At the checkpoint, *we* unloaded the canoes.

object The part of a clause that receives the action of the verb (At the checkpoint, we unloaded *the canoes*) or the part of a phrase that follows a preposition (We dragged them to *the river*).

subject complement A word or word group that follows a linking verb (such as *seems, appears,* or *is* and other forms of *be*) and describes or restates the subject: The tents looked *old and dirty*.

independent (main) clause A word group with a subject and a predicate that can stand alone as a separate sentence. (A predicate is the part of a clause that includes a complete verb and says something about the subject: At the checkpoint, *we unloaded the canoes*.)

relative pronoun A pronoun (such as *who, whom, whose, which,* or *that*) that introduces an adjective clause (a clause that modifies a noun or pronoun).

SUBJECT COMPLEMENT
He assumed *that it did.*

┌──────DIRECT OBJECT──────┐
Hillary claims *no one eats pizza in Italy.* [relative pronoun *that* dropped]

PREP. ┌──────OBJECT OF PREPOSITION──────┐
Gnocchi may be flavored with *whatever fresh herbs are available.*

R2-c Phrases

Like **dependent clauses**, phrases can function as nouns, adjectives, or adverbs in sentences. However, unlike clauses, phrases do not contain both a subject and a verb. (A phrase, of course, cannot stand on its own but occurs as part of an **independent clause**.) The six most common types of grammatical phrases are *prepositional, appositive, participial, gerund, infinitive,* and *absolute.*

Prepositional Phrases. Prepositional phrases always begin with a **preposition** and function as either an adjective or adverb.

Food *in Hunan* is noticeably different from that *in Sichuan.*
ADJECTIVE PHRASE   ADJECTIVE PHRASE

The perfect egg roll is crisp *on the outside* and crunchy *on the inside.*
ADVERB PHRASE   ADVERB PHRASE

Appositive Phrases. Appositive phrases identify or give more information about a noun or pronoun just preceding. They take several forms. A single noun may also serve as an appositive.

The baguette, *the most popular bread in France,* is a loaf about two feet long.

The king of the breakfast rolls, *the croissant,* is shaped like a crescent.

The baker *Marguerite* makes superb croissants.

Participial Phrases. Participles are verb forms used to indicate certain tenses (present: *sipping;* past: *sipped*). They can also be used as verbals — words derived from verbs — and function as adjectives.

At breakfast, we were first served *steaming* coffee and a simple *buttered* roll.

A participial phrase is an adjective phrase made up of a participle and any complements or modifiers it might have. Like participles, participial phrases modify nouns and pronouns in sentences.

Two-thirds of the breakfasts *consumed in the diner* included sausage and eggs.

Prepared in the chef's personal style, the vegetable omelets are served with a cheese sauce *flavored with garlic and herbs.*

---

dependent (subordinate) clause A word group that has a subject, a predicate, and a subordinating word (such as *because*) at the beginning; it cannot stand by itself as a sentence but must be connected to an independent (main) clause: *Although it was raining,* we loaded our gear onto the buses.

independent (main) clause A word group with a subject and a predicate that can stand alone as a separate sentence. (A predicate is the part of a clause that includes a complete verb and says something about the subject: At the checkpoint, *we unloaded the canoes.*)

preposition A word (such as *between, in,* or *of*) that always appears as part of a phrase and indicates the relation between a word in a sentence and the object of the preposition: The water splashed *into* the canoe.

Mopping up the cheese sauce with the last of his roll, Mickey thought to himself, I could get used to this.

Gerund Phrases. Like a participle, a gerund is a verbal. Ending in *-ing*, it even looks like a present participle, but it functions as a noun, filling any noun slot in a clause. Gerund phrases include **complements** and any modifiers of the gerund.

> **complement** A word or word group that describes or restates a subject or an object.

┌SUBJECT┐
Roasting is the quickest way to cook a turkey.

┌————SUBJECT————┐
Preparing a stuffed turkey takes several hours.

You begin by *mixing the dressing.*
　　　　　　　OBJECT OF PREPOSITION

Infinitive Phrases. Like participles and gerunds, infinitives are verbals. The infinitive is the base form of the verb, preceded by *to: to simmer, to broil, to fry*. Infinitives and infinitive phrases function as nouns, adjectives, or adverbs.

Tamales can be complicated *to prepare.*
　　　　　　　　　　ADVERB

To assemble the tamales, begin by cutting the kernels off the corncobs.
　　ADVERB

　　　　　┌————NOUN————┐
Remembering *to save the corn husks* is important.
　OBJECT OF GERUND PHRASE

Anyone's first tamale dinner is a meal *to remember for a long time.*
　　　　　　　　　　　　ADJECTIVE

Absolute Phrases. The absolute phrase does not modify or replace any particular part of a clause; it modifies the whole clause. An absolute phrase includes a noun or pronoun and often includes a past or present participle as well as modifiers. Nearly all modern prose writers rely on absolute phrases. Some style historians consider them a hallmark of modern prose.

Her eyes glistening, Lucy checked out the cases of doughnuts at Krispy Kreme Doughnuts.

She stood patiently in line, *her arms folded to control her hunger, her backpack hanging off one shoulder.*

She walked slowly to a table, *each hand bearing a treasure.*

GL Glossary of Frequently Misused Words

Sometimes writers choose a word that is incorrect, imprecise in meaning, pronounced the same as the correct word (a homophone), or used widely but unacceptable in formal writing situations. In addition, problems can arise with idiomatic phrases, common everyday expressions that may or may not fit, or words whose denotations or connotations do not precisely suit the context of a particular sentence. In general, you should avoid imprecise popular usages in formal writing.

accept/except *Accept* is a verb ("receive with favor"). *Except* may be a verb ("leave out") but is more commonly used as a preposition ("excluding"). Other forms: *acceptance, acceptable; exception.*

None of the composition instructors will *accept* late papers, *except* Mr. Siu.

Her *acceptance* of the bribe *excepts* her from consideration for the position.

adapt/adopt *Adapt* means "adjust to make more suitable." *Adopt* means "take as one's own." Other forms: *adaptable, adaptation; adoption.*

To *adopt* an older child, parents must be willing to *adapt* themselves to the child's needs.

advice/advise *Advice* is a noun; *advise* is a verb. Other forms: *advisable, adviser.*

Everyone *advised* him to heed the expert's *advice.*

affect/effect *Affect* is commonly used as a verb, most often meaning "influence"; in psychology, the noun *affect* is a technical term for an emotional state. *Effect* is generally a noun ("result or consequences"); it is only occasionally used as a verb ("bring about"), although the adjective form (*effective*) is common.

Researchers are studying the *effect* of stress.

How does stress *affect* the human body?

all right *All right* is the preferred spelling, rather than *alright*, which many people regard as unacceptable.

a lot A common expression meaning "a large number," *a lot* is always written as two words. Because it is vague and informal, avoid it in college writing.

among/between Use *among* when you are referring to more than two objects; limit *between* to references to only two objects.

It is hard to choose one winner *among* so many highly qualified candidates for the scholarship.

Between the two extreme positions lies a vast middle ground.

amount/number   *Amount* refers to the quantity of a unit ("amount of water," "amount of discussion"), whereas *number* refers to the quantity of individual items ("number of papers," "number of times"). In general, use *amount* only with a singular noun.

anxious/eager   *Anxious* means "nervous" or "worried"; *eager* means "looking forward [impatiently]." Avoid using *anxious* to mean *eager.*

The students were *eager* to learn their grades.

They were *anxious* they wouldn't pass.

between/among   See among/between.

capital/capitol   *Capital* is the more common word and has a variety of meanings, among them the principal city in a state or country; *capitol* refers only to a government building.

cite/sight/site   *Cite* as a verb means "refer to as proof" or "summon to appear in court." *Site* is a noun meaning "place or location." *Sight* may be a verb or a noun and always refers to seeing or what is seen ("a sight for sore eyes").

Can you *cite* your sources for these figures?

A new dormitory will be built at this *site.*

When she *sighted* the speeding car, the officer *cited* the driver for recklessness.

complement/compliment   *Complement* refers to completion, the making of a satisfactory whole, whereas *compliment* indicates admiration or praise; both can be used as either nouns or verbs. *Complementary* means "serving to complete" or "contrasting in color"; *complimentary* means "given free."

The dean *complimented* the school's recruiters on the full *complement* of students registered for the fall.

The designer received many *compliments* on the way the elements of the room *complemented* one another.

Buy a new refrigerator and receive a *complimentary* ice maker in a *complementary* color.

could of/should of/would of In standard speech, "could have," "should have," and "would have" sound very much like "could of," "should of," and "would of"; however, substituting *of* for *have* in this construction is too casual for written work. The same holds true for "might of," "must of," and "will of."

council/counsel *Council* is a noun ("an assembly of people who deliberate or govern"). *Counsel* is a verb meaning "advise" or a noun meaning "advice." Other forms: *councilor* ("member of a council"); *counselor* ("one who gives advice").

The *council* on drug abuse has issued guidelines for *counseling* troubled students.

Before voting on the important fiscal issue, City *Councilor* Lopez sought the *counsel* of her constituents.

desert/dessert As a noun or an adjective, *desert* (dez´ ert) means "a dry, uncultivated region"; as a verb, *desert* (di zurt´) means "abandon." A *dessert* is a sweet dish served at the end of a meal.

The hunters were alone in the arid *desert, deserted* by their guides.

After a heavy meal, sherbet is the perfect *dessert.*

eager/anxious See **anxious/eager.**

effect/affect See **affect/effect.**

emigrant/immigrant An *emigrant* moves out of a country; an *immigrant* moves into a country. Other forms: *emigrate, emigration, émigré; immigrate, immigration.*

Congress passed a bill to deal with illegal *immigrants* living in the United States.

Members of her family *emigrated* from Cuba to Miami and Madrid.

etc. An abbreviation of the Latin words *et cetera* ("and other things"), *etc.* should never be preceded by *and* in English. Also be careful to spell the abbreviation correctly (*not* "ect."). In general, use *etc.* sparingly, if at all, in college writing.

except See **accept/except.**

> **count noun** A noun that names people and things that can be counted: one *teacher*, two *teachers*; one *movie*, several *movies*.

fewer/less Use *fewer* when referring to count nouns; reserve *less* for amounts you cannot count.

The new cookies have *fewer* calories than the other brand because they contain *less* sugar.

fortuitous/fortunate Often used incorrectly, the adjective *fortuitous* means "by chance" or "unplanned" and should not be confused with *fortunate* ("lucky").

Because the two candidates wished to avoid each other, their *fortuitous* meeting in the parking lot was **not** a *fortunate* event for either party.

hisself/theirselves In nonstandard speech, "hisself" is sometimes used for *himself* and "theirselves" for *themselves*, but such usage is not acceptable in written work.

hopefully In conversation, *hopefully* is often used as a convenient shorthand to suggest that some outcome is generally to be hoped for ("Hopefully, our nominee will win the election"); this usage, however, is not acceptable in most written work. Better substitutes include *I hope, let's hope, everyone hopes*, and *it is to be hoped*, depending on your meaning. The adverb *hopefully* ("full of hope") should always modify a specific verb or adverb.

I *hope* my brother will win the election.

We should all *hope* his brother will win the election.

Her sister is *hopeful* that she will win the election.

The candidate inquired *hopefully* about the results.

immigrant See **emigrant/immigrant**.

its/it's *Its* is a possessive pronoun; *it's* is the contraction of *it is*.

This job has *its* advantages.

When *it's* well grilled, there's nothing like a steak.

lay/lie The verb *lay*, meaning "put, place," is **transitive** (forms of *lay* are *lay, laid, laid*). The verb *lie*, meaning "recline," is **intransitive** (forms of *lie* are *lie, lay, lain*). Writers may incorrectly use *laid* as the past tense of *lie*, or *lay* as the present tense of *lie*. Other forms: *laying, lying*.

The lion *lies* in wait for the approach of its prey.

Joseph *laid* down his shovel, took a shower, and *lay* down for a nap.

transitive verb A verb that needs an object — something that receives the action of the verb — to make its meaning complete.

intransitive verb A verb that does not need an object to make its meaning complete.

less/fewer See **fewer/less**.

literally *Literally* means "exactly as stated, actually" and is often used to suggest that a cliché has in fact come true. However, to say, "The movie made my hair literally stand on end" is to misuse the word (although a person who suffered a fatal heart attack brought on by a fearful shock might correctly be said to have *literally* died of fright).

loose/lose *Lose* is a verb ("mislay, fail to maintain"); *loose* is most often used as an adjective ("not fastened tightly").

A *loose* board may make someone *lose* his or her balance.

number/amount See **amount/number**.

persecute/prosecute *Persecute* means "mistreat or oppress"; *prosecute* most often means "bring a legal suit or action against."

A biased majority can easily *persecute* minority groups.

The law may *prosecute* only those who are indicted.

prejudice/prejudiced *Prejudice* is a noun or a verb. When used adjectivally, it should take the form of the past tense of the verb: *prejudiced*.

We should fight *prejudice* wherever we find it.

He was *prejudiced* against the candidate because she spoke with an accent.

principal/principle *Principal* implies "first in rank, chief," whether it is used as an adjective ("the principal cities of the Midwest") or a noun ("the principal of a midwestern high school"). *Principle* is generally a noun meaning "a basic law or truth."

In *principle,* you are correct.

The *principle* of free speech will be the *principal* topic of discussion.

prosecute/persecute See **persecute/prosecute**.

sensual/sensuous Both *sensual* and *sensuous* suggest the enjoyment of physical pleasure through the senses. However, *sensual* generally implies self-indulgence, particularly in terms of sexual activity; *sensuous* has a more positive meaning and suggests the ability to appreciate intellectually what is received through the senses. Other forms: *sensuality; sensuousness.*

When drunk, the emperor gave himself up to brutal *sensuality.*

Anyone can enjoy a *sensuous* spring night.

set/sit The difference between the verbs *sit* and *set* is similar to that between *lie* and *lay: Sit* is generally intransitive ("rest on one's buttocks"), and *set* is transitive ("put [something] in a certain place"). *Set* also has a number of uses as a noun. The past tense and past **participle** forms of *sit* are both *sat;* these forms for *set* are both *set.*

He would rather *sit* than stand and would rather lie than *sit.*

He *set* his suitcase on the ground and then *sat* on it.

participle A verb form showing present tense (*dancing, freezing*) or past tense (*danced, frozen*) that can also act as an adjective.

should of See **could of/should of/would of**.

sight/site See **cite/sight/site**.

stationary/stationery *Stationary* is an adjective meaning "fixed, remaining in one place" ("Concrete will make the pole stationary"). *Stationery* refers to writing paper. One way to keep the distinction in mind is to associate the *er* in *paper* with that in *stationery*.

that/which When used as a subordinating conjunction, *that* always introduces a **restrictive word group**; *which* is generally used for **nonrestrictive word groups**. Although it is acceptable to use *which* before a restrictive word group, *that* is generally preferred to make it clear that the clause is restrictive. (See the discussion of restrictive and nonrestrictive word groups in P1-c and P2-b, and the review of sentence structure and sentence elements on p. H-115.)

Her first bid for the Senate was the only election *that* she ever lost.

Her first bid for the Senate, *which* was unsuccessful, brought her to prominence.

The Senate election *that* resulted in her defeat took place in 1968.

their/there/they're *Their* is a possessive pronoun; *there* specifies a place or functions as an expletive; and *they're* is a contraction of *they are*.

The coauthors say *there* are no copies of *their* script in *their* office, but *they're* not telling the truth.

theirselves See **hisself/theirselves**.

to/too/two *To* is a preposition, *too* is an adverb, and *two* is generally an adjective. The most common error here is the substitution of *to* for *too*.

It is *too* early *to* predict either of the *two* scores.

unique To be precise, *unique* means "one of a kind, like no other." Careful writers do not use it loosely to mean simply "unusual or rare." Nor can it correctly take a comparative form ("most unique"), although advertisers sometimes use it this way.

Her generosity is not *unique*, although today it is increasingly rare.

This example of Mayan sculpture is apparently *unique;* none other like it has so far been discovered.

used to In colloquial speech, *used to* often sounds like "use to." However, *used to* is the correct form for written work.

subordinating conjunction A word or phrase (such as *although, because, since*, or *as soon as*) that introduces a dependent clause and relates it to an independent clause.

restrictive word group A group of words, not set off by commas, that provides information essential to defining or identifying the noun or pronoun it modifies.

nonrestrictive word group A group of words, set off by commas, that provides extra or nonessential information and could be eliminated without changing the meaning of the noun or pronoun it modifies.

My grandfather *used to* be a Dodgers fan until the team moved to Los Angeles.

weather/whether *Weather* is a noun ("atmospheric conditions"); *whether* is a conjunction.

The *weather* forecast indicates *whether* there will be sun or rain.

which See **that/which.**

who's/whose *Who's* is the contraction of *who is* or *who has*; *whose* is a possessive pronoun.

Who's up next?

She's the only student *who's* done her work correctly.

Whose work is this?

The man *whose* job I took has retired.

would of See **could of/should of/would of.**

Acknowledgments

Text Credits

Sherman Alexie. "A Good Story." From *The Lone Ranger and Tonto Fistfight in Heaven* by Sherman Alexie. Copyright © 1993, 2005 by Sherman Alexie. Used by permission of Grove/Atlantic, Inc.

Mirko Bagaric. "A Case for Torture" from *The Age*, May 17, 2005. Copyright © 2005 by Mirko Bagaric. Reprinted with permission of the author and *The Age*.

La Shawn Barber. "Interracial Marriage: A Slippery Slope?" from Townhall.com, June 11, 2007. Copyright © 2007. Reproduced by permission of the author.

David Castelvecchi. "Carbon Tubes, But Not Nano." First published in *Science News*, 74 (5), 9-9. Retrieved October 11, 2008 from Academic Search Complete database. Reprinted with permission of *Science Now*.

Helena Catt. "Now or Never." A paper delivered in the symposium Citizenship: Learning by Doing. Sixth Child and Family Policy Conference. University of Otago, Dunedin, July 2005. Copyright © Helena Catt. Reproduced by permission of the author.

Amanda Coyne. Excerpt from "The Long Good-Bye: Mother's Day in Federal Prison." Copyright © 1997 by Harper's Magazine. All rights reserved. Reproduced from May issue by special permission.

Annie Dillard. Pages 45–49 from *An American Childhood* by Annie Dillard. Copyright © 1987 by Annie Dillard. Reprinted with the permission of HarperCollins Publishers and Russell & Volkening as agent for the author.

Ross Douthat. "Thinking about Torture." Posted on http://rossdouthat.theatlantic.com/archives/2008/12/think_about_torture.php. December 16, 2008. Copyright © 2008 Ross Douthat. Reproduced by permission of the author.

John T. Edge. "I'm Not Leaving Until I Eat This Thing." Originally published in the *Oxford American* (September/October 1999). Copyright © 1999 by John T. Edge. Reprinted with the permission of the author.

Trey Ellis. "When the Walls Came Tumbling Down." From *The New York Times*, June 15, 2008 issue. © 2008 The New York Times All rights reserved. Used by permission and protected by the Copyright Laws of the United States. The printing, copying, redistribution, or retransmission of the Material without express written permission is prohibited. www.nytimes.com

Richard Estrada. "Sticks and Stones and Sports Team Names." From *The Washington Post*, October 29, 1995 issue. © 1995 The Washington Post. All rights reserved. Used by permission and protected by the Copyright Laws of the United States. The printing, copying, redistribution, or retransmission of the Material without express written permission is prohibited. www.washingtonpost.com

Amitai Etzioni. "Working at McDonald's." Copyright © 1986 by Amitai Etzioni. Author of *The Spirit of Community*. Director, George Washington University Center for Communication Policy Studies. Reproduced with the permission of the author.

Richard A. Friedman. "Born to Be Happy, Through a Twist of Human Hard Wire." From *The New York Times*, December 31, 2002 issue, page F5. © 2002 The New York Times. All rights reserved. Used by permission and protected by the Copyright Laws of the United States. The printing, copying, redistribution, or retransmission of the Material without express written permission is prohibited. www.nytimes.com

Amy Goldwasser. "What's the Matter with Kids Today?" This article first appeared in Salon.com, at www.Salon.com. An online version remains in the Salon archives. www.salon.com/mwt/feature/2008/03/14/kids_and_internet. Reprinted with permission.

Erica Goode. "The Gorge-Yourself Environment." From *The New York Times*, July 22, 2003 issue, page F1. © 2003 The New York Times. All rights reserved. Used by permission and protected by the Copyright Laws of the United States. The printing, copying, redistribution, or retransmission of the Material without express written permission is prohibited. www.nytimes.com

Glenn Greenwald. "Committing War Crimes for the 'Right' Reasons." This article first appeared in Salon.com, at www.Salon.com. An online version remains in the Salon archives. www.salon.com/opinion/greenwald/2008/12/17/douthat. Reprinted with permission.

Jeremy Hsu. "The Secrets of Storytelling: Why We Love a Good Yarn." Published in *Scientific American Mind*, August 2008. Copyright © 2008 Jeremy Hsu. Reprinted by permission of the author. www.sciam.com/article.cfm?id=the-secrets-of-storytelling&page=4.

Ann Hulbert. "*Juno* and the Culture Wars." Originally published by Slate. Copyright © 2007 by Ann Hulbert. Reprinted with permission of The Wylie Agency LLC.

Kermit D. Johnson. "Inhuman Behavior." From the April 18, 2006 issue of the *Christian Century*. Copyright © 2006 by the Christian Century. Reprinted by permission of the Christian Century.

Martin Luther King Jr. Excerpt from "Letter from Birmingham Jail." Copyright © 1963 Dr. Martin Luther King Jr.; copyright renewed 1991 Coretta Scott King. Reprinted by arrangement with the Heirs to the estate of Martin Luther King, Jr., c/o Writers House as agent for the proprietor New York, NY.

Stephen King. "Why We Crave Horror Movies." Copyright © Stephen King. All rights reserved. Originally appeared in *Playboy* (1982). Reprinted With Permission.

Jeffrey Kluger. "What Makes Us Moral." From *Time*, December 3, 2007. Copyright Time Inc. Reprinted by permission. *Time* is a registered trademark of Time, Inc. All rights reserved.

Karen Kornbluh. "Win-Win Flexibility." Originally published in *The Atlantic Monthly* (January/February 2003). From New America Foundation, June 29, 2005. Copyright 2005. Reprinted with the permission of the author.

462 (left) Ozier Muhammad / The New York Times / Redux; (right) Peter DaSilva / The New York Times / Redux; **467** Ozier Muhammad / The New York Times / Redux; **471** Courtesy of Jeremy Hsu; **472** iStock; **477** CNN ImageSource; **478** (top) USA TODAY. Reprinted with Permission; (bottom) The New York Times Agency; **497** (top and middle) Courtesy of John Bruno and Elizabeth Selig, (bottom left) NOAA / Florida Keys National Marine Sanctuary Staff; (bottom right) NOAA / David Burdick; **516** (top) Fuminaro Sato / The New York Times / Redux; (bottom) Courtesy of Fanfics.org; **547** Missouri History Museum, St. Louis. Photo by J.A. Scholten; **549** The Granger Collection, New York; **554** Library of Congress; **557** Ulf Andersen / Getty Images; **616** Library of Congress; **624–25** From *Newsweek*, February 8, 1999, © 1999 Newsweek. Inc. All rights reserved. Photo © Jeanne Friebert / Sipa Press; **626** From *Home Repair Handbook* (Menlo Park, Calif.: Sunset, 1999), pp. 156–157; **673** © Bo Saunders / Corbis; **674** Courtesy of WWF; **677, 683** Library of Congress; **678** (top) Grant Wood, American, 1891–1942, *American Gothic*, 1930, Oil on beaverboard, 30 11/16 × 25 11/16 in. (78 × 65.3 cm) unframed, Friends of American Art Collection, 1930.934, The Art Institute of Chicago. Photography © The Art Institute of Chicago. All rights reserved by the Estate of Nan Wood Graham / Licensed by VAGA, New York, NY; **678, 682** The Gordon Parks Foundation; **686** (top) Library of Congress; (bottom) Agency: Freight Train; Photographer: Dan Bishop; Model: Jemme, Ford Models; **687** (top) Carlos Cortinas – Art Director, Glen Day – Writer; (bottom) Pepsico & TBWA / Chiat / Day; **696** (bottom) U.S. Department of Commerce; **697** (left) U.S. Department of Education; (right) Centers for Disease Control and Prevention; **699** (top) JH Pete Carmichael / Getty Images; (bottom) Lalo Alcaraz © 2002. Dist. By Universal Press Syndicate. Reprinted with permission. All rights reserved; **700** (bottom) Microsoft product screen shot reprinted with permission from Microsoft Corporation; **702** Courtesy Stanford Law School; **706** Microsoft product screen shot reprinted with permission from Microsoft Corporation; **741, 744, 746, 747** Courtesy of EBSCO Publishing.

Author and Title Index

Subject Index

preparing for, 814–15
quotation, commenting on, 820–21
reading exam, 815–16
summary of specific source, 818
synthesizing information, 822
essays, titles, quotation marks for, H-78
et al., 766, 779
etc., H-134
ethnography, subjects for, 68
evaluations, 384–445
about service experience, 851
alternate forms of, 417–18
audience for, 389, 420, 423–24
collaborative activities, 386–87, 425
in college courses, 384
in community, 422
connecting to, 398, 406, 414–15
design elements and visuals,
401, 427, 439–41
editing and proofreading, 441–42
combining sentences, 442
comparisons, checking, 441
in essay exams, 823–24
features of, 387–88
Guide to Writing, chart, 420
invention and research, 421–28
argument, developing, 426
concession or refutation,
considering, 426
counterarguments, developing, 426
purpose for writing, defining, 428
reader's objections, anticipating, 426
research, 422, 427
subject, choosing, 421–23
subject, exploring further, 423–25
subject, testing, 425
thesis statement, tentative, 428
planning and drafting, 429–37
comparing and contrasting, 432–34
counterarguments, 430
Critical Reading Guide, 436–37
ending, 430–31
first draft, 432–34
goal setting, 429
opening strategies, 429
outlining, 431–32
praise and criticism, balancing,
433–34
purpose for writing, clarifying, 429
reasons and support, presenting,
430
sources, summarizing, 434–35
subject, presenting, 429–30
purpose for writing, 388–89, 420

readings
"'Children Need to Play, Not Compete'
by Jessica Statsky: An Evaluation,"
(Romano), 402–9, 415, 429–30,
433–35, 443–44
"Grading Professors" (Kim), 389–94,
399, 415, 429–30, 433, 659
"*Juno* and the Culture Wars" (Hulbert),
389–401, 415, 429–30, 433–34
"Myth of Multitasking, The" (Rosen),
410–17, 433
revising, 437–39
outline, using, 437
troubleshooting draft, 438–39
thinking critically about, 444–45
topics for essays, considering, 401,
409, 422–23
in workplace, 422
Writer at Work (Christine Romano),
443–44
writing process, reflecting on, 444–45
writing strategies
alternative judgments, acknowledging,
400, 408
alternative judgments, refuting, 416–17
authority or expert information, 416
comparisons, 399
concessions, making, 388
counterarguments, 388, 400, 408,
416–17, 443–44
forecasting topic, 408–9
judgment in, 387–88, 399, 407–8,
415–16
quoting, paraphrasing, summarizing,
407–8
readable plan, 388, 400, 408–9, 417
reader's objections, anticipating, 408
reframing, 416–17
rhetorical situation, 398–99, 401, 406
subject, presenting, 387, 398–99,
406–7, 415
supporting evidence, types of, 415–16
thesis statements, 387, 399, 408
topic sentences, 409
transitions (words or phrases), 400, 409
evaluative annotation, 801–2
evidence, supporting
anecdotes as, 666–67
authority or expert information
as, 665–66
in evaluations, 415–16, 426
examples as, 663
in reasoned arguments, 289, 300
reasons, presenting, 662–63

in speculation about causes, 459
statistics as, 664–65
in stories, analysis of, 506–7, 514–15,
529, 531–35
textual evidence as, 514–15, 529,
531–35, 667–68
types of, 289, 300, 415
writing strategies — quoting, paraphrasing, summarizing, 514–15
exact words, use in sentences, H-51–54
examples
appositives, use with, 171
believability, testing for, 595
dashes to set off, 415
in explanations of concepts, 157, 167
in parentheses, 415
in reasoned arguments, 289
in speculation about causes, 468–69
thesis, asserting with, 663
except/accept, H-132
exclamation points
with quotation marks, 119, 761, H-77
use of, H-84
exclamations, H-118
expert information. *See* authority or expert
information
explanations, dashes for emphasis, H-74
explanations of concepts, 127–83
about service experience, 850–51
alternate forms of, 159
audience for, 131, 165
collaborative activities, 166
in community, 127, 155, 163
connecting to, 140, 145, 155
design elements and visuals, 142, 158–59,
167, 177
editing and proofreading, 180–81
features of, 129–31
Guide to Writing, chart, 161
invention and research, 162–68
concept for essay, identifying, 162–65
concept for essay, testing, 165–66
design elements, 167
explanatory strategies, considering,
166–67
purpose for writing, 167
research, 164, 166
thesis statement, 167–68
planning and drafting, 168–74
appositives, use of, 170–71
Critical Reading Guide, 173–74
ending, 169, 176
first draft, 170
goal setting, 168

Index for ESL Writers

Submitting Your Essays for Publication

We hope that we'll be able to include many new essays by students in the next editions of *The St. Martin's Guide to Writing* and its companion collections. Please let us see the best essays you've written using *The Guide*. Send them with this submission form and copies of the agreement form on the back of this page (one for each essay you submit) to English Editor — Student Essays, Bedford/St. Martin's, 33 Irving Place, 10th Floor, New York, NY 10003, or submit them online at bedfordstmartins.com/theguide.

PAPER SUBMISSION FORM

Student's Name _____

Instructor's Name _____

School _____

Department _____

Writing Assignment (circle one)

Remembering an Event	Proposing a Solution
Writing Profiles	Justifying an Evaluation
Explaining a Concept	Speculating about Causes
Finding Common Ground	Analyzing Stories
Arguing a Position	

Agreement Form

I hereby assign to Bedford/St. Martin's ("Bedford") all of my right, title and interest throughout the world, including without limitation, all copyrights, in and to my essay, _____, and any notes and drafts pertaining to it (the sample essay and such materials being referred to as the "Essay").

I understand that Bedford in its discretion has the right but not the obligation to publish the Essay in any form(s) or format(s) that it may desire; that Bedford may edit, revise, condense, or otherwise alter the Essay as it deems appropriate in order to prepare the same for publication. I understand that Bedford has the right to use and to authorize the use of my name as author of the Essay in connection with any work that contains the Essay (or a portion of it).

I represent that the Essay is wholly original and was completely written by me, that publication of it will not infringe upon the rights of any third party, and that I have not granted any rights in it to any third party.

In the event Bedford determines to publish any part of the Essay in one of its print books, I will receive one free copy of the work in which it appears.

Student's signature _____

Name _____ Date _____

Permanent address _____

_____

Phone number(s) _____

E-mail address(es) _____

A Note to the Student:

When a writer creates something — a story, an essay, a poem — he or she automatically possesses all of the rights to that piece of writing, no trip to the U.S. Copyright Office needed. When a writer — an historian, a novelist, a sportswriter — publishes his or her work, he or she normally transfers some or all of those rights to the publisher, by formal agreement. The form above is one such formal agreement. By entering into this agreement, you are engaging in a modern publishing ritual — the transfer of rights from writer to publisher. If this is your first experience submitting something for publication, you should know that you are in good company: every student who has published an essay in one of our books entered into this agreement, and just about every published writer has entered into a similar one.

Thank you for submitting your essay.